Eighth Edition

CompTIA®
NETWORK+
GUIDE TO
NETWORKS

Jill West

Jean Andrews, Ph.D.

Tamara Dean

 CENGAGE

Australia • Brazil • Mexico • Singapore • United Kingdom • United States

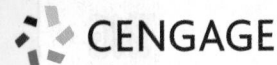

Network+ Guide to Networks,
Eighth Edition
Jill West/Jean Andrews/Tamara Dean

SVP, GM Skills: Jonathan Lau

Product Team Manager: Kristin McNary

Associate Product Manager: Amy Savino

Executive Director of Development: Marah Bellegarde

Senior Product Development Manager: Leigh Hefferon

Senior Content Developer: Michelle Ruelos Cannistraci

Development Editor: Ann Shaffer

Product Assistant: Jake Toth

Marketing Director: Michele McTighe

Production Director: Patty Stephan

Senior Content Project Manager: Brooke Greenhouse

Production Service/Composition: SPi Global

Senior Designer: Diana Graham

Cover image: iStockPhoto.com/ayvengo

For product information and technology assistance, contact us at **Cengage Customer & Sales Support, 1-800-354-9706.**

For permission to use material from this text or product, submit all requests online at **www.cengage.com/permissions**.
Further permissions questions can be e-mailed to **permissionrequest@cengage.com**

Library of Congress Control Number: 2018932044

ISBN: 978-1-3375-6933-0

Cengage
20 Channel Center Street
Boston, MA, 02210
USA

Cengage is a leading provider of customized learning solutions with employees residing in nearly 40 different countries and sales in more than 125 countries around the world. Find your local representative at **www.cengage.com.**

Cengage products are represented in Canada by Nelson Education, Ltd.

To learn more about Cengage, visit **www.cengage.com**

Purchase any of our products at your local college store or at our preferred online store **www.cengagebrain.com**

Notice to the Reader

Publisher does not warrant or guarantee any of the products described herein or perform any independent analysis in connection with any of the product information contained herein. Publisher does not assume, and expressly disclaims, any obligation to obtain and include information other than that provided to it by the manufacturer. The reader is expressly warned to consider and adopt all safety precautions that might be indicated by the activities described herein and to avoid all potential hazards. By following the instructions contained herein, the reader willingly assumes all risks in connection with such instructions. The publisher makes no representations or warranties of any kind, including but not limited to, the warranties of fitness for particular purpose or merchantability, nor are any such representations implied with respect to the material set forth herein, and the publisher takes no responsibility with respect to such material. The publisher shall not be liable for any special, consequential, or exemplary damages resulting, in whole or part, from the readers' use of, or reliance upon, this material.

Some of the product names and company names used in this book have been used for identification purposes only and may be trademarks or registered trademarks of their respective manufacturers and sellers.

Windows® is a registered trademark of Microsoft Corporation. Microsoft.is registered trademark of Microsoft Corporation in the United States and/or other countries.

Cengage is an independent entity from Microsoft Corporation and not affiliated with Microsoft in any manner.

Printed in the United States of America
Print Number: 01   Print Year: 2018

Brief Contents

Table of Contents

Wireless Networking **303**

CHAPTER 7

Virtualization and Cloud Computing **371**

CHAPTER 11

Network Performance and Recovery 615

Preface

Knowing how to install, configure, and troubleshoot a computer network is a highly marketable and exciting skill. This book first introduces the fundamental building blocks that form a modern network, such as hardware, topologies, and protocols, along with an introduction to the OSI model. It then provides in-depth coverage of the most important concepts in contemporary networking, such as TCP/IP, Ethernet, wireless transmission, virtual networks, cloud computing, segmentation, security, and troubleshooting. After reading this book and completing the end-of-chapter exercises, you will be prepared to select the network design, hardware, and software that best fits your environment. You will also have the skills to build a network from scratch and maintain, upgrade, troubleshoot, and manage an existing network. Finally, you will be well-prepared to pass CompTIA's Network+ N10-007 certification exam.

This book explains technical concepts logically and in a clear, approachable style. In addition, concepts are reinforced by real-world examples of networking issues from a professional's standpoint. Each chapter opens with an "On the Job" story from a network engineer, technician, or administrator. These real-world examples, along with Applying Concepts activities, Hands-On Projects, and Capstone Projects in each chapter, make this text a practical learning tool. The numerous tables and color illustrations, along with the glossary, appendices, and study questions, make the text a valuable reference for any networking professional.

Intended Audience

This text is intended to serve the needs of students and professionals who are interested in mastering fundamental, vendor-independent networking concepts. No previous networking experience is necessary to begin learning from this text, although knowledge of basic computer principles is helpful. Those seeking to pass CompTIA's Network+ certification exam will find the text's content, approach, and numerous study questions especially helpful. For more information on CompTIA® Network+ certification, visit CompTIA's website at *comptia.org*.

The text's pedagogical features are designed to provide a truly interactive learning experience, preparing you for the challenges of the highly dynamic networking industry. In addition to the information presented in the text, each chapter includes Applying Concepts activities and Hands-On Projects that guide you through software and hardware configuration in a step-by-step fashion. At the end of each chapter, you will also find Capstone Projects that place you in the role of network admin, requiring you to apply concepts presented in the chapter in various virtualized and emulated environments.

Chapter Descriptions

The following list summarizes the topics covered in each chapter of this book:

Chapter 1, "Introduction to Networking," begins by answering the question "What is a network?" Next, it presents the fundamental types of networks and describes the devices and topologies that create a network. This chapter also introduces the OSI model, best practices for safety when working with networks, and the seven-step troubleshooting model.

Chapter 2, "Network Infrastructure and Documentation," begins with a tour through a campus network's data rooms, from the ISP's entry point through to the users' endpoints. The chapter introduces best practices for managing network and cabling equipment, and explains issues related to managing the environment in which networking equipment operates. This chapter also describes characteristics of network documentation, and explains how to create a network diagram that can be used in network troubleshooting. It ends with a discussion on how to create and follow appropriate change management procedures in an enterprise network environment.

Chapter 3, "Addressing on Networks," describes addressing standards used by devices on a network at various layers of the OSI model, including MAC addresses at the Data Link layer, IP addresses at the Network layer, and ports and sockets at the Transport layer. It also explains how host names and domain names work. The chapter concludes with an introduction to commands used in troubleshooting networks.

Chapter 4, "Network Protocols and Routing," describes the functions of the core TCP/IP protocols, including the common IPv4 and IPv6 routing protocols. The chapter explores in-depth how routers work and how various internal and external gateway protocols select and manage routes between networks. It also explains multiple TCP/IP utilities used for network discovery and troubleshooting.

Chapter 5, "Network Cabling," discusses basic data transmission concepts, including throughput, bandwidth, multiplexing, and common transmission flaws. Next, it describes copper cables, fiber-optic cables, and Ethernet standards, comparing the benefits and limitations of different networking media. The chapter then concludes with an examination of common cable problems and the tools used for troubleshooting those problems.

Chapter 6, "Wireless Networking," examines how nodes exchange wireless signals and identifies potential obstacles to successful wireless transmission. The chapter explores wireless technologies that support the IoT (Internet of Things). It then describes WLAN (wireless LAN) architecture and specifies the characteristics of popular WLAN transmission methods. In this chapter, you will also learn how to install and configure wireless access points and clients, manage wireless security concerns, and evaluate common problems experienced with wireless networks.

Chapter 7, "Virtualization and Cloud Computing," identifies features and benefits of virtualization and cloud computing, and then explains methods for encrypting data to keep it safe at rest, in use, and in motion. The chapter also explores options for remotely connecting to a network, including VPNs and their protocols.

Chapter 8, "Subnets and VLANs," explores the advantages and methods of network segmentation. The chapter examines the purposes of subnets and the related calculations. It then describes techniques for segmenting through the use of VLANs and explains advanced features of switches, including VLAN management.

Chapter 9, "Network Risk Management," covers common security risks and vulnerabilities on a network, including risks associated with people, technology, and malware infections. Here you'll also learn how to assess a network's weaknesses, how to apply appropriate physical security measures, and how to harden devices on the network. Finally, this chapter teaches you about the kinds of information you should include in security policies for users.

Chapter 10, "Security in Network Design," examines security devices specifically designed to protect a network, and then looks more deeply at how to configure switches on a network for optimized performance and security. The chapter breaks down AAA (authentication, authorization, and accounting) processes that control users' access to network resources and looks closely at the partnership between authentication and directory services. The chapter closes with a discussion of specific concerns relating to securing wireless networks.

Chapter 11, "Network Performance and Recovery," presents basic network management concepts and describes how to utilize system and event logs to evaluate, monitor, and manage network performance. The chapter explores redundancy and backup methods that maximize the availability of network resources. It concludes by describing components of a reliable disaster recovery plan and a defensible incident response plan.

Chapter 12, "Wide Area Networks," expands on your knowledge of networks by examining WAN (wide area network) characteristics and technologies, as well as common problems with ISP connections. The chapter compares WAN technologies at Layer 1, such as ISDN, DSL, cable broadband, and T-carriers, and those at Layer 2, including frame relay, ATM, and MPLS, so that you'll understand how each technology works and what makes each one unique. It then concludes with an exploration of common wireless WAN technologies.

The three appendices at the end of this book serve as references for the networking professional:

Appendix A, "CompTIA Network+ N10-007 Certification Exam Objectives," provides a complete list of the latest CompTIA Network+ certification exam objectives, including the percentage of the exam's content that each domain represents and which chapters and sections in the text cover material associated with each objective.

Appendix B, "Visual Guide to Connectors," provides a visual connector reference chart for quick identification of connectors and receptacles used in contemporary networking.

Appendix C, "CompTIA Network+ Practice Exam," offers a practice exam containing 100 questions similar in content and presentation to the multiple-choice questions you will find on CompTIA's Network+ examination.

Features

To aid you in fully understanding networking concepts, this text includes many features designed to enhance your learning experience.

- *On the Job stories*—Each chapter begins with a real-world story giving context for the technology and concepts presented, providing insight into a variety of modern computing environments from the various perspectives of many different professionals in the IT industry.
- *Chapter Objectives*—Each chapter lists the concepts to be mastered within that chapter. This list serves as a quick reference to the chapter's contents and a useful study aid.
- *Applying Concepts activities*—Embedded within each chapter are activities with step-by-step instructions to help you apply concepts as you learn them.
- *Colorful illustrations, photos, tables, and bullet lists*—Numerous full-color illustrations and photos of network media, protocol behavior, hardware, topology, software screens, peripherals, and components help you visualize common network elements, theories, and concepts. In addition, the many tables and bulleted lists provide details and comparisons of both practical and theoretical information.
- *OSI layer icons*—These icons provide visual reinforcement of the link between concepts and the relevant layers of the OSI model. A thorough understanding of where concepts sit on the OSI model makes managing and troubleshooting networks more effective and efficient.
- *CompTIA Network+ Exam Tips and Notes*—Each chapter's content is supplemented with Note features that provide additional insight and understanding, while CompTIA Network+ Exam Tips guide you in your preparations for taking the CompTIA Network+ certification exam.
- *Legacy Networking features*—Older technology covered by the CompTIA Network+ exam provides historical reference to current technology.
- *Key Terms and Glossary*—Highlighted key terms emphasize the core concepts of networking and are defined in the convenient Glossary.

- *Chapter Summaries*—Each chapter's text is followed by a summary of the concepts introduced in that chapter. These summaries help you revisit the ideas covered in each chapter.
- *Review Questions*—The end-of-chapter assessment begins with a set of review questions that reinforce the ideas introduced in each chapter. Many questions are situational. Rather than simply asking you to repeat what you learned, these questions help you evaluate and apply the material you learned. Answering these questions will help ensure that you have mastered the important concepts and provide valuable practice for taking CompTIA's Network+ exam.
- *Hands-On Projects*—Although it is important to understand the theory behind networking technology, nothing beats real-world experience. To this end, each chapter provides several Hands-On Projects aimed at providing you with practical software and hardware implementation experience as well as practice in applying critical thinking skills to the concepts learned throughout the chapter.
- *Capstone Projects*—Each chapter concludes with two or three in-depth projects where you implement the skills and knowledge gained in the chapter through real design and implementation scenarios in a variety of computing environments. With the help of sophisticated virtualization and emulation products you can get free online, the Capstone Projects introduce you to a multitude of real-world software, hardware, and other solutions that increase your familiarity with these products in preparation for addressing workforce challenges.

New to This Edition

- Content maps completely to CompTIA's Network+ N10-007 exam for productive exam preparation.
- New arrangement of content consolidates similar concepts for efficient coverage, allowing for deeper investigation of particularly rich concepts and skills that are emphasized in the latest CompTIA Network+ N10-007 exam, including a stronger emphasis on security, troubleshooting, and virtualization, with added coverage of VLANs, IoT, and fiber-optic technology.
- Interactive learning features throughout each chapter make essential information easily accessible with insightful diagrams, useful tables for quick reference, and bulleted lists that present condensed information in easy-to-digest chunks.
- Applying Concepts activities embedded in each chapter help solidify concepts as you read through the chapter and provide immediate practice of relevant skills.
- New and updated skills-based projects encourage hands-on exploration of chapter concepts. These projects include thought-provoking questions that encourage critical thinking and in-depth evaluation of the material. The software tools used in the projects are included in Windows or freely available online, and hardware requirements are kept to a minimum, making these projects accessible to more students and more schools.

- Capstone Projects at the end of each chapter challenge you to explore concepts and apply skills with real-world tools. Many Capstone Projects employ Cisco's network simulator, Packet Tracer, so you can practice setting up a network from start to finish, including device configuration, subnetting, and extensive use of the command line.
- Supplemental steps in many projects guide you in creating a customized wiki to document information learned and projects completed. The final project gives tips for organizing this wiki as a way to display your new skills for job interviews.

Text and Graphic Conventions

Wherever appropriate, additional information and exercises have been added to this text to help you better understand the topic at hand. The following labels and icons are used throughout the text to alert you to additional materials:

Note

The Note icon draws your attention to helpful material related to the subject being described.

Network+ Exam Tip (i)

The CompTIA Network+ Exam Tip icon provides helpful pointers when studying for the exam.

OSI model icons highlight the specific layer(s) of the OSI model being discussed, and indicate when the layers of interest change throughout the chapter.

7	APPLICATION
6	PRESENTATION
5	SESSION
4	TRANSPORT
3	NETWORK
2	DATA LINK
1	PHYSICAL

Hands-On Projects

Each Hands-On Project in this book is preceded by a description of the project. Hands-On Projects help you understand the theory behind networking with activities using the latest network software and hardware.

Capstone Projects

Capstone Projects are more in-depth assignments that require a higher level of concept application. They challenge you to demonstrate a solid understanding and application of skills required for the CompTIA Network+ exam and a career in networking.

 ## Certification

Each main section of a chapter begins with a list of all relevant CompTIA Network+ objectives covered in that section. This unique feature highlights the important information at a glance and helps you better anticipate how deeply you need to understand the concepts covered.

Instructor's Materials

The instructor's materials provide everything you need for your course in one place. This collection of book-specific lecture and class tools is available online. Please visit *login.cengage.com* and log in to access instructor-specific resources on the Instructor Companion Site, which includes the Instructor's Manual, Solutions Manual, test creation tools, PowerPoint Presentations, Syllabus, and figure files.

- **Electronic Instructor's Manual**. The Instructor's Manual that accompanies this textbook provides additional instructional materials to assist in class preparation, including suggestions for lecture topics.
- **Solutions Manual**. The instructor's resources include solutions to all end-of-chapter material, including review questions and projects.
- **Cengage Testing Powered by Cognero**. This flexible, online system allows you to do the following:
  - Author, edit, and manage test bank content from multiple Cengage solutions.
  - Create multiple test versions in an instant.
  - Deliver tests from your LMS, your classroom, or wherever you want.
- **PowerPoint Presentations**. This book comes with a set of Microsoft PowerPoint slides for each chapter. These slides are meant to be used as a teaching aid for classroom presentations, to be made available to students on the network for chapter review, or to be printed for classroom distribution. Instructors are also at liberty to add their own slides for other topics introduced.
- **Figure Files**. All the figures and tables in the book are included as a teaching aid for classroom presentation, to make available to students for review, or to be printed for classroom distribution.

MindTap

MindTap for West/Andrews/Dean's *Network+ Guide to Networks, Eighth Edition* is a personalized, fully online digital learning platform of content, assignments, and services that engages students and encourages them to think critically, while allowing you to easily set your course through simple customization options. MindTap is designed to help students master the skills they need in today's workforce. Research shows employers need critical thinkers, troubleshooters, and creative problem solvers to stay relevant in our fast paced, technology-driven world.

MindTap helps you achieve this with assignments and activities that provide hands-on practice, real-life relevance, and certification test prep. Students are guided through assignments that help them master basic knowledge and understanding before moving on to more challenging problems.

The live virtual machine labs provide real-life application and practice as well as more advanced learning. Students work in a live environment via the Cloud with real servers and networks that they can explore. Traditional labs using school computers, networks, hardware, and other tools are included as interactive PDF files. These traditional labs tackle hands-on skills, troubleshooting, critical thinking, and strategies for designing and implementing new and upgraded networks in real-life environments. The IQ certification testprep engine allows students to quiz themselves on specific exam domains, and the pre- and post-course assessments measure exactly how much they have learned. Readings, lab simulations, capstone projects, and whiteboard videos support the lecture, while "In the News" assignments encourage students to stay informed of current developments in the networking and IT industries.

MindTap is designed around learning objectives and provides the analytics and reporting to easily see where the class stands in terms of progress, engagement, and completion rates. Use the content and learning path as is or pick and choose how our materials will wrap around yours.

Students can access eBook content in the MindTap Reader, which offers highlighting, note-taking, search and audio (students can listen to text), as well as mobile access. Learn more at http://www.cengage.com/mindtap/.

Instant Access Code: (ISBN: 9781337569415)
Printed Access Code: (ISBN: 9781337569422)

Bloom's Taxonomy

Bloom's Taxonomy is an industry-standard classification system used to help identify the level of ability that learners need to demonstrate proficiency. It is often used to classify educational learning objectives into different levels of complexity. Bloom's Taxonomy reflects the "cognitive process dimension." This represents a continuum of increasing cognitive complexity, from remember (lowest level) to create (highest level).

There are six categories in Bloom's Taxonomy as seen in Figure A. In all instances, the level of coverage for each domain in *Network+ Guide to Networks, Eighth Edition* meets or exceeds the Bloom's Taxonomy level indicated by CompTIA for that objective. See Appendix A for more detail.

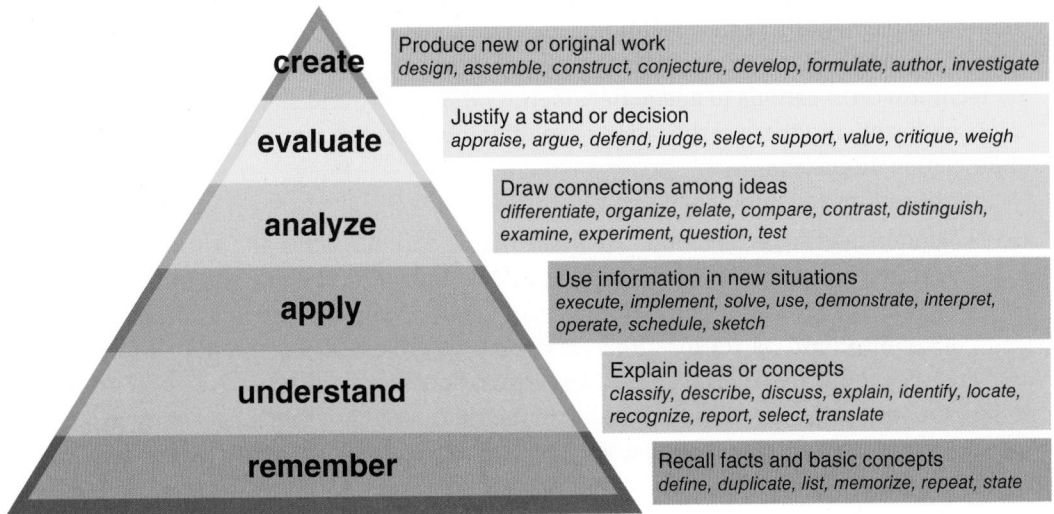

State of the Information Technology (IT) Field

Organizations depend on computers and information technology to thrive and grow. Globalization, or connecting with customers and suppliers around the world, is a direct result of the widespread use of the Internet. Rapidly changing technology further affects how companies do business and keeps the demand for skilled and certified IT workers strong across industries. Every sector of the economy requires IT professionals who can establish, maintain, troubleshoot, and extend their business systems.

The latest *Occupational Outlook Handbook* from the Bureau of Labor Statistics (part of the U.S. Department of Labor) reports that there were more than 390,000 network and computer systems administrator positions in 2016, the most recent year for which this information is available, with a predicted increase of 6 percent between 2016 and 2026. Median pay for jobs in this sector is almost $80,000 annually.

In any industry, a skilled workforce is important for continually driving business. Finding highly skilled IT workers can be a struggle for employers, given that technologies change approximately every two years. With such a quick product life cycle, IT workers must strive to keep up with these changes to continually bring value to their employers.

Certifications

Different levels of education are required for the many jobs in the IT industry. While the level of education and type of training required varies from employer to employer, the need for qualified technicians remains a constant. As technology changes and advances in the industry evolve, many employers prefer candidates who already have the skills to implement these new technologies. Traditional degrees and diplomas do not identify the skills that a job applicant possesses. Companies are relying increasingly on technical certifications to adequately identify the quality and skill qualifications of a job applicant, and these certifications can offer job seekers a competitive edge over their competition.

Certifications fall into one of two categories:

- Vendor-neutral certifications are those that test for the skills and knowledge required in specific industry job roles and do not subscribe to a vendor's specific technology solutions. Some examples of vendor-neutral certifications include all of the CompTIA certifications *(comptia.org)*, Project Management Institute's certifications *(pmi.org)*, and ISACA's certifications *(isaca.org)*.
- Vendor-specific certifications validate the skills and knowledge necessary to be successful while utilizing a specific vendor's technology solution. Some examples of vendor-specific certifications include those offered by Microsoft *(microsoft.com)*, Red Hat *(redhat.com)*, Oracle *(education.oracle.com)*, and Cisco *(learningnetwork.cisco.com)*.

As employers struggle to fill open IT positions with qualified candidates, certifications are a means of validating the skill sets necessary to be successful within organizations. In most careers, salary and compensation are determined by experience and education, but in the IT field, the number and type of certifications an employee earns also determine salary and wage increases. For example, according to CompTIA, the U.S. Department of Defense and companies such as Apple, Cisco, Dell, HP, and Intel recommend or require their networking technicians attain CompTIA Network+ certification. Global Knowledge Training reports that certified IT staff earn, on average, $8,400 or 11.7 percent more than non-certified IT staff. According to the same report, nearly two-thirds of IT professionals in networking reported pursuing additional training in 2016 for the purpose of obtaining additional certifications.

Certification provides job applicants with more than just a competitive edge over their noncertified counterparts competing for the same IT positions. Some institutions of higher education grant college credit to students who successfully pass certification exams, moving them further along in their degree programs. Certification also gives individuals who are interested in careers in the military the ability to move into higher positions more quickly.

CompTIA.

Becoming a CompTIA Certified IT Professional is Easy

It's also the best way to reach greater professional opportunities and rewards.

Why Get CompTIA Certified?

Growing Demand

Labor estimates predict some technology fields will experience growth of over 20% by the year 2020.* CompTIA certification qualifies the skills required to join this workforce.

Higher Salaries

IT professionals with certifications on their resume command better jobs, earn higher salaries and have more doors open to new multi-industry opportunities.

Verified Strengths

91% of hiring managers indicate CompTIA certifications are valuable in validating IT expertise, making certification the best way to demonstrate your competency and knowledge to employers.**

Universal Skills

CompTIA certifications are vendor neutral—which means that certified professionals can proficiently work with an extensive variety of hardware and software found in most organizations.

 **Learn**  **Certify**  **Work**

Learn more about what the exam covers by reviewing the following:

- Exam objectives for key study points.
- Sample questions for a general overview of what to expect on the exam and examples of question format.
- Visit online forums, like LinkedIn, to see what other IT professionals say about CompTIA exams.

Purchase a voucher at a Pearson VUE testing center or at CompTIAstore.com.

- Register for your exam at a Pearson VUE testing center:
- Visit pearsonvue.com/CompTIA to find the closest testing center to you.
- Schedule the exam online. You will be required to enter your voucher number or provide payment information at registration.
- Take your certification exam.

Congratulations on your CompTIA certification!

- Make sure to add your certification to your resume.
- Check out the CompTIA Certification Roadmap to plan your next career move.

Learn more: Certification.CompTIA.org/networkplus

* Source: CompTIA 9th Annual Information Security Trends study: 500 U.S. IT and Business Executives Responsible for Security
** Source: CompTIA Employer Perceptions of IT Training and Certification

Career Planning

Finding a career that fits a person's personality, skill set, and lifestyle is challenging and fulfilling, but can often be difficult. What are the steps individuals should take to find that dream career? Is IT interesting to you? Chances are, if you are reading this book, this question has already been answered. What is it about IT that you like? The world of work options in the IT industry is vast. Some questions to ask yourself: Are you a person who likes to work alone, or do you like to work in a group? Do you like speaking directly with customers, or do you prefer to stay behind the scenes? Does your lifestyle encourage a lot of travel, or do you need to stay in one location? All these factors influence your job decisions. Inventory assessments are a good first step to learning more about yourself, your interests, work values, and abilities. A variety of websites can offer assistance with career planning and assessments.

What's New with CompTIA Network+ Certification

With its N10-007 Network+ exam, CompTIA has emphasized foundational network concepts and the latest network technologies that can serve as a launching pad for a career in networking, security, or other specialties. There's a stronger emphasis on security, virtualization, and troubleshooting. Some objectives have been added, updated, or expanded, such as coverage of IoT (Internet of Things), fiber-optic technology, and VLANs. A few older technologies have been dropped from the objectives. However, bear in mind that some legacy protocols and standards appear in the objectives' list of acronyms, and the CompTIA Network+ exam could refer to them.

As with the previous Network+ exam, the N10-007 version includes many scenario-based questions. Mastering, rather than simply memorizing, the material in this text will help you succeed on the exam and on the job.

Here are the domains covered on the new CompTIA Network+ exam:

Domain	% of Examination
Domain 1.0 Networking Concepts	23%
Domain 2.0 Infrastructure	18%
Domain 3.0 Network Operations	17%
Domain 4.0 Network Security	20%
Domain 5.0 Network Troubleshooting and Tools	22%

About the Authors

Jill West brings a unique cross-section of experience in business, writing, and education to the development of innovative educational materials. She has taught multiple ages and content areas using a flipped classroom, distance learning, and educational counseling. Jill currently teaches at Georgia Northwestern Technical College, and she has over a decade's experience working with Jean Andrews in textbook and digital content development, co-authoring *Network+ Guide to Networks, Eighth Edition, A+ Guide to IT Technical Support, Ninth Edition*, and the *Lab Manual for A+ Guide to Hardware, Ninth Edition*. Jill and her husband Mike live in northwest Georgia where they homeschool their four children.

Jean Andrews has more than 30 years of experience in the computer industry, including more than 13 years in the college classroom. She has worked in a variety of businesses and corporations designing, writing, and supporting application software; managing a PC repair help desk; and troubleshooting wide area networks. She has written numerous books on software, hardware, and the Internet, including the best-selling *A+ Guide to IT Technical Support, Ninth Edition, A+ Guide to Hardware, Ninth Edition*, and *A+ Guide to Software, Ninth Edition*. She lives in northern Georgia.

Tamara Dean has worked in the field of networking for nearly 20 years, most recently as a networking consultant, and before that, as the manager of Internet services and data center operations for a regional ISP. She has managed LANs at the University of Wisconsin and at a pharmaceutical firm, worked as a telecommunications analyst for the FCC, and cofounded a local radio station. Well published in networking, Ms. Dean also authored *Guide to Telecommunications Technology* for Cengage Learning.

Acknowledgments

It's stunning to see how many people contribute to the creation of a textbook. We're privileged and humbled to work with an amazing team of folks who consistently demonstrate professionalism and excellence. First, thank you to Ann Shaffer, Developmental Editor, for smoothing out awkward phrases, encouraging us through long nights and intense deadlines, and suggesting good movies to look forward to after the book is finished. Thank you to Michelle Ruelos Cannistraci, Senior Content Developer, for steady and attentive leadership. Thank you to Brooke Greenhouse, Senior Content Project Manager, for your flexibility and commitment to excellence. Thank you to Amy Savino, Associate Product Manager, for your enthusiastic vision and support. Thank you to all of the following for your attention to detail, resourceful solutions, and creative ideas: Kristin McNary, Product Team Manager; Jake Toth, Product Assistant; and Cassie Cloutier, Associate Marketing Manager. A special thanks to John Freitas, Technical Editor, for your careful review of the entire manuscript.

Many more people contributed time, expertise, and advice during the course of this revision. Every contribution has made this book better than it would have been without your help. Thank you to Jeffrey Johnson, Georgia Northwestern Technical College, for the enlightening tour and computer geek chit-chat. Thank you to Robert Wilson, McCallie School, for the continued tours, stories, and insights. And thanks to all the amazing instructors who have attended our Network+ training sessions and shared their thoughts, creativity, ideas, and concerns. Thank you to each of the reviewers who, driven by your dedication to high-quality education for your students, contributed a great deal of expertise, constantly challenging us to higher levels of insight, accuracy, and clarity. Specifically, thank you to:

Johnathan Yerby, Middle Georgia State University
Ronald Martin, Augusta University Cyber Institute
Terry Richburg, Trident Technical College
Alexey Petrenko, Austin Community College
Joshua Adams, Saint Leo University

To the instructors and learners who use this book, we invite and encourage you to send suggestions or corrections for future editions. Please write to us at *jillwestauthor@ gmail.com*. We never ignore a good idea! And to instructors, if you have ideas that help make a class in CompTIA Network+ preparation a success, please share your ideas with other instructors!

Dedication

This book is dedicated to the covenant of God with man on earth.

Jill West
Jean Andrews, Ph.D.

I'd like to say a personal thank you to my kiddos, Jessica, Sarah, Daniel, and Zack: Thank you for your patience and your hugs and kisses during the long work hours. To my husband, Mike: You mean the world to me. This is your accomplishment, too.

Jill West

Read This Before You Begin

The Applying Concepts activities, Hands-On Projects, and Capstone Projects in this text help you to apply what you have learned about computer networking. Although some modern networking components can be expensive, the projects aim to use widely available and moderately priced hardware and software. The following section lists the minimum hardware and software requirements that allow you to complete all the projects in this text. In addition to the following requirements, students must have administrator privileges on their workstations and, for some projects, on a second workstation, to successfully complete the projects.

Hardware Lab Requirements

- Each student workstation computer requires at least 4 GB of RAM (preferably 8 GB), a recent Intel or AMD processor, and a minimum of 20 GB of free space on the hard disk. Many projects require workstations to have a wired connection to a network, and other projects need a wireless connection.

- Some projects require the use of a second workstation in order to create a network connection between computers. The second computer has the same minimum requirements as the first one. In most cases, this computer could be another student's workstation and the students work in pairs.
- For projects with physical transmission media, students require a networking toolkit that includes the following cable-making supplies: at least 30 feet of Cat 5 or better cabling, at least five RJ-45 plugs, an RJ-45 data/phone jack, a wire cutter, a wire stripper, a crimper, and a punchdown tool.
- For projects with wireless transmission, each class (or each group in the class) should have a wireless SOHO router capable of 802.11n or 802.11ac transmission and compatible wireless NICs in the student workstations.
- For implementing a basic client-server network, a class (or each group in the class) requires a small, consumer-grade switch and two or more Cat 5 or better straight-through patch cables that are each at least 3 feet long.
- One project requires each student to have a smartphone (Android or iPhone). Students can do this project in pairs for those students who don't own a smartphone.
- One project requires a cable modem for the class to examine.
- Many projects require Internet access with a modern browser.

Software Lab Requirements

Most projects are written for workstations running Windows 10. Many include instructions for modifying the steps to work with computers running a different operating system than the one specified in that project, or the steps can be easily adapted. Software requirements include:

- Windows 10 Professional (64-bit) with the Creators Update or better for each student workstation. Most of the steps can be modified for other versions and editions of Windows, including Windows 10 Home and Windows 8.1. Most of the projects can be adapted to work on Linux or macOS workstations.
- The latest version of Chrome, Firefox, or Edge web browser.
- A hypervisor—most projects are written for Oracle VirtualBox or Client Hyper-V (Windows 10 Professional only), and can be adjusted for VMware Workstation Player.
- An installation image for Windows.
- Steps to download installation images for other OSes are given in the projects. These OSes include Ubuntu Desktop, Ubuntu Server, and Kali Linux.
- Other software that will be downloaded include: LastPass, ZenMap, Spiceworks Inventory, FileZilla, Bash on Ubuntu on Windows, Wireshark, LAN Speed Test, Throughput Test, vsftpd, ufw, Wi-Fi analyzer app (on smartphone), NetStress, Packet Tracer, Remote Desktop Manager, Hide.me VPN, ssh, Sandboxie, and Advanced Port Scanner.

Cisco's Packet Tracer is now available free to the public. Instructions for downloading and installing Packet Tracer are given in the first Packet Tracer project in Chapter 6. Abbreviated instructions are also repeated here for convenience, as some instructors might want to preview the emulator:

1. Go to **netacad.com/campaign/ptdt-4** or search for *packet tracer site:netacad.com* for the latest link. Enter your information to enroll in the course.
2. Open the confirmation email, confirm your email address, and configure your account. Click the **Introduction to Packet Tracer** tile.
3. Inside the course, check the Student Resources for the link to download Packet Tracer or begin with the first lessons, which will walk you through the process of installing Packet Tracer. Download the correct version for your computer, and then install Packet Tracer. Note that the download might not complete in the MS Edge browser; if you encounter a problem, try Google Chrome instead. When the installation is complete, run Cisco Packet Tracer.
4. When Packet Tracer opens, sign in with your Networking Academy account that you just created.

## CHAPTER 1

INTRODUCTION TO NETWORKING

After reading this chapter and completing the exercises, you will be able to:

Distinguish between client-server and peer-to-peer networks
- -
Identify types of applications and protocols used on a network
- -
Describe various networking hardware devices and the most common physical topologies
- -
Describe the seven layers of the OSI model
- -
Explain best practices for safety when working with networks and computers
- -
Describe the seven-step troubleshooting model for solving a networking problem

On the Job

I work as a contractor for an organization that uses specialized software to project an image on three screens for a weekly event. The computer is connected to a multimedia transmitter that communicates with receivers connected to each projector. In addition, the projectors are connected via twisted-pair cables and a router so they can be turned on/off from the computer. The configuration had been working well for several years.

Then suddenly one of the screens began to flicker randomly. I checked the software preferences, display settings, and cable connections. Everything appeared to be correct. The next week, the random flicker appeared more frequently. Again, I checked the software and cabling. The following week, the random flicker persisted and the frequency increased. I had to turn off the projector because the flicker was so distracting.

I contacted the company that installed the video system and asked them to perform some hardware troubleshooting. They checked each receiver and transmitter. In addition to checking the software, they connected an I-Pad directly to the problematic projector. After testing several videos, they determined that the projector's HDMI port had gone bad. The projector had to be replaced. Once the new projector was installed, the flickering problem was no longer an issue.

Angela Watkins
Instructor, Computer and Engineering Technology
Spartanburg Community College

Loosely defined, a **network** is a group of computers and other devices (such as printers) that are connected by some type of transmission media. Variations on the elements of a network and the way it is designed, however, are nearly infinite. A network can be as small as two computers connected by a cable in a home office or the largest network of all, the Internet, made up of billions of computers and other devices connected across the world via a combination of cable, phone lines, and wireless links. Networks might link cell phones, personal computers, mainframe computers, printers, corporate phone systems, security cameras, vehicles, and wearable technology devices. They might communicate through copper wires, fiber-optic cable, or radio waves. This chapter introduces you to the fundamentals of networks and how technicians support them.

Network Models

1.5 Compare and contrast the characteristics of network topologies, types, and technologies.

A **topology** describes how the parts of a whole work together. When studying networking, you need to understand both the physical topology and the logical topology of a network:

- *physical topology*—Mostly refers to a network's hardware and how computers, other devices, and cables fit together to form the physical network.

- *logical topology*—Has to do with software, how access to the network is controlled, including how users and programs initially gain access to the network, and how specific resources, such as applications and databases, are shared on the network.

We begin here with a discussion of the network models that help us understand logical topologies and how computers relate to one another in a network. Later in this chapter, you'll learn about network hardware and physical topologies.

Controlling how users and programs get access to resources on a network is a function of the operating systems used on the network. Each OS (operating system) is configured to use one of two models to connect to network resources: the peer-to-peer model or the client-server model. The peer-to-peer model can be achieved using any assortment of desktop, mobile, or tablet operating systems, but the client-server model requires one or more **NOSes (network operating systems)**, which control access to the entire network. Examples of NOSes are Windows Server 2016, Ubuntu Server, and Red Hat Enterprise Linux (Ubuntu and Red Hat are versions of Linux).

Applying Concepts: Explore Network Operating Systems

It's easier to understand what a network operating system is if you've seen one or two in action. For each of the NOSes listed previously (Windows Server 2016, Ubuntu Server, and Red Hat Enterprise Linux), use your favorite search engine to complete the following steps:

1. Search for information about the NOS and write down a short description based on your findings.
2. Search for images of screenshots for the NOS. What are some major elements that you notice on these screens?
3. Find one or two introductory videos for each NOS and watch the videos. What are some similarities between the NOSes? What are some of the differences?

Peer-to-Peer Network Model

Using a **P2P (peer-to-peer) network model**, the operating system of each computer on the network is responsible for controlling access to its resources without centralized control. The computers, called nodes or hosts on the network, form a logical group of computers and users that share resources (see Figure 1-1). Each computer on a P2P network controls its own administration, resources, and security.

Examples of operating systems that might be installed on computers in a peer-to-peer network are Windows, Linux, and macOS on desktop and laptop computers and iOS, Android, and BlackBerry on mobile devices.

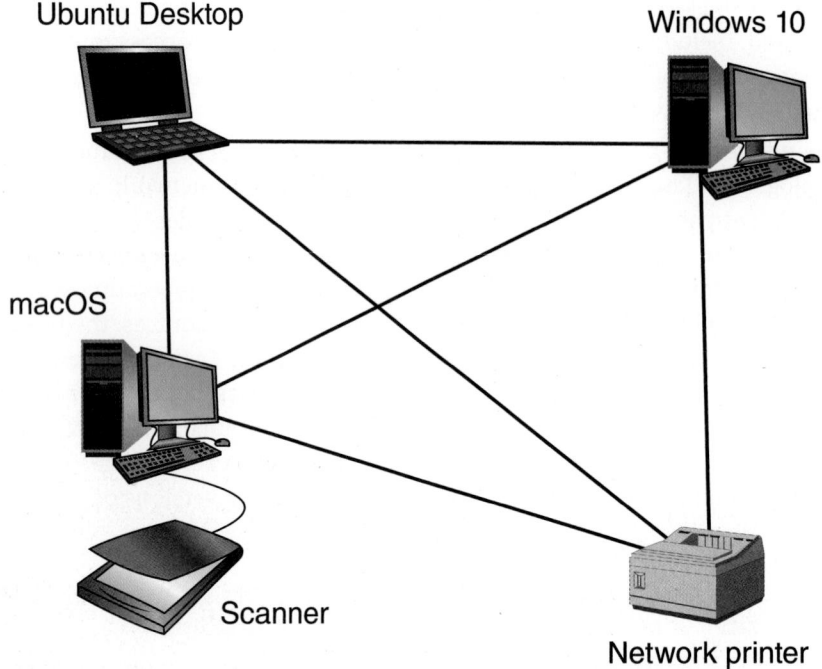

Figure 1-1   In a peer-to-peer network, no computer has more authority than another; each computer controls its own resources, and communicates directly with other computers

Note

When looking at the diagrams in Figure 1-1 and later in Figure 1-2, keep in mind that the connecting lines describe the *logical* arrangement or topology of the group of computers, as opposed to the *physical* arrangement. The physical arrangement in both diagrams may be the same, but the method the OSes use to logically connect differs.

If all computers in a peer-to-peer network are running a Windows operating system, resources can be shared in these ways:

- Using Windows folder and file sharing, each computer maintains a list of users and their rights on that particular computer. Windows allows a user on the network to access local resources based on these assigned rights.
- Using a workgroup, each computer maintains a list of users and their rights on that particular computer. The computer allows a user on the network to access local resources based on the rights given.

- Using a homegroup, each computer shares files, folders, libraries, and printers with other computers in the homegroup. A homegroup limits how sharing can be controlled for individual users because any user of any computer in the homegroup can access homegroup resources.

You can also use a combination of folder and file sharing, workgroups, and homegroups on the same network and even using the same computers. In fact, workgroups and homegroups often coexist on a network. Mixing in folder and file sharing with workgroups and homegroups, however, can get confusing, so it's best to stick with either folder and file sharing or workgroups and homegroups.

Note ✐

This book assumes you are already aware of the knowledge and skills covered in the CompTIA A+ certification objectives. Using and supporting homegroups and sharing folders and files are part of this content. If you need to learn how workgroups, homegroups, and folder and file sharing are configured and supported, see *A+ Guide to IT Technical Support,* by Jean Andrews, Joy Dark, and Jill West.

Generally, if the network supports fewer than 15 computers, a peer-to-peer network is the way to go. The following are advantages of using peer-to-peer networks:

- They are simple to configure. For this reason, they may be used in environments in which time or technical expertise is scarce.
- They are often less expensive to set up and maintain than other types of networks. A network operating system, such as Windows Server 2016, is much more expensive than a desktop operating system, such as Windows 10 Professional.

The following are disadvantages of using traditional peer-to-peer networks:

- They are not scalable, which means, as a peer-to-peer network grows larger, adding or changing significant elements of the network may be difficult.
- They are not necessarily secure, meaning that in simple installations, data and other resources shared by network users can be easily discovered and used by unauthorized people.
- They are not practical for connecting more than a few computers because it's too time consuming to manage the resources on the network. For example, suppose you want to set up a file server. A server is any computer or program that provides a service, such as data or other resources, to other devices. A file server stores files for other computers to access. On this file server, you create a folder named \SharedDocs and create 12 local accounts, one for each of 12 users

who need access to the folder. Then you must set up the workstations with the same local accounts, and the password to each local account on the workstation must match the password for the matching local account on the file server. It can be an organizational nightmare to keep it all straight! If you need to manage that many users and shared resources, it's probably best to implement Windows Server or another NOS.

Client-Server Network Model

In the **client-server network model** (which is sometimes called the client-server architecture or client-server topology), resources are managed by the NOS via a centralized directory database (see Figure 1-2). The database can be managed by one or more servers, so long as they each have a similar NOS installed.

When Windows Server controls network access to a group of computers, this logical group is called a Windows **domain**. The centralized directory database that contains user account information and security for the entire group of computers is called **AD (Active Directory)**. Each user on the network has his/her own domain-level account assigned by the network administrator and kept in Active Directory. This account might be a local account, which is specific to that domain, or a Microsoft account, which links local domain resources with Microsoft cloud resources. A user can sign on to the network from any computer on the network and get access to the resources that Active Directory allows. The process is managed by **AD DS (Active Directory Domain Services)**.

A computer making a request from another is called the **client**. Clients on a client-server network can run applications installed on the desktop and store their own data on local storage devices. Clients don't share their resources directly with each other; instead, access is controlled by entries in the centralized domain database. A client computer accesses resources on another computer by way of the servers controlling this database.

In summary, the NOS (for example, Windows Server 2016, Ubuntu Server, or Red Hat Enterprise Linux) is responsible for:

- Managing data and other resources for a number of clients
- Ensuring that only authorized users access the network
- Controlling which types of files a user can open and read
- Restricting when and from where users can access the network
- Dictating which rules computers will use to communicate
- In some situations, supplying applications and data files to clients

Servers that have an NOS installed require more memory, processing power, and storage capacity than clients because servers are called on to handle heavy processing loads and requests from multiple clients. For example, a server might use a RAID (redundant array of independent disks) configuration of hard drives, so that if one hard drive fails, another hard drive automatically takes its place.

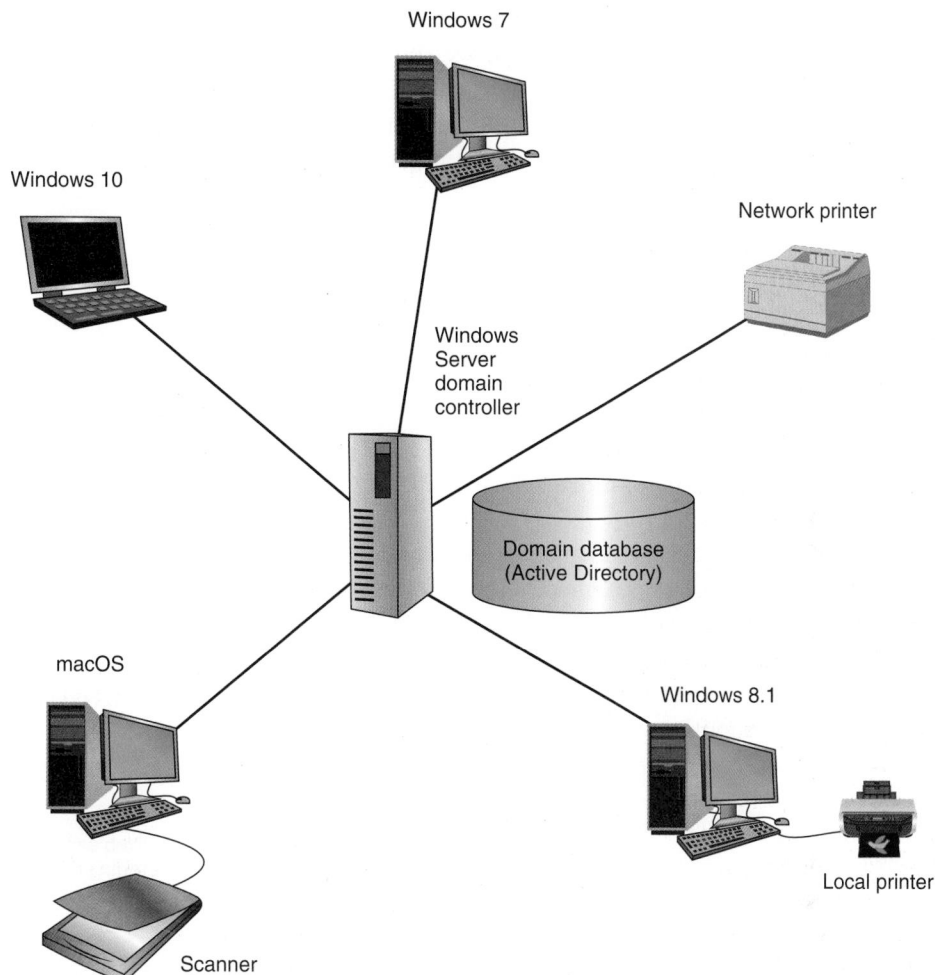

Figure 1-2   A Windows domain uses the client-server model to control access to the network, where security on each computer or device is controlled by a centralized database on a domain controller

Although client-server networks are typically more complex in their design and maintenance than peer-to-peer networks, they offer many advantages over peer-to-peer networks, including:

- User accounts and passwords to the network are assigned in one place.
- Access to multiple shared resources (such as data files or printers) can be centrally granted to a single user or groups of users.
- Problems on the network can be monitored, diagnosed, and often fixed from one location.

- Client-server networks are also more scalable than peer-to-peer networks. In other words, it's easier to add computers and other devices to a client-server network.

We've begun our discussion of network operating systems. Let's look at some of the applications involved in managing the data that travels on a network.

Client-Server Applications

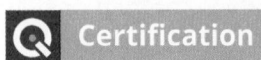

Certification

1.1 Explain the purposes and uses of ports and protocols.

3.4 Given a scenario, use remote access methods.

The resources a network makes available to its users include applications and the data provided by these applications. Collectively, these resources are usually referred to as **network services**. In this section, we'll focus on applications typically found on most networks. These applications, which involve two computers, are known as **client-server applications**. The first computer, a client computer, requests data or a service from the second computer, which is the server. For example, in Figure 1-3, someone uses a web browser to request a web page from a web server.

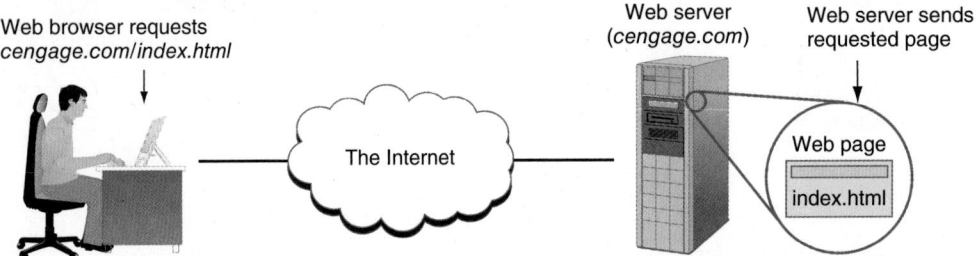

Web browser requests
cengage.com/index.html

The Internet

Web server
(*cengage.com*)

Web server sends
requested page

Web page

index.html

Figure 1-3   A web browser (client application) requests a web page from a web server (server application); the web server returns the requested data to the client

How does the client know how to make the request in a way the server can understand and respond to? These networked devices use methods and rules for communication known as **protocols**. To handle the request for a web page, the client computer must first find the web server. Then, the client and server must agree on the protocols they will use to communicate. Finally, the client makes the request and the server sends its response in the form of a web page. Hardware, the operating systems, and the applications on both computers are all involved in this process.

The computers on a network are able to communicate with each other via the protocols they have in common. The two primary protocols are TCP (Transmission Control Protocol) and IP (Internet Protocol), and the suite of all the protocols an OS uses for communication on a network is the **TCP/IP** suite of protocols.

Here's a brief list of several popular client-server applications and their protocols used on networks and the Internet; we'll look at many of these protocols more closely in later chapters:

- *web service*—A web server serves up web pages to clients. Many corporations have their own web servers, which are available privately on the corporate network. Other web servers are public, accessible from anywhere on the Internet. The primary protocol used by web servers and browsers (clients) is **HTTP (Hypertext Transfer Protocol)**. When HTTP is layered on top of an encryption protocol, such as **SSL (Secure Sockets Layer)** or **TLS (Transport Layer Security)**, the result is **HTTPS (HTTP Secure)**, which gives a secure transmission. The most popular web server application is Apache (see *apache.org*), which primarily runs on UNIX systems, and the second most popular is IIS (Internet Information Services), which is embedded in the Windows Server operating system.

Note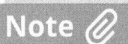

To verify that a web-based transmission is secure, look for "https" in the URL in the browser address box, as in *https://www.wellsfargo.com*.

- *email services*—Email is a client-server application that involves two servers. The client uses **SMTP (Simple Mail Transfer Protocol)** to send an email message to the first server, which is sometimes called the SMTP server (see Figure 1-4). The first server sends the message on to the receiver's mail server, where it's stored until the recipient requests delivery. The recipient's mail server delivers the message to the receiving client using one of two protocols: **POP3 (Post Office Protocol, version 3)** or **IMAP4 (Internet Message Access Protocol, version 4)**. Using POP3, email is downloaded to the client computer. Using IMAP4, the client application manages the email while it's stored on the server. An example of a popular email server application is Microsoft Exchange Server. Outlook, an application in the Microsoft Office suite of applications, is a popular email client application.

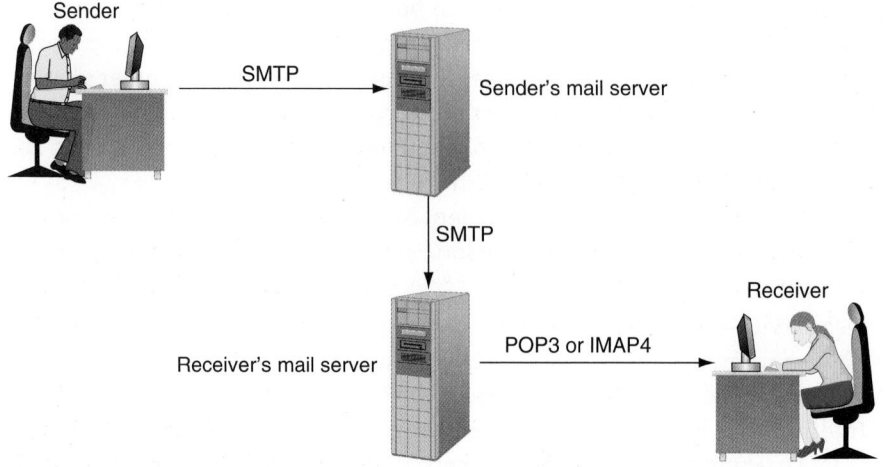

Figure 1-4 SMTP is used to send email to a recipient's email server, and POP3 or IMAP4 is used by the client to receive email

- *FTP service*—FTP is a client-server application that transfers files between two computers, and it primarily uses **FTP (File Transfer Protocol)**. FTP does not provide encryption and is, therefore, not secure. Web browsers can be FTP clients, although dedicated FTP client applications, such as FileZilla (*filezilla-project.org*) and CuteFTP by Globalscape (*cuteftp.com*), offer more features for file transfer than does a browser.

> **Note** 📎
>
> An encrypted and secure file transfer protocol is **SFTP (Secure File Transfer Protocol)**, which is based on the SSH protocol, discussed below.

- *Telnet service*—The **Telnet** protocol is used by the Telnet client-server command-line application to allow an administrator or other user to "remote in" or control a computer remotely. Telnet is included in many operating systems, but transmissions in Telnet are not encrypted, which has caused Telnet to be largely replaced by other, more secure programs, such as the ssh command in the Linux operating system.

> **Note** 📎
>
> The ssh command in Linux uses the **SSH (Secure Shell)** protocol, which creates a secure channel or tunnel between two computers.

- *remote applications*—A **remote application** is an application that is installed and executed on a server and is presented to a user working at a client computer. Windows Server 2008 and later versions include **Remote Desktop Services** to manage remote applications, and versions of Windows Server prior to 2008 provided Terminal Services. Both use RDP (Remote Desktop Protocol) to present the remote application and its data to the client. Remote applications are becoming popular because most of the computing power (memory and CPU speed) and technical support (for application installations and updates and for backing up data) are focused on the server in a centralized location, which means the client computers require less computing power and desk-side support.

- *Remote Desktop*—In Windows operating systems, the Windows Remote Desktop application uses **RDP (Remote Desktop Protocol)** to provide secure, encrypted transmissions that allow a technician to remote in—that is, to access a remote computer from the technician's local computer, as shown in Figure 1-5. For example, when a vendor supports software on your corporate network, the vendor's support technician at the vendor's site can use Remote Desktop to connect to a computer on your corporate network and troubleshoot problems with the vendor's software. The corporate computer serves up its Windows desktop from which the technician can access any resources on your corporate network. In this situation, the vendor's computer is running Remote Desktop as a client and the corporate computer is running Remote Desktop as a server or host.

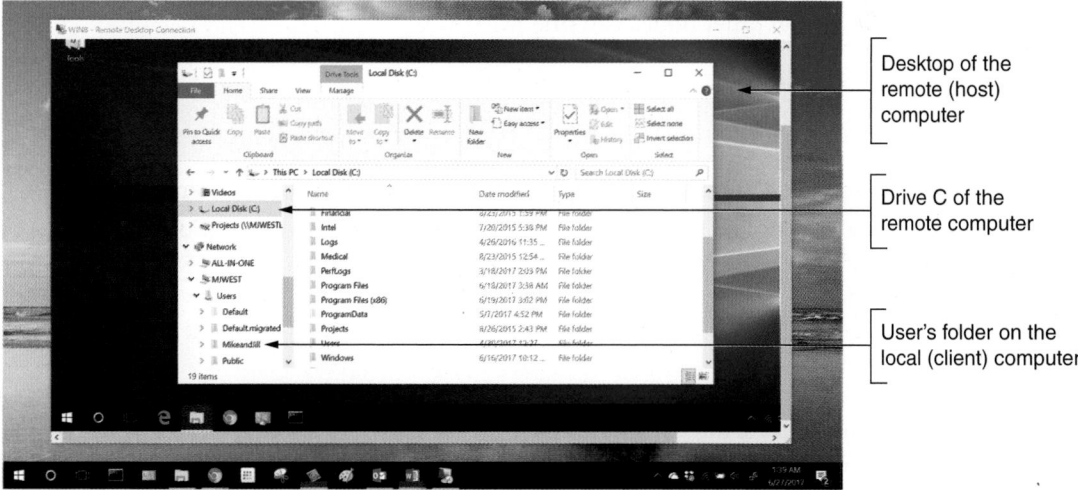

Figure 1-5   Using Remote Desktop, you can access the desktop of the remote computer on your local computer

You can think of applications and their data as the payload traveling on a network and the operating systems as the traffic controllers managing the traffic. The road system itself is the hardware on which the traffic flows. Let's look now at the basics of networking hardware and the physical topologies they use.

Network Hardware

1.5   Compare and contrast the characteristics of network topologies, types, and technologies.

2.2   Given a scenario, determine the appropriate placement of networking devices on a network and install/configure them.

Technically, two computers connected by an ad hoc Wi-Fi connection are a network. But let's start our discussion of networking hardware with the slightly more complex network shown in Figure 1-6. Keep in mind that every node on a network needs a network address so that other nodes can find it.

LANs and Their Hardware

The network in Figure 1-6 is a **LAN (local area network)** because each node on the network can communicate directly with others on the network. LANs are usually contained in a small space, such as an office or building. The five computers and the

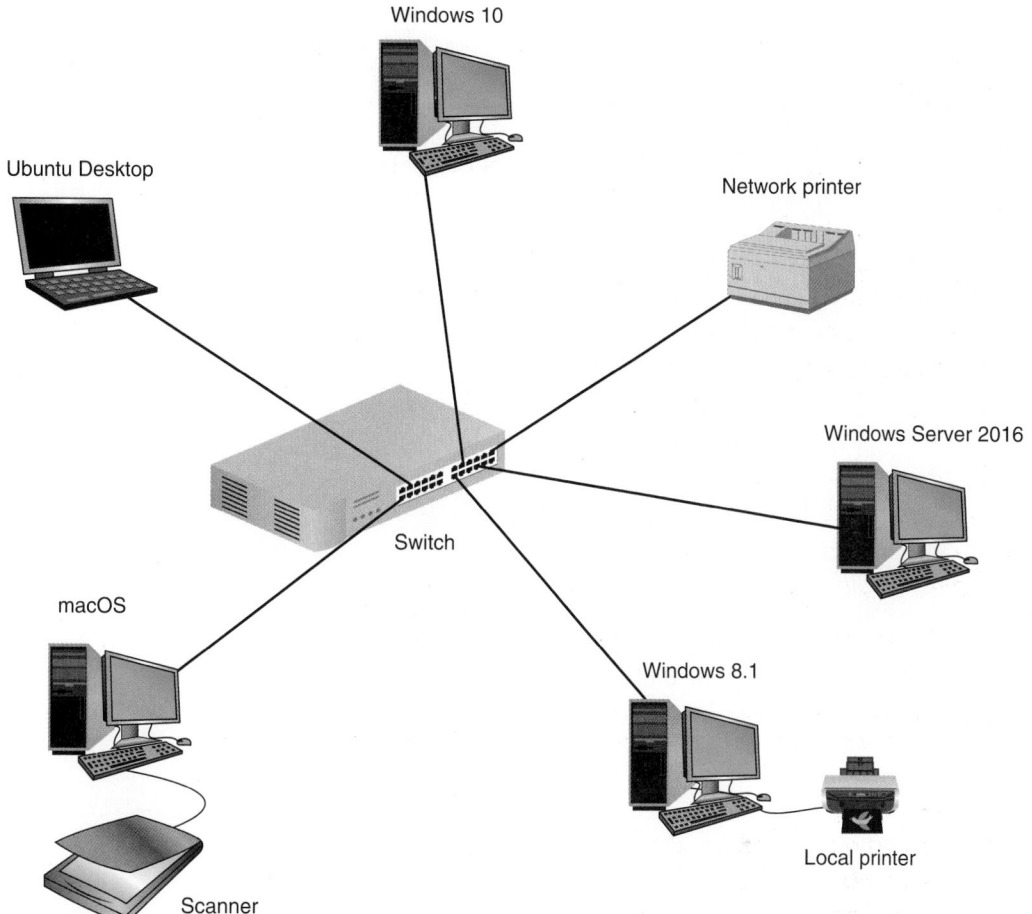

Figure 1-6   This LAN has five computers, a network printer, a local printer, a scanner, and a switch, and is using a star topology

network printer all connect to the switch by way of wired connections. A **switch** (see Figure 1-7) receives incoming data from one of its ports and redirects (switches) it to another port or multiple ports that will send the data to its intended destination(s). The physical topology used by this network is called a **star topology** because all devices connect to one central device, the switch. Compare this to the physical topology of the network shown earlier in Figure 1-1 where each device connects to multiple other devices, which is called a **mesh topology**.

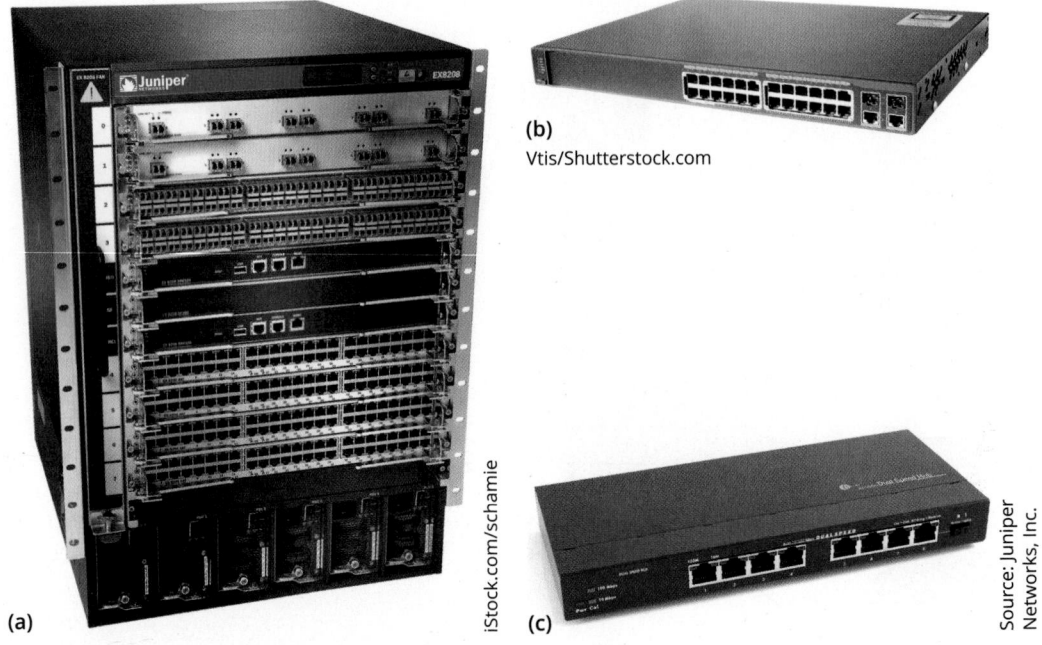

(b)
Vtis/Shutterstock.com

iStock.com/schamie

(a)   **(c)**

Source: Juniper
Networks, Inc.

Figure 1-7   Industrial-grade and consumer-grade switches

Legacy Networking: Hubs

A **hub** is an inefficient and outdated networking device that has been replaced by switches. A hub accepted signals from a transmitting node and repeated those signals to all other connected nodes in a broadcast fashion. On Ethernet networks, hubs once served as the central connection point for a star topology.

On today's Ethernet networks, switches have now replaced hubs. Traffic is greatly reduced with switches because, when a switch receives a transmission from a node, the switch sends it only to the destination node or nodes rather than broadcasting to all nodes connected to the switch.

Computers, network printers, switches, and other network devices have network ports into which you plug a network cable. A network port can be an onboard network port embedded in the computer's motherboard, such as the port on the laptop in Figure 1-8. Another type of port is provided by a **NIC (network interface card)**, also called a network adapter, installed in an expansion slot on the motherboard (see Figure 1-9).

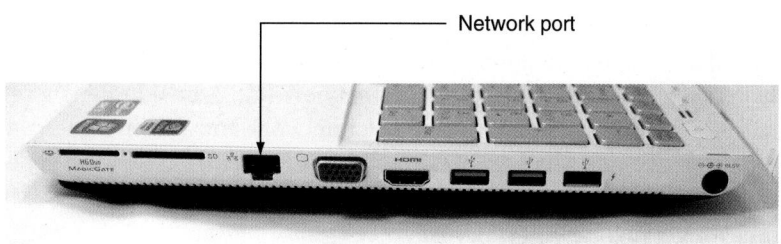

Figure 1-8   A laptop provides an onboard network port to connect to a wired network

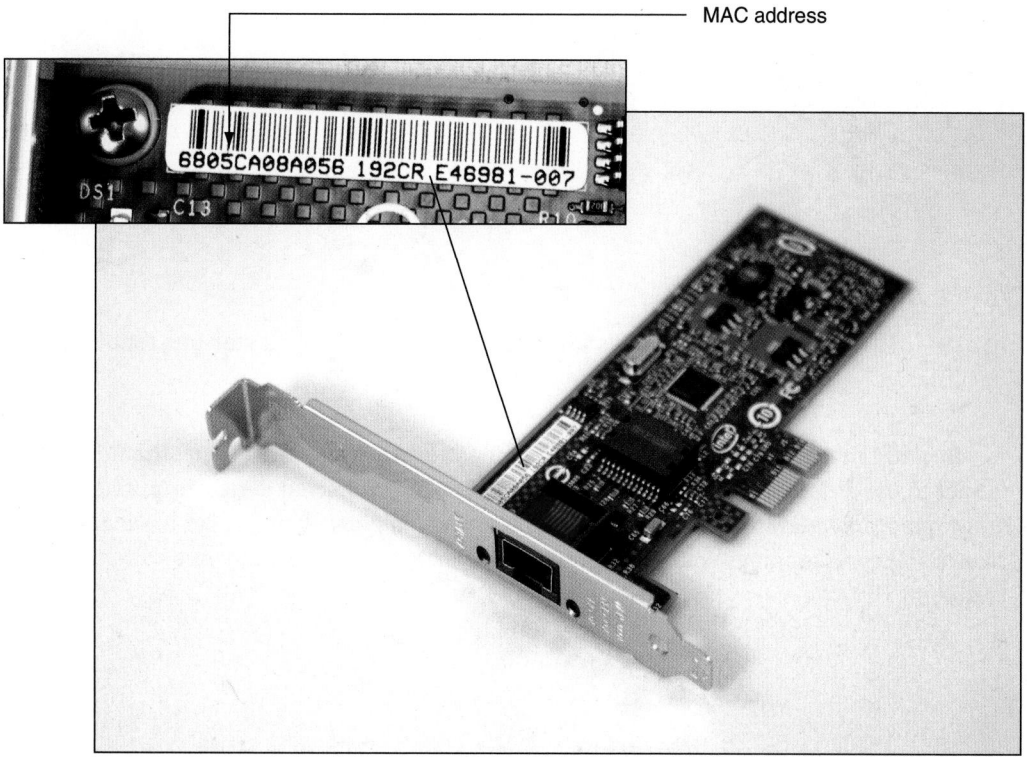

Figure 1-9   This Intel Gigabit Ethernet adapter, also called a network interface card or NIC, uses a PCIe x1 slot on a motherboard

> **Note**
>
> Both onboard and expansion network ports are sometimes called network controllers or network interface controllers (NICs).

A LAN can have several switches. For example, the network in Figure 1-10 has three switches daisy-chained together. The two yellow lines in the figure connecting the three switches represent the backbone of this network. A **backbone** is a central conduit that connects the segments (pieces) of a network and is sometimes referred to as "a network of networks." The backbone might use higher transmission speeds and different cabling than network cables connected to computers because of the heavier traffic and the longer distances it might span.

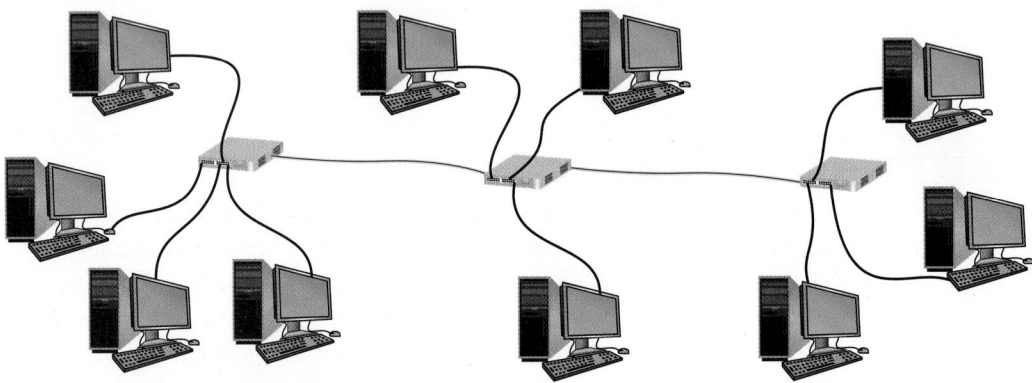

Figure 1-10 This local network has three switches, and is using a star-bus topology

Because the three switches are daisy-chained together in a single line, the network is said to use a **bus topology**. However, each switch is connected to its computers via a star topology. Therefore, the topology of the network in Figure 1-10 is said to be a **star-bus topology**. A topology that combines topologies in this way is known as a **hybrid topology**.

Legacy Networking: Ring Topology

In addition to the bus, star, and mesh topologies, the CompTIA Network+ exam expects you to know about the ring topology, which is seldom used today. In a **ring topology**, nodes are connected in a ring, with one node connecting only to its two neighboring nodes (see Figure 1-11). A node can put data on the ring only when it holds a token, which is a small group of bits passed around the ring. This is similar to saying "I hold the token, so I get to talk now." The ring topology is rarely used today, primarily because of its slow speed.

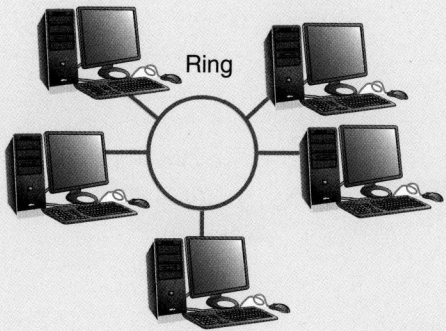

Figure 1-11 Using a ring topology, a computer connects to the two computers adjacent to it in the ring

A LAN needs a way to communicate with other networks, and that's the purpose of a router. A **router** is a device that manages traffic between two or more networks and can help find the best path for traffic to get from one network to another. In **SOHO (small office-home office) networks**, which typically have fewer than 10 computers, a consumer-grade router is used to connect the LAN to the Internet (see Figure 1-12a).

Note 📎

A home network might use a combo device, which is both a router and a switch, and perhaps a wireless access point that creates a Wi-Fi hot spot. For example, the device might provide three network ports and a Wi-Fi hot spot that are part of the local network and one network port to connect to the ISP (Internet service provider) and on to the Internet. In this situation (see Figure 1-12b), the three ports are provided by a switch embedded in the device. The home router belongs to the home's local network on one side and the ISP's local network on the other. Don't confuse this combo device with a dedicated router in which each port connects to a different LAN.

Enterprise and industrial-grade routers can have several network ports, one for each of the networks it connects to. In that case, the router belongs to each of these networks. For example, in Figure 1-13, the router connects three LANs and has a network address that belongs to Network A, another network address that belongs to Network B, and a third network address for Network C.

The fundamental difference between a switch and a router is that a switch belongs only to its local network and a router belongs to two or more local networks. Recall that nodes on a local network communicate directly with one another. However, a host on one LAN cannot communicate with a host on another LAN without a router to manage that communication and stand as a gateway between the networks.

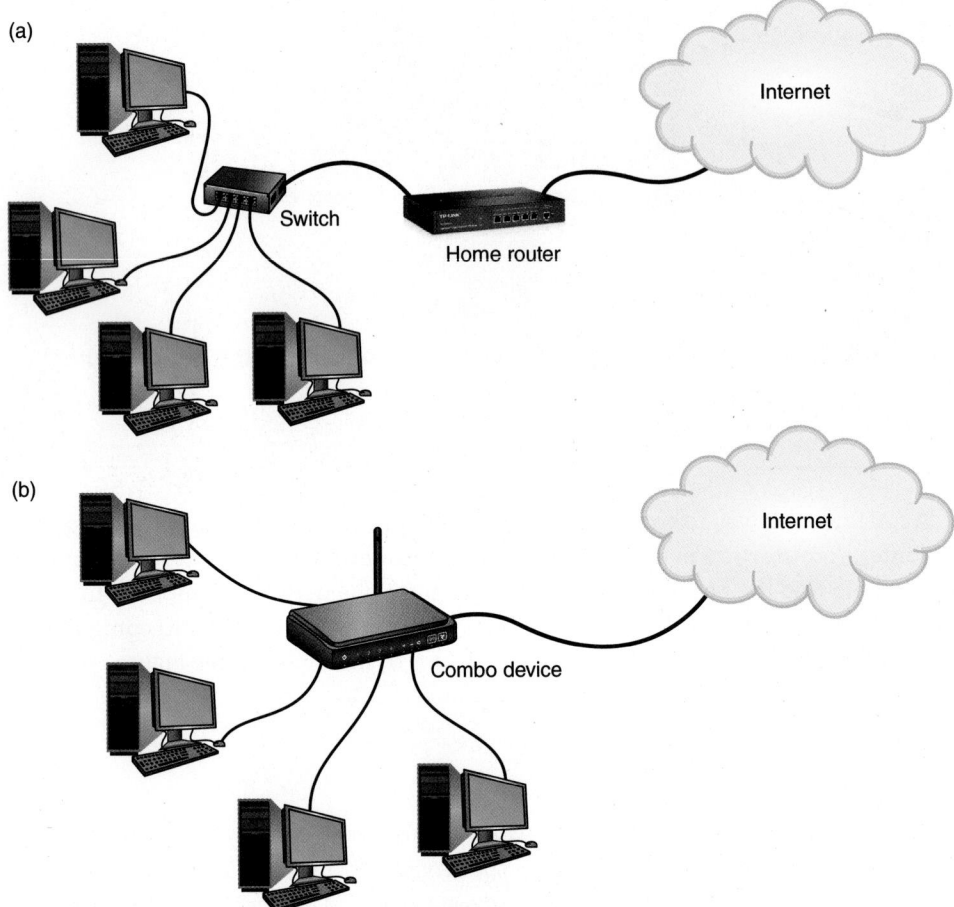

(a)

(b)

Figure 1-12   (a) A router stands between the LAN and the Internet, connecting the two networks; (b) home networks often use a combo device that works as both a switch and a router

---

Note 🖉

We can now make the distinction between the two terms *host* and *node*. A **host** is any computer on a network that hosts a resource such as an application or data, and a **node** is any computer or device on a network that can be addressed on the local network. A client computer or server is both a node and a host, but a router or switch does not normally host resources and is, therefore, merely a node on the network.

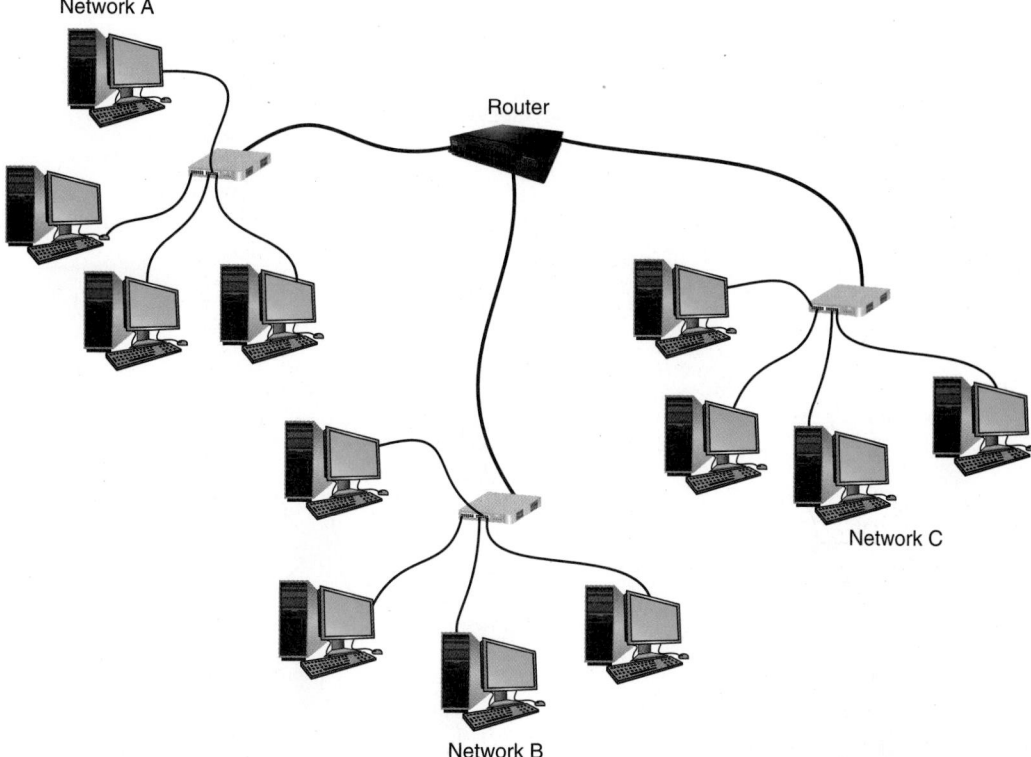

Figure 1-13   Three LANs connected by a router

As you might have already guessed, networked hardware devices on a LAN, such as NICs, switches, and routers, can communicate with each other because of the protocols they have in common. You'll learn more about these protocols in later chapters. For now, let's look at other types of networks besides LANs.

MANs and WANs

A group of LANs that spread over a wide geographical area is called a WAN (wide area network). A group of connected LANs in the same geographical area—for example, a handful of government offices surrounding a state capitol building—is known as a MAN (metropolitan area network) or CAN (campus area network), although in reality you won't often see those terms used or they might be used interchangeably. WANs and MANs often use different transmission methods and media than LANs do. The Internet is the largest and most varied WAN in the world. The smallest network is a PAN (personal area network), which is a network of personal devices, such as the network you use when you sync your smartphone and your computer.

Figure 1-14 shows a WAN link between two local networks bound by routers. For example, a corporation might have an office in San Francisco and another in Philadelphia. Each office has a LAN, and a WAN link connects the two LANs. The WAN link is most likely provided by a third-party service provider.

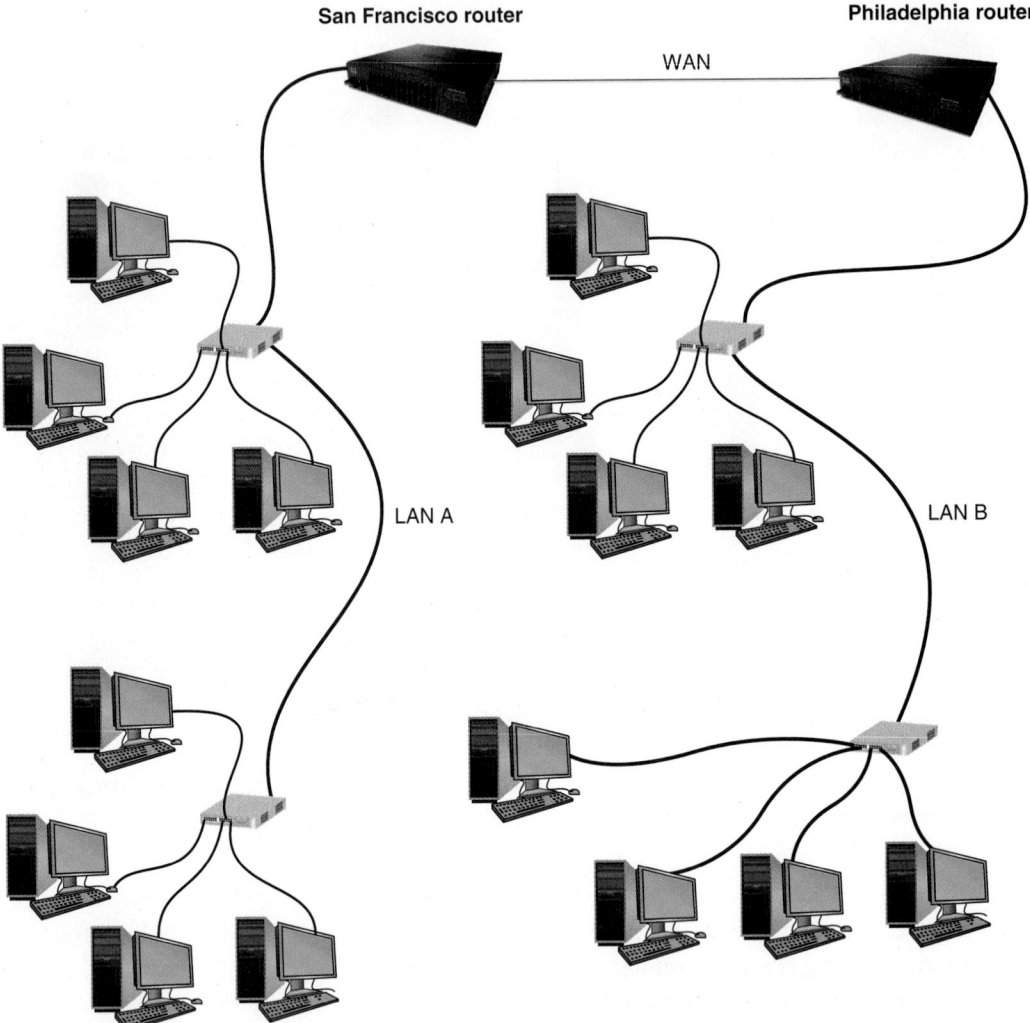

Figure 1-14   A WAN connects two LANs in different geographical areas

You've just learned how operating systems, applications, and hardware create, manage, and use a network. Now let's see, from a bird's-eye view, how they all work together.

The Seven-Layer OSI Model

Q Certification

1.2 Explain devices, applications, protocols, and services at their appropriate OSI layers.

1.3 Explain the concepts and characteristics of routing and switching.

Recall that an application, such as a browser, depends on the operating system to communicate across the network. Operating systems, meanwhile, depend on hardware to communicate across the network (see the left side of Figure 1-15). Throughout the entire process, protocols govern each layer of communication.

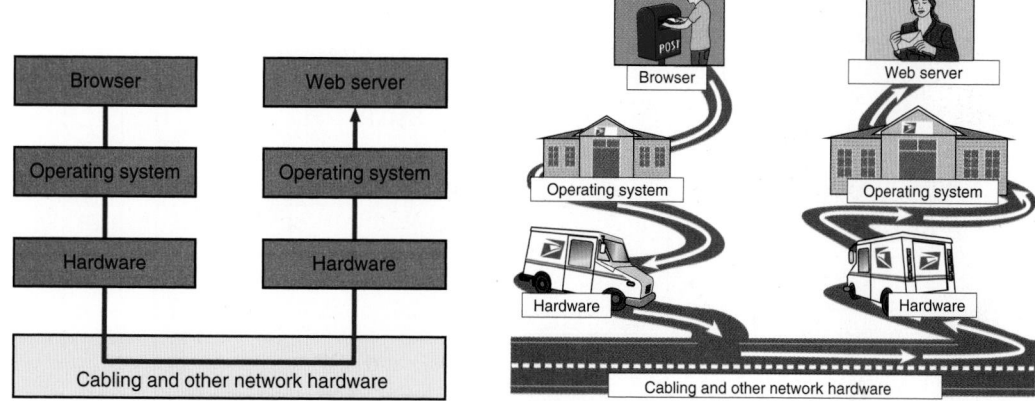

Figure 1-15   A browser and web server communicate by way of the operating system and hardware, similar to how a letter is sent through the mail using the U.S. Postal Service and the road system

To get a better sense of how this works, it's helpful to think of a different type of communication: two people communicating by way of the U.S. Postal Service (see the right side of Figure 1-15). The sender depends on the mailbox to hold her letter until a postal worker picks it up and takes it to the post office. The people at the post office, in turn, depend on truck drivers to transport the letter to the correct city. The truck drivers, for their part, depend on the road system. Throughout the entire process, various protocols govern how people behave. For example, the sender follows basic rules for writing business letters, the mail carriers follow U.S. Postal Service regulations for processing the mail, and the truck drivers follow traffic laws. Think of how complex it might be to explain to someone all the different rules or protocols involved if you were not able to separate or categorize these activities into layers.

Early in the evolution of networking, a seven-layer model was developed to categorize the layers of communication. This model, which is called the **OSI (Open Systems Interconnection) reference model**, is illustrated on the left side of Figure 1-16. It was first developed by the International Organization for Standardization, also called the ISO. (Its shortened name, *ISO,* is derived from a Greek word meaning *equal.*) Network engineers, hardware technicians, programmers, and network administrators still use the layers of the OSI model to communicate about networking technologies. In this book, you'll learn to use the OSI model to help you understand networking protocols and troubleshoot network problems.

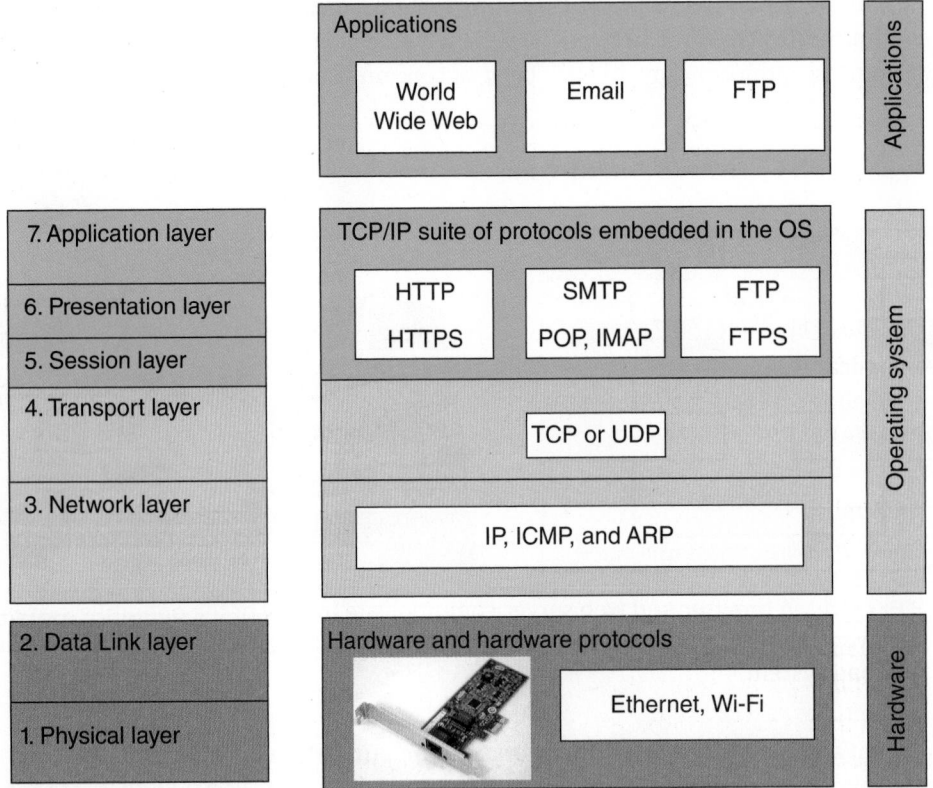

Figure 1-16   How software, protocols, and hardware map to the seven-layer OSI model

---

Network+ Exam Tip ⓘ

The CompTIA Network+ exam expects you to know how to apply the OSI model when troubleshooting network problems.

As you study various protocols used in networking, it will help tremendously to map each protocol onto the OSI model. By doing so, you'll better understand the logistics of which software program or device is initiating and/or receiving the protocol or data and how other protocols are relating to it.

Now let's take a brief look at each layer in the OSI model. The layers are numbered in descending order, starting with Layer 7, the Application layer, at the top. Figure 1-16 guides you through the layers.

> **Note** 📎
>
> You need to memorize the seven layers of the OSI model. Here's a seven-word mnemonic that can help, or you can write your own: **A**ll **P**eople **S**eem **T**o **N**eed **D**ata **P**rocessing.

Layer 7: Application Layer

The **Application layer** in the OSI model describes the interface between two applications, each on separate computers. Earlier in this chapter, you learned about several protocols used at this layer, including HTTP, SMTP, POP3, IMAP4, FTP, Telnet, and RDP. Application layer protocols are used by programs that fall into two categories:

7	APPLICATION
6	PRESENTATION
5	SESSION
4	TRANSPORT
3	NETWORK
2	DATA LINK
1	PHYSICAL

- Application programs that provide services to a user, such as a browser and web server using the HTTP Application layer protocol
- Utility programs that provide services to the system, such as **SNMP (Simple Network Management Protocol)** programs that monitor and gather information about network traffic and can alert network administrators about adverse conditions that need attention

Data that is passed between applications or utility programs and the operating system is called a **payload** and includes control information. The two end-system computers that initiate sending and receiving data are called hosts.

Layer 6: Presentation Layer

In the OSI model, the **Presentation layer** is responsible for reformatting, compressing, and/or encrypting data in a way that the application on the receiving end can read. For example, an email message can be encrypted at the Presentation layer by the email client or by the operating system.

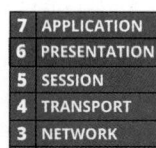

7	APPLICATION
6	PRESENTATION
5	SESSION
4	TRANSPORT
3	NETWORK
2	DATA LINK
1	PHYSICAL

Layer 5: Session Layer

The **Session layer** of the OSI model describes how data between applications is synced and recovered if messages don't arrive intact at the receiving application. For example, the Skype application works with the operating system to establish and maintain a session between two end points for as long as a voice conversation or video conference is in progress.

The Application, Presentation, and Session layers are so intertwined that, in practice, it's often difficult to distinguish between them. Also, tasks for each layer may be performed by the operating system or the application. Most tasks are performed by the OS when an application makes an API call to the OS. In general, an **API (application programming interface) call** is the method an application uses when it makes a request of the OS.

Layer 4: Transport Layer

The **Transport layer** is responsible for transporting Application layer payloads from one application to another. The two main Transport layer protocols are TCP, which guarantees delivery, and UDP, which does not:

- *TCP (Transmission Control Protocol)*—Makes a connection with the end host, checks whether the data is received, and resends it if it is not. TCP is, therefore, called a **connection-oriented protocol**. TCP is used by applications such as web browsers and email. Guaranteed delivery takes longer and is used when it is important to know that the data reached its destination.
- *UDP (User Datagram Protocol)*—Does not guarantee delivery by first connecting and checking whether data is received; thus, UDP is called a **connectionless protocol** or best-effort protocol. UDP is used for broadcasting, such as streaming video or audio over the web, where guaranteed delivery is not as important as fast transmission. UDP is also used to monitor network traffic.

The protocols add their own control information in an area at the beginning of the payload called the **header** to create a message ready to be transmitted to the Network layer. The process of adding a header to the data inherited from the layer above is called **encapsulation**. The Transport layer header addresses the receiving application by a number called a **port**. If the message is too large to transport on the network, TCP divides it into smaller messages called **segments**. In UDP, the message is called a **datagram**.

In our Post Office analogy, you can think of a message as a letter. The sender puts the letter in an envelope and adds the name of the sender and receiver, similar to how the Transport layer encapsulates the payload into a segment or datagram that identifies both the sending and destination applications.

Layer 3: Network Layer

7	APPLICATION
6	PRESENTATION
5	SESSION
4	TRANSPORT
3	NETWORK
2	DATA LINK
1	PHYSICAL

The **Network layer**, sometimes called the Internet layer, is responsible for moving messages from one node to another until they reach the destination host. The principal protocol used by the Network layer is **IP (Internet Protocol)**. IP adds its own Network layer header to the segment or datagram, and the entire Network layer message is now called a **packet**. The Network layer header identifies the sending and receiving hosts by their IP addresses. An **IP address** is an address assigned to each node on a network, which the Network layer uses to uniquely identify them on the network. In our Post Office analogy, the Network layer would be the trucking system used by the Post Office and the IP addresses would be the full return and destination addresses written on the envelope.

IP relies on several supporting protocols to find the best route for a packet when traversing several networks on its way to its destination. These supporting protocols include ICMP (Internet Control Message Protocol) and ARP (Address Resolution Protocol). You'll learn more about these protocols later.

Along the way, if a Network layer protocol is aware that a packet is larger than the maximum size for its network, it will divide the packet into smaller packets in a process called **fragmentation**.

Layer 2: Data Link Layer

7	APPLICATION
6	PRESENTATION
5	SESSION
4	TRANSPORT
3	NETWORK
2	DATA LINK
1	PHYSICAL

Layers 2 and 1 are responsible for interfacing with the physical hardware only on the local network. The protocols at these layers are programmed into the firmware of a computer's NIC and other networking hardware. Layer 2, the **Data Link layer**, is also commonly called the Link layer. The type of networking hardware or technology used on a network determines the Data Link layer protocol used. Examples of Data Link layer protocols are Ethernet and Wi-Fi. (Ethernet works on wired networks and Wi-Fi is wireless.) As you'll learn in later chapters, several types of switches exist. The least intelligent (nonprogrammable) switches, which are called Data Link layer switches or Layer 2 switches, operate at this layer.

Note

The term **firmware** refers to programs embedded into hardware devices. This software does not change unless a firmware upgrade is performed.

The Data Link layer puts its own control information in a Data Link layer header and also attaches control information to the end of the packet in a **trailer**. The entire Data Link layer message is then called a **frame**. The frame header contains the hardware addresses of the source and destination NICs. This address is called a **MAC (Media Access Control) address, physical address, hardware address,** or **Data Link layer address** and is embedded on every network adapter on the globe (refer back to Figure 1-9). The physical addresses are short-range addresses that can only find nodes on the local network.

In our Post Office analogy, a truck might travel from one post office to the next en route to its final destination. The address of a post office along the route would be similar to the physical address of a NIC that a frame reaches as it traverses only one LAN on its way to its destination.

Layer 1: Physical Layer

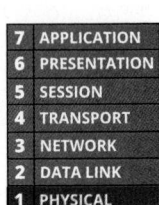

Layer 1, the **Physical layer,** is the simplest layer of all and is responsible only for sending bits via a wired or wireless transmission. These bits can be transmitted as wavelengths in the air (for example, Wi-Fi), voltage on a copper wire (for example, Ethernet on twisted-pair cabling), or light (for example, Ethernet on fiber-optic cabling).

It's interesting to consider that the top layers of the OSI model work the same for both wired and wireless transmissions. In fact, the only layers that must deal with the details of wired versus wireless transmissions are the Data Link layer and Physical layer on the firmware of the NIC. In our Post Office analogy, the Data Link and Physical layers compare with the various road systems a postal truck might use, each with its own speed limits and traffic rules.

Protocol Data Unit or PDU

There are several different names for a group of bits as it moves from one layer to the next and from one LAN to the next. Although technicians loosely call this group of bits a message or a transmission, the technical name is a **PDU (protocol data unit).** Table 1-1 can help you keep all these names straight.

Table 1-1   Names for a PDU or message as it moves from one layer to another

OSI model	Name	Extremely technical name
Layer 7, Application layer Layer 6, Presentation layer Layer 5, Session layer	Payload or data	L7PDU
Layer 4, Transport layer	Segment (TCP) or datagram (UDP)	L4PDU
Layer 3, Network layer	Packet	L3PDU
Layer 2, Data Link layer	Frame	L2PDU
Layer 1, Physical layer	Bit or transmission	L1PDU

Summary of How the Layers Work Together

Now let's tie the layers together, as shown in Figure 1-17. This transmission involves a browser and web server on their respective hosts, a switch, and a router. As you follow the red line from browser to web server, notice the sending host encapsulates the payload in headers and a trailer before sending it, much like an assistant would place the boss's business letter in an envelope before putting it in the mail.

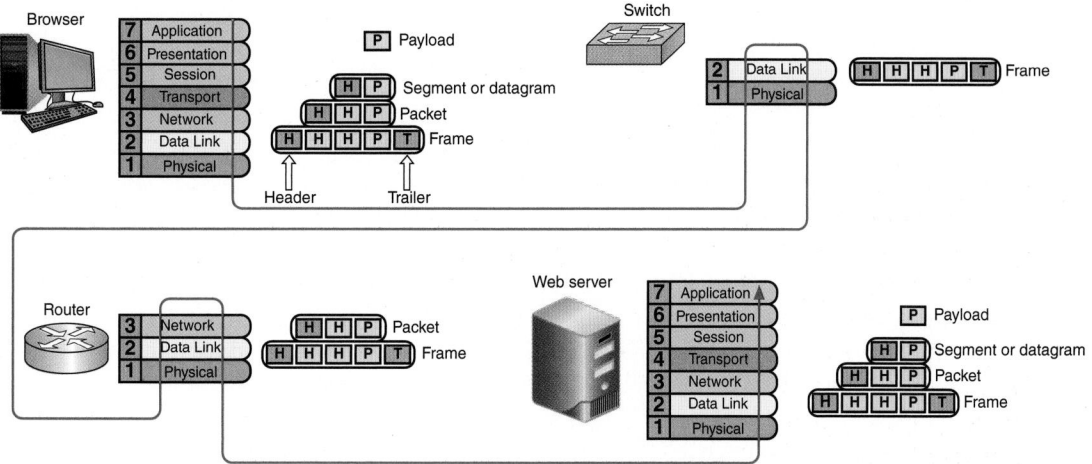

Figure 1-17   Follow the red line to see how the OSI layers work when a browser makes a request to a web server

In the reverse order, the receiving host removes the headers and trailer before the message reaches the web server application, just as the receiver's assistant would remove the letter from the envelope before handing it to the recipient. Removing a header and trailer from a lower layer's PDU is called **decapsulation**.

Note 📎

In conceptual drawings and network maps, symbols are used for switches and routers. In the figure, notice the square symbol representing a switch, and the round symbol, which stands for a router.

The steps listed in Table 1-2 summarize the process illustrated in Figure 1-17.

Table 1-2	Steps through the OSI layers during a browser-to-web server transmission
Sending host	1. The browser, involving the Application, Presentation, and Session layers, creates an HTTP message, or payload, on the source computer and passes it down to the Transport layer.
	2. The Transport layer (TCP, which is part of the OS) encapsulates the payload by adding its own header and passes the segment down to the Network layer.
	3. IP at the Network layer in the OS receives the segment (depicted as two yellow boxes in the figure), adds its header, and passes the packet down to the Data Link layer.
	4. The Data Link layer on the NIC firmware receives the packet (depicted as three yellow boxes in the figure), adds its header and trailer, and passes the frame to the Physical layer.
	5. The Physical layer on the NIC hardware puts bits on the network.
Switch	6. The network transmission is received by the switch, which passes the frame up to the Data Link layer (firmware on the switch), looks at the destination MAC address, and decides where to send the frame.
	7. The pass-through frame is sent to the correct port on the switch and on to the router.
Router	8. The router has two NICs, one for each of the two networks to which it belongs. The Physical layer of the first NIC receives the frame and passes it up to the Data Link layer (NIC firmware), which removes the frame header and trailer and passes the packet up to IP at the Network layer (firmware program or other software) on the router.
	9. This Network layer IP program looks at the destination IP address, determines the next node en route for the packet, and passes the packet back down to the Data Link layer on the second NIC. The Data Link layer adds a new frame header and trailer appropriate for this second NIC's LAN, including the MAC address of the next destination node. It passes the frame to its Physical layer (NIC hardware), which sends the bits on their way.
Destination host	10. When the frame reaches the destination host NIC, the Data Link layer NIC firmware receives it, removes the frame header and trailer, and passes the packet up to IP at the Network layer, which removes its header and passes the segment up to TCP at the Transport layer.
	11. TCP removes its header and passes the payload up to HTTP at the Application layer. HTTP presents the message to the web server.

Note 📎

A four-layer model similar to the OSI model is the TCP/IP model. Using the TCP/IP model, the Application, Presentation, and Session layers are wrapped together and are called the Application layer. The Physical layer is so simple, it's ignored, which makes for four layers: Application layer, Transport layer, Internet layer (the Network layer in the OSI model), and Link layer (the Data Link layer in the OSI model).

So now you have the big picture of networking and how it works. Throughout this book, you will have several opportunities to work with networking equipment such as switches and routers. Before attempting any of these projects, it's important for you to know about safety procedures and policies. In preparation for the work you'll be doing in this book, let's turn our attention to staying safe when working around networks and computers.

Safety Procedures and Policies

3.5   Identify policies and best practices.

As a network and computer technician, you need to know how to protect yourself and sensitive electronic components as you work. Let's look at some best practices for safety.

Emergency Procedures

In case of an emergency, such as a fire alert, you'll need to know the best escape route or emergency exit for you and others around you. Look in the lobby and hallways at your place of work for a posted building layout and fire escape plan so that you are prepared in an emergency. You also need to be aware of emergency exit doors, which are usually labeled with battery-powered, lighted Exit signs and clearly marked on the posted building layout.

Fire Suppression Systems

A company is likely to have a **fire suppression system** in its data center that includes the following:

- *emergency alert system*—These systems vary, but they typically generate loud noise and flashing lights. Some send text and voice message alerts to key personnel, and post alerts by email, network messages, and other means.
- *portable fire extinguishers*—Note that electrical fires require a Class C fire extinguisher, as shown in Figure 1-18.
- *emergency power-off switch*—Don't use a power-off switch unless you really need to; improper shutdowns are hard on computers and their data.
- *suppression agent*—This can consist of a foaming chemical, gas, or water that sprays everywhere to put out the fire.

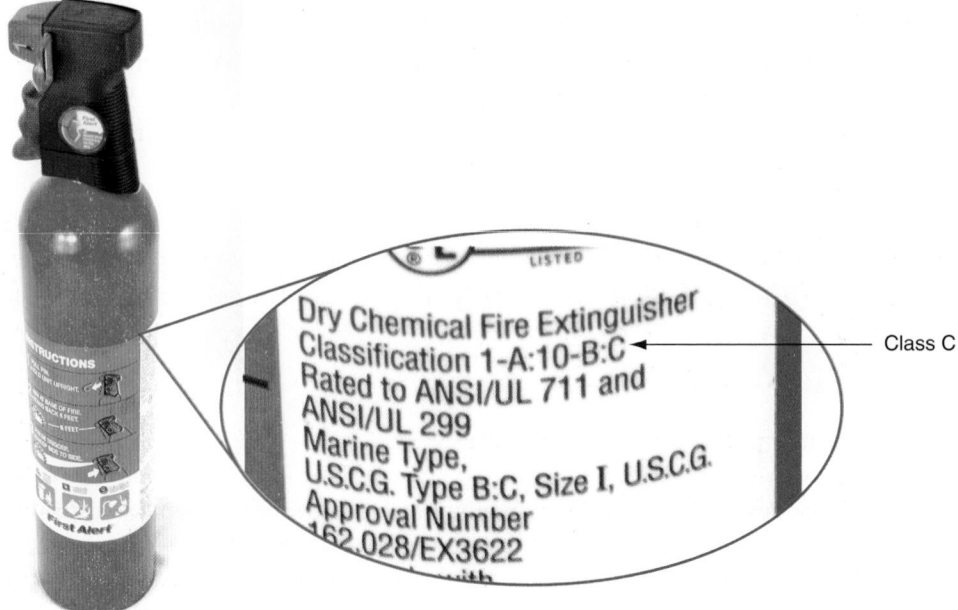

Class C

Figure 1-18 A Class C fire extinguisher is rated to put out electrical fires

Fail Open or Fail Close

What happens to security when a system responsible for security fails? Does the system allow access during the failure (**fail open**) or deny access during the failure (**fail close**)? For example, during a fire alert, using a fail-open policy, all exit doors stay unlocked so that people can safely leave the building and firefighters can enter the building, even though this might present a security risk for thieves entering the building. On the other hand, if firewall software protecting access to a database of customer credit card numbers fails, it might be configured to fail close and to deny access to the database until the software is back online.

A fail-open policy is often based on common sense so as to ensure that, in an emergency, no one is harmed when a system is not working. A fail-close policy is usually based on the need for security to protect private data or other resources.

> **Note** 📎
>
> The term *open* or *close* takes on the opposite meaning when talking about electrical circuits. When a circuit breaker fails, there is a break in the circuit and the circuit is said to be open. The breaker opens the circuit to protect it from out-of-control electricity. Although this sounds like double-talk, an open circuit is, therefore, a fail-close system.

MSDS (Material Safety Data Sheet)

You might need to use cleaning solutions to clean optical discs, tapes and tape drivers, and other devices. Most of these cleaning solutions contain flammable and poisonous materials. Take care when using them so that they don't get on your skin or in your eyes. To find out what to do if you are accidentally exposed to a dangerous solution, look on the instructions printed on the can or check out the material safety data sheet (see Figure 1-19). An **MSDS (material safety data sheet)**, also called an SDS (safety data sheet), explains how to properly handle substances such as chemical solvents and how to dispose of them.

Figure 1-19   Each chemical you use should have a material safety data sheet available

An MSDS includes information such as physical data, toxicity, health effects, first aid, storage, shipping, disposal, and spill procedures. It typically comes packaged with the chemical, but if you can't locate it, you can order one from the manufacturer, or you can find one on the web (see *ilpi.com/msds*).

Safety Precautions

Electrical and tool safety in workplaces is generally regulated by **OSHA (Occupational Safety and Health Administration)**, which is the main federal agency charged with safety and health in the workplace. See *osha.gov*.

OSHA regulations for electrical safety require that electrical devices be turned off and the electrical supply locked out before employees work near these devices. For example, OSHA requires that all devices in a data center cabinet, rack, or panel be turned off and the power locked out before employees work inside of or with these units.

Following are some general OSHA guidelines when using power (electric) tools or other hand tools in the workplace. Your employer can give you more details specific to your work environment:

- Wear **PPE (personal protective equipment)** to protect yourself as you work. For example, wear eye protection where dust or fumes are generated by power tools.
- Keep all tools in good condition and properly store tools not in use. Examine a tool for damage before you use it.
- Use the right tool for the job and operate the tool according to the manufacturer's instructions and guidelines. Don't work with a tool unless you are trained and authorized to use it.
- Watch out for **trip hazards**, so you and others don't stumble on a tool or cord. For example, keep power tool electrical extension cords out from underfoot, and don't leave hand tools lying around unattended.

Lifting Heavy Objects

Back injury, caused by lifting heavy objects, is one of the most common injuries that happens at work. Whenever possible, put heavy objects, such as a large laser printer, on a cart to move them. If you do need to lift a heavy object, follow these guidelines to keep from injuring your back:

1. Decide which side of the object to face so that the load is the most balanced.
2. Stand close to the object with your feet apart.
3. Keeping your back straight, bend your knees and grip the load.
4. Lift with your legs, arms, and shoulders, and not with your back or stomach.
5. Keep the load close to your body and avoid twisting your body while you're holding it.
6. To put the object down, keep your back as straight as you can and lower the object by bending your knees.

Don't try to lift an object that is too heavy for you. Because there are no exact guidelines for when heavy is too heavy, use your best judgment as to when to ask for help.

Protecting Against Static Electricity

Computer components are grounded inside a computer case, and computer power cables all use a three-prong plug for this purpose. The third prong is grounded. **Grounding** means that a device is connected directly to the earth, so that, in the event of a short circuit, the electricity flows into the earth, rather than out of control through the device and back to the power station, which can cause an electrical fire.

In addition, sensitive electronic components (for example, a NIC, motherboard, and memory modules) can be damaged by **ESD (electrostatic discharge)**, commonly known as **static electricity**. Static electricity is an electrical charge at rest. When your body and a component have different static charges and you touch the component, you can discharge up to 1,500 volts of static electricity without seeing a spark or feeling the discharge. However, it only takes 10 volts to damage the component.

Static electricity can cause two types of damage in an electronic component: catastrophic failure and upset failure. A **catastrophic failure** destroys the component beyond use. An **upset failure** can shorten the life of a component and/or cause intermittent errors. Before touching a component, first ground yourself using one of these methods:

- Wear an ESD strap around your wrist that clips onto the chassis (pronounced "chas-ee"), or computer case, which eliminates any ESD between you and the chassis and its components (see Figure 1-20).
- If you don't have an ESD strap handy, be sure to at least touch the case before you touch any component inside the case. This is not as effective as wearing an ESD strap, but can reduce the risk of ESD.
- To protect a sensitive component, always store it inside an antistatic bag when it's not in use.

In addition to protecting against ESD, always shut down and unplug a computer before working inside it.

Troubleshooting Network Problems

5.1   Explain the network troubleshooting methodology.

Troubleshooting is probably the most significant skill you can learn as a network technician. Throughout your career, you'll be called on to troubleshoot problems with networking hardware, operating systems, applications that use the network, and other

Figure 1-20 An ESD strap, which protects computer components from ESD, can clip to the side of the computer chassis and eliminate ESD between you and the chassis

network resources. The CompTIA Network+ exam and this book place a significant emphasis on troubleshooting skills. Troubleshooting will come more easily for you once you get a feel for the big picture of how the process works. The flowchart in Figure 1-21 illustrates the method used by most expert network troubleshooters to solve networking problems.

Study the steps in Figure 1-21 carefully so that you understand how each step feeds into the next, and how the answers for each step build on the information you've

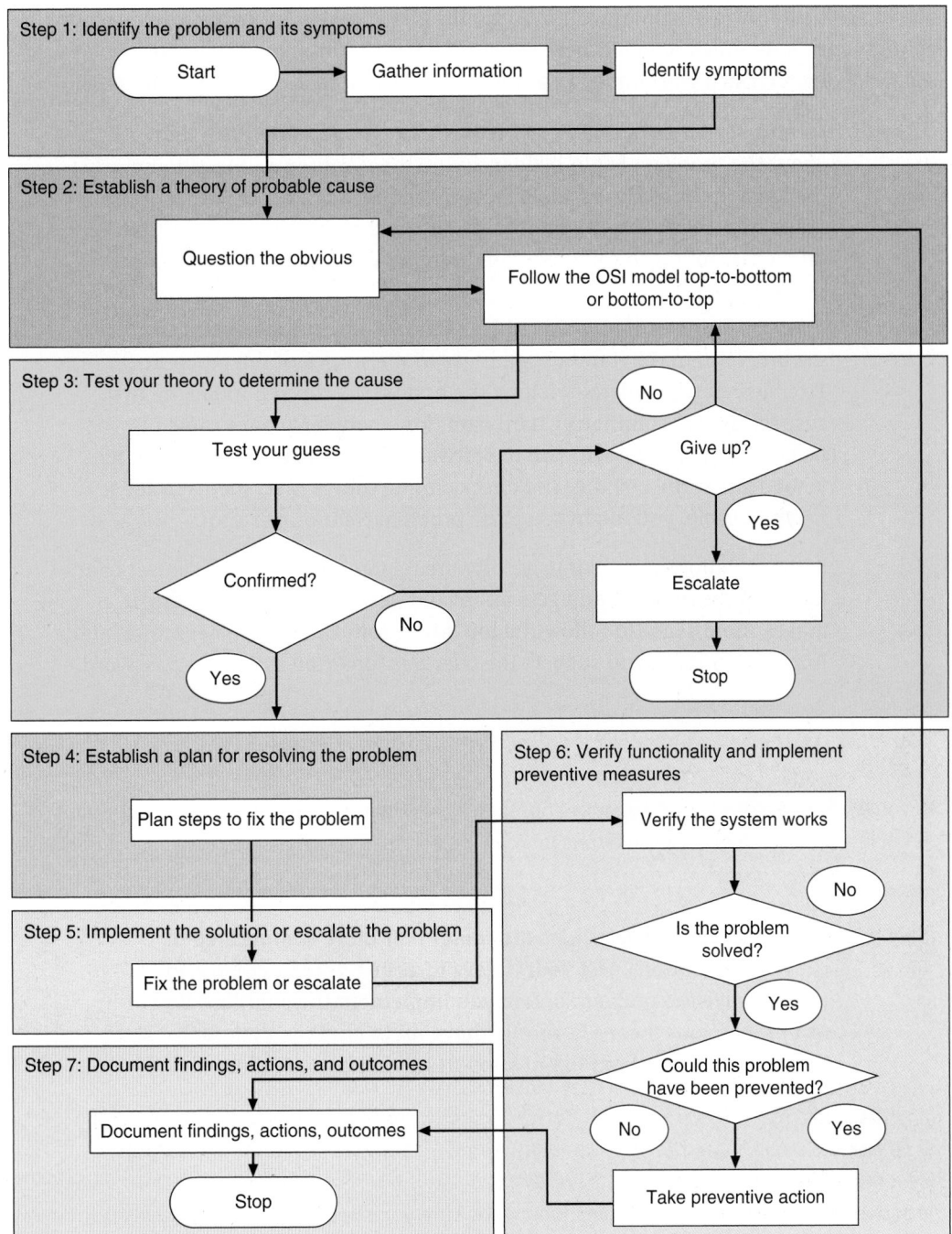

Figure 1-21   General approach to solving network problems

already gathered. Also, it's not uncommon for the Network+ exam to ask you questions about the recommended order of these steps, which step comes next in a given scenario, or which step was missed in a troubleshooting scenario. Here are the steps:

Step 1:   *Identify the problem and its symptoms*—As you gather information about the problem, begin by identifying the symptoms, questioning the user, finding out what has recently changed, and determining the scope of the problem. If possible, duplicate the problem. For multiple problems, approach each problem individually. Solve it before moving on to the next.

Step 2:   *Establish a theory of probable cause*—As you observe the extent of the problem, make your best guess as to the source of the problem. Troubleshooters generally follow the bottom-to-top OSI model by first suspecting and eliminating hardware (for example, a loose cable or failed NIC), before moving on to software as the cause of a problem. As you question the obvious and check simple things first, such as a loose network cable, you might solve the problem right on the spot.

Some situations are obviously software related, such as when a user cannot log on to the network and gets an invalid password message. Here, it makes more sense to follow the top-to-bottom OSI model, beginning at the Application layer, and suspect the user has forgotten his or her password.

Note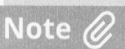

As you work, use a divide-and-conquer approach by eliminating parts of the whole until you zero in on the source of the problem.

Step 3:   *Test your theory to determine the cause*—For more complicated or expensive solutions, test your theory to assure yourself that it will indeed solve the problem before you implement the solution. If your test proves your theory is wrong, move on to another guess or escalate the problem to the next tier of support in your organization.

Note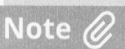

As with any computer-related troubleshooting, be sure you choose the least invasive and least expensive solution first before moving on to more drastic or expensive changes to a computer or the network.

Step 4:   *Establish a plan for resolving the problem*—Changes to a network have the potential for disrupting a lot of people's work. Before you implement a fix, consider the scope of your change, especially how it will affect users, their applications, and their data. Unless the problem poses an emergency, make your changes when the least number of users are on the network.

Step 5:   *Implement the solution or escalate the problem*—Before you make the change, be sure to alert all affected users in advance, create backups of software and data as needed, and save or write down current settings before you change them. Keep good notes as you work, so you can backtrack as necessary. Test your solution thoroughly, and clean up after yourself when you're finished. For major changes, it's often best to roll out changes in stages so as to make sure all is working for a few users before you affect many users.

For complex problems, you might need to escalate the problem to someone with access to more technical resources or with more authority to test or implement a solution. An organization might require that major changes to a network be documented in a change management system.

Step 6:   *Verify functionality and implement preventive measures*—At the time you implement your solution, you'll test the system for full system functionality. It's also a good idea to return a few days later and make sure all is working as you expected. Also consider what you can do to make sure the problem doesn't reappear. For example, is more preventive maintenance required? Do you need to implement network monitoring software?

Step 7:   *Document findings, actions, and outcomes*—Most organizations use a call tracking system (also called help desk software) to document problems and their resolutions. Your organization is likely to expect you to document the name, department, and contact information of the person who originated the call for help; when the call first came in; information about the problem; the symptoms of the problem; the resolution of the problem; the name of the technician who handled the problem; and perhaps the amount of time spent resolving the problem. Your company may also require you to document unique or insightful solutions to problems in your company's knowledge base for you and others to draw from in the future. A **knowledge base** is a collection of accumulated insights and solutions to the problems encountered on a particular network.

Applying Concepts: Troubleshoot a Failed Network Connection

Suppose your computer cannot connect to the Internet. Here's a simple process for troubleshooting this problem that demonstrates all seven steps in the troubleshooting model:

Step 1:   *Identify the problem and its symptoms*—You open your browser on your desktop computer, discover you can't reach any website, and you see an error message on the browser screen. You open File Explorer and find that you can't navigate to resources normally available on your local network.

Step 2:   *Establish a theory of probable cause*—Because a network technician was working near your desk when you left the evening before, you suspect your network cable might have been left unplugged. In the OSI model, you've started at the bottom by suspecting the problem is hardware related.

Step 3:   *Test your theory to determine the cause*—You check the cable and discover it is lying on the floor, not connected to your desktop.

Step 4:   *Establish a plan for resolving the problem*—You decide to plug in the network cable. This is a very simple resolution that does not affect other users. In other situations, your plan might involve informing coworkers of what is about to happen.

Step 5:   *Implement the solution or escalate the problem*—You plug in the cable.

Step 6:   *Verify functionality and implement preventive measures*—You open your browser and find you can surf the web. You verify local network resources are available from File Explorer.

Step 7:   *Document findings, actions, and outcomes*—This simple problem and solution doesn't require documentation. However, network technicians are generally expected to document troubleshooting tasks and solutions.

Chapter Summary

Network Models

- The peer-to-peer model can be achieved using any assortment of desktop, mobile, or tablet operating systems, but the client-server model requires one or more NOSes (network operating systems), which control access to the entire network.

- Peer-to-peer networks are simple to configure and less expensive than other types of networks. However, they are not scalable, not as secure, and not practical for connecting more than a few computers.

- When Windows Server controls network access, the logical group is called a domain.

The centralized directory database that contains user account information and security for the entire group of computers is called AD (Active Directory). Each user on the network has a domain-level account assigned by the network administrator and kept in Active Directory.

Client-Server Applications

- The computers on a network are able to communicate with each other via the protocols they have in common. The two primary protocols are TCP (Transmission Control Protocol) and IP (Internet Protocol), and the suite of all the protocols an OS uses for communication on a network is the TCP/IP suite of protocols.

Network Hardware

- The fundamental difference between a switch and a router is that a switch belongs only to its local network and a router belongs to two or more local networks. A host on one LAN cannot communicate with a host on another LAN without a router to manage that communication and stand as a gateway between the networks.
- A group of LANs that spread over a wide geographical area is called a WAN (wide area network). A group of connected LANs in the same geographical area is known as a MAN (metropolitan area network) or CAN (campus area network). The smallest network is a PAN (personal area network), which is a network of personal devices.

The Seven-Layer OSI Model

- The Application layer describes the interface between two applications, each on separate computers.

- The Presentation layer is responsible for reformatting, compressing, and/or encrypting data in a way that the application on the receiving end can read.
- The Session layer describes how data between applications is synced and recovered if messages don't arrive intact at the receiving application.
- The Transport layer transports Application layer payloads from one application to another. The two main Transport layer protocols are TCP and UDP.
- The Network layer moves messages from one node to another until they reach the destination host.
- Layers 2 and 1 are responsible for interfacing with the physical hardware only on the local network. The protocols at these layers are programmed into the firmware of a computer's NIC and other networking hardware.
- Removing a header and trailer from a lower layer's PDU is called decapsulation.

Safety Procedures and Policies

- In case of an emergency, you'll need to know the best escape route or emergency exit for you and others around you. Also be aware of locations of portable fire extinguishers, and use a Class C fire extinguisher for an electrical fire.
- Whenever possible, put heavy objects on a cart to move them.
- When your body and a component have different static charges and you touch the component, you can discharge up to 1,500 volts of static electricity without seeing a spark or feeling the discharge. However, it only takes 10 volts to damage the component.

Troubleshooting Network Problems

- When troubleshooting problems with networking hardware, operating systems, or applications, follow these steps:
  - Identify the problem and its symptoms
  - Establish a theory of probable cause
  - Test your theory to determine the cause
  - Establish a plan for resolving the problem
  - Implement the solution or escalate the problem
  - Verify functionality and implement preventive measures
  - Document findings, actions, and outcomes

Key Terms

For definitions of key terms, see the Glossary near the end of the book.

AD (Active Directory)
AD DS (Active Directory Domain Services)
API (application programming interface) call
Application layer
backbone
bus topology
CAN (campus area network)
catastrophic failure
client
client-server application
client-server network model
connectionless protocol
connection-oriented protocol
Data Link layer
Data Link layer address
datagram
decapsulation
domain
emergency alert system
encapsulation
ESD (electrostatic discharge)

fail close
fail open
fire suppression system
firmware
fragmentation
frame
FTP (File Transfer Protocol)
grounding
hardware address
header
host
HTTP (Hypertext Transfer Protocol)
HTTPS (HTTP Secure)
hub
hybrid topology
IMAP4 (Internet Message Access Protocol, version 4)
IP (Internet Protocol)
IP address
knowledge base
LAN (local area network)
logical topology
MAC (Media Access Control) address
MAN (metropolitan area network)

mesh topology
MSDS (material safety data sheet)
network
Network layer
network service
NIC (network interface card)
node
NOS (network operating system)
OSHA (Occupational Safety and Health Administration)
OSI (Open Systems Interconnection) reference model
P2P (peer-to-peer) network model
packet
PAN (personal area network)
payload
PDU (protocol data unit)
physical address
Physical layer
physical topology

POP3 (Post Office Protocol, version 3)
port
PPE (personal protective equipment)
Presentation layer
protocol
RDP (Remote Desktop Protocol)
remote application
Remote Desktop Services
ring topology
router
scalable
segment
server
Session layer
SFTP (Secure File Transfer Protocol)
SMTP (Simple Mail Transfer Protocol)
SNMP (Simple Network Management Protocol)
SOHO (small office-home office) network
SSH (Secure Shell)
SSL (Secure Sockets Layer)
star topology
star-bus topology
static electricity
switch
TCP (Transmission Control Protocol)
TCP/IP
Telnet
TLS (Transport Layer Security)
topology
trailer
Transport layer
trip hazard
UDP (User Datagram Protocol)
upset failure
WAN (wide area network)

Review Questions

1. In the client-server model, what is the primary protocol used for communication between a browser and web server?

   a. FTP

   b. TCP

   c. HTTP

   d. SSL

2. Which two encryption protocols might be used to provide secure transmissions for browser and web server communications?

   a. HTTP and HTTPS

   b. SSL and TLS

   c. SSL and HTTP

   d. TCP and UDP

3. Which email protocol allows an email client to download email messages to the local computer?

   a. IMAP4

   b. SMTP

   c. TCP

   d. POP3

4. Which email protocol allows an email client to read mail stored on the mail server?

   a. IMAP4

   b. SMTP

   c. TCP

   d. POP3

5. Which application embedded in Windows operating systems allows remote control of a computer and uses the RDP secure protocol for transmissions?

   a. Telnet

   b. Remote Desktop

   c. SFTP

   d. SSH

6. A network consists of five computers, all running Windows 10 Professional. All the computers are connected to a switch, which is connected to a router, which is connected to the Internet. Which networking model does the network use?

   a. Star-bus

   b. Ring

   c. Hybrid

   d. Peer-to-peer

7. In Question 6, suppose one computer is upgraded from Windows 10 Professional to Windows Server 2016. Which networking model can the network now support that it could not support without the upgrade?
   a. Hybrid
   b. Client-server
   c. Star-bus
   d. Ring

8. A network consists of seven computers and a network printer, all connected directly to one switch. Which network topology does this network use?
   a. Hybrid
   b. Mesh
   c. Star-bus
   d. Star

9. In Question 8, suppose a new switch is connected to the first switch by way of a network cable, and three computers are connected to the new switch. Which network topology is now used?
   a. Hybrid
   b. Mesh
   c. Star-bus
   d. Star

10. Which type of address is used at the Transport layer to identify the receiving application?
   a. IP address
   b. Port
   c. MAC address
   d. Protocol

11. What is the name of the domain controller database that Windows Server 2016 uses to store data about user access and resources on the network?

12. What is the fundamental distinction between a Layer 2 switch and a router?

13. What is the fundamental distinction between a node and a host?

14. What is the fundamental distinction between a MAN and a WAN?

15. What is a message called that is delivered by TCP? What is a message called that is delivered by UDP? At which layer do the two protocols work?

16. At the Network layer, what type of address is used to identify the receiving host?

17. At the Data Link layer, which type of network address is used to identify the receiving node?

18. A computer is unable to access the network. When you check the LED lights near the computer's network port, you discover the lights are not lit. Which layer of the OSI model are you using to troubleshoot this problem? At which two layers does the network adapter work?

19. A user complains that he cannot access a particular website, although he is able to access other websites. At which layer of the OSI model should you begin troubleshooting this problem?

20. A user complains that Skype drops her videoconference calls and she must reconnect. At which layer of the OSI model should you begin troubleshooting? Which OSI layer is responsible for not dropping the Skype connection?

Hands-On Projects

Project 1-1: Set Up a Small Network

For this project, you'll need two Windows 10 computers, a small consumer-grade switch (one that does not require its firmware to be configured), and two regular network cables (a regular network cable is also called a straight-through cable or patch cable). Do the following to set up a small network:

1. Use the network cables to connect each computer to the switch. Make sure the switch has power. Verify the LED lights on the network ports of the computers and switch are lit and/or blinking to verify network connectivity and activity.
2. Open Network and Sharing Center on each computer to verify that Windows sees the computer is connected to the network. (Right-click the network icon in the system tray on the taskbar and click **Open Network and Sharing Center.**)
3. If you don't see connectivity, reset the connection by restarting the computer. You'll learn about easier methods to verify and reset a network connection later.
4. Open File Explorer. In the navigation pane, look in the Network group. You should see the other computer listed. You won't be able to access resources on the other computer unless you share these resources in a homegroup or share a specific folder or file.

Note

You might have to turn on Network Discovery in order to see the other computer. To do this, in the left pane of the Network and Sharing Center, click Change advanced sharing settings. For the current profile (probably the *Guest or Public* profile), select Turn on network discovery. Click Save changes. After completing this project, be sure to revert this setting to *Turn off network discovery* if you use this computer on public networks.

5. Answer the following questions:
   a. Does your network use a client-server or peer-to-peer model?
   b. What is the topology of your network?
   c. If the lights on the switch ports were not lit or blinking, what is your best theory of probable cause? At what layer of the OSI model would this theory be?

Project 1-2: Use Quick Assist

In this chapter, you learned about Remote Desktop and RDP (Remote Desktop Protocol), which IT technicians use to manage remote computers. A similar app, Quick Assist, is also built into Windows, beginning with Windows 10's Anniversary Update. Quick Assist is a client-server application that uses the HTTPS protocol to provide a convenient way for an IT technician, family member, or computer enthusiast to remotely connect to someone else's computer while providing assistance with a computer problem.

Using Quick Assist, the person receiving assistance works at the host computer, which is acting as the server in this client-server application and is serving up its desktop to the other computer. The technician providing assistance works from the client computer, which receives the host computer's desktop. For Quick Assist to work, both computers must be running Windows 10, the technician providing assistance must have a Microsoft account, and the person receiving the connection must agree to it by entering a code generated by the technician's client computer.

> **Note** 📎
>
> Throughout this book, steps are written for Windows 10 Professional with the Creators Update (Version 1703). Many of the projects work equally well on earlier versions of Windows 10 Pro, on Windows 10 Home, and even on Windows 8.1. However, if you're using an edition other than Windows 10 Pro, Version 1703, watch for places where you might need to adapt the steps to fit your OS.

To complete this project, work with a partner where one person acts as a technician giving assistance, and the other acts as a person getting assistance. Quick Assist is designed to help people who are not in the same location work together. So if you and your partner are working on two computers in the same room, pretend you are actually working in remote locations. Perform both sets of steps twice, so you each have the chance to give and get assistance.

To give assistance:

1. Click **Start** and type **Quick Assist**, or open the Windows Accessories folder in the Start menu. Click **Quick Assist** and you see the Quick Assist app, as shown in Figure 1-22.
2. Click **Give assistance**, and sign in with your Microsoft account if necessary. You see a 6-digit security code that is valid for 10 minutes, as shown in Figure 1-23.
3. Do one of the following to share this information with the person you're assisting:
   a. *Copy to clipboard*: Paste the security code and instructions into an email or chat app.
   b. *Send email*: Use Quick Assist to send the security code and instructions directly by email.
   c. *Provide instructions*: Prepare to read aloud the instructions and security code on your screen as you talk the other person through the connection process over the phone.

After the connection is established, your computer displays the screen of the person getting assistance (the host computer), along with a toolbar (see Figure 1-24) that will help you interact with the other computer.

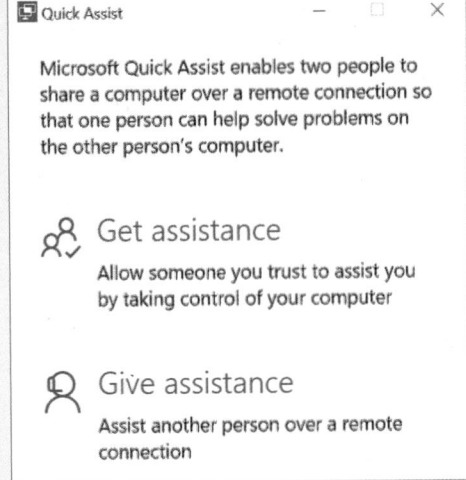

Figure 1-22 Request or offer assistance via a remote connection

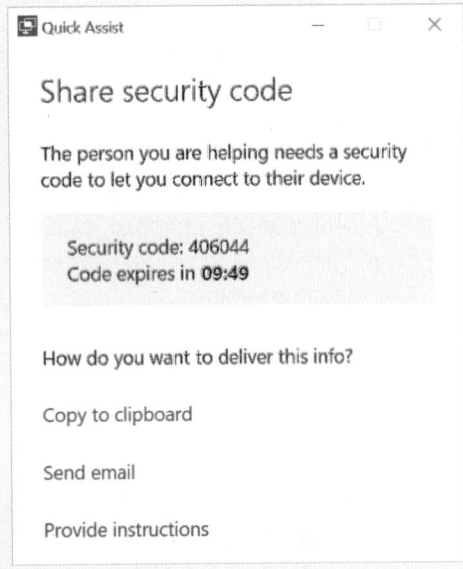

Figure 1-23 Send instructions and the security code to the person receiving assistance

Figure 1-24 During a Quick Assist session, the technician providing assistance has the same rights and privileges as the user account that is signed in on the host computer

To get assistance:

1. Click **Start** and type **Quick Assist**, or open the Windows Accessories folder in the Start menu, and click **Quick Assist**.
2. Click **Get assistance**.
3. Enter the code provided by the technician giving assistance, and click **Submit**.
4. Click **Allow** to give permission for the technician to have access to your computer. After the connection is established, a toolbar appears at the top of your computer screen, as shown in Figure 1-25. During a Quick Assist session, the technician providing assistance has the same rights and privileges as the user account that is signed in on your computer (the host computer). Click **Pause** to temporarily prevent the technician from accessing your computer. Close the toolbar to end the connection.

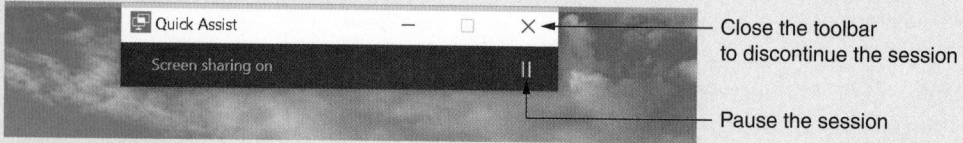

Figure 1-25   **The person receiving assistance maintains control of the screen-sharing session**

Project 1-3: Apply Troubleshooting Methodology

Most likely at this point in your IT career, you've already encountered some challenging troubleshooting scenarios with computers, mobile devices, and perhaps even with networks. Think back to one of the more interesting scenarios you've faced, one where you were able to solve the problem. Take a few moments to write down the symptoms you encountered, the information you gathered, and the questions you asked. Try to remember the sense of confusion or concern that this unknowing created. Then think through what theories you developed on the possible causes of the problem as well as what attempts you made to solve the problem. Write down as many details as you can remember about how you finally discovered the solution, and how you arrived at that conclusion.

Now look back at the troubleshooting flowchart in Figure 1-21. Map your problem-solving experience to the steps shown in the flowchart and include additional details as they come to you. Then answer the following questions:

1. What do you notice about your progression through the OSI model layers? Even without necessarily knowing what the OSI model is, did you naturally take a top-to-bottom or a bottom-to-top approach to the problem?
2. What theories did you test that turned out to be wrong? What information did you learn from those dead ends?
3. Did you involve anyone else in the problem-solving process? If so, who was that person and how did they help?

4. What did you do to test your solution? What measures did you take to ensure the problem didn't happen again?
5. Considering what you've now learned about troubleshooting methodology, what could you have reasonably done differently to discover the solution more quickly?

Project 1-4: IT and Networking Certifications

This book prepares you to take the CompTIA Network+ N10-007 exam, which is considered a fundamental benchmark toward a career in IT. Many other IT certifications also apply to IT and networking. Use the web to research and answer the following questions:

1. Which certification does CompTIA recommend a candidate for the CompTIA Network+ exam to already have?
2. How long does CompTIA recommend you work in networking before you take the CompTIA Network+ exam?
3. Cisco offers a full range of certifications focused on all aspects of networking. How long does Cisco recommend you work in networking before you take the CCNA Routing and Switching exam for certification? Include the web address of your source along with your answer.
4. How long does Cisco recommend you work in networking before you take the CCIE Routing and Switching exam? Include the web address of your source along with your answer.
5. Microsoft offers a group of certifications collectively called the MCSE (Microsoft Certified Solutions Expert). What are the current MCSE certifications? Include the web address of your source along with your answer.
6. Search online for a job opening in IT networking in your geographical area and save or print the job description and requirements. (Excellent sites that post IT jobs are Indeed.com and Monster.com.) Answer the following questions about the job:
   a. Which degrees are required or recommended?
   b. What types of skills are required or recommended?
   c. Which IT certifications are required or recommended?

Capstone Projects

In Capstone Project 1-1, you will set up a VM (virtual machine) using Client Hyper-V, and in Capstone Project 1-2, you set up a VM using Oracle VirtualBox. We will continue to build your virtual network of VMs in later chapters. Client Hyper-V and VirtualBox are client hypervisors, which is software used to manage VMs installed on a workstation. If you don't want to use Client Hyper-V or VirtualBox as your hypervisor of choice, you can substitute another client hypervisor, such as VMware Player, which can be downloaded free from *vmware.com*. Most of the future VM projects in this book can be completed using any of these three hypervisors.

Note that Windows Hyper-V and Oracle VirtualBox don't play well on the same computer and can cause problems, such as failed network connectivity. For that reason, don't install Hyper-V and VirtualBox on the same computer. If you must choose only one hypervisor because you only have one computer available, you'll find that future projects will usually work best using VirtualBox.

Capstone Project 1-1: Set Up a Virtual Machine Using Hyper-V

In this project, you use Hyper-V, which is software embedded in Windows 10 Professional, 64-bit version, to create and manage VMs (virtual machines) and virtual networks on a single workstation. You'll first enable the workstation UEFI to support virtualization and enable Hyper-V, and then create a VM in Hyper-V. Then you will install an OS in the VM. Your instructor will provide access to the Windows operating system installation files used in the VM.

Using a Windows 10 Pro, 64-bit version, computer, follow these steps to enable virtualization in UEFI, enable Hyper-V, and configure a virtual switch for the virtual network:

1. For Hyper-V to work, HAV (hardware-assisted virtualization) must be enabled in UEFI setup. If you are not sure it is enabled, click **Start** and **Power**. Hold down the **Shift** key and click **Restart**. When the computer reboots, click **Troubleshoot, Advanced options**, and **UEFI Firmware settings**. The computer reboots again, this time into UEFI setup. Make sure hardware-assisted virtualization is enabled. For the system shown in Figure 1-26, that is done on the CPU Configuration screen. Also make sure that any subcategory items under HAV are enabled. Save your changes, exit UEFI setup, and allow the system to restart to Windows.

Figure 1-26 Virtualization must be enabled in UEFI setup for Client Hyper-V to work

Source: ASUS

2. Hyper-V is disabled in Windows 10 Pro by default. To enable it, right-click **Start** and click **Apps and Features**. Scroll down and click **Programs and Features** under *Related settings*. Then click **Turn Windows features on or off**. Check **Hyper-V** and click **OK**. When Windows finishes applying changes, click **Restart now** for the changes to take effect.

3. Launch the **Hyper-V Manager** application from the *Windows Administrative Tools* folder on the Start menu. In the Hyper-V Manager left pane, select the name of the host computer, which will be listed underneath *Hyper-V Manager.*

4. To make sure your VMs have access to the network or the Internet, you need to first install a virtual switch in Hyper-V. To create a new virtual network switch, click **Virtual Switch Manager** in the Actions pane.

5. In the Virtual Switch Manager dialog box, verify **New virtual network switch** is selected in the left pane. To bind the virtual switch to the physical network adapter so the VMs can access the physical network, select **External** in the right pane. Then click **Create Virtual Switch.** In the next dialog box, make sure **Allow management operating system to share this network adapter** is checked and click **Apply.** In the Apply Networking Changes dialog box, click **Yes.** Your virtual LAN now has a virtual switch. Close the Virtual Switch Manager dialog box.

> **Note** 📎
>
> Your instructor might have special instructions for the following steps. Check with your instructor before proceeding.

To create a VM, follow these steps:

6. In the Actions pane, click **Quick Create**. Use these parameters for the new VM:
   - Enter a name for your VM, such as VM1 or VM_Lab_A.
   - Click **Change installation source** and select either a .iso or .vhdx file, depending on what installation media your instructor gave you.

> **Note** 📎
>
> A .iso file is a Disc Image File, which is a virtual DVD or CD. A .vhdx file is a virtual hard disk.

   - Make sure Windows Secure Boot is enabled.
   - Specify the VM can use the new virtual switch you created earlier.
   - Click **Create Virtual Machine**.

7. After the VM is created, you can edit its settings if required by your instructor, or click **Connect** and then click **Start**. If you used an ISO file as the installation source, when you see *Press any key to boot from CD or DVD*, press the spacebar so the VM will boot from the ISO file. Figure 1-27 shows where a Windows 10 installation has begun. Follow the prompts on-screen and make any adjustments to default settings as directed by your instructor.

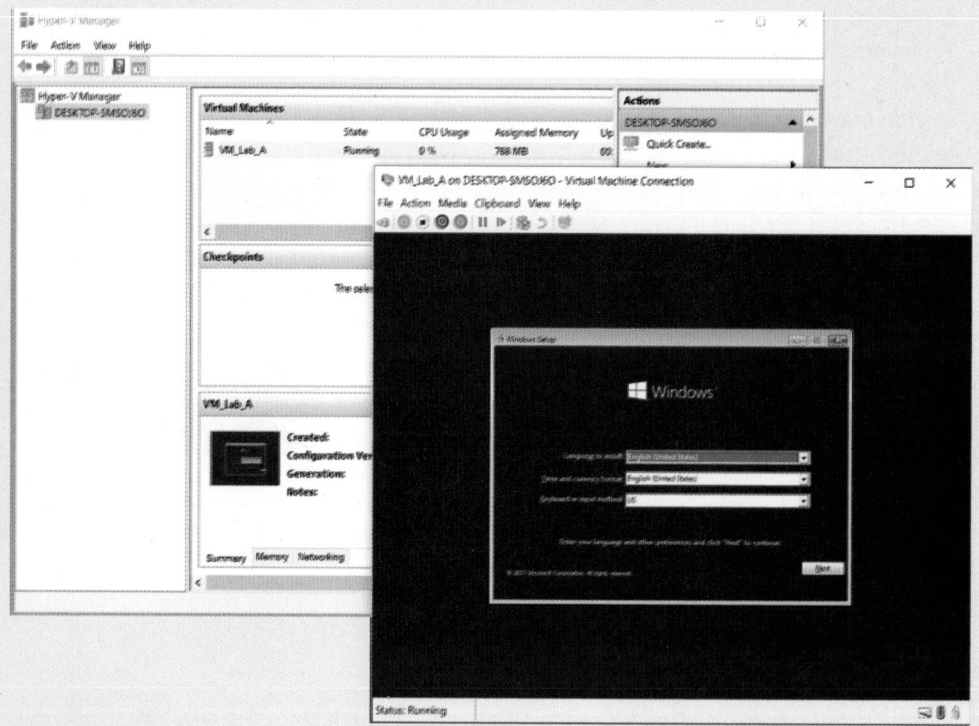

Figure 1-27 Windows 10 setup is running in the VM managed by Hyper-V

Note

If you have trouble booting to the ISO file, consider increasing the VM's available memory in the Settings menu. For example, 64-bit Windows installs more easily with 4 GB of RAM rather than the minimum 2 GB. Keep in mind, though, that any RAM dedicated to a running VM is not available to the host machine.

8. After you have installed Windows in the VM, open the Edge browser to confirm the VM has a good Internet connection.

In later chapters, you'll continue to build your virtual network and install resources in the VMs on your network.

Capstone Project 1-2: Set Up a Virtual Machine Using Oracle VirtualBox

Using any edition of Windows 10, you can download and install Oracle VirtualBox and use this free hypervisor to create virtual machines and a virtual network. Have available an ISO file to install the Windows operating system in the VM. Follow these steps:

1. If you are using a 64-bit host computer and want to install a 64-bit OS in the VM, HAV (hardware-assisted virtualization) must be enabled in UEFI setup. If you are not sure it is enabled, click **Start** and **Power**. Hold down the **Shift** key and click **Restart**. When the computer reboots, click **Troubleshoot, Advanced options**, and **UEFI Firmware settings**. The computer reboots again, this time into UEFI setup. Make sure hardware-assisted virtualization is enabled. For the system shown earlier in Figure 1-26, that's done on the CPU Configuration screen. Also make sure that any subcategory items under HAV are enabled. Save your changes, exit UEFI setup, and allow the system to restart to Windows.

2. Go to **virtualbox.org/wiki/Downloads** and download the **VirtualBox platform package** for Windows hosts to your desktop or other folder on your hard drive. Install the software, accepting default settings during the installation. The Oracle VM VirtualBox Manager window opens (see Figure 1-28).

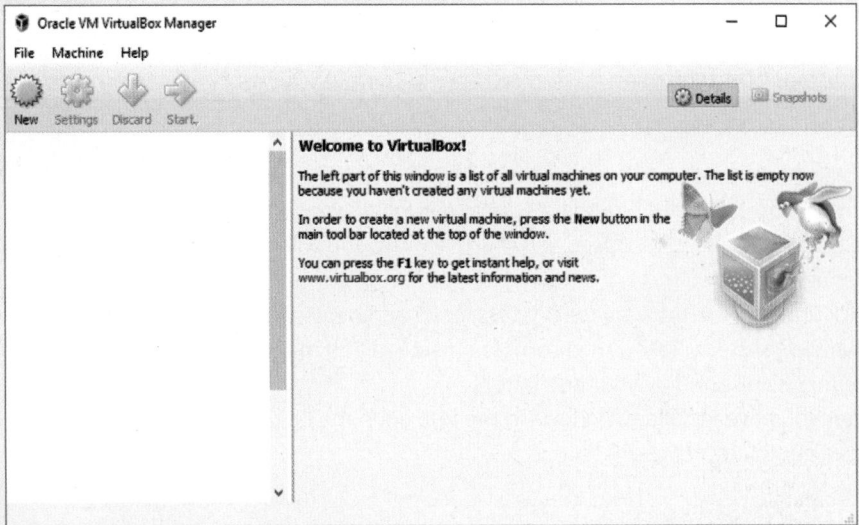

Figure 1-28   Use the VirtualBox Manager to create and manage virtual machines

Source: Oracle Corporation

3. To create a virtual machine using VirtualBox, click **New** in the toolbar and follow the wizard to create a VM. Select a name for your VM, for example VM1 or VM_Lab_A, and select the Windows OS you will install in it. You can accept all default settings for the VM unless directed otherwise by your instructor.

4. With the VM selected, click **Settings** in the VirtualBox Manager window. In the VM's Settings box, click **Storage** in the left pane.

5. In the Storage Tree area, to the right of *Controller: SATA*, click the **Adds optical drive** icon, which looks like a CD with a plus (+) symbol, as shown in Figure 1-29.

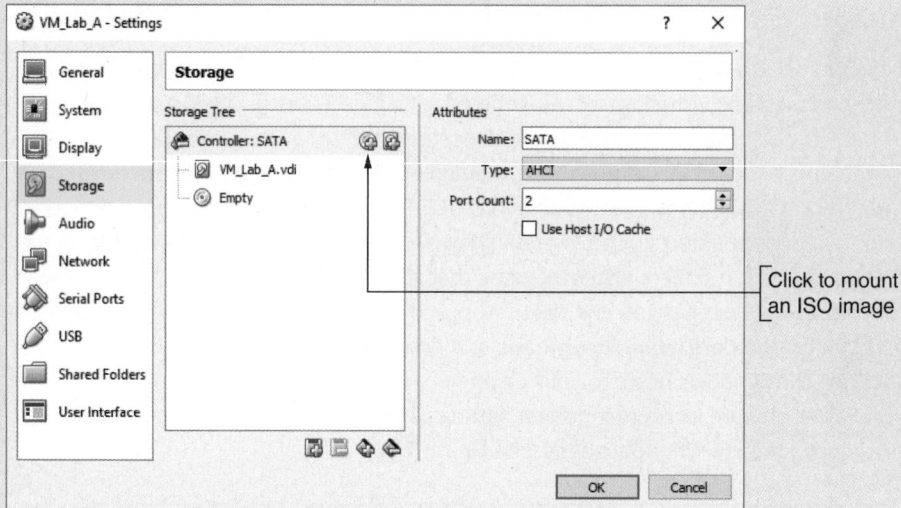

Figure 1-29   Storage Tree options allow you to mount an ISO image as a virtual CD in the VM

Source: Oracle Corporation

6. A dialog box appears. Click **Choose disk.** Browse to the location of the ISO file that contains the Windows operating system setup files made available by your instructor. Select the ISO file, click **Open,** and then click **OK.** You will now return to the VirtualBox Manager window.
7. Click **Start** on the toolbar. Your VM starts up and begins the process of installing the operating system. Follow the prompts on-screen and make any adjustments to default settings as directed by your instructor.
8. After you have installed Windows in the VM, open the Edge browser to confirm the VM has a good Internet connection.

> **Note** 🔗
>
> If you have trouble booting to the ISO file, consider increasing the VM's available memory in the Settings menu. For example, 64-bit Windows installs more easily with 4 GB of RAM rather than the minimum 2 GB. Keep in mind, though, that any RAM dedicated to a running VM is not available to the host machine.

In later chapters, you'll continue to build your virtual network and install resources in the VMs on your network.

## CHAPTER 2

NETWORK INFRASTRUCTURE AND DOCUMENTATION

After reading this chapter and completing the exercises, you will be able to:

Identify and describe network and cabling equipment in commercial buildings and work areas

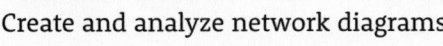

Create and analyze network diagrams

Explain operating procedures, inventory management, labeling conventions, and business documents for a typical network

Track the progress of changes made to a network

On the Job

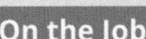

Over the years, our need for localized services or "remote" backups has steadily increased. Part of the solution has been to convert several of our larger wiring closets into small server rooms to host the additional equipment. We place climate monitors in these locations to help monitor temperature and humidity conditions. These monitors report climate conditions via SNMP to our network monitoring system. The network monitoring system then sends notifications to IT staff members if the temperature moves out of a threshold range.

One summer, we placed one of these temperature monitors in a closet where servers had recently been added, and things were good. A few months later, as the temperature cooled outside, we started getting alarms about temperature spikes. The spikes were small at first, but increased as the temperature outside dropped. That was kind of odd.

A little investigation revealed that although the server room had air conditioning, the room's temperature was not managed independently of the nearby offices. As autumn weather cooled the offices in the building, the staff would turn on the heat, warming themselves and, unfortunately, the servers. A tweak of the air conditioning layout quickly resolved this issue and things were once again good.

Robert Wilson
Information Systems Director, McCallie School

Just as a building architect must decide where to place walls and doors, where to install electrical and plumbing systems, and how to manage traffic patterns through rooms to make a building more livable, a network architect must consider many factors regarding hardware and software when designing a network. You've already learned about physical and logical network models, the OSI model, and the hosts, routers, and switches that manage data on the network. This chapter details the structural hardware necessary to connect and support these hosts, routers, and switches and connect them to the outside world. You'll learn about cabling, racks, equipment that monitors the environment, and other equipment that supports the physical network in a building or on a campus.

You'll also learn how critical it is to maintain good network documentation, so you can keep track of the complexities of a typical modern network. Finally, you'll learn how to implement clear policies for managing changes to a network. In later chapters, you will dig deeper into the various layers of network components, including the details of cabling and wireless networking.

Components of Structured Cabling

 **Certification**

7	APPLICATION
6	PRESENTATION
5	SESSION
4	TRANSPORT
3	NETWORK
2	DATA LINK
1	PHYSICAL

2.1   Given a scenario, deploy the appropriate cabling solution.

2.2   Given a scenario, determine the appropriate placement of networking devices on a network and install/configure them.

2.3   Explain the purposes and use cases for advanced networking devices.

2.5   Compare and contrast WAN technologies.

3.1   Given a scenario, use appropriate documentation and diagrams to manage the network.

5.2   Given a scenario, use the appropriate tool.

5.3   Given a scenario, troubleshoot common wired connectivity and performance issues.

If you were to tour hundreds of data centers and equipment rooms at established enterprises—that is, large organizations or businesses—you would see similar equipment and cabling arrangements. That's because organizations tend to follow a single cabling standard formulated by **TIA (Telecommunications Industry Association)** and its former parent company **EIA (Electronic Industries Alliance)**. This standard, known as the TIA/EIA-568 Commercial Building Wiring Standard, or **structured cabling**, describes uniform, enterprise-wide cabling systems, regardless of who manufactures or sells the various parts used in the system.

Network+ Exam Tip ⓘ

TIA and EIA are commonly referred to collectively with the acronym TIA/EIA. Occasionally, including on the CompTIA Network+ exam, you might see the acronyms reversed, as follows: EIA/TIA.

EIA was actually dissolved in 2011. Oversight of the relevant standards was assigned to ECA, the Electronic Components, Assemblies, Equipment & Supplies Association. The standards brand name EIA, however, continues to be used.

The structured cabling standard describes the best way to install networking media to maximize performance and minimize upkeep. The principles of structured cabling apply no matter what type of media, transmission technology, or networking speeds are involved. Structured cabling is based on a hierarchical design and assumes a network is set up in a star topology.

From the Demarc to a Workstation

Imagine you're a network technician touring the network on a school or corporate campus where you've just been hired. To get the lay of the land, your trained eye would be on the lookout for the main components that make up the network infrastructure. These components include the demarc, MDF, and locations of various IDFs strategically branched throughout campus. Figure 2-1 diagrams the main components you would look for in a network. Figure 2-2 shows a cross-section view of one building.

Data Rooms, Racks, and Other Equipment

A network begins at the demarc and ends at a workstation. We begin our tour of the physical network where it begins—at the demarcation point in the entrance facility.

Tour Stop 1: Entrance Facility in Building A

- *entrance facility*—This is the location where an incoming network, such as the Internet, connects with the school or corporate network. For large networks, the entrance facility might be an equipment room or data closet. For small networks, it might simply be equipment and cabling mounted to the side of a building.

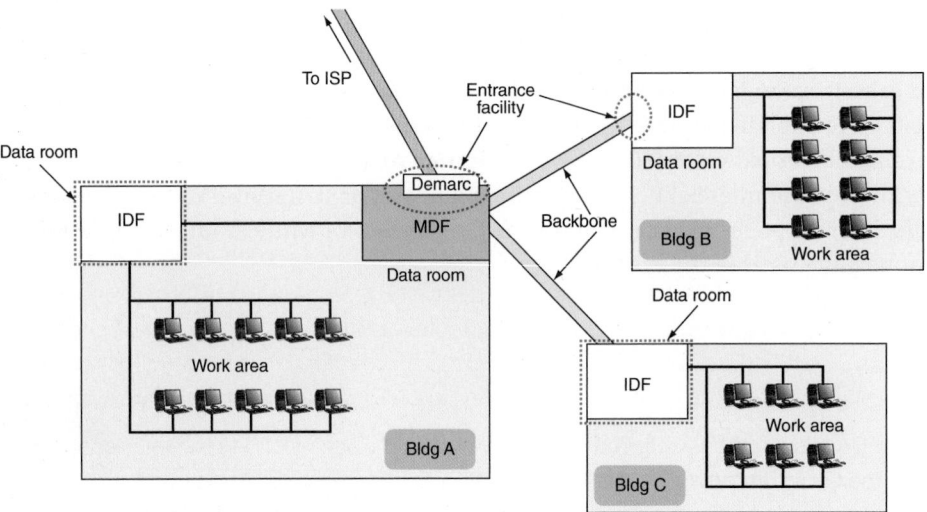

Figure 2-1   TIA/EIA structured cabling in a campus network with three buildings

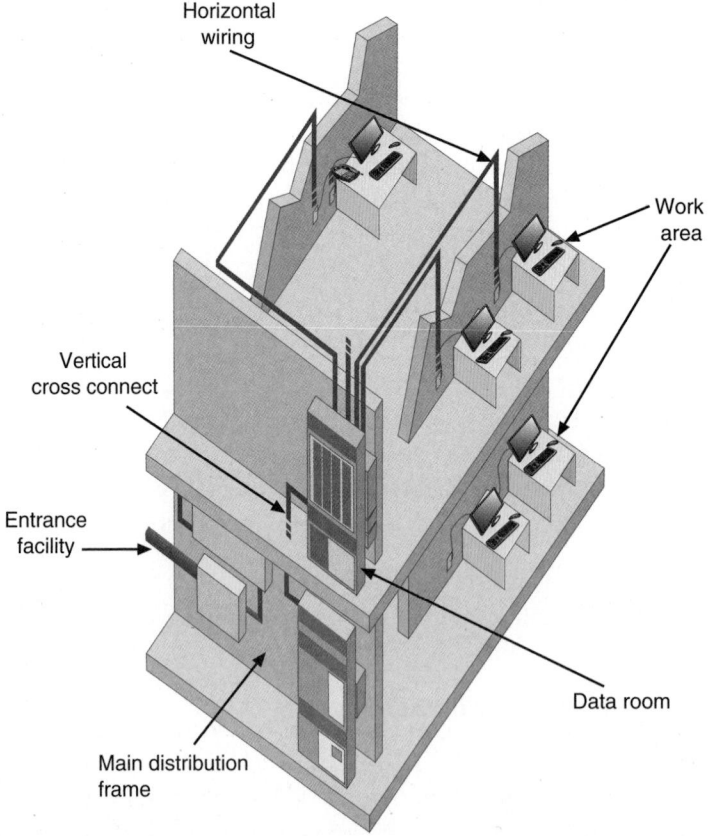

Figure 2-2   TIA/EIA structured cabling inside a building

The entrance facility is where a telecommunications service provider (whether it is a local phone company, Internet service provider, or long-distance carrier) accepts responsibility for the external connection. It contains a service provider's equipment, such as cabling and protective boxes. The most important device that belongs to the service provider in the entrance facility is the demarc.

- *demarc (demarcation point)*—For most situations, the device that marks where a telecommunications service provider's network ends and the organization's network begins (see Figure 2-3) is the demarc, or demarcation point. For example, an ISP (Internet service provider) might be responsible for fiber-optic cabling to your building to connect to your LAN. The device where the WAN ends and the LAN begins is the demarc. The service provider is responsible for its network beyond the demarc, and, in most cases, the organization is responsible for devices and services on the campus side of the demarc.

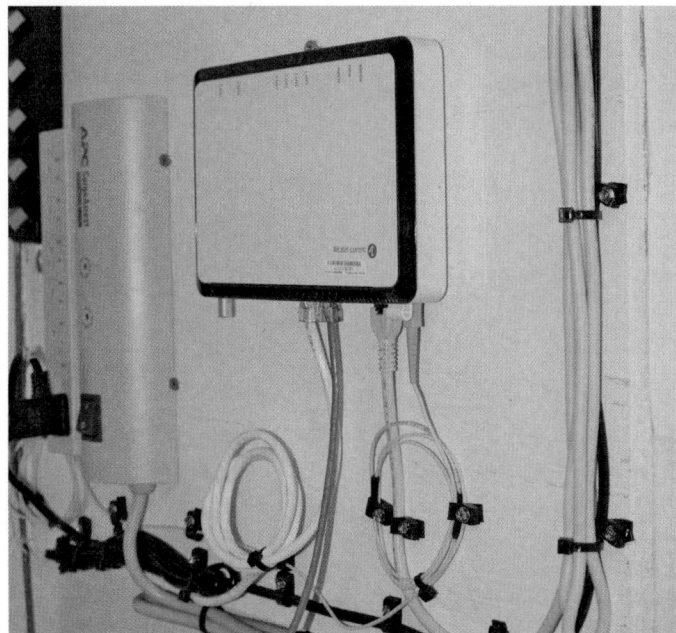

Figure 2-3   Demarc for Internet service to a campus network; this demarc is located inside a small data room and is mounted to a wall near two racks that house routers, switches, servers, and UPSes

- *MDF (main distribution frame or main distribution facility)*—Also known as the MC (main cross-connect), the MDF is the centralized point of interconnection for an organization's LAN or WAN. In practice, the term *MDF* can refer either to the racks holding the network equipment or the room that houses both the racks and the equipment. The MDF and the entrance facility might be in the same data room, or they could be in separate rooms, depending on the layout of the building.

Connections branching out from the MDF include Ethernet cables connecting to nearby work areas, large cables running to IDFs (discussed later in this list) in other buildings or on other floors of the same building, and the incoming connection from the service provider's facility. Imagine a star topology with the MDF at the center, as shown in Figure 2-4. Besides serving as a connection for cables, an MDF might contain the demarc (or an extension from the demarc, if the demarc itself is located outside the building), a transceiver that converts the incoming signal from the ISP into Ethernet, other connectivity devices (such as switches and routers), network servers, and transmission media (such as fiber-optic cable, which is capable of the greatest throughput). Often, it also houses an organization's main servers.

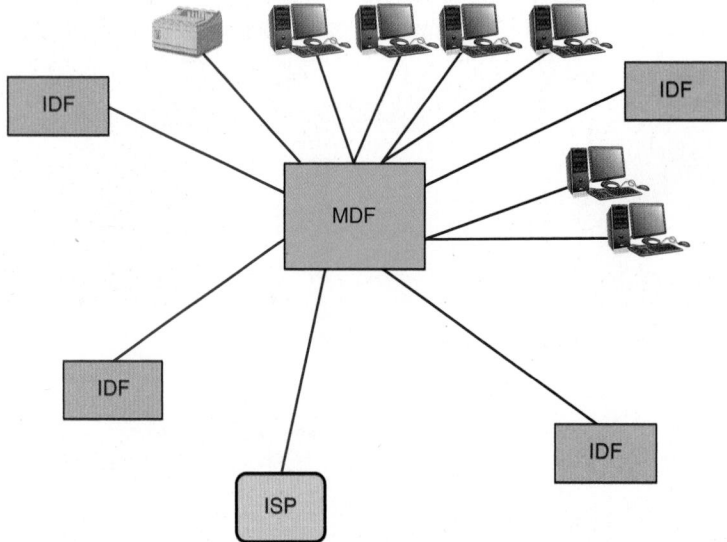

Figure 2-4   The MDF connects to the ISP, IDFs on campus, and nearby workstations

- *data room*—Also called data closet, data center, equipment room, or telecommunications room, a data room is the enclosed space that holds network equipment. These spaces might have requirements for size, clearance around equipment, wall materials, and physical security (such as a locked door). Larger data centers and smaller data closets both require good cooling and ventilation systems for maintaining a constant temperature, as you read about in the *On the Job* story at the beginning of this chapter.
- *racks*—A large data center can contain rows of racks to hold various network equipment. Rack systems make good use of space in data rooms and ensure adequate spacing, access, and ventilation for the devices they house.
- ***patch panel***—This is a panel of data receptors which can be mounted to a wall or a rack and which provides a central termination point when many patch cables

converge in a single location. Figure 2-5 shows the front side of a patch panel. Figure 2-6 shows the rear side of a patch panel that is not yet filled.

Figure 2-5   Patch panel on rack

Empty slots available for more connectors

Figure 2-6   Rear side of a partially filled patch panel, looking in from the back side of the rack

- *VoIP telephone equipment*—**VoIP (Voice over IP)**, also known as IP telephony, is the use of any network (either public or private) to carry voice signals using TCP/IP protocols. In one or more data rooms on a campus network, you might find a **VoIP gateway** device, which converts signals from a campus's analog phone equipment into IP data that can travel over the Internet, or which converts VoIP data from an internal IP network to travel over a phone company's analog telephone lines. You might also find **VoIP PBX (private branch exchange)** equipment. This is a dedicated telephone switch or a virtual switching device that connects and manages calls within a private organization, and manages call connections that exit the network through a VoIP gateway. Internally, this equipment connects to **VoIP endpoints**, which might be telephones sitting at each user's location or applications hosted on a user's computer or other device. See Figure 2-7 for two sample VoIP network layouts.

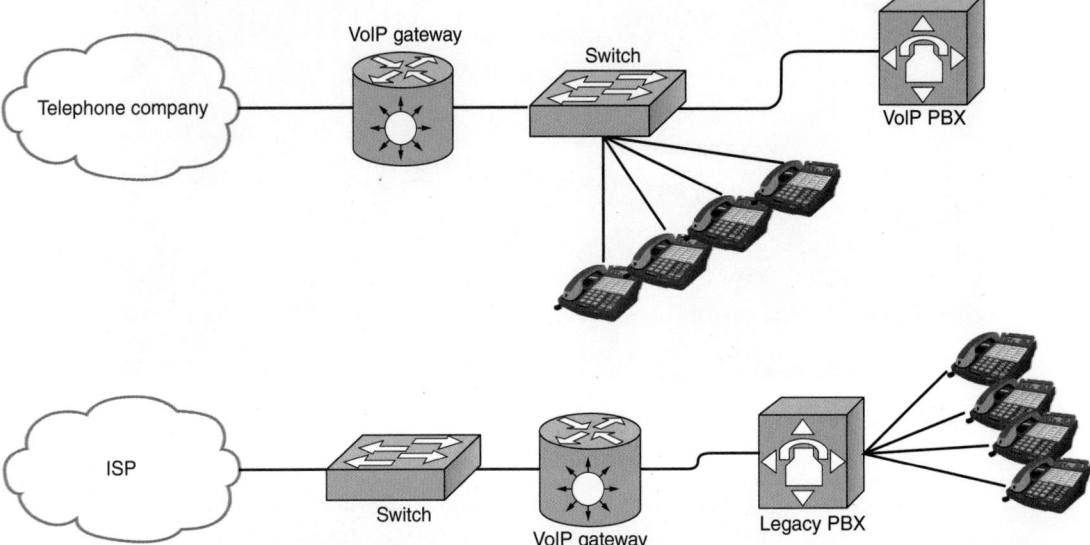

Figure 2-7   VoIP equipment can connect VoIP phones to an analog telephone line or an analog phone system to the Internet; there are pros and cons to each approach

Legacy Networking: Punchdown Blocks

The precursor to the patch panel is another kind of termination point, the punchdown block. This is a panel of voice or data receptors into which twisted-pair wire is inserted, or punched down, using a **punchdown tool**, to complete a circuit. The type of punchdown block used on data networks is known as a **110 block**. 110 blocks are more suitable for data connections than the older **66 block**, which was used primarily for telephone connections. (The numerals 66 and 110 refer to the model numbers of the earliest blocks.) 110 blocks are still available in several different capacities. If you do come across 110 blocks in the field, be careful not to untwist twisted-pair cables more than one-half inch before inserting them into the punchdown block. Figure 2-8 shows a punchdown block.

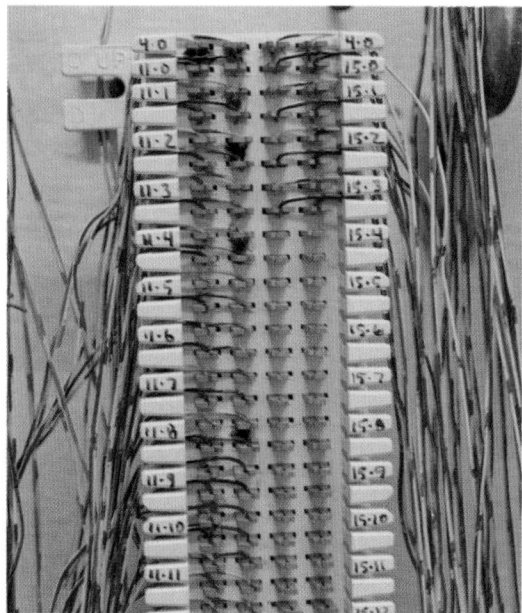

Figure 2-8   Punchdown block on wall

Tour Stop 2: Data Room in Building B

- *IDF (intermediate distribution frame)*—The IDF provides an intermediate connection between the MDF and end-user equipment on each floor and in each building. Again, the term *IDF* can refer either to the racks holding the network equipment or the room that houses both the racks and the equipment. There is only one MDF per campus, but there can be many IDFs connecting internal portions of the network. The TIA/EIA standard specifies at least one IDF per floor, although large organizations may have several data rooms or closets per floor to better manage the data feed from the main data facilities. Connections from the IDF branch out to workstations in an extended star topology, as shown in Figure 2-9.

Tour Stop 3: Work Areas in All Three Buildings

- *work area*—This area encompasses workstations, printers, and other network devices, and all the patch cables, wall jacks, and horizontal cabling necessary to connect these devices to a data room.
- *wall jacks*—A work area often contains wall jacks. The TIA/EIA standard calls for each wall jack to contain at least one voice and one data outlet, as pictured in Figure 2-10. Realistically, you will encounter a variety of wall jacks. For example, in a student computer lab lacking phones, a wall jack with a combination of voice and data outlets is unnecessary.

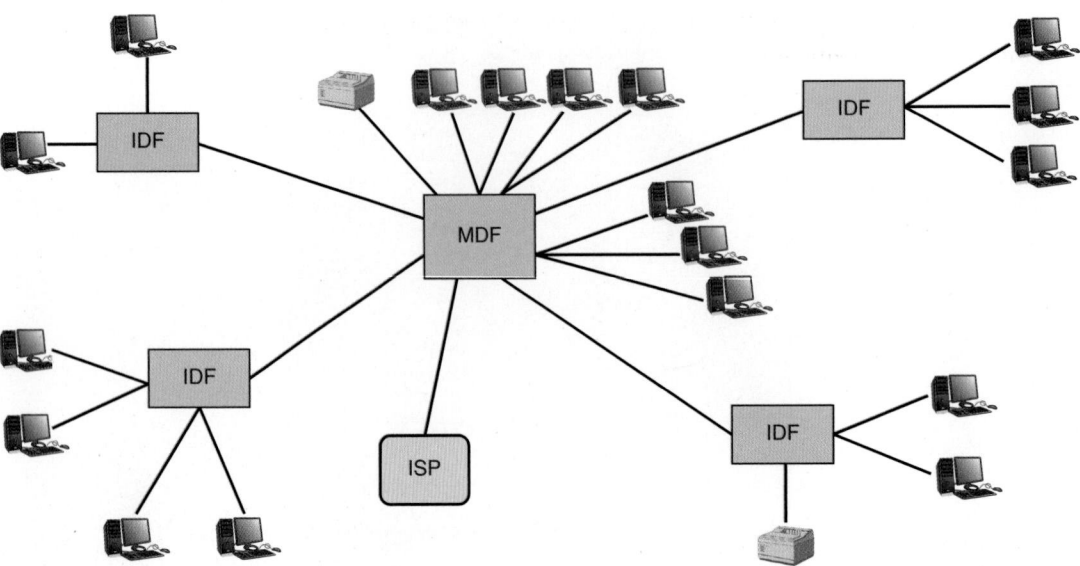

Figure 2-9 Workstations branching off of IDFs that branch off an MDF create an extended star topology

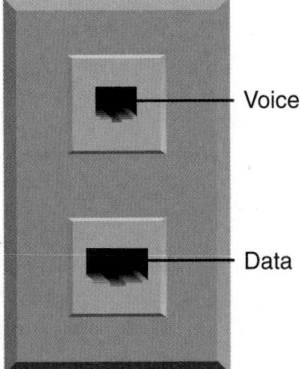

Figure 2-10 A standard TIA/EIA outlet

Rack Systems

By this point in your tour, you've seen a few racks. Generally, racks come in two-post and four-post varieties, though six-post racks are also available. They can also be open-framed, which provides greater accessibility, or enclosed, which provides greater protection. Figure 2-11 shows examples of open two-post racks and enclosed four-post racks.

The side posts in a rack provide bracketing for attaching devices, such as routers, servers, switches, patch panels, audiovisual equipment, or telephony equipment. This equipment often comes with attached or attachable brackets, called rack ears, for securing the device to the posts, as shown in Figure 2-12. Post holes can be round or square, threaded or nonthreaded. Square-hole racks are the most recent attachment innovation, allowing for bolt-free mounting.

Craig Cozart/Getty Images
Two-post rack

Four-post rack
iStock.com/amoklv

Figure 2-11   Open two-post racks and enclosed four-post racks

Rack ear

Figure 2-12   Attach network equipment to rack systems by inserting bolts through rack ears

Racks may be wall- or ceiling-mounted, freestanding on the floor, or bolted to the floor. Other features might include power strips, rack fans for cooling, cable trays, or drawers. Carefully consider a rack's dimensions when purchasing racks, as follows:

- *height*—Rack height is measured in rack units (RU or U) with the industry standard being 42U tall—about 6 feet. Half-racks are usually 18U–22U tall.
- *width*—Equipment racks come in a standard 19-inch frame, meaning that the front is 19 inches wide. You might also come across 23-inch racks.
- *depth*—Rack depths vary considerably between manufacturers.

> **Note** 📎
>
> It's impractical to install a separate console for every device on a rack. Typically, racks have one or more **KVM (keyboard, video, and mouse) switches**, which connect to a single console to provide a central control portal for all devices on the rack. Figure 2-13 shows a console that is held in a pull-out tray and that attaches to multiple KVM switches installed in this rack.

Figure 2-13   Here, a single console uses five KVM switches to access and configure multiple devices in a row of racks

Minimizing cable clutter can help prevent airflow blockages and heat buildup. In a typical rack system, airflow through the chassis is designed to move from front to back. In data centers containing multiple rows of racks, a hot aisle/cold aisle layout, as shown in Figure 2-14, pulls cool air from vents in the floor or from nearby, low-lying wall vents into the rows of racks. The hot air aisles are used to direct the heated air away from the racks into exhaust vents for cooling.

Cabling

As you traveled from the entrance facility, demarc, and MDF, then walked through a couple of buildings locating each IDF, and viewed each work area with their workstations, you noticed a variety of cabling types. Some cables are very thin, the Ethernet cables look familiar, and some cables are wrapped in dark insulation and are inches thick. Let's consider each of these cabling types as we work our way back to where we started our network tour. Then we'll explore cable management techniques before rounding

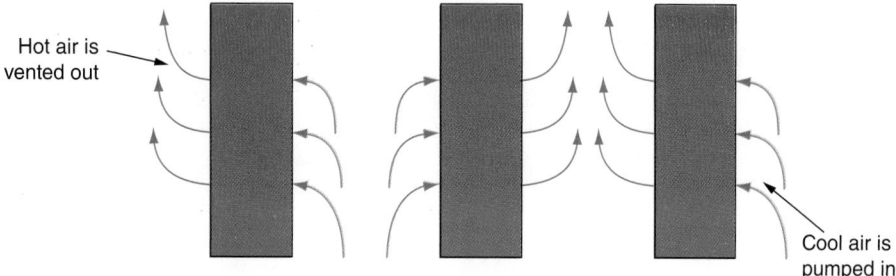

Figure 2-14   Hot aisle/cold aisle rack layout

out this part of the chapter with a discussion of the environmental and security needs of our network hardware.

Types of Cables

Structured cabling standards allow for three basic types of cable installations: patch, horizontal, and backbone cabling.

- *patch cable*—A patch cable is a relatively short (usually between 3 and 25 feet) length of cabling with connectors at both ends.
- *horizontal cabling*—This is the cabling that connects workstations to the closest data room and to switches housed in the room. The maximum allowable distance for horizontal cabling is 100 m. This span includes 90 m to connect the network device in the data room to a data jack on the wall in the work area, plus a maximum of 10 m to connect the wall jack to a workstation. Figure 2-15 depicts an example of a horizontal cabling configuration. Figure 2-16 illustrates a cable installation using UTP from the data room to the work area. Notice the patch panels in the figure.

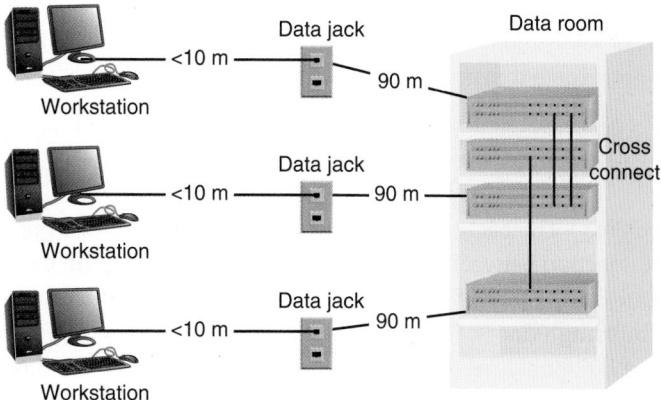

Figure 2-15   Horizontal cabling from a switch in a data room to workstations

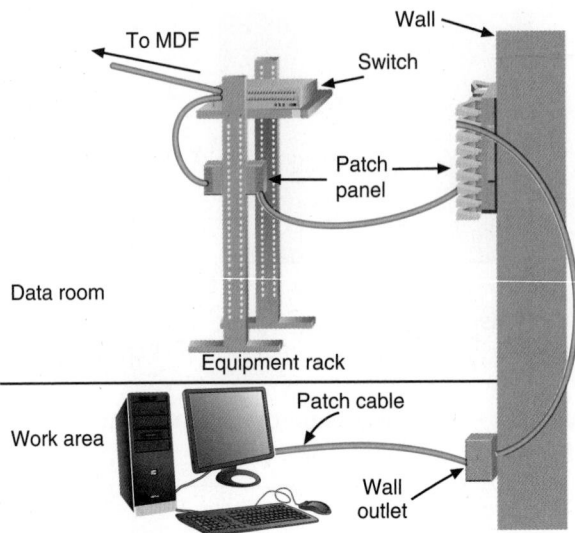

Figure 2-16   A typical UTP cabling installation

> **Note** 📎
>
> TIA/EIA recognizes three possible cabling types for horizontal cabling: UTP, STP, or fiber-optic cable. **UTP (unshielded twisted pair)** cable is a type of copper-based cable that consists of one or more insulated twisted-pair wires encased in a plastic sheath. Figure 2-17 shows three grades of UTP cables used with Ethernet. The second cable in the figure is terminated with an RJ-45 connector. **STP (shielded twisted pair)** cable is a type of copper-based cable containing twisted-pair wires that are not only individually insulated, but also surrounded by a shielding made of a metallic substance such as foil. **Fiber-optic cable** is a form of cable that contains one or several glass or plastic fibers in its core and comes in two types: SMF (single-mode fiber) or MMF (multimode fiber). Copper-based cable transmits data via electric signals, and fiber-optic cable transmits data via pulsing light sent from a laser or LED (light-emitting diode).

- *backbone cabling*—The backbone consists of the cables or wireless links that provide interconnection between the entrance facility and MDF, and between the MDF and IDFs. One component of the backbone is the vertical cross connect, which runs between a building's floors. For example, it might connect an MDF and IDF or two IDFs within a building. Especially on large, modern networks, backbones are often composed of fiber-optic cable. The cables can be thickly insulated and usually are run through flexible plastic sleeving or sturdier conduit, which are pipes installed overhead or through walls or sometimes underground, as shown in Figure 2-18.

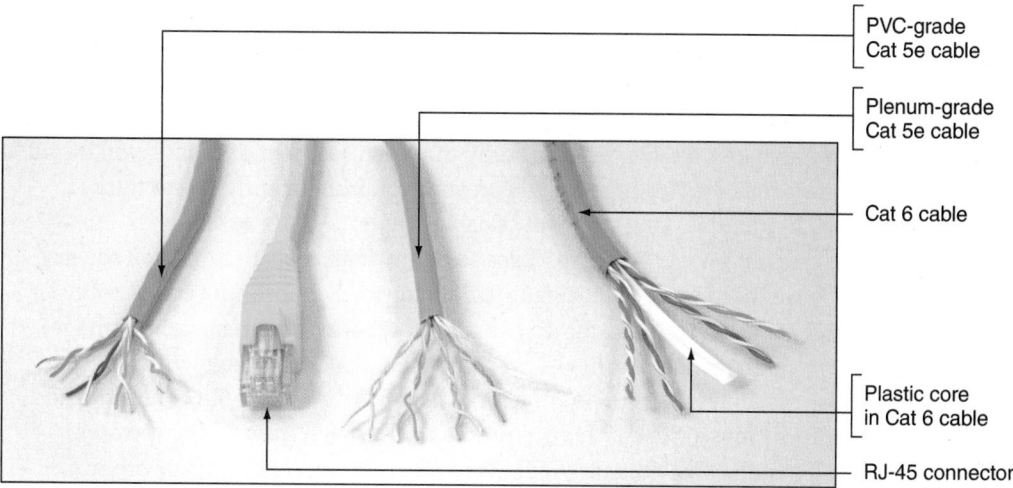

PVC-grade
Cat 5e cable

Plenum-grade
Cat 5e cable

Cat 6 cable

Plastic core
in Cat 6 cable

RJ-45 connector

Figure 2-17 UTP (unshielded twisted-pair) cables and RJ-45 connector used for local wired networks

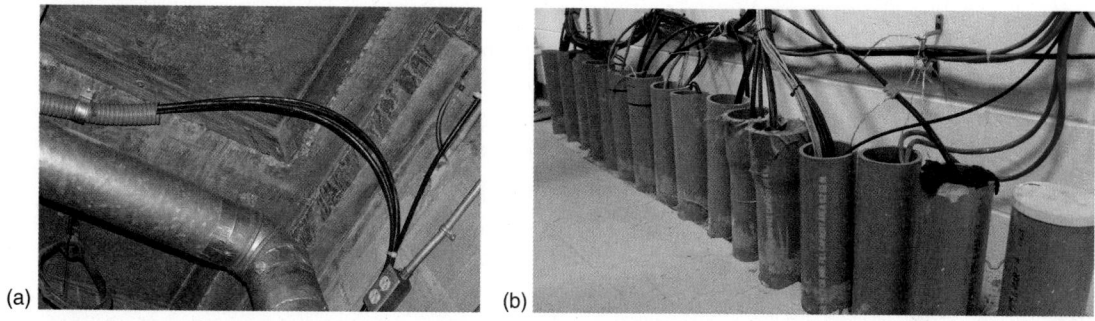

(a)   (b)

Figure 2-18 Sleeving and conduit help protect cabling from damage, but it might also invite rodent traffic and damage along the cables if not properly sealed

Expert network technicians know that many network problems are the result of poor cable installations; they pay very close attention to the quality of cable connections and cable management. Let's look at some standards for cable management in a building or enterprise.

Cable Management

As a network professional, you will likely occasionally add new cables to a data room, repair defective cable ends, or install a data outlet. Following are some cable installation tips that will help prevent Physical layer failures:

- *termination*—When terminating twisted-pair cabling, don't leave more than 1 inch of exposed (stripped) cable before a twisted-pair termination. Doing so increases the possibility of transmission interference between wires, a phenomenon called **crosstalk**.

- *bend radius*—Each type of cable has a prescribed bend radius, which is the radius of the maximum arc into which you can loop a cable without impairing data transmission. Generally, a twisted-pair cable's bend radius is equal to or greater than four times the diameter of the cable. Be careful not to exceed it.
- *verify continuity*—Use a cable tester to verify that each segment of cabling you install transmits data reliably. This practice will prevent you from later having to track down errors in multiple, long stretches of cable.
- *cinch cables loosely*—Avoid cinching cables so tightly with cable ties that you squeeze their outer covering, a practice that leads to difficult-to-diagnose data errors.
- *protect cables*—Avoid laying cable across a floor where it might sustain damage from rolling chairs or foot traffic. At the very least, cover the cable with a cable protector or cord cover. When possible, install cable through cable conduits and seal the ends of these pipes to reduce the risk of damage from pests or water.
- *avoid EMI*—Install cable at least 3 feet away from fluorescent lights or other sources of **EMI (electromagnetic interference)**, which is a type of interference that can be caused by motors, power lines, televisions, copiers, fluorescent lights, or other sources of electrical activity. This will reduce the possibility of noise (interference) that can affect your network's signals.
- *plenum cabling*—If you run cable in the **plenum**, the area above the ceiling tile or below the subflooring, make sure the cable sheath is plenum-rated, and consult with local electric installation codes to be certain you are installing it correctly. A plenum-rated cable is coated with a flame-resistant jacket that produces less smoke than regular cable coated with **PVC (polyvinyl chloride)**, which is made from a cheaper plastic that is toxic when burned. Figure 2-17, shown earlier, includes both a PVC cable and a plenum-grade cable, although the differences are not visibly obvious.
- *grounding*—Pay attention to grounding requirements and follow them religiously.
- *slack in cable runs*—Measure first, measure again, and always leave some slack in cable runs. Stringing cable too tightly risks connectivity and data transmission problems.
- *cable trays*—Use cable management devices such as cable trays and brackets (see Figure 2-19), braided sleeving, and furniture grommets, but don't overfill them.
- *patch panels*—Use patch panels to organize and connect lines. A patch panel does nothing to the data transmitted on a line other than pass the data along through the connection. But patch panels do help keep lines organized as they run from walls to racks to network devices, and they make it easy to switch out patch cables of variable lengths when devices are moved or changed.
- *company standards and stock*—Besides adhering to structured cabling hierarchies and standards, you or your network manager should specify standards for the types of cable used by your organization and maintain a list of approved cabling vendors. Keep a supply room stocked with spare parts so you can easily and quickly replace defective parts.

Figure 2-19   Cable management brackets installed on a rack

- *documentation*—Follow these guidelines to manage documentation at your cabling plant:
  - Keep your cable plant documentation in a centrally accessible location. Make sure it includes locations, installation dates, lengths, and grades of installed cable. You'll learn more about what to include in this documentation later in this chapter.
  - Label every data jack or port, patch panel or punchdown block, connector or circuit. You'll learn more about labeling later in this chapter.
  - Use color-coded cables for different purposes and record the color schemes in your documentation. Cables can be purchased in a variety of sheath colors, as shown in Figure 2-20. For example, you might want to use red for patch cables, green for horizontal cabling, purple for DMZ lines, and yellow for vertical (backbone) cabling.
  - Be certain to update your documentation as you make changes to the network. The more you document, the easier it will be to troubleshoot, move, or add cable segments in the future.

Monitoring the Environment and Security

Due to the sensitive nature of the equipment mounted on racks, environmental and security monitoring are both critical preventive measures. Data rooms are often serviced by HVAC systems that are separate from the rest of the building. The *On the Job* story at the beginning of this chapter gave a good example of why this is necessary. Specialized products are available that monitor the critical factors of a data room's environment. For example, ITWatchDogs offers several environmental monitoring products that can alert technicians to unacceptable temperature, humidity, or airflow conditions, and can also send text or email alerts when a secure door is left open,

Figure 2-20   Different colors of cables can indicate the general purpose of each cable

when the power supply is compromised, or even when light and sound conditions are unacceptable.

These alarms can be programmed to escalate as the severity of the situation increases, alerting higher-level staff if the problem is not resolved. Increasing humidity, for example, is caused by rising levels of water in the air, which can damage sensitive electronic equipment. Of even greater concern is the source of that moisture, which could pose a safety hazard if, say, water is leaking into the room. The monitoring system will likely also record the information so technicians can review recent data to look for patterns of fluctuations.

Security is also a vital priority with data rooms and rack equipment. Every data room should be secured behind a locked door with only limited IT personnel having copies of the keys. Never leave the room unlocked, even for a few moments. Many companies place security cameras to monitor any data room entrance—or at least to monitor any access point leading to the area where the data room is located—to serve as a deterrent to tampering, and to provide critical information should a break-in ever occur.

We've now completed our tour of the campus network. You saw where the Internet connection comes in through the demarc, proceeds to the MDF, and on out to various IDFs throughout campus. You also learned about different types of cables and the planning that goes into good cable installations. With all this equipment on a network, IT staff need good documentation to track the equipment, software, special configurations, and relevant vendors. This next section explores the types of network documentation you might create, reference, and update while working on a network.

Network Documentation

Q Certification

3.1   Given a scenario, use appropriate documentation and diagrams to manage the network.

3.5   Identify policies and best practices.

5.2   Given a scenario, use the appropriate tool.

As you work on a network, you collect a lot of valuable information in your mind. Until we develop good mind-reading technology, documentation is the most reliable way to keep this information safe in case you should be hit by the proverbial bus. Even without a catastrophic event, good documentation makes communication with your coworkers more efficient. It speeds up troubleshooting efforts, and puts information at your fingertips when you face similar problems or challenges in the future.

Let's begin our exploration of network documentation by looking first at the big picture of a network. We'll then dig into more detailed documentation, and end this chapter with a discussion on how to track changes on a network.

Network Diagrams

You've already learned about the importance of knowledge bases and how to document problem resolutions in a call tracking system. Recall that a knowledge base is a collection of accumulated insights and solutions to the problems encountered on a network. Another critically useful form of documentation is **network diagrams**, which are graphical representations of a network's devices and connections. These diagrams may show physical layout, logical topology, IP address reserves, names of major network devices, and types of transmission media. In Figure 2-21, you can see an example of a simple network diagram showing the physical topology of a small network. Figure 2-22 shows the same network's logical topology.

A network diagram is often the product of network mapping, which is the process of discovering and identifying the devices on a network. Several programs are available to assist in detecting, identifying, and monitoring the devices on your network. One of the simpler and most popular tools is **Nmap** (see Figure 2-23). Nmap was originally designed for Linux as a command-line utility, but has since been expanded for compatibility on several other OSes. It's now available in a GUI form called Zenmap (see Figure 2-24). At the end of this chapter, you will install and use Zenmap to discover devices on a network. Network mapping is a fascinating field of study in its own right, and its relevance and importance will only increase as the complexity of today's networks increases. Every network technician can benefit from understanding some general concepts related to network mapping.

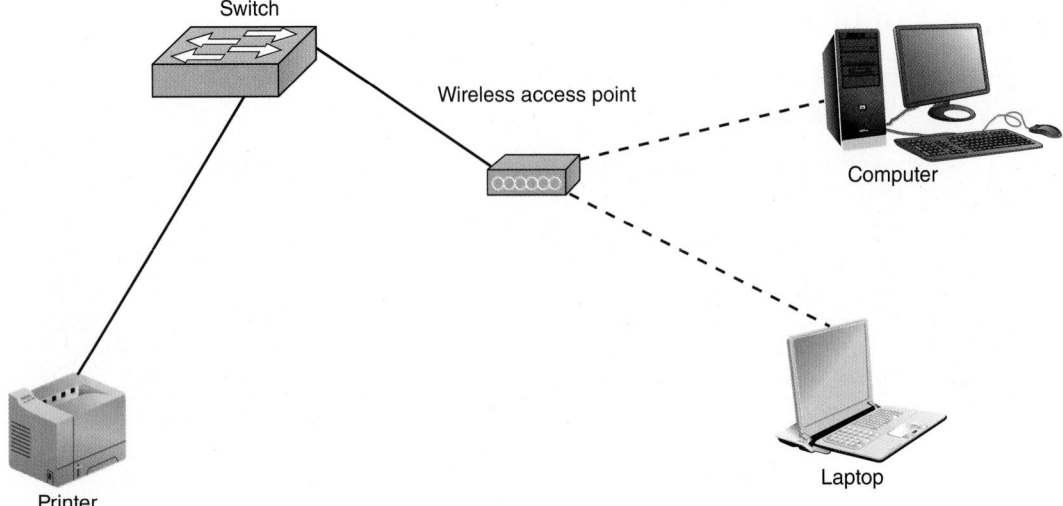

Figure 2-21   A small network's physical topology

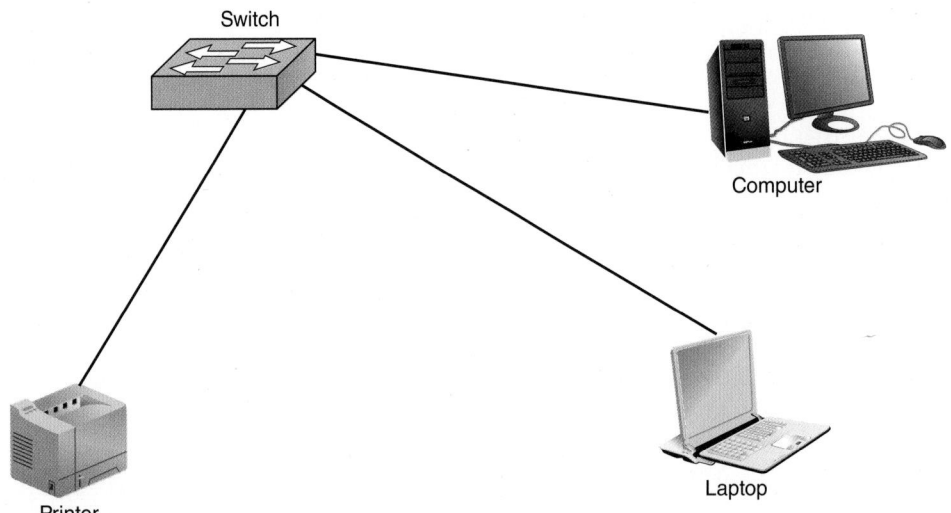

Figure 2-22   A small network's logical topology

You could sketch a diagram or map of your networked devices in a notebook, or you could draw it on your computer using a graphics program. However, many people use software designed for diagramming networks, such as Edraw, SmartDraw, Gliffy, Microsoft Visio, or Network Notepad. Such applications come with icons that represent different types of devices and connections.

Cisco Systems long ago set the standard for the diagram symbols used to represent routers, switches, firewalls, and other devices. These symbols are widely accepted and

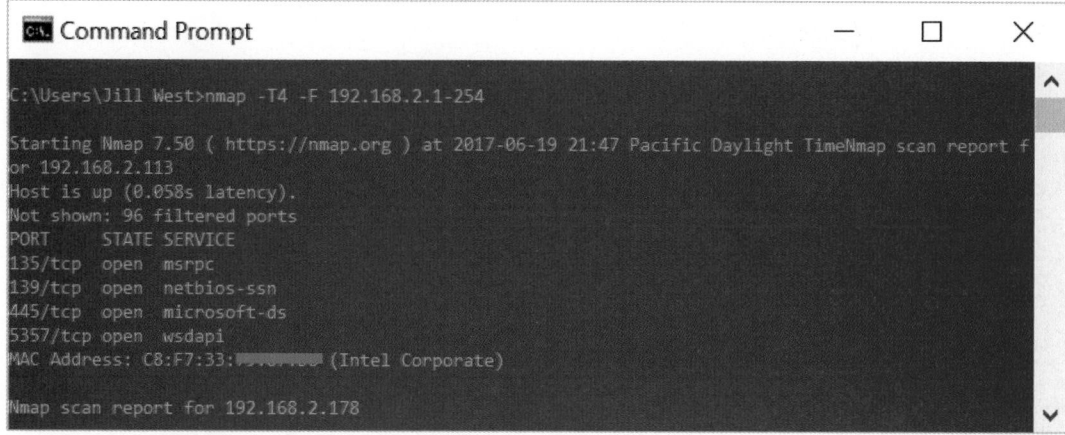

Figure 2-23   Nmap output in Command Prompt
Source: Insecure.org

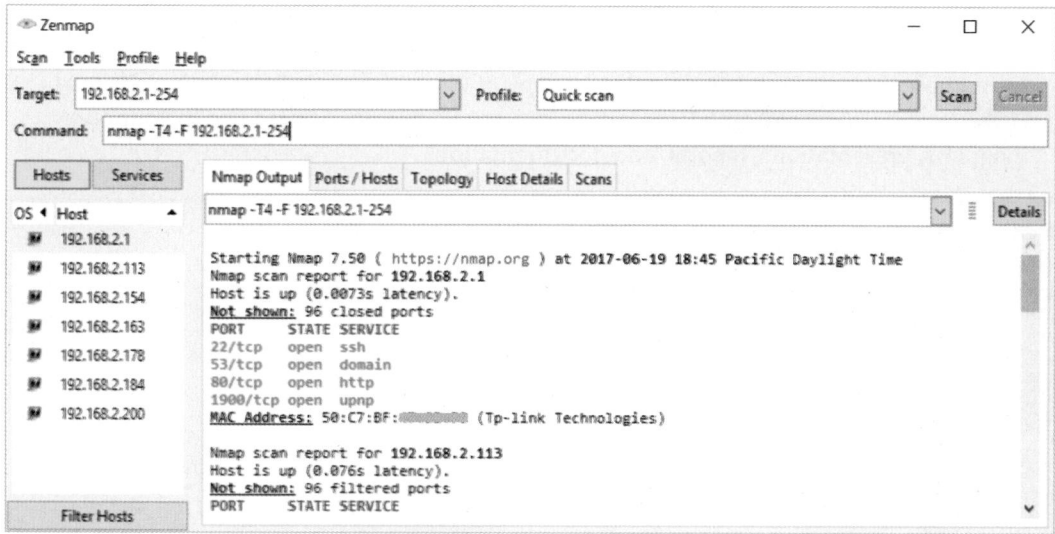

Figure 2-24   Zenmap graphical interface
Source: Insecure.org

understood in the networking field. Figure 2-25 shows a simplified network diagram that uses standard icons based on Cisco's iconography, with each device labeled. Notice that a router is represented by a hockey-puck shape with two arrows pointing inward and two arrows pointing outward. A switch is represented by a small rectangular box, which contains four arrows pointing in opposite directions. A wireless access point is also a rectangular box, but with squiggly lines on the front, and a firewall is a brick wall symbol. The Internet or an undefined portion of a network is represented by a cloud.

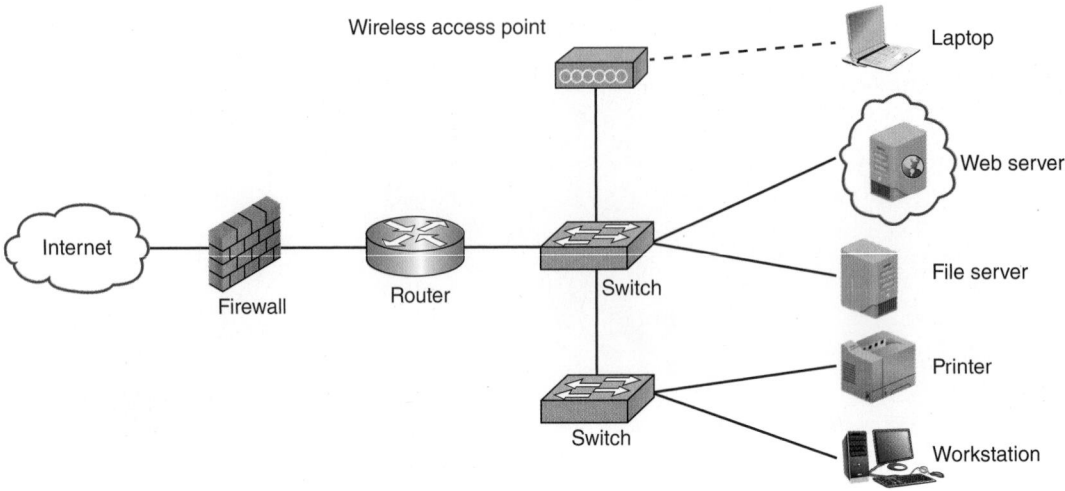

Figure 2-25   Network diagram using Cisco symbols

There are hundreds of Cisco symbols you might encounter when working with network diagrams. Table 2-1 shows several of the most common symbols that we'll use throughout this text. You can download a copy of Cisco's symbols from their website at *cisco.com/c/en/us/about/brand-center/network-topology-icons.html* to use in your own diagrams, presentations, reports, and documentation.

Table 2-1   Network topology icons

Icon	Device	Icon	Device
	Router		Workstation
	Switch		Printer
	Wireless router		Laptop
	Firewall		Cellular phone

Table 2-1 Network topology icons *(continued)*

Icon	Device	Icon	Device
	Hub		IP phone
	Relational database		Radio tower
	File server		Generic building
	Web server		Cloud

Applying Concepts: Create a Network Diagram

Drawing network diagrams will help you more easily visualize all the various devices and connections on a network. You can choose from several very good, free diagram apps. Here, you'll use one of these apps, Draw.io, to create your own network diagram. Complete the following steps:

1. In your browser, go to **draw.io** and select a location to save your diagrams, as shown in Figure 2-26. You might already have an account with Google Drive, Dropbox, or one of the other online storage options, which will simplify this process for you. If you don't want to use one of these online options, click **Device** to download the file to your hard drive when you're finished with it.
2. Click **Create New Diagram**. Give the diagram a name, such as **Ch02_NW1**, and click **Create**. You then see the screen shown in Figure 2-27.
3. Click a shape in the left pane to insert it onto the canvas, or drag and drop a shape from the left pane to the canvas. When you do, the format panel on the right changes and gives you many formatting options appropriate to that shape. Experiment with some of the settings, including color, fill, outline, opacity, text options, and arrangement.
4. Add a few more shapes and experiment with layers, labels, connections, and waypoints.
   a. To add a label, select a shape and start typing. Select the shape and click the **Text** tab to change the location of that label and other attributes.

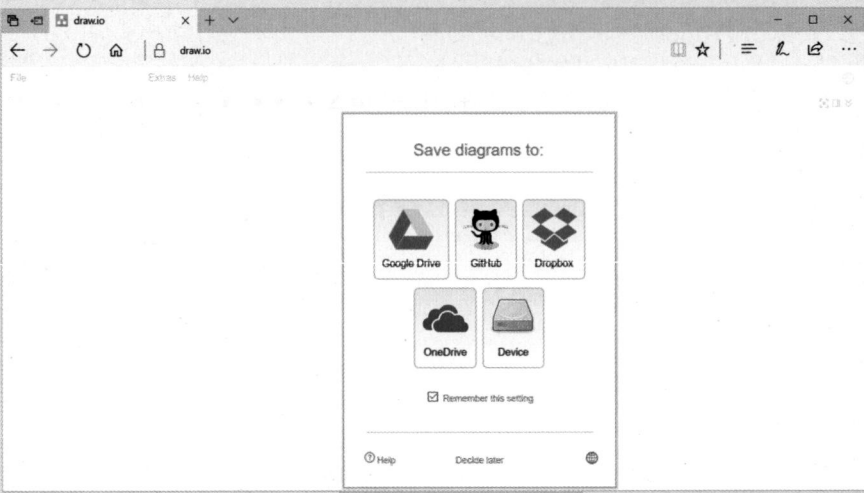

Figure 2-26   Use an account you already have, or store diagrams on your computer

Source: JGraph Ltd.

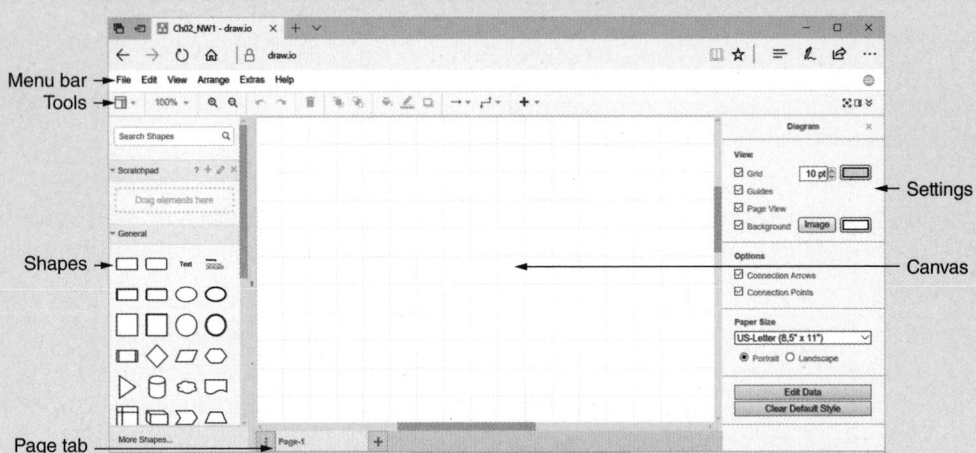

Figure 2-27   A new diagram begins with a blank canvas

Source: JGraph Ltd.

   b. To create a connection, move the mouse pointer over a shape, click a blue X, and drag the new connection to another location on the canvas. Attach the connection to another shape by dropping it on a blue X on the second shape.

   c. A waypoint is an intermediate point along a connection. To adjust waypoints, select a connection and drag any point on the connection to a different place on the canvas. You can change the waypoint style and endpoint styles on the Style tab.

5. Delete the objects currently on your canvas. You can delete items one at a time, or press **Ctrl+A** to select all of them and press **Delete**.
6. At the bottom of the left pane, click **More Shapes**. The Shapes dialog box opens.
7. In the Networking group, select **Cisco**, and then click **Apply**.
8. In the left pane, scroll down to the Cisco groups. Explore the many icons available here so you have a general understanding of what is included in each group.
9. Recreate the small network shown in Figure 2-28. The solid lines show logical device connections, and the cloud represents the Internet. The colored boxes show the groupings of different subnets.

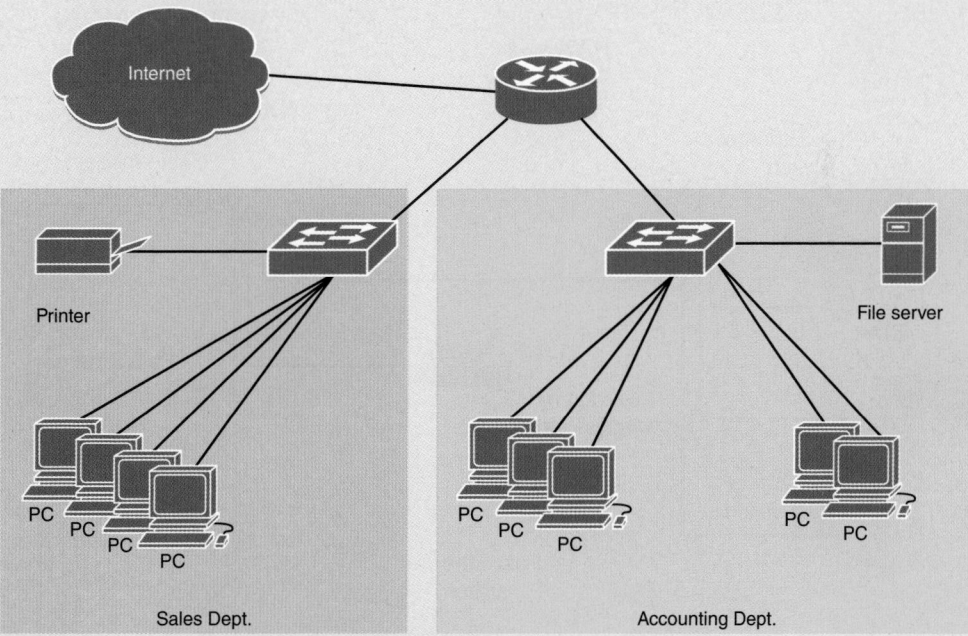

Internet

Printer

File server

PC
PC
PC
PC

PC
PC
PC

PC
PC

Sales Dept.

Accounting Dept.

Figure 2-28   Draw this network diagram

10. Export your final diagram as a .png file and save it to your local hard drive.

> **Note**
>
> Not every device on a network is shown in every diagram of that network. For example, in Figure 2-28, there's no firewall pictured. And yet, there would certainly be at least one firewall in place. The items that are shown in the diagram are selected specifically to illustrate one or a few aspects of the network.

Most network diagrams provide broad snapshots of a network's physical or logical topology. This type of view is useful for planning where to insert a new switch or determining how particular routers, gateways, and firewalls interact. However, if you're a technician looking for a fault in a client's wired connection to the LAN, a broad overview might be too general. In that case, you'll need a **wiring schematic**, which is a graphical representation of a network's wired infrastructure. In its most detailed form, it shows every wire necessary to interconnect network devices and the locations of those wires. Some less-detailed wiring schematics might use a single line to represent the group of wires necessary to connect several clients to a switch. Figure 2-29 provides an example of a wiring schematic for a small office network that relies on cable broadband service to access the Internet.

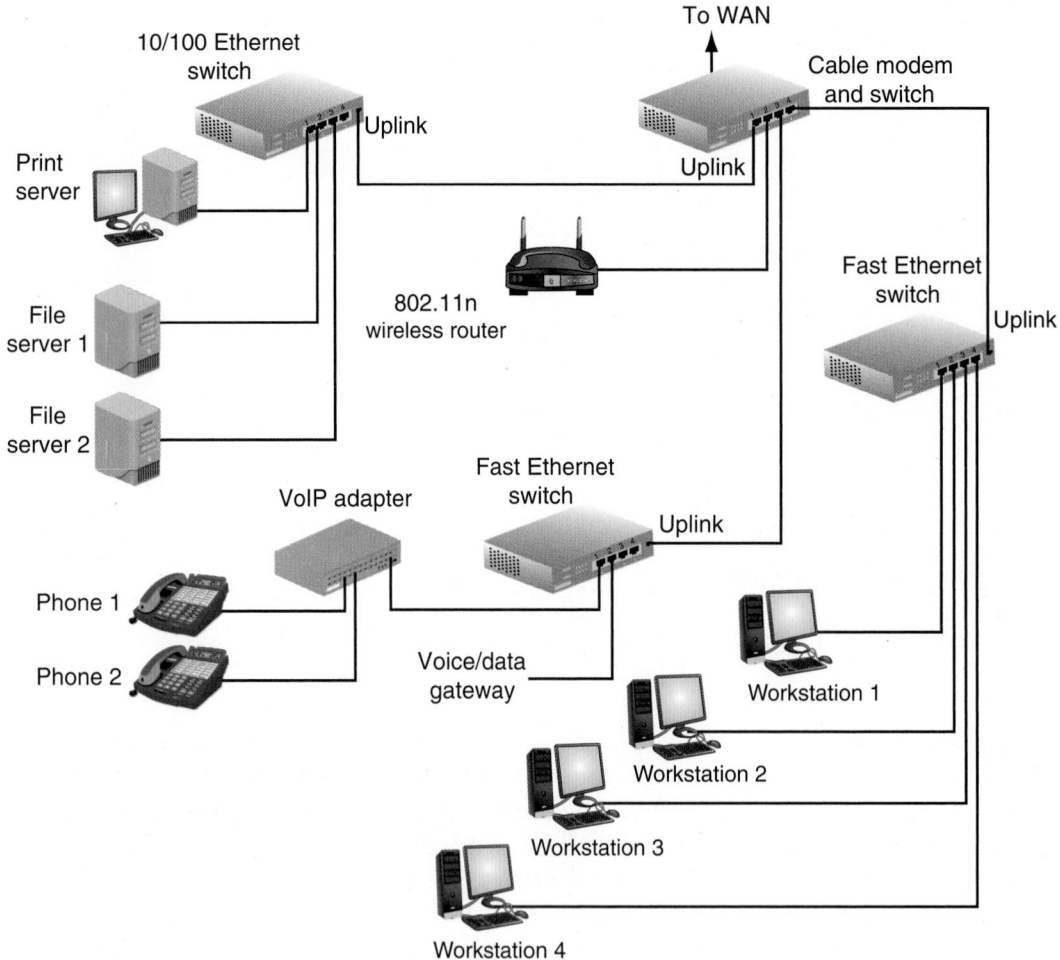

Figure 2-29   Wiring schematic

One more diagram type you will come across is the **rack diagram**. These drawings show the devices stacked in a rack system and are typically drawn to scale. You can see a simple rack diagram in Figure 2-30. Rack diagrams are helpful when planning a rack installation. They're also invaluable for tracking and troubleshooting equipment installed in a rack. Many of the drawing tools used to draw network diagrams, such as Draw.io, include the symbols needed for drawing simple rack diagrams as well.

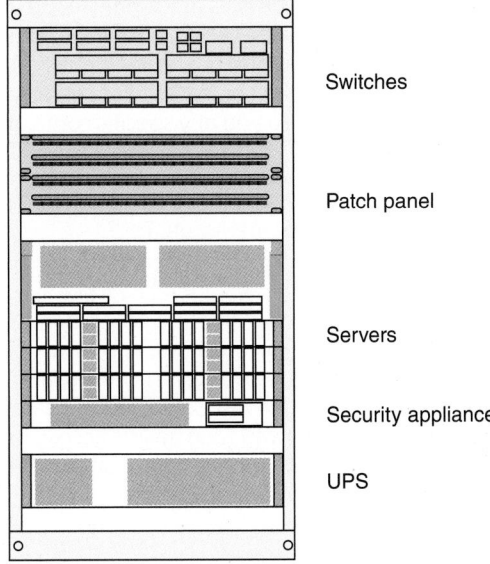

Figure 2-30   Typical devices installed on a rack

Network diagrams give you a visual overview of a network. However, it's impossible for a diagram to include all the information needed for good network documentation. Next, we look at other types of network documentation and consider ways to keep this information up-to-date.

Operating Procedures

Essential documentation covers logical and physical connections on a network; inventory management; IP address utilization; vendors (such as contact information, warranty information, service agreements, and troubleshooting instructions); and internal operating procedures, policies, and standards. The way you gather, format, and store your network documentation can vary. When creating new documentation, take some time to brainstorm all the elements you want to include, and consider how you'll keep each of these documents updated. Use Table 2-2 to help develop your ideas.

Table 2-2   Items to consider covering in network documentation

Type	What to cover
Hardware	*Includes:* Devices, racks, jacks, patch panels, switches, ports, MDF/IDF, floor plans, power and water shutoff locations
	For example: Devices: How many of the following devices are connected to your network: switches, routers, firewalls, access points, servers, UPSes, printers, backup devices, and clients? Where are they located? Are they physical or virtual? If physical, what are their model numbers and vendors? Are they owned or leased? For servers, specify each type of server hosted on each physical device and any specific configurations of those servers.
Software	*Includes:* Operating systems (and their configurations), applications (and their configuration), Active Directory (security groups, domains, etc.)
	For example: Which applications are used by clients and servers? What software is required by different departments? Where do you store the applications? From where do they run? Also keep records of leases, product keys, licenses, and licensing restrictions. **Licensing restrictions** might define who is allowed to use an application and for how long, how many users are allowed to install or access it, whether the application can be made available over a company's network or the Internet, and how many backup copies of the application may be stored.
Network configuration	*Includes:* Protocols, backups, passwords, IP addressing (static, DHCP scopes), subnets, VLANs, server roles, access methods, transmission details
	For example: Describe how backups are made, what information is included, where they are stored, and how to restore from backup.
Contacts	*Includes:* Vendors, decision makers, team members, utilities (alarm, electric, water)
	For example: Include a list of all vendors with contact information, lists of services provided, maintenance agreements, warranties or support subscriptions, and any special troubleshooting instructions from the vendor (or references to where to find that information).
Special instructions	*Includes:* Who to contact in an emergency, how to access backup information, how to meet the requirements of various privacy, security, and safety restrictions
	For example: Medical data is protected by HIPAA (Health Insurance Portability and Accountability Act of 1996). In the event of a network failure or intrusion, certain steps must be taken to notify appropriate parties, minimize data exposure, and remediate any damage.

> **Caution** ⚠
>
> Obviously, you need to keep password documentation very secure. However, multiple people should have access to it. Otherwise, if the network admin is suddenly incapacitated, you might be unable to retrieve high-security passwords. A password manager, such as KeePass or LastPass, can be invaluable in this situation.

If you have not already collected and centrally stored the answers to the items just listed, it could take the efforts of several people and several weeks to compile them, depending on the size and complexity of your network. This evaluation would require visits to data rooms, an examination of servers and desktops, a review of receipts for software and hardware purchases, and, potentially, the use of a protocol analyzer or network management software package. Still, all this effort would save you work in the future.

As you compile the information, organize it into a database that can be easily updated and searched. That way, staff can access the information in a timely manner and keep it current. Your company might provide an internal website or database for this purpose, or you can use a wiki. A **wiki** is a website that can be edited by users. You can add files and photos, easily create links between pages, group pages by different criteria, and make choices about which users have which privileges on the site. At the end of this chapter, you'll create your own wiki to track information from some of the projects in this text.

> **Caution** ⚠
>
> If you use a digital format to store your network documentation, consider that this information might be lost or temporarily inaccessible if your network suffers a catastrophic failure. Keep digital backups securely stored off-site, perhaps in the cloud. Also, keep up-to-date, printed copies in multiple, secure locations.

At some point you need to test how thorough and clear your documentation is. Perhaps the CFO, an executive from another department, or a carefully selected consultant can sort through the information, asking questions and pointing out areas of misunderstanding or gaps in coverage. When hiring new technicians, refer them often to your documentation and ask for feedback on how easily they can make sense of it. Also devote a certain amount of time on a regular basis to updating your documentation.

Inventory Management

The process of designing, implementing, and maintaining an entire network is called the **system life cycle**. A major part of this process is the removal and disposal of outdated assets, and the addition of compatible, updated devices. This is much easier to oversee and accomplish when you know what devices you have on your network. The term **inventory management** refers to the monitoring and maintaining of all the assets that make up a network. You might create your own documentation for this, such as a spreadsheet or a database, or you might use an inventory management application with features designed to simplify this process. The first step in inventory management is to list all the components on the network, which include:

- *hardware*—Configuration files, model number, serial number, location on the network, and technical support contact
- *software*—Version number, vendor, licensing, and technical support contact

Inventory management documentation simplifies maintaining and upgrading a network because it ensures that you know what the network includes. For example, if you discover that a router purchased two years ago requires an upgrade to its operating system software to fix a security flaw, you will also need to know how many routers are installed, where they are installed, and whether any have already received the software upgrade. Up-to-date inventory management documentation allows you to avoid searching through old invoices and troubleshooting records to answer these questions.

In addition, inventory documentation provides network administrators with information about the costs and benefits of certain types of hardware or software. For example, if you conclude that 20 percent of your staff's troubleshooting time is spent on one flawed brand of hard drive, inventory documentation can reveal how many hard drives you would need to replace if you chose to replace those components, and whether it would make sense to replace the entire installed base. Some inventory management applications can also track the length of equipment leases and alert network managers when leases will expire.

> **Note** 📎
>
> The term *inventory management* originally referred to an organization's system for keeping tabs on every piece of equipment it owned. This function was usually handled through the Accounting Department. Some of the accounting-related tasks included under the original definition for inventory management, such as managing the depreciation on network equipment or tracking the expiration of leases, apply to inventory management in networking as well.

Labeling and Naming Conventions

Maintaining up-to-date records about your network devices will reduce your workload and make troubleshooting easier and more efficient. Adequate recordkeeping also saves money by preventing unnecessary purchases. The secret to keeping track of devices is naming them systematically, and then labeling them with those names. A good naming convention can serve double duty by including essential information about the device. Consider the following tips:

- Use names that are as descriptive as possible (without giving away too much information to potential hackers).
- Only include fields that are absolutely essential in identifying the device.
- Don't overcomplicate the name with useless or redundant information.
- Pay attention to any established naming convention already in use by your employer. For example, existing acronyms for the various departments in your corporation are more recognizable for employees.
- Think big-picture-down-to-details when designing device name fields, such as starting with the building name, then floor, then data room number, then rack number. If your company has national locations or international locations, certain names may need to include codes for continent, country, state, city, and so on. Think in terms of "top-down" or "outside-in" and be consistent.
- Consider any security risks from the details you might include in your naming convention. Make sure naming and labeling information is stored behind locked doors and inside secure databases. Don't use names that identify the location (physical or digital) of sensitive information that might alert an attacker to a highly desirable target, such as customer credit card information or protected patient data. When needed, use more obscure names that won't easily attract attention.

Applying Concepts: Examine a Naming Convention

A good naming convention will save you a lot of time that would otherwise be lost looking up device names. Consider the following device names:

002-09-03-01-03
phx-09-nw-01-rtr3

The first name is simply a string of numbers, which many people would have a hard time recognizing as meaningful information. A numeric system like this would force new employees to spend too much time decoding device names.

The second name is easier to interpret on the fly. Some of the numbers have been replaced with abbreviated names, locations, and other identifying information. The first field tells you that the device is located in Phoenix, which is abbreviated as phx. The second field (09) refers to the floor number, so using a number is unavoidable. The third field (nw) refers to the data room's location within the building (the northwest corner) rather than the data room's number, which would also be onerous to memorize. The fourth field contains the rack number (01), and the final field (rtr3) identifies the type of device (a router) and the number of the router (3).

> **Note** 📎
>
> When designing a naming convention, be sure to include enough digits in each field to allow for future expansion. A two-digit field is much more limited than a three- or four-digit field. One digit will work fine for numbering the racks in a small data closet, which can't possibly hold 10 racks. But if you're numbering employees or workstations, your company may quickly outgrow a two-digit workstation field.

Not every company needs long device names; and small devices, such as the ports on a switch, aren't big enough to accommodate long names. For example, when labeling ports on a patch panel or switch in a data room, a connection type (vertical versus horizontal, storage versus workstation, etc.) and possibly a room number may suffice. For jacks on a wall, consider names such as the employee's job title, desk location, or something similar. Avoid using employee names because many of those will change over the lifetime of the device. Ultimately, the name of the game is *consistency*.

A word to the wise network technician: Learn to view good labeling as a beautiful thing! For the meticulous technician, labeling can become an art form. Here are some tips to get started:

- As discussed earlier, you can use color-coded cables for different general purposes. However, don't rely on the cable colors alone; use labels on ports or tags on cables to identify each cable's specific purpose, as shown in Figure 2-31.

(a)   (b)

Figure 2-31   Labels on ports and tags on cables

- In addition to labeling cables, also label the ports and jacks that cables connect to. Place the labels directly on patch panels, switches, routers, wall plates, and computers, and be sure that labels are used to identify systems, circuits, and connections.

- Where labels won't fit on the device itself, draw a simple diagram of the device that indicates the purpose of each port, slot, and connector, such as the example in Figure 2-32.

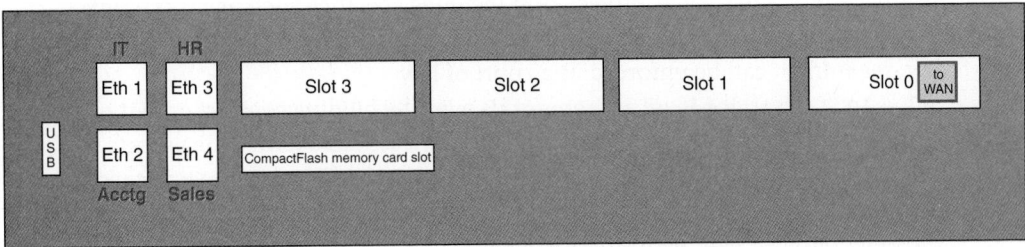

Figure 2-32   Simple diagram of a Cisco router with red labels identifying how five ports are used

- A portable label maker is indispensable for creating labels. Choose labels that are durable and that are designed to stick to plastic and metal, not paper. Keep your label maker handy in your toolbox as you work. Whenever you find a device, wall jack, or port not labeled and you are able to identify its purpose, take the time to label it correctly. Others in your organization will soon see you as the "label champion."

Business Documents

Aside from the documentation you create to track network assets and resources, you will also encounter a variety of standard business documents in the course of your work as a network technician. These documents help define who is responsible for various devices, applications, and expenses. For example, if your organization shares space or networking equipment with another organization, or if your organization leases equipment from a vendor, written documents will define each entity's responsibilities. Although you won't likely be held responsible for creating these documents, it's helpful to be familiar with their purpose and structure, especially if you're involved in making decisions about equipment purchases or software subscriptions:

- *RFP*—An **RFP (request for proposal)** is a request to vendors to submit a proposal for a product or service your company wants to purchase. Key parts of an RFP include why your company requires the product or service, how the product or service will be used, how and when the proposals will be evaluated, and a list of items a vendor should include in its proposal (for example, a detailed description of its product or service, technical support, user training, and initial and ongoing costs).
- *MOU*—An **MOU (memorandum of understanding)** documents the intentions of two or more parties to enter into a binding agreement, or contract, and is sometimes used between an informal handshake and the legally binding signatures on contracts. The MOU can be helpful in pushing along contract negotiations and in defining specific concerns of each party, but it is usually not a legally binding document,

does not grant extensive rights to either party, provides no legal recourse, and is not intended to provide thorough coverage of the agreement to come.

- *SOW*—An **SOW (statement of work)** documents in detail the work that must be completed for a particular project, and includes specifics such as tasks, deliverables, standards, payment schedule, and work timeline. An SOW is legally binding, meaning it can be enforced in a court of law.

- *SLA*—An **SLA (service-level agreement)** is a legally binding contract or part of a contract that defines, in plain language and in measurable terms, the aspects of a service provided to a customer, such as the service provided by an ISP. Details specified might include contract duration (minimum or maximum), guaranteed uptime, problem management, performance benchmarks, and termination options.

- *MSA*—An **MSA (master service agreement)** is a contract that defines the terms of future contracts between parties, such as payment terms or arbitration arrangements.

- *MLA*—An **MLA (master license agreement)** grants a license from a creator, developer, or producer, such as a software producer, to a third party for the purposes of marketing, sublicensing, or distributing the product to consumers as a stand-alone product or as part of another product.

> **Note** 📎
>
> It's important to understand the specifics covered—and *not* covered—in a particular document before signing it. For example, although the typical MOU is not intended to serve as a binding contract, there are circumstances under which it could be binding, especially if money is exchanged. Be sure to consult an attorney for advice regarding concerns you might have about any document before you sign it.

Change Management

 **Certification**

3.1 Given a scenario, use appropriate documentation and diagrams to manage the network.

3.3 Explain common scanning, monitoring, and patching processes and summarize their expected outputs.

Network conditions are always in a state of flux. Technology advances, vendors come and go, responsibilities and needs of users change, and attacks from malware and hackers can expose vulnerabilities that require attention. Managing change while maintaining your network's efficiency and availability requires good planning. Even a simple change can result in lengthy downtimes if not instituted properly. Network users need to know when to expect certain network resources to be unavailable. This way, they can plan ahead so as not to lose productivity time. Changes, especially those that affect many users or expensive equipment, must be carefully planned and thoroughly documented. And in most cases, these changes will need to be approved before they can be performed.

The following section describes some of the most common types of software and hardware changes, from installing patches to replacing a network backbone, and explains how to implement those changes. After that, you look at the change management documentation that might be required for an enterprise-scale network.

Software and Hardware Changes

You might be called on to implement the following four types of software changes:

- *patch*—A software **patch** is a correction, improvement, or enhancement to software. It corrects a bug, closes a vulnerability, or adds minor enhancements to only part of the software, leaving most of the code untouched. The process of monitoring the release of new patches, testing them for use on networked devices, and installing them is called **patch management**.
- *upgrade*—A software **upgrade** is a major change to a software package that enhances the functionality and features of the software, while also correcting bugs and vulnerabilities.
- *rollback*—A software **rollback** is the process of reverting to a previous version of software after attempting to patch or upgrade it.
- *installation*—New software, such as CRM (customer relationship management) software for sales reps or a financial software package for accountants, must be installed on the relevant devices and incorporated with network resources.

Hardware changes could be something as simple as replacing a hard drive or as intensive as upgrading a campus's network backbone cabling. Typical hardware changes include adding new security cameras, replacing old workstations, installing new printers, and upgrading IP phone hardware.

Applying Concepts: Steps to Change Software or Hardware

Although the specifics vary for each type of software or hardware change, the general steps can be summarized as follows:

1. Generally, don't allow patches to be automatically installed in the OS, application, or device. When you're responsible for a computer or network, you need to fully understand the impact of any change before you allow that change.

2. Determine whether the patch or upgrade is necessary. Patches to plug security holes are almost always necessary; however, adding new features or functionality to software might cause more work than it's worth in time and money.

3. Read the vendor's documentation regarding the patch or upgrade to learn its purpose, and make sure you understand how it will affect the system, whether or not it is compatible with current hardware and software, and how to apply or undo the change.

4. Before deploying the patch or upgrade, test it in a testing lab to make sure it acts as expected. A testing lab is a small network that is segmented from the rest of the network, and contains computers, called test beds, that represent the typical hardware and OS configurations in your network, as well as any specialized equipment your company uses (for example, printers, bar-code readers, and biometric devices, such as fingerprint readers or retina scanners) that might interact with the proposed new software or hardware. Also determine whether and how the change can be reversed, in case troubles arise. Document your findings.

5. Determine whether the change should apply to some or all users, network segments, or devices. Also decide whether it will be distributed centrally or machine by machine.

6. Schedule the change for completion during off-hours (unless it is an emergency). The time period in which a change will be implemented is called the maintenance window. Everyone responsible for those who might be affected by a disruption in service (for example, the technical staff or directors of user departments) must be informed of and agree to the maintenance window in advance.

7. Immediately before the change is made, inform system administrators, help desk personnel, and affected users about the change and the maintenance window.

> **Note** 📎
>
> If problems arise as the maintenance is in progress and you realize that you are about to exceed the maintenance window, be sure to inform technical staff and users of the anticipated delay and what to expect.

8. Back up the current system, software, or hardware configuration before making any modifications. You can typically copy the configuration of a router, switch, or server to a USB flash drive, backup media, or network share.

9. If necessary, throughout the maintenance window, prevent users from accessing the system or the part of the system being altered.

10. Keep the installation instructions and vendor documentation handy as you implement the change.

11. After the change is implemented, test the system in real time, even though you have already tested it in the testing lab. Exercise the software as a typical user would. For hardware devices, put a higher load on the device than it would incur during normal use in your organization. Note any unintended or unanticipated consequences of the modification.

12. If the change was successful, reenable access to the system. If it was unsuccessful, revert to the previous version of the software or hardware.

13. Inform system administrators, help desk personnel, and affected users when the change is complete. If you had to reverse it, make this known and explain why.

14. Record your change in the change management system, as described later in this chapter.

Regardless of how hard you try to make hardware and software changes go smoothly, eventually you will encounter a situation when you must roll back your changes. Although no hard-and-fast rules for rollbacks exist, Table 2-3 summarizes some basic suggestions. Bear in mind that you must always refer to the software vendor's documentation to reverse an upgrade. If you must roll back a network operating system upgrade, you should also consult with experienced professionals about the best approach for your network environment.

Table 2-3 Reversing a software upgrade

Type of upgrade	Options for reversing
Operating system patch	Use the patch's automatic uninstall utility.
Client software upgrade	Use the upgrade's automatic uninstall utility, or reinstall the previous version of the client on top of the upgrade.
Shared application upgrade	Use the application's automatic uninstall utility, or maintain a complete copy of the previous installation of the application and reinstall it over the upgrade.
Operating system upgrade	Prior to the upgrade, make a complete backup of the system; to roll back, restore the entire system from the backup; uninstall an operating system upgrade only as a last resort.

Note

When replacing a device or a component in a device (for example, a hard drive), keep the old component for a while, especially if it is the only one of its kind at your organization. Not only might you need to put it back in the device, but you might also need to refer to it for information.

Hardware and software are not the only types of changes you might need to implement and manage. Other types include changes to the network (such as when connecting to a new ISP), the environment (such as when installing a new HVAC system), and documentation procedures (such as when upgrading to a more automated call tracking system). The same change management principles apply to any type of change:

- Process all changes through the proper channels
- Minimize negative impacts on business processes
- Plan thoroughly to maximize the chances of a successful change on the first attempt
- Document each change throughout the process

Change Management Documentation

Generally, the larger an organization, the more documentation is necessary when making hardware and software changes. Required processes and how these processes are documented are designed to protect the person making the change, users, managers, and the organization so that changes don't unnecessarily disrupt normal work flow or put undue responsibility for a problem on any one person. Here is a list of what you may need to do:

1. *Submit a change request document*—Find out who in the organization is responsible for submitting such a document. For example, the lead accountant might be considered the owner of an accounting application, and is therefore the only one allowed to request an upgrade to the application. On the other hand, IT personnel might be able to request a security patch be applied to the same application. In this case, the change request document might include items listed in Table 2-4.

Table 2-4   Parts of a change request document

Information	Example
Person submitting the change request and person who must authorize the change	The network administrator is submitting the request and the director of IT must approve it.
Type of change	Software patch
Reason for change	To fix a bug
Configuration procedures	An upgraded application might require new data file templates be built, settings defined for an entire department of users, or existing data be converted to a new format.
Potential impact	Ten users in the Accounting Department will need three hours of training.
Grounds for rollback	The new application doesn't work as expected and the Accounting Department head decides it's best to go back to the old way of doing things.
Notification process	Management and users will be informed of the change through email.
Timeline for the change	Anticipated downtime is two hours.

2. *Understand and follow the approval process*—The manager of a department might be able to approve a minor change to an application, hardware device, or OS, whereas major changes might need to go through a review board process. You might be expected to provide additional documentation during this review process. The complexity of the approval process is usually determined by the cost and time involved in making the change, the number of users affected, the potential risk to their work productivity, and the difficulty of rolling back the change. Sometimes a change request is entered into a change management database where many people can access the request, enter supporting documentation and questions, and weigh in with their opinions regarding the change.

Note 📎

Minor changes, such as applying a security patch to an application that involves only a few users, are sometimes made without going through an official change request process, but are usually documented in some way, such as a technician making entries in the change management database before and after the change is made.

3. *The change is project-managed*—After a major change is approved, a change coordinator is usually assigned to the project. This coordinator is a project manager responsible for overseeing all aspects of the change including user training; coordinating between departments involved in the change; documenting how and when notification of the change will happen; negotiating with users, management, and the IT Department regarding the authorized downtime for the change to happen; communicating with management regarding any unforeseen problems that arise during the change; and managing the budget for the change. Technicians and the network administrator work closely with the change coordinator during the change process.

4. *Provide additional documentation*—Depending on the organization, other required documentation might include testing documentation (for example, test data, testing scenarios, and software and hardware used for the testing), step-by-step procedures for applying the change, vendor documentation and vendor contact information, and locations of configuration backups and of backups that will be used in the event of a rollback. Network administrators should pay particular attention to updating their own documentation regarding the network, including updating the network map you learned about earlier in this chapter. These network documentation updates might include:

    - Network configuration (for example, the network was segmented with three new VLANs and subnets added)
    - IP address utilization (for example, the IP address ranges used in the three new subnets)

- Additions to the network (for example, new routers and switches were installed to accommodate new VLANs to handle additional network traffic)
- Physical location changes (for example, 20 workstations, a switch, and two printers were moved to a different building on the corporate campus)

5. *Close the change*—After the change is implemented and tested and users have settled into the change without problems, the change is officially closed. Sometimes the change coordinator will call a debriefing session where all involved can evaluate how well the change went and what can be done to improve future changes.

Chapter Summary

Components of Structured Cabling

- Organizations tend to follow a single cabling standard formulated by TIA (Telecommunications Industry Association) and its former parent company EIA (Electronic Industries Alliance). This standard, known as the TIA/EIA-568 Commercial Building Wiring Standard, or structured cabling, describes uniform, enterprise-wide cabling systems, regardless of who manufactures or sells the various parts used in the system.

- A network begins at the demarc and ends at a workstation. For most situations, the demarc is the device that marks where a telecommunications service provider's network ends and the organization's network begins.

- Horizontal cabling connects workstations to the closest data room and to switches housed in that room. The backbone consists of the cables or wireless links that provide interconnection between the entrance facility and MDF, and between the MDF and IDFs.

- Data rooms are often serviced by HVAC systems that are separate from the rest of the building. Specialized products are available that monitor the critical factors of a data room's environment.

Network Documentation

- Network diagrams may show physical layout, logical topology, IP address reserves, names of major network devices, and types of transmission media.

- When creating new documentation, take some time to brainstorm all the elements you want to include, and consider how you'll keep each of these documents updated.

- Inventory management simplifies maintaining and upgrading the network chiefly because you know what the system includes. In addition, inventory management documentation provides network administrators with information about the costs and benefits of certain types of hardware or software.

- The secret to keeping track of devices is naming them systematically, and then labeling them with those names.

- It's important to understand the specifics covered—and *not* covered—in a particular document before signing it.

Change Management

- Four types of software changes include a patch, upgrade, rollback, and installation. Typical hardware changes include adding new security cameras, replacing old workstations, installing new printers, and upgrading IP phone hardware.

- Generally, the larger an organization, the more documentation is necessary when making hardware and software changes. Required processes and how these processes are documented are designed to protect the person making the change, users, managers, and the organization so that changes don't unnecessarily disrupt normal work flow or put undue responsibility for a problem on any one person.

Key Terms

For definitions of key terms, see the Glossary near the end of the book.

110 block
66 block
crosstalk
demarc (demarcation point)
EIA (Electronic Industries Alliance)
EMI (electromagnetic interference)
entrance facility
fiber-optic cable
IDF (intermediate distribution frame)
inventory management
KVM (keyboard, video, and mouse) switch
licensing restrictions
MDF (main distribution frame or main distribution facility)

MLA (master license agreement)
MOU (memorandum of understanding)
MSA (master service agreement)
network diagram
Nmap
patch
patch management
patch panel
plenum
punchdown tool
PVC (polyvinyl chloride)
rack diagram
RFP (request for proposal)
rollback
SLA (service-level agreement)

SOW (statement of work)
STP (shielded twisted pair)
structured cabling
system life cycle
TIA (Telecommunications Industry Association)
upgrade
UTP (unshielded twisted pair)
VoIP (Voice over IP)
VoIP endpoint
VoIP gateway
VoIP PBX (private branch exchange)
wiki
wiring schematic

Review Questions

1. A technician from your ISP has arrived to help you troubleshoot a weak WAN connection. To what location do you take her?
   a. IDF
   b. Work area
   c. CEO's office
   d. Entrance facility

2. A transceiver was recently damaged by a lightning strike during a storm. How might you decide whether the ISP is responsible for replacing this device, or whether your company must foot the bill?
   a. Look at whether the device is located on the ISP's side of the demarc.
   b. Look at the manufacturer information on the device's label.
   c. Look at purchase records for the device to determine when it was acquired.
   d. Look at what kinds of cables are connected to this device.

3. Which of the following devices are you likely to find in the MDF? Choose all that apply.
   a. Routers
   b. Switches
   c. Network printer
   d. KVM switch

4. Which device converts signals from a campus's analog phone equipment into IP data that can travel over the Internet?
   a. VoIP PBX
   b. VoIP endpoint
   c. VoIP gateway
   d. VoIP switch

5. If you're shopping for a rack switch, what component on the switch tells you it can be mounted to a rack?
   a. AC adapter
   b. Rack ears
   c. Padded feet
   d. Large fans

6. You need to connect a new network printer to a nearby wall jack. What kind of cable should you use?
   a. Fiber-optic cable
   b. Patch cable
   c. Backbone cable
   d. Plenum-rated cable

7. You've decided to run an Nmap scan on your network. What app could you open to perform this task? Choose all that apply.
   a. Zenmap
   b. Microsoft Edge
   c. Command Prompt
   d. PowerShell

8. What type of diagram shows a graphical representation of a network's wired infrastructure?
   a. Rack diagram
   b. Wiring schematic
   c. Network map
   d. Network topology

9. Which of these is considered a secure place to store a list of documented network passwords?
   a. The CEO's smartphone
   b. A sticky note under the keyboard
   c. A password manager
   d. The MDF

10. What is the first step of inventory management?
    a. Interview users.
    b. Back up network data.
    c. List an administrative account's username and password for each device on a network.
    d. List all components on the network.

11. There is only one _____ per network, but there can be many _____ connecting internal portions of the network.

12. Why is it important to use a structured cabling standard when installing and managing cabling systems?

13. Why is it important to use plenum-rated cabling in the area above the ceiling tile?

14. What is the unit of measurement that defines the space available in a rack? How tall are standard racks?

15. Why is it important to minimize cable clutter in a rack?

16. What are some elements that are typically included in network diagrams?

17. How can you go about gathering the information needed to assemble a thorough operations manual?

18. List some good names for devices on your home network or on the network in your school's lab. Demonstrate the use of best practices when creating a naming scheme for devices on a computer network.

19. For what time period should you schedule a network change?

20. In a large organization, how do you typically request permission to perform a network change?

Hands-On Projects

Project 2-1: Tour MDF and IDF Data Rooms

The equipment and spaces discussed in this chapter come alive when you can see them in real-life situations. Ideally, you would connect with IT departments at schools and businesses in your area and tour their networking facilities so you can see these things for yourself. Additionally, your instructor might be able to give you a tour of the network equipment at your school. In preparation for these real-life tours or as a suitable replacement for them if necessary, find and watch video tours online of various MDF and IDF facilities. Complete the following steps:

1. Do an online search for video tours of MDF and IDF facilities. Good search terms include: "MDF IDF tour," "main distribution frame tour," "data room tour," and "MDF data room." Look for videos that show you around the MDF or IDF data room, identifying major components and their connections. The best tour videos include a walk to other buildings on the network's campus.

2. Answer the following questions:

   a. List the videos you watched. Include a URL for each video, or an explanation of how to find it on a particular website.

   b. What network components were shown?

   c. What are three things you learned about the layout of the room, what equipment is there, or how the equipment is installed?

Project 2-2: Create a Password Manager Account

Throughout this text, you will create several accounts at different websites in order to access tools for various projects. As you learned in the chapter, a password manager can help you document those passwords and store them securely.

In this project, you create a LastPass account where you can store all your account information for the projects in this book. LastPass provides a free subscription option, and you can access your information from any device. If you want, you can also store account information for your other school and personal accounts in LastPass. Just remember to always keep your master password secure.

> **Note** 📎
>
> You'll learn more about how to create a secure password later. For now, keep in mind that the longer the password, the better. A simple and memorable way to do this is to think of an obscure line from a favorite song or movie, and use several words of that line to create your master password. Here's an example: *SpockTransmitNow*.

Complete the following steps to create your password manager account online:

1. Go to **lastpass.com** and click **Log In**. On the Log In page, click **Create an account now**.
2. Enter your email address and create a master password (the longer, the better—just make sure you can remember it because there is only one, somewhat unreliable way to recover the account if you forget the password). When you are ready, agree to the terms and privacy policy, and click **Continue**.
3. Confirm your password and click **Confirm**.
4. Click **Log In** at the top of the page and log into your new LastPass account.
5. The LastPass vault is shown in Figure 2-33. Click through each menu option in the left pane.

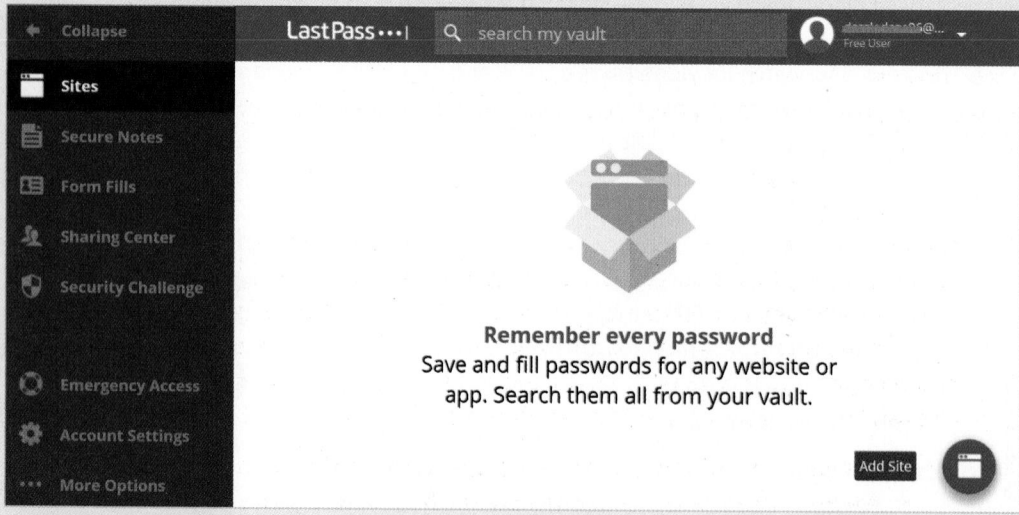

Figure 2-33   Store passwords, notes, and form information in your LastPass vault

Source: LogMeIn, Inc.

6. When you get to Account Settings, scroll down to *SMS Account Recovery* and click **Update Phone**. Add a phone number where you can receive a recovery text message should you forget your master password. The phone must be in your possession to complete this step. Send the test code to your phone and verify your phone in LastPass after you receive the code. Close the *update_phone* tab in your browser. Close the *Account Settings* dialog box.

> **Note** 📎
>
> Whenever you change your phone number, be sure to update this information in LastPass right away.

7. Click the **Add Site** button, as shown in the lower right corner of Figure 2-33. Enter information for a site you visit often, such as a social media site or an email service. If you want, you can make up information for this entry. You can delete it later after you've added some sites from other projects.
8. If you added a real account for a real website, move the mouse pointer over the site's tile and click **Launch** to automatically open and sign in to that site.
9. Log out of LastPass in your browser. Always remember to log out of your account before walking away from your computer. Store a copy of your master password in a very secure place, such as a lockbox in your home, a safe deposit box at a bank, or an encrypted file on your computer.

> **Note** 📎
>
> You can download and install LastPass as an extension in your favorite browser on a computer that you own. LastPass is compatible with Chrome, Firefox, Safari, Opera, and Edge. You can also install the LastPass app on your smartphone (Android, iPhone, and Windows Phone).

> **Caution** ⚠
>
> No password manager is 100 percent reliably secure. Hackers target these services, and occasionally they're successful. LastPass, however, is one of the most reliable password managers currently available for free. KeePass is another good one.
>
> No password manager is secure if you leave your account open on a computer or device you're not using, or if you write your master password where someone else can find it. Follow these guidelines consistently:
>
> - Always log out of your password manager account when you're not using it.
> - Always close browser windows where you have been signed into a secure account of any kind.
> - Always lock or sign out of Windows before walking away from your computer.

Project 2-3: Create a Wiki

One way to collect information from members of your team is to use a wiki creator to build your own wiki. There are many good wiki tools that require a purchase or subscription, such as Google Sites and SharePoint. These paid apps provide impressive features that really shine when you're collaborating with several people or making your wiki public as part of your business front. A free app such as *Wikidot.com*, though, can give you all the features you need for tracking your own project information in this book. And it will help you better understand which features are most important to you.

> **Note** 📎
>
> Websites change. These steps were accurate at the time this text was written. However, you might need to adjust these steps to account for future changes.

Complete the following steps to create your own wiki:

1. Go to **wikidot.com** and create an account. Store your account information in your Last-Pass account.
2. Open your confirmation email and activate your Wikidot account.
3. Once inside your Wikidot account, click on the **Sites** tab. Scroll down and click **Create site** in the left pane.
4. Add information for your wiki. Give it a name and web address, and choose the Standard Template.

> **Note** 📎
>
> You can choose any template for a later wiki, or change the template for this wiki after completing this project.

5. Select an access policy. Unless directed otherwise by your instructor, choose the **Private** option.
6. Confirm that you have read and agreed to the Terms of Service, and then click **Get my Wikidot site**. Your Wikidot site is created with generic information that will help you get started, as shown in Figure 2-34.

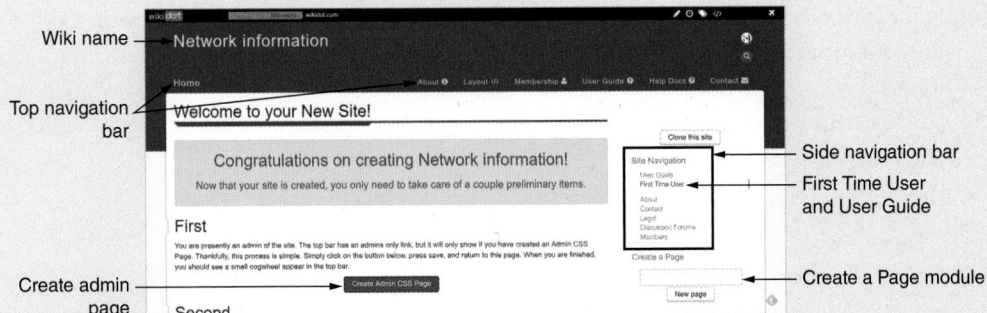

Wiki name

Top navigation bar

Create admin page

Side navigation bar

First Time User and User Guide

Create a Page module

Figure 2-34   Use a wiki to collect network information that all your team members can access
Source: Wikidot Inc.

7. To see the admin link in the top navigation bar, click **Create Admin CSS Page** in the *First* section on the welcome page. Without making any edits to the page, click **Save** at the bottom of the page. There should now be a gear icon in the top navigation bar, as shown in Figure 2-35. If you click on it, you can see the admin navigation menu. We'll come back to that soon.

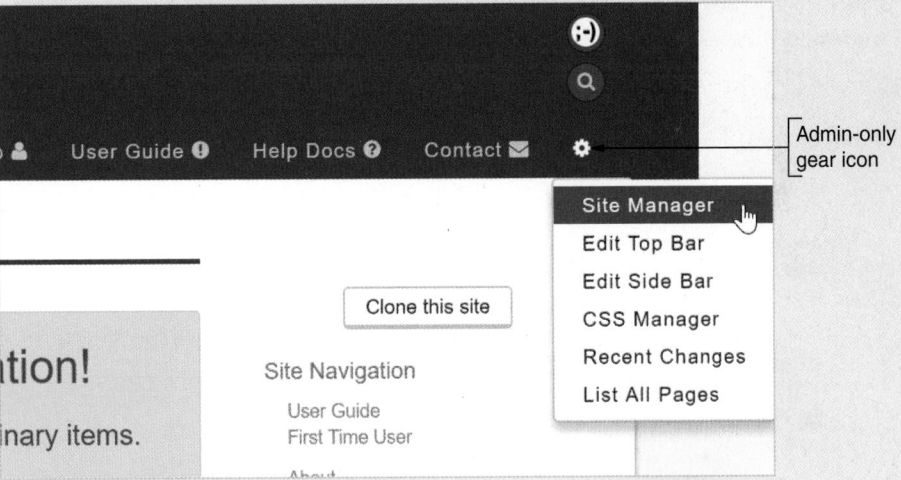

Admin-only gear icon

Figure 2-35   The gear icon accesses the admin navigation menu
Source: Wikidot Inc.

8. Skim through the First Time User page and the User Guide to understand how to create pages and categories and how to use modules.

9. Click each tab along the top navigation bar and skim the contents: **Home**, **About**, **Layout**, **Membership**, **User Guide**, **Help Docs**, and **Contact**. This will help you become familiar with the pages included in this template.

10. Click the **Home** link to go back to the Home page. At the bottom of the page, click **Edit**, as shown in Figure 2-36.

What are you waiting for?

Give Wikidot a shot. Press the button below to clone this template and get started!

Clone this site

page revision: 0, last edited: 14 Jun 2017, 20:49 (3 hours ago)
Stop watching site jillwest.wikidot.com [?]

| Edit | Tags | History | Files | Print | Site tools | + Options |

Figure 2-36　**Page tools at the bottom of each page**
Source: Wikidot Inc.

11. In the Header box, change the text *Welcome to Wikidot* (See Figure 2-37) to say **This is my Wikidot.** Save your changes.

Edit Home

Title　Home

Header
```
[[div class="row"]]
[[div class="col-lg-5 col-md-6"]]
+ Welcome to Wikidot.

This site runs on Wikidot, one of the world's largest wiki farms. But, Wikidot is more than just a wiki, as you'll disc
free and professional websites, each doing something special.
```

Content
```
[[div class="feature feature-center"]]
[[div class="row"]]
[[div class="col-lg-12"]]
+ Whatever your web project, Wikidot helps you make it better.
```

Figure 2-37　**Make changes to the text on any page**
Source: Wikidot Inc.

12. Click the **About** link to go to the About page. In the side navigation bar, in the *Create a Page* module, type **Virtualization:VMclients** (see Figure 2-38). Notice that there is no space before or after the colon. This will create a new page named *VMclients* in the category *Virtualization*. Click **New page**.

13. Type the information for the Capstone Project you completed in Chapter 1, as shown in Figure 2-39. Click **Save**.

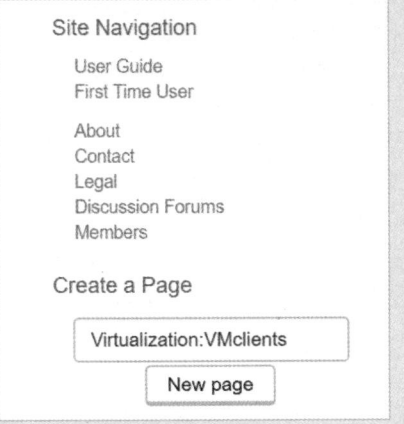

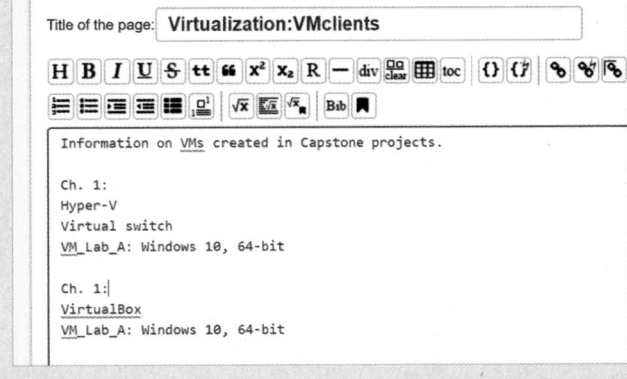

Figure 2-38   Create a new category and page in a wiki

Source: Wikidot Inc.

Figure 2-39   Add information for Hyper-V or for VirtualBox

Source: Wikidot Inc.

14. To see a list of all pages in your wiki, click the gear icon in the top bar, and then click **List All Pages**. Make sure you see your Virtualization:VMclients page listed. You will continue to add pages and content in later chapters.
15. Click the gear icon and click **Site Manager** to go to the Dashboard.
16. In the left pane, click **Security** and then click **Access policy**. The page jumps to the Membership section, but you can scroll back up to see your current access policy. Scroll down and notice in the blue box that you can apply for a free educational upgrade. This is optional and is not required for this project.
17. Click through the other settings and options and make changes as desired. When you're finished, click your wiki's name in the upper-left corner next to the Wikidot logo to return to your wiki.

Project 2-4: Install and Use Zenmap

In this activity, you install Zenmap, the GUI version of Nmap for Windows, and use it to scan your computer and your local network.

> **Note**
>
> Websites change. These steps were accurate at the time this text was written. However, you might need to adjust these steps to account for future changes.

Complete the following steps:

1. Go to **nmap.org** and click **Download**. Scroll down to the Windows section, which might look similar to Figure 2-40.

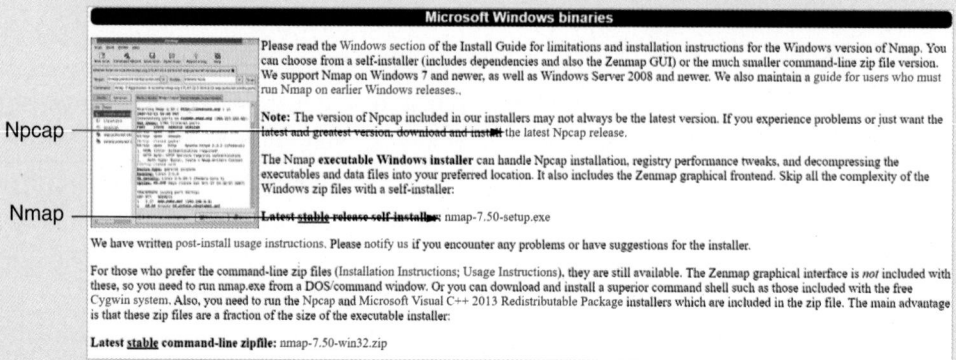

Figure 2-40 Download and install Npcap first, and then download and install Nmap

Source: Insecure.org

2. Before installing Zenmap, you need to install the most recent version of Npcap, which is a packet sniffing library for Windows. Click **the latest Npcap release** link, and then click the most recent **Npcap installer** link. At the time of this writing, the listed version was 0.92. Go to the download location and run the program to install Npcap. Respond to any system warnings. When you see the Installation Options dialog box, make sure that **Install Npcap in WinPcap API-compatible Mode** is checked, as shown in Figure 2-41. Otherwise, accept all default settings during installation.

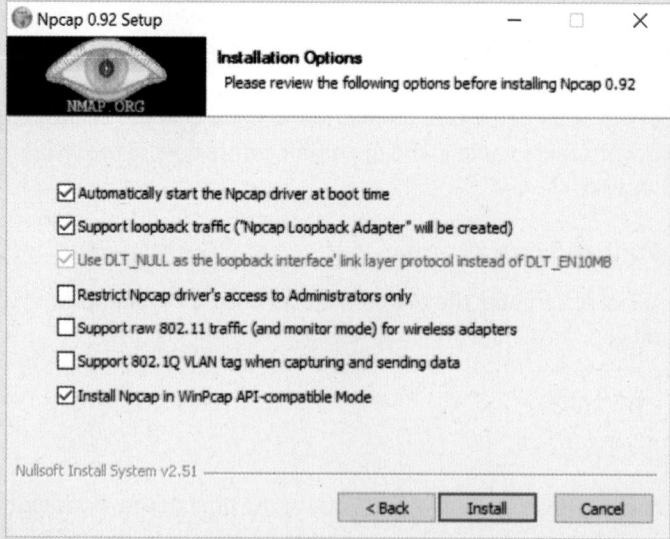

Figure 2-41 WinPcap API-compatible Mode is a legacy option required for some programs to access the driver

Source: Insecure.org

3. In your browser, click **Back** to return to the Windows section on the Download page. Click the **Latest stable release self-installer** link. At the time of this writing, the download file was called **nmap-7.50-setup.exe**. Go to the download location and run the program to install Nmap. Respond to any system warnings and accept all default settings during installation. If you get a message asking whether to reinstall Npcap, click **No** if the new installation would use an older version of Npcap than the one you just installed. For example, in Figure 2-42, the currently installed version is 0.92. Nmap is requesting to install version 0.91, which is an older version. We want the newer version to stay in place, so we clicked No.

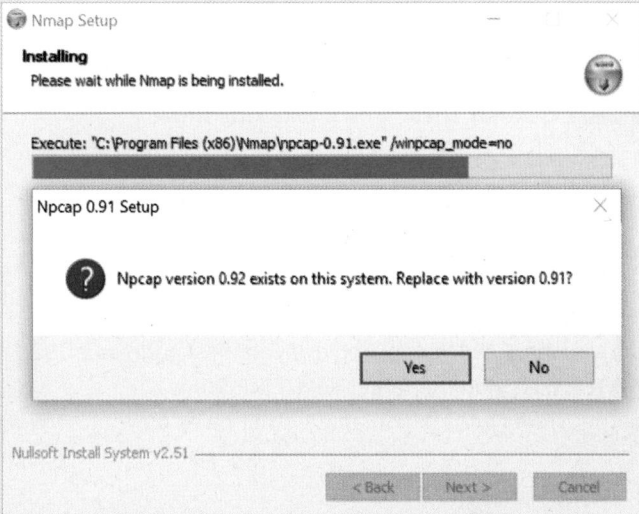

Figure 2-42   Keep the latest version of Npcap that you installed earlier
Source: Insecure.org

4. Once the installation is complete, close all open windows, and then open Zenmap from your desktop. Start with a quick scan of your local computer. In the Target field, enter **localhost,** and in the Profile field, select **Quick scan**. Click **Scan**. The scan shows a list of ports on your computer and the services assigned to them, similar to the results shown in Figure 2-43.

In the following steps, you'll try a scan of your local network and see how the output changes. This time you will target all IP addresses in the same range as your computer's IP address. The easiest way to do this is to first determine your computer's IP address.

5. Open a Command Prompt or PowerShell window and enter the command **ipconfig.** Find the IPv4 address for the active network connection and write it down if necessary.

6. Go back to Zenmap. In the Target field, type your local computer's IPv4 address. However, so that you can scan a range of IP addresses, replace the final block of digits

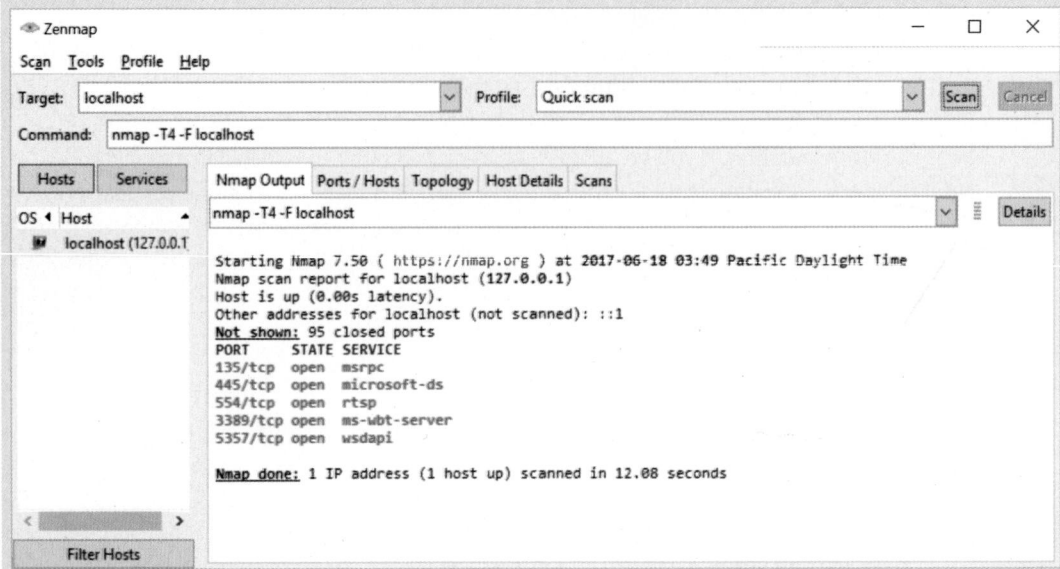

Figure 2-43 Zenmap localhost scan output

Source: Insecure.org

in your IPv4 address with **1-254.** For example, if your IPv4 address is 192.168.1.106, you would enter **192.168.1.1-254** in the Target field. Click **Scan.**

7. This time the output shows information about other hosts on your network as well as the information you've already seen for your own computer. Scroll through the output and answer the following questions:

   a. How many IP addresses were scanned? How many hosts are up?

   b. Compared with the information you saw earlier about your own computer, what different information is revealed about the other hosts?

   c. Find a host with open ports reported and list the ports and their services in your answer. What other information is provided about that host?

Note

You'll learn more about ports, IP addresses, and MAC addresses later.

In Project 2-3, you created a wiki to track information about your work in this course. You started a category called Virtualization and recorded information about the VM you created in Chapter 1. App installations for projects is another kind of information we want to track in the wiki.

8. Go to your Wikidot site and click **User Guide** in the top navigation bar. In the side navigation bar, in the *Create a Page* module, type **Applications:Zenmap**. This will

create a new page named *Zenmap* in a new category named *Applications*. Click **New page**.

9. Under "Create a new page," type some information about your Zenmap installation. What is Zenmap? On which computer did you install Zenmap? What problems did you run into, and what solutions did you come up with? What information did you learn about your network from running scans in Zenmap? When you are finished, click **Save**.

10. Click the gear icon and click **List All Pages** to confirm your new page was created. In a later chapter, we'll streamline your navigation bars and pages.

Capstone Projects

Capstone Project 2-1: Create a VM and Install Ubuntu Desktop

In the Capstone Projects of Chapter 1, you created a virtual machine using Windows 10 Client Hyper-V and/or Oracle VirtualBox. In this Capstone Project, you create a second VM in your virtual network and install Ubuntu Desktop in the VM. In Chapter 4, you'll install Ubuntu Server in your network. For these VM projects, you can use your choice of hypervisor.

Using one of the same computers that you used in Capstone Project 1-1 or 1-2 that has Client Hyper-V or Oracle VirtualBox installed, depending on which hypervisor you prefer, follow these steps:

1. Go to **ubuntu.com** and download the Ubuntu Desktop OS to your hard drive. This is a free download, so you can decline to make any donations. The file that downloads is an ISO file. Ubuntu is a well-known version of Linux and offers both desktop and server editions.

2. Open the Oracle VM VirtualBox Manager or Hyper-V Manager. Following the directions in the Chapter 1 Capstone Projects, create a new VM named VM2, VM_Lab_B, or something similar. Note that if you're using Hyper-V Manager and you use the Quick Create option, uncheck the box that says *This virtual machine will run Windows* before clicking *Change installation source*. Mount the ISO file that contains the Ubuntu Desktop download to a virtual DVD in your VM.

3. Start the VM and install Ubuntu Desktop, accepting all default settings (see Figure 2-44). When given the option, don't install any extra software bundled with the OS. You'll need to restart the VM when the installation is finished.

4. To verify you have an Internet connection, open the Mozilla Firefox browser and surf the web.

5. Good network technicians must know how to use many operating systems. Poke around in the Ubuntu Desktop interface and get familiar with it. You can also search the web for tutorials and YouTube videos on how to use Ubuntu Desktop. What can you do with the Dashboard icon at the top of the left sidebar?

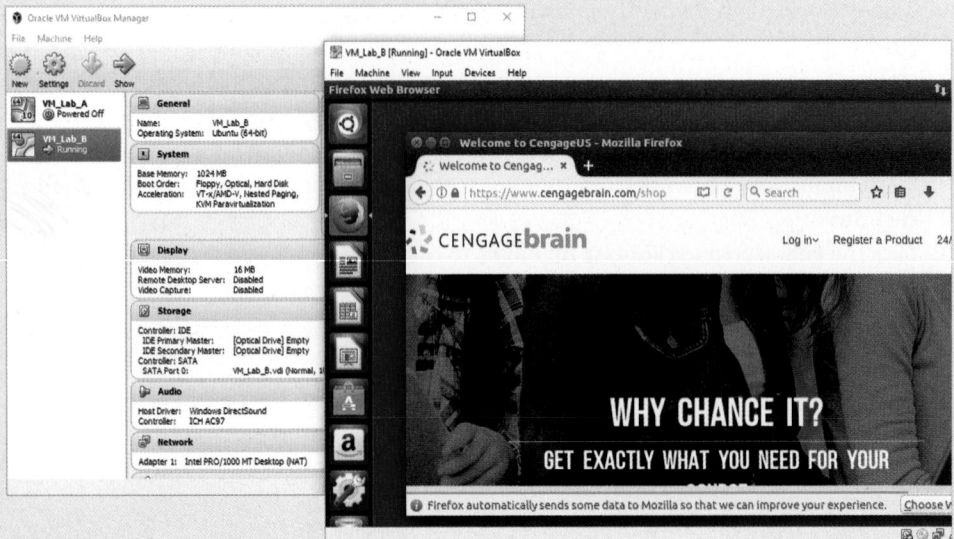

Figure 2-44   Ubuntu Desktop is installed in a VM in Oracle VirtualBox

Source: Canonical Group Limited and Oracle Corporation

6. When you're ready to shut down your VM, click the gear icon in the upper-right corner of the Ubuntu Desktop screen and click **Shut Down** in the menu that appears.

7. Before you walk away from this project, take a moment to add the new information to your VMclients page in your wiki. Go to the Virtualization:VMclients page, click **Edit** at the bottom of the page, and add the new VM to your list. Include the chapter number, hypervisor used, VM computer name, and VM operating system. Also note any additional information that you might find helpful when you return to this VM in the future. When you're finished, click **Save**.

Capstone Project 2-2: Download and Use Spiceworks

In Hands-On Project 2-4, you downloaded and used Zenmap, the Nmap GUI, to collect data about the devices on your network. Another popular program for taking inventory of network devices is Spiceworks Inventory. You might be familiar with Spiceworks Help Desk for its ticket-tracking features. Spiceworks Inventory is software that is included in the Help Desk installation and supports inventory management so that you can track the devices on your network, monitoring software licenses, cloud services, IP address assignments, and more. A third Spiceworks product is Network Monitor, which includes some powerful network mapping and monitoring functionality. In this project, you download and install Spiceworks Inventory, scan your network, and view a network map. Complete the following steps:

1. To begin, go to the Spiceworks website at **spiceworks.com**. Download and install Spiceworks Inventory. You'll have to create an account to download the package, so be sure to record your new account information in LastPass. During installation, accept the

default port 80. Decline Nmap and WinPCap because you already installed those programs when you installed Zenmap, which typically includes more recent versions than
Spiceworks does. Accept all other defaults during the installation process.

2. When the installation is complete, close the setup window. Spiceworks opens in a
    browser. If it doesn't, click **Spiceworks Desktop** on the Start menu. Sign in with your
    Spiceworks account.

3. Fill in your information on the *Personalize this install of Spiceworks* page and click **Save**.
    (You can keep the name "Bruce Wayne" if you like, but make sure you use your real
    email address.)

4. First you need to discover network devices, so click the **Discover & Monitor My Devices**
    button.

5. Enter domain credentials if you have them. Otherwise, select **I don't have any** for
    Windows and Mac/Linux/Unix, and then click **Go to Inventory**. An example of the scan
    results is shown in Figure 2-45.

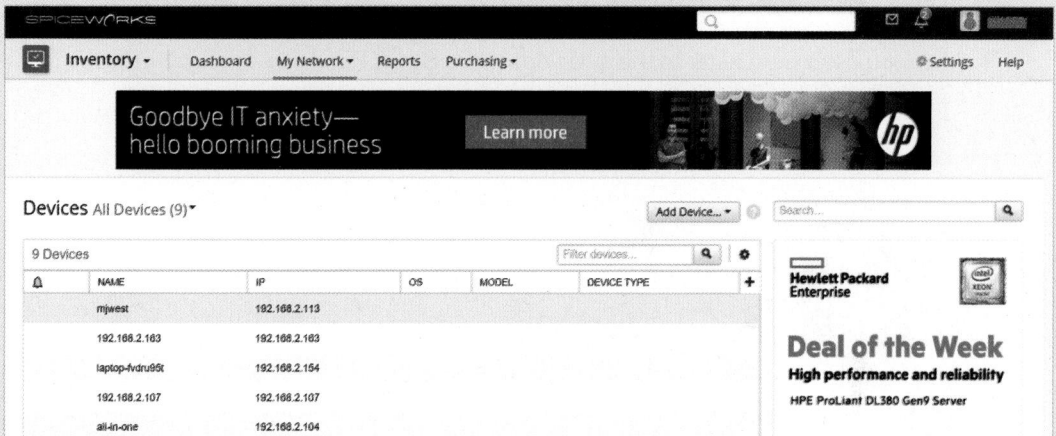

Figure 2-45   Scan results will likely be incomplete unless you're using an administrative
domain account

Source: Spiceworks Inc.

6. In our example, Spiceworks was able to resolve a few device names already. Depending
    on the type of credentials you used, your device scan might have been more or less suc-
    cessful, but that's fine for the level of work you'll be doing in this project. Take a couple
    of minutes to explore the results of your scan and answer the following questions:

    a. How many devices were successfully inventoried?

    b. Click on one of the devices to select it, preferably one that has more information
       listed than just an IP address. Scroll down to where you can see the *General Info* tab
       for the selected device. What information is reported here?

    c. Click on the other tabs, such as *Configuration* and *Software*. What other information
       can you see about this device? If no other information is listed, what are three or four
       interesting items that you *could* see if your scan results were more thorough?

7. At the top of the page, click **Dashboard**. Skim through the various items listed here to see what kinds of information you could collect and monitor with Spiceworks.

8. At the top of the page, click **My Network** and **Scan**. Spiceworks automatically selects an IP address range. Enter any additional credentials, and click **Start Scan**.

9. Spiceworks will probably report that it has some login errors that need fixing. Scroll down and click **Skip this step** to choose not to address the errors at this time.

10. Under *Explore Your Device Inventory*, click **Go**, and then click **View Your Devices**. What new information do you see in these results, if any?

11. At the top of the page, click **My Network** and **Network Map**. Enable Flash if necessary. After the map is created, answer the following questions:

   a. How many devices appear on the Network Map?

   b. What is the IP address of your network's default gateway? How did you identify this device on your map?

12. Finally, add one more page to your wiki for this new app installation. Name the new page **Applications:SpiceWorks**. Add important information to the page about your experience installing SpiceWorks, what you learned, and what you might need to remember when you use it next. Refer to the questions at the end of Hands-On Project 2-4 if you need more ideas on what information to include.

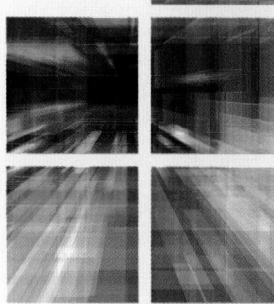

## CHAPTER 3

ADDRESSING ON NETWORKS

After reading this chapter and completing the exercises, you will be able to:

Find the MAC address of a computer and explain its function in network communications

Configure TCP/IP settings on a computer, including IP address, subnet mask, default gateway, and DNS servers

Explain the purpose of ports and sockets, and identify the ports of several common, network protocols

Describe domain names and the name resolution process

Use command-line tools to troubleshoot common network problems

On the Job

While I was working as a junior project manager in the Technology Solutions Department for a large corporation, I was assigned to work on a network infrastructure project. At the time, I had no training as a network engineer, and was instead responsible for small- to medium-sized technology projects as they related to a business unit that spanned five states. For this new project, our goal was to change the network's topology in a way that would allow the network to grow over time for the least amount of money, and to keep the network up to date with the latest trends within the industry.

As with most projects, a budget was set at the beginning. This budget allowed us to hire a professional vendor to complete the wiring and cabling installations. The network engineers who worked for the vendor were experts on everything related to wiring and cabling. However, before they could get very far, our budget was aggressively reduced. Suddenly, we could no longer afford the cabling experts. Instead, senior managers decided that work would be completed by our company's own junior IT technicians, people who were better suited to printer paper jam resolution than recabling an entire network. They knew nothing about hierarchical cable structure, maximum cable distances, or endpoint terminations.

This ignorance of basic networking standards had dire consequences on our project's budget and timeline. But the problem wasn't just that the IT people doing the work lacked the proper knowledge. As the project manager, with no systematic knowledge of networking standards, I was also hampered in my ability to keep things on track.

Part of a successful project manager's job is recognizing the need for subject matter experts, or at least being able to understand where to find key pieces of information related to the project and then interpreting that information as it relates to the project. In my case, a simple understanding of a set of telecommunications standards, or TIA/EIA-568, would have been indispensable in completing the network topology change project.

Our in-house team began the project on a vacant floor that was to become new employee office space. We unknowingly exceeded cable runs, terminated wall outlet connection points incorrectly, and generally did a poor installation job. Only after new client computers were installed and exhibited a variety of connection issues did we realize our installation was most likely the culprit. We soon understood that our lack of prior planning and our ignorance of industry standards were to blame. Through painful trial and error, we gained an in-depth knowledge of telecommunications structured cabling and the tools needed to implement a network topology change, but with the cost of this knowledge, was a lot of time on a ladder removing ceiling tiles and working late into the night to ensure clients were able to effectively run their applications at the start of the next workday.

Tom Johnson
Segment Account Manager, Defense Industry

In Chapter 1, you learned that the OSI model can be used to describe just about every aspect of networking. You saw firsthand the usefulness of working your way up or down the seven layers of the OSI model to troubleshoot networking problems. In Chapter 2, you toured the elements of a typical network infrastructure and saw the importance of documentation in maintaining and troubleshooting a network. In this chapter, you will learn the several methods used to address and find software, computers, and other devices on a network. We'll take a bottom-up approach to the OSI model as we explore these topics, starting at the Data Link layer and working our way up to the Application layer. (The lowest OSI layer, the Physical layer, does not require a network address.) At the end of this chapter, you will learn how to troubleshoot addressing problems by using common command-line utilities.

Addressing Overview

 **Certification**

7	APPLICATION
6	PRESENTATION
5	SESSION
4	TRANSPORT
3	NETWORK
2	DATA LINK
1	PHYSICAL

1.2 Explain devices, applications, protocols, and services at their appropriate OSI layers.

In Chapter 1, you learned that addressing methods operate at the Data Link, Network, Transport, and Application layers of the OSI model so that one host or node can find another on a network. Here's a quick overview of the four addressing methods, starting at the bottom of the OSI model:

- *Data Link layer MAC address*—A MAC address is embedded on every NIC on the globe and is assumed to be unique to that NIC. A MAC address is 48 bits, written as six hex numbers separated by colons, as in 00:60:8C:00:54:99. Nodes on a LAN find each other using their MAC addresses.
- *Network layer IP address*—An IP address is assigned to nearly every **interface**, which is a network connection made by a node on a network. An IP address can be used to find any computer in the world if the IP address is public on the Internet. Applications such as browsers can store and retrieve IP addresses. But for routing purposes, an IP address is used only at the Network layer.

    There are two types of IP addresses:

    - *IPv4*—**IPv4 (Internet Protocol version 4)** addresses have 32 bits and are written as four decimal numbers called **octets**, for example, 92.106.50.200. Each octet, when written in binary, consists of exactly 8 bits. For example, the octet 92 can be written as 0101 1100.

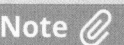 **Note**

A binary number is a number written in the base-2 number system, which uses only the numerals 0 and 1.

    - *IPv6*—**IPv6 (Internet Protocol version 6)** addresses have 128 bits and are written as eight blocks of hexadecimal numbers, for example, 2001:0DB8:0B80:00 00:0000:00D3:9C5A:00CC. Each block contains 16 bits.

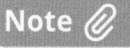 **Note**

A hexadecimal number (also called a hex number) is a number written in the base-16 number system, which uses the 16 numerals 0, 1, 2, 3, 4, 5, 6, 7, 8, 9, A, B, C, D, E, and F.

- *Transport layer ports*—A port is a number used by the Transport layer to find an application. It identifies one application among several that might be running on a host. For example, a web server application is usually configured to listen for incoming requests at port 80.
- *Application layer FQDNs, computer names, and host names*—Every host on a network is assigned a unique character-based name called the **FQDN (fully qualified domain name)**, for example, *susan.mycompany.com, ftp.mycompany. com,* and *www.mycompany.com.* Collectively, the last two parts of a host's name (for example, mycompany.com) are called the **domain name**, which matches the name of the organization's domain or network. The first part (for example, susan, ftp, and www) is the **host name**, which identifies the individual computer on the network. Ftp is the host name usually given to an FTP server, and www is typically the host name assigned to a computer running a web server.

> **Note**
>
> Technically, an FQDN ends in a period: *ftp.mycompany.com.*
> However, in most applications, the terminal period is understood even when it is not typed or shown on the screen.

> **Note**
>
> When a technician refers to a host name, you can assume she's actually referring to the FQDN unless stated otherwise.

> **Note**
>
> The organization responsible for tracking the assignments of IP addresses, port numbers, and domain names is **IANA (Internet Assigned Numbers Authority)** (pronounced "I–anna"). IANA is a department of **ICANN (Internet Corporation for Assigned Names and Numbers)**. ICANN is a nonprofit organization charged with setting many policies that guide how the Internet works. For more information, see *iana.org* and *icann.org.* At *icann.org,* you can download helpful white papers that explain how the Internet works.

Now that you have the big picture of how addressing happens at each layer of the OSI model, let's dig into the details of how it all works, beginning with MAC addresses at the bottom of the model.

MAC Addresses

 **Certification**

7	APPLICATION
6	PRESENTATION
5	SESSION
4	TRANSPORT
3	NETWORK
2	DATA LINK
1	PHYSICAL

1.2 Explain devices, applications, protocols, and services at their appropriate OSI layers.

You can find a network adapter's MAC address stamped directly onto the NIC's circuit board or on a sticker attached to some part of the NIC, as shown in Figure 3-1. Later in this chapter, you'll learn to use TCP/IP utilities to report the MAC address.

MAC addresses contain two parts, are 48 bits long, and are written as hexadecimal numbers separated by colons—for example, 00:60:8C:00:54:99. The first 24 bits (six hex characters, such as 00:60:8C in our example) are known as the **OUI (Organizationally Unique Identifier)**, which identifies the NIC's manufacturer. A manufacturer's OUI is assigned by the IEEE (Institute of Electrical and Electronics Engineers). If you know a computer's MAC address, you can determine which company manufactured its NIC by looking up its OUI. The IEEE maintains a database of OUIs and their manufacturers, which is accessible via the web. At the time of this writing, the database search page could be found at *http://standards.ieee.org/regauth/oui/index.shtml*.

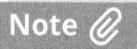 **Note**

Links to websites given in this book might become outdated as websites change. If a given link doesn't work, try a Google search on the item to find the new link.

Figure 3-1   NIC with MAC address

Source: D-Link of North America

The last 24 bits make up the **extension identifier** or **device ID** and identify the device itself. Manufacturers assign each NIC a unique extension identifier, based on the NIC's model and manufacture date, so that, in theory, no two NICs share the same MAC address.

IP Addresses

 **Certification**

7	APPLICATION
6	PRESENTATION
5	SESSION
4	TRANSPORT
3	NETWORK
2	DATA LINK
1	PHYSICAL

1.3 Explain the concepts and characteristics of routing and switching.

1.4 Given a scenario, configure the appropriate IP addressing concepts.

1.8 Explain the functions of network services.

As we move up to Layer 3, recall that IP addresses identify nodes at the Network layer. Whereas MAC addresses are used for communication inside a network, an IP address is required in order for a device to communicate outside its local network through a gateway device such as a router.

You can permanently assign a **static IP address** to a device, or you can config-ure the device to request and receive (or lease) a **dynamic IP address** from a DHCP server each time it connects to the network. A **DHCP (Dynamic Host Configuration Protocol)** server manages the dynamic distribution of IP addresses to devices on a net-work. You'll learn more about DHCP later in this chapter. For now, let's look at this and related TCP/IP settings on a Windows 10 computer:

1. In Control Panel, open the **Network and Sharing Center**. Click **Change adapter settings**.

Note 📎

It's a bit of a challenge to find Control Panel in Windows 10 with the Creators Update. Click **Start**, scroll down and click **Windows System**, and then click **Control Panel**.

You can pin Control Panel to the Start menu or to your taskbar at the bottom of your screen to make it more accessible in the future. To do this, go to Control Panel in the Start menu again, right-click it, and click **Pin to Start** to pin it to the Start menu. Alternatively, instead of clicking *Pin to Start*, point to **More**, and click **Pin to taskbar**. You'll see the Control Panel icon listed in your taskbar items, as shown in Figure 3-2. Notice in the figure, Command Prompt is also pinned to the taskbar.

When Control Panel is used for projects in this book, steps are written for the Large icons view. This generally makes the most important items for technicians easier to access. To change the view in Control Panel, click the View by drop-down menu in the top right corner of the window. Windows will usually remember the last view that you used the next time you open Control Panel.

Command Prompt

Control Panel

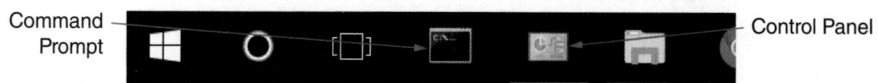

Figure 3-2 Pin Control Panel and Command Prompt to your taskbar for easy access

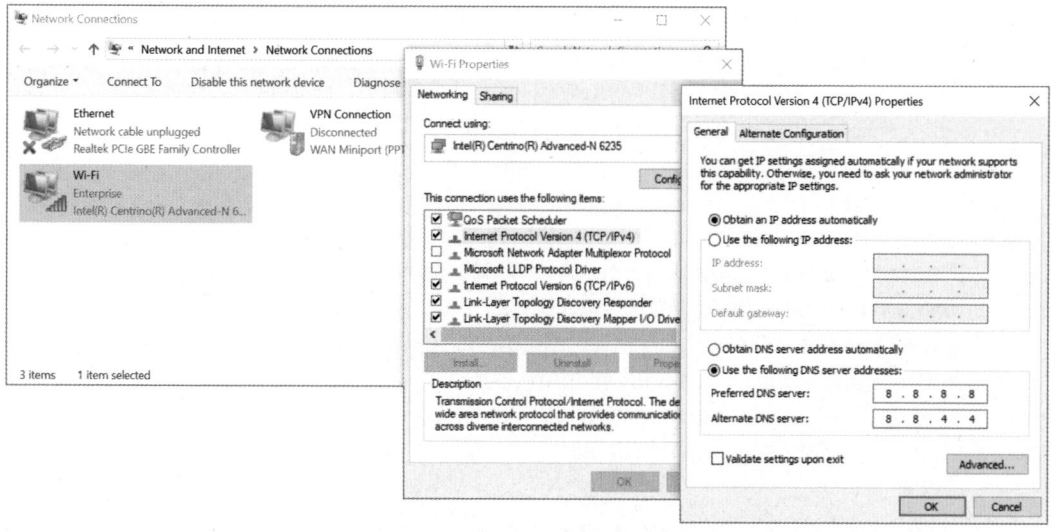

Figure 3-3 Configure TCP/IP for a network interface by using static or dynamic IP addressing

2. Right-click the network connection and click **Properties**. In the connection's properties dialog box, click **Internet Protocol Version 4 (TCP/IPv4)**, and then click **Properties**. See Figure 3-3.

3. Here you can select *Obtain an IP address automatically* for dynamic IP addressing to be assigned by a DHCP server, or you can manually assign a static IP address, subnet mask, and default gateway. Notice you can also configure TCP/IP to obtain DNS server addresses from the DHCP server, or you can manually assign DNS server addresses.

Here's a brief explanation of these settings:

- *gateway*—A computer, router, or other device that a host uses to access another network. The **default gateway** is the gateway device that nodes on the network turn to first for access to the outside world.

- *subnet mask*—Also called a **netmask**; a 32-bit number that helps one computer find another. The 32 bits are used to indicate what portion of an IP address is the network portion, called the **network ID** or network address, and what part is the host portion, called the **host ID** or **node ID**. Using this information, a computer can determine if another computer with a given IP address is on its own or a different network.

> **Note** ✐
>
> Technically, there is a subtle distinction between the meanings of the terms *subnet mask* and *netmask*. A **subnet** is a smaller network within a larger network. A netmask indicates the bits of an IP address that identify the larger network, while the subnet mask indicates the bits of an IP address that identify a smaller subnet within the larger network. Most of the time, however, these two terms are used interchangeably. You'll learn more about subnets in a later chapter.

- *DNS server*—Servers that are responsible for tracking computer names and their IP addresses. Later in the chapter, you will learn more about the various types of DNS servers and how they work together.

You can use the **ipconfig** utility in a Command Prompt window to find out the current TCP/IP settings. This is especially helpful when using DHCP, because an automatically assigned IP address is not reported in the IPv4 properties dialog box. You'll learn more about this utility later in this chapter.

Applying Concepts: Command-Line Interface Options in Windows 10

In Windows, commands such as `ipconfig` can be entered at a **CLI (command-line interface)** that does not provide the Windows graphics normally offered in a GUI (graphical user interface). Network technicians need to be comfortable with the CLI because it is quicker and often more powerful and flexible than a GUI. In Windows 10, a CLI can be accessed through Command Prompt, PowerShell, or the new **WSL (Windows Subsystem for Linux)**. WSL is a Linux shell that allows users to interact with underlying Windows functions and system files. It's not a VM, and it's not a fully separate operating system. You'll install and use WSL in a project at the end of this chapter. For now, let's look at options for opening a Command Prompt window:

1. To open a regular Command Prompt window in Windows 10, click **Start**, scroll down and click **Windows System**, and then click **Command Prompt**.

2. To open a Command Prompt window with administrative privileges (called an **elevated Command Prompt**), click **Start**, scroll down and click **Windows System**, right-click **Command Prompt**, point to **More**, and then click **Run as administrator**.

Thankfully, there are faster ways to access a Command Prompt window:

- Press the **Windows** key or click **Start**, type **command** or **cmd**, and press **Enter** or click **Command Prompt**.

- Pin the Command Prompt icon to the taskbar, as we did earlier for Control Panel.

- Right-click **Start** to see the Quick Links menu. By default, in Windows 10 with the Creators Update, Windows PowerShell is listed in this menu instead of Command Prompt. However, you can change this setting. From the Quick Links menu, click **Settings**. This opens the Settings app. Click **Personalization**, and then click **Taskbar**. Scroll down and click to turn off **Replace Command Prompt with Windows PowerShell in the menu when I right-click the start button or press Windows key+X**, as shown in Figure 3-4.

3. You'll learn to use several commands later in the chapter. For now, enter the **exit** command to close the Command Prompt window.

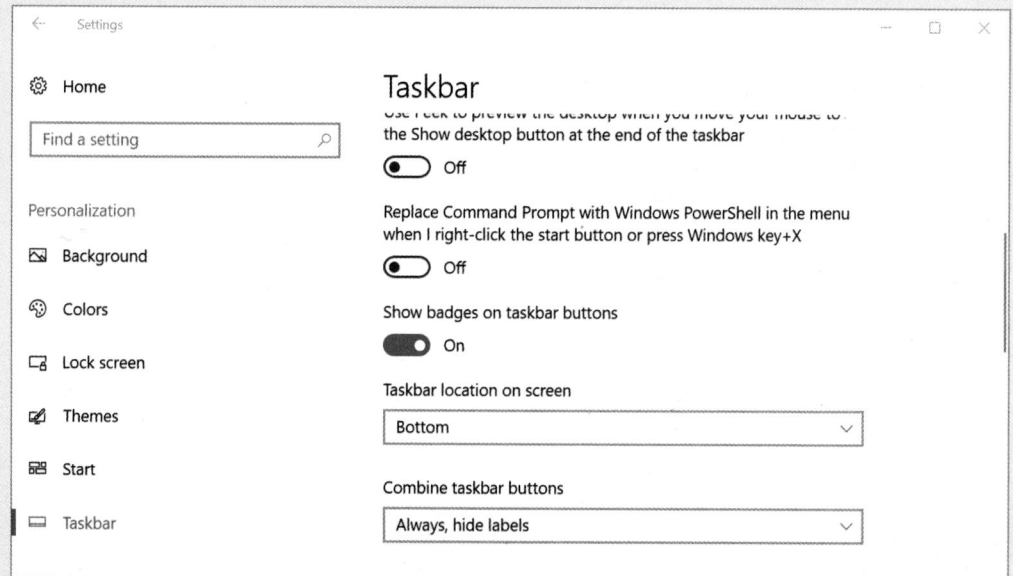

Figure 3-4 Choose a CLI to be listed in the Quick Links menu, which appears when you right-click Start or when you press Win + X on your keyboard

Recall that networks may use two types of IP addresses: IPv4 addresses, which have 32 bits, and IPv6 addresses, which have 128 bits. In the next section, you will learn how IPv4 addresses are formatted and assigned. Then you will learn how IPv6 addresses are formatted and assigned.

IPv4 Addresses

A 32-bit IP address is organized into four groups of 8 bits each, which are presented as four decimal numbers separated by periods, such as 72.56.105.12. Each of these four groups is called an octet. The largest possible 8-bit number is 11111111, which is equal to 255 in decimal. So, the largest possible IP address in decimal is 255.255.255.255, which in binary is 11111111.11111111.11111111.11111111. Each of the four octets can be any number from 0 to 255, making a total of about 4.3 billion IPv4 addresses (256 × 256 × 256 × 256). Some IP addresses are reserved, so these numbers are approximations.

Let's begin our discussion of IPv4 addresses by looking at how they are formatted.

Format of IPv4 Addresses

The first part of an IP address identifies the network, and the last part identifies the host. When using **classful addressing**, which is an older method of managing IP address ranges, the dividing line between the network and host portions is determined by the numerical range the IP address falls in. Classful IPv4 addresses are divided into five classes: Class A, Class B, Class C, Class D, and Class E. Table 3-1 shows the range for each class of IPv4 addresses that are available for public use. And Figure 3-5 shows how Classes A, B, and C are divided into the network and host portions.

Class A, B, and C licensed IP addresses are available for use on the Internet and are therefore called **public IP addresses**. To conserve its public IP addresses, a company can use **private IP addresses** on its private networks—that is, networks that do not directly connect to the Internet. IANA recommends that the following IP addresses be used for private networks:

- 10.0.0.0 through 10.255.255.255
- 172.16.0.0 through 172.31.255.255
- 192.168.0.0 through 192.168.255.255

Table 3-1   IP address classes

Class	Network octets*	Approximate number of possible networks	Approximate number of possible IP addresses in each network
A	1.x.y.z to 126.x.y.z	126	16 million
B	128.0.x.y to 191.255.x.y	16,000	65,000
C	192.0.0.x to 223.255.255.x	2 million	254

*An x, y, or z in the IP address stands for an octet that is used to identify hosts on the network

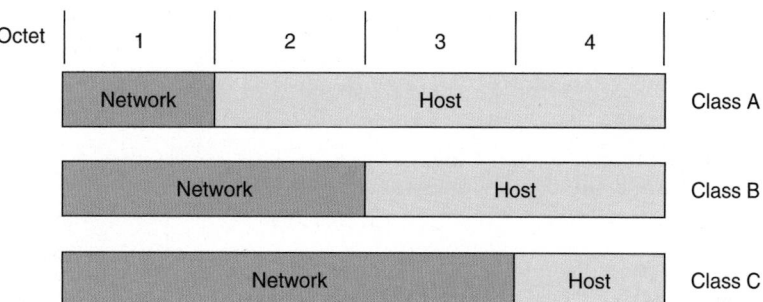

Figure 3-5 The network portion and host portion for each class of IP addresses

Class D and Class E IP addresses are not available for general use. Class D addresses begin with octets 224 through 239 and are used for **multicast** transmissions, in which one host sends messages to multiple hosts. An example of this is when a host transmits a videoconference over the Internet to multiple participants. Class E addresses, which begin with 240 through 254, are reserved for research. Additionally, the IP addresses listed in Table 3-2 are reserved for special use by TCP/IP and should not be assigned to a device on a network.

Table 3-2 Reserved IP addresses

IP address(es)	Function
255.255.255.255	Used for broadcast messages by TCP/IP background processes. A **broadcast** message is read by every node on the network.
0.0.0.0	Currently unassigned
127.0.0.1 through 127.255.255.254	Used for research or can indicate your own computer, in which case it is called the **loopback address**. Later in this chapter, you will learn to use the loopback address to verify that TCP/IP is configured correctly on a computer when it can talk to and hear itself on the loopback interface.
169.254.0.1 through 169.254.255.254	Used to create an **APIPA (Automatic Private IP Addressing)** address when a computer configured for DHCP first connects to the network and is unable to lease an IPv4 address from the DHCP server.

Network+ Exam Tip (i)

APIPA is known to show up often on the CompTIA Network+ exam.

DHCP (Dynamic Host Configuration Protocol)

Recall that static IP addresses are manually assigned by the network administrator, whereas dynamic IP addresses are automatically assigned by a DHCP server each time a computer connects to the network. Because it can become unmanageable to keep up with static IP address assignments, most network administrators choose to use dynamic IP addressing.

Applying Concepts: Configure a DHCP Server

Each type of DHCP server software is configured differently. Generally, you define a range of IP addresses, called a **DHCP scope** or **DHCP pool**, to be assigned to clients when they request an address. For example, Figure 3-6 shows a screen provided by the firmware utility for a home router, which is also a DHCP server. Using this screen, you set the starting IP address (192.168.2.100 in the figure) and the ending IP address (192.168.2.199 in the figure) of the DHCP scope. The scope includes the following additional information, called **scope options**:

- a time limit, called a **lease time**
- the default gateway's IP address
- the primary and secondary DNS server addresses

When other nodes on the network frequently need to know the IP address of a particular client, you can have DHCP offer that client the same IP address every time it requests one. The DHCP server recognizes this client based on its MAC address, so this reserved IP address is called a variety of names: **MAC reservation**, **IP reservation**, or **DHCP reservation**. For example, a network printer should consistently use the same IP address so that computers on the network can always find it. In Figure 3-7, which shows the management interface for a TP-Link SOHO router, an OKI Data network printer has a reserved IP address of 192.168.2.200.

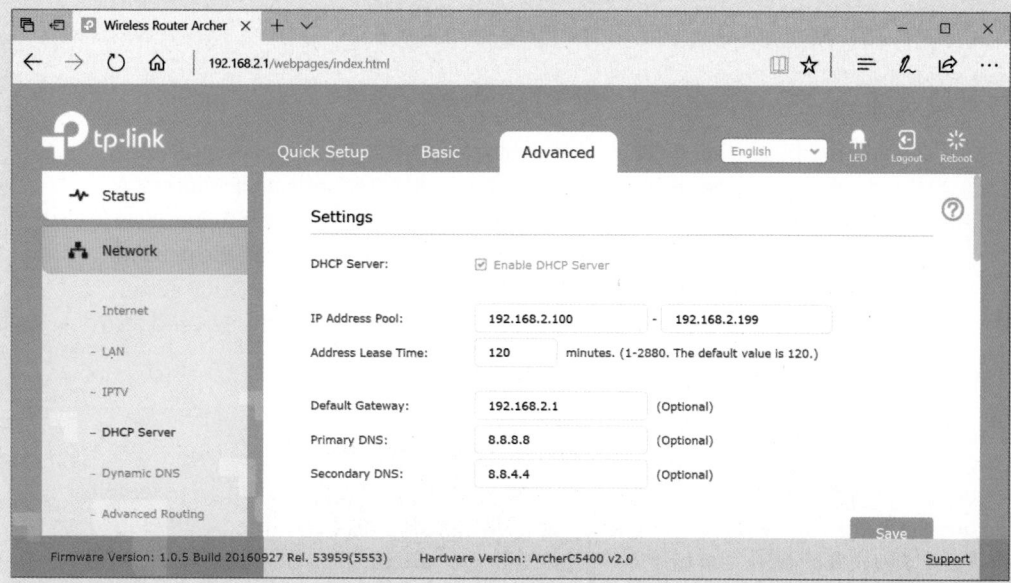

Figure 3-6   Set a range of IP addresses on a DHCP server
Source: TP-Link Technologies Co., Ltd.

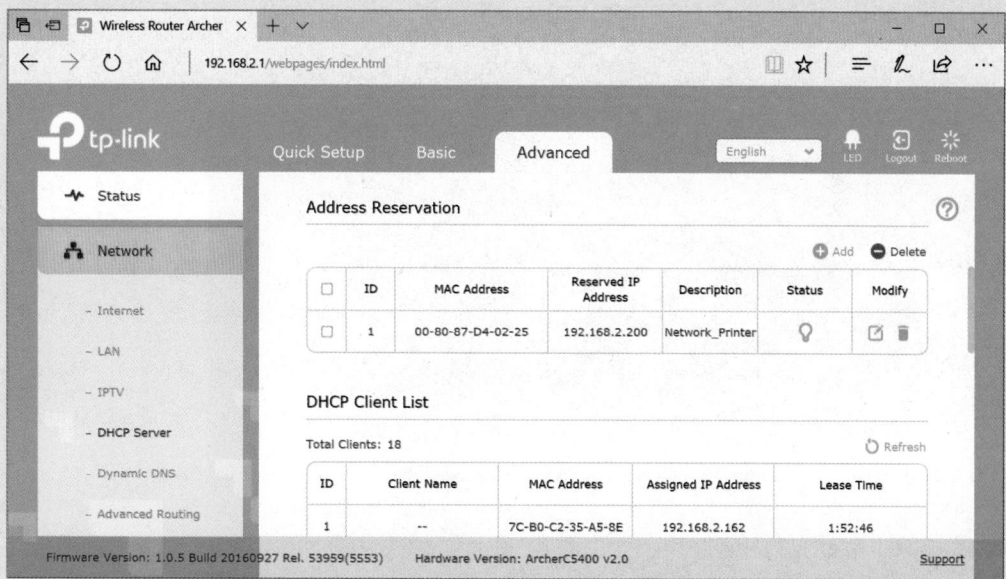

Figure 3-7   Reserve an IP address for one or more network clients, such as a network printer
Source: TP-Link Technologies Co., Ltd.

Note

A reserved IP address is not quite the same thing as a static IP address. A reserved IP address is offered to the client by DHCP when the client requests an IP address. A static IP address is configured on the client itself so that the client never requests an IP address from DHCP in the first place. If you have one or more clients on the network with static IP addresses, you need to configure an **IP exclusion** on the DHCP server. This excludes one or more IP addresses from the IP address pool so the server doesn't offer those IP addresses to other clients.

In Linux systems, you configure the DHCP software by editing a text file. For example, the text file for one Linux distro's DHCP server is dhcpd.conf, which is stored in the /etc/dhcp directory. Figure 3-8 shows the text file as it appears in vim, which is a Linux text editor. A # at the beginning of a line identifies the line as a comment line (a line that is not executed). The range of IP addresses that will be assigned to clients in Figure 3-8 is 10.254.239.10 to 10.254.239.20, which consists of 11 IP addresses.

DHCP for IPv4 servers listen at port 67 and DHCPv4 clients receive responses at port 68. When using DHCP for IPv6, which is called **DHCPv6**, DHCP servers listen at port 546 and clients receive responses at port 547.

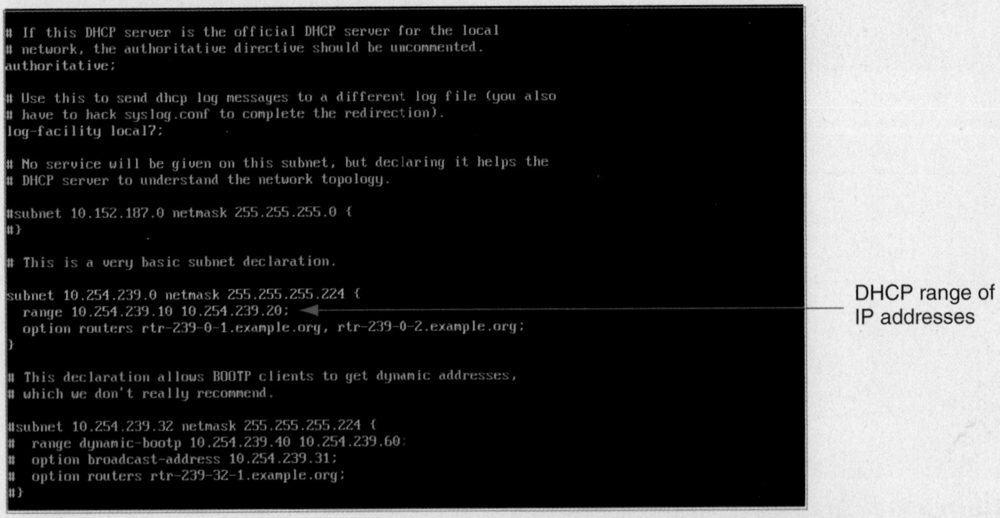

```
# If this DHCP server is the official DHCP server for the local
# network, the authoritative directive should be uncommented.
authoritative;

# Use this to send dhcp log messages to a different log file (you also
# have to hack syslog.conf to complete the redirection).
log-facility local7;

# No service will be given on this subnet, but declaring it helps the
# DHCP server to understand the network topology.

#subnet 10.152.187.0 netmask 255.255.255.0 {
#}

# This is a very basic subnet declaration.

subnet 10.254.239.0 netmask 255.255.255.224 {
  range 10.254.239.10 10.254.239.20;          ◄——
  option routers rtr-239-0-1.example.org, rtr-239-0-2.example.org;
}

# This declaration allows BOOTP clients to get dynamic addresses,
# which we don't really recommend.

#subnet 10.254.239.32 netmask 255.255.255.224 {
#   range dynamic-bootp 10.254.239.40 10.254.239.60;
#   option broadcast-address 10.254.239.31;
#   option routers rtr-239-32-1.example.org;
#}
```

DHCP range of IP addresses

Figure 3-8   Edit a text file in Linux to set an IP address range for a DHCP server

Source: Canonical Group Limited

Address Translation

NAT (Network Address Translation) is a technique designed to conserve the number of public IP addresses needed by a network. A gateway device that stands between a private network and other networks substitutes the private IP addresses used by computers on the private network with its own public IP address when these computers need access to other networks or the Internet. The process is called **address translation**. Besides requiring only a single public IP address for the entire private network, another advantage of NAT is security; the gateway hides the entire private network behind this one address.

How does the gateway know which local host is to receive a response from a host on the Internet? **PAT (Port Address Translation)** assigns a separate TCP port to each session between a local host and an Internet host. See Figure 3-9. When the Internet host responds to the local host, the gateway uses PAT to determine which local host is the intended recipient.

Two variations of NAT you need to be aware of are:

- *SNAT*—Using **SNAT (Static Network Address Translation or Source Network Address Translation)**, the gateway assigns the same public IP address to a host each time it makes a request to access the Internet. Small home networks with only a single public IP address provided by its ISP use SNAT.
- *DNAT or Destination NAT*—Using **DNAT (Destination Network Address Translation)**, hosts outside the network address a computer inside the network by a predefined public IP address. When a message sent to the public IP address reaches the router managing DNAT, the destination IP address is changed to the private IP address of the host inside the network. The router must maintain a translation table of public IP addresses mapped to various hosts inside the network.

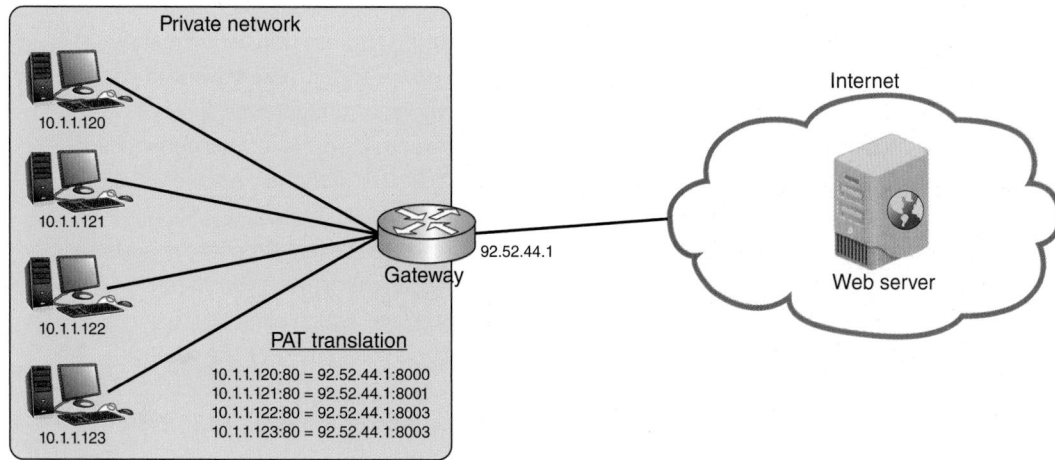

Figure 3-9 PAT (Port Address Translation)

Figure 3-10 contrasts SNAT and DNAT. SNAT changes the *source* IP addresses of *outgoing* messages and is used to reduce the number of public IP addresses needed by a network. DNAT changes the *destination* IP address of *incoming* messages and is often used by large organizations that provide services to the Internet. The various servers can use private IP addresses for security and also to allow network administrators more freedom to manage these servers. For example, they can switch a web server to a backup computer while doing maintenance on the primary server by simply making a change in the router's DNAT settings, redirecting a public IP address to the backup computer.

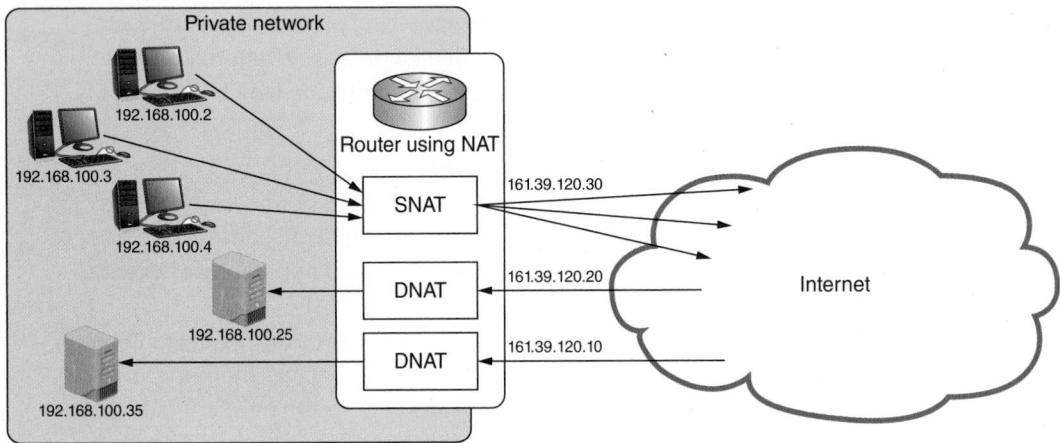

Figure 3-10 SNAT for outgoing messages, and DNAT for incoming messages

Applying Concepts: Configure Address Translation Using NAT

For simple default gateways such as a home router, configuring address translation means making sure NAT is turned on. That's about all you can do. However, for more advanced gateways, such as an industrial-grade Cisco router or Linux server, you configure the NAT software by editing NAT translation tables stored on the device. For example, suppose your network supports a web server available to the Internet, as shown in Figure 3-11. On the web, the website is known by the public IP address 69.32.208.74. Figure 3-12 shows the sample text file required to set up the translation tables for DNAT to direct traffic to the web server at private IP address 192.168.10.7. Note that any line that begins with an exclamation mark (!) is a comment.

The first group of lines defines the router's outside interface, which connects with the outside network, and is called the serial interface. The second group defines the router's inside Ethernet interface. The last line that is not a comment line says that when clients from the Internet send a request to IP address 69.32.208.74, the request is translated to the IP address 192.168.10.7.

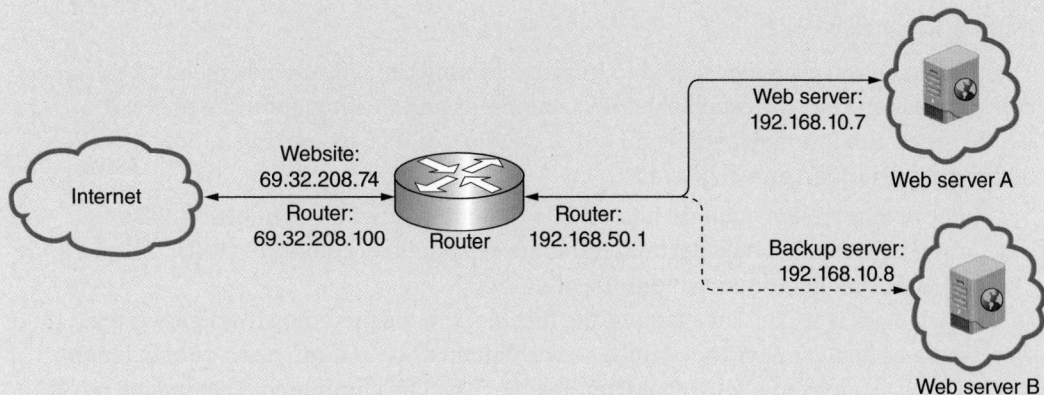

Figure 3-11   Messages to the website are being routed to web server A

```
interface serial 0/0
  ip address 69.32.208.100 255.255.255.0
  ip nat outside

!--- Defines the serial 0/0 interface as the router's NAT outside interface
!--- with an IP address of 69.32.208.100

interface ethernet 1/1
  ip address 192.168.50.1 255.255.255.0
  ip nat inside

!--- Defines the Ethernet 1/1 interface as the router's NAT inside interface
!--- with an IP address of 192.168.50.1


ip nat inside source static 192.168.10.7 69.32.208.74

!--- States that source information about the inside host will be translated
!--- so the host's private IP address (192.168.10.7) will appear as the
!--- public IP address (69.32.208.74). Both ingoing and outgoing traffic
!--- exchanged with the public IP address will be routed to the host at the
!--- private IP address.
```

Figure 3-12   NAT translation table entry in Linux

At the end of this chapter, you'll create your own NAT translation table entry using this example as a template. To help you better understand where the IP addresses in a translation table entry come from, answer the following questions about the information in Figures 3-11 and 3-12:

1. What is the router's outside interface IP address?
2. What is the router's inside interface IP address?
3. What is the website's public IP address?
4. What is the private IP address of the active web server?

IPv6 Addresses

The IPv6 standards were developed to improve routing capabilities and speed of communication over the established IPv4 standards and to allow for more public IP addresses on the Internet. Let's begin our discussion of IPv6 by looking at how IPv6 addresses are written and displayed:

- Recall that an IPv6 address has 128 bits that are written as eight blocks (also called quartets) of hexadecimal numbers separated by colons, like this: 2001:0000:0B80:0000:0000:00D3:9C5A:00CC.
- Each block is 16 bits. For example, the first block in the preceding IP address is the hexadecimal number 2001, which can be written as 0010 0000 0000 0001 in binary.
- Leading zeroes in a four-character hex block can be eliminated. This means our sample IP address can be written as 2001:0000:B80:0000:0000:D3:9C5A:CC.
- If blocks contain all zeroes, they can be eliminated and replaced by double colons (::). To avoid confusion, only one set of double colons is used in an IP address. This means our sample IP address can be written two ways:

  ○ 2001::B80:0000:0000:D3:9C5A:CC

  ○ 2001:0000:B80::D3:9C5A:CC

In this example, the preferred method is the second one (2001:0000:B80::D3:9C5A:CC) because the address contains the fewest zeroes.

The way computers communicate using IPv6 has changed the terminology used to describe TCP/IP communication. Here are a few terms used in the IPv6 standards:

- A link, sometimes called the local link, is any LAN bounded by routers.
- An interface is a node's attachment to a link. The attachment can be physical using a network adapter or wireless connection, or logical, such as with a virtual machine.
- When a network is configured to use both IPv4 and IPv6 protocols, the network is said to be dual stacked. However, if packets on this network must traverse other networks where dual stacking is not used, the solution is to use tunneling, which is a method of transporting IPv6 packets through or over an IPv4 network. Because the Internet is not completely dual stacked, tunneling is always used for IPv6 transmission on the Internet.
- The last 64 bits, or four blocks, of an IPv6 address identify the interface and are called the interface ID or interface identifier. These 64 bits uniquely identify an interface on the local link.
- Neighbors are two or more nodes on the same link.

Types of IPv6 Addresses

IPv6 classifies IP addresses differently than IPv4. IPv6 supports these three types of IP addresses, classified by how the address is used:

- *unicast address*—Specifies a single node on a network. Figure 3-13 diagrams the two types of unicast addresses:

○ *global address*—Can be routed on the Internet and is similar to public IPv4 addresses. Most begin with the prefix 2000::/3, although other prefixes are being released. The /3 indicates that the first three bits are fixed and are always 001. Looking at Figure 3-13, notice the 16 bits reserved for the **subnet ID**, which can be used to identify a subnet on a large corporate network.

○ *link local address*—Can be used for communicating with nodes in the same link, and is similar to an autoconfigured APIPA address in IPv4. It begins with FE80::/10. The first 10 bits of the reserved prefix are fixed (1111 1110 10), and the remaining 54 bits in the 64-bit prefix are all zeroes. Therefore, a link local address prefix is sometimes written as FE80::/64, as shown in Figure 3-13. Link local addresses are not allowed past the local link or on the Internet.

- *multicast address*—Delivers packets to all nodes in the targeted, multicast group.
- *anycast address*—Identifies multiple destinations, with packets delivered to the closest destination. For example, a DNS server might send a DNS request to a group of DNS servers that have all been assigned the same anycast address. A router handling the request examines routes to all the DNS servers in the group and routes the request to the closest server.

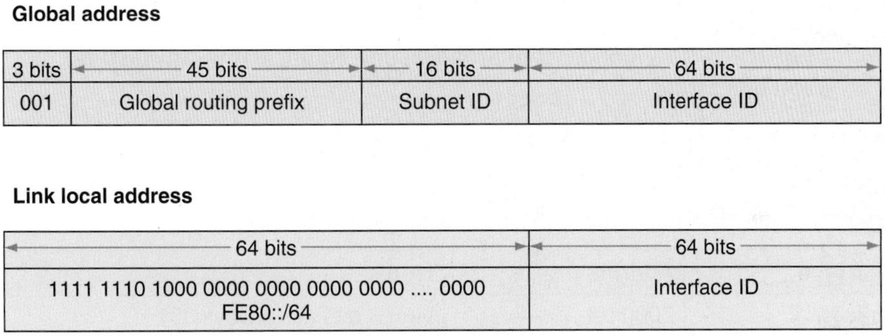

Global address

3 bits	45 bits	16 bits	64 bits
001	Global routing prefix	Subnet ID	Interface ID

Link local address

64 bits	64 bits
1111 1110 1000 0000 0000 0000 0000 .... 0000 FE80::/64	Interface ID

Figure 3-13   Two types of IPv6 addresses

Recall that with IPv4 broadcasting, messages are sent to every node on a network. However, IPv6 reduces network traffic by eliminating broadcasting. The concepts of broadcasting, multicasting, anycasting, and unicasting are depicted in Figure 3-14 for easy comparison. In the figure, each green dot is the sending node. The cream dots are the intended recipients. The blue dots are other nodes on the network and do not receive the transmission.

Table 3-3 lists some currently used address prefixes for IPv6 addresses. Notice in the table the unique local unicast addresses, which work on local links and are similar to IPv4 private IP addresses. You can expect more prefixes to be assigned as they are needed.

You can use the `ipconfig` command to view IPv4 and IPv6 addresses assigned to all network connections on a computer. For example, in Figure 3-15, four IP addresses have been assigned to the physical connections on a laptop.

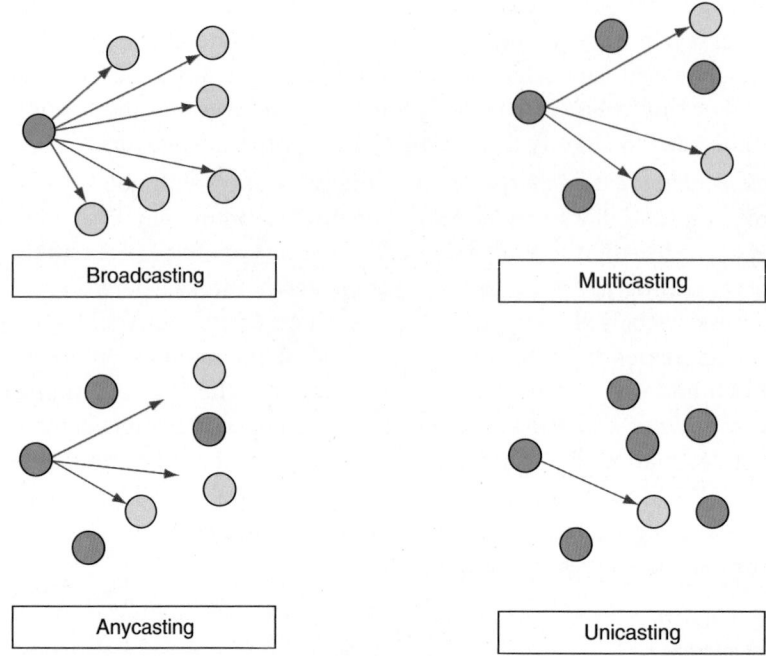

Figure 3-14   Concepts of broadcasting, multicasting, anycasting, and unicasting

Table 3-3   Address prefixes for types of IPv6 addresses

IP address type	Address prefix	Notes
Global unicast	2000::/3	First 3 bits are always 001
Link local unicast	FE80::/64	First 64 bits are always 1111 1110 1000 0000 0000 0000 0000
Unique local unicast	FC00::/7	First 7 bits are always 1111 110
	FD00::/8	First 8 bits are always 1111 1101
Multicast	FF00::/8	First 8 bits are always 1111 1111

IPv6 Autoconfiguration

IPv6 addressing is designed so that a computer can autoconfigure its own link local IP address without the help of a DHCPv6 server. This is similar to how IPv4 uses an APIPA address. Here's what happens with autoconfiguration when a computer using IPv6 first makes a network connection:

Step 1—The computer creates its IPv6 address. It uses FE80::/64 as the first 64 bits, called the prefix. Depending on how the OS is configured, the last 64 bits (called the interface ID) can be generated in two ways:

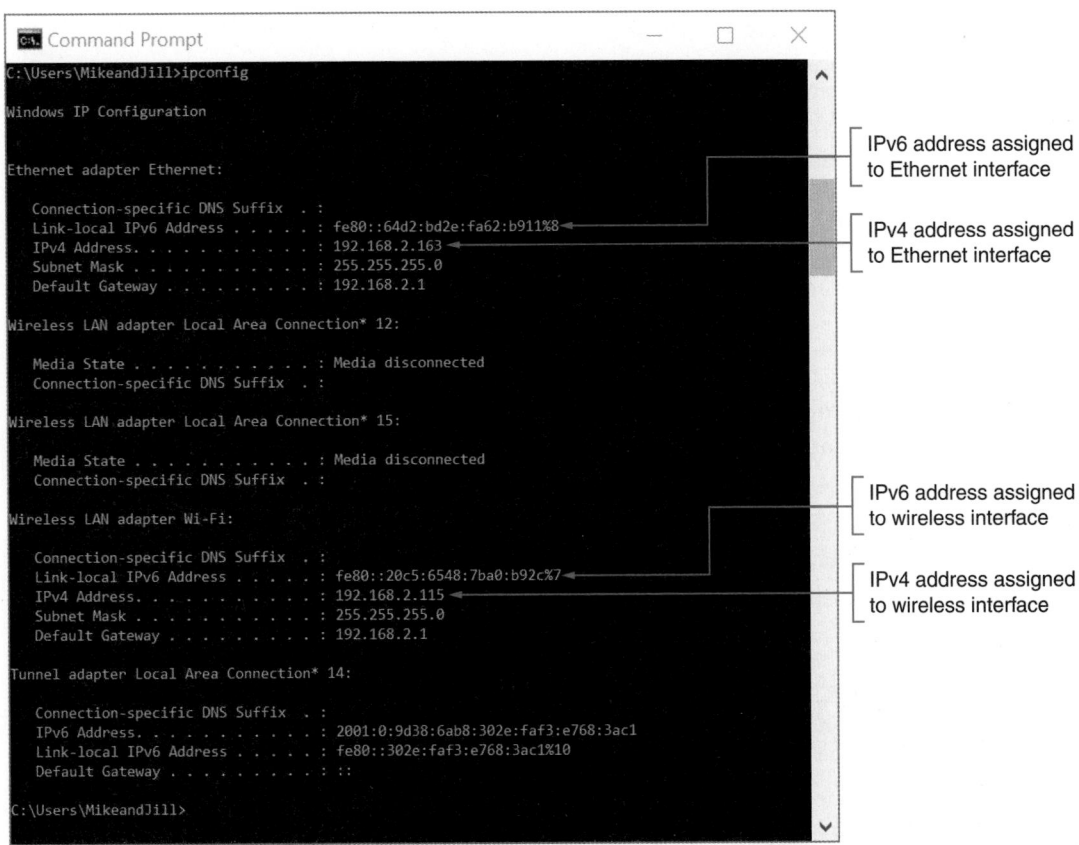

Figure 3-15   The `ipconfig` command shows IPv4 and IPv6 addresses assigned to this computer

- *The 64 bits are randomly generated*—In this case, the IP address is called a temporary address and is never registered in DNS or used to generate global addresses for use on the Internet. The IP address changes often to help prevent hackers from discovering the computer. This is the default method used by Windows 10.
- *The 64 bits are generated from the network adapter's MAC address*—MAC addresses consist of 48 bits and must be converted to the 64-bit standard, called the **EUI-64 (Extended Unique Identifier-64)** standard. To generate the interface ID, the OS takes the 48 bits of the device's MAC address, inserts a fixed 16-bit value in the middle of the 48 bits, and inverts the value of the seventh bit.

Step 2—The computer checks to make sure its IP address is unique on the network.

Step 3—The computer asks if a router on the network can provide configuration information. This message is called a **RS (router solicitation)**. If a router responds with DHCP information in what's called a **RA (router advertisement)** message, the computer uses whatever information this might be, such as the IP addresses of DNS servers or the network prefix. The process is called prefix discovery and the computer uses the prefix to generate its own link local or global IPv6 address by appending its interface ID to the prefix.

Because a computer can generate its own link local or global IP address, a DHCPv6 server usually serves up only global IPv6 addresses to hosts that require static address assignments. For example, web servers and DNS servers can receive their static IPv6 addresses from a DHCPv6 server.

Note 📎

On larger networks, IP address infrastructure can quickly become overwhelming. An **IPAM (IP address management)** system, whether as a standalone product or embedded in another product such as Windows Server, provides a way to plan, deploy, and monitor a network's IP address space. IPAM tools can automatically detect IP address ranges, assignments, reservations, and exclusions, integrate this information with data from DNS records, and provide constant monitoring for growth, security, and troubleshooting purposes.

Now we move up to Layer 4 of the OSI model, where ports are used to identify an application when it receives communication from a remote host.

Ports and Sockets

 **Certification**

7	APPLICATION
6	PRESENTATION
5	SESSION
4	TRANSPORT
3	NETWORK
2	DATA LINK
1	PHYSICAL

1.1 Explain the purposes and uses of ports and protocols.

1.8 Explain the functions of network services.

A port is a number assigned to a **process**, such as an application or a service, that can receive data. Whereas an IP address is used to find a computer, a port is used to find a process running on that computer. TCP and UDP ports ensure that data is transmitted to the correct process among multiple processes running on the computer. If you compare network addressing with the addressing system used by the postal service, and you equate a host's IP address to the address of a building, then a port is similar to an apartment number within that building.

A **socket** consists of both a host's IP address and a process's TCP or UDP port, with a colon separating the two values. For example, the standard port for the Telnet service is TCP 23. If a host has an IP address of 10.43.3.87, the socket address for Telnet running on that host is 10.43.3.87:23.

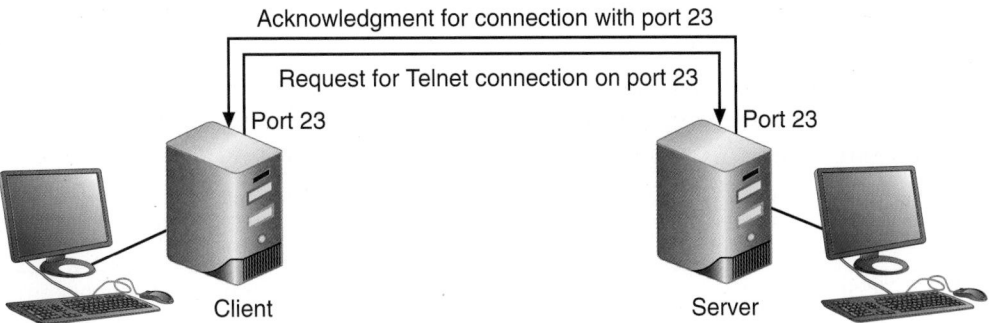

Figure 3-16   A virtual connection for the Telnet service

When the host receives a request to communicate on TCP port 23, it establishes or opens a **session**, which is an ongoing conversation, with the Telnet service. At that point, the socket is said to be open. When the TCP session is complete, the socket is closed or dissolved. You can think of a socket as a virtual circuit between a server and client (see Figure 3-16).

Port numbers range from 0 to 65535 and are divided by IANA into three types:

- *well-known ports*—Range from 0 to 1023 and are assigned by IANA to widely used and well-known utilities and applications, such as Telnet, FTP, and HTTP. Table 3-4 lists some of the most common well-known ports used by TCP and/or UDP.
- *registered ports*—Range from 1024 to 49151 and can be used temporarily by processes for nonstandard assignments for increased security. Default assignments of these registered ports must be registered with IANA.
- *dynamic and private ports*—Range from 49152 to 65535 and are open for use without restriction.
  - *dynamic port*—Number assigned by a client or server as the need arises. For example, if a client program has several open sockets with multiple servers, it can use a different dynamic port number for each socket.
  - *private port*—Number assigned by a network administrator that is different from the well-known port number for that service. For example, the administrator might assign a private port number other than the standard port 80 to a web server on the Internet so that several people can test the site before it's made available to the public. To reach the web server, a tester must enter the private port number in the browser address box along with the web server's IP address.

Network+ Exam Tip ⓘ

To prepare for the CompTIA Network+ exam, you need to memorize all the well-known ports listed in Table 3-4. Some of these protocols are discussed in detail in later chapters. We've put them all together in Table 3-4 for easy reference.

Table 3-4 Well-known TCP and UDP ports

Port	Process name	Protocol used	Used for:
20	FTP-DATA	TCP	File transfer—data
21	FTP	TCP	File transfer—control (an FTP server listens at port 21 and sends/receives data at port 20)
22	SSH	TCP	Secure communications between computers
22	SFTP	TCP	Encrypted file transfer using SSH
23	TELNET	TCP	Unencrypted control of remote computers
25	SMTP	TCP	Outgoing email messages
53	DNS	TCP and UDP	Name resolution
67	DHCP	UDP	Distribution of IP addresses on a network—client to server messages
68	DHCP	UDP	Distribution of IP addresses on a network—server to client messages
69	TFTP	UDP	Simple file transfer
80	HTTP	TCP and UDP	Requests between web servers and web clients
110	POP3	TCP	Incoming email messages (downloaded messages)
123	NTP	UDP	Network time synchronization
143	IMAP4	TCP	Incoming email messages (messages stored on server)
161	SNMP	TCP and UDP	Management of network devices
389	LDAP	TCP and UDP	Access to network-based directories
443	HTTPS	TCP	Secure implementation of HTTP
445	SMB	TCP	Network file sharing
636	LDAPS	TCP and UDP	Secure access to network-based directories
1720	H.323	TCP	Creation of connections for multimedia session
3389	RDP	TCP	Encrypted control of remote computers
5060	SIP	UDP	Creation of unencrypted connections for multimedia session
5061	SIP	UDP	Creation of encrypted connections for multimedia session

In Chapter 1, you learned about most of the protocols listed in Table 3-4. A few of them have already been covered in this chapter. Here's a brief description of the ones not yet covered:

- *TFTP (Trivial File Transfer Protocol)*—Most commonly used by computers (without user intervention) as they are booting up to request configuration files from another computer on the local network. TFTP uses UDP, whereas normal FTP uses TCP.
- *NTP (Network Time Protocol)*—A simple protocol used to synchronize clocks on computers throughout a network. The genius of NTP is how it can almost completely account for the variable delays across a network, even on the open Internet. Not every network has its own time server, but those that do can maintain accuracy to within a millisecond of each other and are closely synced to the UTC (Coordinated Universal Time).
- *LDAP (Lightweight Directory Access Protocol)*—A standard protocol for accessing network-based directories. **LDAPS (Lightweight Directory Access Protocol over SSL)** uses SSL to encrypt its communications. You'll learn more about LDAP and LDAPS in a later chapter.
- *SMB (Server Message Block)*—First used by earlier Windows OSes for file sharing on a network. UNIX uses a version of SMB in its Samba software, which can share files with other operating systems, including Windows systems.
- *SIP (Session Initiation Protocol)*—A signaling protocol that is used to make an initial connection between hosts but that does not participate in data transfer during the session. After SIP establishes the connection, other protocols kick in—for example, RTP (Real-time Transport Protocol or Real-time Protocol) that transports streaming audio and video data for VoIP calls.
- *H.323*—Another signaling protocol used to make a connection between hosts prior to communicating multimedia data. H.323 has largely been replaced by SIP, which is easier to use.

Domain Names and DNS (Domain Name System)

 **Certification**

7	APPLICATION
6	PRESENTATION
5	SESSION
4	TRANSPORT
3	NETWORK
2	DATA LINK
1	PHYSICAL

1.8   Explain the functions of network services.

Host names and domain names were created because character-based names are easier for humans to remember than numeric IP addresses. Recall that an FQDN is a host name and a domain name together, such as *www.cengage.com*. The last part of an FQDN (*com* in our example) is called the **TLD (top-level domain)**.

Domain names must be registered with an Internet naming authority that works on behalf of ICANN. Table 3-5 lists some well-known ICANN-approved TLDs. Of these, no restrictions exist on the use of the .com, .org, and .net TLDs, but ICANN does restrict what type of hosts can be associated with the .arpa, .mil, .edu, and .gov TLDs. A complete list of current TLDs can be found at *iana.org/domains/root/db/*.

Table 3-5 Some well-known top-level domains

Domain suffix	Type of organization
ARPA	Reverse lookup domain (special Internet function)
COM	Commercial
EDU	Educational
GOV	Government
ORG	Noncommercial organization (such as a nonprofit agency)
NET	Network (such as an ISP)
MIL	United States military organization
BIZ	Businesses
INFO	Unrestricted use

Note

A registry, also known as a domain name registry operator, is an organization or country that is responsible for one or more TLDs and that maintains a database or registry of TLD information. A domain name registrar such as *godaddy.com* is an organization accredited by registries and ICANN to lease domain names to companies or individuals, following the guidelines of the TLD registry operators.

While FQDNs are convenient for humans, a computer must convert the FQDN to an IP address before it can find the referenced computer. Suppose you type an FQDN into a browser address bar; how does your computer figure out the IP address for that web server? To answer this question, you need to learn about **name resolution**, which is the process of discovering the IP address of a host when its FQDN is known.

In the mid-1980s, **DNS (Domain Name System or Domain Name Service)** was designed to associate computer names with IP addresses. DNS is an Application layer client-server system of computers and databases made up of these elements, which we will explore in more detail in the following sections:

- *namespace*—The entire collection of computer names and their associated IP addresses stored in databases on DNS name servers around the globe
- *name servers*—Computers that hold these databases, organized in a hierarchical structure
- *resolvers*—A DNS client that requests information from DNS name servers

Namespace Databases

DNS namespace databases are stored on thousands of servers around the world, rather than being centralized on a single server or group of servers. In other words, DNS doesn't follow a centralized database model, but rather a distributed database model. Because data is distributed over thousands of servers, DNS will not fail catastrophically if one or a handful of servers experiences errors.

Each organization that provides host services (for example, websites or email) on the public Internet is responsible for providing and maintaining its own DNS authoritative servers for public access, or they can use a third-party or cloud-hosted DNS server. An **authoritative server** is the authority on computer names and their IP addresses for computers in their domains. The domains (for example, *cengage.com* and *course.com*) that the organization is responsible for managing are called collectively a **DNS zone**. A large organization can keep all its domains in a single zone, or it can subdivide its domains into multiple zones to make each zone easier to manage.

Name Servers

An organization might have these four common types of DNS servers:

- *primary DNS server*—The authoritative name server for the organization, which holds the authoritative DNS database for the organization's zones. This server is contacted by clients, both local and over the Internet, to resolve DNS queries for the organization's domains.
- *secondary DNS server*—The backup authoritative name server for the organization. When a secondary DNS server needs to update its database, it makes the request to the primary server for the update; this process is called a zone transfer.
- *caching DNS server*—A server that accesses public DNS data and caches the DNS information it collects. This server receives DNS queries from local network clients and works to resolve them by contacting other DNS servers for information. Caching DNS servers do not store zone files (which is why they must rely on their caches and resolution efforts), and therefore do not participate in zone transfers, which further helps to reduce network traffic on the intranet.
- *forwarding DNS server*—An optional server that receives queries from local clients but doesn't work to resolve the queries. Typically, a forwarding server will maintain its own DNS cache from previous queries, and so it might already have the information the client needs. If not, the forwarding server forwards the query to another server to resolve. Several forwarding servers might be strategically placed throughout the organization's network to reduce network traffic on slow links.

 **Note**

The primary and secondary DNS servers listed in a client's IP configuration are not the same as an organization's primary and secondary authoritative DNS servers. The client's configuration is referring to the network's caching or forwarding servers.

Any of these DNS server types can coexist on the same machine, depending on the needs of the network. For example, a primary DNS server for one zone might be a secondary DNS server for a different zone within the organization. A primary DNS server might also serve as a caching server for its local network clients (although for security purposes, this is not recommended). A caching server might also rely on forwarding for certain clients or certain types of traffic.

DNS name servers are organized in the hierarchical structure shown in Figure 3-17. At the root level, 13 clusters of **root servers** hold information used to locate the TLD (top-level domain) servers. These TLD servers hold information about the authoritative servers owned by various organizations.

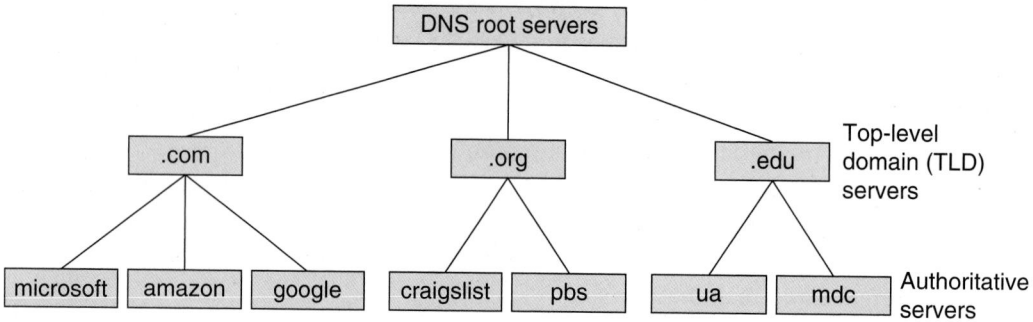

Figure 3-17   Hierarchy of name servers

To understand how these servers interact, let's look at an example. Suppose an employee at Cengage, using a computer in the *cengage.com* domain, enters *www.mdc.edu* in her web browser address box. The browser makes an API call to the DNS resolver, a TCP/IP component in the OS, for the IP address of the *www.mdc.edu* host.

 **Note**

Recall that an application uses an API call to request the operating system perform a service or task.

Here are the steps to resolve the name, which are also illustrated in Figure 3-18:

Step 1—The resolver on the client computer first searches its DNS cache, a database stored on the local computer, for the match. If it can't find the information there, the resolver sends a DNS message or query to its local DNS server. In this example, let's assume this caching server doesn't yet know the IP address of the *www.mdc.edu* host.

> **Note** @
>
> DNS messages are Application layer messages that use UDP at the Transport layer. Communication with DNS servers occur on port 53.

Steps 2 and 3—The local name server queries a root server with the request. The root server responds to the local name server with a list of IP addresses of TLD name servers responsible for the .edu suffix.

Steps 4 and 5—The local name server makes the same request to one of the TLD name servers responsible for the .edu suffix. The TLD name server responds with the IP address of the *mdc.edu* authoritative server.

Steps 6 and 7—The local name server makes the request to the authoritative name server at Miami Dade Community College, which responds to the Cengage name server with the IP address of the *www.mdc.edu* host.

Step 8—The local name server responds to the client resolver with the requested IP address. Both the Cengage name server and the Cengage client computer store the information in their DNS caches, and, therefore, don't need to ask again until that information expires.

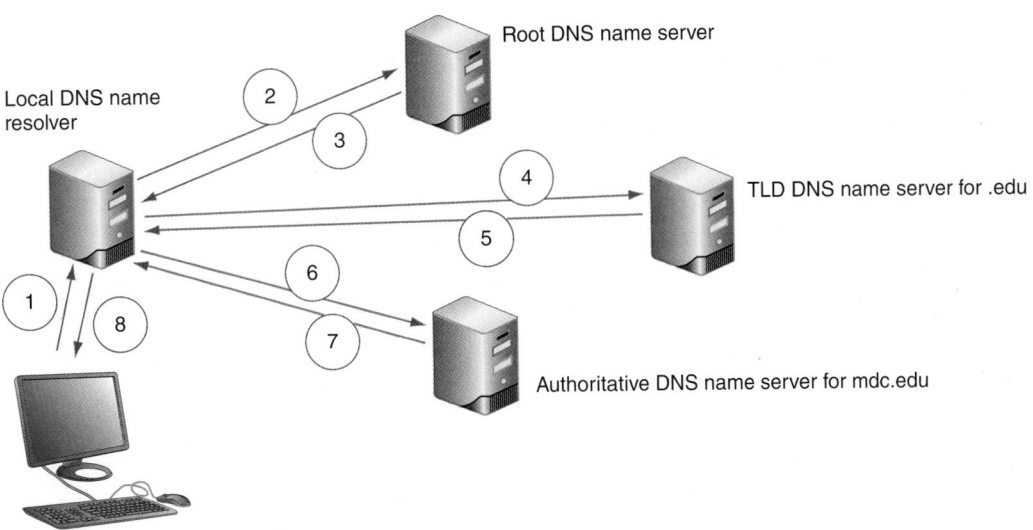

Figure 3-18   Queries for name resolution of *www.mdc.edu*

Requests sometimes involve additional name servers. Following are a few ways the process can get more complex:

- A client's local caching server typically is not the same machine as the authoritative name server for the organization's domain. Instead, the caching server exists only to resolve names for its own local clients.
- Name servers within a company might not have access to root servers. The local name server might forward the query to the name server at the company's ISP (Internet service provider), which might forward the query to a name server elsewhere on the Internet. This name server might query a root server; however, if any name server in the process has the requested information, it responds without the involvement of a root server, TLD name server, or authoritative name server.
- A TLD name server might be aware of an intermediate name server rather than the authoritative name server. When the local name server queries this intermediate name server, it might respond with the IP address of the authoritative name server.

Notice in these steps, the local name server kept working until the FQDN resolution was made, but other servers only aided in the process. Here we can see there are two types of DNS requests:

- *recursive query*—A query that demands a resolution or the answer "It can't be found." For example, the initial request the resolver makes to the local server is a recursive query. The local server must provide the information requested by the resolver, as in "The buck stops here."
- *iterative query*—A query that does not demand resolution. For example, when the local server issues queries to other servers, the other servers only provide information if they have it.

Resource Records in a DNS Database

Namespace databases are stored in DNS zone files, which keep information in various types of **resource records**. A DNS administrator needs to be familiar with these types of records, each designed to hold specific types of information:

- *A (Address) record*—Stores the name-to-address mapping for a host. This resource record provides the primary function of DNS—to match host names to IP addresses, using IPv4 addresses.
- *AAAA (Address) record* (*called a "quad-A record"*)—Holds the name-to-address mapping for IPv6 addresses.
- *CNAME (Canonical Name) record*—Holds alternative names for a host. These names can be used in place of the **canonical name**, which is the complete and properly formatted name, such as *www.mycompany.com*.
- *PTR (Pointer) record*—Used for reverse lookups, which provide a host name when you know its IP address. PTR records are usually created by ISPs and stored in a specially formatted reverse lookup zone file, or **reverse zone**. Reverse zones

differ from a typical forward lookup zone file, or **forward zone**, that holds A records, in that the IP addresses must be stored in reverse—with the last octet listed first—plus the domain *.in-addr.arpa*. For example, the IP address 1.2.3.4 would be stored in a PTR record as *4.3.2.1.in-addr.arpa*.

- *NS (Name Server) record*—Indicates the authoritative name server for a domain. It's mostly used for delegating subdomains to other name servers.
- *MX (Mail Exchanger) record*—Identifies an email server and is used for email traffic.
- *SRV (Service) record*—Identifies the hostname and port of a computer that hosts a specific network service besides email, such as FTP or SIP.
- *TXT (Text) record*—Holds any type of free-form text. It might contain text designed to be read by humans regarding network, server, or accounting issues. Most often it's used by:
  - *SPF (Sender Policy Framework)*—A validation system that helps fight spam by identifying the email servers allowed to send email on behalf of a domain.
  - *DKIM (DomainKeys Identified Mail)*—An authentication method that uses encryption to verify the domain name of an email's sender.

Network+ Exam Tip ⓘ

The CompTIA Network+ exam expects you to know about the eight types of DNS resource records in the preceding list.

Table 3-6 lists some sample zone file entries. Each line, or record, contains the text *IN*, which indicates the record can be used by DNS servers on the Internet.

In an actual DNS zone file, each resource record begins with a **TTL (Time to Live)** field that identifies how long the record should be saved in a cache on a server. Administrators can set the TTL based on how volatile is the DNS data (in other words, how often the administrator expects the IP addresses to change). TTL information is included in zone transfers.

DNS Server Software

By far, the most popular DNS server software is BIND (Berkeley Internet Name Domain), which is free, open-source software that runs on Linux, UNIX, and Windows platforms. **Open source** is the term for software whose code is publicly available for use and modification. You can download the BIND software from *isc.org*. Most Linux and UNIX distributions include BIND in the distribution.

Many other DNS server software products exist. For example, the Windows Server operating system has a built-in DNS service called Microsoft DNS Server,

Table 3-6 Zone file records used to configure a DNS server

Record	Description
`www.example.com IN A 92.100.80.40`	Maps the server named www in the example.com domain to the IP address 92.100.80.40
`www.example.com IN AAAA 2001:db8:cafe:f9::d3`	Maps a name to an IPv6 address
`demo.example.com IN CNAME www.example.com`	Says that the *www.example.com* host can also be addressed by its alias name *demo.example.com*
`40.80.100.92.in-addr-arpa IN PTR www.example.com`	Used for reverse lookup—that is, to find the name when you know the IP address. Note the IP address is reversed and *in-addr-arpa* is appended to it.
`www.example.com IN NS ns1.otherdns.com`	Directs DNS queries to a third-party, authoritative DNS server

`example.com IN MX 10`
 	
`mail.us.example.com`
 	
`example.com IN MX 20`
 	
`mail2.us.example.com`
	Tells email servers the preferred routes to take, ordered by best route, when sending email to the *example.com* domain

`_sip._udp.example.com IN`
 	
`SRV 0 75 5060`
 	
`fastsip.example.com`
 	
`_sip._udp.example.com IN`
 	
`SRV 0 25 5060`
 	
`slowsip.example.com`
	Directs SIP traffic (_sip.) to two SIP servers (fastsip.example.com and *slowsip.example.com*) using UDP (_udp.) at the Transport layer and the well-known SIP port (5060). The priority for both is 0 (the highest priority). However, the traffic load is distributed more heavily on the faster server (75) and more lightly on the slower server (25).

`example.com IN TXT v=spf1` `include:outlook.com ~all`	Adds the outlook.com email server as an approved sender for the example.com domain. The phrase v=spf1 defines the SPF version.

which partners closely with AD (Active Directory) services. A wise network administrator knows that DNS authoritative records must be accessible to Internet users, but Active Directory must be highly secured. The solution is to handle internal and external DNS queries by different DNS servers, or, less ideally, by a single DNS server that is specially configured to keep internal and external DNS zones separate.

In Figure 3-19, you can see two firewalls, one protecting the external DNS server and another one in front of the internal DNS server. A **firewall** is a dedicated device or software on a computer that selectively filters or blocks traffic between networks.

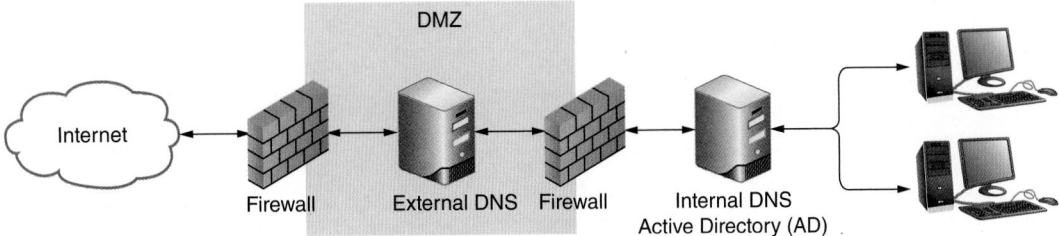

Figure 3-19 DNS services handled by two different servers so that the internal network remains protected

You will learn more about firewalls in later chapters. For now, note that all firewalls are porous to some degree in that they always let *some* traffic through; the question is what kind of traffic they allow—some of this filtering is accomplished by opening or closing the ports you learned about earlier in this chapter. The external DNS server is behind a more porous firewall, which allows greater exposure to the Internet so that certain permissible traffic can pass. The internal DNS server is better protected behind the second, more hardened firewall, which is stricter about the types of traffic allowed. The area between the two firewalls is called a **DMZ** or **demilitarized zone**. In this scenario, all DNS requests from the inside network that require external resolution are forwarded to the external DNS server, which also handles incoming queries from the Internet. Internal DNS requests are handled by AD's DNS server, which is kept secure from the Internet.

Troubleshooting Address Problems

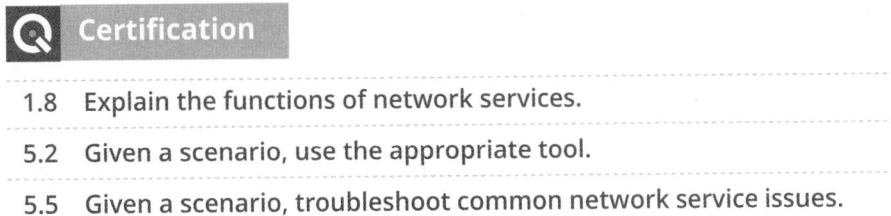

1.8   Explain the functions of network services.

5.2   Given a scenario, use the appropriate tool.

5.5   Given a scenario, troubleshoot common network service issues.

Now that you are familiar with the basics of network addressing, you can learn how to solve problems with network connections. Event Viewer is one of the first places to start looking for clues when something goes wrong with a computer. It can provide a lot of valuable information about the problems the computer is experiencing, and might even make suggestions for what to do next. For example, consider the printer error shown in Figure 3-20.

When Event Viewer doesn't give the information you need, move on to the TCP/IP troubleshooting commands discussed next.

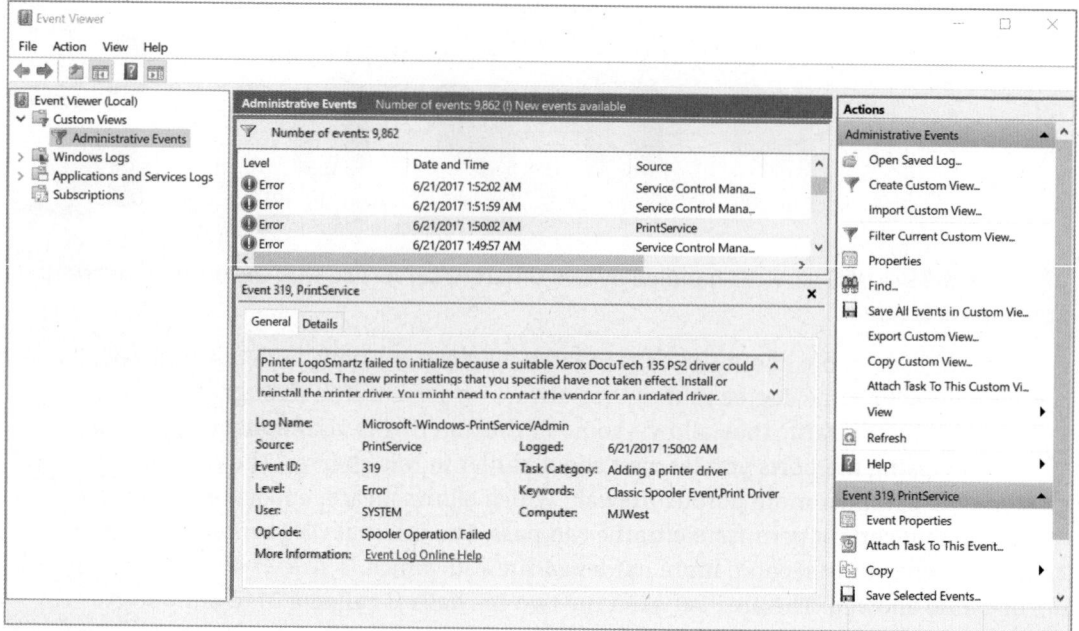

Figure 3-20 Event Viewer provided the diagnosis of a problem and recommended steps to fix the problem

---

Note 📎

Earlier in the chapter, you learned to access the command prompt in Windows. On a Linux system, you'll need to open a shell prompt. The steps for accessing a shell prompt vary depending on the Linux distribution that you're using. For Ubuntu Desktop, use either of the following options:

- Press **Ctrl+Alt+T** on your keyboard.
- Click the **Dash** icon at the top of the left sidebar, type **terminal**, and click **Terminal** (see Figure 3-21).

To close the shell prompt, click the red **X** icon or enter the `exit` command.

Troubleshooting Tools

Command-line tools are a great way to get a look "under the hood" when something is going wrong on your network. Some of the most helpful tools are `ping`, `ipconfig` (Windows only), `ifconfig` (Linux only), `nslookup`, and `dig` (Linux only). Let's see what each of these tools can do. As you read, consider practicing the commands at a Windows command prompt or Linux shell prompt.

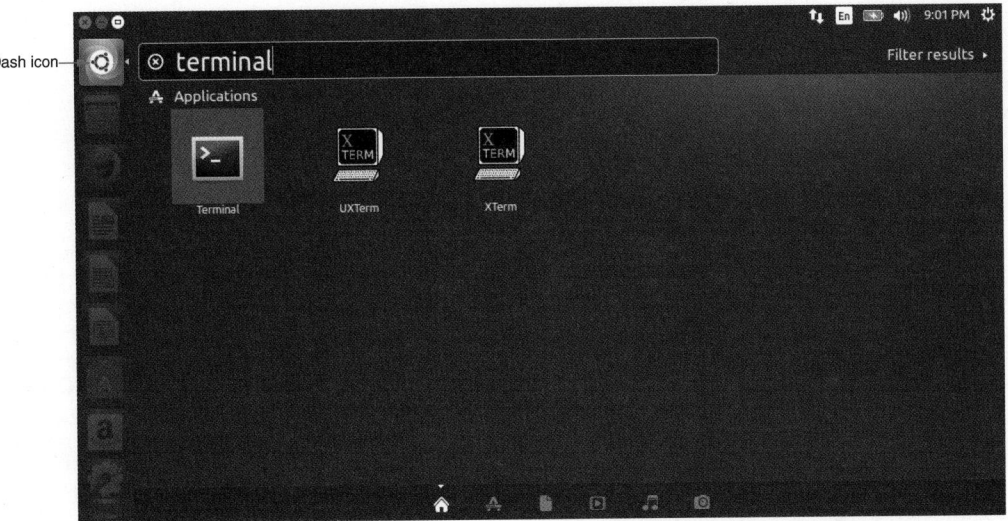

Dash icon

Figure 3-21   In Ubuntu, use the Dash icon to search for applications and files

Source: Canonical Group Ltd.

ping

The utility **ping (Packet Internet Groper)** is used to verify that TCP/IP is installed, bound to the NIC, configured correctly, and communicating with the network. Think about how a whale sends out a signal and listens for the echo. The nature of the echo can tell the whale a lot of information about the object the original signal bumped into. The ping utility starts by sending out a signal called an echo request to another computer, which is simply a request for a response. The other computer then responds to the request in the form of an echo reply. The protocol used by the echo request and echo reply is **ICMP (Internet Control Message Protocol)**, a lightweight protocol used to carry error messages and information about a network.

The first tool you should use to test basic connectivity to the network, Internet, and specific hosts is `ping`. The `ping` command has several options or parameters, and a few of them are listed here:

```
ping [-a] [-t] [-n] [-?] [IP address] [host name] [/?]
```

Table 3-7 gives some examples of how these options can be used. IPv6 networks use a version of ICMP called **ICMPv6**. Here are two variations of `ping` for different operating systems, which can be used with IPv6 addresses:

- `ping6`—On Linux computers running IPv6, use `ping6` to verify whether an IPv6 host is available. When you ping a multicast address with `ping6`, you get responses from all IPv6 hosts on that subnet.
- `ping -6`—On Windows computers, use `ping` with the -6 parameter. The `ping -6` command verifies connectivity on IPv6 networks.

Table 3-7   Options for the ping command

Sample ping commands	Description
ping www.google.com	Ping a host using its host name to verify you have Internet access and name resolution. *Google.com* is a reliable site to use for testing. See the results in Figure 3-22.
ping 8.8.8.8	Ping an IP address on the Internet to verify you have Internet access. The address 8.8.8.8, which is easy to remember, points to Google's public DNS servers.
ping -a 8.8.8.8	Test for name resolution and display the host name to verify DNS is working.
ping 92.10.11.200	In this example, 92.10.11.200 is the address of a host on another subnet in your corporate network. This ping shows if you can reach that subnet.
ping 192.168.1.1	In this example, 192.168.1.1 is the address of your default gateway. This ping shows if you can reach it.
ping 127.0.0.1	Ping the loopback address, 127.0.0.1, to determine whether your workstation's TCP/IP services are running.
ping localhost	This is another way of pinging your loopback address.
ping -? or ping/?	Display the help text for the ping command, including its syntax and a full list of parameters.
ping -t 192.168.1.1	Continue pinging until interrupted. To display statistics, press CTRL+Break. To stop pinging, press CTRL+C.
ping -n 2 192.168.1.1	Define the number of echo requests to send. By default, ping sends four echo requests. In this example, we have limited it to two.

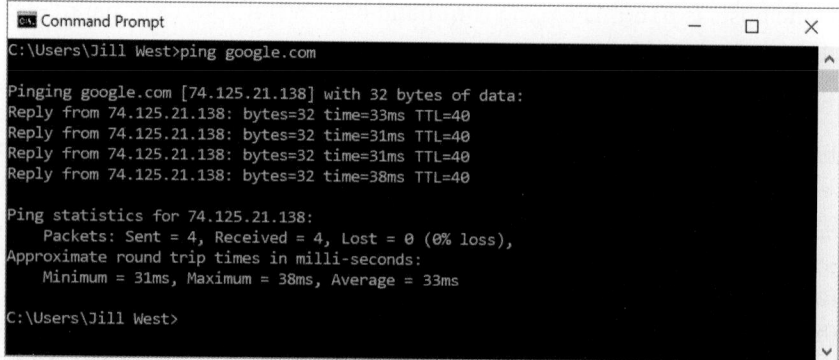

Figure 3-22   Results of a successful ping

> **Note**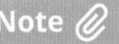
>
> In Windows, the -6 parameter is not necessary when pinging an IPv6 address (as opposed to pinging a host name) because the format of the address itself specifies that an IPv6 host is being pinged.

- For the ping6 and ping -6 commands to work over the Internet, you must have access to the IPv6 Internet. Your ISP might provide native IPv6 connectivity, or you might be able to use an IPv6 tunnel provided by an IPv6 tunnel broker service, such as IPv6 Tunnel Broker (*tunnelbroker.net*), offered by Hurricane Electric, or SixXS (*sixxs.net/main*).
- Try pinging Google's IPv6 DNS server, as follows:

ping -6 2001:4860:4860::8888

- Figure 3-23 shows the results on a computer with an ISP that does provide access to the IPv6 Internet; the IPv6 ping was successful after a short delay.

```
Command Prompt                                    —    □    ×

C:\Users\MikeandJill>ping -6 2001:4860:4860::8888

Pinging 2001:4860:4860::8888 with 32 bytes of data:
Request timed out.
Reply from 2001:4860:4860::8888: time=146ms
Reply from 2001:4860:4860::8888: time=135ms
Reply from 2001:4860:4860::8888: time=159ms

Ping statistics for 2001:4860:4860::8888:
    Packets: Sent = 4, Received = 3, Lost = 1 (25% loss),
Approximate round trip times in milli-seconds:
    Minimum = 135ms, Maximum = 159ms, Average = 146ms

C:\Users\MikeandJill>
```

Figure 3-23   After an initial delay, the ping -6 was successful

ipconfig

The ipconfig command shows current TCP/IP addressing and domain name information on a Windows computer. You can also use ipconfig to change some of these settings. Here are two ways to use ipconfig:

- In a Command Prompt window, enter the **ipconfig** command to view IP configuration information (see Figure 3-24). Notice which local connections are available on your computer and which ones are currently connected. Also locate your active connection's IPv4 or IPv6 address, subnet mask, and default gateway.
- The ipconfig command shows an abbreviated summary of configuration information. To see a more complete summary, use the command **ipconfig /all**. See Figure 3-25 for an example.

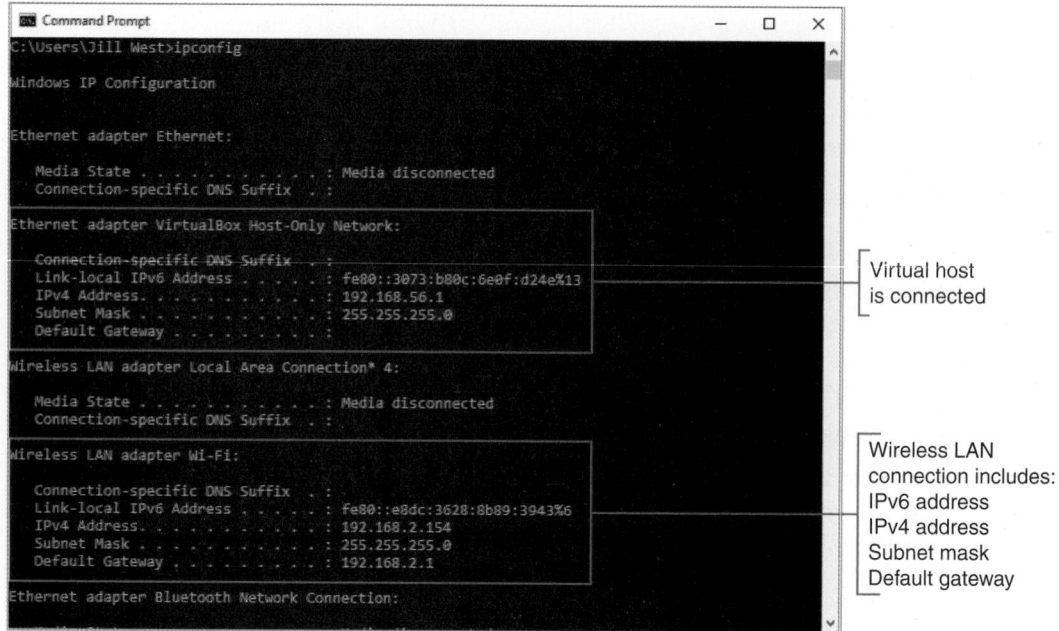

Figure 3-24   This computer is connected to two different network interfaces, one of which is a virtual network inside VirtualBox

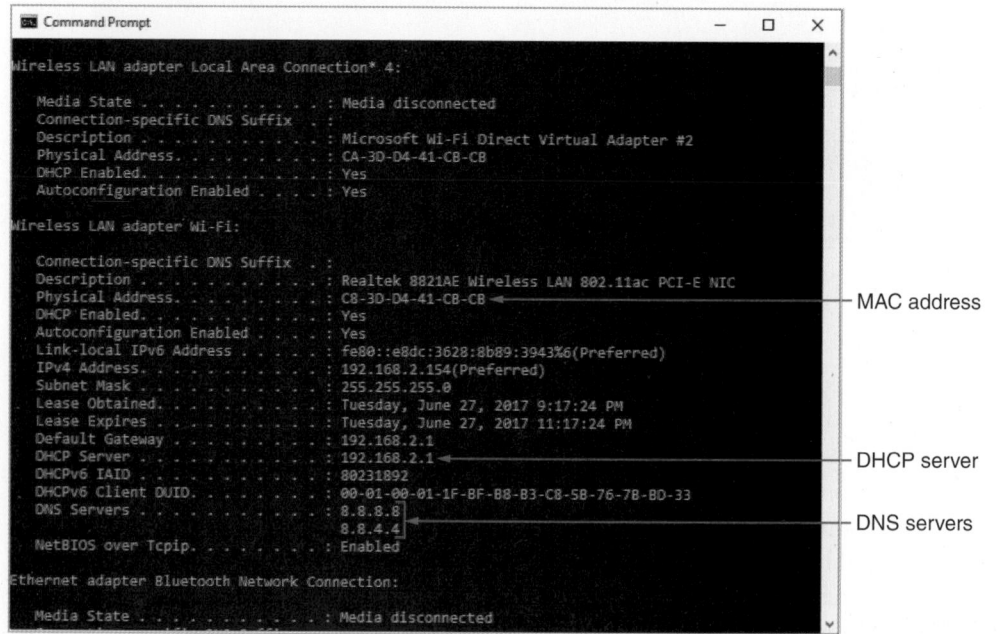

Figure 3-25   `ipconfig /all` gives a great deal more information than `ipconfig` by itself

Table 3-8 describes some popular parameters for the ipconfig command. Notice that, with the ipconfig command, you need to type a forward slash (/) before a parameter, rather than a hyphen as you do with the ping command.

Table 3-8   **Examples of the ipconfig command**

ipconfig command	Description
ipconfig /? or ipconfig -?	Displays the help text for the ipconfig command, including its syntax and a full list of parameters.
ipconfig /all	Displays TCP/IP configuration information for each network adapter.
ipconfig /release	Releases the IP address when dynamic IP addressing is being used. Releasing the IP address effectively disables the computer's communications with the network until a new IP address is assigned.
ipconfig /release6	Releases an IPv6 IP address.
ipconfig /renew	Leases a new IP address (often the same one you just released) from a DHCP server. To solve problems with duplicate IP addresses, misconfigured DHCP, or misconfigured DNS, reset the TCP/IP connection by entering these two commands: ipconfig /release ipconfig /renew
ipconfig /renew6	Leases a new IPv6 IP address from a DHCPv6 server.
ipconfig /displaydns	Displays information about name resolutions that Windows currently holds in the DNS resolver cache.
ipconfig /flushdns	Flushes—or clears—the name resolver cache, which might solve a problem when the browser cannot find a host on the Internet or when a misconfigured DNS server has sent wrong information to the resolver cache.

ifconfig

On UNIX and Linux systems, use the **ifconfig** utility to view and manage TCP/IP settings. As with ipconfig on Windows systems, you can use ifconfig to view and modify TCP/IP settings and to release and renew the DHCP configuration.

Note

Remember that Linux and UNIX commands are case sensitive. Be sure to type ifconfig and not Ifconfig.

If your Linux or UNIX system provides a GUI (graphical user interface), first open a shell prompt from the desktop. At the shell prompt, you can use the `ifconfig` commands listed in Table 3-9.

Table 3-9 Some `ifconfig` commands

`ifconfig` command	Description
`ifconfig`	Displays basic TCP/IP information and network information, including the MAC address of the NIC.
`ifconfig -a`	Displays TCP/IP information associated with every interface on a Linux device; can be used with other parameters. See Figure 3-26.
`ifconfig down`	Marks the interface, or network connection, as unavailable to the network.
`ifconfig up`	Reinitializes the interface after it has been taken down (via the `ifconfig down` command), so that it is once again available to the network.
`man ifconfig`	Displays the manual pages, called man pages, for the `ifconfig` command, which tells you how to use the command and about command parameters (similar to the `ipconfig /?` command in Windows).

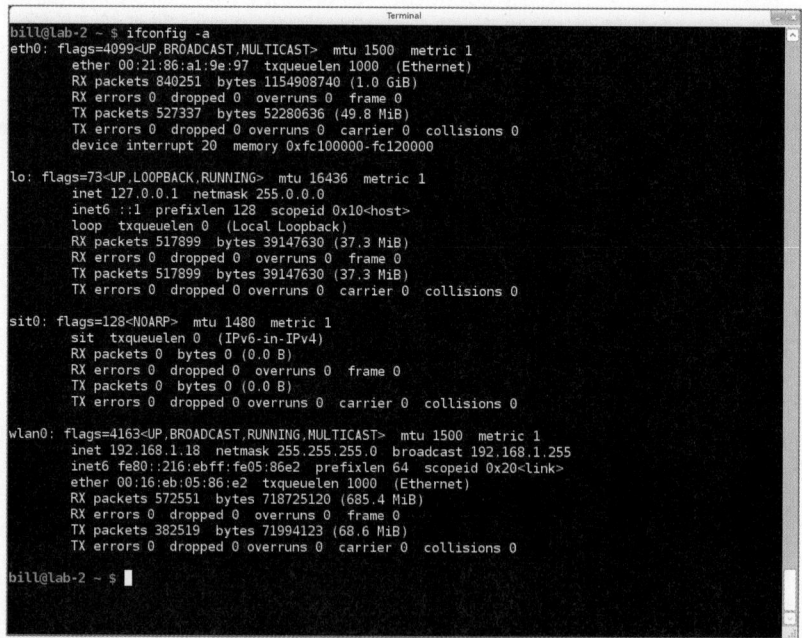

Figure 3-26 Detailed information available through `ifconfig -a`
Source: The Linux Foundation

Note

Other `ifconfig` parameters, such as those that apply to DHCP settings, vary according to the type and version of the UNIX or Linux system you use.

nslookup

The **nslookup (name space lookup)** utility allows you to query the DNS database from any computer on the network and find the host name of a device by specifying its IP address, or vice versa. This is useful for verifying that a host is configured correctly or for troubleshooting DNS resolution problems. For example, if you want to find out whether the host named *cengage.com* is operational, enter the command `nslookup cengage.com`.

Figure 3-27 shows the result of running a simple `nslookup` command. Notice that the command provides the target host's IP address as well as the name and address of the primary DNS server for the local network that provided the information.

To find the host name of a device whose IP address you know, you need to perform a reverse DNS lookup: `nslookup 69.32.208.74`. In this case, the response would include the FQDN of the target host and the name and address of the primary DNS server that made the response.

The nslookup utility is available in two modes: interactive and noninteractive. `Nslookup` in noninteractive mode gives a response for a single `nslookup` command.

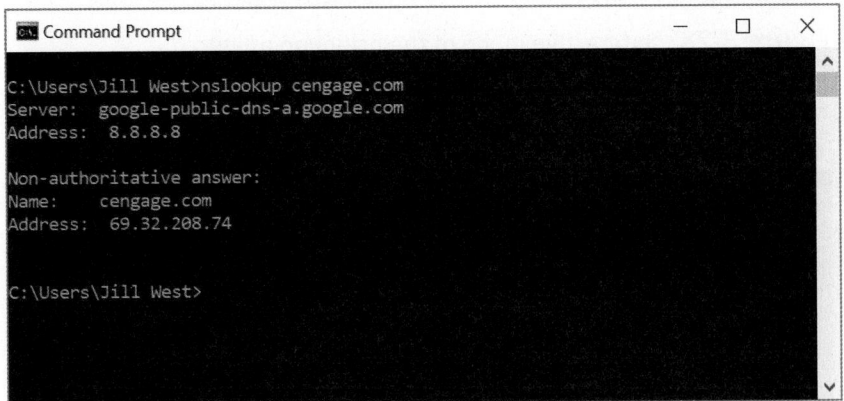

Figure 3-27   `nslookup` shows DNS server and web host information

This is fine when you're investigating only one server, or when you're retrieving single items of information at a time. To test multiple DNS servers at one time, use the nslookup utility in interactive mode, which makes available more of the utility's options. To launch interactive mode, enter the **nslookup** command without any parameters.

As shown in Figure 3-28, after you enter this command, the command prompt changes to a greater-than symbol (>). You can then use additional commands to find out more about the contents of the DNS database. For example, on a computer running UNIX, you could view a list of all the host name and IP address correlations on a particular DNS server by entering the command `ls`.

You can change DNS servers from within interactive mode with the `server` subcommand and specifying the IP address of the new DNS server. Assign a new DNS server, such as OpenDNS's server, with the command: `server 208.67.222.222` (see Figure 3-29).

To exit nslookup interactive mode and return to the normal command prompt, enter `exit`.

Many other nslookup options exist. To see these options on a UNIX or Linux system, use the `man nslookup` command. On a Windows-based system, use the `nslookup/?` command.

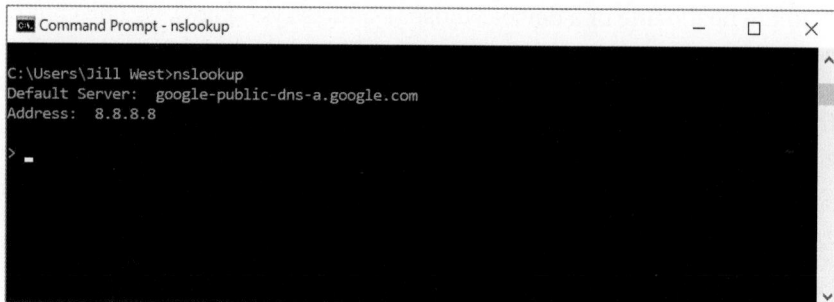

Figure 3-28   Interactive mode of the nslookup utility

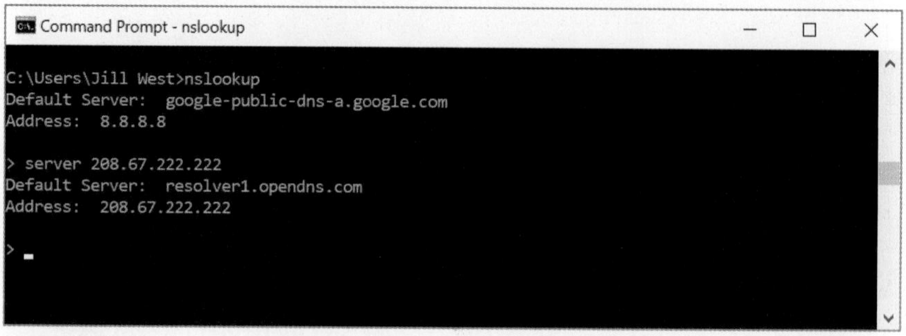

Figure 3-29   The `server` subcommand can be used to change DNS servers

dig

The **dig (domain information groper)** utility is available on Linux and macOS and provides more detailed domain information than nslookup. Use dig to query DNS nameservers for information about host addresses and other DNS records. dig is newer than nslookup; it uses more reliable sources of information to output its results and makes more advanced options available for complex queries. For a time, nslookup in Linux was deprecated in favor of dig (and a related command, host), but has since been resurrected because it's considered easier to use than dig. Some sample dig commands are covered in Table 3-10.

Table 3-10 Sample dig commands

Sample dig commands	Description
dig google.com	Performs a DNS lookup on a domain name.
dig @8.8.8.8 google.com	Specifies a name server in the *google.com* domain.
dig @8.8.8.8 google.com MX	Requests a list of all A records in the *google.com* domain on a specific name server.
dig google.com ANY	Requests a list of all record types in the *google.com* domain.
dig -x 74.125.21.102	Performs a reverse lookup on a Google IP address.
man dig	Displays the man page for the dig command.

Common Network Issues

At this point, you already understand a great deal about how a network works and what resources it needs to function well. Let's look at some common network problems to see how these concepts start to come together.

Incorrect time

When a single computer keeps showing the wrong time after powering on, a good IT technician first suspects a dead CMOS battery. When devices in a domain consistently sync to the wrong time, technicians start wondering from where those devices are getting their time information. Recall that NTP relies on a time server, either on the local network or on the Internet, to sync time settings across devices. This only works when the time source is reliable.

You can check a domain computer's time source from a Command Prompt window. Enter the command w32tm /query /source. If your computer is not a member of a domain, you can determine and adjust the time server your computer syncs to when it connects to the Internet with the following steps:

1. Right-click the time and date in the system tray and click **Adjust date/time**. Make sure *Set time automatically* is turned **On**.

2. Scroll down and click **Additional date, time & regional settings**. The Clock, Language, and Region window opens in Control Panel.
3. Click **Set the time and date, Internet Time**, and **Change settings**. The Internet Time Settings dialog box opens, as shown in Figure 3-30.
4. Click the drop-down arrow to select a different time server, preferably one that is close to you geographically. **Click Update now**, and then click **OK**.

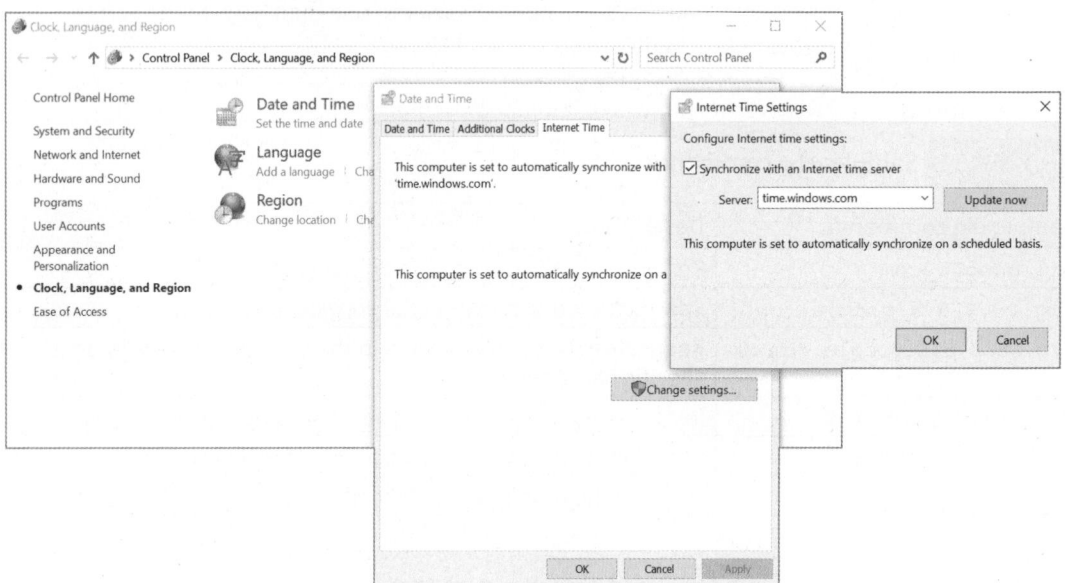

Figure 3-30 Change the time server your computer uses to synchronize its system time

DHCP Issues

When a DHCP server gives a client an IP address, it sets a time limit, or lease time, on the IP address. At the end of the lease, the IP address assignment expires. By default, this time limit is usually anywhere from 120 minutes to 8 days, depending on the device and software used. Because DHCP has a limited scope from which to draw IP addresses, the limited lease helps ensure that IP addresses are available to new clients when needed. If the lease is set too long, the network tends to suffer from an exhausted DHCP scope, meaning the available IP addresses get used up and no new clients can connect to the network. If the lease is set too short, clients' IP addresses expire quickly and new leases must be negotiated, which increases network traffic and disrupts network availability to clients.

If you're getting DHCP errors, or if multiple clients are having trouble connecting to the network, check the settings on your DHCP server. Make sure the DHCP scope is large enough to account for the number of clients the network must support, including clients that aren't active but still have an IP address leased out. A stable network with little client turnover, such as in a small office, can handle a longer lease time—perhaps months—even with a limited DHCP scope. On larger networks, especially those where many client devices log on and off frequently (such as in a popular coffee shop, a school cafeteria, or a busy sales office), a shorter lease time will increase the available IP addresses at any given moment.

Network Connection Configuration Issues

An IP address alone is not enough to get a computer connected to a network. Here are some common configuration errors:

- *incorrect netmask*—A computer needs a netmask to identify which bits in its IP address identify the network portion and which bits identify its own host ID. An incorrect netmask will result in a failed or extremely limited connection to the network. Depending on the exact misconfiguration, the computer might have outgoing connectivity with other network devices and even with the Internet. But most other network devices won't be able to find the misconfigured node for purposes of normal network communication.
- *incorrect gateway*—An incorrect IP address for the default gateway can have the opposite effect: The incorrectly configured client might be able to communicate directly with devices on its network, but it will not be able to communicate with any devices outside the local network.
- *duplicate IP address*—This error message indicates that two devices on the same network are trying to use the same IP address. Usually this happens when at least one node is configured with a static IP address, and (1) another node is configured with the same static IP address, or (2) this IP address was not reserved in DHCP and the server is attempting to assign the IP address to another node.

When a computer is struggling to establish a network connection, check its TCP/IP configuration settings. You learned how to do this earlier in the chapter. For convenience, here are the steps again to access this information:

1. Open the Network and Sharing Center and click **Change adapter settings**.
2. Right-click the active network connection and click **Properties**.
3. Click **Internet Protocol Version 4 (TCP/IPv4)**, and click **Properties**.

If the computer is not obtaining an IP address and related information from a DHCP server, the static settings might be using the wrong information. Try switching to DHCP, at least temporarily. If a static assignment is necessary, you can check a working computer on the network to determine the correct subnet mask and default gateway address.

- *names not resolving*—Suppose you have a static IP address, netmask, and default gateway all configured correctly, you open a browser to check the connection, and you can't get to a web page. You open a Command Prompt window, ping the gateway, and ping Google's public DNS server, and everything is working. But you still can't navigate to websites. Most likely, you're experiencing a DNS problem. When you set a static IP address, you also must set addresses for the primary and backup DNS servers. This is an easy detail to overlook. On the other hand, if you're using DHCP and still experiencing problems with names not resolving, your default DNS servers might be down. Consider changing to a public, cloud-hosted DNS server. Many public DNS servers are available free online, such as the following:

a. Google (*developers.google.com/speed/public-dns*): 8.8.8.8 and 8.8.4.4
b. OpenDNS Home (*opendns.com*): 208.67.222.222 and 208.67.220.220
c. Norton ConnectSafe: 199.85.126.10 and 199.85.127.10, or see their website (*dns.norton.com*) for more options

Some of these DNS servers also block known malware, adult content, and advertisements.

Chapter Summary

Addressing Overview

- The organization responsible for tracking the assignments of domain names, port numbers, and IP addresses is IANA (Internet Assigned Numbers Authority).

MAC Addresses

- MAC addresses contain two parts, are 48 bits long, and are written as hexadecimal numbers separated by colons. The first 24 bits are known as the OUI (Organizationally Unique Identifier), which identifies the NIC's manufacturer.

IP Addresses

- IP addresses identify nodes at the Network layer. An IP address is required in order for a device to communicate with an outside network through a gateway device such as a router.
- The first part of an IPv4 address identifies the network, and the last part identifies the host.

- A DHCP scope is a range of addresses to be assigned to clients when they request an IPv4 address.
- A gateway device that stands between a private network and other networks substitutes the private IP addresses used by computers on the private network with its own public IP address when these computers need access to other networks or the Internet. This process is called address translation.
- The IPv6 standards were developed to improve routing capabilities and speed of communication over the established IPv4 standards and to allow for more public IP addresses on the Internet.
- A unicast address specifies a single node on an IPv6 network.
- IPv6 addressing is designed so that a computer can autoconfigure its own link local IP address without the help of a DHCPv6 server.

Ports and Sockets

- A port is a number assigned to a process, such as an application or service, that can receive data. TCP and UDP ports ensure that data is transmitted to the correct process among multiple processes running on the computer.

Domain Names and DNS (Domain Name System)

- Name resolution is the process of discovering the IP address of a host when its FQDN is known.

- A large organization can keep all its domains in a single zone, or it can subdivide its domains into multiple zones to make each zone easier to manage.

- At the root level of the DNS hierarchical structure are 13 clusters of root servers used to locate the TLD (top-level domain) servers. These TLD servers hold information about the authoritative servers, which are the authority on computer names and their IP addresses for computers in their domains.

- Namespace databases are stored in DNS zone files, which keep information in various types of resource records.

- By far, the most popular DNS server software is BIND (Berkeley Internet Name Domain), which is free, open-source software that runs on Linux, UNIX, and Windows platforms.

Troubleshooting Address Problems

- Event Viewer is one of the first places to start looking for clues when something goes wrong with a computer.

- Some of the most helpful command-line tools are `ping`, `ipconfig` (Windows only), `ifconfig` (Linux only), `nslookup`, and `dig` (Linux only).

- The utility ping (Packet Internet Groper) is used to verify that TCP/IP is installed, bound to the NIC, configured correctly, and communicating with the network.

- The `ipconfig` command shows current TCP/IP addressing and domain name information on a Windows computer.

- On UNIX and Linux systems, use the ifconfig utility to view and manage TCP/IP settings.

- The nslookup (name space lookup) utility allows you to query the DNS database from any computer on the network and find the host name of a device by specifying its IP address, or vice versa.

- The dig (domain information groper) utility is available on Linux and macOS and provides more detailed domain information than `nslookup`.

- If your computer is not a member of a domain, you can determine and adjust the time server your computer syncs to when it connects to the Internet.

- Make sure the DHCP scope is large enough to account for the number of clients the network must support, including clients that aren't active but still have an IP address leased out.

- If the computer is not obtaining an IP address and related information from a DHCP server, the static settings might be using the wrong information. Try switching to DHCP, at least temporarily.

Key Terms

For definitions of key terms, see the Glossary near the end of the book.

A (Address) record

AAAA (Address) record

address translation

anycast address

APIPA (Automatic Private IP
   Addressing)

authoritative server

broadcast

broadcast domain

caching DNS server

canonical name

classful addressing

CLI (command-line
   interface)

CNAME (Canonical Name)
   record

default gateway

device ID

DHCP (Dynamic Host
   Configuration Protocol)

DHCP pool

DHCP reservation

DHCP scope

DHCPv6

dig (domain information
   groper)

DKIM (DomainKeys
   Identified Mail)

DMZ (demilitarized zone)

DNAT (Destination Network
   Address Translation)

DNS (Domain Name System
   or Domain Name Service)

DNS zone

domain name

dual stacked

dynamic IP address

elevated Command Prompt

EUI-64 (Extended Unique
   Identifier-64)

exhausted DHCP scope

extension identifier

firewall

forward zone

forwarding DNS server

FQDN (fully qualified
   domain name)

gateway

global address

H.323

host ID

host name

IANA (Internet Assigned
   Numbers Authority)

ICANN (Internet
   Corporation for Assigned
   Names and Numbers)

ICMP (Internet Control
   Message Protocol)

ICMPv6

ifconfig

interface

interface ID

IP exclusion

IP reservation

IPAM (IP address
   management)

ipconfig

IPv4 (Internet Protocol
   version 4)

IPv6 (Internet Protocol
   version 6)

iterative query

LDAP (Lightweight Directory
   Access Protocol)

LDAPS (Lightweight
   Directory Access Protocol
   over SSL)

lease time

link

link local address

local link

loopback address

MAC reservation

MX (Mail Exchanger) record

multicast

multicast address

name resolution

NAT (Network Address
   Translation)

neighbors

netmask

network ID

node ID

NS (Name Server) record

nslookup (name space
   lookup)

NTP (Network Time
   Protocol)

octet

open source

OUI (Organizationally
   Unique Identifier)

PAT (Port Address
   Translation)

ping (Packet Internet
   Groper)

primary DNS server

private IP address

process

PTR (Pointer) record

public IP address

RA (router advertisement)

recursive query

registered port

resource record

reverse zone

root server

RS (router solicitation)

scope options

secondary DNS server
session
SIP (Session Initiation
   Protocol)
SMB (Server Message Block)
SNAT (Static Network
   Address Translation or
   Source Network Address
   Translation)

SPF (Sender Policy
   Framework)
socket
SRV (Service) record
static IP address
subnet
subnet ID
subnet mask
TFTP (Trivial File Transfer

   Protocol)
TLD (top-level domain)
TTL (Time to Live)
TXT (Text) record
tunneling
unicast address
well-known port
WSL (Windows Subsystem
   for Linux)

Review Questions

1. Which part of a MAC address is unique to each manufacturer?
   a. The network identifier
   b. The OUI
   c. The device identifier
   d. The physical address

2. What type of device does a computer turn to first when attempting to make contact with a host with a known IP address on another network?
   a. Default gateway
   b. DNS server
   c. Root server
   d. DHCP server

3. What decimal number corresponds to the binary number 11111111?
   a. 255
   b. 256
   c. 127
   d. 11,111,111

4. Suppose you send data to the 11111111 11111111 11111111 11111111 IP address on an IPv4 network. To which device(s) are you transmitting?
   a. All devices on the Internet
   b. All devices on your local network
   c. The one device that is configured with this IP address
   d. No devices

5. When your computer first joins an IPv6 network, what is the prefix of the IPv6 address the computer first configures for itself?
   a. FF00::/8
   b. 2001::/64
   c. 2001::/3
   d. FE80::/10

6. If you are connected to a network that uses DHCP, and you need to terminate your Windows workstation's DHCP lease, which command would you use?
   a. `ipconfig /release`
   b. `ipconfig /renew`
   c. `ifconfig /release`
   d. `ifconfig /renew`

7. Which of these commands is available only in Linux?
   a. `ping`
   b. `ipconfig`
   c. `dig`
   d. `nslookup`

8. Which computers are the highest authorities in the Domain Name System hierarchy?
   a. Authoritative name servers
   b. Root servers
   c. Top-level domain servers
   d. Primary DNS servers

9. You have just brought online a new secondary DNS server and notice your network-monitoring software reports a significant increase in network traffic. Which two hosts on your network are likely to be causing the increased traffic and why?

    a. The caching and primary DNS servers, because the caching server is requesting zone transfers from the primary server

    b. The secondary and primary DNS servers, because the secondary server is requesting zone transfers from the primary server

    c. The root and primary DNS servers, because the primary server is requesting zone transfers from the root server

    d. The web server and primary DNS server, because the web server is requesting zone transfers from the primary DNS server

10. Which type of DNS record identifies an email server?

    a. AAAA record

    b. CNAME record

    c. MX record

    d. PTR record

11. What is the range of addresses that might be assigned by APIPA?

12. You are the network manager for a computer training center that allows students to bring their own laptops to class for learning and taking notes. Students need access to the Internet, so you have configured your network's DHCP server to issue IP addresses automatically. Which DHCP option should you modify to make sure you are not wasting addresses used by students who have left for the day?

13. You have decided to use SNAT and PAT on your small office network. At minimum, how many IP addresses must you obtain from your ISP for all five clients in your office to be able to access servers on the Internet?

14. How many bits does an IPv6 address contain?

15. FTP sometimes uses a random port for data transfer, but an FTP server always, unless programmed otherwise, listens to the same port for session requests from clients. What port does an FTP server listen on?

16. You issue a transmission from your workstation to the following socket on your LAN: 10.1.1.145:110. Assuming your network uses standard port designations, what Application layer protocol handles your transmission?

17. Suppose you want to change the default port for RDP as a security precaution. What port does RDP use by default, and from what range of numbers should you select a private port number?

18. You have just set up a new wireless network at your house, and you want to determine whether your Linux laptop has connected to it and obtained a valid IP address. What command will give you the information you need?

19. While troubleshooting a network connection problem for a coworker, you discover the computer is querying a nonexistent DNS server. What command-line utility can you use to assign the correct DNS server IP address?

20. When running a scan on your computer, you find that a session has been established with a host at the address 208.85.40.44:80. Which Application layer protocol is in use for this session? What command-line utility might you use to determine which computer is the host?

Hands-On Projects

Project 3-1: Identify a NIC Manufacturer

Wireshark is a free, open-source network protocol analyzer that can help demystify network messages and help make the OSI model a little more tangible for you. In Chapter 4, you'll install Wireshark and practice capturing some of the hundreds of packets that cross a network connection every minute.

Most of these packets include the MAC addresses of the sender, the receiver, or both. When collecting network data on Wireshark using the default settings, some of the OUIs are automatically resolved, telling you the manufacturer of each device. In Figure 3-31, you can see where Wireshark has identified the manufacturer—Intel—of a laptop NIC on this network.

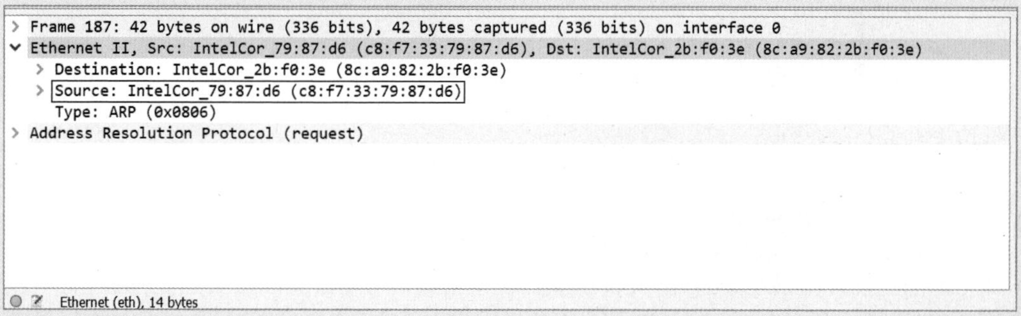

```
> Frame 187: 42 bytes on wire (336 bits), 42 bytes captured (336 bits) on interface 0
v Ethernet II, Src: IntelCor_79:87:d6 (c8:f7:33:79:87:d6), Dst: IntelCor_2b:f0:3e (8c:a9:82:2b:f0:3e)
  > Destination: IntelCor_2b:f0:3e (8c:a9:82:2b:f0:3e)
  > Source: IntelCor_79:87:d6 (c8:f7:33:79:87:d6)
    Type: ARP (0x0806)
> Address Resolution Protocol (request)



  ◯ ⌇  Ethernet (eth), 14 bytes
```

Figure 3-31   Wireshark capture shows that the destination node's NIC is made by Intel
Source: The Wireshark Foundation

Sometimes, however, you might be working with physical addresses provided by a command output, or you might need a little more information than what is provided by a Wireshark capture. For these situations, use an online MAC address lookup table such as Wireshark's OUI Lookup Tool.

1. In your browser, go to **wireshark.org/tools/oui-lookup**
   Notice earlier in Figure 3-31 that the MAC address of the Source device is located inside the black box. The first three bytes of this address, c8:f7:33, make up the OUI of the device's manufacturer. Type those numbers into Wireshark's OUI Lookup Tool and click **Find**. What results did you get?

Note 📎

If you were pulling OUIs from your own Wireshark capture or command-line output, you could copy and paste one or more OUIs into the website search box.

You can perform the same lookup using output from a Command Prompt window:

2. Open a Command Prompt window and enter `ipconfig/all` to identify the NIC's physical address.

3. To select and copy this information into your Clipboard, first press **Ctrl+M** to enable marking, and then select the first three bytes of the physical address for the active network connection. Press **Ctrl+C**.

4. Click in the search box on Wireshark's website, press **Ctrl+V** to paste the information into the Wireshark Lookup Tool, and click **Find**. Who is the manufacturer of your NIC?

Project 3-2: Change IPv6 Autoconfiguration Settings

By default, when configuring an IPv6 address, Windows 10 generates a random number to fill out the bits needed for the NIC portion of the IPv6 address. This security measure helps conceal your device's MAC address, and further protects your privacy by generating a new number every so often. There may be times, however, when you need your system to maintain a static IPv6 address. To do this, you can disable IPv6 autoconfiguration using the netsh utility in an elevated Command Prompt window. Do the following:

1. Open an elevated Command Prompt window.

2. Enter `ipconfig/all`. What is your computer's current IPv6 address and MAC address? Carefully compare the two addresses. Are they in any way numerically related?

3. To disable the random IP address generation feature, enter the command:

   ```
   netsh interface ipv6 set global
   randomizeidentifiers=disabled
   ```

4. To instruct Windows to use the EUI-64 standard instead of the default settings, use this command:

   ```
   netsh interface ipv6 set privacy
   state=disabled
   ```
   Figure 3-32 shows where both commands were entered and accepted.

5. Enter `ipconfig /all` again. What is your computer's new IPv6 address? How closely does this number resemble the MAC address?

   Notice in the second half of the IPv6 address, after *FE80::*, that the fixed value FF FE has been inserted halfway through the MAC address values. The host portion of the IPv6 address might use a slightly different value than the OUI in the MAC address because the seventh bit of the MAC address is inverted.

6. Re-enable random IPv6 address generation with these two commands:

   ```
   netsh interface ipv6 set global
   randomizeidentifiers=enabled
   netsh interface ipv6 set privacy
   state=enabled
   ```

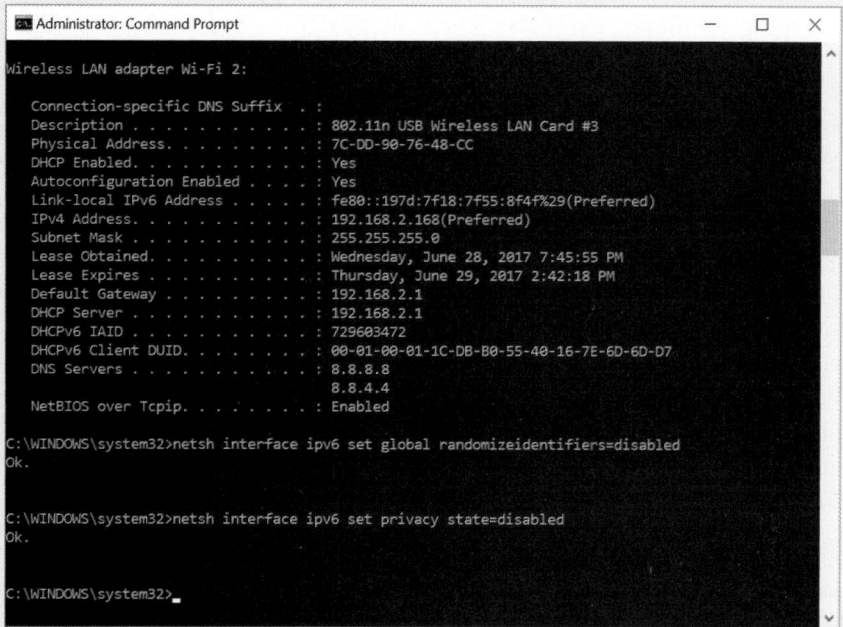

```
Administrator: Command Prompt                                    —    □    ×

Wireless LAN adapter Wi-Fi 2:

   Connection-specific DNS Suffix  . :
   Description . . . . . . . . . . . : 802.11n USB Wireless LAN Card #3
   Physical Address. . . . . . . . . : 7C-DD-90-76-48-CC
   DHCP Enabled. . . . . . . . . . . : Yes
   Autoconfiguration Enabled . . . . : Yes
   Link-local IPv6 Address . . . . . : fe80::197d:7f18:7f55:8f4f%29(Preferred)
   IPv4 Address. . . . . . . . . . . : 192.168.2.168(Preferred)
   Subnet Mask . . . . . . . . . . . : 255.255.255.0
   Lease Obtained. . . . . . . . . . : Wednesday, June 28, 2017 7:45:55 PM
   Lease Expires . . . . . . . . . . : Thursday, June 29, 2017 2:42:18 PM
   Default Gateway . . . . . . . . . : 192.168.2.1
   DHCP Server . . . . . . . . . . . : 192.168.2.1
   DHCPv6 IAID . . . . . . . . . . . : 729603472
   DHCPv6 Client DUID. . . . . . . . : 00-01-00-01-1C-DB-B0-55-40-16-7E-6D-6D-D7
   DNS Servers . . . . . . . . . . . : 8.8.8.8
                                        8.8.4.4
   NetBIOS over Tcpip. . . . . . . . : Enabled

C:\WINDOWS\system32>netsh interface ipv6 set global randomizeidentifiers=disabled
Ok.


C:\WINDOWS\system32>netsh interface ipv6 set privacy state=disabled
Ok.


C:\WINDOWS\system32>_
```

Figure 3-32   Command Prompt outputs a confirmation for each `netsh` command entered

Project 3-3: Manage a DNS Cache

You have learned that clients as well as name servers store DNS information to associate names with IP addresses. In this project, you view the contents of a local DNS cache, clear it, and view it again after performing some DNS lookups. Then you change DNS servers and view the DNS cache once again.

1. To view the DNS cache, open an elevated Command Prompt window and enter the following command: `ipconfig /displaydns`
2. If this computer has been used to resolve host names with IP addresses—for example, if it has been used to retrieve email or browse the web—a list of locally cached resource records appears. Read the file to see what kinds of records have been saved, using the scroll bar if necessary. How many are A (Host) records and how many are a different type, such as CNAME?
3. Clear the DNS cache with this command: `ipconfig /flushdns`

    The operating system confirms that the DNS resolver cache has been flushed. One circumstance in which you might want to empty a client's DNS cache is if the client needs to reach a host whose IP address has changed (for example, a website whose server was moved to a different hosting company). As long as the DNS information is locally cached, the client will continue to look for the host at the old location. Clearing the cache allows the client to retrieve the new IP address for the host.

4. View the DNS cache again with the command: `ipconfig /displaydns`
   Because you just emptied the DNS cache, you see a message indicating that Windows could not display the DNS resolver cache. (See Figure 3-33.)

5. Open a browser window and go to **cengage.com**. Next, go to **google.com**. Finally, go to **loc.gov**.

6. Return to the Command Prompt window and view the DNS cache containing the new list of resource records using this command: `ipconfig /displaydns`

7. Scroll up through the list of resource records and note how many associations were saved in your local DNS cache after visiting just three websites. How many hosts are identified for each site you visited? What type of record is most common? What other situations can you think of, other than wanting to reach a host that has moved to a different address, in which you might want to clear your DNS cache?

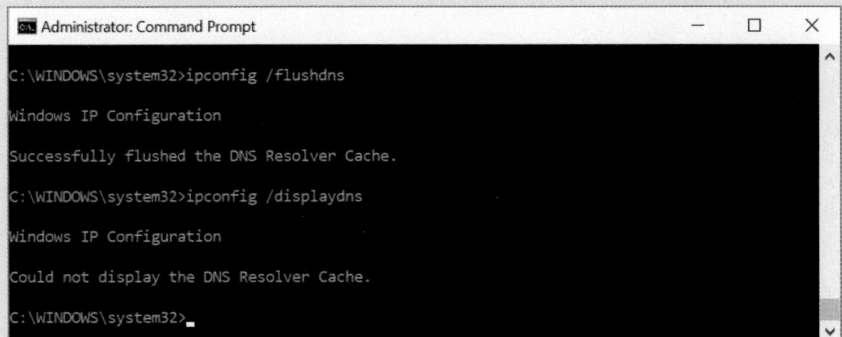

Figure 3-33   This DNS cache is empty

By default, DHCP supplies the IP addresses of DNS servers when you first connect to a network. When traveling, you can still use your organization's DNS servers, even when they are far away from your laptop. Doing so means you don't have to rely on DNS servers provided by a public hot spot, which might be controlled by hackers.

Follow these steps to view or change the name server information on a Windows 10 workstation:

8. Open the Network and Sharing Center and click **Change adapter settings**.

9. Right-click the connection you want to configure, and click **Properties** on the shortcut menu. Respond to the UAC box if necessary.

10. On the Networking tab under *This connection uses the following items*, select **Internet Protocol Version 4 (TCP/IPv4)**, and click **Properties**. The Internet Protocol Version 4 (TCP/IPv4) Properties dialog box opens.

11. To change the default settings and specify the DNS server for your workstation, rather than allowing DHCP to supply the DNS server address, on the General tab, click **Use the following DNS server addresses**.

12. Enter the IP address for your primary DNS server in the Preferred DNS server space and the address for your secondary DNS server in the Alternate DNS server space. For the purposes of this project, if your instructor has not specified another pair of DNS servers, you can point to Google's public DNS servers. Use **8.8.8.8** as the Preferred DNS server and **8.8.4.4** as the Alternate DNS server. Click **OK**,

13. Now that you have changed your DNS servers, do you still have DNS data stored in your DNS cache? To find out, return to the Command Prompt window and view the DNS cache to see what records are still there. Then close all windows, saving your changes.

Project 3-4: Create a NAT Translation Table Entry

Your corporation hosts a website at the static public IP address 92.110.30.123. A router directs this traffic to a web server at the private IP address 192.168.11.100. However, the web server needs a hardware upgrade and will be down for two days. Your network administrator has asked you to configure the router so that requests to the IP address 92.110.30.123 are redirected to the backup server for the website, which has the private IP address 192.168.11.110. The router's inside Ethernet interface uses IP address 192.168.11.254 and its outside interface uses the IP address 92.110.30.65. Answer the following questions about the new static route you'll be creating:

1. What is the router's outside interface IP address?
2. What is the router's inside interface IP address?
3. What is the website's public IP address?
4. What is the private IP address of the backup web server?

Use the example given in Figure 3-12 earlier in the chapter as a template to create the NAT translation table entries for the address translation. For the subnet masks, use the default subnet mask for a Class C IP address license. Include appropriate comment lines in your table.

Capstone Project 3-1: Set Up an FTP Server

In this project, you return to the small network you created in Chapter 1, Project 1-1. You'll install and use FTP. Recall that FTP is a client-server application in which the first computer, the client, requests data or a service from the second computer, the server.

Designate one computer as computer A, the server, and the other computer as computer B, the client. Do the following using computer A:

1. Create a folder named **Normal Users** and create a file in the folder named **Normal Users.txt**. Later, any files or folders you want on your FTP site can be stored in this folder.

2. Connect Computer A to the Internet so you can get the FileZilla software. Go to **filezilla-project.org** and download the free FileZilla Server software to your desktop. As you do so, be sure to not accept other free software the site offers.

3. Install FileZilla Server, accepting all default settings, which places a shortcut on your desktop and sets the FTP service to start automatically.

4. After the installation is complete, the *Enter server to administrate* dialog box appears (see Figure 3-34). Enter an administration password and be sure to record this password in a **Secure Note**, using the **Server** type, in your LastPass account. Also note the Host is *localhost*, which refers to your loopback interface.

5. Because you're running only one FTP server on computer A, check the **Always connect to this server** check box. When you click **Connect**, the FileZilla Server window opens. You can also open this window by using the shortcut on your desktop. You can now disconnect Computer A from the Internet and reconnect it to your switch.

6. You're now ready to configure your FTP server. To set up a user group, click **Edit, Groups**. In the right pane under Groups, click **Add**. In the *Add user group* dialog box, type **Normal Users** and click **OK**.

7. In the left pane, under Page, click **Shared folders**.

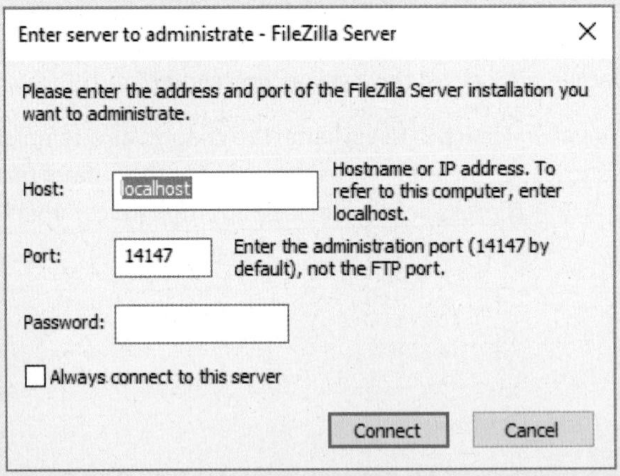

Enter server to administrate - FileZilla Server	✕

Please enter the address and port of the FileZilla Server installation you want to administrate.

Host:	localhost	Hostname or IP address. To refer to this computer, enter localhost.
Port:	14147	Enter the administration port (14147 by default), not the FTP port.
Password:		

☐ Always connect to this server

[Connect] [Cancel]

Figure 3-34 Enter the admin password that will be used to log on and manage the FileZilla FTP server

Source: FileZilla

8. Under Directories, click **Add**. Select the **Normal Users** folder and click **OK**. The folder is listed in the middle pane.

9. Under Directories, select the **Normal Users** directory and then click **Set as home dir**. Click **OK**.

10. Next, click **Edit, Users**, and create a new user named **User1**. Put the user in the **Normal Users** group.

11. In the Account settings pane, check **Password** and assign the password **password**. Click **OK**.

12. To verify the service is working, let's use the FTP client commands embedded in Windows on Computer A. As you work, watch the dialog recorded in the FileZilla Server window (see Figure 3-35). Open a Command Prompt window and enter the commands listed in Table 3-11.

Table 3-11	Commands for Capstone Project 3-1
Command	**Explanation**
`ftp localhost`	Connect to the FTP service
`User1`	Enter your user ID
`password`	Enter the password
`dir`	List the contents of the shared folder
`quit`	Close the FTP session

13. In the FileZilla Server window, click **Edit**, then click **Settings**. Under General settings, note that the server is listening at port 21. Click **Cancel**, then close the FileZilla Server window.

14. The server software is still running as a background service, listening at port 21 for clients to initiate a session. To see the service running, open the Windows Services console. To do this, right-click **Start**, click **Run**, type **services.msc**, and press **Enter**. In the Services console, verify that the *FileZilla Server FTP server* service is running and set to start automatically each time the computer starts. Close the Services console.

15. To find out the IP address of computer A, in the Command Prompt window, enter **ipconfig**. What is the IP address?

Using computer B, you're now ready to test the FTP client. Do the following:

16. Open a Command Prompt window and ping computer A. The output should show replies from computer A, indicating connectivity.

17. Now try the same commands as in step 12, using the IP address of computer A in the first command line. Most likely, you will not be able to connect because the firewall on computer A blocks incoming connections on port 21 by default. Be sure to end with the **quit** command.

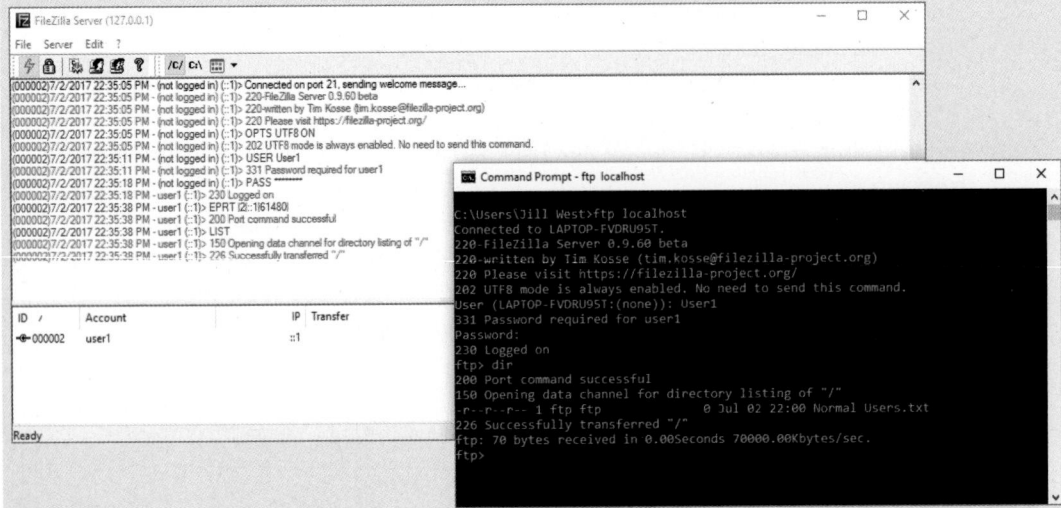

Figure 3-35   Use the FileZilla Server window to monitor real-time activity on the FTP server

Source: FileZilla

On computer A, do the following to open port 21:

18. In the Network and Sharing Center, click **Windows Firewall**. In the Windows Firewall window, click **Advanced settings**. In the left pane, click **Inbound Rules** and then click **New Rule** in the right pane. Create a new rule that opens the TCP local port 21, and name the rule **FTP Server**.

On computer B, you should now be able to open an FTP session with computer A. Do the following:

19. Using the commands listed in step 12 and the IP address of computer A, open the session and verify you can see the contents of the shared folder. If you see a Windows Security Alert, allow access. You might have to restart the session to try again at this point. Once you see the Normal Users.txt file in the directory listing, quit the session and close the Command Prompt window.

> **Note**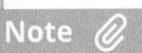
>
> If you want to again block FTP in Windows Firewall on Computer B, open the Network and Sharing Center, click **Windows Firewall**, click **Allow an app or feature through Windows Firewall**, click **Change settings**, and click to deselect **File Transfer Program**. Click **OK**.
>
> If you want to disable the FTP Server firewall rule on Computer A, open the Network and Sharing Center, click **Windows Firewall**, click **Advanced settings**, click **Inbound Rules**, click to select **FTP Server**, and in the left pane click **Disable Rule**.
>
> Close all open windows.

Capstone Project 3-2: Install and Use WSL (Windows Subsystem for Linux)
WSL runs on any 64-bit Windows 10 system with the Anniversary Update (version 1607) or later. You must first turn on Developer Mode, and then enable the Windows Subsystem for Linux (Beta) feature. As its name suggests, this feature is still in beta as Microsoft continues to resolve many bugs and gaps in compatibility. Complete the following steps to enable Windows Subsystem for Linux and install Ubuntu Bash on a Windows 10 system:

1. First, turn on Developer Mode.
   a. Open the **Settings** app and click **Update & security**. In the left pane, scroll down and click **For developers**.
   b. Select **Developer mode**, as shown in Figure 3-36. Click **Yes** to turn on Developer Mode and close the Settings app.

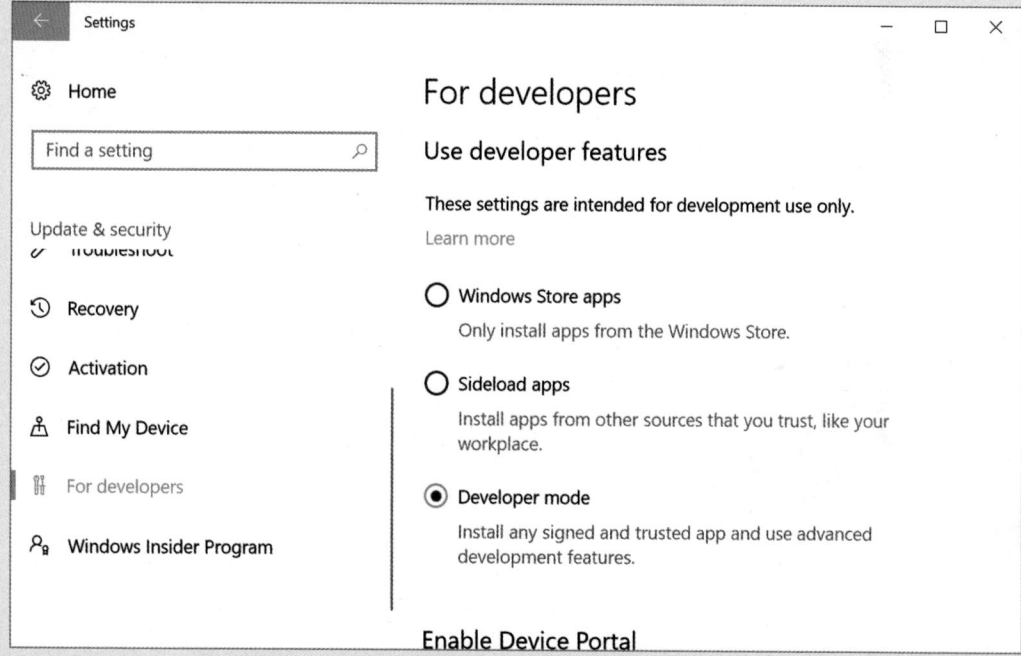

Figure 3-36   Turn on Developer Mode from the Settings app

2. Enable Windows Subsystem for Linux.
   a. Open **Control Panel** and click **Programs and Features**. In the left pane, click **Turn Windows features on or off**.
   b. Scroll down and click **Windows Subsystem for Linux (Beta)**, as shown in Figure 3-37. Click **OK**.

> **Notes**
>
> To open Turn Windows features on or off directly, you can also click Start, begin typing **turn Windows**, then click **Turn Windows features on or off**.

  c. Restart the computer when the changes are complete to finish enabling Windows Subsystem for Linux.

3. Now that you have enabled Windows Subsystem for Linux, you can install a version of Linux designed to run on Windows. This version is called *Bash on Ubuntu on Windows*. To install and run Bash on Ubuntu on Windows from the command prompt, do the following:

  a. Open a Command Prompt window and enter the command `bash` (see Figure 3-38). Note that the first time you enter the `bash` command, Windows downloads and installs Bash on Ubuntu on Windows.

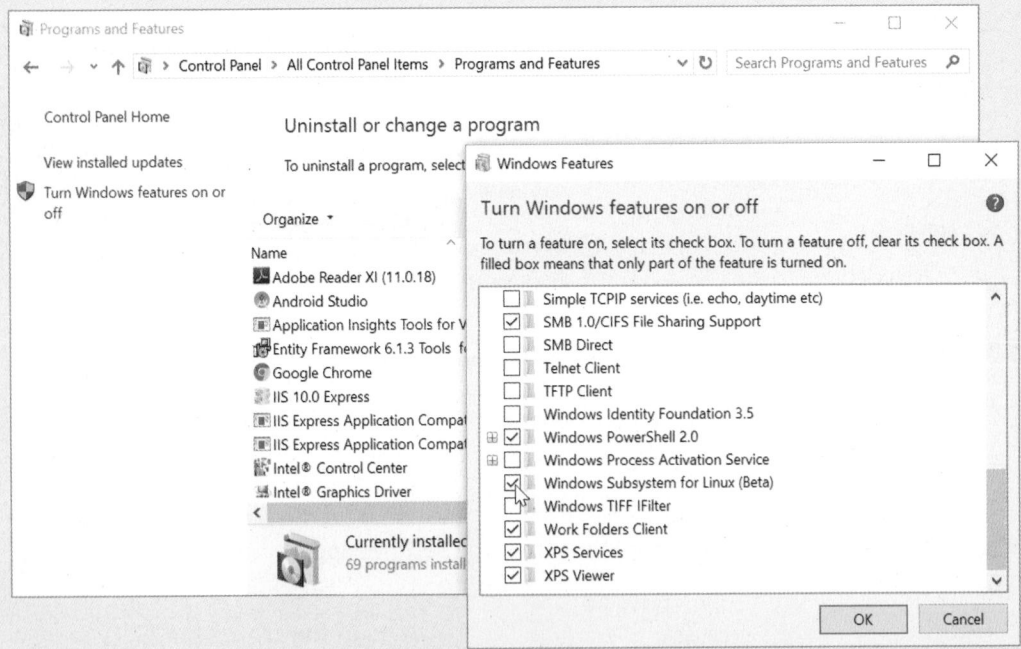

Figure 3-37 Turn on the Windows Subsystem for Linux (Beta) feature

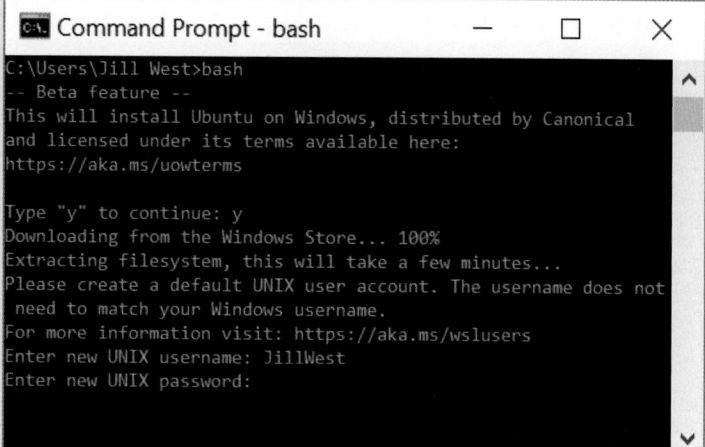

Figure 3-38   The first time you enter the `bash` command, Windows will download and install Ubuntu on Windows

b. Enter **y** to accept the installation terms. Bash on Ubuntu on Windows downloads from the Windows Store, and then is extracted and installed. This might take several minutes.

c. Enter a new UNIX username at the prompt. This username can be different from your Windows username.

d. Enter a password at the next prompt. The cursor will not move as you type the password. Re-enter the password at the next prompt. Add this information as a Secure Note in your LastPass vault.

e. After the installation is complete, Windows switches to the Bash on Ubuntu on Windows environment with its shell prompt within the Command Prompt window, as shown in Figure 3-39.

f. You can continue to interact with Bash on Ubuntu on Windows from the Command Prompt window, or you can open Bash on Ubuntu on Windows in a separate window. To do this, click **Start**, and then click **Bash on Ubuntu on Windows** in the Start menu. You can also open Bash from within PowerShell. See Figure 3-40 to compare the three windows.

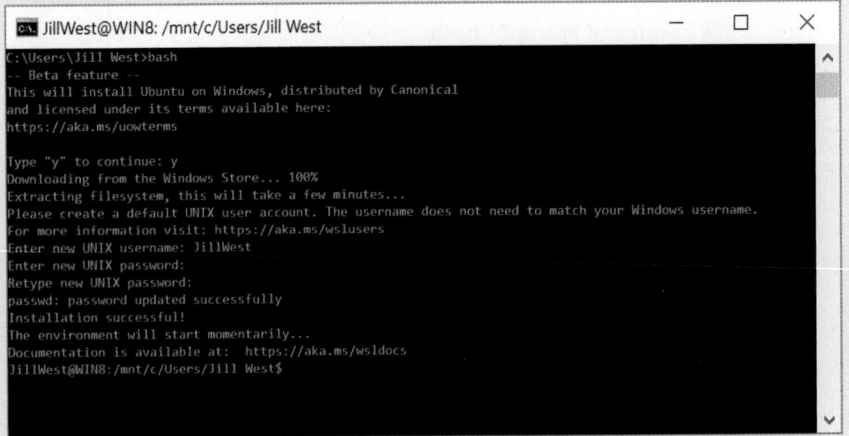

Figure 3-39   Bash on Ubuntu on Windows is installed and provides a shell prompt

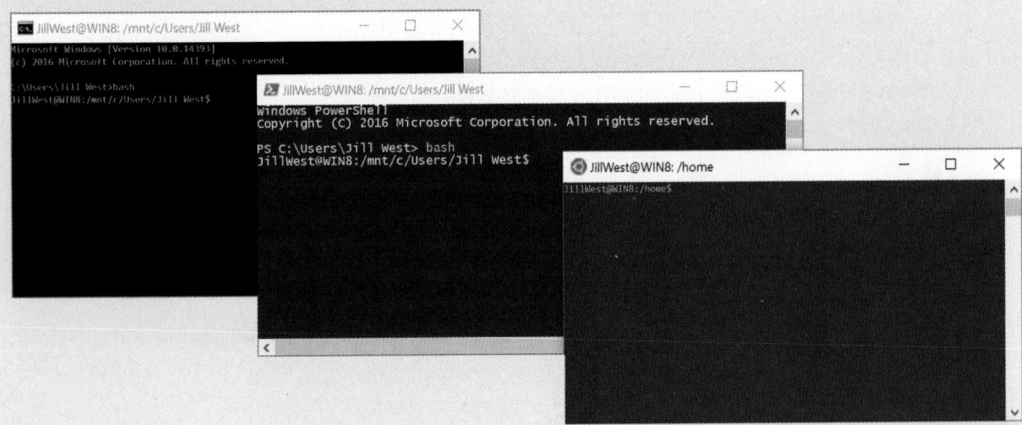

Figure 3-40   Bash on Ubuntu can be accessed from Command Prompt, PowerShell, or its own app, Bash on Ubuntu on Windows

At this point, many of the Linux commands you have become familiar with will work as usual at the Ubuntu shell prompt. The commands interact with the underlying Windows system files, and changes to those files can be monitored through other Windows tools.

## CHAPTER 4

NETWORK PROTOCOLS AND ROUTING

After reading this chapter and completing the exercises, you will be able to:

Describe the functions of core TCP/IP protocols

Identify how each protocol's information is formatted in a TCP/IP message

Explain how routers manage internetwork communications

Employ various TCP/IP utilities for network discovery and troubleshooting

On the Job

I woke up to a message from an on-call engineer, Bill, saying, "Help, I am out of ideas for DNS troubleshooting!" Twenty minutes later, as I walked into the office, he recited a chaotic list of all the troubleshooting steps he took and every possible problem that could have caused the issue at hand. We took a walk to the vending machines so I could get caffeine and the story.

Dying server hardware forced Bill to move a number of services to new hardware. DNS was scheduled to be last, as the configuration was simple, and moving it was supposed to be a quick and easy task. Everything seemed to work fine, but queries for all of the Internet and a test internal domain were not being answered. The OS configuration and DNS server settings all seemed fine, but no matter what we tweaked, the service did not work right.

Because Bill knew more about DNS than I did, there was little reason for a detailed walk-through of the configurations. I took a quick look, in hope of finding something obvious that he had missed, but the configuration was sound. Because no trivial fix was available, I reverted to basic troubleshooting mode and started to work through a simple list of items to check: "ping localhost, ping the interface, ping the router, and a host beyond it...."

The last check returned "connect: Network is unreachable." A quick glance at the routing table explained the issue: There was no default route. Without a way to forward traffic, no host outside of a few statically defined internal networks were reachable, including all of the root DNS servers.

The fix was simple and, once the service was restored, I helped a bit with moving other services. Another set of eyes is an invaluable asset during late-night work, and I had to work off all that caffeine.

Marcin Antkiewicz

In Chapter 1, you learned that a protocol is a rule that governs how computers on a network exchange data and instructions, and then in Chapter 2, you learned about network infrastructure equipment. In Chapter 3, you learned how the Data Link, Network, Transport, and Application layer protocols navigate that infrastructure and use various types of addresses as they determine where to send transmitted application data and instructions. You've also learned about the tasks associated with each layer of the OSI model, such as formatting, addressing, and error correction. All these tasks are governed by protocols.

This chapter focuses on how application data and instructions make the trip from one host to another at the Transport, Network, and Data Link layers. You will learn how protocol messages are constructed at each of these layers, and you will explore the basics of how routers work, primarily at the Network layer. Finally, you will learn how to troubleshoot route issues between hosts.

TCP/IP Core Protocols

 **Certification**

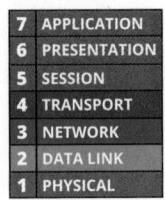

7	APPLICATION
6	PRESENTATION
5	SESSION
4	TRANSPORT
3	NETWORK
2	DATA LINK
1	PHYSICAL

1.1   Explain the purposes and uses of ports and protocols.

1.3   Explain the concepts and characteristics of routing and switching.

2.2   Given a scenario, determine the appropriate placement of networking devices on a network and install/configure them.

2.4   Explain the purposes of virtualization and network storage technologies.

5.2   Given a scenario, use the appropriate tool.

TCP/IP is a suite of protocols, or standards, that includes TCP, IP (IPv4 and IPv6), UDP, ARP, and many others. In this part of the chapter, we'll begin with an examination of message headers used at the Transport layer. We'll then work our way down the layers in the OSI model, looking at each layer's headers (and Layer 2's trailer) along the way. First, let's summarize what you've learned so far about headers and trailers as illustrated in Figure 4-1 and described in the following list:

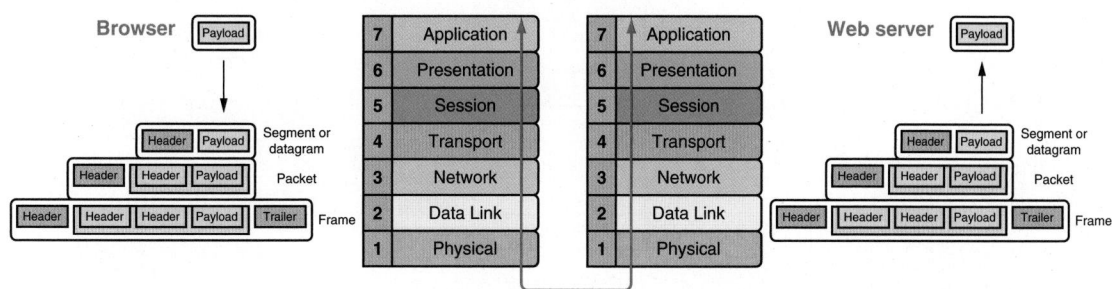

Figure 4-1   Each layer adds its own data and addresses its transmission to the corresponding layer in the destination device

- *Layers 7, 6, and 5*—Data and instructions, known as the payload, are generated by an application running on the source host. For example, in Figure 4-1, the payload is created by the browser as data passes from the highest layer of the OSI model, down on through the next two highest layers.
- *Layer 4*—A Transport layer protocol, usually either TCP or UDP, adds a header to the payload. This header includes a port number to identify the receiving application on the destination host. The entire message then becomes a segment (when using TCP) or datagram (when using UDP).
- *Layer 3*—The Network layer adds its own header to the passed-down segment or datagram. This header identifies the IP address of the destination host and the message is called a packet.
- *Layer 2*—The packet is passed to the Data Link layer on the NIC, which encapsulates this data with its own header and trailer, creating a frame. This layer's frame includes a physical address used to find a node on the local network.
- *Layer 1*—The Physical layer on the NIC receives the frame and places the actual transmission on the network.

The receiving host de-encapsulates the message at each layer in reverse order and then presents the payload to the receiving application.

In transit, the transmission might pass through any number of connectivity devices, such as switches and routers. Connectivity devices are specialized devices that allow two or more networks or multiple parts of one network to connect and exchange data. Each device is known by the topmost OSI layer header it reads and processes, as shown in Figure 4-2. For example, if a switch reads and processes the Data Link layer header but passes the message along without reading higher-layer headers, it is known as a Layer 2 switch. On the other hand, a router that reads and processes the Network layer header and leaves alone the Transport layer header is known as a Layer 3 device.

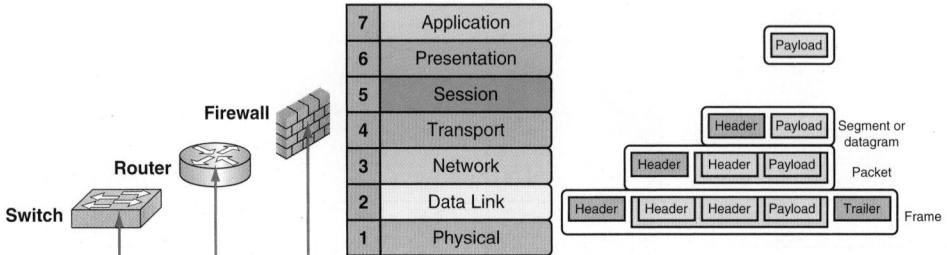

Figure 4-2   Connectivity devices are known by the highest OSI layer they read and process

With our quick review in hand, let's examine the details of the core TCP/IP protocols, beginning with TCP.

TCP (Transmission Control Protocol)

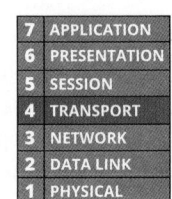

Recall that TCP operates in the Transport layer of the OSI model and provides reliable data delivery services. Let's compare TCP to making a phone call, as we look at the three characteristics of TCP in its role as a reliable delivery protocol:

- *connection-oriented*—Before TCP transmits data, it ensures that a connection or session is established, similar to making sure someone is listening on the other end of a phone call before you start talking. TCP uses a three-step process called a **three-way handshake** to establish a TCP connection. This process is described in detail later in this section. Only after TCP establishes this connection does it transmit the actual data, such as an HTTP request for a web page.
- *sequencing and checksums*—In the analogy of a phone call, you might ask the other person if he can hear you clearly, and repeat a sentence as necessary. In the same vein, TCP sends a character string called a **checksum**; TCP on the destination host then generates a similar string. If the two checksums fail to match, the destination host asks the source to retransmit the data. In addition, because messages don't always arrive in the same order they were created, TCP attaches a chronological sequence number to each segment so the destination host can, if necessary, reorder segments as they arrive.

- *flow control*—You might slow down your talking over the phone if the other person needs a slower pace in order to hear every word and understand your message. Similarly, flow control is the process of gauging the appropriate rate of transmission based on how quickly the recipient can accept data. For example, suppose a receiver indicates its buffer can handle up to 4000 bytes. The sender will issue up to 4000 bytes in one or many small packets and then pause, waiting for an acknowledgment, before sending more data.

TCP manages all these elements—the three-way handshake, checksums, sequencing, and flow control—by posting data to fields in the TCP header at the beginning of a TCP segment.

Fields in a TCP Segment

Figure 4-3 lists the items, called fields, included in a TCP segment. Each block shown in the figure represents a series of bits, with each row representing 32 bits. If you were to string the rows alongside each other, in order from top to bottom, you would create one, long series of bits. This is a TCP segment. All the fields except the last one, the data field, are part of the TCP header. The content of the data field is the entire message sent from the layer above the Transport layer.

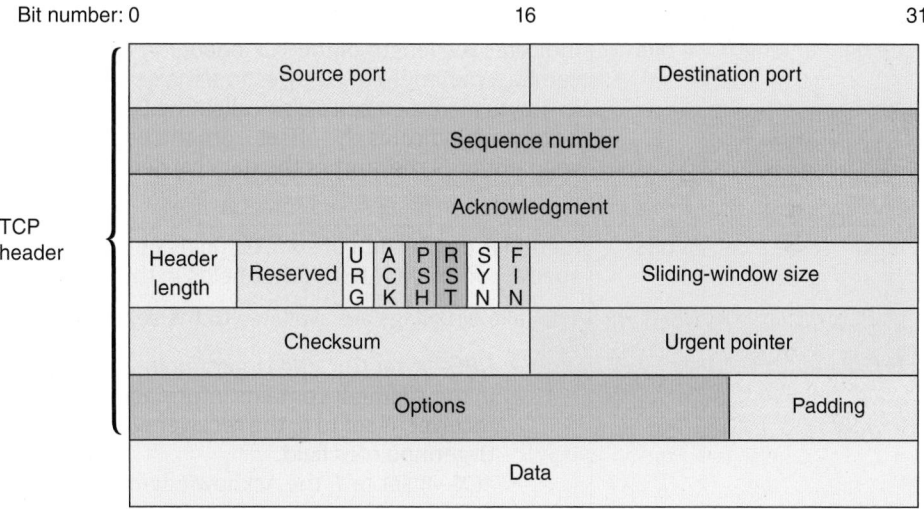

Figure 4-3   A TCP segment

Note

Headers are constructed in groups of 32 bits called words. Each word consists of 4 bytes, called blocks, of 8 bits each. This explains why diagrams of headers, such as the one in Figure 4-3, are always depicted in 32-bit groups.

The fields shown in Figure 4-3 are defined in Table 4-1. Remember, the data field in the bottom row is not part of the TCP header. When the TCP segment is sent down to the Network layer (Layer 3), the entire segment becomes the data portion of an IP message. This payload is then encapsulated in an IP packet.

Table 4-1   Fields in a TCP segment

Field		Length	Function
Header	Source port	16 bits	Indicates the port at the source node. Recall that a port is the number that identifies a process on a host. The port allows a process to be available for incoming or outgoing data.
	Destination port	16 bits	Indicates the port at the destination node.
	Sequence number	32 bits	Identifies the data segment's position in the stream of data segments being sent.
	Acknowledgment number	32 bits	Confirms receipt of data via a return message to the sender.
	TCP header length	4 bits	Indicates the length of the TCP header in bytes. The header can be a minimum of 20 bytes to a maximum of 60 bytes in 4-byte increments. It's also called the Data offset field because it indicates the offset from the beginning of the segment until the start of the data carried by the segment.
	Reserved	6 bits	Indicates a field reserved for later use.
	Flags	6 bits	Identifies a collection of six 1-bit fields or flags that signal special conditions about other fields in the header. The following flags are available to the sender: • *URG*—If set to *1*, the Urgent pointer field later in the segment contains information for the receiver. If set to *0*, the receiver will ignore the Urgent pointer field. • *ACK*—If set to *1*, the Acknowledgment field earlier in the segment contains information for the receiver. If set to *0*, the receiver will ignore the Acknowledgment field. • *PSH*—If set to *1*, data should be sent to an application without buffering. • *RST*—If set to *1*, the sender is requesting that the connection be reset.

Table 4-1   Fields in a TCP segment *(continued)*

Field	Length	Function
		• *SYN* —If set to *1*, the sender is requesting a synchronization of the sequence numbers between the two nodes. This code indicates that no payload is included in the segment, and the acknowledgment number should be increased by 1 in response. • *FIN* —If set to *1*, the segment is the last in a sequence and the connection should be closed.
Sliding-window size (or window)	16 bits	Indicates how many bytes the sender can issue to a receiver before acknowledgment is received. This field performs flow control, preventing the receiver's buffer from being deluged with bytes.
Checksum	16 bits	Allows the receiving node to determine whether the TCP segment became corrupted during transmission.
Urgent pointer	16 bits	Indicates a location in the data field where urgent data resides.
Options	0–32 bits	Specifies special options, such as the maximum segment size a network can handle.
Padding	Variable	Contains filler bits to ensure that the size of the TCP header is a multiple of 32 bits.
Data	Variable	Contains data sent by the source host. The data field is not part of the TCP header—it is encapsulated by the TCP header. The size of the data field depends on how much data needs to be transmitted, the constraints on the TCP segment size imposed by the network type, and the limitation that the segment must fit within an IP packet at the next layer.

Now let's see how the fields in the TCP header are used to perform a three-way handshake to establish a TCP session.

TCP Three-Way Handshake

The TCP three-way handshake establishes a session before TCP transmits the actual data, such as an HTTP request for a web page. Think about how a handshake works when meeting a new acquaintance. You reach out your hand, not knowing how the other person will respond. If the person offers his hand in return, the two of you grasp hands and you can then proceed with the conversation. Figure 4-4 shows the three transmissions in a TCP handshake, which are summarized in the following list:

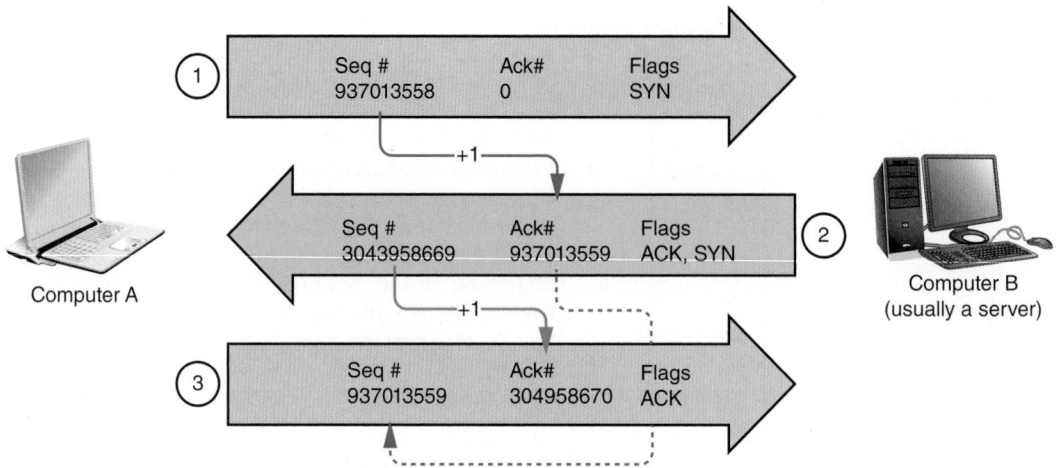

Figure 4-4 The three-way handshake process establishes a TCP session

Step 1, SYN (request for a connection)—Computer A issues a message to computer B with the following information:

- In its Sequence number field, computer A selects and sends a random number that will be used to synchronize communication. In Figure 4-4, for example, this number is 937013558.
- Its SYN bit is set to 1, which means the SYN flag is activated. This indicates the desire to communicate and synchronize sequence numbers. It's as if computer A is offering a hand to computer B to see if there will be a response.
- The ACK bit is usually set to 0 for this first transmission because there is no information yet from computer B to acknowledge.

Step 2, SYN/ACK (response to the request)—When computer B receives this message, it responds with a segment containing the following information:

- The ACK and SYN bits are both set to 1, essentially saying, "Yes, I'm here *and* I'm listening."
- The Acknowledgment number field contains a number that equals the sequence number computer A originally sent, plus 1. As Figure 4-4 illustrates, computer B sends the number 937013559. In this manner, computer B signals to computer A that it has received the request for communication and further, it expects computer A to respond again with the sequence number 937013559.
- In its Sequence number field, computer B sends its own random number (in Figure 4-4, this number is 3043958669).

Step 3, ACK (connection established)—Computer A issues a segment with the following information:

- The sequence number is 937013559 because this is what computer B indicated it expects to receive.
- The Acknowledgment number field equals the sequence number that computer B sent, plus 1. In our example, this number is 3043958670.
- The ACK bit is set to 1.

The connection has now been established, and in the next message, computer A will begin data transmission.

> **Note** 📎
>
> The ISN (Initial Sequence Number) of the first SYN message in the three-way handshake appears to be random, but in reality, it is calculated by a specific, clock-based algorithm, which varies by operating system. The existence of these algorithms and their predictability is actually a security loophole that hackers can use to undermine a host's availability for connections.

Up until this point, no payload has been included in any of the three initial messages, and the sequence numbers have increased by exactly 1 in each acknowledgment. After these three transmissions, the payload or data is sent. This can be done in a single message for a small amount of data, such as a web page request, or fragmented over several messages, such as the data for the web page itself.

At this point, the sequence numbers will each be increased by the number of bits included in each received segment, as confirmation that the correct length of message was received. In the example shown in Figure 4-4, computer A will send the next message, which will include the payload (such as an HTTP request) from a higher layer. Suppose that computer A's web page request message, the fourth message in this session, is 725 bits long. Computer B will receive this message, count the bits, and add 725 to the sequence number (937013559) of the received message. This new number, 937014284, becomes the acknowledgment number for the return message (which would be the fifth message in the session).

The two hosts continue communicating in this manner until computer A issues a segment whose FIN bit is set to 1, indicating the end of the transmission.

Applying Concepts: Examine a Sample TCP Header

In Capstone Project 4-2, you'll capture and examine a TCP segment using Wireshark. Now that you know the function of each TCP segment field, you will be able to interpret the segment's contents. Let's practice with an example. Figure 4-5 shows a sample TCP header.

```
Transmission Control Protocol, Src Port: http (80), Dst Port: 1958 (1958), Seq: 3043958669, Ack: 937013559,  Len: 0
    Source port : http (80)
    Destination port: 1958 (1958)
    Sequence number: 3043958669
    Acknowledgment number: 937013559
    Header length: 24 bytes
⊟Flags:_ 0xx0012 (SYN, ACK)
        0... .... = Congestion Window Reduced (CWR): Not set
        .0.. .... = ECN-Echo: Not set
        ..0. .... = Urgent: Not set
        ...1 .... = Acknowledgment: Set
        .... 0... = Push: Not set
        .... .0.. = Reset: Not set
        .... ..1. = Syn: Set
        .... ...0 = Fin: not set
    window size: 5840
    Checksum: 0x206a (correct)
⊟Options: (4bytes)
        Maximum segment size: 1460 bytes
```

Figure 4-5   TCP segment header

Suppose the segment in Figure 4-5 was sent from computer B to computer A. Table 4-2 interprets the rows shown in Figure 4-5, beginning with the second row, which is labeled "Source port."

Table 4-2   Translation of TCP field data

Field name	TCP header data
Source port	The segment was issued from computer B's port 80, the port assigned to HTTP by default.
Destination port	The segment is addressed to port 1958 on computer A.
Sequence number	The segment is identified by sequence number 3043958669.
Acknowledgment number	By containing a value other than zero, this field informs computer A that its last communication was received. Computer B is indicating that the next segment it receives from computer A should have the sequence number of 937013559, which is the same as this segment's acknowledgment number.
Header length	The TCP header is 24 bytes long—4 bytes larger than its minimum size, which means that some of the available options were specified or the padding space was used.
Flags: Congestion Window Reduced (CWR) and ECN-Echo	These optional flags can be used to help TCP react to and reduce traffic congestion. They are only available when TCP is establishing a connection. However, in this segment, they are not activated.

Table 4-2 Translation of TCP field data *(continued)*

Field name	TCP header data
Flags: Acknowledgment and Syn	Of all the possible flags in the Figure 4-5 segment, only the ACK and SYN flags are set. This means that computer B is acknowledging the last segment it received from computer A and also negotiating a synchronization scheme for sequencing.
Window size	The window size is 5840, meaning that computer B can accept 5840 bytes of data from computer A before Computer A should expect an acknowledgment.
Checksum	The valid outcome of the error-checking algorithm used to verify the segment's header is 0x206a. When computer A receives this segment, it will perform the same algorithm, and if the result matches, it will know the TCP header arrived without damage.
Maximum segment size	The maximum TCP segment size for this session is 1460 bytes.

Note

A computer doesn't "see" the TCP segment as it's organized and formatted in Figure 4-5. The information in Figure 4-5 was generated by a **protocol analyzer**, which is a program that collects and examines network messages. In this case, we used Wireshark, which translates each message into a user-friendly format. From the computer's standpoint, the TCP segment arrives as a series of bits: 0s and 1s. The computer relies on TCP standards to determine how to interpret each bit in the segment based on its location and value. You'll install and use the Wireshark protocol analyzer in a project at the end of this chapter.

TCP is not the only core protocol at the Transport layer. A similar but less complex protocol, UDP, is discussed next.

UDP (User Datagram Protocol)

UDP (User Datagram Protocol) is an unreliable, connectionless protocol. The term *unreliable* does not mean that UDP can't be used reliably. Instead, it means that UDP does not guarantee delivery of data, and no connection is established by UDP before data is transmitted. UDP provides no handshake to establish a connection, acknowledgment of transmissions received, error checking, sequencing, or flow control and is, therefore,

7	APPLICATION
6	PRESENTATION
5	SESSION
4	TRANSPORT
3	NETWORK
2	DATA LINK
1	PHYSICAL

more efficient and faster than TCP. Instead of conversing with someone on a phone call, this would be more like talking on a radio show where you send out your signal whether anyone is listening or not. UDP is useful when a great volume of data must be transferred quickly, such as live audio or video transmissions over the Internet. It's also used for small requests, such as DNS, or in situations when the data changes often and speed is more important than complete accuracy, such as when gaming over the network.

In contrast to a TCP header's 10 fields, the UDP header contains only four fields: Source port, Destination port, Length, and Checksum. Use of the UDP Checksum field is optional on IPv4 networks, but required for IPv6 transmissions. Figure 4-6 depicts a UDP datagram. Contrast its header with the much larger TCP segment header shown earlier in Figure 4-3.

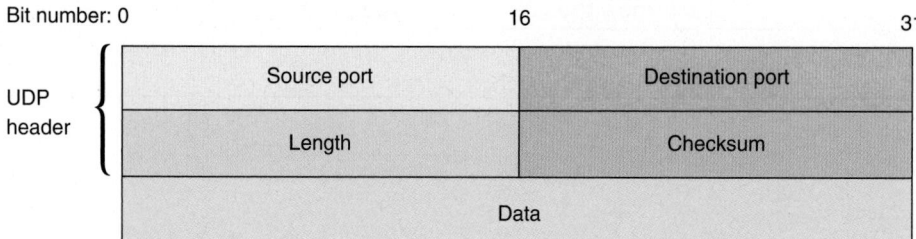

Figure 4-6   A UDP datagram

> **Note** 📎
>
> Application layer protocols can work in conjunction with UDP to emulate some of the reliability normally provided by TCP. For example, RTP (Real-time Transport Protocol, or Real-time Protocol), which is used to transmit audio and video on the web, operates at the Application layer of the OSI model and relies on UDP at the Transport layer. It applies sequence numbers to indicate the order in which messages should be assembled at their destination. These sequence numbers also help to indicate whether messages were lost during transmission.

Now that you understand the functions of and differences between TCP and UDP at Layer 4, you are ready to learn more about IP (Internet Protocol) at Layer 3.

IP (Internet Protocol)

IP (Internet Protocol) belongs to the Network layer of the OSI model. It specifies where data should be delivered, identifying the data's source and destination IP addresses. IP is the protocol that enables TCP/IP to internetwork—that is, to traverse more than one LAN segment and more than one type of network through a router.

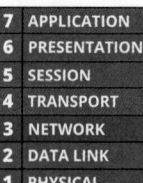

As you know, at the Network layer of the OSI model, data is organized in packets. The IP packet acts as an addressed envelope for data and contains information necessary for routers to transfer data between different LAN segments, getting data where it needs to go.

IP is a connectionless protocol, meaning IP does not establish a session to send its packets. Each IP packet travels separately from all other packets in its series, where some messages might take a different route than others, even though they're going to the same place. Once IP delivers the message to the correct host, it depends on TCP to ensure the messages are put back in the right order, if that's necessary. It also relies on either TCP or UDP to ensure each message reaches the correct application on the receiving host.

As you already know, two versions of IP are used on networks today. IPv4, which was introduced to the public in 1981, is still the standard on most networks. IPv6 was released in 1998 and offers better security, better prioritization provisions, more automatic IP address configurations, and additional IP addresses. Most new applications, servers, clients, and network devices support IPv6. However, due to the cost of upgrading infrastructure, many organizations have hesitated to transition their networks from IPv4.

As a network support technician, you need to know how to support both versions of IP. Let's first see how IPv4 packets are constructed and then we'll discuss IPv6 packets.

IPv4 Packets

Figure 4-7 depicts an IPv4 packet. Its fields are explained in Table 4-3. Note that the data field in the bottom row of the table does not belong to the IPv4 header.

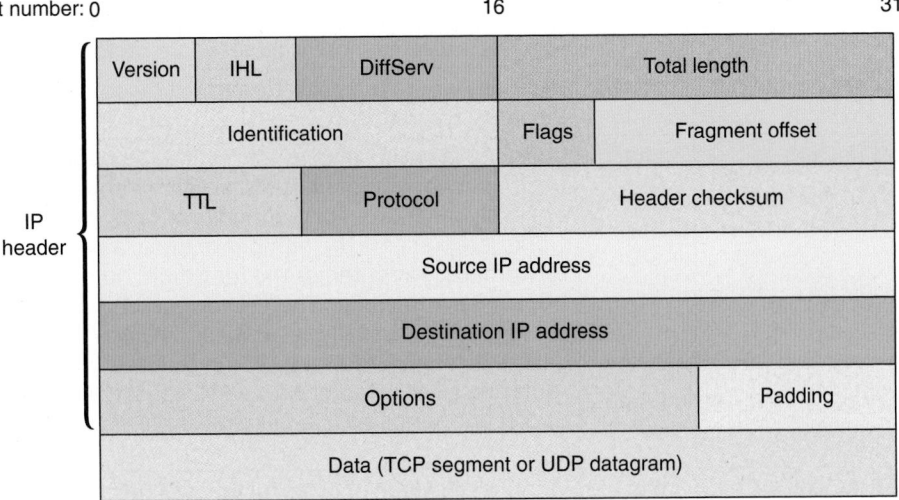

Figure 4-7   An IPv4 packet

Table 4-3 Fields in an IPv4 packet

Field		Length	Function
Header	Version	4 bits	Identifies the version number of the protocol—for example, IPv4 or IPv6. The receiving workstation looks at this field first to determine whether it can read the incoming data. If it cannot, it will reject the packet.
	IHL (Internet header length)	4 bits	Indicates the length of the IP header in bytes. The header can be a minimum of 20 bytes to a maximum of 60 bytes in 4-byte increments. It's also called the Data offset field because it indicates the offset from the beginning of the packet until the start of the data carried by the packet.
	DiffServ (Differentiated services)	8 bits	Informs routers the level of precedence they should apply when processing the incoming packet. Differentiated services allows up to 64 values and a wide range of priority-handling options.
	Total length	16 bits	Identifies the total length of the IP packet, including the header and data, in bytes. An IP packet, including its header and data, cannot exceed 65,535 bytes.
	Identification	16 bits	Identifies the message to which a packet belongs and enables the receiving host to reassemble fragmented messages. This field and the following two fields, Flags and Fragment offset, assist in reassembly of fragmented packets. IP packets that are larger than what the network allows are fragmented into smaller packets for transmission.
	Flags	3 bits	Indicates whether a message is fragmented and, if it is fragmented, whether this packet is the last fragment. The first bit is reserved for future use. When the second bit is set, it prevents the packet from being fragmented. A value of 1 in the third bit indicates more fragments are on the way.
	Fragment offset	13 bits	Identifies where the packet fragment belongs in the series of incoming fragments.
	TTL (Time to Live)	8 bits	Indicates the maximum duration that the packet can remain on the network before it is discarded. Although this field was originally meant to represent units of time, on modern networks it represents the number of times a packet can still be forwarded by a router, or the maximum number of router **hops** it has remaining. The TTL for packets varies and can be configured; it is usually set at 32 or 64. Each time a packet passes through a router, its TTL is reduced by 1. When a router receives a packet with a TTL equal to 0, it discards that packet and sends a *TTL expired* message via ICMP back to the source host.
	Protocol	8 bits	Identifies the type of protocol that will receive the packet (for example, TCP, UDP, or ICMP).

Table 4-3   Fields in an IPv4 packet *(continued)*

Field		Length	Function
	Header checksum	16 bits	Allows the receiving host to calculate whether the IP header has been corrupted during transmission. If the checksum accompanying the message does not match the calculated checksum when the packet is received, the packet is presumed to be corrupt and is discarded.
	Source IP address	32 bits	Indicates the IP address of the source host.
	Destination IP address	32 bits	Indicates the IP address of the destination host.
	Options	Variable	May contain optional routing and timing information.
	Padding	Variable	Contains filler bits to ensure that the header is a multiple of 32 bits.
Data		Variable	Includes the data originally sent by the source host, plus any headers from higher layers. The data field is not part of the IP header—it is encapsulated by the IP header.

Applying Concepts: Examine a Sample IPv4 Header

Let's examine the IPv4 header shown in the Wireshark capture in Figure 4-8. The fields are explained in Table 4-4, beginning with the Version field.

```
⊟Internet Protocol, Src Addr: 140.147.249.7 (140.147.249.7), Dst Addr: 10.11.11.51 (10.11.11.51)
      Version: 4
      Header length: 20 bytes
   ⊞Differentiated Services Field: 0x00 (DSCP 0x00: Default; ECN 0x00)
      Total Length: 44
      Identification: 0x0000 (0)
   ⊟Flags: 0x04
         .1.. = Don't fragment: Set
         ..0. = More fragments: Not set
      Fragment offset: 0
      Time to live: 64
      Protocol: TCP (0x06)
      Header checksum: 0x9ff3 (correct)
      Source: 140.147.249.7 (140.147.249.7)
      Destination: 10.11.11.51 (10.11.11.51)
```

Figure 4-8   IPv4 packet header

Table 4-4   Explanation of IPv4 header fields listed in Figure 4-8

Field name	IPv4 header data
Version	The transmission relies on version 4 of the Internet Protocol.
Header length	The packet has a header length of 20 bytes. Because this is the minimum size for an IP header, you can deduce that the packet contains no options or padding.
Differentiated Services Field	No options for priority handling are set, which is not unusual in routine data exchanges such as requesting a web page.
Total Length	The total length of the packet is 44 bytes. This makes sense when you consider that its header is 20 bytes and the TCP segment that it encapsulates is 24 bytes. Considering that the maximum size of an IP packet is 65,535 bytes, this is a very small packet.
Identification	This field uniquely identifies the packet. This packet, the first one issued from computer B to computer A in the TCP connection exchange, is identified in hexadecimal notation as 0x0000 or simply 0.
Flag: Don't fragment and Fragment offset	The Don't fragment option is set to 1, so we know this packet is not fragmented. And because it's not fragmented, the Fragment offset field does not apply and is set to 0.
Time to live	This packet's TTL is set to 64. If the packet were to keep traversing networks, it would be allowed 64 more hops before it was discarded.
Protocol	This field indicates that a TCP segment is encapsulated within the packet. TCP is always indicated by the hexadecimal string of 0x06.
Header checksum	This field provides the correct header checksum answer, which is used by the recipient of this packet to determine whether the header was damaged in transit.
Source and Destination	These last two fields show the IPv4 addresses for the packet's source and destination, respectively.

IPv6 Packets

Due to the added information it carries, IPv6 uses a different packet format than IPv4. The fields in an IPv6 packet header are shown in Figure 4-9 and described in Table 4-5. Remember that the data field in the bottom row does not belong to the IPv6 header.

If you compare the fields and functions listed in Table 4-5 with those listed for the IPv4 packet in Table 4-3, you'll notice some similarities and some differences. For example, both packets begin with a 4-bit Version field. Other fields, such as the TTL in IPv4 and the hop limit in IPv6, are similar, but slightly different. One striking difference between the two versions is that IPv6 packets accommodate the much longer IPv6 addresses. Also, there is no Fragment offset field in IPv6 packets. This is because IPv6 hosts adjust their packet sizes to fit the requirements of the network before sending IPv6 messages.

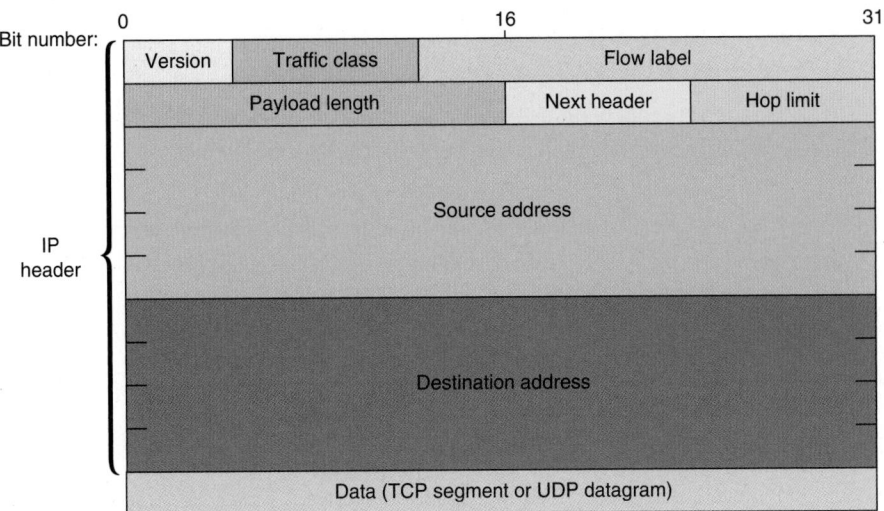

Figure 4-9   An IPv6 packet

Table 4-5   Fields in an IPv6 packet

Field		Length	Function
Header	Version	4 bits	Indicates which IP version the packet uses.
	Traffic class	8 bits	Identifies the packet's priority. It is similar to, but not the same as, the DiffServ field in IPv4 packets.
	Flow label	20 bits	Indicates which flow, or sequence of packets from one source to one or multiple destinations, the packet belongs to. Routers interpret flow information to ensure that packets belonging to the same transmission arrive together. Flow information may also help with traffic prioritization.
	Payload length	16 bits	Indicates the size of the payload, or data, carried by the packet. Unlike the Total length field in IPv4 packets, the Payload length in IPv6 packets does not refer to the size of the whole packet.
	Next header	8 bits	Identifies the type of header that immediately follows the IP packet header, usually TCP or UDP.
	Hop limit	8 bits	Indicates the number of times the packet can be forwarded by routers on the network, similar to the TTL field in IPv4 packets. When the hop limit reaches 0, the packet is discarded.
	Source address	128 bits	Indicates the full IP address of the source host.
	Destination address	128 bits	Indicates the full IP address of the destination host.
Data		Variable	Includes the data originally sent by the source host, plus any headers from higher layers. The data field is not part of the IPv6 header—it is encapsulated by the IPv6 header.

Applying Concepts: Examine a Sample IPv6 Header

Figure 4-10 shows the contents of an actual IPv6 packet header captured by Wireshark, and Table 4-6 breaks down what it all means. This packet formed part of a message issued by ping.

```
⊟ Internet Protocol Version 6, Src: 2001:470:1f10:1a6::2 (2001:470:1f10:1a6::2), Dst: 2001:470
  ⊞ 0110 .... = Version: 6
  ⊞ .... 0000 0000 .... .... .... .... .... = Traffic class: 0x00000000
    .... .... .... 0000 0000 0000 0000 0000 = Flowlabel: 0x00000000
    Payload length: 64
    Next header: ICMPv6 (0x3a)
    Hop limit: 64
    Source: 2001:470:1f10:1a6::2 (2001:470:1f10:1a6::2)
    Destination: 2001:470:1f10:1a6::1 (2001:470:1f10:1a6::1)
```

Figure 4-10   IPv6 packet header

Table 4-6   Explanation of IPv6 header fields listed in Figure 4-10

Field name	IPv6 header data
Version	Version 6 of the Internet Protocol is used, expressed in binary format as 0110.
Traffic class and Flowlabel	Both of these fields are set to 0x00000000, which means neither field has a specified value. Routers receiving a packet that lacks Traffic class or Flow label information will not prioritize the packet or make any guarantees that it will reach its destination at the same time as any other packets. For many types of traffic, this is perfectly acceptable.
Payload length	This packet carries 64 bits of data. Considering that IPv6 packets can carry payloads as large as 64 KB, this is a very small packet.
Next header	The data in this packet's payload belongs to an ICMPv6 transmission.
Hop limit	This packet can be forwarded by routers up to 64 times before it is discarded.
Source and Destination	These last two fields show the IPv6 addresses for the packet's source and destination, respectively.

IP is the primary Network layer protocol, but another Layer 3 protocol, ICMP, also plays a significant role on both IPv4 and IPv6 networks. Let's see how ICMP works, and then we'll round out our list of protocols with ARP and Ethernet at Layer 2.

ICMP (Internet Control Message Protocol)

Whereas IP helps direct data to its correct destination, ICMP (Internet Control Message Protocol) is a Network layer, core protocol that reports on the success or failure of data delivery. It can indicate when part of a network is

7	APPLICATION
6	PRESENTATION
5	SESSION
4	TRANSPORT
3	NETWORK
2	DATA LINK
1	PHYSICAL

congested, when data fails to reach its destination, and when data has been discarded because the allotted Time to Live has expired (that is, when the data has traveled its allotted number of hops). ICMP announces these transmission failures to the sender, but does not correct errors it detects—those functions are left to higher-layer protocols, such as TCP. However, ICMP's announcements provide critical information for trouble-shooting network problems. ICMP messages are generated automatically by network devices, such as routers, and by utilities, such as ping.

Because it operates at Layer 3 alongside IP, ICMP messages contain both an IP header and an ICMP header. Figure 4-11 depicts an ICMP header that is inserted after the ICMP message's IP header. The fields are explained in Table 4-7. Note that the data field in the bottom row of the table does not belong to the ICMP header.

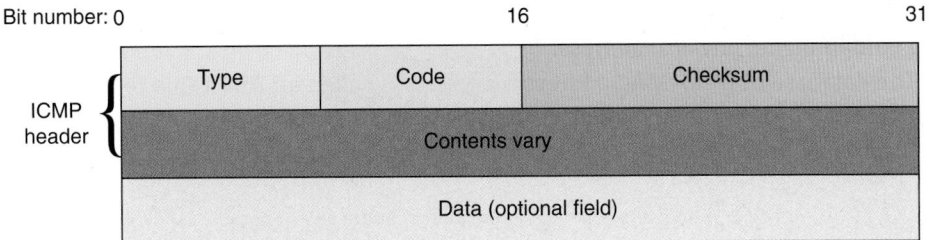

Figure 4-11   An ICMP packet

Table 4-7	An ICMP packet		
Field		**Length**	**Function**
Header	Type	8 bits	Indicates the type of ICMP message, such as Destination Unreachable.
	Code	8 bits	Indicates the subtype of the message, such as Destination host unknown.
	Checksum	16 bits	Allows the receiving node to determine whether the ICMP packet became corrupted during transmission.
	Rest of header	32 bits	Varies depending on message type and subtype.
	Data	Variable	Usually contains the IP header and first 8 bytes of the data portion of the IP packet that triggered the ICMP message.

IPv6 relies on ICMPv6 (Internet Control Message Protocol for use with IPv6) to perform the functions that ICMPv4 and ARP perform in IPv4 networks. This includes detecting and reporting data transmission errors, discovering other nodes on a net-work, and managing multicasting. To understand the different purposes of ICMPv4 and ICMPv6, let's take a closer look at ARP on IPv4 networks.

ARP (Address Resolution Protocol) on IPv4 Networks

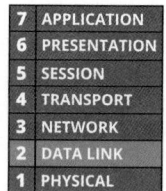

ARP (Address Resolution Protocol) works in conjunction with IPv4 to discover the MAC address of a node on the local network and to maintain a database that maps local IP addresses to MAC addresses. ARP is a Layer 2 protocol that uses IP in Layer 3. It's sometimes said to function at Layer 2.5 because it touches information (IP addresses and MAC addresses) at both layers. However, it operates only within its local network bound by routers.

ARP relies on broadcasting, which transmits simultaneously to all nodes on a particular network segment. For example, if one node needs to know the MAC address of another node on the same network, the first node issues a broadcast message to the network, using ARP, that essentially says, "Will the computer with the IP address 1.2.3.4 please send me its MAC address?" The node with the IP address 1.2.3.4 then transmits a reply containing its physical address.

The database of IP-to-MAC address mappings is called an **ARP table** or ARP cache, and is kept on a computer's hard drive. Each OS can use its own format for the ARP table. A sample ARP table is shown in Figure 4-12.

```
IP Address          Hardware Address    Type

123.45.67.80        60:23:A6:F1:C4:D2   Static
123.45.67.89        20:00:3D:21:E0:11   Dynamic
123.45.67.73        A0:BB:77:C2:25:FA   Dynamic
```

Figure 4-12   Sample ARP table

ARP tables might contain two types of entries: dynamic and static. **Dynamic ARP table entries** are created when a client makes an ARP request for information that could not be satisfied by data already in the ARP table; once received, the new information is recorded in the table for future reference. **Static ARP table entries** are those that someone has entered manually using the ARP utility. This ARP utility, accessed via the `arp` command in both Windows and Linux, provides a way of obtaining information from and manipulating a device's ARP table.

To view a Windows workstation's ARP table, open a Command Prompt window and enter the command `arp -a`. Figure 4-13 shows sample results of this command run on a home network. The first line contains the interface IP address, which is the local computer's address. The columns and rows below it contain the addresses of other nodes on the network, along with their physical addresses (MAC addresses) and record types.

Ethernet

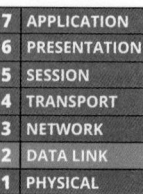

The most important Data Link layer standard, Ethernet, is adaptable, capable of running on a variety of network media, and offers excellent throughput at a reasonable cost. Because of its many advantages, Ethernet is, by far, the most popular network technology used on modern LANs.

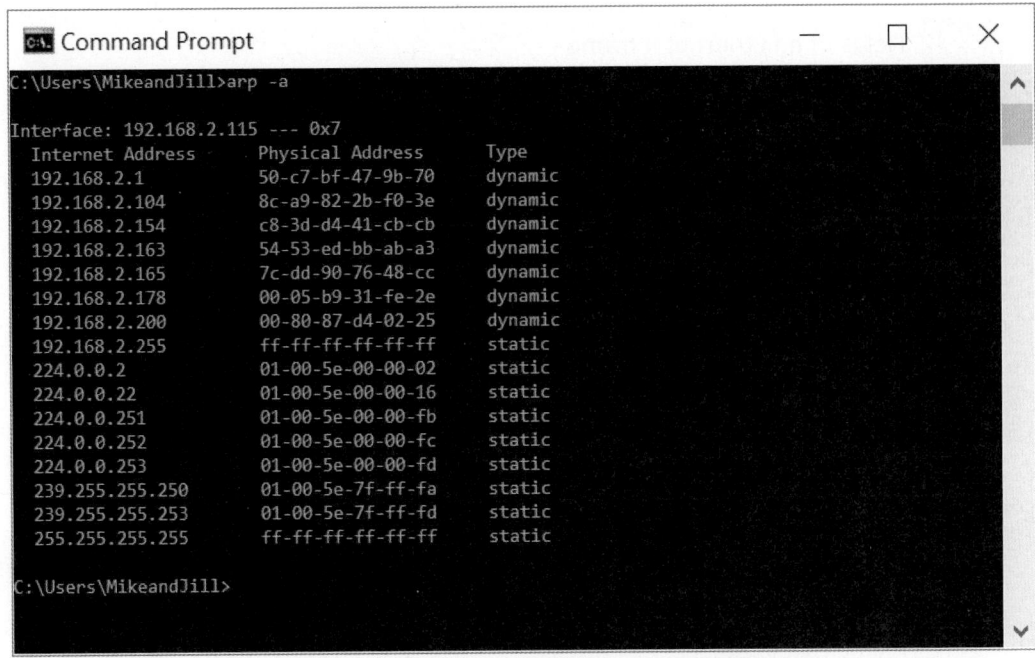

Figure 4-13   The `arp -a` command lists devices on the network

Ethernet II is the current Ethernet standard and was developed by DEC, Intel, and Xerox (abbreviated as DIX) before IEEE began to standardize Ethernet.

Unlike higher-layer protocols, Ethernet adds both a header and a trailer to the payload it inherits from the layer above it. This creates a frame around the payload. Figure 4-14 depicts an Ethernet II frame, and the details of the Ethernet II frame fields are listed in Table 4-8.

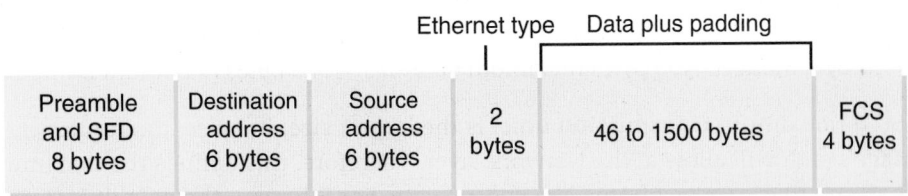

Figure 4-14   Ethernet II frame

Notice in Table 4-8 that the preamble and SFD fields are not included when calculating a frame's size. Most protocol analyzers such as Wireshark can't capture these first two fields (and sometimes not even the FCS), as this data is removed from incoming transmissions by the hardware before it becomes visible to any but the most sophisticated capture tools.

Table 4-8   Fields of an Ethernet II frame

Field name		Length	Description
Preamble		7 bytes	Synchronizes the recipient's receiver clock.*
SFD (start frame delimiter)		1 byte	Indicates the frame is about to begin.*
Header	Destination address	6 bytes	Provides the recipient's MAC address.
	Source address	6 bytes	Provides the sender's MAC address.
	Type field	2 bytes	Specifies the upper-layer protocol carried in the frame. For example, an IP packet has 0x0800 in the Type field.
Data		46 bytes to 1500 bytes	If the data is not at least 46 bytes, padding is added to meet the minimum.
Trailer	FCS (frame check sequence)	4 bytes	Ensures that the data at the destination exactly matches the data issued from the source using the CRC (cyclic redundancy check) algorithm.

*Not included when calculating a frame's total size

Together, the header and the FCS make up the 18-byte "frame" around the data. The data portion of an Ethernet frame may contain from 46 to 1500 bytes of information. Therefore, we can calculate the minimum and maximum frame sizes:

- 18-byte frame + 46 bytes minimum data size = 64 bytes minimum frame size
- 18-byte frame + 1500 bytes maximum data size = 1518 bytes maximum frame size

MTU (maximum transmission unit) is the largest size, in bytes, that routers in a message's path will allow at the Network layer. Therefore, this defines the maximum payload size that a Layer 2 frame can encapsulate. For Ethernet, the default MTU is 1500 bytes, a value that is generally considered the Internet standard. However, other Layer 2 technologies might allow higher MTUs, or require lower MTUs. Because of the overhead present in each frame and the time it takes for the NIC to manage a frame, the use of larger frame sizes on a network generally results in faster throughput.

There are a couple of notable exceptions to Ethernet frame size limitations:

- Ethernet frames on a VLAN (virtual LAN) can have an extra 4-byte field between the Source address field and the Type field, which is used to manage VLAN traffic. If this field exists, the maximum frame size is 1522 bytes. You'll learn more about VLANs later.

- Some special-purpose networks use a proprietary version of Ethernet that allows for a **jumbo frame**, in which the MTU can be as high as 9198 bytes, depending on the type of Ethernet architecture used.

Note

You might have noticed that the maximum size of an IP packet is 65,535 bytes, while the maximum size of a Network layer PDU being transmitted over an Ethernet network is only 1500 bytes. Why the discrepancy?

Fragmentation is the process of dividing packets that are too large for a network's hardware into smaller packets that can safely traverse the network. In an IPv4 network, routers examine incoming packets to determine if the packet size is larger than the outgoing interface's MTU and if the packet is allowed to be fragmented. A packet that meets these two conditions will be divided into smaller packets, each with its own header that indicates its position in the series of fragments.

Fragmentation slows down network communications, so ideally, MTUs are set at a level that works for all devices along the message's path. TCP also helps avoid fragmentation by negotiating an MSS (maximum segment size), which defines the maximum size of the Transport layer PDU, at the beginning of a session.

Legacy Networking: Collisions and CSMA/CD

When IEEE released the first Ethernet standard in 1980, it was officially called IEEE 802.3 CSMA/CD, and was unofficially called Ethernet. A CSMA/CD frame used a slightly different layout than the Ethernet II frame layout used on today's networks. The earlier frame was called an 802.3 frame, and the current Ethernet II frame is called a DIX frame. CSMA/CD networks often used a hub at the Physical layer of the OSI model.

All nodes connected to a hub compete for access to the network. The MAC (media access control) method used by nodes for arbitration on the network is **CSMA/CD (Carrier Sense Multiple Access with Collision Detection)**. Take a minute to think about the full name *Carrier Sense Multiple Access with Collision Detection*:

- *Carrier Sense* refers to an Ethernet NIC listening and waiting until no other nodes are transmitting data.
- *Multiple Access* refers to several nodes accessing the same network media.
- *Collision Detection* refers to what happens when two nodes attempt a transmission at the same time.

When the transmissions of two nodes interfere with each other, a **collision** happens. After a collision, each node waits a random amount of time and then resends the transmission. A **collision domain** is the portion of a network in which collisions can occur. Hubs connecting multiple computers in a star-bus topology resulted in massive collisions.

> **Note** 🖇
>
> Recall that structured cabling guidelines provide detailed recommendations on the maximum distances cable segments can run between nodes. It's interesting to note that these maximum cable lengths are partly determined by CSMA/CD. If a cable is too long, the entire message can be transmitted before a collision can be detected. In this case, the node does not know to resend the corrupted transmission.
>
> To ensure that any collisions are detected, frames are made large enough to fill the entire cable during transmission. It might seem odd to think about a transmission "filling a cable," but think about water going through a water hose. You can turn on the spigot and run the water for a very short time. The water runs through the hose to the other end but the hose isn't filled all at the same time. Only if you leave the water running long enough, will water start coming out the other end while it's still entering the hose at the spigot. With a long enough transmission, a similar thing happens on a cable—the beginning of the message starts arriving at its destination before the end of the message has been completely transmitted.

> **Network+ Exam Tip** ⓘ
>
> The CompTIA Network+ exam expects you to be able to contrast a broadcast domain and a collision domain, and you're now ready to do that. Both types of domains are defined by the group of nodes that transmissions can reach. Transmissions in a broadcast domain reach all nodes on a LAN, but are not forwarded by routers. Therefore, routers define the borders of a broadcast domain, which is, by definition, a LAN.
>
> In contrast, transmissions in a collision domain reach only those nodes directly connected to a hub. Therefore, the hub defines the borders of its collision domain. Figure 4-15 illustrates the difference between broadcast domains and a collision domain.

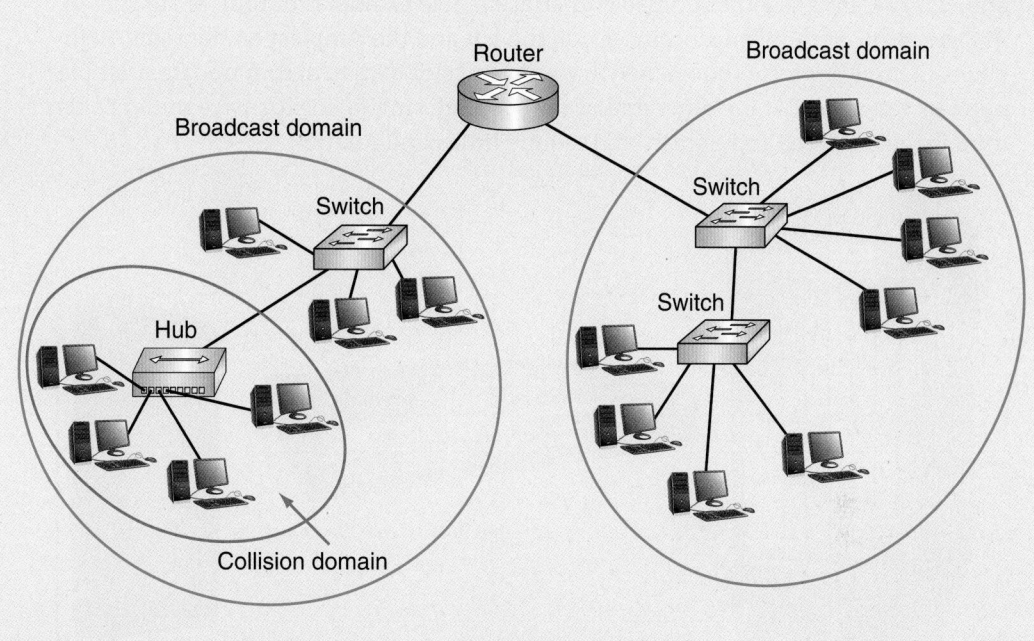

Figure 4-15 Broadcast domains and a collision domain

Routers and How They Work

 Certification

7	APPLICATION
6	PRESENTATION
5	SESSION
4	TRANSPORT
3	NETWORK
2	DATA LINK
1	PHYSICAL

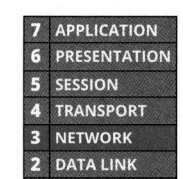

1.3 Explain the concepts and characteristics of routing and switching.

2.2 Given a scenario, determine the appropriate placement of networking devices on a network and install/configure them.

2.3 Explain the purposes and use cases for advanced networking devices.

5.2 Given a scenario, use the appropriate tool.

Returning to the Layer 3 discussions of how packets traverse networks, you're now ready to learn more about how routers work. A router joins two or more networks and passes packets from one network to another. Routers are responsible for determining the next network to which a packet should be forwarded on its way to its destination. A typical router has an internal processor, an operating system, memory, input and output jacks for different types of network connectors (depending on the network type), and, usually, a management console interface. Three examples of routers are shown in Figure 4-16, with the most complex on the left and the simplest on the right. High-powered, multiprotocol routers may have several slot bays to accommodate multiple network interfaces. At the other end of the scale are simple, inexpensive routers often used in small offices and homes, and require little configuration.

Figure 4-16 ISP, business, and consumer routers
Source: Courtesy of Juniper Networks, Inc (left and center images). Courtesy of NETGEAR (right image).

A router's strength lies in its intelligence. Although any one router can be specialized for a variety of tasks, all routers can do the following:

- Connect dissimilar networks, such as a LAN and a WAN, which use different types of routing protocols.
- Interpret Layer 3 and often Layer 4 addressing and other information (such as quality of service indicators).
- Determine the best path for data to follow from point A to point B. The **best path** is the most efficient route to the message's destination calculated by the router, based upon the information the router has available to it.
- Reroute traffic if the path of first choice is down but another path is available.

In addition to performing these basic functions, routers may perform any of the following optional functions:

- Filter broadcast transmissions to alleviate network congestion.
- Acting as a simple firewall, prevent certain types of traffic from getting to a network, enabling customized segregation and security.
- Support simultaneous local and remote connectivity.
- Provide high network fault tolerance through redundant components such as power supplies or network interfaces.
- Monitor network traffic and report statistics.
- Diagnose internal or other connectivity problems and trigger alarms.

Routers are often categorized according to their location on a network or the Internet and the routing protocols they use. The various categories are described in the following list and diagrammed in Figure 4-17:

- **Core routers**, also called **interior routers**, are located inside networks within the same autonomous system. An **AS (autonomous system)** is a group of networks, often on the same domain, that are operated by the same organization. For example, Cengage, the company that published this book, might have several LANs that all fall under its domain, with each LAN connected to the others by core routers. An AS is sometimes referred to as a trusted network because the entire domain is under the organization's control. Core routers communicate only with routers within the same AS.
- **Edge routers**, or **border routers**, connect an autonomous system with an outside network, also called an untrusted network. For example, the router that connects a business with its ISP is an edge router.
- **Exterior router** refers to any router outside the organization's AS, such as a router on the Internet backbone. Sometimes a technician might refer to her own edge router as an exterior router because it communicates with routers outside the AS. But keep in mind that every router communicating over the Internet is an edge router for some organization's AS, even if that organization is a large telecommunications company managing a portion of the Internet backbone.

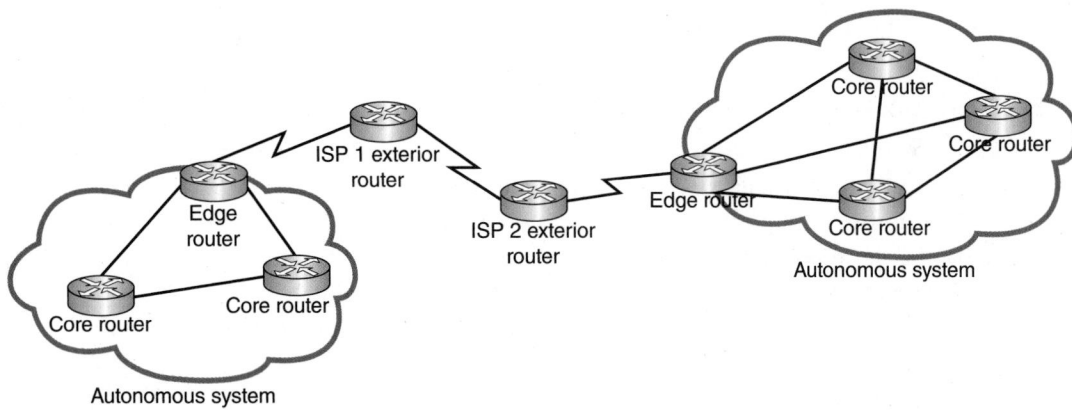

Figure 4-17   Core, edge, and exterior routers

On small office or home office LANs, routers are simple to install: Plug in the network cable from the cable modem connected to your ISP on one port and connect your computer(s) to your LAN through another port or by a wireless connection. Turn on the router and computer, and use a web-based utility program on the router to set it up.

However, high-powered, multiprotocol routers can be a challenge to install on sizable networks. Typically, an engineer must be very familiar with routing technology to figure out how to place and configure a router to the best advantage. If you plan to specialize in network design or management, you should research router types and their capabilities further.

Multilayer Switches

A **Layer 3 switch** is a switch that is capable of interpreting Layer 3 data and works much like a router. It supports the same routing protocols and makes routing decisions. Layer 3 switches were designed to work on large LANs, similar to core routers, except they're faster and less expensive. The primary difference is the way the hardware is built, but, in fact, it's often difficult to distinguish between a Layer 3 switch and a router. In some cases, the difference comes down to what the manufacturer has decided to call the device in order to improve sales.

7	APPLICATION
6	PRESENTATION
5	SESSION
4	TRANSPORT
3	NETWORK
2	DATA LINK
1	PHYSICAL

Layer 4 switches also exist and are capable of interpreting Layer 4 data. They operate anywhere between Layer 4 and Layer 7 and are also known as content switches or application switches. Among other things, the ability to interpret higher-layer data enables switches to perform advanced filtering, keep statistics, and provide security functions.

The features of Layer 3 and Layer 4 switches vary widely depending on the manufacturer and price and can cost significantly more than Layer 2 switches. This variability is exacerbated by the fact that key players in the networking trade have not agreed on standards for these switches. They are typically used as part of a network's backbone and are not appropriate on a single LAN. In general, however, Layer 4, Layer 3, and Layer 2 switches are all optimized for fast Layer 2 data handling.

As you learn more about how routers work, keep in mind that Layer 3 and Layer 4 switches can work the same way.

Routing Tables

A **routing table** is a database that holds information about where hosts are located and the most efficient way to reach them. A router has two or more network ports and each port connects to a different network; each network connection is assigned an interface ID, and logically, the router belongs to every network it connects to. A router relies on its routing table to identify which network a host belongs to and which of the router's interfaces points toward the best next hop to reach that network.

7	APPLICATION
6	PRESENTATION
5	SESSION
4	TRANSPORT
3	NETWORK
2	DATA LINK
1	PHYSICAL

For example, in Figure 4-18, suppose a workstation in LAN A wants to print to the network printer in LAN D. The following steps describe how routing tables would be used in this transmission:

Step 1—Workstation 1 issues a print command to a network printer. IP on the workstation recognizes that the IP address of the printer is on a different LAN than the workstation and forwards the transmission through switch A to its default gateway, router A.

Step 2—Router A examines the destination IP address in the packet's header and searches its routing table to determine which network and router the message

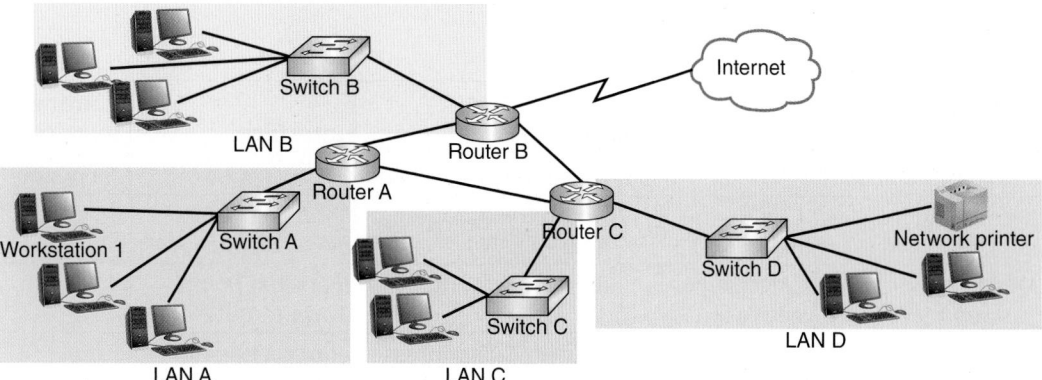

Figure 4-18   Routers rely on routing tables to locate destination hosts

should go to. As shown in Table 4-9, each row in the routing table describes one route, including a destination network and how to get there. Here's a breakdown of how the search process happens:

- Router A examines all rows in its routing table. In each row, it uses information in the first two columns, the destination network's IP address and netmask, to calculate the range of IP addresses included in that network.
- If the message's destination IP address fits in the calculated range for a route, the router then reads the IP address of the gateway in the third column. This gateway is the next hop router. It also reads in the fourth column the interface it will use to send the message out.
- If it finds more than one possible route, the router uses **routing metrics** (information about each route) in the last column to determine which route is most efficient. The smaller the metrics number, the better the route. Notice in Figure 4-18 and in Table 4-9 that two routes can reach the network printer on LAN D. Of these two routes, the router would select the one with the lower metrics value. You'll learn more about routing metrics later in this chapter.
- If it doesn't find a matching entry, the router looks for 0.0.0.0 in the first column. This route is the **default route**—the route to use if no other route is a match. Recall from the On the Job story at the beginning of this chapter, the default route was missing in the routing table. The gateway in the third column of this route is called the **gateway of last resort**, which is the router that accepts unroutable messages from other routers.
- If no default route is defined, the router will drop the message.

So in our scenario, router A finds two matches with LAN D's network information, and chooses the best of these two options based on their respective routing metrics. Router A then determines that it should send the message out the port that faces router C.

Table 4-9   Portions of router A's routing table

Destination network ID	Netmask	Gateway	Interface	Routing metrics
Matching information		*Forwarding information*		*Tie breaker*
LAN A's IP address	LAN A's netmask	None (This is router A's own LAN.)	Port that points toward switch A	1
LAN B's IP address	LAN B's netmask	Router B's IP address	Port that points toward router B	4
LAN C's IP address	LAN C's netmask	Router C's IP address	Port that points toward router C	5
LAN D's IP address	LAN D's netmask	Router B's IP address	Port that points toward router B	10
LAN D's IP address	LAN D's netmask	Router C's IP address	Port that points toward router C	5
IP address on the Internet	That host's netmask	Router B's IP address	Port that points toward router B	23
0.0.0.0 (any network)*	0 (any netmask)	Router B's IP address**	Port that points toward router B	3

*This row is the default route.

**This router is router A's gateway of last resort.

> *Step 3*—Before it forwards the message, router A decreases the number of hops tallied in the TTL field of the packet header. It then sends the message to router C.

> *Step 4*—Router C decreases the packet's hop count by 1, reads the packet's destination IP address, searches its routing table for matching network information, and determines the message is destined for its own LAN D. It sends the message to switch D on LAN D.

> *Step 5*—Using its ARP table, switch D matches the destination IP address with the printer's MAC address. If switch D didn't have a matching entry in its ARP table for

Note 📎

What's the difference between a default gateway, a default route, and a gateway of last resort?

- Most hosts have a default gateway—a router or Layer 3 switch—where they send all routable messages. Hosts can't communicate with other networks without a default gateway.
- Most routers have a default route as a backup route when no other route can be determined.
- The default route points to a gateway of last resort. A router's gateway of last resort is where it sends messages addressed to networks the router can't find in its routing table.

the network printer's IP address, it would use an ARP broadcast to request the printer's MAC address. Switch D then delivers the transmission to the printer, which picks up the message, and begins printing.

Routing Path Types

Routing paths are determined in one of two ways: static or dynamic routing.

- *static routing*—A network administrator configures a routing table to direct messages along specific paths between networks. For example, it's common to see a static route between a small business and its ISP. However, static routes can't account for occasional network congestion, failed connections, or device moves, and they require human intervention.
- *dynamic routing*—A router automatically calculates the best path between two networks and accumulates this information in its routing table. If congestion or failures affect the network, a router using dynamic routing can detect the problems and reroute messages through a different path. When a router is added to a network, dynamic routing ensures that the new router's routing tables are updated.

The `route` Command

The `route` **command** allows you to view a host's routing table. Here are some variations for different operating systems:

- *Linux or UNIX*—Enter `route` at the shell prompt.
- *Windows*—Enter `route print` at the command prompt.
- *Cisco's IOS*—Enter `show ip route` at the CLI in enable mode. You'll have a chance to practice using Cisco commands in a few projects in later chapters.

Routing tables on workstations typically contain no more than a few, unique entries, including the default gateway and loopback address. However, routing tables on Internet backbone routers, such as those operated by ISPs, maintain hundreds of thousands of entries.

Routing Metrics

Finding the best route or best path for messages to take across networks is one of the most valued and sophisticated functions performed by a router. Some examples of routing metrics used to determine the best path may include:

- Hop count, which is the number of network segments crossed
- Theoretical bandwidth and actual throughput on a potential path
- Delay, or **latency**, on a potential path, which results in slower performance
- Load, which is the traffic or processing burden sustained by a router in the path
- MTU, which is the largest IP packet size in bytes allowed by routers in the path without fragmentation (excludes the frame size on the local network)

- **Routing cost**, which is a value assigned to a particular route as judged by the network administrator; the more desirable the path, the lower its cost
- Reliability of a potential path, based on historical performance
- A network's topology

Routing Protocols to Determine Best Paths

To determine the best path, routers communicate with each other through **routing protocols**. Routing protocol messages, similar to scouting parties exploring unknown terrain, go forth to collect data about current network status and contribute to the selection of best paths. Routers use this data to create their routing tables. Keep in mind that routing protocols are not the same as routable protocols such as IP, although routing protocols might piggyback on IP to reach their destinations. Also, the various routing protocols operate at different layers of the OSI model—usually, either Layer 3, Layer 4, or Layer 7. However, for the purposes of our discussion, we're primarily considering the effects that routing protocols have on Layer 3 routing activities.

Routers rate the reliability and priority of a routing protocol's data based on these criteria:

- *AD (administrative distance)*—Each routing protocol is assigned a default AD, which is a number indicating the protocol's reliability, with lower values being given higher priority. This assignment can be changed by a network administrator when one protocol should take precedence over a previously higher-rated protocol on that network.
- *convergence time*—Routing protocols are also rated on the time it takes to recognize a best path in the event of a change or network outage.
- *overhead*—A routing protocol is rated on its overhead, or the burden placed on the underlying network to support the protocol.

The most common routing protocols are summarized in Table 4-10 and are described in more detail in the following sections. Additional routing protocols exist, but their discussions exceed the scope of this book.

Table 4-10   Summary of common routing protocols

Routing protocol	Type	Algorithm used
RIP (Routing Information Protocol)	IGP	Distance-vector
RIPv2 (Routing Information Protocol, version 2)	IGP	Distance-vector
OSPF (Open Shortest Path First)	IGP	Link-state
IS-IS (Intermediate System to Intermediate System)	IGP	Link-state
EIGRP (Enhanced Interior Gateway Routing Protocol)	IGP	Advanced distance-vector
BGP (Border Gateway Protocol)*	EGP	Advanced distance-vector or path vector

*CompTIA classifies BGP as a "hybrid routing protocol."

Interior and Exterior Gateway Protocols

As you examine Table 4-10, you can see that a routing protocol is classified as IGP or EGP. Here's an explanation of the two types, which are diagrammed in Figure 4-19:

- **IGPs (interior gateway protocols)** are routing protocols used by core routers and edge routers within autonomous systems. IGPs are often grouped according to the algorithms they use to calculate best paths:

  - **Distance-vector routing protocols** calculate the best path to a destination on the basis of the distance to that destination. Some distance-vector routing protocols factor only the number of hops to the destination, whereas others take into account route latency and other network traffic characteristics. Distance-vector routing protocols periodically exchange their route information with neighboring routers. However, routers relying on this type of routing protocol must accept the data they receive from their neighbors and cannot independently assess network conditions two or more hops away. RIP, RIPv2, and EIGRP are distance-vector routing protocols.

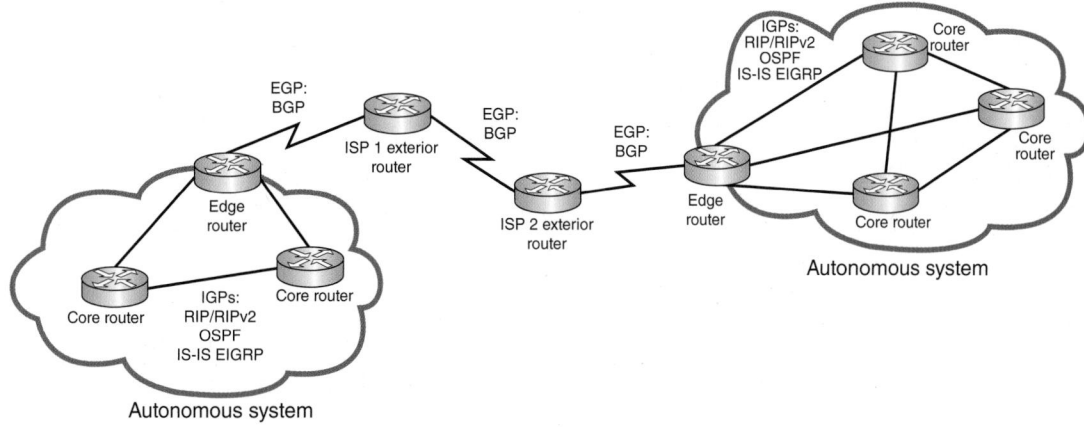

Figure 4-19   BGP is the only routing protocol that communicates across the Internet

- Link-state routing protocols enable routers to communicate beyond neighboring routers, after which each router can independently map the network and determine the best path between itself and a message's destination node. These protocols tend to adapt more quickly to changes in the network, but can also be more complex to configure and troubleshoot. OSPF and IS-IS are link-state routing protocols.
- EGPs (exterior gateway protocols) are routing protocols used by edge routers and exterior routers to distribute data outside of autonomous systems. The one EGP protocol we discuss in this chapter, which is the only EGP currently in use, is BGP.

Note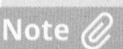

An older routing protocol named Exterior Gateway Protocol is obsolete. However, the generic term *exterior gateway protocol* now refers to any routing protocol that routes information between autonomous systems.

Let's look at the details of these routing protocols, beginning with RIP and RIPv2, which are both outdated but still in use on many networks because of their simplicity and compatibility with older routers.

Legacy Networking: RIP (Routing Information Protocol) and RIPv2

RIP (Routing Information Protocol), a distance-vector routing protocol, is the oldest routing protocol. Here are some notable considerations when using RIP on a network.
Advantages:

- *simplicity*—Quick and easy configuration.
- *stability*—Prevents routing loops from continuing indefinitely by limiting the number of hops a message can take between its source and its destination to 15. If the number of hops in a path exceeds 15, the network destination is considered unreachable.

Disadvantages:

- *limited metrics*—Only considers the number of hops between nodes when determining the best path.
- *excessive overhead*—Broadcasts routing tables every 30 seconds to other routers, regardless of whether the tables have changed.
- *poor convergence time*—Might take several minutes for new information to propagate to the far reaches of the network.
- *limited network size*—Does not work well in very large network environments where data might have to travel through more than 15 routers to reach its destination (for example, on a metro network).
- *slower and less secure*—Outdated by newer routing protocols.

Developers have improved RIP since its release in 1988 and informally renamed the original RIP as RIPv1 (Routing Information Protocol version 1). The latest version, **RIPv2 (Routing Information Protocol version 2)**, generates less broadcast traffic and functions more securely than RIPv1. Still, RIPv2 cannot exceed 15 hops, and it is also considered an outdated routing protocol.

OSPF (Open Shortest Path First)

OSPF (Open Shortest Path First) is an IGP and a link-state routing protocol used on core or edge routers. It was introduced as an improvement to RIP and can coexist with RIP or RIPv2 on a network. Characteristics include the following:

- *supports large networks*—Imposes no hop limits on a transmission path.
- *complex algorithms*—Calculates more efficient best paths than RIP. Under optimal network conditions, the best path is the most direct path between two points. If excessive traffic levels or an outage prevent data from following the most direct path, a router might determine that the most efficient path actually goes through additional routers.
- *shared data*—Maintains a database of the other routers' links. If OSPF learns of the failure of a given link, the router can rapidly compute an alternate path.
- *low overhead, fast convergence*—Demands more memory and CPU power for calculations, but keeps network bandwidth to a minimum with a very fast convergence time, often invisible to users.
- *stability*—Uses algorithms that prevent routing loops.
- *multi-vendor routers*—Supported by all modern routers. It is commonly used on autonomous systems that rely on a mix of routers from different manufacturers.

IS-IS (Intermediate System to Intermediate System)

Another IGP, which is also a link-state routing protocol, is **IS-IS (Intermediate System to Intermediate System)**. IS-IS uses a best-path algorithm similar to OSPF's. It was originally codified by ISO, which referred to routers as "intermediate systems," thus the protocol's name. Unlike OSPF, however, IS-IS is designed for use on core routers only. Also, IS-IS is not handcuffed to IPv4 like OSPF is, so it's easy to adapt to IPv6. Service providers generally prefer to use IS-IS in their own networks because it's more scalable than OSPF, but OSPF is still more common.

EIGRP (Enhanced Interior Gateway Routing Protocol)

EIGRP (Enhanced Interior Gateway Routing Protocol), an IGP, was developed in the mid-1980s by Cisco Systems. It is an advanced distance-vector protocol that combines some of the features of a link-state protocol and so is sometimes referred to as a hybrid protocol. With a fast convergence time and low network overhead, it's easier to configure and less CPU-intensive than OSPF. EIGRP also offers the benefits of supporting multiple protocols and limiting unnecessary network traffic between routers.

Originally, EIGRP was proprietary to Cisco routers. In 2013, parts of the EIGRP standard were released to the public so that networks running routers from other vendors can now use EIGRP. It accommodates very large and heterogeneous networks, but it is still optimized for Cisco routers and not many manufacturers have made the transition. On LANs that use Cisco routers exclusively, EIGRP is generally preferred over OSPF.

BGP (Border Gateway Protocol)

The only current EGP is **BGP (Border Gateway Protocol)**, which has been dubbed the "protocol of the Internet." Whereas OSPF and IS-IS scouting parties only scout out their home territory, a BGP scouting party can go cross-country. BGP spans multiple autonomous systems and is used by edge and exterior routers on the Internet. Here are some special characteristics of BGP:

- *path-vector routing protocol*—Communicates via BGP-specific messages that travel between routers over TCP sessions.
- *efficient*—Determines best paths based on many different factors.
- *customizable*—Can be configured to follow policies that might, for example, avoid a certain router, or instruct a group of routers to prefer one particular route over other available routes.

BGP is the most complex of the routing protocols mentioned in this chapter. If you maintain networks for an ISP or large telecommunications company, you will need to understand BGP.

Network+ Exam Tip ⓘ

BGP considers many factors to determine best paths, and is more complex than other distance-vector routing protocols. In fact, its adaptability has earned it the official classification of advanced distance-vector routing protocol. You might also sometimes see BGP classified as a path-vector protocol because it maintains dynamic path information beyond the device's neighboring routers. However, because of its complexity and the number of factors it can consider when calculating best paths, the CompTIA Network+ exam classifies BGP as a **hybrid routing protocol**, implying that it exhibits characteristics of both distance-vector and link-state routing protocols.

Troubleshooting Route Issues

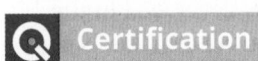 Certification

1.3 Explain the concepts and characteristics of routing and switching.

4.2 Explain authentication and access controls.

4.4 Summarize common networking attacks.

5.2 Given a scenario, use the appropriate tool.

5.5 Given a scenario, troubleshoot common network service issues.

As with any type of communication, many potential points of failure exist in the TCP/IP transmission process. The number of points increases with the size of the network and the distance of the transmission. Fortunately, TCP/IP comes with a complete set of utilities that can help you track down most TCP/IP-related problems without using expensive software or hardware to analyze network traffic. You should be familiar with the purposes of the following tools and their parameters, not only because the CompTIA Network+ certification exam covers them, but also because you will regularly need these tools in your work with TCP/IP networks.

Troubleshooting Tools

You've already learned about seven very important TCP/IP utilities—ping, ipconfig, ifconfig, nslookup, dig, arp, and route. The following sections present additional TCP/IP utilities that can help you discover information about your node and network, and concludes with a summary of all these utilities along with a few troubleshooting scenarios.

netstat

The **netstat** utility displays TCP/IP statistics and details about TCP/IP components and connections on a host. Information that can be obtained from the netstat command includes:

- the port on which a TCP/IP service is running
- which network connections are currently established for a client
- how many messages have been handled by a network interface since it was activated
- how many data errors have occurred on a particular network interface

For example, suppose you are a network administrator in charge of maintaining file, print, and web servers for an organization. You discover that your web server, which has multiple processors, sufficient hard disk space, and multiple NICs, is suddenly taking twice as long to respond to HTTP requests. Besides checking the server's memory resources and its software for indications of problems, you can use netstat to determine the characteristics of traffic going into and out of each NIC. Perhaps you discover that one NIC is consistently handling 80 percent of the traffic instead of only half. You might run hardware diagnostics on the NIC, and discover that its onboard processor is failing, making it much slower than the other NIC.

Table 4-11 shows some parameters you can use with netstat in Windows. You can also use netstat on Linux machines with a different set of parameters.

Table 4-11	`netstat` command options

netstat command	Description
`netstat`	Lists all active TCP/IP connections on the local machine, including the Transport layer protocol used (usually just TCP), messages sent and received, IP address, and state of those connections.
`netstat -n`	Lists current connections, including IP addresses and ports.
`netstat -f`	Lists current connections, including IP addresses, ports, and FQDNs.
`netstat -a`	Lists all current TCP connections and all listening TCP and UDP ports.
`netstat -e`	Displays statistics about messages sent over a network interface, including errors and discards.
`netstat -s`	Displays statistics about each message transmitted by a host, separated according to protocol type (TCP, UDP, IP, or ICMP).
`netstat -r`	Displays routing table information.
`netstat -o`	Lists the PID (process identifier) for each process using a connection and information about the connection.
`netstat -b`	Lists the name of each process using a connection and information about the connection. Requires an elevated Command Prompt.

Note

Command parameters can be combined into a single command. For example, entering the command `netstat -an` will display the IP addresses and ports of active TCP connections and also listening TCP and UDP ports.

tracert or traceroute

The Windows **tracert** utility uses ICMP echo requests to trace the path from one networked node to another, identifying all intermediate hops between the two nodes. Linux, UNIX, and macOS systems use UDP datagrams or, possibly, TCP SYN messages, for their **traceroute** utility, but the concept is still the same.

Note

Traceroute can be configured to use TCP or ICMP messages. See the traceroute man pages to learn how to configure this and many other options.

Both traceroute and tracert utilities employ a trial-and-error approach to discover the nodes at each hop from the source to the destination, as described here:

- Traceroute sends UDP messages to a random, unused port on the destination node, and listens for an ICMP "Port Unreachable" error message in response from that node.
- Tracert sends an ICMP echo request to the destination node and listens for an ICMP echo reply from that node.
- Both utilities limit the TTL of these repeated trial messages, called **probes**, thereby triggering routers along the route to return specific information about the route being traversed. In fact, by default they send three probes with each iteration so averages can be calculated from the three responses at each step.

Study Figure 4-20 to see how a trace works with `traceroute`.

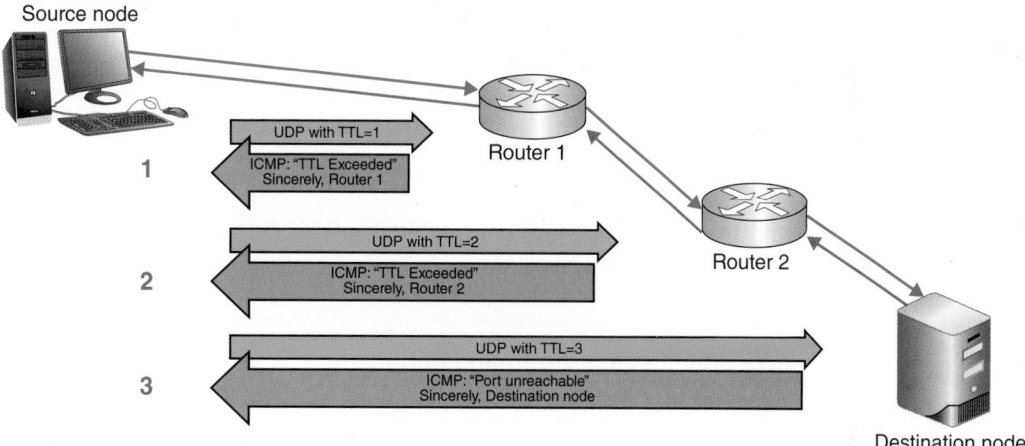

Figure 4-20   The traceroute utility uses error messages from routers to map nodes on a route

Step 1—The first three UDP datagrams transmitted have their TTL set to 1. Because the TTL determines how many more network hops a datagram can make, datagrams with a TTL of 1 expire as they hit the first router. When they expire, an ICMP error message is returned to the source—in this case, the node that began the trace.

Step 2—Using the return messages, the trace now knows the identity of the first router. It then transmits a series of datagrams with a TTL of 2 to determine the identity of the second router.

Step 3—The process continues for the next router in the path, and then the fourth, fifth, and so on, until the destination node is reached. The trace also returns the amount of time it took for the datagrams to reach each router in the path.

This process is identical for `tracert` in Windows except for two modifications. First, the probes sent from the source are ICMP echo request messages. (Each message is still limited by the specific TTL restrictions.) Second, the final reply from the destination node is an ICMP echo reply rather than an ICMP port unreachable error message.

> ### Applying Concepts: Trace the Route to *Google.com*
>
> You can perform a trace using an IP address or a host name. On a UNIX or Linux system, the command syntax would be:
>
> > `traceroute 8.8.8.8` or `traceroute google.com`
>
> Because `tracert` is installed by default on Windows, use a Windows machine for this exercise instead:
>
> 1. On a Windows system, perform a trace on one of Google's public DNS servers with the command `tracert 8.8.8.8`. How many hops were traced? What is the IP address of the final hop?
> 2. Use `tracert` to perform a trace on Google's web server with the command `tracert google.com`. How many hops were traced this time? What is the IP address of the final hop? Why is this IP address different than the IP address of the final hop in the previous step?

The `traceroute` or `tracert` command has several available parameters. Table 4-12 describes some of the more popular ones.

Table 4-12   `traceroute` and `tracert` command options

Command	Description

`traceroute -n google.com`
or
`tracert -d google.com`
	Instructs the command to not resolve IP addresses to host names.

`traceroute -m 12 google.com`
or
`tracert -h 12 google.com`
	Specifies the maximum number of hops when attempting to reach a host; this parameter must be followed by a specific number. Without this parameter, the command defaults to 30.

`traceroute -w 2 google.com`
or
`tracert -w 2000 google.com`
	Identifies a timeout period for responses; this parameter must be followed by a variable to indicate the number of seconds (in Linux) or milliseconds (in Windows) that the utility should wait for a response. The default time is usually between 3 and 5 seconds for Linux and 4000 milliseconds (4 seconds) for Windows.

`traceroute -f 3 google.com`	Sets the first TTL value and must be followed by a variable to indicate the number of hops for the first probe. The default value is 1, which begins the trace at the first router on the route. Beginning at later hops in the route can more quickly narrow down the location of a network problem. `tracert` does not have a corresponding parameter for this function.

Table 4-12   `traceroute` and `tracert` command options *(continued)*

Command	Description
`traceroute -I google.com`	Instructs the command to use ICMP echo requests instead of UDP datagrams.
`traceroute -T google.com`	Instructs the command to use TCP SYN probes instead of UDP datagrams.
`traceroute -4 google.com` or `tracert -4 google.com`	Forces the command to use IPv4 packets only.
`traceroute -6 google.com` or `tracert -6 google.com`	Forces the command to use IPv6 packets instead of IPv4. The other parameters can be added to these IPv6 commands and function essentially the same as they do in IPv4.

Note that a trace test might stop before reaching the destination. This usually happens for one of three reasons: (1) the device the trace is attempting to reach is down, (2) it's too busy to process lower-priority messages such as UDP or ICMP, or (3) a firewall blocks UDP and ICMP transmissions, especially if it receives several in a short period of time. If you are trying to trace a route to a host situated behind a firewall, you can try using TCP in `traceroute`. Otherwise, your efforts might be thwarted. (Because `ping` uses ICMP transmissions, the same limitations exist for that utility.)

One possible work-around for firewall-imposed limitations on multiple UDP or ICMP probes in a short period of time is to add more of a delay between the probe repetitions. This can be done with the `-z` parameter followed by the number of seconds (up to 10) for the minimum wait time between probes. This option, like many others, is only available for `traceroute`, not `tracert`.

Note 📎

Many Linux distributions, like Ubuntu, do not include the traceroute utility by default. You will have to install traceroute to use it on those systems. You might find in its place a simpler utility called tracepath. The `tracepath` command does not provide as many options as `traceroute`. However, it is based on the same principles, and might be sufficient to save you the time of installing the traceroute package.

A trace cannot detect router configuration problems or predict variations of routes over a period of time. Therefore, a trace is best used on a network with which you are already familiar. The traceroute or tracert utility can help you diagnose network congestion or network failures. You can then use your judgment and experience to compare the actual test results with what you anticipate the results should be.

pathping

The Windows utility **pathping** combines elements of both ping and tracert to provide deeper information about network issues along a route. It sends multiple pings to each hop along a route, then compiles the information into a single report. To see a sample of the type of information `pathping` provides, try the following command:

```
pathping google.com
```

Note

Remember that you can stop a command while it's running by pressing CTRL+C.

Table 4-13 gives some `pathping` examples.

Table 4-13   `pathping` command options

`pathping` command	Description
`pathping -n google.com`	Instructs the command to not resolve IP addresses to host names.
`pathping -h 12 google.com`	Specifies the maximum number of hops the messages should take when attempting to reach a host (the default is 30); this parameter must be followed by a specific number of hops.
`pathping -p 2000 google.com`	Identifies the wait time between pings; this parameter must be followed by a variable to indicate the number of milliseconds to wait. The default time is 4000 milliseconds (4 seconds).
`pathping -q 4 google.com`	Limits the number of queries per hop; must be followed by a variable to indicate the number of queries allowed. By default, `pathping` sends 100 pings per hop, which tends to take a long time to run.

Note

Linux offers its own version of the pathping utility, called mtr, which is short for "my traceroute." Even though it's named after `traceroute`, it actually functions more like `pathping`, by combining traits of both `ping` and `traceroute`. Like `traceroute`, `mtr` might not be installed by default on several Linux distributions. Ubuntu, for example, includes a non-GUI "tiny" version of `mtr` called `mtr-tiny`.

tcpdump

The **tcpdump** utility is a free, command-line packet sniffer that runs on Linux and other Unix operating systems. Earlier in this chapter, you learned about the protocol analyzer Wireshark. A **packet sniffer** is very similar and many people use the terms interchangeably. In essence, the difference between a packet sniffer and a protocol analyzer is the level of interpretation and analysis the tool provides for the data captured from the network interface.

Like Wireshark, `tcpdump` captures traffic that crosses a computer's network interface. The output can be saved to a file that you can filter or play back. Because of its robust configuration options and straightforward, command-line interface, it's a popular tool among security professionals and hackers alike. When used on a network device, such as a router or switch, `tcpdump` can become a very powerful tool indeed.

You must either use the `sudo` command or log in as root to access `tcpdump`. To do this, either enter `sudo` before each `tcpdump` command, or at the shell prompt, enter `sudo su root`, which changes you over to the root account. Table 4-14 gives some `tcpdump` examples.

Table 4-14   `tcpdump` command options

`tcpdump` command	Description
`tcpdump not port 22 or` `tcpdump not port 23`	Filters out SSH or Telnet packets, which is helpful when running `tcpdump` on a remotely accessed network device.
`tcpdump -n`	Instructs the command to not resolve IP addresses to host names.
`tcpdump -c 50`	Limits the number of captured packets to 50.
`tcpdump -i any`	Listens to all network interfaces on a device.
`tcpdump -D`	Lists all interfaces available for capture.
`tcpdump port http`	Filters out all traffic except HTTP.
`tcpdump -w capture.cap`	Saves the file output to a file named capture.cap.
`tcpdump -r capture.cap`	Reads the file capture.cap and outputs the data in the terminal window. This file can also be read by applications like Wireshark.

Solving Common Routing Problems

You can use the tools presented in this chapter to troubleshoot and solve several common problems on your network. Table 4-15 gives a brief summary of all the command-line utilities we've covered so far and how they can help you.

Table 4-15   Command-line utilities

Command	Common uses
`arp`	Provides a way of obtaining information from and manipulating a device's ARP table.
`dig`	Queries DNS servers with more advanced options than `nslookup`.
`ipconfig` or `ifconfig`	Provides information about TCP/IP network connections and the ability to manage some of those settings.

(continues)

Table 4-15 Command-line utilities *(continued)*

Command	Common uses
netstat	Displays TCP/IP statistics and details about TCP/IP components and connections on a host.
nmap	Detects, identifies, and monitors devices on a network.
nslookup	Queries DNS servers and provides the ability to manage the settings for accessing those servers.
pathping (mtr on Linux/UNIX/ macOS)	Sends multiple pings to each hop along a route, then compiles the information into a single report.
ping	Verifies connectivity between two nodes on a network.
route	Displays a host's routing table.
tcpdump	Captures traffic that crosses a computer's network interface.
traceroute or tracert	Traces the path from one networked node to another, identifying all intermediate routers between the two nodes.

Using what you've learned, let's explore a few common network problems and how to solve them.

Duplicate MAC Addresses

Devices on separate networks can have the same MAC address without causing any problems. Even if duplicate MAC addresses need to communicate with each other across separate networks, the fact that MAC addresses exist at Layer 2 means that the MAC addresses themselves are not transmitted outside of their local network. However, two devices on the *same* network with the same MAC address *is* a problem.

Because MAC addresses are assigned statically by the manufacturer, you might wonder how two devices could possibly have the same MAC address. Sometimes manufacturers (by accident or by neglect) reuse the same MAC address for two or more devices. Additionally, a MAC address can be impersonated, which is a security risk called **spoofing**. On a network where access is limited to certain devices based on their MAC address, an attacker can spoof an approved device's MAC address and gain access to the network. This is a relatively easy attack to carry out, which is why MAC address filtering is not considered a reliable way to control access to a network.

Most of the time, though, duplicate MAC addresses only cause intermittent connectivity issues for the computers involved in the duplication. Here's how the situation develops:

Step 1—Each computer regularly broadcasts its IP address and the duplicated MAC address so devices on the network can update their ARP tables.

Step 2—Those other devices, in response, update their records to point toward one computer, and then the other computer, and then back to the first one, and so on, depending upon the latest transmission they received.

Step 3—Sometimes devices will send communications to the correct computer, and sometimes their records will be wrong.

Thankfully, duplicate MAC addresses are a relatively rare problem. It happens most often when managing multiple virtual devices on a large network, and in those cases, it's typically due to human error. Most switches will detect the problem and produce helpful error messages of some kind. Then it's a matter of tracking down which virtual devices have the same MAC address and updating each device's configuration.

Hardware Failure

When a router, switch, NIC, or other hardware goes down, your job as a network technician includes identifying the location of the hardware failure. Even on smaller networks, it can be a challenge to determine exactly which device is causing problems. Though you could manually check each device on your network for errors, you might be able to shorten your list with a little detective work first. Here's how:

1. Use `tracert` or `traceroute` (depending on your OS) to track down malfunctioning routers and other devices on larger networks. Because ICMP messages are considered low priority, be sure to run the command multiple times and compare the results before drawing any conclusions.
2. Keep in mind that routers are designed to route traffic to other destinations. You might get more accurate `tracert` or `traceroute` feedback on a questionable router if you target a node on the other side of that router rather than aiming for the router itself.
3. As you hone in on the troublesome device, use `ping` to test for network connectivity.

Discovering Neighbor Devices

Routers learn about all the devices on their networks through a process called **neighbor discovery**. This process can go awry when changes are made to the network, or when a problem is developing but is only producing sporadic symptoms.

On IPv4 networks, neighbor discovery is managed by ARP with help from ICMP. The `arp` command can be used on IPv4 devices to diagnose and repair problems with ARP tables. If you notice inconsistent connectivity issues related to certain addresses, you might need to flush the ARP table on any device experiencing the problem. This forces the device to repopulate its ARP table in order to correct any errors.

IPv6 devices use NDP (Neighbor Discovery Protocol) in ICMPv6 messages to automatically detect neighboring devices, and to automatically adjust when neighboring nodes fail or are removed from the network. NDP eliminates the need for ARP and some ICMP functions in IPv6 networks, and is much more resistant to hacking attempts than ARP.

Chapter Summary

TCP/IP Core Protocols

- TCP/IP is a suite of protocols that includes TCP, IP (IPv4 and IPv6), UDP, ARP, and many others.

- TCP operates at the Transport layer of the OSI model and provides reliable data delivery services.

- UDP is an unreliable, connectionless protocol, meaning it does not guarantee delivery of data, and no connection is established by UDP before data is transmitted.

- IP belongs to the Network layer of the OSI model. It specifies where data should be delivered, identifying the data's source and destination IP addresses.

- ICMP is a Network layer, core protocol that reports on the success or failure of data delivery. It announces transmission failures to the sender, but does not correct errors it detects.

- ARP works in conjunction with IPv4 to discover the MAC address of a node on the local network and to maintain a database that maps local IP addresses to MAC addresses.

- Ethernet is a Data Link layer standard that is adaptable, capable of running on a variety of network media, and offers excellent throughput at a reasonable cost.

Routers and How They Work

- A router joins two or more networks and passes packets from one network to another. Routers are responsible for determining the next network to which a packet should be forwarded on its way to its destination.

- A Layer 3 switch is a switch that is capable of interpreting Layer 3 data and works much like a router. Layer 4 switches also exist and are capable of interpreting Layer 4 data.

- A router relies on its routing table to identify which network a host belongs to and which of the router's interfaces points toward the best next hop to reach that network.

- Routing paths are determined by static routing, which are routes configured by a network administrator, or dynamic routing, which are routes automatically calculated by the router to provide the best path between two networks.

- The `route` command allows you to view a host's routing table.

- Routers use routing metrics to determine the best route for messages to take across networks. This is one of the most valued and sophisticated functions performed by a router.

- To communicate with each other, routers use routing protocols that are similar to scouting parties, exploring unknown terrain and collecting data about current network status.

- Interior gateway protocols are used by core routers and edge routers within an autonomous system, while exterior gateway protocols communicate between autonomous systems.

Troubleshooting Route Issues

- TCP/IP comes with a complete set of utilities to help you track down most TCP/IP-related problems without using expensive software or hardware to analyze traffic.
- Helpful TCP/IP utilities include ping, ipconfig, ifconfig, nslookup, dig, arp, route, netstat, tracert, traceroute, pathping, and tcpdump.
- When a router, switch, NIC, or other hardware goes down, your job as a network technician includes identifying the location of the hardware failure. Even on smaller networks, you might need some good detective work to determine exactly which device is causing problems.

Key Terms

For definitions of key terms, see the Glossary near the end of the book.

AD (administrative distance)

ARP (Address Resolution Protocol)

ARP table

AS (autonomous system)

best path

BGP (Border Gateway Protocol)

border router

checksum

collision

collision domain

convergence time

core router

CSMA/CD (Carrier Sense Multiple Access with Collision Detection)

default route

distance-vector routing protocol

dynamic ARP table entry

dynamic routing

edge router

EGP (exterior gateway protocol)

EIGRP (Enhanced Interior Gateway Routing Protocol)

Ethernet II

exterior router

gateway of last resort

hop

hop limit

hybrid routing protocol

IGP (interior gateway protocol)

interior router

internetwork

IS-IS (Intermediate System to Intermediate System)

jumbo frame

latency

Layer 3 switch

Layer 4 switch

link-state routing protocol

MTU (maximum transmission unit)

neighbor discovery

netstat

OSPF (Open Shortest Path First)

packet sniffer

pathping

probe

protocol analyzer

RIP (Routing Information Protocol)

RIPv2 (Routing Information Protocol version 2)

route command

routing cost

routing metric

routing protocol

routing table

spoofing

static ARP table entry

static routing

tcpdump

three-way handshake

traceroute

tracert

Review Questions

1. Which protocol's header would a Layer 4 device read and process?
   a. IP
   b. TCP
   c. ARP
   d. HTTP

2. What field in a TCP segment is used to determine if an arriving data unit exactly matches the data unit sent by the source?
   a. Source port
   b. Acknowledgment number
   c. DiffServ
   d. Checksum

3. At which OSI layer does IP operate?
   a. Application layer
   b. Transport layer
   c. Network layer
   d. Data Link layer

4. Which OSI layer is responsible for directing data from one LAN to another?
   a. Transport layer
   b. Network layer
   c. Data Link layer
   d. Physical layer

5. What kind of route is created when a network administrator configures a router to use a specific path between nodes?
   a. Trace route
   b. Static route
   c. Default route
   d. Best path

6. When a router can't determine a path to a message's destination, where does it send the message?
   a. Default gateway
   b. Routing table
   c. Administrative distance
   d. Gateway of last resort

7. A routing protocol's reliability and priority are rated by what measurement?
   a. Routing table
   b. MTU
   c. Latency
   d. AD

8. Which routing protocol does an exterior router use to collect data to build its routing tables?
   a. RIPv2
   b. BGP
   c. OSPF
   d. IP

9. What is the Internet standard MTU?
   a. 65,535 bytes
   b. 1,522 bytes
   c. 1,500 bytes
   d. 9,198 bytes

10. Which two protocols manage neighbor discovery processes on IPv4 networks?
    a. ICMP and ARP
    b. IPv4 and IPv6
    c. TCP and UDP
    d. BGP and OSPF

11. What three characteristics about TCP distinguish it from UDP?

12. What process is used to establish a TCP connection?

13. What is the difference between dynamic ARP table entries and static ARP table entries?

14. Which two fields in an Ethernet frame help synchronize device communications but are not counted toward the frame's size?

15. What four functions do all routers perform?

16. What database does a router consult before determining the most efficient path for delivering a message?

17. Give three examples of routing metrics used by routers to determine the best of various available routing paths.

18. List three IGPs (interior gateway protocols).

19. Which Linux utility provides output similar to Wireshark's?

20. Which protocol is supported by ICMPv6 to facilitate neighbor discovery on an IPv6 network?

Hands-On Projects

Project 4-1: Repair a Duplicate IP Address

ARP can be a valuable troubleshooting tool for discovering the identity of a machine whose IP address you know, or for identifying two machines assigned the same IP address. Let's see what happens when two devices on the network are assigned the same IP address. First you change the IP address of a local Windows machine to match an IP address of another device—in other words, you "break" the computer. Then you see how the arp command helps you diagnose the problem.

1. Open a Command Prompt window and enter the command **arp -a.** Your device's IP address is listed as the Interface address at the top of the list. Write down this IP address and the address of another device on the network.

2. Open the Network and Sharing Center, click **Change adapter settings,** right-click the active network connection, and click **Properties.** If necessary, enter an administrator password in the UAC box and click **Yes.**

3. Select Internet Protocol Version 4 (TCP/IPv4) and click **Properties.** Set the IP address to match the other device's IP address that you wrote down in Step 1. The system automatically assigns the Subnet mask, as shown in Figure 4-21. Click **OK,** press **Tab,** and then click **Close**.

4. Back at the command prompt, enter **ipconfig /all.**

5. Find the appropriate network connection and identify your computer's current IPv4 address. Has your computer identified the duplicate IP address problem yet? How do you know? Your computer might also have autoconfigured another IP address. If so, what address did your computer resort to?

6. In the window on the left side of Figure 4-22, you can see a warning that the IP address is a duplicate. The system also shows a preferred IPv4 address of 169.254.143.79, which is an APIPA address. How can you tell this is an APIPA address?

7. To confirm the duplication of IP addresses, enter the command **arp -a.** You can see in Figure 4-22 that the local computer's IPv4 address listed on the left matches another IP address in the ARP table on the right, and again you see the APIPA address assigned to the local interface. What are two ways to solve this problem?

8. Open the Internet Protocol Version 4 (TCP/IPv4) Properties dialog box again and select the option **Obtain an IP address automatically,** then click **OK.** Close the connection's

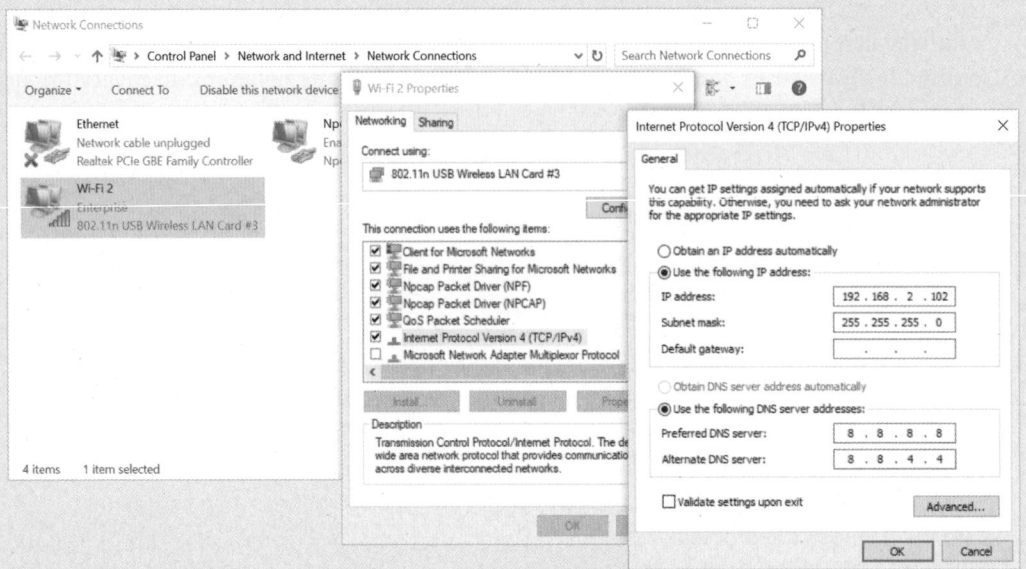

Figure 4-21   The subnet mask is assigned automatically

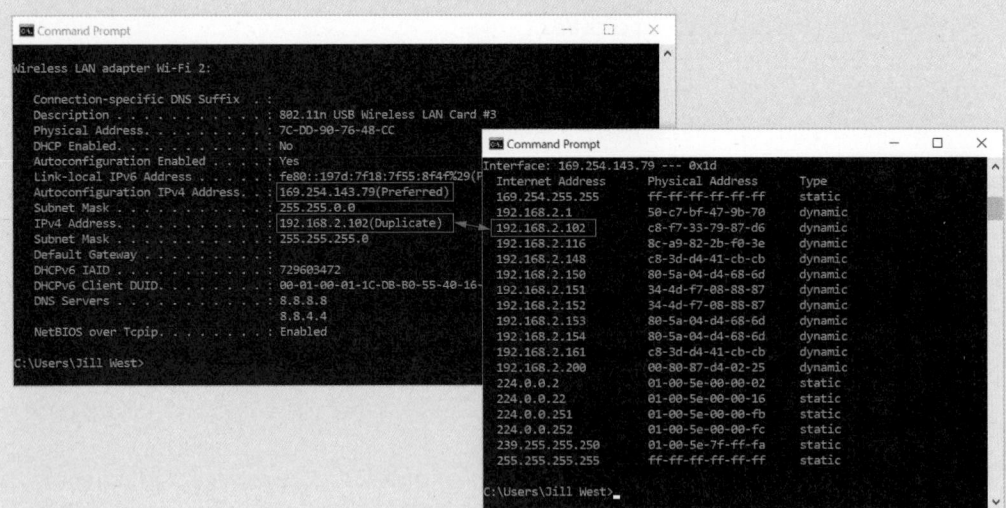

Figure 4-22   The computer automatically configured an APIPA address

properties dialog box, the Network Connections window, and the Network and Sharing Center window.

9. Run the `ipconfig` command or the `arp -a` command to confirm that a unique IP address has been assigned. What is the new IP address?

10. Close the Command Prompt window.

Project 4-2: Redirect Command Output to a Text File

Sometimes when you're using a command such as `pathping`, the sheer volume of output can be daunting to work with. There's no way to search through the output for specific information, and you can only expand the Command Prompt window so far. One solution to this problem is to redirect the command output to a text file where you can search the text, copy and paste text, and save the output for future reference. To accomplish this feat, you'll need to add a redirection operator to the command whose output you want to export to a text file. Complete the following steps:

1. First, try this simple command:

   `ipconfig > ipconfigtest.txt`

   In this case, you have run the `ipconfig` command and redirected the output to a text file named ipconfigtest.txt. By default, the file is saved to the current default folder, for example, C:\Users\JillWest.

2. To specify the location of the file when you create it, add the path to the file in the command line. For example, to save the file to the desktop, use the following command (substitute the correct file path to your desktop):

   `ipconfig > C:\Users\`*`Username`*`\Desktop\ipconfigtest.txt`

3. If you already have a file on the desktop by that name, the file will be overwritten with the new data. What if you would rather append data to an existing file? In this case, use the >> operator. Enter this command (substitute the correct file path to your desktop):

   `ipconfig >> C:\Users\`*`Username`*`\Desktop\ipconfigtest.txt`

   Now the new output will appear at the end of the existing file, and all the data is preserved within this single file. This option is useful when collecting data from repeated tests or from multiple computers, where you want all the data to converge into a single file for future analysis.

4. Where do command parameters fit when redirecting output? Let's use the `netstat` command to show the IP address and port of each TCP and UDP connection on the computer. In the following command, substitute the correct file path to your desktop to output the data to a new file:

   `netstat -an > C:\Users\`*`Username`*`\Desktop\connections.txt`

   Notice that any parameters you want to use should be inserted after the command itself and before the redirection operator.

5. Include a space in the filename by putting quotation marks around the entire filename *and* location:

   `ping 8.8.8.8 > "C:\Users\`*`Username`*`\Desktop\find google.txt"`

   What do you do if you've already run a command, and you desperately want to save some of the data from the output? In Windows 10, you can perform a normal copy-and-paste operation in the Command Prompt window, but you first must instruct Command Prompt to accept keyboard shortcut commands. Complete these steps to see how this works:

6. Run the command `ipconfig /all.` The new output populates your Command Prompt window.
7. Right-click the Command Prompt window title bar, point to **Edit**, and click **Mark.**
8. Scroll to where you want to begin collecting the copy. Press and hold the mouse button, drag the mouse to highlight all the text you want to copy, and release. Then press **Enter**. The text is copied to the Clipboard.
9. Go to any text editor program and paste the selected text into your document.

Project 4-3: Create a Routing Table Entry in Windows

A computer's routing table can be viewed and modified using the `route` command at an elevated Command Prompt. Complete the following steps:

1. In this chapter, you used both `route print` and `netstat -r` to view the routing table. Because you'll need the `route` command to modify the routing table, open an elevated Command Prompt window and enter the **route print** command to view the routing table.

   The list of interfaces on your computer should look familiar—you saw these when you ran `ipconfig` in Chapter 3. Several of the IPv4 routes on your routing table should look familiar as well. 127.0.0.1 is your loopback address, and the surrounding 127.x.y.z routes refer to reserved addresses in that domain. In Figure 4-23, you can see that this computer's IP address is 192.168.2.170. You can also see surrounding reserved addresses for that private domain. 224.0.0.0 is reserved for multicasting, and 255.255.255.255 for certain broadcast messages.

   In the IPv6 section on your computer, ::1/128 is the loopback address. FE80::/64 is the link local address, and an FE80 address is the IPv6 address assigned to your computer. FF00::/8 is the multicast address.

2. Now add an entry to the routing table that will reroute messages destined for the private network 172.16.50.0/24 to another internal IP address, 192.168.10.8. Enter the following command:

   `route add 172.16.50.0 mask 255.255.255.0 192.168.10.8`

3. Now all messages generated by this routing table's local host and addressed to an IP address in the network 172.16.50.0/24 will instead be routed to the host at 192.168.10.8. You can see in Figure 4-24 where this new entry has been inserted. Run **route print** again on your computer to confirm your entry was recorded.

4. Windows resets its routing table during reboot, so add the **–p** parameter after the word `route` in the command from Step 2 to make the static route persist beyond reboot. (See Figure 4-25.)

5. Delete the route you just added with the following command:

   `route delete 172.16.50.0`

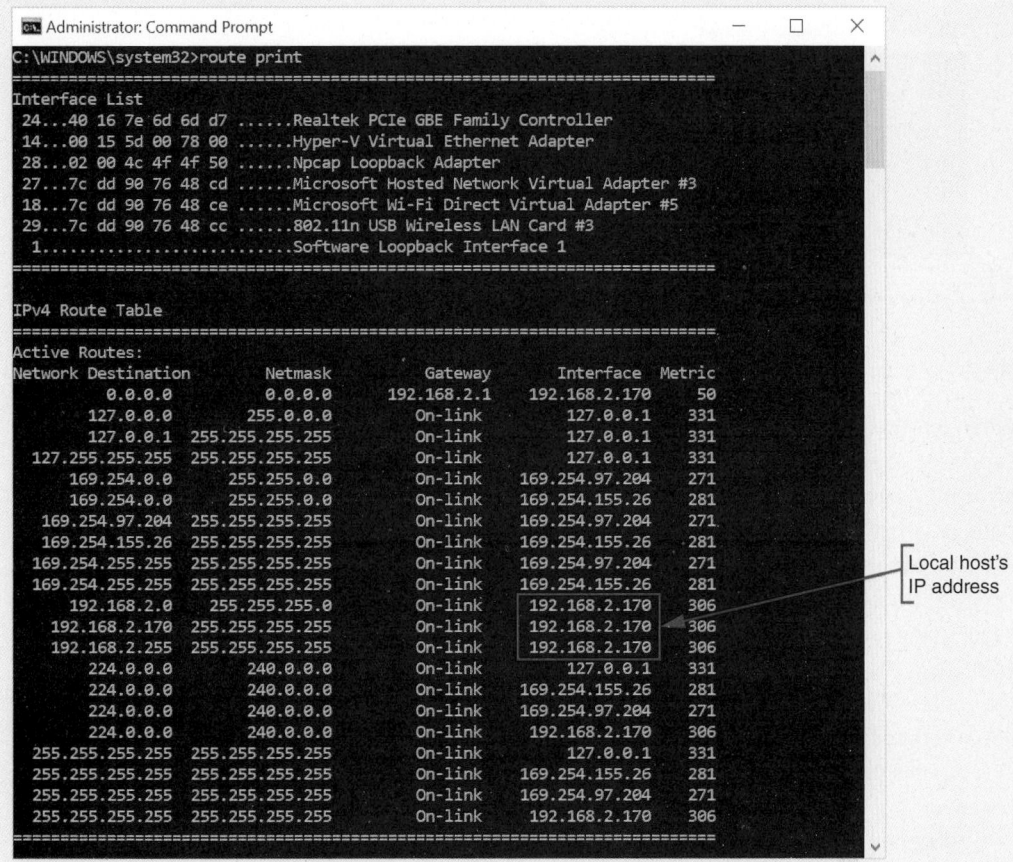

```
Administrator: Command Prompt                                              —    □    ✕

C:\WINDOWS\system32>route print
===========================================================================
Interface List
 24...40 16 7e 6d 6d d7 ......Realtek PCIe GBE Family Controller
 14...00 15 5d 00 78 00 ......Hyper-V Virtual Ethernet Adapter
 28...02 00 4c 4f 4f 50 ......Npcap Loopback Adapter
 27...7c dd 90 76 48 cd ......Microsoft Hosted Network Virtual Adapter #3
 18...7c dd 90 76 48 ce ......Microsoft Wi-Fi Direct Virtual Adapter #5
 29...7c dd 90 76 48 cc ......802.11n USB Wireless LAN Card #3
  1...........................Software Loopback Interface 1
===========================================================================

IPv4 Route Table
===========================================================================
Active Routes:
Network Destination        Netmask          Gateway       Interface  Metric
          0.0.0.0          0.0.0.0      192.168.2.1   192.168.2.170     50
        127.0.0.0        255.0.0.0         On-link         127.0.0.1    331
        127.0.0.1  255.255.255.255         On-link         127.0.0.1    331
  127.255.255.255  255.255.255.255         On-link         127.0.0.1    331
      169.254.0.0      255.255.0.0         On-link    169.254.97.204    271
      169.254.0.0      255.255.0.0         On-link    169.254.155.26    281
   169.254.97.204  255.255.255.255         On-link    169.254.97.204    271
   169.254.155.26  255.255.255.255         On-link    169.254.155.26    281
  169.254.255.255  255.255.255.255         On-link    169.254.97.204    271
  169.254.255.255  255.255.255.255         On-link    169.254.155.26    281
      192.168.2.0    255.255.255.0         On-link     192.168.2.170    306
    192.168.2.170  255.255.255.255         On-link     192.168.2.170    306
    192.168.2.255  255.255.255.255         On-link     192.168.2.170    306
        224.0.0.0        240.0.0.0         On-link         127.0.0.1    331
        224.0.0.0        240.0.0.0         On-link    169.254.155.26    281
        224.0.0.0        240.0.0.0         On-link    169.254.97.204    271
        224.0.0.0        240.0.0.0         On-link     192.168.2.170    306
  255.255.255.255  255.255.255.255         On-link         127.0.0.1    331
  255.255.255.255  255.255.255.255         On-link    169.254.155.26    281
  255.255.255.255  255.255.255.255         On-link    169.254.97.204    271
  255.255.255.255  255.255.255.255         On-link     192.168.2.170    306
===========================================================================
```

Local host's IP address

Figure 4-23   Several of the active routes on this computer involve its own IP address

```
IPv4 Route Table
===========================================================================
Active Routes:
Network Destination        Netmask          Gateway       Interface  Metric
          0.0.0.0          0.0.0.0      192.168.2.1   192.168.2.170     50
        127.0.0.0        255.0.0.0         On-link         127.0.0.1    331
        127.0.0.1  255.255.255.255         On-link         127.0.0.1    331
  127.255.255.255  255.255.255.255         On-link         127.0.0.1    331
      169.254.0.0      255.255.0.0         On-link    169.254.97.204    271
      169.254.0.0      255.255.0.0         On-link    169.254.155.26    281
   169.254.97.204  255.255.255.255         On-link    169.254.97.204    271
   169.254.155.26  255.255.255.255         On-link    169.254.155.26    281
  169.254.255.255  255.255.255.255         On-link    169.254.97.204    271
  169.254.255.255  255.255.255.255         On-link    169.254.155.26    281
      172.16.50.0    255.255.255.0     192.168.10.8    192.168.2.170     51
      192.168.2.0    255.255.255.0         On-link     192.168.2.170    306
    192.168.2.170  255.255.255.255         On-link     192.168.2.170    306
```

Figure 4-24   The static route has been successfully added

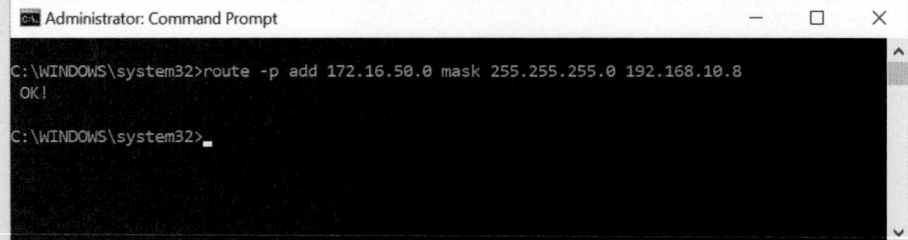

Figure 4-25   The -p parameter will ensure this route persists through reboot

Project 4-4: Create a Path MTU Black Hole

When a router receives a message that is too large for the next segment's MTU, the router is supposed to respond with an ICMP error message to the sender. Sometimes, though, these error messages are not returned correctly. This can result in an MTU black hole along the path, where messages are being lost for no apparent reason.

You can use the ping command to determine the largest size message that can successfully traverse a path to its destination by adjusting the buffer size of the ICMP echo message. Using too large of a buffer will prevent the messages from returning in response to your ping. Start with a smaller buffer and work your way up to determine the largest MTU the route can handle. The ping parameters needed in Windows are –f (do not fragment the IP packet) and –l (packet or buffer size is specified following the lowercase L).

What is the largest MTU that can be used to reach the *cengage.com* host from your computer without creating an MTU black hole? To find out, complete the following steps:

1. Ping *cengage.com* using an IP packet size of 1024.
2. What is the ping command you used?
3. Keep increasing the packet size until the packet does not return. Do not allow the packet to be fragmented.
4. What is the largest MTU that gets through?
5. What error message appears when an MTU error occurs?

Capstone Projects

Capstone Project 4-1: Set Up Ubuntu Server in a VM

In the Chapter 1 Capstone Projects, you created a virtual machine using Oracle VirtualBox or Windows 10 Client Hyper-V. In Chapter 2, Capstone Project 2-1, you added a second VM, this one running Ubuntu Desktop. In this Capstone Project, you create a third VM and install Ubuntu Server in the VM. You also learn how to use some Linux commands. In Chapter 5, you'll set up an FTP server in Ubuntu Server and make FTP services available to other computers in your network.

Using the same computer that you used in Capstone Project 1-1 or 1-2 (which should have Oracle VirtualBox or Client Hyper-V installed), follow these steps:

1. Go to **ubuntu.com/server** and download the Ubuntu Server OS to your hard drive. If you're given the choice of multiple versions, choose the newest version. The file that downloads is an ISO file.

2. Open the Oracle VM VirtualBox Manager or Hyper-V Manager. Following the directions in the Chapter 1 Capstone Projects, create a new VM named VM3, VM_Lab_C, or something similar. Note that if you're using Hyper-V Manager and you use the Quick Create option, uncheck the *This virtual machine will run Windows* box before clicking *Change installation source*. Mount the ISO file that contains the Ubuntu Server download to a virtual DVD in your VM.

Note

Ubuntu Server is only available as a 64-bit OS. To install a 64-bit guest OS in a VM, the host OS must also be 64-bit.

---

3. Start the VM and install Ubuntu Server, accepting all default settings. Be sure to record your Ubuntu hostname, username, and password in your LastPass account. When given the option, decline to install any extra software bundled with the OS other than standard system utilities.

4. After you restart the VM, Ubuntu Server launches, which does not have a GUI interface. You should see the shell command interface, as shown in Figure 4-26.

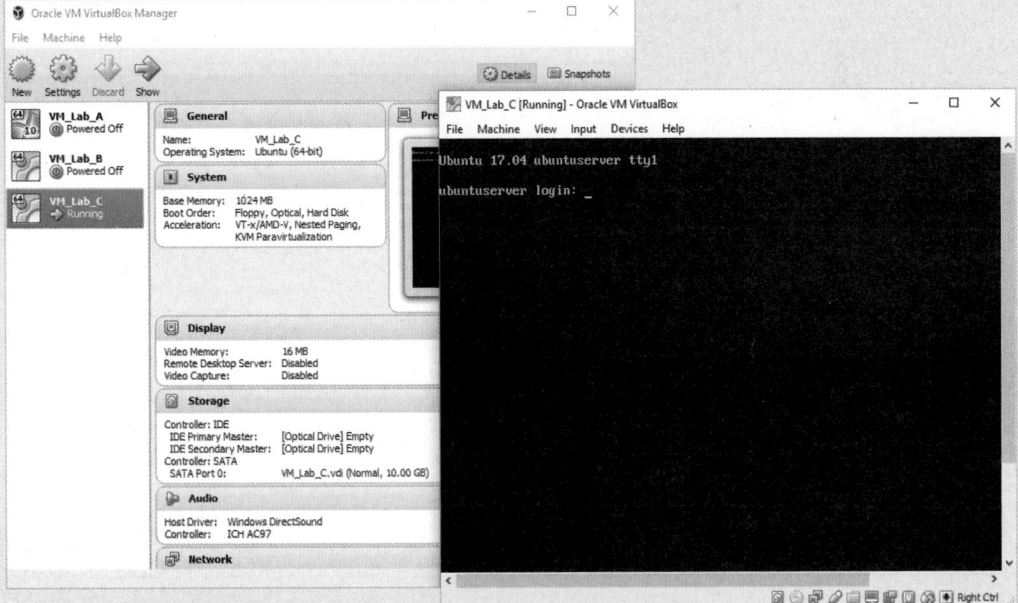

Figure 4-26   Ubuntu Server is installed in a VM in VirtualBox

Source: Canonical Group Limited and Oracle Corporation

5. First, enter your username and press **Enter.** Then enter your password and press **Enter.** You're now logged in to your Ubuntu Server. The shell shows the shell prompt, which usually includes your username and current directory followed by a $.

6. Practice using Ubuntu Server by entering in order each of the commands listed in Table 4-16. As you do so, you'll examine the directory structure, create a new directory, and put a blank file in it.

Table 4-16   Practice Linux commands in Ubuntu Server

Step	Command	Description
1	pwd	Displays the full path to the current directory. When you first log in to a system, that directory is /home/*username*.
2	mkdir mydir	Creates a directory named mydir. The directory is created in the current directory. You must have permission to edit the current directory.
3	dir	Lists files and directories in the current directory. In Linux, a directory is treated more like a file than a Windows directory.
4	cd mydir	Goes to the directory you just created in the /home/*username* directory.
5	touch myfile	Creates a blank file named myfile in the current directory.
6	ls	Similar to dir, lists current directory contents.
7	cd ..	Moves up one level in the directory tree.
8	cd /etc	Changes directory to the /etc directory, where text files are kept for configuring installed programs.
9	ls	Examines the contents of the /etc directory.
10	cd /home	Changes directory to the /home directory.
11	ping 127.0.0.1	Pings the loopback address. Pinging continues until you stop it by pressing CTRL+C.
12	**CTRL+C**	Breaks out of a command or process; use it to recover after entering a wrong command or to stop a command that requires you manually halt the output.
13	ifconfig	Displays TCP/IP configuration data.
14	man ifconfig	Displays the page from the Linux Manual about the ifconfig command.
15	df	Displays the amount of free space on your hard drive.
16	exit	Logs out; the login shell prompt appears, where you can log in again. Enter your username and password to log in again.
17	sudo poweroff	Shuts down the VM. You'll need to enter your password and then the system shuts down.

7. Add the new VM's information to your VMclients page in your wiki. On the Virtualization:VMclients page, click **Edit** at the bottom of the page, and add the new VM to your list. Include the chapter number, hypervisor used, VM computer name, and VM operating system. Also note any additional information that you might find helpful when you return to this VM in the future such as how to view the Linux Manual or how to shut down the system. When you're finished, click **Save**.

Capstone Project 4-2: Install and Use Wireshark

Wireshark is a free, open-source network protocol analyzer that can help demystify network messages for you and help make the OSI model easier to understand. For some students, using Wireshark for the first time can be an epiphany experience. It allows you to study the OSI layers, all the information that is added to every message, and all the messages that have to go back and forth just to bring up a web page or simply to connect to the network. It all becomes much more real when you see how many messages Wireshark collects during even a short capture.

   We will install Wireshark in this project and take a first look at how it works. In a later chapter, we'll dig deeper into Wireshark's capabilities.

1. Open a browser and go to **wireshark.org**. Download and install the current stable release, using the appropriate version for your OS. At the time of this writing, the current stable release is 2.4.2. If you're using the same computer you used for Chapter 2, Project 2-4, the Wireshark installer should recognize that you already have Npcap installed and will not offer to install WinPcap. If you're using a different computer, accept the WinPcap option and complete the WinPcap installation when prompted. In the Wireshark setup window, you do *not* need USBPcap. Reboot your computer to complete the Wireshark installation.

> **Note** 📎
>
> WinPcap is a Windows service that does not come standard in Windows, but is required to capture live network data.

2. When installation is complete, open **Wireshark**. Note that while the Wireshark Legacy app might also have been installed on your computer, we'll use the Wireshark app for this and later projects.

3. In the Wireshark Network Analyzer window, select your network interface from the list. Then click the shark-fin icon to start the capture, as shown in Figure 4-27.

4. While the capture is running, open your browser and navigate to **cengage.com**. Then open a Command Prompt window and enter `ping 8.8.8.8`. Click the red box on the command ribbon to stop the capture.

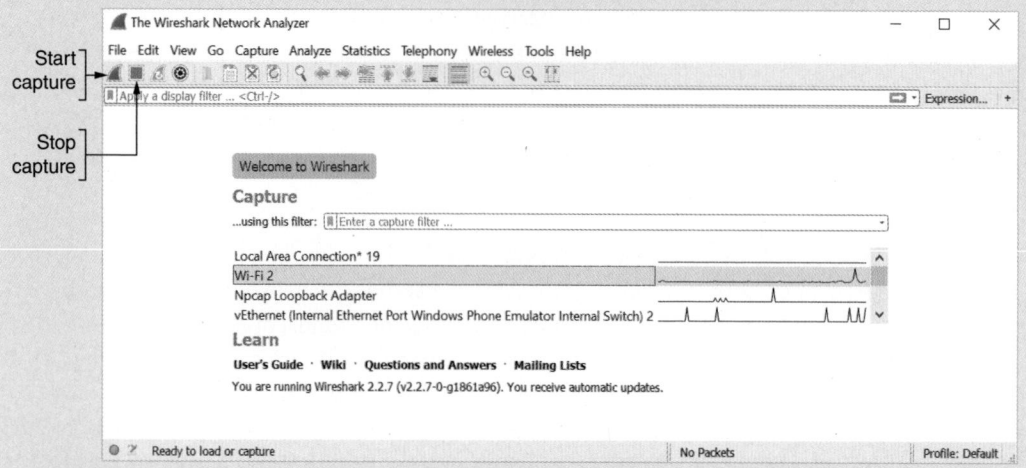

Figure 4-27   The Wireshark Network Analyzer window
Source: The Wireshark Foundation

Take a look at some of the items you've captured. You can adjust the pane sizes by grabbing a border between them and dragging. Expand the top pane so you can see more of the captured messages at one time. Let's start to decode this blur of numbers and letters.

5. Notice the column headers along the top of the capture, as shown in Figure 4-28. Of particular interest are the Source and Destination columns, the Protocol column, and the Info column. Find a UDP message that has an IPv4 Source address and click on it. In the middle pane, click on each line to expand that layer's information. What pieces of information stand out to you? Which device on your network do you think sent this message, and which device(s) received it?

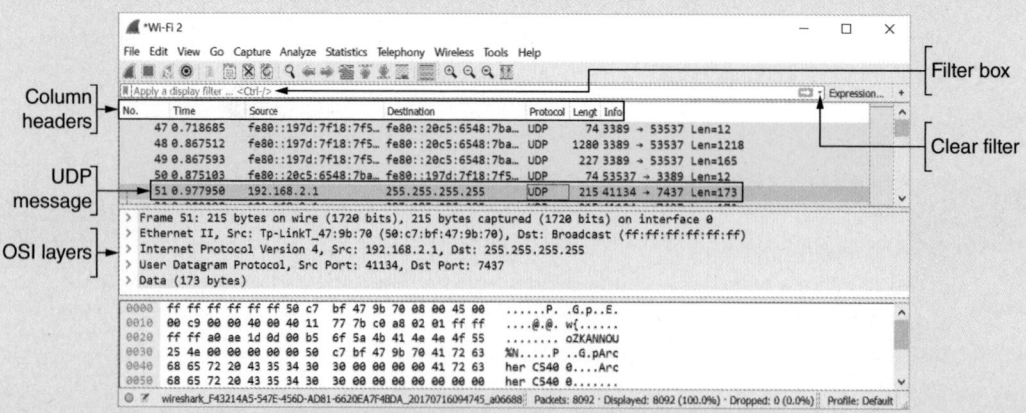

Figure 4-28   A Wireshark capture
Source: The Wireshark Foundation

Color highlighting can help you easily spot different protocols. Notice in Figure 4-29 that TCP messages are a light lavender color, ARP messages are a yellowish color, and DNS messages are a light bluish color. You can see the protocol names in the Protocol column.

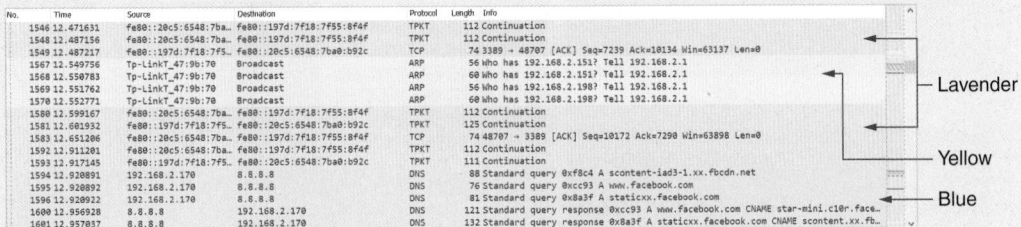

Figure 4-29   Different highlight colors correspond to different protocols
Source: The Wireshark Foundation

> **Note**
>
> The TPKT (ThroughPacket) protocol listed in Figure 4-29 is another kind of Transport layer protocol, one which piggybacks on TCP. TPKT is often used by RDP (Remote Desktop Protocol). It makes sense to see TPKT messages in this Wireshark capture because we ran Wireshark through a remote desktop connection on a lab computer across the room.

6. To see a list of currently assigned highlight colors and to adjust these assignments, on the main toolbar, click **View** and then click **Coloring Rules**. Here, you can change the priority for matching protocols within a message to colors in the output pane (because more than one protocol is used in each message), and you can assign colors that are easier to spot. In Figure 4-30, the background color for ICMP is changed to a bright green. When you're happy with your color selections, click **OK**.

7. To filter for a particular kind of message in your capture, type the name of the protocol in the Filter box (identified in Figure 4-28). Figure 4-31 shows a filter for ICMP messages, which are currently highlighted in bright green. These ICMP messages were generated when pinging another host on the network. Try filtering for other protocols discussed in this and earlier chapters, and see how many different types you can find in your capture. Click the red X to clear filters between searches. Which protocols did you find?

8. To compare which OSI layers are represented by each of these protocols, apply a slightly more complicated filter where you can see both HTTP messages and ICMP messages in the same search. Enter the following phrase into the Filter box: **http or icmp**.

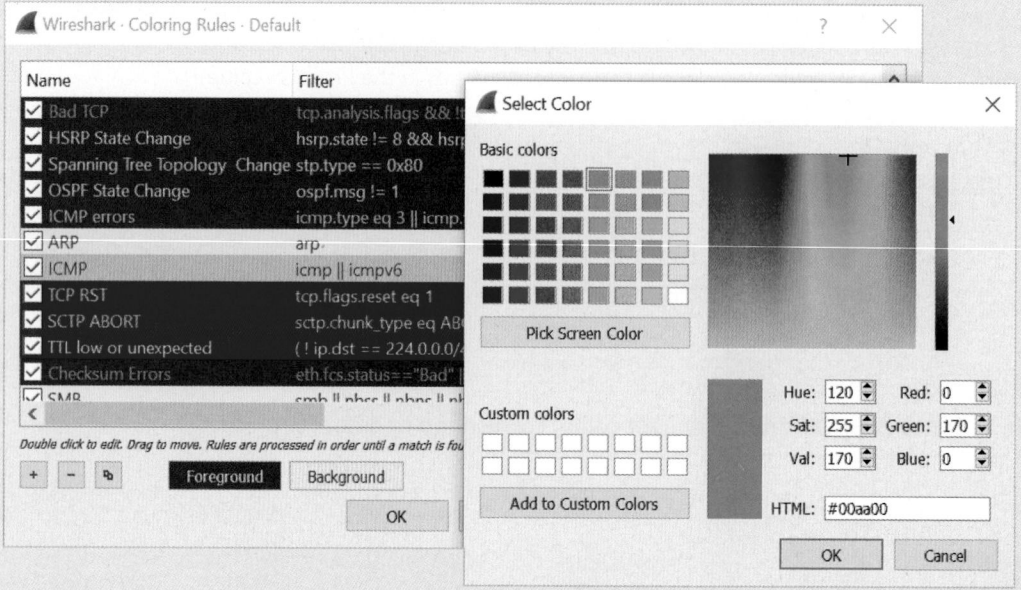

Figure 4-30   Choose colors that are easier to spot

Source: The Wireshark Foundation

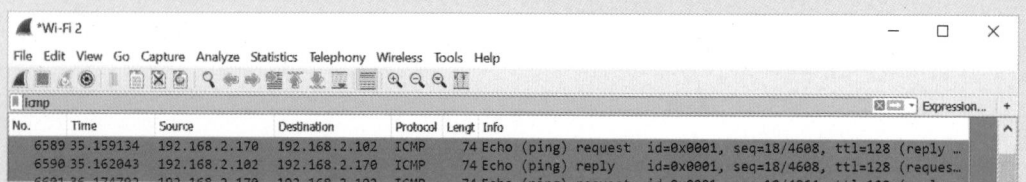

Figure 4-31   Use a filter to narrow your search

Source: The Wireshark Foundation

9. Click on an ICMP message and count the layers of information available in the middle pane. In Figure 4-32, there are four layers of information, which correspond to Layer 2 (Frame and Ethernet II) and Layer 3 (Internet Protocol Version 4 and Internet Control Message Protocol).

10. Examine an HTTP message. Figure 4-33 shows five layers of information in the middle pane. This time, Layer 7 (Hypertext Transfer Protocol) and Layer 4 (Transmission Control Protocol) are represented, in addition to Layer 3 (Internet Protocol Version 4) and Layer 2 (Ethernet II and Frame).

11. Recall that TCP is a connection-oriented protocol. You can filter a capture to follow a TCP stream so you can see how these messages go back and forth for a single session. Clear your filter box, and then find a TCP message. Right-click it, point to **Follow**, and click **TCP Stream** (see Figure 4-34). Next, click **Close** to close the Follow TCP Stream window and notice that Wireshark has filtered the capture for this stream's messages.

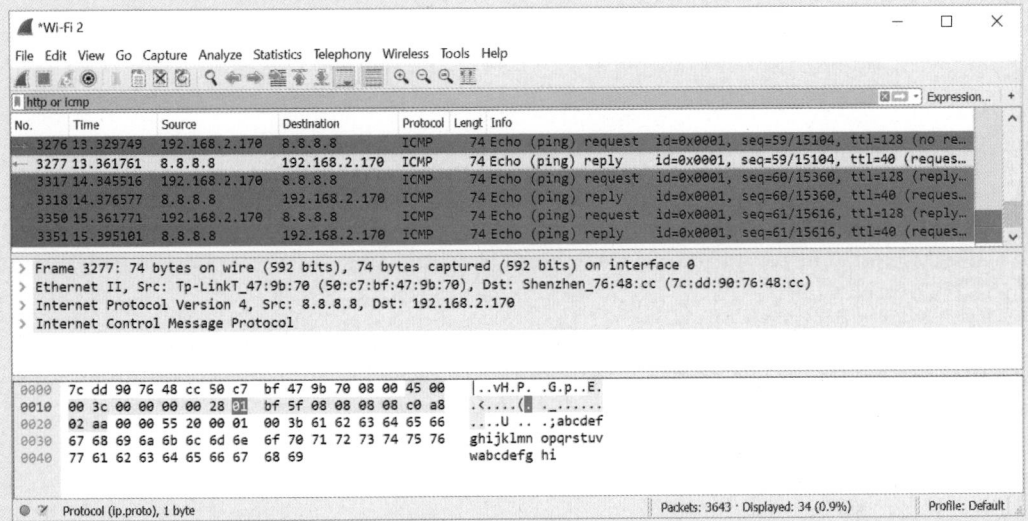

Figure 4-32   Use the middle pane to dig into each layer's headers

Source: The Wireshark Foundation

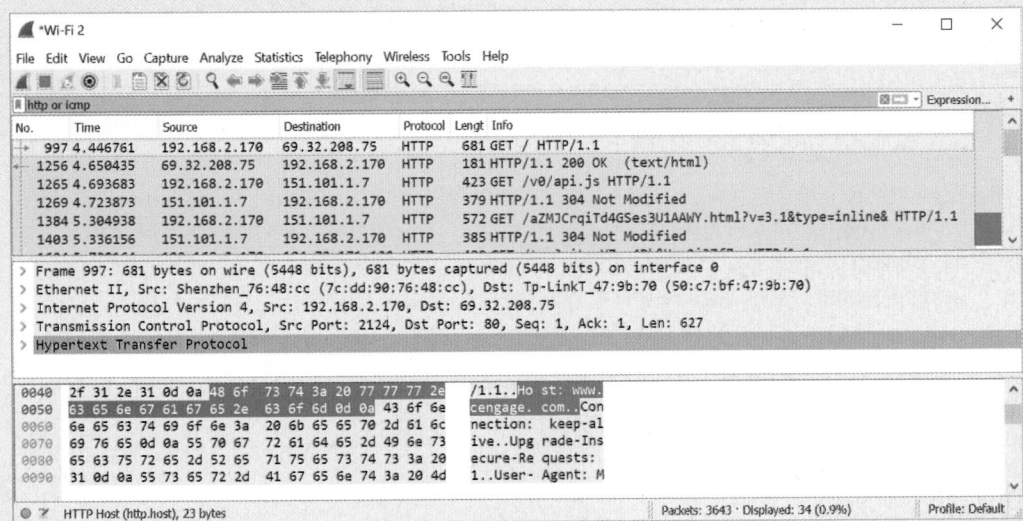

Figure 4-33   This HTTP message uses TCP at the Transport layer to contact a Cengage web server

Source: The Wireshark Foundation

12. In the Info column, you can see both SYN and ACK flags, which you learned about in this chapter. What is the purpose of these messages? Scroll to the bottom of the TCP stream. What flag indicates the stream is ending?

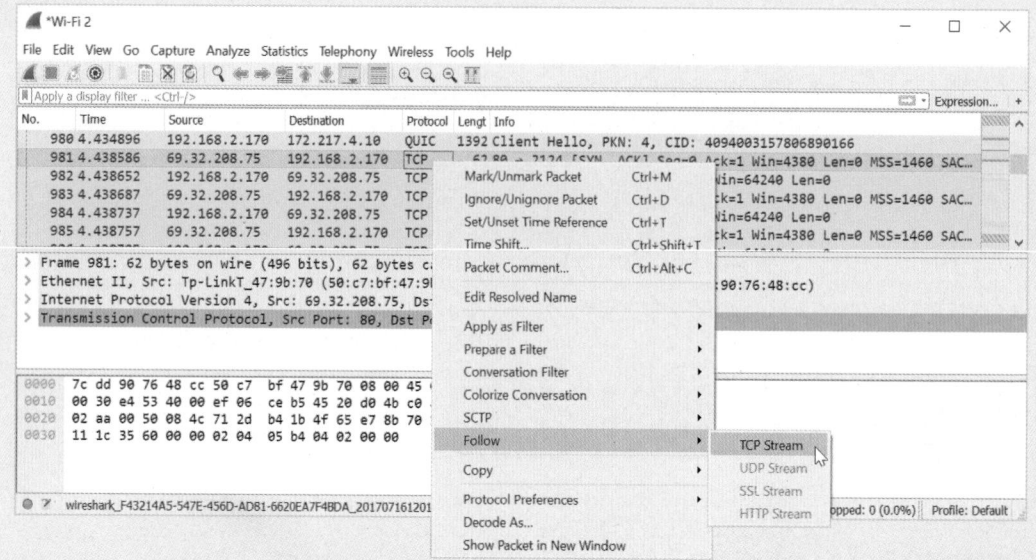

Figure 4-34   Follow the conversation in a TCP stream

Source: The Wireshark Foundation

13. Click on any message that includes a Source or Destination MAC address on the Ethernet II line of output in the middle pane. What protocol is listed for the message you selected? Was Wireshark able to resolve the name of the manufacturer for this device? If so, what is it?

14. In your wiki, add a new page titled **Applications:Wireshark**. Indicate the chapter and project number for this installation, the computer you used for this project, a brief description of what you learned, and any other information you might find helpful when using Wireshark later. We'll return to Wireshark in a later chapter.

## CHAPTER 5

NETWORK CABLING

After reading this chapter and completing the exercises, you will be able to:

Explain basic data transmission concepts, including throughput, bandwidth, multiplexing, and common transmission flaws

Identify and describe the physical characteristics and official standards of coaxial cable, twisted-pair cable, and fiber-optic cable, and their related connectors

Compare the benefits and limitations of various networking media

Select and use the appropriate tool to troubleshoot common cable problems

On the Job

I was asked to consult on a network problem concerning slow speeds and dead network jacks. The business was located in a building that was configured for two rental spaces with a single entrance. After entering the front door, I encountered a door to one set of offices on the right and the same on the left. Straight ahead was a door to the mechanical rooms.

When I removed the wall plates, I found that the installer had untwisted the pairs by at least one inch on all of the jacks. On some of the nonfunctional wall jacks, the pairs were untwisted three inches or more and stuffed haphazardly into the wall box.

The next mystery was the single 12-port switch, which didn't make sense because I was now able to achieve link on 19 wall sockets. This meant that it was time to start removing ceiling tiles and following wires. Fortunately, all of the wires came together in a bundle that exited into the ceiling above the entryway. From there, most of the bundle turned and went toward the mechanical room, where the fiber-modem and 12-port switch were located. Unfortunately, a few of the wires went toward the other rental space. The other set of offices was not currently rented, and so was not accessible without contacting the landlord. The landlord was hesitant to give access to the other space. He insisted that the problem could not have anything to do with the wiring in that part of the building because his nephew, who was an electrician, had done all of the network cabling in the building. Instead, the landlord insisted that the tenants must have messed up the wall jacks on their side.

After tracing cable after cable above the suspended ceiling, I finally found another network switch hiding on top of one of the ceiling tiles. All of the cable terminations had around two inches of the pairs untwisted to make it easier to install the RJ-45 terminals.

I reconnected all the wall jacks and replaced all of the terminals on the cables at the hidden switch. All of the client's wall jacks were now able to achieve link and connect, transferring at 100 Mbps full-duplex.

Todd Fisher Wallin
Operations Coordinator, Driftless Community Radio

Just as highways and streets provide the foundation for automobile travel, networking media provides the physical foundation for data transmission. Networking media is the physical or atmospheric paths that signals follow. The first networks used thick coaxial cables. Today's local area networks use copper or fiber cabling, or wireless transmissions. Wireless networking is covered in a later chapter.

Networks are always evolving to meet the demand for greater speed, versatility, and reliability, and networking media technologies change rapidly. Understanding the characteristics of various networking media is critical to designing and troubleshooting networks. You also need to know how data is transmitted over these various media types. This chapter discusses the details of data transmission and physical networking media. You'll learn what it takes to make data transmission dependable and how to correct some common transmission problems.

Transmission Basics

 **Certification**

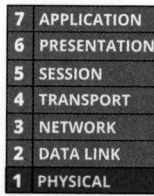

7	APPLICATION
6	PRESENTATION
5	SESSION
4	TRANSPORT
3	NETWORK
2	DATA LINK
1	PHYSICAL

3.3 Explain common scanning, monitoring, and patching processes and summarize their expected outputs.

5.3 Given a scenario, troubleshoot common wired connectivity and performance issues.

The transmission techniques in use on today's networks are complex and varied. Through minor tweaks and major renovations, network administrators constantly seek ways to maximize the efficiency of their networks. Let's first look at what measurements indicate network efficiency, and then we'll explore obstacles to good network performance. Optimizing network performance is discussed in later chapters.

Throughput and Bandwidth

A networking professional often needs to measure two transmission characteristics:

- *bandwidth*—The amount of data that could theoretically be transmitted during a given period of time. In an analogy, the bandwidth of a three-lane freeway is the number of vehicles that can pass a checkpoint in one minute when traffic is bumper-to-bumper and traveling at the maximum speed limit. In practice, that bandwidth never happens. Still, we could increase potential bandwidth by adding more lanes to the freeway. At the same time, consider that adding too many lanes for the amount of anticipated traffic, so that some lanes are never used, would be a waste of resources.
- *throughput (also called payload rate or effective data rate)*—The measure of how much data is actually transmitted during a given period of time. In our analogy, throughput measures the actual traffic on the three-lane freeway that passes in one minute. Using all the available bandwidth results in more accidents and traffic jams than if bandwidth exceeds actual throughput by a little. However, this beneficial effect is limited—providing a *lot* more potential bandwidth than actual throughput does not achieve additional improvement in performance unless you need to account for regular spikes in traffic.

In networking, throughput and bandwidth are commonly expressed as bits transmitted per second, called **bit rate**, such as 1000 bits per second or 1 Kbps (1 kilobit per second). Table 5-1 summarizes the terminology and abbreviations used when discussing different throughput and bandwidth amounts.

Table 5-1   Throughput and bandwidth measures

Quantity	Prefix	Abbreviation
1 bit per second	n/a	1 bps = 1 bit per second
1000 bits per second	kilo	1 Kbps = 1 kilobit per second
1,000,000 bits per second	mega	1 Mbps = 1 megabit per second
1,000,000,000 bits per second	giga	1 Gbps = 1 gigabit per second
1,000,000,000,000 bits per second	tera	1 Tbps = 1 terabit per second

As an example, a low-cost residential broadband Internet connection might be rated for a maximum bandwidth of 3 Mbps, but actual throughput is usually lower. This explains why providers often advertise "*up to* 3 Mbps." A LAN that achieves a throughput of 1 Gbps might require a bandwidth transmission rate of 1.25 Gbps because of the overhead in Ethernet frames. Applications that require significant throughput include videoconferencing and telephone signaling. By contrast, instant messaging and email, for example, require much less throughput.

Note 🖉

Be careful not to confuse bits and bytes when discussing throughput:

- Data storage quantities are typically expressed in multiples of bytes.
- Data transmission quantities (in other words, throughput) are more commonly expressed in multiples of bits per second.

When representing different data quantities, a small *b* represents bits, whereas a capital *B* represents bytes. To put this into context, a dial-up modem might transmit data at 56.6 Kbps (kilobits per second), while a data file might be 56 KB (kilobytes) in size.

Another difference between data storage and data throughput measures is that with data storage, the prefix *kilo* means 2 to the 10th power, or 1024, not 1000.

Transmission Flaws

On a busy network, why is actual throughput less than the potential bandwidth of the network? Three factors that can degrade network performance are noise, attenuation, and latency.

Noise

Noise can degrade or distort a signal and, on a network, is measured in dB (decibels). Two common sources of noise are:

- *EMI (electromagnetic interference)*—Caused by motors, power lines, televisions, copiers, fluorescent lights, microwave ovens, manufacturing machinery, and other sources of electrical activity (including a severe thunderstorm). One type of EMI is **RFI (radio frequency interference)**, or electromagnetic interference caused by radio waves. (Often, you'll see EMI referred to as EMI/RFI.) Strong broadcast signals from radio or TV antennas can generate RFI.
- *crosstalk*—Occurs when a signal traveling on one wire or cable infringes on the signal traveling over an adjacent wire or cable, as shown in Figure 5-1.

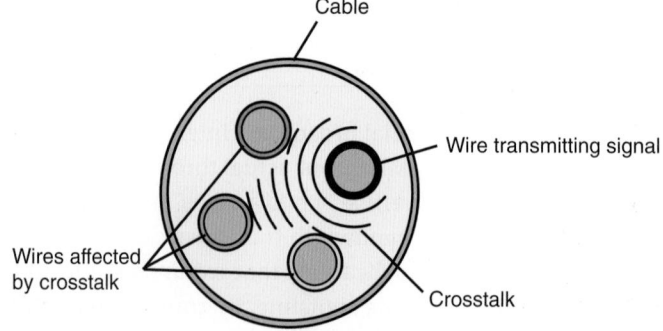

Figure 5-1   Crosstalk between wires in a cable

The resulting noise, or crosstalk, is equal to a portion of the second line's signal. If you've ever been on a traditional, landline phone and heard the conversation on a second line in the background, you have heard the effects of crosstalk.

In data networks, crosstalk can be extreme enough to prevent the accurate delivery of data. Three common types are:

- *alien crosstalk*—Crosstalk that occurs between two cables
- *NEXT (near end crosstalk)*—Crosstalk that occurs between wire pairs near the source of a signal
- *FEXT (far end crosstalk)*—Crosstalk measured at the far end of the cable from the signal source

In every signal, a certain amount of noise is unavoidable. However, engineers have devised a number of ways to limit the potential for noise to degrade a signal. One way is simply to ensure that the strength of the signal exceeds the strength of the noise. Proper cable design and installation are also critical for protecting against noise effects.

Attenuation

Another transmission flaw is **attenuation**, or the loss of a signal's strength as it travels away from its source. Just as your voice becomes fainter as it travels farther, so do signals fade with distance. To compensate for attenuation, signals are boosted en route using a **repeater**, which regenerates a digital signal in its original form without the noise it might have previously accumulated. Figure 5-2 shows a digital signal distorted by noise and then regenerated by a repeater. A switch on an Ethernet network works as a multiport repeater, as the bits transmitted "start over" at each port on the switch.

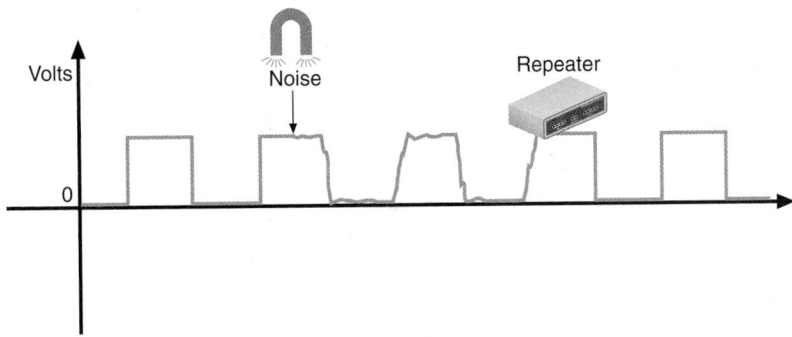

Figure 5-2   A digital signal distorted by noise and then repeated

Latency

Although electrons travel rapidly, they still have to travel, and a brief delay takes place between the instant when data leaves the source and when it arrives at its destination. Recall that this delay is called latency.

The length of the cable affects latency, as does the existence of any intervening connectivity device, such as a router. Different devices affect latency to different degrees. For example, modems, which convert, or modulate, both incoming and outgoing signals for transmission over a network, increase a connection's latency far more than switches, which simply repeat a signal. The most common way to measure latency on data networks is by calculating a packet's **RTT (round trip time)**, or the length of time it takes for a packet to go from sender to receiver, then back from receiver to sender. RTT is usually measured in milliseconds.

Latency causes problems when a receiving node is expecting some type of communication, such as the rest of a data stream it has begun to accept. If packets experience varying amounts of delay, they can arrive out of order—a problem commonly called **jitter**, or more precisely, PDV (packet delay variation). This might cause streaming video or voice transmissions to pause repeatedly, jump around, or stall out completely. Another latency-related problem occurs if the node does not receive the rest of the data stream within a given time period, and therefore assumes no more data is coming. In this case, transmission errors are returned to the sender.

While noise, attenuation, and latency degrade a network's efficiency, there are some changes you can make to the network to increase efficiency. First, let's consider settings on a device's NIC.

Duplex, Half-Duplex, and Simplex

Network connections perform best when network devices are properly configured. Two important NIC settings include the direction in which signals travel over the media and the number of signals that can traverse the media at any given time. These two settings are combined to create different methods of communication:

- *full-duplex*, *also called duplex*—Signals are free to travel in both directions over a medium simultaneously. As an analogy, talking on the telephone is a full-duplex transmission because both parties in the conversation can speak at the same time. Modern NICs use full-duplex by default.
- *half-duplex*—Signals may travel in both directions over a medium but in only one direction at a time. For example, an apartment building's intercom system might be half-duplex if only one person can speak at a time.
- *simplex*—Signals may travel in only one direction, and is sometimes called one-way, or unidirectional, communication. Broadcast radio and garage door openers are examples of simplex transmissions.

In Windows, you can use Device Manager to configure a NIC, including speed and duplex settings. For example, notice in Figure 5-3 that you can choose Full Duplex, Half Duplex, or Auto Negotiation, which allows the NIC to select the best link speed and duplex that is also supported by a neighboring device. However, if you specify a particular speed and duplex that's not supported by the neighboring device, the result is a **speed and duplex mismatch** and, therefore, slow or failed transmissions.

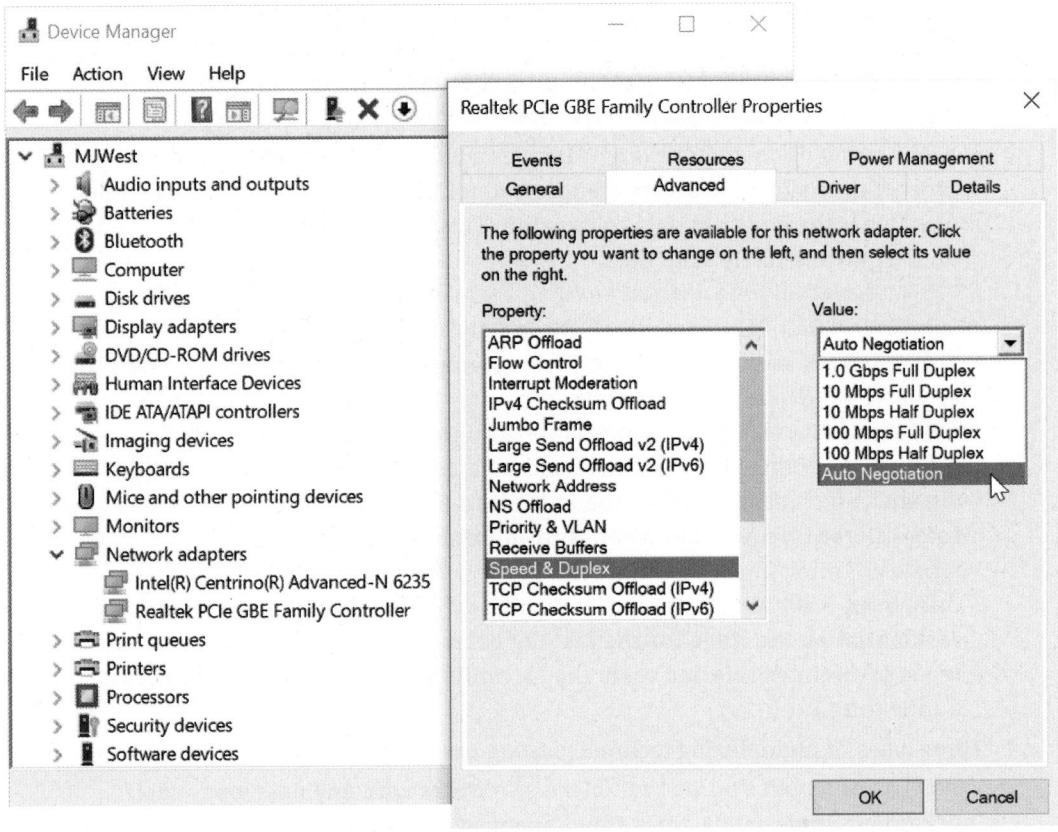

Figure 5-3   A network adapter's Speed & Duplex configuration can be changed

Multiplexing

Duplexing allows a signal to travel in both directions in a cable at one time. This might be achieved by pairing two wires together inside the cable, where one wire transmits and the other receives. Or it might be accomplished by transmitting two or more signals on the same wire. A form of transmission that allows multiple signals to travel simultaneously over one medium is known as **multiplexing**.

Networks rely on multiplexing to increase the amount of data that can be transmitted in a given timespan over a given bandwidth. To carry multiple signals, the medium's channel is logically separated into multiple smaller channels, or subchannels. Many different types of multiplexing are available, and the type used in any given situation depends on what the media, transmission, and reception equipment can handle. For each type of multiplexing, a device that can combine many signals on a channel, a multiplexer (mux), is required at the transmitting end of the channel. At the receiving end, a demultiplexer (demux) separates the combined signals.

Different types of multiplexing manipulate the signals in different ways. Three common types of multiplexing used on copper lines are:

- *TDM (time division multiplexing)*—Divides a channel into multiple intervals of time, or time slots. Time slots are reserved for their designated nodes regardless of whether the node has data to transmit. This can be inefficient if some nodes on the network rarely send data.

- *STDM (statistical time division multiplexing)*—Assigns time slots to nodes (similar to TDM), but then adjusts these slots according to priority and need. This approach uses all slots rather than leaving some unused, which maximizes available bandwidth on a network.

- *FDM (frequency division multiplexing)*—Assigns different frequencies to create multiple frequency bands, each used by a subchannel, so that multiple signals can transmit on the line at the same time. Signals are modulated into different frequencies, then multiplexed to simultaneously travel over a single channel, and demultiplexed at the other end. Telephone companies once used FDM for all phone lines and now still use multiplex signals on residential phone lines for the last leg before entering a residence. (The last leg is sometimes referred to as the last mile even though it's not necessarily a mile long.)

Three types of multiplexing technologies are used with fiber-optic cable:

- *WDM (wavelength division multiplexing)*—Works with any fiber-optic cable to carry multiple light signals simultaneously by dividing a light beam into different wavelengths, or colors, on a single fiber. The technology works similar to how a prism divides white light into various colors. Original WDM provided only two wavelengths or channels per strand of fiber.

- *DWDM (dense wavelength division multiplexing or dense WDM)*—Increases the number of channels provided by normal WDM to between 80 and 320 channels. Dense WDM can be amplified en route and is typically used on high-bandwidth or long-distance WAN links, such as the connection between a large ISP and its (even larger) NSP (network service provider).

- *CWDM (coarse wavelength division multiplexing or coarse WDM)*—Lowers cost by spacing frequency bands wider apart to allow for cheaper transceiver equipment. Coarse WDM multiplexers typically can support 4, 8, 16, or 18 channels per fiber, as you can see on this manufacturer's website in Figure 5-4. The effective distance of coarse WDM is more limited because the signal is not amplified.

Monitoring and optimizing network performance is a substantial part of network administration. We'll revisit this topic more extensively later.

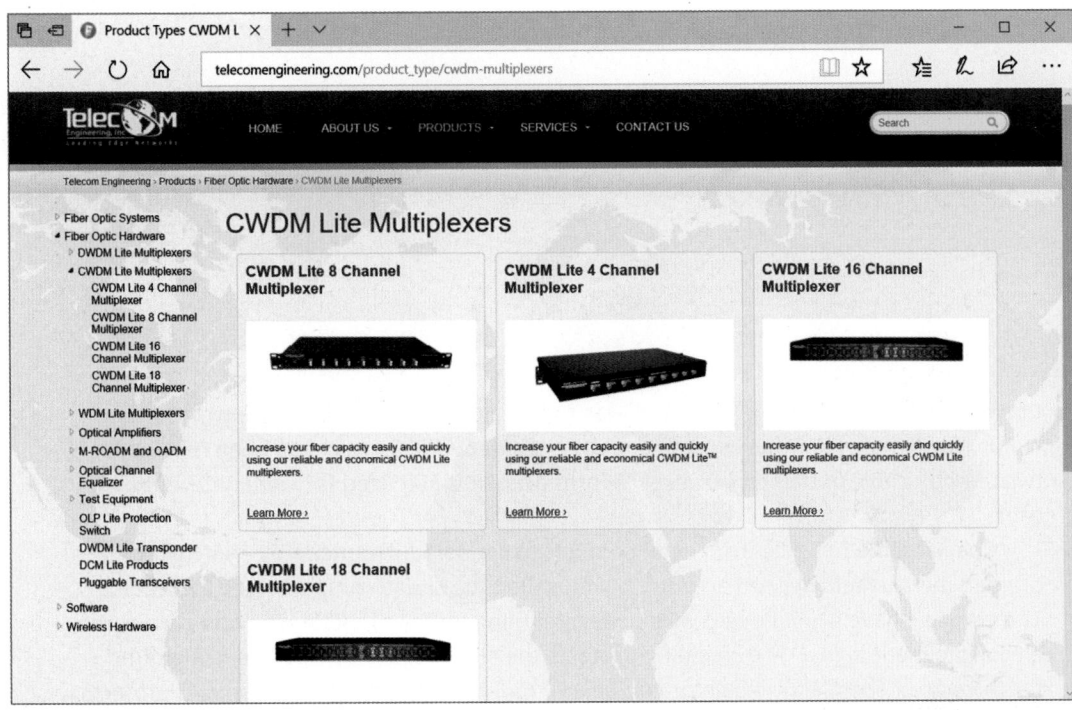

Figure 5-4   CWDM multiplexers come in 4-channel, 8-channel, 16-channel, and 18-channel varieties

Source: Telecom Engineering, Inc.

Copper Cable

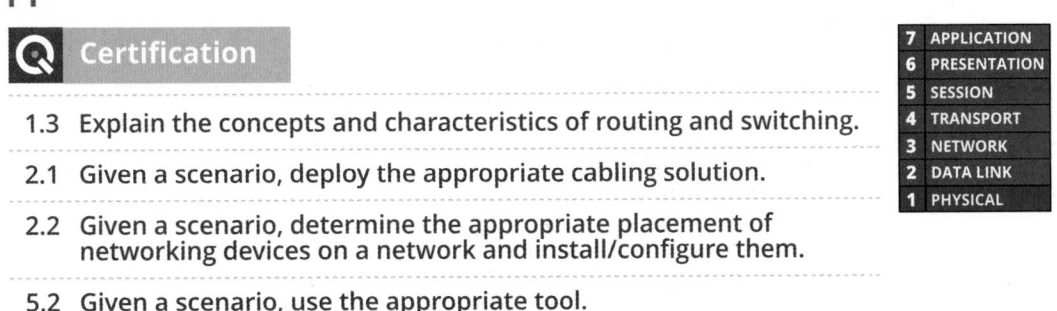

Certification

7	APPLICATION
6	PRESENTATION
5	SESSION
4	TRANSPORT
3	NETWORK
2	DATA LINK
1	PHYSICAL

1.3   Explain the concepts and characteristics of routing and switching.

2.1   Given a scenario, deploy the appropriate cabling solution.

2.2   Given a scenario, determine the appropriate placement of networking devices on a network and install/configure them.

5.2   Given a scenario, use the appropriate tool.

5.3   Given a scenario, troubleshoot common wired connectivity and performance issues.

Now that you understand some of the basics of data transmission on a network, you're ready to learn about different types of transmission media. Let's begin with some bare-bones details about an outdated media: coaxial cable.

Network+ Exam Tip ⓘ

The CompTIA Network+ exam expects you to know the characteristics and limitations of each type of media, how to install and design a network with each type, how to troubleshoot networking media problems, and how to provide for future network growth with each option.

Legacy Networking: Coaxial Cable

Coaxial cable, called "coax" for short, was the foundation for Ethernet networks in the 1980s. You'll most likely never see a coaxial cable network, as coax has been replaced by twisted-pair cable and fiber; however, a form of coax is still used for cable Internet and cable TV.

Coaxial cable has a central metal core (often copper) surrounded by an insulator, a braided metal shielding, and an outer cover, called the sheath or jacket (see Figure 5-5). The core can have a solid metal wire or several thin strands of metal wire and carries the electromagnetic signal. The shielding protects the signal against noise and is a ground for the signal. The plastic insulator can be PVC (polyvinyl chloride) or Teflon and protects the core from the metal shielding because if the two made contact, the wire would short-circuit. The sheath protects the cable from physical damage and might be PVC or a more expensive fire-resistant plastic.

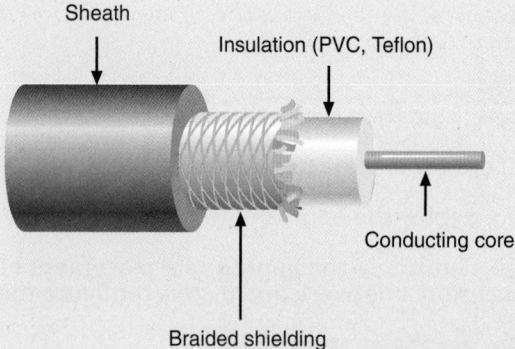

Sheath

Insulation (PVC, Teflon)

Conducting core

Braided shielding

Figure 5-5   Coaxial cable

Coaxial cabling comes in hundreds of specifications, which are all assigned an RG specification number. (RG stands for *radio guide,* which is appropriate because coaxial cabling can be used by radio frequencies in broadband transmission.) The RG ratings measure the materials used for shielding and conducting cores, which in turn influence their transmission characteristics, such as impedance (the resistance that contributes to controlling the signal, as expressed in ohms), attenuation, and throughput.

Each type of coax is suited to a different purpose. When discussing the size of the conducting core in a coaxial cable, we refer to its AWG (American Wire Gauge) size. The larger the AWG size, the smaller the diameter of the core wire. Table 5-2 lists the two most common coaxial cable specifications still in use today.

Table 5-2	Coaxial cable specifications		
Type	**Impedance**	**Core**	**Uses**
RG-59	75 ohms	20 or 22 AWG core, usually made of braided copper	Still used for relatively short connections, for example, when distributing video signals from a central receiver to multiple monitors within a building. RG-59 is less expensive than the more common RG-6, but suffers from greater attenuation.
RG-6	75 ohms	18 AWG conducting core, usually made of solid copper	Used to deliver broadband cable Internet service and cable TV, particularly over long distances. Cable Internet service entering your home is RG-6.

Network+ Exam Tip ⓘ

The CompTIA Network+ exam expects you to know about RG-59 and RG-6 cables, F-connectors, and BNC connectors.

These two coaxial cable types, RG-6 and RG-59, can terminate with one of two connector types:

- **F-connectors** attach to coaxial cable so that the pin in the center of the connector is the conducting core of the cable. Therefore, F-connectors require that the cable contain a solid metal core. After being attached to the cable by crimping or compression, connectors are threaded and screwed together like a nut-and-bolt assembly. A male F-connector, or plug, attached to coax is shown in Figure 5-6. A corresponding female F-connector, or jack, would be coupled with the male connector. F-connectors are most often used with RG-6 cables.

Figure 5-6 F-connector

Source: MCM Electronics, Inc.

- A **BNC connector** is crimped, compressed, or twisted onto a coaxial cable. BNC stands for *Bayonet Neill-Concelman,* a term that refers to both an older style of connection and its two inventors. (Sometimes the term *British Naval Connector* is also used.) A BNC connector connects to another BNC connector via a turn-and-lock mechanism—this is the bayonet coupling referenced in its name. Unlike an F-connector, a male BNC connector provides its own conducting pin. BNC connectors are used with RG-59 coaxial cables, and less commonly, with RG-6. Figure 5-7 shows a BNC connector. Today, F-connectors are much more common.

Igor Smichkov/Shutterstock.com

Figure 5-7　BNC connector

> ### Note 📎
>
> When sourcing connectors for coaxial cable, you need to specify the type of cable you are using. For instance, when working with RG-6 coax, choose an F-connector made specifically for RG-6 cables. That way, you'll be certain that the connectors and cable share the same impedance rating. If impedance ratings don't match, data errors will occur and transmission performance will suffer.

Next, you'll learn about a medium you're more likely to find on modern LANs: twisted-pair cable.

Twisted-Pair Cable

Twisted-pair cable consists of color-coded pairs of insulated copper wires, each with a diameter of 0.4 to 0.8 mm (approximately the diameter of a sewing pin). Every two wires are twisted around each other to form pairs, and all the pairs are encased in a plastic sheath, as shown in Figure 5-8.

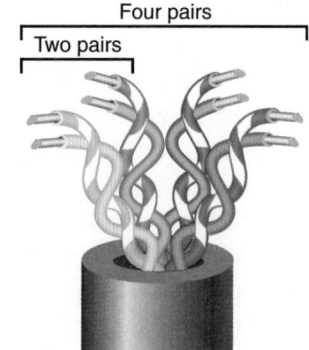

Four pairs

Two pairs

Figure 5-8　Twisted-pair cable

> **Note** 🖇
>
> The terms *wire* and *cable* are used synonymously in some situations. Strictly speaking, however, *wire* is a subset of *cabling* because the *cabling* category may also include fiber-optic cable, which is almost never called *wire*. The exact meaning of the term *wire* depends on context. For example, if you said, in a somewhat casual way, "We had 6 gigs of data go over the wire last night," you would be referring to whatever transmission media helped carry the data—whether fiber, radio waves, or copper cable.

Twisted-pair cabling in Ethernet networks contains four wire pairs. On **Fast Ethernet** networks, which have a maximum speed of 100 Mbps, one pair sends data, another pair receives data, and the other two pairs are not used for data transmission. Networks using **Gigabit Ethernet** and higher standards, with a speed of at least 1000 Mbps, use all four pairs for both sending and receiving. You'll learn more about Ethernet standards later in this chapter.

> **Note** 🖇
>
> The more twists per foot in a pair of wires, the more resistant the pair will be to crosstalk or noise. Higher-quality, more-expensive twisted-pair cable contains more twists per foot. The number of twists per meter or foot is known as the **twist ratio**. Because twisting the wire pairs more tightly requires more cable, however, a high twist ratio can result in greater attenuation. For optimal performance, cable manufacturers must strike a balance between minimizing crosstalk and reducing attenuation.

In 1991, the TIA/EIA organizations finalized their specifications for twisted-pair wiring in a standard called "TIA/EIA 568." The TIA/EIA 568 standard divides twisted-pair wiring into several categories. The categories you will see most often are Cat (category) 3, 5, 5e, 6, 6a, and 7, all of which are described in Table 5-3. (Cat 4 cabling exists, too, but it is rarely used.) Modern LANs use Cat 5e or higher wiring, which is the minimum required to support Gigabit Ethernet. Cat 6 and above are certified for multigigabit transmissions, although Cat 6 cable has shorter distance limitations when supporting 10G.

In Figure 5-9, notice the reference on the cable to UTP. All twisted-pair cable falls into one of two classifications: STP (shielded twisted pair) or UTP (unshielded twisted pair). Let's look at characteristics of each type.

Table 5-3   Twisted-pair cabling standards

Standard		Maximum supported throughput	Band-width/ signal rate	Description
Cat 3 (Category 3)		10 Mbps	Up to 16 MHz	Used for 10-Mbps Ethernet or 4-Mbps Token Ring networks. Rarely found on any modern network.
Cat 5 (Category 5)		100 Mbps	100 MHz	Required minimum standard for Fast Ethernet.
Gigabit Ethernet	Cat 5e (Enhanced Category 5)	1000 Mbps (1 Gbps)	350 MHz	A higher-grade version of Cat 5 wiring that contains high-quality copper, offers a higher twist ratio, and uses advanced methods for reducing crosstalk.
	Cat 6 (Category 6)	10 Gbps	250 MHz	Includes a plastic core to prevent crosstalk between twisted pairs in the cable. Can also have foil insulation that covers the bundle of wire pairs, and a fire-resistant plastic sheath.
	Cat 6a (Augmented Category 6)	10 Gbps	500 MHz	Reduces attenuation and crosstalk and allows for potentially exceeding traditional network segment length limits. Can reliably transmit data at multigigabit per second rates. Backward compatible with Cat 5, Cat 5e, and Cat 6 cabling, which means that it can replace lower-level cabling without requiring connector or equipment changes.
	Cat 7 (Category 7) Not included in TIA/EIA standards	10 Gbps	600 MHz	Supports higher frequencies because each wire pair is wrapped in its own shielding, then packaged in additional shielding beneath the sheath. Requires more sophisticated connectors, either GG45, which is backward compatible with RJ-45, or TERA, which is not. It's larger and less flexible than earlier versions, and is also less common.
	Cat 7a (Augmented Category 7) Not included in TIA/EIA standards	40–100 Gbps	1000 MHz	ISO standards for Cat 7a cabling are still being drafted and simulations conducted.

> **Note** 📎
>
> To identify the category of a twisted-pair cable, check for information stamped on the jacket, as shown in Figure 5-9.

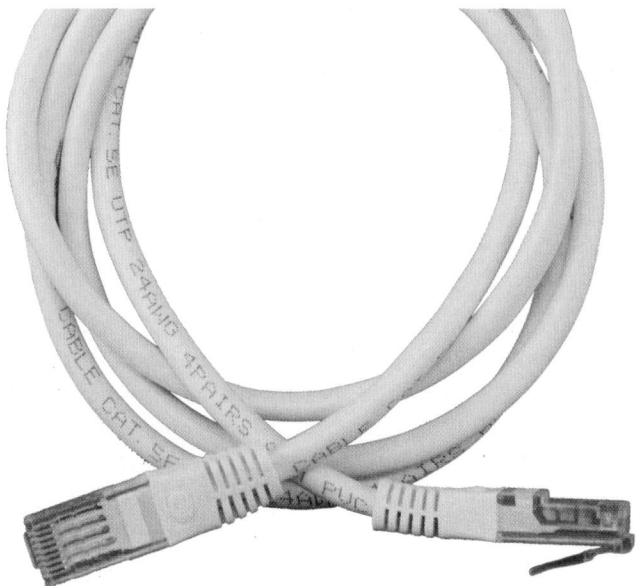

Figure 5-9   This data cable is Cat 5e

STP (Shielded Twisted Pair)

Recall that STP (shielded twisted pair) cable consists of twisted-pair wires that are not only individually insulated, but also surrounded by a shielding made of a metallic substance such as a foil. Some STP cables use a braided copper shielding. The shielding acts as a barrier to external electromagnetic forces, thus preventing them from affecting the signals traveling over the wire inside the shielding. It also contains the electrical energy of the signals inside. The shielding must be grounded to enhance its protective effects and prevent reflection issues. The effectiveness of STP's shield depends on these characteristics:

- level and type of environmental noise
- thickness and material used for the shield
- grounding mechanism
- symmetry and consistency of the shielding

Figure 5-10 depicts an STP cable.

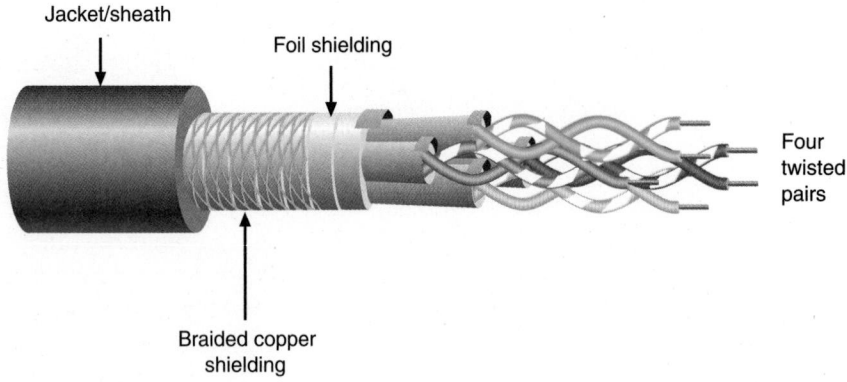

Figure 5-10   STP cable

UTP (Unshielded Twisted Pair)

UTP cabling consists of one or more insulated wire pairs encased in a plastic sheath. As its name implies, UTP does not contain additional shielding for the twisted pairs. As a result, UTP is both less expensive and less resistant to noise than STP, and is more popular than STP, primarily because of its lower cost. Figure 5-11 depicts three types of UTP cable: PVC-grade Cat 5e, plenum-grade Cat 5e, Cat 6 with its plastic core, and a UTP cable with an RJ-45 connector attached. Recall that a plenum-grade cable's jacket is flame-resistant, while the PVC cable's coating is toxic when burned.

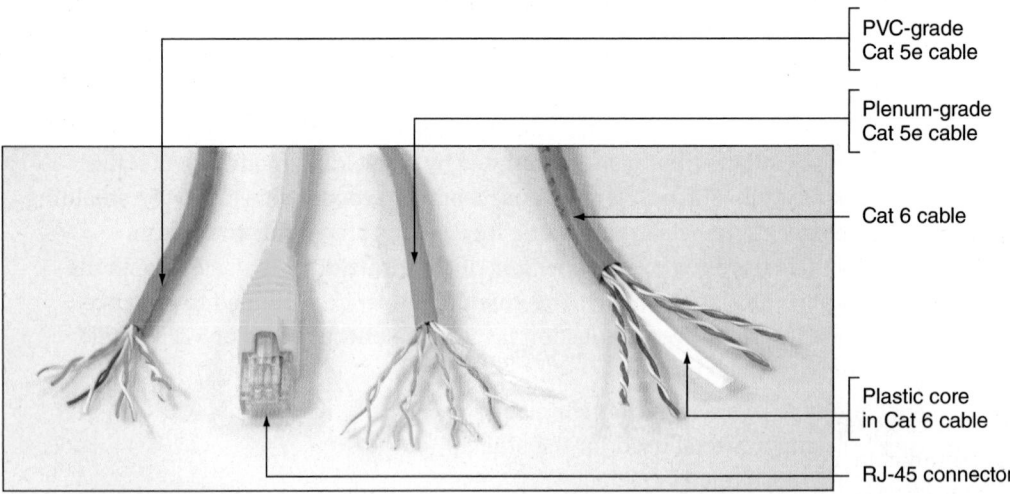

Figure 5-11   Various UTP cables and RJ-45 connector

Comparing STP and UTP

STP and UTP share several characteristics. The following list highlights their similarities and differences:

- *throughput*—STP and UTP can both transmit data at 10 Mbps, 100 Mbps, 1 Gbps, and 10 Gbps, depending on the grade of cabling and the transmission method in use.
- *cost*—STP and UTP vary in cost, depending on the grade of copper used, the category rating, and any enhancements. Typically, STP is more expensive than UTP because it contains more materials and it has a lower demand. It also requires grounding, which can lead to more expensive installation. High-grade UTP can be expensive, too, however.
- *connector*—STP and UTP use **RJ-45 (registered jack 45)** modular connectors and data jacks, which look similar to analog telephone connectors and jacks. However, telephone connections follow the **RJ-11 (registered jack 11)** standard. Figure 5-12 shows a close-up of an RJ-45 connector for a cable containing four wire pairs. For comparison, this figure also shows a traditional RJ-11 phone line connector. Most types of Ethernet that rely on twisted-pair cabling use RJ-45 connectors.

Figure 5-12   RJ-45 and RJ-11 connectors

- *noise immunity*—Because of its shielding, STP is more noise resistant than UTP. On the other hand, noise on UTP cable can be reduced with filtering and balancing techniques.
- *size and scalability*—The maximum segment length for both STP and UTP is 100 m, or 328 feet, on Ethernet networks that support data rates from 1 Mbps to 10 Gbps.

Cable Pinouts

Proper cable termination is a basic requirement for two nodes on a network to communicate. Poor terminations, as you read in the *On the Job* story at the beginning of this chapter, can lead to loss or noise—and consequently, errors—in a signal. Closely following termination standards, then, is critical.

TIA/EIA has specified two different methods of inserting twisted-pair wires into RJ-45 plugs: **TIA/EIA 568A** and **TIA/EIA 568B** (also known as T568A and T568B, respectively). Functionally, there is very little difference between these two standards. You only have to be certain that you use the same standard on every RJ-45 plug and jack on your network, so data is transmitted and received correctly. T568B is more common and is likely what you'll find on home and business networks. However, the federal government requires T568A on all federal contracts.

Figure 5-13 depicts pin numbers and assignments (called **pinouts**) for both standards. *Tx* refers to transmit, and *Rx* refers to receive. Standard pinouts are designed with the avoidance of crosstalk in mind.

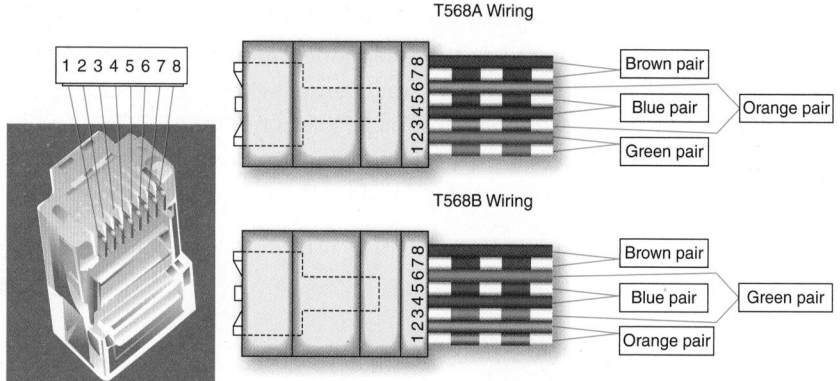

Pin #	T568A Color	T568B Color	Fast Ethernet function	Gigabit Ethernet function
1	White/green	White/orange	Tx+	Bidirectional+
2	Green	Orange	Tx−	Bidirectional−
3	White/orange	White/green	Rx+	Bidirectional+
4	Blue	Blue	*Unused*	Bidirectional+
5	White/blue	White/blue	*Unused*	Bidirectional−
6	Orange	Green	Rx−	Bidirectional−
7	White/brown	White/brown	*Unused*	Bidirectional+
8	Brown	Brown	*Unused*	Bidirectional−

Figure 5-13 T568A and T568B standard terminations for Fast Ethernet and Gigabit Ethernet

With Fast Ethernet, only the orange and green pairs are used: one pair transmits and one pair receives. The difference between pinouts in T568A and T568B is that these two pairs are reversed. For Gigabit Ethernet, all four pairs are used for transmitting and receiving. This more efficient use of wires helps account for the higher bandwidth of Gigabit.

The most common type of networking cable is a **straight-through cable**, also called a **patch cable**. To create one, terminate the RJ-45 plugs at both ends of the cable identically, following one of the TIA/EIA 568 standards. It's called a straight-through cable because it allows signals to pass "straight through" from one end to the other.

> **Note** 📎
>
> A **loopback adapter** attaches to a port, such as an RJ-45 port, or a cable connector. It crosses the transmit line with the receive line to create a closed loop, tricking a host into thinking it's connected to a network as it "hears" its own data transmission. This is one way to test a port or cable for connectivity. See Figure 5-14. Inserting a loopback plug directly into a port will test for a bad port, and inserting a cable connector into a loopback jack will additionally test the cable for continuity (but not performance).
>
> You'll create your own loopback plug and jack in projects at the end of this chapter.

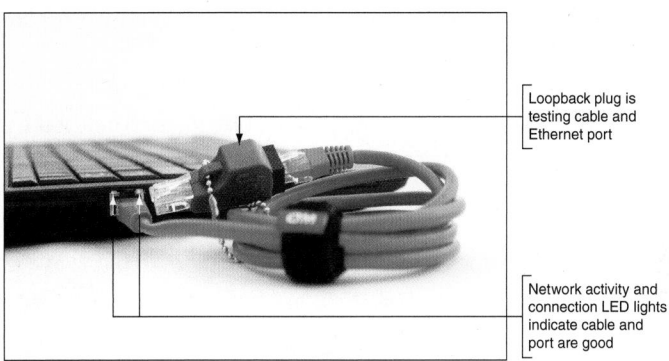

Loopback plug is testing cable and Ethernet port

Network activity and connection LED lights indicate cable and port are good

Figure 5-14   Here, a loopback plug verifies the cable and network port are good

Legacy Networking: Crossover Cable

With older networking devices that did not support Gigabit Ethernet, each wire could only be used to either transmit or receive, not both. A straight-through cable was always used to connect two unlike devices—for example, to connect a PC transmitting on the wire a switch received on, or a switch transmitting on the wire a router received on. When you needed to connect two like devices (for example, a switch to a switch), a problem occurred because the two switches were both transmitting on the same wire and both listening to receive on the same wire. The solution was to use a crossover cable. A **crossover cable** has the transmit and receive wires reversed and was used to connect a PC to a PC or a switch to a switch. See Figure 5-15. Notice in the figure a crossover cable was also needed to connect a PC to a router because legacy routers are expected to connect only to switches.

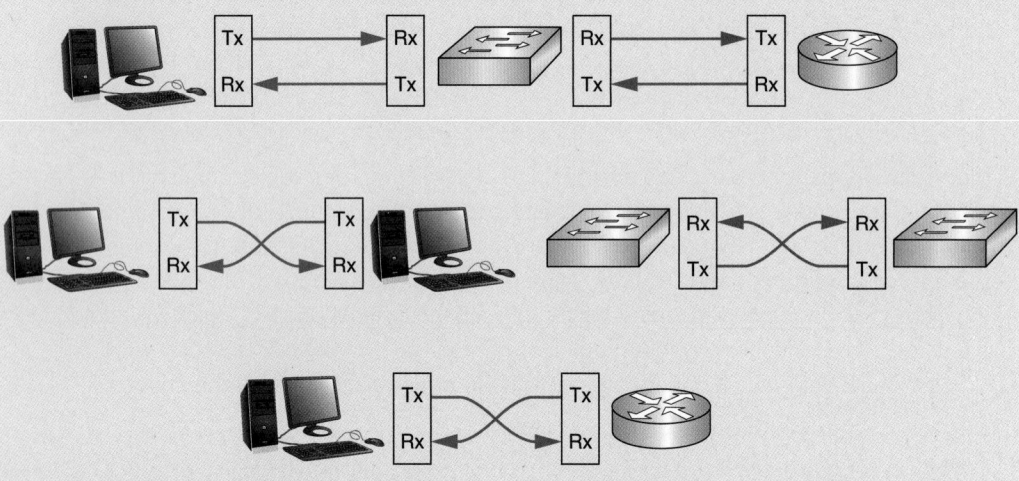

Figure 5-15   On legacy networks, straight-through cables connect unlike devices and crossover cables connect like devices

Modern devices have an autosense function that enables them to detect the way wires are terminated in a plug and then adapt their transmit and receive signaling accordingly. This means crossover cables are now largely obsolete, except when they are needed to support older devices.

In a straight-through cable, each wire connects to the same pin on each end. For example, the orange/white wire goes *straight through* from pin 1 to pin 1. In a crossover cable, the transmit and receive wires are reversed, as shown in Figure 5-16. The diagram on the left in Figure 5-16 has the orange and green pairs reversed and will work with Fast Ethernet because this Ethernet standard requires only two pairs. The diagram on the right in Figure 5-16 has all four pairs reversed (blue, orange, green, and brown pairs) and will work with Gigabit Ethernet because Gigabit Ethernet transmits on four pairs.

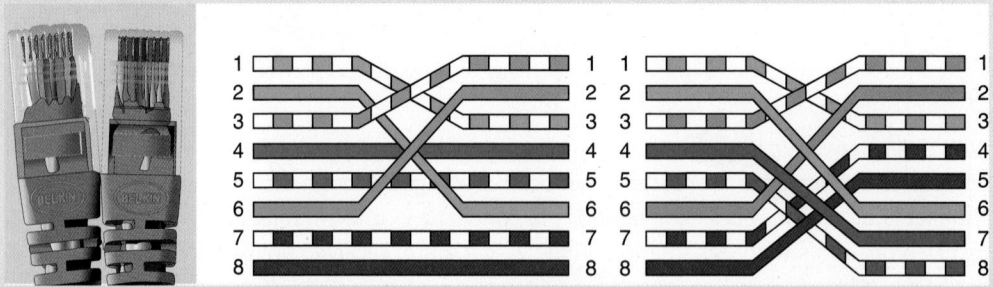

Figure 5-16   Two crossed pairs in a crossover cable are compatible with Fast Ethernet; four crossed pairs are compatible with Gigabit Ethernet

Network+ Exam Tip ⓘ

One potential cause of NEXT (near end crosstalk) is an improper termination—for example, one in which wire insulation has been damaged, where wire pairs have been untwisted too far, or where straight-through or crossover standards have been mismatched. This last problem can happen when the TX (transmission) and RX (receive) wires are crossed, which, on the CompTIA Network+ exam, is called a **TX/RX reverse**.

Rollover Cable

Whereas a crossover cable reverses the transmit and receive wire pairs, a rollover cable reverses all the wires without regard to how they are paired. With a rollover cable, it's as if the cable terminations are a mirror image of each other, as shown in Figure 5-17. Rollover cables, also called console cables, are used to connect a computer to the console port of a router. Routers have two different kinds of ports: Ethernet ports and the console port. **Ethernet ports** allow for network communications and are the type of port used to create LANs through the router. A router's **console port** is used to communicate with the router itself, such as when making configuration changes to the device.

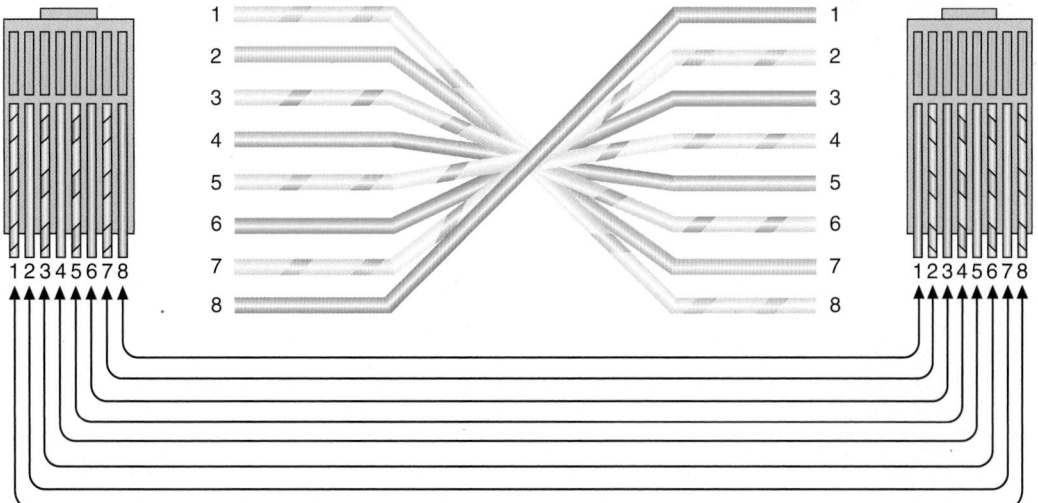

Figure 5-17   RJ-45 terminations on a rollover cable

Legacy Networking: Serial Cables and Connectors

Occasionally, you might encounter a router, switch, or server with an older console port, called a serial port. Serial ports and serial cables follow the TIA/EIA standards known as RS-232 (Recommended Standard 232). Different connector types comply with this standard, including RJ-45 connectors, **DB-9 connectors**, and **DB-25 connectors**. You are already familiar with RJ-45 connectors. Figure 5-18 illustrates male DB-9 and DB-25 connectors. The arrangement of the pins on both connectors resembles a sideways letter D. The DB-9 connector on the left side of the figure contains 9 contact points, and, as you can guess, the DB-25 connector on the right side of the figure contains 25.

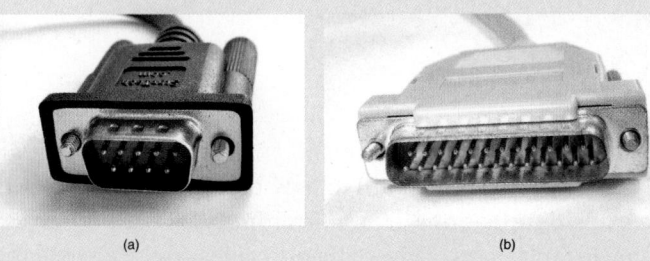

(a)   (b)

Figure 5-18   DB-9 and DB-25 connectors

Serial cables are also used for monitors, printers, and other peripheral devices. When selecting a serial cable for a specific use, check the devices for male or female connections, and also check both ends of the cable to ensure it meets the requirements of the devices you're connecting.

Caution ⚠

The fact that a serial cable terminates in an RJ-45 connector does not mean it will work if plugged into a device's RJ-45 Ethernet port! When using a serial cable with an RJ-45 connector, be certain to plug it into the appropriate serial interface. In many situations, using an incorrect cable type can cause damage to sensitive equipment.

Network+ Exam Tip ⓘ

We've discussed several copper cable connectors in this section. You can see a list of all the ones you'll need to know for the CompTIA Network+ exam, along with images to help you identify them visually, in Appendix B.

Applying Concepts: Terminate Twisted-Pair Cable

It's likely that at some point you will have to replace an RJ-45 connector on an existing cable, such as when a wire inside the cable is damaged or if pins in the connector are bent. This section describes how to terminate twisted-pair cable. The tools you'll need—a wire cutter, wire stripper, and crimper—are pictured in Figures 5-19, 5-20, and 5-21, respectively. Alternatively, you can use a single device that contains all three of these tools. A wire cutter makes a clean cut through a cable, while a wire stripper pulls off the protective covering without damaging the wires inside. A **crimper** pushes on the pins inside an RJ-45 connector so they pierce the wire's insulation, thus creating contact between the two conductors. You'll also need an RJ-45 connector, which might come with a boot. A boot is a plastic cover to protect the wires where they enter the connector.

iStock.com/David White

Figure 5-19   Wire cutter

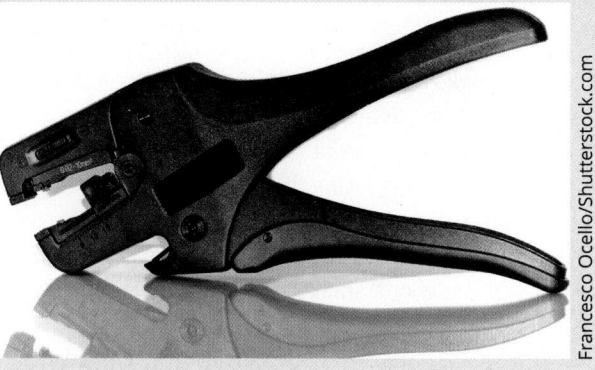

Francesco Ocello/Shutterstock.com

Figure 5-20   Wire stripper

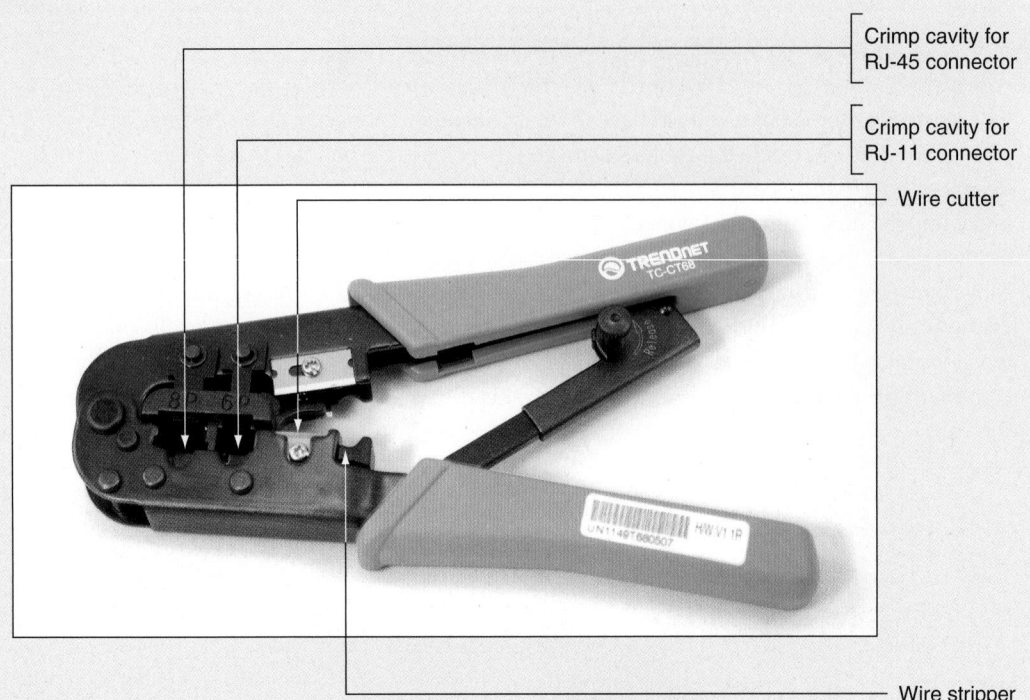

Crimp cavity for
RJ-45 connector

Crimp cavity for
RJ-11 connector

Wire cutter

Wire stripper

Figure 5-21   This crimper can crimp RJ-45 and RJ-11 connectors

Following are the steps to create a straight-through patch cable using Cat 5e twisted-pair cabling. To create a crossover cable or rollover cable, you would simply reorder the wires in Step 4 to match Figure 5-16 or Figure 5-17, respectively. The process of fixing wires inside the connector is called crimping, and it is a skill that requires practice—so don't be discouraged if the first cable you create doesn't reliably transmit and receive data. You'll get more practice terminating cables in two Hands-On projects at the end of this chapter. To create a straight-through patch cable using Cat 5e twisted-pair cabling:

1. Using the wire cutter, make a clean cut at both ends of the twisted-pair cable. Cut the cable the length you want the final cable to be, plus a few extra inches. If you're using a boot, slide one onto each end of the cable with the smaller opening facing the length of the cable and the larger opening facing the cut end that you're terminating.

2. Using the wire stripper, remove the sheath off of one end of the twisted-pair cable, beginning at approximately 1 inch from the end. This is easier if you first score the sheath with a pair of scissors or a small knife. Be careful to neither damage nor remove the insulation that's on the twisted-pair wires inside.

3. In addition to the four wire pairs, inside the sheath you'll find a string. This string, known as a strip string or rip cord, is included to make it possible to remove an additional length of the outer sheath beyond the point where your cutting tool might have

nicked the wire pairs. Use a pocketknife, wire cutters, or scissors to start a new cut at the edge of the sheath, then pull the string through the cut to expose an additional inch of the inner wires, as shown in Figure 5-22. Cut off the excess string and sheath.

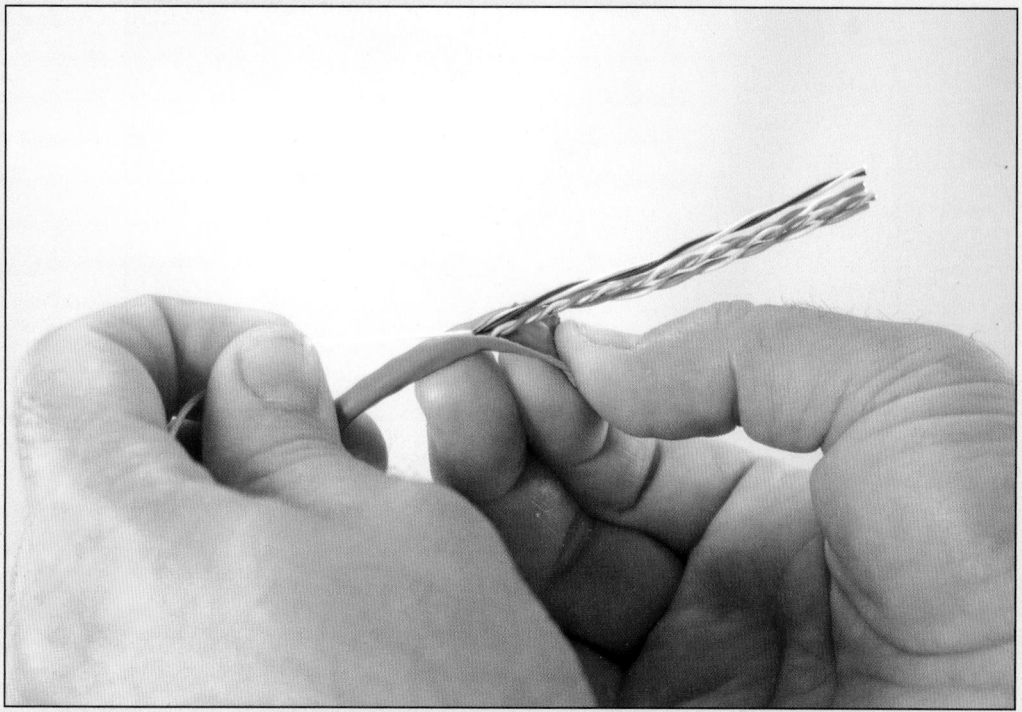

Figure 5-22   Pull back the sheath, then cut off the extra sheath and string

4. Carefully unwind each pair and straighten each wire. Make a clean cut evenly across the wires about an inch from the opening in the sheath.
5. To make a straight-through cable, align all eight wires on a flat surface, one next to the other, ordered according to their colors and positions listed earlier in Figure 5-13. It might be helpful first to groom—or pull steadily across the length of—the unwound section of each wire to straighten it out and help it stay in place.
6. Measure 1/2 inch from the end of the wires, and cleanly cut the wires straight across at this length. As you can see in Figure 5-23, it might help to hold the RJ-45 connector next to the wires to determine how short to cut the wires.
7. Keeping the wires in line and in order, gently slide them into their positions in the RJ-45 plug. The plug should be positioned with the flat side facing toward you and the pin side facing away from you, so the appropriate wires enter the correct slots for the wiring standard. The sheath should extend into the plug about 3/8 of an inch.
8. After the wires are fully inserted, place the RJ-45 plug in the crimping tool and press firmly to crimp the wires into place. Be careful not to rotate your hand or the wire as you do this, otherwise only some of the wires will be properly terminated.

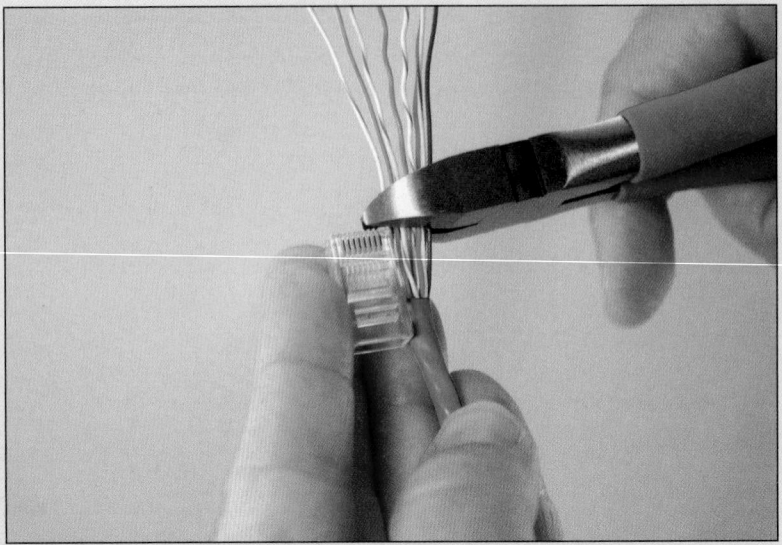

Figure 5-23   Straighten the wires, arrange them in order, and cut them to the appropriate length

9. Remove the RJ-45 connector from the crimping tool. Look through the clear plastic connector to make sure each wire appears to be in contact with its pin (see Figure 5-24). It might be difficult to tell simply by looking at the connector. To test the connection, try to pull the plug off the wire. If it comes out, start over. However, the real test is whether your cable will successfully transmit and receive signals. If the connection appears solid, slide the boot over the connector so it fits snugly over the clip.

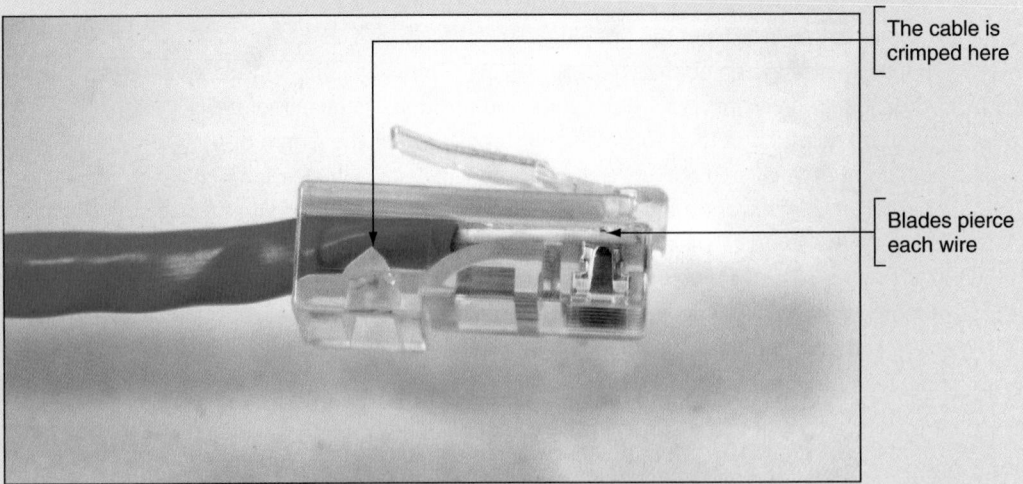

The cable is crimped here

Blades pierce each wire

Figure 5-24   Blades in the connector pierce the insulation of each individual copper wire

10. Repeat Steps 2 through 9 for the other end of the cable. After completing Step 9 for the other end, you will have created a straight-through patch cable.

Even after you feel confident making your own cables, it's a good idea to verify that they can transmit and receive data at the necessary rates using a cable tester. Cable testing is discussed later in this chapter.

PoE (Power over Ethernet)

In 2003, IEEE released its **802.3af** standard, which specifies a method for supplying electrical power over twisted-pair Ethernet connections, also known as **PoE (Power over Ethernet)**. Although the standard is relatively new, the concept is not. In fact, home telephones receive power from the telephone company over the line that enters a residence. This power is necessary for dial tone and ringing.

On an Ethernet network, carrying power over network connections can be useful for nodes that are located far from traditional power receptacles or need a constant, reliable power source. The amount of power provided is relatively small—15.4 watts for standard PoE devices and 25.5 watts for the newer **PoE+** devices, defined by the **802.3at** standard. But that's enough to power a wireless access point, an IP telephone, or a security camera mounted high on a wall.

The PoE standard specifies two types of devices:

- *PSE (power sourcing equipment)*—The device that supplies the power
- *PDs (powered devices)*—Devices that receive power from the PSE

PoE requires Cat 5 or better copper cable. Inside the cable, electric current may run over an unused pair of wires or over the pair of wires used for data transmission. The standard allows for both approaches; however, on a single network, the choice of current-carrying pairs should be consistent between all PSEs and PDs.

A switch or router that is expected to provide power over Ethernet must support the technology. The switch shown in Figure 5-25 indicates PoE is available on all 8 of its ports.

Figure 5-25   PoE-capable switch

Also, the end node must be capable of receiving PoE. The PSE device first determines whether a node is PoE-capable before attempting to supply it with power. While the security camera in Figure 5-26 includes an optional power adapter connector, its Ethernet connector is designed to receive PoE instead.

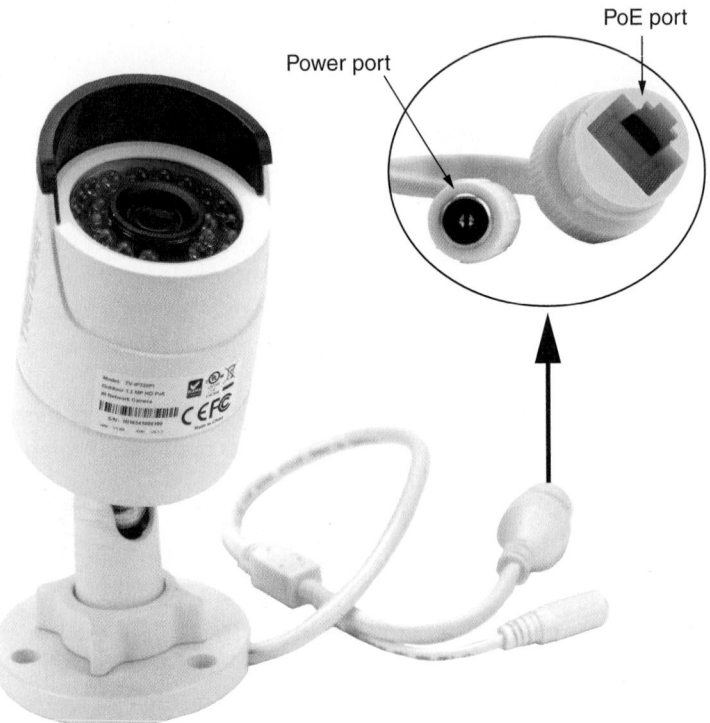

Figure 5-26   PoE-capable security camera

Let's look at how these devices might be arranged on a network. The top part of Figure 5-27 shows a PoE-capable switch providing power and data connections to a PoE-capable security camera.

On networks that demand PoE but don't have PoE-capable equipment, you can add PoE adapters, like the one shown in Figure 5-28. One type of adapter, called an injector or midspan and shown in the bottom left of Figure 5-27, connects to a non-PoE switch or router to inject power onto the network. Another type of adapter, called a splitter and shown in the bottom right of Figure 5-27, attaches to a non-PoE client, such as an outdoor camera, to receive power over the Ethernet connection. Use either one or both, depending on the needs of the devices being installed.

We've explored copper cabling at the Physical layer, but the Data Link layer is also affected by the physical media that makes up a network. Let's see how this works.

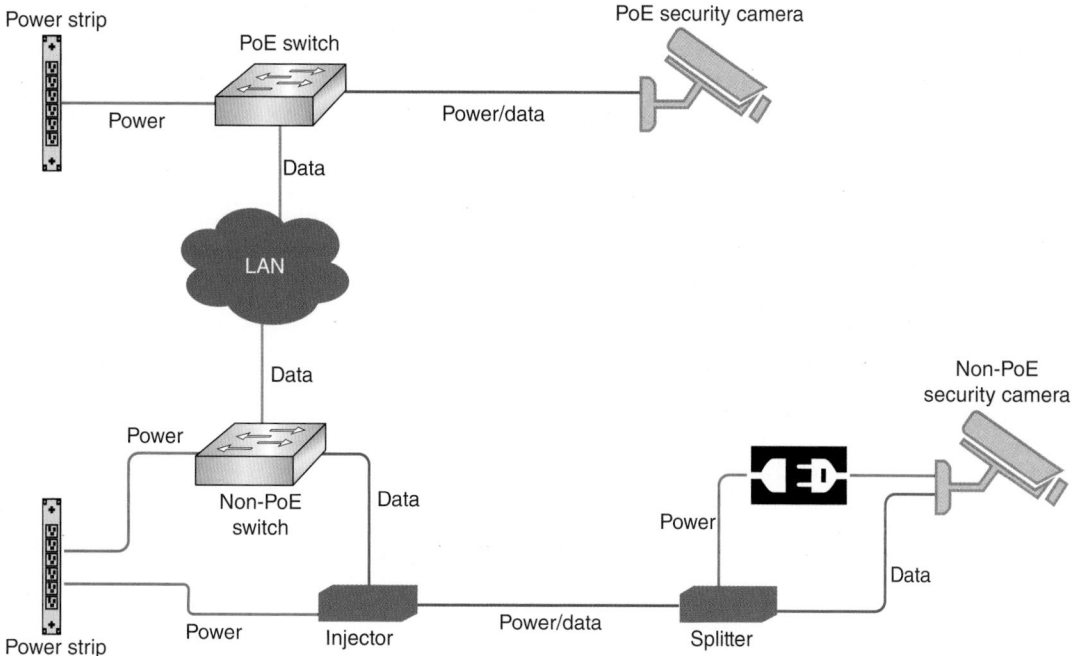

Figure 5-27   PoE adapters can add PoE functionality to non-PoE devices on a network

Source: D-Link North America

Figure 5-28   Power and data separately enter this
PoE injector through ports shown on the right, and
exit together through the port shown on the left

Ethernet Standards for Twisted-Pair Cable

A cable's category (such as Cat 5e or Cat 6) determines the fastest network
speed it can support. This is a Layer 1 characteristic. A device's NIC is
also rated for maximum network speeds, which are defined by various
Ethernet standards. Although Ethernet is generally thought of as a Layer
2 protocol, it also has Layer 1 functions that determine a transmission's

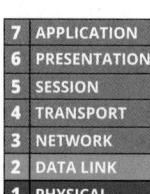

7	APPLICATION
6	PRESENTATION
5	SESSION
4	TRANSPORT
3	NETWORK
2	DATA LINK
1	PHYSICAL

frequency and other electrical characteristics. Part of the function of this layer is to provide signaling between two nodes as they negotiate a common language by which to communicate. Other familiar Layer 2 technologies, such as USB and Wi-Fi, also include Physical layer components. As for Ethernet, most LANs today use devices and NICs that can support Fast Ethernet and Gigabit Ethernet. When they first connect, devices auto-negotiate for the fastest standard they have in common. However, the network must be wired with cabling that is capable of supporting those speeds. Table 5-4 lists the various Ethernet standards supported by the different categories of twisted-pair cabling.

Table 5-4   **Ethernet standards used with twisted-pair cabling**

Standard	Maximum transmission speed (Mbps)	Maximum distance per segment (m)	Physical media	Pairs of wires used for transmission
100Base-T Fast Ethernet	100	100	Cat 5 or better	2 pair
1000Base-T Gigabit Ethernet	1000	100	Cat 5 or better (Cat 5e is preferred)	4 pair
10GBase-T 10-Gigabit Ethernet	10,000	100	Cat 6a or Cat 7 (Cat 7 is preferred)	4 pair

Network+ Exam Tip ⓘ

Memorize every detail in Table 5-4. You'll need them to pass the exam.

Note ✐

Two new standards were recently ratified by IEEE:

- *2.5GBase-T*—2500 Mbps, requires Cat 5e or better
- *5GBase-T*—5000 Mbps, requires Cat 6 or better

These new standards provide intermediate steps between Gigabit Ethernet and 10-Gigabit Ethernet. A network can support a variety of Ethernet standards at once. When matched with the proper twisted-pair category of cable, it's possible to progressively upgrade a network, one device or NIC at a time.

The fastest Ethernet standard is 10GBase-T, which achieves dramatic transmission rates on twisted-pair cabling that is comparable to fiber-optic cabling, and is less expensive than fiber-optic. Still, as with other twisted-pair Ethernet standards, the maximum segment length for 10GBase-T is 100 meters. This limitation means that 10GBase-T is not appropriate for long-distance WANs, but could easily allow the use of converged services, such as video and voice, at every desktop in a LAN.

Now that you've learned about the capabilities of copper wires to conduct signals, let's explore the possibilities when light signals are transmitted over glass fibers.

Fiber-Optic Cable

 **Certification**

		7 APPLICATION
		6 PRESENTATION
		5 SESSION
2.1	Given a scenario, deploy the appropriate cabling solution.	4 TRANSPORT
		3 NETWORK
2.2	Given a scenario, determine the appropriate placement of networking devices on a network and install/configure them.	2 DATA LINK
		1 PHYSICAL
5.2	Given a scenario, use the appropriate tool.	
5.3	Given a scenario, troubleshoot common wired connectivity and performance issues.	

Fiber-optic cable, or simply *fiber,* contains one or several glass or plastic fibers at its center, or **core**. Data is transmitted through the central fibers via pulsing light typically sent from one of two possible sources:

- *laser*—An intense, focused light that can travel extremely long distances with very high data throughput
- *LED (light-emitting diode)*—A cool-burning, long-lasting technology used on shorter fiber-optic connections, such as between floors in a building or between a switch and a router

Surrounding the fibers is a layer of glass or plastic called **cladding**. The cladding is less dense than the glass or plastic in the strands and so reflects light back to the core in patterns that vary depending on the transmission mode. This reflection allows the fiber to bend around corners without diminishing the integrity of the light-based signal (although bend radius limitations do apply).

Outside the cladding, a plastic buffer protects the cladding and core. Because the buffer is opaque, it also absorbs any light that might escape. To prevent the cable from stretching, and to protect the inner core further, strands of Kevlar (a polymeric fiber) surround the plastic buffer. Finally, a plastic sheath covers the strands of Kevlar. Figure 5-29 shows a fiber-optic cable with multiple, insulated fibers. The clear strands you see protruding from each line are not the actual cores—these are the visible cladding around each core. The core itself is microscopic in width.

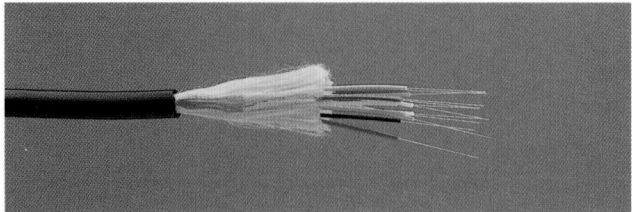

Figure 5-29   A fiber-optic cable

Source: Optical Cable Corporation

Like twisted-pair and coaxial cabling, fiber-optic cabling comes in a number of different varieties, depending on its intended use and the manufacturer. For example, fiber-optic cables used to connect the facilities of large telephone and data carriers may contain as many as 1000 fibers and be heavily sheathed to prevent damage from extreme environmental conditions. At the other end of the spectrum, fiber-optic patch cables for use on LANs might contain only two strands of fiber and be pliable enough to wrap around your hand.

Because each strand of glass in a fiber-optic cable transmits in one direction only—in simplex fashion—two strands are needed for full-duplex communication. One solution is to use a zipcord cable, in which two strands are combined side by side in conjoined jackets, as depicted in Figure 5-30. You'll find zipcords where fiber-optic cable spans relatively short distances, such as connecting a server and switch. A zipcord may come with one of many types of connectors on its ends, as described later in this section.

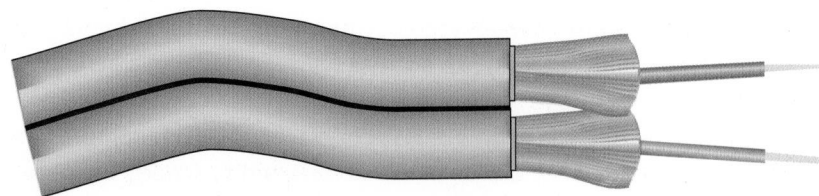

Figure 5-30   Zipcord fiber-optic patch cable

Fiber-optic cable is the industry standard for high-speed networking and provides the following benefits over copper cabling:
- Extremely high throughput
- Very high resistance to noise
- Excellent security
- Ability to carry signals for much longer distances before requiring repeaters

The most significant drawback to fiber is that it is more expensive than twisted-pair cable. Also, fiber-optic cable requires special equipment for splicing, or joining, which means that quickly repairing a fiber-optic cable in the field (given little time or resources) can be difficult. Fiber's characteristics are summarized in the following list:

- *throughput*—Fiber has proved reliable in transmitting data at rates that can reach 100 gigabits (or 100,000 megabits) per second per channel. Fiber's amazing throughput is partly due to the physics of light traveling through glass. Unlike electrical pulses traveling over copper, light experiences virtually no resistance. Therefore, light-based signals can be transmitted at faster rates and with fewer errors than electrical pulses. In fact, a pure glass strand can accept up to 1 billion laser light pulses per second. Its high throughput capability makes it suitable for network backbones and for supporting applications that generate a great deal of traffic, such as video or audio conferencing.

- *cost*—Fiber-optic cable is the most expensive transmission medium. Because of its cost, most organizations find it impractical to run fiber to every desktop. Not only is the cable itself more expensive than copper cabling, but fiber-optic transmitters and connectivity equipment can cost as much as five times more than those designed for UTP networks. In addition, hiring skilled fiber cable installers costs more than hiring twisted-pair cable installers.

- *noise immunity*—Because fiber does not conduct electrical current to transmit signals, it is unaffected by EMI. Its impressive noise resistance is one reason why fiber can span such long distances.

- *size and scalability*—Depending on the type of fiber-optic cable used, segment lengths vary from 2 to 40,000 meters. The maximum limit is due primarily to **optical loss**, or the degradation of the light signal after it travels a certain distance away from its source (just as the light of a flashlight dims after a certain number of feet). Optical loss accrues over long distances and grows with every connection point in the fiber network. Dust or oil in a connection (for example, from people handling the fiber while splicing it) can further exacerbate optical loss. The distance a cable can carry light depends partly on the light's wavelength. It also depends on whether the cable is single mode or multimode.

SMF (Single Mode Fiber)

SMF (single mode fiber) consists of a narrow core of 8 to 10 microns in diameter. Laser-generated light travels a single path over the core, reflecting very little. Because it reflects little, the light does not disperse as the signal travels along the fiber. This continuity allows SMF to accommodate the highest bandwidths and longest distances (without requiring repeaters) of all network transmission media. Figure 5-31 depicts a simplified version of how signals travel over single mode fiber.

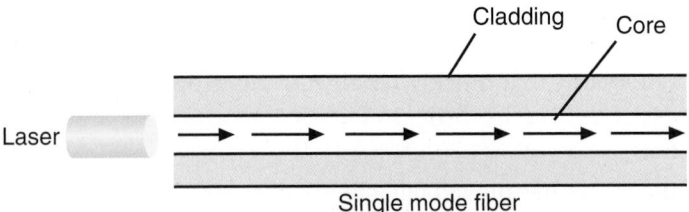

Figure 5-31   Transmission over single mode fiber-optic cable

The Internet backbone depends on single mode fiber. However, because of its relatively high cost, SMF is rarely used for short connections, such as those between a server and switch.

MMF (Multimode Fiber)

MMF (multimode fiber) contains a core with a larger diameter than SMF, usually 50 or 62.5 microns, over which many pulses of light generated by a laser or LED light source travel at various angles. Signals traveling over multimode fiber experience greater attenuation than those traversing single mode fiber. Therefore, MMF is not suited to distances longer than a few kilometers. On the other hand, MMF is less expensive to install and, therefore, typically used to connect routers, switches, and servers on the backbone of a network or to connect a desktop workstation to the network. Figure 5-32 depicts a simplified view of how signals travel over multimode fiber.

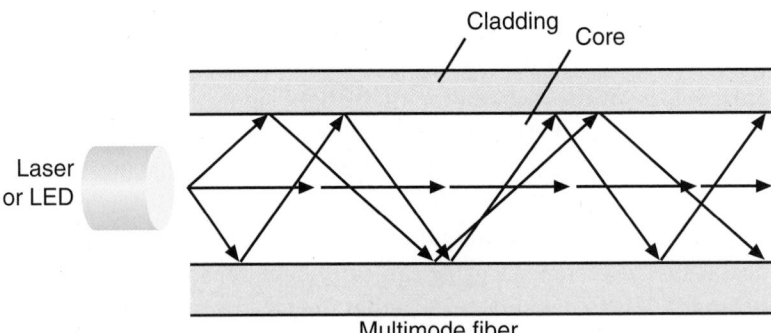

Figure 5-32   Transmission over multimode fiber-optic cable

The transition between SMF and MMF cabling might occur at an **FDP (fiber distribution panel)**, which is usually a case on a rack where fiber cables converge, connect with each other, and connect with fiber optic terminal equipment from the ISP. Splices at the FDP (or elsewhere on the network) might be accomplished by joining two fiber cables in a permanent bond, or various connectors might be used to create temporary splices.

Although a bit more sensitive to error than terminating copper cable, you can also terminate fiber-optic cable. A typical fiber termination kit might include the following tools:
- *fiber stripper*—strips off the outer layers of a fiber-optic cable
- *fiber cleaver*—cuts a clean slice through the fiber strands

If you don't have this equipment on hand, prepare for the CompTIA Network+ exam by watching a few videos on the web that demonstrate the process and the tools used. For the exam, you need to know what these tools are, but you do not need to know how to terminate fiber-optic cable.

Fiber Connectors

Just as fiber cables are classified by SMF or MMF, fiber-cable connectors are also grouped along these lines. MMF connectors can be classified by the number of fibers, and SMF connectors are classified by the size and shape of the ferrule. The **ferrule** is the extended tip of a connector that makes contact with the receptacle in the jack or other connector, as you can see in Figure 5-33.

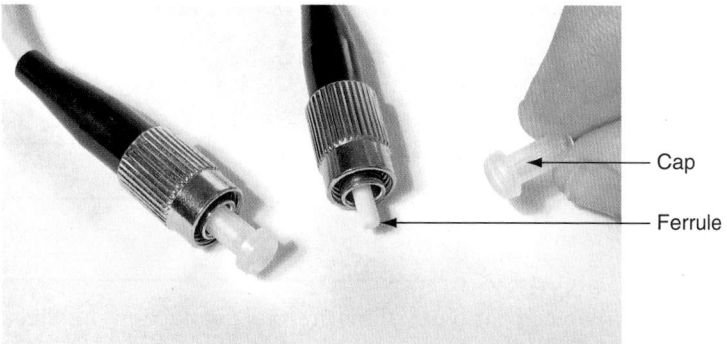

Cap

Ferrule

Figure 5-33   A cap protects the ferrule when the connector is not in use

SMF connectors are designed to reduce back reflection, which is the return of the light signal back into the fiber that is transmitting the signal. Back reflection is measured as optical loss in dB (decibels). Shapes and polishes currently used on SMF ferrules to reduce back reflection include:

- *UPC (Ultra Polished Connector)*—Extensive polishing of the tips creates a rounded surface on a **UPC (Ultra Polished Connector)**, which allows the two internal fibers to meet and increases efficiency over older types of connections.

- *APC (Angle Polished Connector)*—The latest advancement in ferrule technology uses the principles of reflection to its advantage. The **APC (Angle Polished Connector)** still uses a polished curved surface, but the end faces are placed at an angle to each other. The industry standard for this angle is 8 degrees.

> **Note**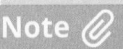
>
> UPC adapters and connectors are often blue and APC adapters and connectors are often green. But not always.

You can see the two current types of ferrule shapes in Figure 5-34. The red arrows indicate the back reflection for each connection. Notice how the APC connection reflects any signal loss in a different direction than the source of the signal. Back reflection worsens in UPC connections over time, but APC connections are not as sensitive to degradation from repeatedly disconnecting and reconnecting cables.

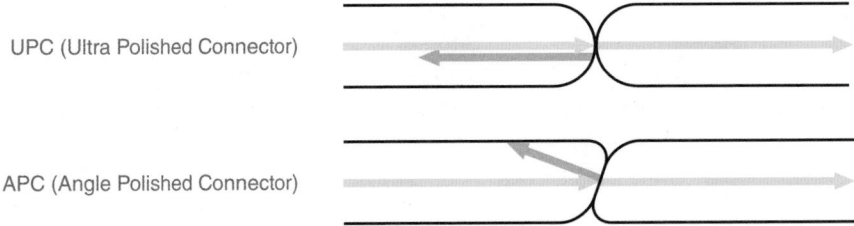

Figure 5-34   Two current types of mechanical connections in fiber-optic connectors

Table 5-5 summarizes the fiber connectors you'll need to know for the CompTIA Network+ exam. SMF connectors are typically available with a 1.25-mm ferrule or a 2.5-mm ferrule, though other sizes can be found. The most common 1.25-mm ferrule connector is **LC (local connector)**. Two 2.5-mm ferrules are **SC (subscriber connector or standard connector)** and **ST (straight tip)**. The most common type of MMF connector is **MTRJ (Mechanical Transfer-Registered Jack)**.

Table 5-5   Characteristics of fiber connectors

Photo	Connector	Polish	Ferrule characteristics	Full-duplex?
	LC	UPC, APC	1.25 mm	Yes
	ST	UPC	2.5 mm	No
	SC	UPC, APC	2.5 mm	Can be
	MTRJ	N/A	2 fibers	Yes

Source: Senko Advanced Components, Inc.

Older fiber networks might use ST or SC connectors. However, LC and MTRJ connectors are now more common because of their smaller sizes, which allows for a higher density of connections at each termination point. The MTRJ connector is unique in that it contains two strands of fiber in a single ferrule. With two strands per ferrule, a single MTRJ connector provides full-duplex signaling. SC and LC connectors are also available in full-duplex mode.

Media Converters

As long as networks contain both copper and fiber media, some kind of conversion must take place. A **media converter** is hardware that enables networks or segments running on different media to interconnect and exchange signals. For example, suppose an Ethernet segment leading from your company's data center uses fiber-optic cable to connect to a workgroup switch that only accepts twisted-pair (copper) cable. In that case, you could use a media converter to interconnect the switch with the fiber-optic cable. The media converter completes the physical connection and also converts the electrical signals from the copper cable to light wave signals that can traverse the fiber-optic cable, and vice versa. Such a media converter is shown in Figure 5-35.

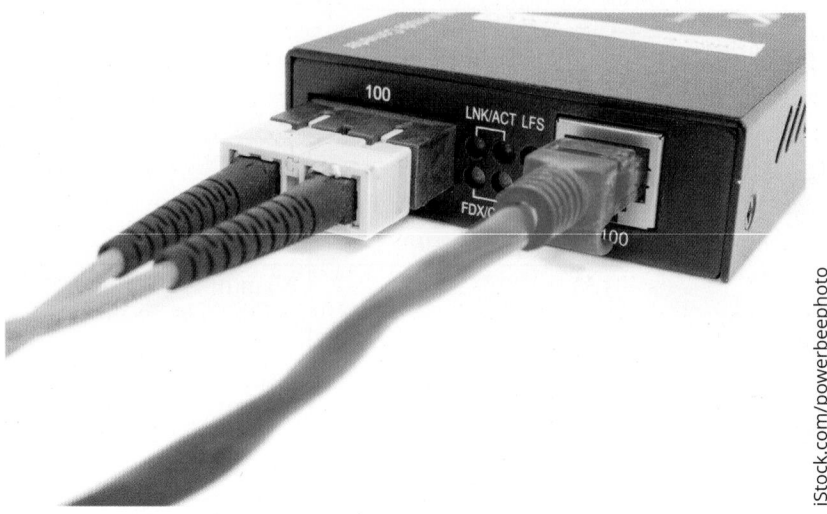

iStock.com/powerbeephoto

Figure 5-35   Copper wire-to-fiber media converter

You must select the correct media converter for the type of fiber being connected, whether it's SMF to copper or MMF to copper. Converters are also needed to connect networks using MMF with networks using SMF. Figure 5-36 shows a converter that connects single mode and multimode portions of a network.

Fiber Transceivers

Suppose you are purchasing a switch that will be part of a network for a new, fast-growing business. The current requirements for the switch might be two fiber-optic connections for the network backbone and 24 RJ-45 Gigabit Ethernet connections for clients and servers. For the future, however, you are considering fiber-optic connectivity to every desktop.

Rather than ordering a switch that contains exactly the currently needed number and type of onboard interfaces, you could order a switch that allows you to change and upgrade its interfaces at any time. These switches contain sockets where one of many types of modular interfaces, called **transceivers**, can be plugged in. Such transceivers are easily inserted into the

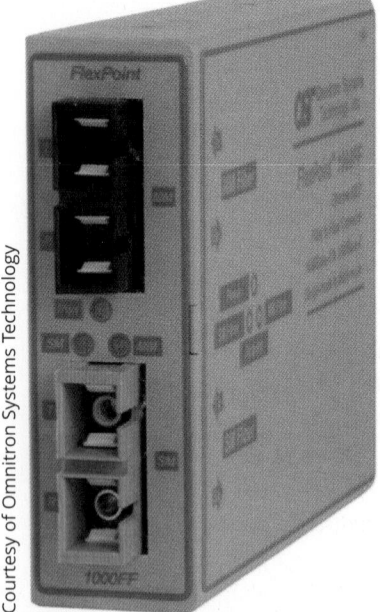

Courtesy of Omnitron Systems Technology

Figure 5-36   Single mode to multimode converter

sockets to connect with its motherboard and upgraded later as technology improves. A hardware component that can be changed in this manner, without disrupting operations, is called **hot-swappable**. Using hot-swappable transceivers means you don't have to purchase a new switch, open the chassis of the existing switch (causing network downtime and risking hardware damage), or even turn off the switch to upgrade the network. Modular interfaces can also be installed on some expansion board NICs and media converters.

GBIC (Gigabit interface converter), pronounced *jee-bick*, is a standard type of transceiver designed in the 1990s for Gigabit Ethernet connections. GBICs might contain RJ-45 ports for copper cables or SC ports for fiber-optic connections. Figure 5-37 shows a GBIC that can be used on a 1000Base-SX network.

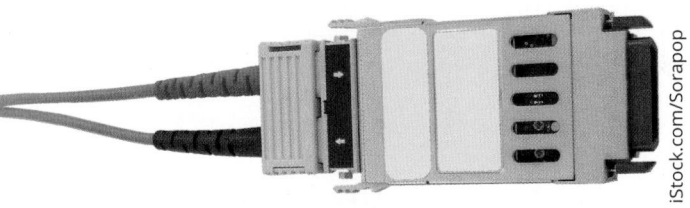

iStock.com/Sorapop

Figure 5-37   GBIC (Gigabit interface converter) with dual SC ports

Newer transceivers that have made the GBIC obsolete include:

- *SFP (small form-factor pluggable)*—Provides the same function as GBICs and is more compact, allowing more ports per linear inch. Also known as mini GBICs or SFP GBICs. Typically used for 1 Gbps connections, but theoretically capable of 5 Gbps.
- *XFP (10 Gigabit small form-factor pluggable)*—Supports up to 10 Gbps and is slightly larger than SFP with lower power consumption than SFP+.
- *SFP+*—Developed later than XFP and is the same module size as SFP; theoretical maximum transmission speed is 16 Gbps.
- *QSFP (quad small form-factor pluggable)*—Complies with the 802.3ba standard, squeezing four channels in a single transceiver and supporting data rates up to 40 Gbps (4 x 10 Gbps).
- *QSFP+*—Generally the same technology as QSFP while supporting data rates over 40 Gbps. Highest speed format at the time of this writing is QSFP28 with a total theoretical maximum data rate of 112 Gbps (4 x 28 Gbps).

- *CFP (centum form-factor pluggable)*—Intended for 100-Gbps network connections, with each succeeding generation (CFP, CFP2, CFP4) becoming smaller and more energy-efficient. *Centum* is Latin for 100.

To avoid a transceiver mismatch, these devices must be paired based on supported speeds and protocols. Also consider the cable connectors you'll be using. Most modern transceivers support LC or, occasionally, RJ-45 connectors.

Figure 5-38 shows two SFPs. The black dust plug on the left side of the bottom transceiver is covering two ports for fiber-optic cable connectors, one for transmitting and another for receiving data. Figure 5-39 shows two transceivers installed in a

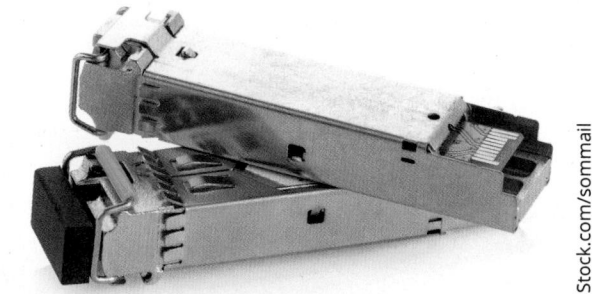

iStock.com/sommail

Figure 5-38   These SFPs slide into a switch to add fiber-optic connectivity

iStock.com/FactoryTh

Figure 5-39   This media converter supports both SFP+ and XFP

media converter. The transceiver on the left is an SFP+, and the transceiver on the right is an XFP.

Notice that all these transceivers include two ports. Full-duplex communication is achieved by sending data on one port, and receiving data through the other. A newer technology allows **bidirectional** transmission on both ports, which means each fiber cable carries data in both directions. These newer devices are called bidirectional transceivers or **BiDi transceivers**. (BiDi is pronounced *bye-dye*.) They use WDM technology to separate the data traveling in each direction on different wavelengths of light, and so sometimes they're called WDM transceivers. To work, they must be deployed in pairs with a BiDi transceiver on each end of the cable. BiDi transceivers are more expensive than their duplex cousins, but reduce by half the amount of fiber cabling needed for the same data throughput, making them more economical.

Installing a transceiver of any of these types is simply a matter of sliding it into a compatible socket on the connectivity device. Most transceivers come with a tab or latch system to lock them into place. They are also keyed so that they will slide into the socket only when aligned properly. The switch or router need not be powered down when you add or remove transceivers. However, do not attach cables before inserting a transceiver, and always remove the cables before removing a transceiver. Figure 5-40 illustrates how a fiber-optic SFP is installed in a switch.

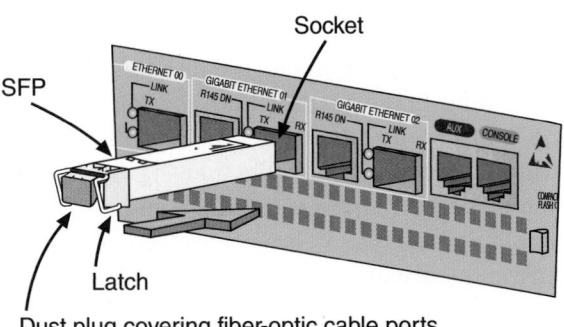

Figure 5-40   Installing an SFP in a switch

Some transceivers contain management interfaces separate from the switch's configuration utility. For example, a 10-Gbps SFP+ on a router could have its own IP address. A network administrator could use the Telnet utility to connect to the transceiver and configure its ports for a particular speed or routing protocol without accessing the router's operating system.

> **Note** 📎
>
> A helpful tool when testing a transceiver's functionality or checking for a mismatch is a loop-back adapter. Recall from earlier in this chapter that a loopback adapter can create a closed loop to trick a device into thinking it's connected to a network. A loopback adapter can do much the same thing with a transceiver, although a fiber-optic loopback adapter is specifically needed for use on a fiber connector. Figure 5-41 shows a fiber-optic loopback adapter with two LC fiber-cable connectors.

Figure 5-41   Fiber-optic loopback adapter

Ethernet Standards for Fiber-Optic Cable

7	APPLICATION
6	PRESENTATION
5	SESSION
4	TRANSPORT
3	NETWORK
2	DATA LINK
1	PHYSICAL

Long before IEEE developed a 10GBase-T standard for twisted-pair cable, it had established standards for achieving high data rates over fiber-optic cable. In fact, fiber optic is the best medium for delivering high throughput. Table 5-6 lists various Ethernet standards established by IEEE for fiber-optic cabling. Notice in the table that Gigabit Ethernet has two standards and 10-Gigabit Ethernet has six standards that use fiber-optic cables. As we saw when discussing transceivers, even faster Ethernet networks are on the way. IEEE has recently ratified standards for 40- and 100-Gigabit Ethernet.

For the Network+ exam, you only need to know the two standards for Gigabit Ethernet. Here are some important details about these standards:

- 1000Base-LX is the more common fiber version of Gigabit Ethernet and uses long wavelengths (hence the *L* in its name *LX*) of 1300 nanometers. (A nanometer equals 0.000000001 meters, or about the width of six carbon atoms in a row.) Because of its long segments, it's used for long backbones connecting buildings in a MAN or for connecting an ISP with its telecommunications carrier.

Table 5-6   Ethernet standards using fiber-optic cable

Standard		Maximum transmission speed (Mbps)	Maximum distance per segment (m)	Physical media
Gigabit Ethernet	1000Base-LX	1000	550 for MMF, 5000 for SMF	MMF or SMF
	1000Base-SX	1000	Up to 550, depending on modal bandwidth and fiber core diameter	MMF
10-Gigabit Ethernet	10GBase-SR and 10GBase-SW	10,000	Up to 300, depending on modal bandwidth and fiber core diameter	MMF
	10GBase-LR and 10GBase-LW	10,000	10,000	SMF
	10GBase-ER and 10GBase-EW	10,000	40,000	SMF

- 1000Base-SX is also a form of Gigabit Ethernet, is less expensive to install than 1000Base-LX, and uses shorter wavelengths of 850 nanometers (hence the *S* in its name *SX*). The maximum segment length for 1000Base-SX depends on two things: the diameter of the fiber and the modal bandwidth used to transmit signals. **Modal bandwidth** is a measure of the highest frequency of signal a multimode fiber can support over a specific distance and is measured in MHz-km. It is related to the distortion that occurs when multiple pulses of light, although issued at the same time, arrive at the end of a fiber at slightly different times. The higher the modal bandwidth, the longer a multimode fiber can carry a signal reliably. Table 5-7 shows some sample segment maximums for 1000Base-SX installations. Only one repeater may be used between segments. Therefore, 1000Base-SX is best suited for shorter network runs than 1000Base-LX—for example, connecting a data center with a data closet in an office building.

Table 5-7   1000Base-SX segment lengths

Multimode fiber diameter	Maximum segment length
50 microns	550 m
62.5 microns	275 m

Common Fiber Cable Problems

7	APPLICATION
6	PRESENTATION
5	SESSION
4	TRANSPORT
3	NETWORK
2	DATA LINK
1	PHYSICAL

Working with fiber cable presents a set of troubleshooting challenges that don't arise when you are working with copper cables. Problems that are unique to fiber cable include:

- *fiber type mismatch*—This term is misleading because a fiber type mismatch is actually more of a fiber core mismatch. Connecting an SMF cable to an MMF cable will prevent the transmission from traversing the connection successfully, though some of the signal can get through. However, even same-mode cables can be mismatched, if the cores have different widths. A cable with a 50-micron core, for example, should not be connected to a cable with a 62.5-micron core, even though they're both MMF.
- *wavelength mismatch*—SMF, MMF, and POF (Plastic Optical Fiber) each use different wavelengths for transmissions. A wavelength mismatch occurs when transmissions are optimized for one type of cable but sent over a different type of cable.
- *dirty connectors*—If fiber connectors get dirty or just a little dusty, signal loss and other errors can start to cause problems. Always keep protectors on fiber connectors and dust covers over fiber jacks when they're not in use.

Troubleshooting Tools

 **Certification**

7	APPLICATION
6	PRESENTATION
5	SESSION
4	TRANSPORT
3	NETWORK
2	DATA LINK
1	PHYSICAL

5.2 Given a scenario, use the appropriate tool.

5.3 Given a scenario, troubleshoot common wired connectivity and performance issues.

Symptoms of cabling problems can be as elusive as occasional lost packets or as obvious as a break in network connectivity. You can start troubleshooting a network connection problem by checking the network connection LED status indicator lights on the network ports of the devices involved. A steady light indicates connectivity and a blinking light indicates activity. A red or amber light, as shown in Figure 5-42, might indicate a problem. Check the device NICs and make sure cable connections are solid.

If all the devices check out and you suspect a cabling issue, you need to know which tools are designed to analyze and isolate problems related to particular types of network media. Several tools are available, ranging from simple continuity testers that indicate whether a cable is faulty, to sophisticated cable performance testers that graphically depict a cable's attenuation and crosstalk characteristics over the length of the cable. Knowing the specific tool to use for a particular troubleshooting scenario

Figure 5-42   Status indicator lights for an onboard network port

can help you quickly zero in on the problem and the solution. The following sections describe a variety of cable troubleshooting tools, their functions, and their relative costs.

Toner and Probe Kit

Ideally, you and your networking colleagues would label each port and wire termination in a data room so that problems and changes can be easily managed. However, because of personnel changes and time constraints, a data room might be disorganized and poorly documented. If this is the case where you work, a tone generator and a tone locator can help you determine where a wire, possibly out of hundreds, terminates:

- *tone generator (or toner)*—A small, electronic device that issues a signal on a wire
- *tone locator (or probe)*—A device that emits a tone when it detects electrical activity on a wire

They are sold together as a set, often called a **toner and probe kit** or just **toner probe** (see Figure 5-43).

Place the tone generator at one end of a wire using the appropriate connector. Swipe the tone locator over each of the terminations you suspect to be the other end of that wire. You can verify the location of the wire's termination when you hear the tone.

Figure 5-44 depicts the use of a tone generator and a tone locator. Work by trial and error, guessing which termination corresponds to the wire over which you've generated a signal until the tone locator indicates the correct choice.

Connectors to
connect to cable
or wire

Toner

Probe

Figure 5-43 A toner and probe kit by Fluke Corporation

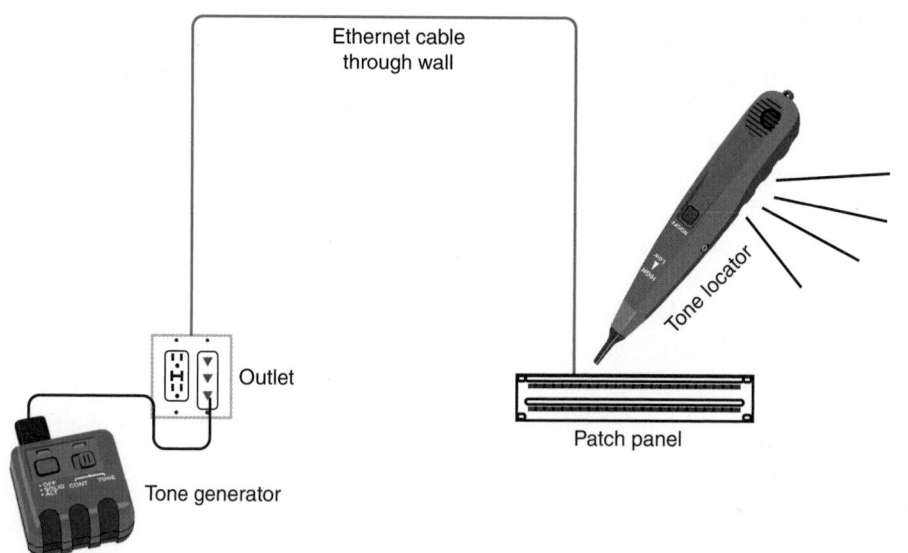

Ethernet cable
through wall

Tone locator

Outlet

Patch panel

Tone generator

Figure 5-44 A toner and probe kit locates the termination of a wire

Tone generators and tone locators cannot be used to determine any characteristics about a wire, such as whether it's defective or whether its length exceeds IEEE standards for a certain type of network. They are only used to determine where a wire terminates.

Multimeter

A **multimeter** is a simple instrument that can measure many characteristics of an electric circuit, including its resistance, voltage, and impedance (see Figure 5-45). Although you could use separate instruments for measuring impedance, resistance (opposition to electrical current), and voltage on a wire, it is more convenient to have one instrument that accomplishes all these functions.

Figure 5-45   A multimeter

Impedance is the telltale factor for ascertaining where faults in a cable lie. A certain amount of impedance is required for a signal to be properly transmitted and interpreted. However, very high or low levels of impedance can signify a damaged wire, incorrect pairing, or a termination point. In other words, changes in impedance can indicate where current is stopped or inhibited.

As a network professional, you might use a multimeter to do the following:

- Measure voltage to verify that a cable is properly conducting electricity—that is, whether its signal can travel unimpeded from one node on the network to another.
- Check for the presence of noise on a wire (by detecting extraneous voltage).
- Test for short or open circuits in the wire (by detecting unexpected resistance or loss of voltage).

    ○ A **short circuit** is an unwanted connection, such as when exposed wires touch each other.

    ○ An **open circuit** is one where needed connections are missing, such as when a wire breaks.

Cable Continuity Tester

In troubleshooting a Physical layer problem, you might find the cause of a problem by simply testing a cable's **continuity**—that is, whether it is carrying a signal to its destination. Tools used to test the continuity of the cable might be called cable checkers, **continuity testers**, or cable testers. The term **cable tester**, however, is a general term that might also refer to more sophisticated tools which measure cable performance.

A cable continuity tester (see Figure 5-46) is battery operated and has two parts:

- The base unit connects to one end of the cable and generates voltage.
- The remote unit connects to the other end of the cable and detects the voltage.

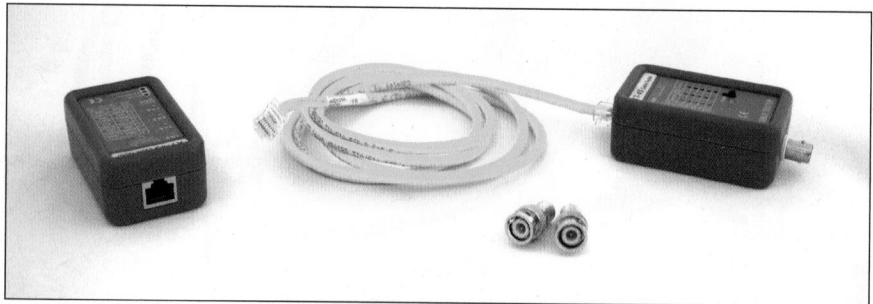

Figure 5-46 Use a cable tester pair to determine the type of cable and if the cable is good

Most cable testers provide a series of lights that signal pass/fail or other information, and some units also emit an audible tone. Here are some additional characteristics to consider when selecting a cable tester:

- Some continuity testers will verify that the wires in a UTP or STP cable are paired correctly following TIA/EIA 568 standards and that they are not shorted, exposed, or crossed. It might seem like mixing colors wouldn't matter on a cable so long as both ends of the cable match. However, an incorrect pinout can cause excessive crosstalk issues, voltage spikes, reduced performance, and problematic connections, especially with older devices. Make sure that the cable tester you purchase can test the type of network you use—for example, 100Base-T or 1000Base-T Ethernet.
- Continuity testers for fiber-optic cables issue light pulses on the fiber and determine whether they reach the other end of the fiber. Some continuity testers offer the ability to test both copper and fiber-optic cables.
- Most continuity testers are portable and lightweight, and typically use one 9-volt battery. A continuity tester can cost between $10 and $300 and can save many hours of work. Popular manufacturers of these cable testing devices include Belkin, Fluke, and Paladin.

Note

Do not use a continuity tester on a live network cable. Disconnect the cable from the network, and then test its continuity.

Cable Performance Tester

Whereas continuity testers can determine whether a single cable is carrying current, more sophisticated equipment is needed to measure the overall performance of a cabling structure. A device used for this sophisticated testing is called a **cable performance tester**, line tester, certifier, or network tester. It allows you to perform the same continuity and fault tests as a continuity tester, but can also be used to:

- Measure the distance to a connectivity device, termination point, or damage in a cable
- Measure attenuation along a cable
- Measure NEXT (near end crosstalk) between wires as well as alien cross talk
- Measure termination resistance and impedance
- Issue pass/fail ratings for Cat 3, Cat 5, Cat 5e, Cat 6, Cat 6a, or Cat 7 standards
- Store and print cable testing results or directly save data to a computer database

- Graphically depict a cable's attenuation and crosstalk characteristics over the length of the cable

A sophisticated performance tester will include a **TDR (time domain reflectometer)**. A TDR issues a signal on a cable and then measures the way the signal bounces back (or reflects) to the TDR. Bad connectors, crimps, bends, short circuits, cable mismatches, bad wiring, or other defects modify the signal's amplitude before it returns to the TDR, thus changing the way it reflects. The TDR analyzes the return signal, and based on its condition and the amount of time the signal took to return, determines cable imperfections.

Performance testers for fiber-optic connections use **OTDRs (optical time domain reflectometers)**. Rather than issue an electrical signal over the cable as twisted-pair cable testers do, an OTDR transmits light-based signals of different wavelengths over the fiber. Based on the type of return light signal, the OTDR can do the following:

- Accurately measure the length of the fiber
- Determine the location of faulty splices, breaks, bad or mismatched connectors, or bends
- Measure attenuation over the cable

Because of their sophistication, performance testers for both copper and fiber-optic cables cost significantly more than continuity testers. A high-end unit could cost up to $40,000, while a very low-end unit could sell for a few hundred dollars. On the left side of Figure 5-47, you can see an example of a high-end cable performance tester that is capable of measuring the characteristics of both copper and fiber-optic cables.

OPM (Optical Power Meter)

An **OPM (optical power meter)**, also called a **light meter**, measures the amount of light power transmitted on a fiber-optic line. The device must be calibrated precisely, following highly accurate optical power standards set by the NIST (National Institute of Standards and Technology), which is a nonregulatory agency of the U.S. Department of Commerce. However, the surrounding room temperature, connection type, and skill of the technician conducting the test all affect the accuracy of the final test results.

A simple light meter is pictured on the right side of Figure 5-47. More sophisticated and accurate meters are available at much higher price points.

As we conclude our exploration of various cable testing tools, consider that the time it takes to test a cable before installation could save many hours of troubleshooting after the network is in place. Whether you make your own cables or purchase cabling from a reputable vendor, test the cable to ensure that it meets your network's required standards. Just because a cable is labeled "Cat 6a," for example, does not necessarily mean that it will live up to that standard.

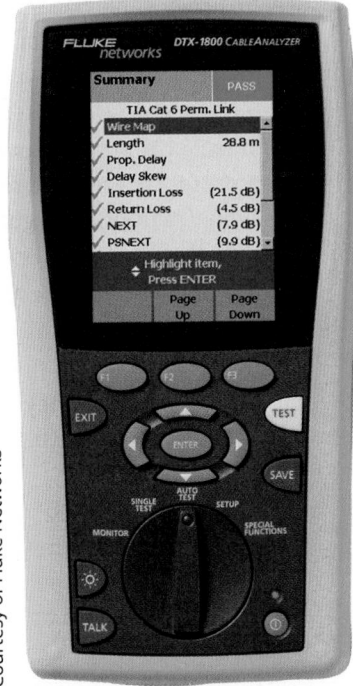 

Courtesy of Fluke Networks

Figure 5-47   (a) On the left, the DTX-1800 device by Fluke Networks is a high-end cable performance tester designed to certify structured cabling (b) The optical power meter on the right is a more budget-friendly device that measures light power transmitted on a fiber-optic line

Chapter Summary

Transmission Basics

- Bandwidth is the amount of data that could theoretically be transmitted during a given period of time, while throughput is the measure of how much data is actually transmitted during a given period of time.

- Noise can degrade or distort a signal. Attenuation is the loss of a signal's strength as it travels away from its source.

- Latency is the brief delay between the time when data is transmitted and when it is received.

- Duplex signals are free to travel in both directions over a medium simultaneously. Specifying a speed or duplex setting on a NIC that is not supported by a neighboring device results in a speed and duplex mismatch and, therefore, slow or failed transmissions.

- To carry multiple signals, a medium's channel is logically separated into multiple smaller channels, or subchannels, by varying each signal's time slot (TDM or STDM), frequency (FDM), or wavelength (WDM, DWDM, or CWDM).

Copper Cable

- Today's networks might use RG-59 coaxial cable for short connections, such as distributing video signals to multiple monitors in a building, or RG-6 coaxial cable to deliver broadband cable Internet service and cable TV.

- Twisted-pair cable consists of color-coded pairs of insulated copper wires, each with a diameter of 0.4 to 0.8 mm. On Fast Ethernet networks, one pair sends data, another pair receives data, and the other two pairs are not used for data transmission. Networks using Gigabit Ethernet and higher standards use all four pairs for both sending and receiving.

- STP cable's shielding acts as a barrier to external electromagnetic forces, thus preventing them from affecting the signals traveling over the wire inside the shielding.

- UTP cable is both less expensive and less resistant to noise than STP, and is more popular than STP, primarily because of its lower cost.

- STP and UTP both use RJ-45 modular connectors and data jacks, which look similar to analog telephone connectors and jacks.

- TIA/EIA has specified two different methods of inserting twisted-pair wires into RJ-45 plugs: TIA/EIA 568A and TIA/EIA 568B. Functionally, there is very little difference between these two standards; however, the same standard should be used throughout a network so data is transmitted and received correctly.

- A crossover cable has the transmit and receive wires reversed and was used to connect a PC to a PC or a switch to a switch.

- A router's console port is used with a console cable, or rollover cable, to communicate with the router itself, such as when making configuration changes to the device.

- DB-9 and DB-25 connectors comply with the RS-232 standard.

- A crimper pushes on the pins inside an RJ-45 connector so they pierce the wire's insulation, thus creating contact between the two conductors.

- IEEE's 802.3af and 802.3at standards specify a method for supplying a small amount of power over twisted-pair Ethernet cables, a technology known as PoE (Power over Ethernet).

- A device's NIC is rated for maximum network speeds defined by various Ethernet standards that operate at Layer 2. However, the network must be wired with cabling that is capable of supporting those speeds.

Fiber-Optic Cable

- Data is transmitted through the central fibers of fiber-optic cable via pulsing light sent from a laser or an LED source.

- Laser-generated light travels over a single path inside SMF cables, reflecting very little. This continuity allows SMF to accommodate the highest bandwidths and longest distances of all network transmission media.

- MMF contains a core with a larger diameter than SMF over which many pulses of light generated by a laser or LED light source travel at different angles.

- Older fiber networks might use ST or SC connectors. However, LC and MTRJ connectors are now more common because of their smaller sizes.

- A media converter is hardware that enables networks or segments running on different media to interconnect and exchange signals.

- Some switches and routers contain sockets where one of many types of modular interfaces, called transceivers, can be plugged in. Such transceivers are easily inserted into the sockets without disrupting operations and can be upgraded later as technology improves.

- 1000Base-LX is the more common fiber version of Gigabit Ethernet and uses long wavelengths, while 1000Base-SX is also common, is less expensive to install, and uses shorter wavelengths.

- Cabling problems unique to fiber include fiber type mismatch, wavelength mismatch, and dirty connectors.

Troubleshooting Tools

- Start troubleshooting a network connection problem by checking the network connection LED status indicator lights on the network ports of the devices involved.

- A tone generator issues a signal on a wire that can be detected by a tone locator, which emits an audible tone when the electrical signal is nearby.

- A multimeter can measure many characteristics of an electric circuit, including its resistance, voltage, and impedance.

- A cable continuity tester is battery operated and has two parts: the base unit that connects to one end of the cable and generates a voltage, and the remote unit that connects to the other end of the cable and detects the voltage to determine continuity of wired connections inside the cable.

- A sophisticated cable performance tester will include a TDR (time domain reflector) that issues a signal on a cable and then measures the way the signal bounces back, detecting types and locations of cable defects.

- An OPM (optical power meter) measures the amount of light power transmitted on a fiber-optic line.

Key Terms

For definitions of key terms, see the Glossary near the end of the book.

100Base-T
1000Base-LX
1000Base-SX
1000Base-T
10GBase-T
802.3af
802.3at
alien crosstalk
APC (Angle Polished
  Connector)

attenuation
bandwidth
BiDi transceiver
bidirectional
bit rate
BNC connector
cable performance tester
cable tester
Cat 3 (Category 3)
Cat 5 (Category 5)

Cat 5e (Enhanced
  Category 5)
Cat 6 (Category 6)
Cat 6a (Augmented
  Category 6)
Cat 7 (Category 7)
Cat 7a (Augmented
  Category 7)
CFP (centum form-factor
  pluggable)

cladding
coaxial cable
console port
continuity
continuity tester
core
crimper
crossover cable
CWDM (coarse wavelength division multiplexing or coarse WDM)
DB-9 connector
DB-25 connector
duplex
DWDM (dense wavelength division multiplexing or dense WDM)
Ethernet port
F-connector
Fast Ethernet
FDM (frequency division multiplexing)
FDP (fiber distribution panel)
ferrule
FEXT (far end crosstalk)
full-duplex
GBIC (Gigabit interface converter)
Gigabit Ethernet
hot-swappable
jitter
LC (local connector)
LED (light-emitting diode)

light meter
loopback adapter
media converter
MMF (multimode fiber)
modal bandwidth
MTRJ (Mechanical Transfer-Registered Jack)
multimeter
multiplexing
NEXT (near end crosstalk)
open circuit
OPM (optical power meter)
optical loss
OTDR (optical time domain reflectometer)
patch cable
pinout
PoE (Power over Ethernet)
PoE+
probe
QSFP (quad small form-factor pluggable)
QSFP+
repeater
RFI (radio frequency interference)
RG-6 (radio guide 6)
RG-59 (radio guide 59)
RJ-11 (registered jack 11)
RJ-45 (registered jack 45)
RTT (round trip time)
SC (subscriber connector or standard connector)

SFP (small form-factor pluggable)
SFP+
short circuit
SMF (single mode fiber)
speed and duplex mismatch
ST (straight tip)
STDM (statistical time division multiplexing)
straight-through cable
TDM (time division multiplexing)
TDR (time domain reflectometer)
throughput
TIA/EIA 568A
TIA/EIA 568B
tone generator
tone locator
toner
toner and probe kit
toner probe
transceiver
twist ratio
twisted-pair
TX/RX reverse
UPC (Ultra Polished Connector)
WDM (wavelength division multiplexing)
XFP (10 Gigabit small form-factor pluggable)

Review Questions

1. Which transmission characteristic is never fully achieved?
   a. Latency
   b. Throughput
   c. Bit rate
   d. Bandwidth

2. Which kind of crosstalk occurs between wire pairs near the source of the signal?
   a. Alien
   b. TX/RX reverse
   c. FEXT
   d. NEXT

3. Which kind of multiplexing assigns slots to nodes according to priority and need?
   a. WDM (wavelength division multiplexing)
   b. STDM (statistical time division multiplexing)
   c. TDM (time division multiplexing)
   d. CWDM (coarse wavelength division multiplexing)

4. What kind of cable uses BNC connectors? Which connector is likely to be used by cable TV?
   a. Coaxial cable, F-connector
   b. Twisted-pair cable, RJ-11
   c. Copper cable, RJ-45
   d. Fiber-optic cable, MTRJ

5. Which of these categories of twisted-pair cable can support Gigabit Ethernet?
   a. Cat 5, Cat 6, Cat 7
   b. Cat 5e, Cat 6, Cat 3
   c. Cat 5e, Cat 6a, Cat 7
   d. Cat 6, Cat 7a, Cat 5

6. Suppose you're creating patch cables to be used in a government office. What color wire goes in the first pin?
   a. White/orange
   b. White/green
   c. Brown
   d. Blue

7. What is the earliest twisted-pair cabling standard that meets the minimum requirements for 10GBase-T transmissions?
   a. Cat 5e
   b. Cat 5
   c. Cat 6a
   d. Cat 7

8. What type of fiber cable problem is caused when pairing a 50-micron core cable with a 62.5-micron core cable?
   a. Dirty connectors
   b. Wavelength mismatch
   c. Fiber type mismatch
   d. TX/RX reverse

9. Which part of a toner and probe kit emits an audible tone when it detects electrical activity on a wire pair?
   a. TDR
   b. Tone generator
   c. Tone locator
   d. Toner

10. Which fiber connector contains two strands of fiber in each ferrule?
    a. MTRJ
    b. SC
    c. ST
    d. LC

11. How is latency measured, and in what unit?

12. What is a twist ratio, and why is it important?

13. What fiber is used in fiber-optic cabling to protect the inner core and prevent the cable from stretching?

14. What characteristic of optical transmissions is primarily responsible for the distance limitations of fiber-optic cabling?

15. Why is SMF more efficient over long distances than MMF?

16. Why do APC ferrules create less back reflection than UPC ferrules?

17. Which fiber transceiver is the same size as SFP transceivers, but can support network speeds over 10 Gbps?

18. Suppose you're assisting with a cable installation using fiber-optic cabling that will support Gigabit Ethernet. You're approved to install segments up to 4000 m in length. What kind of cable are you using?

19. What is the difference between short circuits and open circuits?

20. What kind of tool can measure the distance to the location of damage in a cable?

Hands-On Projects

Project 5-1: Create a Loopback Plug

In this chapter, you practiced terminating an Ethernet cable by attaching an RJ-45 connector. You also learned that a loopback plug crosses the transmit line with the receive line to trick a device into thinking it's connected to a network. You can create your own loopback plug by altering the pinout on the connector and forcing the transmissions to loop back in on themselves. A loopback plug is helpful for determining if a NIC on a workstation or a port on a switch is working or not.

To make your own loopback plug, you'll need a 6-inch length of UTP cabling (Cat 5 or Cat 5e), an unused RJ-45 plug, wire cutters, and a cable crimper.

1. Cut to loosen the cable's covering, then slide the covering off the cable and flatten out the wire pairs. Do not untwist the wire pairs. Select one wire pair (one solid and one striped) and lay the other pairs aside because you won't need them.
2. Untwist the wires on each end an inch or less and straighten out the tips. If needed, give each wire a clean cut to make sure the two wires on each end are even with each other.
3. Insert one end of the twisted pair into the RJ-45 plug, making sure the solid color wire goes into slot 1, and the striped wire goes into slot 2. Push the wires all the way into the slots.
4. Loop the wire pair around and insert the other end into the plug. The solid color wire goes into slot 3, and the striped wire goes into slot 6. (Slots 4, 5, 7, and 8 are not needed unless you'll be testing Gigabit Ethernet equipment.)
5. Push the wires all the way in, and use the crimper to secure the wires in the plug. If a boot came with the plug, you can insert it over the wire loop and push it all the way through to cover the wire/plug connection, as shown in Figure 5-48.

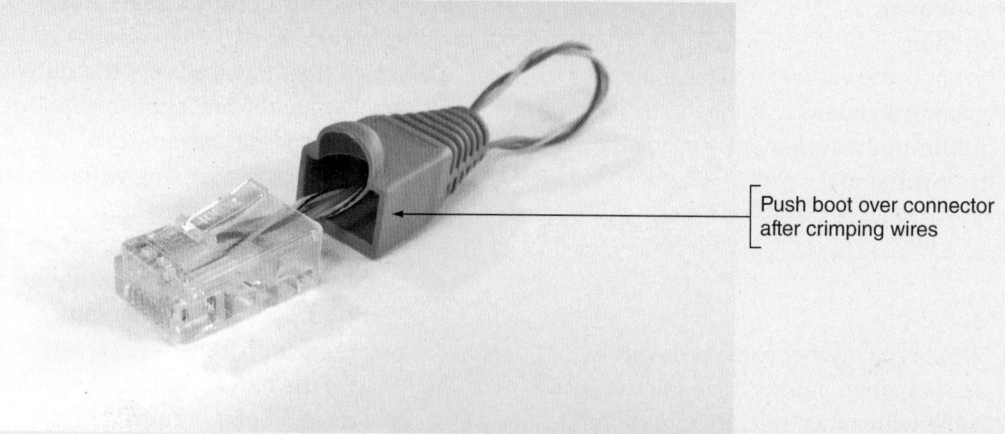

Push boot over connector after crimping wires

Figure 5-48   Adding the boot to the loopback plug is optional

6. Insert the loopback plug into a device's Ethernet port that is known to be working correctly and has LED indicator lights. If the port's link indicator lights up (this might take a minute), you've successfully created a loopback plug.

> **Note** 📎
>
> If you want to include the other two pins in the adapter so you can test VoIP and similar Gigabit Ethernet equipment, you'll need to use a second twisted pair from your original cable. Before crimping, insert one end of the second pair into the plug. Press the solid color wire into slot 4 and the striped wire into slot 5. Loop the wire around and press the solid color wire into slot 7 and the striped wire into slot 8. Crimp, and you're done.

Project 5-2: Create a Loopback Jack

A loopback plug can be used to test a port on a switch or a workstation's NIC. A loopback jack, however, can be used to test a cable or to identify which port a cable is connected to. This is especially helpful when the cable is already run through the wall or is tangled up with other cables.

Creating a loopback plug is pretty straightforward, and wiring a loopback jack is even easier. For this project, you'll need a 2-inch length of UTP cabling (Cat 5 or Cat 5e), an unused RJ-45 data/phone jack (these are very inexpensive and easily found at many home improvement stores), and a punchdown tool.

1. Cut to loosen the cable's covering, slide the covering off the cable, select one wire pair, and untwist it completely. Lay the other pairs aside because you won't need them.
2. Turn the jack so the slots are easily accessible. Take a single wire and press one end into the slot next to the "A–green/white" icon. Press the other end into the slot with the "A–orange/white" icon.

> **Note** 📎
>
> There is some variation in how RJ-45 jacks are designed. If these generic directions don't match the jack you're using, check the documentation that came with the jack.

3. Take the other, single wire, press one end into the slot next to the "A–orange" icon, and press the other end into the slot next to the "A–green" icon. In some cases, depending on the actual jack you use, the two wires will create an "X" shape through the center of the jack between the slots, as shown in Figure 5-49. With other jacks, the wires might cross over each other on one side only.

Figure 5-49 With this jack, the wires cross in the middle

4. Use the punchdown tool to punch the wires all the way into their respective slots. The punchdown tool will also clip the excess length off the wires. Make sure to orient the punchdown tool so the cutting side will slice the outside length of the wire and not the inside length. If a cover came with the jack, place it over the wires.

5. To test your loopback jack, plug a patch cable you know to be good into a device's Ethernet port that you know works, then plug the jack onto the other end of the cable. Wait up to a minute to give the link sufficient time to be established. If the port's link indicator lights up, you've successfully created a loopback jack.

For storage, you can plug your loopback plug into your loopback jack (see Figure 5-50), giving you a handy two-in-one tool for your toolkit.

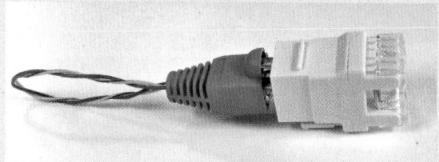

Figure 5-50 Attach the plug and jack together to protect their connections when storing them

Project 5-3: Latency Around the World

In this chapter, you learned that latency is the delay caused by the time it takes messages to travel over network media from one place to another. This concept is easy to see in the real world, where it takes longer, for example, for you to travel across the country than it does to go to the grocery store. Even though network messages travel much faster than a car or a jet plane, it still takes time for them to get from one place to another.

Complete the following steps to see how distance affects a message's RTT (round trip time):

1. Open a Command Prompt window and run `tracert` on a website whose servers are located on a different continent from you, across one ocean. If you're located in the

> **Note**
>
> For an Ubuntu or other Linux installation, use `traceroute` rather than `tracert` for this project. But you first must install the traceroute utility. On Ubuntu, run this command:
>
> `sudo apt-get install traceroute`

Midwest or Eastern United States, for example, you can run the command **tracert london.edu** (London Business School). If you are on the West Coast, however, you might get more useful results for this step by targeting a server across the Pacific Ocean, such as **tracert www.tiu.ac.jp** (Tokyo International University). What command did you use?

2. Examine the output and find the point in the route when messages started jumping across the ocean. By what percentage does the RTT increase after the jump compared with before it? You can see an example in Figure 5-51.

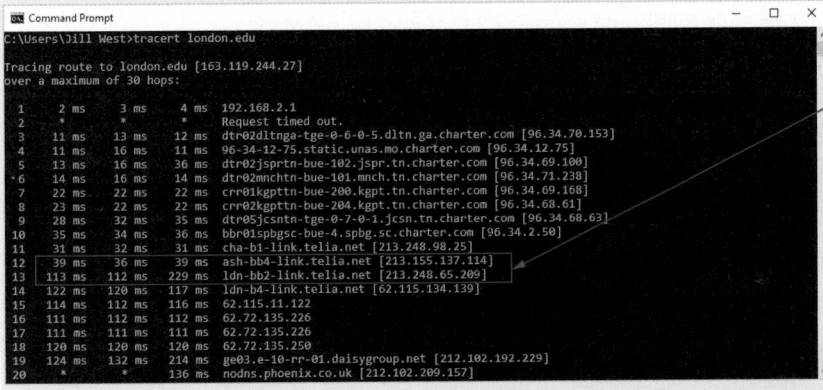

The first router in this box is located in Ashburn, VA, and is the last U.S. router listed.

The second router in this box is located in London, England, and is the first European router listed.

Figure 5-51   The latency time increases significantly as the messages start to cross the ocean

To calculate the percentage for this jump, you would select a time from just after the jump (229, for example) and divide it by a time from just before the jump (such as 39), then multiply by 100 percent: 229/39 × 100% = 587%. In this case, the sample data would yield a 587 percent increase. It takes nearly six times as long for a message to go round-trip across the Atlantic from the United States to London, England (the location of this first European router) as it does for a message to travel round trip between two servers that are both located on the U.S. East Coast (this local computer, and the last U.S. router in the route).

3. Choose a website whose servers are on a continent even farther away from you. For example, if you are in the United States, you could trace the route to the University of Delhi in India at the address du.ac.in. What command did you use? How many hops did it take until the route crossed an ocean? What other anomalies do you notice about this global route?

4. Choose one more website as close to directly across the globe from you as possible. U.S. locations might want to use the University of Western Australia at uwa.edu.au. What command did you use? How many hops are in the route? Did the route go east or west around the world from your location? How can you tell?

5. Scott Base in Antarctica runs several webcams from various research locations. Run a trace to the Scott Base website at **antarcticanz.govt.nz**. What's the closest router to Scott Base's web server that your trace reached? If you can't tell from the command output where the last response came from, go to **iplocation.net** in your browser. Enter the final IP address to determine that router's location.

6. Think about other locations around the world that might be reached through an interesting route. Find a website hosted in that location and trace the route to it. Which website did you target? Where is it located? What are some locations along the route of your trace?

7. Try the `ping` command on several of these same IP addresses. Did it work? Why do you think this is the case?

Project 5-4: Test a LAN's Speed and Throughput

A variety of software and web-based tools are available to help you establish baseline measurements—and later, detect fluctuations and problems—in the efficiency of your network and Internet connections. This project walks you through two different tests you can perform on your school's lab network or at home on your own LAN. You'll need two computers with either Windows 10 or macOS installed and connected to the same network.

TotuSoft's LAN Speed Test is a simple, free program that only needs access to a shared folder on the local area network in order to test throughput speeds on the network. The Public Users folder on another workstation meets this requirement.

To test a wired network connection, make sure both your computer and the target computer have a wired connection to the network (rather than a Wi-Fi connection), and then complete the following steps:

1. Go to **totusoft.com**, download the latest version of **LAN Speed Test (Lite)**, and run the downloaded .exe file. The app will automatically detect your own computer's IP address.

2. Find a shared folder on another workstation or a server on your network, as shown in Figure 5-52. Select the folder as the target, accept the default settings, and start the test.

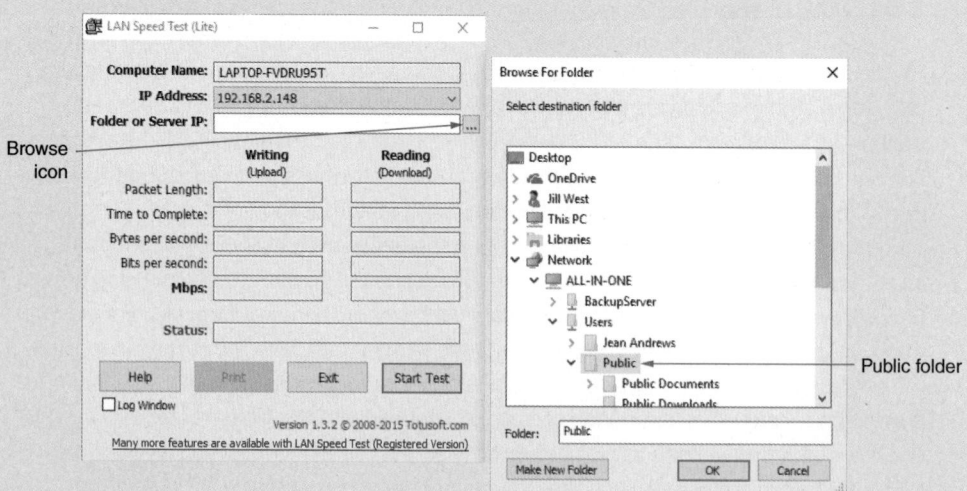

Figure 5-52   Browse to a public folder on another computer on your network

Source: TotuSoft

3. Accept the default settings for the test, including file size and the option to delete the file after the test is finished. Click **Ok**.

4. When the test has finished running, answer the following questions:

    a. What network media connects your computer to your network?

    b. How do your test results compare with the various Ethernet standards discussed in the chapter?

    c. If your test results differ from the standards you were expecting, how do you explain these results?

TamoSoft, another security and network monitoring software company, offers a free Throughput Test that works on both wired and wireless LAN connections. Complete the following steps:

5. Go to **tamos.com** and look for the Throughput Test in the Download Area. Download and install it on two computers on the same LAN, accepting default settings in the setup wizard.

> **Note** 📎
>
> If Run Server and Run Client are not visible at the top of the Start menu, scroll down and click to expand TamoSoft Throughput Test. Then click Run Server or Run Client, respectively.

6. One computer will act as the client and one as the server.

    a. On the server computer, click **Start** and, in the Start menu, click **Run Server**. If necessary, click **Yes** in the UAC dialog box.

    b. On the client computer, click **Start** and, in the Start menu, click **Run Client**. If necessary, click **Yes** in the UAC dialog box.

7. On the computer acting as the server, note its IP address, which is reported automatically in the TamoSoft Throughput Test window. Accept all the default settings. Nothing more is needed on this end of the connection because the server only needs to listen for the client.

8. On the computer acting as the client, enter the server's IP address, then click **Connect**. Figure 5-53 shows the server and client consoles side by side.

9. In the Chart pane, TCP and UDP throughput are monitored. Upstream refers to traffic moving from the client computer to the server computer. Downstream refers to traffic moving from the server computer to the client computer. Other charts include Loss and RTT. Let the test run for a while, then click **Disconnect**. Examine the results, and answer the following questions.

    a. On the Throughput chart, what was the highest reading obtained, and what kind of traffic was it?

    b. On the Loss chart, were there any significant loss results, and what kind of traffic was involved? What theories do you have about why this might be? Where would you look next to resolve this problem?

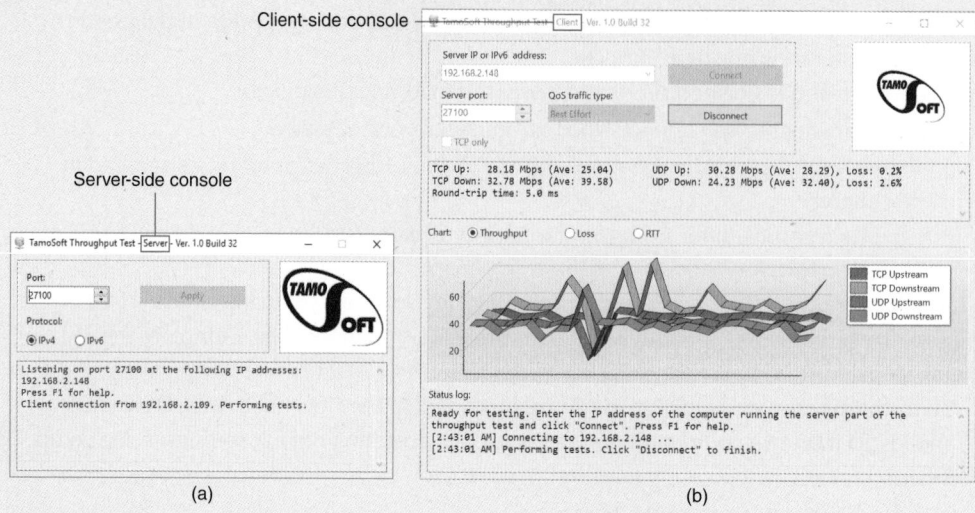

Figure 5-53   Server (a) and client (b) consoles for Throughput Test, with results showing on the client side

Source: TamoSoft

    c. On the RTT (round trip time) chart, were there any spikes? Do you notice any correlation between the timing of the spikes on this chart and the timing of problem indicators on the other two charts?
10. Document both of these software installations in your wikidot website.

Capstone Projects

Capstone Project 5-1: Set Up an FTP Server in Ubuntu Server

In Chapter 4, in Capstone Project 4-1, you installed Ubuntu Server in a VM and learned to use some Linux commands in Ubuntu. In this Capstone Project, you set up an FTP server on the Ubuntu Server VM. Follow these steps:

1. Using the same VM you created in Capstone Project 4-1, log on to Ubuntu Server with your username and password. Refer to your LastPass vault if you don't remember that information.

2. To install a program, you need to have the security privileges of a superuser. In Linux, the superuser is named *root*. You can apply root privileges to any command by preceding the command with the sudo command. To use root privileges to install the FTP program named vsftpd, enter this command:

```
sudo apt-get install vsftpd
```

Note 🖉

If you get an error message saying the vsftpd package can't be located, you might need to update your apt-get package list. To do so, enter the command `sudo apt-get update`, and then try the vsftpd installation again.

3. Respond to the prompts and then wait for the package to install.
4. Now you need to configure the FTP program by editing the vsftpd.conf text file stored in the /etc directory. Before you edit the file, go to the /etc directory and make a backup copy of the file just in case you need it later:

```
cd /etc
sudo cp vsftpd.conf vsftpd.backup
```

5. Ubuntu has several available text editors; we'll use the vim editor. First install the editor:

```
sudo apt-get install vim
```

6. Now edit the FTP configuration file:

```
sudo vim vsftpd.conf
```

Here are a few tips on using the vim editor. You can find out more about it by doing a Google search:
- Use the arrow keys to move over the file.
- To edit the file, type **i** to enter Insert mode. INSERT appears at the bottom of your VM screen.
- To leave Insert mode, press **Escape**.
- To save your changes, type **:w**.
- To exit without saving your changes, type **:q**.
- To save your changes and exit, type **:wq**.

7. Using vim, find and, if necessary, change three lines in the config file to create the settings listed in Table 5-8. Part of the file, including the three lines, is shown in Figure 5-54.

Table 5-8 Check these settings in the vsftpd.conf file

Setting	Description
anonymous_enable=NO	Disable anonymous logins.
local_enable=YES	If you see a # at the beginning of this line, delete it to uncomment the line and allow local users to log in.
write_enable=YES	If you see a # at the beginning of this line, delete it to allow users to write to a directory.

```
# Example config file /etc/vsftpd.conf
#
# The default compiled in settings are fairly paranoid. This sample file
# loosens things up a bit, to make the ftp daemon more usable.
# Please see vsftpd.conf.5 for all compiled in defaults.
#
# READ THIS: This example file is NOT an exhaustive list of vsftpd options.
# Please read the vsftpd.conf.5 manual page to get a full idea of vsftpd's
# capabilities.
#
#
# Run standalone?  vsftpd can run either from an inetd or as a standalone
# daemon started from an initscript.
listen=NO
#
# This directive enables listening on IPv6 sockets. By default, listening
# on the IPv6 "any" address (::) will accept connections from both IPv6
# and IPv4 clients. It is not necessary to listen on *both* IPv4 and IPv6
# sockets. If you want that (perhaps because you want to listen on specific
# addresses) then you must run two copies of vsftpd with two configuration
# files.
listen_ipv6=YES
#
# Allow anonymous FTP? (Disabled by default).
anonymous_enable=NO
#
# Uncomment this to allow local users to log in.
local_enable=YES
#
# Uncomment this to enable any form of FTP write command.
#write_enable=YES
#
# Default umask for local users is 077. You may wish to change this to 022,
# if your users expect that (022 is used by most other ftpd's)
#local_umask=022

"vsftpd.conf" 155L, 5850C                                        1,1            Top
```

Figure 5-54 Part of the vsftpd.conf text file
Source: Canonical Group Limited

8. Exit the vim editor, saving your changes. Restart the FTP service using this command:

   `sudo service vsftpd restart`

9. To test your FTP server using the local machine, enter **`ftp 127.0.0.1`**. Then enter your username and password for your Ubuntu Server account. Next enter the **`dir`** command to see a list of directories and files. You should see the mydir directory that you created in your /home/*username* directory when doing Capstone Project 4-1. Type **`bye`** to disconnect from the FTP server.

10. To find out the IP address of the server, type **`ifconfig`**.

11. Go to another computer on your local network or in your virtual network and use the commands from Step 9 to connect to your FTP server, this time using the IP address of your server rather than the loopback address. Here are some caveats, potential problems, and possible solutions to consider for this step:

    • Your installation of Ubuntu Server might not allow FTP traffic through its firewall. You'll learn about the default Ubuntu Server firewall, iptables, in Chapter 10. For now, let's enable the simpler firewall, ufw (Uncomplicated Firewall), and open the required FTP ports. Enter these commands:

      ```
      sudo ufw enable
      sudo ufw allow 20/tcp
      sudo ufw allow 21/tcp
      sudo ufw status
      ```

- Confirm that ufw is active and that ports 20 and 21 are allowed. Reboot the server with the command `sudo reboot`. Run `ifconfig` on the FTP server to determine its new IP address, and then repeat Step 9 on the FTP client.

- If you're using VirtualBox for either the server or the client, you must first enable Bridged mode on each VM's network adapter, which you'll learn more about in Chapter 7. To do this, first power down all VirtualBox VMs. Select the Ubuntu Server VM, click **Settings**, and click **Network**. On the Adapter 1 tab, click the drop-down menu for *Attached to*, and select **Bridged Adapter**. Click **OK**. Repeat these steps for one or more VMs you want to use as an FTP client machine. Start the server and client VMs, run `ifconfig` on Ubuntu Server to determine its new IP address, and then repeat Step 9 on the FTP client.

- If you're using a Windows machine for the client, either virtual or physical, you should be able to log onto the FTP server from the Windows Command Prompt. However, you might run into a firewall problem when you attempt to run the `dir` command. Windows Command Prompt uses an older and less secure process for transferring FTP data, which often snags on modern firewalls. If Windows asks for permission to allow FTP traffic through the firewall, giving your approval should allow the `dir` output through. Another option is to use File Explorer instead. Open a File Explorer window, and in the address bar, type **ftp://*username*@ubuntuserver** and press **Enter**. You'll be prompted for login information, and then you should see the mydir directory that you created in your /home/*username* directory when doing Capstone Project 4-1.

Be sure to make some notes on your wikidot VMclients page regarding any adjustments you made for this step to work. Also list any web pages or tips you learned in researching and resolving any other errors you encountered.

> **Note**
>
> If you want to transfer files with FTP commands, use the `get` and `put` commands.

12. If you've not done so already, return to your wikidot **Virtualization:VMclients** page and update your notes for each VM you adjusted during this project. List any changes you made to settings and installations. You might also consider creating a new page where you collect Linux commands that you're learning in these projects. The best learning happens when you're troubleshooting problems that crop up, and taking good notes will help you retain more of this valuable information.

Capstone Project 5-2: Decode a TCP Segment in a Wireshark Capture

In Chapter 4, you walked through a TCP segment to interpret the fields included in its header. You also installed Wireshark and examined several messages in your capture. In this project, you'll pull these concepts together and use Wireshark to capture your own DNS messages, examine TCP headers in a TCP stream, and practice interpreting the information that you find.

1. Open Wireshark and snap the window to one side of your screen. Open a browser and snap that window to the other side of your screen, so you can see both windows.

> **Note** 📎
>
> In Windows, you can quickly snap a window to one side of your screen by holding down the Win key on your keyboard, pressing either the left or right arrow key, then releasing both keys. Alternately, you can drag a window to one edge of your screen until it snaps into position.

2. Start the Wireshark capture on your active network connection. In the browser, navigate to **google.com**. Once the page loads, stop the Wireshark capture. You'll have fewer messages to sort through if you can do this entire process fairly quickly.

3. Somewhere in your capture, a DNS message will show the original request to resolve the name *google.com* to its IP address. A series of TCP messages will then show the three-way handshake, along with the rest of the data transmission. Because your transmission has to do with requesting a secure web page using HTTPS, you need to filter to port 443. Apply the following filter to your capture to expose the messages involved with your website request: **dns or tcp.port eq 443**

4. This filter helps reduce the number of messages to the ones you actually want to see. But you'll still probably have to scroll through your results to find exactly the right DNS message that started this process. You'll see DNS in the Protocol field, and something to the effect of "Standard query" and "www.google.com" in the Info field, as shown in Figure 5-55. Notice that in this capture, both the primary (8.8.8.8) and the secondary (8.8.4.4) DNS servers made a DNS query to resolve the domain name.

5. Once you've located the message querying the DNS server, click on it and examine the details of the message in the second pane. Answer the following questions:
   a. What is the OUI of the source's NIC?
   b. Which IP version was used?
   c. If the message used IPv4, what was the TTL? If IPv6, what was the hop limit?
   d. Did the message use TCP or UDP?
   e. What is the source port? The destination port?

6. Now check your filter results for the first [SYN] message after this DNS request. Open the TCP segment header in the second pane, and answer the following questions:
   a. What is the sequence number?
   b. Which flags are set in the TCP segment?

   If you're using the default settings in Wireshark, you probably found a sequence number of 0. That's because Wireshark shows relative sequence numbers instead of the actual

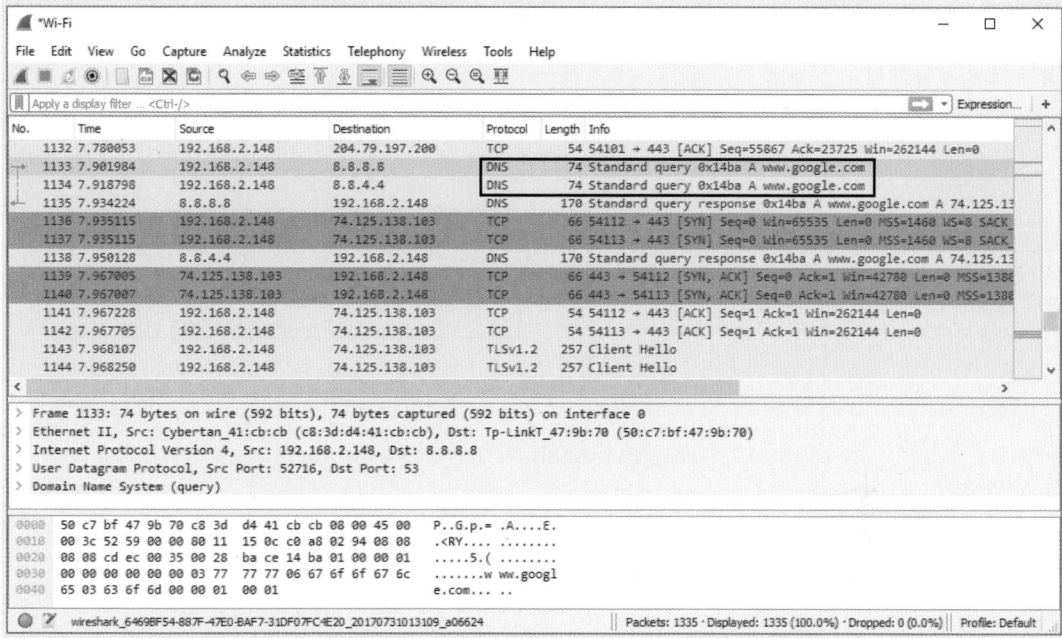

Figure 5-55   This DNS message is a request to resolve the domain name *www.google.com*

Source: The Wireshark Foundation

numbers used in the segments themselves. Relative numbers are easier for humans to keep up with, but they provide no security in that they're very predictable. Random numbers, on the other hand, are more difficult to fake.

7. To find the actual sequence number assigned to this segment, click on the sequence number field in the second pane, then find the corresponding value now highlighted in the third pane. The actual value is presented in hexadecimal format.

8. To switch the output to show actual sequence numbers (in decimal form) in your capture, click on the **Edit** menu, click **Preferences,** expand the **Protocols** list, scroll down and click **TCP,** and uncheck **Relative sequence numbers.** Then click **OK.** Notice in Figure 5-56 that the actual sequence and acknowledgment numbers are now shown in the Wireshark capture.

9. Apply another filter layer to show only the messages for this TCP conversation. Right-click the **[SYN]** message you selected earlier, point to **Follow,** and click **TCP Stream.** Close the Follow TCP Stream dialog box that opens, as you will be examining data in the actual capture.

10. Immediately after that initial [SYN] message, locate the [SYN, ACK] message and answer the following questions:

   a. What is the source IP address? The destination IP address?

   b. What is the sequence number? The acknowledgment number?

   c. Which flags are set in the TCP segment?

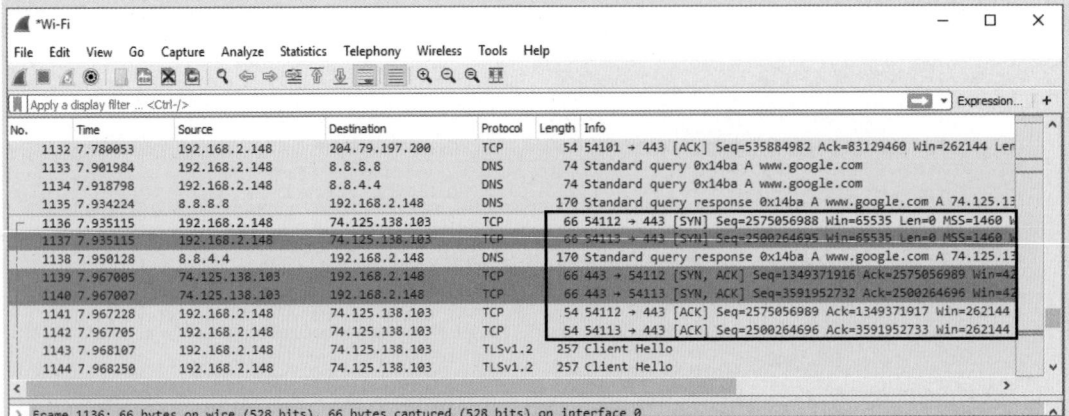

Figure 5-56   The captured messages now show the actual numbers used in the Seq and Ack fields

Source: The Wireshark Foundation

11. Locate the third message in this three-way handshake, the [ACK] message, and answer the following questions:

a. What is the source IP address? The destination IP address?

b. What is the sequence number? The acknowledgment number?

c. Which flags are set in the TCP segment?

12. The three-way handshake establishes the session, but the conversation continues as the web server begins to respond to your browser's request for the web page. First, Google's server redirects the conversation to a secure website using HTTP over SSL/TLS. Look for a series of messages listing TLS in the Protocol field. Locate the Client Hello and Server Hello messages, as shown in Figure 5-57. A few lines below that, locate

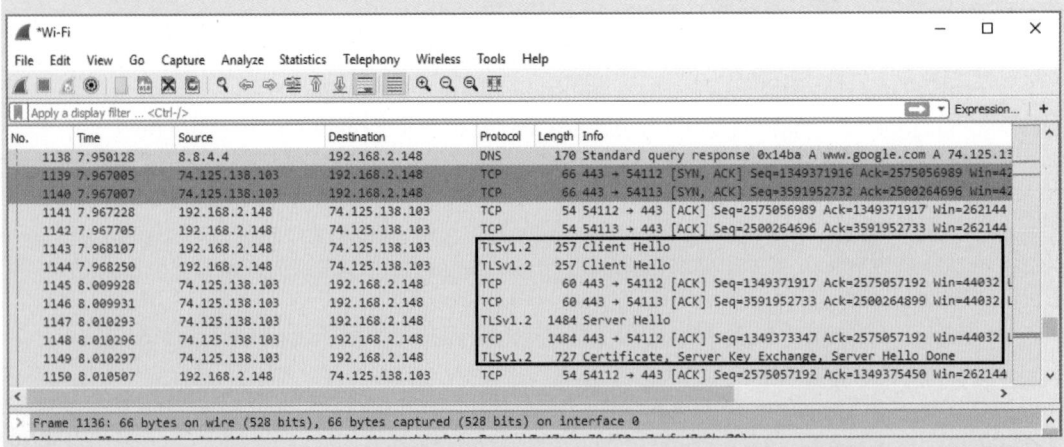

Figure 5-57   The web server establishes a secure link with the web client

Source: The Wireshark Foundation

the Certificate and Server Key Exchange message where the server completes its Hello process. You'll learn more about encryption keys in Chapter 7.

13. Soon after this key exchange, you'll see several messages using the TLS protocol that are labeled Application Data. Look at the Length field for these messages. What is the size of the longest message listed?

14. Click on one of the longest messages, and answer the following questions:

   a. List the types of headers included in this message, in order.

   b. What is the source IP address? The destination IP address?

   c. Which flags are set in the TCP segment?

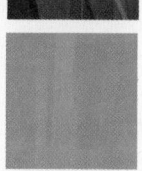

## CHAPTER 6

WIRELESS NETWORKING

After reading this chapter and completing the exercises, you will be able to:

Identify and describe various types of wireless networking characteristics

- -

Explain the various wireless standards that support the Internet of Things

- -

Explain 802.11 standards and innovations

- -

Implement a Wi-Fi network

- -

Secure a Wi-Fi network

- -

Troubleshoot a Wi-Fi network

- -

On the Job

I've installed wireless network equipment for the past 15 years. Our company builds and repairs computers and installs wireless networks and surveillance systems in office buildings, warehouses, and homes. We work with both directional wireless and open-space, broadcast wireless.

When installing a wireless AP, we're always careful to take note of any device specifications, such as the AP's range, and we have to consider what obstacles are in the device's line of sight. We evaluate any walls, ceilings, and other obstacles that come in between the source of the wireless signal and the various locations of receiving devices, such as printers, computers, and cell phones.

One installation comes to mind that really baffled us. It was an older home here in Dalton, Georgia, and was built around the early 1900s.

The house wasn't huge, and we installed an AP in the kitchen area. We initially tested the signal in the kitchen and, as expected, received 4 bars of signal strength. Next, we walked into the living room, which was just on the other side of the wall from the kitchen. In the living room, however, we barely received 1 bar.

We put in a higher wattage output AP and upon repeating the test, we still just received 1 bar in the living room. As part of our investigation, we went into the attic and discovered that this wall between the kitchen and the living room was built of plaster instead of sheetrock. Further investigation revealed that underneath the plaster was a layer of chicken wire. A little research revealed that in the old days, some walls incorporated chicken wire in the internal structure to hold the plaster against the wall. This wall was like a fortress, blocking our wireless signal.

We installed a second AP in another room to solve the problem. The moral to this story is, when installing wireless, beware of what an impact a single wall can have, especially in older homes.

Scott Merritt, Service Mgr.
Dalton Computer Services, Inc.

For decades, radio and TV stations have transmitted analog signals through the air. Air provides an intangible means of transporting data over networks and is often used in conjunction with wired technologies.

This chapter first looks at how wireless transmissions work, regardless of the type of wireless technology used. These wireless characteristics apply to satellite, Bluetooth, Wi-Fi, cellular, and other wireless signals. Some of these wireless signals, such as satellite and cellular, can travel long distances and will be discussed in more detail later. This chapter explores how to set up, manage, secure, and troubleshoot local wireless networks that you might find in an enterprise setting or that you might set up in your own home.

Characteristics of Wireless Transmissions

 **Certification**

7	APPLICATION
6	PRESENTATION
5	SESSION
4	TRANSPORT
3	NETWORK
2	DATA LINK
1	PHYSICAL

1.6   Given a scenario, implement the appropriate wireless technologies and configurations.

2.2   Given a scenario, determine the appropriate placement of networking devices on a network and install/configure them.

5.4   Given a scenario, troubleshoot common wireless connectivity and performance issues.

In previous chapters, you learned about signals that travel over a physical medium, such as a copper or fiber-optic cable. LANs that transmit signals through the air via RF (radio frequency) waves are known as **WLANs (wireless local area networks)**. Wireless transmission media is now common in business and home networks and necessary in some specialized network environments. Wired and wireless signals share many similarities, including use of the same Layer 3 and higher protocols, for example. However, the nature of the atmosphere makes wireless transmission vastly different from wired transmission at lower OSI layers. Let's look at what wireless signals are, and then we'll see how they're transmitted.

The Wireless Spectrum

All wireless signals are carried through the air by electromagnetic waves. The **wireless spectrum**, commonly called the airwaves, is the frequency range of electromagnetic waves used for data and voice communication. As defined by the FCC (Federal Communications Commission), which controls its use, the wireless spectrum spans frequency ranges or **bands** between 9 kHz and 300 GHz. (A hertz or Hz is one cycle per second.) Table 6-1 lists the frequency ranges from low to high used by wireless technologies discussed in this and other chapters. Notice in the table that several of the bands cover a frequency range that is further subdivided into channels. Some bands have only a single frequency, called a fixed frequency, for that band.

Table 6-1   Frequency ranges of wireless technologies listed from low to high frequencies

| Technologies | Frequency range (band) kHz, MHz, or GHz | | Description |
	Low	High	
RFID	125 kHz	134.2 kHz	The lowest of several frequency ranges for RFID and approved for global use
NFC	13.56 MHz		Fixed frequency
Z-Wave	90.842 MHz		Fixed frequency
Cellular	824 MHz	896 MHz	Commonly called the 800 band
RFID	858 MHz	930 MHz	One of several bands assigned to RFID
Cellular	1850 MHz	1990 MHz	Commonly called the 1900 band
Wi-Fi; 802.11b/g/n	2.4 GHz	2.4835 GHz	11 or 14 channels
ZigBee	2.4 GHz	2.4835 GHz	16 channels
Bluetooth	2.4 GHz	2.4835 GHz	79 channels
RFID	2.446 GHz	2.454 GHz	Highest frequency range for RFID
ANT+	2.457 GHz		Fixed frequency
Wi-Fi; 802.11a/n/ac	5.1 GHz	5.8 GHz	24 channels
IR	300 GHz	300,000 GHz	10 channels plus 4 near-infrared channels

Figure 6-1 shows where these bands fit in the wireless spectrum. Frequency bands used for AM, FM, and satellite communications are included in Figure 6-1 for comparison and to show where potential overlap of signals might occur.

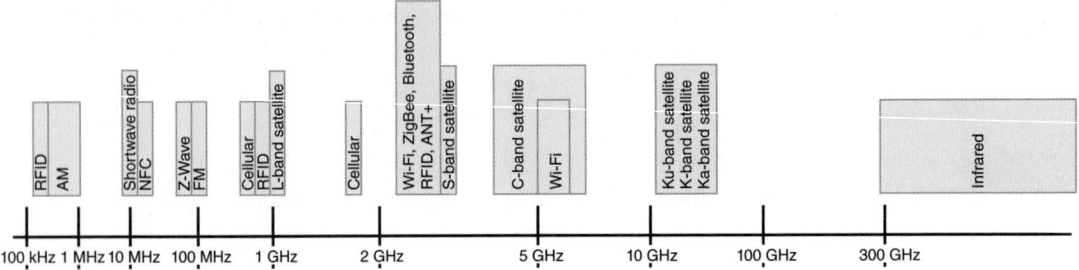

Figure 6-1   The wireless spectrum

 **Note**

The airwaves are considered a natural resource. In the United States, the FCC grants organizations in different locations exclusive rights to use each frequency and specifies which frequency ranges can be used for what purposes. Other countries have similar regulatory agencies. The ITU (International Telecommunication Union) is a United Nations agency that sets standards for international telecommunications including wireless frequency allocations and satellite orbits. Some bands can only be used with a license (for example, a band devoted to television, FM, or AM). Others, such as Wi-Fi bands, are available for public use. In the case of Wi-Fi, this means you can own and use a Wi-Fi device without acquiring a license granted by the FCC to use the band.

Notice in Figure 6-1 that Wi-Fi, Bluetooth, ZigBee, ANT+, as well as some satellite signals share the frequency ranges around 2.4 GHz. How do these technologies share these airwaves without one signal interfering with another? Let's explore how channels are managed to reduce interference caused by overlapping channels.

Channel Management

A band used by a wireless device is defined by its overall frequency range. To allow multiple devices to share the same band, the band is subdivided into channels and channels are further subdivided into narrowband channels. Most wireless devices implement one of two technologies to take advantage of the frequencies within its band to avoid interference:

- *FHSS (frequency hopping spread spectrum)*—Short bursts of data are transmitted on a particular frequency within the band and the next burst goes to the next frequency in the sequence. **Frequency hopping** can happen hundreds of times a second. FHSS is cheaper to implement than DSSS and performs better than DSSS in crowded, indoor environments.

- *DSSS (direct sequence spread spectrum)*—Data streams are divided and encoded into small chunks, called chips, which are spread over all available frequencies within one of three, wide channels, all at the same time. The process of dividing and encoding the data is called chipping, and the spreading ratio used to transform the data is called the chipping code, which is unique to each device. DSSS uses the available bandwidth more efficiently than FHSS and tends to have a higher throughput.

Here's a breakdown of how each wireless standard in the 2.4 GHz range uses its allotted band. You'll learn more about each of these standards later in this chapter.

- Wi-Fi, commonly used for wireless Internet access, uses DSSS. In the United States, the FCC has defined 11 channels within the 2.4-GHz band for Wi-Fi and 24 channels in the 5-GHz band. (Other countries might have 14 Wi-Fi channels for the 2.4-GHz band.) In the United States, each channel is 20 MHz wide. A Wi-Fi **AP (access point)**, which is the central connectivity device for Wi-Fi clients on a network, is manually configured to use a selected group of channels. Wi-Fi client devices scan the entire band for active channels.
- Bluetooth, commonly used to connect wireless personal devices, uses FHSS to take advantage of the 79 channels allocated to the Bluetooth band. In a network of Bluetooth devices (called a piconet), one device is designated the master and provides a clock the other devices use to coordinate their channel hopping. Because Bluetooth transmissions are constantly hopping channels, interference and collisions are unlikely to cause significant problems.
- ZigBee, commonly used in industrial, scientific, and medical devices, uses DSSS and 16 channels.
- ANT+, commonly used in activity monitoring devices, uses a fixed frequency, and, therefore, does not use DSSS or FHSS.

Even with the frequency spread of FHSS or DSSS to avoid interference, collisions can still happen. Each technology has a procedure to follow when it senses a collision. For example, when a Bluetooth device senses a collision with a Wi-Fi channel, it backs off using the frequencies in that Wi-Fi channel for a short time, giving Wi-Fi the opportunity to finish its transmission, as shown in Figure 6-2. Wi-Fi devices use a "listen before transmit" strategy to find a silent channel. More details about how Wi-Fi handles collisions is covered later in the chapter.

Antennas

The air provides no fixed path for signals to follow, so signals travel without guidance. Contrast this to wired media, such as UTP or fiber-optic cable, which do provide a fixed signal path. The lack of a fixed path requires wireless signals to be transmitted, received, controlled, and corrected differently than wired signals. Part of this work is done at a hardware level.

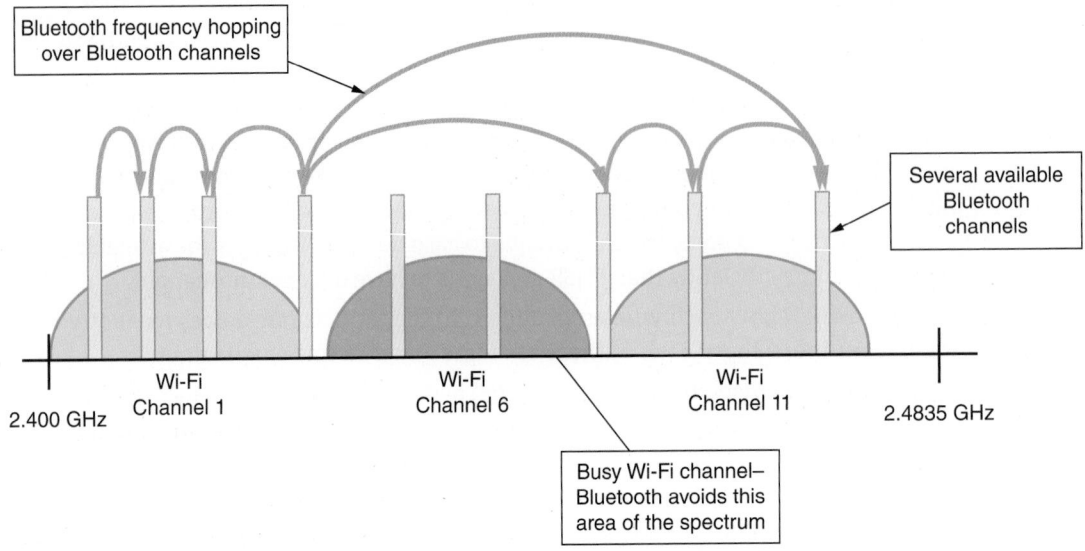

Figure 6-2   Bluetooth frequency hopping avoids a busy Wi-Fi channel

Just as with wired signals, wireless signals originate from electrical current traveling along a conductor. The electrical signal travels from the transmitter to an antenna, which then emits the signal as a series of electromagnetic waves into the atmosphere. The signal moves through the air until it reaches its destination. At the destination, another antenna accepts the signal, and a receiver converts it back to current. Figure 6-3 illustrates this process.

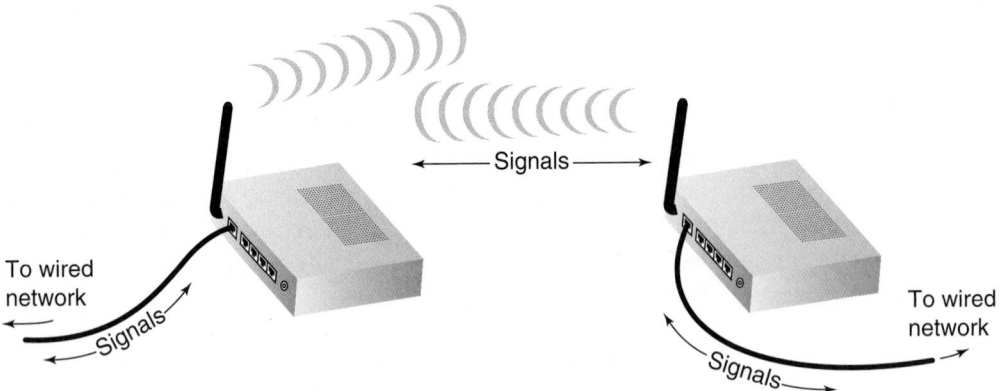

Figure 6-3   Wireless transmission and reception

Notice that antennas are used for both the transmission and reception of wireless signals. As you might expect, to exchange information, two antennas must be tuned to the same frequency in order to use the same channel.

Each type of wireless service requires an antenna specifically designed for that service. The service's specifications determine the antenna's power output, frequency, and radiation pattern. An antenna's **radiation pattern** describes the relative strength over a three-dimensional area of all the electromagnetic energy the antenna sends or receives. Radiation patterns can be used to classify antennas into two basic categories:

- *unidirectional antenna* (*also called a directional antenna*)—Issues wireless signals along a single direction. This type is used when the source needs to communicate with one destination, as in a point-to-point link, or in a specific area. A satellite downlink (for example, the kind used to receive digital TV signals) uses directional antennas.
- *omnidirectional antenna*—Issues and receives wireless signals with equal strength and clarity in all directions. This type is used when many different receivers must be able to pick up the signal in many directions, or when the receiver's location is highly mobile. TV and radio stations use omnidirectional antennas, as do most towers that transmit cellular signals.

The geographical area that an antenna or wireless system can reach is known as its **range**. Receivers must be within the range to receive accurate signals consistently. Even within an antenna's range, however, signals may be hampered by obstacles and rendered unintelligible.

Signal Propagation

Propagation refers to the way in which a wave travels from one point to another. Ideally, a wireless signal would travel directly in a straight line from its transmitter to its intended receiver. This type of propagation, known as **LOS (line of sight)**, maximizes distance for the amount of energy used and results in reception of the clearest possible signal. However, because the atmosphere is an unguided medium and the path between a transmitter and a receiver is not always clear, wireless signals do not usually follow a straight line.

> **Note** 📎
>
> Satellite and infrared transmissions require a clear line of sight. However, some signals might be blocked in what appears to be a clear line of sight. For example, many energy-efficient windows are covered with a film that filters out certain layers of sunlight. Even though you can see through the window, a satellite signal, such as an XM radio satellite signal, might not be able to get through.

When an obstacle stands in a signal's way, the signal might pass through the object, it might be absorbed by the object, or it might be subject to any of the following phenomena, depending upon the object's geometry and its constituent materials:

- *fading*—As a signal runs into various obstacles, its energy will gradually fade, which causes the strength of the signal that reaches the receiver to be lower than the transmitted signal's strength. Excessive fading can cause dropped connections or slow data transmission.

- *attenuation*—As with wired signals, wireless signals also experience attenuation. After a signal is transmitted, the farther it moves away from the transmission source, the more it weakens. Similar to wired transmission, wireless signals can be amplified by increasing the power of the transmission or extended by repeating the signal from a closer broadcast point called a **wireless range extender**, such as the one designed for a home network shown in Figure 6-4.

Figure 6-4   Wi-Fi range extender

- *interference*—Electromagnetic waves in the atmosphere can interfere with wireless communications similar to how EMI (electromagnetic interference) affects wired transmissions. Because wireless signals cannot depend on a conduit or shielding to protect them from extraneous EMI, they are more vulnerable to noise than wired transmissions are. The proportion of noise to the strength of a signal is called the **SNR** or S/N **(signal-to-noise ratio)**. Signals traveling through areas in which many wireless communications systems are in use—for example, the center of a metropolitan area—are the most apt to suffer from interference.
- *refraction*—As a wave travels into and through a different transmission medium, such as when traveling through glass or other solids, the wave's direction, speed, and wavelength are altered, or refracted. Imagine how light waves are altered when entering the water in a pool. If you're underwater looking back at the surface, the image you see is distorted.
- *reflection*—The wave encounters an obstacle and reflects, or bounces back, toward its source. A wireless signal will bounce off objects whose dimensions

are large compared with the signal's average wavelength. In the context of a wireless LAN, whose wavelengths are approximately 12 cm, such objects include walls, floors, ceilings, and the Earth—anything with a large, flat surface. In addition, signals reflect more readily off conductive materials, such as metal, than off insulators, such as concrete.

- *scattering*—When a wireless signal encounters an object that has small dimensions compared with the signal's wavelength, it's diffused or scattered in multiple directions. Scattering is also related to the roughness of the surface a wireless signal encounters. The rougher the surface, the more likely a signal is to scatter when it hits that surface. In an office building, objects such as chairs, books, and computers cause scattering of wireless LAN signals. For signals traveling outdoors, rain, mist, hail, and snow may all cause scattering.

- *diffraction*—A wireless signal is diffracted, or split into secondary waves, when it encounters an obstruction. The secondary waves continue to propagate in the direction in which they were split. If you could see wireless signals being diffracted, they would appear to be bending around the obstacle. Objects with sharp edges—including the corners of walls and desks—cause diffraction.

Wireless signals follow a number of different paths to their destination. Such signals are known as multipath signals. Figure 6-5 illustrates multipath signals caused by reflection, scattering, and diffraction.

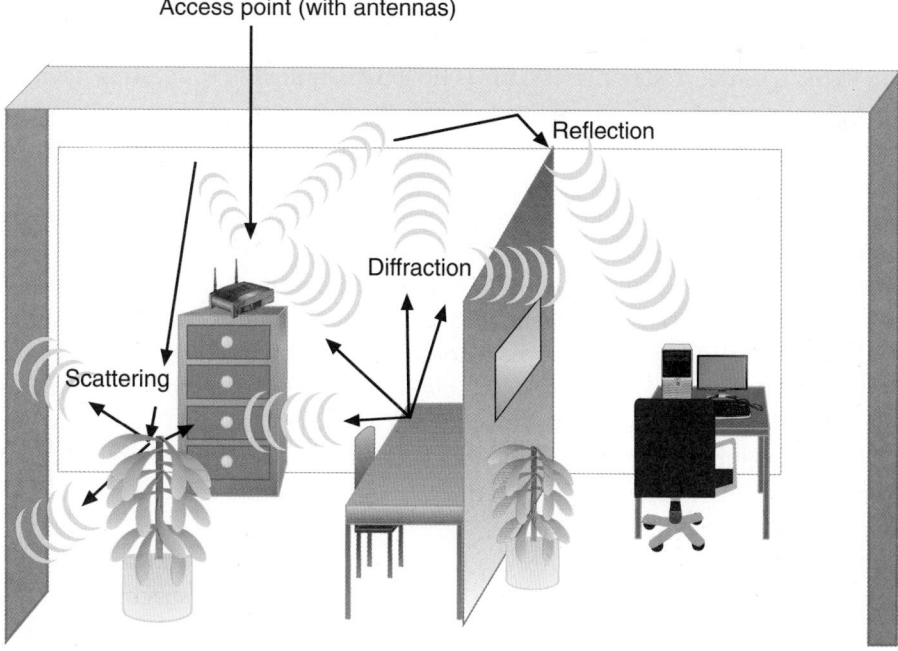

Figure 6-5   Multipath signal propagation

The multipath nature of wireless signals is both a blessing and a curse. On one hand, because signals bounce off obstacles, they have a better chance of reaching their destination. The downside to multipath signaling is that, because of their various paths, multipath signals travel different distances between their transmitter and a receiver. Thus, multiple instances of the same signal can arrive at a receiver at different times. This might cause signals to be misinterpreted, resulting in data errors. Error-correction algorithms detect the errors and sometimes the sender must retransmit the signal. The more errors that occur, the slower the throughput.

Many standards have been developed to account for—and even take advantage of—the various characteristics of wireless transmissions. The best known is IEEE's 802.11 standards, also known as Wi-Fi. Before we dig into a more extensive discussion of Wi-Fi, let's first take a look at a growing subset of wireless transmissions.

Wireless Standards for the IoT (Internet of Things)

Certification

1.5 Compare and contrast the characteristics of network topologies, types, and technologies.

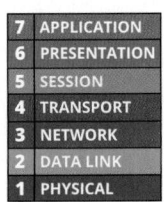

7	APPLICATION
6	PRESENTATION
5	SESSION
4	TRANSPORT
3	NETWORK
2	DATA LINK
1	PHYSICAL

Up to this point, we've primarily discussed how to connect computers of all types—desktops, laptops, smartphones, and tablets—to a local network and beyond to the Internet. Today, networking is no longer limited to computing devices. All sorts of things can be connected to a network, from toasters, refrigerators, bathroom scales, and garage doors to watches, lamps, cars, and even the kitchen sink. This **IoT (Internet of Things)** is made up of any device that can be connected to the Internet—that is, any sensor, computer, or wearable device that talks to other devices over a network.

One of the fastest-growing areas of IoT is personal monitoring devices, such as health monitors, exercise equipment, GPS locators, and smartwatches. Another exploding IoT market interconnects smart home devices. You might already be familiar with Amazon Echo, Apple HomePod, or Google Home. These voice-controlled speakers and their embedded personal assistant apps (such as Alexa, Siri, and Google Assistant) can interlink a plethora of devices, from locks and lights to security cameras and coffee pots (see Figure 6-6). All these connected devices within a home create a type of LAN called a HAN (home area network).

Similarly, a mini-version of a LAN is a PAN (personal area network), and the purely wireless version is a **WPAN (wireless PAN)**, as defined in the 802.15 specifications. These standards include short-range wireless technologies such as Bluetooth and ZigBee. PANs rarely exceed about 10 meters in any direction, and usually only contain a

Figure 6-6   A voice-controlled speaker and personal assistant app can manage many smart home devices

iStock.com/Chesky_W

few personal devices, such as a PC, smartphone, USB printer, and perhaps a Bluetooth headset or an infrared, wireless mouse.

Several wireless standards have been pulled into the service of these emerging IoT technologies. The most common wireless technologies used to connect WPAN and HAN devices are discussed next. Due to the innovative nature and limited scope of some of these protocols, the familiar OSI model layers don't neatly apply. Many of these protocols are designed to function primarily at the Physical and Data Link layers. But some of them interact more extensively with devices and users, all the way up to the Application layer.

ZigBee

Based on the 802.15.4 standard, ZigBee is a low-powered, battery-conserving wireless technology. It is designed to handle small amounts of data and is therefore ideal for use in ISM (industrial, scientific, and medical) sensors. ZigBee is also used in IoT devices for purposes such

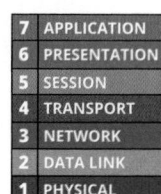

7	APPLICATION
6	PRESENTATION
5	SESSION
4	TRANSPORT
3	NETWORK
2	DATA LINK
1	PHYSICAL

as building automation, HVAC control, AMR (Automatic Meter Reading), and fleet management. The protocol is known for its relative simplicity and reliability when compared to other technologies such as Bluetooth, and its level of security, which is accomplished through the use of 128-bit AES encryption. You'll learn more about encryption types later.

Z-Wave

7	APPLICATION
6	PRESENTATION
5	SESSION
4	TRANSPORT
3	NETWORK
2	DATA LINK
1	PHYSICAL

Similar to ZigBee, **Z-Wave** is a smart home protocol that provides two basic types of functions: signaling, to manage wireless connections, and control, to transmit data and commands between devices. A Z-Wave network controller, called a hub, receives commands from a smartphone or computer and relays the commands to various smart devices on its network. You can see several of these hubs pictured in Figure 6-7. Devices on the network are identified by a 1-byte Node ID, and the entire network has a 4-byte Network ID. Multiple Z-Wave networks can coexist in the same space because the Network ID prevents communication outside of a device's Z-Wave network. This protocol also uses AES-128 encryption for high-security devices, such as door locks.

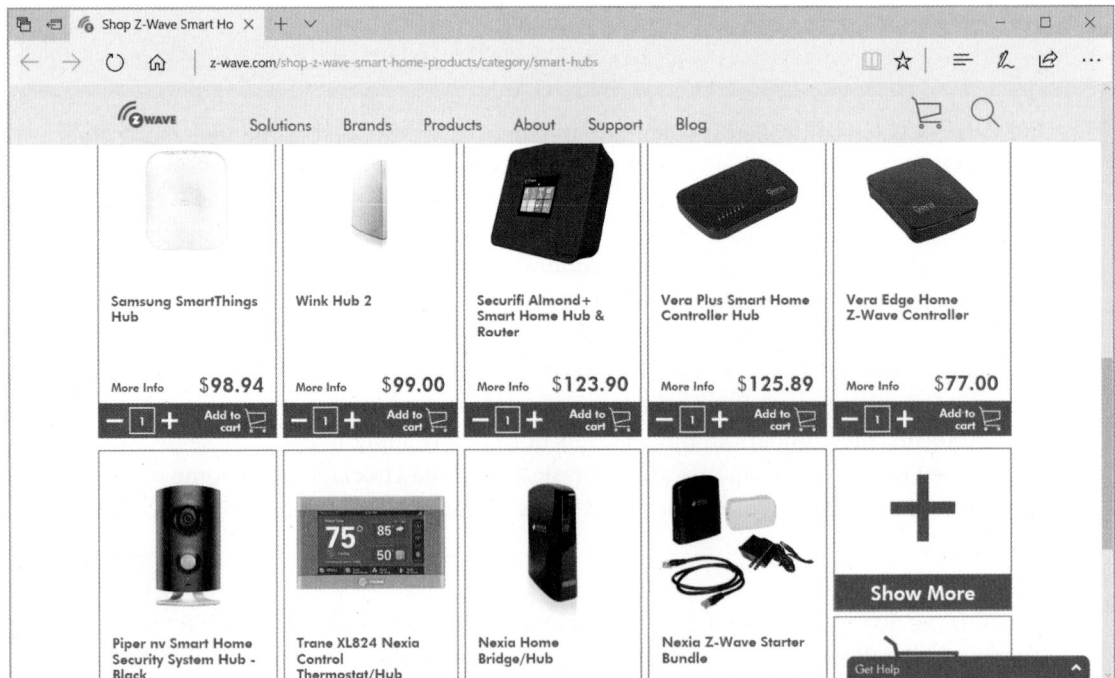

Figure 6-7 A variety of Z-Wave hubs are available from several different manufacturers

Source: Sigma Designs, Inc.

Z-Wave transmissions have a range of up to 100 m per hop, and can tolerate up to four hops through repeaters. Z-Wave–controlled devices can serve as repeaters on a Z-Wave mesh network, mapping and selecting routes between nodes based on the latency of so-called healing messages. The healing process allows a node to reach another node indirectly over a longer distance, and is resistant to changes or failures in network connections. However, due to the nature of how Z-Wave collects data on node locations, the protocol assumes that node locations are static. Smaller, mobile devices, such as remote controls, don't participate in the routing process or serve as repeaters. Likewise, battery-powered devices, which rely on sleep mode to conserve battery power, don't function as repeaters, either, because their sleep mode interferes with the device's ability to receive and respond to unsolicited routing messages.

Bluetooth

7	APPLICATION
6	PRESENTATION
5	SESSION
4	TRANSPORT
3	NETWORK
2	DATA LINK
1	PHYSICAL

Bluetooth, defined by IEEE 802.15.1 specifications, is named after a medieval king of Denmark named Harald Bluetooth, who fought to merge several Danish tribes under a single government. Like its namesake, **Bluetooth** technology unites separate entities. To be precise, it unites mobile devices, PCs, and accessories under a single communications standard. Bluetooth operates in the radio band of 2.4 GHz to 2.4835 GHz and, as you learned earlier in the chapter, hops between frequencies within that band (up to 1600 hops/sec) to help reduce interference. Most Bluetooth devices require close proximity to form a connection, with the exact distance requirements depending on the class of Bluetooth device. Class 1 devices provide the greatest flexibility, with their ability to maintain a reliable connection up to 100 meters apart. Table 6-2 describes the three classes along with their power output. Bluetooth power output is measured in mW (milliwatts), which is one-thousandth of a watt. (Compare this with a 60-watt light bulb, and you'll get an idea of how tiny this amount of power is.)

Table 6-2   Bluetooth power classes

Class	Maximum power output	Typical range	Purpose
1	100 mW	Up to 100 m	Used for industrial purposes
2	2.5 mW	Up to 10 m	Used for mobile devices
3	1 mW	Up to 1 m	Rarely used

These days, most new computers come with an integrated Bluetooth adapter. A plethora of Bluetooth electronic accessories are available, from wearable technology like headsets and watches to highly responsive gaming equipment or high-throughput media players. Manufacturers of Bluetooth devices must obtain approval from the Bluetooth SIG (Special Interest Group) before selling a new Bluetooth device, which must meet high standards defined by SIG. The various protocols integrated into Bluetooth span all layers of the OSI model, from the Physical layer up through the Application layer, depending on the device.

Before you can connect two Bluetooth devices, they must be **paired**, as shown in Figure 6-8. This pairing process involves four, simple steps:

- Turn on the Bluetooth antenna for each device (if it is not turned on by default).
- Make at least one of the devices discoverable.
- On the other device, select the discoverable device to connect to.
- Enter a PIN if required.

Figure 6-8   The flashing red light indicates this Bluetooth device is in discoverable mode for pairing with a smartphone or MP3 player

Bluetooth interfaces are susceptible to a range of security risks, especially undesired Bluetooth connections such as bluejacking, in which a connection is used to send unsolicited data, and bluesnarfing, in which a connection is used to download data without permission. Wireless security concerns are discussed more extensively later in this chapter.

ANT+

ANT+ (pronounced *ant plus*) technology is based on the ANT protocol, which is an ad-hoc wireless protocol operating at about 2.4 GHz. This is one less acronym to learn, as the term ANT simply refers to the insect, which is small in size and a tenacious worker. The ANT

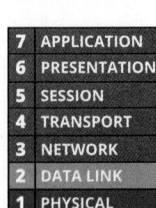

protocol was originally developed in 2004 by the ANT Wireless division of Dynastream Innovations. The company is currently owned by Garmin. While ANT+ is a proprietary protocol, it is also open-source and therefore used by many manufacturers in addition to Garmin.

ANT+ gathers and tracks information from sensors that are typically embedded in heart rate monitors, GPS devices, and other activity monitoring devices. Garmin's smartwatches, for example, track an athlete's activity levels and geographic movement, and then wirelessly sync this data to the person's smartphone, computer, and web-based accounts such as Strava (a social media site for athletic activities) or Facebook. Unlike Bluetooth, ANT+ can also sync data from multiple devices for the same activity, such as a smartwatch, smartphone, bicycle computer (like the one shown in Figure 6-9), or fitness equipment such as a treadmill.

Figure 6-9   A cycling computer can track location, speed, elevation, and more

iStock.com/piola666

RFID (Radio Frequency Identification)

7	APPLICATION
6	PRESENTATION
5	SESSION
4	TRANSPORT
3	NETWORK
2	DATA LINK
1	PHYSICAL

RFID (Radio Frequency Identification) uses electromagnetic fields to store data on a small chip in an RFID tag, which includes an antenna that can both transmit and receive, and possibly a battery. The tag holds 1 to 8 KB of data, such as a serial number, credit card information, or medical data, which it can transmit to a nearby reader. Tag and reader combinations come in three general types:

- *ARPT (Active Reader Passive Tag)*—When prompted by an active reader, a passive tag pulls power from the reader's radio waves to power its transmission. These tags only work within a few centimeters of the reader.
- *PRAT (Passive Reader Active Tag)*—A battery-powered tag actively transmits its credentials at regular time intervals. Battery-powered tags don't require such close proximity to function—the most sophisticated devices work up to 200 m away.
- *ARAT (Active Reader Active Tag)*—An active reader interacts with a battery-powered tag.

RFID is commonly used for inventory management. Because the tag does not need to be precisely positioned close to the reader, an employee can quickly scan a shelf of several items to determine what's in stock and what needs to be re-ordered without having to scan each individual item. The same technology can be used to speed up a customer's checkout time. Perhaps you've seen advertisements for grocery stores that don't require customers to run each item through a laser scanner. RFID allows the reader to identify every purchase in the customer's bag all at one time. An RFID tag might also be embedded in the customer's credit card, allowing for so-called "contactless" payment.

Caution ⚠

The prevalence of RFID chips in credit cards has contributed to the upsurge of a type of fraud called skimming. The culprit installs a card reader, or skimmer, on a payment terminal, such as a gas pump or ATM. The skimmer collects data stored on the magnetic strips or on RFID chips in cards used at that terminal. Physical contact is required to collect data from a magnetic strip, but the RFID chip can transmit data to a skimmer several inches away. The criminal returns later to collect the device along with the stolen data it has accumulated.

Always examine a payment terminal for signs of tampering. If it looks different than nearby terminals, a skimmer might be cleverly disguised right in front of you, such as the one shown in Figure 6-10. The skimmer is designed to detach easily so the thief can retrieve it quickly, so pull on the payment terminal a little to see if anything budges. Consider googling for images of credit card skimmers, ATM skimmers, and gas pump skimmers. The more familiar you are with what to look for, the safer you'll be. If you see something suspicious, call the police and don't use that terminal.

In a similar scam, thieves steal information from your credit card while it sits snugly in your wallet. A thief can swipe an RFID reader near the victim's pocket or bag and collect information from enclosed RFID credit cards, which is called electronic pickpocketing. Many manufacturers sell RFID-blocking wallets of varying quality and effectiveness. You can also wrap your wallet or cards in a layer of aluminum foil. In all circumstances, pay close attention to the people who stand near you in checkout lines, shopping areas, restaurants, and other public spaces.

Skimmer

Figure 6-10   **Skimmers on payment terminals can be surprisingly difficult to spot**

Note 📎

Most newer credit cards contain a different kind of chip called an EMV (Europay, Master-card, and Visa) chip. EMV chips perform a small amount of processing with each transaction where a unique transaction number is generated any time the chip is activated. This means that, even if a thief captures your payment information at the point of sale, the transaction number can't be used again. EMV chips also require physical contact in order to be activated, which eliminates the risk of information being transmitted wirelessly from the card.

However, some EMV credit cards also include RFID technology for contactless payments, which can still transmit your credit card information to a snooping thief. Also, thieves can still use stolen credit card information for "card-not-present" fraud, such as online purchases.

NFC (Near-Field Communication)

7	APPLICATION
6	PRESENTATION
5	SESSION
4	TRANSPORT
3	NETWORK
2	DATA LINK
1	PHYSICAL

If you've ever shared your virtual business card or a photo with a friend by tapping your smartphones together, you've used NFC. **NFC (near-field communication)** is a form of RFID and transfers data wirelessly over very short distances (usually 10 cm or less). A tiny antenna embedded in the device sends its radio signal at a fixed frequency of 13.56 MHz. The signal can also be transmitted one way by an NFC tag, or smart tag, such as when employees need to access a secure area of a building. Other uses of NFC tags include ticketing, cashless payment, shopping loyalty or membership programs, identification, data sharing, and PC logon capabilities.

NFC tags, such as the ones shown in Figure 6-11, require no power source other than the receiving device's power field. The NFC tag collects power from the smartphone or other device by magnetic induction, which is a form of wireless power transmission. Once power is introduced to the NFC tag by the receiving device's proximity, the tag transmits its data, up to 32 KB depending upon the tag's type. The four tag types are listed in Table 6-3.

Figure 6-11   These programmable NFC tags have sticky backs for attaching to a flat surface like a wall, desk, or car dashboard

Table 6-3   Four types of NFC tags

Tag type	Storage	Speed	Configuration
Type 1	96 bytes—2 Kb	106 Kbps	User-configured for read/write or read-only
Type 2	48 bytes—2 Kb	106 Kbps	
Type 3	Up to 1 Mb	212 Kbps	Manufacturer-configured for read/write or read-only
Type 4	Up to 32 Kb	106 Kbps—424 Kbps	

NFC tags are very inexpensive and can be purchased blank, ready to be loaded and integrated into posters, stickers, business cards, keychains, prescription bottles, or equipment labels. They can be programmed to transmit stored data, launch apps, direct a browser to a web page, or change device settings. This makes them useful even for casual, personal use, such as changing your phone's settings when you pass through your front door at home or when you get into your car.

Wireless USB

7	APPLICATION
6	PRESENTATION
5	SESSION
4	TRANSPORT
3	NETWORK
2	DATA LINK
1	PHYSICAL

Based on the UWB (Ultra-Wideband) radio platform, Certified W-USB (Wireless USB) products mimic wired USB 2.0 connections with similar speeds, security, ease of use, and compatibility. UWB radios transmit in the range between 3.1 and 10.6 GHz, a relatively uncrowded band that is also commonly used for wireless media streaming. More recent developments for wireless USB include devices that use the Wi-Fi frequencies of 2.4 and 5 GHz or the WiGig protocol's faster throughput in the 60-GHz band.

Figure 6-12 shows a wireless USB mouse and dongle, which is the part that plugs into a USB port on a computer. Like other WPAN technologies, wireless USB requires little power and operates within about a 10-m range.

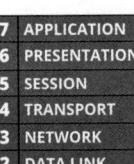

Figure 6-12   This mouse uses wireless USB to communicate with the computer and infrared to detect movement over a solid surface

IR (Infrared)

7	APPLICATION
6	PRESENTATION
5	SESSION
4	TRANSPORT
3	NETWORK
2	DATA LINK
1	PHYSICAL

IR (Infrared or infrared radiation) technology has found new life in the world of IoT, where it's used primarily to collect data through various sensors. IR exists just below the spectrum that is visible to the human eye, with longer wavelengths than red light. An LED in a device creates the invisible radiation, which is then detected by a sensor's semiconductor material that converts the signals into electrical current. IR sensors are used to collect information such as:

- Presence or level of liquid, based on the quality of a reflection
- Variations in reflections from skin caused by variations in blood flow, which can be used to monitor heart rate
- Proximity to the device, which can trigger an action such as steering a vehicle away from an obstacle
- Commands from a control device, such as a game or TV remote control

Nearby light sources or dust in the air can reduce the accuracy of collected data. IR requires a nearly unobstructed line of sight between the transmitter and receiver—some devices use a scatter mode that reflects IR signals off nearby surfaces in order to circumvent some obstacles, but IR cannot pass through these obstacles. This limitation can actually be used to increase the security of IR transmissions.

The mouse in Figure 6-12 emits infrared radiation through a small opening on the bottom to detect movement over a mousepad or other solid surface. IR is also commonly used in remote controls such as the one that comes with the projector shown in Figure 6-13. Infrared standards are defined by the IrDA (Infrared Data Association). Its website is *irda.org*.

Figure 6-13 This remote control contains an IR transceiver to communicate with the projector

Now that you've explored some of the short-range wireless technologies used by IoT, you're ready to learn more about Wi-Fi and the 802.11 standards that support both IoT and WLANs. We'll begin with a discussion of the most common Wi-Fi standards.

802.11 WLAN Standards

7	APPLICATION
6	PRESENTATION
5	SESSION
4	TRANSPORT
3	NETWORK
2	DATA LINK
1	PHYSICAL

WLANs work at OSI Layers 1 and 2. They support the same TCP/IP higher-layer OSI protocols (such as IP, TCP, and UDP) and operating systems (such as UNIX, Linux, or Windows) as wired LANs. This compatibility ensures that wireless and wired transmission methods can be integrated on the same network.

The most popular OSI Physical and Data Link layer standards used by WLANs is Wi-Fi. **Wi-Fi** (short for *wireless fidelity*) is a collection of wireless standards and their amendments, extensions, and corrections developed by IEEE's 802.11 committee. Notable wireless standards developed by the IEEE 802.11 committee and its task groups are 802.11b, 802.11a, 802.11g, 802.11n, and 802.11ac.

The 802.11 standards vary at the Physical layer. In addition, 802.11n and later standards modify the way frames are used at the **MAC sublayer**, which is the lower portion of the Data Link layer that is specifically involved with managing MAC addresses in message frames.

Layer 2's other sublayer is called the **LLC sublayer**. ("LLC" stands for "logical link control.") The LLC sublayer is primarily concerned with multiplexing, flow and error control, and reliability.

Table 6-4 summarizes the technical details of the 802.11 standards and is followed by a more detailed description of each standard.

Table 6-4   Technical details for 802.11 wireless standards

Standard		Frequency band	Max. theoretical throughput	Geographic range
802.11b		2.4 GHz	11 Mbps	100 m
802.11a		5 GHz	54 Mbps	50 m
802.11g		2.4 GHz	54 Mbps	100 m
802.11n		2.4 GHz or 5 GHz	600 Mbps	Indoor: 70 m Outdoor: 250 m
802.11ac	Wave 1 (3 data streams)	5 GHz	1.3 Gbps	Indoor: 70 m Outdoor: 250 m
	Wave 2 (4 data streams)		3.47 Gbps	
	Wave 3 (8 data streams)		6.93 Gbps	

- *802.11b*—In 1999, the IEEE released its 802.11b standard, which separates the 2.4-GHz band into 22-MHz channels. Among all the 802.11 standards, 802.11b was the first to take hold. It is also the least expensive of all the 802.11 WLAN technologies. However, most network administrators have replaced 802.11b with a faster standard, such as 802.11n.
- *802.11a*—Although the 802.11a task group began its standards work before the 802.11b group, 802.11a was released *after* 802.11b. The higher throughput of 802.11a, as compared with 802.11b, is attributable to its use of higher frequencies, its unique method of modulating data, and more available bandwidth. Perhaps most significant is that the 5-GHz band is not as congested as the 2.4-GHz band. Thus, 802.11a signals are less likely to suffer interference. However, higher-frequency signals require more power to transmit, and they travel shorter distances than lower-frequency signals. As a result, 802.11a networks require a greater density of access points to cover the same distance that 802.11b networks cover. The additional access points, as well as the nature of 802.11a equipment, make this standard more expensive than either 802.11b or 802.11g. For this and other reasons, 802.11a is rarely preferred.
- *802.11g*—IEEE's 802.11g WLAN standard is designed to be just as affordable as 802.11b while increasing its maximum theoretical throughput with different data modulation techniques. In addition, 802.11g benefits from being compatible with 802.11b networks. This was a significant advantage at the time when network administrators were upgrading their wireless access points to the 802.11g technology while still needing to offer wireless access to their older computers.
- *802.11n*—In 2009, IEEE ratified the 802.11n standard. However, it was in development for years before that, and as early as mid-2007, manufacturers were selling 802.11n-compatible transceivers in their networking equipment. The primary goal of IEEE's 802.11n committee was to create a wireless standard that provided much higher effective throughput than the earlier 802.11 standards, and they succeeded. 802.11n boasts a maximum throughput of 600 Mbps, making it a realistic platform for telephone and video signals. IEEE also specified that the 802.11n standard must be backward compatible with the 802.11a, b, and g standards. This is made possible because 802.11n uses both the 2.4-GHz and the 5.0-GHz frequency bands.
- *802.11ac*—Officially approved in early 2014, 802.11ac operates on the 5-GHz band and exceeds benchmarks set by earlier standards by increasing its useful

bandwidth and amplitude. 802.11ac is the first Wi-Fi standard to approach Gigabit Ethernet capabilities, providing better support for more wireless clients at a time. In fact, 802.11ac access points function more like a switch than a hub in that they can handle multiple transmissions at one time over the same frequency spectrum. This new standard is being deployed in three waves, with Wave 1 and Wave 2 devices already available at the time of this printing.

Note 🖉

The actual geographic range of any wireless technology depends on several factors, including the power of the antenna, physical barriers or obstacles between sending and receiving nodes, and interference in the environment. Therefore, although a technology is rated for a certain average geographic range, it might actually transmit signals in a shorter or longer range at various times under various conditions.

A more relevant measure of an AP's performance in a particular environment is how well it saturates its range with a strong, fast signal. This is one of the primary advantages of 802.11ac over 802.11n: The newer standard does a better job of providing faster transmissions throughout its geographic range. So, for example, at 75 m, the signal from an 802.11ac AP will be much stronger than the signal from an 802.11n AP under the same conditions.

Regardless of the standard followed, all 802.11 networks share many features and innovations in common. All 802.11 networks follow the same access method, for example, as described in the following section. In addition, some newer innovations give the later standards a significant performance edge over earlier standards.

Access Method

You've learned that the Data Link layer, specifically the MAC sublayer, is responsible for appending physical addresses to a data frame and for governing multiple nodes' access to a single medium. Like 802.3 (Ethernet), 802.11 appends 48-bit physical addresses to a frame to identify its source and destination. The use of the same physical addressing scheme allows 802.11 networks to be easily combined with other IEEE 802 networks, including Ethernet (802.3) networks. However, 802.11 networks use a different access method than Ethernet networks do.

Wireless devices are not designed to transmit and receive simultaneously and so cannot prevent collisions. Instead, 802.11 standards specify the use of **CSMA/CA (Carrier Sense Multiple Access with Collision Avoidance)** to access a shared medium, as illustrated in Figure 6-14 and described next. Compared with CSMA/CD (Carrier Sense Multiple Access with Collision Detection), CSMA/CA minimizes the potential for collisions, but cannot detect the occurrence of a collision and so cannot take steps to recover from the collisions that do occur.

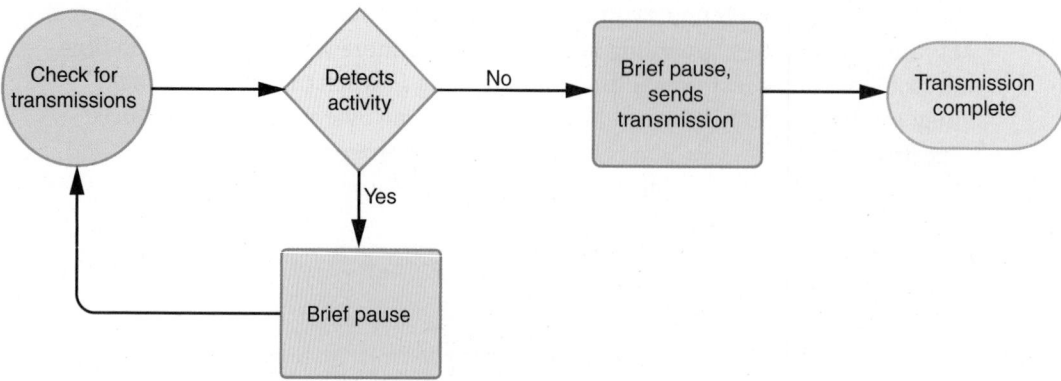

Figure 6-14   CSMA/CA uses ACK messages to confirm successful transmission

Step 1:   Using CSMA/CA, a node on an 802.11 network checks for existing wireless transmissions (the green circle in Figure 6-14) before it begins to send data.

- If the source node detects no transmission activity on the network, it waits a brief, random amount of time, and then sends its transmission.
- If the source does detect activity, it waits a brief period of time before checking the channel again.

Step 2:   The destination node receives the transmission and, after verifying its accuracy, issues an ACK (acknowledgment) packet to the source.

- If the source receives this acknowledgment, it assumes the transmission was properly completed.
- Interference or other transmissions on the network could impede this exchange. If, after transmitting a message, the source node fails to receive acknowledgment from the destination node, it assumes its transmission did not arrive properly, and it begins the CSMA/CA process anew.

The use of ACK packets to verify every transmission means that 802.11 networks require more overhead than 802.3 networks. A wireless network with a theoretical maximum throughput of 10 Mbps will, in fact, transmit less data per second than a wired Ethernet network with the same theoretical maximum throughput.

Nodes that are physically located far apart from each other on a wireless network present a particular challenge in that they are too far apart to collaborate in preventing collisions. This is called the hidden node problem, where a node is not visible to other nodes on the other side of the coverage area. One way to ensure that packets are not inhibited by other transmissions is to reserve the medium for one node's use. In 802.11, this can be accomplished through the optional **RTS/CTS (Request to Send/Clear to Send)** protocol. Figure 6-15 illustrates the CSMA/CA process when using RTS/CTS.

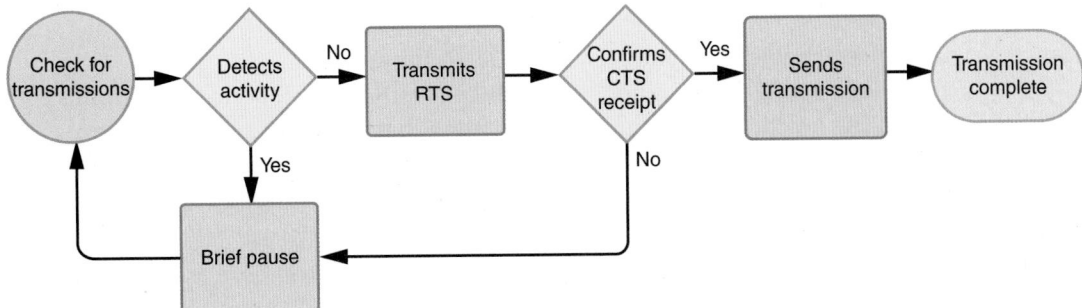

Figure 6-15   CSMA/CA with the optional RTS/CTS protocol

When using RTS/CTS, a source node issues an RTS signal to the access point requesting the exclusive opportunity to transmit. If the access point agrees by responding with a CTS signal, the access point temporarily suspends communication with all nodes in its range and waits for the source node to complete its transmission. When used, RTS/CTS decreases network efficiency. However, it can be worthwhile when transmitting large packets.

Association

Suppose you bring your laptop to a local Internet café, turn it on, and soon your laptop prompts you to log on to the café's wireless network to gain access to the Internet through its hot spot. This seemingly simple process, known as **association**, involves a number of packet exchanges between the café's access point and your computer. Association is another function of the MAC sublayer described in the 802.11 standard.

As long as a wireless node is on and has its wireless protocols running, it periodically surveys its surroundings for evidence of an access point, a task known as **scanning**. A node can use either active scanning or passive scanning:

- *active scanning*—The wireless client takes the initiative:
  - ○ The computer transmits a special frame, known as a **probe**, on all available channels within its frequency range.
  - ○ An AP detects the probe frame and issues a probe response containing all the information a computer needs to associate with the AP, including a status code and node ID, or station ID, for that computer.
  - ○ The computer can agree to associate with that AP. The final decision to associate with an AP, at least for the first time, usually requires the consent of the user.
  - ○ The two nodes begin communicating over the frequency channel specified by the AP.

- *passive scanning*—The AP takes the initiative:
  - A wireless-enabled computer listens on all channels within its frequency range for a special signal, known as a **beacon frame**, issued periodically from an AP. The beacon frame contains information that a wireless node requires to associate itself with the AP, including the network's transmission rate and the **SSID (service set identifier)**, a unique character string used to identify an access point.
  - The computer—usually with the consent of the user—can choose to associate with the AP.
  - The two nodes agree on a frequency channel and begin communicating.

When setting up a WLAN, most network administrators use the AP's configuration utility to assign a unique SSID, rather than the default SSID provided by the manufacturer. The default SSID often contains the name of the manufacturer and perhaps even the model number of the access point, which can give hackers a head-start on cracking into the network. Changing the SSID contributes to better security and easier network management, though you should keep the following tips in mind:

- Disguise the nature of the network identified by the SSID to avoid giving hackers more information than necessary. For example, it's probably not a good idea to name the Accounting Department's access point "Acctg."
- Minimize confusion for employees by using easily recognized—though uncommon—SSIDs. The point of this is to increase security on client devices as they travel to other areas, so they don't inadvertently attempt to connect to networks with an identical name.

IEEE terminology includes a couple of notable variations to the standard SSID configuration:

- *BSS (basic service set)*—A group of nodes that share an access point. The identifier for this group of nodes is known as a **BSSID (basic service set identifier)**.
- *ESS (extended service set)*—A group of access points connected to the same LAN. BSSes that belong to the same ESS share a special identifier, called an **ESSID (extended service set identifier)**. Within an ESS, a client can associate with any one of many APs that use the same ESSID. This allows users to roam about a large office space without losing wireless network service. In practice, many networking professionals don't distinguish between the terms *SSID* and *ESSID*. They simply configure every access point in a group or LAN with the same SSID.

Figure 6-16 illustrates a network with only one BSS; Figure 6-17 shows a network encompassing multiple BSSes that form an ESS.

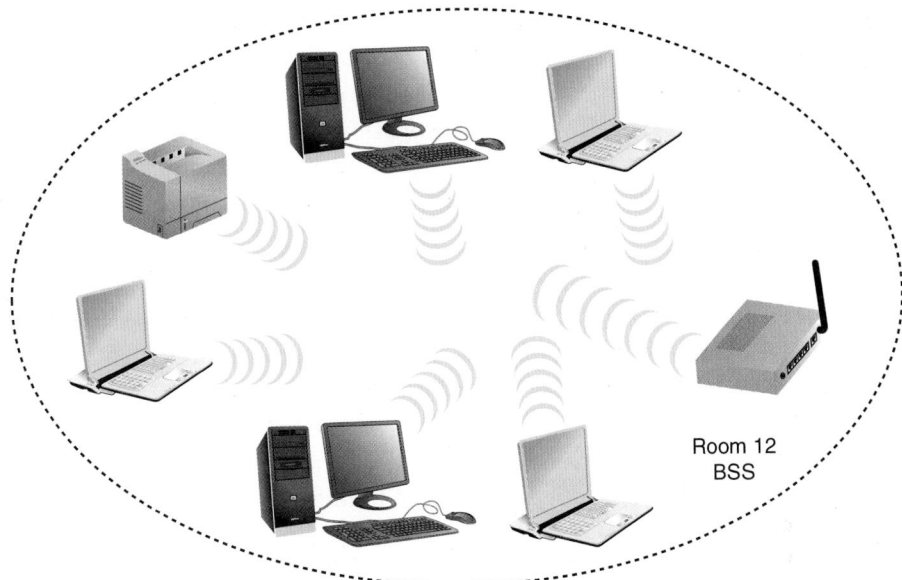

Figure 6-16   A network with a single BSS

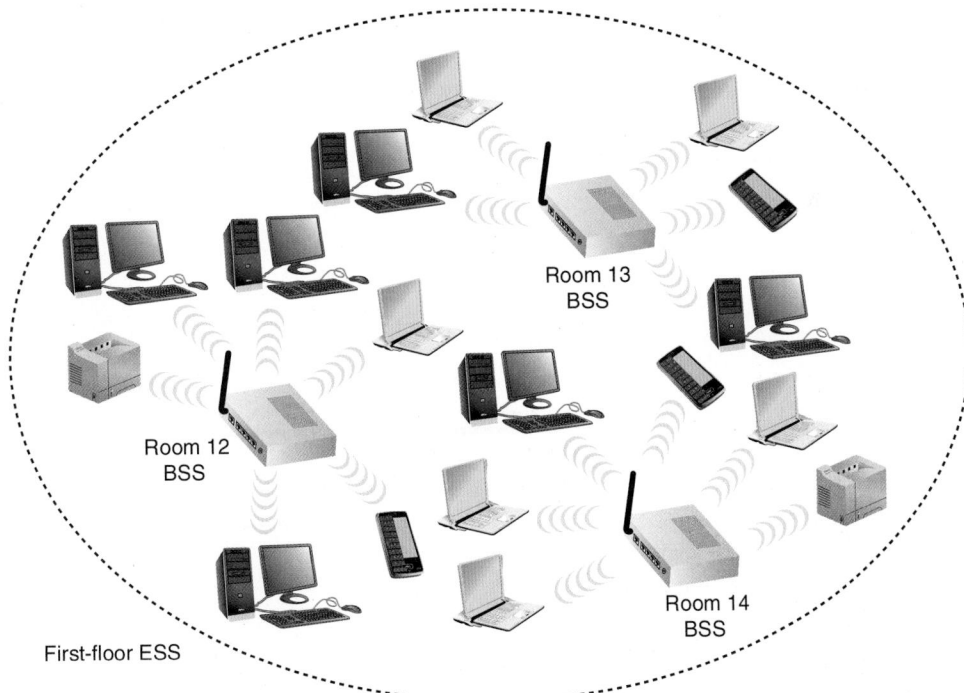

Figure 6-17   A network with multiple BSSes forming an ESS—devices can be moved from one room to the next without losing network connectivity

As devices are moved between BSSes within a single ESS, connecting to a different AP requires **reassociation**. This is an automatic process that occurs when:

- A mobile user moves out of one AP's range and into the range of another.
- The initial AP is experiencing a high rate of errors. On a network with multiple APs, network managers can take advantage of the nodes' scanning feature to automatically balance transmission loads between access points.

IEEE 802.11 Frames

You have learned about some types of overhead required to manage access to the 802.11 wireless networks—for example, ACKs, probes, and beacons. For each of these functions, the 802.11 standard specifies a specific frame type at the MAC sublayer. These multiple frame types are divided into three groups:

- *management frames*—Involved in association and reassociation; examples of this type of frame include probe and beacon frames. (Details of management frames are beyond the scope of this book.)
- *control frames*—Related to medium access and data delivery; examples of this type of frame include ACK and RTS/CTS frames. (Details of control frames are beyond the scope of this book.)
- *data frames*—Responsible for carrying data between nodes. An 802.11 data frame is illustrated in Figure 6-18. Compare the 802.11 data frame with the Ethernet data frame also shown in Figure 6-18. As you can see in the figure, the 802.11 data frame carries significant overhead—that is, it includes a large quantity of fields in addition to the data field.

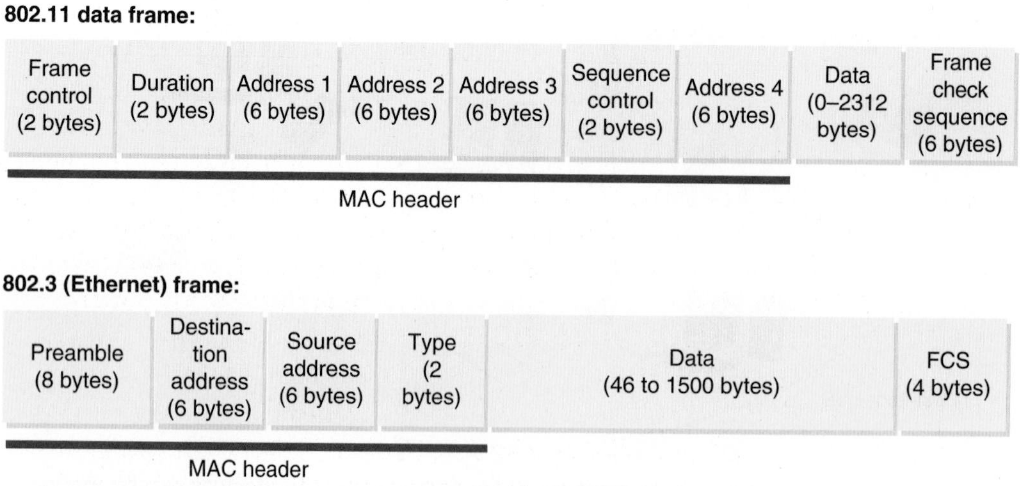

802.11 data frame:

Frame control (2 bytes)	Duration (2 bytes)	Address 1 (6 bytes)	Address 2 (6 bytes)	Address 3 (6 bytes)	Sequence control (2 bytes)	Address 4 (6 bytes)	Data (0–2312 bytes)	Frame check sequence (6 bytes)

MAC header

802.3 (Ethernet) frame:

Preamble (8 bytes)	Destination address (6 bytes)	Source address (6 bytes)	Type (2 bytes)	Data (46 to 1500 bytes)	FCS (4 bytes)

MAC header

Figure 6-18   Basic 802.11 data frame compared with an 802.3 Ethernet frame

The 802.11 data frame's fields are summarized in Table 6-5.

Table 6-5   Fields in an 802.11 data frame

	Field name	Length	Description
Header	Frame control	2 bytes	Holds information about the protocol in use, the type of frame being transmitted, whether the frame is part of a larger, fragmented packet, whether the frame is one that was reissued after an unverified delivery attempt, what type of security the frame uses, and so on.
	Duration	2 bytes	Indicates how long the field's transmission will take so other nodes know when the channel will be available again.
	Address 1	6 bytes	Source address.
	Address 2	6 bytes	Transmitter address.
	Address 3	6 bytes	Receiver address.
	Sequence control	2 bytes	Indicates how a large packet is fragmented.
	Address 4	6 bytes	Destination address.
Data		0–2312 bytes	Includes the data originally sent by the source host, plus headers from higher layers. The Data field is not part of the frame header or trailer—it is encapsulated by the frame.
Trailer	Frame check sequence	6 bytes	Uses a cyclical code to check for errors in the transmission.

Notice that the 802.11 data frame contains four address fields; by contrast, the 802.3 (Ethernet) frame has only two. The transmitter and receiver addresses refer to the access point or another intermediary device (if used) on the wireless network.

Another unique characteristic of the 802.11 data frame is its Sequence Control field. This field is used to indicate how a large packet is fragmented—that is, how it is subdivided into smaller packets for more reliable delivery. Recall that on wired TCP/IP networks, error checking occurs at the Transport layer of the OSI model and packet fragmentation, if necessary, occurs at the Network layer. However, in 802.11 networks, error checking and packet fragmentation are handled at the MAC sublayer of the Data Link layer.

By handling fragmentation at a lower layer, 802.11 makes its transmission—which is less efficient and more error-prone—transparent to higher layers. This means 802.11 nodes are more easily integrated with 802.3 networks and prevent the 802.11 conversations of an integrated network from slowing down the 802.3 conversations.

802.11 Innovations

Although some of their Physical layer services vary, all the 802.11 standards use half-duplex signaling. In other words, a wireless node using one of the 802.11 techniques can either transmit or receive, but cannot do both simultaneously unless the node has more than one transceiver installed. Some wireless access points can simulate full-duplex signaling by using multiple frequencies. But the transmission for each antenna is still only half-duplex.

Despite this physical limitation, beginning with 802.11n, several innovations have been implemented that contribute to making later 802.11 standards much faster and much more reliable:

- *MIMO (multiple input-multiple output)*—First available in 802.11n, multiple antennas on the access point and on a client device process incoming or outgoing data simultaneously. Figure 6-19 shows an 802.11n/802.11ac dual band SOHO router with three antennas. There are some multiantenna 802.11g devices available, but these antennas take turns processing the data stream. 802.11n/ac devices, however, simultaneously process data through two or more antennas. As you learned earlier, wireless signals propagate in a multipath fashion. Therefore, multiple signals cannot be expected to arrive at the same receiver in concert. MIMO uses this phenomenon to its advantage by adjusting either the phase or amplitude of signals from each antenna. This improves the transmission in two ways:

  ○ *signal quality and range*—Spatial diversity of the different antennas eliminates noise in the transmission, which also increases the distance it can effectively travel. Each antenna receives a slightly different version of the signal, and the strengths of each signal are summed.

  ○ *signal capacity*—Spatial multiplexing adds a new data stream between each additional pair of antennas, thereby increasing the amount of data being transmitted and received. This effect increases linearly with the addition of each pair of antennas.

Figure 6-19 Dual band SOHO router with three antennas

Source: *amazon.com*

- *MU-MIMO (multiuser MIMO)*—Related to MIMO, MU-MIMO is an even newer technology implemented by 802.11ac Wave 2 products that allows multiple antennas to service multiple clients simultaneously. This feature reduces congestion and thereby contributes to even faster data transmission. As with MIMO, however, a MU-MIMO access point can only be used at full capacity when the client devices also support MU-MIMO technology.
- *channel bonding*—In 802.11n, two adjacent 20-MHz channels can be combined, or bonded, to make a 40-MHz channel, as shown in Figure 6-20. In fact, bonding two 20-MHz channels more than doubles the bandwidth available in a single 20-MHz channel. That's because the small amount of bandwidth normally reserved as buffers against interference at the top and bottom of the 20-MHz channels can be assigned to carry data instead. Because the 5-GHz band contains more channels and is less crowded (at least, for now), it's better suited to channel bonding than the 2.4-GHz band, which is another factor contributing to 802.11ac's improved performance over 802.11n. The newer 802.11ac standard takes channel bonding to a higher level by supporting 20-, 40-, and 80-MHz channels, with optional use of 160-MHz channels.

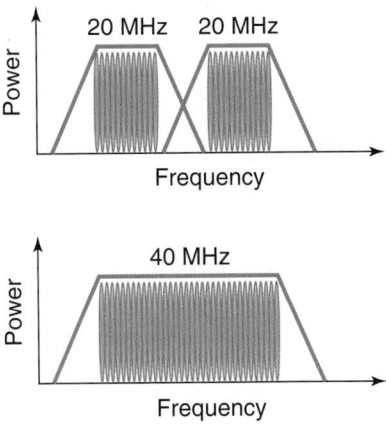

Figure 6-20   Channel bonding

- *frame aggregation*—Beginning with 802.11n, networks can use one of two techniques for combining multiple data frames into one larger frame: A-MSDU (Aggregated Mac Service Data Unit) or A-MPDU (Aggregated Mac Protocol Data Unit). 802.11ac uses A-MPDU for all transmissions by default. Both approaches combine multiple frames to reduce overhead. To understand how frame aggregation works, suppose three small data frames are combined into one larger frame. Each larger frame will have only one copy of the same addressing information that would appear in the smaller frames. Proportionally, the header fields take up less of the aggregated frame's space. In addition, replacing four small frames with one large frame means an access point and client will have to exchange one-quarter the number of messages to negotiate media access and error control. Maximum frame sizes for both 802.11n and 802.11ac are shown in Table 6-6. Compare these numbers to the maximum 802.11b/a/g frame size of 4095 bytes.

Table 6-6 Maximum frame sizes using frame aggregation

Wi-Fi standard	A-MSDU	A-MPDU
802.11n	7935 bytes	65,535 bytes
802.11ac	11,454 bytes	4,692,480 bytes

Figure 6-21 illustrates the lowered overhead accomplished by both A-MSDU and A-MPDU. The advantage of A-MSDU over A-MPDU is that more of the frame's information is combined with other frames transmitted at the same time. The potential disadvantage to using larger frames is the increased probability of errors when transmitting larger blocks of data. Therefore, the advantage of A-MPDU is that each frame added to the mix retains some of its error checking data, resulting in greater reliability.

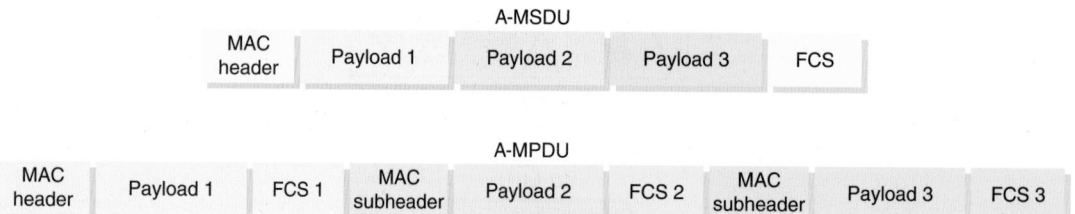

Figure 6-21   A-MSDU and A-MPDU aggregated frames

Note that not all the techniques listed here are used in every 802.11n or 802.11ac implementation. Further, reaching maximum throughput depends on the number and type of these strategies used. It also depends on whether the network uses the 2.4-GHz (for 802.11n) or the 5-GHz band. Considering these factors, an 802.11n network's actual throughputs vary between 65 Mbps and 500 Mbps, while an 802.11ac Wave 2 network's actual throughputs have been documented, at the time of this writing, as high as 891 Mbps *per client* at short-range distances.

As mentioned earlier, 802.11n and 802.11ac are compatible with all three earlier versions of the 802.11 standard. In mixed environments, however, some of the new standards' techniques for improving throughput will not be possible. To ensure the fastest data rates on your 802.11n LAN, it's optimal to use only 802.11n-compatible devices. 802.11ac can be implemented more gradually, with both 802.11n and 802.11ac devices in operation at the same time.

Implementing a Wi-Fi Network

 **Certification**

7	APPLICATION
6	PRESENTATION
5	SESSION
4	TRANSPORT
3	NETWORK
2	DATA LINK
1	PHYSICAL

1.5   Compare and contrast the characteristics of network topologies, types, and technologies.

1.6   Given a scenario, implement the appropriate wireless technologies and configurations.

2.2   Given a scenario, determine the appropriate placement of networking devices on a network and install/configure them.

2.3   Explain the purposes and use cases for advanced networking devices.

3.5   Identify policies and best practices.

4.4   Summarize common networking attacks.

5.4   Given a scenario, troubleshoot common wireless connectivity and performance issues.

Now that you understand how wireless signals are exchanged, what can hinder them, and which Physical and Data Link layer standards they follow, you are ready to put these ideas into practice. This section first describes the WLAN topologies and how to design small WLANs, which are the types you might use at home or in a small office. Then we'll walk through installing and configuring access points and clients on larger wireless networks.

Wireless Topologies

Because they are not bound by cabling paths between nodes and connectivity devices, wireless networks are not laid out using the same topologies as wired networks. They have their own topologies:

- *ad hoc*—A small number of nodes closely positioned transmit directly to each other without an intervening connectivity device, as shown in Figure 6-22.
- *infrastructure*—An intervening connectivity device, a WAP (wireless access point) or AP (access point), as shown in Figure 6-23, accepts wireless signals from multiple nodes and retransmits them to the rest of the network. To cover its intended range, an access point must have sufficient power and be strategically placed so that all connected nodes can communicate with it.
- *mesh*—Several access points work as peer devices on the same network, as illustrated in Figure 6-24, where the AP devices cooperate to provide more fault-tolerant network access to clients. A **wireless controller** might be used only initially to configure the APs, or the APs might remain connected to the wireless

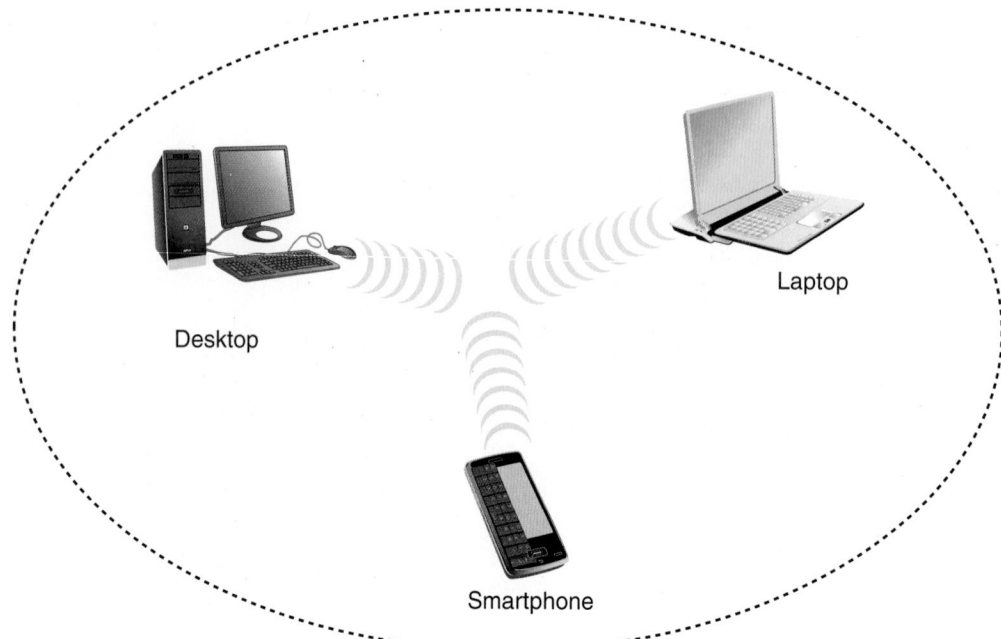

Figure 6-22   An ad hoc WLAN

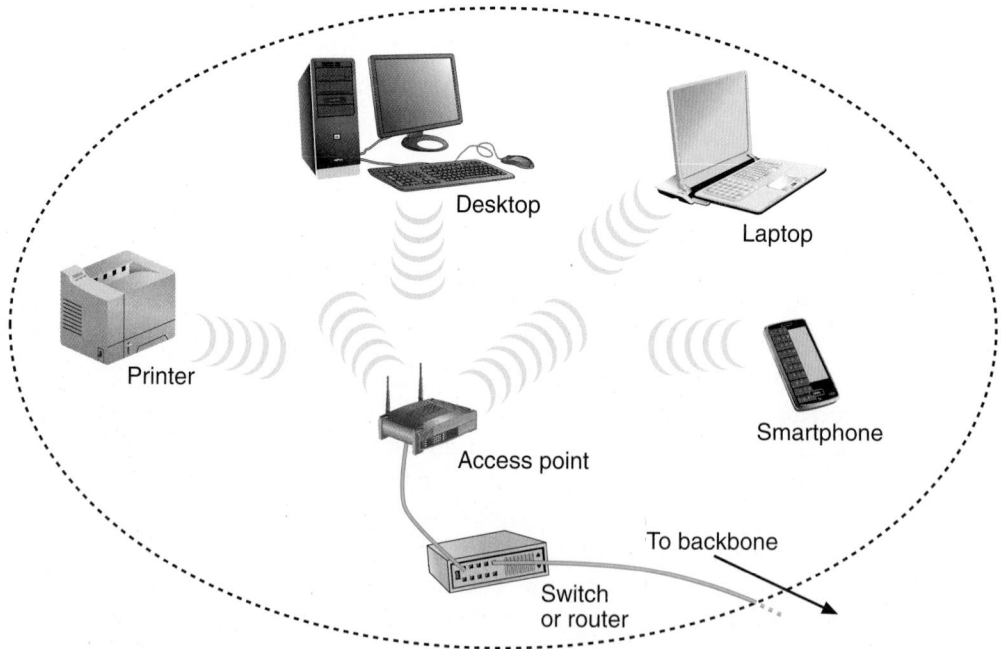

Figure 6-23   An infrastructure WLAN

controller for continued management. A wireless controller might be a physical device installed locally, such as the one shown in Figure 6-25, or it might be cloud-based, VM-based, or embedded in one of the APs.

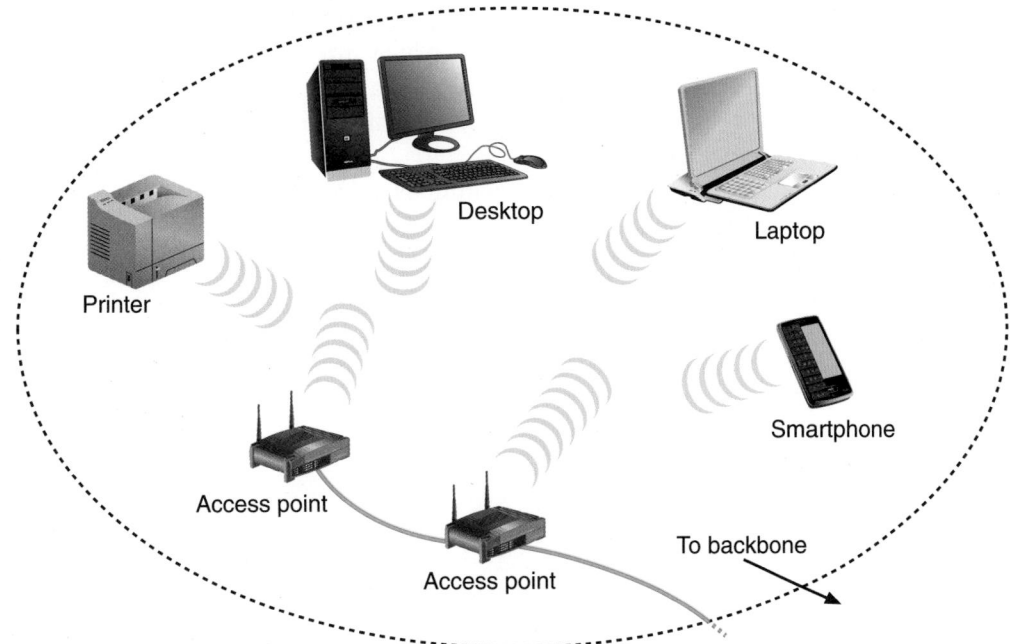

Figure 6-24   A mesh WLAN

Figure 6-25   Use a wireless controller to configure, deploy, and manage APs

Centralized wireless management is made possible by a lightweight wireless protocol, such as Cisco's proprietary **LWAPP (Lightweight Access Point Protocol)**, or Cisco's newer **CAPWAP (Control and Provisioning of Wireless Access Points)**, both of which direct all wireless frames to the controller by adding extra headers to the frames. The wireless controller can provide centralized authentication for wireless clients, load balancing, and channel management so that neighboring APs don't try to use overlapping channels. The controller manages AP redundancy by directing wireless traffic to alternate APs when an AP fails. Wireless controllers can also detect the presence of unauthorized APs, called **rogue access points**, by recognizing when an unauthorized AP attempts to connect to the network.

In addition to connecting multiple nodes within a LAN, wireless technology can be used to connect two different parts of a LAN or two separate LANs. Such connections typically use a fixed link with directional antennas between two access points, as shown in Figure 6-26.

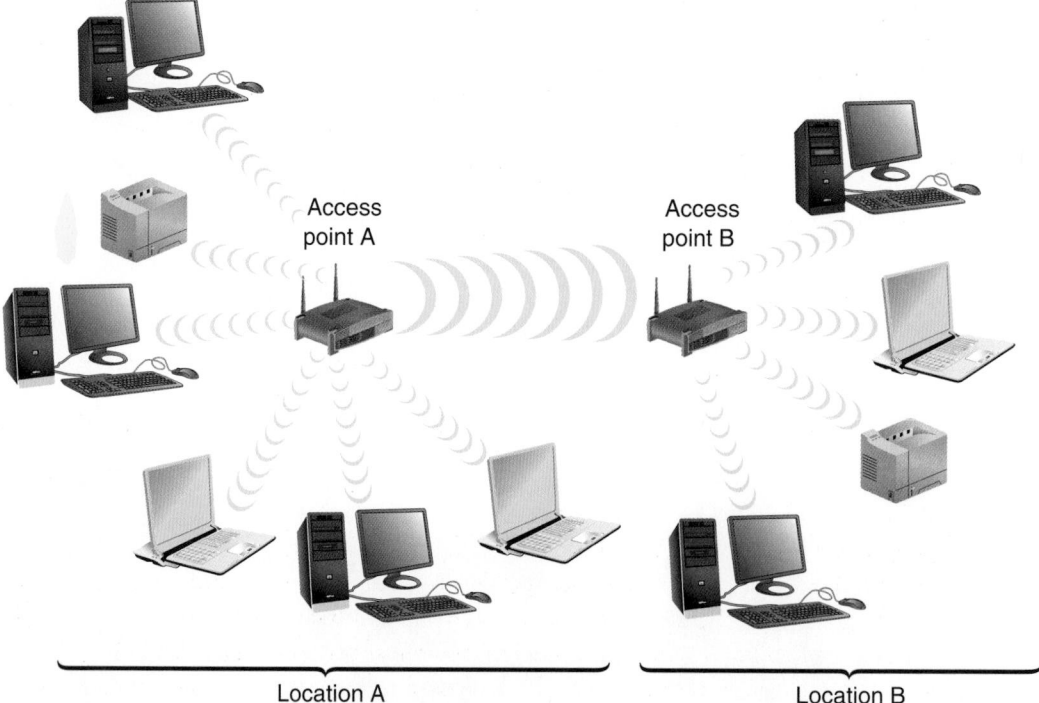

Figure 6-26   Wireless LAN connection

Because point-to-point links only have to transmit in one general direction, they can apply more energy to signal propagation through a unidirectional antenna, such as the one in Figure 6-27. This allows them to achieve a greater transmission distance than mobile wireless links can offer. For example, access points connecting two WLANs could be located up to 1000 feet apart.

Figure 6-27   An outdoor unidirectional antenna that transmits across a nearby football field

Determine the Design

Most small, wireless LANs use the infrastructure topology, requiring one or more APs. A home or small office network, called a SOHO network, might call for only one AP. This device often combines switching, routing, and other network functions as well. In this case, the device is more accurately called a wireless router or SOHO router, and connects wireless clients to the LAN in addition to serving as their gateway to the Internet. Figure 6-28 illustrates the typical arrangement of a home or small office WLAN, and is described next.

- The ISP's signal comes into the premises through a cable or DSL modem.
- The modem connects to the SOHO router using an RJ-45 cable. This cable is inserted into the SOHO router's WAN port, which is set apart from the other data ports and might be labeled "Internet" or remain unlabeled. Notice the yellow port on the router in Figure 6-29.

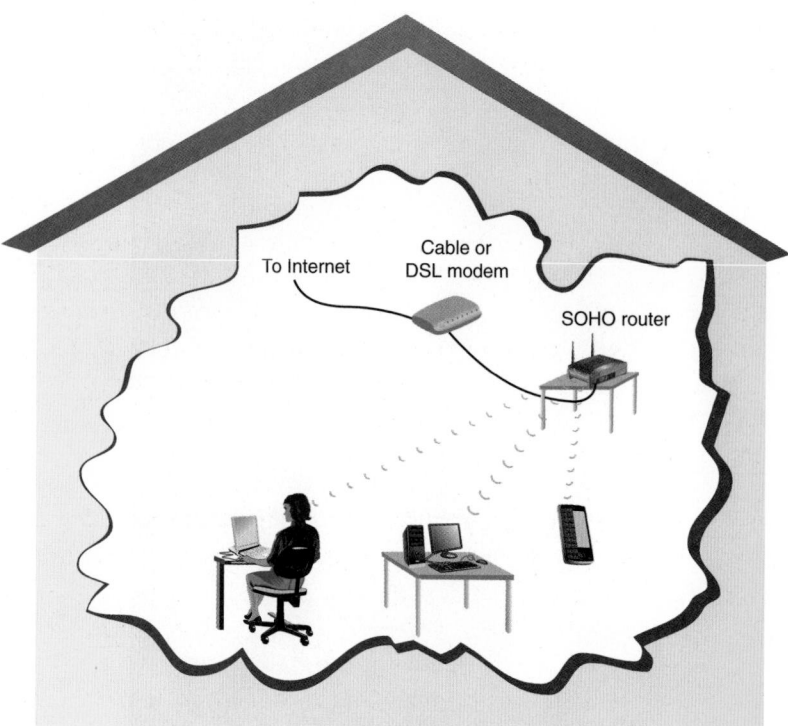

Figure 6-28 Home or small office WLAN arrangement

- The additional ports allow for wired access to the router, which contains switch hardware inside the device to manage connected devices. An AP that does not include routing or switching functions would lack these extra ports and act much like a wireless hub.

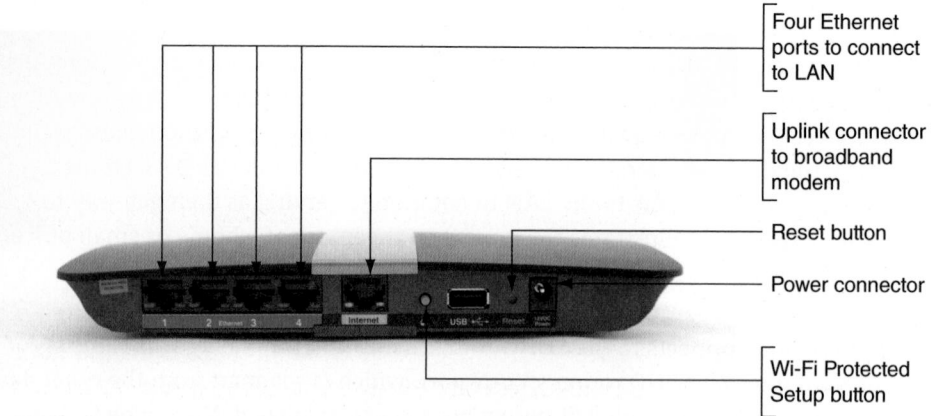

Four Ethernet ports to connect to LAN

Uplink connector to broadband modem

Reset button

Power connector

Wi-Fi Protected Setup button

Figure 6-29 Connectors and ports on the back of a Cisco SOHO router

Consider these factors when deciding where to install a WLAN's access point:

- *distance*—Consider typical distances between the AP and its clients, and distance restrictions for the 802.11 standard your AP is using. If your small office spans three floors, and clients are evenly distributed among the floors, you might choose to situate the AP on the second floor.
- *type and number of obstacles*—Consider the type and number of obstacles between the AP and it clients. If your three-story building is constructed like a bunker with massive concrete floors, you might consider installing a separate AP on each floor. If a building or office space is long and narrow, you might need two APs—one at each end of the building. Remember from the *On the Job* story at the beginning of this chapter, sometimes obstacles can be more consequential than they at first appear.
- *coverage*—Place the AP in a high spot, such as on a shelf or rack or in a drop ceiling.
- *interference*—Make sure the AP is not close to potential sources of interference, including cordless phones, fluorescent lights, or microwave ovens.

Larger WLANs warrant a more systematic approach to access point placement. Before placing APs in every data room, it's wise to conduct a site survey. A **site survey** assesses client requirements, facility characteristics, and coverage areas to determine an AP arrangement that will ensure reliable wireless connectivity within a given area.

Suppose you are the network manager for a large organization whose wireless clients are distributed over six floors of a building. On two floors, your organization takes up 2000 square feet of office space, but on the other four floors, your offices are limited to only 200 square feet. In addition, clients move between floors regularly, and the lobby-level floor has less wireless traffic than the others. Other building occupants are also running wireless networks. Let's see what activities might contribute to a thorough site survey in this situation:

- Study building blueprints to identify potential obstacles, clarify the distances your network needs to span on each floor, and anticipate wireless demand from devices that tend to occupy each floor during the course of business.
- Consider whether Wi-Fi access points will be used as **wireless bridges** to extend wired access to remote areas of the network, as shown in Figure 6-30. The throughput demands of a wireless bridge can be significantly higher than typical Wi-Fi clients.
- Determine whether certain floors require multiple APs. Visually inspecting the floors will also help determine coverage areas and best AP locations.
- Measure the signal coverage and strength from other WLANs to inform your decision about the optimal strength and frequency for your wireless signals.
- Test proposed access point locations. In testing, a "dummy" AP is carried from location to location while a wireless client connects to it and measures its range and throughput. (Some companies sell software specially designed to conduct such testing.)

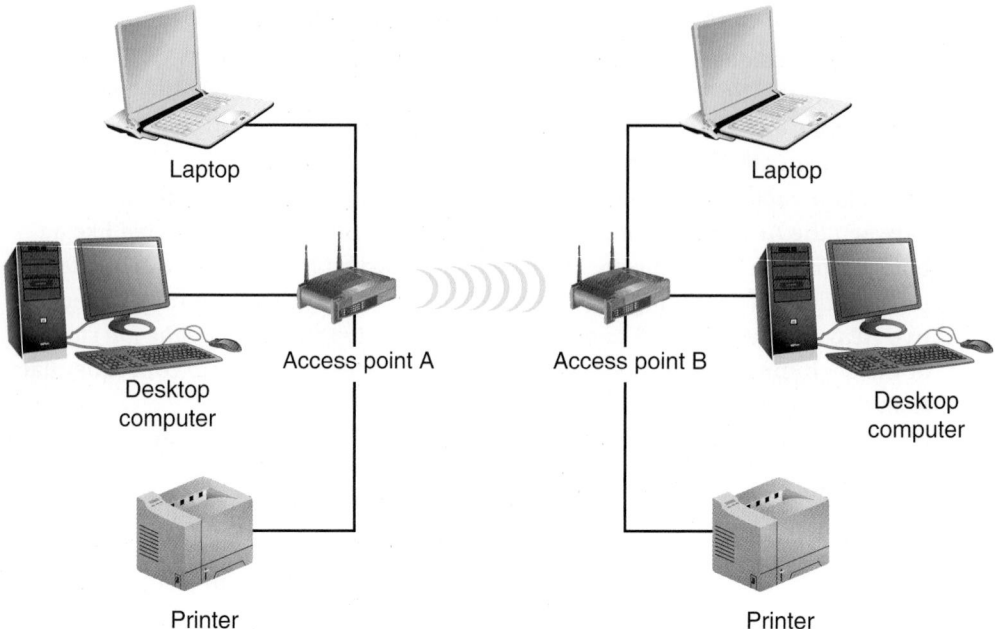

Figure 6-30   A wireless bridge provides remote wired access

- Test wireless access from the farthest corners of your space. This testing will reveal unforeseen obstacles, such as EMI issued from lights or heavy machinery.
- Consider the materials used in objects that aren't always present in the environment, such as stocked inventory in a warehouse.
- Consider how the wireless portions of the LAN will integrate with the wired portions. Access points connect the two.

The site survey can be completed more efficiently with the use of wireless survey tools such as site survey software. Fluke Networks offers AirMagnet, for example. Another option is inSSIDer by MetaGeek. After the initial setup, you can use these programs to monitor WLAN performance and possible interference or intrusion by other wireless signals in the area. Many of these programs, for example, offer a heat map feature that maps Wi-Fi signals and other noise in your location. An accurate heat map can also pinpoint gaps in Wi-Fi coverage, called dead zones, throughout the building to ensure that employee productivity isn't adversely affected by dropped Wi-Fi connections or unnecessarily slow connections.

After a site survey has identified and verified the optimal quantity and location of access points, you are ready to install them. Recall that to ensure seamless connectivity from one coverage area to another, all APs must belong to the same ESS and share an ESSID. Configuring APs, including assigning ESSIDs, is described in the next section.

Figure 6-31 shows an example of an enterprise WLAN.

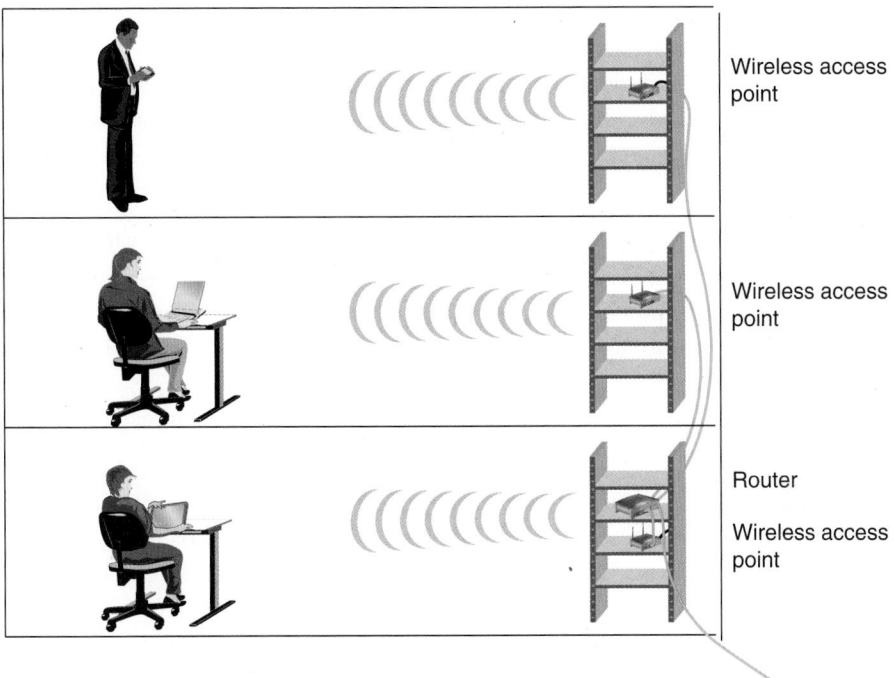

Figure 6-31 An enterprise-scale WLAN

Configure Wi-Fi Connectivity Devices

You have learned that access points provide wireless connectivity for mobile clients on an infrastructure WLAN. APs vary in which wireless standards they support, their antenna strength, and other features, such as support for voice signals or the latest security measures. You can buy a small AP or SOHO router for less than $50. More sophisticated or specialized APs—for example, those designed for outdoor use, as on city streets or at train platforms—cost much more. However, as wireless network-ing has become commonplace, even the least expensive devices are increasingly sophisticated.

The setup process for a SOHO router is similar regardless of the manufacturer or model. The variables you will set during installation include:

- Administrator password
- SSID
- Whether or not the SSID is broadcast
- Security options such as type and credentials needed to associate with the AP
- Whether or not DHCP is used; note that most network administrators do not configure their wireless access point as a DHCP server and, in fact, doing so when another DHCP server is already designated will cause addressing problems on the network

In the Hands-On Projects at the end of this chapter, you will have the chance to install and configure a SOHO router.

If something goes awry during your SOHO router configuration, you can force a reset of all the variables you changed. Wireless routers feature a reset button on their back panel. The following steps describe how to reset a SOHO router:

1. Disconnect all data cables and unplug the power cable.
2. Using the end of a paper clip, depress the reset button while you plug the power cable back in.
3. Continue holding down the button for at least 30 seconds (the required duration varies among manufacturers; check your router's documentation for the duration yours requires).
4. Release the button; at this point, the router's values should be reset to the manufacturer's defaults.

After successfully configuring your SOHO router, you are ready to introduce it to the network. In the case of a small office or home WLAN, this means using a patch cable to connect the device's WAN port to your modem's LAN port. Afterward, clients should be able to associate with the access point and gain Internet access. The following section describes how to configure clients to connect to your WLAN.

Configure Wi-Fi Clients

Wireless access configuration varies from one type of client to another. A gaming or media device will require a slightly different process than a laptop or tablet. The specific steps vary by device type and manufacturer. In general, as long as an AP is broadcasting its SSID, clients in its vicinity will detect it and offer the user the option to associate with it. If the AP uses encryption, you will need to provide the right credentials to associate with it successfully. Later in this chapter, you'll have the chance to change some of the settings on a wireless Windows client.

In an enterprise environment, configuring clients for wireless access to the network can entail a much more involved, two-part process:

- *on-boarding*—Users or network technicians install a specific app, called an agent, on a user's device, whether the device is a smartphone, laptop, or tablet. This gives the device trusted access to certain portions of the network. Access to email services, file-sharing services, and certain network administrative features might all be controlled by the device's permission levels enabled by on-boarding that device.
- *off-boarding*—The reverse procedure involves removing the agent. For security purposes, network administrators need a feature that allows them to do this remotely, in case a device is lost or stolen. This feature, called a **remote wipe**, clears a device of all important information, permissions, and apps without having physical access to the device. It might even allow you to completely disable the device, making any network or data access impossible.

Applying Concepts: Explore a Linux Wireless Interface

As with Windows operating systems, most Linux and UNIX clients provide a graphical interface for configuring their wireless interfaces. Because each version differs somewhat from the others, describing the steps required for each graphical interface is beyond the scope of this book. However, **iwconfig**, a command-line utility for viewing and setting wireless interface parameters, is common to nearly all versions of Linux and UNIX. The following steps, which can be performed on a Linux machine or a Linux VM, provide a basic primer for using the `iwconfig` command:

1. Make sure your wireless NIC is installed and that your Linux or UNIX workstation or host machine is within range of a working AP. You must also be logged into Linux or UNIX as root or a user with root-equivalent privileges. (Recall that the root user on UNIX or Linux systems is comparable to an administrative user on Windows systems.)
2. Open Terminal and enter **iwconfig**. The output should look similar to that shown in Figure 6-32.

```
% iwconfig

lo          no wireless extensions.


eth0        no wireless extensions.


eth1        IEEE 802.11abgn  ESSID:"CLASS_1"

            Mode:Managed  Frequency:2.412 GHz  Access Point: 00:0F:66:8E:19:89

            Bit Rate:54 Mb/s    Tx-Power:14 dBm

            Retry long limit:7   RTS thr:off   Fragment thr:off

            Power Management:on

            Link Quality=60/70  Signal level=-50 dBm

            Rx invalid nwid:0  Rx invalid crypt:0  Rx invalid frag:0

            Tx excessive retries:0  Invalid misc:747   Missed beacon:0
```

Figure 6-32   Output from the iwconfig command

3. Here's a brief description of the output:
   - lo indicates the loopback interface
   - eth0 represents an interface that is not wireless (that is, a wired NIC)

- eth1 represents the wireless interface; on your computer, the wireless NIC might have a different designation.
- `iwconfig` also reveals characteristics of the AP's signal, including its frequency, power, and signal level

4. For more detailed information about this command, enter `man iwconfig`. Using the `iwconfig` command, you can modify the SSID of the access point you choose to associate with, as well as many other variables. Some examples are detailed in Table 6-7. The syntax of the following examples assumes your workstation has labeled your wireless NIC eth1.

Table 6-7   Sample `iwconfig` commands

Command	Description
`iwconfig eth1 essid CLASS_1`	Instructs the wireless interface to associate with an AP whose SSID (or ESSID, as shown in this command) is CLASS_1.
`iwconfig eth1 mode Managed`	Instructs the wireless interface to operate in infrastructure mode (as opposed to ad hoc mode).
`iwconfig eth1 channel auto`	Instructs the wireless interface to automatically select the best channel for wireless data exchange.
`iwconfig eth1 freq 2.422G`	Instructs the wireless interface to communicate on the 2.422-GHz frequency.
`iwconfig eth1 key 6e225e3931`	Instructs the wireless interface to use the hexadecimal number 6e225e3931 as its key for secure authentication with the AP. (6e225e3931 is only an example; on your network, you will choose your own key.)

In this and the previous section, you have learned how to configure wireless clients and access points. Optimized configurations help increase network efficiency as well as securing network resources from damage or intrusion. The following section explains some key points about securing a wireless network.

Wi-Fi Network Security

 **Certification**

4.2   Explain authentication and access controls.

4.3   Given a scenario, secure a basic wireless network.

4.4   Summarize common networking attacks.

As you have learned, most organizations use one or more of the 802.11 protocol standards on their WLANs. By default, the 802.11 standard does not offer any security. The client only needs to know the access point's SSID, which many access points broadcast. Network administrators may prevent their access points from broadcasting the SSIDs, making them harder to detect. However, this does not provide true security. Two solutions to this problem are authentication and encryption:

- **Authentication** is the process of comparing and matching a client's credentials with the credentials in a client database to enable the client to log on to the network. The authentication process can be somewhat strengthened by using **MAC filtering**, or MAC address filtering, which prevents the AP from authenticating any device whose MAC address is not listed by the network administrator. (MAC filtering can also be instituted on a switch instead of an AP.) It can be time consuming, however, to maintain a current list of all approved MAC addresses, and MAC addresses are easily impersonated.

- **Encryption** is the use of an algorithm to scramble data into a format that can be read only by reversing the algorithm—that is, by decrypting the data. The purpose of encryption is to keep information private. Many forms of encryption exist, with some being more secure than others.

You'll learn more about the underlying processes of authentication and encryption in later chapters. Here, we'll explore techniques specific to securing wireless networks with authentication and encryption.

Legacy Networking: WEP (Wired Equivalent Privacy)

For some measure of security, 802.11 allows for optional encryption using the **WEP (Wired Equivalent Privacy)** standard. When configuring WEP, you establish a character string that is required to associate with the access point, also known as the network key. The user must provide the correct key before the client can gain access to the network via the access point. The network key can be saved as part of the client's wireless connection's properties. WEP uses keys both to authenticate network clients and to encrypt data in transit.

The first implementation of WEP allowed for 64-bit network keys, and current versions of WEP allow for more secure, 128-bit or even 256-bit network keys. Still, WEP's use of the shared key for authenticating all users and for exchanging data makes it more susceptible to discovery than a dynamically generated, random, or single-use key. Even 128-bit network keys can be cracked in a matter of minutes. Moreover, because WEP operates in the Physical and Data Link layers of the OSI model, it does not offer end-to-end data transmission security. WEP was replaced with a quick-fix improvement called WPA, which was later improved yet again with WPA2. Both of these standards are discussed next.

WPA/WPA2 (Wi-Fi Protected Access)

A significant disadvantage to WEP is that it uses the same network key for all clients and the key is static, which means it won't change without intervention. Due to this inherent insecurity, a replacement security technology was developed, called **WPA (Wi-Fi Protected Access or Wireless Protected Access)**, which dynamically assigns every transmission its own key. The encryption protocol used in WPA was replaced by a stronger encryption protocol for the updated version, called **WPA2**, which can be enabled on most consumer-grade APs. WPA2 includes support for the previously released WPA protocol. The most secure Wi-Fi communication is made possible by combining a RADIUS server with WPA or WPA2, known as WPA-Enterprise or WPA2-Enterprise, respectively. You'll learn about RADIUS servers later.

Some additional security options you might want to enable on your wireless network include:

- Many establishments—and homeowners, for that matter—create a separate **guest network** through their Wi-Fi router/access point. This is a smart security precaution, as it gives guests access to Internet service through an open network without opening the doors to the entire LAN on that router. Parents, also, might want to give their children use of an SSID with more limited network access in order to enforce household rules regarding Internet use.
- If you do provide a guest network, either at home or at a business, be sure to set up a **captive portal**. This is the first page a new client sees in the browser when connecting to the guest network, and usually requires the user to agree to a set of terms and conditions before gaining further access to the guest network. The captive portal should remind users of the following:

  ○ They are connecting to a network that does not provide user authentication or data encryption. This means data is not secure when transmitted over this connection.
  ○ They should be careful about what data they transmit, even over email, while using the guest network.
  ○ They should take extra care to avoid engaging in any illegal activity through the network connection, as that activity could be traced back to your public IP address.

Security Threats to Wi-Fi Networks

Wireless transmissions are particularly susceptible to eavesdropping. You already learned about the dangers of bluejacking and bluesnarfing with Bluetooth connections. Several additional security threats to wireless networks are discussed in the following list:

- *war driving*—A hacker searches for unprotected wireless networks by driving around with a laptop or smartphone configured to receive and capture wireless data transmissions. (The term is derived from the term *war dialing*, which is a similar tactic involving old, dial-up modems.) War driving is surprisingly effective for obtaining private information. Years ago, the hacker community publicized the vulnerabilities of a well-known store chain, which were discovered while war driving. The retailer used wireless cash registers to help customers make purchases when the regular, wired cash registers were busy. However, the wireless cash registers transmitted purchase information, including credit card numbers and customer names, to network APs in cleartext. By chance, a person in the parking lot who was running a protocol analyzer program on his laptop obtained several credit card numbers in a very short time. The person alerted the retailer to the security risk (rather than exploiting the information he gathered). Needless to say, after the retailer discovered its error, it abandoned the use of wireless cash registers until after a thorough evaluation of its data security.

- *war chalking*—Once hackers discover vulnerable access points, they make this information public by drawing symbols with chalk on the sidewalk or wall within range of a wireless network. The symbols, patterned after marks that hobos devised to indicate hospitable places for food or rest, indicate the access point's SSID and whether it's secured. Alternatively, many websites offer maps of these open networks, as reported by war drivers.

- *evil twin*— Clients running Linux, macOS, or a modern version of Windows will first attempt to associate with a known access point. This feature can result in network devices connecting to rogue access points, or access points installed without the authorization of the network administrator. One type of rogue access point, an evil twin, can be used to trick a device into connecting to the wrong network. Suppose another user brings his own AP to a café and its signal is twice as strong as the café's AP. Your laptop will automatically recognize the other user's stronger AP as the best option. If the user has configured his AP with the same SSID as the café's, and if you've configured your laptop to trust that SSID, your laptop might complete association to this evil twin AP without your knowledge. The person controlling the evil twin could then steal your data or gain access to another network that trusts your system. Note that a user can create a rogue access point inadvertently, too—for example, by bringing an AP to work, using software to turn a workstation into an AP, or creating a hot spot with a smartphone. As a network technician, check regularly for evil twins or other rogue access points within your network's geographical area. Especially be on the lookout for access points that show a stronger signal than your corporate AP because Windows lists SSIDs by signal strength, and users are accustomed to selecting the SSID at the top of the list.

- *WPA attack*—These attacks, also called WPA cracking, involve an interception of the network keys communicated between clients and access points.

- *WPS attack*—WPS (Wi-Fi Protected Setup) is a user-friendly—but not very secure—security setting available on some consumer-grade APs. Part of the security involves requiring a PIN (personal identification number) in order to access the AP's settings or to associate a new device with the network. The problem is that the PIN can be easily cracked through a **brute force attack**, which means simply trying numerous possible character combinations to find the correct combination. This gives the attacker access to the network's WPA2 key. The PIN feature in WPS should be disabled if possible.

Applying Concepts: Examine Wireless Security Settings

Now that you understand some of the security options available for a wireless network connection, let's explore how to check the current settings on your AP and change them if necessary.

Using a Windows 10 computer that is connected to a local network via Wi-Fi, complete the following steps:

1. Right-click the Wi-Fi connection icon in the taskbar and click **Open Network and Sharing Center**.
2. Under *View your active networks*, click the Wi-Fi connection, then click **Wireless Properties**.
3. In the Wireless Network Properties dialog box, look for the following information on both the Connection and the Security tabs.

   a. What are the network's Name and SSID?
   b. Is the connection configured to connect automatically when the wireless network is in range?
   c. What are the network's Security and Encryption types?

Troubleshooting Wi-Fi Networks

 Certification

5.2 Given a scenario, use the appropriate tool.

5.4 Given a scenario, troubleshoot common wireless connectivity and performance issues.

You've already learned about several tools used to test copper and fiber-optic cables in Ethernet networks. Cable continuity and performance testers, of course, will tell you nothing about the wireless connections, nodes, or access points on a network. For that, you need tools that contain wireless NICs and run wireless protocols. As you learned earlier in the chapter, you can start gathering information about a wireless environment by viewing the wireless network connection properties on your workstation. However, this tells you only a little about your wireless environment—and it only applies to one workstation. To get the full picture of your wireless environment, you need to use more advanced wireless network tools, as described in the following section.

Wi-Fi Network Tools

Many applications can scan for wireless signals over a certain geographical range and discover all the access points and wireless nodes transmitting in the area. This is useful for determining whether an access point is functioning properly, whether it is positioned correctly so that all the nodes it serves are within its range, and whether nodes and access points are communicating over the proper channels within a frequency band. Here are two tools you should have in your toolkit:

- *spectrum analyzer*—A device that can assess the quality of a wireless signal. Spectrum analysis is useful, for example, to ascertain where interference is greatest.
- *Wi-Fi analyzer*—Software that can evaluate Wi-Fi network availability as well as help optimize Wi-Fi signal settings or help identify Wi-Fi security threats. Identifying the wireless channels being used nearby helps you optimize the wireless channel utilization in your vicinity.

Software tools that can perform wireless network assessment are often available for free and might be provided by the access point's manufacturer. Following is a list of specific capabilities common to wireless network testing tools:

- Identify transmitting APs, nodes, and the channels over which they are communicating
- Measure signal strength from and determine the range of an AP
- Indicate the effects of attenuation, signal loss, and noise
- Interpret signal strength information to rate potential AP locations
- Ensure proper association and reassociation when moving between APs
- Capture and interpret traffic exchanged between APs and nodes
- Measure throughput and assess data transmission errors
- Analyze the characteristics of each channel within a frequency band to indicate the clearest channels

Applying Concepts: Wi-Fi Analyzer on Your Smartphone

You can turn your smartphone into a Wi-Fi analyzer by installing a free or inexpensive app through your phone's app store. These days, such apps are easy to find, easy to use, and provide useful information without much hassle. In this project, you install a Wi-Fi analyzer app on your phone and try it out on your home or school Wi-Fi network. These instructions are specific to an Android smartphone installing the Wifi Analyzer app, but you can adjust the steps to work for other smartphones and different apps.

1. On an Android smartphone, go to the Play Store and search for the app called **Wifi Analyzer**. The app used in this specific example was created by farproc, but you can choose a different app if you want to.

2. Install the app and open it. You can look at the Online Help page at this time, or you can wait until later.

3. At the time of this writing, the Wifi Analyzer is programmed to automatically start scanning for Wi-Fi signals. It provides a live feed of signal strength and channel coverage for the wireless networks in its reach. You can see in Figure 6-33 that several home networks were available at the time of the scan, with several of these using various overlapping channels. The local networks provided the strongest signals.

Wireless networks perform best when using channels not used by nearby networks. For this reason, it's best to program the network for channels at the beginning, center, and end of the channel bandwidth. For example, recall that 2.4-GHz-band devices offer up to 14 channels, although most only offer 11 channels, especially in the United States. In the United States, then, neighboring Wi-Fi networks typically use channels 1, 6, and 11 in order to minimize overlap. When all 14 channels are available, such as in many parts of Europe, the channel spread might still be 1-6-11 to maximize compatibility with devices from other areas of the world, or it might instead be 1-5-9-13 to maximize use of the available bandwidth.

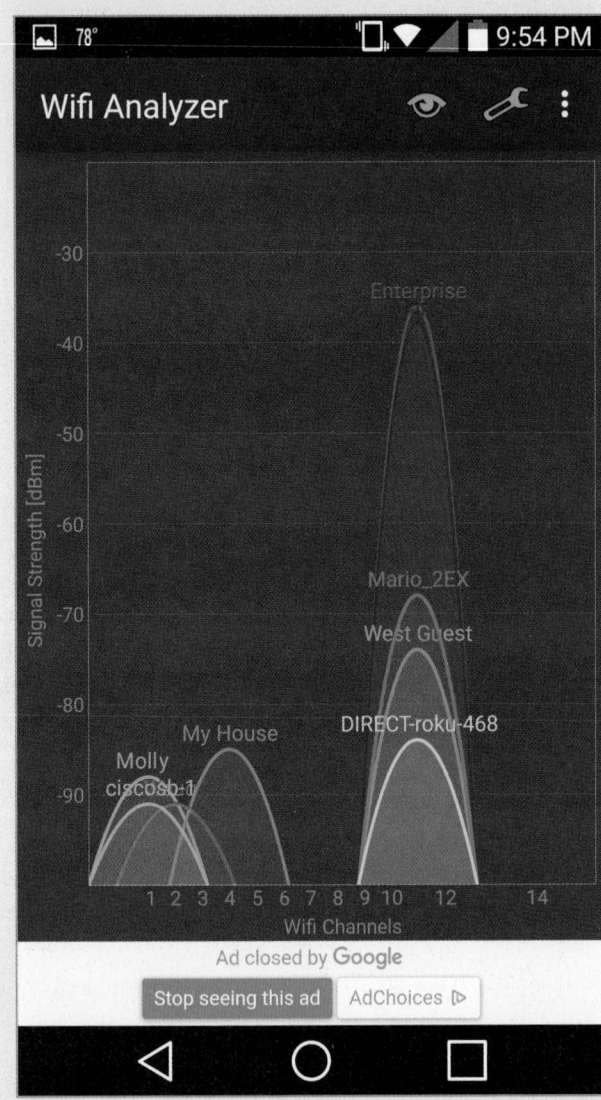

Figure 6-33   The Wifi Analyzer app detected several home networks nearby

Source: Wifi Analyzer

If your wireless network is programmed for the same channel as your neighbor's wireless network, you will get better performance if you change your network's channel to part of the channel range not currently in use in your vicinity.

4. What channel is your network programmed to?

5. The Wifi Analyzer app provides some interesting features, including a signal meter, as shown on the left side of Figure 6-34, and a list of other hosts on the smartphone's LAN, as shown on the right side of Figure 6-34. Notice in the list of LAN neighbors that device MAC addresses and manufacturers are also listed. Take a few minutes to explore your wireless analyzer app's features. What features and information did you find? What changes might you want to make to your Wi-Fi network's settings to increase its performance or security?

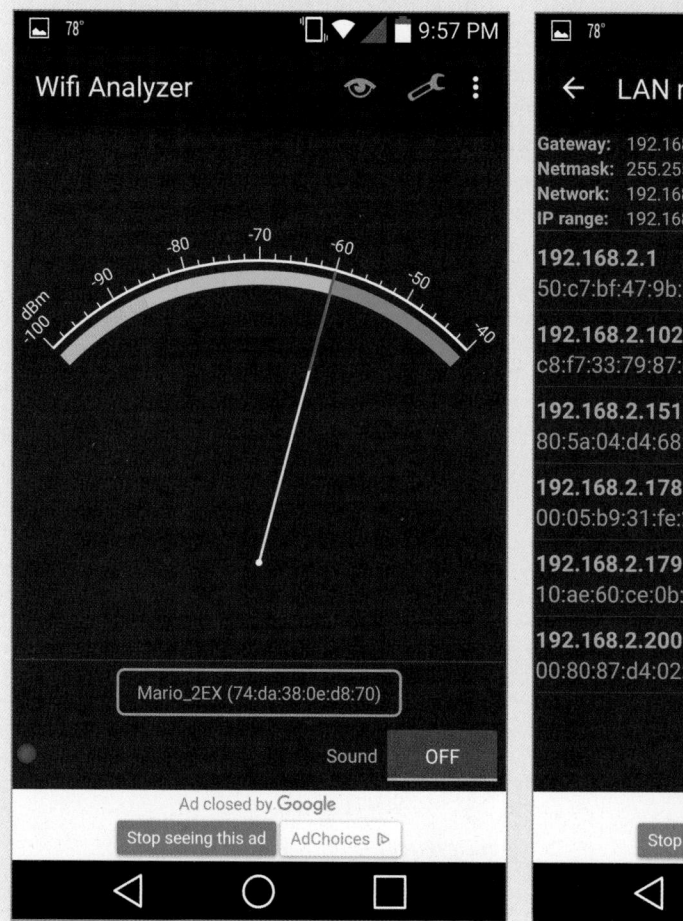

Figure 6-34   Readings from the Wifi Analyzer app

Source: Wifi Analyzer

Avoid Pitfalls

You might have had the frustrating experience of not being able to log on to a network, even though you were sure you'd typed in your username and password correctly. Maybe it turned out that your Caps Lock key was on, changing your case-sensitive password. Or maybe you were trying to log on to the wrong server. On every type of network, many variables must be accurately set on clients, servers, and connectivity devices in order for communication to succeed. Wireless networks add a few more variables. Following are some wireless configuration pitfalls to avoid:

- *wrong SSID*—Your wireless client must select the correct SSID. As you have learned, you may instruct clients to search for any available access point (or clients might be configured to do this by default). However, if the access point does not broadcast its SSID, or if your workstation is not configured to look for access points, you will have to enter the SSID during client configuration. Also, bear in mind that SSIDs are case sensitive. That is, *CLASS_1* does not equal *Class_1*.
- *security type mismatch*—Your wireless client must be configured to use the same type of encryption as your access point. Most of the time, this is negotiated automatically between the AP and the client. To configure the security type manually on a Windows 10 client, open the Network and Sharing Center, click Change adapter settings, right-click the active connection and click Status, and then open the connection's properties dialog box. Click the Security tab to change the security type, encryption type, or network security key, as shown in Figure 6-35.

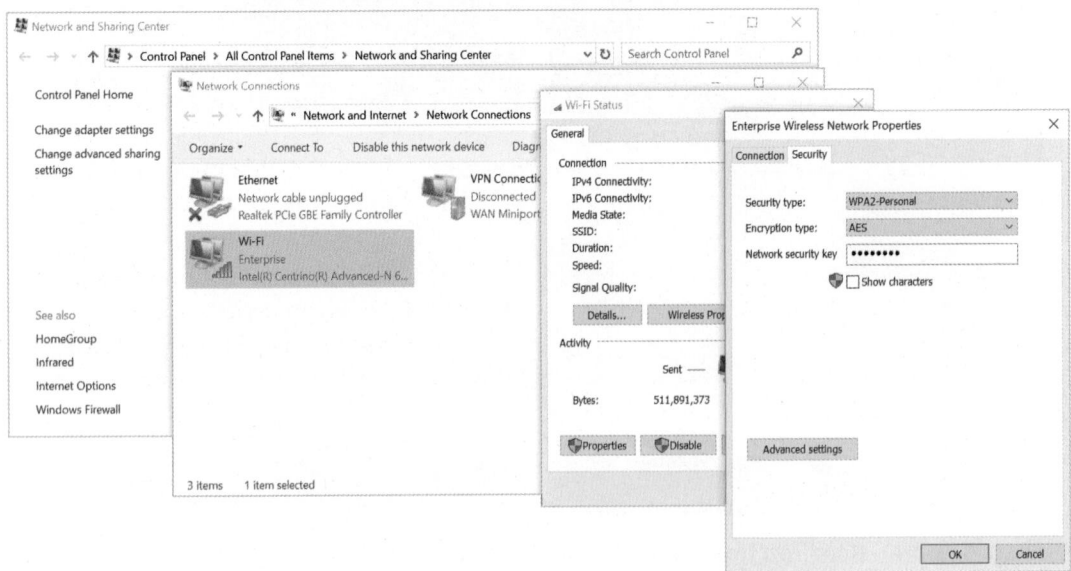

Figure 6-35   Adjust a network connection's security settings

- *wrong passphrase*—Similarly, you must use a security key, or passphrase, that matches the access point's. If incorrect, your client cannot authenticate with the access point.

- *overlapping channels or mismatched frequencies*—You have learned that the access point establishes the channel and frequency over which it will communicate with clients. Clients, then, automatically sense the correct channel and frequency. However, if you have instructed your client to use only a channel or frequency different from the one your access point uses, association will fail to occur. Similarly, using channels or frequencies that are too close to each other on the frequency spectrum can interfere with each other's transmissions.

- *mismatched standards (802.11 b/a/g/n/ac)*—If your access point is set to communicate only via 802.11ac, even if the documentation says it supports 802.11n and 802.11ac, clients must also follow the 802.11ac standard. Clients might also be able to detect and match the correct type of 802.11 standard. However, if they are configured to follow only one standard, they will never find an access point broadcasting via a different standard.

- *incorrect antenna placement*—On a network, many factors can cause data errors and a resulting decrease in performance. Be sure to check the recommended geographic range for your AP, and keep clients well within that distance. If a client is too far from an AP, communication might occur, but data errors become more probable. Also remember to place your antenna in a high spot for best signal reception.

- *interference*—If intermittent and difficult-to-diagnose wireless communication errors occur, interference might be the culprit. Check for sources of EMI, such as fluorescent lights, heavy machinery, cordless phones, and microwaves in the data transmission path.

- *simultaneous wired and wireless connections*—A workstation is designed to transmit either via a wired or a wireless connection, but not both at the same time. When troubleshooting connection issues, consider whether the computer is making conflicting attempts to communicate with the network through both types of connections. You can resolve the issue by disabling the Wi-Fi adapter or by unplugging the Ethernet cable.

- *problems with firmware updates*—Updates to a NIC or access point's firmware can help patch vulnerabilities and increase functionality. The flip side of this issue, however, is that updates should be tested before being rolled out system-wide.

- *unoptimized access point power levels*—Each access point's power level, or the strength of the signal the access point emits, should be optimized for the geographic area covered by that AP. Power levels that are too low will result in dropped signals as clients roam to the peripheral areas of the AP's range. However, maxed out power levels will result in too much overlap between AP coverage areas, causing clients from other coverage areas to attempt to connect with APs that are farther away but transmitting the stronger signal. Begin with a 50 percent power setting, and make incremental changes as needed to optimize the amount of overlap between APs. Also keep in mind that even if a client can receive a signal from a high-powered AP installed on the other end of the building, the return signal from the client might not be reliably strong enough to reach the AP, which is called a near-far effect.

- *incorrect antenna type*—You might think that omnidirectional antennas would nearly always be the best choice when setting up Wi-Fi coverage. The idea is to place the AP in the center of its coverage area, then send the signal out in all directions. However, in many situations, installing unidirectional antennas instead will enhance a signal's availability, directing the signal right where you need it while not wasting a signal in areas where you don't. For example, suppose a company installs an omnidirectional antenna near a factory's 30-foot-high ceiling. Because the antenna's signal is broadcast in all directions from its location, distributing its signal strength in a spherical shape, the best possible signal would only be available to workers who could walk on the ceiling—obviously, that's not a viable situation. To be useful, the signal needs to be directed down to the floor. A unidirectional antenna, in this case, can be positioned up high and pointed down to create a dome-shaped coverage that spreads out as it nears the plant floor, as shown in Figure 6-36.

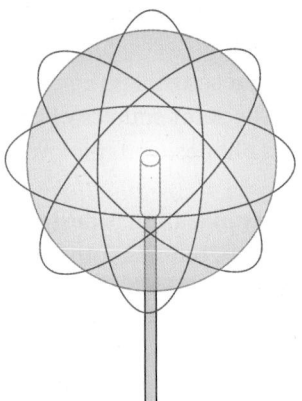

An omnidirectional antenna placed high near a ceiling broadcasts a signal in all directions, but the signal is mostly inaccessible to workers on the floor

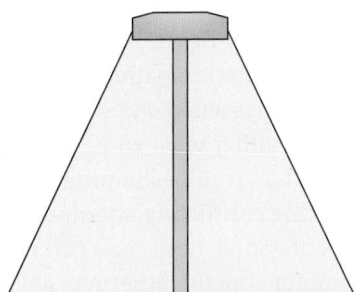

A unidirectional antenna can be positioned near the ceiling, but aimed at the floor, giving workers substantial access to its signal

Figure 6-36 A unidirectional antenna provides more efficient signal coverage in this situation

- *client saturation or overcapacity*—APs vary in the number of device connections they can handle at any given time. A SOHO network's AP might take 10–15 devices before becoming overwhelmed, whereas a high-powered, commercial AP can handle a much larger client load without exceeding its bandwidth saturation limitations. The 802.11ac standard also provides this advantage, in that this newest standard expands available bandwidth while also managing that bandwidth more efficiently to support more clients. Keep in mind, when shopping for a new AP, that the actual, effective capacity in the real world will be significantly less than the AP's advertised capacity.

Applying Concepts: Snail-Speed Wi-Fi

Your company recently rented new office space across town to make room for expansion in the Accounting Department, and part of your responsibility with the new acquisition was to install three new 802.11ac APs. You completed the job just before the weekend, at the same time as the 19 accounting employees finished setting up their file cabinets and reception area furniture. Some of your fellow IT technicians completed workstation setup that same day; most of the workstations are connected to the network via Wi-Fi due to restrictions imposed by your company's contract with the property owner. Today, Monday, the accounting personnel report for work at the new building.

At first, the new location's network seems to be working fine. The local network is communicating well with the home office's network, and everyone has access to all the files they need on the file servers. As everyone gets settled in for the day and starts their Monday duties, however, the network slows to a snail's pace. It's not long before you start to get complaints about emails being delayed, files not being accessible, and print jobs to network printers getting lost. You make a beeline across town to figure out what's wrong.

During the course of your investigation, you find that all the hosts on the local network are accessible. However, you find it odd that even though your ping tests are usually successful, sometimes they aren't. You know the APs are all new devices, and you double-check their configurations to try to determine a common source for all the problems you've noted. Here's a summary of the results you've gathered:

- All three APs are active and communicating successfully with your laptop.
- All three APs are configured with identical SSIDs and other settings.
- For good measure, you also walk around the office space with your wireless analyzer to confirm there are no significant dead zones or interference.

Why are wireless transmissions being lost in transit? Below are several possible resolutions. Select the best one and explain your reasoning:
- a. One of the APs is faulty and not processing transmissions. It should be removed and replaced.
- b. The NICs in the employees' workstations were damaged during the move. Probably several just need to be reseated while some might need to be replaced.
- c. The APs should not have the same SSID. Rename each AP so their SSIDs don't match.
- d. Three APs are insufficient for the wireless load of the Accounting Department. More APs should be added.

e. The APs are all part of the same LAN and should be separated into separate LANs.

f. The workstation computers are programmed to search for and connect with the wrong SSID, or the network keys are entered wrong. Every workstation's wireless interface settings should be checked.

g. The APs are all programmed to use the same channel. They should be programmed for different channels.

Chapter Summary

Characteristics of Wireless Transmissions

- LANs that transmit signals through the air via RF (radio frequency) waves are known as WLANs (wireless local area networks).
- The wireless spectrum, commonly called the airwaves, is the frequency range of electromagnetic waves used for data and voice communications.
- To allow multiple devices to share the same band, the band is subdivided into channels and channels are further subdivided into narrowband channels.
- An antenna's radiation pattern describes the relative strength over a three-dimensional area of all the electromagnetic energy the antenna sends or receives.
- Propagation refers to the way in which a wave travels from one point to another.

Wireless Standards for the IoT (Internet of Things)

- The IoT (Internet of Things) is made up of any device that can be connected to the Internet—that is, any sensor, computer, or wearable device that talks to other devices over a network.

- Based on the 802.15.4 standard, ZigBee is a low-powered, battery-conserving wireless technology. It is designed to handle small amounts of data and is therefore ideal for use in ISM (industrial, scientific, and medical) sensors.
- Similar to ZigBee, Z-Wave is a smart home protocol that provides two basic types of functions: signaling, to manage wireless connections, and control, to transmit data and commands between devices.
- Bluetooth operates in the radio band of 2.4 GHz to 2.4835 GHz and hops between frequencies within that band (up to 1600 hops/sec) to help reduce interference.
- ANT+ (pronounced *ant plus*) technology is based on the ANT protocol, which is an ad-hoc wireless protocol operating at about 2.4 GHz.
- RFID (Radio Frequency Identification) uses electromagnetic fields to store data on a small chip in an RFID tag, which includes an antenna that can both transmit and receive, and possibly a battery.
- NFC (near-field communication) is a form of RFID that transfers data wirelessly over very short distances (usually 10 cm or less).

- Like other WPAN technologies, wireless USB requires little power and operates within about a 10-m range.
- IR (Infrared or infrared radiation) technology has found new life in the world of IoT, where it's used primarily to collect data through various sensors. IR exists just below the spectrum that is visible to the human eye, with longer wavelengths than red light.

802.11 WLAN Standards

- The most popular OSI Physical and Data Link layer standards used by WLANs is Wi-Fi. Wi-Fi (short for *wireless fidelity*) is a collection of wireless standards and their amendments, extensions, and corrections developed by IEEE's 802.11 committee.
- Compared with CSMA/CD (Carrier Sense Multiple Access with Collision Detection), CSMA/CA (Carrier Sense Multiple Access with Collision Avoidance) minimizes the potential for collisions, but cannot detect the occurrence of a collision and so cannot take steps to recover from the collisions that occur.
- Association is another function of the MAC sublayer described in the 802.11 standard.
- There are some types of overhead required to manage access to the 802.11 wireless networks—for example, ACKs, probes, and beacons. For each of these functions, the 802.11 standard specifies a specific frame type at the MAC sublayer.
- MIMO and MU-MIMO access points can only be used at full capacity when the client devices also support MIMO or MU-MIMO technology, respectively.

Implementing a Wi-Fi Network

- Because they are not bound by cabling paths between nodes and connectivity devices, wireless networks are not laid out using the same topologies as wired networks. They have their own topologies.
- Most small, wireless LANs use the infrastructure topology, requiring one or more APs. A home or small office network, called a SOHO network, might call for only one AP. This device often combines switching, routing, and other network functions as well.
- APs vary in which wireless standards they support, their antenna strength, and other features, such as support for voice signals or the latest security measures. However, the setup process for a SOHO router is similar regardless of the manufacturer or model.
- In general, as long as an AP is broadcasting its SSID, clients in its vicinity will detect it and offer the user the option to associate with it. If the AP uses encryption, you will need to provide the right credentials to associate with it successfully.

Wi-Fi Network Security

- Authentication is the process of comparing and matching a client's credentials with the credentials in a client database to enable the client to log on to the network. Encryption is the use of an algorithm to scramble data into a format that can be read only by reversing the algorithm—that is, by decrypting the data.
- WPA (Wi-Fi Protected Access or Wireless Protected Access) dynamically assigns every transmission its own key. The encryption protocol used in WPA was replaced by a stronger encryption protocol for the updated version, called WPA2, which can be enabled on most consumer-grade APs.
- Wireless transmissions are particularly susceptible to eavesdropping.

Troubleshooting Wi-Fi Networks

- Many applications can scan for wireless signals over a certain geographical range and discover all the access points and wireless nodes transmitting in the area. This is useful for determining whether an access point is functioning properly, whether it is positioned correctly so that all the nodes it serves are within its range, and whether nodes and access points are communicating over the proper channels within a frequency band.

- On every type of network, many variables must be accurately set on clients, servers, and connectivity devices in order for communication to succeed. Wireless networks add a few more variables.

Key Terms

For definitions of key terms, see the Glossary near the end of the book.

802.11a
802.11ac
802.11b
802.11g
802.11n
ad hoc
ANT+
AP (access point)
association
authentication
band
beacon frame
Bluetooth
brute force attack
BSS (basic service set)
BSSID (basic service set identifier)
captive portal
CAPWAP (Control and Provisioning of Wireless Access Points)
channel bonding
CSMA/CA (Carrier Sense Multiple Access with Collision Avoidance)
data frame
diffraction
DSSS (direct sequence spread spectrum)

encryption
ESS (extended service set)
ESSID (extended service set identifier)
evil twin
fading
FHSS (frequency hopping spread spectrum)
frequency hopping
guest network
infrastructure
interference
IoT (Internet of Things)
IR (infrared)
iwconfig
LLC sublayer
LOS (line of sight)
LWAPP (Lightweight Access Point Protocol)
MAC filtering
MAC sublayer
mesh
MIMO (multiple input-multiple output)
MU-MIMO (multiuser MIMO)
NFC (near-field communication)
off-boarding

omnidirectional antenna
on-boarding
paired
probe
propagation
radiation pattern
range
reassociation
reflection
refraction
remote wipe
RFID (Radio Frequency Identification)
rogue access point
RTS/CTS (Request to Send/ Clear to Send)
scanning
scattering
site survey
SNR (signal-to-noise ratio)
spectrum analyzer
SSID (service set identifier)
unidirectional antenna
war driving
WEP (Wired Equivalent Privacy)
Wi-Fi

Wi-Fi analyzer
wireless bridge
wireless controller
wireless range extender
wireless spectrum

WLAN (wireless local area
    network)
WPA (Wi-Fi Protected
    Access or Wireless
    Protected Access)

WPA2
WPAN (wireless PAN)
Z-Wave

Review Questions

1. What is the lowest layer of the OSI model at which wired and wireless transmissions share the same protocols?
   a. Layer 4
   b. Layer 3
   c. Layer 2
   d. Layer 1

2. What technology does Bluetooth use to take advantage of the 79 channels allocated to the Bluetooth band?
   a. ZigBee
   b. DSSS
   c. RTS/CTS
   d. FHSS

3. Which one of the following wireless transmission types requires a clear LOS to function?
   a. Bluetooth
   b. NFC
   c. Infrared
   d. Wi-Fi

4. Which Bluetooth class has the highest power output?
   a. Class 1
   b. Class 2
   c. Class 3
   d. They all have equal power output

5. A hacker takes advantage of an open Bluetooth connection to send a virus to a user's smartphone. What kind of security breach has occurred?
   a. Data breach
   b. Bluejacking

   c. War driving
   d. Bluesnarfing

6. A user swipes her smartphone across a tag on a poster to obtain showtimes for a movie she wants to see later that evening. What wireless technology transmitted the data?
   a. NFC
   b. Bluetooth
   c. Z-Wave
   d. ANT+

7. Which 802.11 standard functions in both the 2.4-GHz and 5-GHz bands?
   a. 802.11g
   b. 802.11ac
   c. 802.11b
   d. 802.11n

8. Which Carrier Sense technology is used on wireless networks to reduce collisions?
   a. CSMA/CD
   b. 802.11
   c. CSMA/CA
   d. SSID

9. You've just completed a survey of the wireless signals traversing the airspace in your employer's vicinity, and you've found an unauthorized AP with a very strong signal near the middle of the 100-acre campus. What kind of threat do you need to report to your boss?
   a. Rogue AP
   b. War driving
   c. Bluesnarfing
   d. Hidden node

10. You just settled in for some study time at the local coffee shop, and you pause long enough to connect your smartphone to the Wi-Fi so you can listen to some music while you study. As you're about to sign in, you realize that you clicked on an SSID called "Free Coffee and Internet." What kind of security trap did you almost fall for?
    a. Guest network
    b. Bluejacking
    c. Evil twin
    d. Brute force attack

11. To exchange information, two antennas must be tuned to the same _____.

12. Which kind of antenna is used in a point-to-point link, especially over long distances?

13. When a wireless signal encounters a large obstacle, what happens to the signal?

14. Signals traveling through areas in which many wireless communications systems are in use will exhibit a lower _____ due to the higher proportion of noise.

15. Which Wi-Fi frequency band offers 24 unlicensed communications channels in the United States?

16. Why do wireless networks experience a greater reduction in throughput compared with wired networks?

17. Which IoT wireless standard is used to sync data from a smartwatch, bike computer, and smart phone to a single user account?

18. 802.11ac provides an advantage over 802.11n by incorporating increased channel bonding capabilities. What size bonded channels does 802.11ac support?

19. What feature of a site survey maps the Wi-Fi signals and other noise in your location?

20. You're setting up a home network for your neighbor, who is a music teacher. She has students visiting her home regularly for lessons and wants to provide Internet access for their parents while they're waiting on the children. However, she's concerned about keeping her own data private. What wireless feature can you configure on her AP to meet her requests?

Hands-On Projects

Project 6-1: Configure a SOHO Router

In this project, you configure a SOHO router, which includes routing, switching, wireless access functions, and other network services in a single device. Configuration steps on various SOHO wireless connectivity devices differ, but they involve a similar process and require you to modify the same variables. Always follow the manufacturer's directions rather than the general directions given here.

This project assumes that the router is brand new or that it has been reset so any previous configuration has been erased. (To reset the router manually, use the end of a paper clip or pen to press and hold the reset button on the back of the router for up to 30 seconds.) You'll also need the router's default IP address, admin username, and admin password. To find this information, look in the router's documentation, look for a sticker on the router itself, or search online for your model and brand of router. This project assumes you are working on a Windows 10 workstation logged on as a user with administrative privileges.

1. Connect the computer to the router with a patch cable plugged into a network (Ethernet) port on the router (see Figure 6-37). Then plug the router into a power outlet and turn it on.

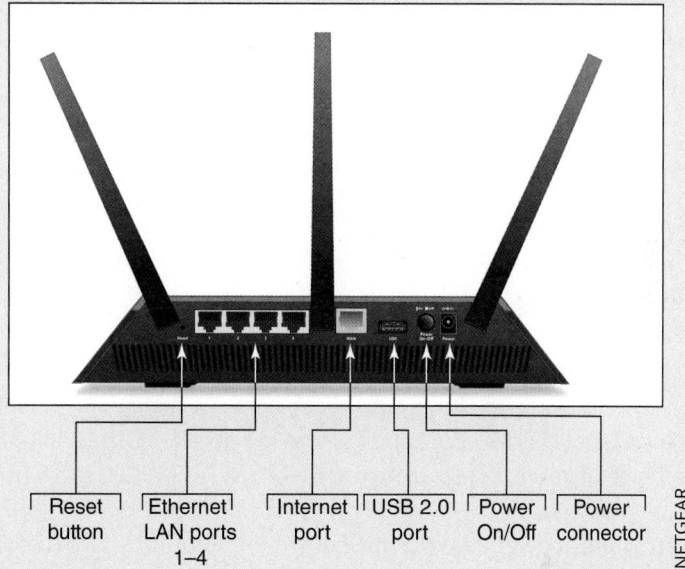

Reset button   Ethernet LAN ports 1–4   Internet port   USB 2.0 port   Power On/Off   Power connector   NETGEAR

Figure 6-37   **Connections and ports on the back of a NETGEAR router**

2. Connect the ISP modem or other device to the router's Internet port, and connect any other devices on the network that require a wired connection.

3. Firmware on the router (which can be flashed for updates) contains a configuration program that you can access using a web browser from anywhere on the network. In your browser address box, type the IP address of the router (for many routers, that address is 192.168.1.1) and press **Enter**. Sign in using the default admin username and password. For our router, the default username and password are both **admin**, although yours might be different. What is the IP address and sign-in information for your router?

4. The main setup page appears. The setup program will take you through the process of configuring the router. After you've configured the router, you might have to turn your cable or DSL modem off and then turn it back on so that it correctly syncs up with the router. Figure 6-38 shows the main page for a router that has already been configured. For most situations, the default settings on this and other pages should work without any changes. What basic steps did the setup program have you follow to configure the router?

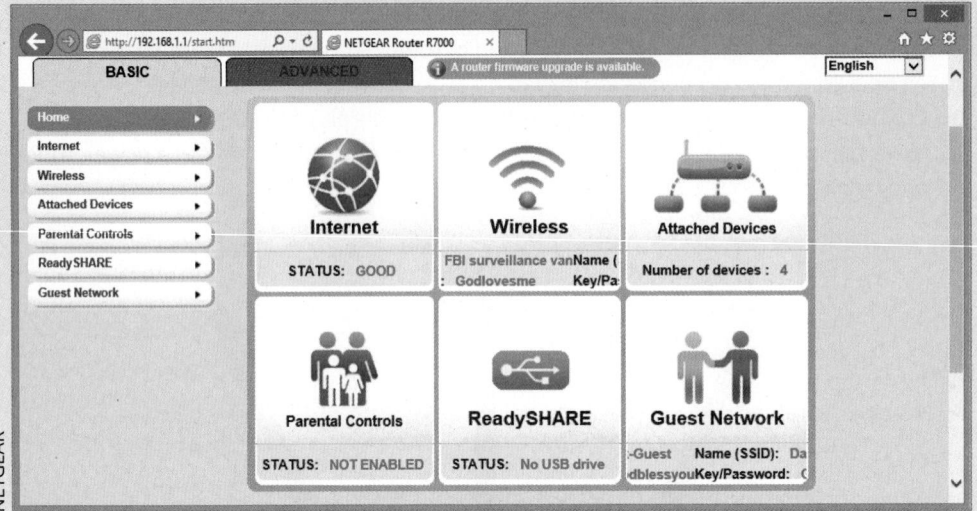

NETGEAR

Figure 6-38   Main page for router firmware setup

5. It's extremely important to protect access to your network and prevent others from hijacking your router. If you have not already done so, change the default password so that others cannot change your router setup. In Figure 6-38, the BASIC tab is selected. Most of the settings you'll want to adjust are on the ADVANCED tab for this router. To change the password on the router shown in the figure, you would click **ADVANCED, Administration**, and **Set Password**. What are the steps for your router? Record your new router password in your LastPass vault along with any other helpful information about your router, such as its management IP address.

6. Spend some time examining the various features of your router. If you make any changes that you want to keep, be sure to save them. What is the public IP address of the router on the ISP network? Why is it necessary for the router to have two IP addresses? When finished, you can sign out now or stay signed in for the next project.

Project 6-2: Modify SOHO Router Settings for Wireless Connections

Now that you have installed your new SOHO router, you're ready to modify its configuration through the administrator interface. This project picks up where Project 6-1 left off and requires the same Windows 10 computer connected to one of the router's data ports.

1. Sign in to your router's administrative interface. Refer to your LastPass vault if you need help remembering this information.

2. Access the wireless settings page. Review the settings that appear on this page, including the SSID. You might have assigned an SSID in Project 6-1 during the initial setup. If not, assign an SSID and security key now. Record this information in your LastPass vault.

3. Answer the following questions:

   a. Which 802.11 standards will this router use to communicate with wireless clients?

   b. Which channel is selected by default?

c. Why do you think this channel was selected, and how do you think you can change it?

d. Is the SSID set to broadcast or not?

e. What would happen if you disabled the broadcast?

f. Would clients still be able to communicate with the router?

4. Disconnect the patch cable between your computer and the router.

5. Click the **Network** icon in your taskbar. Windows displays a list of wireless networks that are broadcasting availability. List the top three networks that are available.

6. Select the name of your wireless network. If you are comfortable with automatically connecting to this network in the future, check **Connect automatically** and then click **Connect**. Because you are attempting to connect to a secured network, Windows will prompt you for the security key. Refer to your notes in LastPass if you need help remembering this information.

7. After connecting, open a browser and navigate to **speedtest.net** or a similar speed test website. Run a speed test to determine your connection's download and upload speeds, respectively. What are your test results?

Project 6-3: Optimize Wireless Security on a SOHO Router

Properly securing a wireless access point is not the kind of chore most home users think to do. Some IT students have actually created businesses securing home networks for their neighbors, friends, and family. In this project, you work with AP settings that increase a home wireless network's security. These steps are specific to a Linksys router, but can easily be adapted for other consumer-grade AP brands.

1. On your (or a friend's, with their permission) home network, sign in to the router's configuration console. If no factory settings have been changed yet, you can use the default access credentials provided by the manufacturer.

2. As you make changes, be sure to write down access information for the network owner. Provide instructions on where to keep this information safe, such as locked up in a safe or stored at a separate location. Ideally, you would walk the network owner through the process of setting up a password manager using a tool such as LastPass or KeePass.

3. On the wireless settings page, change the SSID to a name that is unique and completely unrelated to the brand or type of router being used or to the names of the residents.

4. Whether the SSID is broadcast or not is a personal preference. It's more convenient to broadcast the SSID and does not seriously affect the network's security. Save your changes.

5. On the wireless security page, check the security mode. Select **WPA Auto** if available, otherwise select **WPA2**. The encryption type should be **AES** unless older devices are in use, in which case you'll have to resort to the **TKIP or AES** setting. These protocols are explained in Chapter 10.

6. Change the security key to a nondictionary code that includes both letters and numbers, and at least 10 digits. The more digits, the more secure the key. A long security key is more secure than a completely random but short one, so consider using a line from a favorite song with a couple of numbers and symbols thrown in. Save your changes.

7. On the administration page, set the admin password to a phrase that, again, includes both letters and numbers, the longer the better. Also disable Remote Management. Save your changes.

8. Go to each device that is used regularly on the network and force each device to "forget" the network so the previous settings will be removed from the device. Reconnect each device to the network with the new settings.

Project 6-4: Establish a Wireless Network Baseline

One of the first pieces of information you'll want to have handy when troubleshooting wireless issues is a baseline with which to compare current conditions at the time of the problem. Free software like NetStress can help you gather this kind of information while your network is working well.

You'll need two Windows computers (use Windows 10 or 8.1) on the same LAN to complete this project. Both computers must be connected wirelessly to the LAN. You'll also need an Ethernet patch cable to create a wired connection for one computer.

1. Go to **nutsaboutnets.com** and look for the free **NetStress** download. At the time of this writing, the download is available at the address **nutsaboutnets.com/netstress**. Download and install the NetStress application on two different computers that are connected to the same LAN. One computer will function as the transmitter computer, and the other will function as the receiver. During installation, you might see some messages. If so, respond as follows:

   - If you get a warning that the app you're trying to install isn't a verified app from the Store, click **Install anyway**.
   - If you get a UAC warning, click **Yes**.
   - If you see a Setup dialog box warning that the application requires Microsoft.NET Framework 2.0 first be installed on your machine, click **OK**. The .NET Framework should already be available on your computer, but you might need to activate it before continuing with the NetStress installation. To do this, open **Control Panel** and click **Programs and Features**. Click **Turn Windows features on or off**. Click to select **.NET Framework 3.5 (includes .NET 2.0 and 3.0)**, and then click **OK**. Windows might need to download files from Windows Update in order to continue. When the Windows features changes are finished, click **Close.** Return to the NetStress setup wizard and complete installation.

2. Open the **NetStress** application on both computers. In the Select Network Interface (local host) box, click on your wireless interface and click **OK**. If you get any Windows Security Alerts, click **Allow access** to allow access through your firewall.

3. On the Transmitter computer, click the blinking **Remote Receiver IP** button at the top of the window. In the Select Remote Receiver window, select or type the IP address of the Receiver computer and click **OK**.

4. In the menu bar, click **Start**.

5. Allow the test to run for a couple of minutes, then click **Stop** in the menu bar.

6. Using **Snipping Tool**, which is a screen capture application embedded in Windows, take a screenshot of the results of your test on the Receiver computer. Be sure to get results for both the **Timecourse (Total)** tab and the **Timecourse (TCP)** tab. Save your screenshots in a location where you can find them easily in a few minutes.

7. Connect one of the computers to the router/AP with an Ethernet cable and rerun the test for a couple of minutes again. Take a screenshot of these results as well, then answer the following questions:

   a. On the Receiver, what were the average TCP and Total throughputs when both computers were using wireless interfaces?

   b. On the Receiver, what were the average TCP and Total throughputs when one computer was using a wired interface?

   c. How can you explain the differences?

8. Make some notes about these installations on your Wikidot website.

Capstone Projects

Capstone Project 6-1: Install and Use Packet Tracer

If you plan to pursue networking or security as your area of specialty in IT, you might consider earning a few Cisco networking certifications after you complete your CompTIA Network+ certification. The Cisco Networking Academy website provides many useful tools for advancing your networking education. One of those tools is a network simulator called Packet Tracer.

In this Capstone Project, you download and install Packet Tracer, take a tour of the simulator interface, and create a very basic network using simulated devices in Packet Tracer. This version of Packet Tracer is free to the public, and your school does not have to be a member of Cisco's Networking Academy for you to download and use it. In later projects, we'll return to Packet Tracer to build more complex networks and even learn some basic Cisco IOS commands. Cisco IOS (Internetworking Operating Systems) is the operating system used on Cisco networking devices, such as routers and switches (with minor variations in the specific IOS for each different type of device). Many other manufacturers of networking devices use the same or similar commands, and those that use different commands typically use very similar functions, even if they call it something a little different.

To get the Packet Tracer download, you must first sign up for the free Introduction to Packet Tracer online course on the Cisco Networking Academy website. Complete the following steps to create your account:

1. In your browser, navigate to **netacad.com/campaign/ptdt-4**. If the course is not listed on this page, do a search for *packet tracer site:netacad.com* and follow links to "Download Packet Tracer" or "Introduction to Packet Tracer" to find the current Packet Tracer introduction course. Enter your name, email, and text verification to enroll in the course.

2. Open the confirmation email and confirm your email address. Configure your account, and save your account information in your LastPass vault. You will need this information again.

3. If desired, you can answer the NetAcad survey questions now, or wait until later. When you're ready, click on the **Introduction to Packet Tracer** tile.

Now you're ready to download and install Packet Tracer. If you need help with the download and installation process, launch the course and navigate to Chapter 1, Section 1.2, Topic 1.1.2 for additional guidance. Complete the following steps:

4. Inside the course, check the Student Resources to find the link to download Packet Tracer. Download the correct version for your computer, and then install Packet Tracer. Note that the download might not complete in the MS Edge browser; if you encounter a problem, try Google Chrome instead. When the installation is complete, run **Cisco Packet Tracer**.

5. When Packet Tracer opens, sign in with your Networking Academy account that you just created. If you see a Windows Security Alert, allow access through your firewall. Cisco Packet Tracer opens. The interface window is shown in Figure 6-39.

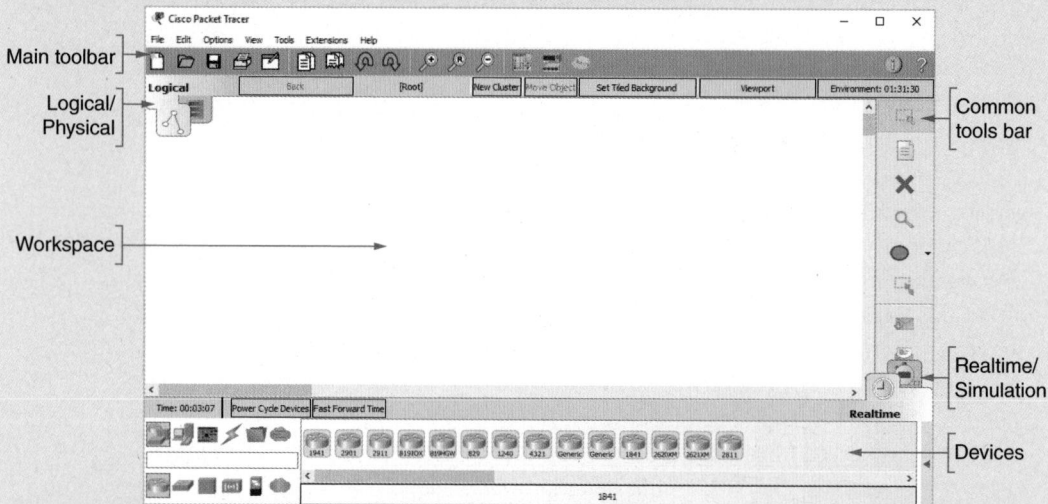

Figure 6-39   Explore the Packet Tracer window
Source: Cisco Systems, Inc.

The Introduction to Packet Tracer course presents an excellent introduction to Packet Tracer and provides lab activities. Packet Tracer Activities are interactive labs in which you download a start file, make the changes instructed in the lab, and then grade the activity in Packet Tracer. Complete the following steps to access your course:

6. Return to the Networking Academy website (**netacad.com**), sign in if necessary, click **Launch Course** on the Introduction to Packet Tracer tile, and then click **Launch Course** again. You've already downloaded Packet Tracer, so you can skip Chapter 1.

7. Complete Chapters 2, 3, and 4, including their videos and labs, and complete the Packet Tracer Basics Quiz at the end of Chapter 4. The other chapters provide excellent

information on Packet Tracer but are not required for this project. Answer the following questions along the way:

a. What is a simple PDU in Packet Tracer?

b. What is a .pka file?

c. Which window shows instructions for a lab activity?

d. What color is a console cable in Packet Tracer?

e. When configuring a switch in a Packet Tracer activity, if the Config tab and CLI tab are both locked, what device do you need to use to configure the switch?

f. Which Packet Tracer feature do you think will be most helpful for you in learning how to manage a network?

8. Record some notes in your Wikidot website about your Packet Tracer installation. Also make some notes about how to use Packet Tracer. This will make it feel more familiar the next time you use it.

Capstone Project 6-2: Check a Router's Compatibility for New Firmware

Some wireless routers are designed with many security features and require no special firmware to enable a second (or more) SSID, guest network, or captive portal. In some cases, however, you might be able to install DD-WRT on a router to add desired features. DD-WRT is open source, Linux-based firmware that can be installed on many routers or access points to expand their capabilities.

The functions available in this firmware are dependent upon the extent of its compatibility with the device on which you install it. In this activity, you check a router's information against the Router Database on the DD-WRT website to see which version of the firmware the router can support. Then you check the Database Report to see which of the firmware's features are compatible with your router. This project does *not* include installing the firmware, as the process tends to be very specific to the hardware and other variables, and requires more advanced understanding of installation challenges and troubleshooting skills.

To complete this project, you will need a SOHO router, such as Linksys, Asus, or Netgear, manufactured for any 802.11 standard through ac. Complete the following steps:

1. Examine the device itself and locate the router's model number. What is the model number?

2. Go to DD-WRT's website at **dd-wrt.com** and navigate to the **Router Database**. Enter your router's model number to search the database.

Caution ⚠

If at some point you decide to attempt downloading and installing DD-WRT, it is especially important to ensure you're obtaining the download from a reputable source, such as the one mentioned here. Many rogue versions exist that could cause a great deal of damage to your system and data.

3. Some routers require a license to use DD-WRT, in which case you'd have to purchase a license for your router. Some routers are not supported at all, while some are labeled as "works in progress," meaning support for that router is in the works but no release date is scheduled. Most routers, however, are supported. If yours is, click the correct router in the list. If your router is not supported, do a search for **Linksys WRT320N** and answer the remaining questions for this router. Which downloads did the database report for your router?

4. For some routers, multiple variations of DD-WRT are available. These variations provide different features and require different levels of expertise to administer. If you see a **Build variations** link under *Additional Information*, click it. If your router's listing does not provide this kind of information, do a search for **Linksys WRT320N** and answer the remaining questions for this router. What are some known issues reported for the router? Are there any warnings listed on the Build variations page?

5. Continue browsing through the Build Features table, which you accessed in the previous step through the DD-WRT Wiki link for Build variations. Which variations are supported by your router *and* provide each of the following features, respectively? (Hint: You'll need to cross-reference this table with the database report for your router to make sure you're only listing variations that are compatible with your router. This table might contain variations that were not listed for your router.) Provide a brief description of what functions or options each feature can provide.

   a. Access restrictions

   b. Chillispot

   c. Kaid, Xlink Kai, or some other form of Kaid

   d. OpenVPN

   e. Repeater

   f. Samba/CIFS client

   g. Wake On LAN

   h. Wiviz

Installing the DD-WRT firmware to your router is accomplished through a process called flashing, and is beyond the scope of this book. If you're using an old router that you can afford to risk bricking (which means to ruin the device to the point where it is no longer functional, effectively turning it into a brick), you might want to try it. But be sure to do your research first! The DD-WRT Wiki is chock-full of helpful articles to walk you through the process with your specific router. Once installed, even the most basic DD-WRT variation can provide helpful features such as repeater functionality (greatly expanding the reach of your Wi-Fi network) and access restrictions (increasing the control you have over who can do what on your network).

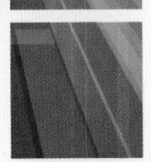

## CHAPTER 7

VIRTUALIZATION AND CLOUD COMPUTING

After reading this chapter and completing the exercises, you will be able to:

Describe and explain virtualization technologies, including how virtual machines connect with a network and how networking infrastructure devices can be virtualized

Describe cloud computing categories and models, and discuss concerns regarding cloud connectivity and security

Secure network connections using encryption protocols

Configure remote access connections between devices

On the Job

In a classroom environment, it can be difficult to provide a real-world experience for students to learn. Virtualization has provided an excellent opportunity for teachers to provide students a way to practice installing operating systems, test theories, and troubleshoot issues that may arise with these systems.

After years of using VirtualBox for our operating systems class, my colleagues and I decided that we needed to address a few drawbacks to our system. For starters, it was becoming very time-consuming to move from virtual machine to virtual machine to grade, install updates, and change passwords. Another issue had to do with the fact that the labs students complete on the virtual machines build upon each other. If a student's virtual machine became corrupted, the student would have to start all over. To prevent this, we needed an easy method to maintain an operational backup copy of each virtual machine. We decided to fix these problems by running all the virtual machines from a central location.

We purchased a Dell server, installed Server 2012 with Hyper-V, attached one NIC to the school's network, and ran all updates. We assigned the second NIC the network name *Corp2012*. Then we attached Corp2012 to a switch wired to each PC in the lab. This separation of duties ensured that the students' virtual machines did not connect to the school's network, thereby keeping the physical server secure from outside viruses that could potentially stage an attack by way of the workstations. Students are required to work in a virtual environment; but this environment must be totally isolated to ensure the security of the school network and the physical server.

Finally, using Hyper-V, we created the virtual machines and connected them to the Corp2012 network. The students could then use Remote Desktop to access their individual virtual machines.

Moving from one workstation to another for grading and other tasks is now a thing of the past. We can manage all virtual machines on the Hyper-V server using Remote Desktop from the Instructor machine. The instructor can sit at one machine and remote into each student's virtual server one at a time. Backing up each student's virtual machine is a simple matter of using VSS (Volume Shadow Copy Service) in Hyper-V. VSS can be configured to create backups of a virtual machine at regular intervals. We have it set up to create backups after each class period so if a virtual drive becomes corrupt, students can use the backup rather than having to start over. All in all, we've saved the instructors and students a lot of time and effort.

June West
Spartanburg Community College

Computer networking is really all about accessing resources while also keeping those resources safe. Networking technology is changing constantly to keep up with a fast-paced world. In the midst of all this change, network administrators are charged with making sure resources are both accessible and secure. These resources may be physical or virtual, on the local network, or somewhere else in the world.

In this chapter, we'll explore various ways of making local and remote resources available on a network in ways that are both secure and reliable. You will learn about the flexibility of virtualization, which is a cost-effective way of expanding network resources, as well as the growing fields of cloud computing and remote access, which make network resources available across long distances. These IT innovations touch nearly every industry. Let's begin this chapter with a discussion of the expansion of available resources made possible by virtualization.

Virtualization

 **Certification**

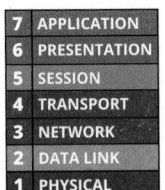

1.3   Explain the concepts and characteristics of routing and switching.

2.4   Explain the purposes of virtualization and network storage technologies.

Beginning with the first chapter in this text, you've created and worked with a variety of virtual machines, or VMs, in several of the Capstone Projects. On a Windows computer, you used Hyper-V or VirtualBox to create workstation and server VMs, and you installed both Windows and Linux operating systems on those VMs. By this point, you've had the opportunity to become familiar with the process and some of the terms involved in working with virtualization technology. Now let's take a closer look at exactly what you've been accomplishing in these projects.

Virtualization is a virtual, or logical, version of something rather than the actual, or physical, version. For example, when you create an Ubuntu server VM on a Windows PC, the Windows machine is the physical computer, or **host**, and the Ubuntu machine is a logical computer, or **guest**, that is hosted by the physical computer. The Ubuntu operating system acts as if it is installed on a separate, physical machine. How is this possible?

The key is a type of software known as a hypervisor. A **hypervisor** creates and manages a VM, and manages resource allocation and sharing between a host and any of its guest VMs. Together, all the virtual devices on a single computer share the same CPU, hard disks, memory, and physical network interfaces. Yet each VM can be configured to use a different operating system, and can emulate a different type of CPU, storage drive, or NIC, than the physical computer it resides on. Meanwhile, to users, a VM appears and acts no differently from a physical computer running the same software. Figure 7-1 illustrates some of the elements of virtualization.

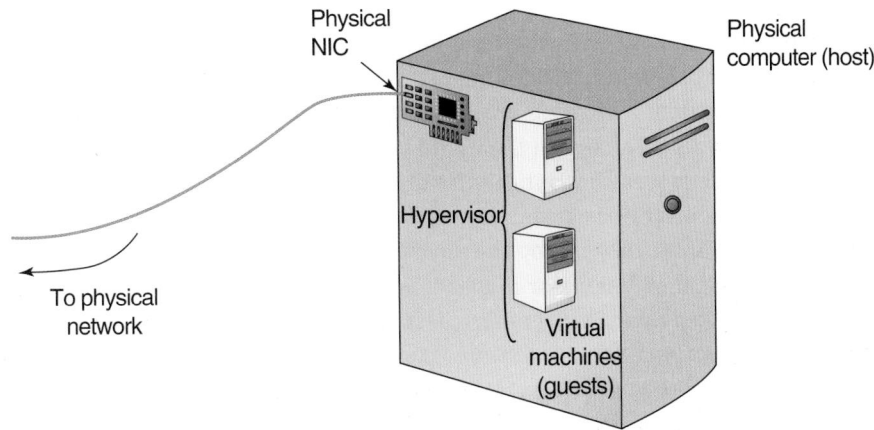

Figure 7-1   Elements of virtualization

There are two types of hypervisors: Type 1 and Type 2. The differences are diagrammed in Figure 7-2 and explained next.

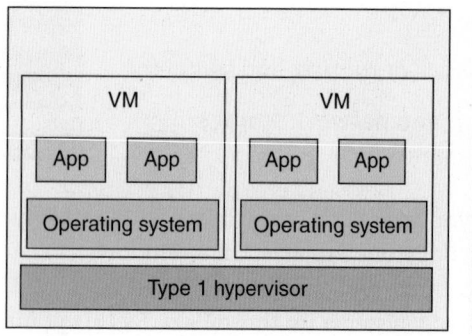 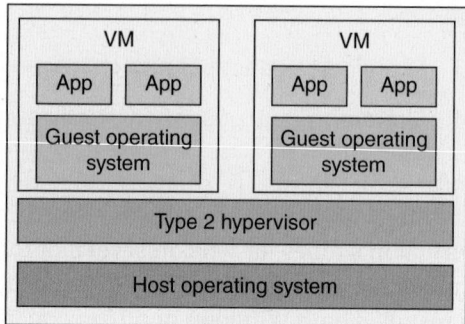

Figure 7-2   Type 1 and Type 2 hypervisors

- *Type 1 hypervisor*—Installs on a computer before any OS and is therefore called a bare-metal hypervisor. It partitions the hardware computing power to multiple VMs, each with their own OS. Popular examples include XenServer by Citrix, ESXi by VMware, and Hyper-V by Microsoft.
- *Type 2 hypervisor*—Installs in a host OS as an application and is called a hosted hypervisor. Client Hyper-V and VirtualBox, which you've seen in the Capstone Projects, are examples of Type 2 hypervisors, as are the popular VMware Player and Linux KVM. A Type 2 hypervisor is not as powerful as a Type 1 hypervisor because it is dependent on the host OS to allot its computing power. VMs hosted by a Type 2 hypervisor also are not as secure or as fast as a Type 1 hypervisor's VMs.

A VM's software and hardware characteristics are assigned when it is created in the hypervisor. As you have learned, these characteristics can differ completely from those of the host machine. Keep in mind that a VM is entirely a logical entity—it's not confined to the features of the local hardware in the same way that a physical machine is. You can customize the VM with a guest operating system, amount of memory, hard disk size, and processor type, to name just a few options. Figure 7-3 shows a screen from the VMware VM creation wizard that allows you to specify the amount of memory allocated to a VM. Notice in the figure you could click on other devices in the hardware list, such as processors, optical disc drives, and the network adapter, to make changes to those specifications as well.

While there are limits imposed by the physical hardware, such as total available RAM or storage space, the hypervisor makes it possible for a VM guest to function differently than the host machine or other guest machines. As you learn more about virtualization, train yourself to notice how logical functions operate on a different layer, or plane, than what might be implied by the physical hardware.

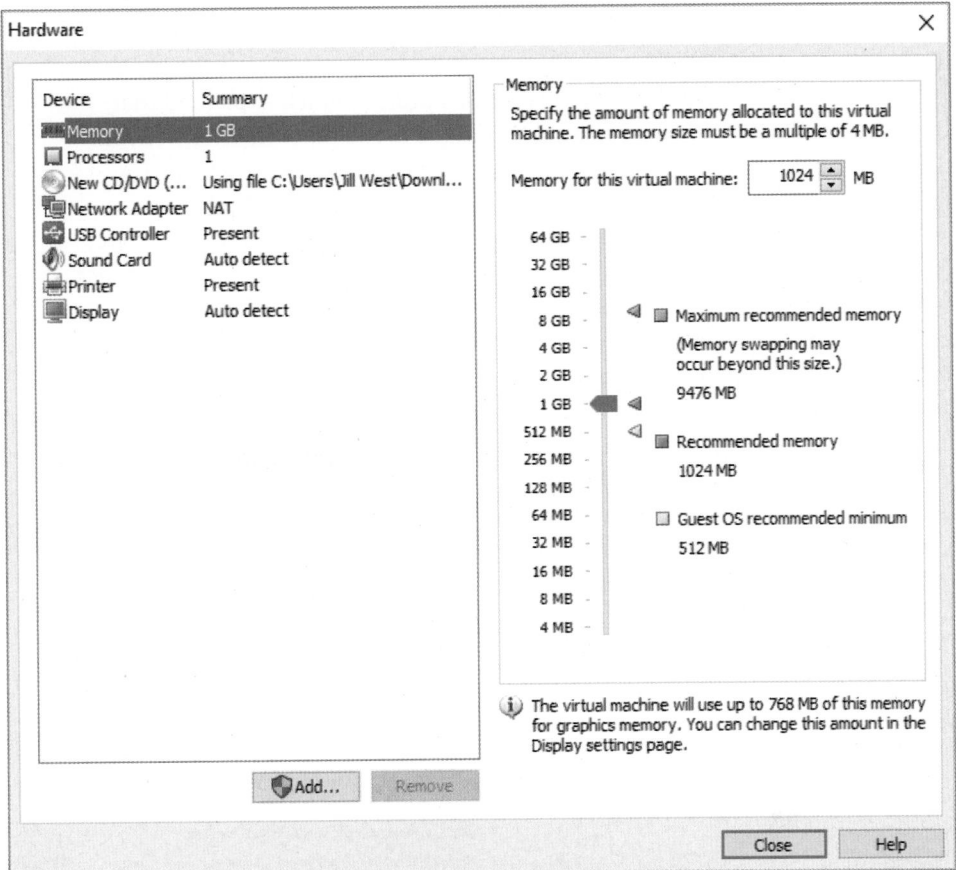

Figure 7-3   Specifying a VM's memory in VMware

Source: VMware, Inc.

Think about the foundation of a house—in many cases, a foundation is made of cement blocks, it usually reaches deep into the ground, and it defines the outline of the house to be built above it. Looking only at the foundation, however, would not necessarily indicate how many floors the house will have, what colors the walls will be, or what materials will be used on the inside or the outside. On a single foundation, you might even build two townhouses or four apartments. Similarly, the physical hardware of a computer defines some outer limits of capabilities, such as how much RAM is available to all running VMs or how much storage space is available for all VM-associated data. However, within those limits, you can create many virtual machines with a variety of characteristics. These VMs are managed by the hypervisor without being directly defined by the hardware supporting it all.

Network Connection Types

In Chapter 5's Capstone Project 5-1, you set up an FTP server in an Ubuntu Server VM. You might remember the troubleshooting tips for this project which explained that, if you were using VirtualBox, you had to enable Bridged mode on each VM's network adapter. Let's talk about what that means.

Every VM has its own virtual network adapter, or **vNIC (virtual NIC)**, that can connect the VM to other machines, both virtual and physical. Just like a physical NIC, a vNIC operates at the Data Link layer and provides the computer with network access. Each VM can have several vNICs, no matter how many NICs the host machine has. The maximum number of vNICs on a VM depends on the limits imposed by the hypervisor. For example, VirtualBox allows up to eight vNICs per VM. Upon creation, each vNIC is automatically assigned a MAC address.

Figure 7-4 shows a dialog box from the VMware wizard that allows you to customize properties of a virtual workstation's vNIC. One of many options you can configure for each vNIC is its inbound and outbound transmission speeds. For example, you could select transmission speeds that simulate a T1 or cable broadband connection, which you'll learn more about later.

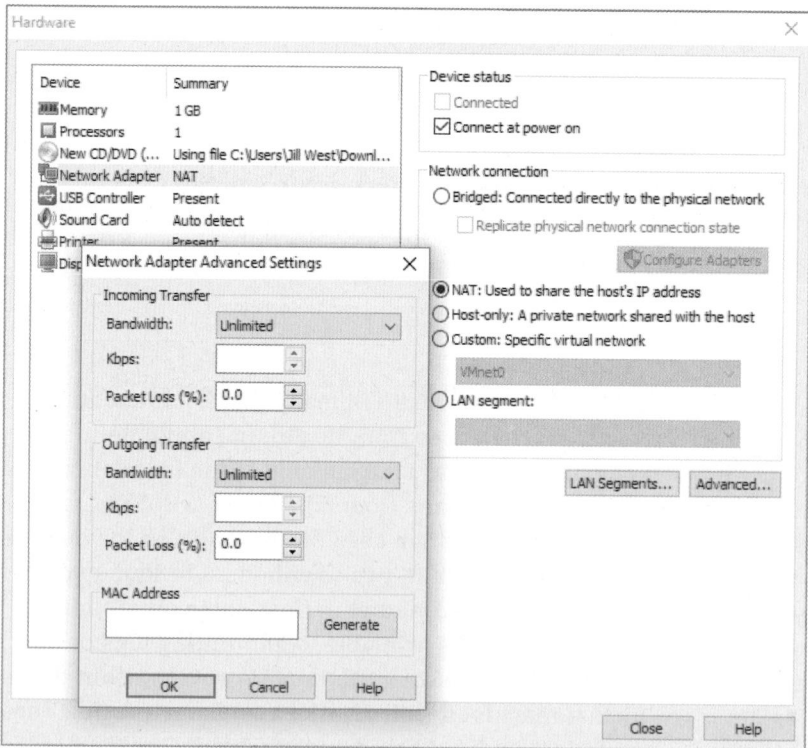

Figure 7-4   Customizing vNIC properties in VMware

Source: VMware, Inc.

As soon as the virtual machine's vNIC is selected, the hypervisor creates a connection between that VM and the host. Depending on the hypervisor, this connection might be called a bridge or a switch. This **vSwitch (virtual switch)** or bridge is a logically defined device that operates at the Data Link layer to pass frames between nodes. Thus, it can allow VMs to communicate with each other and with nodes on a physical LAN or WAN.

One host can support multiple virtual switches, which are controlled by the hypervisor. Figure 7-5 illustrates a host machine with two physical NICs that supports several virtual machines and their vNICs. A virtual switch connects the vNICs to the network.

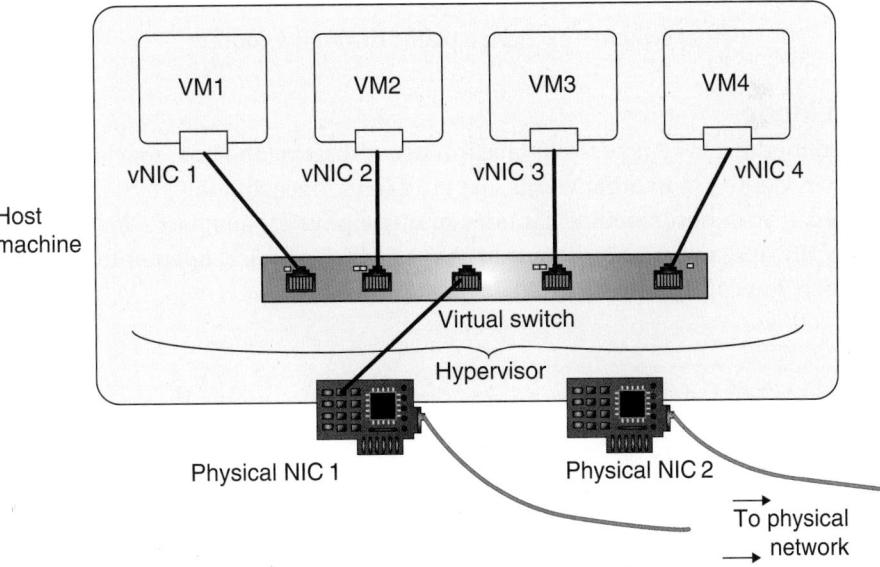

Figure 7-5   Virtual servers on a single host connect with a virtual switch

VMs can go through a virtual switch on the host computer to reach the physical network and can communicate with physical or virtual routers, other network devices, and other hosts on the local or another network. For example, in Figure 7-6 a VM on Host A can communicate with a VM on Host B.

The way a vNIC is configured determines whether the VM is joined to a virtual network or attempts to join the physical LAN that the host machine is connected to. These various configurations are called networking modes, the most common of which are bridged, NAT, and host-only, as described next. These descriptions are specific to the Type 2 hypervisors you've been using in your projects. However, Type 1 hypervisors offer these and other network configurations as well.

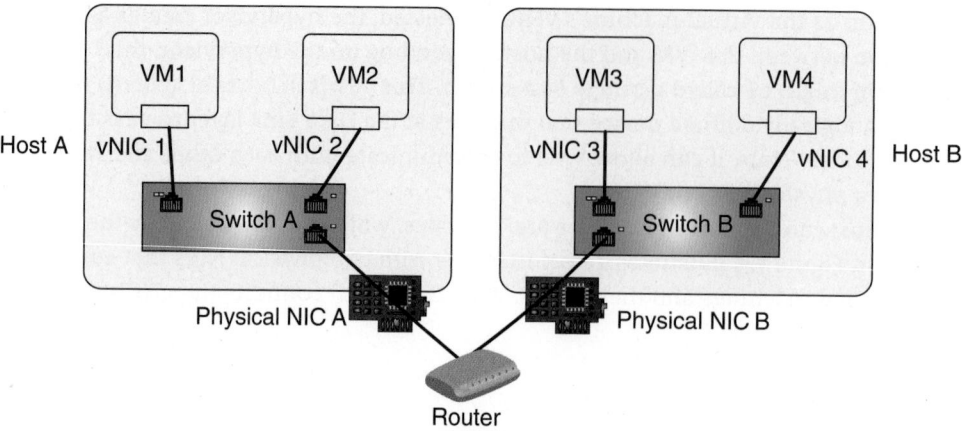

Figure 7-6 Virtual switches exchange traffic through a router

Bridged Mode

In **bridged mode**, a vNIC accesses a physical network using the host machine's NIC, as shown in Figure 7-7. In other words, the virtual interface and the physical interface are bridged. If your host machine contains multiple physical adapters—for example, a wireless NIC and a wired NIC—you can choose which physical adapter to use as the bridge when you configure the virtual adapter.

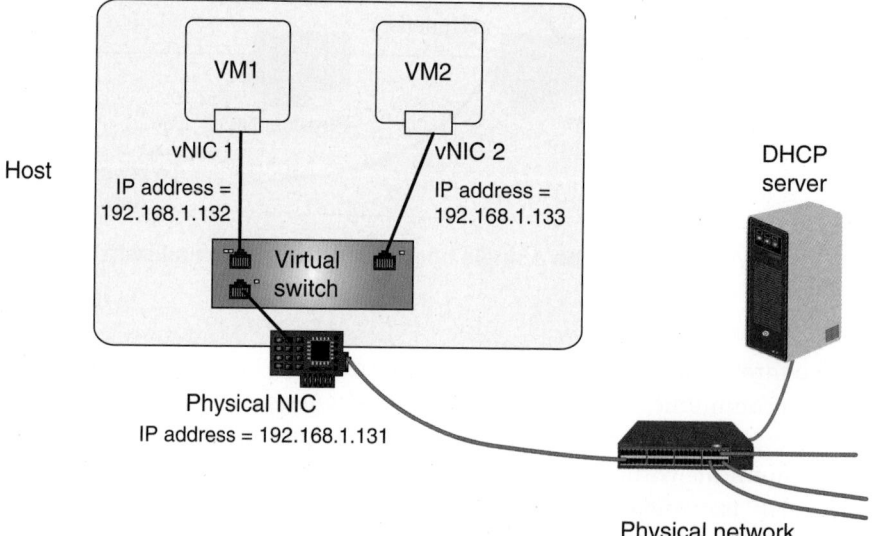

Figure 7-7 This vNIC accesses the physical network directly in bridged mode

Although a bridged vNIC communicates through the host's adapter, it obtains its own IP address, default gateway, and subnet mask from a DHCP server on the physical LAN. For example, suppose your DHCP server is configured to assign addresses in the range of 192.168.1.120 through 192.168.1.254 to nodes on your LAN. The router might assign your host machine's physical NIC an IP address of 192.168.1.131. A guest on your host might obtain an IP address of 192.168.1.132. A second guest on that host might obtain an IP address of 192.168.1.133, and so on.

When connected using bridged mode, a VM appears to other nodes as just another client or server on the network. Other nodes communicate directly with the computer without realizing it is virtual.

Note 📎

In VMware and VirtualBox, you can choose the bridged connection type when you create or configure the virtual adapter. In KVM, you create a bridge between the VM and your physical NIC when you modify the vNIC's settings. In Hyper-V, you create a bridged connection type by assigning VMs to an external network switch. Additionally, bridged mode is the most common networking mode for VMs hosted by Type 1 hypervisors such as XenServer. Figure 7-8 shows the Hardware dialog box that appears while creating a virtual machine in VMware with the Bridged network connection type selected.

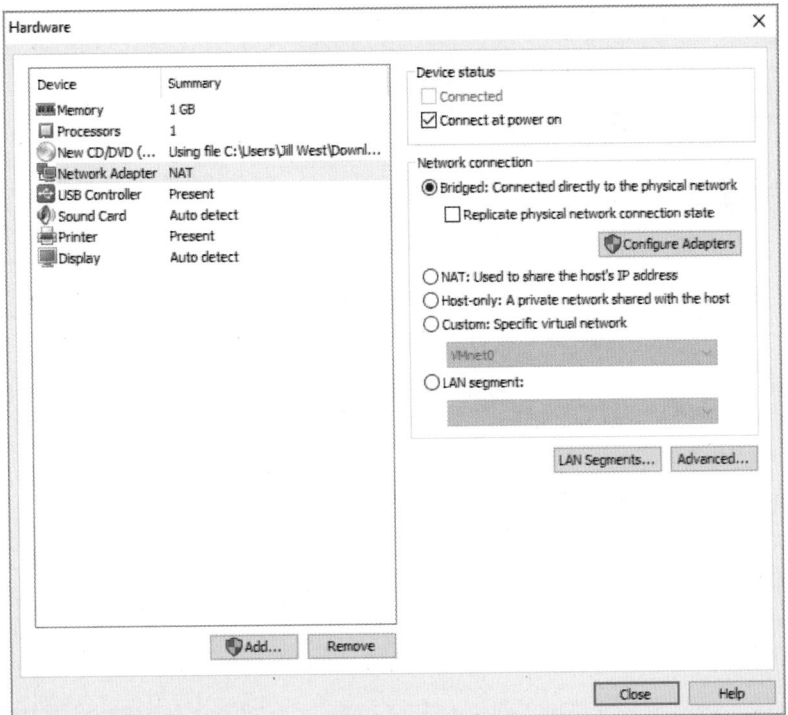

Figure 7-8 Selecting the Bridged option for a vNIC in VMware

Source: VMware, Inc.

VMs that must be available at a specific IP address, such as mail servers or web servers, should be assigned bridged network connections. However, VMs that other nodes do not need to access directly can be configured to use the NAT networking mode.

NAT Mode

In **NAT mode**, a vNIC relies on the host machine to act as a NAT device. In other words, the VM obtains IP addressing information from its host, rather than a server or router on the physical network. To accomplish this, the hypervisor acts as a DHCP server. A vNIC operating in NAT mode can still communicate with other nodes on the network and vice versa. However, other nodes communicate with the host machine's IP address to reach the VM; the VM itself is invisible to nodes on the physical network. Figure 7-9 illustrates a VM operating in NAT mode.

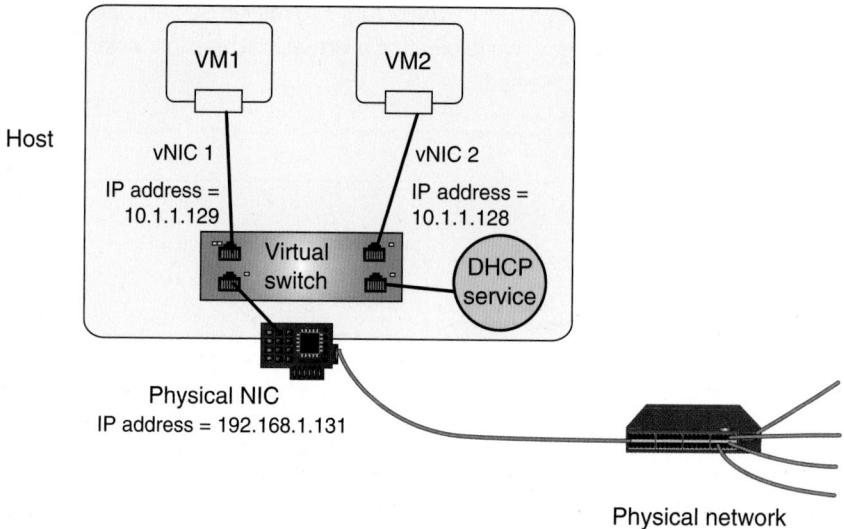

Figure 7-9   The vNIC accesses the physical network via NAT in NAT mode

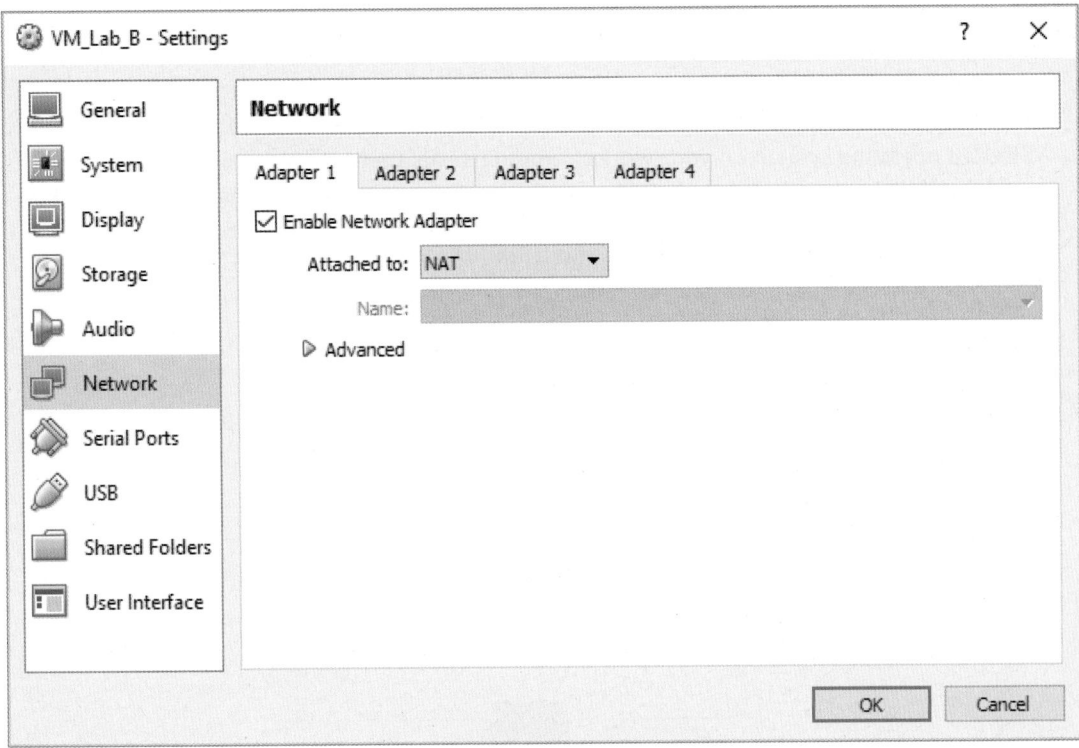

Figure 7-10   Selecting the NAT option for a vNIC in VirtualBox
Source: VMware, Inc.

Once you have selected the NAT configuration type, you can configure the pool of IP addresses available to the VMs on a host. For example, suppose, as shown in Figure 7-9, your host machine has an IP address of 192.168.1.131. You might configure your host's DHCP service to assign IP addresses in the range of 10.1.1.120 through 10.1.1.254 to the VMs you create on that host. Because these addresses will never be evident beyond the host, you have flexibility in choosing their IP address range.

The NAT network connection type is appropriate for VMs that do not need to be accessed at a known address by other network nodes. For example, virtual workstations that are mainly used to run stand-alone applications, or serve as test beds to test applications or operating system installations, are good candidates for NAT network connections.

Host-Only Mode

In **host-only mode**, VMs on one host can exchange data with each other and with their host, but they cannot communicate with any nodes beyond the host. In other words, the vNICs never receive or transmit data via the host machine's physical NIC. In host-only mode, as in NAT mode, VMs use the DHCP service in the host's virtualization software to obtain IP address assignments.

Figure 7-11 illustrates how the host-only option creates an isolated virtual network. Host-only mode is appropriate for test networks or if you simply need to install a different operating system on your workstation to use an application that is incompatible with your host's operating system. For example, suppose a project requires you to create diagrams in Microsoft Visio and your workstation runs Red Hat Linux. You could install a Windows 10 VM solely for the purpose of installing and running Visio.

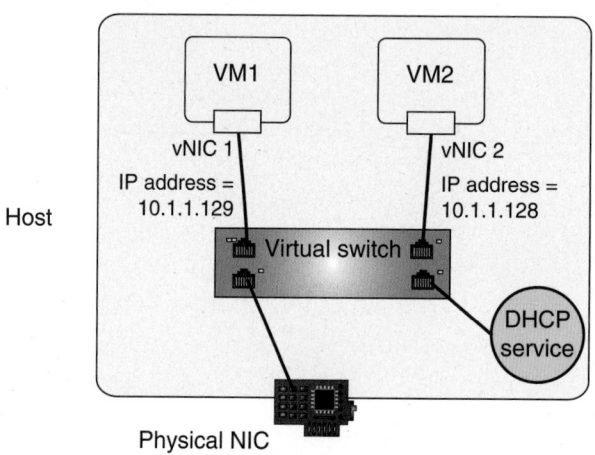

Figure 7-11 vNICs in a host-only network can only talk to other VMs running on that host

Obviously, because host-only mode prevents VMs from exchanging data with a physical network, this configuration cannot work for virtual servers that need to be accessed by clients across a LAN. Nor can it be used for virtual workstations that need to access LAN or WAN services, such as email or web pages. Host-only networking is less commonly used than NAT or bridged mode networking.

Note 📎

You can choose host-only networking when you create or configure a VM in VMware or VirtualBox. In Hyper-V, the host-only connection type is created by assigning VMs to a private virtual network. In KVM, host-only is not a predefined option, but can be assigned to a vNIC via the command-line interface.

Virtualization software gives you the flexibility of creating several different networking types on one host machine. For example, on one host you could create a host-only network to test multiple versions of Linux. On the same host, you could create a group of Windows Server 2016 machines that are connected to your physical LAN using the bridged connection type. Or, rather than specifying one of the four networking connection types described previously, you could also create a VM that contains a vNIC but is not connected to any nodes, whether virtual or physical. Preventing the VM from communicating with other nodes keeps it completely isolated. This might be desirable when testing unpredictable software or an image of untrusted origin.

Pros and Cons of Virtualization

Virtualization offers several advantages, including the following:

- *efficient use of resources*—Physical clients or servers devoted to one function typically use only a fraction of their capacity. Without virtualization, a company might purchase five computers to run five different services—for example, an email server, a file server, two web servers, and a database server. Each service might demand no more than 10–20 percent of its computer's processing power and memory. With virtualization, however, a single, powerful computer can support all five services. This creates a significant single point of failure, however, if this one server goes down for any reason. Therefore, in actual practice, most of these network services are also duplicated across multiple physical servers.

- *cost and energy savings*—Organizations save money by purchasing fewer and less expensive physical machines. They also save electricity because there are fewer and more efficient computers drawing power and less demand for air conditioning in the computer room. Some institutions with thousands of users, such as Stanford University, are using virtualization as a way to conserve energy and are promoting it as part of campus-wide sustainability efforts. Thin clients, for example, are very small, energy-efficient computers that can be used to populate large computer labs on a college campus. Thin clients connect to a central server to perform most of their processing functions. When a user signs in to a domain account on the thin client, the thin client then contacts the server for all other functions. The server hosts the thin client's software, including the operating system and most or all applications. In other words, the thin client's entire desktop is virtualized and hosted by the server.

- *fault and threat isolation*—In a virtual environment, the isolation of each guest system means that a problem with one guest does not affect the others. For example, an instructor might create multiple instances of an operating system and applications on a single computer that's shared by several classes. This allows each student to work on his own instance of the OS environment. Any configuration errors or changes he makes on his guest machine will not affect other students. In another example, a network administrator who wants to try a beta version of an application might install that application on a guest machine rather than the host, in case the untested software causes problems. Furthermore, because a VM is granted limited access to hardware resources, security attacks on a guest pose less risk to a host or the physical network to which it's connected.

- *simple backups, recovery, and replication*—Virtualization software enables network administrators to save backup images of a guest machine. The images can later be used to recreate that machine on another host or on the same host. This feature allows for simple backups and quick recovery, such as for the classroom scenario you read about in this chapter's *On the Job story*. It also makes it easy to create multiple, identical copies of one VM, called clones. Some virtualization programs allow you to save image files of VMs that can be imported into a competitor's virtualization program.

Not every type of client or server is a good candidate for virtualization, however. Potential disadvantages to creating multiple guests on a single host machine include the following:

- *compromised performance*—When multiple VMs contend for finite physical resources, one VM could monopolize those resources and impair the performance of others on the same computer. In theory, careful management and resource allocation should prevent this. In practice, however, it is unwise to force a critical application—for example, a factory's real-time control systems or a hospital's emergency medical systems—to share resources and take that risk. Imagine a brewery that uses computers to measure and control tank levels, pressure, flow, and temperature of liquid ingredients during processing. These functions are vital for product quality and safety. In this example, where specialty software demands real-time, error-free performance, it makes sense to devote all of a computer's resources to this set of functions, rather than share that computer with the brewery's human resources database server, for example. In addition to multiple guest systems vying for limited physical resources, a hypervisor also requires some overhead.

- *increased complexity*—Although virtualization reduces the number of physical machines to manage, it increases complexity and administrative burden in other ways. For instance, a network administrator who uses virtual servers and switches must thoroughly understand virtualization software. In addition, managing addressing and switching for multiple VMs is more complex than doing so for physical machines. (You will learn more about these techniques later in this chapter.) Finally, because VMs are so easy to set up, they might be created capriciously or as part of experimentation, and then forgotten. As a result, extra VMs might litter a server's hard disk, consume resources, and unnecessarily complicate network management. By contrast, abandoned physical servers might only take up rack space.

- *increased licensing costs*—Because every instance of commercial software requires its own license, every VM that uses such software comes with added cost. In some cases, the added cost brings little return. For example, a software developer might want to create four instances of Windows Server on a single computer to test new software using four testing procedures on four different OS installation configurations. To comply with Microsoft's licensing restrictions, the developer will have to purchase four licenses for Windows Server. Depending on the developer's intentions, it might make more sense, instead, to share one installation of Windows Server and separate the four testing procedures by using four different logon IDs. Alternatively, the developer could save the initial VM image and start over fresh for each test.
- *single point of failure*—If a host machine fails, all its guest machines will fail, too. As mentioned earlier, an organization that creates VMs for its email server, file server, web servers, and database server on a single physical computer would lose all those services if the computer went down. Wise network administrators implement measures such as clustering and automatic failover to prevent that from happening.

Most of the potential disadvantages in this list can be mitigated through thoughtful design and virtualization control. Similarly, the same advantages and disadvantages of client virtualization apply to virtualizing other network devices. Next, let's look at what can be accomplished when virtualization technology is used elsewhere on the network.

NFV (Network Functions Virtualization)

We've seen how a single workstation can host many VM workstations or servers, each with its own network connection, operating system, and applications. Networking devices can also be virtualized. For example, instead of purchasing an expensive hardware firewall to protect a LAN, suppose you were to install a firewall's operating system in a VM on an inexpensive server. Suppose you also install a router VM on that server instead of purchasing an expensive hardware router. You've now provided your network with two sophisticated, virtualized devices—a **virtual firewall** and a **virtual router**—on one, inexpensive server instead of paying for two, expensive, dedicated devices.

Note

To clarify, a software firewall is merely an application, like Windows Firewall. It's very limited in scope and features, and only services a single client. A dedicated firewall device, such as those made by Fortinet, Cisco, or Palo Alto Networks, services an entire network (or portion of a network). It has many more features than a firewall app, and runs on its own OS.

A virtual firewall emulates a hardware firewall, and is hosted in a virtualized environment. An example would be the pfSense VMware Ready Virtual Firewall Appliance by Netgate. Another example is Barracuda's NextGen Firewall F-Series, which is compatible with VMware, XenServer, KVM, and Hyper-V and also provides protection for cloud-based portions of the network. There must be a hypervisor present (usually Type 1) for a virtual firewall to exist.

These distinctions apply to other devices as well, such as routers, switches, and load balancers.

Now replicate these savings over dozens of devices for a large network, and you can begin to see some of the advantage of virtualizing network functions. Other advantages include the following:

- Virtual devices can be quickly and sometimes automatically migrated, or moved, from one server to another in the event of a hardware failure or maintenance.
- Resources, such as hardware, energy usage, and physical space, are utilized more efficiently.
- Services can be easily scaled to meet the changing needs of a network.

Merging physical and virtual network architecture is called **NFV (Network Functions Virtualization)**. NFV provides flexible, cost-saving options for many types of network devices, including virtual servers, data storage, load balancers, and firewalls. However, there are a few caveats and considerations to keep in mind:

- You'll need licenses for each of the virtualized devices as well as for the Type 1 hypervisor that will host them. Fortunately, the cost of these licenses amounts to a fraction of the cost of similarly featured hardware devices.
- The interaction between physical and virtual devices introduces a small degree of latency as data passes through the hypervisor and its connections. Usually, this delay is negligible. However, it might be a relevant consideration in some cases.
- Even some of the most die-hard virtualization fans are uncomfortable using a virtual firewall to protect the entire network. The server hosting a virtual firewall occasionally needs to be restarted in the course of regular maintenance or some kind of failure, and in that event, the hosted firewall goes down with the server. Instead, many network admins believe that virtual firewalls are only appropriate for securing virtual-only portions of the network, or serving as a backup to physical firewall devices.

SDN (Software-Defined Networking)

As network infrastructures become more complex, configuring all these networking devices—both virtual and physical—to create and manage the network infrastructure presents a growing challenge. **SDN (software-defined networking)** is a centralized approach to networking that removes most of the decision-making power from network devices and instead handles that responsibility at a software level with a product called an SDN controller, or network controller. The **SDN controller** integrates configuration and management control of all network devices, both physical and virtual, into one cohesive system that is overseen by the network administrator through a single dashboard. Instead of reconfiguring each network device individually, the SDN controller can be used to reconfigure groups of network devices all at one time. It can even make configuration changes automatically in response to changing network conditions. Let's look at a couple of figures to explore the concepts at work here.

On the left side of Figure 7-12, you see a traditionally configured network infrastructure. Each physical and virtual device, whether it's a router, switch, firewall, or load balancer, makes its own decisions about where transmissions should be sent based upon the protocols and other configurations on that device. That decision-making process is called the **control plane**. The outcome of those decisions—actual transmissions on the network—is called the **data plane**. Traditionally, each device handles its own control plane and data plane.

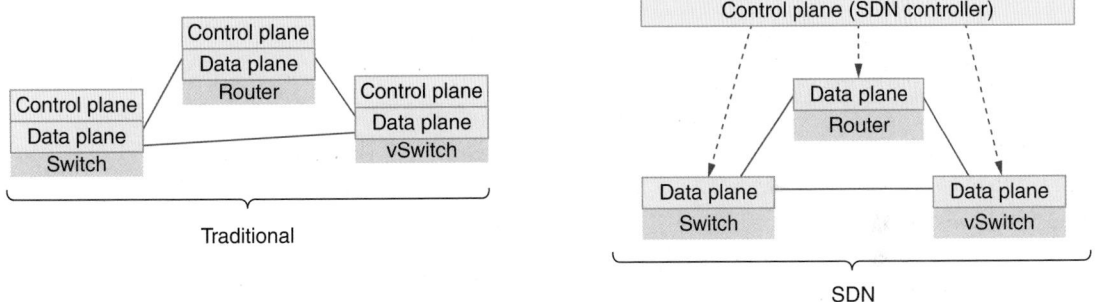

Figure 7-12 Individual control planes in a traditional network versus a centralized control plane in an SDN network

On the right side of Figure 7-12, you see an implementation of SDN. Instead of each device making its own decisions, the SDN controller manages these decisions for the devices and then tells the devices what to do with data traversing the network. What's more, the SDN controller can be programmed to change the rules for those decisions in order to adapt to changing network conditions.

For example, if a streaming video call needs additional bandwidth, the SDN controller can temporarily assign a higher priority to that traffic across the network, and then cancel that configuration when the call is finished. At no point in this process does a network administrator have to access any networking device's management console to make any changes to the device's configuration. The SDN controller handles all the changes at a more abstracted level, and informs the affected networking devices of what to do with the relevant data on the physical level.

The network devices essentially become "dumb" devices, without needing any particular knowledge of overarching network needs or protocols. This hardware is significantly less expensive than their more sophisticated counterparts and in the marketplace, they're often called white box switches. In essence, networking devices in an SDN-controlled environment function only at Layer 1 in the OSI model, while the SDN controller can manage functionality at all the other OSI layers. Figure 7-13 illustrates the relationship between the physical devices that send and receive transmissions over the network, the SDN controller that coordinates these transmissions, and the applications continuing to function at the top of the stack.

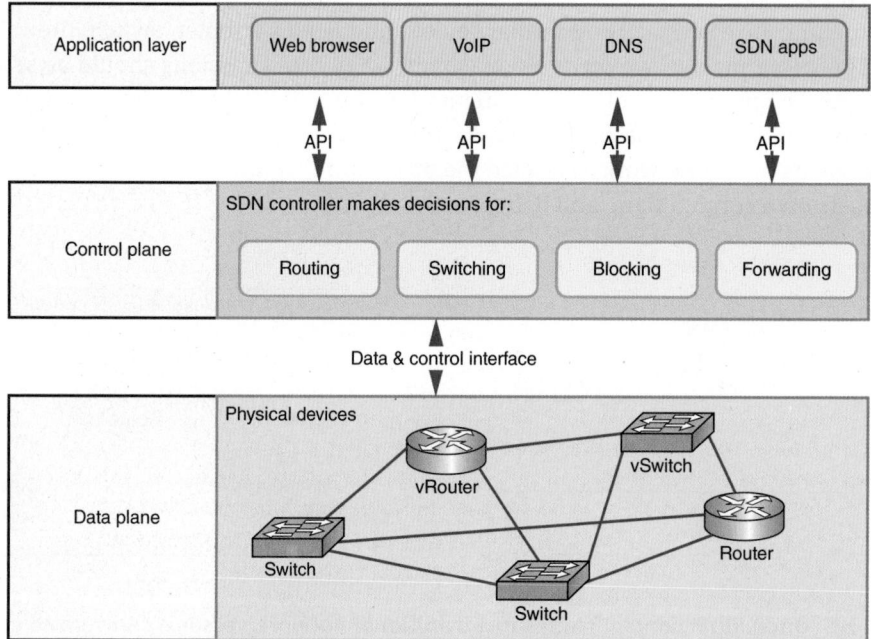

Figure 7-13 Physical and virtual network devices operate only on Layer 1's data plane, while the SDN controller takes over decision-making functions at Layers 2 and up

As you can see, one of the primary advantages to separating the control plane from the data plane is to provide network technicians with more centralized control of network settings and management—physical and virtual devices can all be managed from a central interface. SDN also creates the potential to implement more sophisticated network functions while using less-expensive devices. Several vendors offer SDN controller software, including VMware, Cisco, HP, IBM, and Juniper. Open-source SDN controllers include OpenDaylight, Beacon, and OpenShift.

In recent years, SDN architecture has been expanding to include management of network resources that are hosted in places other than an organization's own network.

All these resources can be centrally managed by a network's administrator through the framework of SDN software. In the next section, you learn how network resources can be leased from third-party providers and accessed over the Internet. Virtualization technologies lay the groundwork for a burgeoning IT industry: cloud computing.

Cloud Computing

 **Certification**

7	APPLICATION
6	PRESENTATION
5	SESSION
4	TRANSPORT
3	NETWORK
2	DATA LINK
1	PHYSICAL

1.7   Summarize cloud concepts and their purposes.

On network diagrams, the Internet is frequently drawn as a cloud, where you can access information stored on web servers around the world. The image captured something essential about modern networking, and now **cloud computing** refers to the flexible provision of data storage, applications, or services to clients over the Internet. You might already be familiar with cloud storage services such as Dropbox, OneDrive, and Google Drive, which let you store your own data on web-based servers. Web-based email is another example of cloud computing. Most cloud service providers use virtualization software to supply multiple platforms to multiple users. For example, industry leaders Rackspace (in its Private, Public, or Hybrid Cloud products) and Amazon (in its Elastic Compute Cloud, or EC2, service) use Xen virtualization software by Citrix to create virtual environments for their customers.

Cloud computing covers a broad range of services from hosting websites and database servers to providing virtual servers for collaboration or software development. All these services have the following features in common:

- *on-demand*—Services, applications, and storage in a cloud are available to users at any time, upon the user's request.
- *cross-platform*—Clients of all types, including smartphones, laptops, desktops, thin clients, and tablet computers, can access services, applications, and storage in a cloud, no matter what operating system they run or where they are located, as long as they have a network connection.
- *consolidated*—Host computers in the cloud provide multiple virtual machines, resources such as disk space, applications, and services that are pooled, or consolidated. For example, a single cloud computing provider can host hundreds of websites for hundreds of different customers on just a few servers. This is called a multi-tenant service model.
- *metered*—Everything offered by a cloud computing provider, including applications, desktops, storage, and other services, is measured. A provider might limit or charge by the amount of bandwidth, processing power, storage space, or client connections available to customers.

- *elastic*—Services and storage capacity can be quickly and dynamically—sometimes even automatically—scaled up or down. In other words, they are elastic. The elasticity of cloud computing means that storage space can be increased or reduced, and that applications and clients can be added or removed, as needed. For example, if your database server in the cloud is running out of hard disk space, you can upgrade your subscription to expand it yourself, without your having to alert the service provider. The amount of space you can add and the flexibility with which it can be added depend on your agreement with the service provider.

Let's consider a scenario where cloud computing enables a company to partner with people who are scattered across the globe. Suppose an organization that develops graphic design software employs dozens of creative and highly skilled developers on a project, and these developers, half of them working from home, are located in six different countries. How can these employees, located so far away from the central office and from each other, collaborate successfully?

The company contracts with a cloud services organization to host its servers, making the company's test platform easily accessible to any of its employees via the Internet. The company's developers can load any kind of software on the servers, test it from afar, and share this content with distant members of the team. If additional hard disk space is needed, that resource can be dynamically allocated. This means the disk space reserved for the software can be increased automatically as the need arises, and then later when it's no longer needed, that space can be freed up again for other developers. In addition, the cloud services provider makes sure the servers are secure and regularly backed up. Cloud computing removes from the company's IT personnel the burden of managing the servers so they can focus on other priorities. Figure 7-14 illustrates some of the benefits of cloud computing for this organization.

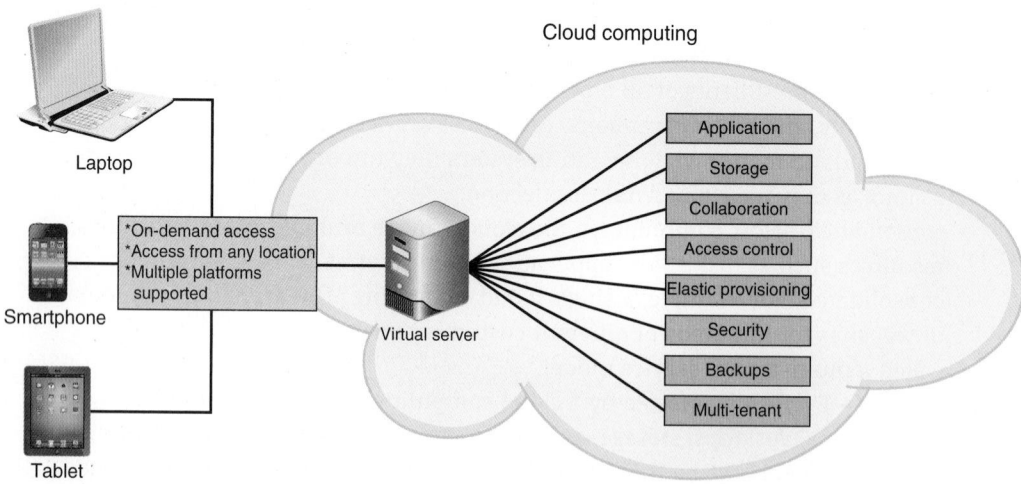

Figure 7-14 Characteristics of cloud computing

Cloud Computing Categories

Cloud computing service models are categorized by the types of services they provide. NIST (National Institute of Standards and Technology) has developed a standard definition for each category, which varies by the division of labor implemented. For example, as shown in Figure 7-15, an organization is traditionally responsible for their entire network, top to bottom. In this traditional arrangement, the organization maintains its own network infrastructure devices, manages its own network services and data storage, and purchases licenses for its own applications. Three of the many types of cloud computing service models are illustrated in Figure 7-15. These common types incrementally increase the amount of management responsibilities outsourced to cloud computing vendors.

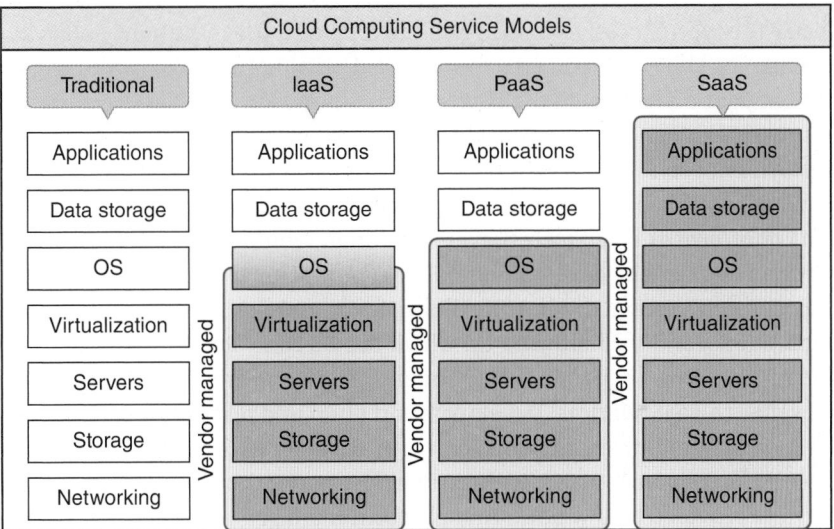

Figure 7-15 At each progressive level of these cloud computing service models, the vendor takes over more computing responsibility for the organization

To understand the various service models, it's helpful to compare them to the many ways to acquire a pizza for dinner. On the traditional end of the scale, you can make the pizza yourself. On the other end of the scale, you can have someone else make it and serve it to you. Let's check out each service model in Figure 7-15, and explore their differences using a pizza analogy:

- *traditional*—All the hardware, software, and everything else is located and managed at your location. This would be like making your own pizza from scratch at home. You provide all the ingredients, bake it in your own oven, and eat it at your own table. For example, you install Microsoft Office on your laptop and keep all your documents on your hard drive. You can work with Office and your documents without being connected to the Internet.

- *IaaS (Infrastructure as a Service)*—Hardware services are provided virtually, including network infrastructure devices such as virtual servers and end user interfaces such as **HVDs (hosted virtual desktops)**. HVDs are desktop operating environments running on a different physical computer than the one the user interacts with. These devices rely on the network infrastructure at the vendor's site, but customers are responsible for their own application installations, data management and backup, and possibly operating systems. For example, customers might use the vendor's servers to store data, host websites, and provide email, DNS, or DHCP services, but could provide their own NOS licenses and productivity software, such as customer tracking, sales management, and an office suite.

    In our pizza analogy, this would be like a take-and-bake restaurant. You decide the type of crust you want and the toppings; the restaurant puts it all together for you. Then you take the unbaked pizza home, bake it yourself, and eat it at your own table. In the IT world, AWS (Amazon Web Services) is a good example of an IaaS. Amazon provides the processing power, storage space, and deployment services. You create VMs and choose OSes to install on them. You load applications, databases, etc., and run Internet and other network services on them.

- *PaaS (Platform as a Service)*—Developers often require access to multiple platforms during the development process. A **platform** in this context includes the operating system, the runtime libraries or modules the OS provides to applications, and the hardware on which the OS runs. Rather than purchasing and maintaining a separate device for each platform, another option is to subscribe to PaaS services. Developers can build and test their applications within these virtual, online environments, which are tailored to the specific needs of the project. Alternatively, an organization's entire network might be built on platform services provided by a vendor. Any platform managed by a vendor resides on the vendor's hardware and relies on their uptime and accessibility to meet performance parameters. However, the customers are responsible for their own applications and/or data storage, including maintaining backups of the data.

    In our pizza analogy, this is the delivery option. You decide on the crust and toppings, the restaurant bakes it for you, and then they bring it to your front door within 30 minutes. You provide your own table and do the cleanup after dinner. Google Cloud Platform (*cloud.google.com*) is a good example of PaaS. They offer pre-built VMs where you can immediately start installing and testing software.

- *SaaS (Software as a Service)*—Applications are provided through an online user interface and are compatible with a variety of devices and operating systems. Online email services such as Gmail and Yahoo! are good examples of SaaS, as are CRM (customer relationship management) apps, such as Salesforce and Zoho. Google offers an entire suite of virtual software applications through Google Drive and their other embedded products. Except for the interface itself (the device and whatever browser software is required to access the website), the vendor provides every level of support from network infrastructure through data storage and application implementation.

Here we see the full capability of pizza provider services. The restaurant provides the crust and all the ingredients, bakes it for us, and serves it directly to the table that they also have provided. We had to get ourselves to the restaurant, but we didn't need to bring anything to make it all work (except our payment, of course), and they do the cleanup after we leave. This is similar to applications you run online, like email, office productivity apps, or CRM software.

- *XaaS (Anything as a Service or Everything as a Service)*—In this broader model, the "X" represents an unknown, just as it does in algebra. (And you thought you would never again use algebra.) Here, the cloud can provide any combination of functions depending on a client's exact needs. This includes, for example, monitoring, storage, applications, and virtual desktops.

Note 📎

Another SaaS implementation that doesn't quite fit the official definition of SaaS is rentable software, or software by subscription. Many companies are moving toward this **subscription model**, such as Adobe and Microsoft. When you buy an annual subscription to Office 365, for example, you install the software on your own computer and you must therefore provide your own hardware with a functioning OS. However, the downloadable software is available in formats that are compatible with multiple OSes, and in many cases, the license provides for installation on multiple devices. In this specific case, the SaaS also can include data storage by connecting the licensed account with OneDrive, a virtual data storage service.

Consider the service models as they're shown in Figure 7-16. The smaller, upper end of the pyramid indicates how little a SaaS customer needs to understand and interact with a cloud provider's infrastructure in order for the customer to perform his work. In contrast, an IaaS customer interacts more heavily with her service provider's infrastructure for every aspect of her computing needs. IaaS is much more pervasively integrated with a client's computer network than is SaaS.

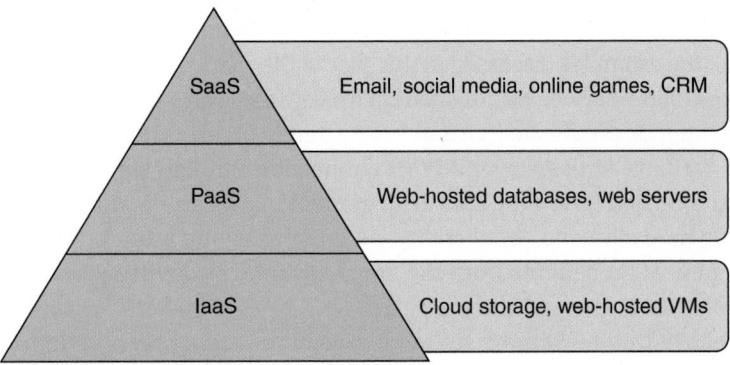

Figure 7-16   IaaS customers must understand more about a cloud provider's hardware infrastructure than SaaS customers

At the same time, consider how accessible each type of cloud service is to end users. In Figure 7-17, the triangle is upside-down. End users, the largest group of cloud computing consumers, can easily access and use SaaS products without much setup, whereas IaaS products require extensive preparation by a much smaller group of more skilled network architects and administrators, who provide systems for their end users. In the middle of this pyramid is PaaS, which is typically used by application developers, both professionals and laypersons, for testing their products. Customers at the lower layers of this pyramid build products that support customers at the higher layers, such as when a company subscribes to an IaaS product, on which it offers its own PaaS products to its own unique market of customers.

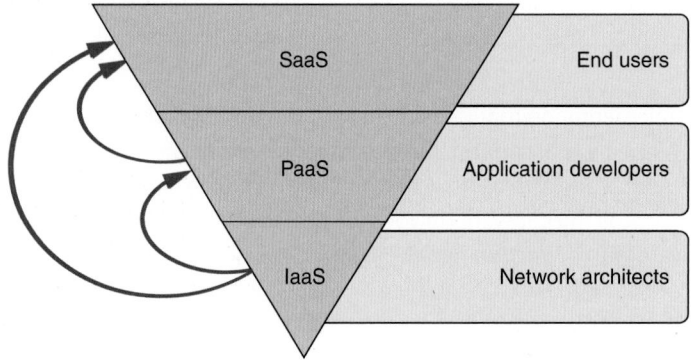

Figure 7-17 SaaS are more immediately accessible to a wide market of end users than other categories of cloud services

Deployment Models

Cloud services are delivered in a variety of deployment models, depending on who manages the cloud and who has access to it. The main deployment models you are likely to encounter are:

- *public cloud*—Service provided over public transmission lines, such as the Internet. Most of the examples discussed in this part of the chapter take place in public clouds.
- *private cloud*—Service established on an organization's own servers in its own data center, or established virtually for a single organization's private use and made available to users over a WAN connection through some type of remote access. If hosted internally, this arrangement allows an organization to use existing hardware and connectivity, potentially saving money. If hosted virtually, the organization benefits from the usual advantages of virtual services, such as scalability and accessibility.
- *community cloud*—Service shared between multiple organizations, but not available publicly. Organizations with common interests, such as regulatory

requirements, performance requirements, or data access, might share resources in this way. For example, a medical database might be made accessible to all hospitals in a geographic area. In that case, the community cloud could be hosted internally by one or more of the organizations involved, or hosted by a third-party provider. But it would not be made available to the public.

- *hybrid cloud*—A combination of the other service models into a single deployment, or a collection of services connected within the cloud. In the real world, the hybrid cloud infrastructure is a common result of transitory solutions. (In IT, "solution" refers to a product, service, or combination of products and services, and often includes extra features such as ongoing customer service.) An example of a hybrid cloud by design might arise when a company stores data in a private cloud, but uses a public cloud email service.

Cloud Connectivity and Security

While cloud computing offers many significant advantages and opportunities for expansion, there are some drawbacks worth considering. Dependence on the Internet means dependence on your network's connection to the ISP and reliance on other third parties as well. Potential risks and limitations include:

- ISP's uptime
- ISP-imposed bandwidth limitations
- Cloud provider's uptime
- Cloud provider's backup and security systems
- Misconfiguration that exposes one client's data to another client
- Unauthorized access to data by cloud provider employees or by illegitimate users
- Breaches of confidentiality agreements when data is stored online
- Data security regulations (such as for healthcare, financial, or government entities)
- Questions over ownership of intellectual property stored in the cloud (for example, photos or comments made on social media websites, or files saved in online storage accounts)
- Questions over data maintenance if a payment is not made on time
- Risks to the network, proprietary data, or customer information caused by BYOC (bring your own cloud) services on users' personal devices
- Reduced consumer confidence, fines, lawsuits, and possibly criminal charges when cloud breaches occur

One way to reduce the inherent risks of cloud computing is to use encryption, which is discussed in the next section. Another way is to carefully choose the method by which your network connects to your cloud resources. Business requirements, risk management, and cost all factor into this decision. Cloud providers will often offer attractive SLAs (service-level agreements) based upon their own technology's availability. However, the WAN connection that links their resources with your network is just as important. To this end, organizations generally have a 4-tiered array of options:

- *Internet*—Provides the simplest and cheapest option, but with high and unpredictable latency as well as significant security concerns.
- *remote access connections*—Uses tunneling or terminal emulation technologies to increase security. You'll learn more about remote access options later in this chapter.
- *leased line*—Relies on private WAN options to reserve a dedicated amount of bandwidth between the cloud provider and the customer's premises. Depending on the respective locations of provider and customer, this might require the cooperation of multiple ISPs in order to reach the cloud provider's servers. Hybrid pay-per-use models are available where the customer reserves a portion of anticipated bandwidth needs, and then is invoiced for additional bandwidth used during the pay period.
- *dedicated connection*—Maximizes predictability and minimizes latency, and of course comes with a high price tag. Some of the larger cloud service providers maintain multiple **PoP (Points of Presence)** around the world. This means the provider rents space at a data center facility, called a **colocation facility** or carrier hotel that is shared by a variety of providers. In many cases, ISPs can provide dedicated access from a customer's premises to a cloud provider's PoP. This is more cost effective when an organization subscribes to multiple cloud providers who all use the same colocation. Amazon's AWS Direct Connect and Microsoft's Azure ExpressRoute both offer dedicated connection services.

As you can see, security with cloud computing services is a significant concern with some unique challenges. To address these concerns, data is often encrypted. In this next section, you'll learn how encryption protocols work to help secure data transmitted over these remote connections and in many other kinds of situations where data security is critical.

Encryption Protocols

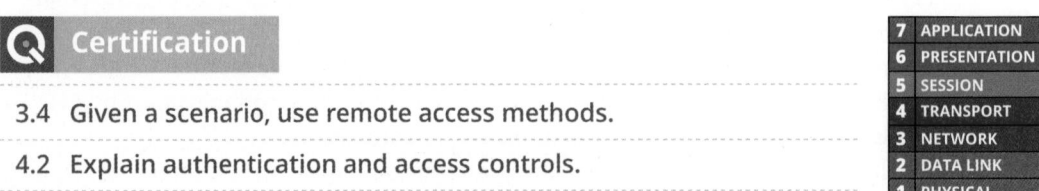

Data exists generally in three states: at rest, in use, and in motion.

- *at rest*—Data is most secure when it's stored on a device that is protected by a firewall, anti-malware software, and physical security (such as being inside a locked room). However, these protections are no guarantee. Additional protections include storing portions of the data in separate locations so that no single portion is meaningful on its own.

- *in use*—For data to be used, it must be accessible, which brings inherent risk. Tightly controlling access to the data and reliable authentication of users help reduce these risks. You'll learn more about access control and authentication methods later.
- *in motion*—This is when data is most vulnerable. Especially when data must leave your own, trusted network, it's exposed to a multitude of potential gaps, intrusions, and weak links. As you've seen in earlier chapters, wireless transmissions, especially, are susceptible to interception. And wired transmissions also risk exposure. The number of devices, organizations, and transmission methods involved in sending a single email across the Internet highlights the need for a layer of security that travels with the data.

Encryption is the last means of defense against data theft. In other words, if an intruder has bypassed all other methods of security, including physical security (for instance, he has broken into the data center) and network design security (for instance, he has defied a firewall's packet-filtering techniques or removed encapsulated frames from transmissions), data may still be safe if it is encrypted. Encryption protocols use a mathematical code, called a cipher, to scramble data into a format that can be read only by reversing the cipher—that is, by deciphering, or decrypting, the data. The purpose of encryption is to keep information private. Many forms of encryption exist, with some being more secure than others. Even as new forms of encryption are developed, new ways of cracking their codes emerge, too.

To protect data at rest, in use, and in motion, encryption methods are primarily evaluated by three benchmarks:

- *confidentiality*—Data can only be viewed by its intended recipient or at its intended destination.
- *integrity*—Data is not modified in the time after the sender transmits it and before the receiver picks it up.
- *availability*—Data is available and accessible to the intended recipient when needed, meaning the sender is accountable for successful delivery of the data.

Together, these three principles form the standard security model called the **CIA (confidentiality, integrity, and availability) triad**. Encryption can happen at various layers of the OSI model. Let's first begin with a brief description of what key encryption is, and then we'll explore some of the most common encryption protocols used to protect data stored on or traveling across networks. We'll start at Layer 3 and then work our way up the OSI layers.

Key Encryption

The most popular kind of encryption encodes the original data's bits using a **key**, or a random string of characters—sometimes several times in different sequences—to scramble the data and from it, generate a unique and consistently sized data block called ciphertext. The key is created according to a specific set of rules, or algorithms.

Key encryption can be separated into two categories, private key and public key encryption, as described next:

- *private key encryption*—Data is encrypted using a single key that only the sender and the receiver know. Private key encryption is also known as **symmetric encryption** because the same key is used during both the encryption and decryption of the data. A potential problem with private key encryption is that the sender must somehow share the key with the recipient without it being intercepted.

- *public key encryption*—Data is encrypted with a private key known only to the user, and decrypted with a mathematically related public key that can be made available through a third-party source, such as a public key server. This ensures data integrity, as the sender's public key will only work if the data has not been tampered with. Alternatively, data can be encrypted with the public key, and then can only be decrypted with the matching private key. This ensures data confidentiality, as only the intended recipient (the owner of the keys) can decrypt the data. A public key server is a publicly accessible host (such as a server on the Internet) that freely provides a list of users' public keys, much as a telephone book provides a list of peoples' phone numbers. The combination of a public key and a private key is known as a key pair. Because public key encryption requires the use of two different keys, one to encrypt and the other to decrypt, it is also known as **asymmetric encryption**.

With the abundance of private and public keys, not to mention the number of places where each may be kept, users need simple and secure key management. One answer to this problem is to use digital certificates. A person or a business can request a **digital certificate**, which is a small file containing that user's verified identification information and the user's public key. The digital certificate is issued, maintained, and validated by an organization called a **CA (certificate authority)**. The use of certificate authorities to associate public keys with certain users is known as **PKI (Public-key Infrastructure)**.

> **Note** ✐
>
> Digital certificates are primarily used to certify and secure websites where financial and other sensitive information is exchanged, but they're also used for other types of websites and to secure email communications, to authenticate client devices in a domain, or to authenticate users to a network. When surfing the web, at some point you might have gotten an error that said the website's SSL certificate was untrusted. This means the website's digital certificate used by the encryption protocol SSL (which was formerly used to secure HTTP) was not signed by a trusted CA or associated with a trusted root certificate.

The next two sections detail specific protocols, including SSL, that are used to encrypt data as it is transmitted over a network. The first encryption protocol in our list, IPsec, operates at the Network layer.

IPsec (Internet Protocol Security)

7	APPLICATION
6	PRESENTATION
5	SESSION
4	TRANSPORT
3	NETWORK
2	DATA LINK
1	PHYSICAL

IPsec (Internet Protocol Security) is an encryption protocol suite that defines a set of rules for encryption, authentication, and key management for TCP/IP transmissions. It is an enhancement to IPv4 and is native to IPv6. IPsec works at the Network layer of the OSI model—it adds security information to the headers of all IP packets and encrypts the data payload.

IPsec creates secure connections in five steps, as follows:

1. *IPsec initiation*—Noteworthy traffic, as defined by a security policy, triggers the initiation of the IPsec encryption process.

2. *key management*—Through a **key management** process, two nodes agree on common parameters for the keys they will use. This phase primarily includes two services:
   - *IKE (Internet Key Exchange)*—Negotiates the exchange of keys, including authentication of the keys; the current version is IKEv2, which you'll see again in the discussion on VPNs later in this chapter
   - *ISAKMP (Internet Security Association and Key Management Protocol)*—Works within the IKE process to establish policies for managing the keys

3. *security negotiations*—IKE continues to establish security parameters and associations that will serve to protect data while in transit.

4. *data transfer*—After parameters and encryption techniques are agreed upon, a secure channel is created, which can be used for secure transmissions until the channel is broken. Data is encrypted and then transmitted. Either **AH (authentication header)** encryption or **ESP (Encapsulating Security Payload)** encryption may be used. Both types of encryption provide authentication of the IP packet's data payload through public key techniques. In addition, ESP encrypts the entire IP packet for added security.

5. *termination*—IPsec requires regular reestablishment of a connection to minimize the opportunity for interference. The connection can be renegotiated and reestablished before the current session times out in order to maintain communication.

IPsec can be used with any type of TCP/IP transmission and operates in two modes:
   - *transport mode*—Connects two hosts.
   - *tunnel mode*—Runs on routers or other connectivity devices in the context of VPNs.

SSL (Secure Sockets Layer) and TLS (Transport Layer Security)

7	APPLICATION
6	PRESENTATION
5	SESSION
4	TRANSPORT
3	NETWORK
2	DATA LINK
1	PHYSICAL

SSL (Secure Sockets Layer) and TLS (Transport Layer Security) are both methods of encrypting TCP/IP transmissions—including web pages and data entered into web forms—en route between the client and server using public key encryption technology. The two protocols can work side by side and are widely known as SSL/TLS or TLS/SSL. All browsers today (for example, Google Chrome, Mozilla Firefox, Apple's Safari, Microsoft Edge, and Internet Explorer) support SSL/TLS to create secure transmissions of HTTP sessions.

SSL was originally developed by Netscape and operates in the Application layer. Since that time, the IETF (Internet Engineering Task Force), which is an organization of volunteers who help develop Internet standards, has standardized the similar TLS protocol. TLS operates in the Transport layer and uses slightly different encryption algorithms than SSL, but otherwise is essentially the updated version of SSL. SSL has now been deprecated and should be disabled whenever possible, leaving the more secure TLS to provide protection. In reality, you'll often see them both enabled for backward compatibility.

As you recall, HTTP uses TCP port 80, whereas HTTPS (HTTP Secure) uses SSL/TLS encryption and TCP port 443, rather than port 80. Each time a client and server establish an SSL/TLS connection, they establish a unique session, or an association between the client and server that is defined by an agreement on a specific set of encryption techniques. The session allows the client and server to continue to exchange data securely as long as the client is still connected to the server. A session is created by a handshake protocol, one of several protocols within SSL/TLS, and perhaps the most significant. As its name implies, the **handshake protocol** allows the client and server to introduce themselves to each other and establishes terms for how they will securely exchange data.

This handshake conversation is similar to the TCP three-way handshake you've already learned about. Given the scenario of a browser accessing a secure website, the SSL/TLS handshake works as follows:

Step 1—The browser, representing the client computer in this scenario, sends a **client_hello** message to the web server, which contains information about what level of security the browser is capable of accepting and what type of encryption the browser can decipher. The client_hello message also establishes a randomly generated number that uniquely identifies the client and another number that identifies the session.

Step 2—The server responds with a **server_hello** message that confirms the information it received from the browser and agrees to certain terms of encryption based on the options supplied by the browser. Depending on the web server's preferred encryption method, the server might choose to issue to the browser a public key or a digital certificate.

Step 3—If the server requests a certificate from the browser, the browser sends it. Any data the browser sends to the server is encrypted using the server's public key. Session keys used only for this one session are also established.

After the browser and server have agreed on the terms of encryption, the secure channel is in place and they begin exchanging data.

A variant of TLS is **DTLS (Datagram Transport Layer Security)**, which is designed specifically for streaming communications. As the name implies, DTLS relies on UDP instead of TCP, which minimizes delays. However, applications using DTLS must provide their own means of packet reordering, flow control, and reliability assurance. DTLS includes security levels that are comparable to TLS and is commonly used by delay-sensitive applications such as VoIP and tunneling applications such as VPN. You'll learn more about VPNs later in this chapter.

Note

Transmissions over secure connections, such as when using HTTPS websites, might be intercepted but cannot be read. For example, suppose you are using unsecured Wi-Fi at a coffee shop and log on to Facebook from your laptop browser. Without TLS protecting your logon information, anyone lounging nearby can hack into, read, and steal your unencrypted wireless transmissions.

Some online activities, however, such as online banking, should never be performed on unsecure Wi-Fi hot spots. Despite the security provided by these encryption techniques, other steps of the process can break down. One example might include browsing an insecure portion of a website (HTTP) for part of the browsing session, which provides a brief opportunity for your browser to be hijacked by a hacker and sent to what looks like the official logon page, but really is not.

Applying Concepts: Browser Security

You can change the settings in your browser to make sure you're using the latest version of TLS. On a Windows machine, changes you make to one browser for these settings will affect other browsers installed on your computer. Complete the following steps:

1. To open Internet Explorer, first open **Microsoft Edge**. In Microsoft Edge, click **Settings and more**, and then click **Open with Internet Explorer**. Alternatively, press **Win+R** and enter **iexplore**.
2. In Internet Explorer, click the **Tools** icon. Click **Internet options**.
3. On the Advanced tab, scroll down to the Security section. Which SSL/TLS options are currently enabled?
4. Disable **SSL 3.0** and **TLS 1.0.** Make sure **TLS 1.1** and **TLS 1.2** are enabled. If you regularly use an unsecured wireless network like at a coffee shop or a restaurant, also select **Warn if changing between secure and not secure mode** so you'll be notified when interacting with an unsecured website. See Figure 7-18. Click **OK**.

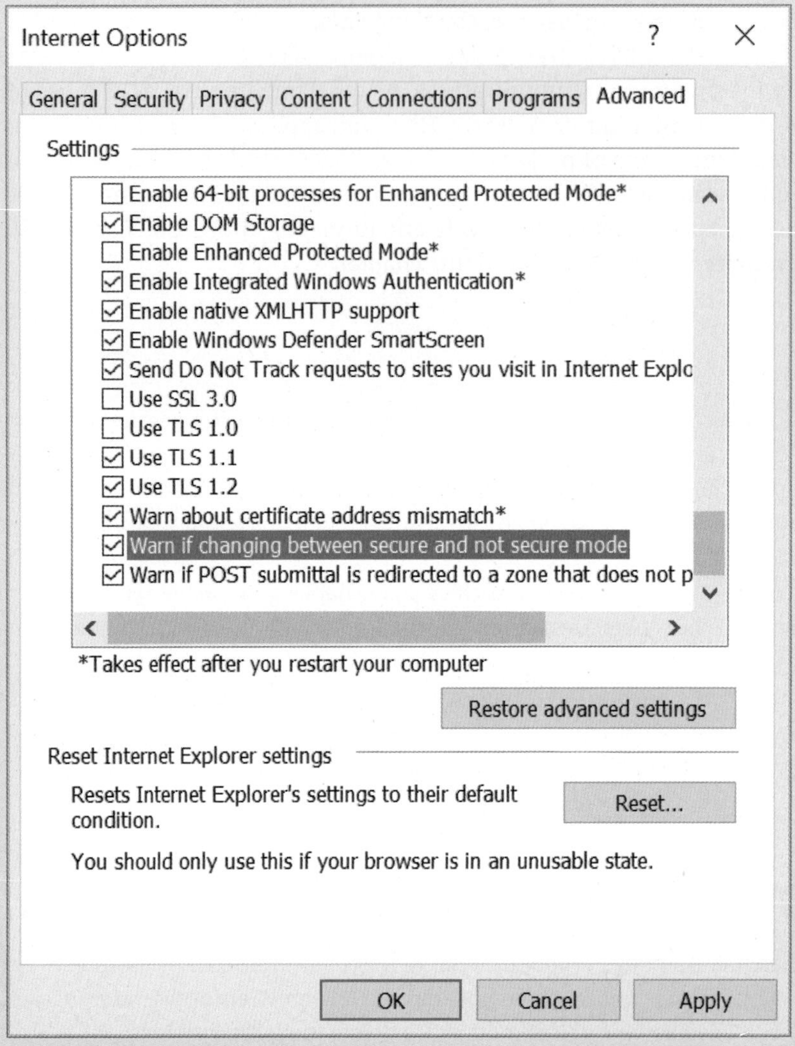

Internet Options   ?   ✕

General | Security | Privacy | Content | Connections | Programs | **Advanced**

Settings

☐ Enable 64-bit processes for Enhanced Protected Mode*
☑ Enable DOM Storage
☐ Enable Enhanced Protected Mode*
☑ Enable Integrated Windows Authentication*
☑ Enable native XMLHTTP support
☑ Enable Windows Defender SmartScreen
☑ Send Do Not Track requests to sites you visit in Internet Explo
☐ Use SSL 3.0
☐ Use TLS 1.0
☑ Use TLS 1.1
☑ Use TLS 1.2
☑ Warn about certificate address mismatch*
☑ Warn if changing between secure and not secure mode
☑ Warn if POST submittal is redirected to a zone that does not p

*Takes effect after you restart your computer

[Restore advanced settings]

Reset Internet Explorer settings

Resets Internet Explorer's settings to their default condition.   [Reset...]

You should only use this if your browser is in an unusable state.

[OK]   [Cancel]   [Apply]

Figure 7-18   TLS 1.1 and TLS 1.2 provide the best security for surfing online

Note

Some browsers will prevent navigation to unsecured websites when the warning option is checked as previously instructed. This is a good thing if you're using a questionable network. But if you have trouble navigating to unsecured sites you feel comfortable with, you'll need to go back and uncheck this option in Internet options.

> **Caution**
>
> When visiting secure websites, it's important to notice if you have a secure connection with a trusted website before entering personal information on that site. Internet Explorer, for example, shows a padlock icon when the site's certificate has been identified and confirmed. This visual is still no guarantee, however, as scammers are now figuring out how to impersonate HTTPS websites' credentials.

5. In Internet Explorer, navigate to **paypal.com**. What is the exact address shown in the address box after the page loads in the browser?
6. Use the mouse pointer to point to the padlock icon. What CA verified the legitimacy of the website?
7. Click the padlock icon. What additional information is provided about the website?

Now that you understand a little about encryption and related security concerns, you're ready to dive into remote connection technologies that require encryption for security.

Remote Access

 **Certification**

7	APPLICATION
6	PRESENTATION
5	SESSION
4	TRANSPORT
3	NETWORK
2	DATA LINK
1	PHYSICAL

1.3   Explain the concepts and characteristics of routing and switching.

2.3   Explain the purposes and use cases for advanced networking devices.

2.5   Compare and contrast WAN technologies.

3.4   Given a scenario, use remote access methods.

3.5   Identify policies and best practices.

As a remote user, you can connect to a network and its resources via remote access, which is a service that allows a client to connect with and log on to a server, LAN, or WAN in a different geographical location. After connecting, a remote client can access files, applications, and other shared resources, such as printers, like any other client on the server, LAN, or WAN. To communicate via remote access, the client and host need a transmission path plus the appropriate software to complete the connection and exchange data.

All types of remote access techniques connecting to a network require some type of **RAS (remote access server)** to accept a remote connection and grant it privileges to the network's resources. Also, software must be installed on both the remote client and the remote access server to negotiate and maintain this connection.

There are two types of remote access servers:

- *dedicated devices*—Devices such as Cisco's AS5800 access servers are dedicated solely as an RAS to run software that, in conjunction with their operating system, performs authentication for clients. An ISP might use a dedicated device to authenticate client computers or home routers to access the ISP resources and the Internet. See Figure 7-19.

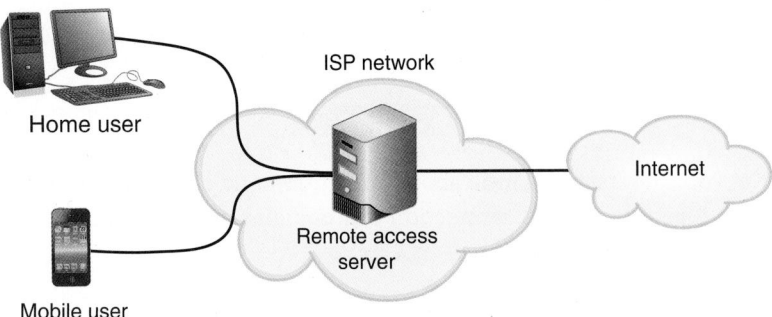

Figure 7-19 An ISP uses a remote access server to authenticate subscribers to its services, including access to the Internet

- *software running on a server*—The remote access service might run under a network operating system to allow remote logon to a corporate network. For example, DirectAccess is a service first introduced in Windows Server 2008 R2 that can automatically authenticate remote users and computers to the Windows domain and its corporate network resources. See Figure 7-20.

Several types of remote access methods exist. Three of the most common, which we'll explore in greater depth throughout this section, are:

- Point-to-point remote access over a dedicated (usually leased) line, such as DSL or T1 access to an ISP.
- Terminal emulation, also called remote virtual computing, which allows a remote client to take over and command a host computer. Examples of terminal emulation software are Telnet, SSH, Remote Desktop, and VNC (Virtual Network Computing). We'll discuss all of these in more detail soon.
- **VPN (virtual private network)**, which is a virtual connection that remotely accesses resources between a client and a network, two networks, or two hosts over the Internet or other types of networks.

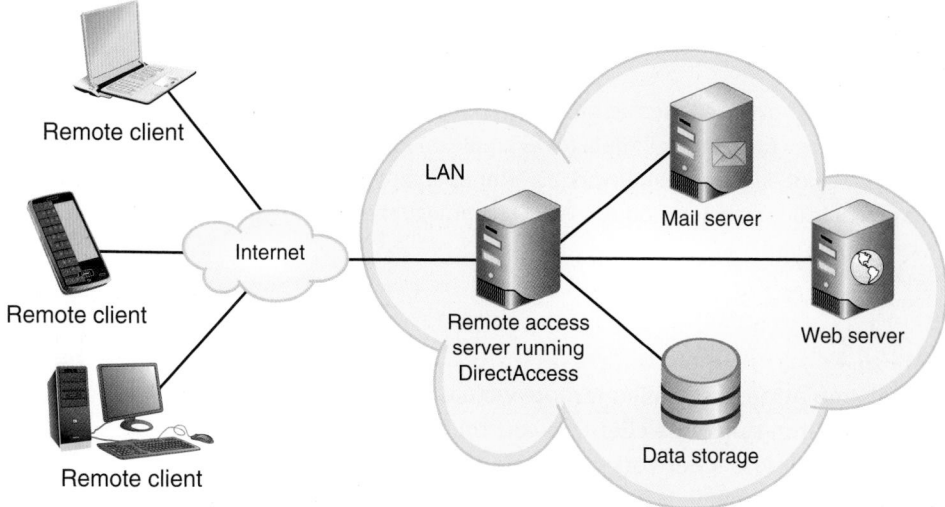

Figure 7-20   DirectAccess authenticates users to the Windows domain

Security and privacy are of utmost concern when managing and using remote access connections. To this end, data is often encrypted before it is transmitted over the remote connection. Some remote access protocols natively include encryption functionality, whereas other remote access methods must be paired with a specific encryption protocol, such as the ones you learned about earlier in this chapter.

Point-to-Point Remote Access Protocols

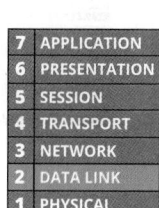

7	APPLICATION
6	PRESENTATION
5	SESSION
4	TRANSPORT
3	NETWORK
2	DATA LINK
1	PHYSICAL

Clients and remote access servers require an agreed-to protocol to establish a session and exchange data. An older protocol of this type is SLIP (Serial Line Internet Protocol), which is rarely used today. It does not support encryption, can carry only IP packets (but not other Network layer protocols), and works strictly on serial connections such as dial-up or DSL. SLIP has been replaced by PPP as the preferred communications protocol for remote access point-to-point connections.

PPP (Point-to-Point Protocol) is a Data Link layer protocol that directly connects two WAN endpoints. One example might be when a DSL or cable modem connects to a server at the ISP. PPP headers and trailers create a PPP frame that encapsulates Network layer packets. The frames total only 8 or 10 bytes, the difference depending on the size of the FCS field (recall that the FCS field ensures the data is received intact). Here's what PPP can do:

- Negotiate and establish a connection between the two endpoints.
- Use an authentication protocol, such as MS-CHAPv2 or EAP, to authenticate a client to the remote system.
- Support several Network layer protocols, such as IP, that might use the connection.
- Encrypt the transmissions, although PPP encryption is considered weak by today's standards.

Terminal Emulation

7	APPLICATION
6	PRESENTATION
5	SESSION
4	TRANSPORT
3	NETWORK
2	DATA LINK
1	PHYSICAL

Terminal emulation, also called remote virtual computing, allows a user on one computer, called the client, to control another computer, called the host or server, across a network connection. Examples of command-line software that can provide terminal emulation include Telnet and SSH, and some GUI-based software examples are Remote Desktop for Windows, join.me, VNC, and TeamViewer. A host may allow clients a variety of privileges, from merely viewing the screen to running programs and modifying data files on the host's hard disk. After connecting, if the remote user has sufficient privileges, she can send keystrokes and mouse clicks to the host and receive screen output in return. In other words, to the remote user, it appears as if she is working on the LAN- or WAN-connected host. For example, a traveling salesperson can use her laptop to "remote in" to her desktop computer at corporate headquarters. This way, she can remotely update a workbook stored on her desktop computer using Excel, also installed on the desktop.

Telnet

As you've learned, the Telnet protocol is a terminal emulation utility used by Telnet client/server applications that allow an administrator or other user to control a computer remotely. For example, if you were a network administrator working at one building on your school's campus and had to modify the configuration on a router in another building, you could use Telnet to access the router and run commands to change configuration settings. However, Telnet provides little security for establishing a connection (poor authentication) and no security for transmitting data (no encryption).

SSH (Secure Shell)

SSH (Secure Shell) is a collection of protocols that does both authentication and encryption. With SSH, you can securely log on to a host, execute commands on that host, and copy files to or from that host. SSH encrypts data exchanged throughout the session. It guards against a number of security threats, including unauthorized access to a host, IP spoofing, interception of data in transit (even if it must be transferred via intermediate hosts), and **DNS spoofing**, in which a hacker forges name server records to falsify his host's identity. Depending on the version, SSH may use Triple DES, AES, Blowfish, or other, less-common encryption schemes or techniques.

Network+ Exam Tip (i)

After completing your Network+ certification, you might consider studying for the Security+ certification. CompTIA's Security+ exam covers a broad range of foundational topics in the area of IT security, including the encryption techniques listed here for SSH. This essential understanding of security concerns, techniques, and concepts will serve you well no matter which area of IT you choose to specialize in.

SSH was developed by SSH Communications Security, and use of their SSH implementation requires paying for a license. However, open-source versions of the protocol suite, such as OpenSSH, are available for most computer platforms.

To form a secure connection, SSH must be running on both the client and server. Like Telnet, the SSH client is a utility that can be run at the shell prompt on a UNIX or Linux system or at the command prompt on a Windows-based system. Other versions of the program come with a graphical interface. The SSH suite of protocols is included with all modern UNIX and Linux distributions and with macOS Server and macOS client operating systems. For Windows-based computers, you need to download a freeware SSH client, such as PuTTY (*putty.org*). You can see in Figure 7-21 that PuTTY supports several connection types, including both SSH and Telnet. PuTTY can also be run from the command line.

SSH allows for password authentication or authentication using public and private keys. For authentication using keys, you first generate a public key and a private key on your client workstation by running the `ssh-keygen` command (or by choosing the correct menu options in a graphical SSH program). The keys are saved in two different, encrypted files on your hard disk. Next, you will transfer the public key to an authorization file on the host to which you want to connect. When you connect to the host via SSH, the client and host exchange public keys, and if both can be authenticated, the connection is completed.

SSH listens at port 22, and is highly configurable. For example, you can choose among several types of encryption methods and it can also be configured to perform **port forwarding**, which means it can redirect traffic that would normally use an insecure port (such as FTP) to a SSH-secured port. This allows you to use SSH for more than simply logging on to a host and manipulating files. With port forwarding, you could, for example, exchange HTTP traffic with a web server via a secured SSH connection. Later in this chapter, you'll configure port forwarding on a SOHO router. And at the end of this chapter in Capstone Project 7-1, you'll use SSH in Ubuntu.

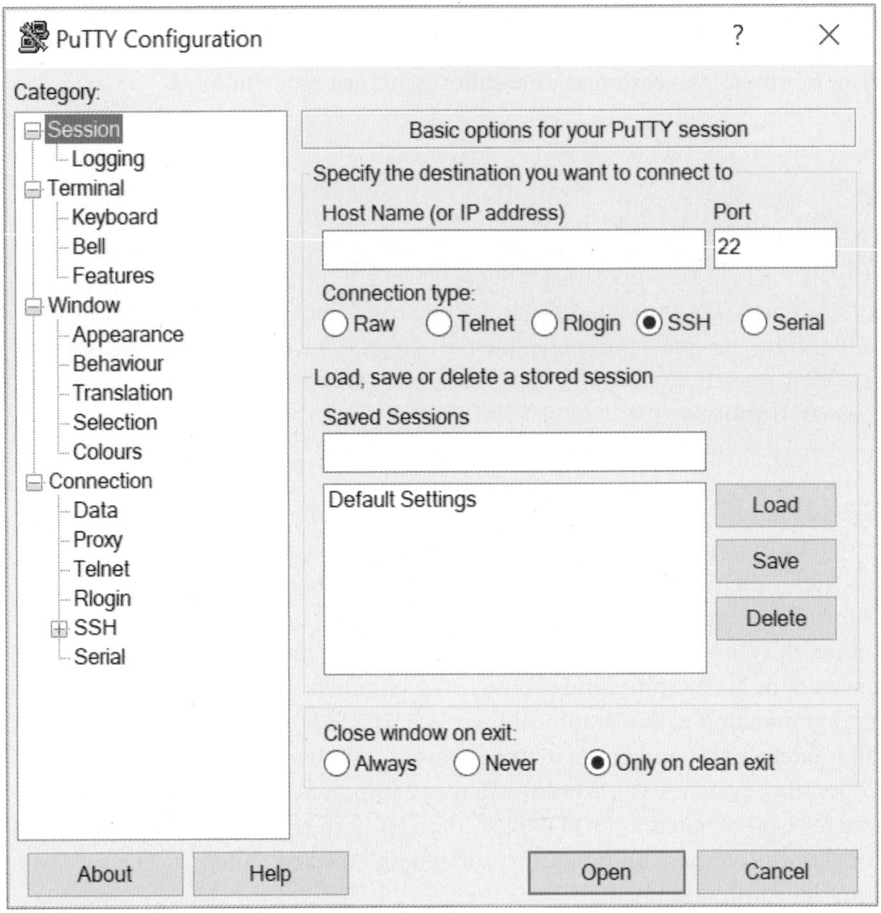

Figure 7-21 On a Windows computer, use an app like PuTTY to create a SSH connection to another computer

Source: PuTTY

RDP (Remote Desktop Protocol) and VNC (Virtual Network Computing)

7	APPLICATION
6	PRESENTATION
5	SESSION
4	TRANSPORT
3	NETWORK
2	DATA LINK
1	PHYSICAL

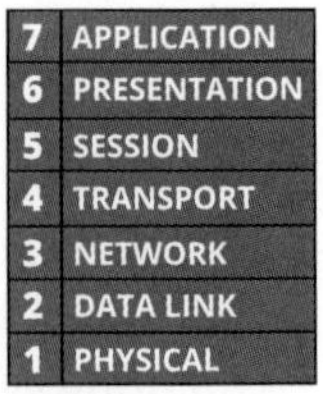

Recall that RDP (Remote Desktop Protocol) is a Microsoft proprietary protocol used by Windows Remote Desktop and Remote Assistance client/server utilities to connect to and control a remote computer. Similarly, **VNC (Virtual Network Computing** or Virtual Network Connection) uses the cross-platform protocol RFB (remote frame buffer) to remotely control a workstation or server. VNC is slower than Remote Desktop and requires more network bandwidth. However, because VNC is open source, many companies have developed their own software that can:

- Run OSes on client computers
- Remotely access computers, tablets, and smartphones
- Remotely control media equipment and surveillance systems

Applying Concepts: Configure Port Forwarding

To allow a Remote Desktop connection over the Internet, the router must be configured to forward RDP traffic (port 3389) to the correct computer. In this project, you learn how to set up port forwarding for RDP on a SOHO router. At the end of the chapter, you will configure a pair of computers for an RDP connection.

Note that the router would need a static IP address from the ISP to reliably use RDP over the Internet. This project is designed to show you how to configure port forwarding and will not require you to use RDP over an Internet connection.

Complete the following steps:

1. On the host computer (the computer to receive the connection), configure a static, private IP address. You learned how to do this as part of Hands-On Project 4-1. Write down the static IP address.
2. Open a web browser, navigate to your router's administration website, and log on.
3. Look for a port forwarding or port range forwarding option on the router's admin interface. For the Linksys router in Figure 7-22, for example, this feature is accessed under the Applications & Gaming tab. For the TP-Link router in Figure 7-23, this feature is accessed on the Advanced tab under NAT Forwarding > Virtual Servers.

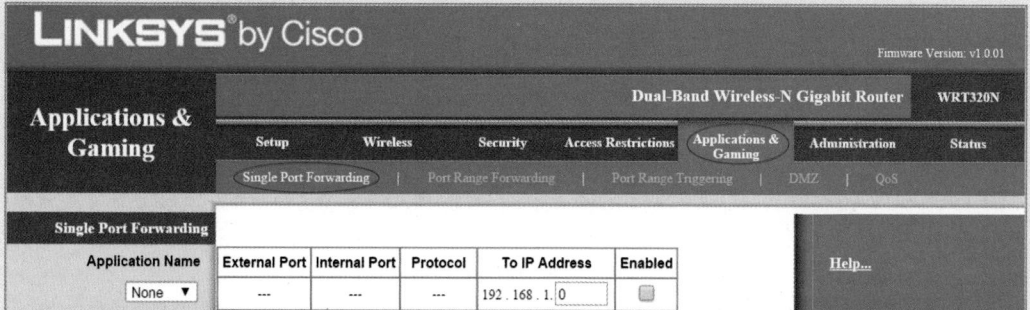

Figure 7-22   This Linksys router's port forwarding feature is configured on the Applications & Gaming tab

Source: Cisco Systems, Inc.

4. Add a port forwarding entry. Type **RDP** for the service type, and **3389** for both the external and internal ports. For Protocol, select **Both** or **All** so both TCP and UDP 3389 ports will be linked. In the *To IP Address* or *Internal IP* column, type the IP address of the host computer, then enable the entry.
5. Save the settings.

Caution

As a general rule, do not leave port forwarding enabled unless you're using it.

Figure 7-23   This TP-Link router's port forwarding feature is configured on the Advanced tab in the NAT forwarding section of the menu bar
Source: TP-Link Technologies Co., Ltd.

6. Because we won't actually be using RDP over the Internet, delete the port forwarding entry.

Server applications such as Remote Desktop listen for network activity from clients. If you want these server applications to be available at all times, you can set your network adapter properties to enable WoL (Wake on LAN). WoL causes the host computer to turn on from a powered-off state when it detects a specific type of network activity. To do this, the network adapter retains power and listens for network activity. System administrators might also use utilities to remotely wake a computer to perform routine maintenance.

Follow these steps to set up the Wake-on-LAN feature:

1. Boot the computer and access its UEFI setup utility. For Windows 10 computers, you can do this from within Windows. Click **Start** and **Power**. Hold down the **Shift** key and click **Restart**. When the computer reboots, click **Troubleshoot, Advanced options**, and **UEFI Firmware settings**. The computer reboots again, this time into UEFI setup.
2. In UEFI setup, locate the Wake-on-LAN feature and enable it. Save the setting change and reboot the machine.
3. Open a Command Prompt window and enter `ipconfig /all` to determine the computer's IP address. Close the Command Prompt window.
4. Next, you'll enable Wake-on-LAN in Windows. Open the **Network and Sharing Center**.
5. In the left pane, click **Change adapter settings**. Right-click the network adapter for the wired connection and click **Properties**.
6. Click **Configure** and then click the **Power Management** tab.
7. Make sure the **Allow the computer to turn off this device to save power** option is selected. This enables Power Management in Windows.
8. Check **Allow this device to wake the computer** and click **OK**.

Management URL Using HTTPS

In the past, when setting up a new SOHO router or other networking device, the user had to download and install a setup program from the manufacturer. Increasingly, networking devices are configured through a connected computer's browser that navigates to a management URL, where the user can make changes directly to the device. In the port forwarding Applying Concepts project, you used a web browser to configure a SOHO router (refer back to Figures 7-22 and 7-23). You also used a browser to configure a SOHO router in Hands-On Project 6-1 in Chapter 6. To do this, you entered the router's IP address into the address bar. All of the device's configurations were completed through the web browser. Ideally, these device consoles will require an encrypted connection over HTTPS, although this is not always the case.

7	APPLICATION
6	PRESENTATION
5	SESSION
4	TRANSPORT
3	NETWORK
2	DATA LINK
1	PHYSICAL

Out-of-Band Management

Telnet, SSH, RDP, VNC, and a management URL all rely on the existing network infrastructure for a network administrator to remotely control the device. Before he or she can configure these devices, they must already be booted up, and they must already have configuration software installed. This is called in-band management, and inherently limits troubleshooting capabilities. Out-of-band management, however, relies on a dedicated connection (either wired or wireless) between the network administrator's computer and each critical network device, such as routers, firewalls, servers, power supplies, applications, and security cameras. These dedicated connections allow network administrators to remotely:

7	APPLICATION
6	PRESENTATION
5	SESSION
4	TRANSPORT
3	NETWORK
2	DATA LINK
1	PHYSICAL

- Power up a device
- Change firmware settings
- Reinstall operating systems
- Monitor hardware sensors
- Troubleshoot boot problems
- Limit network users' access to management functions
- Manage devices even when other parts of the network are down

Out-of-band management solutions come in an array of options, from basic reboot abilities to full-scale device management. A remote management card is attached to the network device's console port, or sometimes the remote management card is built into the device. A dial-in modem—either through a wired phone line or through a cellular connection—might be attached to the device to provide backup CLI access in the event of a catastrophic network shutdown. A single device, such as a console server or console router, provides centralized management of all linked devices.

Remote File Access

7	APPLICATION
6	PRESENTATION
5	SESSION
4	TRANSPORT
3	NETWORK
2	DATA LINK
1	PHYSICAL

Although not technically a form of terminal emulation, FTP (File Transfer Protocol) does provide remote file access. Now that you understand more about how encryption can secure transmissions, you're ready to learn about some remote file access options related to FTP. Recall that FTP is a utility that can transfer files to and from a host computer running FTP server software. You learned how to use FTP in Windows in Capstone Project 3-1 in Chapter 3, and you learned how to set up an FTP server in Linux in Capstone Project 5-1 in Chapter 5. The FTP app that you installed in Chapter 5 was called vsftpd, which stands for *very secure FTP daemon*. Three related technologies include the following:

- *FTPS (FTP Security or FTP Secure)*—An added layer of protection for FTP using SSL/TLS that can encrypt both the control and data channels. Recall that FTP listens at port 21, which is the command channel. Data is usually transferred over port 20, which is the data channel. FTPS is typically configured to listen at port 21, like FTP, but requires two data channels. By default, those data channels are at ports 989 and 990. However, FTPS can also be configured to negotiate its data ports within a predefined range each time it makes a connection. FTPS can be difficult to configure through a firewall. You can configure the vsftpd app to support FTPS, as they are both based on the original FTP standards.

- *SFTP (Secure FTP)*—A file-transfer version of SSH that includes encryption and authentication, and is sometimes inaccurately called FTP over SSH or SSH FTP. Note that SFTP is an extension of the SSH protocol, not of FTP. Unlike FTP or FTPS, which use a control channel and one or two data channels, SFTP uses only a single connection—both inbound and outbound communications are usually configured to cross SSH's port 22. SFTP and FTPS are incompatible with each other. While SFTP uses a similar acronym to vsftpd, these two standards also are not compatible with each other. However, SFTP is supported by Linux and UNIX servers.

- *TFTP (Trivial FTP)*—A simple version of FTP that includes no authentication or security for transferring files and uses UDP at the Transport layer (unlike FTP, which relies on TCP at the Transport layer). TFTP requires very little memory and is most often used by machines behind the scenes to transfer boot files or configuration files. It's not safe for communication over the Internet, is not capable of giving users access to directory information, and limits file transfers to 4 GB. TFTP listens at port 69 and negotiates a data channel for each connection.

VPNs (Virtual Private Networks)

7	APPLICATION
6	PRESENTATION
5	SESSION
4	TRANSPORT
3	NETWORK
2	DATA LINK
1	PHYSICAL

A VPN is a network connection encrypted from end to end that creates a private connection to a remote network. A VPN is sometimes referred to as a tunnel. For example, a national insurance provider uses VPNs to securely connect its agent offices across the country with its databases at the national headquarters. By relying on the public transmission networks already in place, VPNs avoid the expense of having to lease private point-to-point connections between each office and the national headquarters. Based on the kinds of endpoints they connect, VPNs can be loosely classified according to three models:

- *site-to-site VPN*—Tunnels connect multiple sites on a WAN, as shown in Figure 7-24. At each site, a VPN gateway on the edge of the LAN establishes the secure connection. Each gateway is a router or remote access server with VPN software installed and encrypts and encapsulates data to exchange over the tunnel. Meanwhile, clients, servers, and other hosts on the protected LANs communicate through the VPN gateways as if they were all on the same, private network and do not themselves need to run special VPN software. Site-to-site VPNs require that each location have a static public IP address.

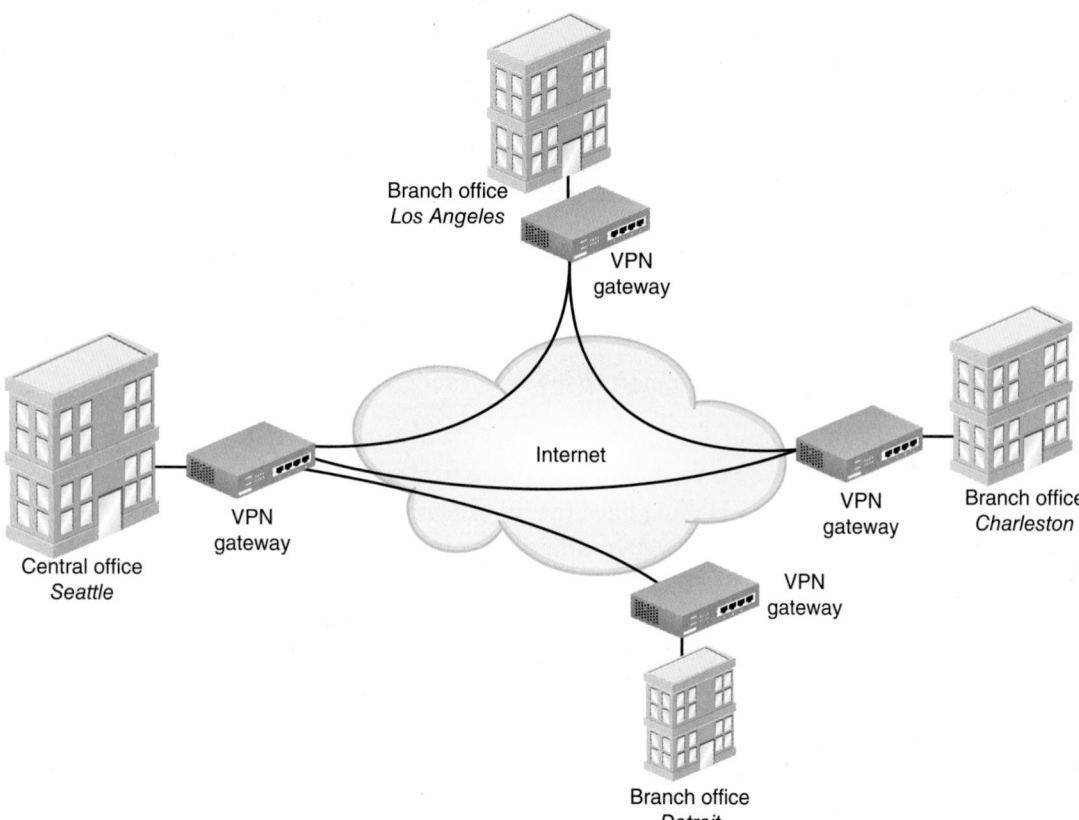

Figure 7-24   A VPN gateway connects each site to one or more other sites

- *client-to-site VPN*, *also called host-to-site VPN or remote-access VPN*—Remote clients, servers, and other hosts establish tunnels with a private network through a VPN gateway at the edge of the LAN, as shown in Figure 7-25. Each remote client on a client-to-site VPN must run VPN software to connect to the VPN gateway. The tunnel created between them encrypts and encapsulates data. This is the type of VPN typically associated with remote access. As with site-to-site VPNs, clients and hosts on the protected LAN communicate with remote clients by way of the VPN gateway and are not required to run VPN software. To establish a client-to-site VPN, only the VPN gateway location needs a static public IP address.

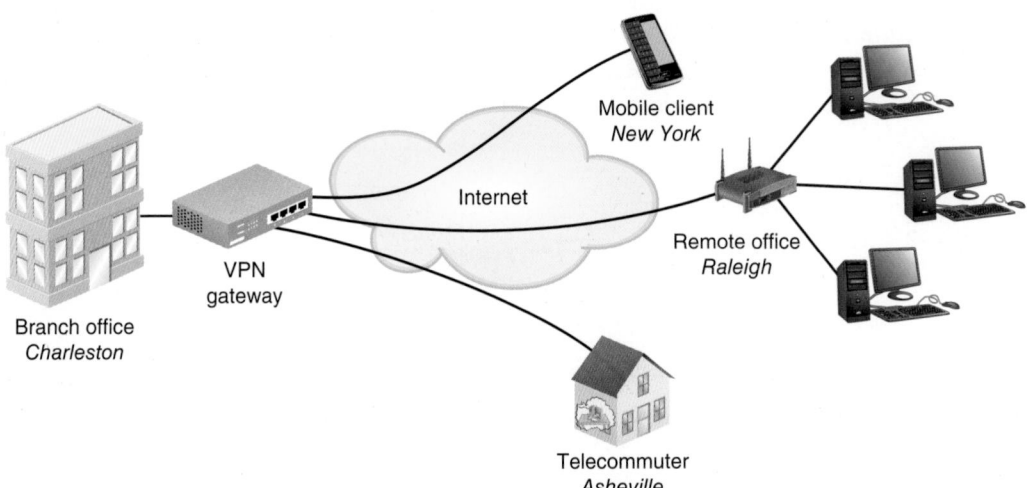

Figure 7-25 Remote clients connect to the LAN through the VPN gateway

- *host-to-host VPN*—Two computers create a VPN tunnel directly between them. Both computers must have the appropriate software installed, and they don't serve as a gateway to other hosts on their respective networks. In a host-to-host VPN, usually the site that receives the VPN connection (such as a home network) needs a static public IP address. Another option, however, is to subscribe to a service such as Dynamic DNS by Oracle (*dyn.com/dns*), which automatically tracks dynamic IP address information for subscriber locations.

The beauty of VPNs is that they can be tailored to a customer's distance, user, and bandwidth needs, so, of course, every configuration is unique. However, all share the characteristics of privacy achieved over public transmission facilities using encapsulation and, usually, encryption.

The software or hardware required to establish VPNs is typically inexpensive, and in some cases, is included in the OS or a networking device's hardware. Many routers and firewalls have embedded VPN solutions. A router-based VPN is the most common implementation of VPNs on UNIX-based networks, as opposed to the server-based VPNs that Windows networks often use. Third-party solutions also work with Windows, UNIX, Linux, and macOS Server network operating systems.

For large organizations where more than a few simultaneous VPN connections must be maintained, a specialized device known as a **VPN concentrator** can be used as the VPN server (see Figure 7-26). A VPN concentrator performs the following tasks:

- Authenticates VPN clients
- Establishes tunnels for VPN connections
- Manages encryption for VPN transmissions

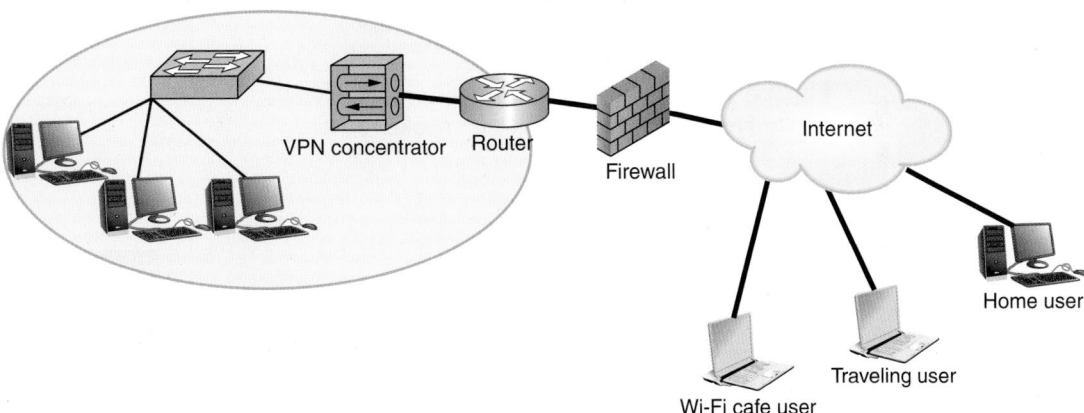

Figure 7-26 Placement of a VPN concentrator on a LAN

The two primary encryption techniques used by VPNs today are IPsec and SSL, which you learned about earlier in this chapter. Most VPN concentrators support either standard.

An enterprise-wide VPN can include elements of both the client-to-site and site-to-site models. A particular type of enterprise VPN using Cisco devices, called **DMVPN (Dynamic Multipoint VPN)**, dynamically creates VPN tunnels between branch locations as needed rather than requiring constant, static tunnels for site-to-site connections. In this configuration, as shown in Figure 7-27, a hub router sits at the headquarters location, and each remote office has a spoke router. Usually, when hosting enterprise VPN connections, the involved gateways all need static IP addresses from the ISP. With DMVPN, however, only the hub router needs a static public IP address. The spoke routers can communicate with the hub router to create VPN tunnels as needed, even from a spoke router to a spoke router.

A DMVPN configuration is achieved through creative adaptation and use of VPN tunneling protocols, discussed next.

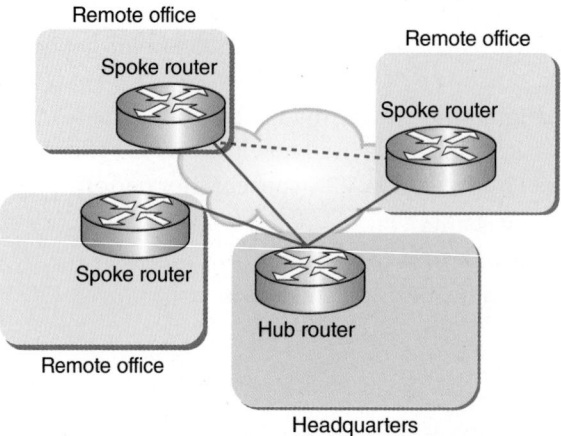

Figure 7-27 VPN tunnels are automatically created as needed, even between spoke routers

VPN Tunneling Protocols

To ensure a VPN can carry all types of data in a private manner over any kind of connection, special VPN protocols encapsulate higher-layer protocols in a process known as tunneling. Recall that IPv6 hosts can tunnel through an IPv4 network and vice versa. The same process is used by VPN protocols to create a virtual connection, or tunnel, between two VPN endpoints.

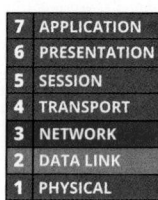

To understand how a VPN tunnel works, imagine a truck being transported across a river on a ferry. The truck is carefully loaded, tethered, and covered, and then it's carried across the water to its destination. At its destination, the cover and tethers are removed and the cargo is unloaded. The truck can then drive on down the road as it was originally designed to function. Similarly, with VPN tunneling protocols, complete frames are encrypted, encapsulated, and transported inside normal IP packets and Data Link layer frames. In other words, a frame travels across the network as the payload inside another frame. Once the frame is released on the other side of the tunnel, it acts as it would have on the network where it originated, allowing the user to access network resources as if she were locally logged onto the network.

Many VPN tunneling protocols operate at the Data Link layer to encapsulate the VPN frame inside a Network layer packet. Some VPN tunneling protocols work instead at Layer 3, which enables additional features and options, especially for site-to-site VPN traffic. Most tunneling protocols rely on an additional encryption protocol to provide data security. Figure 7-28 shows a PPP frame encapsulated in a VPN frame that is encrypted by IPsec.

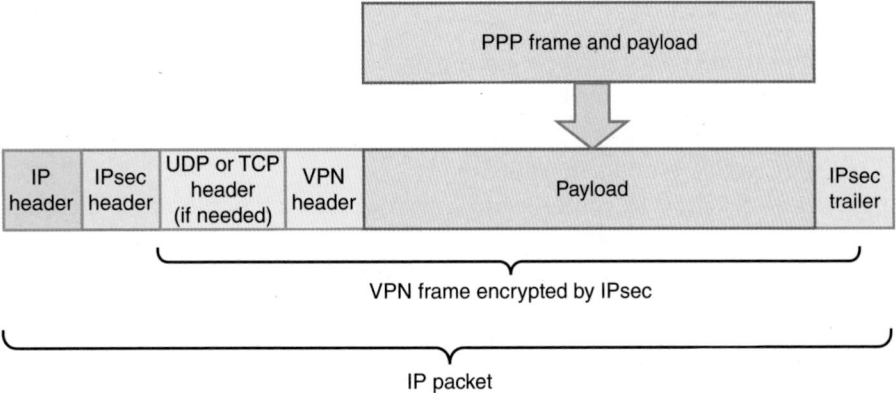

Figure 7-28   The VPN frame, such as GRE or L2TP, is encapsulated inside the Network layer packet

Some common VPN tunneling protocols are described in the following list:

- **PPTP (Point-to-Point Tunneling Protocol)** is an older, Layer 2 protocol developed by Microsoft that encapsulates VPN data frames. It uses TCP segments at the Transport layer. PPTP supports the encryption, authentication, and access services provided by the VPN server; however, PPTP itself is outdated and is no longer considered secure.

- **L2TP (Layer 2 Tunneling Protocol)** is a VPN tunneling protocol based on technology developed by Cisco and standardized by the IETF. L2TP encapsulates PPP data in a similar manner to PPTP, but differs in a few key ways. Unlike PPTP, L2TP is a standard accepted and used by multiple vendors, so it can connect a VPN that uses a mix of equipment types—for example, a Juniper router, a Cisco router, and a NETGEAR router. Also, L2TP can connect two routers, a router and a remote access server, or a client and a remote access server. Typically, L2TP is implemented with IPsec for security, and this L2TP/IPsec combination is considered secure and acceptable for most situations.

- **GRE (Generic Routing Encapsulation)**, developed by Cisco, is a Layer 3 protocol used to transmit PPP, IP, and other kinds of messages through a tunnel. Like L2TP, GRE is used in conjunction with IPsec to increase the security of the transmissions.

- **OpenVPN** is an open-source VPN protocol that uses a custom security protocol called OpenSSL for encryption. OpenVPN has the ability to cross many firewalls where IPsec might be blocked. It is both highly secure and highly configurable.

- **IKEv2**, which as you learned earlier is a component of the IPsec protocol suite, offers fast throughput and good stability when moving between wireless hotspots. It's compatible with a wide variety of devices and is often recommended by VPN providers as the most secure option among the VPN protocols they support.

Remote Access Policies

A good remote access policy protects a company's data, network, and liability, no matter what type of remote access is involved. Here are some common requirements:

- Devices used for remote access must be kept up to date with patches, anti-malware software, and a firewall.
- Device access must be controlled by a strong password or biometric measures, such as fingerprint, retina, or face recognition. The device should lock down automatically after only a few minutes of inactivity.
- Passwords must be strong and must be changed periodically. Password best practices are discussed further in later chapters.
- Passwords cannot be shared, even with a family member.
- The device's internal and external storage devices must be encrypted. Note that some countries require that encrypted storage devices be decrypted or that encryption keys be filed with authorities. Employees who travel abroad should account for this when deciding what data to transport.
- Company and customer data that is accessed, transferred, stored, or printed must be kept secure.
- The loss or theft of any devices used for remote access or to process remotely accessed data (such as a printer) must be reported to the company immediately (or within a reasonable time frame, such as 72 hours).
- Encrypted VPN software must be used to remotely access company network resources. Typically, these options are clearly defined in the policy.
- While remotely connected to the company network, the device must not be connected to the open Internet or any other network not fully owned and controlled by the employee. This restriction is usually built into enterprise VPN solutions.
- Remote sessions must be terminated when not in use. In most cases, remote sessions should be configured to time out automatically as a precaution.

Chapter Summary

Virtualization

- Virtualization is a virtual, or logical, version of something rather than the actual, or physical, version. A hypervisor is software that creates and manages a VM, and manages resource allocation and sharing between a host and any of its guest VMs.

- VMs can go through a virtual switch on the host computer to reach the physical network and can communicate with physical or virtual routers, other network devices, and other hosts on the local or another network. The way a vNIC is configured determines whether the VM is joined to a virtual network or attempts

- to join the physical LAN that the host machine is connected to.

- Although a bridged vNIC communicates through the host's adapter, it obtains its own IP address, default gateway, and subnet mask from a DHCP server on the physical LAN.

- In NAT mode, a vNIC relies on the host machine to act as a NAT device. In other words, the VM obtains IP addressing information from its host, rather than a server or router on the physical network.

- In host-only mode, VMs on one host can exchange data with each other and with their host, but they cannot communicate with any nodes beyond the host.

- Although virtualization reduces the number of physical machines, it increases complexity and administrative burden in other ways.

- NFV (Network Functions Virtualization) provides flexible, cost-saving options for many types of network devices, including virtual servers, data storage, load balancers, and firewalls.

- SDN (software-defined networking) is a centralized approach to networking that removes most of the decision-making power from network devices. That responsibility is instead handled at a software level with a product called an SDN controller.

Cloud Computing

- Cloud computing covers a broad range of services from hosting websites and database servers to providing virtual servers for collaboration or software development.

- Cloud computing service models are categorized by the types of services they provide. NIST (National Institute of Standards and Technology) has developed a standard definition for each category, which varies by the division of labor implemented. Three common cloud computing service models, IaaS, PaaS, and SaaS, incrementally increase the amount of management responsibilities outsourced to cloud computing vendors.

- Cloud services are delivered in a variety of deployment models, depending on who manages the cloud and who has access to it. The main deployment models you are likely to encounter are public cloud, private cloud, community cloud, and hybrid cloud.

- One way to reduce the inherent risks of cloud computing is to use encryption. Another way is to carefully choose the method by which your network connects to your cloud resources.

Encryption Protocols

- Data exists generally in three states: in motion, in use, and at rest. Encryption is the last means of defense against data theft.

- The most popular kind of encryption encodes the original data's bits using a key, or a random string of characters— sometimes several times in different sequences—to scramble the data and from it, generate a unique and consistently sized data block called ciphertext. The key is created according to a specific set of rules, or algorithms.

- IPsec (Internet Protocol Security) is an encryption protocol suite that defines a set of rules for encryption, authentication, and key management for TCP/IP transmissions. It works at the Network layer of the OSI model—it adds security information to the headers of all IP packets and encrypts the data payload.

- SSL (Secure Sockets Layer) and TLS (Transport Layer Security) are both methods of encrypting TCP/IP transmissions—including web pages and data entered into web forms—en route between the client and server using public key encryption technology.

Remote Access

- As a remote user, you can connect to a network and its resources via remote access, which is a service that allows a client to connect with and log on to a server, LAN, or WAN in a different geographical location. After connecting, a remote client can access files, applications, and other shared resources, such as printers, like any other client on the server, LAN, or WAN.
- PPP (Point-to-Point Protocol) is a Data Link layer protocol that directly connects two WAN endpoints.
- Terminal emulation, also called remote virtual computing, allows a user on one computer, called the client, to control another computer, called the host or server, across a network connection.
- The Telnet protocol is a terminal emulation utility used by Telnet client/server applications that allow an administrator or other user to control a computer remotely.

- SSH (Secure Shell) is a collection of protocols that does both authentication and encryption.
- RDP (Remote Desktop Protocol) is a Microsoft proprietary protocol used by Windows Remote Desktop and Remote Assistance client/server utilities to connect to and control a remote computer. Similarly, VNC (Virtual Network Computing) uses the cross-platform protocol RFB (remote frame buffer) to remotely control a workstation or server.
- Increasingly, networking devices are configured through a connected computer's browser that navigates to a management URL, where the user can make changes directly to the device.
- Out-of-band management relies on a dedicated connection with each critical network device, such as routers, firewalls, servers, power supplies, applications, and security cameras.
- Three remote file access technologies related to FTP include FTPS, SFTP, and TFTP.
- A VPN is a network connection encrypted from end to end that creates a private connection to a remote network.
- To ensure a VPN can carry all types of data in a private manner over any kind of connection, special VPN protocols encapsulate higher-layer protocols in a process known as tunneling.
- Regardless of the type of remote access made available to employees, a good remote access policy further protects a company's data, network, and liability.

Key Terms

For definitions of key terms, see the Glossary near the end of the book.

AH (authentication header)
asymmetric encryption
bridged mode
CA (certificate authority)
CIA (confidentiality, integrity, and availability) triad
client_hello
client-to-site VPN
cloud computing
colocation facility
community cloud
console router
console server
control plane
data plane
digital certificate
DMVPN (Dynamic Multipoint VPN)
DNS spoofing
DTLS (Datagram Transport Layer Security)
ESP (Encapsulating Security Payload)
FTPS (FTP Security or FTP Secure)
GRE (Generic Routing Encapsulation)
guest
handshake protocol
host
host-only mode

HVD (hosted virtual desktop)
hybrid cloud
hypervisor
IaaS (Infrastructure as a Service)
IKE (Internet Key Exchange)
IKEv2
in-band management
IPsec (Internet Protocol Security)
ISAKMP (Internet Security Association and Key Management Protocol)
key
key management
L2TP (Layer 2 Tunneling Protocol)
management URL
NAT mode
NFV (Network Functions Virtualization)
OpenVPN
out-of-band management
PaaS (Platform as a Service)
PKI (Public-key Infrastructure)
platform
PoP (Point of Presence)
port forwarding
PPP (Point-to-Point Protocol)

PPPoE (PPP over Ethernet)
PPTP (Point-to-Point Tunneling Protocol)
private cloud
private key encryption
public cloud
public key encryption
RAS (remote access server)
remote access
SaaS (Software as a Service)
SDN (software-defined networking)
SDN controller
server_hello
site-to-site VPN
subscription model
symmetric encryption
Type 1 hypervisor
Type 2 hypervisor
virtual firewall
virtual router
virtualization
VNC (Virtual Network Computing)
vNIC (virtual NIC)
VPN (virtual private network)
VPN concentrator
vSwitch (virtual switch)
XaaS (Anything as a Service or Everything as a Service)

Review Questions

1. What software allows you to define VMs and manage resource allocation and sharing among them on a host computer?
   a. Hypervisor
   b. NFV (Network Functions Virtualization)
   c. SDN (software-defined networking)
   d. Terminal emulation

2. What virtual, logically defined device operates at the Data Link layer to pass frames between nodes?
   a. Virtual firewall
   b. Virtual switch
   c. Virtual router
   d. Virtual load balancer

3. With which network connection type does the VM obtain IP addressing information from its host?
   a. Bridged mode
   b. Managed mode
   c. NAT mode
   d. Host-only mode

4. Which cloud computing services model gives software developers access to multiple operating systems for testing?
   a. IaaS
   b. PaaS
   c. SaaS
   d. XaaS

5. What service in Windows Server 2016 authenticates remote users and computers to the Windows domain and its corporate network resources?
   a. Active Directory
   b. Group Policy
   c. DirectAccess
   d. RAS (Remote Access Service)

6. Which remote access protocol is used over an Ethernet network?
   a. PPPoE
   b. RAS

   c. PPP
   d. SLIP

7. Which encryption protocol does GRE use to increase the security of its transmissions?
   a. SSL
   b. SFTP
   c. IPsec
   d. SSH

8. Which tunneling protocol is a component of the IPsec protocol suite?
   a. L2TP
   b. OpenVPN
   c. PPTP
   d. IKEv2

9. Which encryption benchmark ensures data is not modified after it's transmitted and before it's received?
   a. Confidentiality
   b. Integrity
   c. Availability
   d. Symmetric

10. Which remote file access protocol is an extension of SSH?
    a. SFTP
    b. TFTP
    c. FTPS
    d. HTTPS

11. List two advantages to using virtualization on a network.

12. How does a vNIC get a MAC address?

13. Which Transport layer protocol does PPTP use?

14. Which secured tunneling protocol might be able to cross firewalls where IPsec is blocked?

15. Which type of hypervisor is installed on bare metal?

16. When surfing online, you get some strange data on an apparently secure website, and you realize you need to

check the legitimacy of the site. What kind of organization issues digital certificates for websites?

17. Which current protocol is used to create secure transmissions for HTTP browsing sessions?

18. What kind of device can be used to configure and manage physical and virtual networking devices across the network?

19. Which terminal emulation protocol is similar to RDP but is open source?

20. Which port must be open for RDP traffic to cross a firewall?

Hands-On Projects

Project 7-1: Use Remote Desktop

The host or server computer is the computer that serves up Remote Desktop to client computers. To prepare your host computer, you need to configure the computer for static IP addressing and also configure the Remote Desktop service. The following steps are specific to a Windows 10 (Professional or Enterprise) machine, but can be adapted to Windows 8.1:

1. Configure the host computer for static IP addressing. As a reminder, you learned how to do this as part of Hands-On Project 4-1. To determine what IP address to use, open a Command Prompt window and enter `ipconfig`. Use the current IP address for the static IP address.

Note 📎

Alternately, instead of configuring static IP addressing, you can find and write down the computer's name. To do this, open the Settings app, click System, and click About.

2. To turn on the Remote Desktop service on the host computer, open the **Settings** window and in the left pane, click **About**. Scroll down to Related settings, and click **System info**. In the left pane of the System window, click **Remote settings**. The System Properties dialog box appears with the Remote tab selected. In the Remote Desktop area, check **Allow remote connections to this computer**.

3. Users who have administrative privileges are allowed to use Remote Desktop by default, but other users need to be added. If you need to add a user, click **Select Users** and follow the directions on-screen. Then close all windows.

4. Verify that Windows Firewall is set to allow Remote Desktop activity to this computer. To do this, open the **Network and Sharing Center** and click **Windows Firewall**. In the left pane, click **Allow an app or feature through Windows Firewall**.

5. The Allowed apps window appears. Scroll down to Remote Desktop and adjust the settings as needed to match the settings in Figure 7-29. Click **OK** to apply any changes. You will learn more about Windows Firewall later.

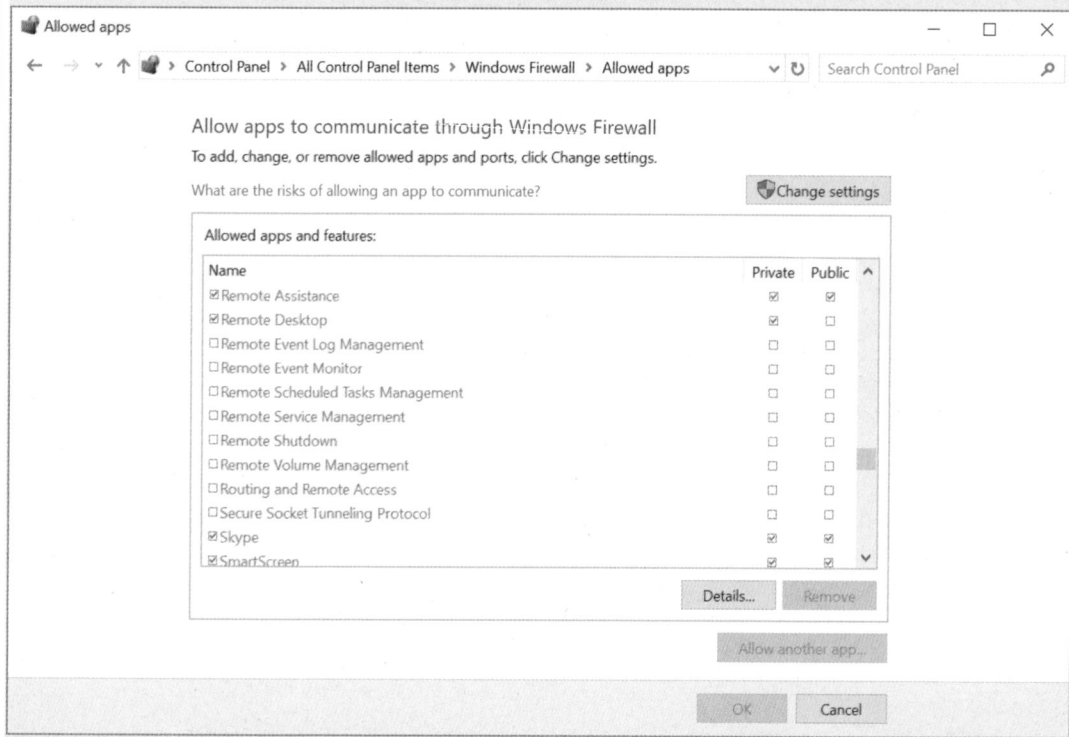

Figure 7-29 **Allow Remote Desktop communication through Windows Firewall on the host computer**

You are now ready to test Remote Desktop by attempting to access another computer somewhere on your local network. First, let's verify you have Remote Desktop working on your local network. Note that any version of Windows 7, 8.1, or 10 can serve as a client computer (the computer viewing the host computer's desktop) for a Remote Desktop connection. The following steps are written specifically for Windows 10.

Follow these steps to use Remote Desktop on the client computer:

6. Press **Win+R**, type **mstsc** in the search box, and press **Enter**. This is easier to remember if you know that Remote Desktop Services used to be called Microsoft Terminal Services; mstsc (Microsoft Terminal Services Client) is the client portion. Alternately, you can click **Start**, scroll down and click **Windows Accessories**, and then click **Remote Desktop Connection**.

7. Enter the IP address or the host name of the computer to which you want to connect. If you decide to use a host name, begin the host name with two backslashes, as in \\CompanyFileServer.

8. If you plan to transfer files from one computer to the other, click **Show Options** and then click the **Local Resources** tab, as shown in the left side of Figure 7-30. Under *Local devices and resources*, click **More**. The box on the right side of Figure 7-30 appears.

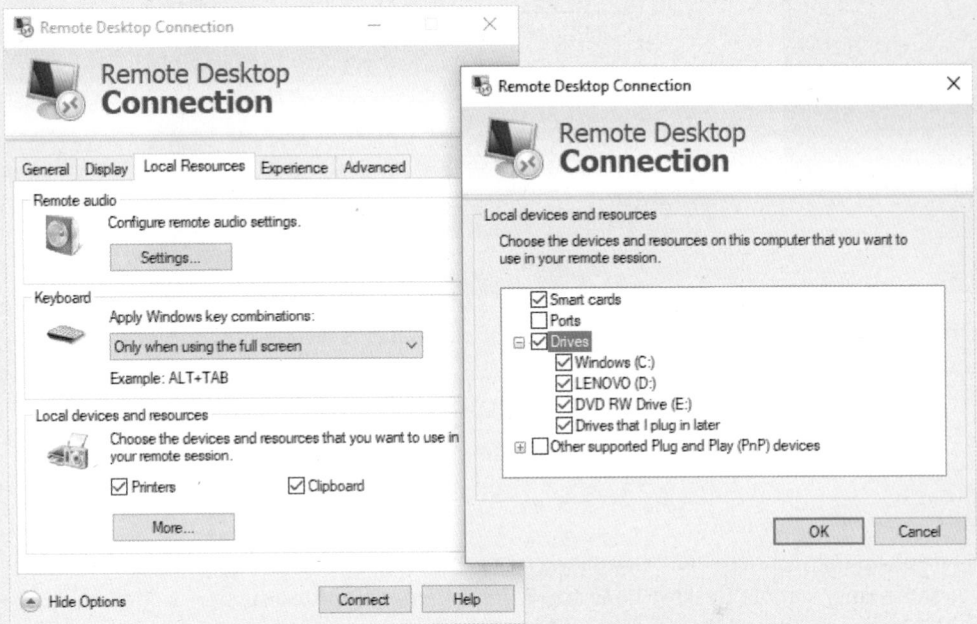

Figure 7-30   Allow drives to be shared using the Remote Desktop Connection

9. Check **Drives**, click **OK**, and then click **Connect** to make the connection. If a warning box appears, click **Connect** again.

10. Log on using a username and password for the remote computer. If a warning box appears saying the identity of the remote computer cannot be verified, click **Yes** to continue with the connection.

11. The desktop of the remote computer appears in a window, as shown in Figure 7-31. When you click this window, you can work with the remote computer just as if you were sitting in front of it, except the response time will be slower. To move files back and forth between computers, use File Explorer on the remote computer. Files on your local computer and on the remote computer will appear in File Explorer on the remote computer's screen in the This PC group. For example, in Figure 7-31, you can see drive C: on each computer labeled in the figure. To close the connection to the remote computer, log off the remote computer or close the Remote Desktop Connection window.

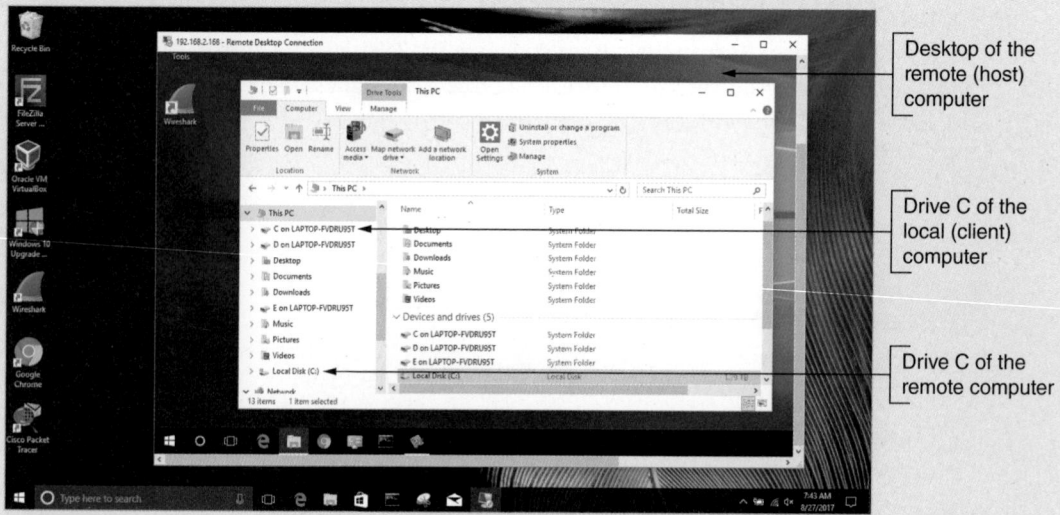

Figure 7-31   The desktop of the remote, host computer is visible on your local, client computer

Note 📎

Even though Windows normally allows more than one user to be logged on at the same time, Remote Desktop does not. When a Remote Desktop session is opened, all local users on the host computer are logged off.

Project 7-2: Use Remote Desktop Manager

In the previous project, you created a Remote Desktop connection between two computers. In the real world, you might need to manage several remote connections of several types, such as RDP, FTP, TeamViewer, VNC, VPN, and so on. RDM (Remote Desktop Manager) by Devolutions, Inc., can corral all these remote connections into a single interface.

In this project, you use the same two computers you used for Project 7-1. Complete the following steps to set up Remote Desktop Manager on the computer that will manage the connections, called the client computer for the purposes of this project:

1. On the client computer, navigate to the Devolutions, Inc., website at **remotedesktopmanager.com** and click the **Download** link. Download and install the Free Edition of Remote Desktop Manager. During installation, use the **Typical** setup type and accept all other default settings. (You can adjust the Shortcuts options if you'd like.) Also complete installation of Visual C++ if required. When installation is complete, launch the application.

2. Create a free online account to register for Remote Desktop Manager Online (also free). Record your account information in your LastPass vault. Activate your account when you receive the confirmation email, then complete registration for the software you just downloaded, and log on. Alternately, you can choose to register later and complete the registration process within 30 days.

RDM can manage many different types of remote sessions, including Citrix, FTP, Spiceworks, TeamViewer, VPN, Telnet, SSH, and many others. For this project, you'll use Remote Desktop to create a session with the same host computer you used in Project 7-1. Complete the following steps to create the RDP connection through RDM:

3. Make sure the host computer is turned on.

4. On the client computer, in the RDM center pane, click the **Dashboard** tab and then click **Add Session**. Click **Microsoft Remote Desktop (RDP)** then click **OK**. Name the session **RDP to lab computer** or something similar that makes sense to you. Enter the name of the computer, and enter a valid username and password. Click **OK**.

5. Click **Open Session**. As you can see, RDM allowed you to create the Remote Desktop connection through the application's interface instead of needing to open Remote Desktop on the client computer. This might seem insignificant until you consider how this single interface can provide some consistency when working with multiple kinds of remote connections to multiple host and client devices.

6. Click **Close Session** to disconnect the computers.

7. In RDM on the client computer, click the **New Entry** plus-sign icon at the top of the screen. Choose a different type of remote connection to create between the two computers, or create a new connection with a different computer. Build that entry and create that connection as well. You might need to download and install some software (such as TeamViewer) or make some configuration changes, depending upon which option you choose.

8. Make notes on your Wikidot website about the Remote Desktop Manager application installed in this project. Be sure to include information about which computer(s) you've configured connections for in RDM.

Note

TeamViewer is an easy and free app to work with for creating remote connections. You've also learned how to create FileZilla and FTP connections. Alternatively, your instructor might want you to use a different program, such as Telnet or SSH.

Project 7-3: Explore VM Network Configuration Options in Oracle VirtualBox

Earlier in this book, you had the opportunity to create at least one VM using Oracle VirtualBox. The instructions for this project are specific to VirtualBox, although they can be adapted to Hyper-V or VMware. The instructions also assume you have Windows 10 installed on the VM, although again, the steps could be adapted to another OS.

In this project, you will explore the network settings for the VM, practice communicating between the VM and the host machine, and practice communicating between the VM and a host on the Internet. The host computer, which is the physical computer, should be connected to the Internet. Complete the following steps:

1. Open **VirtualBox** and start the **Windows 10 VM**.
2. Open a Command Prompt window and enter `ipconfig` to determine the VM's IPv4 address, subnet mask, and default gateway. Write down this information.
3. Check the VM's connection to the Internet by pinging one of Google's DNS servers with the command `ping 8.8.8.8`. Was the ping successful?
4. Open the Command Prompt window on the host computer, the physical PC hosting the VirtualBox VM. Enter `ipconfig` to determine the host machine's IPv4 address, subnet mask, and default gateway. Write down this information.
5. How does the host computer's address information compare with the VM's information? Both computers should have a default subnet mask of 255.255.255.0, which means both computers have a Class C IPv4 address. Look at the first three octets of each computer's IPv4 address. Do they match? If so, they're on the same subnet. If not, the computers are on different subnets. Are these two computers on the same subnet?
6. Return to the Oracle VM VirtualBox Manager window. Right-click the VM in the left pane and click **Settings**.
7. In the Settings window, click **Network** in the left pane and then make sure the **Adapter 1** tab is selected, as shown in Figure 7-32. Notice in this figure that the adapter is configured to use NAT.

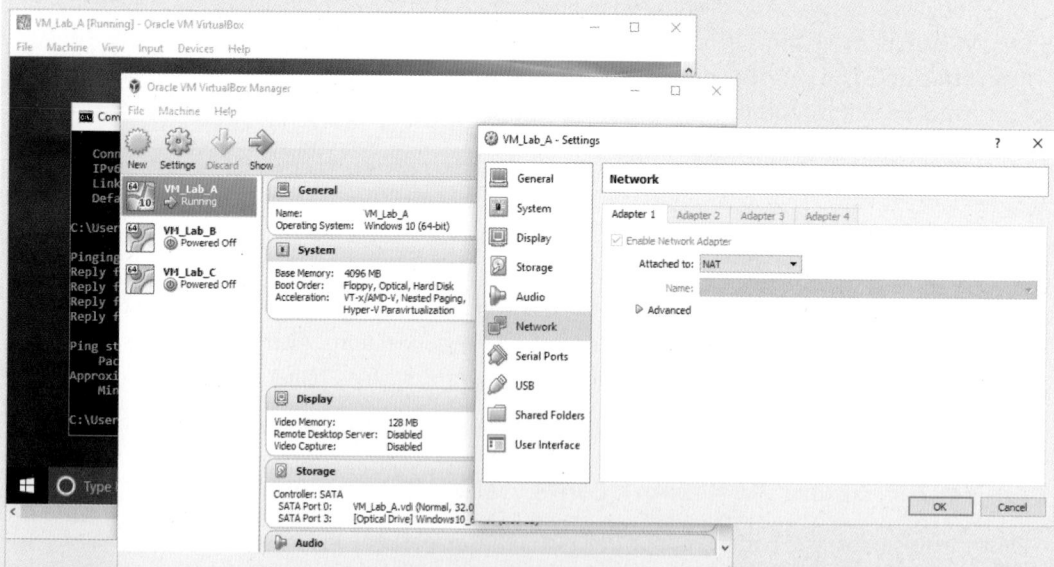

Figure 7-32   The NAT option is selected here

Source: VMware, Inc.

8. Click the **Attached to** down arrow, click **Bridged Adapter**, and then click **OK**.

9. Return to the VM's window. You see a message indicating that the VM has detected a network change, and is requesting permission to find PCs and other devices and content on the network. Click **Yes**.

10. Repeat the `ipconfig` command. What are the IPv4 address, subnet mask, and default gateway now? How does this information compare with the host PC's information? Are the two computers on the same subnet now?

11. On the VM, ping Google's DNS server again. Was the ping successful?

12. On the Oracle VM VirtualBox Manager window, return to the **VM's Settings**, **Network** menu, click the **Attached to** down arrow, click **Internal Network**, and then click **OK**.

13. On the VM, repeat `ipconfig` and `ping` Google's DNS server again. What changed?

14. Change the VM's *Attached to* setting to **NAT** and click **OK**. On the VM, repeat `ipconfig` and `ping` Google's DNS server again. What changed?

15. Close all windows on the VM, shut down the VM, and close all windows on the host machine.

Project 7-4: Create a VPN Connection

For this project, you will download and install a free VPN client app, and use the app to surf online. Complete the following steps:

1. In your browser, go to **hide.me** and click **Pricing**. Register for the free tier of service. When you receive the invitation email, activate your account. Be sure to record your account information in your LastPass vault.

2. In your account dashboard, download the VPN client to your computer and install it.

3. After installation, sign in to the app using the hide.me account that you created in Step 1. Once you've signed in, click **Settings** at the bottom of the hide.me VPN dialog box. Then answer the following questions, checking each of the tabs for relevant information:

   a. What is a Kill Switch?

   b. Which setting disables local network connectivity during the VPN connection?

   c. What is the default MTU size?

   d. Which VPN protocol does hide.me use by default?

4. Close the Settings dialog box. In the hide.me VPN dialog box (see Figure 7-33), what is your current IP address?

5. Click **Connect**. It might take several minutes to complete the connection. Once you are connected, what is your new IP address?

   If you get an error message, or if the app gets stuck for more than 10 minutes, complete the following steps to create a new rule in Windows Firewall that will allow hide.me to create a VPN connection.

   a. Press **Win+R** and enter **WF.msc**. The Windows Firewall with Advanced Security window opens.

   b. In the left pane, click **Inbound Rules**. In the right pane, click **New Rule**.

   c. Make sure **Program** is selected, then click **Next**.

   d. Select **This program path**, and then click **Browse**. Navigate to the location of the installed hide.me app. If you're not sure where the app is installed, use Cortana to

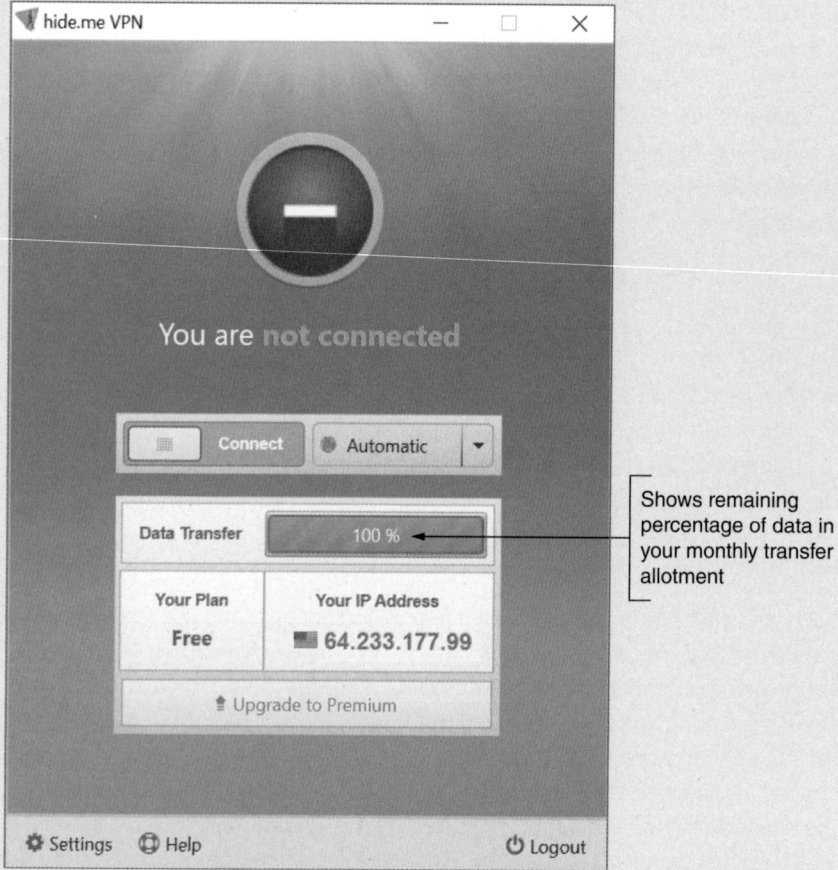

Figure 7-33   The hide.me VPN client application
Source: eVenture Ltd.

search for **hide.me VPN**, right-click the app in the search results, and click **Open file location**. Use this file path to locate the hide.me app in the New Inbound Rule Wizard window. By default, our app was installed at the following location:

This PC > Local Disk (C:) > ProgramData > Microsoft > Windows > Start Menu > Programs > hide.me VPN

e. Once you've located the hide.me app, select it and click **Open**. Then click **Next**.

f. Select **Allow the connection if it is secure**, and then click **Next** three times.

g. Deselect **Domain** and **Public** so only **Private** is selected. Click **Next**.

h. Name the rule **hide.me VPN**. Click **Finish**. The new rule is listed at the top of the Inbound Rules pane. Close the Windows Firewall with Advanced Security window and try again to create a VPN connection through the **hide.me** VPN app.

6. Open a browser and navigate to a couple of websites. When you're finished, what is the new remaining Data Transfer level?

7. Click **Logout**. Make notes on your Wikidot website about this new app installation.

Capstone Projects

Capstone Project 7-1: Use SSH in Ubuntu

In this project, you will learn to use SSH in Ubuntu. Using the Ubuntu VMs you created in Capstone Projects 2-1 and 4-1, follow these steps to create a SSH connection.

On the VM that has Ubuntu Server installed, do the following:

1. Start the VM and log on. Refer to your LastPass vault if you don't remember your logon information.
2. SSH is included in Ubuntu Server but is not installed. Enter this command to install and start SSH: `sudo apt-get install ssh`
3. Enter the command `ifconfig` and write down the IP address of the Ubuntu Server VM.

On the VM that has Ubuntu Desktop installed, do the following:

4. Start the VM and log on. Refer to your LastPass vault if you don't remember your logon information.
5. Open a shell prompt, and enter the command `ifconfig`. Note the IP address of the Ubuntu Desktop VM.
6. Enter the `ssh` command with the IP address of the Ubuntu Server VM. For example, if the server IP address is 192.168.1.147, enter this command:

   `ssh 192.168.1.147`

   If your username on the Ubuntu Server machine is not the same as your username on the Ubuntu Desktop machine, you'll need to add a bit more information to this command in order to remote into the server. Try this command instead:

   `ssh server_username@server_ipaddress`

   For example, if the server IP address is 192.168.1.147 and the server username is jillwest, enter this command:

   `ssh jillwest@192.168.1.147`

7. Enter your password on the server to log on to the server using SSH. You now have a SSH session established between the Ubuntu Desktop VM and the Ubuntu Server VM.
8. Enter the `dir` command. What directory is the server's current default directory?
9. Enter the `ifconfig` command. Which IP address is displayed in the command output: the Ubuntu Desktop VM's address or the Ubuntu Server VM's address?
10. When you're finished using the SSH session, break the session using the `exit` command.
11. To shut down each VM, enter the `sudo poweroff` command in each VM.
12. Add some notes to your Wikidot website about the SSH installation on the Ubuntu Server VM.

Capstone Project 7-2: Build a Packet Tracer Network

In Capstone Project 6-1 in Chapter 6, you installed Packet Tracer and completed several chapters in the Introduction to Packet Tracer course. In this project, you will begin to build your own network from scratch, and you'll continue building on this network in future chapters. Look back at your notes on your Wikidot website if you need help remembering details about what you learned in the earlier project.

On the same computer that you used for Capstone Project 6-1, complete the following steps:

1. Open **Packet Tracer**.
2. Add one **Generic router** to the workspace.
3. Add two **2960 switches** to the workspace.
4. Add two **Generic workstations** to the workspace.
5. Arrange these devices in a pyramid shape, with the workstations at the bottom, the switches in the middle, and the router at the top. See Figure 7-34 to get an idea of the correct layout. Use the **Copper Straight-Through** connection to connect each of these devices as described next:

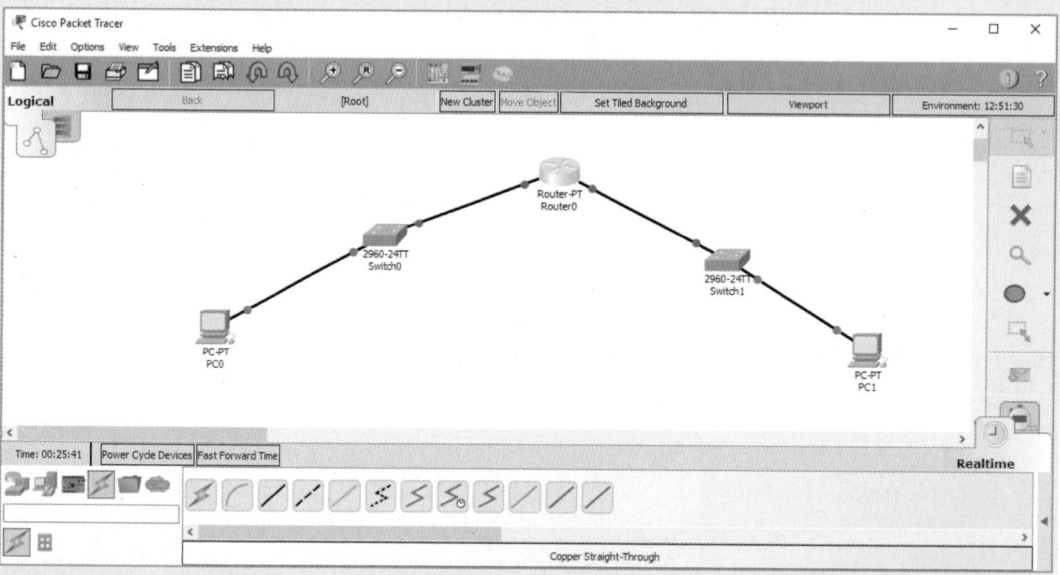

Figure 7-34   Lay out the devices in a pyramid shape
Source: Cisco Systems, Inc.

   a. On each workstation, connect the Ethernet cable to the **FastEthernet0** interface.
   b. On each switch, connect the Ethernet cable from the workstation to the **FastEthernet0/1** interface. Connect the Ethernet cable from the router to the **FastEthernet0/2** interface.
   c. On the router, connect Switch0 to the **FastEthernet0/0** interface and connect Switch1 to the **FastEthernet1/0** interface.
   d. Wait a few minutes for the workstation-to-switch connections to turn green on both ends of each connection.

The router and the switch have to be configured for the connections to come up:

6. Click the **Router0** to open the configuration window. Click the **Config** tab. As you make changes, notice the commands that show up in the Equivalent IOS Commands pane at the bottom of the window.

7. Click the **FastEthernet0/0** interface. Make the following changes to the interface's configuration:
   Port Status: **On**
   IP Address: **192.168.0.1**
   Subnet Mask: **255.255.255.0**

8. Click the **FastEthernet1/0** interface. Make the following changes to the interface's configuration:
   Port Status: **On**
   IP Address: **172.16.0.1**
   Subnet Mask: **255.255.0.0**

9. Close the **Router0** window, and wait a few minutes for the switch-to-router connections to turn green on both ends of each connection.

10. Click **PC0** to open the configuration window. Click the **Desktop** tab, and then click **IP Configuration**. Make the following changes to the workstation's configuration:
    IP Configuration: **Static**
    IP Address: **192.168.0.100**
    Subnet Mask: **255.255.255.0**
    Default Gateway: **192.168.0.1**

11. Close the IP Configuration window by clicking the small, blue **X** in the upper right corner. Then click **Command Prompt**. Enter `ipconfig` to confirm the network configuration is correct.

12. Close **Command Prompt** and close the **PC0** window.

13. Click **PC1** to open the configuration window. Click the **Desktop** tab, and then click **IP Configuration**. Make the following changes to the workstation's configuration:
    IP Configuration: **Static**
    IP Address: **172.16.0.100**
    Subnet Mask: **255.255.0.0**
    Default Gateway: **172.16.0.1**

14. Close the IP Configuration window by clicking the small, blue **X** in the upper right corner. Then click **Command Prompt**. Enter `ipconfig` to confirm the network configuration is correct.

15. Enter the command `ping 192.168.0.100`. Was the ping successful? If so, then you have successfully begun building your Packet Tracer network. If not, troubleshoot your network to determine where the problem is and fix it.

16. In the main Packet Tracer window, open the **Simulation Panel** (click **View**, **Simulation Mode**, or press **Shift+S**). In the PC1 configuration window, run the ping again. Move or minimize the PC1 configuration window so you can see the devices in the workspace. In the Simulation Panel, click **Auto Capture / Play** and see what happens. When you're ready, click a PDU message on the network to examine its details and to see an explanation of each step in the process.

17. When you've explored the PDU messages, close the **Simulation Panel**, close **Command Prompt**, and close the **PC1** window.

18. Add a **Note** to each connection that lists its IP address, subnet mask, and default gateway if relevant. Figure 7-35 shows an example for the router.

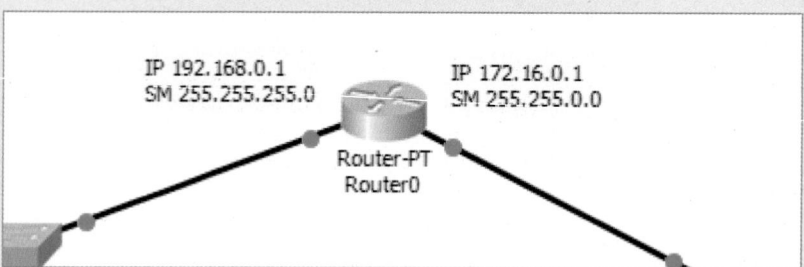

Figure 7-35   Good documentation makes troubleshooting easier later
Source: Cisco Systems, Inc.

19. Click **File**, **Save**, and save your Packet Tracer file in a safe place for future projects.

20. Add installation information to the Packet Tracer page on your Wikidot website, along with any notes that you think might be helpful to you for the next Packet Tracer project. When you're finished, close Packet Tracer.

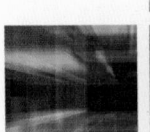

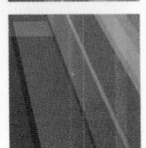

SUBNETS AND VLANs

After reading this chapter and completing the exercises, you will be able to:

Explain the purposes of network segmentation

Calculate and implement subnets

Explain how VLANs work and how they're used

I recently provided the technical expertise to build a new FM radio station in rural Wisconsin. In addition to specifying and installing microphones, speakers, and sound boards, I also designed and created the station's network. Within the station's building, the network connects studios, office computers, and a VoIP (Voice over IP) telephone system. Beyond the building, the network sends the station's broadcast signal to its antenna.

When I set up the radio station network, I decided to separate different kinds of network traffic. To do this, I chose to create VLANs, rather than creating multiple physical networks, for several reasons, not the least of which is the cost of acquiring and maintaining multiple network switches. Managing multiple subnets on a single device has simplified deployment and long-term maintenance.

The VLANs are set up as follows:

- VLAN 101 (IP address subnet 10.10.1.0/24) is the transmitter network.
- VLAN 201 (IP address subnet 10.20.1.0/24) is the studio network.
- VLAN 301 (IP address subnet 10.30.1.0/24) is the office network.
- VLAN 401 (IP address subnet 10.40.1.0/24) is the telephone network.

Using VLANs allows the station to keep general Internet traffic off the latency-sensitive studio subnet. The systems on the studio subnet include the audio automation players and the analog-to-digital audio encoders. These computers receive and send digital audio over the network and demand timely delivery of packets. Further, these computers do not need to access Internet resources. We chose to isolate these systems from the others using VLANs (and access lists) to help guarantee the timely delivery of audio data.

Meanwhile, placing our VoIP telephones on a separate VLAN prevents studio audio traffic, as well as the general office and Internet traffic, from interfering with the telephone system traffic.

David Klann
WDRT 91.9FM

Network segmentation takes the divide-and-conquer approach to network management. When done well, it increases both performance and security on a network. A network can be segmented physically by creating multiple LANs or logically through the use of VLANs (virtual LANs). Either way, the larger broadcast domain is divided into smaller segments, and the IP address space is subdivided as well.

In this chapter, you'll learn about two important concepts that enable and support network segmentation: subnets and virtual LANs (or VLANs). Fundamentally, a subnet is a group of IP addresses, and a VLAN is a group of ports on a switch. Subnets and VLANs usually work together, but you'll learn about each of them separately first.

Before we get into how subnetting works, let's step back to briefly look at why you might want to segment a network using either multiple LANs or multiple VLANs. Then we'll explore the important role that subnetting plays in network segmentation. And finally, we'll look at how VLANs work and the unique flexibility they offer.

Network Segmentation

4.6   Explain common mitigation techniques and their purposes.

When a network is segmented into multiple smaller networks, traffic on one network is separated from another network's traffic and each network is its own broadcast domain. A network administrator might separate a network's traffic into smaller portions to accomplish the following:

- *enhance security*—Transmissions in broadcast domains are limited to each network so there's less possibility of hackers or malware reaching remote, protected networks in the enterprise domain. At the same time, other devices, such as a web server, can be made more accessible to the open Internet than the rest of the network. For example, a DMZ (demilitarized zone) can provide an area of the network with less stringent security for these purposes.
- *improve performance*—Segmenting limits broadcast traffic by decreasing the size of each broadcast domain. The more efficient use of bandwidth results in

better overall network performance. The *On the Job* story at the beginning of this chapter gave an excellent example of how this applies in a real-world situation.

- *simplify troubleshooting*—When troubleshooting, rather than examining the whole network for errors or bottlenecks, the network administrator can narrow down the problem area to a particular, smaller network. For example, suppose a network is subdivided with separate smaller networks for Accounting, Human Resources, and IT. One day there's trouble transmitting data only to a certain group of users—those on the Accounting network. This fact gives the network administrator some significant insight into the nature of the problem.

Networks are commonly segmented according to one of the following groupings:

- *geographic locations*—For example, the floors of a building connected by a LAN, or the buildings connected by a WAN
- *departmental boundaries*—For example, the Accounting, Human Resources, and Sales departments
- *device types*—For example, printers, desktops, and IP phones

As we explore options for network segmentation throughout this chapter, keep in mind that there are a variety of ways to go about separating broadcast domains on a network. Each segmentation method addresses different needs, offering varying capabilities and limitations. The OSI model also plays a part in network segmentation. You can use physical devices at Layer 1 to create separate LANs. At Layer 2, you can create virtual LANs, which you'll learn more about later in this chapter. And at Layer 3, you can use subnetting to organize devices within the available IP address space, whether the LANs are defined physically or virtually. Figure 8-1 can help you visualize the relationship between these various concepts.

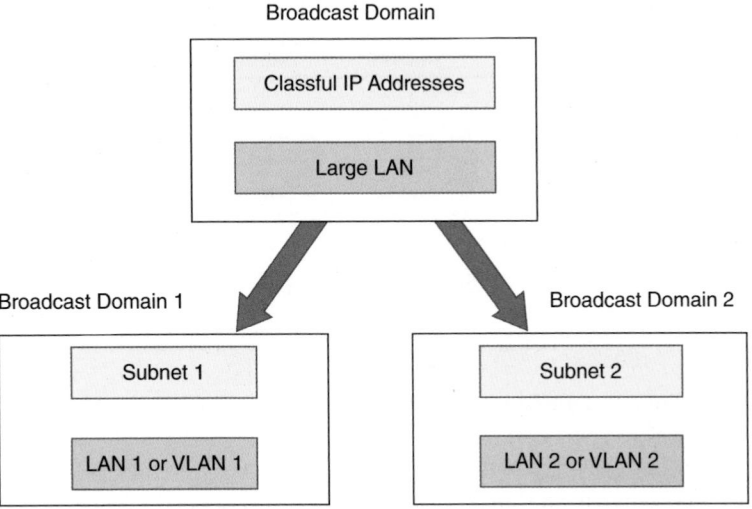

Figure 8-1 Network segmentation divides a large broadcast domain into smaller broadcast domains

Regardless of how you go about segmenting a network, you'll need to find the right balance between separating and connecting devices within each network portion. Let's begin with a discussion of how subnetting complements physical segmentation.

Subnets

Certification

7	APPLICATION
6	PRESENTATION
5	SESSION
4	TRANSPORT
3	NETWORK
2	DATA LINK
1	PHYSICAL

1.4 Given a scenario, configure the appropriate IP addressing components.

1.8 Explain the functions of network services.

Suppose a company's network has grown from 20 or 30 computers and other devices to a few hundred computers and other devices. The network began as a single LAN with computers connected by a few Layer 2 switches where one switch connected to a router, and then on to the ISP. See Figure 8-2. Because there is only a single LAN or broadcast domain, any host on the network can communicate directly with any other host, and the one router serves as the default gateway for the whole network. The entire LAN has one pool of IP addresses, for example, 192.168.89.0/24, with a subnet mask of 255.255.255.0.

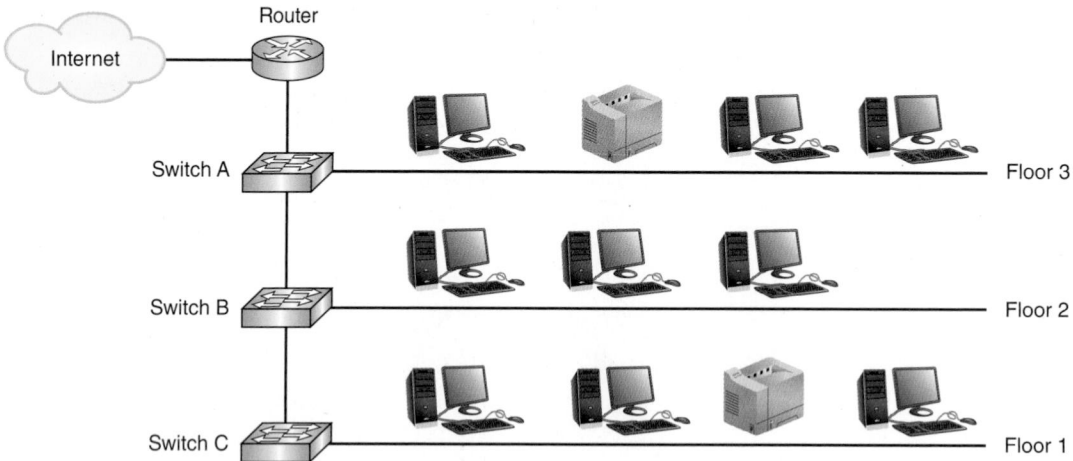

Figure 8-2 A single LAN with some switches and a router

As the network grows, you'll need to better manage network traffic by segmenting the network so that each floor contains a separate LAN, or broadcast domain. One way to accomplish this is to install a router on each floor, as illustrated in Figure 8-3. As you know, routers don't forward broadcast traffic. You can think of a router as a broadcast boundary, and fundamentally, routers are tools you can use to divide and conquer network traffic. However, you also need to manage the IP address space at a logical layer. To do this, you need to configure (either manually or through the DHCP server) the clients on each subnet so they know which devices are on their own subnet and which devices are not. And you need to configure each router to ensure that it serves as the default gateway for its LAN and forwards traffic to the other two LANs as necessary.

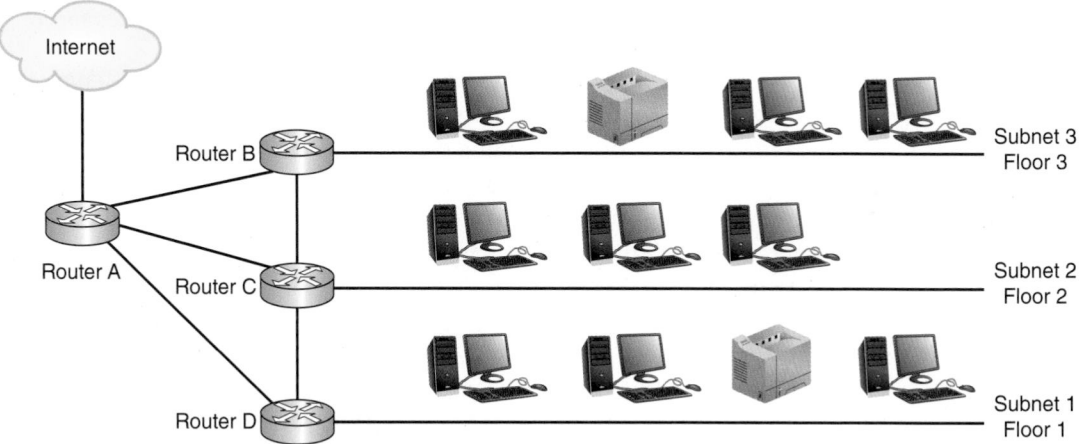

Figure 8-3   A separate subnet for each floor

At this point, you have three separate and smaller LANs, or subnets, within the larger network. However, a device on Subnet 2, for example, doesn't yet know that devices on Subnet 3 aren't still sharing the same LAN. How do you divide the pool of IP addresses so that a computer on Subnet 2 knows to send transmissions for devices on other subnets to the default gateway instead of trying to communicate with them directly? The solution is to divide your pool of IP addresses into three groups, or subnets, one for each LAN or floor of the building. This technique is called subnetting.

Subnetting helps solve the fundamental problem with classful addressing: too many host addresses assigned to each classful network, resulting in available addresses being used up too quickly. For example, a single Class B network can have up to 65,534 IP addresses and hosts all on the one LAN. Imagine the challenges involved in managing such a highly populated LAN, not to mention the poor performance that would result. Subnetting helps us manage IP address space more efficiently. Also, though it might not be obvious at this point, using well-chosen subnets provides the following benefits:

- Network documentation is easier to manage.
- Problems are easier to locate and resolve.

- Routers can more easily manage IP address spaces that don't overlap.
- Routing is more efficient on larger networks when IP address spaces are mathematically related at a binary level.

How Subnet Masks Work

A device uses a subnet mask to determine which subnet or network it belongs to. Let's review a little of what you've already learned regarding IP addresses and subnet masks. Recall that an IPv4 address has 32 bits and is divided into two parts: the network portion, which identifies the network and is called the network ID, and the host portion, which identifies the host and is called the host ID.

When a computer is ready to send a transmission to another host, it first compares the bits in its own network ID to the bits in the network ID of the destination host. If the bits match, the remote host is on the sending computer's own network, and it sends the transmission directly to that host. If the bits don't match, the destination host is on another network, and the computer sends the transmission to the default gateway on its network. The gateway is responsible for sending the transmission toward the correct network.

> **Note**
>
> You might sometimes find the term *network ID* used interchangeably with the terms *network number* or *network prefix*.

How does a computer know how many bits of its IP address is the network ID? The subnet mask gives that information. Recall that an IPv4 subnet mask is 32 bits long. The number of 1s in the subnet mask determines the number of bits in the IP address that belong to the network ID. For example, suppose a computer has an IP address of 192.168.123.132 and its subnet mask in decimal is 255.255.255.0. To identify the bits that make up the network ID, first convert these numbers to binary, as follows:

- IP address 192.168.123.132 in binary:

  11000000.10101000.01111011.10000100
- Subnet mask 255.255.255.0 in binary:

  11111111.11111111.11111111.00000000

> **Note**
>
> In this example and in many others in this chapter, a red font is used for the network ID portion of an IP address.

Applying Concepts: Binary Calculations

You won't be allowed to use a calculator during the CompTIA Network+ exam, but when calculating conversions on the job, using a calculator can make the task much simpler. Take, for example, the decimal number 131. Complete the following steps to convert it to a binary number using the Windows 10 Calculator:

1. Open the Calculator app. Click the menu icon, and then click **Programmer**. Verify that the **DEC** option is selected.
2. Type **131**. Other formats of this number are listed automatically. The binary equivalent of the decimal number 131, which is 1000 0011, appears next to the BIN option.
3. Select the **BIN** option, as shown in Figure 8-4, and type a binary number to convert it to a decimal number.

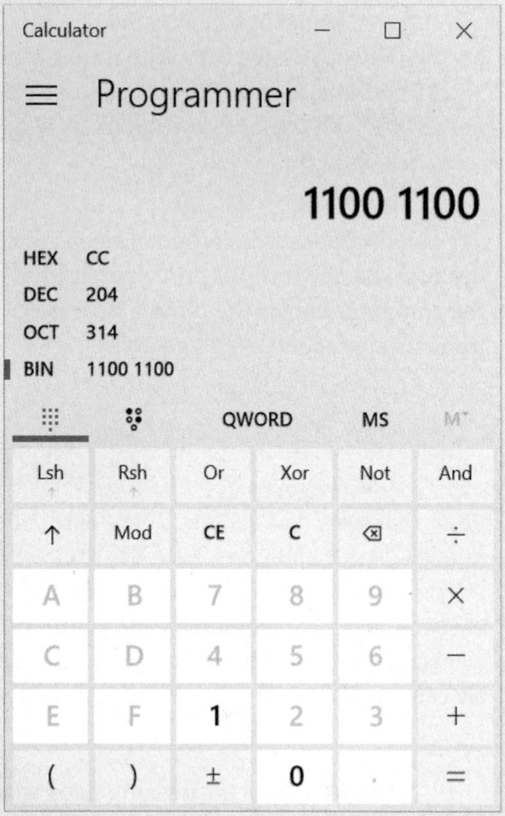

If you're connected to the Internet and using a web browser, you can quickly convert binary and decimal numbers using Google calculator:

4. Go to **google.com**, and then type the number you want to convert, along with the desired format, in the search text box. For example, to convert the

Figure 8-4   Use the Windows Calculator app to convert between decimal and binary

decimal number 131 into binary form, enter **131 in binary**. You see the following result: 131 = 0b10000011. The prefix "0b" (that's a zero, not the letter O) indicates that the number is in binary format. Notice that Google assumes a number is in decimal form unless stated otherwise.
5. To convert a binary number into decimal form, type 0b (again, that's the number zero, not the letter O) before the binary number. For example, entering **0b10000011 in decimal** returns the decimal number 131.

To best prepare yourself for the CompTIA Network+ exam, consider performing all of these calculations manually and using the calculator only to check your results. If your manual calculations don't match the calculator's computations, make sure you investigate carefully to see where you made a mistake. Repeat until your calculations are consistently correct.

A subnet mask is always a series of 1s followed by a series of 0s. The 1s mark the network portion of an IP address and the 0s mark the host portion. Therefore, the network ID portion of the IP address in our example is 24 bits, or the first three octets: 192.168.123. The host portion is the last octet: 132. Putting them together and using red for the network ID, we can write this IP address as 192.168.123.132.

By convention, you see 0s used to complete the four octets when referring to the network ID and the host portion of an IP address separately, like this:

- Network ID: 192.168.123.0
- Host portion: 0.0.0.132

Now suppose this computer needs to communicate with a host at 192.168.30.140. Because the network IDs don't match (that is, 192.168.123 does not match 192.168.30), the computer knows the remote host is not on its own network and sends the transmission to its default gateway.

Legacy Networking: Classful Addressing in IPv4

Recall that every IPv4 address can be associated with a network class—A, B, C, D, or E (though Class D and E addresses are reserved for special purposes). Classful addressing is the simplest type of IPv4 addressing and uses only whole octets for the network ID and host portions. In our earlier example of 192.168.123.132, the network ID consists of three whole octets, and is, therefore, an example of classful addressing. Table 8-1 lists how the 32 bits are allocated with classful addressing for Classes A, B, and C.

Table 8-1   Classful addressing uses whole octets for the network ID

Class	Network portion in red n=network ID bit h=host address bit	Bits in network ID	Bits in host portion
A	nnnnnnnn.hhhhhhhh.hhhhhhhh.hhhhhhhh	8	24
B	nnnnnnnn.nnnnnnnn.hhhhhhhh.hhhhhhhh	16	16
C	nnnnnnnn.nnnnnnnn.nnnnnnnn.hhhhhhhh	24	8

When using classful IPv4 addressing, the last octet of a network ID is always equal to 0 (and may have additional, preceding octets equal to 0). For example, the network ID for a Class A network might be 92.0.0.0, and the network ID for a Class B network might be 147.12.0.0. Also, a workstation cannot be assigned the same address as the network ID, which explains why the last octet of a host's IP address is almost never 0.

Although classful addressing rules no longer restrict addressing options on modern networks, we still use the classes as a starting point for IPv4 subnet calculations.

Each network class is associated with a default subnet mask, as shown in Table 8-2. For example, by default, a Class A address's first octet (or 8 bits) represents network information. That means that if you work on a network whose hosts are configured with a subnet mask of 11111111 00000000 00000000 00000000, or 255.0.0.0, you know that the network is using Class A addresses.

Table 8-2   Default IPv4 subnet masks

Network class	Default subnet mask (binary)	Number of bits used for network information	Default subnet mask (dotted decimal)
A	11111111 00000000 00000000 00000000	8	255.0.0.0
B	11111111 11111111 00000000 00000000	16	255.255.0.0
C	11111111 11111111 11111111 00000000	24	255.255.255.0

Applying Concepts: Use the Logical ANDing Function to Calculate a Network ID

To calculate a host's network ID given its IPv4 address and subnet mask, computers follow a logical process of combining bits known as **ANDing**. In ANDing, a bit with a value of 1 combined, or anded, with another bit with a value of 1 results in a 1. A bit with a value of 0 anded with any other bit results in a 0. If you think of 1 as "true" and 0 as "false," the logic of ANDing makes sense: ANDing a true statement to a true statement still results in a true statement. But ANDing a true statement to a false statement results in a false statement.

ANDing logic is demonstrated in Table 8-3, which provides every possible combination of having a 1 or 0 bit in an IPv4 address or subnet mask.

Table 8-3   ANDing

IP address bit	1	1	0	0
Subnet mask bit	1	0	1	0
Resulting bit	1	0	0	0

A sample IPv4 host address, its default subnet mask, and its network ID are shown in Figure 8-5 in both binary and dotted decimal notation. Notice that the address's fourth octet could have been composed of any combination of 1s and 0s, and the network ID's fourth octet would still be all 0s.

	IP address:	11000000	00100010	01011001	01111111	192.34.89.127
AND	Subnet mask:	11111111	11111111	11111111	00000000	255.255.255.0
Equals	Network ID:	11000000	00100010	01011001	00000000	192.34.89.0

Figure 8-5 Example of ANDing a host's network ID

Figure 8-5 shows how ANDing logic is applied to an IPv4 address plus a default subnet mask. It works the same way for networks that are subnetted with classless subnet masks, discussed later in this chapter.

CIDR (Classless Interdomain Routing)

You can't just look at an IP address and immediately see how many of its bits are network bits and how many are host bits. Instead, you can use a subnet mask to determine this information. Another option is to use **CIDR (Classless Interdomain Routing)**, devised by the IETF in 1993. This shorthand method for identifying network and host bits in an IP address is also known as **CIDR notation** or slash notation. (Note that CIDR is pronounced *cider*.)

CIDR notation takes the network ID or a host's IP address and follows it with a forward slash (/), which is then followed by the number of bits that are used for the network ID. For example, this private IP address could be written as 192.168.89.127/24, where 24 represents the number of 1s in the subnet mask and therefore the number of bits in the network ID. In CIDR terminology, the forward slash, plus the number of bits used for the network ID—for example, /24—is known as a **CIDR block**.

The next section describes how to calculate IPv4 subnets, and how to determine the range of usable host addresses on a subnet, as well as the subnet masks the host addresses use. Later in the chapter, you will learn how subnetting differs in IPv6.

IPv4 Subnet Calculations

Subnetting, which alters the rules of classful IPv4 addressing, is called **classless addressing**. To create a subnet, you borrow bits that would represent host information in classful addressing and use those bits instead to represent network information. By doing so, you increase the number of bits available for the network ID, and you also reduce the number of bits available for identifying hosts. Consequently, you increase the number of networks and reduce the number of usable host addresses in each network or subnet. The more bits you borrow for network information, the more subnets you can have, but the fewer hosts each subnet can have.

For example, suppose you have a network with one router, and then you add a second router to divide your local network into two LANs. The network ID of the original network is 192.168.89.0 and its subnet mask is 255.255.255.0. Let's create two subnets of IP addresses, one for each LAN. The results of each of the following steps are shown in Table 8-4:

1. *Borrow from host bits*—Currently, the network ID is 24 bits. First convert it to binary:

   - Network ID 192.168.89.0 in binary:

     11000000.10101000.01011001.00000000

   Borrow one bit from the host portion to give to the network ID, which will then have 25 bits (notice one additional red bit). Here, the borrowed bit is formatted in red and is also underlined:

   - 11000000.10101000.01011001.<u>0</u>0000000

   How many subnets can you now have? The underlined red bit can be a 0 or a 1, which gives you the possibility of two subnets.

2. *Determine the subnet mask*—Recall that the subnet mask marks the bits in an IP address that belong to the network ID. Therefore, the subnet mask for both subnets is:

   - 11111111.11111111.11111111.10000000 or decimal 255.255.255.128

   To calculate that last octet, you convert binary 10000000 to decimal, which is 128. You can use a calculator to do the conversion or manually calculate it.

3. *Determine the network IDs*—Recall that in the network ID, the underlined red bit can be a 1 or 0. Therefore, the network ID for each subnet is:

   - Subnet 1: 11000000.10101000.01011001.00000000 or decimal 192.168.89.0
   - Subnet 2: 11000000.10101000.01011001.10000000 or decimal 192.168.89.128

   In CIDR notation, the network ID for each subnet is:

   - Subnet 1: 192.168.89.0/25
   - Subnet 2: 192.168.89.128/25

4. *Determine the ranges of IP addresses*—Start with the range of IP addresses for subnet A. For host addresses, use the 7 bits in the last octet. (The first bit for this octet is always 0 and belongs to the network ID.) Start counting in binary and converting to decimal:

   - 00000000 is not used because it's the network ID for this subnet
   - 00000001 or decimal 1
   - 00000010 or decimal 2
   - 00000011 or decimal 3
   - ...
   - 01111110 or decimal 126
   - 01111111 or decimal 127, which is used for broadcasting rather than as a host address

   Therefore, the range of host IP addresses for subnet A is 192.168.89.1 through 192.168.89.126.

For subnet B, the first bit of the last octet is 1 and the range of host addresses is as follows:

- 10000000 is not used because it's the network ID for this subnet
- 10000001 in decimal: 129
- 10000010 in decimal: 130
- 10000011 in decimal: 131
- ...
- 11111110 in decimal: 254
- 11111111 in decimal: 255 is not used because it's used for broadcasting

Therefore, the range of host IP addresses for subnet B is 192.168.89.129 through 192.168.89.254.

Table 8-4   Steps to divide IP addresses for network ID 192.168.89.0 into two subnets

Step 1: Borrow from host bits.				
Network ID	192	168	89	0
In binary	11000000	10101000	01011001	00000000
Borrow 1 bit	11000000	10101000	01011001	00000000
Step 2: Determine the subnet mask.				
In binary	11111111	11111111	11111111	10000000
In decimal	255	255	255	128
Step 3: Determine the network IDs.				
Network ID 1	11000000	10101000	01011001	00000000
In decimal	192	168	89	0
In CIDR notation	192.168.89.0/25			
Network ID 2	11000000	10101000	01011001	10000000
In decimal	192	168	89	128
In CIDR notation	192.168.89.128/25			
Step 4: Determine range of host IP addresses.				
Subnet 1:				
First host, binary	11000000	10101000	01011001	000000001
First host, decimal	192	168	89	1
Last host, binary	11000000	10101000	01011001	01111110
Last host, decimal	192	168	89	126
Subnet 2:				
First host, binary	11000000	10101000	01011001	10000001
First host, decimal	192	168	89	129
Last host, binary	11000000	10101000	01011001	11111110
Last host, decimal	192	168	89	254

Now you're ready to move on to a more complicated example, performing calculations using formulas, without so much binary involved. Suppose you want to divide your local network, which has a network ID of 192.168.89.0, into six subnets to correspond to your building's six floors. The following steps walk you through the process:

1. *Decide how many bits to borrow*—How many bits must you borrow from the host portion of the IP addresses in order to get six subnets? Use this formula to determine the number of bits:

$$2^n = Y$$

   - *n* equals the number of bits that must be switched from the host address to the network ID.
   - *Y* equals the number of subnets that result.

   Because you want six separate subnets (meaning that Y, in this case, is 6), the equation becomes $2^n = 6$.

   Experiment with different values for *n* until you find a value large enough to give you at least the number of subnets you need. For example, you know that $2^2 = 4$; however, 4 is not high enough. Instead consider that $2^3 = 8$; this will give you enough subnets to meet your current needs and allow room for future growth. Now that *n* equals 3, you know that three bits in the host addresses of your Class C network must change to network ID bits. You also know that three bits in your subnet mask must change from 0 to 1.

2. *Determine the subnet mask*—As you know, the default subnet mask for a Class C network is 255.255.255.0, or 11111111 11111111 11111111 00000000. In this default subnet mask, the first 24 bits indicate the position of network information.

   Changing three of the default subnet mask's bits from host to network information gives you the subnet mask 11111111 11111111 11111111 11100000. In this modified subnet mask, the first 27 bits indicate the bits for the network ID. Note that for this Class C network whose network ID is 192.168.89.0, the slash notation would now be 192.168.89.0/27 because 27 bits of the subnets' addresses are used to provide network information.

   Converting from binary to the more familiar dotted decimal notation, this subnet mask becomes 255.255.255.224. When you configure the TCP/IP properties of clients on your network, as shown in Figure 8-6, you would specify this new subnet mask.

> **Note** ✎
>
> When examining the subnet mask for a network, if any octet is not 255 or 0, you know that this network is a subnet and classful addressing is not used. The unusual octet (224 in our example) is often called the *interesting octet*. Subtract the interesting octet value from 256 and you get what is called the **magic number**. In this example, the magic number is 256 − 224 = 32. This magic number can be used to calculate the network IDs in all the subnets of the larger network, which you'll see next.

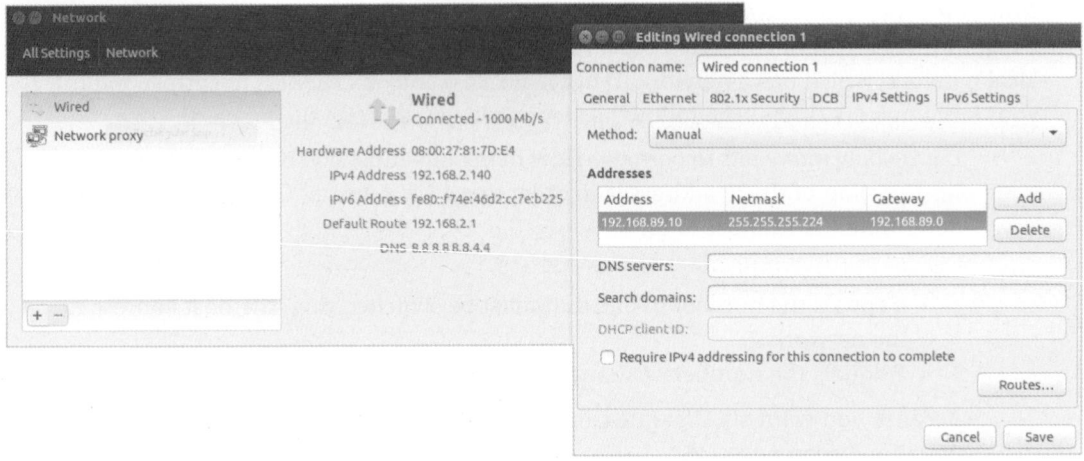

Figure 8-6   TCP/IPv4 client configuration for a subnet in Ubuntu Desktop
Source: Canonical Group Limited

3. *Calculate the network ID for each subnet*—The first three octets of the network ID for the Class C network 192.168.89.0 is the same for all eight possible subnets. The network IDs differ in the last octet. Use the magic number to calculate them as follows:

   - Subnet 1 Network ID: 192.168.89.0
   - Subnet 2 Network ID: 192.168.89.0   + 32 yields 192.168.89.32
   - Subnet 3 Network ID: 192.168.89.32   + 32 yields 192.168.89.64
   - Subnet 4 Network ID: 192.168.89.64   + 32 yields 192.168.89.96
   - Subnet 5 Network ID: 192.168.89.96   + 32 yields 192.168.89.128
   - Subnet 6 Network ID: 192.168.89.128 + 32 yields 192.168.89.160
   - Subnet 7 Network ID: 192.168.89.160 + 32 yields 192.168.89.192
   - Subnet 8 Network ID: 192.168.89.192 + 32 yields 192.168.89.224

   This method of adding on the same number over and over is called skip-counting.

4. *Determine the IP address range for each subnet*—Recall that you have borrowed 3 bits from what used to be host information in the IP address. That leaves 5 bits instead of 8 available in the last octet of your Class C addresses to identify hosts. To calculate the number of possible hosts, keep in mind that each of the 5 bits has two possibilities, a 1 or a 0. Therefore, the number of host addresses is 2 x 2 x 2 x 2 x 2, or 32 host addresses. But you can't use two of these addresses for hosts because one is used for the network ID (the one where all five bits are 0 in binary) and one for the broadcast address (the one where all five bits are 1 in binary). That leaves you 30 host addresses in each subnet.

As a shortcut to calculating the number of hosts, you can use the formula:

$$2^h - 2 = Z$$

- h equals the number of bits remaining in the host portion.
- Z equals the number of hosts available in each subnet.

So, $2^5 - 2$ yields 30 possible hosts per subnet.

In this example, you can have a maximum of 8 (number of subnets) × 30 (number of hosts per subnet), or 240, unique host addresses on the entire, larger network. Each time you subnet a network, you lose two possible host addresses with each subnet. This overhead is the price you pay for subnetting a network, in exchange for the advantages you gain.

Once you know the network ID of the subnets, calculating the address range of hosts in a subnet is easy. For example, take subnet 5. The network ID is 192.168.89.128. Because you won't use the network ID for a host address, you start with the next value and keep going until you reach the broadcast address for the subnet, yielding for this particular subnet a total of 30 addresses. Therefore, the address range for subnet 5 is 192.168.89.129 through 192.168.89.158. (The last value 158 is 128 + 30.)

Note

If you're having trouble coming up with the broadcast address for a subnet, look at the network ID of the next subnet and drop back one address. For example, the network ID for subnet 6 is 192.168.89.160. One address below that address is 192.168.89.159, which is the broadcast address for subnet 5. Notice that in binary, this last octet 159 ends with five 1s in the host portion of the IP address: 10011111.

Table 8-5 lists the network ID, broadcast address, and the range of usable host addresses for each of the eight subnets in this sample Class C network. Together, the existing network ID plus the additional bits used for subnet information are sometimes called the extended network prefix.

Table 8-5   Subnet information for eight possible subnets in a sample IPv4 Class C network

Subnet number	Network ID (extended network prefix)	Range of host addresses	Broadcast address
1	192.168.89.0 or 11000000 10101000 01011001 00000000	192.168.89.1-30	192.168.89.31 or 11000000 10101000 01011001 00011111
2	192.168.89.32 or 11000000 10101000 01011001 00100000	192.168.89.33-62	192.168.89.63 or 11000000 10101000 01011001 00111111

(continues)

Table 8-5	Subnet information for eight possible subnets in a sample IPv4 Class C network *(continued)*		
Subnet number	Network ID (extended network prefix)	Range of host addresses	Broadcast address
3	192.168.89.64 or 11000000 10101000 01011001 01000000	192.168.89.65-94	192.168.89.95 or 11000000 10101000 01011001 01011111
4	192.168.89.96 or 11000000 10101000 01011001 01100000	192.168.89.97-126	192.168.89.127 or 11000000 10101000 01011001 01111111
5	192.168.89.128 or 11000000 10101000 01011001 10000000	192.168.89.129-158	192.168.89.159 or 11000000 10101000 01011001 10011111
6	192.168.89.160 or 11000000 10101000 01011001 10100000	192.168.89.161-190	192.168.89.191 or 11000000 10101000 01011001 10111111
7	192.168.89.192 or 11000000 10101000 01011001 11000000	192.168.89.193-222	192.168.89.223 or 11000000 10101000 01011001 11011111
8	192.168.89.224 or 11000000 10101000 01011001 11100000	192.168.89.225-254	192.168.89.255 or 11000000 10101000 01011001 11111111

Note

You can also calculate the magic number by raising 2 to the power of the number of bits in the host portion of the subnet mask. Use this formula:

$$2^h = \text{magic number}$$

In this example, the host portion has 5 bits. Therefore, the magic number is $2^5 = 32$. You can then use this number to determine the number of network IDs in subnets.

Subnet Mask Tables

Class A, Class B, and Class C networks can all be subnetted. But because each class reserves a different number of bits for network information, each class has a different number of host information bits that can be used for subnet information. The number of hosts and subnets on your network will vary depending on your network class and the way you use subnetting. Several websites provide excellent tools that can help you calculate subnet information. One such site is *subnetmask.info*. Other websites and apps can give you practice calculating subnets in preparation for your certification exams. Check out the website *subnettingquestions.com* in your browser or the /24 Subnetting Practice app on both Android and iPhone.

Table 8-6 lists the numbers of subnets and hosts that can be created by subnetting a Class B network. Notice the range of subnet masks that can be used instead of the default Class B subnet mask of 255.255.0.0. Also compare the listed numbers of hosts per subnet to the 65,534 hosts available on a Class B network that does not use subnetting.

Table 8-6   IPv4 Class B subnet masks

Subnet mask	CIDR notation	Number of subnets on network	Number of hosts per subnet
255.255.128.0 or 11111111 11111111 10000000 00000000	/17	2	32,766
255.255.192.0 or 11111111 11111111 11000000 00000000	/18	4	16,382
255.255.224.0 or 11111111 11111111 11100000 00000000	/19	8	8190
255.255.240.0 or 11111111 11111111 11110000 00000000	/20	16	4094
255.255.248.0 or 11111111 11111111 11111000 00000000	/21	32	2046
255.255.252.0 or 11111111 11111111 11111100 00000000	/22	64	1022
255.255.254.0 or 11111111 11111111 11111110 00000000	/23	128	510
255.255.255.0 or 11111111 11111111 11111111 00000000	/24	256	254
255.255.255.128 or 11111111 11111111 11111111 10000000	/25	512	126
255.255.255.192 or 11111111 11111111 11111111 11000000	/26	1024	62
255.255.255.224 or 11111111 11111111 11111111 11100000	/27	2048	30
255.255.255.240 or 11111111 11111111 11111111 11110000	/28	4096	14
255.255.255.248 or 11111111 11111111 11111111 11111000	/29	8192	6
255.255.255.252 or 11111111 11111111 11111111 11111100	/30	16,384	2

Table 8-7 lists the numbers of subnets and hosts that can be created by subnetting a Class C network. Notice that a Class C network allows for fewer subnets than a Class B network. This is because Class C addresses have fewer host information bits that can be borrowed for network information. In addition, fewer bits are left over for host information, which leads to a lower number of hosts per subnet than the number available to Class B subnets.

Table 8-7   IPv4 Class C subnet masks

Subnet mask	CIDR notation	Number of subnets on network	Number of hosts per subnet
255.255.255.128 or 11111111 11111111 11111111 10000000	/25	2	126
255.255.255.192 or 11111111 11111111 11111111 11000000	/26	4	62
255.255.255.224 or 11111111 11111111 11111111 11100000	/27	8	30
255.255.255.240 or 11111111 11111111 11111111 11110000	/28	16	14
255.255.255.248 or 11111111 11111111 11111111 11111000	/29	32	6
255.255.255.252 or 11111111 11111111 11111111 11111100	/30	64	2

Subnetting Questions on Exams

Although it's impossible to know for sure, you're likely to see two types of subnet calculation problems on the CompTIA Network+ exam:

- Given certain network requirements (such as required number of hosts or required number of subnets), calculate possible subnets and host IP address ranges.
- Given an IP address, determine its subnet's network ID, broadcast address, and first/last host addresses.

You've already seen steps for solving the first type of problem using a Class C network ID. Now let's look at another example of the same type of problem, but this time we'll begin with a Class B network ID. Then we'll look at an example of the second type of subnetting problem.

Applying Concepts: Calculate IPv4 Subnets and Host IP Address Ranges

Suppose your organization uses the Class B network ID of 172.20.0.0 for its entire network and wants to create 15 subnets. Do the following steps, answering the questions as you go:

1. You first need to decide how many bits to borrow from the host address bits. Recall that you can use the formula $2^n = Y$. For the new subnets, how many bits must be borrowed from the host address portion? How many bits total will be used for identifying a host's subnet?
2. You can now calculate the subnet mask. The default subnet mask for a Class B network is 255.255.0.0, and so the third octet is the one that will change. What is the subnet mask for these subnets, written in decimal?

3. The magic number will tell you by what amount to skip-count when you're listing the subnets' network IDs. There are two ways to calculate the magic number: subtract the interesting octet's value from 256, or use the formula 2^h. What is the magic number you can use to calculate the network IDs?

4. Now you can calculate the network IDs for each subnet. Begin with the original network ID. Then in the third octet, count up by the magic number with each iteration. The last subnet's network ID will be equal to 256 minus the magic number, because you can't use 256 itself in any IP address. What is the CIDR notation for the first subnet's network ID? For the second subnet's network ID? For the last subnet's network ID?

5. If 20 bits are used to identify the network and subnet, that leaves 12 bits to identify each host. Using the formula $2^h - 2 = Z$, how many host addresses are possible in each subnet? (You might need a calculator for this step, which is why it's unusual to see an exam question where you're working with bits in the third octet.)

6. The range of available host addresses consists of all the possible IP addresses between the network ID and the broadcast address (which is 1 below the network ID for the next subnet). What is the range of host addresses for the first subnet? For the second subnet? For the last subnet?

Now you're ready to work through the other type of subnetting problem that you'll likely see on your CompTIA Network+ exam: calculating a host's network information.

Applying Concepts: Calculate an IPv4 Host's Network Information

Let's now work backwards in our calculations by beginning with one host's IP address information. Suppose a server on your network displays the following IPv4 network configuration:

IPv4 address: 192.168.89.130
Subnet mask: 255.255.255.224

Your task is to determine the network ID of the subnet this server is located on, the broadcast address, and the range of available host addresses on this subnet. Do the following steps, answering the questions as you go:

1. We don't necessarily need to use binary for these calculations. So long as the interesting octet is at the end of the subnet mask, we can easily find the magic number and go from there. As with our earlier calculations, you need to subtract

the interesting octet's value from 256 to get the magic number. What is the magic number?

2. If the interesting octet is located at the end of the subnet mask, you can assume the first three octets of the IP address identify the classful network ID before this network was subnetted. This network ID also serves as the network ID for the first subnet. What is the network ID of the first subnet?

3. You can now use the magic number to calculate the remaining subnets' network IDs. What is the second subnet's network ID? What is the final subnet's network ID?

4. To narrow this down to our server's subnet, we need to either skip-count up from a lower numbered subnet or skip-count down from a higher numbered subnet. Either way will work. We're looking for a network ID that is as close to the server's IP address as possible without going over. What is the server's subnet's network ID?

5. You can look at the next higher subnet's network ID and subtract 1 to determine the broadcast address of the server's subnet. What is the broadcast address?

6. Finally, any IP address between the subnet's network ID and its broadcast address is the range of available host IP addresses. What is this range?

If the subnet mask's interesting octet is in the third octet's location, you can convert the subnet mask to binary, determine how many bits are used for the network portion (n) and the host portion (h), and then use the formula 2^h to calculate the magic number. You can also convert the network portion of the binary address into decimal to determine the initial subnet's network ID. From there, use the magic number to calculate the other network IDs, broadcast addresses, and ranges of host IP addresses.

Network+ Exam Tip ⓘ

If these calculation processes seem overwhelming, you're not alone. Many people have developed a variety of handy shortcuts for calculating subnets. In a Hands-On Project at the end of this chapter, you'll see how to use a shortcut to answer each of the two primary types of subnetting exam questions. If these shortcuts don't resonate with you, you can search online to find a shortcut that does click. There are many options, and sometimes it's just a matter of finding the approach that is easiest for you to remember and work with.

Implement Subnets

Now that you've calculated the subnets for the scenarios presented earlier in the chapter, how do you implement them? Figure 8-7 shows the subnets assigned to the three LANs you saw earlier in Figure 8-3. Also in Figure 8-7, you can see the IP address of the default gateway for each LAN, which is the IP address assigned to the router's interface on the LAN. Note that only three of the eight possible subnets listed earlier in Table 8-5 are used.

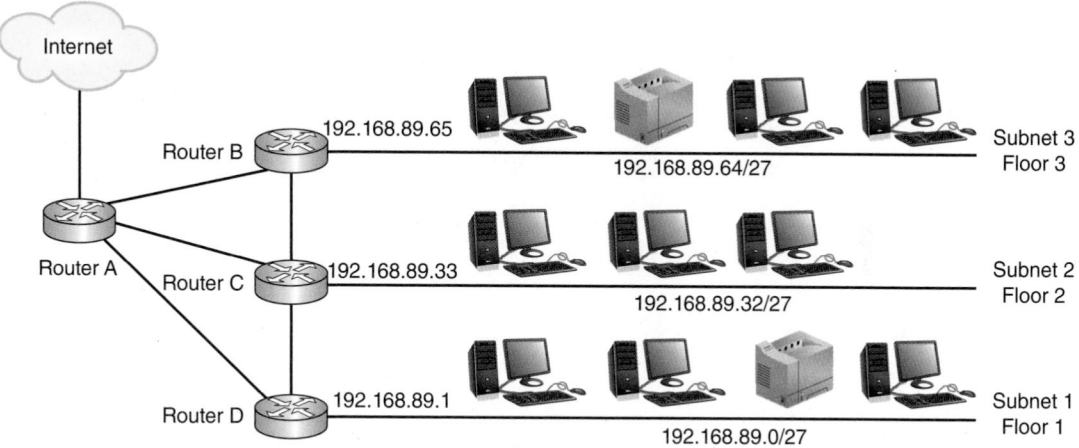

Figure 8-7 Subnets 1, 2, and 3 and their respective default gateways

Figure 8-8 illustrates another scenario in which an enterprise network uses the same Class C range of private addresses that begin with 192.168.89. The network administrator has subnetted this Class C network into six (of eight possible) smaller networks. As you know, routers connect different networks via their physical interfaces. In the case of subnetting, each subnet corresponds to a different network interface, or port, on the router.

The administrator must program each interface on the router with the network ID and subnet mask for its subnet or LAN. Though tedious on larger networks, static IP addressing can also be used on network hosts. Figure 8-9a shows the TCP/IPv4 properties dialog box of an Ubuntu workstation on the first subnet, and Figure 8-9b shows the static configuration for a Windows workstation on the second subnet. As shown in the figure, the first IP address in the range of host addresses for the subnet is assigned to the router's interface on the subnet, which serves the subnet as its default gateway. This convention varies between organizations, though. Some network admins prefer to use the last available host address in a range for the default gateway.

For dynamic IP addressing, the administrator programs each subnet's DHCP server with the network ID, subnet mask, range of IP addresses, and default gateway for the subnet. In many cases, however, it's cost prohibitive to create a separate DHCP

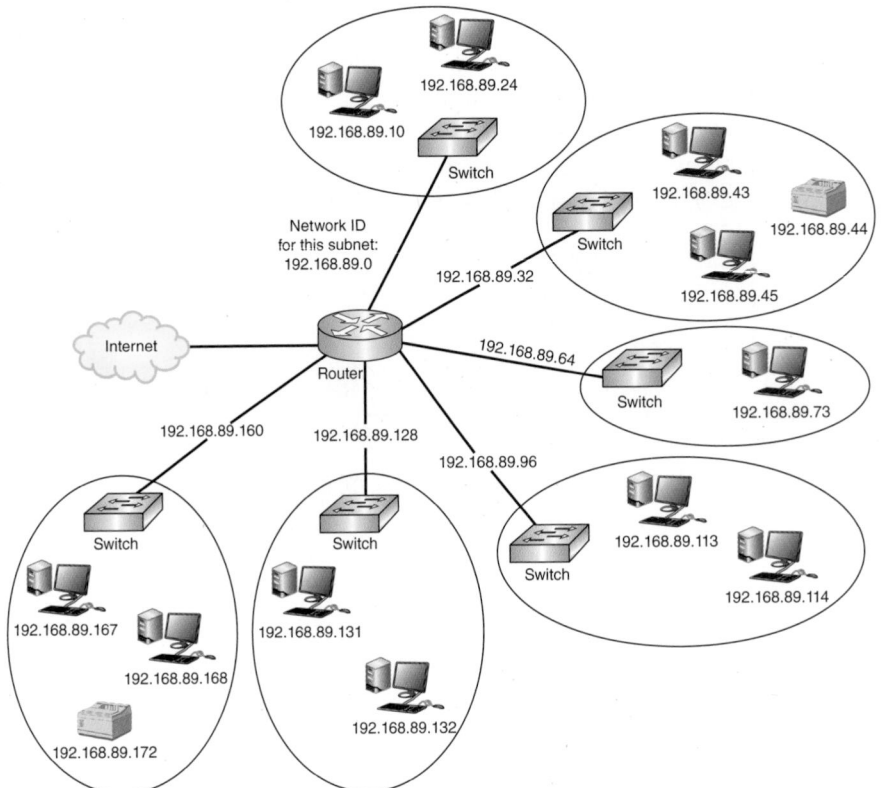

Figure 8-8   One router connecting several LANs, each assigned a subnet

server for each subnet. As we see here, some types of broadcast traffic, such as DHCP messages, need to travel beyond the subnet's broadcast domain in order to access centralized network services. A centrally managed DHCP server can provide DHCP assignments to multiple subnets (and VLANs) with the help of a **DHCP relay agent**. The following steps describe this process:

Step 1—A router, firewall, or Layer 3 switch programmed to support relay agent software receives the DHCP request from a client in one of its local broadcast domains.

Step 2—The Layer 3 device creates a message of its own and routes this transmission to the specified DHCP server in a different broadcast domain.

Step 3—The DHCP server notes the relay agent's IP address and assigns the DHCP client an IP address on the same subnet.

On some Cisco products, a more robust command, **ip helper-address**, can be configured to create and send helper messages that support several types of

Internet Protocol Version 4 (TCP/IPv4) Properties ✕

General

You can get IP settings assigned automatically if your network supports this capability. Otherwise, you need to ask your network administrator for the appropriate IP settings.

○ Obtain an IP address automatically

◉ Use the following IP address:

IP address:	192 . 168 . 89 . 50
Subnet mask:	255 . 255 . 255 . 224
Default gateway:	192 . 168 . 89 . 33

○ Obtain DNS server address automatically

◉ Use the following DNS server addresses:

| Preferred DNS server: | 192 . 168 . 89 . 2 |
| Alternate DNS server: | . . . |

☐ Validate settings upon exit   [Advanced...]

[OK]   [Cancel]

Editing Wired connection 1

Connection name: [Wired connection 1]

General Ethernet 802.1x Security DCB **IPv4 Settings** IPv6 Settings

Method: [Manual ▾]

Addresses

| Address | Netmask | Gateway | [Add] |
| 192.168.89.10 | 255.255.255.224 | 192.168.89.0 | [Delete] |

DNS servers: [ ]

Search domains: [ ]

DHCP client ID: [ ]

☐ Require IPv4 addressing for this connection to complete

[Routes...]

[Cancel] [Save]

(a)   (b)

Figure 8-9 Static IP configurations for workstations on two subnets
Source: Canonical Group Limited

UDP traffic, including DHCP, TFTP, DNS, and TACACS+ (which you'll learn more about later).

VLSM (Variable Length Subnet Mask)

Traditional subnetting reduces the waste of IP addresses, but results in multiple subnets that are all the same size. This uniformity in subnet size can be inefficient in complex networks. **VLSM (Variable Length Subnet Mask)** allows subnets to be further subdivided into smaller and smaller groupings until each subnet is about the same size as the necessary IP address space. This is often referred to as "subnetting a subnet."

To understand how this works, consider a pizza being shared by members of a young family. Dad might need a very large slice of the pizza, while Mom prefers a medium slice, and the children each need smaller slices. Similarly, with VLSM, some subnets can have larger "slices" of the network, while other subnets (such as a two-point connection between two routers) can be limited to only a few host addresses. See Figure 8-10.

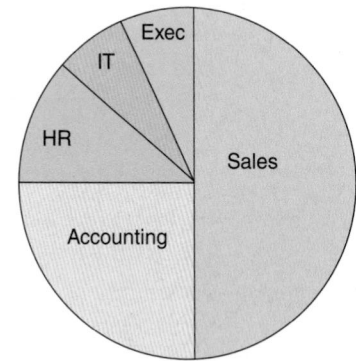

Figure 8-10 VLSM creates subnets of various sizes

To create VLSM subnets, you create the largest subnet first. Then you create the next largest subnet, and the next one and so on, until you have divided up all the remaining space. In this way, you ensure that the largest subnets get the space they need, and the smallest subnets are also sized appropriately. Let's work through an example.

Suppose you need to configure the subnets shown in Table 8-8 using the 192.168.10.0/24 IP address space. The Sales department needs the most number of hosts. At the other end of the spectrum, your WAN links only need two hosts each. The other subnets fall somewhere in the middle.

Table 8-8   Subnets of various sizes needed on the network

Subnet	Included hosts	Number of hosts	CIDR notation (as calculated next)
1	Sales	120	192.168.10.0 /25
2	Accounting	58	192.168.10.128 /26
3	HR	25	192.168.10.192 /27
4	IT	6	192.168.10.224 /29
5	Executives	5	192.168.10.232 /29
6	WAN link	2	192.168.10.240 /30
7	WAN link	2	192.168.10.244 /30

Step 1—Determine the appropriate subnet mask and other network information for the largest subnet. By borrowing one bit from the host bits, we get the following available subnets:

Subnet 1: 192.168.10.0 /25
Subnet 2: 192.168.10.128 /25

Step 2—We assign the first of these subnets to the Sales department. Now we can use the second subnet for further calculations.

Step 3—Determine the appropriate subnet mask and other network information for the next largest subnet. By borrowing one more bit from the host bits, we get the following available subnets:

Subnet 2: 192.168.10.128 /26
Subnet 3: 192.168.10.192 /26

Step 4—We assign the first of these subnets to the Accounting department. Now we can use the remaining subnet for further calculations.

Step 5—Determine the appropriate subnet mask and other network information for the next largest subnet. By borrowing one more bit from the host bits, we get the following available subnets:

Subnet 3: 192.168.10.192 /27
Subnet 4: 192.168.10.224 /27

Step 6—We assign the first of these subnets to the Human Resources department. Now we use the other subnet for further calculations.

Step 7—The next two departments are about the same size, and will each fit within a /29 subnet. By borrowing two more bits from the host bits this time, we get the following available subnets:

> Subnet 4: 192.168.10.224 /29
> Subnet 5: 192.168.10.232 /29
> Subnet 6: 192.168.10.240 /29
> Subnet 7: 192.168.10.248 /29

Step 8—We assign the first two of these subnets to the IT department and the Executive suite. Now we use one of the other subnets for further calculations.

Step 9—The last two required subnets only need two host addresses each, and will each fit within a /30 subnet. By borrowing one more bit from the host bits to further subdivide Subnet 6, and renumbering the remaining space to be Subnet 8 (which will be reserved for future use on our network), we get the following available subnets:

> Subnet 6: 192.168.10.240 /30
> Subnet 7: 192.168.10.244 /30
> Subnet 8: 192.168.10.248 /29

Step 10—We assign each of these subnets to a WAN link, with the final subnet left over for future use.

Figure 8-11 shows the mathematically determined distribution, with each department allocated the IP address space it needs.

This is an efficient way to define IP address spaces on a network. However, in reality, it's not a good idea to configure subnets so tightly. In this case, for example, there's very little room for growth. Most companies should allow for significant growth, especially as technology continues to expand the need for IP addresses on a network.

One way to prepare for this growth is to begin with a larger IP address space. For example, you might start with a /23 or even a /22 network. Then subdivide from there, giving each subnet significantly more host addresses than it currently needs. This works for private IP addresses, but not so much for public IP addresses. Another way to account for future growth is to convert the network to IPv6 addressing instead of IPv4. Let's take a look at how IPv6 subnetting works.

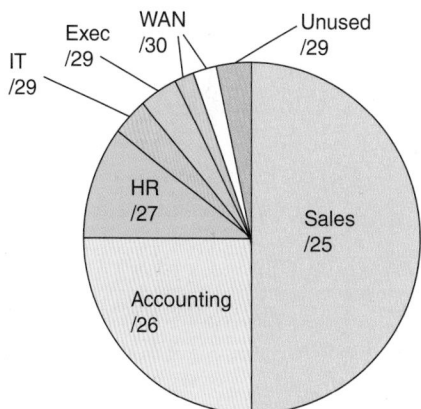

Figure 8-11 Actual subnet allocations

Subnets in IPv6

Recall that IPv6 addresses are composed of 128 bits, compared with IPv4's 32-bit addresses. That means 2^{128} addresses are available in IPv6, compared with IPv4's 2^{32} available addresses. Given so many addresses, an ISP can offer each of its customers an entire IPv6 subnet, or thousands of addresses, rather than a handful of IPv4 addresses that must be shared among all the company's nodes. In this case, subnetting helps network administrators manage the enormous volume of IPv6 addresses.

Subnetting in IPv6 is simpler than subnetting in IPv4, and differs from IPv4 in substantial ways:

- IPv6 addressing uses no classes. There are no IPv6 equivalents to IPv4's Class A, Class B, or Class C networks. Every IPv6 address is classless.
- IPv6 does not use subnet masks.
- A single IPv6 subnet is capable of supplying 18,446,744,073,709,551,616 IPv6 addresses.

Let's see how these numbers pan out. Recall that a unicast address is an address assigned to a single interface on the network. Also recall that every unicast address can be represented in binary form, but is more commonly written as eight blocks of four hexadecimal characters separated by colons. For example, 2608:FE10:1:AA:002:50FF:FE2 B:E708 is a valid IPv6 address. Now let's divide that address into parts:

- The last four blocks, which equate to the last 64 bits, identify the interface. (On many IPv6 networks, those 64 bits are based on the interface's EUI-64 version of each device's MAC address.)
- The first four blocks or 64 bits normally identify the network and serve as the network prefix, also called the **site prefix** or **global routing prefix**, as shown in Figure 8-12. In the IPv6 address 2608:FE10:1:AA:002:50FF:FE2B:E708, the site prefix is 2608:FE10:1:AA and the interface ID is 002:50FF:FE2B:E708. You might see site prefixes represented as, for example, 2608:FE10:1:AA::/64, where the number of bits that identify the network follow a slash.

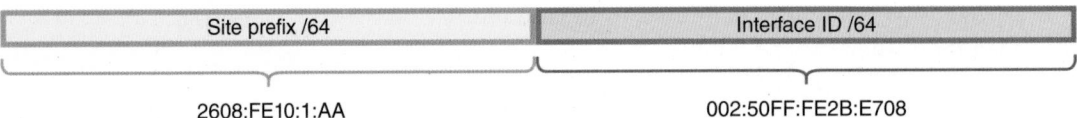

Figure 8-12   Network prefix and interface ID in an IPv6 address

- The fourth hexadecimal block in the site prefix can be altered to create subnets within a site. Let's take a closer look at how that block fits into the big picture.

As shown in Figure 8-13, an RIR (regional Internet registry) might assign an ISP a block of addresses that share a 32-bit routing prefix, such as 2608:FE10::/32. That ISP, in turn, might assign a very large organization a block of addresses that share the same 48-bit site prefix, such as 2608:FE10:1::/48, and smaller business customers might receive a 56-bit site prefix, such as 2608:FE10:1:AA::://56, or a 64-bit site prefix, such as 2608:FE10:1:AA::/64.

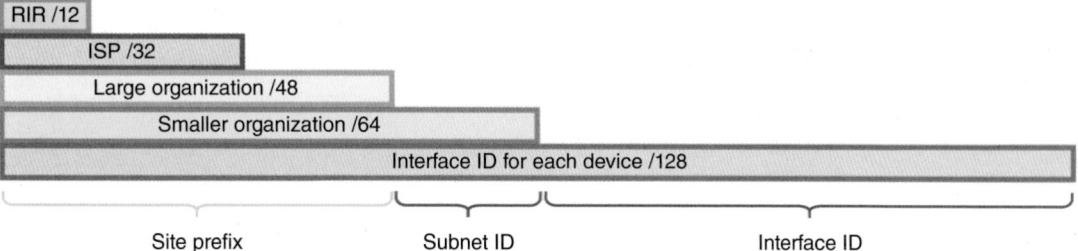

Figure 8-13   Hierarchy of IPv6 routes and subnets

The subnet ID is one block long, which is four hexadecimal characters, or 16 bits in binary. An organization with a /48 site prefix can use all 16 bits to create up to 65,536 subnets. A /56 site prefix can create up to 256 subnets, and a /64 site prefix has only the single subnet, which contains over 18 quintillion possible host addresses, which is more than twice the estimated number of grains of sand in all the beaches and deserts of the earth. As you can see, IPv6 allows for a huge number of potential hosts on a single network.

Let's take our sample network with a site prefix of 2608:FE10:1/48, and see what happens with the next block of bits at a binary level. In binary, that fourth block, the Subnet ID, could be all zeroes:

0000 0000 0000 0000
Or it could be all 1s:

1111 1111 1111 1111
And then there's every possible combination in between:

0000 0000 0000 0001
0000 0000 0000 0010
0000 0000 0000 0011
0000 0000 0000 0100

...
1111 1111 1111 1100
1111 1111 1111 1101
1111 1111 1111 1110
That's 65,536 possible subnets. A sample network with a site prefix of 2608:FE10:1:AA/56 can work with eight of those bits to create 256 possible subnets:

0000 0000

0000 0001

0000 0010

...

1111 1101

1111 1110

1111 1111

Sometimes organizations further subdivide this block into site, sub-site, and subnet IDs. For example, consider Figure 8-14, where the Subnet ID block is managed at two different levels: the first half for sub-sites (such as offices in different states or different cities), and the second half for subnets within each site (such as floors in a building or departments located at each site).

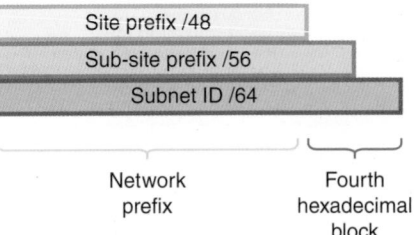

Figure 8-14   The Subnet ID block can be used to identify subsites within an organization

Calculating subnets can feel overwhelming when you're first learning how to work with these numbers. The key here is practice. Find a subnet calculation system that works for you, and then practice often. Rest assured that you don't have to be a "math" person to learn these skills.

Now that you have learned how subnets, which are implemented at the Network layer, function differently in IPv4 and IPv6 addressing, you're ready to explore network segmentation that happens at the Data Link layer: VLANs.

VLANs (Virtual Local Area Networks)

 **Certification**

7	APPLICATION
6	PRESENTATION
5	SESSION
4	TRANSPORT
3	NETWORK
2	DATA LINK
1	PHYSICAL

1.3 Explain the concepts and characteristics of routing and switching.

4.4 Summarize common networking attacks.

4.6 Explain common mitigation techniques and their purposes.

5.3 Given a scenario, troubleshoot common wired connectivity and performance issues.

Let's begin with a discussion about the similarities and differences between subnets and VLANs. As you've learned, a subnet groups IP addresses so that clients on a large network can be logically organized into smaller networks. As you've also seen, this is often accomplished by adding routers (or Layer 3 switches) to the network or by using multiple ports on a single router (or Layer 3 switch). This creates multiple LANs within the larger network, with subnets organizing the available IP address space.

By contrast, a **VLAN (virtual local area network or virtual LAN)** groups ports on a Layer 2 switch so that some of the local traffic on the switch is forced to go through a router, thereby limiting the traffic to a smaller broadcast domain. As virtual LANs, VLANs abstract the broadcast domain from the networking hardware. This is similar to how VMs abstract computing functions from a computer's hardware. When using VLANs, the boundaries of the broadcast domain can be virtually defined anywhere within a single physical LAN.

Recall the example given earlier in this chapter of a large network on three floors of a building, as shown earlier in Figure 8-2. Rather than placing new routers on each floor of the building, you could use managed switches and VLANs to segment the network. For example, suppose you segment the network by department in the company rather than by floors in the building, as shown in Figure 8-15. To do this, you would install managed switches to replace the original switches if necessary. (It may not be necessary, because many enterprise switches these days have built-in VLAN functionality.) Next, you assign each host to a specific VLAN. You do this by configuring the switch port that each host is connected to.

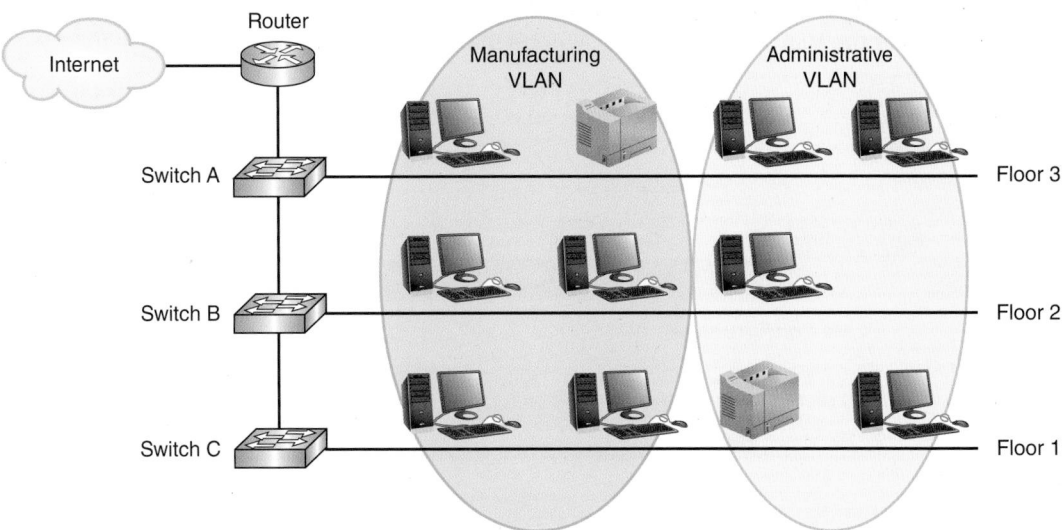

Figure 8-15   A simple VLAN design

Although you can add routers to separate a large LAN into manageable smaller LANs, reasons for using VLANs to do the job instead include:

- Isolating connections with heavy or unpredictable traffic patterns, such as when separating heavy VoIP traffic from other network activities
- Identifying groups of devices whose data should be given priority handling, such as executive client devices or an ICS (industrial control system) that manages a refrigeration system or a gas pipeline
- Containing groups of devices that rely on legacy protocols incompatible with the majority of the network's traffic, such as a legacy SCADA (supervisory control and data acquisition) system monitoring an oil refinery

- Separating groups of users who need special or limited security or network functions, such as when setting up a guest network
- Configuring temporary networks, such as when making specific network resources available to a short-term project team
- Reducing the cost of networking equipment, such as when upgrading a network design to include additional departments or new types of network traffic

Managed Switches

An **unmanaged switch** provides plug-and-play simplicity with minimal configuration options and has no IP address assigned to it. Unmanaged switches are not very expensive, but their capabilities are limited and they cannot support VLANs. **Managed switches**, on the other hand, can be configured via a command-line interface or a web-based management GUI (see Figure 8-16), and sometimes can be configured in groups. Usually, they are also assigned IP addresses for the purpose of continued management. VLANs can only be implemented through managed switches, whose ports can be partitioned into groups. Figure 8-17 shows the switch ports that are configured for the VLANs listed on the switch's management interface in Figure 8-16.

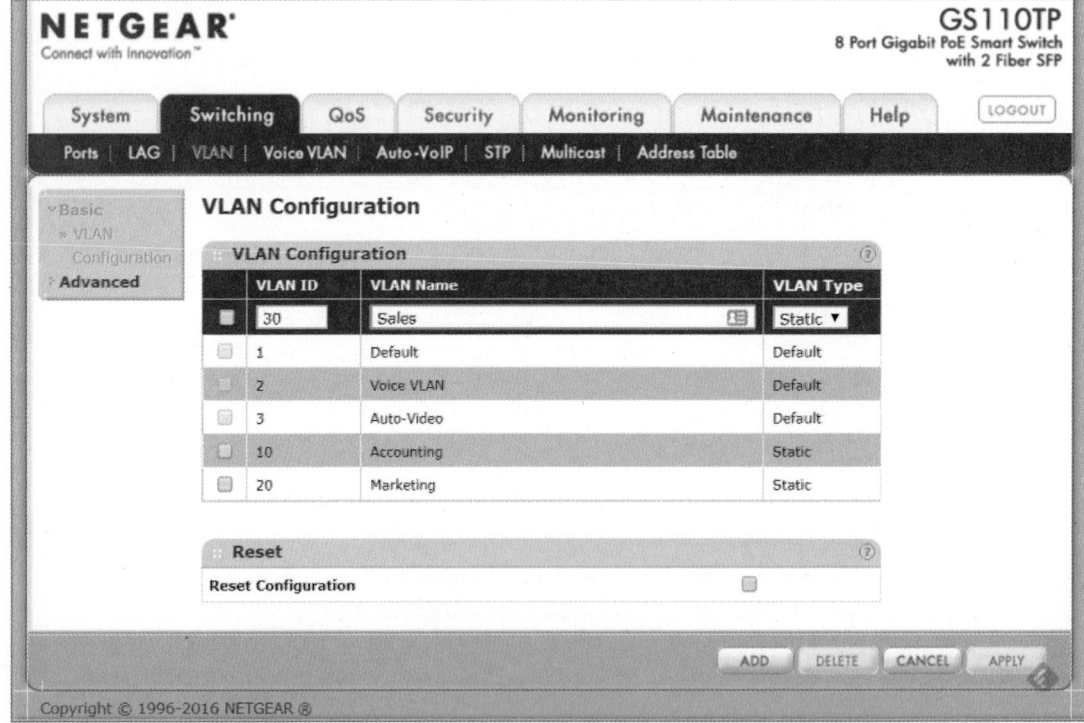

Figure 8-16   Configure VLANs on a managed switch's management interface

Source: Netgear

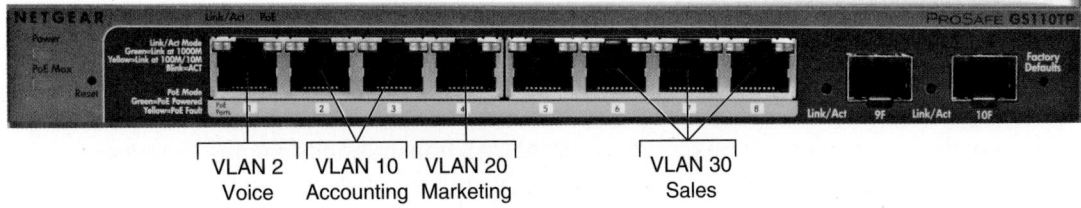

Figure 8-17   Each port on a managed switch might be configured for a different VLAN

Recall that switches are Layer 2 devices. (There are, of course, Layer 3 switches. However, these devices function as routers at Layer 3, not as switches.) By sorting traffic based on Layer 2 information, VLANs create two or more broadcast domains from a single broadcast domain, which is also a Layer 2 construct. Let's look at some illustrations to see how this works. Figure 8-18 shows how a normal Layer 2 switch operates. This switch manages all network traffic on the LAN unless a host on the network wants to communicate with a host on another network, and then that traffic goes through the router.

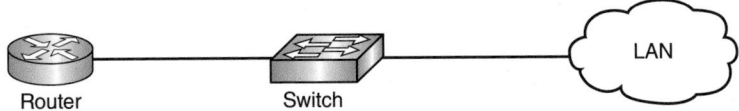

Figure 8-18   A switch connecting a LAN to a router

Figure 8-19 shows what happens when ports on a managed switch are partitioned into two VLANs. Traffic within each VLAN still goes through the switch as normal to reach other devices on the same VLAN. Traffic to hosts on other networks still goes through the router. However, traffic between hosts on VLAN 1 and VLAN 2 must now also go through the router, which is called inter-VLAN routing. This simple VLAN configuration, where one router connects to a switch that supports multiple VLANs, is sometimes called an ROAS ("router-on-a-stick").

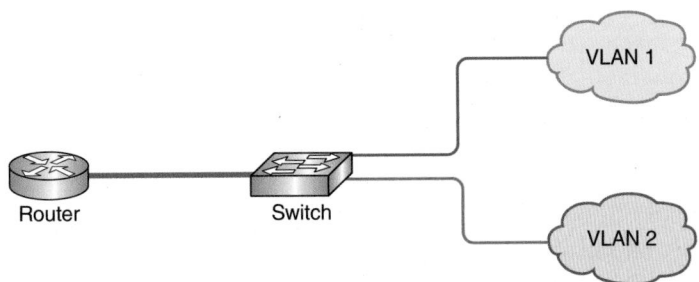

Figure 8-19   A managed switch with its ports partitioned into two groups, each belonging to a different VLAN

To visualize what happens with the actual hardware, take a look at Figure 8-20. Here you can see that several ports on the switch are assigned to VLAN 1 or VLAN 2. The ports for a VLAN don't have to be next to each other—each port is individually configured to belong to a specific VLAN. Any device that is connected to a VLAN-configured port is automatically considered to be part of that VLAN. All transmissions coming from the connected client will be associated with the VLAN configured on the switch port.

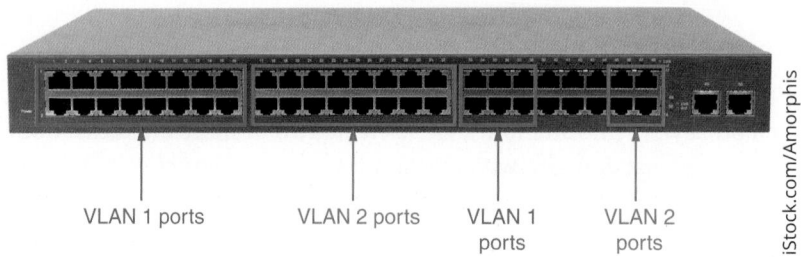

Figure 8-20   Each port on a switch can be assigned to a different VLAN

To identify the transmissions that belong to each VLAN, the switch adds a **tag** to Ethernet frames that identifies the port through which they arrive at the switch. This VLAN identifier is specified in the **802.1Q** standard, which is the IEEE standard that defines how VLAN information appears in frames and how switches interpret that information. Note that the 802.1Q standard is sometimes referred to as dot1q. Also, the port information required by this standard is sometimes referred to as the 802.1Q tag or dot1q tag.

Figure 8-21 shows where the 802.1Q tag is inserted in the Ethernet frame's header. The tag travels with the transmission until it reaches a router or the switch port connected to the destination device, whichever comes first. At that point, the tag is stripped from the frame. If the frame is being routed to a new VLAN, the router adds a new tag at this point, which is then removed once the frame reaches its final switch port. In most cases, neither the sending device nor the receiving device is aware of the VLAN infrastructure.

You've seen that a switch can support more than one VLAN. Similarly, a VLAN can include ports from more than one switch. Suppose we add a couple of more switches to the LAN, as in Figure 8-22. Switch B's ports in our example network can be configured with the same or different VLANs as the ports on Switch A. Traffic from one device on VLAN 1 connected to Switch A can travel to another device on VLAN 1 connected to Switch B as local traffic because they're in the same VLAN-defined broadcast domain. However, devices on separate VLANs—even if they're connected to the same switch— can't talk to each other without going through the router. Therefore, transmissions from a device on VLAN 1 connected to Switch B must go through the router in order to reach a device on VLAN 3, even though both devices are plugged into the same switch.

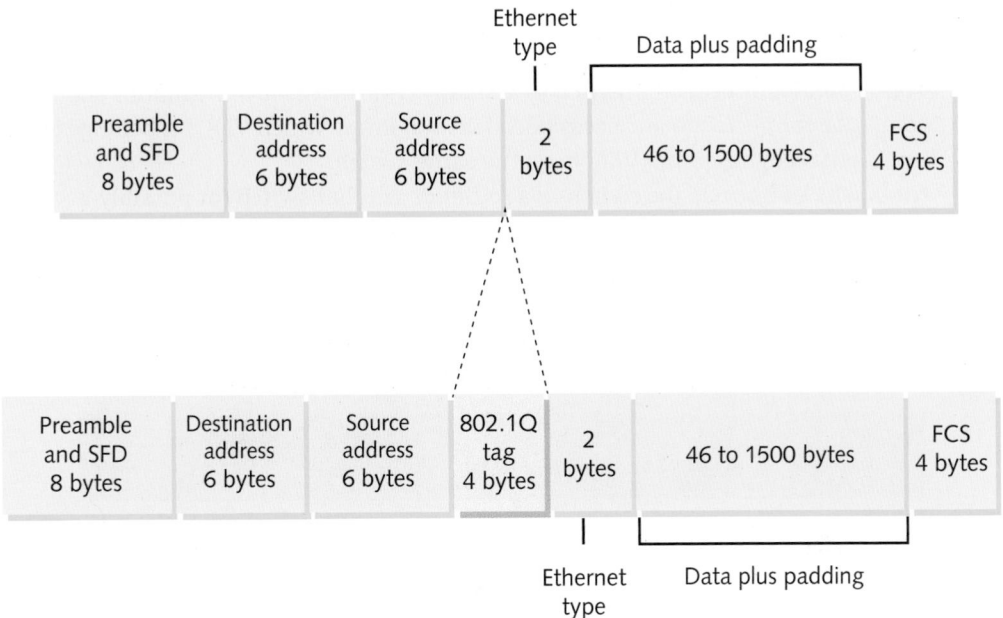

Figure 8-21   The 802.1Q VLAN tag is inserted after the Source address field in an Ethernet frame

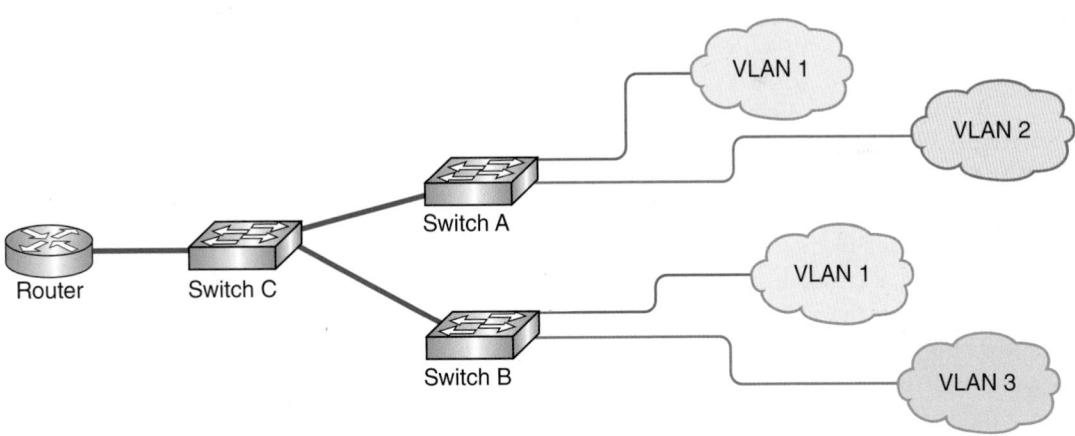

Figure 8-22   Three switches on a LAN with multiple VLANs

Switch Ports and Trunks

Notice in Figure 8-22 that Switch A is connected to devices on two VLANs, and it's also connected to Switch C. These are two very different types of connections. Ports connected to client devices are usually configured to support traffic for only one VLAN. However, the port that connects to Switch C must be able to carry traffic for multiple

VLANs. Therefore, each port on a switch that supports VLANs is configured as one of two types of VLAN ports:

- *access port*—Connects the switch to an endpoint, such as a workstation. The computer connected to an access port does not know which VLAN it belongs to, nor can it recognize other VLANs on the same switch.
- *trunk port*—Connects the switch to a router or another switch (or possibly a server). This interface manages traffic from multiple VLANs (see Figure 8-23). A trunk line (or just "trunk") is a link between two trunk ports.

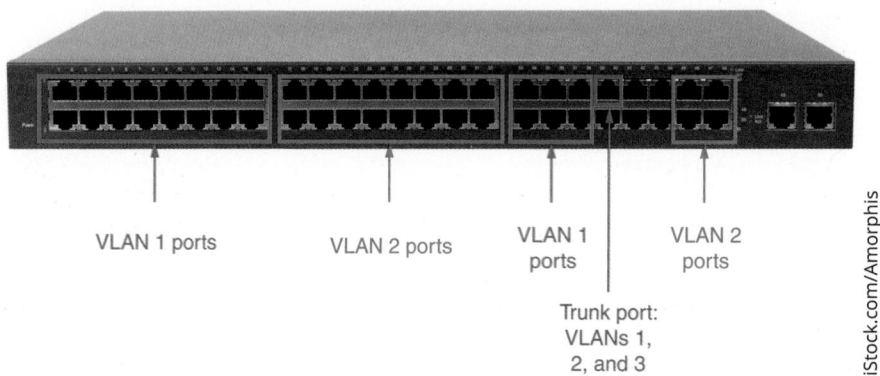

iStock.com/Amorphis

Figure 8-23   A trunk port supports traffic from multiple VLANs

A single switch can support traffic belonging to several VLANs across the network, thanks to the technique known as **trunking**. The term *trunk* originated in the telephony field, where it refers to an aggregation of logical connections over one physical connection. For example, a trunk carries signals for many residential telephone lines in the same neighborhood over one cable. Similarly, in the context of switching, a trunk is a single physical connection between networking devices through which many logical VLANs can transmit and receive data. Figure 8-24 shows the relative location of access ports, trunk ports, and trunk lines on our sample network.

Trunking protocols assign and interpret the VLAN tags in Ethernet frames, thereby managing the distribution of frames through a trunk. The most popular protocol for exchanging VLAN information over trunks is Cisco's **VTP (VLAN Trunk Protocol)**. VTP allows changes to a VLAN database on one switch, called the stack master, to be communicated to all other switches in the network. This provides network administrators with the ability to centrally manage all VLANs by making changes to a single switch. Other switches besides the stack master in the same VTP domain can also communicate VLAN updates, such as the addition of a new VLAN.

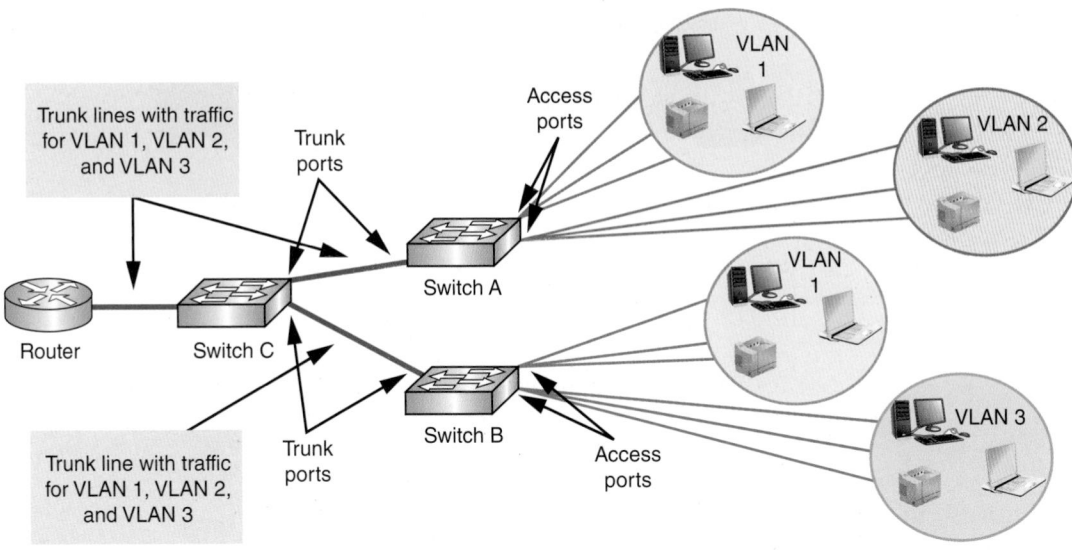

Figure 8-24   Each trunk line carries traffic for multiple VLANs

VLANs and Subnets

In most situations, each VLAN is assigned its own subnet of IP addresses. This means that the subnet, working at Layer 3, includes the same group of hosts as the VLAN, working at Layer 2. For example, our sample network (shown earlier in Figure 8-22 and again here in Figure 8-25) is divided into three subnets where VLAN 1 = Subnet 1, VLAN 2 = Subnet 2, and VLAN 3 = Subnet 3. As traffic from each VLAN reaches the router, the router sees three logical, virtual LANs connected to a single router port, as you can see in Figure 8-26.

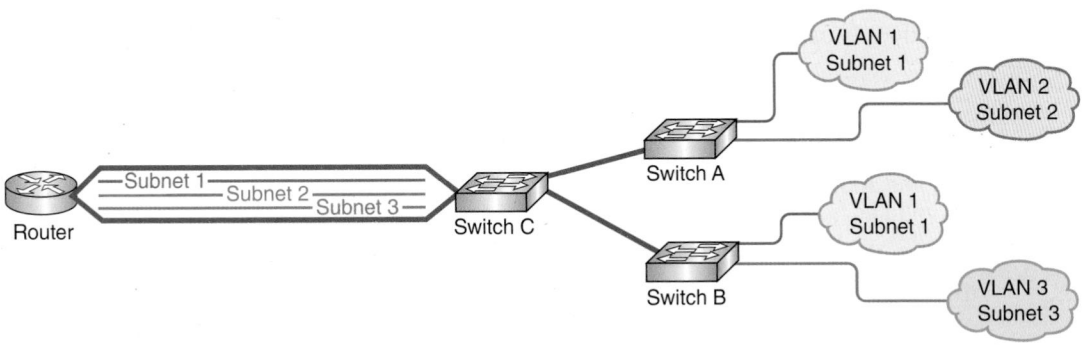

Figure 8-25   Three subnets are connected to a single router interface

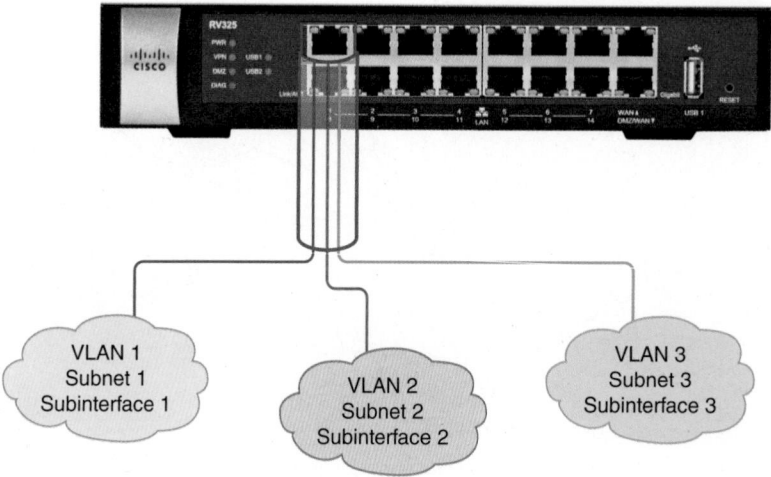

Figure 8-26   One router interface is configured to support three different subnets

Also, each VLAN and subnet combination acts as a single broadcast domain. Although it is possible to do otherwise, network administrators find life much easier when they adhere to the following rule:

1 broadcast domain = 1 VLAN = 1 subnet

So how do VLAN clients get the appropriate IP address assignments from the subnet's range of addresses portioned to each VLAN? One way to do this is to run a DCHP server for the entire network and use a DHCP relay agent to help sort DHCP requests by subnet, as described earlier in this chapter. If instead the router is providing DHCP services through this one interface, then the interface must be logically divided into three sub-interfaces. Each sub-interface is then configured with its own, subnetted range of IP addresses. In a project at the end of this chapter, you get practice doing exactly this using a router in Packet Tracer.

Types of VLANs

Different types of IP addresses serve different purposes (such as private, public, loopback, and APIPA IP addresses). The same is true of VLANs. Here are common VLAN types you'll likely come across when managing a network:

- *default VLAN*—Typically preconfigured on a switch and initially includes all the switch's ports. Other VLANs might be preconfigured as well, depending on the device and manufacturer. The default VLAN cannot be renamed or deleted; however, ports in the default VLAN can be reassigned to other VLANs.
- *native VLAN*—Receives all untagged frames from untagged ports. By default, this is the same as the default VLAN. However, this configuration poses a

security risk when untagged traffic is allowed to travel in a VLAN-managed network. To protect the network from unauthorized traffic, the native VLAN should be changed to an unused VLAN so that untagged traffic essentially runs into a dead-end. To do this on a Cisco switch, for example, use the command `switchport trunk native vlan`. On a Juniper switch, the native VLAN is configured with the command `set port-mode trunk` followed by `set native-vlan-id`. Each switch port can be configured for a different native VLAN using these commands. However, switch ports on each end of a trunk should agree on the native VLAN assignment. If the ports don't agree, this is called a **native VLAN mismatch**, or just **VLAN mismatch**, and will result in a configuration error.

- *data VLAN (or user VLAN)*—Carries user-generated traffic, such as email, web browsing, or database updates.
- *management VLAN*—Can be used to provide administrative access to a switch. By default, this might be the same as the default VLAN; however, this poses a security risk and should be changed.
- *voice VLAN*—Supports VoIP traffic, which requires high bandwidths, priority over other traffic, flexible routing, and minimized latency.

In addition to defining the types of traffic handled by a VLAN, you can also specify security parameters, filtering instructions (if the switch should not forward any frames from a certain VLAN, for example), performance requirements for certain ports, and network addressing and management options. Options vary according to the switch manufacturer and model. In Capstone Projects at the end of this chapter, you will have the opportunity to create and configure VLANs on switches in your Packet Tracer network.

View Configured VLANs

Once you create a VLAN, you also maintain it via the switch's software. Figure 8-27 illustrates the result of a `show vlan` command on a Cisco switch on a large, enterprise network. The `show vlan` command is used to list the current VLANs recognized by a switch. Other manufacturers' switch software include similar maintenance commands.

Figure 8-27 lists 18 VLANs configured on the network. Let's analyze what all this output tells us:

- The first half of the command output shows each VLAN's number, name, status, and which ports belong to it. For example, VLAN number 18, which is named "VLAN0018," is active and contains the ports "Gi1/3" and "Gi2/3." A port called "Gi1/3," in this case, refers to the third port on the first Gigabit Ethernet module of this switch.
- VLAN number 1 and VLANs 1002 through 1005 are defaults pre-established on the Cisco switch. Other than VLAN 1, these default VLANs are not currently in use.
- The second half of the command output provides additional information about each VLAN, including the type of network it operates on. In this example, all

```
VLAN    Name                              Status      Ports
----    --------------------------------  ---------   -------------------------------
1       default                           active      Te1/1, Te1/2, Gi1/5, Gi1/6
                                                      Te2/1, Te2/2, Gi2/5, Gi2/6
                                                      Gi4/3, Gi5/12, Gi6/12, Gi6/19
                                                      Gi8/11, Gi8/19, Gi9/4
5       VLAN0005                          active
13      VLAN0013                          active      Gi3/2, Gi3/3, Gi3/4, Gi8/12
14      VLAN0014                          active      Gi4/1, Gi4/2, Gi4/4, Gi9/12
16      VLAN0016                          active      Gi5/8
18      VLAN0018                          active      Gi1/3, Gi2/3
19      VLAN0019                          active      Gi5/11, Gi6/11
104     VLAN0104                          active      Gi1/4, Gi2/4, Gi3/5, Gi3/6
                                                      Gi4/5, Gi4/6, Gi5/1, Gi5/2
                                                      Gi5/3, Gi5/4, Gi5/5, Gi5/6
                                                      Gi5/7, Gi5/9, Gi5/10, Gi5/13
                                                      Gi5/14, Gi5/15, Gi5/16, Gi5/17
                                                      Gi5/18, Gi5/19, Gi5/20, Gi5/21
                                                      Gi5/22, Gi5/23, Gi5/24, Gi6/1
                                                      Gi6/2, Gi6/3, Gi6/4, Gi6/5
                                                      Gi6/6, Gi6/7, Gi6/9, Gi6/10
                                                      Gi6/13, Gi6/14, Gi6/15, Gi6/16
                                                      Gi6/17, Gi6/18, Gi6/20, Gi6/21
                                                      Gi6/22, Gi6/23, Gi6/24, Gi7/6
                                                      Gi7/8, Gi7/11, Gi7/12, Gi7/19
                                                      Gi8/8, Gi8/24, Gi9/1, Gi9/2
                                                      Gi9/3, Gi9/13
105     VLAN0105                          active      Gi7/24, Gi9/5, Gi9/6, Gi9/7
                                                      Gi9/8, Gi9/10, Gi9/11, Gi9/14
                                                      Gi9/16, Gi9/18, Gi9/19, Gi9/20
                                                      Gi9/21, Gi9/22, Gi9/23, Gi9/24
                                                      Gi10/1, Gi10/2, Gi10/4, Gi10/5
                                                      Gi10/6, Gi10/8, Gi10/9, Gi10/10
                                                      Gi10/11, Gi10/12, Gi10/13
                                                      Gi10/14, Gi10/15, Gi10/16
                                                      Gi10/17, Gi10/18, Gi10/19
                                                      Gi10/20, Gi10/21, Gi10/22
                                                      Gi10/23, Gi10/24
106     VLAN0106                          active      Gi6/8
107     VLAN0107                          active      Gi7/1, Gi7/2, Gi7/3, Gi7/4
                                                      Gi7/5, Gi7/7, Gi7/9, Gi7/10
                                                      Gi7/13, Gi7/14, Gi7/16, Gi7/17
                                                      Gi7/18, Gi7/21, Gi7/22, Gi8/1
                                                      Gi8/2, Gi8/3, Gi8/4, Gi8/5
                                                      Gi8/6, Gi8/7, Gi8/9, Gi8/10
                                                      Gi8/13, Gi8/14, Gi8/16, Gi8/17
                                                      Gi8/18, Gi8/21, Gi8/22
108     VLAN0108                          active      Gi7/15, Gi7/20, Gi7/23, Gi8/15
                                                      Gi8/20, Gi8/23
109     VLAN0109                          active
601     VLAN0601                          active
1002    fddi-default                      act/unsup
1003    token-ring-default                act/unsup
1004    fddinet-default                   act/unsup
1005    trnet-default                     act/unsup

VLAN    Type   SAID        MTU    Parent  RingNo  BridgeNo  Stp   BrdgMode  Trans1  Trans2
----    -----  ----------  -----  ------  ------  --------  ----  --------  ------  ------
1       enet   100001      1500   -       -       -         -     -         0       0
5       enet   100005      1500   -       -       -         -     -         0       0
13      enet   100013      1500   -       -       -         -     -         0       0
14      enet   100014      1500   -       -       -         -     -         0       0
16      enet   100016      1500   -       -       -         -     -         0       0
18      enet   100018      1500   -       -       -         -     -         0       0
19      enet   100019      1500   -       -       -         -     -         0       0
104     enet   100104      1500   -       -       -         -     -         0       0
105     enet   100105      1500   -       -       -         -     -         0       0
106     enet   100106      1500   -       -       -         -     -         0       0
107     enet   100107      1500   -       -       -         -     -         0       0
108     enet   100108      1500   -       -       -         -     -         0       0
109     enet   100109      1500   -       -       -         -     -         0       0
601     enet   100601      1500   -       -       -         -     -         0       0
1002    fddi   101002      1500   -       -       -         -     -         0       0
1003    tr     101003      1500   -       -       -         -     -         0       0
1004    fdnet  101004      1500   -       -       -         ieee  -         0       0
1005    trnet  101005      1500   -       -       -         ibm   -         v       0
```

Figure 8-27   Output of the show vlan command on a Cisco switch

VLANs that are active and not pre-established defaults use Ethernet, which is indicated by the *enet* type.

- Each VLAN is assigned a different SAID (security association identifier), which indicates to other connectivity devices which VLAN a transmission belongs to. By default, Cisco switches assign a VLAN the SAID of 100,000 plus the VLAN number.
- In this example, each VLAN is configured to transmit and receive frames with an MTU (maximum transmission unit) size of 1500 bytes, which is the default selection. Rarely do network administrators change this variable.

Troubleshoot and Secure VLANs

Configuration errors are a common cause of VLAN problems. The `show vlan` command discussed earlier in this chapter yields information that can help you identify misconfigurations. Start by checking the configuration against your documentation and then check physical connections. If that doesn't work, consider these common configuration errors:

- *incorrect port mode*—Switch ports connected to endpoints, such as workstations and servers, should nearly always use access mode. Switch ports connected to other network devices should be configured in trunk mode only if that connection must support multiple VLANs.
- *incorrect VLAN assignment*—This can happen due to a variety of situations, including misconfigurations of the client authentication process in which a VLAN is assigned to the device before the authentication process is complete.
- *VLAN isolation*—By grouping certain nodes into a VLAN, you are not merely including those nodes—you are also excluding other groups of nodes. This means you can potentially cut off an entire group from the rest of the network. VLANs must be connected to and configured on a router or Layer 3 switch to allow different VLANs to exchange data outside their own broadcast domain.

Hackers sometimes take advantage of the way VLANs are tagged to implement an attack called **VLAN hopping**. The attacker generates transmissions that appear, to the switch, to belong to a protected VLAN, then crosses VLANs to access sensitive data or inject harmful software. There are two approaches to VLAN hopping:

- *double tagging*—The hacker stacks VLAN tags in Ethernet frames. When the first, legitimate tag is removed by a switch, the second, illegitimate tag is revealed, tricking a switch into forwarding the transmission on to a restricted VLAN.
- *switch spoofing*—An attacker connects to a switch and then makes the connection look to the switch as if it's a trunk line. The switch might auto-configure its port into trunk mode when it detects trunk mode on the other end of the connection. A hacker can then feed his own VLAN traffic into that port and access VLANs throughout the network.

The following mitigation efforts will reduce the risk of VLAN hopping:

- Don't use the default VLAN.
- Change the native VLAN to an unused VLAN ID.
- Disable auto-trunking on switches that don't need to support traffic from multiple VLANs.
- On switches that do carry traffic from multiple VLANs, configure all ports as access ports unless they're used as trunk ports.
- Specify which VLANs are supported on each trunk instead of accepting a range of all VLANs.
- Use physical security methods such as door locks to restrict access to network equipment.

Chapter Summary

Network Segmentation

- When a network is segmented into multiple smaller networks, traffic on one network is separated from another network's traffic and each network is its own broadcast domain.

Subnets

- Subnetting helps solve the fundamental problem with classful addressing: too many host addresses assigned to each classful network, resulting in available addresses being used up too quickly.

- When a computer is ready to send a transmission to another host, it first compares the bits in its own network ID to the bits in the network ID of the destination host. If the bits match, the remote host is on the sending computer's own network, and it sends the transmission directly to that host. If the bits don't match, the destination host is on another network, and the computer sends the transmission to the default gateway on its network.

- CIDR notation takes the network ID or a host's IP address and follows it with a forward slash (/), which is then followed by the number of bits that are used for the network ID.

- To create a subnet, you borrow bits that would represent host information in classful addressing and use those bits instead to represent network information. By doing so, you increase the number of bits available for the network ID, and you also reduce the number of bits available for identifying hosts. Consequently, you increase the number of networks and reduce the number of usable host addresses in each network or subnet.

- Class A, Class B, and Class C networks can all be subnetted. But because each class reserves a different number of bits for network information, each class has a different number of host information bits that can be used for subnet information.

- There are generally two types of subnet calculation problems you're likely to see on the CompTIA Network+ exam: Calculate possible subnets or calculate subnet information for a single IP address.

- For dynamic IP addressing, the administrator programs each subnet's DHCP server with the network ID, subnet mask, range of IP addresses, and default gateway for the subnet.
- VLSM (Variable Length Subnet Mask) allows subnets to be further subdivided into smaller and smaller groupings until each subnet is about the same size as the IP address space that is needed. This is often referred to as "subnetting a subnet."
- Subnetting in IPv6 is simpler than subnetting in IPv4. The subnet ID portion of an IPv6 address is one block long, which is four hexadecimal characters, which is 16 bits in binary.

VLANs (Virtual Local Area Networks)

- A VLAN (virtual local area network or virtual LAN) groups ports on a switch so that some of the local traffic on the switch is forced to go through a router, thereby limiting the traffic to a smaller broadcast domain. As virtual LANs, VLANs abstract the broadcast domain from the networking hardware similar to how VMs abstract computing functions from a computer's hardware.
- Managed switches can be configured via a command-line interface or a web-based management GUI, and sometimes can be configured in groups. VLANs can only be implemented through managed switches, whose ports can be partitioned into groups.
- A single switch can support traffic belonging to several VLANs across the network, thanks to a technique known as trunking. A trunk is a single physical connection between networking devices through which many logical VLANs can transmit and receive data.
- In most situations, each VLAN is assigned its own subnet of IP addresses. This means that the subnet, working at Layer 3, includes the same group of hosts as the VLAN, working at Layer 2.
- Just as different types of IP addresses serve different purposes (such as private, public, loopback, and APIPA IP addresses), so do different types of VLANs.
- Once you create a VLAN, you also maintain it via the switch's software. The `show vlan` command is used to list the current VLANs recognized by a switch. Other manufacturers' switch software includes similar maintenance commands.
- Hackers sometimes take advantage of the way VLANs are tagged to implement an attack called VLAN hopping, in which the attacker generates transmissions that appear, to the switch, to belong to a protected VLAN. The attacker can then cross VLANs to access sensitive data or inject harmful software.

Key Terms

For definitions of key terms, see the Glossary near the end of the book.

802.1Q	CIDR block	global routing prefix
access port	CIDR notation	ip helper-address
ANDing	classless addressing	magic number
CIDR (Classless Interdomain Routing)	default VLAN	managed switch
	DHCP relay agent	native VLAN

native VLAN mismatch
site prefix
tag
trunk port
trunking

unmanaged switch
VLAN (virtual
    local area network or
    virtual LAN)
VLAN hopping

VLAN mismatch
VLSM (Variable
    Length Subnet Mask)
VTP (VLAN
    Trunk Protocol)

Review Questions

1. How many bits of a Class A IP address are used for host information?
   a. 8 bits
   b. 16 bits
   c. 24 bits
   d. 32 bits

2. What is the formula for determining the number of possible hosts on a network?
   a. $2^n = Y$
   b. $2^n - 2 = Y$
   c. $2^h = Z$
   d. $2^h - 2 = Z$

3. Which of the following is *not* a good reason to segment a network?
   a. To limit access to broadcast domains
   b. To reduce the demand on bandwidth
   c. To increase the number of networking devices on a network
   d. To narrow down the location of problems on a network

4. What is the least number of bits you would need to borrow from the network portion of a Class B subnet mask to get at least 130 hosts per subnet?
   a. None
   b. Eight
   c. Nine
   d. Ten

5. What do well-chosen subnets accomplish?
   a. IP address spaces overlap for easier management.
   b. Network documentation is easier to manage.

   c. Routing efficiency is decreased by ensuring IP address spaces are not mathematically related.
   d. Problems affect the entire network, making them more difficult to pin down.

6. Which formulas can be used to calculate the magic number? Choose two.
   a. 256 – the interesting octet
   b. $2^h - 2$
   c. 2^n
   d. 2^h

7. Which hexadecimal block in an IPv6 address is used for the Subnet ID?
   a. The first one
   b. The third one
   c. The fourth one
   d. The eighth one

8. While designing your network's VLAN topology, your team has decided to use a centrally managed DHCP server rather than creating a separate DHCP server for each VLAN. What software will you need in order to make the central DHCP server accessible across VLANs?
   a. DHCP relay agent
   b. DHCP server
   c. Hypervisor
   d. Virtual router

9. Which port mode on a switch enables that port to manage traffic for multiple VLANs?
   a. Console
   b. Ethernet

c. Access

d. Trunk

10. Which IEEE standard determines how VLANs work on a network?

   a. 802.1x

   b. 802.11

   c. 802.3af

   d. 802.1Q

11. What is the network ID with CIDR notation for the IP address 172.16.32.108 whose subnet mask is 255.255.255.0?

12. Suppose your company has leased one Class C license, 120.10.10.0, and wants to sublease the first half of these IP addresses to another company. What is the CIDR notation for the subnet to be subleased? What is the subnet mask for this network?

13. Subnetting operates at Layer _____ while VLANs function at Layer _____.

14. Which VLAN on a switch manages untagged frames?

15. An attacker configures a VLAN frame with two tags instead of just one. The first tag directs the frame to the authorized VLAN. After the frame enters the first VLAN, the switch appropriately removes the tag, then discovers the next tag, and sends the frame along to a protected VLAN, which the attacker is not authorized to access. What kind of attack is this?

16. What area of a network can provide less stringent security so a web server is more accessible from the open Internet?

17. On which networking device do you configure VLANs?

18. Which IP addressing technique subnets a subnet to create subnets of various sizes?

19. Which VLAN is designed to support administrative access to networking devices?

20. Which Cisco command lists configured VLANs on a switch?

Hands-On Projects

Project 8-1: Calculate Subnets

In this chapter, you saw how to calculate subnets for both Class B and Class C networks. In this project, you work with a Class B private network. Complete the steps as follows:

1. Your employer is opening a new location, and the IT director has assigned you the task of calculating the subnet numbers for the new LAN. You've determined that you need 50 subnets for the Class B network beginning with the network ID 172.20.0.0. How many host bits will you need to use for network information in the new subnets?

2. After the subnetting is complete, how many unused subnets will be waiting on hold for future expansion, and how many possible hosts can each subnet contain?

3. What is the new subnet mask?

4. Complete Table 8-9.

Table 8-9 Calculate subnets

Subnet number	Extended network prefix	Range of host addresses	Broadcast address
1	172.20.0.0	172.20.0.1 through 172.20.3.254	
2	172.20.4.0	_____ through 172.20.7.254	
3		172.20.8.1 through _____	172.20.11.255
4			
5			
...	...	...	...
50			

5. What is the CIDR notation for this network?
6. What is the broadcast address of the subnet for the host at 172.20.6.139?
7. Is the host at 172.20.11.250 on the same subnet as the host at 172.20.12.3? How do you know?

Project 8-2: Shortcuts to Subnet Calculations

There are many handy shortcuts you can find online for calculating subnets more quickly and easily. On the job, it would probably be best to use a subnet calculator, such as the one at *subnet-calculator.com*, to better ensure you don't make any time-consuming mistakes in your calculations. However, on the Network+ certification exam, subnetting shortcuts can help you get to an answer without wasting much of your limited time.

To use this shortcut method, you'll first draw a series of numbers. This might look confusing at first, but hang in there. It should make sense by the end. Complete the following steps:

1. Write one row of eight numbers from right to left, starting with 1 on the right, then 2, then 4, and so on, doubling each number as you move left. See the top row in Figure 8-28.

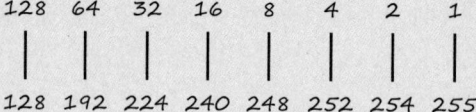

Figure 8-28 Write these numbers and connect the number in each row

2. Below this first row, write another row of eight numbers from right to left, this time starting with 255 on the right. Subtract the number directly above 255 to get the next number, 254. Subtract the number directly above 254 to get 252, and so on. You know you've done it correctly if the left-most number in both rows is 128. (After you've done this a few times, you'll likely have these numbers memorized.) When you're finished, draw a line connecting the corresponding numbers in each row, as shown in Figure 8-28.

3. Above the top row, write another row of eight numbers, but this time work left to right. Start with 2 on the left, and double each number as you move to the right. See the top row in Figure 8-29.

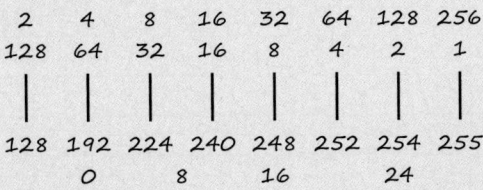

Figure 8-29 You don't have to memorize these numbers, just memorize the pattern of how to get them and where to write them

4. Below the bottom row, write four more numbers from left to right. Start with 0 on the left, then skip-count by 8s, as shown in Figure 8-29.

You're now ready to use your shortcut to calculate subnets. Let's start with the Class C network at 192.168.15.0 and create at least 15 subnets with at least 10 hosts each.

5. On the row immediately above the vertical lines, find the lowest number that covers the needed hosts and circle it, as shown in Figure 8-30. This is your magic number. In Figure 8-30, the magic number is 16.

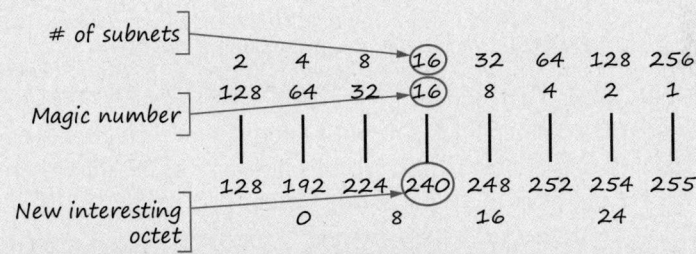

Figure 8-30 Circle the magic number, the number of subnets, and the new subnet octet

6. Circle the number directly above the magic number, as shown in Figure 8-30. This tells you how many subnets you'll be creating.

7. Circle the number directly below the magic number, as shown in Figure 8-30. This is the new interesting octet in the subnet mask. What is the subnet mask for the subnets in this scenario?

8. To calculate the subnets' network IDs, start with the original network IP address 192.168.15.0. In the fourth octet, skip-count by the magic number as high as you can go without going over 255. Add this information to Table 8-10 in the Network ID column.

Table 8-10	Subnetting practice	
Network ID	**Host IP range**	**Broadcast address**
192.168.15.0	192.168.15.1 – 192.168.15.14	192.168.15.15
192.168.15.16		

9. Fill in the rest of Table 8-10. Recall that you can subtract 1 from a network ID to get the previous subnet's broadcast address. The host IP address range consists of all numbers between the network ID and the broadcast address.

The bottom row in our shortcut helps you solve the other type of subnetting problem you learned about in this chapter: finding network information when given a single host's IP address and subnet mask. Note that this system only works as described here for IP addresses using 24 or more bits in the network ID portion.

Let's practice one. Suppose you're told that 192.168.89.130/27 is a host's CIDR notation. How do you find the host's network ID, broadcast address, and the range of host addresses in the same subnet? Complete the following steps:

10. Write the host's IP address directly below the lowest row in your shortcut, with one octet per number on the last row. See Figure 8-31.
11. Draw a line to connect each pair of corresponding numbers. See Figure 8-31.
12. The CIDR number in this scenario is /27. Looking at the four multiples of 8 above the IP address in Figure 8-31, circle the largest of these without going over the CIDR number. In this case, it's 24. See Figure 8-32.
13. Start counting at the multiple of 8 that you circled. Count up with each jump that you make from left to right along the second row. And stop when you reach the CIDR number for this host. Follow along in Figure 8-33 for this example. Point to the multiple of 8 that you circled and say "24." Say "25" when you jump to 128 in the second row. Say "26"

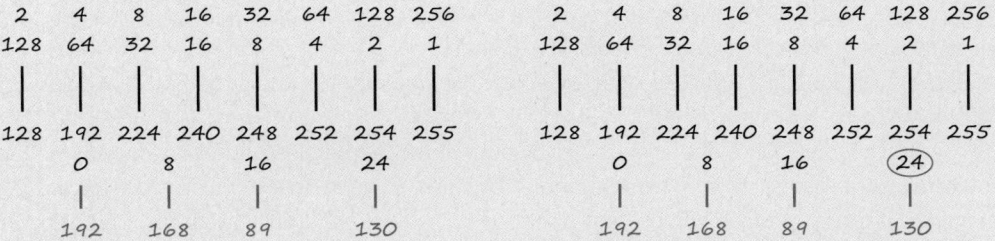

Figure 8-31 Write the host's IP address at the bottom and draw lines to connect the numbers

Figure 8-32 Circle the largest multiple of 8 without going over the CIDR number

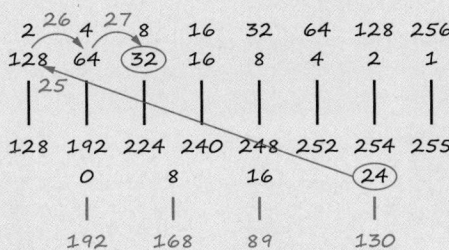

Figure 8-33 Count up with each jump along the second row

when you jump to 64 in the second row. Say "27" when you jump to 32 in the second row. Because 27 is the CIDR number for the host address, this is where you stop. Circle the number you stopped on, which in this case is 32. This is the magic number.

14. If more than 8 bits were used for the host portion, this method would not work. However, because 8 or fewer bits are used for the host portion, you can assume that the starting network ID for these subnets is the first three octets of the host's IP address with 0 in the final octet. This means you can now fill in enough information about this host's subnet and the surrounding subnets to find the information you need. Complete only the needed portions of Table 8-11. To simplify things, the table only includes enough subnets to allow you to work one subnet beyond the host's subnet.

Table 8-11 More subnetting practice

Network ID	Host IP range	Broadcast address
192.168.89.0	xxxxxxx	xxxxxxx
	xxxxxxx	xxxxxxx
	xxxxxxx	xxxxxxx
	xxxxxxx	xxxxxxx
	xxxxxxx	xxxxxxx

How well did these shortcuts help you? If it clicked for you, great! Keep practicing with these methods and you might even learn it well enough to do most of it in your head. If it didn't work for you, do a Google search for *subnetting shortcuts* and find a method that does work for you.

Several good websites and apps can give you a variety of practice subnet questions so you can become especially comfortable with calculating subnets. Do a Google search for *subnetting practice*, or try an app on your phone, such as /24 Subnetting Practice by Zerones, available on both Android and iPhone. A good subnetting practice app like /24 Subnetting Practice will give you options on the types of problems to work with (see Figure 8-34a), will tell you the correct answer (see Figure 8-34b), and will explain why that answer is correct (see Figure 8-34c).

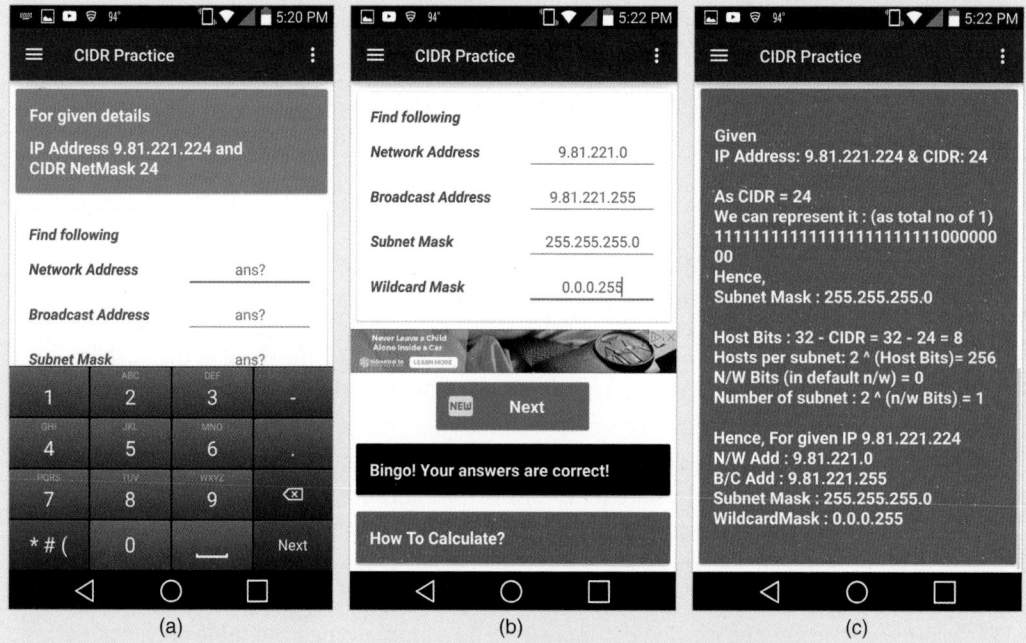

(a)   (b)   (c)

Figure 8-34   **Practice subnetting problems on your smartphone**
Source: Zerones

Project 8-3: Configure VLANs Using a Switch's GUI

As you saw in the chapter, some switches allow you to configure VLANs through a graphical user interface instead of through a command-line interface. In this project, you use an online switch simulator to practice configuring VLANs on a Linksys switch. Complete the following steps:

1. In your browser, go to **ui.linksys.com**. Scroll down to find the **LGS528P** switch and click on it. At the time of this writing, the web address is *ui.linksys.com/LGS528P*. If you can't find this switch, look for another enterprise-grade switch.

2. Click the latest version available for this switch. At the time of this writing, the version is **V1.0.1.4**.

3. Click **Log In**. You do not need a username or password.

4. Take a few minutes to explore the switch's management interface. Answer the following questions:

   a. How many ports does it have?

   b. What is the switch's current IPv4 address? Why does this switch have an IP address at all?

   c. How many VLANs are currently configured on the switch? Which one is the default VLAN?

5. If you're not already there, click the **Configuration** tab and then click **VLAN Management**.

6. Click the **Edit** button. Select **VLAN 2** and name it **Accounting**. Click **Apply**, and then click **Close**. Because this is a simulator, the changes are not saved.

7. Click the **Add** button. Make sure **Single VLAN** is selected. Create your own VLAN with an ID number and name. Click **Apply** and then click **Close**.

8. In the left pane under VLAN Management, click **Interfaces**. Note that all interfaces are currently configured for trunk mode. At the bottom of the list, click **Edit**. Select a port, make sure **Access** mode is selected, click **Apply**, and then click **Close**.

Although none of the changes you make in this simulator are saved, it's still a good way to help you visualize what kinds of changes this switch is capable of supporting. Other manufacturers also offer simulators for some of their devices.

Capstone Projects

Here you have a golden opportunity to explore nearly all the main concepts you learned in this chapter by making some additions and configurations to your Packet Tracer network. To allow you to make the most of this opportunity, this chapter includes a third Capstone Project.

Capstone Project 8-1: Add Subnets to Your Packet Tracer Network

In Chapter 6, Capstone Project 6-1, you installed Packet Tracer. In Chapter 7, Capstone Project 7-2, you began building a Packet Tracer network. In this project, you will calculate subnet information for nine subnets, which you will then configure on your network in Packet Tracer. Then in Capstone Projects 8-2 and 8-3, you will configure VLANs on the Packet Tracer network.

Let's begin by adding a few more devices to your network. Complete the following steps:

1. In Packet Tracer, open your Packet Tracer file from Capstone Project 7-2.

2. Add the following new devices:

   a. Three new **Generic routers**

   b. Four new **2960 switches**

   c. Four new **Generic workstations**

Arrange the devices as shown in Figure 8-35. You might need to shift the original devices over so you can see the entire network. Don't worry about configuring any of the devices yet.

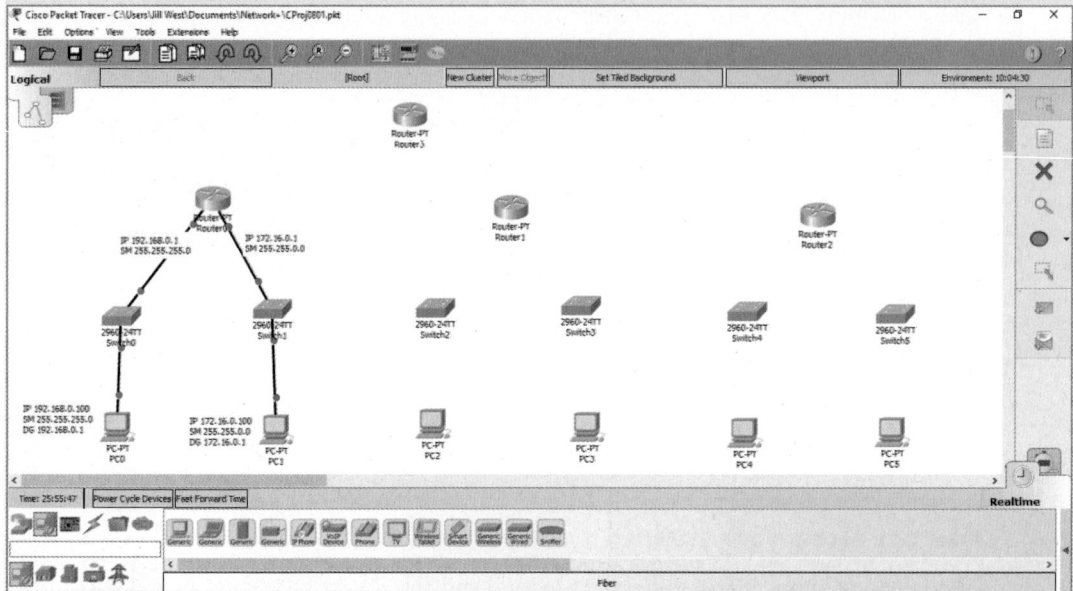

Figure 8-35   Add more devices to your Packet Tracer network
Source: Cisco Systems, Inc.

3. Connect the new devices to each other using the **Copper Straight-Through** cable as described next:

   a. On each workstation, connect the Ethernet cable to the **FastEthernet0** interface.

   b. On each switch, connect the Ethernet cable from the workstation to the **FastEthernet0/1** interface. Connect the Ethernet cable from the switch to its router to the switch's **FastEthernet0/2** interface.

   c. On Router1, connect Switch2 to the **FastEthernet0/0** interface and connect Switch3 to the **FastEthernet1/0** interface.

   d. On Router2, connect Switch4 to the **FastEthernet0/0** interface and connect Switch5 to the **FastEthernet1/0** interface.

   e. Wait a few minutes for the workstation-to-switch connections to turn green on both ends of each connection.

4. Use a **Fiber** cable to connect the **FastEthernet4/0** port on Router0 to the **FastEthernet4/0** port on Router3. Repeat with Router1 (**FastEthernet4/0**) to Router3 (**FastEthernet5/0**). Note that any connection to a router will remain red until the ports are configured. Also notice that you've now used up the existing fiber connections available on Router3, so you need to add a new interface module.

5. Click **Router3**. On the Physical tab, scroll to the right and click the power switch to turn the router off. Drag and drop a **PT-ROUTER-NM-1FFE MODULE** to an open slot in the Physical Device View, as shown in Figure 8-36. Turn the power back on. Close the Router3 window.

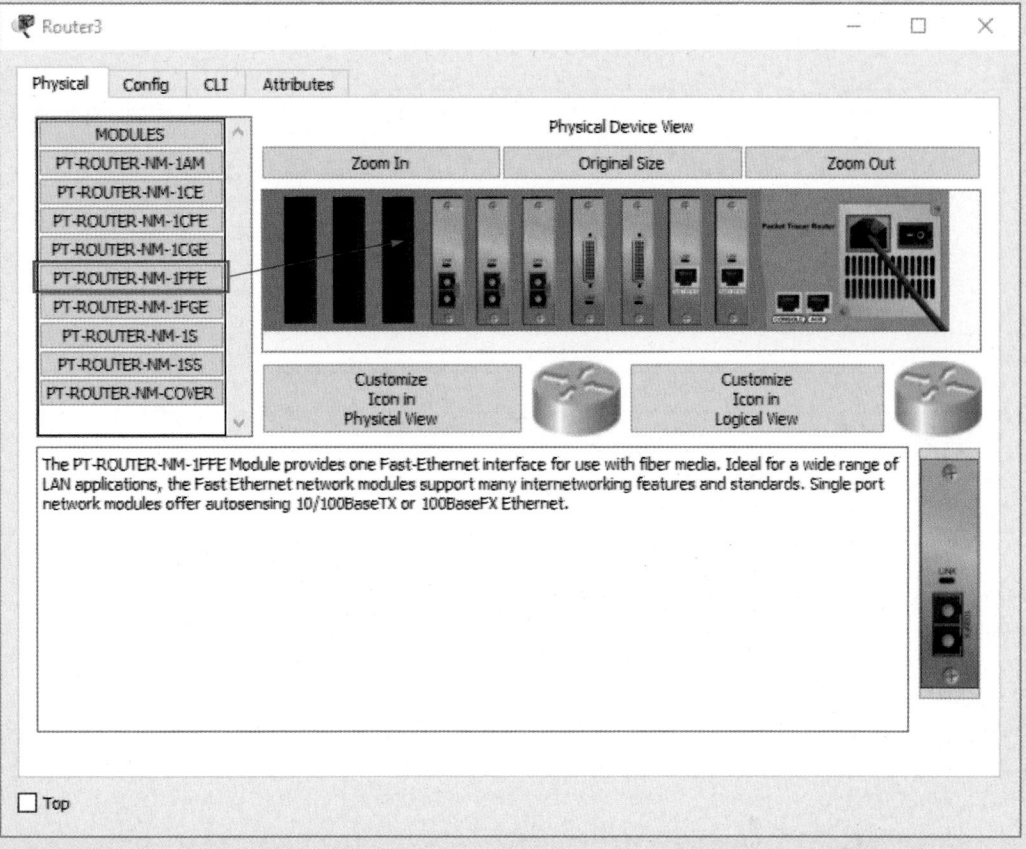

Figure 8-36   Add a new Fast-Ethernet interface for fiber media to the router

Source: Cisco Systems, Inc.

6. Use a **Fiber** cable to connect the **FastEthernet4/0** port on Router2 to the **FastEthernet6/0** port on Router3.

Now you're ready to calculate the subnets you'll use in your Packet Tracer network. Answer the following questions:

7. You'll need a different subnet for each connection to a router or each connection between routers. How many subnets will you need altogether?

8. Using the formula $2^n = Y$, how many bits will you need to borrow from the host portion of the IP address?

9. What will your new subnet mask be?

10. What is the magic number for these calculations?

11. How many possible hosts can each subnet have?

12. Fill in the Network ID column in Table 8-12 with the first several subnets for this network. The first one is filled in for you. The table only covers the subnets you'll need for this project.

13. Fill in the Broadcast address column in Table 8-12.

14. Fill in the Range of host addresses column in Table 8-12.

Table 8-12   Subnet information for Packet Tracer network

Subnet number	Network ID	Range of host addresses	Broadcast address
1	192.168.43.0		
2			
3			
4			
5			
6			
7			
8			
9			

Three of these subnets only need two host addresses, because they connect only two routers. Let's take the first subnet here and divide it again into three additional, smaller subnets. Answer the following questions:

15. If you borrow one more bit from the host portion of the IP address in Subnet 1, how many smaller subnets will this create? Is this enough?

16. If you borrow two more bits from the host portion of the IP address in Subnet 1, how many smaller subnets will this create? Is this enough?

17. What's the new subnet mask for these smaller subnets?

18. How many hosts can each of these smaller subnets have?

19. Fill in Table 8-13 with the smaller subnets' information. The first one is filled in for you.

Table 8-13   Smaller subnets for router-to-router connections

Subnet number	Network ID	Range of host addresses	Broadcast address
1A	192.168.43.0	192.168.43.1 – 192.168.43.2	192.168.43.3
1B			
1C			
1D			

Let's look at where each of these subnet assignments belong on your network in Packet Tracer. Complete the following steps:

20. Each of the smaller subnets will be assigned to a connection between two routers. Each router interface will be assigned a host IP address within that smaller subnet. Notice in Table 8-14 how the IP addresses for these smaller subnets are assigned to each router's interfaces (Fa4/0 for Routers 0, 1, and 2, and all three interfaces for Router3).

Table 8-14	IP address assignments for device interfaces			
Device	Interface	IP address	Subnet mask	Default gateway
Router0	Fa0/0	192.168.43.17		N/A
	Fa1/0			N/A
	Fa4/0	192.168.43.1		N/A
Router1	Fa0/0			N/A
	Fa1/0			N/A
	Fa4/0	192.168.43.5		N/A
Router2	Fa0/0			N/A
	Fa1/0			N/A
	Fa4/0	192.168.43.9		N/A
Router3	Fa4/0	192.168.43.2		N/A
	Fa5/0	192.168.43.6		N/A
	Fa6/0	192.168.43.10		N/A
PC0	Fa0	192.168.43.30	255.255.255.240	192.168.43.17
PC1	Fa0			
PC2	Fa0			
PC3	Fa0			
PC4	Fa0			
PC5	Fa0			

21. Subnet 2 is assigned to PC0's subnet. Notice in Table 8-14 that PC0's default gateway is the first usable host address in the subnet, and PC0's interface has the last usable host address in the subnet. Also, PC0's default gateway address is the IP address of Router0's interface (Fa0/0) on that subnet.

22. Repeat this pattern and assign the following subnets to each PC, filling in the relevant information for that workstation and its router in Table 8-14.

    a. Subnet 3 is assigned to PC1.

    b. Subnet 4 is assigned to PC2.

    c. Subnet 5 is assigned to PC3.

    d. Subnet 6 is assigned to PC4.

    e. Subnet 7 is assigned to PC5.

Now you're ready to configure these subnets on your network in Packet Tracer. Complete the following steps:

23. Click **Router0** and click the **Config** tab. Configure each of the three connected interfaces with the information listed for Router0 in Table 8-14, and turn on any connected ports that are not already on. Update the on-screen notes to reflect these changes and make new notes as needed.

24. Repeat Step 23 for each of the other three routers.

25. Click **PC0**, click the **Desktop** tab, and click **IP Configuration**. Configure the IP Address, Subnet Mask, and Default Gateway information listed for PC0 in Table 8-14. Update the on-screen notes to reflect these changes and make new notes as needed.

26. Repeat Step 25 for each of the other workstations.

27. If any link does not turn green, troubleshoot the configuration to find the problem. Most of the time, the problem is a typo or forgetting to turn on a port. After all the links turn green, start pinging various interfaces from different workstations to confirm all the connections are configured correctly. To run ping from any PC, click the PC, and then click the **Desktop** tab. Click **Command Prompt** and run your pings from here. For example, can you ping PC0 from PC5? Can you ping all three of Router3's interfaces from PC3? What problems did you find from your ping tests, and how did you fix them?

28. Click **File, Save As,** and save this Packet Tracer file in a safe place for future projects.

29. Add installation information to the Packet Tracer page on your Wikidot website, along with any notes that you think might be helpful to you for the next Packet Tracer project. When you're finished, close **Packet Tracer** or continue to Capstone Project 8-2.

Capstone Project 8-2: Add VLANs to Your Packet Tracer Network

This Capstone Project picks up where Capstone Project 8-1 left off. In this project, you create VLANs on switches in your Packet Tracer network, and test the connections to see which devices can communicate with each other and which ones can't at each successive configuration. Feel free to experiment beyond the tests we suggest. You might even want to create a copy of your Packet Tracer file so you can experiment more extensively, or create your own, unique network with different configurations.

Let's begin by creating a pair of simple VLANs on Switch0. For this project, you use the switch's configuration interface. In Capstone Project 8-3, you'll learn to use the CLI for both a switch and a router. After completing Capstone Project 8-1, complete the following steps:

1. In Packet Tracer, open your Packet Tracer file from Capstone Project 8-1.

2. On the far-left side of the workspace, add three more PCs as shown in Figure 8-37. If you need to create more space on that side of the workspace, use the **Select** tool from the Common tools bar on the right. Press and hold the mouse button and drag the mouse pointer to select all items on the screen, release the mouse button, then click any selected object to move the entire group.

3. Connect each of these PCs to the switch using the following interfaces and **Copper Straight-Through** cables:
   - PC6 to FastEthernet0/3
   - PC7 to FastEthernet0/4
   - PC8 to FastEthernet0/5

4. Now you're ready to configure the switch. As you make configuration changes, remember to watch the commands that Packet Tracer automatically generates for you. Click **Switch0**, and then click the **Config** tab. In the left pane, click **VLAN Database**.

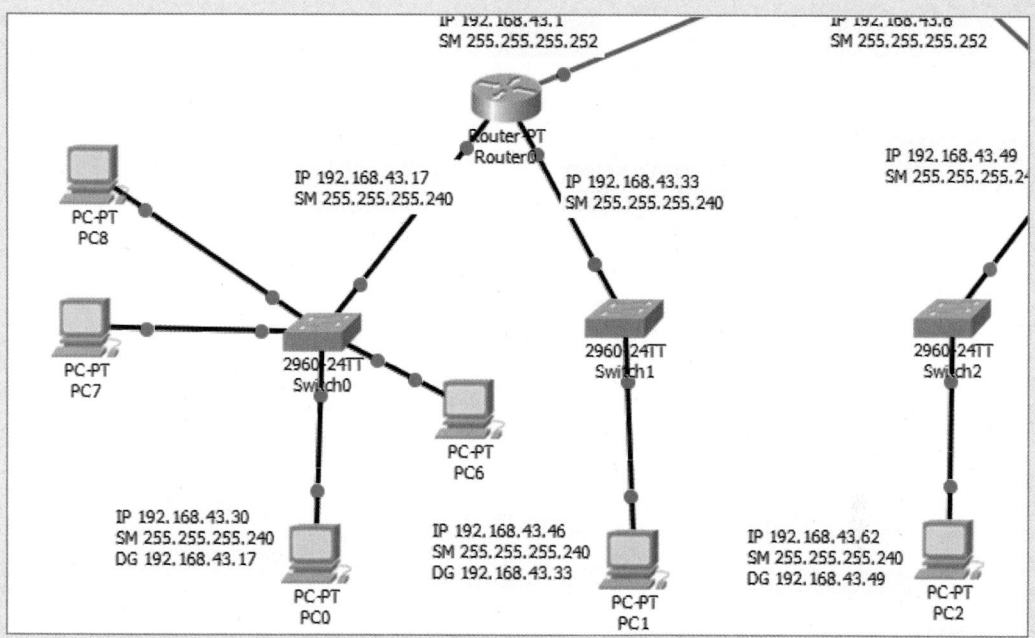

Figure 8-37 **Four workstations for two VLANs on one switch**

Source: Cisco Systems, Inc.

5. Create two VLANs: one for Accounting, and one for Sales. Recall that VLAN 1 already exists as the default VLAN, so be sure to start with VLAN 2. Enter the following information for the first new VLAN, and then click **Add**:
   VLAN Number: **2**
   VLAN Name: **Accounting**

6. Enter the following information for the second new VLAN, and then click **Add**:
   VLAN Number: **3**
   VLAN Name: **Sales**

7. Confirm that both new VLANs appear in the middle pane. What is the full list of VLANs now included in the middle pane?

8. You've created each of the VLANs, and now you need to configure ports for each VLAN. In the left pane, click **FastEthernet0/1**. What mode and VLAN is this port already configured for?

> **Note** 📎
>
> If at any point you need to check which interface a particular connection is using on a device, float your cursor over the connection. Packet Tracer will show the interface in use on each end.

9. Make sure **Access** is selected, and then change the VLAN to **2:Accounting**. What command did Packet Tracer use to configure this interface for VLAN 2?

10. Repeat this process for the other three PCs connected to Switch0. Use the following information:

    FastEthernet0/3 (connected to PC6): **Access** mode, VLAN **2**

    FastEthernet0/4 (connected to PC7): **Access** mode, VLAN **3**

    FastEthernet0/5 (connected to PC8): **Access** mode, VLAN **3**

11. To confirm your configurations are correct, click the **CLI** tab. The current prompt should be `Switch (config-if)#`. This says you're configuring a switch, and you're in interface configuration mode. Enter the command `exit` to return to global configuration mode. The prompt should now be `Switch (config)#`. Enter the command `do show vlan`. The output should look like Figure 8-38. If it doesn't, troubleshoot the steps you've taken so far to see what needs to be changed. Press **Tab** to return to the prompt.

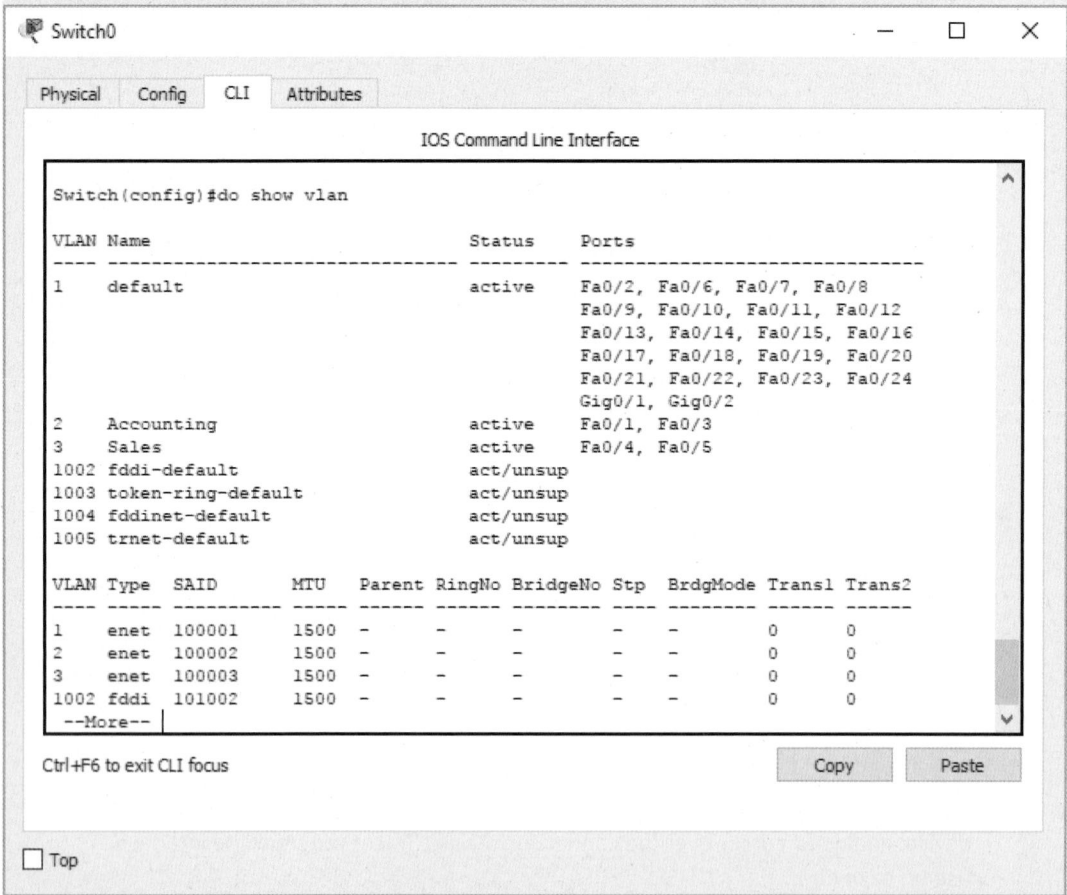

Figure 8-38 Two new VLANS have two ports each

Source: Cisco Systems, Inc.

12. Before you leave the switch to work on the PCs, you need to save the configurations you've completed so far. To do this, you need to leave global configuration mode and use privileged EXEC mode instead. Enter the command **exit**, enter the command **copy run start**, and then press **Enter** again. Close the Switch0 window.

13. VLANs are configured on a switch; however, you still need to configure IP addresses on the PCs. Refer to Capstone Project 8-1 if you need help remembering how to configure a static IP address on a PC. For this step, you'll initially leave all four PCs on the same subnet even though they're on different VLANs. Use **192.168.43.17** as the default gateway for all three PCs, and use the following information:

    PC6: **192.168.43.29 255.255.255.240**
    PC7: **192.168.43.20 255.255.255.240**
    PC8: **192.168.43.19 255.255.255.240**

14. First, test the communication between the two PCs that are on the same VLAN and on the same subnet. Click **PC0** and ping PC6 at **192.168.43.29**. Does it work? Why do you think this is?

15. Now ping across VLANs, which in this case, are still on the same subnet. From PC0, ping PC7 at **192.168.43.20**. Does it work? Why do you think this is?

16. Configure the router to send traffic between VLANs. To do this, you have to configure a sub-interface on the router for each VLAN. Basically, this means you're dividing the one physical interface into two logical interfaces. But first, you have to remove the IP address configuration on the physical interface so you can use this IP address space for the sub-interfaces. Click **Router0** and then click the **Config** tab. In the left pane, click **FastEthernet0/0**. Delete the IP address and subnet mask information.

17. Now click the **CLI** tab. Enter the commands listed in Table 8-15 to configure a sub-interface for each VLAN using two subnets of the original subnet for this network.

Table 8-15   Create sub-interfaces on the router's physical interface

Command	Purpose
`interface fastethernet0/0.2` and press **Enter** again	Creates the sub-interface and enters interface configuration mode
`encapsulation dot1Q 2`	Sets encapsulation
`ip address 192.168.43.25 255.255.255.248`	Assigns network information to the sub-interface
`exit`	Returns to global configuration mode
`interface fastethernet0/0.3` and press **Enter** again	Creates the sub-interface and enters interface configuration mode
`encapsulation dot1Q 3`	Sets encapsulation
`ip address 192.168.43.17 255.255.255.248`	Assigns network information to the sub-interface
`exit`	Returns to global configuration mode
`exit` and press **Enter**	Returns to privileged EXEC mode
`copy run start` and press **Enter**	Saves the current settings

18. Now, because you've adjusted the subnetting for these devices, go back to each of the four PCs and update their IP configuration information to reflect the correct subnet and the correct default gateway, as needed. Also update your notes for all involved devices as needed. Ping from PC0 to PC7. Does it work now? Why do you think this is?

19. Click **File**, **Save As**, and save this Packet Tracer file in a safe place for future projects.

20. Add installation information to the Packet Tracer page on your Wikidot website, along with any notes that you think might be helpful to you for the next Packet Tracer project. When you're finished, close **Packet Tracer** or continue to Capstone Project 8-3.

Capstone Project 8-3: Configure VLANs in Packet Tracer Using the CLI

This Capstone Project picks up where Capstone Project 8-2 left off. In Capstone Project 8-2, you created two VLANs on one switch. For the most part, when possible, you used the Configuration GUI to make these changes. This time, let's work on a different subnet, add a second switch, configure DHCP services for both VLANs, and do all of this from the networking devices' CLIs. This might seem intimidating, but don't worry; after completing this chapter, you have the skills to succeed at this project.

Complete the following steps:

1. In Packet Tracer, open your Packet Tracer file from Capstone Project 8-2.

2. Scroll to the right side of the network. Add a switch and three more PCs, positioned as shown in Figure 8-39.

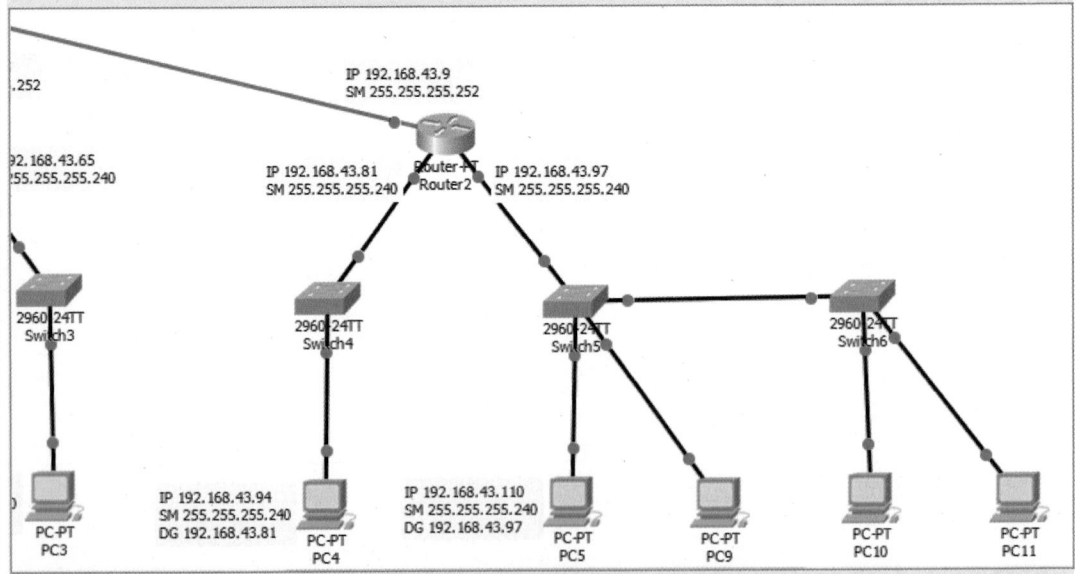

Figure 8-39   These two switches on the right will support two VLANs

Source: Cisco Systems, Inc.

3. Connect each of the devices to the following interfaces using **Copper Straight-Through** cables:
   - Switch5 (**FastEthernet0/24**) to Switch6 (**FastEthernet0/24**)
   - PC9 to Switch5 (**FastEthernet0/3**)
   - PC10 to Switch6 (**FastEthernet0/1**)
   - PC11 to Switch6 (**FastEthernet0/3**)

   Technically, you should have used a Crossover cable to connect the two switches to each other. However, the link worked. Why do you think this is?
4. Configure two VLANs with one PC from each switch on each VLAN. Click **Switch5** and click the **CLI** tab. Press **Enter**.
5. Here, you're starting out in user EXEC mode. To access privileged mode, which allows you to carry out administrative tasks, enter the command `enable`.
6. Enter the command `configure terminal`. This takes you into global configuration mode, which you saw earlier in this project.
7. Enter the commands listed in Table 8-16 to create and name two VLANs.

Table 8-16   Create and name two VLANs

Command	Purpose
`vlan 10`	Creates VLAN 10 and enters VLAN configuration mode for that VLAN
`name HR`	Assigns VLAN 10 the name HR
`vlan 11`	Creates VLAN 11 and enters VLAN configuration mode for that VLAN
`name IT`	Assigns VLAN 11 the name IT
`exit`	Returns to global configuration mode

Note

Spaces are not allowed in the VLAN name. The VLAN name is not used by other switches or nodes, but is a convenient reference for network administrators.

8. Enter the commands listed in Table 8-17 to assign a port to each of the two VLANs. When you're finished, close the switch's window.
9. Repeat Steps 4 – 8 for Switch6.

   Now you have the VLANs configured on both switches. Let's shift to the router to configure inter-VLAN routing and DHCP services. Complete the following steps:

10. Click **Router2** and then click the **Config** tab. In the left pane, click **FastEthernet0/0**. Delete the IP address and subnet mask information.
11. Click the **CLI** tab. Enter the commands listed in Table 8-18 to configure a sub-interface for each VLAN using two subnets of the original subnet for this network.

Table 8-17   Assign a port to each VLAN

Command	Purpose
`interface fastethernet0/1`	Enters interface configuration mode for FastEthernet0/1
`switchport mode access`	Sets access mode for this port
`switchport access vlan 10`	Assigns this port to VLAN 10
`exit`	Returns to global configuration mode
`interface fastethernet 0/3`	Enters interface configuration mode for FastEthernet0/3
`switchport mode access`	Sets access mode for this port
`switchport access vlan 11`	Assigns this port to VLAN 11
`exit`	Returns to global configuration mode
`interface fastethernet0/24`	Enters interface configuration mode for FastEthernet0/24
`switchport mode trunk` and press **Enter**	Sets trunk mode for this port, which is connected to the other switch
`exit`	Returns to global configuration mode
Switch5 only: `interface fastethernet0/2`	Enters interface configuration mode for FastEthernet0/2
Switch5 only: `switchport mode trunk` and press **Enter**	Sets trunk mode for this port, which is connected to the router
Switch5 only: `exit`	Returns to global configuration mode
`do show vlan`	Shows configured VLANs and associated ports—confirm that VLAN 10 and VLAN 11 are configured correctly, then press **Tab**
`exit` and press **Enter**	Returns to privileged EXEC mode
`copy run start` and press **Enter**	Saves the current settings

Table 8-18   Create two sub-interfaces, each with their own subnet

Command	Purpose
`enable`	Enters privileged EXEC mode
`configure terminal`	Enters global configuration mode
`interface fastethernet1/0.10` and press **Enter** again	Creates the sub-interface and enters interface configuration mode
`encapsulation dot1Q 10`	Sets encapsulation

Table 8-18 Create two sub-interfaces, each with their own subnet (*continued*)

Command	Purpose
`ip address 192.168.43.97 255.255.255.248`	Assigns network information to the sub-interface
`exit`	Returns to global configuration mode
`interface fastethernet1/0.11` and press **Enter** again	Creates the sub-interface and enters interface configuration mode
`encapsulation dot1Q 11`	Sets encapsulation
`ip address 192.168.43.105 255.255.255.248`	Assigns network information to the sub-interface
`exit`	Returns to global configuration mode

12. Next, configure DHCP on the router. Enter the commands listed in Table 8-19. When you're finished, close the router's window.

Table 8-19 Configure DHCP pools on a router

Command	Purpose
`ip dhcp pool FIRST`	Creates the first DHCP pool and enters DHCP configuration mode
`network 192.168.43.96 255.255.255.248`	Defines network information for the DHCP pool
`default-router 192.168.43.97`	Defines the default router for the DHCP pool
`ip dhcp pool SECOND`	Creates the second DHCP pool and enters DHCP configuration mode
`network 192.168.43.104 255.255.255.248`	Defines network information for the DHCP pool
`default-router 192.168.43.105`	Defines the default router for the DHCP pool
`exit`	Returns to global configuration mode
`exit` and press **Enter**	Returns to privileged EXEC mode
`copy run start` and press **Enter**	Saves the current settings

13. Test your DHCP configurations. Click on **PC5, Desktop**, and **IP Configuration**. This PC is currently configured with a static IP address. Select **DHCP** and wait while the DHCP request is resolved. What network information was assigned to PC5?

14. Repeat Step 13 for the other three PCs on these VLANs. What network information was assigned to PC9, PC10, and PC11?

15. Ping PC9 from PC5. Does it work? Why do you think this is?

16. Ping PC10 from PC5. Does it work? Why do you think this is?

17. Click **File**, **Save As**, and save this Packet Tracer file in a safe place for future projects.

18. Add installation information to the Packet Tracer page on your Wikidot website, along with any notes that you think might be helpful to you for the next Packet Tracer project. When you're finished, close **Packet Tracer**.

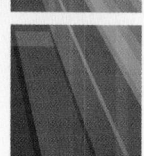

CHAPTER 9

NETWORK RISK MANAGEMENT

After reading this chapter and completing the exercises, you will be able to:

Identify people, technology, and malware security risks to a network

Describe tools used to evaluate the security of a network

Discuss physical security methods that prevent and detect intrusions

Configure devices on a network for increased security

Describe various security policies and explain how they can guide users' activities on a network

---

On the Job

Security often involves synthesizing tidbits of information from many disparate sources in order to form an accurate picture of what has happened. My team once responded to a report that desktop computers at a biomedical corporation were crashing. Their hard drives had been erased, apparently, by a virus that circumvented the company's antivirus protections.

While examining an affected PC, we noticed that a few processes were still running—thanks to the fact that the operating system generally won't allow the deletion of files that are in use. Among these processes were several instances of svchost.exe. Closer examination revealed that one of these had the same name as the legitimate Windows executable, but was in fact an impostor: A saboteur was at work.

497

Using a disassembler, we determined that the Trojan checked a folder on a server every minute for the presence of a command file. It would then execute the contents of the command file. We built a program to monitor that directory and archive copies of any files that appeared; our program also recorded the user account that put the file there and the name of the system from which this was done.

The account had domain administrator privileges, and this led us to examine the domain's logon scripts, where we found the code that installed the Trojan on users' workstations. We wrote a second program to record the MAC address of the system when it registered its name with the DHCP server and inspect the ARP tables from the network's switches in order to find the physical port to which it was connected. Then, with a building wiring diagram, we were able to track the culprit to a specific cubicle.

Finding the source of this problem involved knowledge about network infrastructure, operating systems, administration techniques, programming, and reverse engineering. This is an extreme example, to be sure, but real-world security problems seldom confine themselves to a single technical area of specialization.

Peyton Engel
Technical Architect, CDW Corporation

In the early days of computing, when secured mainframes acted as central hosts and data repositories were accessed only by dumb terminals with limited rights, network security was all but unassailable. As networks have become more geographically distributed and heterogeneous, however, the risk of their misuse has also increased. Consider the largest, most heterogeneous network in existence: the Internet. Because it contains billions of points of entry, millions of servers, and billions of miles of transmission paths, it leads to millions of attacks on private networks every day. The threat of an outsider accessing an organization's network via the Internet, and then stealing or destroying data, is very real.

In this chapter, you will learn about numerous threats to your network's data and infrastructure, how to manage those vulnerabilities, and, perhaps most important, how to convey the importance of network security to the rest of your organization through an effective security policy. Later, we will continue the discussion of network security and go behind the scenes with ways to secure network access and activity. If you choose to specialize in network security, consider attaining CompTIA's Security+ certification, which requires deeper knowledge of the topics covered in this text.

Security Risks

Q Certification

3.5   Identify policies and best practices.

4.4   Summarize common networking attacks.

4.6   Explain common mitigation techniques and their purposes.

5.5   Given a scenario, troubleshoot common network service issues.

Different types of organizations have various levels of network security risks. For example, if you work for a large savings and loan institution that allows its clients to view their current loan status online, you must consider a number of risks associated with data and access. If someone obtained unauthorized access to your network, all of your customers' personal financial data could be vulnerable. On the other hand, if you work for a local car wash that uses its internal LAN only to track assets and sales, you may be less concerned if someone gains access to your network because the implications of unauthorized access or use of sensitive data, called a **data breach**, are less dire. When considering security risks, the fundamental questions are: "What is at risk?" and "What do I stand to lose if it is stolen, damaged, or eradicated?"

To understand how to manage network security, you first need to know how to recognize threats to your network. And to do that, you must be familiar with the terms coined by network security experts. A **hacker**, in the original sense of the word, is someone who masters the inner workings of computer hardware and software in an effort to better understand them. To be called a hacker used to be a compliment, reflecting extraordinary computer skills. Today, *hacker* is used more generally to describe individuals who gain unauthorized access to systems or networks with or without malicious intent. Hacking might also refer to finding a creative way around a problem, increasing functionality of a device or program, or otherwise manipulating resources beyond their original design, and has even come to be used in reference to noncomputer related scenarios, such as *life hacking* or *guitar hacks*.

Interestingly, hackers are categorized according to their intent and the prior approval of the organizations whose networks they're hacking. Consider the following categories:

- *white hat hacker*—These IT security experts are hired by organizations to assess their security and risks. They're sometimes called ethical hackers. Their goal is to identify security vulnerabilities of all kinds so the organization can make changes to increase their security. The extent of their efforts is usually clearly defined in a written contract before they begin their testing, and their activities are limited by existing laws and restrictions. At no point is private data compromised outside of that trusted relationship.

- *black hat hacker*—These groups or individuals use their skills to bypass security systems to cause damage, steal data, or compromise privacy. They're not concerned with legal restrictions, and are intent on achieving personal gain or executing a personal agenda against an individual or an organization. Some black hat hackers and groups are also available for hire to serve someone else's agenda.
- *gray hat hacker*—These hackers abide by a code of ethics all their own. Although they might engage in illegal activity, their intent is to educate and assist. For example, a computer hobbyist who hacks a local business's weak Wi-Fi password, and then reports that weakness to the business owners without damaging or stealing the company's data, has engaged in gray hat hacking. Gray hats are vulnerable to legal prosecution, and therefore often go to a great deal of effort to remain anonymous.

As you can see, some people attempting to break through a network's security are doing so with the organization's permission and cooperation. In these cases, the goal is to find weaknesses in the security system so that those security gaps can be closed and therefore better protect the network and its resources.

A weakness of a system, process, or architecture that could lead to compromised information or unauthorized access is known as a **vulnerability**. The act of taking advantage of a vulnerability is known as an **exploit**. For example, you've already learned about the possibility for unauthorized, or rogue, access points to make themselves available to wireless clients as an evil twin. Once unsuspecting clients associate with such access points, the hacker can steal data in transit or access information on the client's system. The evil twin masquerades as a valid access point, using the same SSID (service set identifier) and potentially other identical settings. This exploit takes advantage of a vulnerability inherent in wireless communications in which SSIDs are openly broadcast and Wi-Fi clients scan for connections.

A **zero-day exploit**, or zero-day attack, is one that takes advantage of a software vulnerability that hasn't yet or has only very recently become public. Zero-day exploits are particularly dangerous because the vulnerability is exploited before the software developer has the opportunity to provide a solution for it or before the user applies the published solution. For example, Microsoft schedules regular security updates to Windows on the second Tuesday of each month, called Patch Tuesday. Hackers can use this information to identify unannounced vulnerabilities in Windows, and then immediately proceed to attack unpatched machines. Due to the quick timing of these attacks, the day after Patch Tuesday is informally dubbed Exploit Wednesday. Most current vulnerabilities, however, are well known. Throughout this chapter, you will learn about several kinds of exploits and how to prevent or counteract security threats.

As you read about each vulnerability, think about whether it applies to your network (and if so, how damaging it might be), how an exploit of the vulnerability could be prevented, and how it relates to other security threats. Keep in mind that malicious and determined intruders may use one technique, which then allows them to use a second technique, which then supports a third technique, and so on. For example, a hacker might discover someone's username by watching her log on to the network; the hacker might then use a password-cracking program to access the network, where he might plant a program that generates an extraordinary volume of traffic that essentially disables the network's connectivity devices. None of the risks discussed in this chapter stand alone. Any risk can open the door to further exploitation.

People Risks

By some estimates, human errors, ignorance, and omissions cause more than half of all security breaches sustained by networks. Human error accounts for so many security breaches because taking advantage of people is often an easy way to circumvent network security. End-user awareness and training can be a monumental task that requires regular attention and due diligence. Ultimately, it is the company's responsibility to ensure that its employees adhere to applicable standards and policies. An uninformed employee's inadvertent missteps that cause a data breach can result in extreme litigation expenses for a company.

One of the most common methods by which an intruder gains access to a network is to simply ask users for their passwords. For example, the intruder might pose as a technical support analyst who needs to know the password to troubleshoot a problem. This strategy is called **social engineering** because it involves manipulating social relationships to gain access. Common types of social engineering include the following:

- *phishing*—An electronic communication that appears to come from a legitimate person or organization and requests access or authentication information. For example, a hacker might send an email asking you to submit your username and password to a website whose link is provided in the message, claiming that it's necessary to verify your account with a particular online retailer. Phishing emails are extremely effective, especially the more sophisticated ones. When well-executed, these emails can trick even a savvy IT security professional. An example of a phishing email is shown in Figure 9-1.
- *baiting*—A malware-infected file, such as a free music download, or device, such as a USB flash drive, is seemingly left unguarded for someone to take and attempt to use on their own computer. The malware then infects the computer and gives the attacker access to the victim's computer, data, or online accounts.
- *quid pro quo*—A free gift or service is offered in exchange for private information or "temporary" access to the user's computer system. This tactic is surprisingly effective with employees who have not been adequately trained to detect social engineering attempts.
- *tailgating*—A person posing as an employee or a delivery or service provider follows an authorized employee into a restricted area. For example, a delivery person carrying a large box might ask someone to "hold the door," which gives this person access through an otherwise secure door. A friendly sounding conversation with an employee as they walk into a building might get an intruder past the front desk security. It might feel rude to deny someone's request for assistance in holding open a secure door, but not everyone who is nice has good intentions.

From: Microsoft Outlook' [mailto:ikennyandkelly@example.example.com]
Sent: Thursday, March 9, 2017 11:25 AM

Subject: FINAL NOTICE : (One Step Validation Process 03-09-2017)

 Office 365

Dear User,,

Your Microsoft Outlook Account Requires an Urgent Validation to ensure it would not be
deactivated within 24 hours.

Proceed to Microsoft Outlook Validation page by clicking on the icon below to get started

 Get Started

Thank you for using Microsoft Outlook.

Figure 9-1 Phishing emails often include legitimate-looking logos, buttons, instructions, and fine print

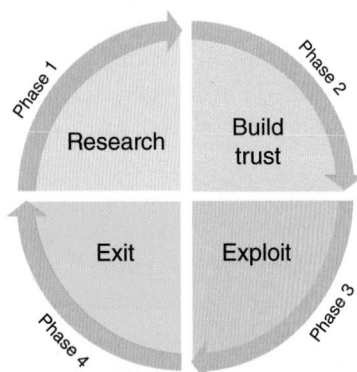

Figure 9-2 This cycle might happen quickly over a few seconds, or take much longer, even several years

Hackers use psychological insights to develop and refine their techniques. The more you understand their processes—and teach your coworkers about these techniques—the more effectively you can defend against them. Figure 9-2 shows the typical social engineering attack cycle. Phase 1, research, is the most important, and often requires the most time investment. Attackers build familiarity by initially asking for seemingly benign information. As they gather more data, they use these tidbits to build trust and gain access to more private information. This is Phase 2, building trust.

Phase 3, exploit, is the point of action on the part of the victim that gives the attacker the access he desires. This might be as simple as holding the door open, or more involved, such as divulging trade secrets with someone the victim believes to be a colleague. Finally, in Phase 4, exit, the attacker executes an exit strategy in such a way that does not leave evidence or raise suspicion. The attacker might then repeat the cycle, gaining deeper access until his objective is achieved.

The most important defense against social engineering is employee training, along with frequent reminders and tips regarding the latest scams. However, this preventative measure doesn't address another kind of risk associated with people: insider threats. An insider is someone who is or was trusted by an organization, such as an employee, former employee, contractor, or other associate. Sometimes trusted people have or develop malicious intent, which is called an **insider threat**. These attackers pose a particularly high risk to an organization due to their knowledge of the company's systems, procedures, and layers of security.

Whether people-related risks come from malicious insiders or naïve, trusted users, companies can take measures to reduce these risks, such as the following:

- Background checks for new hires and, where relevant, for contractors
- **Principle of least privilege**, meaning employees and contractors are only given enough access and privileges to do their jobs, and these privileges are terminated as soon as the person no longer needs them
- Checks and balances on employee behavior, such as scheduled access, mandatory vacations, and job rotations
- **DLP (data loss prevention)** solution that identifies sensitive data on the network and prevents it from being copied, such as downloading to a flash drive, or transmitted off the network, such as emailing or posting to cloud storage

Technology Risks

This section describes security risks inherent in all seven layers of the OSI model. Attacks on transmission media, NICs, network access methods (for example, Ethernet), switches, routers, access points, and gateways require more technical sophistication than those that take advantage of human errors. For instance, to eavesdrop on transmissions passing through a switch, an intruder must use a device such as a protocol analyzer, connected to one of the switch's ports. Because a router connects one type of network to another, an intruder might take advantage of the router's security flaws by sending a flood of TCP/IP transmissions to the router, thereby disabling it from carrying legitimate traffic.

7	APPLICATION
6	PRESENTATION
5	SESSION
4	TRANSPORT
3	NETWORK
2	DATA LINK
1	PHYSICAL

The following risks are inherent in network hardware and design:

- *spoofing attack*—MAC addresses can be impersonated in an attack called spoofing. Other types of spoofing attacks involve impersonating IP addresses. IP address spoofing can result in DoS (denial of service) attacks or modified DNS messages. Let's look at each of these types of attacks.
- *DoS (denial of service) attack*—A **DoS (denial-of-service) attack** occurs when a legitimate user is unable to access normal network resources, such as a web server, because of an attacker's intervention. Most often, this type of attack is achieved by flooding a system with so many requests for services that it can't respond to any of them, as shown in Figure 9-3. As a result, all data transmissions are disrupted. This incursion is a relatively simple attack to launch (for example, a hacker could create a looping program that sends thousands of email messages

to your system per minute). DoS attacks can also result from malfunctioning software. Because DoS attacks are so common, let's look at several DoS subtypes.

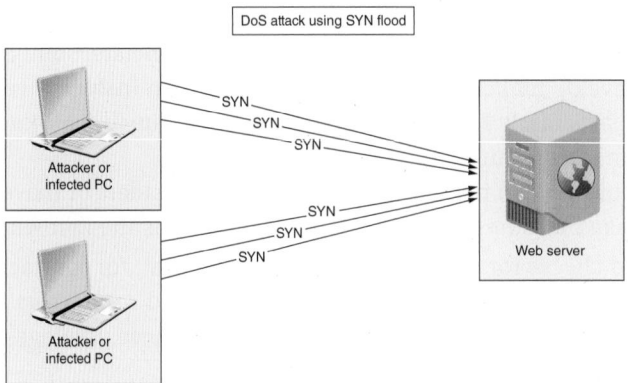

Figure 9-3 A simple DoS attack flooding a web server with SYN requests

○ *DDoS (distributed DoS) attack*—Whereas a DoS attack comes from one or a few sources owned by the attacker, DDoS attacks are orchestrated through many sources, as shown in Figure 9-4. Most of these machines are zombies, which means the owners are unaware that their computers are being used in the coordinated attack. Malware, called a bot, is installed on each machine and gives the bot herder, or central controller, remote control of the computer.

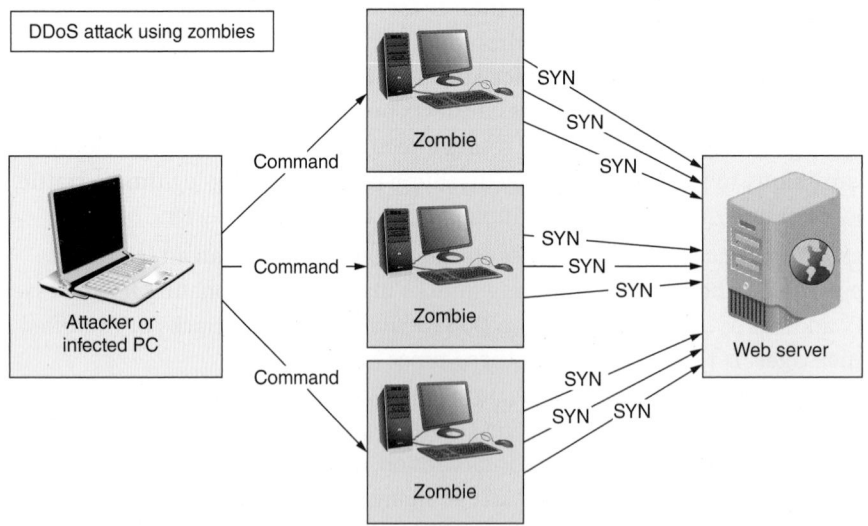

Figure 9-4 A SYN flood coordinated through several malware-infected, zombie computers

Many people believe their computers are not at high risk of security compromise because they don't keep valuable information on the computer. They don't realize their computing resources are also a target. Computers can be requisitioned as part of a botnet, also called a zombie army, in coordinated DDoS attacks without the owners' knowledge or consent, and these botnets are sometimes made available for hire on the black market. The traffic spike caused by so many attackers is much more difficult to defend against than an attack from a single source. Effective firewalls can greatly reduce the chances of a computer being drafted into illegal botnets.

○ **DRDoS (distributed reflection DoS) attack**—A DRDoS attack (or distributed reflective DoS attack) is a DDoS attack bounced off of uninfected computers, called reflectors, before being directed at the target. This is achieved by spoofing the source IP address in the attack to make it look like all the requests for response are being sent by the target, then all the reflectors send their responses to the target, thereby flooding the target with traffic, as shown in Figure 9-5.

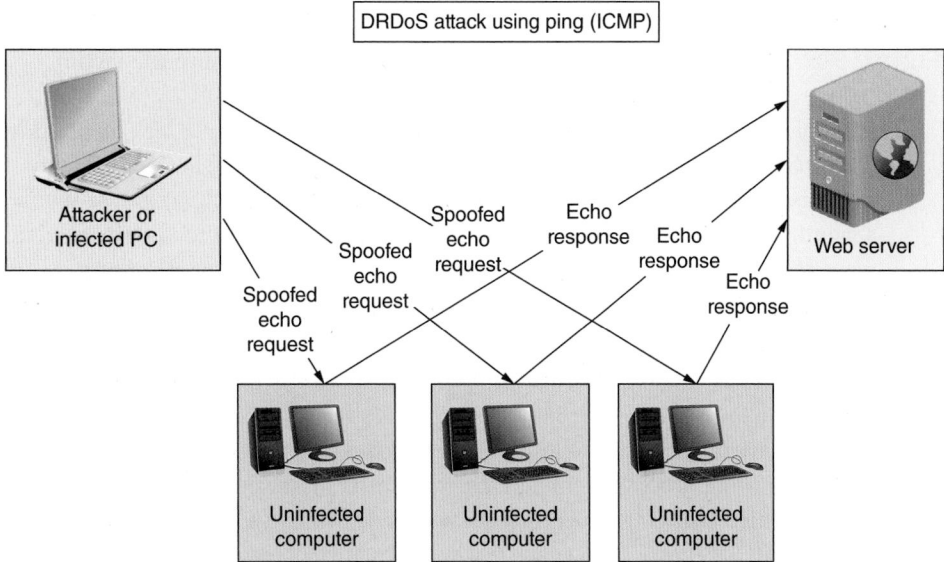

Figure 9-5   Spoofed ICMP echo requests appear to come from the victim computer

○ **amplified DRDoS attack**—A DRDoS attack can be amplified when conducted using small, simple requests that trigger very large responses from the target, as shown in Figure 9-6. Several protocols lend themselves to being used in these kinds of attacks, such as DNS, NTP, ICMP, SNMP, and LDAP.

○ **PDoS (permanent DoS) attack**—A PDoS attack damages a device's firmware beyond repair. This is called "bricking" the device because it effectively turns the device into a brick. PDoS attacks usually target routers or switches.

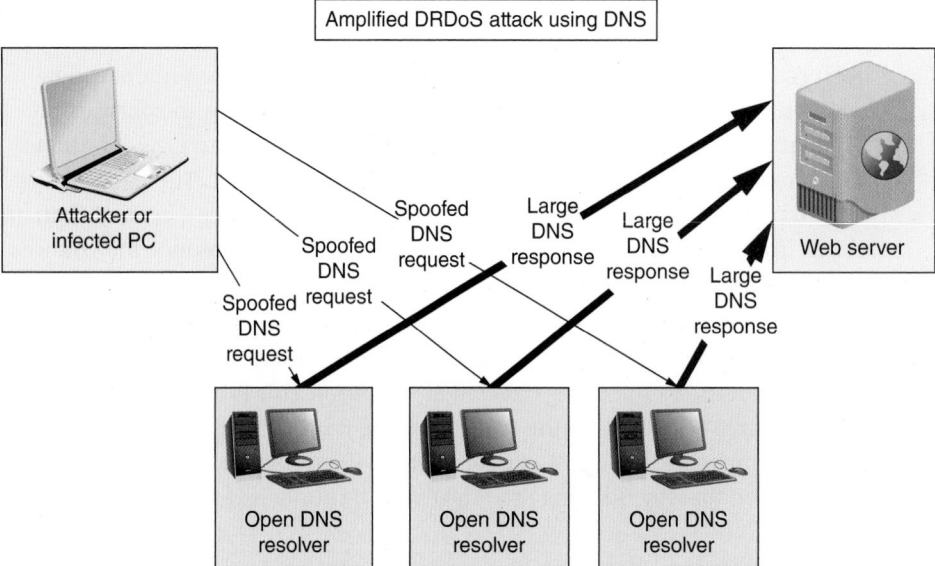

Figure 9-6   Spoofed DNS requests prompt large responses sent to the victim

- *friendly DoS attack*—An unintentional DoS attack, or friendly attack, is not done with malicious intent. An example might be when a website is flooded with an unexpectedly high amount of shopping traffic during a flash sale, or when a significant event is reported on the news and people flood to certain, related websites, especially if a specific website was mentioned in news reports.

- *DNS poisoning, or DNS spoofing*—By altering DNS records on a DNS server, an attacker can redirect Internet traffic from a legitimate web server to a phishing website, which is called **DNS poisoning** or DNS spoofing. Because of the way DNS servers share their cached entries, poisoned DNS records can spread rapidly to other DNS servers, ISPs, home and business networks, and individual computers. In fact, intentional DNS spoofing is one way China maintains its so-called "Great Firewall," which blocks its citizens from accessing websites such as YouTube, Pinterest, and Facebook. However, in 2010, China's DNS records somehow leaked into neighboring countries' DNS root servers. The altered DNS records started spreading around the world, blocking Internet traffic in other countries from accessing popular websites and redirecting that traffic to Chinese servers.

- *ARP poisoning*—Similar to DNS caches, ARP tables can be altered. ARP works in conjunction with IPv4 to discover the MAC address of a node on the local network. This information is stored in a database called the ARP table or ARP cache, which maps IP addresses to MAC addresses on the LAN. However, ARP performs no authentication, and so is highly vulnerable to attack. When attackers use faked ARP replies to alter ARP tables in the network, the attack is called **ARP poisoning**, or ARP spoofing. ARP vulnerabilities contribute to the feasibility of several other exploits, including DoS (denial-of-service) attacks, MitM (man-in-the-middle) attacks, which is described next, and MAC flooding. MAC flooding involves overloading a switch with ARP replies.

- *MitM (man-in-the-middle) attack*—A **MitM (man-in-the-middle) attack** relies on intercepted transmissions and can take several forms. In all these forms, a person redirects and captures secure transmissions as they occur. For example, in the case of an evil twin attack, which is a type of MitM attack, a hacker could intercept transmissions between clients and a rogue access point. Through these captured transmissions, the attacker can learn users' passwords or even supply users with a phony website that looks valid but presents clickable options capable of harming their systems.

- *rogue DHCP server*—Default trust relationships between one network device and another might allow a hacker to access the entire network because of a single flaw. For example, DHCP messages are allowed to flow freely through ports on switches so that clients can request and receive DHCP assignments. A **rogue DHCP server** running on a client device, however, could be used to implement a MitM attack by configuring the attacker's IP address as the victim computers' default gateway. Alternatively, the attacker could give her IP address as the DNS server and then spoof websites. DHCP messages should be monitored by a security feature on switches called **DHCP snooping**, in which any switch ports connected to clients are not allowed to transmit DHCP messages that should only come from a trusted DHCP server. In Figure 9-7, you can see that the Layer 3 switch trusts the DHCP offer made by the DHCP server, and this offer can be forwarded to the workgroup switches. A DHCP offer from the attacking computer on the bottom right of the figure, however, will not be trusted. DHCP snooping is configured on a switch using the `ip dhcp snooping` command.

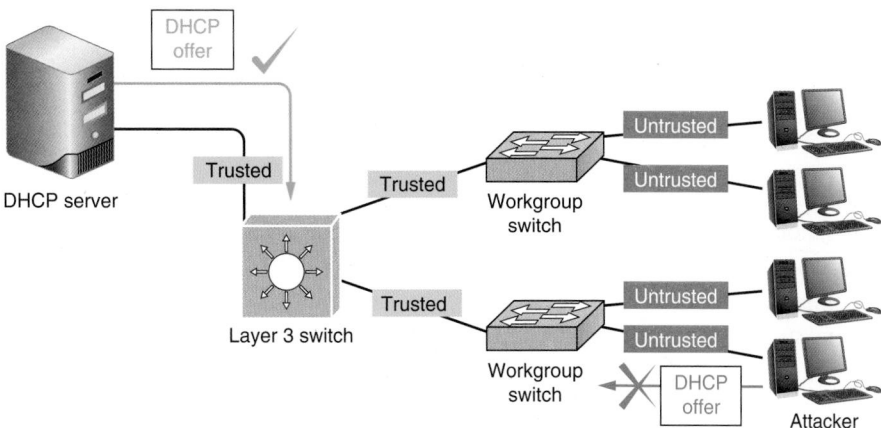

Figure 9-7   DHCP offer messages can only enter a trusted port on a switch, not an untrusted port

- *deauth (deauthentication) attack*—When a Wi-Fi client is legitimately connected to a wireless access point, the AP or the client can send a deauthentication frame to tell the other device that the authentication session is being terminated. This can happen for any number of reasons, including inactivity, the client is leaving the area, the AP is overwhelmed with too many clients, or an unspecified reason. These frames are unencrypted and are easily spoofed. In a **deauth (deauthentication) attack**, the attacker sends these faked deauthentication frames to the AP, the client, or both (or as a broadcast to the whole wireless network) to trigger the deauthentication process and knock one or more clients off the wireless network. This is essentially a Wi-Fi DoS attack in that valid users are prevented from having normal access to the network. At minimum, it can be a frustrating experience for users. In the hands of a skilled attacker, further information can be collected for more destructive attacks, such as a MitM attack.
- *insecure protocols and services*—Certain TCP/IP protocols are inherently insecure. For example, IP addresses can be falsified, checksums can be thwarted, UDP requires no authentication, and TCP requires only weak authentication. FTP is notorious for its vulnerabilities. In a well-known exploit, **FTP bounce**, hackers take advantage of this insecure protocol. When a client running an FTP utility requests data from an FTP server, the client normally specifies its own IP address and FTP's default port number. However, it is possible for the client to specify any port on any host's IP address. By commanding the FTP server to connect to a different computer, a hacker can scan the ports on other hosts and transmit malicious code. To thwart FTP bounce attacks, most modern FTP servers will not issue data to hosts other than the client that originated the request. Other insecure protocols include HTTP (use HTTPS with SSL/TLS instead), Telnet (use along with IPsec), SLIP (use PPP instead), TFTP (use SFTP instead), SNMPv1, and SNMPv2 (use SNMPv3 instead).
- *back doors*—Software might contain **back doors**, which are security flaws that allow unauthorized users to gain access to the system. Unless the network administrator performs regular updates, a hacker might exploit these flaws. Legacy systems are particularly notorious for leaving these kinds of gaps in a network's overall security net.

Malware Risks

Malware (short for *malicious software*) refers to any program or piece of code designed to intrude upon or harm a system or its resources. Included in this category are viruses, Trojan horses, worms, bots, and ransomware. You can find lists online of recent outbreaks of malware, such as the report shown in Figure 9-8 from Symantec's website (*symantec. com/security_response/landing/threats.jsp*). Several types are described in the following list:

- *virus*—A program that replicates itself with the intent to infect more computers, either through network connections when it piggybacks on other files or through the exchange of external storage devices. A virus might damage files or systems, or it might simply annoy users by flashing messages or pictures on the screen, for example.

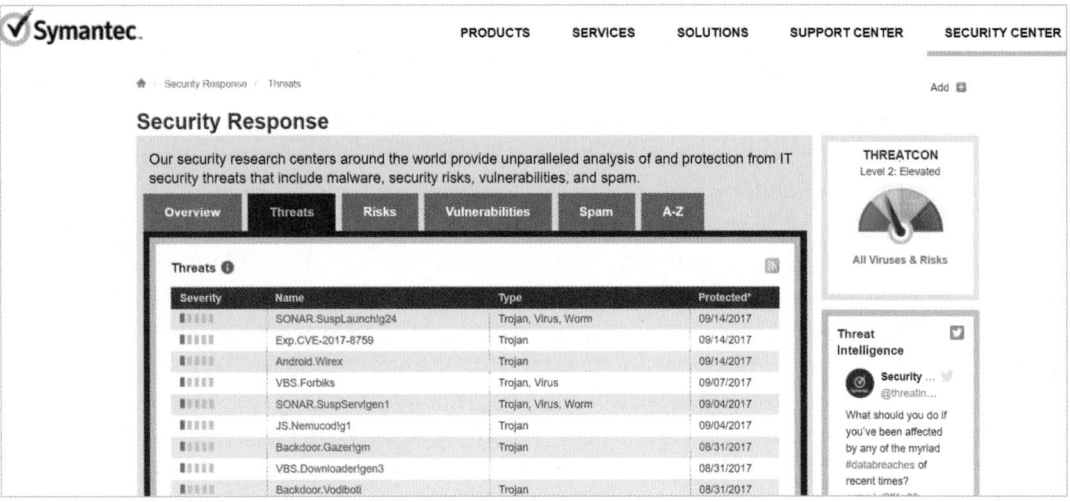

Figure 9-8   Security professionals track the emergence of new threats

Source: Symantec Corporation

- *Trojan horse (or Trojan)*—A program that disguises itself as something useful but actually harms your system; named after the famous wooden horse in which soldiers were hidden. Because Trojan horses do not replicate themselves, they are not considered viruses. An example of a Trojan horse is an executable file that someone sends you over the Internet, promising that the executable will install a great new game, when in fact it erases data on your hard disk or mails spam to all the users in your email program's address book.
- *worm*—A program that runs independently of other software and travels between computers and across networks. They may be transmitted by any type of file transfer, including email attachments. Worms do not alter other programs in the same way that viruses do, but they can carry viruses. Because they can transport and hide viruses, you should be concerned about picking up worms when you exchange files on the Internet, via email, or on flash drives.
- *bot* (short for robot)—A process that runs automatically, without requiring a person to start or stop it. Bots can be beneficial or malicious. Especially when used for ill intent, it does not require user interaction to run or propagate itself. Instead, it connects to a central server (called a command-and-control server, or C&C server) which then commands an entire botnet of similarly infected devices. Bots can be used to damage or destroy a computer's data or system files, issue objectionable content, launch DoS attacks, or open back doors for further infestation. Bots are especially difficult to contain because of their fast, surreptitious, and distributed dissemination.

- *ransomware*—A program that locks a user's data or computer system until a ransom is paid. In most cases, the infection encrypts data on the computer, and can also encrypt data on backup devices, removable storage devices, and even cloud storage accounts connected to the computer, such as Dropbox or OneDrive. The victim receives a message, such as the one shown in Figure 9-9, with the demand for payment and instructions on how to make the payment, usually through untraceable online payment systems. The amount of ransom varies, and for large organizations, has reached well into the millions of dollars. To add a sense of urgency, some ransomware starts deleting data at certain time increments, showing a countdown clock to the next scheduled deletion. In addition, some ransomware threatens to send the user's files to email contacts stored on the computer. Even if victims pay the ransom, they don't always get their data back. Currently, the only mostly reliable defense is to make manual backups of data on a regular basis *and* disconnect the backup media from the computer between backups.

Figure 9-9 This version of the Jigsaw ransomware threatens to send all the user's data to all contacts collected from the computer

Source: New Jersey Cybersecurity & Communications Integration Cell

Certain characteristics can make malware harder to detect and eliminate. Some of these characteristics, which can be found in any type of malware, include the following:

- *encryption*—Some malware is encrypted to prevent detection. Most anti-malware software searches files for a recognizable string of characters that identify the virus. However, encryption can thwart the anti-malware program's attempts to detect it.
- *stealth*—Some malware disguises itself as legitimate programs or replaces part of a legitimate program's code with destructive code.
- *polymorphism*—Polymorphic malware changes its characteristics (such as the arrangement of bytes, size, and internal instructions) every time it's transferred to a new system, making it harder to identify.
- *time dependence*—Some malware is programmed to activate on a particular date. This type of malware can remain dormant and harmless until its activation date arrives. Time-dependent malware can include **logic bombs**, or programs designed to start when certain conditions are met. (Logic bombs can also activate when other types of conditions, such as a specific change to a file, are met, and they are not always malicious.)

Malware can exhibit more than one of the preceding characteristics. The Natas virus, for example, combines polymorphism and stealth techniques to create a very destructive virus. Hundreds of new viruses, worms, Trojan horses, bots, and ransomware are unleashed on the world's computers each month. Although it is impossible to keep abreast of every virus in circulation, you should at least know where you can find out more information about malware. An excellent resource for learning about new malware, their characteristics, and ways to get rid of them is Symantec's website, shown earlier in Figure 9-8, and McAfee's Virus Information Library at *home.mcafee.com/virusinfo/*.

Security Assessment

 Certification

3.3   Explain common scanning, monitoring, and patching processes and summarize their expected outputs.

4.6   Explain common mitigation techniques and their purposes.

5.2   Given a scenario, use the appropriate tool.

Before spending time and money on network security, first examine your network's security risks. Consider the effect that a loss or breach of data, applications, or access would have on your network. The more serious the potential consequences, the more attention you need to pay to security.

Every organization should assess its security risks by conducting a **posture assessment**, which is a thorough examination of each aspect of the network to determine how it might be compromised. A threat's consequences might be severe, potentially resulting in a network outage or the dispersal of top-secret information, or it might be mild, potentially resulting in a lack of access for one user or the dispersal of a relatively insignificant piece of corporate data. The more devastating a threat's effects and the more likely it is to happen, the more rigorously your security measures should address it.

Posture assessments should be performed at least annually and preferably quarterly. They should also be performed after making any significant changes to the network. If your IT Department has sufficient skills and time for routine posture assessments, they can be performed in-house. A qualified consulting company can also assess the security of your network. If the company is accredited by an agency that sets network security standards, the assessment qualifies as a **security audit**.

Certain customers—for example, a military agency—might require your company to pass an accredited security audit before they'll do business with you. Regulators require some types of companies, such as accounting firms, to host periodic security audits. But even if an audit is optional, the advantage of having an objective third party analyze your network is that they might find risks you overlooked because of your familiarity with your environment. Security audits might seem expensive, but if your network hosts confidential and critical data, they are well worth the cost.

In this section of the chapter, you'll first learn about various scanning tools used for posture assessments and security audits. Then you'll see how you can bait hackers so you can learn more about their activities.

Scanning Tools

To ensure that your security efforts are thorough, it helps to think like a hacker. During a posture assessment, for example, you might use some of the same methods a hacker uses to identify cracks in your security architecture. In fact, security experts often conduct simulated attacks on a network to determine its weaknesses. Let's look at three types of attack simulations:

- *vulnerability scanning, or vulnerability assessment*—This technique is used to identify vulnerabilities in a network. It's often performed by a company's own staff, and does not attempt to exploit any vulnerabilities. Vulnerability scanning might also be the first step in other attack simulations or in a real attack. During attack simulations, there are two types of vulnerability scans:
  - *authenticated*—In this case, the attacker is given the same access to the network as a trusted user would have, such as an employee or an intruder who has somehow hacked into a user's account.
  - *unauthenticated*—In this case, the attacker begins on the perimeter of the network, looking for vulnerabilities that do not require trusted user privileges.

- *penetration testing*—This attack simulation uses various tools to find network vulnerabilities, as in vulnerability scanning, and then attempts to exploit those vulnerabilities.
- *red team-blue team exercise*—During this exercise, the red team conducts the attack, and the blue team attempts to defend the network. Usually the red team is a hired attacker, such as a consultant or security organization, and the blue team is the company's own IT, security, and other staff. In some cases, the blue team has no warning of the impending attack in order to better evaluate day-to-day defenses. The red team relies heavily on social engineering to attempt to access the company's private data, accounts, or systems without getting caught. The company's detection and response to the attack is the primary focus, rather than the technical vulnerabilities of the network itself.

Scanning tools provide hackers—and you—with a simple and reliable way to discover crucial information about your network, including, but not limited to, the following:

- Every available host
- Services, including applications and versions, running on every host
- Operating systems running on every host
- Open, closed, and filtered ports on every host
- Existence, type, placement, and configuration of firewalls
- Software configurations
- Unencrypted, sensitive data

Used intentionally on your own network, scanning tools improve security by pointing out insecure ports, software and firmware that must be patched, permissions that should be restricted, and so on. They can also contribute valuable data to asset management and audit reports. Let's look at three popular scanning tools you can use:

- *Nmap*—The scanning tool Nmap and its GUI version Zenmap are designed to scan large networks quickly and provide information about a network and its hosts. Nmap began as a simple **port scanner**, which is an application that searches a device for open ports indicating which insecure service might be used to craft an attack. For example, if a server's port 23 is open, Telnet can be used to remote into the target device and take control of it. Developers later expanded Nmap's capabilities to include gathering information about hosts and their software. When running Nmap, you can choose what type of information to discover, thereby customizing your scan results. In a project at the end of this chapter, you'll use another app, Advanced Port Scanner, to find open protocol ports on your network.
- *Nessus*—Developed by Tenable Security (*tenable.com*), Nessus performs even more sophisticated vulnerability scans than Nmap. Among other things, Nessus can identify unencrypted, sensitive data, such as credit card numbers, saved on your network's hosts. The program can run on your network or from off-site servers continuously maintained and updated by the developer.

- *Metasploit*—This popular penetration testing tool combines known scanning and exploit techniques to explore potentially new attack routes. For example, Figure 9-10 shows a Metasploit scan using HTTP, SMTP, and SMB probes; the application also employs Nmap, Telnet, FTP, and UDP probes. Notice that the scan successfully identified the administrative username and password for this home network's SOHO router.

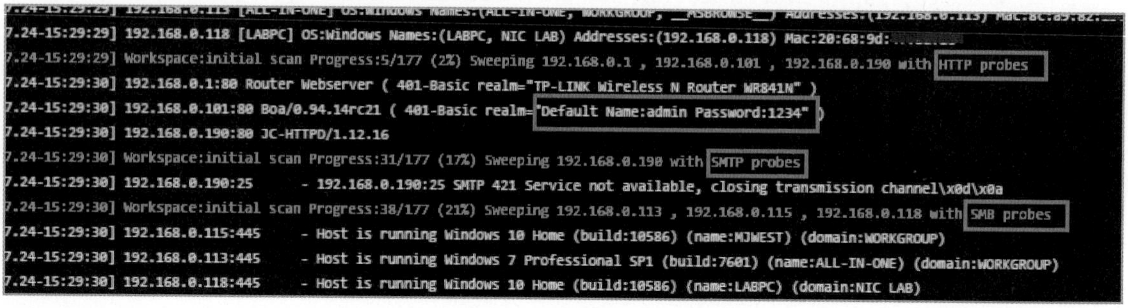

Figure 9-10   Metasploit detected a SOHO router's administrative username and password
Source: Rapid7 LLC

Used by hackers—or, more likely, bots—these tools can obviously lead to compromised security. In other words, each of these tools has legitimate uses as well as illegal uses. However, even if the scanning tools are used against you, you can learn from them. For example, a properly configured firewall will collect information about scanning attempts in its log. By reviewing the log, you will discover what kinds of exploits could be—or have been—attempted against your network. Therefore, another way to learn about hackers is to lure them to your network on purpose, as described next.

Honeypots and Honeynets

Staying a step ahead of hackers and constantly evolving exploits requires vigilance. Those who want to learn more about hacking techniques or nab a hacker in the act might create a **honeypot**, or a decoy system that is purposely vulnerable and filled with what appears to be sensitive (though false) content, such as financial data. To lure hackers, the system might be given an enticing name, such as one that indicates a name server or a storage location for confidential data. Once hackers access the honeypot, a network administrator can use monitoring software and logs to track the intruder's moves. In this way, the network administrator might learn about new vulnerabilities that must be addressed on his real networked hosts.

To fool hackers and gain useful information, honeypots cannot appear too blatantly insecure, and tracking mechanisms must be hidden. In addition, a honeypot must be isolated from secure systems to prevent a savvy hacker from using it as an intermediate host for other attacks. In more elaborate setups, several honeypots might be connected to form a **honeynet**. Honeypot software options include KFSensor (*keyfocus.net*), Canary (*canary.tools*), and Honeyd (*honeyd.org*).

Honeypots and honeynets can provide unique information about hacking behavior and, if configured well, are low maintenance sources of information with few false positives. But in practice, security researchers or those merely curious about hacking trends are more likely than overworked network administrators to establish and monitor these decoy systems.

Now that you understand the variety of risks facing networks and several ways of identifying these risks on a specific network, you are ready to learn about techniques for securing the network's physical devices.

Physical Security

4.1   Summarize the purposes of physical security devices.

Physical access to all of a network's critical components must be restricted and controlled. Consider the damage that could be done if an intruder were able to steal devices, directly connect his own computer to unprotected console ports, damage or destroy expensive equipment, or simply reset these devices by pressing the physical reset button. Only trusted networking staff should have access to secure computer rooms, data rooms, network closets, storage rooms, entrance facilities, and locked equipment cabinets. Furthermore, only authorized staff should have access to the premises, such as offices and data centers, where these rooms are located.

Preventative measures such as locked doors can make it more difficult for unauthorized people to get into these areas. However, it's also important to have good detection measures in place for those times when someone is able to breach a secured perimeter. Let's look at physical security methods you can use for both prevention and detection.

Prevention Methods

If computer rooms are not locked, intruders may steal equipment or sabotage software or hardware. For example, a malicious visitor could slip into an unsecured computer room and take control of a server where an administrator is logged on, then steal data or reformat the server's hard drive. Although a security policy defines who has access to the computer room, locking the locations that house networking equipment is necessary to keep unauthorized individuals out. Door access controls range from a simple deadbolt to more sophisticated options, as described here:

- *keypad or cipher lock*—Electronic keypads, also called **cipher locks**, are physical or electronic locks that require a code to open the door, which can reduce the inherent risk of lost keys. Changing the cipher lock's code regularly can also help increase security. Cipher locks are not designed solely for physical security, such as on an outside door, so much as for the purpose of controlling access to an area, such as an indoor data room, by logging who comes and goes, enabling or disabling unescorted entry, scheduling open access times, and even responding to access made under duress (with a special hostage code that trips an alarm when entered). Figure 9-11 shows one example of a cipher lock.

- *key fob*—A **key fob** provides remote control over locks and security systems. You probably have a key fob like the one shown in Figure 9-12 that you use to remotely lock or unlock your car doors. To reduce the number of devices you need to carry, many lock types allow you to use a key fob app installed on a smartphone.

iStock.com/richterfoto

Figure 9-11 A cipher lock can document who enters an area and when

iStock.com/bluestocking

Figure 9-12 A key fob can remotely lock and unlock doors, and often includes a panic button

- *access badge*—Most companies require employees to have some kind of ID **badge** that identifies the person by name and perhaps includes a photo, title, and other information. Additionally, many organizations provide electronic access badges, or **smart cards**. When the smart card is swiped through a reader, the door unlocks and the person's access to the secured area is time stamped and logged in a database. These badges can be programmed to allow their owner access to some, but not all, rooms in a building. Figure 9-13 depicts a typical badge access security system.
- *proximity card*—Some badges, such as the one in Figure 9-14, are actually proximity cards (also called prox cards), which do not require direct contact with a proximity reader in order to be detected. In fact, a reader can be concealed inside a wall or other enclosure and requires very little maintenance. With a typical range of about 5–10 cm, the card can be detected even while it's still inside a wallet or purse, or it can be incorporated or duplicated in a key fob.
- *biometrics*—A more expensive physical security solution involves biorecognition access, in which a device scans an individual's unique physical characteristics, called **biometrics**, such as the color patterns in her iris or the geometry of her hand, to verify her identity. Organizations might use biometric devices to regulate entrance through gates or other physical barriers to their campuses. See Figure 9-15.

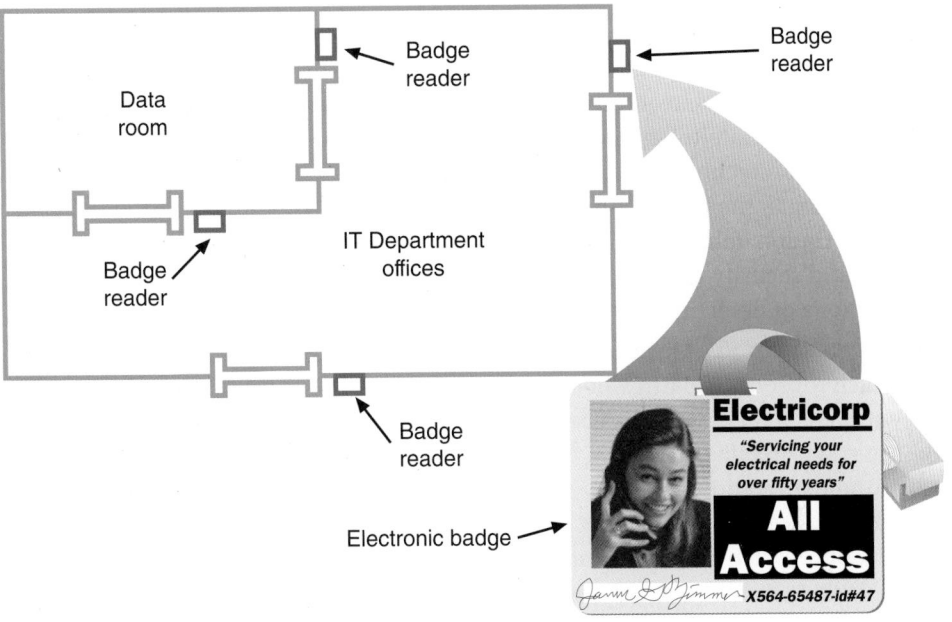

Figure 9-13   Badge access security system

Figure 9-14   A proximity card does not require physical contact with a proximity reader

Figure 9-15   Fingerprint scanner

> **Caution** ⚠️
>
> Consider that a door might not be the only way to enter a room with sensitive equipment. Drop ceilings, also called suspended ceilings, can provide easy access to someone determined to get around a locked door. Secured rooms should be completely surrounded by impenetrable walls, ceilings, and floors. If a data room does have a drop ceiling, make sure the walls are extended all the way up to the true ceiling beyond the drop ceiling grid.

Detection Methods

Despite all precautions, sometimes breaches do occur. The key to protecting sensitive data and systems is to detect intrusions as quickly as possible and be prepared to respond appropriately. Beyond detecting the presence of an intruder, however, security detection technologies have expanded to detect other types of events as well. For example, the temperature of vaccines in transit, the movement of delivery and transportation vehicles, and the expiration of food items can all be monitored for the safety and security of the people who use these items. The following list explores some methods of detecting physical intrusions and other kinds of events:

- *motion detection*—**Motion detection** technology, which triggers an alarm when it detects movement within its field of view, has been around for a long time. Sensors like the one in Figure 9-16 are often found even in home security systems. The latest motion detectors can discern between different types of motion, such as small animals, blowing plants, or walking humans, to reduce false alarms. Motion sensors might be configured to record date and time of motion detection, or trigger lights, alarms, or video cameras.

Figure 9-16   Motion detectors trigger an alarm when movement is detected

- *video surveillance*—Many IT departments use video surveillance systems, called **CCTV (closed-circuit TV)**, to monitor activity in secured data rooms. IP cameras can be placed in data centers, computer rooms, data rooms, and data storage areas, as well as facility entrances. Figure 9-17 shows the management interface for one of these cameras. The cameras might run continuously, or they might be equipped with motion detectors to start recording when movement occurs within their viewing area.

  IT technicians might also be called upon to install and service a video surveillance system for the entire company (see Figure 9-18). The video footage generated from these cameras is contained within a secure segment of the network, and is usually saved for a period of time in case it's needed later in a security breach investigation or prosecution.

- *tamper detection*—Many devices that need protection can't be kept within a secure area. For example, utility meters, parking meters, entry doors, ATMs, network cables, and even security cameras are potential targets. **Tamper detection** sensors on these devices can detect physical penetration, temperature extremes, input voltage variations, input frequency variations, or certain kinds of radiation. This might trigger defensive measures such as an alarm or shutdown, or it might activate a video camera or other security system. Another tamper detection option is a sticker or latch, as shown in Figure 9-19. Any damage to the sticker or latch tells you the device was tampered with.

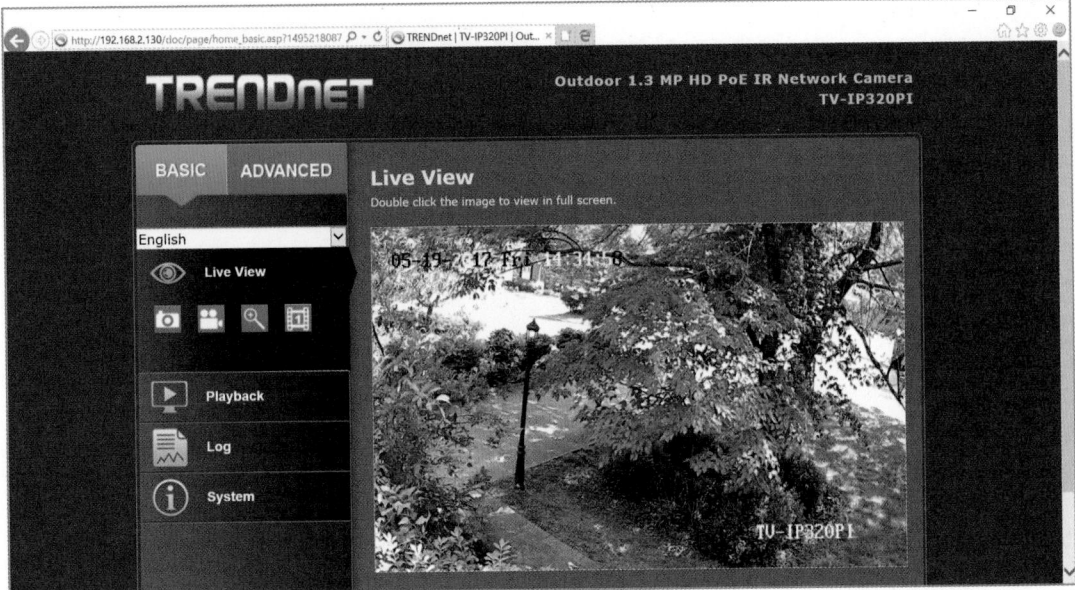

Figure 9-17   This small IP camera can be monitored through a browser or smartphone app

Source: TRENDNet

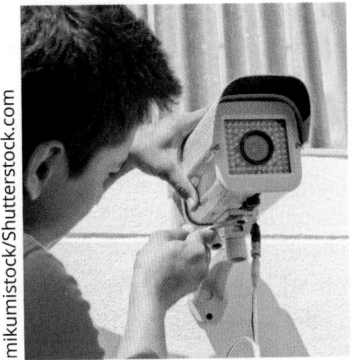

Figure 9-18   IT personnel might be responsible for the installation and maintenance of a CCTV network

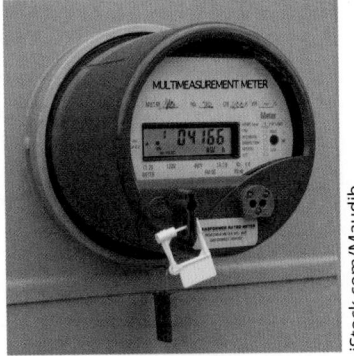

Figure 9-19   A single-use, plastic security seal

- *asset tracking*—**Asset tracking tags** can be used to monitor the movement and condition of equipment, inventory, and people. Whether a simple barcode or a wireless-enabled transmitter, such as the RFID label on the box in Figure 9-20, asset tracking enables constant or periodic collection of information. This data is then reported to a central management application for monitoring, logging, and reporting. As wireless technologies have improved, these asset tracking systems have grown beyond Wi-Fi-dependent systems, which tend to be expensive and require frequent battery replacement for each asset being tracked. Today, these systems often use Bluetooth, RFID (such as NFC), cellular, and GPS wireless technologies. These technologies are sometimes also combined with cloud technology, to provide deeper insights through data analytics, and with IoT technology, to increase the security of IoT networks.

Figure 9-20 The RFID label on this box allows the delivery service to track its progress

As with other security measures, the most important way to ensure physical security is to plan for it. You can begin your planning by asking questions related to physical security checks in your security audit. Consider the following questions:

- Which rooms contain critical systems or data and must be secured?
- Through what means might intruders gain access to the facility, computer room, data room, network closet, or data storage areas (including doors, windows, adjacent rooms, ceilings, large vents, temporary walls, hallways, and so on)?
- How and to what extent are authorized personnel granted entry? Do they undergo background or reference checks? Is their need for access clearly justified? Are their hours of access restricted? Who ensures that lost keys or ID badges are reported?
- Are employees instructed on how to ensure security after entering or leaving secured areas (for example, by not propping open doors)?
- Are authentication methods (such as ID badges) difficult to forge or circumvent?
- Do supervisors or security personnel make periodic physical security checks?
- Are all combinations, codes, or other access means to computer facilities protected at all times, and are these combinations changed frequently?
- What is the plan for documenting and responding to physical security breaches?

Device Hardening

 Certification

4.5 Given a scenario, implement network device hardening.

4.6 Explain common mitigation techniques and their purposes.

Besides securing network devices from external tampering, you can take many steps to secure the device from network- or software-supported attacks as well. These practices are called **device hardening**. There are many layers of defense you can implement, although the options vary from one device to another. In this chapter, we examine device hardening practices that apply generically to many types of devices. Later we'll explore device hardening techniques that are specific to switches and routers.

Updates and Security Patches

Updates to applications, operating systems, and device firmware address several issues, including fixing bugs, adding new features, and closing security gaps. In this chapter, we're most concerned with security issues. Because of the urgency of protecting networks and data from being compromised, security gaps are often addressed in smaller, more frequent updates called patches. Let's consider a situation where a single, failed patch compromised the personal identification information of more than 100 million people.

In September 2017, Equifax (one of the three major consumer credit reporting agencies) announced a major data breach where hackers accessed confidential information repeatedly from mid-May through July of that year. Names, Social Security numbers, birthdates, addresses, and, in some cases, driver's license numbers for approximately 143 million people, mostly U.S. residents, were compromised. That's nearly half of the U.S. population. For about 209,000 of those people, credit card numbers were also stolen. How did this happen?

Details are still emerging at the time of this writing. However, reports currently indicate that a web server bug had been discovered months earlier in an open-source software package used by Equifax. The bug allowed extensive back-door access to web servers run by major banking, government, retail, and other organizations. While a patch was issued by the software developer one day after the bug was discovered, security professionals suspect that Equifax either failed to apply the patch or inadequately implemented the patch in their systems before the breach occurred. The investigation is still ongoing to determine exactly where the system broke down and who is responsible. To learn more about recent developments on this story, do a Google search for "Equifax breach technical details" or something similar. Look for authoritative news sources that specialize in the IT industry, such as *krebsonsecurity.com*, *techradar.com*, or *computerworld.com*, and also look for government websites with official, public notices.

Caution ⚠

To help protect your personal and financial information, experts recommend that you check your credit report at least once a year. U.S. residents can do this for free at *annualcreditreport .com*, a federal government approved site sponsored by all three major credit reporting agencies (Equifax, Experian, and TransUnion). Type that address directly into your browser's address bar to make sure you don't end up on a spoofed website. You can order a free, annual report from each of the three agencies through this site, either all at once or spaced throughout the year.

If you're concerned about any indications of fraud on your account, you can contact one of these agencies to report the fraud and try to resolve the problem. You can also place a temporary fraud alert on your account for 90 days or more at no charge. A fraud alert notifies potential creditors to take extra security precautions before approving a new line of credit on your account.

The process of properly managing and applying security patches includes the following:

- *discovery*—In this first phase, you investigate what's on your network, so that you can protect it. Good documentation will help indicate whether a newly discovered vulnerability and its patch applies to your network, how extensively the issue affects your systems, how urgent the change is, and what you'll need to do to implement the patch correctly.
- *standardization*—Updating OS and application versions consistently across the network will simplify the change process for future updates.
- *layered security*—The term "layered security" refers to multiple defenses applied to a single network. For layered security to be effective, you need to understand how these various solutions interact, and look for any gaps in coverage.
- *vulnerability reporting*—Identifying and prioritizing relevant security issues and patch releases is essential. In some organizations, one or more staff members take primary responsibility for this task. Network administrators can also subscribe to reporting services from vendors, third parties, and government organizations.
- *implementation*—Implementing patches includes validating, prioritizing, testing, and applying them. Careful implementation is especially important with security patches, which, as you have seen, can serve a critical role in protecting a business's interests. Performing patch rollouts in phases, or tiers, requires formal change management processes.
- *assessment*—In this phase, you evaluate the success of patch implementation and the overall effectiveness of the patch. Was the patch applied everywhere it was needed? Is it working as expected? Can you detect any further gaps in security?
- *risk mitigation*—In some cases, it may not be possible to apply a patch where needed. For example, a new patch might not be compatible with legacy software on a server. In this case, the server can't support the patch without compromising the needed software. To lessen the resulting risk, you should apply other layers of protection to the affected devices and applications.

Note 🖉

Opinions about how to handle firmware updates vary widely. Some network admins take the approach, "If it ain't broke, don't fix it." That is, they don't upgrade firmware unless they see a pressing reason to do so. Others prefer to address firmware upgrades routinely, alongside other routine updates. Customer support technicians often tell clients to update the firmware on their device and then call back if there's still a problem. On the job, be sure to research firmware upgrades thoroughly before deciding whether to implement them. If at all possible, perform the firmware upgrade locally rather than remotely. And be prepared to troubleshoot unexpected problems after the upgrade.

Administrative Credentials

Most devices that can be configured through a management interface come with a default access account. Often, the username, if there is one, is something like "admin." The password might be "password," "admin," or "1234." Because these default credentials are so commonly used, they're also extremely insecure. Surprisingly, many network administrators—even in large organizations—never take the time to change these credentials to something more difficult to crack. When configuring a device, make it a habit to change the default administrative credentials before you do anything else, and record this information in a safe place. When you do so, avoid common usernames and passwords. You'll learn more about how to create secure passwords later in this chapter.

Caution ⚠

Be careful to configure secure usernames and passwords on *all* devices connected to any part of your network, even if the device itself seems to be an insignificant security threat, such as the chiller for an HVAC system or security cameras in a CCTV (closed-circuit TV) network. Any access point into the network can be used to compromise the network's data or other resources.

Recall that many devices are managed through remote access connections, the most common of which is SSH. Also recall that SSH keys can be used to authenticate devices making the remote connection. This is especially helpful for power users such as system administrators or when using SSH connections for automated processes such as file transfers, financial transactions, or configuration updates.

Over long-distance connections, using SSH keys is more secure than using passwords because a securely encrypted key is more difficult to crack than a password. However, just like usernames and passwords, these authentication credentials should be changed from the provider's default settings. To do this, first remove the existing keys with the `rm` command. Then generate a new key pair with the `ssh-keygen` command. Figure 9-21 shows the PuTTY Key Generator, which can also be used to create SSH key pairs.

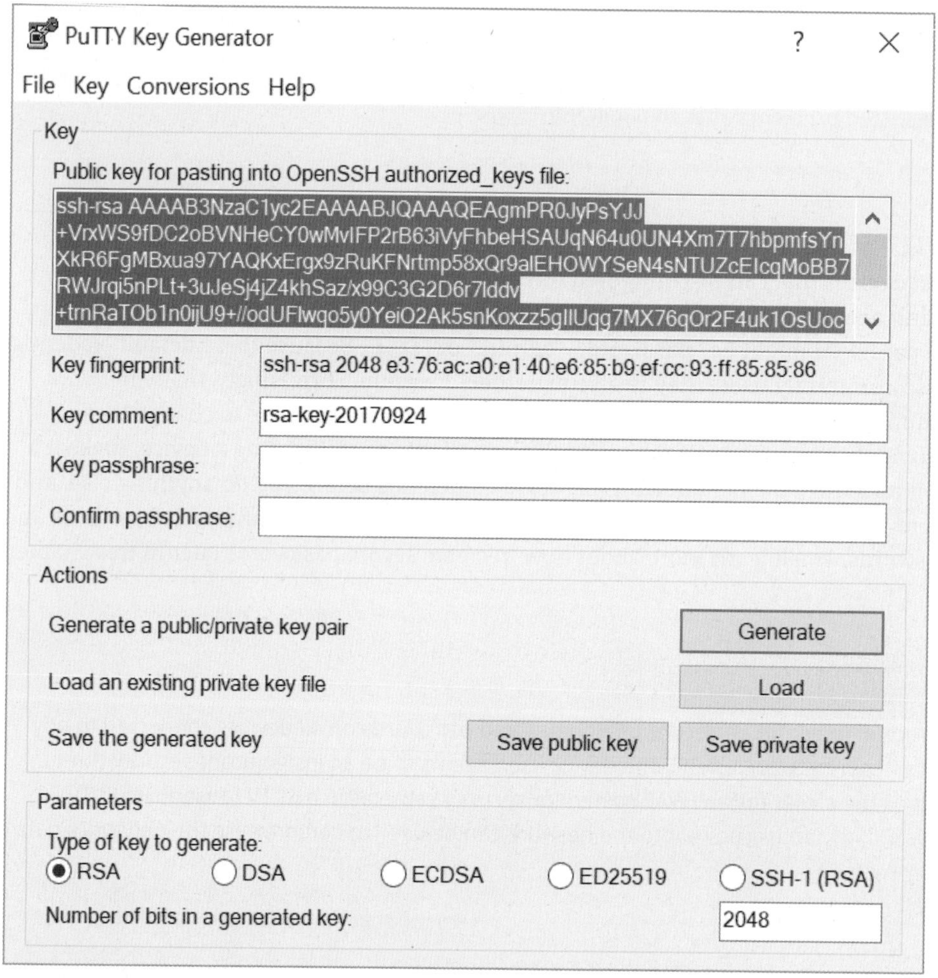

Figure 9-21   Use the PuTTY Key Generator to create a public/private key pair
Source: PuTTY

Many devices offer the option to configure several administrative accounts with varying levels of access. Additionally, user accounts on an enterprise's domain might be capable of accessing different features within a device's management interface. For example, a support technician in a company might be given an admin account with the ability to configure certain features on a single device or on all similar devices within a domain, such as workstations or certain servers. A high-level network administrator might, instead, have a domain admin account, which allows the person to make changes to Active Directory on a server, access private customer information in a database, or recover from a backup after a system failure.

The most privileged of these account types is called a **privileged user account**. Security precautions for this type of account include the following:

- *limited use*—These accounts should only be used when those higher privileges are necessary to accomplish a task. Even those employees who have a privileged user account should also have a lower-level account for normal activities. In fact, anyone who has a user account of any kind should be given only the least amount of access needed to do a specific job.
- *limited location*—Many companies require the privileged user account be accessed only on location so that no one, not even a legitimate network administrator, can access the device remotely and make high-level changes. One advantage to this restriction is that access credentials for this account will never be cached on a workstation or other end user device.
- *limited duration*—Privileged user accounts should be carefully accounted for and disabled as soon as they're not needed, such as when an employee is terminated.
- *limited access*—The passwords for these accounts should be especially secure and difficult to crack. Passwords should also be stored securely, and when possible, multi-factor authentication should be required, which you'll learn more about later.
- *limited privacy*—A privileged user account can be used for destructive activity— whether malicious or not. For that reason, every user action in these accounts should be recorded and monitored by someone other than the owner of that account. Privileged user monitoring software is available from companies such as Imperva (*imperva.com*), ManageEngine (*manageengine.com*), and Splunk (*splunk.com*).

Services and Protocols

Imagine that a hacker wants to bring a library's database and mail servers to a halt. Suppose also that the library's database is public and can be searched by anyone on the web. The hacker might begin by scanning for ports on the database server to determine which ports are open to certain processes or services. If she found an open port on the server, the hacker might connect to the system and deposit a program that would, a few days later, damage operating system files. Or, she could launch a heavy stream of traffic that overwhelms the database server and prevents it from functioning. She might also use her newly discovered access to determine the root password on the system, gain access to other systems, and launch a similar attack on the library's mail server, which is attached to the database server. In this way, even a single mistake on one server (not protecting an open port) can open vulnerabilities on multiple systems.

Insecure services and protocols, such as Telnet and FTP, should be disabled in a system whenever possible. Leaving these software ports open and services running practically invites an intrusion because it's so easy to crack into a system through these open doors. To protect devices from these threats, follow these guidelines:

- Use secure protocols, such as SSH and SFTP, instead of insecure protocols, such as Telnet and FTP.
- Disable any running services on a computer that are not needed. You can Google your OS and "unneeded services" to determine which services are most likely good candidates for disabling.
- Minimize the number of startup programs to include only those apps that you really need.
- Close TCP/IP ports on the local firewall that are not used for ongoing activities.
- Disable unneeded connection technologies, such as Bluetooth, Wi-Fi, NFC, and IR.
- Remove known networks if they're no longer needed.
- Disable or uninstall applications that are no longer needed.

Hashing

Hashing means to transform data through an algorithm that generally reduces the amount of space needed for the data. Hashing is not the same thing as encryption, though it's often listed as a type of encryption and does, in a similar manner, transform data from one format to another. Encrypted data can be decrypted, but hashed data cannot. Hashing is mostly used to ensure data integrity—that is, to verify the data has not been altered, which is similar to the purpose of a checksum. However, hashes can play a critical role in a good encryption protocol.

If a secure algorithm is used, hashing is nearly impossible to reverse. Instead, you can take known data, hash it using the same hashing function, and compare the new hash with the stored, hashed data. If the hashes match, this indicates the known data is exactly the same as the original data. If the output does not match, this indicates the hashed data has likely been altered.

The most commonly used hashing algorithm today is some form of **SHA (Secure Hash Algorithm)**. You might hear this pronounced "shaw" or "shay." The primary advantage of SHA over older hashing algorithms is its resistance to collisions. A collision is when two different data sources result in the same hash. A prevalence of collisions from a hashing algorithm essentially defeats the purpose of hashing. However, the added security to avoid collisions means the hashing process takes longer than with less secure options. There are several versions of SHA:

- *SHA-0*—The original version of SHA was developed by the NSA and was later dubbed SHA-0. It used a 160-bit hash function.
- *SHA-1*—The original version was quickly replaced by the next, slightly modified version, SHA-1, due to an undisclosed flaw in SHA-0. SHA-1 has also since been retired in favor of the next two iterations of SHA, although many systems still rely on the easily cracked SHA-1.
- *SHA-2*—Also designed by the NSA, SHA-2 supports a variety of hash sizes, the most popular of which are SHA-256 (with a 256-bit hash) and SHA-512 (with a

512-bit hash). Note that the 2 in SHA-2 refers to the version number, whereas the larger numbers in SHA-256 and SHA-512 refer to the length of the hash functions.

- *SHA-3*—The most recent iteration of SHA, SHA-3 was developed by private designers for a public competition in 2012. SHA-3 is very different in design from SHA-2, even though it uses the same 256- and 512-bit hash lengths.

SHA-2 and SHA-3 are often implemented together for increased security. It's also common for data to be hashed in multiple passes, along with encryption passes layered in to the process.

What does hashing have to do with device hardening? Consider the following options:

- Passwords are often stored in hashed form to prevent them from being read even if they were to be accessed. Using a highly secure hash algorithm nearly guarantees that stolen passwords will be useless to the thief.
- Entire files can also be hashed. File hashing is accomplished by applying a hash algorithm to all the data in a file. Some sites provide file hashes of files you might download from their site. If you hash your downloaded file and the hash matches the provider's hash, then you can be fairly confident the file has not been infected or corrupted.

Applying Concepts: Hash a Text String

Several hashing tools are available free online. One website, *onlinemd5.com*, lets you choose between three hashing algorithms: MD5 (an older, outdated hashing algorithm), SHA-1, and SHA-256. Complete the following steps:

1. In your browser, go to **onlinemd5.com**. The first tool shown on this page can hash an entire file, but we want to practice with smaller portions of text. Scroll down to the *MD5 & SHA1 Hash Generator For Text* box.
2. **MD5** should be selected by default. Type a string of text into the box and watch the hash output calculate automatically as you type. What do you notice about the length of the string hash as you enter each additional letter?
3. Copy the final string hash into a text document for later comparison. Windows Notepad works well for this purpose.
4. Select **SHA1** and copy the new string hash into your text document for comparison.
5. Select **SHA-256** and copy the new string hash into your text document for comparison. Which string hash is longer? Why do you think that is?
6. Now type a lot more text into the hash generator. What happens to the string hash?
7. Now change exactly one letter in the hash generator's input text. What happens to the string hash?

You can also use the command line in Windows PowerShell, macOS Terminal, and Linux Terminal to hash an entire file. Search online for the commands used for each CLI listed in Table 9-1, and write the correct commands in the Command column.

Table 9-1   Hashing commands in Windows, macOS, and Linux

OS	Task	Command
Windows	Hash a file using MD5	
Windows	Hash a file using SHA-1	
Windows	Hash a file using SHA-256 (default)	
macOS	Hash a file using MD5	
macOS	Hash a file using SHA-1 (default)	
macOS	Hash a file using SHA-256	
Linux	Hash a file using MD5	
Linux	Hash a file using SHA-1	
Linux	Hash a file using SHA-256	

Anti-Malware Software

You might think that you can simply install a virus-scanning program on your network and move to the next issue. In fact, protection against harmful code involves more than just installing anti-malware software. It requires choosing the most appropriate anti-malware program for your environment, monitoring the network, continually updating the anti-malware program, and educating users.

Even if a user doesn't immediately notice malware on her system, the harmful software generally leaves evidence of itself, whether by changing the operation of the machine or by announcing its signature characteristics in the malware code. Although the latter can be detected only via anti-malware software, users can typically detect the operational changes without any special software. For example, you might suspect a virus on your system if any of the following symptoms arise:

- Unexplained increases in file sizes
- Significant, unexplained decline in system or network performance (for example, a program takes much longer than usual to start or to save a file)
- Unusual error messages with no apparent cause
- Significant, unexpected loss of system memory
- Periodic, unexpected rebooting
- Fluctuations in display quality

When implementing anti-malware software on a network, one of your most important decisions is where to install the software. Some scenarios include:

- *host-based*—If you install anti-malware software on every desktop, you have addressed the most likely point of entry, but ignored the most important files that might be infected—those on the server. Host-based anti-malware also provides insufficient coverage when a significant portion of the network is virtualized.

- *server-based*—If the anti-malware software resides on the server and checks every file and transaction, you will protect important files, but slow your network performance considerably.
- *network-based*—Securing the network's gateways, where the Internet connects with the interior network, can provide a formidable layer of defense against the primary source of intrusion—the Internet. However, this does nothing to prevent users from putting the network at risk with infected files on flash drives, laptops, or smartphones.
- *cloud-based*—Many anti-malware solutions already employ cloud-based resources within their programming. And cloud-based anti-malware provides the same kinds of benefits as other cloud-based solutions, such as scalability, cost efficiency, and shared resources. These cloud vendors are still working out bugs, and it can be a challenge to ensure that coverage soaks the entire network with no blind spots. Cloud solutions also increase the amount of Internet traffic in order to perform their duties.

To find a balance between sufficient protection and minimal impact on performance, you must examine your network's vulnerabilities and critical performance needs. However, be aware that anti-malware is not a completely reliable form of protection. Other methods of device hardening are more effective, especially when multiple layers of security are put in place.

Security Policies for Users

Ⓠ Certification

3.5   Identify policies and best practices.

4.4   Summarize common networking attacks.

4.6   Explain common mitigation techniques and their purposes.

Most network security breaches begin or continue due to human error. This section describes hardening techniques designed to minimize break-ins by communicating with and managing the users in your organization with well-planned security policies.

A **security policy** for network users identifies your security goals, risks, levels of authority, designated security coordinator and team members, responsibilities for each team member, and responsibilities for each employee. In addition, it specifies how to address security breaches. It should not state exactly which hardware, software, architecture, or protocols will be used to ensure security, nor how hardware or software will be installed and configured. These details change from time to time and should be shared only with authorized network administrators or managers.

Security Policy Goals

Before drafting a security policy, you should understand why the security policy is necessary and how it will serve your organization. Typical goals for security policies include:

- Ensure that authorized users have appropriate access to the resources they need.
- Prevent unauthorized users from gaining access to the network, systems, programs, or data.
- Protect sensitive data from unauthorized access, both from within and from outside the organization.
- Prevent accidental damage to hardware or software.
- Prevent intentional damage to hardware or software.
- Create an environment in which the network and systems can withstand and, if necessary, quickly respond to and recover from any type of threat.
- Communicate each employee's responsibilities with respect to maintaining data integrity and system security.
- For each employee, obtain a signed consent to monitoring form, which is a document that ensures employees are made aware that their use of company equipment and accounts can be monitored and reviewed as needed for security purposes.

or that each employee is responsible for signing in his or her visitors at the front desk and obtaining a temporary badge for them. Aspects of security policies that are not related to computers are beyond the scope of this chapter, however.

After defining the goals of your security policy, you can devise a strategy to attain them. First, you might form a committee composed of managers and interested parties from a variety of departments, in addition to your network administrators. The more decision makers you include, the more effective the policy created by the committee will ultimately be. This committee can assign a security coordinator, who will then drive the creation of the security policy.

Note 📎

To increase the acceptance of your security policy in your organization, tie security measures to business needs and clearly communicate the potential effects of security breaches. For example, if your company sells clothes over the Internet, make sure users and managers understand that a two-hour outage (as could be caused by a hacker who uses IP spoofing to gain control of your systems) could cost the company $100,000 in lost sales. With this under-standing, employees are more likely to embrace the security policy.

A security policy must address an organization's specific risks. To understand your risks, you should conduct a posture assessment that identifies vulnerabilities and rates both the severity of each threat and its likelihood of occurring, as described earlier in this chapter. After you have identified risks and assigned responsibilities for managing them, you are ready to outline the policy's content, as described through the rest of this chapter. Although compiling all this information might seem daunting, the process ensures that everyone understands the organization's stance on security and the reasons it is so important.

BYOD (Bring Your Own Device)

BYOD (bring your own device) refers to the practice of allowing people to bring their smartphones, laptops, or other technology into a facility for the purpose of performing work or school responsibilities. Variations on this theme include the following:

- *BYOA (bring your own application)*—Employees or students supply their choice of software on a computer or mobile device.
- *BYOC (bring your own cloud)*—Employees or students supply their choice of cloud application or storage.

- *BYOT (bring your own technology)*—A generic reference that includes the other BYO options.
- *CYOD (choose your own device)*—Employees or students are allowed to choose a device from a limited number of options, usually supplied by the company or school.

Organizations offering BYOD options need to detail what is allowed and what isn't, what reimbursements or allowances the company might offer, what restrictions will keep the organization's data and networks safe, and what configurations to the device are needed in order to comply with the policy. BYOD practices can be cheaper for organizations to implement and tend to improve efficiency and morale for employees and students. However, security and legal compliance concerns must be sufficiently addressed in clearly defined BYOD policies.

Part of a BYOD policy might include on-boarding and off-boarding procedures. Recall that the process of configuring wireless clients for network access is called on-boarding. These configurations can be handled automatically by **MDM (mobile device management)** software. MDM works with all common mobile platforms and their service providers, and can add or remove devices remotely. Examples of MDM software include VMware's AirWatch (*air-watch.com*) and Cisco's Meraki Systems Manager (*meraki.cisco.com*).

MDM software can automate enrollment, enforce password policies and other security restrictions, encrypt data on the device, sync data across corporate devices, wipe the device, and monitor the device's location and communications. The best MDM packages include granular control over these options. For example, an administrator might configure the software to remove corporate data from all devices while leaving personal data untouched. A less intrusive option is MAM (mobile application management), which targets specific apps on a device rather than controlling the entire device.

AUP (Acceptable Use Policy)

An **AUP (acceptable use policy)** explains to users what they can and cannot do while accessing a network's resources. It also explains penalties for violations, and might describe how these measures protect the network's security. Employers should never assume that employees inherently know what is acceptable use of company IT resources and what is not. Detailing this information clarifies expectations for everyone. Some of the restrictions might include the following:

- Don't do anything illegal.
- Don't try to circumvent network security restrictions.
- Don't market products or services to other network users.
- Don't forward spam email.
- Don't violate the rights of any person or organization.

- Don't violate copyright, trade secret, patent, intellectual property, or other regulations. This includes but is not limited to:
  - Don't install, use, or distribute pirated materials.
  - Don't copy, digitize, or distribute copyrighted materials.
- Don't export software, technical information, or encryption technology.

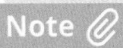

Note

International and regional export controls limit what software, data, technology, and devices can cross certain political boundaries. For example, you might need an export license to travel internationally with encrypted data, and some countries might require that you decrypt data before entering the country. In some countries, authorities might confiscate devices temporarily or permanently. For this reason, you should never carry confidential data about patients, clients, or customers internationally.

- Always sign off or lock a device when not in use.
- Use company resources to fulfill job obligations, and not for personal tasks that should be performed outside of business hours using the employee's own resources.
- Be aware that activities on the network can be and are monitored and may be formally audited.
- Immediately report any suspected compromise of confidential data or customer privacy.

NDA (Non-Disclosure Agreement)

A security policy should also define what *confidential* and *private* means to the organization. This is often done in an **NDA (non-disclosure agreement)**. In general, information is confidential if it could be used by other parties to impair an organization's functioning, decrease customers' confidence, cause a financial loss, damage an organization's status, or give a significant advantage to a competitor. However, if you work in an environment such as a hospital, where most data is sensitive or confidential, your security policy should classify information in degrees of sensitivity that correspond to how strictly its access is regulated. For example, top-secret data may be accessible only by the organization's CEO and vice presidents, whereas confidential data may be accessible only to those who must modify or create it (for example, doctors or hospital accountants).

> **Note**
>
> Any information covered by an NDA might also be protected from international export.

Password Policy

Choosing a secure password is one of the easiest and least expensive ways to help guard against unauthorized access. Unfortunately, too many people prefer to use an easy-to-remember password. If your password is obvious to you, however, it might also be easy for a hacker to figure out. The following guidelines for creating passwords should be part of your organization's security policy. It is especially important for network administrators to choose difficult passwords, and also to keep passwords confidential and change them frequently.

Tips for making and keeping passwords secure include the following:

- Always change system default passwords after installing new software or equipment. For example, after installing a router, the default administrator's password on the router might be set by the manufacturer to *password*, with this information printed on a sticker on the bottom of the device.

- Do not use familiar information, such as your name, nickname, birth date, anniversary, pet's name, child's name, spouse's name, user ID, phone number, address, favorite color, favorite hobby, or any other words or numbers that others might associate with you.

- Do not use any word that might appear in a dictionary, even an "urban" or "slang" dictionary. Hackers can use programs that try a combination of your user ID and every word in a dictionary to gain access to the network. This is known as a **dictionary attack**, and it is typically the first technique a hacker uses when trying to guess a password (besides asking the user for her password).

- Make the password longer than eight characters—the longer, the better. Recall that, in a brute force attack, a hacker attempts numerous possible character combinations until the correct combination is found. A shorter password is more vulnerable to a brute force attack than a longer one is. To maximize the benefit of a longer password, consider the following tips:

  - Choose a combination of letters and numbers; however, don't use common replacements of certain numbers for certain letters as hackers already know to look for these and they're harder for you to remember

  - Use a combination of uppercase and lowercase letters, preferably in a random pattern instead of starting with a capital letter

  - Add special characters, such as exclamation marks or hyphens, if allowed

- Do not repeat words or number sequences
- Do not use a single letter, number, or symbol more than twice in succession (such as "passwordddddddddd")
- Do not use easily recognized phrases such as a line from a famous song, poem, or movie

> **Note**
>
> Current research indicates that a long, random string of words, such as *correcthorsebatterystaple*, is easier to remember, more secure, and takes longer to crack than a seemingly randomized series of letters, numbers, and symbols that is short enough for a human to remember. The idea is to combine length with randomness in a way that works well for human memory and is challenging for computers to crack.

- Do not write down your password or share it with others, including coworkers or family members. Never store passwords in a web browser. Many browsers store these passwords in plaintext and can be easily hacked.
- Change your password at least every 60 days or more frequently. If you are a network administrator, establish controls through directory services that force users to change their passwords at least every 60 days.
- Do not reuse passwords after they have expired.
- Use different passwords for different applications. For example, choose separate passwords for your email account, online banking, VPN connection, and so on. That way, if someone learns one of your passwords, he won't be able to use the same information to access all your secured accounts.
- Make it easier to keep a secure record of long, random passwords by installing and using password management software such as LastPass or KeePass (*keepass.info*). These programs can generate unique strings of random letters, numbers, and symbols for each password, and store them securely in an encrypted database which is accessible from multiple devices through a single, master password. This way, users only need to remember one, well-formed password that is sufficiently long and random to help maximize security of their password database.

Password guidelines should be clearly communicated to everyone in your organization through your security policy. Although users might grumble about designing memorable but secure, long, random passwords and changing their passwords frequently, you can assure them that the company's financial, proprietary, and personnel data is safer as a result.

Note 📎

Even if data is encrypted, at some point data is accessed, stored, or otherwise manipulated in its unencrypted form, and this is when vulnerability is greatest. This threat is called endpoint vulnerability because data is exposed in its unencrypted form at an endpoint of use, such as when a password is entered on a user's smartphone. For example, suppose a user has taken all precautions to create a long, complex password for his online bank account. The bank's website stores his account access information in an encrypted database. However, if the user then writes his password on a sticky note and hides it under his keyboard on his desk, his highly secured bank account is still extremely vulnerable to thieves.

Applying Concepts: Create a Secure Master Password in LastPass

In Chapter 2, you created an account in LastPass, a password manager, which you have continued to use for several projects throughout this book. Recall that in Chapter 2, you were advised to create a long master password using a line from a song or movie to make it easier to remember. Although this is a quick way to encourage someone to use a more secure password than what most users use, for a password manager's master password or for any kind of secure user or administrative account, you can certainly do better. It's now time to create a more secure master password for your LastPass account. Complete the following steps:

1. Review the list of tips in this section for creating a secure password. How does your current master password compare to the advice described in these steps?
2. In your browser, go to the website **howsecureismypassword.net.** Enter your current master password to see how long it would take a hacker to crack your password based on its length. What time frame does the site report?

Caution ⚠

Be sure to type the howsecureismypassword.net address directly into your browser's address bar. Do not click on a link to this website from another website, from a Google search, or from a navigation suggestion. The official How Secure Is My Password website is safe to use because the password you type into the calculator is never transmitted off your local computer. The calculations are all performed locally in your browser. To be certain of this, you can navigate to the website, disconnect your computer from the Internet, and then enter your passwords to check their security level. However, many phishing websites spoof the How Secure Is My Password website, and are designed specifically to trick you into typing your most secure passwords into their web pages.

3. Considering the tips listed earlier for creating a secure password, make some changes to your current master password. Enter the new password into the **howsecureismypassword .net** website. Keep making changes and testing your changes until you get calculation results showing at least 1 million years to crack the password and you've used as many of the earlier tips as you can. Make sure you use a combination of letters, numbers, and symbols that you can remember without keeping a written copy of the password with you. What time frame does the site report for your new password?

4. Change your master password in LastPass to your new, secure password.

5. Determine one or two safe locations where you can keep a recorded copy of your master password, such as written on a note that you keep in a locked box or safe deposit box, or in an encrypted file on your computer. Record your master password in this safe place for your reference if you later forget your master password. Be sure to always keep this note or file secure—do not leave it sitting out for any length of time thinking you'll put it away "later" because "later" might not happen soon enough.

6. Consider who might need access to your passwords should you become incapacitated. Would your parents or siblings need access to this information, or perhaps a spouse, partner, or older child? In LastPass, set up Emergency Access for this trusted person using their email address. Decide what period of time this person should have to wait from the time access is requested until LastPass approves access. During this wait time, if you are not actually incapacitated, you can decline their request to access your vault.

Privileged User Agreement

A **PUA (privileged user agreement)**, or privileged access agreement, addresses the specific concerns related to privileged access given to administrators and certain support staff. For example, a doctor who has access to HIPAA-protected patient information must sign a privileged user agreement that defines what he can and can't do with that patient data, and what special precautions he must take to protect the patient's privacy. Certain checks and balances must also be maintained and defined in the PUA. For example, the person who can authorize vendor payments should not be the same person who creates vendor accounts.

The privileged user agreement outlines guidelines, rules, restrictions, and consequences of violations, all of which help minimize the risk involved in allowing privileged access to some users. When accessing a privileged account, the user is advised to stay signed into the account only as long as is necessary to perform the needed tasks, and then sign off, not relying on the time-out feature to sign her off. Privileged users need more frequent training and reminders to avoid falling for social engineering attacks of various types. And in many cases, activity in privileged accounts will be specially monitored through a PAM (privileged account management) tool, such as BeyondTrust's PowerBroker (*beyondtrust.com*) or CyberArk's Privileged Account Security Solution (*cyberark.com*).

Anti-Malware Policy

Anti-malware software alone will not keep your network safe from malicious code. Because most malware infections can be prevented by applying a little technology and forethought, it's important that all network users understand how to prevent the spread of malware. An anti-malware policy provides rules for using anti-malware software, as well as policies for installing programs, sharing files, and using external storage such as flash drives. To be most effective, an anti-malware policy should be authorized and supported by the organization's management. Suggestions for anti-malware policy guidelines include the following:

- Every computer in an organization should be equipped with malware detection and cleaning software that regularly scans for malware. This software should be centrally distributed and updated to stay current with newly released malware.
- Users should not be allowed to alter or disable the anti-malware software.
- Users should know what to do in case their anti-malware program detects malware. For example, you might recommend that the user stop working on his computer, and instead call the help desk to receive assistance in disinfecting the system.
- An anti-malware team should be appointed to focus on maintaining the anti-malware measures. This team would be responsible for choosing anti-malware software, keeping the software updated, educating users, and responding in case of a significant malware outbreak.
- Users should be prohibited from installing any unauthorized software on their systems. This edict might seem extreme, but in fact users downloading programs (especially games) from the Internet are a common source of malware. If your organization permits game playing, you might institute a policy in which every game must first be checked for malware and then installed on a user's system by a technician.
- System-wide alerts should be issued to network users notifying them of a serious malware threat and advising them how to prevent infection, even if the malware hasn't been detected on your network yet.

When drafting an anti-malware policy, bear in mind that these measures are not meant to restrict users' freedom, but rather to protect the network from damage and downtime. Explain to users that the anti-malware policy protects their own data as well as critical system files. If possible, automate the anti-malware software installation and operation so that users barely notice its presence. Do not rely on users to run their anti-malware software each time they insert a USB drive or open an email attachment because they will quickly forget to do so.

Chapter Summary

Security Risks

- A weakness of a system, process, or architecture that could lead to compromised information or unauthorized access is known as a vulnerability. The act of taking advantage of a vulnerability is known as an exploit.

- End-user awareness and training can be a monumental task that requires regular attention and due diligence. Ultimately, it is the company's responsibility to ensure that its employees adhere to applicable standards and policies.

- A DoS (denial-of-service) attack occurs when a legitimate user is unable to access normal network resources, such as a web server, because of an attacker's intervention. Most often, this type of attack is achieved by flooding a system with so many requests for services that it can't respond to any of them.

- Malware (short for malicious software) refers to any program or piece of code designed to intrude upon or harm a system or its resources. Included in this category are viruses, Trojan horses, worms, bots, and ransomware.

Security Assessment

- Every organization should assess its security risks by conducting a posture assessment, which is a thorough examination of each aspect of the network to determine how it might be compromised.

- Penetration testing uses various tools to find network vulnerabilities, as in vulnerability scanning, and then attempts to exploit those vulnerabilities.

- Those who want to learn more about hacking techniques or nab a hacker in the act might create a honeypot, or a decoy system that is purposely vulnerable and filled with what appears to be sensitive (though false) content, such as financial data.

Physical Security

- Physical access to all of a network's critical components must be restricted and controlled. Consider the damage that could be done if an intruder were able to steal devices, directly connect his own computer to unprotected console ports, damage or destroy expensive equipment, or simply reset these devices by pressing the physical reset button.

- Most companies require employees to have some kind of ID badge that identifies the person by name and perhaps includes a photo, title, and other information. Additionally, many organizations provide electronic access badges, or smart cards.

- Asset tracking tags can be used to monitor the movement and condition of equipment, inventory, and people. Whether a simple barcode or a wireless-enabled transmitter, asset tracking enables constant or periodic collection of information.

Device Hardening

- Besides securing network devices from external tampering, you can take many steps to secure the device from network- or software-supported attacks as well. These practices are called device hardening.

- Because of the urgency of protecting networks and data from being compromised, security gaps are often addressed in smaller, more frequent updates called patches.

- Most devices that can be configured through a management interface come with a default access account. When configuring a device, make it a habit to change the default administrative credentials before you do anything else.

- Insecure services and protocols, such as Telnet and FTP, should be disabled in a system whenever possible.

- Hashing means to transform data through an algorithm that generally reduces the amount of space needed for the data. If a secure algorithm is used, hashing is nearly impossible to reverse.

- Protection against harmful code involves choosing the most appropriate anti-malware program for your environment, monitoring the network, continually updating the anti-malware program, and educating users.

Security Policies for Users

- A security policy for network users identifies your security goals, risks, levels of authority, designated security coordinator and team members, responsibilities for each team member, and responsibilities for each employee. In addition, it specifies how to address security breaches.

- Security policies help ensure that authorized users have appropriate access to the resources they need. They also help prevent unauthorized users from gaining access to the network, systems, programs, or data.

- BYOD (bring your own device) refers to the practice of allowing employees or students to bring their smartphones, laptops, or other technology for the purpose of performing work or school responsibilities.

- An AUP (acceptable use policy) explains to users what they can and cannot do while accessing a network's resources and also explains penalties for violations. It might also describe how these measures protect the network's security.

- Information is confidential if it could be used by other parties to impair an organization's functioning, decrease customers' confidence, cause a financial loss, damage an organization's status, or give a significant advantage to a competitor. However, in an environment where most data is sensitive or confidential, your security policy should classify information in degrees of sensitivity that correspond to how strictly its access is regulated.

- Choosing a secure password is one of the easiest and least expensive ways to help guard against unauthorized access. Unfortunately, too many people prefer to use an easy-to-remember password.

- A PUA (privileged user agreement), or privileged access agreement, addresses the specific concerns related to privileged access given to administrators and certain support staff.

- Anti-malware software alone will not keep your network safe from malicious code. Because most malware infections can be prevented by applying a little technology and forethought, it's important that all network users understand how to prevent the spread of malware.

Key Terms

For definitions of key terms, see the Glossary near the end of the book.

amplified DRDoS attack
ARP poisoning
asset tracking tag
AUP (acceptable use policy)
back door
badge
biometrics
BYOD (bring your own device)
CCTV (closed-circuit TV)
cipher lock
data breach
DDoS (distributed DoS) attack
deauth (deauthentication) attack
device hardening
DHCP snooping
dictionary attack
DLP (data loss prevention)
DNS poisoning

DoS (denial-of-service) attack
DRDoS (distributed reflection DoS) attack
exploit
FTP bounce
hacker
hashing
honeynet
honeypot
insider threat
key fob
logic bomb
malware
MDM (mobile device management)
MitM (man-in-the-middle) attack
motion detection
NDA (non-disclosure agreement)

PDoS (permanent DoS) attack
penetration testing
phishing
port scanner
posture assessment
principle of least privilege
privileged user account
PUA (privileged user agreement)
ransomware
rogue DHCP server
security audit
security policy
SHA (Secure Hash Algorithm)
smart card
social engineering
tamper detection
virus
vulnerability
vulnerability scanning
zero-day exploit

Review Questions

1. Your organization has just approved a special budget for a network security upgrade. What procedure should you conduct in order to make recommendations for the upgrade priorities?
   a. Data breach
   b. Security audit
   c. Exploitation
   d. Posture assessment

2. Which type of DoS attack orchestrates an attack using uninfected computers?
   a. DDoS (Distributed DoS) attack
   b. Spoofing attack

   c. DRDoS (Distributed Reflection DoS) attack
   d. PDoS (Permanent DoS) attack

3. A company accidentally sends a newsletter with a mistyped website address. The address points to a website that has been spoofed by hackers in order to collect information from people who make the same typo. What kind of attack is this?
   a. Phishing
   b. Baiting
   c. Quid pro quo
   d. Tailgating

4. A former employee discovers six months after he starts work at a new company that his account credentials still give him access to his old company's servers. He demonstrates his access to several friends to brag about his cleverness and talk badly about the company. What kind of attack is this?
   a. Principle of least privilege
   b. Insider threat
   c. Vulnerability
   d. Denial of service

5. A spoofed DNS record spreads to other DNS servers. What is this attack called?
   a. ARP poisoning
   b. DHCP snooping
   c. MitM attack
   d. DNS poisoning

6. Which of these attacks is a form of Wi-Fi DoS attack?
   a. Rogue DHCP server
   b. FTP bounce
   c. Deauthentication attack
   d. Amplified DRDoS attack

7. Leading up to the year 2000, many people expected computer systems the world over to fail when clocks turned the date to January 1, 2000. What type of threat was this?
   a. Ransomware
   b. Logic bomb
   c. Virus
   d. Worm

8. What kind of attack simulation detects vulnerabilities and attempts to exploit them?
   a. Red team-blue team exercise
   b. Vulnerability scanning

   c. Security audit
   d. Penetration testing

9. Which of the following is considered a secure protocol?
   a. FTP
   b. SSH
   c. Telnet
   d. HTTP

10. A company wants to have its employees sign a document that details some project-related information that should not be discussed outside the project's team members. What type of document should they use?
    a. AUP
    b. NDA
    c. MDM
    d. BYOD

11. What is the difference between a vulnerability and an exploit?

12. What are the four phases in the social engineering attack cycle?

13. List five subtypes of DoS attacks.

14. What type of scanning might identify that Telnet is running on a server?

15. Give an example of biometric detection.

16. What unique characteristic of zero-day exploits make them so dangerous?

17. What characteristic of ARP makes it particularly vulnerable to being used in a DoS attack?

18. A neighbor hacks into your secured wireless network on a regular basis, but you didn't give him the password. What loophole was most likely left open?

19. Which form of SHA was developed by private designers?

20. Why might organizations be willing to take on the risk of BYOD?

Hands-On Projects

Project 9-1: Secure a Workstation

Securing a workstation is one of the most important tasks you will perform when setting up security for an organization or individual. A few simple tweaks to a computer's security policy will greatly improve its resistance to attack.

On a computer running Windows 10 Pro, follow these steps to require that a user press Ctrl+Alt+Del to log on:

1. Press **Win+R**, and in the Search box, type **netplwiz** and press **Enter**. Write down the usernames displayed in the User Accounts dialog box.
2. Click the **Advanced** tab and under Secure sign-in, check **Require users to press Ctrl+Alt+Delete**. Why does this setting help increase the workstation's security?
3. Apply the changes and restart the computer to confirm the change.

Follow these steps to secure the computer using a screen saver and sleep mode:

4. Open Settings, click **Accounts**, and click **Sign-in options**. Under Require sign-in, select **When PC wakes up from sleep**.
5. Return to the Settings Home window, click **System**, and click **Power & sleep**. Set the Screen timeouts and Sleep timeouts as desired.
6. Return to the Settings Home window, click **Personalization**, and click **Lock screen**. Scroll down and click **Screen saver settings**. Select a screen saver to activate the screen saver function.
7. Set a wait time. For optimal security, this should be a low number. Check **On resume, display logon screen**. Click **OK** and close all windows.

Follow these steps to require that all users have a password:

8. Press **Win+R**, and in the Search box, type **gpedit.msc** and then press **Enter**. The Local Group Policy Editor window opens.
9. Navigate to **Computer Configuration, Windows Settings, Security Settings, Account Policies, Password Policy**.
10. Change the Minimum password length policy to a value higher than zero. How many characters did you require?

Project 9-2: Research Kali Linux

Kali Linux is a unique distribution of Linux in that it is designed specifically for enhancing the security of a network. The operating system can be run from a flash drive or CD, and includes an impressive array of security tools. In this project, you research the features of Kali Linux. In Capstone Project 9-2, you will install Kali Linux in a VM. Complete the following steps:

1. Spend some time researching Kali Linux to answer the following questions:
   a. Who develops Kali Linux? What distribution was the predecessor to Kali Linux?
   b. What is the main purpose(s) of the Kali Linux distribution?

    c. What are the installation options for Kali Linux? For example, can you use a USB flash drive? Can you dual-boot Kali Linux next to other operating systems? Which ones?

    d. For which hypervisors does Kali Linux offer custom images? What tools must be added to a VirtualBox Kali Linux VM to provide proper integration with the host machine?

    e. What hypervisor comes already installed in Kali Linux?

    f. What are the categories of tools available in Kali Linux?

    g. On the Downloads page, which hashing algorithm does the website use to confirm the validity of the Kali download files?

Remember that hacking a network without the owner's express permission is highly illegal. If you download and use Kali Linux, be sure to keep it inside your own network. Capstone Project 9-2 will give you an opportunity to explore the features of Kali Linux.

Project 9-3: Install and Play with Sandboxie

A sandbox provides an isolated space on your computer to run questionable software or multiple instances of the same software, or to access websites that might present a threat to your computer's system. Web browsers themselves act as simple sandboxes, but you can create a safer environment with a dedicated sandbox program. Sandboxie is a popular sandbox program for Windows that is also free. In this project, you install Sandboxie and explore some of its features. Complete the following steps:

1. Using an administrator account on a Windows machine, go to **sandboxie.com**. Download and install the latest, free version of Sandboxie. Accept all default settings. When Sandboxie opens, click **OK** to apply software compatibility configuration settings.

2. Read the Getting Started tutorial and follow the instructions for opening a sandboxed web browser, downloading a file, and deleting the sandbox contents. Here are a few pointers:

    a. The browser might be slow to open and slow to respond.

    b. Once it opens, use the mouse to point to the edge of the browser window. What visual cue notifies you that the browser is running in a sandbox?

    c. When you're instructed to download a file, you can search for an image related to your favorite hobby and download a copy to your computer.

3. Close the Sandboxie Control window.

4. You saw during the tutorial how to open the sandboxed web browser from the Sandboxed Web Browser icon on the desktop. This time, open a web browser from the browser's own desktop icon. To do this, the browser's shortcut icon must be saved to the Desktop, or you can open the app's file location from the Start menu. Then right-click the browser's icon and click **Run Sandboxed**. Make sure DefaultBox is selected, then click **OK**.

5. Open a second window of the same browser, but this time open it normally—that is, not in the Sandboxie sandbox.

6. Use the mouse to point to each of the browser icons in the taskbar at the bottom of your screen. What characters in the title of the sandboxed preview window indicate that window is sandboxed?

7. Close the sandboxed browser. Add a page to your Wikidot website and make some notes about this installation.

Project 9-4: Download and Use Advanced Port Scanner

In this chapter, you learned that one way to secure a device is to close unneeded software ports in the operating system. Advanced Port Scanner is a free tool that scans a network for open ports and reports on the applications using those ports. In this project, you will download and use Advanced Port Scanner. Complete the following steps:

1. In your browser, go to **advanced-port-scanner.com**, download the app's software, and then install it using the default settings. Run Advanced Port Scanner when the installation is complete.

2. When Advanced Port Scanner opens, the IP address range for your network should be listed automatically. If not, you can check your current IP address using Command Prompt and use that information to insert the correct IP address range yourself. When you're ready, click the **Scan** button. The results of a scan on a home network are shown in Figure 9-22.

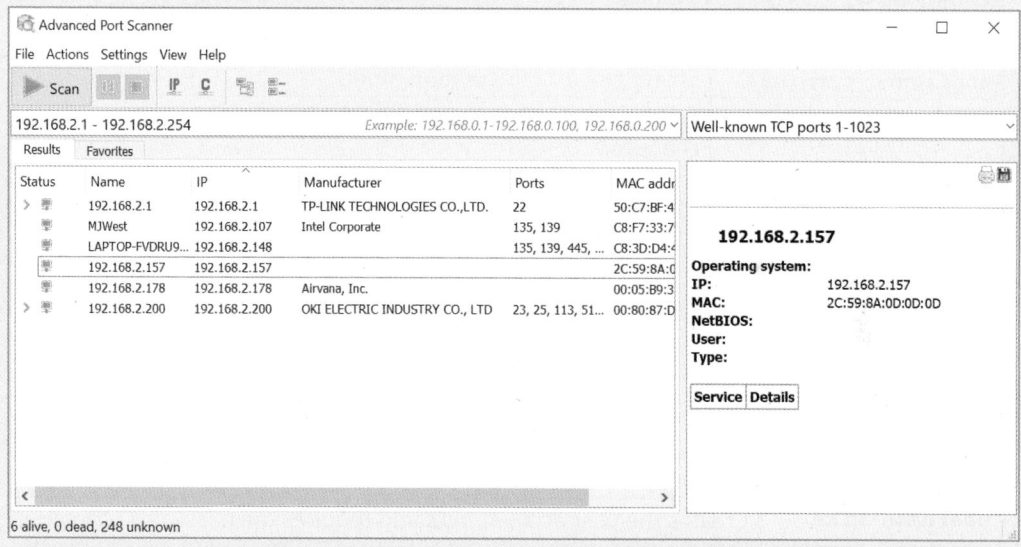

Figure 9-22   Open ports found by Advanced Port Scanner
Source: Famatech

3. When the scan is complete, look at the ports reported for each device. Which ports for insecure protocols are listed, such as port 21 for FTP? Are there any ports that stand out to you as being open unnecessarily?

4. Select another computer on the network besides your local device. Click **Actions**, point to **Tools**, and click **Ping**. What happens? What other commands are available in Advanced Port Scanner?

5. Add a page to your Wikidot website and make some notes about this installation.

Capstone Projects

Capstone Project 9-1: Configure Router Passwords in Packet Tracer

When configuring a networking device, one of the very first tasks should be to change the default administrative credentials. In this project, you will use the CLI to configure user accounts and passwords for a router in your Packet Tracer network. Complete the following steps:

1. In Packet Tracer, open your Packet Tracer file from Capstone Project 8-3.
2. Click **Router3**, and click the **CLI** tab. Press **Enter** to continue.
3. Enter the commands listed in Table 9-2 to change the router's default name.

Table 9-2   Change a router's hostname

Command	Purpose
`enable`	Enables privileged EXEC mode
`configure terminal`	Enters global configuration mode
`hostname R3`	Renames the router from the default to R3. Notice the prompt changes.

4. What prompt do you see now?
5. Now you're ready to create a username and password, which will be required to sign into the router's management interface. Enter the commands listed in Table 9-3.

Table 9-3   Set a username and password and check the configuration

Command	Purpose
`username mike password cengage`	Creates the user account *mike* and requires the password *cengage* for that account
`line console 0`	Accesses the console port configuration interface
`login local`	Configures the router to require a locally configured username and password to log into the router's management interface
Ctrl + Z	Returns to privileged EXEC mode
Enter	
`logout`	Logs out of the router's interface
Enter	Logs back into the router's interface using the new username *mike* and password *cengage*
`mike`	
`cengage`	

6. Let's take a look at the configured username and password in the running-config file. Enter the commands listed in Table 9-4.

Table 9-4 View configurations in the running-config file

Command	Purpose
`enable`	Enables privileged EXEC mode
`show running-config`	Lists the configurations in the running-config file

Note 📎

Press Enter to advance one line at a time in the running-config file.
Press Space to advance one page at a time.
When you're finished, press Ctrl+C to exit the running-config file.

7. What username and password are shown in the running-config file? Why is this a problem?
8. Passwords should never be stored in plain text. Let's look at another way to create a password so the password will be stored more securely. Enter the commands listed in Table 9-5.

Table 9-5 Set a username and secret password and confirm configurations

Command	Purpose
`configure terminal`	Enters global configuration mode
`username jill secret cengage`	Creates the user account *jill* and requires the secret password *cengage* for that account
Ctrl + Z	Returns to privileged EXEC mode
Enter	
`show running-config`	Lists the configurations in the running-config file

9. What usernames and passwords are shown in the running-config file now? The password for both accounts is *cengage*. Why do these passwords look different in the running-config file?
10. While we're at it, let's also set two more passwords. Either one of these passwords could be required in order to enable privileged EXEC mode (although in reality, only the last enable password will continue to work). The difference is that one password will be stored in plain text, and the other will be hashed. Enter the commands listed in Table 9-6.

Table 9-6 Set a password and a secret password that can enable privileged EXEC mode

Command	Purpose
`configure terminal`	Enters global configuration mode
`enable password networkplus`	Requires the password *networkplus* in order to enable privileged EXEC mode
`enable secret comptia`	Requires the password *comptia* in order to enable privileged EXEC mode
Ctrl + Z	Returns to privileged EXEC mode
Enter	
`show running-config`	Lists the configurations in the running-config file

11. What enable passwords are shown in the running-config file?
12. You can hash existing passwords on a router, rather than having to go back and reconfigure each insecure password. Enter the commands listed in Table 9-7.

Table 9-7 Hash existing passwords

Command	Purpose
`configure terminal`	Enters global configuration mode
`service password-encryption`	Encrypts any unencrypted passwords
Ctrl + Z	Returns to privileged EXEC mode
Enter	
`show running-config`	Lists the configurations in the running-config file

13. What do you notice now about the two enable passwords? What about the two user account passwords?
14. Compare the complexity of the codes for the passwords that were originally stored in plain text with the passwords that were originally hashed. The secret passwords show a much more complex code. Notice the 5 in front of the secret passwords, which indicates the MD5 hash was used. Also notice the 7 in front of the other passwords. These Type 7 passwords are easily cracked. In your browser, go to **packetlife.net/toolbox** and click **Type 7 Reverser**. Copy and paste the Type 7 password string for each of the Type 7 passwords in Packet Tracer into the Type 7 hash box on the website. Note that you will need to select and then right-click each string instead of using the Ctrl + C shortcut to copy each string into your Clipboard. After pasting each string into the hash box, click **Reverse**. Do the values match your original plain text passwords? What happens when you paste a Type 5 password string into the hash box?

15. To save these configurations, enter the command `copy run start`, and then press **Enter** again.

16. Make some notes on your Wikidot website about your activities in Packet Tracer for this project.

Capstone Project 9-2: Install Kali Linux in a VM

In Project 9-2 in this chapter, you researched Kali Linux, which is a Linux distro that comes loaded with dozens of penetration testing tools. In this project, you download the Kali Linux image file and install it in a VM.

Caution ⚠️

It's highly illegal to perform penetration testing procedures on a network that you do not own or have specific permission to test. If you choose to use the penetration testing tools included in Kali Linux, this is best done on your own, home network where you own the networking equipment and pay the bill yourself.

If you use a network that you do not own, be sure to obtain explicit permission from the network owner, preferably in writing, signed, and dated. If you practice using the pen testing tools in a school lab, be sure to follow your instructor's directions carefully.

Penetration testing a network you don't own without the owner's permission can incur multiple federal felony charges, even if the network owner is a relative or friend. Please be absolutely certain you have permission *in writing* **before using the Kali Linux pen testing tools.**

Complete the following steps:

1. In your browser, go to **kali.org**. Find the downloads for the Kali Virtual Images. Download the appropriate Kali image for the hypervisor you're using for this project. The light image is sufficient for this project.

2. Import the Kali Linux image into your hypervisor by following these steps, which differ from the way you created VMs previously:

   - In VirtualBox, click **File, Import Appliance**. Locate the downloaded image, and click **Open**. Accept the default settings and click **Import** to complete the process. You might need to disable USB 2.0 support in order to start the VM in VirtualBox. If so, open the VM's Settings window, click **USB**, and select the **USB 1.1 (OHCI) Controller**, as shown in Figure 9-23.

   - In VMware, you first have to unzip the downloaded image. However, this requires an extraction app from 7-zip.org. Alternatively, you might be able to use the VirtualBox image. When you're ready, in VMware click **Open a Virtual Machine**, locate

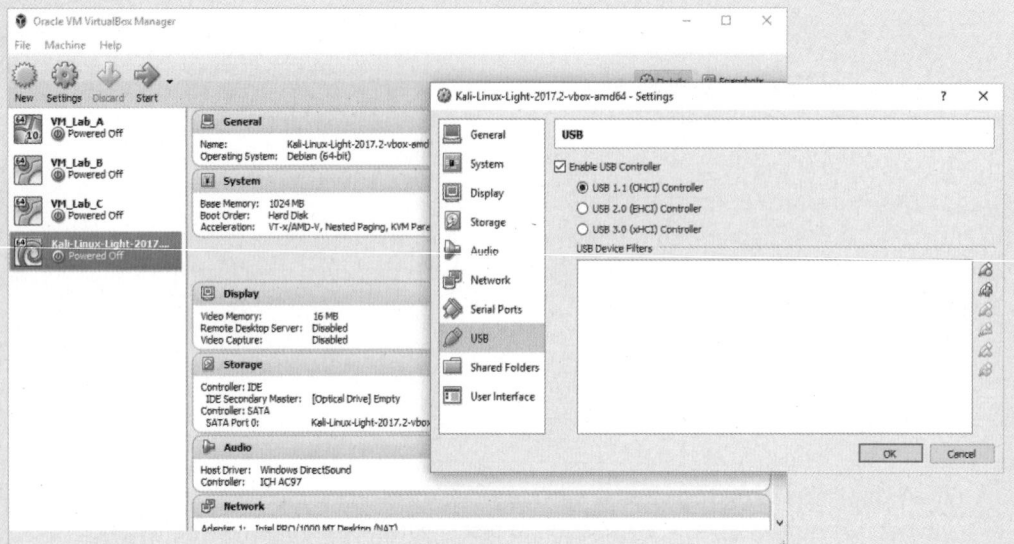

Figure 9-23 In VirtualBox, select the USB 1.1 controller

Source: Oracle Corporation

the downloaded image, and click **Open**. Accept the default settings to complete the process.

- In Hyper-V, you first have to unzip the downloaded image. However, this requires an extraction app from 7-zip.org. When you're ready, click **Import Virtual Machine**, click **Next**, locate the file, and continue through the steps on-screen. Alternatively, you might prefer to install the Kali Linux ISO into a new VM as you have done with other projects in this text. Either approach will likely require some troubleshooting, so be sure to search online for help if you get stuck.

3. Start and sign in to the Kali Linux VM. The virtual images of Kali Linux are all configured with the default username **root** and password **toor**.

4. For this project, we'll take a quick tour around the Kali Linux desktop, as shown in Figure 9-24. You can explore the tools on your own if you want to. Make sure that you own the network you're penetration testing, or make sure you have *written* permission from the network owner before using any of the tools provided in Kali Linux.

   Answer the following questions:

   - Open the File System window. What three places are listed by default? Close the File System window.
   - Open the Terminal Emulator window. What is the default command prompt?
   - Ping Google's public DNS server (8.8.8.8). Is the ping successful? Press Ctrl+C to stop the output. Close the Terminal window.
   - Click **Applications** at the top of the screen. How many categories of tools are available?

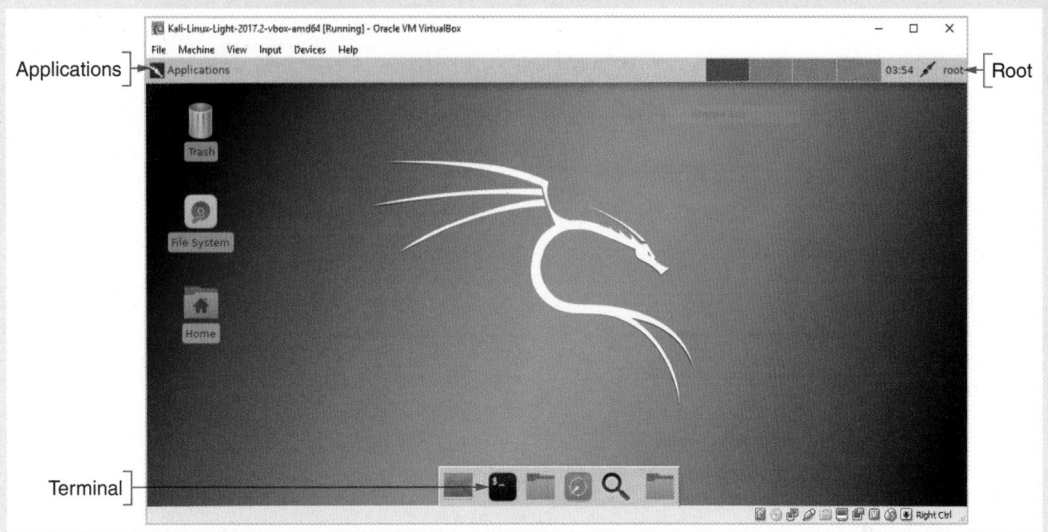

Applications

Root

Terminal

Figure 9-24   The Kali Linux desktop in a VirtualBox VM

Source: Offensive Security

- You have already used one of these tools in earlier labs. What is the first category nmap is listed under?
- Click **root** at the top of the screen and click **Shut Down** to power down the VM.

5. Add some notes to your Wikidot website about the new VM installation.

## CHAPTER 10

SECURITY IN NETWORK DESIGN

After reading this chapter and completing the exercises, you will be able to:

Describe the functions and features of various network security devices

Implement security precautions on a switch

Track the processes of authentication, authorization, and auditing on a network

Explain the available options in network access control methods

Configure various security measures on a wireless network

On the Job

I was the network administrator and entire IT department for a mortgage company owned by a bank, which I'll call Bank A. Much of my job focused on certain legal and financial processes that had to run at different intervals, ranging from daily to quarterly. To facilitate these processes, I created static routes that allowed for the direct encrypted transfer of files from the mortgage company's servers to Bank A's servers.

Eventually, our company was purchased by another bank, which I'll call Bank B. Naturally, many of our legal and financial processes had to change. This in turn necessitated numerous changes to the network. Working with Bank B's IT department, I began updating Access Control Lists, and providing detailed information to our third-party Intrusion Prevention Service to make sure legitimate business was not accidently blocked. We tested firewalls, ACLs, VPNs, batch processes, static routes and were confident that everything had been implemented successfully. It took coordination from three teams of people working over two weeks and weekends, but we got everything ready by the time the acquisition was announced. Everything went smoothly. The people at the mortgage company saw no changes to their work. The people at Bank B received all the files that they needed in the correct formats.

Fast-forward two months. I was working off-site, and my phone starts ringing nonstop. Some files needed to be transferred to a federal agency within hours or the mortgage company would be fined hundreds of thousands of dollars. No person at the mortgage company had permission or knowledge to investigate the issue. I had to pull off the interstate, find a coffee shop with Internet access, and get to work solving the problem.

Eventually we figured out the issue was a static route associated with a quarterly process that we had overlooked. I started by calling the people at Bank A to ask if they could detect any network traffic trying to reach a specific IP address. After some digging around, they found traffic from the mortgage company's network being refused by a decommissioned server. To fix the problem, I configured new static routes and the files made it in on time by less than an hour.

Johnathan Yerby, Ph.D.
Middle Georgia State University

In the previous chapter, we began our discussion of network security with an exploration of threats to the network, physical security, and security policies for users. A typical network user will likely be exposed to all of these things at some point in a non-IT career. In this chapter, we dig in behind-the-scenes to see what security precautions IT professionals need to implement on a network to help keep it secure.

We'll begin with a discussion of network security devices, which is a category that includes far more than just firewalls. We'll continue our discussion of device hardening by examining security precautions needed on network switches. Then we'll explore the complementary processes of network access control and authentication, both on wired and wireless networks.

Network Security Devices

 **Certification**

1.3   Explain the concepts and characteristics of routing and switching.

2.2   Given a scenario, determine the appropriate placement of networking devices on a network and install/configure them.

2.3   Explain the purposes and use cases for advanced networking devices.

Many devices on a network are designed specifically with network security in mind. Others primarily serve non-security purposes, and yet are outfitted with significant security features and abilities. Proxy servers and ACLs on network devices are examples of non-security devices with security features, while firewalls and IDS/IPS systems are the network's specialized security devices. Using multiple options for network security results in layered security, as you saw in the *On the Job* story at the beginning of this chapter, and provides more protection than any one type of device or defense can provide on its own. Therefore, many of these options are often used in combination. Let's look at how each of these components contribute to security in network design.

Proxy Servers

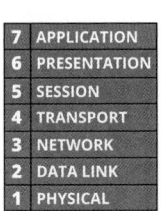

One approach to enhancing network security is adding a proxy server. A **proxy server**, or proxy, acts as an intermediary between the external and internal networks, screening all incoming and outgoing traffic. Proxy servers manage security at the Application layer of the OSI model. Although proxy servers only provide low-grade security relative to other security devices, they can help prevent an attack on internal network resources such as web servers and web clients.

To understand how they work, think of the secure data on a server as the president and the proxy server as the secretary of state. Rather than have the president risk his safety by leaving the country, the secretary of state travels abroad, speaks for the president, and gathers information on the president's behalf. In fact, foreign leaders may never actually meet the president. Instead, the secretary of state acts as his proxy. In a similar way, a proxy server represents a private network to another network (usually the Internet).

Although a proxy server appears to the outside world as an internal network server, in reality it is merely another filtering device for the internal LAN. One of its most important functions is preventing the outside world from discovering addresses on the internal network. For example, suppose your LAN uses a proxy server, and you want to send an email message from your workstation inside the LAN to a colleague via the Internet. The following steps describe the process:

Step 1:   Your message goes to the proxy server. Depending on the configuration of your network, you might or might not have to log on separately to the proxy server first.

Step 2: The proxy server repackages the data frames that make up the message so that, rather than your workstation's IP address being the source, the proxy server inserts its own IP address as the source.

Step 3: The proxy server passes your repackaged data to a packet-filtering firewall, which you'll learn more about later in this chapter.

Step 4: The firewall verifies that the source IP address in your packets is valid (that it came from the proxy server) and then sends your message to the Internet.

Examples of proxy server software include Squid (*squid-cache.org*) and, for Windows only, WinGate by Qbik (*wingate.com*), which includes firewall features as well. Figure 10-1 depicts how a proxy server might fit into a network design.

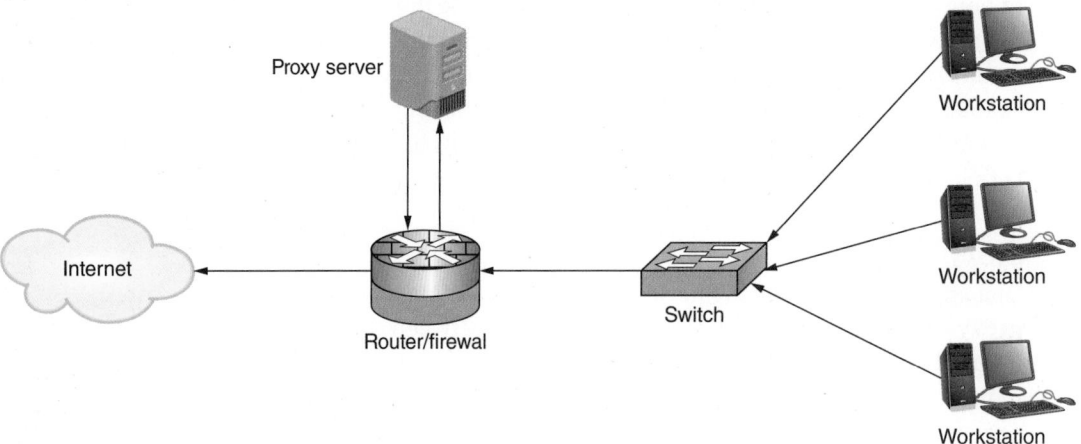

Figure 10-1   A proxy server is used to connect to the Internet

You might have noticed that proxy services sound suspiciously similar to NAT, which you learned about earlier. However, they differ significantly. You've already learned that proxy servers can provide some content filtering, which is possible because they function at the Application layer rather than at the lower, Network layer. Proxy servers can also improve performance for users accessing resources external to their network by caching files. For example, a proxy server situated between a LAN and an external web server can be configured to save recently viewed web pages. The next time a user on the LAN wants to view one of the saved web pages, content is provided by the proxy server. This eliminates the time required to travel over a WAN connection and retrieve the same content multiple times from the external web server.

Whereas proxy servers access resources on the Internet for a client, a reverse proxy provides services to Internet clients from servers on its own network. In this case, the reverse proxy provides identity protection for the server rather than the client, as well as some amount of Application layer firewall protection. Reverse proxies are particularly useful when multiple web servers are accessed through the same public IP address.

> **Note**
>
> Often, firewall and proxy server features are combined in one device. In other words, you might purchase a firewall that can block certain types of traffic from entering your network (a firewall function), and also modify the addresses in the packets leaving your network (a proxy function).

ACLs (Access Control Lists) on Network Devices

7	APPLICATION
6	PRESENTATION
5	SESSION
4	TRANSPORT
3	NETWORK
2	DATA LINK
1	PHYSICAL

Before a hacker on another network can gain access to files on your network's server, he must traverse one or more switches and routers. Although devices such as firewalls, described later in this chapter, provide more tailored security, manipulating switch and router configurations affords a small degree of security, especially when these devices sit on or near the edge of a network where they can control access to the network. This section describes a fundamental way to control traffic through routers, Layer 3 switches, and firewalls.

A router's main function is to examine packets and determine where to direct them based on their Network layer addressing information. Thanks to a router's **ACL (access control list)**, or access list, routers can also decline to forward certain packets depending on their content. An ACL acts like a filter to instruct the router to permit or deny traffic according to one or more of the following variables:

- Network layer protocol (for example, IP or ICMP)
- Transport layer protocol (for example, TCP or UDP)
- Source IP address
- Destination IP address (which can restrict or allow certain websites)
- TCP or UDP port number

Each time a router receives a packet, it examines the packet and refers to its ACL to determine whether the packet meets criteria for permitting or denying travel on the network. See Figure 10-2. Each statement or test in the ACL specifies either a permit or deny flag. The router starts at the top of the list and makes a test based on the first statement. If a packet's characteristics match a permit statement, the packet moves on to the network. If the packet's characteristics match a deny statement, the packet is immediately discarded. If the packet's characteristics don't match the statement, the router moves down the list to the next statement in the ACL. If the packet does not match any criteria given in the statements in the ACL, the packet is dropped (as shown by the last "No" value in Figure 10-2). This last decision is called the **implicit deny** rule, which ensures that any traffic the ACL does not explicitly permit is denied by default.

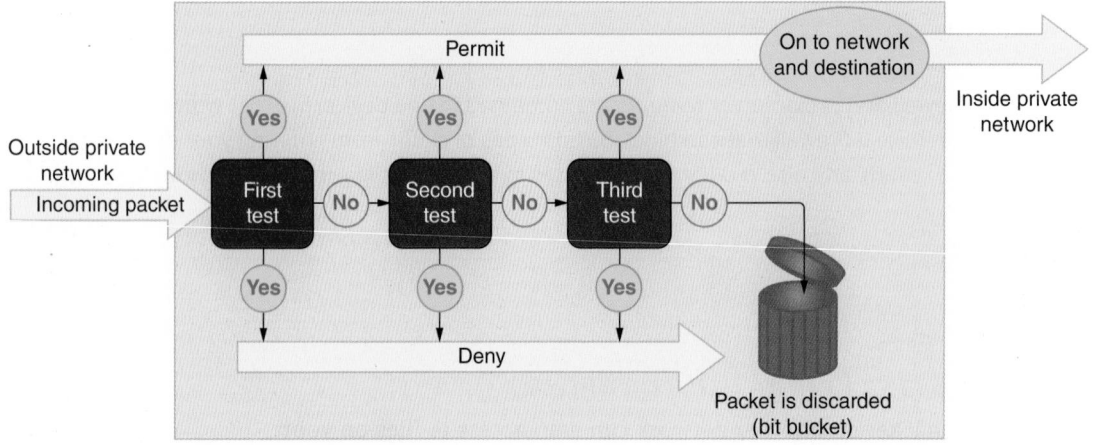

Figure 10-2   A router uses an ACL to permit or deny traffic to or from a network it protects

On most routers, each interface must be assigned a separate ACL, and different ACLs may be associated with inbound and outbound traffic. When ACLs are installed on routers, each ACL is assigned a number or name.

The access-list command is used to assign a statement to an already-installed ACL. The command must identify the ACL and include a permit or deny argument. Here are a few sample commands used to create statements in the ACL that controls incoming traffic to a router. The ACL is named acl_2:

- To permit ICMP traffic from any IP address or network to any IP address or network:

```
access-list acl_2 permit icmp any any
```

- To deny ICMP traffic from any IP address or network to any IP address or network:

```
access-list acl_2 deny icmp any any
```

- To permit TCP traffic from 2.2.2.2 host machine to 5.5.5.5 host machine:

```
access-list acl_2 permit tcp host 2.2.2.2 host 5.5.5.5
```

- To permit TCP traffic from 2.2.2.2 host machine to 3.3.3.3 host machine to destination web port 80 (the "eq" parameter says "equal to" and "www" is a keyword that stands for port 80):

```
access-list acl_2 permit tcp host 2.2.2.2 host 3.3.3.3 eq www
```

Statements can also specify network segments (groups of IP addresses) by using a network address for the segment and a wildcard mask. The bits in a wildcard mask work opposite of how bits in a subnet mask work. A 0 in the wildcard mask says to match the IP address bits to the network address given, and 1 says you don't care what the IP address bits are. For example, a wildcard mask of 0.0.0.255 can be written as

00000000.00000000.00000000.11111111, which says the first three octets of an IP address must match the given network address, and the last octet can be any value. The following command permits TCP traffic to pass through when the first three octets of an IP address are 10.1.1, and the last octet can be any value:

```
access-list acl_2 permit tcp 10.1.1.0 0.0.0.255
```

Note

In ACL statements, `any` is equivalent to using a wildcard mask of 255.255.255.255, which allows all IP addresses to pass through.

An access list is not automatically installed on a router. If you don't configure an ACL, the router allows all traffic through. Once you create an ACL and assign it to an interface, you have explicitly permitted or denied certain types of traffic. Naturally, the more statements or tests a router must scan (in other words, the longer the ACL), the more time it takes a router to act, and, therefore, the slower the router's overall performance.

When troubleshooting a problematic connection between two hosts, or between some applications or ports on two hosts, consider that the problem might be a misconfigured ACL. For example, suppose you can successfully ping a host, but `telnet` and `tracert` attempts cannot connect with the same host. You can use a process of elimination on the device's various ACLs to identify the incorrect ACL settings and correct the problem. Common errors include listing the ACL statements in the wrong order, using the wrong criteria when defining a rule, and constructing a rule incorrectly.

Firewalls

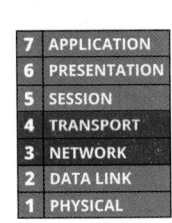

A firewall is a specialized device or software that selectively filters or blocks traffic between networks. A firewall protects a network by blocking certain traffic from traversing the firewall's position, similar to a bouncer checking IDs at the entrance to a private club. While firewalls include filtering from ACLs, they also offer a wide variety of other methods to evaluate, filter, and control network traffic.

A firewall might be placed internally, residing between two interconnected private networks. More commonly, the firewall is placed on the edge of the private network, monitoring the connection between a private network and a public network (such as the Internet), as shown in Figure 10-3. This is an example of a **network-based firewall**, so named because it protects an entire private network. Figure 10-4 shows dedicated firewall appliances that might be purchased for a medium-sized or large corporation's network. You'll also see firewall features integrated in routers, switches, and other network devices. Other types of firewalls, known as **host-based firewalls**, only protect the computer on which they are installed.

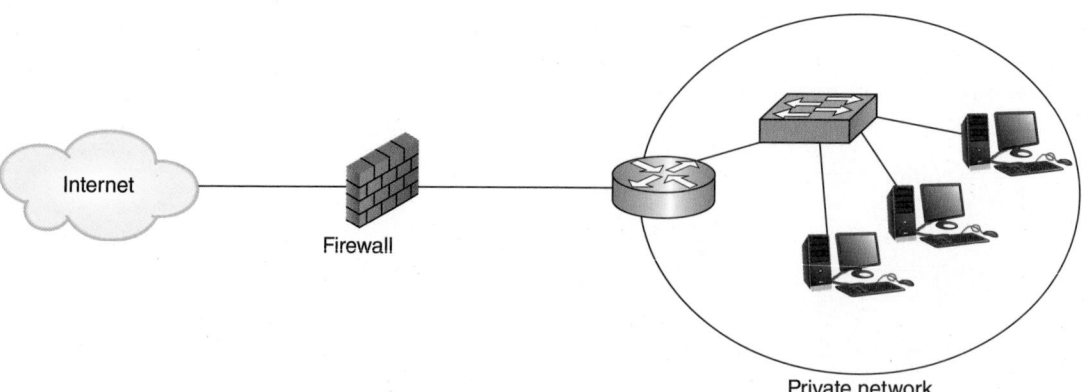

Figure 10-3   Placement of a firewall between a private network and the Internet

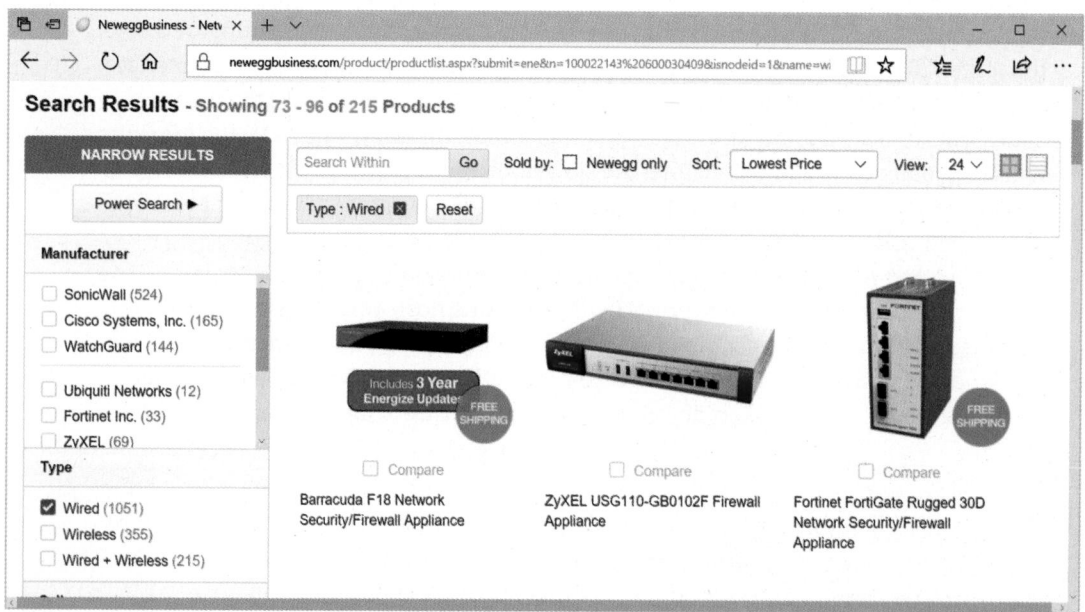

Figure 10-4   A dedicated firewall device

Source: Newegg Business, Inc.

Network+ Exam Tip ⓘ

Many types of firewalls exist, and they can be implemented in many different ways. To understand secure network design and to qualify for CompTIA Network+ certification, you should recognize which functions firewalls can provide, where they can be placed on a network, and how to determine what features you need in a firewall.

The simplest form of a firewall is a packet-filtering firewall, which is a network device or application that examines the header of every packet of data it receives on any of its interfaces (called inbound traffic), as shown in Figure 10-5. The firewall refers to its ACL to determine whether that type of packet is authorized to continue to its destination, regardless of whether that destination is on the internal LAN or on an external network. If a packet does not meet the filtering criteria, the firewall blocks the packet from continuing. However, if a packet does meet filtering criteria, the firewall allows that packet to pass through to the network the firewall protects. This is a common feature of SOHO routers and in fact, nearly all routers can be configured to act as packet-filtering firewalls via ACLs.

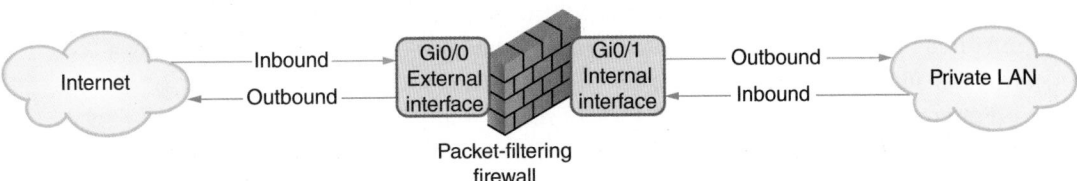

Figure 10-5   Arrows pointing toward the firewall are inbound for that device

Figure 10-5 shows the firewall filtering traffic that comes into the LAN from the Internet, and also traffic that goes out of the LAN to the Internet. One possible reason for blocking Internet-bound traffic is to stop worms from spreading. For example, if you're running a web server, which in most cases only needs to respond to incoming requests and does not need to initiate outgoing requests, you could configure a packet-filtering firewall to block certain types of outgoing transmissions initiated by the web server. In this way, you help prevent spreading worms that are designed to attach themselves to web servers and propagate themselves to other computers on the Internet.

Often, firewalls ship with a default configuration designed to block the most common types of security threats. In other words, the firewall may be preconfigured to accept or deny certain types of traffic. However, many network administrators choose to customize the firewall settings, for example, blocking additional ports or adding criteria for the type of traffic that may travel into or out of ports. Some common criteria by which a packet-filtering firewall might accept or deny traffic include the following:

- Source and destination IP addresses
- Source and destination ports (for example, ports that supply TCP/UDP connections, FTP, Telnet, ARP, ICMP, and so on)
- Flags set in the TCP header (for example, SYN or ACK)
- Transmissions that use the UDP or ICMP protocols
- A packet's status as the first packet in a new data stream or a subsequent packet
- A packet's status as inbound to or outbound from your private network

Based on these options, a network administrator could configure his firewall, for example, to prevent any IP address that does not begin with "10.121," the network ID of the addresses on his network, from accessing the network's router and servers.

Furthermore, he could disable—or block—certain well-known ports, such as the insecure NetBIOS ports (137, 138, and 139). Blocking ports prevents *any* user from connecting to and completing a transmission through those ports. This technique is useful to further guard against unauthorized access to the network. In other words, even if a hacker could spoof an IP address that began with *10.121*, he could not access the NetBIOS ports (which are notoriously insecure) on the firewall.

Ports can be blocked not only on firewalls, but also on routers, servers, or any device that uses ports. For example, if you established a web server for testing but did not want anyone in your organization to connect to your test web pages through a browser, you could block port 80 on that server. Be careful, however, when opening or blocking ports used by multiple protocols or types of connections, such as SSH's port 22. An incorrectly configured firewall is an easy thing to overlook when, for example, troubleshooting a newly installed application on a host.

For greater security, you can choose a firewall that performs more complex functions than simply filtering packets. Among the factors to consider when making your decision are the following:

- Does the firewall support encryption?
- Does the firewall support user authentication?
- Does the firewall allow you to manage it centrally and through a standard interface?
- How easily can you establish rules for access to and from the firewall?
- Does the firewall support filtering at the highest layers of the OSI model, not just at the Data Link and Transport layers? For example, **content-filtering firewalls** can block designated types of traffic based on application data contained within packets. A school might configure its firewall to prevent responses from a website with questionable content from reaching the client that requested the site.
- Does the firewall provide internal logging and auditing capabilities, such as IDS or IPS? IDS and IPS are described later in this chapter.
- Does the firewall protect the identity of your internal LAN's addresses from the outside world?
- Can the firewall monitor packets according to existing traffic streams? A **stateful firewall** is able to inspect each incoming packet to determine whether it belongs to a currently active connection (called a stateful inspection) and is, therefore, a legitimate packet. A **stateless firewall** manages each incoming packet as a stand-alone entity without regard to currently active connections. Stateless firewalls are faster than stateful firewalls, but are not as sophisticated.

A SOHO wireless router typically acts as a firewall and includes packet-filtering options. At the other end of the spectrum, devices made by Cisco or Fortinet for enterprise-wide security are known as security appliances and can perform several functions, such as encryption, load balancing, and IPS, in addition to packet filtering. Examples of software that enable a computer to act as a packet-filtering firewall include **iptables** (a command-line firewall utility for Linux systems), ZoneAlarm, and Comodo Firewall. Some operating systems, including Windows 10, include firewall software. You'll explore Windows Firewall in the next section, and in a project at the end of this chapter, you'll practice using iptables in Ubuntu Server.

Applying Concepts: Windows Defender Firewall

Follow these steps to find out how to configure Windows Defender Firewall on a Windows 10 computer:

1. Open Windows Defender Firewall from Control Panel, as shown in Figure 10-6.

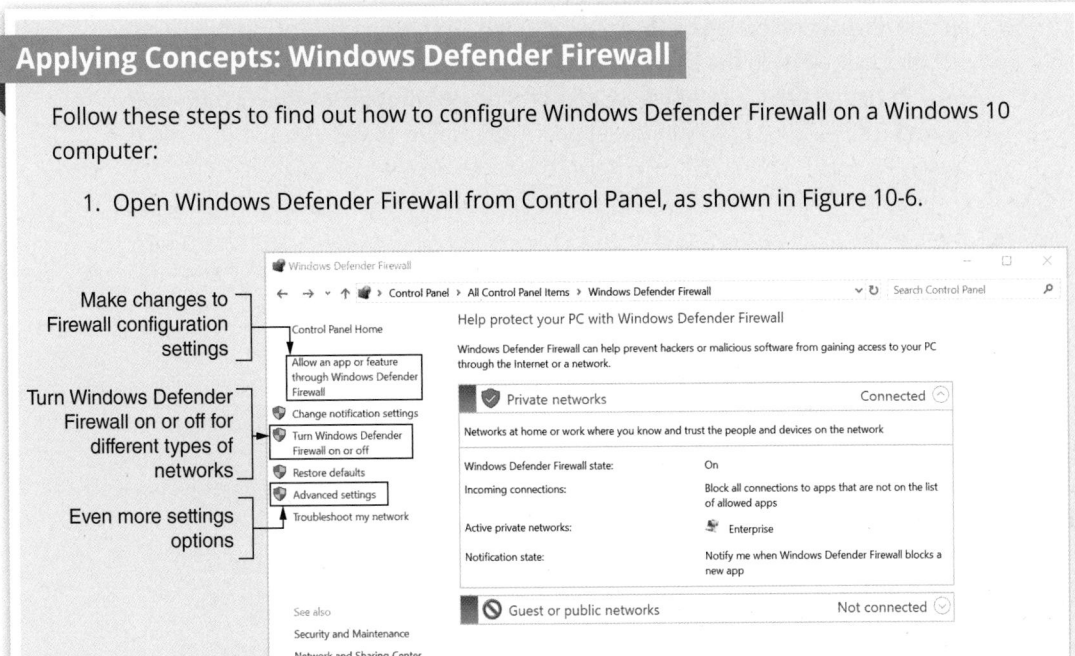

Figure 10-6   Windows Defender Firewall shows the computer is currently connected to a private network

2. To control firewall settings for each type of network location, in the left pane click **Turn Windows Defender Firewall on or off**. The Customize Settings window appears (see Figure 10-7). Notice in the figure that Windows Defender Firewall is turned on for each network location type.

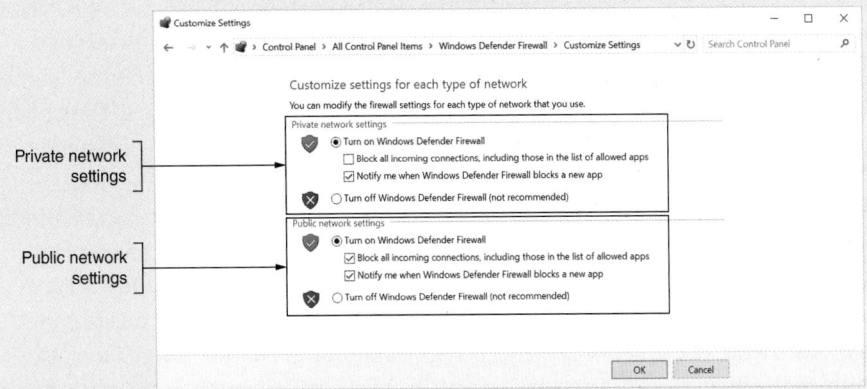

Figure 10-7   Customize settings for a private or public network

3. To allow no exceptions through the firewall on a private network or public network, check **Block all incoming connections, including those in the list of allowed apps.** After you have made your changes, click **OK.**

4. You can allow an exception to your firewall rules. To change the programs allowed through the firewall, in the left pane of the Windows Defender Firewall window (shown earlier in Figure 10-6), click **Allow an app or feature through Windows Defender Firewall.** The Allowed apps window appears (see Figure 10-8).

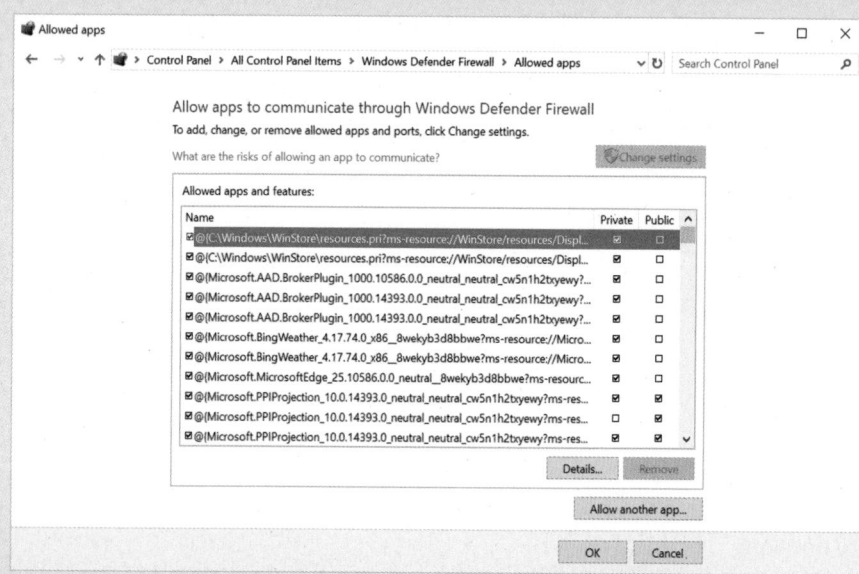

Figure 10-8   Allow apps to communicate through the firewall

5. Scroll down to find the app you want to allow to initiate a connection from a remote computer to this computer, and then, in the right side of the window, click the **Private** check box and/or the **Public** check box to indicate which type of network location the app is allowed to use. If you don't see your app in the list, near the bottom of the window click **Allow another app** to see more apps or to add your own. (If the option is gray, click **Change settings** to enable it.) When you are finished making changes, click **OK** to return to the Windows Defender Firewall window.

6. For even more control over firewall settings, in the Windows Defender Firewall window, click **Advanced settings**. The Windows Defender Firewall with Advanced Security window opens. In the left pane, select **Inbound Rules** or **Outbound Rules**. A list of apps appears in the middle pane. Right-click an app and select **Properties** from the shortcut menu. The Properties dialog box gives full control of how exceptions get through the firewall, including which users, protocols, ports, and remote computers can use each opening (see Figure 10-9).

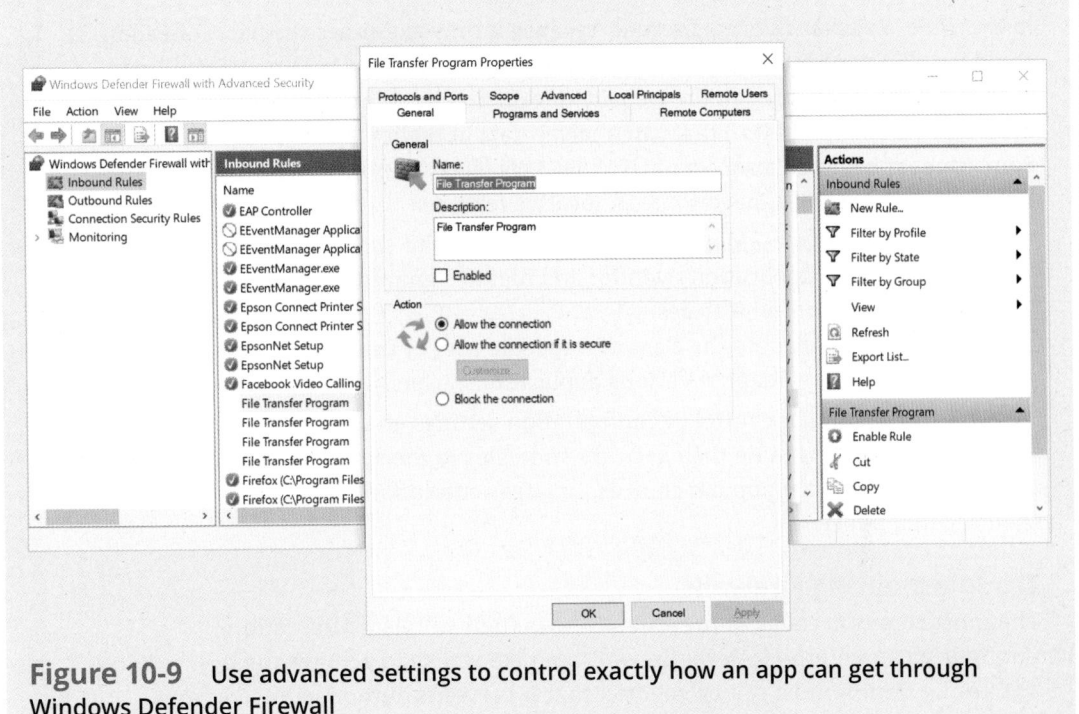

Figure 10-9   Use advanced settings to control exactly how an app can get through Windows Defender Firewall

UTM (Unified Threat Management)

In response to the increasing complexity of threats against computing resources, vendors of firewalls and their related products continue to improve and innovate. One such innovation is **UTM (Unified Threat Management)**, which is a security strategy that combines multiple layers of security appliances and technologies into a single safety net. A UTM solution can provide a full spread of security services managed from a single point of control. One disadvantage to this arrangement is that the "total" really is the sum of its parts. So, if one layer of coverage in a UTM is low quality, overall protection is significantly compromised. UTM, due to its multiplicity of features, also requires a great deal of processing power. Because this is less of a challenge today than it was in the past, UTM is regaining ground as a leading security strategy, especially for small- to medium-sized businesses that benefit the most from devices needing little configuration or management.

NGFW (Next Generation Firewalls)

Because simple packet-filtering firewalls operate at the Network layer of the OSI model and examine only network addresses, they cannot distinguish between a user who is trying to breach the firewall and a user who is authorized to do so. For example, your organization might host a web server, which necessitates accepting requests for port 80 on that server.

7	**APPLICATION**
6	**PRESENTATION**
5	**SESSION**
4	**TRANSPORT**
3	**NETWORK**
2	**DATA LINK**
1	**PHYSICAL**

In this case, a packet-filtering firewall, because it only examines the packet header, could not distinguish between a harmless web browser and a hacker attempting to manipulate her way through the website to gain access to the network. For more thorough security, a firewall that can analyze data at higher layers is required. Sometimes considered a subset of UTM, **NGFWs (Next Generation Firewalls)**, also called **Layer 7 firewalls**, have some innovative features:

- *application aware*—Monitor and limit the traffic of specific applications, including the application's vendor and digital signature. This includes built-in Application Control features.
- *user aware*—Adapt to the class of a specific user or user group.
- *context aware*—Adapt to various applications, users, and devices.

This more granular control of configuration settings enables network administrators to fine-tune their security strategies to the specific needs of their companies. NGFWs are popular choices for larger enterprises that need to customize their security policies.

Troubleshooting Firewalls

The most common cause of firewall failure is firewall misconfiguration. Configuring an enterprise-level firewall can take weeks to achieve the best results. The configuration must not be so strict that it prevents authorized users from transmitting and receiving necessary data, yet not so lenient that you unnecessarily risk security breaches.

Further complicating the matter is that you might need to create exceptions to the rules. For example, suppose that your human resources manager is working from a conference center in Salt Lake City while recruiting new employees, and needs to access the Denver server that stores payroll information. In this instance, the Denver network administrator might create an exception to allow transmissions from the human resources manager's workstation's IP address to reach that server. In the networking profession, creating an exception to the filtering rules is called "punching a hole" in the firewall.

IDS (Intrusion Detection System)

7	APPLICATION
6	PRESENTATION
5	SESSION
4	TRANSPORT
3	NETWORK
2	DATA LINK
1	PHYSICAL

An **IDS (intrusion detection system)** is a stand-alone device, an application, or a built-in feature running on a workstation, server, switch, router, or firewall. It monitors network traffic, generating alerts about suspicious activity (see the right side of Figure 10-10). Whereas a router's ACL or a firewall acts like a bouncer at a private club who checks everyone's ID and ensures that only club members enter through the door, an IDS is generally installed to provide security monitoring inside the network, similar to security personnel sitting in a private room monitoring closed-circuit cameras in the club and alerting other security personnel when they see suspicious activity. These days, IDS most commonly exists as an embedded feature in UTM solutions or NGFWs.

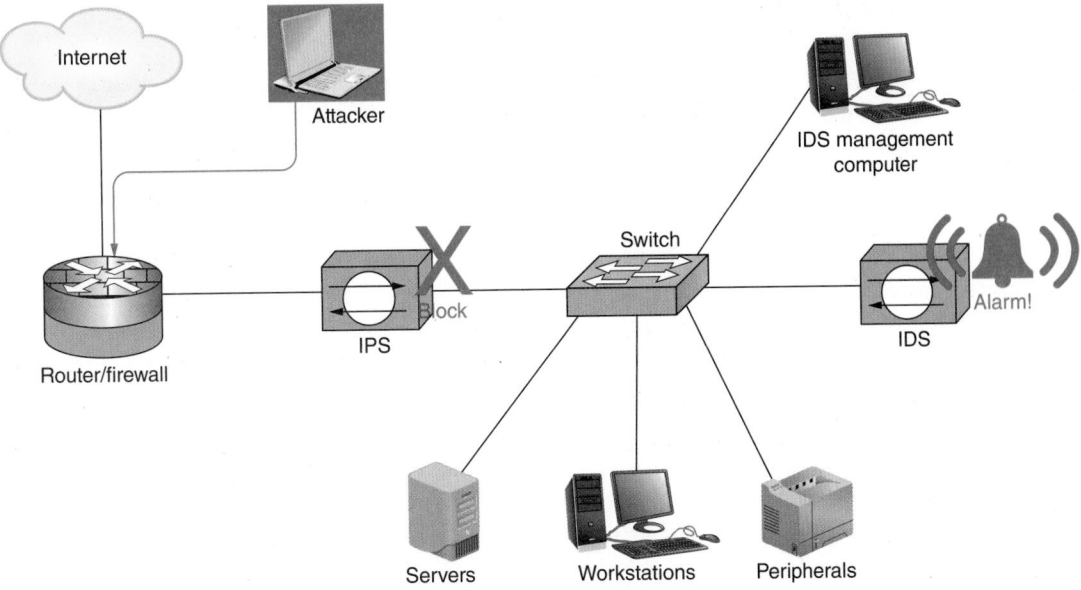

Figure 10-10   An IDS detects traffic patterns, while an IPS can intercept traffic that might threaten a corporate network

An IDS uses two primary methods for detecting threats on the network:

- *statistical anomaly detection*—Compares network traffic samples to a predetermined baseline in order to detect anomalies beyond certain parameters.
- *signature-based detection*—Looks for identifiable patterns, or **signatures**, of code that are known to indicate specific vulnerabilities, exploits, or other undesirable traffic on the organization's network (such as games). To maintain effectiveness, these signatures must be regularly updated in a process called **signature management**. This also includes retiring irrelevant signatures and selecting the signatures most relevant to a specific network's needs in order to most efficiently use memory and processing resources when scanning network traffic.

The most thorough security employs both of the IDS implementations listed as follows in order to detect a wider scope of threats and provide multiple levels of defense:

- An **HIDS (host-based intrusion detection system)** runs on a single computer to detect attacks to that one host. For example, an HIDS might detect an attempt to exploit an insecure application running on a server or repeated attempts to log on to the server. An HIDS solution might also include **FIM (file integrity monitoring)**, which alerts the system of any changes made to files that shouldn't change, such as operating system files. FIM works by generating a baseline checksum of the monitored files, and then recalculating the checksum at regular intervals to determine if anything has changed.

- An **NIDS (network-based intrusion detection system)** protects a network or portion of a network, and is usually situated at the edge of the network or in a network's protective perimeter, known as the DMZ, or demilitarized zone. Here, it can detect many types of suspicious traffic patterns, such as those typical of denial-of-service or smurf attacks.

An NIDS sits off to the side of network traffic and is sent duplicates of packets traversing the network. One technique that an NIDS might use to monitor traffic carried by a switch is port mirroring. In **port mirroring**, also called SPAN (switched port analyzer), one port on a switch is configured to send a copy of all the switch's traffic to the device connected to that port. The device runs a monitoring program, which can now see all traffic the switch receives. This monitoring program can be located on either the local network or at a remote location.

One drawback to using an IDS is the number of false positives it can generate. For instance, it might interpret as a security threat the multiple logon attempts of a legitimate user who's forgotten his password. If the IDS is configured to alert the network manager each time such an event occurs, the network manager might be overwhelmed with such warnings and eventually ignore all the IDS's messages. Therefore, to be useful, IDS software must be thoughtfully customized. In addition, to continue to guard against new threats, IDS software must be updated and rules of detection reevaluated regularly.

Major vendors of networking hardware, such as Cisco, Juniper Networks, and Symantec, sell IDS-equipped devices. However, most IDS solutions these days are software-based and can be installed on a variety of network-connected machines. Examples of popular, open-source IDS software include Suricata (*suricata-ids.org*) and the very popular Snort (*snort.org*).

IPS (Intrusion Prevention System)

Although an IDS can only detect and log suspicious activity, an **IPS (intrusion prevention system)** stands in-line between the attacker and the targeted network or host, and can prevent traffic from reaching that network or host (see the left side of Figure 10-10). If an IDS is similar to security personnel using closed-circuit cameras to monitor a private club, an IPS would be similar to security personnel walking around in the club available to escort unruly patrons to the exit door. IPSes were originally designed as a more comprehensive traffic analysis and protection tool than firewalls. However, firewalls have evolved, and as a result, the differences between a firewall and an IPS have diminished.

7	APPLICATION
6	PRESENTATION
5	SESSION
4	TRANSPORT
3	NETWORK
2	DATA LINK
1	PHYSICAL

Because an IPS stands in-line with network traffic, it can stop that traffic. For example, if an IPS detects a hacker's attempt to flood the network with traffic, it can prevent that traffic from proceeding to the network. Thereafter, the IPS might quarantine that malicious user based on the sending device's IP address. At the same time, the IPS continues to allow valid traffic to pass.

As with IDS, an **NIPS (network-based intrusion prevention system)** can protect entire networks while an **HIPS (host-based intrusion prevention system)** protects a specific host. Using NIPS and HIPS together increases the network's security. For example, an HIPS running on a file server might accept a hacker's attempt to log on if the hacker is posing as a legitimate client. With the proper NIPS, however, such a hacker would likely never get to the server. Like an IDS, an IPS requires careful configuration to avoid an abundance of false alarms.

Both an IDS and IPS can be placed inside a network or on the network perimeter. Notice in Figure 10-11 an NIPS is used to monitor and protect traffic in the DMZ, and a second NIPS is positioned inside the private network on the perimeter of segment A to monitor and protect traffic on this one network segment. In the figure, you can see that HIPS software is also running on a server.

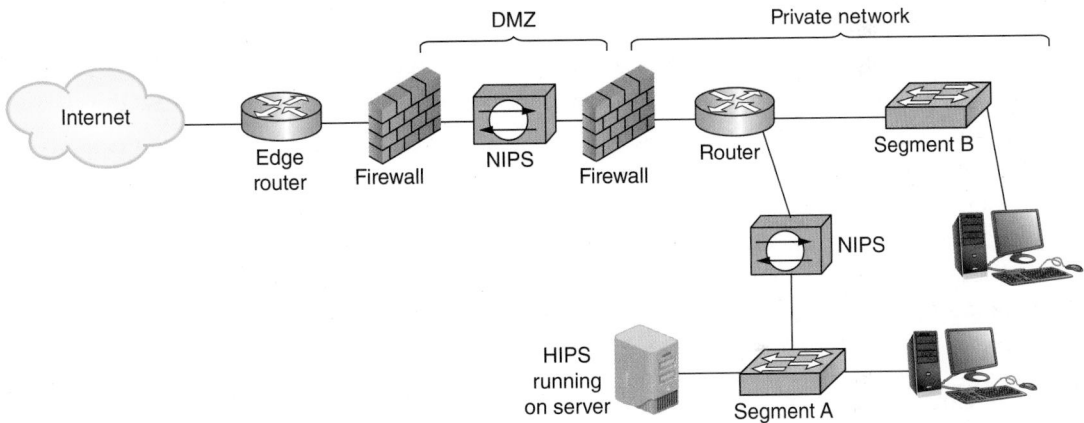

Figure 10-11   Placement of IPS devices and software on a network

Now that you have seen the main devices used on a network to protect its resources, let's look briefly at how the information from those devices is managed.

SIEM (Security Information and Event Management)

IDS, IPS, firewalls, and proxy servers all generate a great deal of data that is stored in logs and must be monitored and analyzed in order to be of particular use in real time. **SIEM (Security Information and Event Management)** systems can be configured to evaluate all of this data, looking for significant events that require attention from the IT staff according to predefined rules. When one of these rules is triggered, an **alert** is generated and logged by the system. If programmed to do so, a **notification** is then sent to IT personnel via email, text, or some other method. The challenge is to find the right balance between sensitivity and workload. For example, a SIEM that isn't sensitive enough will miss critical events that require response. However, a few hundred notifications per day will quickly overwhelm IT staff; they can't possibly respond to so many alerts and will eventually start ignoring them.

The SIEM's effectiveness is partly determined by how much storage space is allocated for the generated data, and by the number of events it processes per second. As for the amount of data storage space, consider all the devices, such as switches, routers, servers, and security systems, that will feed data to the SIEM, and allow for future growth of this traffic as well.

The network administrator can fine-tune a SIEM's rules for the specific needs of a particular network by defining which events should trigger which responses. The SIEM system can also be configured to monitor particular indicators of anticipated problems or issues. These rules should be reevaluated periodically. Also, network technicians should review the raw data on a regular basis to ensure that no glaring indicators are being missed by existing rules. Examples of SIEM software include AlienVault OSSIM (Open Source SIEM), IBM Security QRadar SIEM, SolarWinds Log & Event Manager, and Splunk ES (Enterprise Security).

We've looked at several network security devices. Switches, however, are sprinkled throughout a network and make up the primary method by which devices access the network. How can switches be configured more securely? Let's find out.

Switch Management

 **Certification**

7	APPLICATION
6	PRESENTATION
5	SESSION
4	TRANSPORT
3	NETWORK
2	DATA LINK
1	PHYSICAL

1.3 Explain the concepts and characteristics of routing and switching.

4.2 Explain authentication and access controls.

4.5 Given a scenario, implement network device hardening.

4.6 Explain common mitigation techniques and their purposes.

You've already learned a lot about how switches work, such as when supporting VLANs on a network. However, the responsibility of switch management extends well beyond the tasks associated with connecting devices and configuring VLANs. As networks rely increasingly on VLANs and other switch-based technologies, managed switches and Layer 3 switches play a much more critical role in an enterprise environment. At the same time, switch security becomes a more important—and more complex—factor in protecting a network's resources.

In this section, we'll look first at how paths between switches are managed, and then we'll examine switch security concerns, both at the Physical layer and the more abstract Data Link and Network layers.

Switch Path Management

Suppose you design an enterprise-wide network with several interconnected switches. To make the network more fault tolerant, you install multiple, or redundant, switches at critical junctures. Redundancy allows data the option of traveling through more than one switch toward its destination and makes your network less vulnerable to hardware malfunctions. For example, if one switch suffers a power supply failure, traffic can reroute through a second switch. Your network might look something like the one pictured in Figure 10-12 where several fast and powerful multilayer switches work together at the core of the network, and workgroup switches connect directly to endpoints. (In reality, of course, many more nodes would connect to both types of switches.)

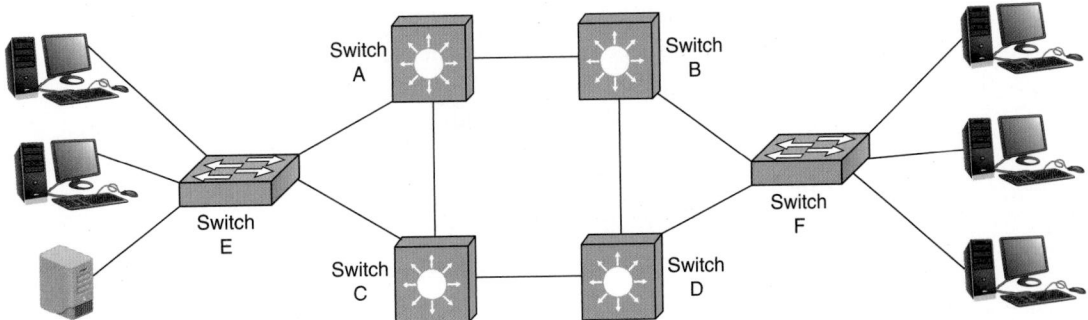

Figure 10-12   Enterprise-wide switched network

A potential problem with the network shown in Figure 10-12 has to do with traffic loops. What if a server attached to switch E issues a broadcast frame, which switch E then reissues to all its ports except the port to which the server is attached? In that case, switch E will issue the broadcast frame to switches A and C, which will then reissue the broadcast frame to switches B and D and to each other, and so on. If not limited in some way, these redundant broadcast transmissions will flood the network, and the high traffic volume will severely impair network performance. To eliminate the possibility of this and other types of traffic loops, **STP (Spanning Tree Protocol)** was developed by Radia Perlman at Digital Equipment Corporation in 1985 and then adopted by the IEEE in 1990.

The first iteration of STP, defined in IEEE standard 802.1D, functions at the Data Link layer. It prevents traffic loops, also called switching loops, by calculating paths that avoid potential loops and by artificially blocking the links that would complete a loop. In addition, STP can adapt to changes in the network. For instance, if a switch is removed, STP will recalculate the best loop-free data paths between the remaining switches.

> **Note** 📎
>
> In the following explanation of STP, you can substitute *switch* wherever the word *bridge* is used. As you have learned, a switch is really just a glorified bridge. STP terminology refers to a Layer 2 device as a *bridge* because STP was designed and created before switches existed.

So how does STP select and enforce switching paths on a network? Consider the following process:

Step 1: STP selects a **root bridge**, or master bridge, which will provide the basis for all subsequent path calculations. Only one root bridge exists on a network. From this root bridge, a series of logical branches, or data paths, emanate like branches on a tree. STP selects the root bridge based on its BID (Bridge ID). The BID is a combination of a 2-byte priority field, which can be set by a network admin, and the bridge's MAC address. To begin with, all bridges on the network share the same priority number, and so the bridge with the lowest MAC address becomes the root bridge by default.

Step 2: STP examines the possible paths between all other bridges and the root bridge, and chooses the most efficient of these paths, called the least cost path, for each of the bridges. To enforce this path, STP stipulates that on any bridge, only one root port, which is the bridge's port that is closest to the root bridge, can forward frames toward the root bridge.

Step 3: STP disables links that are not part of a shortest path. To do this, it enables only the lowest-cost port on each link between two bridges to transmit network traffic. This port is called the designated port. All ports can, however, continue to *receive* STP information.

Figure 10-13 illustrates a switched network with certain paths selected and others blocked by STP. In this drawing, root ports, pointing toward the root bridge, are labeled *RP*. Designated ports, pointing downstream from the root bridge, are labeled *DP*. For example, traffic from the root bridge, switch E, going to switch B would be forwarded through switches C and A. Even though switch B is also connected to switches D and F, STP has limited the logical pathway to only go through switches C and A. Now suppose switch A were to fail. STP would automatically adapt by choosing a different logical pathway for frames destined for switch B.

STP information is transmitted between switches via **BPDUs (Bridge Protocol Data Units)**. To protect the integrity of STP paths and the information transmitted by these BPDUs, some security precautions that must be configured on STP-enabled interfaces include the following:

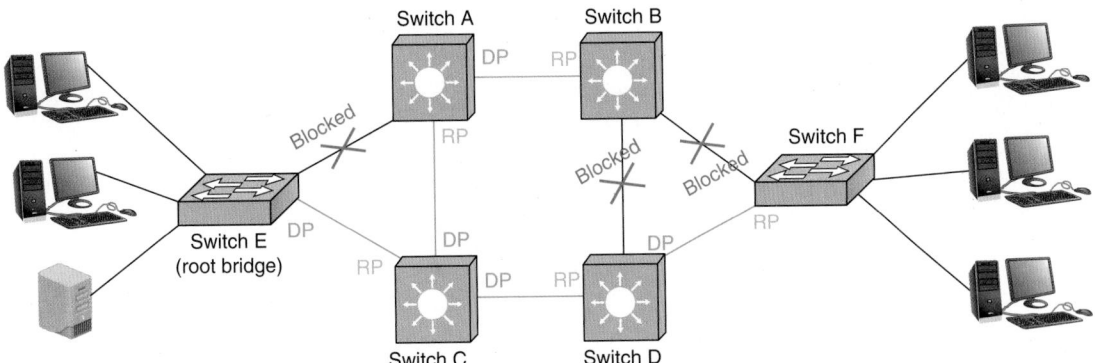

Figure 10-13   *DP* indicates downstream designated ports, and *RP* indicates upstream root ports

- *BPDU guard*—Blocks BPDUs on any port serving network hosts, such as workstations and servers, and thereby ensures these devices aren't considered as possible paths. BPDU guards also enhance security by preventing a rogue switch or computer connected to one of these ports from hijacking the network's STP paths.
- *BPDU filter*—Disables STP on specific ports. For example, you might use a BPDU filter on the demarc, where the ISP's service connects with a business's network, to prevent the ISP's WAN topology from mixing with the corporate network's topology for the purpose of plotting STP paths.
- *root guard*—Prevents switches beyond the configured port from becoming the root bridge. For example, an ISP might configure a root guard on an interface facing a customer's network to ensure that none of the customer's switches becomes the ISP's root bridge.

Network developers have repeatedly modified STP to improve and customize its functioning. The original STP is considered too slow for today's networks. For instance, it could take up to two minutes to detect and account for a link failure. With that kind of lag time, older versions of STP would bog down network transmissions, especially where high-volume, speed-dependent traffic, like telephone or video signals, is involved. Newer versions of STP include the following:

- **RSTP (Rapid Spanning Tree Protocol)**, defined in IEEE's 802.1w standard, and MSTP (Multiple Spanning Tree Protocol), originally defined by the 802.1s standard, can detect and correct for link failures in milliseconds.
- TRILL (Transparent Interconnection of Lots of Links) is a multipath, link-state protocol (using IS-IS) developed by the IETF.
- **SPB (Shortest Path Bridging)** is a descendent of STP and is defined in IEEE's 802.1aq standard. SPB differs from earlier iterations of STP in that it keeps all potential paths active while managing the flow of data across those paths to

prevent loops. By utilizing all network paths, SPB greatly improves network performance.
- Some switch manufacturers, such as Cisco and Extreme Networks, have designed proprietary versions of STP that are optimized to work most efficiently on their equipment.

Protocols designed to replace STP, such as SPB, operate at Layer 3 instead of or in addition to Layer 2, making them more compatible with various types of technologies such as the connection protocols used on storage networks.

When installing switches on your network, you don't need to enable or configure STP (or the more current version that came with your switch). It will come with the switch's operating software and should function smoothly by default and without intervention. However, if you want to designate preferred paths between bridges or choose a special root bridge, for example, STP and its relatives allow you to alter default prioritizations.

Switch Port Security

Unused switch, router, or server ports can be accessed and exploited by hackers if they are not disabled. For example, a router's configuration port could be exploited via Telnet if not adequately secured. Unused physical and virtual ports on switches and other network devices should be disabled until needed. You can do this on Cisco, Huawei, and Arista routers and switches with the shutdown command. To enable them again, use the no shutdown command on Cisco or Arista devices, and use undo shutdown on Huawei devices. On a Juniper device, the corresponding commands are disable and enable, respectively.

Another Cisco command (which is also used on Arista devices) to secure switch access ports is switchport port-security (or just port-security on Huawei switches). This is essentially a MAC filtering function that also protects against MAC flooding, which makes it a type of flood guard. Acceptable MAC addresses are stored in a **MAC address table**, which can be configured manually or dynamically from its default of 1 up to a maximum number of devices as determined by the network administrator. Once the MAC address table is full, a security violation occurs if another device attempts to connect to the port. By default, the switch will shut down the port, or it can be configured to restrict data from the rogue device. Either way, the switch generates an SNMP notification.

On a Juniper switch, the mac-limit command restricts the number of MAC addresses allowed in the MAC address table. Allowed MAC addresses are configured with the allowed-mac command.

Many Huawei, Arista, Juniper, Cisco, and similar devices offer a type of flood guard known as storm control that protects against flooding attacks from broadcast and multicast traffic. Storm control monitors network traffic at one-second intervals to determine if the traffic levels are within acceptable thresholds. Any time traffic exceeds the predefined threshold, all traffic is dropped for the remainder of the time interval.

This feature is managed on all three major vendors' devices using the `storm-control` command (without the hyphen on Huawei devices: `storm control`).

So far in this chapter, we've explored physical security devices and switch hardening. Let's take a step back and look at how access to the network is collectively handled at higher layers of the OSI model.

AAA (Authentication, Authorization, and Accounting)

Q **Certification**

3.5   Identify policies and best practices.

4.2   Explain authentication and access controls.

4.3   Given a scenario, secure a basic wireless network.

4.6   Explain common mitigation techniques and their purposes.

Controlling users' access to a network and its resources consists of three major elements: authentication, authorization, and accounting. Together, this framework is abbreviated as **AAA (authentication, authorization, and accounting)** and is pronounced *triple-A*. The three components required to manage **access control** to a network and its resources are described next:

- *authentication*—Authentication, in this case, user authentication, is the process of verifying a user's credentials (typically a username and password) to grant the user access to secured resources on a system or network. In other words, authentication asks the question, "Who are you?"
- *authorization*—Once a user has access to the network, the **authorization** process determines what the user can and cannot do with network resources. In other words, authorization asks the question, "What are you allowed to do?" Authorization restrictions affect Layer 2 segmentation, Layer 3 filtering, and Layer 7 entitlements. For example, what VLAN are you assigned to? What servers or databases can you access? What commands can you run on a device?
- *accounting*—The **accounting** system logs users' access and activities on the network. In other words, accounting asks, "What did you do?" The records that are kept in these logs are later audited, either internally or by an outside entity, to ensure compliance with existing organizational rules or external laws and requirements.

We now look at each of the three elements of access control in more detail, beginning with authentication.

Authentication

A user can be authenticated to the local device or to the network. With local authentication, a user can, for example, sign in to Windows using a local user account. With network authentication, she can sign in to the network using her network user account that is stored in Active Directory on a Windows domain.

Local Authentication

Local authentication processes are performed on the local device. Usernames and passwords are stored locally, which has both advantages and disadvantages:

- *low security*—Most end user devices are less secure than network servers. A hacker can attempt a brute force attack or other workarounds to access a single device. If those same credentials are used on other devices, then all these devices are compromised. Also, local authentication does not allow for remotely locking down a user account.
- *convenience varies*—For only a handful of devices, managing local accounts can be done a lot more easily than setting up a Windows domain, directory services, and all the supporting configurations. However, once you surpass about a dozen devices, the convenience of local authentication declines considerably.
- *reliable backup access*—In the case of a network failure or server failure, the only workable option is local authentication. For this reason, networking devices and servers should be configured with a local privileged account that is only used when authentication services on the network are unavailable, and of course this account should have very secure credentials.

Applying Concepts: Apply Local Security Policies

With local authentication, you can set security policies to require all local users to have passwords and to rename default user accounts. The **Group Policy** (gpedit.msc) utility is a Windows console that controls what users can do and how the system can be used. Group Policy works by making entries in the Registry; applying scripts to Windows start-up, shutdown, and logon processes; and adjusting security settings. Policies can be applied to the computer or to the user.

Follow these steps to set a few important security policies on a Windows 10 Professional, Enterprise, or Education computer. (Note that Windows 10 Home does not include Group Policy.)

1. Sign in to Windows using an administrator account. Press **Win**+**R** on your keyboard, and then enter **gpedit.msc** to open the Local Group Policy Editor window.
2. To change a policy, first use the left pane to select the appropriate policy group, and then use the right pane to view and edit a policy. Consider making the following important security policy adjustments:
   a. *Change default usernames*—A hacker is less likely to hack into the built-in Administrator account or Guest account if you change the names of these default accounts. To change the name of the Administrator account, select the Security Options group

in the left pane as follows: **Computer Configuration, Windows Settings, Security Settings, Local Policies, Security Options**. See the left side of Figure 10-14. In the right pane, double-click **Accounts: Rename administrator account**. In the Properties dialog box for this policy (see the right side of Figure 10-14), change the name and click **OK**. To change the name of the Guest account, use the policy **Accounts: Rename guest account.**

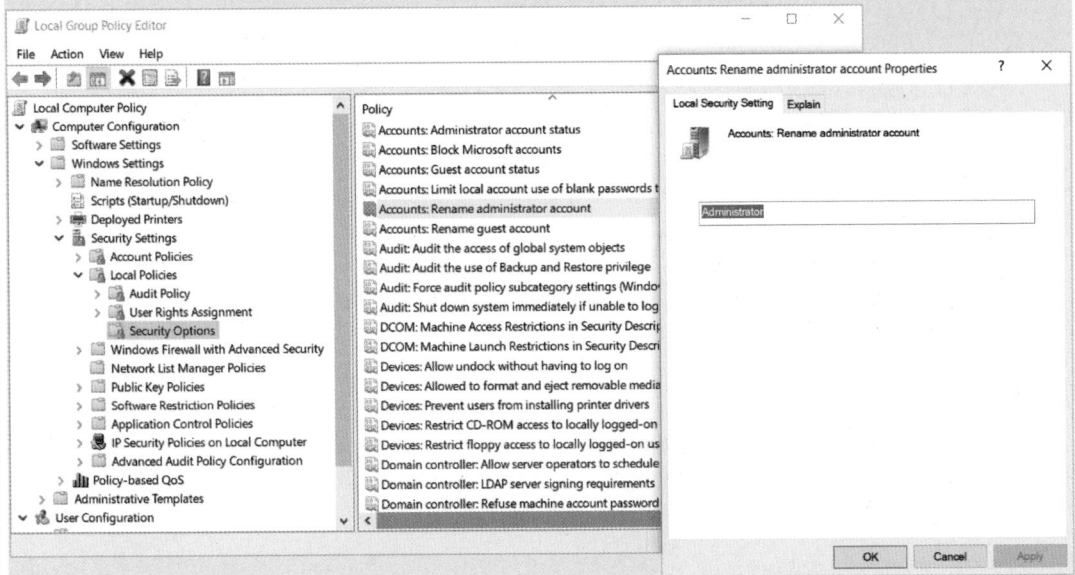

Figure 10-14   Change default user names in the Local Group Policy Editor

b. *Require user passwords*—The **password policy** is probably the most important policy used to secure a system. To require that all user accounts have passwords, select the Password Policy group in the left pane as follows: **Computer Configuration, Windows Settings, Security Settings, Account Policies, Password Policy**. See the left side of Figure 10-15. Use the **Minimum password length** policy and set the minimum length to eight characters or more (see the right side of Figure 10-15).

c. *Allow only a single logon*—By default, Windows allows fast user switching, which means multiple users can log on to Windows at the same time. By disabling this feature, you require a user to save his work and log off the computer in order for another user to sign into it. This frees up computer resources and protects user data. To disable access to this feature and allow only a single logon, select the Logon group in the left pane as follows: **Computer Configuration, Administrative Templates, System, Logon**. Then use the **Hide entry points for Fast User Switching** policy. Enable this policy so that the *Switch user* option is dimmed and not available on the Shut down submenu of the Start menu.

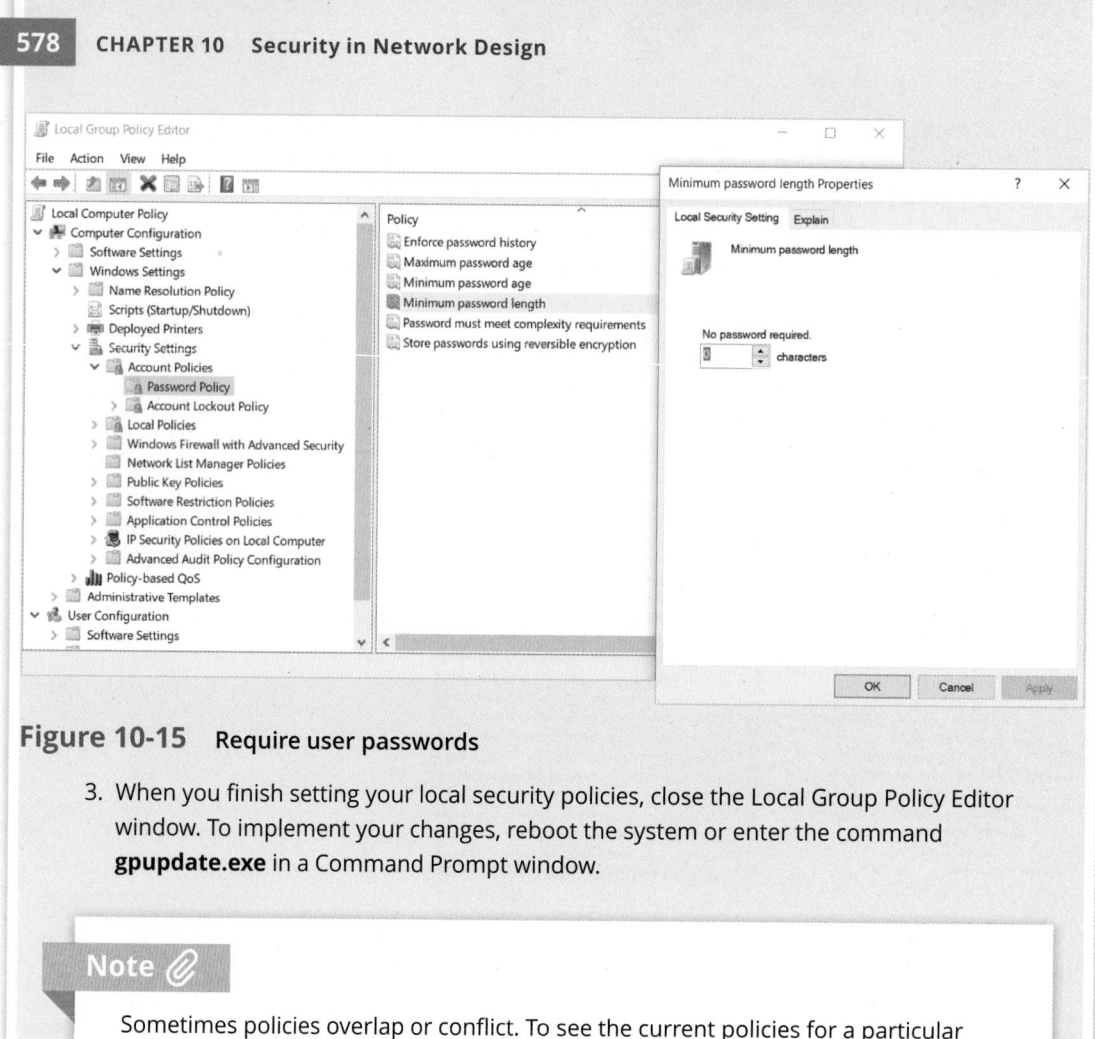

Figure 10-15 Require user passwords

3. When you finish setting your local security policies, close the Local Group Policy Editor window. To implement your changes, reboot the system or enter the command **gpupdate.exe** in a Command Prompt window.

> **Note** 📎
>
> Sometimes policies overlap or conflict. To see the current policies for a particular computer or user, you can use the `gpresult` command in a Command Prompt window. To learn about the appropriate parameters for this command, search the *technet.microsoft.com* website.

With local authentication, every computer (workstation or server) on the network is responsible for securing its own resources. If several users need access to a file server, for example, each user must have a local user account on the file server. This local account and password must match the user account and password that the account holder used to sign in to Windows at his or her workstation. As a network grows, keeping all these local accounts straight can become an administrative nightmare. The time will come when you will want to move on to a Windows domain.

In Windows, you can switch from local authentication to network authentication on the domain using the System Properties dialog box. To make the switch, in the System Properties dialog box (see Figure 10-16), click **Network ID** and then select **This computer is part of a business network; I use it to connect to other computers at work**. Click **Next** and select **My company uses a network with a domain**. When you click **Next**, you are given the opportunity to enter your user name, password, name of the Windows domain, and the name of your computer on the Windows domain. All this information is stored in Active Directory by Windows Server. When you complete the process, the next time you sign in to Windows, you will use the network user name to sign in to the Windows domain. Active Directory then controls the access you have to resources on the network.

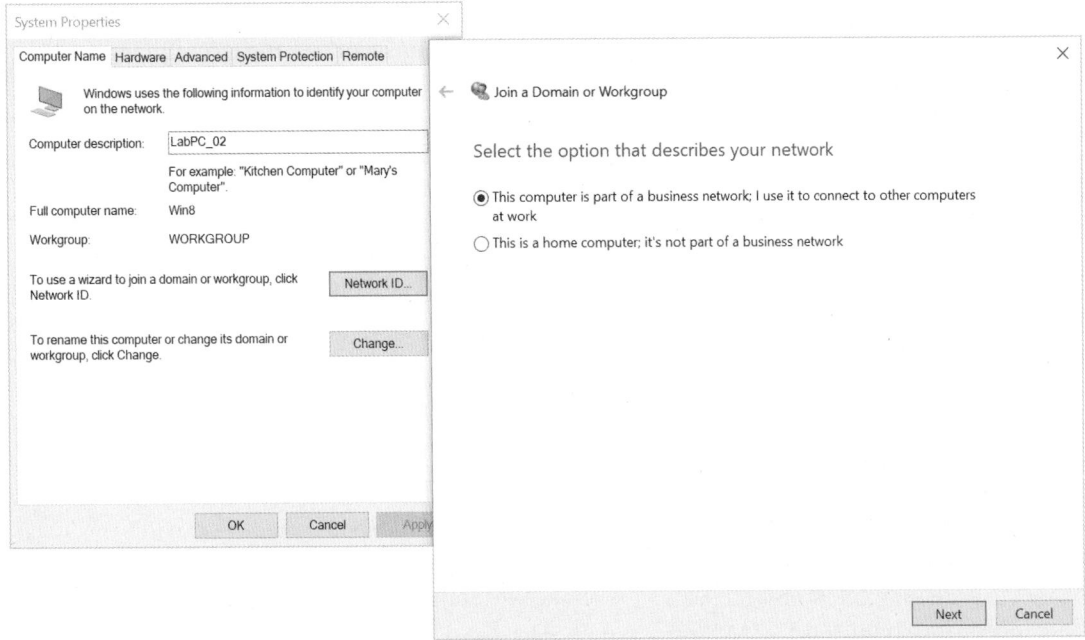

Figure 10-16   Switch from local authentication to authentication on a Windows domain

Network Authentication and Logon Restrictions

Regardless of whether you run your network on a Microsoft, Macintosh, or Linux NOS, you can harden your network by requiring secure passwords to authenticate to the network. The following is a list of additional authentication restrictions that strengthen network security:

- *time of day*—Some user accounts may be active only during specific hours— for example, between 8:00 a.m. and 5:00 p.m. Specifying valid hours for an account can increase security by preventing any account from being used by unauthorized personnel after hours.

- *total time logged on*—Some user accounts may be restricted to a specific number of hours per day of logged-on time. Restricting total hours in this way can increase security in the case of temporary user accounts. For example, suppose that your organization offers an Adobe Photoshop training class to a group of high school students one afternoon, and the Photoshop program and training files reside on your staff server. You might create accounts that could log on for only four hours on that day.
- *source address*—You can specify that user accounts may log on only from certain workstations or certain areas of the network (that is, domains or segments). This restriction can prevent unauthorized use of accounts from workstations outside the network.
- *unsuccessful logon attempts*—Hackers might repeatedly attempt to log on under a valid username for which they do not know the password. As the network administrator, you can set a limit on how many consecutive, unsuccessful logon attempts from a single user ID the server will accept before blocking that ID from even attempting to log on.
- *geographic location*—**Geofencing** determines a client's geographic location to enforce a virtual security perimeter. In other words, the client must be located within a certain area in order to gain access to the network. With geofencing, GPS (global positioning system) or RFID (radio frequency identification) data is sent to the authentication server to report the location of the device attempting to authenticate to the network.

Caution ⚠

A special kind of DoS attack called an authentication attack floods a AAA server with authentication requests that must all be processed and responded to. This can force the server to shut down. By default, a floodguard feature might be configured on the AAA server to reclaim compromised resources. Floodguard settings can be changed with the `floodguard` command.

Authorization

Remember—even the best authentication techniques, including encryption, computer room door locks, security policies, and password rules, make no difference if you authorize the wrong network users access to critical data and programs.

User access to network resources falls into one of these two categories: 1) the privilege or right to execute, install, and uninstall software, and 2) permission to read, modify, create, or delete data files and folders.

The most popular authorization method is **RBAC (role-based access control)**. With role-based access control, a network administrator receives from a user's supervisor a detailed description of the roles or jobs the user performs for the organization. The administrator is responsible for assigning the privileges and permissions necessary for the user to perform only these roles. In addition, all users may require access to certain public resources on the network, for example, a portion of the company website available to all employees. In most cases, these public rights are very limited.

With role-based access control, a network administrator creates user groups associated with these roles and assigns privileges and permissions to each user group. Each user is assigned to a user group that matches a requirement for his job, and in most cases, a user can belong to more than one user group. In some situations, however, a checks and balances safety net is enforced by implementing **role separation**; this means each user can only be a member of a single group in order to perform any tasks at all. If a user is listed in more than one group, all privileges and permissions are locked down for that user.

For Windows, Figure 10-17 shows the Computer Management window where you can see several built-in user groups and the option to create your own, new groups.

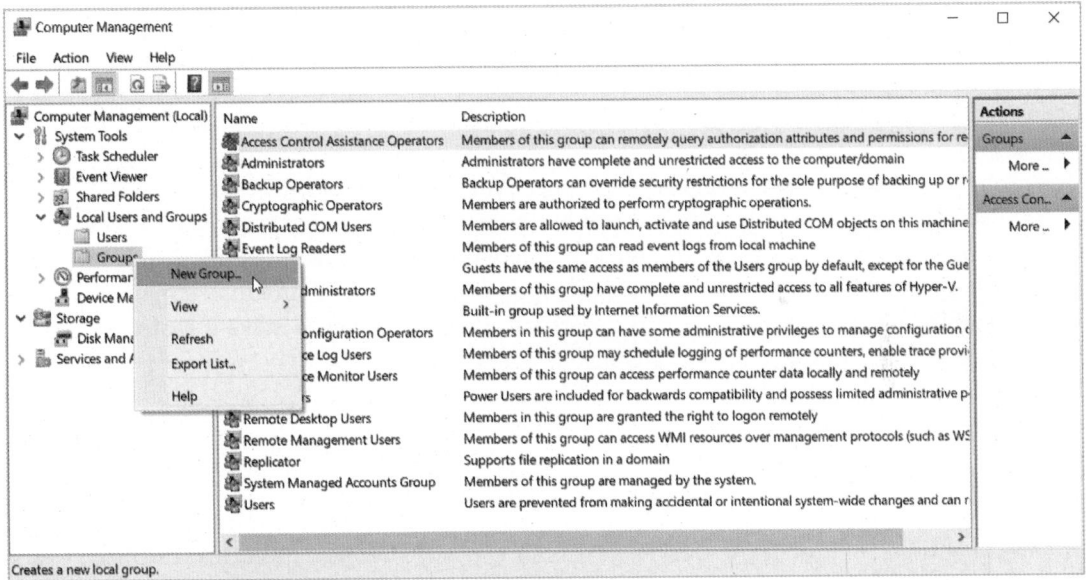

Figure 10-17   Windows allows you to create new groups and add users to these groups

For example, the IT Department at a large university will most likely need more than one person who can create new user IDs and passwords for students and faculty. Naturally, the staff in charge of creating these credentials need the correct privileges to perform this task. You could assign the appropriate rights to each staff member individually, but a more efficient approach is to create a user ID and password management *group*, and put all the IT personnel in that account management group. Later, when someone leaves the IT Department or joins the department, you can easily remove users from or add users to the group.

Windows provides the option to create local groups on individual workstations. Active Directory gives additional options for creating **domain local groups**, which are centrally managed for the entire network.

> **Note** 📎
>
> Two other popular methods of access control in addition to RBAC are DAC and MAC. The least secure of these options is **DAC (discretionary access control)**. This is where users decide for themselves who has access to that user's resources. The most restrictive is **MAC (mandatory access control)**. In this case, resources are organized into hierarchical classifications, such as "confidential" or "top secret." Resources are also grouped into categories, perhaps by department. Users, then, are also classified and categorized. If a user's classification and category matches those of a resource, then the user is given access.

Accounting

Throughout this text, you have been learning about the many logs that systems generate so that an administrator can troubleshoot and audit these systems. With a Linux or Macintosh NOS, most logs are generated as text files. These text files can get quite long and a network administrator is responsible for making sure they don't hog server storage space. In addition, you can install a log file viewer to make it easier to monitor log files for interesting or suspicious events.

> **Note** 📎
>
> Check out Linux commands `tail`, `head`, `grep`, `sed`, and `awk`, which are useful for searching very long log files.

In Windows, you can use Event Viewer to view Windows logs. For example, in Figure 10-18, you can see an Audit Failure event related to an account that failed to log on. As you can see in the figure, Audit events appear in the Windows Logs, Security group of Event Viewer. Also, before these logon events are logged, you must use Group Policy to turn on the feature.

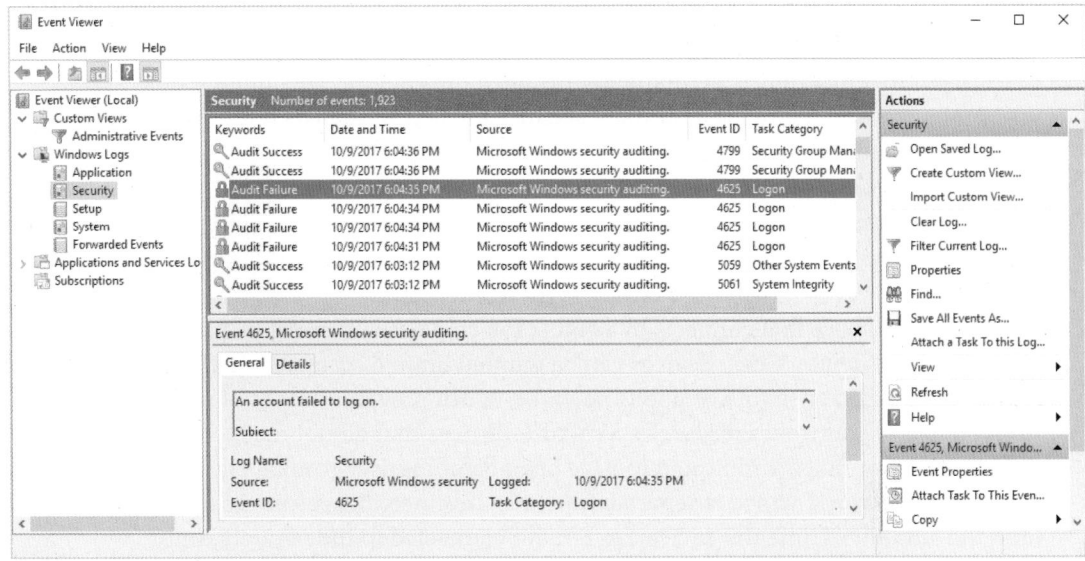

Figure 10-18   Windows Event Viewer displays a security audit event

NAC (Network Access Control) Solutions

As networks continue to grow and get more complex with more organizations implementing BYOD (bring your own device) environments, administrators have struggled with the need to balance network access with network security. These challenges have, in turn, sparked a variety of solutions. To help manage the complexity, a **NAC (network access control)** system takes authentication, authorization, and accounting to a new level. A NAC system employs a set of rules, called **network policies**, which determine the level and type of access granted to a device when it joins a network. A popular NAC solution by Cisco includes Cisco firewalls, routers, switches, and ASA (Adaptive Security Appliance) devices that all collectively perform NAC functions. In addition, Microsoft offers NAP (Network Access Protection) software that functions as a NAC solution in Windows Server.

NAC systems authenticate and authorize devices by verifying that the device complies with predefined security benchmarks, such as whether the device has certain system settings, or whether it has specific applications installed. On some networks, software called an **agent** must be installed on the device before the device can be authenticated. The agent monitors the device's status regarding the security benchmarks to determine the device's compliance. Two types of agents are commonly used:

- A **nonpersistent agent**, or dissolvable agent, remains on the device long enough to verify compliance and complete authentication, and then uninstalls.

Devices might be required to periodically reinstall the agent to complete the authentication process again.

- A **persistent agent** is permanently installed on a device. This more robust program might provide additional security measures, such as remote wipe, virus scans, and mass messaging.

Not all networks require agents. Another option is Active Directory, which allows for **agentless authentication**, in which the user is authenticated to a domain. Active Directory then scans the device to determine compliance with NAC requirements.

Not every device that connects to a NAC-protected network must be preconfigured as an approved device. Guest devices can be granted limited access to network resources in a guest network or public network, which provides a layer of protection from the private network's resources. Similarly, devices that do not meet compliance requirements, or that are indicated to have been compromised, can be placed in a **quarantine network**, which is separate from sensitive network resources and might limit the amount of time the device can remain connected to the network, until remediation steps can be completed.

Access Control Technologies

 **Certification**

2.3 Explain the purposes and use cases for advanced networking devices.

4.2 Explain authentication and access controls.

Of the main three AAA processes, authentication tends to be the most complicated. Let's look more closely at the building blocks that make authentication happen. Authentication protocols are the rules that computers follow to accomplish authentication. Several types of authentication services and protocols exist, and some also incorporate authorization and auditing components. These technologies vary according to which encryption schemes they rely on and the steps they take to verify credentials.

Directory Services

In order for clients to authenticate to network resources (as opposed to individual devices), some sort of directory server on the network must maintain a database of account information, such as usernames, passwords, and any other authentication credentials. Often this is accomplished in AD (Active Directory) or something more Linux-focused like OpenLDAP (*openldap.org*) or 389 Directory Server (*directory.fedoraproject.org*).

All these options are built to be LDAP-compliant. LDAP (Lightweight Directory Access Protocol) is a standard protocol for accessing an existing directory. The mechanisms of LDAP dictate some basic requirements for any directory it accesses, and so there is a lot of commonality in how directory servers are configured, regardless of the software used. LDAP can query the database, which draws information out of the database. It can also be used to add new information or edit existing data.

By default, AD is configured to use the Kerberos protocol, which you'll learn about shortly. However, AD can use LDAP instead or use both side by side. When supporting AD together, Kerberos provides authentication with the database, and then LDAP provides authorization by determining what the user can do while they're on the network. Let's begin our exploration of authentication protocols with some legacy protocols that you might see on the Network+ exam. Then we'll look at Kerberos and some other modern authentication protocols.

Legacy Networking: Outdated Authentication Protocols

As you read about these legacy protocols, notice how the authentication process gradually became more sophisticated and, therefore, somewhat more secure. Four older authentication protocols include the following:

- **PAP (Password Authentication Protocol)**—A client uses PAP to send an authentication request that includes its credentials. The server compares the credentials to those in its user database. If the credentials match, the server responds to the client with an acknowledgment of authentication and grants the client access to secured resources. If the credentials do not match, the server denies the request to authenticate. Figure 10-19 illustrates PAP's two-step authentication process. Thus, PAP is a simple authentication protocol, but is not secure. Also, it sends the client's credentials in cleartext, without encryption.

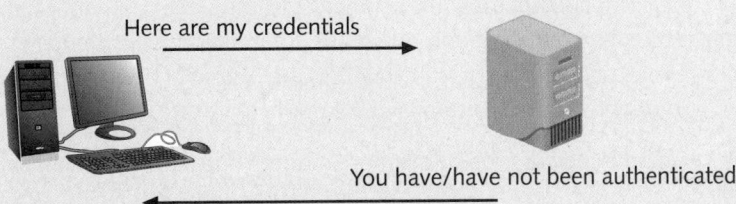

Here are my credentials

You have/have not been authenticated

Figure 10-19   Two-step authentication used in PAP

- **CHAP (Challenge Handshake Authentication Protocol)**—Unlike PAP, CHAP encrypts usernames and passwords for transmission. It also requires three steps to complete the authentication process. Together, these steps use a three-way handshake. Figure 10-20 illustrates the three-way handshake, described next:

1. *challenge*—The server sends the client a randomly generated string of characters.
2. *response*—The client adds its password to the challenge and encrypts the new string of characters. It sends this new string of characters in a response to the server. Meanwhile, the server also concatenates the user's password with the challenge and encrypts the new character string, using the same encryption scheme the client used.
3. *accept/reject*—The server compares the encrypted string of characters it received from the client with the encrypted string of characters it has generated. If the two match, it authenticates the client. But if the two differ, it rejects the client's request for authentication.

Figure 10-20   **Three-way handshake used in CHAP**

- *MS-CHAP (Microsoft Challenge Handshake Authentication Protocol)*—Similar to CHAP, MS-CHAP was developed by Microsoft and used with Windows-based computers. One potential flaw in both CHAP and MS-CHAP authentication is that someone eavesdropping on the network could capture the string of characters that is encrypted with the password, decrypt that string, and obtain the client's password.
- *MS-CHAPv2 (Microsoft Challenge Handshake Authentication Protocol, version 2)*—To address the problems with MS-CHAP, MS-CHAPv2 uses stronger encryption, does not use the same encryption strings for transmission and reception, and requires mutual authentication. In **mutual authentication**, each computer verifies the credentials of the other—for example, the client authenticates the server just as the server authenticates the client. This is more secure than requiring only one of the communicating computers to authenticate the other. You'll still encounter MS-CHAPv2 in the course of business, especially with older VPN systems and in WPA2-Enterprise environments.

Now let's return to our discussion of the more modern and secure authentication options.

Kerberos

Recall that Kerberos is the authentication protocol configured by default on Active Directory. **Kerberos** is a cross-platform authentication protocol that uses key encryption to verify the identity of clients and to securely exchange information after a client logs on to a system. It is an example of a private key encryption service and is considered especially secure. Let's see how this works.

Kerberos does not automatically trust clients. Instead, it requires clients to prove their identities through a third party. This is similar to what happens when you apply for a passport. The government does not simply believe that you are, for example, "Corey Steen," but instead requires you to present proof, such as your birth certificate. In addition to checking the validity of a client, Kerberos communications are encrypted and unlikely to be deciphered by any device on the network other than the client.

To understand specifically how a client uses Kerberos, you need to understand some of the terms used when discussing this protocol:

- *principal*—A Kerberos client or user.
- *KDC (Key Distribution Center)*—The server that issues keys to clients during initial client authentication.
- *ticket*—A temporary set of credentials that a client uses to prove to other servers that its identity has been validated.

Note

A ticket is not the same as a key. Keys belong to the user or server and initially validate the user's and server's identity to each other during the authentication process to create a session. A ticket, however, is used to gain access to another network service, such as email, an internal payroll site, a printer, or a file server. A key is similar to using your credit card to pay for entrance into a carnival or county fair. Your entrance fee includes a time-limited wristband which you can use to obtain a separate ticket for each game, ride, or beverage that you consume during the event. As long as you're at the event for that evening, you can get more tickets by showing your wristband, and each ticket is exchanged for another game, ride, or beverage. However, when you come back the next night, you have to start over by using your credit card to purchase a new wristband.

A Kerberos server runs two services:

- *AS (authentication service)*—Initially validates a client. In our carnival analogy, this would be the box office at the entrance gate.
- *TGS (ticket-granting service)*—Issues tickets to an authenticated client for access to services on the network. This would be the ticket booth inside the fairgrounds, where you show your wristband to get more tickets.

Now that you have learned the basic terms used by Kerberos, you can follow the process it requires for client-server communication. Bear in mind that the purpose of Kerberos is to connect a valid user with a network *service* the user wants to access, such as email, printing, file storage, databases, or web applications. To accomplish this, both the user and the service must register their own keys with the AS ahead of time.

Figure 10-21 shows how TGS works. Suppose the principal (the client) is Jamal. The following steps describe the Kerberos authentication process:

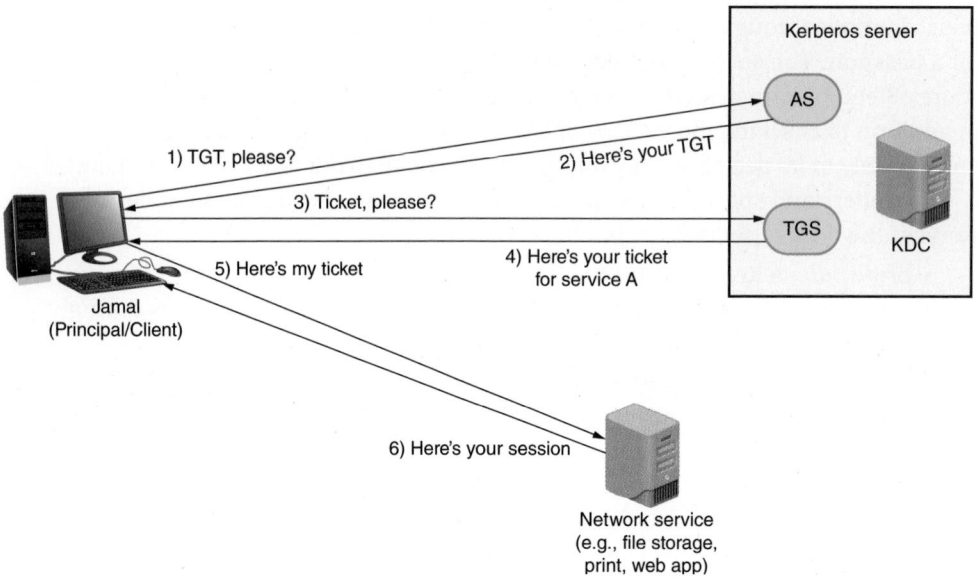

Figure 10-21 The Ticket-Granting Service offers a client a ticket for each network service it needs to access

Step 1: When Jamal first logs on to the network, his computer sends an authentication request to the AS (see Figure 10-22). This request contains Jamal's username, but not his password. However, the time stamp on the request is encrypted with Jamal's password.

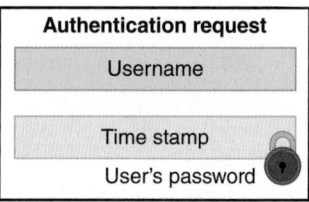

Figure 10-22 Step 1: Authentication request

Step 2: The AS on the KDC first confirms that Jamal is in its database and uses his password (retrieved from its database) to decrypt the timestamp. If all goes well, the AS generates a session key, which is used for encryption and decryption for future communication, and encrypts this key with the user's password (see Figure 10-23). The AS also generates a TGT (Ticket-Granting Ticket), which will expire within a specified amount of time (by default, this limit is 10 hours). The TGT is like the wristband in our carnival analogy. To prevent counterfeiting, the TGT is encrypted with a secret KDC key so that only the KDC can read it and confirm its legitimacy.

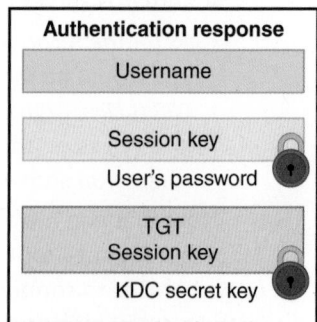

Figure 10-23 Step 2: Authentication response

Step 3: After receiving the TGT, the principal decrypts the session key using the user's password. If the correct password is used and decryption is successful, the principal can then submit a ticket request to the TGS for access to a network service (see Figure 10-24). The request includes the user's name and a time stamp that are both encrypted using the session key. It also includes the fully encrypted TGT, which the principal never decrypted.

Step 4: The TGS validates the TGT and the rest of the request message's contents, and then creates a ticket that allows Jamal to use the network service. This ticket (see Figure 10-25) includes the service's name, a time stamp, and the service's session key, all encrypted using the session key issued to the principal earlier. It also includes information the service will need to confirm the request is valid, including the principal's session key. This part is encrypted using a secret key that the service knows, but the principal does not.

Step 5: Jamal's computer decrypts the information it needs using the session key. It then creates a service request (see Figure 10-26) that contains the encrypted information from the TGS, plus a time stamp encrypted with the session key.

Step 6: The service decrypts the ticket using its own secret key, finds the principal's session key included in the ticket, and then decrypts the remainder of the message to confirm its validity. Finally, the service verifies that the principal requesting its use is truly Jamal as the KDC indicated, and allows access.

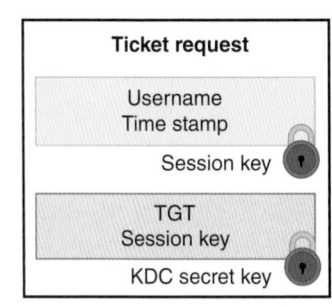

Figure 10-24   Step 3: Ticket request

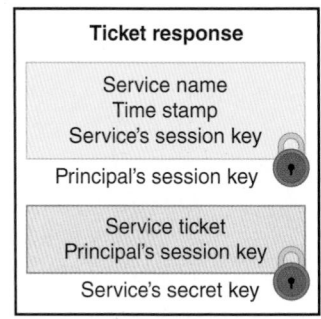

Figure 10-25   Step 4: Ticket response

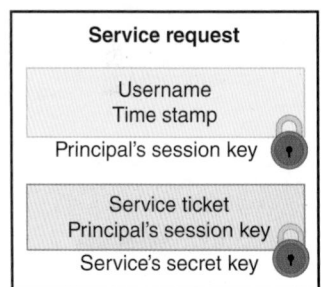

Figure 10-26   Step 5: Service request

Note

Kerberos, which was designed at MIT (Massachusetts Institute of Technology), is named after the three-headed dog in Greek mythology who guarded the gates of Hades. The three heads represent the principal, the network server providing a service, and the KDC. MIT still provides free copies of the Kerberos code. In addition, many software vendors have developed their own versions of Kerberos.

SSO (Single Sign-On)

Kerberos is an example of **SSO (single sign-on)**, a form of authentication in which a client signs on one time to access multiple systems or resources. The primary advantage of single sign-on is convenience. Users don't have to remember several passwords, and network administrators can limit the time they devote to password management. The biggest disadvantage to single sign-on authentication is that once the obstacle of authentication is cleared, the user has access to numerous resources. A hacker needs fewer credentials to gain access to potentially many files or connections.

For greater security, some systems—especially those using SSO—require clients to supply two or more pieces of information to verify their identity. In a **2FA (two-factor authentication)** scenario, a user must provide something and know something. For example, he might have to provide a fingerprint scan as well as know and enter his password.

An authentication process that requires two or more pieces of information is known as **MFA (multifactor authentication)**. There are five categories of authentication factors covered by the CompTIA Network+ exam. These factors, along with some examples of each, are:

- *something you know*—A password, PIN, or biographical data
- *something you have*—An ATM card, smart card, or key
- *something you are*—Your fingerprint, facial pattern, or iris pattern
- *somewhere you are*—Your location in a specific building or secured closet
- *something you do*—The specific way you type, speak, or walk

Multifactor authentication requires at least one authentication method from at least two different categories. For example, logging into a network might require a password, a fingerprint scan, plus a piece of information generated from a security token. A **security token** is a device or application that stores or generates information, such as a series of numbers or letters, known only to its authorized user.

On the left side of Figure 10-27, a smartphone app requests a website-generated QR code to set up a user's account, such as Facebook, for 2FA. Once established, a random code is generated every 30 seconds that must be entered in addition to the user's password in order to access the account. An example of a hardware-based token is the popular SecurID key chain fob from RSA Security, as shown on the right side of Figure 10-27. The SecurID device generates a password that changes every 60 seconds. When logging on, a user provides the number that currently appears on the SecurID fob. Before he is allowed access to secured resources, his network checks with

(a)   (b)

Figure 10-27   a) A smartphone 2FA app;
b) A SecurID fob
Sources: Twilio, Inc. and Courtesy of RSA, the Security Division of EMC

RSA Security's service to verify that the number is correct. Google Authenticator, Google's number generator service, provides free, software-based security tokens.

RADIUS (Remote Authentication Dial-In User Service)

In environments that support many simultaneous connections and several user IDs and passwords, it might make sense to use a centralized service to manage access to resources across all three functions of AAA. By far, the most popular AAA service is **RADIUS (Remote Authentication Dial-In User Service)**. RADIUS is an open-source standard developed by Livingston Enterprises in 1991 and later standardized by the IETF. It runs in the Application layer and can use either UDP or, as of 2012, TCP in the Transport layer. RADIUS treats authentication and authorization as a single process, meaning that the same type of packet is used for both functions, while accounting is a separate process.

RADIUS can operate as a software application on a remote access server or on a computer dedicated to this type of authentication, called a RADIUS server. Because RADIUS servers are highly scalable, many ISPs use a RADIUS server as a central authentication point for wireless, mobile, and remote users. RADIUS services are often combined with other network services on a single machine. For example, an organization might combine a DHCP server with a RADIUS server to manage allocation of addresses and privileges assigned to each address on the network.

Figure 10-28 illustrates a RADIUS server managing network access for local and remote users. RADIUS can run on almost all modern OSes. While RADIUS includes some very sophisticated accounting features, it also only encrypts the password in transmissions, and so is not as secure as TACACS+, discussed next.

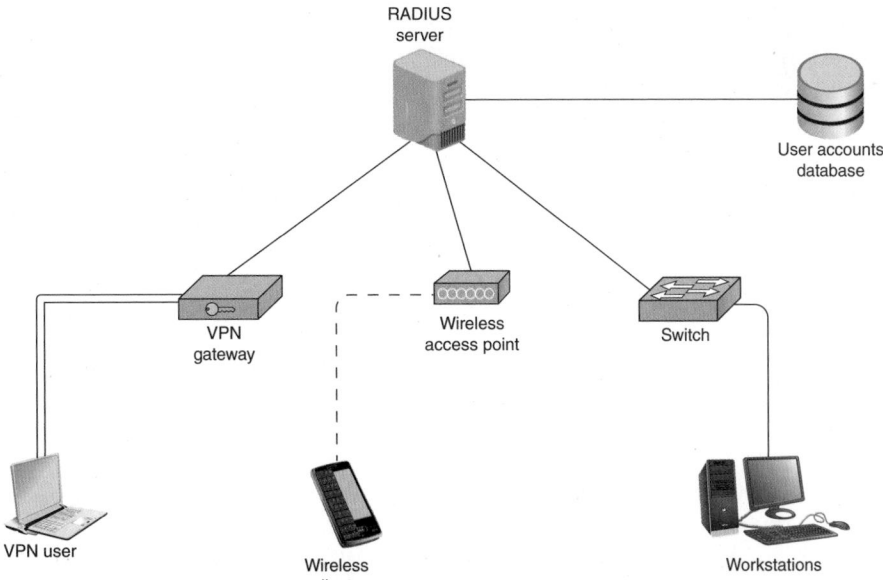

Figure 10-28   A RADIUS server on a network servicing various types of users

> **Note**
>
> A newer protocol called Diameter was first developed in 1998 to replace RADIUS. In geometry, the diameter of a circle is twice its radius; the implication is that the Diameter protocol is twice as good as the RADIUS protocol. While many vendors offer Diameter options on their systems, for the most part, RADIUS is still more widely used.

TACACS+ (Terminal Access Controller Access Control System Plus)

Another AAA protocol, **TACACS+ (Terminal Access Controller Access Control System Plus)**, offers network administrators the option of separating the authentication, authorization, and auditing capabilities. For instance, TACACS+ might provide access and accounting functions, but use another technique, such as Kerberos (discussed earlier in this chapter), to authenticate users. TACACS+ differs from RADIUS in that it:

- Relies on TCP, not UDP, at the Transport layer.
- Was developed by Cisco Systems, Inc., for proprietary use.
- Is typically installed on a router or switch, rather than on a server.
- Is most often used for device administration access control for technicians, although it can be used for network resource access control for users.
- Encrypts all information transmitted for AAA (RADIUS only encrypts the password).

You've now learned a lot about AAA on a network and controlling users' access to network resources. However, special considerations apply when authenticating users over wireless connections. These connections are less controlled and more vulnerable to MitM attacks, spoofing, and other exploits. Let's look at the technologies that have been developed to address these concerns.

Wireless Network Security

 **Certification**

4.2 Explain authentication and access controls.

4.3 Given a scenario, secure a basic wireless network.

In the wireless networking chapter, we began a discussion about wireless network security. You learned about some of the inherent weaknesses of WEP (Wired Equivalent Privacy), and security improvements made through WPA (Wi-Fi Protected Access) and its successor, WPA2. Now that you've learned more about both encryption and authentication, you're ready for a more detailed discussion of wireless network security.

To begin, recall that a significant disadvantage of WEP was that it used a shared encryption key for all clients and the key might never change. In fact, WEP offered two forms of authentication, neither of which is secure:

- *OSA (Open System Authentication)*—No key is used at all. The wireless access client, knowing only the access point's SSID, requests authentication. The AP generates a single-use code for that session only, and the computer accepts the code. However, no encrypted data can be sent over this temporary connection, and any device can be authenticated. In fact, no real authentication occurs.
- *SKA (Shared Key Authentication)*—All wireless access clients use the same key, which can then be used for encrypted transmissions. However, the key can be cracked, compromising the security of all clients on the network.

Due to this inherent insecurity, IEEE devised a new wireless security standard, called 802.11i. This standard included the subset standard WPA, which was later replaced by WPA2. The following sections explore the progressive improvements made to the 802.11i standard.

WPA (Wi-Fi Protected Access)

802.11i incorporates an encryption key generation and management scheme known as **TKIP (Temporal Key Integrity Protocol)**, pronounced *tee-kip*, to improve security for legacy WEP-based devices. TKIP accomplished three significant improvements:

- *message integrity*—Uses a message integrity code, called Michael, that ensures incoming packets are, in fact, coming from their declared source. This is also called packet authentication.
- *key distribution*—Assigns every transmission its own key.
- *encryption*—Includes encryption originally provided by **RC4 (Rivest Cipher 4)**, a now insecure encryption cipher that is still widely used.

In reality, TKIP was a quick fix, designed more as an integrity check for WEP transmissions than as a sophisticated encryption protocol. WPA's TKIP used the same encryption mechanism as WEP but with improved algorithms to wrap the older WEP transmissions in a more securely encrypted transmission. However, you'll still find modern wireless network devices offering TKIP to provide compatibility with older wireless devices.

WPA2 (Wi-Fi Protected Access, Version 2)

The data confidentiality methods used in WPA were replaced by stronger technologies for the updated version, WPA2. **CCMP**, which is short for **Counter Mode with CBC (Cipher Block Chaining) MAC (Message Authentication Code) Protocol**, improves wireless security for newer devices that can use WPA2. Acronyms within acronyms are only the beginning of what makes this protocol so interesting. Whereas TKIP was meant to be backward-compatible as much as possible, CCMP is more future-focused.

CCMP helps ensure data confidentiality with both encryption and packet authentication by providing:

- *message integrity*—CCMP uses CBC-MAC, which ensures incoming packets are, in fact, coming from their declared source, and does so using the block cipher algorithm AES, described next.
- *encryption*—CCMP also uses **AES (Advanced Encryption Standard)**, which provides faster and more secure encryption than TKIP for wireless transmissions. AES relies on a more sophisticated family of ciphers along with multiple stages of data transformation.

> **Note**
>
> Two similar types of cipher algorithms are stream ciphers and block ciphers. The essential difference is that stream ciphers encrypt 1 byte (or possibly 1 bit) at a time, while block ciphers encrypt much larger chunks, or blocks, in each calculation.

Personal and Enterprise

On many wireless routers and access points, you might have noticed options for WPA-Personal and WPA-Enterprise, or WPA2-Personal and WPA2-Enterprise. The Personal versions of WPA and WPA2 are sometimes referred to as WPA-PSK or WPA2-PSK, where **PSK** is short for **Pre-Shared Key**. This is the common configuration on home wireless networks in which you need to enter a passphrase for your device to authenticate to the network. The passphrase and the SSID characters are then used to calculate a unique encryption key for each device.

The Enterprise versions of WPA and WPA2 implement additional security measures. In most cases, a RADIUS server is used in cooperation with an authentication mechanism called EAP. **EAP (Extensible Authentication Protocol)** differs from the authentication protocols discussed previously in that it only provides the framework for authenticating clients and servers. It does not perform encryption or authentication on its own. Instead, it works with other encryption and authentication schemes to verify the credentials of users and devices. For example, EAP can function alongside RADIUS, where EAP organizes communications with the network client device and RADIUS handles the actual authentication on the server. In this case, EAP messages are encapsulated inside RADIUS messages between the network device, such as a switch or access point, and the RADIUS server. Look at Figure 10-29 to see how EAP and RADIUS handle different portions of the interaction.

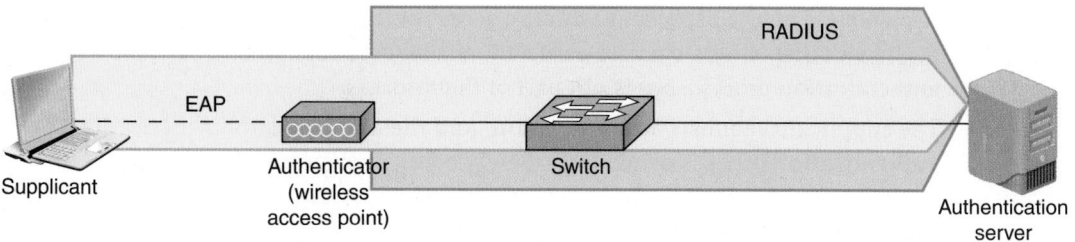

Figure 10-29   EAP messages are encapsulated in RADIUS messages

The three main EAP entities, as shown in Figure 10-29, are:

- *supplicant*—The device requesting authentication, such as a smartphone or laptop
- *authenticator*—The network device that initiates the authentication process, such as a wireless access point
- *authentication server*—The server that performs the authentication

The conversation between these entities looks something like the diagram shown in Figure 10-30. The steps are described next:

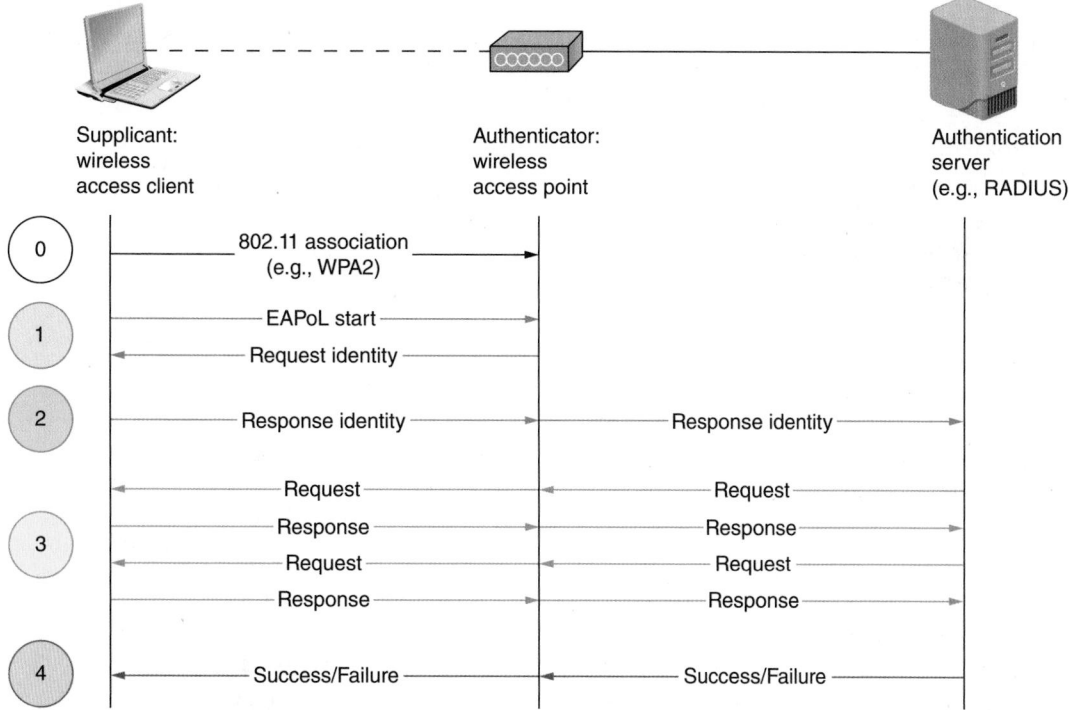

Figure 10-30   If a RADIUS server is used here, EAP communications between the authenticator and the RADIUS server would be encapsulated in RADIUS messages

Step 0: The wireless device associates with the access point, usually with WPA2. We begin with Step 0 here because association is an essential precursor to the authentication process, but is not part of that process.

Step 1: The supplicant requests authentication, and the authenticator initiates the authentication process by asking a newly connected supplicant to verify itself.

Step 2: After the supplicant responds, the authenticator forwards that information to the authentication server, such as a RADIUS server.

Step 3: The server usually sends more than one request in response. In its first request, it asks the supplicant's identity and indicates what type of authentication to use. In subsequent requests, the server asks the supplicant for authentication information to prove the supplicant's identity. The supplicant responds to each of the server's requests in the required format.

Step 4: If the responses match what the server expects, the server authenticates the supplicant. Otherwise, authentication fails.

One of EAP's advantages is its flexibility. It is supported by nearly all modern operating systems and can be used with many different authentication methods. For example, although the typical network authentication involves a user ID and password, EAP also works with biometric methods, such as retina or hand-scanning.

EAP is also adaptable to new technology. EAP was originally designed to work only on point-to-point connections (usually on a WAN) and relied on PPP. However, it was adapted to work on both wired and wireless LANs in the **802.1X** standard, dubbed **EAPoL (EAP over LAN)**. In this case, EAP is carried by Ethernet messages instead of PPP messages. To accomplish this, 802.1X allows only EAPoL traffic over any switch or AP port connected to a wired or wireless client until that client has authenticated with the authentication server. This is called PNAC (port-based network access control), or sometimes port-based authentication. Today, 802.1X is primarily used on wireless LANs.

Several versions and adaptations of EAP exist. The most common versions, including PEAP, EAP-FAST, and EAP-TLS, are the ones you need to know for the Network+ exam.

EAP-TLS

Similar to how HTTPS uses SSL/TLS encryption to secure HTTP transmissions, **EAP-TLS** uses TLS encryption to protect communications. EAP-TLS also uses PKI (public-key infrastructure) certificates to exchange public keys and authenticate both the supplicant and the server through mutual authentication. While these certificates can be a challenge to set up, the resulting authentication strength is often worth the trade-off in convenience. Figure 10-31 shows the addition of a CA (Certificate Authority) to the network to help manage the certificates needed by EAP-TLS.

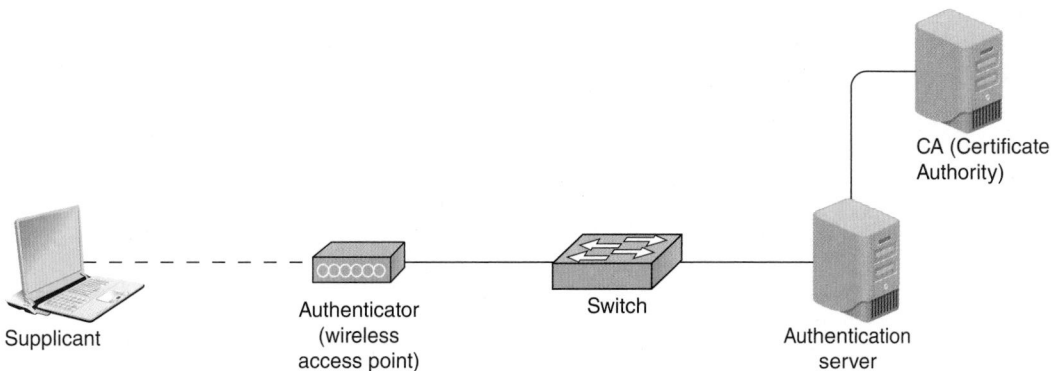

Figure 10-31   EAP-TLS requires a Certificate Authority

PEAP (Protected EAP)

While EAP-TLS is certificate-based, PEAP and EAP-FAST are tunnel-based. **PEAP (Protected EAP)** creates an encrypted TLS tunnel between the supplicant and the server before proceeding with the usual EAP process. As shown in Figure 10-32, PEAP is called the outer method. Then another form of EAP is used for the inner method, which is the process that occurs inside the protected tunnel. The most common inner method is EAP-MSCHAPv2, which runs an MS-CHAPv2 session inside the tunnel, perhaps to a RADIUS server and beyond to Active Directory.

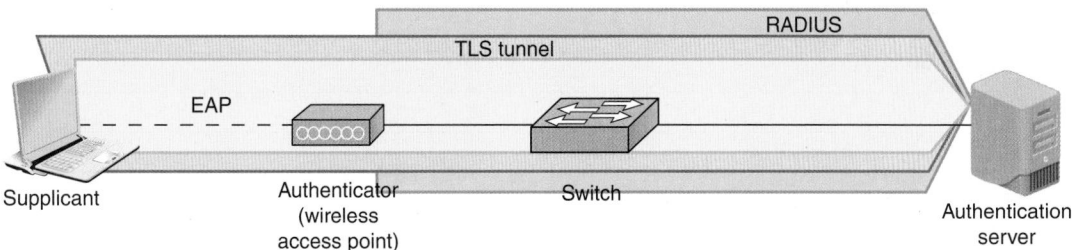

Figure 10-32   PEAP creates an encrypted TLS tunnel

EAP-FAST (EAP-Flexible Authentication via Secure Tunneling)

EAP-FAST (EAP-Flexible Authentication via Secure Tunneling) is also a form of tunneled EAP. It was developed by Cisco and works similarly to PEAP, except faster. The most important difference with EAP-FAST is that it uses PACs (Protected Access Credentials), which are somewhat similar to cookies that websites store on a user's computer to track their activities. A PAC is stored on the supplicant device for speedier establishment of the TLS tunnel in future sessions.

Applying Concepts: Protocol Synopsis

Each of the protocols covered in this and previous chapters plays an important role in securing transmissions between devices and locations. It's important to have the big picture in mind regarding how these protocols interact with each other and the roles they play in various parts of the system when troubleshooting connectivity and security issues.

In this project, you synthesize the major characteristics of each protocol into a single reference table. You can create the following Table 10-1 in a word-processing program or a spreadsheet program. Then refer to Chapters 7 – 10 to fill in the missing pieces. Protocol types include encryption, connection, authentication, tunneling, trunking, hashing, and AAA. Some of the listed protocols are included in more than one of these categories.

Table 10-1 Notable encryption and authentication methods

Security method	Type	Primary use(s)	Notes
IPsec	Encryption	TCP/IP transmissions	
SSL		TCP/IP transmissions	
TLS			Secure transmission of HTTP sessions
PPP	Connection	Remote access	
SSH	Connection, Authentication, Encryption		
RDP			
VNC			
L2TP	Tunneling	VPN	
GRE		VPN	
OpenVPN			
IKEv2			
VTP			
SHA		Data integrity	
LDAP	Authentication	Directory access	
Kerberos		Client validation	Verify the identity of clients and securely exchange information after a client logs on to a system
RADIUS			Central authentication point for network users, including wireless, mobile, and remote users

Security method	Type	Primary use(s)	Notes
Table 10-1 Notable encryption and authentication methods *(continued)*			
TACACS+	AAA (Authentication, Authorization, and Accounting)	Client validation and monitoring	
EAP		Client verification	
802.1X			
AES		Wi-Fi and other uses	

Chapter Summary

Network Security Devices

- A proxy server, or proxy, acts as an intermediary between the external and internal networks, screening all incoming and outgoing traffic. Although proxy servers only provide low-grade security relative to other security devices, they can help prevent an attack on internal network resources such as web servers and web clients.

- Thanks to a router's ACL (access control list), or access list, routers can decline to forward certain packets depending on their content. An ACL acts like a filter to instruct the router to permit or deny traffic.

- A firewall is a specialized device or software that selectively filters or blocks traffic between networks. A firewall might be placed internally, residing between two interconnected private networks. More commonly, the firewall is placed external to the private network, monitoring the connection between a private network and a public network (such as the Internet).

- An IDS (intrusion detection system) is a stand-alone device, an application, or a built-in feature running on a workstation, server, switch, router, or firewall, which is used to monitor network traffic, generating alerts when suspicious activity happens.

- Although an IDS can only detect and log suspicious activity, an IPS (intrusion prevention system) stands in-line between the attacker and the network or host, and can prevent traffic from reaching the protected network or host.

- IDS, IPS, firewalls, and proxy servers all generate a great deal of data that is stored in logs and must be monitored and analyzed in order to be of particular use in real time. SIEM (Security Information and Event Management) systems can be configured to evaluate all of this data, looking for significant events that require attention from the IT staff according to predefined rules.

Switch Management

- STP (Spanning Tree Protocol) prevents traffic loops, also called switching loops, by calculating paths that avoid potential loops and by artificially blocking the links that would complete a loop. In addition, STP can adapt to changes in the network.

- Unused physical and virtual ports on switches and other network devices should be disabled until needed. You can do this on Cisco, Huawei, and Arista routers and switches with the `shutdown` command. On a Juniper device, the corresponding command is `disable`.

AAA (Authentication, Authorization, and Accounting)

- Controlling users' access to a network consists of three major elements: authentication, authorization, and accounting. Together, this framework is abbreviated as AAA (authentication, authorization, and accounting) and is pronounced *triple-A*.

- Local authentication processes are performed on the local device. Usernames and passwords are stored locally, which has both advantages and disadvantages.

- With geofencing, GPS (global positioning system) or RFID (radio frequency identification) data is sent to the authentication server to report the location of the device attempting to authenticate to the network.

- User access to network resources falls into one of these two categories: 1) the privilege or right to execute, install, and uninstall software, and 2) permission to read, modify, create, or delete data files and folders.

- Systems generate many logs that an administrator can use for troubleshooting and auditing.

- A NAC system employs a set of rules, called network policies, which determine the level and type of access granted to a device when it joins a network.

Access Control Technologies

- In order for clients to authenticate to network resources (as opposed to individual devices), some sort of directory server on the network must maintain a database of account information, such as usernames, passwords, and any other authentication credentials. All these options are built to be LDAP-compliant.

- Kerberos is a cross-platform authentication protocol that uses key encryption to verify the identity of clients and to securely exchange information after a client logs on to a system. Kerberos is the authentication protocol configured by default on Active Directory.

- Kerberos is an example of SSO (single sign-on), a form of authentication in which a client signs on one time to access multiple systems or resources. The primary advantage of single sign-on is convenience. The biggest disadvantage to single sign-on authentication is that once the obstacle of authentication is cleared, the user has access to numerous resources.

- By far, the most popular AAA service is RADIUS (Remote Authentication Dial-In User Service). RADIUS is an open-source standard that treats authentication and authorization as a single process, meaning that the same type of packet is used for both functions, while accounting is a separate process.

- TACACS+ (Terminal Access Controller Access Control System Plus), offers network administrators the option of separating the access, authentication, and auditing capabilities. For instance, TACACS+ might provide access and accounting functions, but use another technique, such as Kerberos, to authenticate users.

Wireless Network Security

- WEP offered two forms of authentication, neither of which is secure: OSA (Open System Authentication) and SKA (Shared Key Authentication).
- TKIP was a quick fix, designed more as an integrity check for WEP transmissions than as a sophisticated encryption protocol. WPA's TKIP used the same encryption mechanism as WEP but with improved algorithms to wrap the older WEP transmissions in a more securely encrypted transmission.
- CCMP, which is short for Counter Mode with CBC (Cipher Block Chaining) MAC (Message Authentication Code) Protocol, improves wireless security for newer devices that can use WPA2. Whereas TKIP was meant to be backward-compatible as much as possible, CCMP is more future-focused. CCMP helps ensure data confidentiality with both encryption and packet authentication.

- The Personal versions of WPA and WPA2 are sometimes referred to as WPA-PSK or WPA2-PSK, where PSK is short for Pre-Shared Key. This is the common configuration on home wireless networks in which you need to enter a passphrase for your device to authenticate to the network.
- The Enterprise versions of WPA and WPA2 implement additional security measures. In most cases, a RADIUS server is used in cooperation with an authentication mechanism called EAP. EAP (Extensible Authentication Protocol) only provides the framework for authenticating clients and servers; it does not perform encryption or authentication on its own. Instead, it works with other encryption and authentication schemes to verify the credentials of users and devices.

Key Terms

For definitions of key terms, see the Glossary near the end of the book.

2FA (two-factor authentication)	AES (Advanced Encryption Standard)	BPDU filter
802.1X	agent	BPDU guard
AAA (authentication, authorization, and accounting)	agentless authentication	CCMP (Counter Mode with CBC [Cipher Block Chaining] MAC [Message Authentication Code] Protocol)
access control	alert	
accounting	authentication server	
ACL (access control list)	authenticator	CHAP (Challenge Handshake Authentication Protocol)
	authorization	
	BPDU (Bridge Protocol Data Unit)	content-filtering firewall

DAC (discretionary access control)
domain local group
EAP (Extensible Authentication Protocol)
EAP-FAST (EAP-Flexible Authentication via Secure Tunneling)
EAP-TLS
EAPoL (EAP over LAN)
FIM (file integrity monitoring)
geofencing
Group Policy
HIDS (host-based intrusion detection system)
HIPS (host-based intrusion prevention system)
host-based firewall
IDS (intrusion detection system)
implicit deny
IPS (intrusion prevention system)
iptables
KDC (Key Distribution Center)
Kerberos
Layer 7 firewall
MAC address table
MAC (mandatory access control)
MFA (multifactor authentication)

MS-CHAP (Microsoft Challenge Handshake Authentication Protocol)
MS-CHAPv2 (Microsoft Challenge Handshake Authentication Protocol, version 2)
mutual authentication
NAC (network access control)
network-based firewall
network policy
NGFW (Next Generation Firewall)
NIDS (network-based intrusion detection system)
NIPS (network-based intrusion prevention system)
nonpersistent agent
notification
OSA (Open System Authentication)
PAP (Password Authentication Protocol)
password policy
PEAP (Protected EAP)
persistent agent
port mirroring
principal
proxy server
PSK (Pre-Shared Key)
quarantine network

RADIUS (Remote Authentication Dial-In User Service)
RBAC (role-based access control)
RC4 (Rivest Cipher 4)
role separation
root bridge
root guard
RSTP (Rapid Spanning Tree Protocol)
security token
SIEM (Security Information and Event Management)
signature
signature management
SKA (Shared Key Authentication)
SPB (Shortest Path Bridging)
SSO (single sign-on)
stateful firewall
stateless firewall
STP (Spanning Tree Protocol)
supplicant
TACACS+ (Terminal Access Controller Access Control System Plus)
ticket
TKIP (Temporal Key Integrity Protocol)
UTM (Unified Threat Management)

Review Questions

1. At what layer of the OSI model do proxy servers operate?
   a. Layer 3
   b. Layer 2
   c. Layer 7
   d. Layer 4

2. Which of the following ACL commands would permit web-browsing traffic from any IP address to any IP address?
   a. `access-list acl_2 deny tcp any any`
   b. `access-list acl_2 permit http any any`

   c. `access-list acl_2 deny tcp host`
     `2.2.2.2 host 3.3.3.3 eq www`

   d. `access-list acl_2 permit icmp`
     `any any`

3. What kind of firewall blocks traffic based on application data contained within the packets?

   a. Host-based firewall

   b. Content-filtering firewall

   c. Packet-filtering firewall

   d. Stateless firewall

4. Which of the following features is common to both an NGFW and traditional firewalls?

   a. Application Control

   b. IDS and/or IPS

   c. User awareness

   d. User authentication

5. Which NGFW feature allows a network admin to restrict traffic generated by a specific game?

   a. Content filter

   b. User awareness

   c. Context awareness

   d. Application awareness

6. What software might be installed on a device in order to authenticate it to the network?

   a. Operating system

   b. Security policy

   c. NAC (network access control)

   d. Agent

7. Which of the following is *not* one of the three AAA services provided by RADIUS and TACACS+?

   a. Authentication

   b. Authorization

   c. Access control

   d. Accounting

8. What feature of Windows Server allows for agentless authentication?

   a. AD (Active Directory)

   b. ACL (access control list)

   c. IDS (intrusion detection system)

   d. Network-based firewall

9. Which command on an Arista switch would require an SNMP notification when too many devices try to connect to a port?

   a. `mac-limit`

   b. `switchport port-security`

   c. `storm-control`

   d. `shutdown`

10. Active Directory and 389 Directory Server are both compatible with which directory access protocol?

   a. LDAP

   b. RADIUS

   c. Kerberos

   d. AES

11. What are the two primary features that give proxy servers an advantage over NAT?

12. What kinds of issues might indicate a misconfigured ACL?

13. Any traffic that is not explicitly permitted in the ACL is _____, which is called the _____.

14. What's the essential difference between an IPS and an IDS?

15. What causes most firewall failures?

16. Why is a BPDU filter needed at the demarc?

17. Why do network administrators create domain groups to manage user security privileges?

18. Only one _____ exists on a network using STP.

19. What kind of ticket is held by Kerberos's TGS?

20. EAPoL is primarily used with what kind of transmission?

Hands-On Projects

Project 10-1: Configure RADIUS in Packet Tracer

In Chapter 6, Capstone Project 6-1, you downloaded and installed Packet Tracer. You've continued to build on your Packet Tracer network in Chapters 7, 8, and 9. In this project, you'll configure RADIUS on a new Packet Tracer network. Complete the following steps:

> **Note** 🔗
>
> If you've not been completing the Capstone Projects, prepare for this project by completing Capstone Project 6-1 first.

1. Open Packet Tracer. From the **Network Devices, Wireless Devices** menu, insert a **WRT300N** wireless router.
2. On the wireless router's Config tab, set its LAN-facing IP address to **192.168.5.1/24**.
3. From the **End Devices** menu, insert a generic laptop.
4. On the laptop's Physical tab, replace the Ethernet network module with a wireless module:
   a. Click the laptop's power button to turn off the laptop.
   b. Drag the PT-LAPTOP-NM-1CFE card from the laptop to the MODULES pane. Zoom in if necessary. The card is labeled "FAST ETH0."
   c. Drag the WPC300N module from the MODULES pane to the laptop.
   d. Turn the laptop back on.
   e. A wireless connection is automatically created between the wireless router and the laptop. If not, troubleshoot the problem.
5. Now let's set up some security parameters on the wireless router:
   a. On the wireless router's Config tab on the Wireless page, select **WPA2** authentication.
   b. Set the RADIUS server's IP address to **192.168.5.2**.
   c. Set the shared secret to **networkplus**.
   d. Make sure the encryption type is **AES**.
   e. What has happened to your network devices? Why do you think this is?
6. To solve this problem, you need to create a RADIUS server:
   a. From the **End Devices** menu, insert a generic server.
   b. On the server's Config tab on the FastEthernet0 page, set its IP address to **192.168.5.2/24**.
   c. On the server's Services tab, on the AAA page, turn on the AAA service.
7. In the Network Configuration section, add a new client with the following information:
   a. Client Name: **WRouter0**
   b. Client IP: **192.168.5.1**
   c. Secret: **networkplus**

    d. ServerType: **Radius**

    e. Click **Add**.

8. In the User Setup section, add a new user with the following information:

    a. Username: **User1**

    b. Password: **cengage**

    c. Click **Add**.

9. Using a Copper Straight-Through cable, connect the server's FastEthernet0 port to the wireless router's Ethernet 1 port. Has the wireless connection been reestablished? Why do you think this is?

10. On the laptop's Config tab, on the Wireless0 page, change the following settings:

    a. Authentication: **WPA2**

    b. User ID: **User1**

    c. Password: **cengage**

    d. Close the laptop's configuration window, and the wireless connection should reestablish within a minute or two.

    e. You didn't configure the laptop's user information on the wireless router. How did the router know to accept the laptop as a wireless client?

11. Save your project for use in Project 10-2.

12. Make some notes on your Wikidot website about your activities in Packet Tracer for this project.

Project 10-2: Secure a Basic Wireless Network in Packet Tracer

This project picks up where Project 10-1 left off. In this project, you explore more of the wireless security options available on a wireless router. Using the Packet Tracer network you created in Project 10-1, complete the following steps:

1. On the wireless router's GUI tab, what is the current DHCP pool? What is the client lease time?

2. On the Wireless > Basic Wireless Settings page, change the default SSID to **HappyVintage**.

3. On the Wireless > Wireless Security page, WPA2 Enterprise is already selected. What other security mode option(s) do you have? Which of these security modes is the most secure?

4. AES encryption is selected. What other encryption option(s) do you have? Which of these encryption options is most secure?

5. Close the wireless router's configuration window. What changed on your network? Why do you think this is?

6. On the laptop's Config tab, on the Wireless0 page, change the SSID to **HappyVintage**. What happens on your network?

7. Save your project for future reference.

8. Make some notes on your Wikidot website about your activities in Packet Tracer for this project.

Project 10-3: Configure ACLs in Packet Tracer

In this project, you will create a new network in Packet Tracer, configure an ACL on the router, and then test the connections between devices. Complete the following steps:

1. Create a Packet Tracer network with one 1941 router, two 2960 switches, and four PCs, and create all the needed connections with Copper Straight-Through cables, as shown in Figure 10-33. Connect the switches to the router using GigabitEthernet connections.

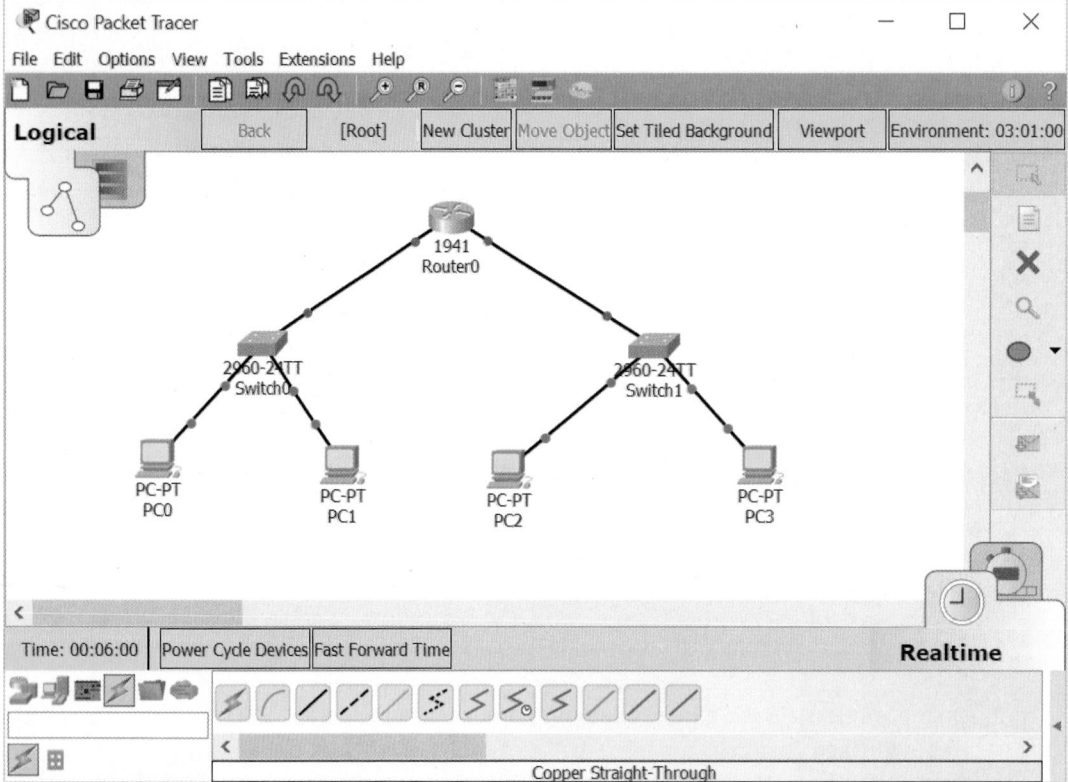

Figure 10-33   Add these devices to your network

Source: Cisco Systems, Inc.

2. The links between PCs and switches should come up automatically. On the router's Config tab, configure each GigabitEthernet interface as follows:
   a. Turn the port on.
   b. Assign a Class C IP address with a /24 subnet mask. Make sure these ports are on different subnets.
3. On each PC, configure an IP address, subnet mask, and default gateway within the appropriate subnet for the router interface it's connected to. For example, if you used 192.168.2.1/24 for Gi0/0 on the router, you could use 192.168.2.10/24 with a default gateway of 192.168.2.1 for one of the PCs on that subnet. As you go, place a note on

the screen for each configured interface so it will be easier for you to keep track of IP address assignments later in this project.

4. Make sure each of the PCs can successfully ping each of the other PCs.
5. On the router's CLI tab, if your configuration access has timed out, press **Enter**, and then enter the commands from Table 10-2. If you're still in interface configuration mode on the CLI tab, enter **exit** once, then begin with the access-list command in Table 10-2.

Table 10-2   Create an ACL on a router

Command	Purpose
`enable`	Enters privileged EXEC mode
`configure terminal`	Enters global configuration mode
`access-list 1 deny host` [*PC0's IP address*]	Denies traffic from PC0
`interface gigabitethernet0/0`	Enters interface configuration mode for GigabitEthernet0/0
`ip access-group 1 in`	Applies access-list 1 to incoming traffic on this interface
`exit`	Returns to global configuration mode
`exit` and press **Enter**	Returns to privileged EXEC mode

6. So far, you've blocked traffic coming to the router's GigabitEthernet0/0 interface from PC0. Let's test your work:
   a. From PC0, ping PC1. Does it work? Why do you think this is?
   b. From PC0, ping PC2. Does it work? Why do you think this is?
   c. From PC2, ping PC0. Does it work? Why do you think this is?
   d. From PC2, ping PC1. Does it work? Why do you think this is?
7. Let's edit the ACL to permit traffic from PC1. On the router's CLI tab, enter the commands from Table 10-3.

Table 10-3   View and edit an ACL on a router

Command	Purpose
`show access-lists`	Shows existing entries in access list 1
`configure terminal`	Enters global configuration mode
`access-list 1 permit host` [*PC1's IP address*]	Permits traffic from PC1
`exit`	Returns to global configuration mode
`show access-lists`	Shows existing entries in access list 1
`exit` and press **Enter**	Returns to privileged EXEC mode
`copy run start` and press **Enter**	Saves the current settings

8. You've now added a new entry to your ACL. Let's test your work:

   a. From PC0, ping PC1. Does it work? Why do you think this is?

   b. From PC0, ping PC2. Does it work? Why do you think this is?

   c. From PC2, ping PC0. Does it work? Why do you think this is?

   d. From PC2, ping PC1. Does it work? Why do you think this is?

9. Save your project for future reference.

10. Make some notes on your Wikidot website about your activities in Packet Tracer for this project.

Project 10-4: Compare Windows Server AD to Azure AD

AD DS (Active Directory Domain Services) has been around since Windows 2000 Server, and took a significant leap forward with Windows Server 2008. However, AD, as it's most commonly called, was not designed to integrate cloud services within its domain. Microsoft's answer to this problem was to introduce Windows Azure Active Directory. Azure is not intended as a replacement for AD, but rather as a supplement. Many of the concepts you've learned about in this book, such as cloud computing and security in network design, have built a solid foundation for you to now begin exploring Azure AD. Complete the following steps:

1. Many employers, when interviewing technicians for job openings, will ask the job applicant what he knows about Active Directory. Just like you need to be familiar with the user interface for Windows, Linux, and macOS, you also should know your way around AD. Spend some time researching online about how AD works and what it does. Watch some videos for basic functions, such as configuring users and user groups.

2. Write a paragraph or two describing what you've learned. As practice for business-quality communications, carefully edit your writing. Use complete sentences, good grammar, and correct spelling.

Note

Some people have a hard time "hearing" their own writing. They use incomplete sentences or poorly constructed sentences without realizing it, and yet they don't make these kinds of mistakes when speaking. If you struggle to write well, consider having someone else read your paragraph back to you out loud so you can hear your own mistakes. You might also copy and paste the text into Google Translate (*translate.google.com*), which can read it back to you. Listen for statements that don't make sense, that didn't say what you intended them to say, or that could be interpreted in many different ways.

3. Spend some time researching Azure and comparing it to Active Directory. What services does Azure offer that are the same as AD? What services does Azure offer that are

different? Which protocols does Azure rely on? What AD limitations does Azure address? Also watch some videos showing how to use Azure.

4. Write two paragraphs describing what you've learned. As practice for business-quality communications, carefully edit your writing. Use complete sentences, good grammar, and correct spelling. Consider drawing a diagram or two to illustrate the information you're sharing.

Capstone Projects

Capstone Project 10-1: Secure Switch Ports in Packet Tracer

In this project, you will create a new network in Packet Tracer and configure port security on the switch. Complete the following steps:

1. Create a Packet Tracer network with one 2960 switch and two PCs, as shown in Figure 10-34. Create the needed connections with Copper Straight-Through cables, connecting PC0 to Switch0's FastEthernet0/1 interface and PC1 to Switch0's FastEthernet0/2 interface. The links between the switch and the PCs should come up automatically.

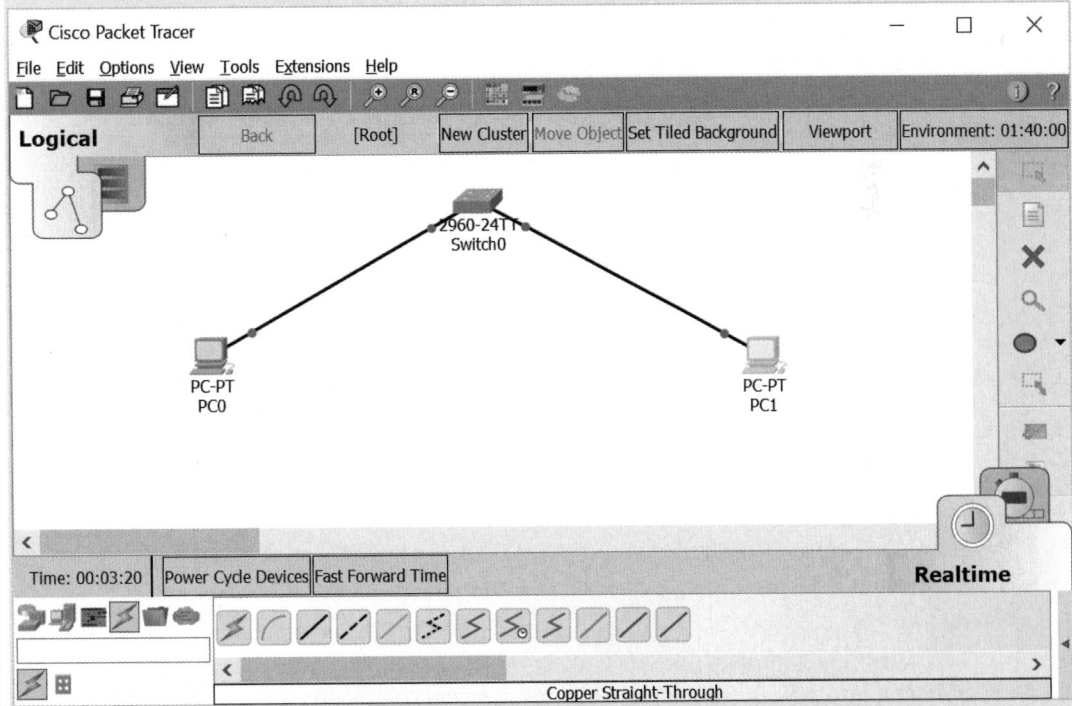

Figure 10-34 Create a new Packet Tracer network
Source: Cisco Systems, Inc.

2. Configure the PCs with the following static IP addresses:
   a. PC0: 192.168.10.10/24
   b. PC1: 192.168.10.20/24
3. Let's see what options are available for port security on the switch's port that faces PC0. On the switch's CLI tab, press **Enter**, then enter the commands from Table 10-4. In Step 4, there are questions for you to answer as you work through the commands in Table 10-4.

Table 10-4   **Explore port security options on a switch**

Command	Purpose
`enable`	Enters privileged EXEC mode
`configure terminal`	Enters global configuration mode
`interface fastethernet0/1`	Enters interface configuration mode for FastEthernet0/1
`switchport port-security ?`	Shows options for the `switchport port-security` command
`switchport port-security mac-address ?`	Shows options for the `switchport port-security mac-address` command
`switchport port-security maximum ?`	Shows options for the `switchport port-security maximum` command
`switchport port-security violation ?`	Shows options for the `switchport port-security violation` command

4. Answer the following questions:
   a. What are the three configuration options for the `switchport port-security` command?
   b. What are the two configuration options for the `switchport port-security mac-address` command?
   c. How many MAC addresses can be allowed using the `switchport port-security maximum` command?
   d. What are the three configuration options for the `switchport port-security violation` command?

Note 📎

When reentering the same or similar commands repeatedly at the IOS CLI, you can press the up arrow on your keyboard to recall recent commands. Then make edits to a recalled command before entering it.

5. Now you're ready to configure port security on the switch's port that faces PC0. But first, you have to configure the port for access mode. On the switch's CLI tab, enter the commands from Table 10-5.

Table 10-5   Configure port security on a switch

Command	Purpose
`switchport mode access`	Sets access mode for this port
`switchport access vlan 1`	Assigns this port to VLAN 1
`switchport port-security`	Enables port security on the port
`switchport port-security maximum 1`	Sets maximum number of MAC addresses allowed on this port (default value is 1)
`switchport port-security violation shutdown`	Requires the port to shut down if port-security is violated (default is shutdown)
`switchport port-security mac-address sticky`	Instructs the port to dynamically learn the MAC addresses of connected devices until maximum number is reached, and to statically remember those MAC addresses, that is, to make them "stick"
`exit`	Returns to global configuration mode
`exit` and press `Enter`	Returns to privileged EXEC mode
`copy run start` and press `Enter`	Saves the current settings

6. Now that you've secured the port and instructed the switch to automatically learn and remember the MAC address of the connected computer, let's check the MAC address table. Enter the command `show mac-address-table`. What MAC address information is listed?

7. The switch has not yet seen any packets from PC0 in order to learn its MAC address. So let's send some packets across the interface from which the switch can collect some information. From PC0, ping PC1. Then rerun the `show mac-address-table` command on the switch. Now what information is listed? What is the type of each entry? Why do you think this is?

8. Let's pretend a hacker gains physical access to the Ethernet cable connected to PC0. She removes the cable from PC0 and connects it to her own laptop. What will happen when she tries to access the network? To find out, do the following:

   a. Delete the cable connecting PC0 to the switch as follows: click the **Delete** button to the right of the workspace, click the cable, then press **Esc** to exit Delete mode. What information is reported on the switch's CLI tab?

   b. Add a laptop to the workspace. Set its static IP address information to 192.168.10.30/24.

   c. Add a Copper Straight-Through connection from the laptop to the switch's FastEthernet0/1 port. Wait for the link to come up. What information is reported on the switch's CLI tab now?

9. The connection is successfully established, but can the hacker do anything on the network? Go to the laptop's Command Prompt interface. Position the laptop's configuration window off to the side of the workspace so you can see the network and enter commands at the same time. Ping PC1. What happens? What information is reported on the switch's CLI tab? What do you think "administratively down" means?

10. The switch has automatically shut down the port in response to the security violation. Let's try to reconnect the legitimate computer. Delete the laptop's connection to the switch, and add a new connection between PC0 and the switch's FastEthernet0/1 port. What happens? Try to ping PC1. What happens?

11. To reenable the connection from PC0, go to the switch's CLI tab. Position the switch's configuration window off to the side of the workspace so you can see the network and enter commands at the same time. Press **Enter** to return to the command prompt, and then enter the commands from Table 10-6. What happens to the connection?

Table 10-6   Restart a switch's port

Command	Purpose
`configure terminal`	Enters global configuration mode
`interface fastethernet0/1`	Enters interface configuration mode for FastEthernet0/1
`shutdown`	Disables the port
`no shutdown` and press `Enter`	Enables the port

12. Ping PC1 from PC0 to confirm the connection is restored. Save your project for future reference.

13. Make some notes on your Wikidot website about your activities in Packet Tracer for this project.

Capstone Project 10-2: Use iptables in Ubuntu Server

In Chapter 4, Capstone Project 4-1, you installed Ubuntu Server in a VM. In Chapter 5, Capstone Project 5-1, you might have enabled a simple Linux firewall called ufw (Uncomplicated Firewall). The default Ubuntu Server firewall, however, is iptables, which you learned about in this chapter.

In this project, you will learn some basic commands in iptables, configure a couple of rules, and save the rules in a file. Complete the following steps:

1. Start your Ubuntu Server VM and log in. Refer to your notes in Wikidot and your account information in LastPass if you need a refresher on where this VM is saved and how to access the user account. You'll need your password several times throughout this project, so keep it handy.

2. Let's begin by looking at what rules are currently in force. Enter the command `sudo iptables -L` and then enter your password. The three chains, or lists of rules, are currently empty. What three chains are listed?

3. Firewall traffic can be set to either accept traffic that doesn't meet a deny rule, which is called implicit allow, or reject traffic that doesn't meet an accept rule, which is called implicit deny. No restrictions are configured by default, so we need to add some. Let's first allow any current connections to continue. Enter the following command, as shown in Figure 10-35:

```
sudo iptables -A INPUT -m conntrack --ctstate ESTABLISHED,RELATED -j
ACCEPT
```

```
Ubuntu 17.04 ubuntuserver tty1

ubuntuserver login: jillwest
Password:
Last login: Tue Oct 10 00:18:46 EDT 2017 on tty1
Welcome to Ubuntu 17.04 (GNU/Linux 4.10.0-19-generic x86_64)

 * Documentation:  https://help.ubuntu.com
 * Management:     https://landscape.canonical.com
 * Support:        https://ubuntu.com/advantage

 * What are your preferred Linux desktop apps?  Help us set the default
   desktop apps in Ubuntu 18.04 LTS:
   - https://ubu.one/apps1804

130 packages can be updated.
72 updates are security updates.


jillwest@ubuntuserver:~$ sudo iptables -L
[sudo] password for jillwest:
Chain INPUT (policy ACCEPT)
target     prot opt source               destination

Chain FORWARD (policy ACCEPT)
target     prot opt source               destination

Chain OUTPUT (policy ACCEPT)
target     prot opt source               destination
jillwest@ubuntuserver:~$ sudo iptables -A INPUT -m conntrack --ctstate ESTABLISHED,RELATED -j ACCEPT
_
```

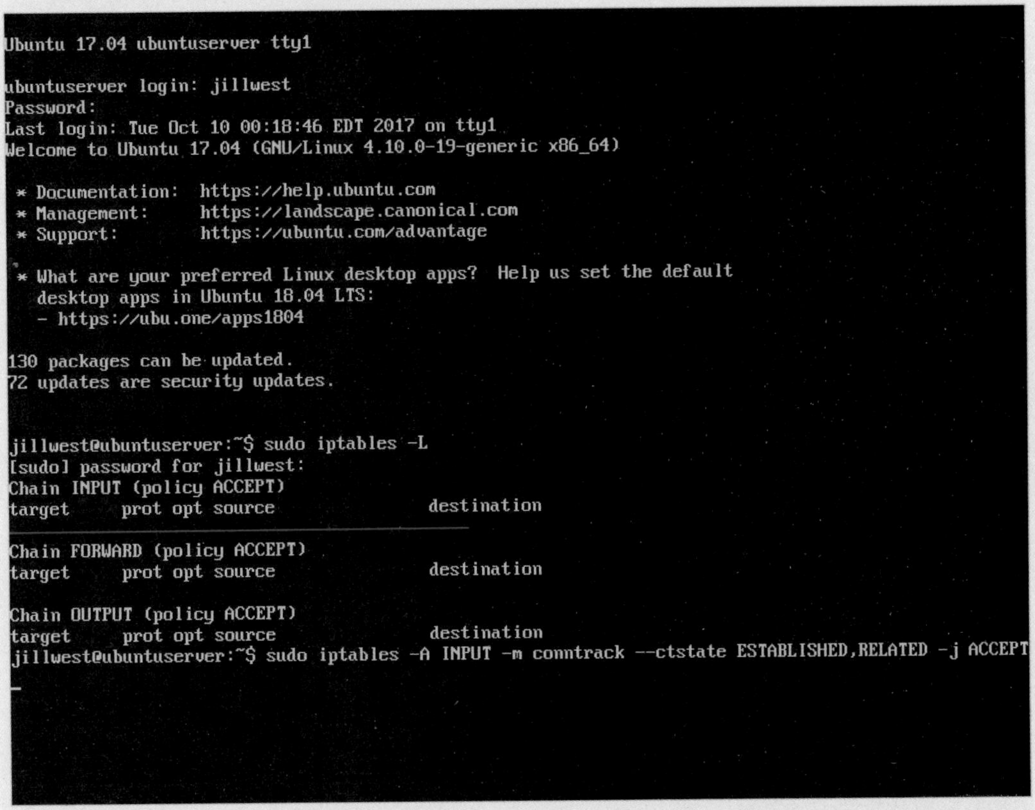

Figure 10-35 Be careful to enter this command exactly as shown on the last line

Source: Canonical Group Limited

4. Enter the `sudo iptables -L` command again to make sure the new rule is listed. Which chain(s) includes the new rule?

5. Next, open port 22 for SSH connections. Enter the following command:

```
sudo iptables -A INPUT -p tcp --dport ssh -j ACCEPT
```

6. The iptables utility automatically knows that SSH runs on port 22 by default, so it opens port 22 when SSH is listed in this command. Sometimes, however, you might want to list the port number itself. Using the command in Step 5 as a guide, what command would you enter to allow HTTP traffic using the port number instead of the protocol name?

7. Now change the default input policy so it will drop any traffic that doesn't match an accept rule. Enter the following command:

   `sudo iptables -P INPUT DROP`

8. Enter the `sudo iptables -L` command again to see your changes. Which chain now has a DROP policy? What policy is listed for the other two chains? Using the command in Step 7 as a guide, what command would you enter to change the default forward policy instead?

9. These policies are not persistent, meaning they will be lost the next time you power off the Ubuntu Server VM. To save these rules, you first have to export the data to a file. Enter the following command, and then enter your password:

   `sudo sh -c "iptables-save > /etc/iptables.rules"`

10. To confirm your file was saved, change to the /etc directory with the command `cd /etc`. Then show the directory's contents with the command `ls`. Is your file listed? What is it called?

11. You won't always have a handy guide to tell you what commands to enter when you want to accomplish a task at the command line. Oftentimes, you have to do some research. The iptables utility has the option to automatically restore the rules from the rules file each time you power on the system. Look online and find the command that makes this possible. What did you find? What does this command do?

12. Use the `sudo poweroff` command to shut down the VM. Make some notes on your Wikidot website about your activities in Ubuntu Server for this project.

## CHAPTER 11

NETWORK PERFORMANCE AND RECOVERY

After reading this chapter and completing the exercises, you will be able to:

Use appropriate tools to monitor device and network events

Adjust device configurations to optimize network performance

Identify methods to increase network availability

Identify best practices for incident response and disaster recovery

Intermittent errors (those that come and go) are among the most difficult to solve, and keeping careful logs of errors is often an essential troubleshooting technique. As an independent contractor for a large telecommunications company, I served on the third and final tier of a help desk that supported an application used by internal customers (company employees) over several wide area networks. The application functioned on more than 100 dedicated circuits that all terminated to feed a large database at corporate headquarters.

Transactions managed by the application were scanned for errors before they were posted to the database. Over time we were able to identify the source of most of these errors as bugs in the application. As we requested fixes from the application developer, we happily saw drastic reductions in the number of errors. However, a few intermittent errors proved to be most difficult to troubleshoot. After eliminating application bugs as the source of the problem, we began to suspect hardware. We carefully logged each error and searched for patterns of consistency: a particular circuit, client computer, branch office, type of transaction, currency, amount of transaction, time of day, and even day of the week. After weeks of logging and searching, we could not uncover a pattern and yet still intermittent errors persisted. Finally, it occurred to us to search for patterns of *no* errors. We went back through our logs and identified about 15 circuits that consistently yielded no errors since we had been keeping logs.

As we worked with the hardware teams, it came to light that these 15 or so circuits all had couplers installed and *none* of the other circuits used couplers. We all felt we had uncovered a significant clue, but still the problem wasn't solved. My team decided to request a network analyzer to monitor problematic circuits. Before we had the analyzer in place, the application developer was finally able to reproduce the problem in the lab by using progressively faster circuits. The application required a buffer on the receiving end, which held incoming data before it was processed by the application. Faster circuits produced a buffer overflow, resulting in corrupted transactions. The mystery was solved. The couplers had managed to slightly reduce performance of the circuits, which allowed the application buffer to keep up with these slightly slower circuits. After weeks of troubleshooting, the solution was a simple programmer fix: Increase the application buffer size.

Jean Andrews
Author and Independent Contractor

Because networks are a vital part of keeping an organization running, you must pay careful attention to measures that keep network resources safe, available, and performing well. Throughout this text, you have learned about building scalable, reliable networks as well as selecting the most appropriate hardware, topologies, and services to operate your network. You have also learned about security measures to guard network access and resources. In this chapter, you will learn how to optimize networks for today's high-bandwidth needs, protect your network's performance from faults and failures, and recover in the event your network experiences a minor outage or a more severe disaster. With proper adjustments, redundancies, and preparations, you can create and maintain a resilient network.

Collecting Network Data

3.1   Given a scenario, use appropriate documentation and diagrams to manage the network.

3.3   Explain common scanning, monitoring, and patching processes and summarize their expected outputs.

5.2   Given a scenario, use the appropriate tool.

5.3   Given a scenario, troubleshoot common wired connectivity and performance issues.

5.5   Given a scenario, troubleshoot common network service issues.

Network management is a general term that means different things to different networking professionals. At its broadest, **network management** refers to the assessment, monitoring, and maintenance of all aspects of a network. It can include controlling user access to network resources, monitoring performance baselines, checking for hardware faults, ensuring optimized QoS (quality of service) for critical applications, maintaining records of network assets and software configurations, and determining what time of day is best for upgrading hardware and software.

Several disciplines fall under the heading of network management. All share the goals of enhancing efficiency and performance while preventing costly downtime or loss. Ideally, network management accomplishes these tasks by helping the administrator predict problems before they occur. For example, a trend in network usage could indicate when a switch will be overwhelmed with traffic. In response, the network administrator could increase the switch's processing capabilities or replace the switch before users begin experiencing slow or dropped connections.

Before you can assess and make predictions about a network's health, however, you must first understand its logical and physical structure and how it functions under typical conditions. And in order to do that, you must be able to collect data about the network's traffic.

Monitoring Tools

A network monitor is a tool that continually monitors network traffic. A similar tool, a protocol analyzer, can monitor traffic at a specific interface between a server or client and the network. In practice, these two terms—network monitor and protocol analyzer—are often used interchangeably. However, they differ significantly when it comes to the kinds of data you can expect to gather with each tool. Think about the difference between monitoring the traffic that a single device encounters on its connection to the network, versus monitoring devices and traffic patterns throughout a particular network. For example, Spiceworks is a type of network monitoring software because it can be configured to monitor multiple devices on a network at one time. Wireshark is a type of protocol analyzer because it monitors traffic on the interface between a single device and the network.

Wireshark or other monitoring applications running on a single computer connected to a switch doesn't see all the traffic on a network—it only sees the traffic the switch sends to it, which includes broadcast traffic and traffic specifically addressed to the one computer (see the computer in the red box on the right in Figure 11-1). To track more of the network traffic, you can use one of these other methods, which are also illustrated in Figure 11-1:

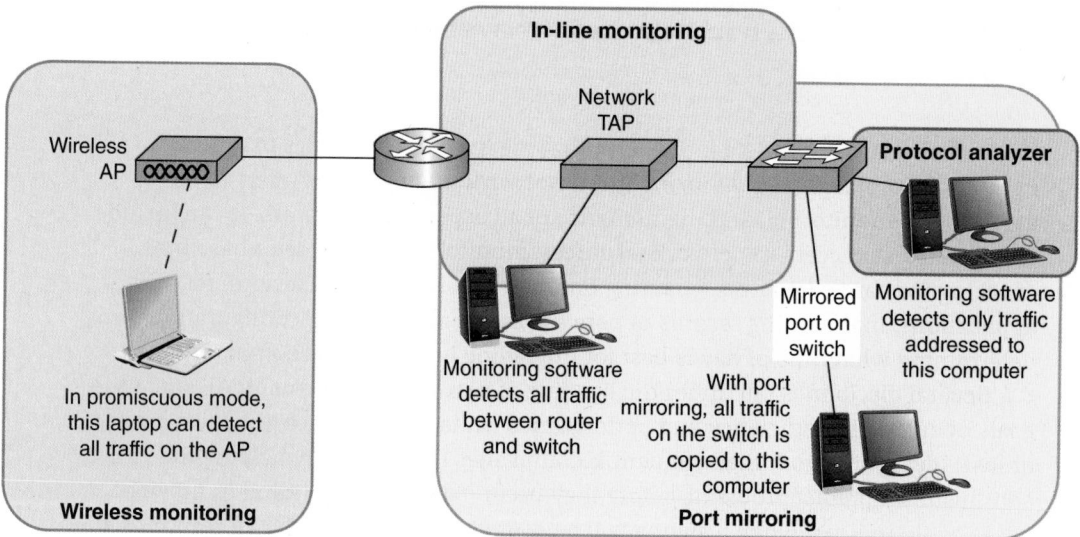

Figure 11-1   Methods to monitor network traffic

- *wireless monitoring*—Run monitoring software on a computer connected wirelessly to the network (see the computer on the left in Figure 11-1). For the computer to "see" all traffic, its network adapter must support promiscuous mode. In promiscuous mode, a device driver directs the NIC to pass all wireless frames to the operating system and on to the monitoring software, not just those broadcasted or intended for the host. Usually promiscuous mode is enabled in the monitoring application. Occasionally you'll need to enable the feature through the OS. (For Windows, use the NIC's properties box from Device Manager.)
- *port mirroring*—Program a switch to use port mirroring, whereby all traffic sent to any port on the switch is also sent to the mirrored port. Then connect the port to a computer running monitoring software.

- *in-line monitoring*—Install a device, called a network TAP (test access point) or packet sniffer, in line with network traffic. As you can see in Figure 11-2, the device usually has four ports:
  - ○ Two ports send and receive all traffic, usually between a switch and a router.
  - ○ A third port mirrors the traffic, sending it to a computer running monitoring software in promiscuous mode, such as Wireshark.
  - ○ The fourth port is used for device configuration.

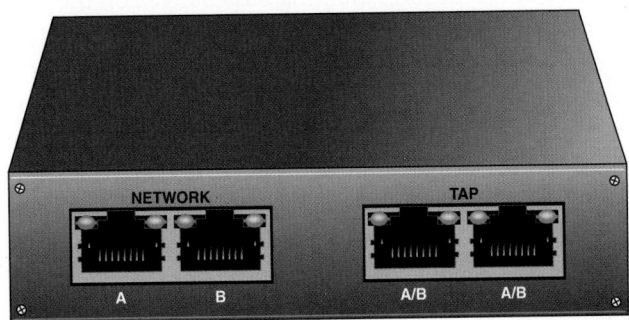

Figure 11-2   Network TAPs are available for both copper and fiber network troubleshooting

Some NOSes come with built-in network monitoring tools. In addition, you can purchase or download free network monitoring tools developed by other software companies. Hundreds of such programs exist. After you have worked with one network monitoring tool, such as Spiceworks, you'll find that other products work in much the same way. Most even use very similar graphical interfaces. All network monitoring tools can perform at least the following functions:

- Set the NIC to run in promiscuous mode so it will pass all traffic it receives to the monitoring software.
- Continuously monitor network traffic on a segment.
- Capture network data transmitted on a segment.
- Capture frames sent to or from a specific node.
- Reproduce network conditions by transmitting a selected amount and type of data.
- Generate statistics about network activity (for example, what percentage of the total frames transmitted on a segment are broadcast frames).

Some network monitoring tools can also perform the following functions:

- Discover all network nodes on a segment.
- Establish a baseline, including performance, utilization rate, and so on.
- Track utilization of network resources (such as bandwidth and storage) and device resources (such as CPU or memory usage) and present this information in the form of graphs, tables, or charts.

- Store traffic data and generate reports.
- Trigger alarms when traffic conditions meet specific thresholds (for example, if usage exceeds 60 percent of capacity).
- Identify usage anomalies, such as top talkers (hosts that send an inordinate amount of data) or top listeners (hosts that receive an inordinate amount of data).

How can capturing data help you solve networking problems? Imagine that traffic on a segment of the network you administer suddenly grinds to a halt one morning at about 8:00 a.m. You no sooner step in the door than everyone from the help desk calls to tell you how slowly the network is running. Nothing has changed on the network since last night when it ran normally, so you can think of no obvious reasons for problems.

At the workstation where you have previously installed a network monitoring tool, you capture all data transmissions for approximately five minutes. You then sort the frames in the network monitoring software, arranging the nodes in order based on the volume of traffic each has generated. You might find that one workstation appears at the top of the list with an excessively high number of bad transmissions. Or, you might discover that a server has been compromised by a hacker and is generating a flood of data over the network. Or possibly your current sampling size doesn't yet reveal any problems, and you run a second, longer capture. Once you know the source of the problem, you know where to look for a resolution.

At the same time, finding the source of the problem requires using the correct tool. A network monitor's data will allow for **traffic analysis**, which examines the flow of network traffic for patterns and exceptions to those patterns. For example, traffic analysis will identify locations of network bottlenecks, such as an outdated device that should be replaced or a network service that needs more resources. A protocol analyzer, however, will dig into the details of specific packets and perform **packet analysis** functions, which identify protocols, errors, and misconfigurations. Both approaches can yield insightful information; however, focusing on the most relevant approach will help you locate the source of the problem more quickly.

Before adopting a network monitor or protocol analyzer, you should be aware of some of the data errors that these tools can distinguish through traffic analysis or packet analysis techniques. The effective utilization of network monitoring tools can help identify and prevent many types of complications, such as the following:

- *runts*—Packets that are smaller than the medium's minimum packet size. For instance, any Ethernet packet that is smaller than 64 bytes is considered a runt.
- *giants*—Packets that exceed the medium's maximum packet size. For example, an Ethernet packet larger than 1518 bytes (or 1522 bytes for VLAN packets) is normally considered a giant.
- *jabber*—A device that handles electrical signals improperly, usually affecting the rest of the network. A network monitor will detect a jabber as a device that is always retransmitting, effectively bringing the network to a halt. A jabber usually results from a bad NIC. Occasionally, it can be caused by outside electrical interference.

- *ghosts*—Frames that are not actually data frames, but aberrations caused by a device misinterpreting stray voltage on the wire. Unlike true data frames, ghosts have an invalid pattern at the beginning of the frame pattern.
- *packet loss*—Packets lost due to an unknown protocol, unrecognized port, network noise, or some other anomaly. Lost packets never arrive at their destination.
- *discarded packets*—Packets that arrive at their destination, but are then deliberately discarded, or dropped, because issues such as buffer overflow, latency, bottlenecks, or other forms of network congestion delayed them beyond their usable time frame. A discarded packet is often referred to as a discard.
- *interface resets*—Repeated resets of the connection, resulting in lower-quality utilization; caused by an interface misconfiguration.

Faults and conditions that exceed certain thresholds can trigger alerts, and those alerts might generate notifications to IT personnel. Depending on the software used, these notifications might be transmitted either by email or text message, also called SMS (Short Message Service), or they can automatically prompt support ticket generation. They can also be recorded by system and event logs. Many devices, such as routers, switches, servers, and workstations, come with embedded event logging tools of various types and will store logs within their own systems. Other tools collect log entries from devices across the network. Let's look at both of these possibilities.

Applying Concepts: Identify a Process Hogging Network Resources

Suppose you notice a sudden decrease in network performance and suspect malware is hogging network resources. Follow these steps to identify a legitimate process or malware that is affecting network performance:

1. Every process is assigned a PID (process identifier). To display the PID associated with each network connection, open an elevated Command Prompt and enter the command `netstat -o`.
2. You can identify the names of the processes for each PID by looking in Task Manager (press **Ctrl** +**Alt** +**Del** and then click **Task Manager**). Click **More details**. On the Processes tab, if the PID column is not showing, right-click a column heading and check **PID**.
3. Alternatively, you can have netstat resolve process names. Enter the command `netstat -b`, which will take longer to run. If you don't recognize a process name, do a quick Google search to learn about it.
4. You might need to forcefully stop an out-of-control process. In most cases, you could do this with the Windows Services console (services.msc). To stop a process that refuses to stop by normal means, you can use the `taskkill` command with the `/f` parameter and the process's PID. For example, if the PID is 2212, enter the command:

```
taskkill /f /pid:2212
```

If that doesn't work, you might first need to take ownership of the process program file. To do this, enter the command `takeown /f <filename>` using the filename listed for the process when you ran the `netstat -b` command.

System and Event Logs

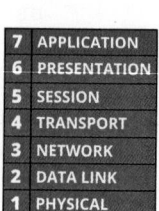

7	APPLICATION
6	PRESENTATION
5	SESSION
4	TRANSPORT
3	NETWORK
2	DATA LINK
1	PHYSICAL

Virtually every condition recognized by an operating system can be recorded. Records of such activities are kept in a log. For example, each time your computer requests an IP address from the DHCP server and doesn't receive a response, this event can be recorded in a log. Likewise, a log entry can be added each time a firewall denies a host's attempt to connect to another host on the network that the firewall defends.

Different operating systems log different kinds of events by default. In addition, network administrators can customize logs by defining conditions under which new entries are created. For example, an engineer might want to know when the relative humidity in a data center exceeds 60 percent. If a device can monitor this information and communicate it in real time to a computer, the results can be written to a log. On Windows-based computers, such a log is known as an **event log** and can be easily viewed with the **Event Viewer** application, as you will see in the following project.

Applying Concepts: Explore Event Viewer in Windows

In this project, you will use the Event Viewer application to explore the event log on a computer running Windows 10. Ideally, the computer will have been used for a while, so the event log contains several entries. It need not be connected to a network. However, you must be logged on to the computer as a user with administrator privileges.

1. Right-click **Start**, and click **Event Viewer**.
2. The Event Viewer window opens, with three panes as shown in Figure 11-3. The center pane lists a summary of administrative events. Notice that events are classified into several types, which might include *Critical, Error, Warning, Information, Audit Success* and, in some cases, *Audit Failure*. The number of events that have been logged in each category is listed to the right of the classification entry. How many Critical and Error events has your workstation logged in the last 24 hours? In the last seven days?
3. If your workstation has logged any critical or error events in the past seven days, click the plus sign next to the event type. A list of events appears. (If you do not have any entries in the Critical or Error categories, click the plus sign next to the event type *Warning* instead.)
4. Notice that each event log entry is identified by an Event ID, its source, and the type of log on which it's recorded. (Event Viewer's default screen lists entries for all types of logs kept by the Windows operating system.) Scroll through the entries until you find

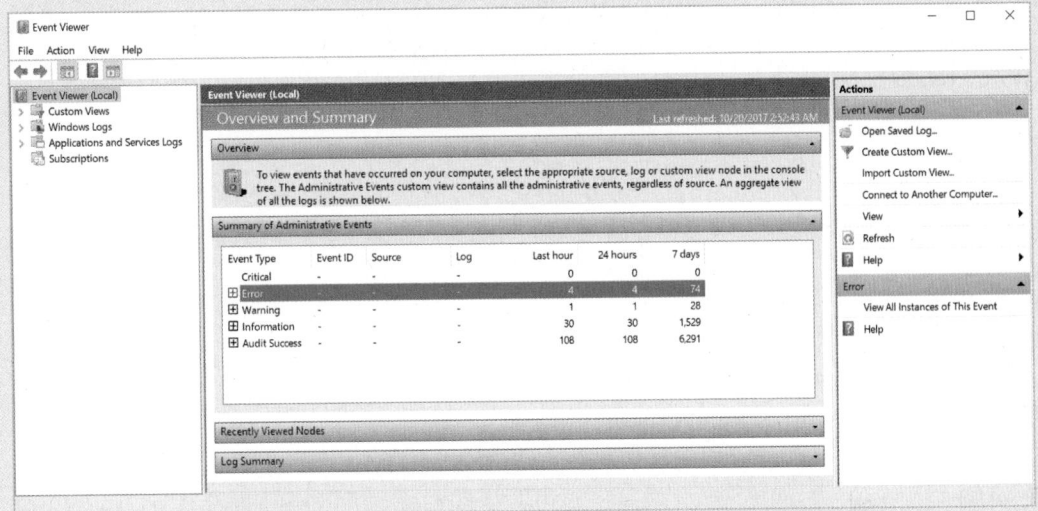

Figure 11-3   Event Viewer logs errors and other activities in Windows

one that was logged by "System"—if possible, one that has occurred more than once in the past seven days. Double-click that entry to read more about it. The Summary page events pane appears in the center of the Event Viewer display (see Figure 11-4).

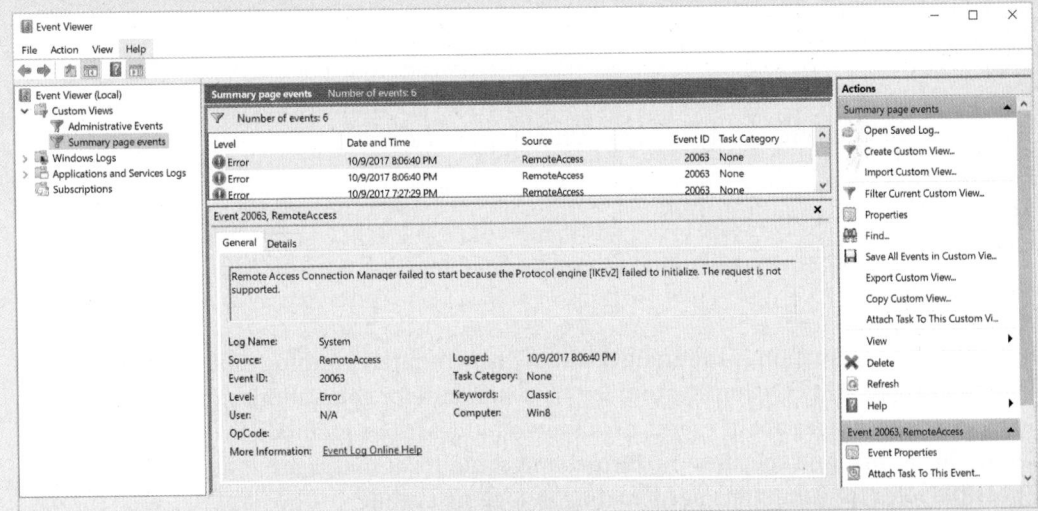

Figure 11-4   This event shows a problem where IKEv2 failed to initialize

5. Notice when these errors were recorded. On the General tab in the lower portion of the middle pane, read a detailed description of the error you chose to view. If you were a network manager, would you choose to be alerted whenever this error occurred on a workstation or server? Why or why not?

6. Now click **Windows Logs** in the left pane of the Event Viewer display to view the different types of logs about Windows events. The Windows Logs listing appears in the center pane, as shown in Figure 11-5.

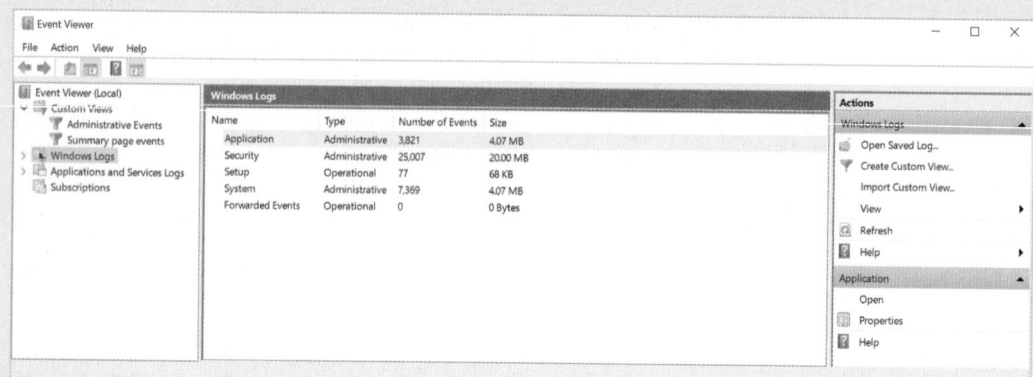

Figure 11-5 Windows Logs listing in Event Viewer

7. Which of the five logs has recorded the highest number of events? How large is that log file?
8. Suppose you want to limit the size of the system log. Right-click the **System** entry in the Windows Logs listing, and then click **Properties** in the shortcut menu that appears.
9. The Log Properties - System (Type: Administrative) dialog box opens. Next to the *Maximum log size (KB)* text box, enter **16000** to limit the log file size to 16 MB.
10. Click **OK** to save your change. If you receive a message that indicates your current log's size exceeds the maximum limit you just entered, click **OK** to accept the recommended practice of enforcing the maximum after the log is cleared.

In Hands-On Project 11-1, you'll learn how to work with the data collected in Windows event logs.

Similar information is routinely recorded by computers running Linux or UNIX via the syslog utility. **Syslog (system log)** is a standard for generating, storing, and processing messages about events on a system. It describes methods for detecting and reporting events and specifies the format and contents of messages. It also defines two possible roles for computers participating in logging events:

- *generator*—The computer that is monitored by a syslog-compatible application and that issues event information
- *collector*—The computer that gathers event messages from generators

The syslog standard also establishes levels of severity for every logged event. For example, "0" indicates an emergency situation, whereas "7" points to specific information that might help in debugging a problem.

Computers running Linux and UNIX record syslog data in a system log. Table 11-1 shows the locations of system logs in some versions of Linux and UNIX.

Table 11-1	Linux and UNIX system log locations
Version type	**System log location**
Newer versions of Linux	/var/log/messages
Older versions of UNIX	/var/log/syslog/
Solaris versions of UNIX	var/adm/messages

Note

To find out where various logs are kept on your UNIX or Linux system, view the /etc/syslog. conf file (on some systems, this is the /etc/rsyslog.conf file). The /etc/syslog.conf file is also where you can configure the types of events to log and what priority to assign each event.

Bear in mind that the syslog utility doesn't alert you to any problems, but it does keep a history of messages issued by the system. It's up to you to monitor the system log for errors, or filter log data to monitor packet flow when troubleshooting a problem or checking for patterns that might indicate developing problems. Most UNIX and Linux desktop operating systems provide a GUI application for easily reviewing and filtering the information in system logs. Other applications are available for sifting through syslog data and generating alerts. In Capstone Project 11-2 at the end of this chapter, you'll view and sort through data in a system log.

Using the information collected in event logs and system logs for fault management requires thoughtful data filtering and sorting. After all, you can't assume that all of the information in these logs points to a problem, even if it is marked with a warning. For example, you might have typed your password incorrectly while trying to log on to your computer, thus generating a log entry. Keep in mind, however, that sometimes seemingly innocuous information turns out to be exactly the data you need to diagnose a problem, as you saw in the *On the Job* story at the beginning of this chapter.

SNMP Logs

You've just learned about logs that are created and managed on individual devices. Organizations often use enterprise-wide network management systems to perform similar logging functions on an entire network. Hundreds of such tools exist. All rely on a similar architecture (see Figure 11-6), in which the following entities work together:

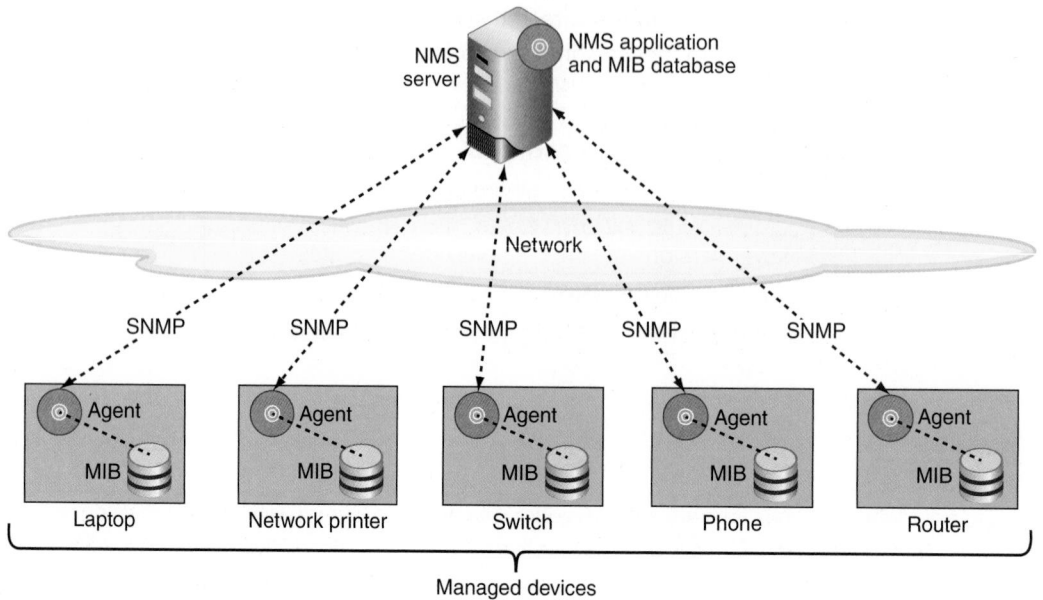

Figure 11-6 Network management architecture

- *NMS (network management system) server*—At least one network management console, which may be a server or workstation, depending on the size of the network, collects data from multiple managed devices at regular intervals in a process called **polling**.
- *managed device*—Any network node monitored by the NMS is a managed device. Each managed device may contain several **managed objects**, which is any characteristic of the device that is monitored, including components such as a processor, memory, hard disk, or NIC, or intangibles such as performance or utilization. Each managed object is assigned an **OID (object identifier)**.
- *network management agent*—Each managed device runs a network management agent, which is a software routine that collects information about the device's operation and provides it to the NMS. For example, on a server, an agent can measure how many users are connected to the server or what percentage of the processor's resources are used at any given time. So as not to affect the performance of a device while collecting information, agents demand minimal processing resources.
- *MIB (Management Information Base)*—The list of objects managed by the NMS, as well as the descriptions of these objects, are kept in the MIB (Management Information Base). The MIB also contains data about an object's performance in a database format that can be mined and analyzed. The MIB is designed in a top-down, hierarchical tree structure, where the root is unnamed.

Agents communicate information about managed devices via any one of several Application layer protocols. On modern networks, most agents use SNMP (Simple Network Management Protocol). Recall that SNMP is part of the TCP/IP suite of protocols and typically runs over UDP on ports 161 and 162 (though it can be configured to run over TCP). Three versions of SNMP exist:

- SNMPv1 (Simple Network Management Protocol version 1)—This is the original version, released in 1988. Because of its limited features, it is rarely used on modern networks.
- SNMPv2 (Simple Network Management Protocol version 2)—This version improved on SNMPv1 with increased performance and slightly better security, among other features.
- SNMPv3 (Simple Network Management Protocol version 3)—This version is similar to SNMPv2, but adds authentication, validation, and encryption for messages exchanged between managed devices and the network management console.

SNMPv3 is the most secure version of the protocol. However, some administrators have hesitated to upgrade to SNMPv3 because it requires more complex configuration. Therefore, SNMPv2 is still widely used. Most, but not all, network management applications support multiple versions of SNMP.

There are a few, key SNMP messages used to communicate between the NMS and managed devices. As you can see in the following list, most of these conversations are initiated by the NMS:

- *SNMP Get Request*—The NMS sends a request for data to the agent on a managed device. See the left side of Figure 11-7.
- *SNMP Get Response*—The agent sends a response with the requested information.
- *SNMP Get Next*—The NMS might then request the next row of data in the MIB database.
- *SNMP Walk*—With this one command, the NMS can issue the equivalent of a sequence of SNMP Get Next messages to walk through sequential rows in the MIB database.
- *SNMP Trap*—An agent can be programmed to detect certain abnormal conditions that prompt the generation of SNMP Trap messages, where the agent sends the NMS unsolicited data once the specified conditions on the managed device are met (see the right side of Figure 11-7). For example, on a Cisco server, you could use the command `snmp trap link-status` to instruct the SNMP agent to send an alert if or when an interface fails. The trap can later be disabled with the command `no snmp trap link-status`. SNMP Trap messages can alert network administrators of unresponsive services or devices, power supply issues, high temperatures, and tripped circuit breakers, which allows technicians to identify and address the problems quickly—hopefully before users start to notice the problem. An unresponsive service like DHCP, for example, could be restarted remotely. A report of a tripped circuit breaker prevents further investigation into why a specific device isn't responsive.

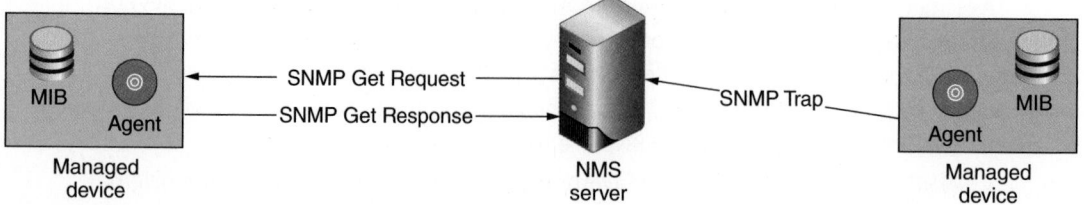

Figure 11-7 Most SNMP conversations are initiated by the NMS server, except when a managed device sends an SNMP Trap message

Network+ Exam Tip ⓘ

When using UDP, SNMP agents receive requests from the NMS on port 161. The NMS receives agent responses and traps on its port 162. SNMP messages can be secured with TLS, in which case agents receive requests on port 10161 and the NMS receives responses and traps on port 10162.

After data is collected, the network management application can present an administrator with several ways to view and analyze the data. For example, a very common way to analyze data is by a line graph. Alternatively, a popular way to view data is in the form of a map that shows fully functional links or devices in green, partially (or less than optimally) functioning links or devices in yellow, and failed links or devices in red. An example of the type of map generated by a network performance monitor is shown in Figure 11-8.

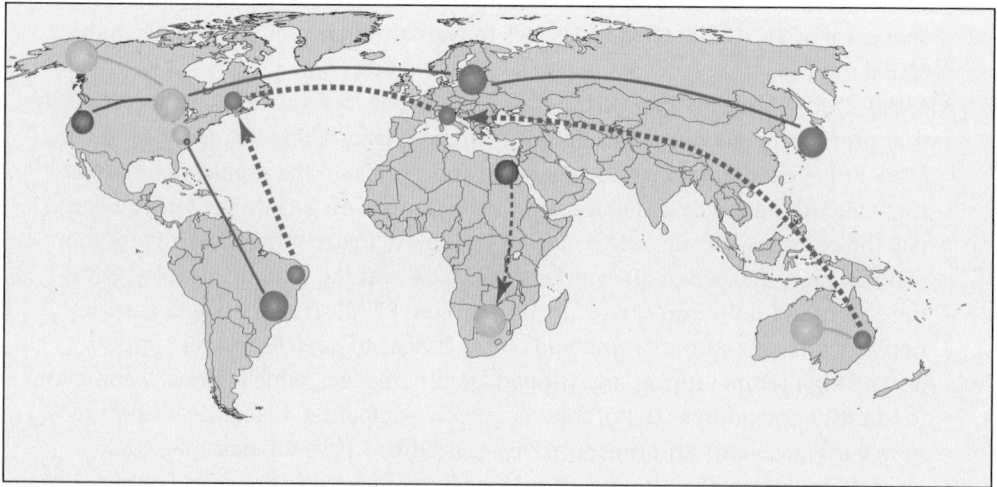

Figure 11-8 Map showing network status

Because of their flexibility, sophisticated network management applications are also challenging to configure and fine-tune. You have to be careful to collect only useful data and not an excessive amount of routine information. For example, on a network with dozens of routers, collecting SNMP-generated messages that essentially say "I'm still here" every five seconds would result in massive amounts of insignificant data. A glut of information makes it difficult to ascertain when a router in fact requires attention. Instead, when configuring a network management application to poll a router, you might choose to generate an SNMP-based message only when the router's processor is operating at 75 percent of its capacity, or to measure only the amount of traffic passing through a NIC every five minutes.

When it comes to monitoring network performance, data creation is the easy part. The challenge, as you'll see next, is to identify and efficiently analyze useful and relevant data.

Performance Baselines

To identify when there's a problem on the network, you must first know what is normal for that network. A **baseline** is a report of the network's normal state of operation and might include a range of acceptable measurements. Baseline measurements are obtained by analyzing network traffic information and might include information on the utilization rate for your network backbone, number of users logged on per day or per hour, number of protocols that run on your network, statistics about errors (such as runts, jabbers, or giants), frequency with which networked applications are used, or information regarding which users take up the most bandwidth. The graph in Figure 11-9 shows a sample baseline for daily network traffic over a six-week period.

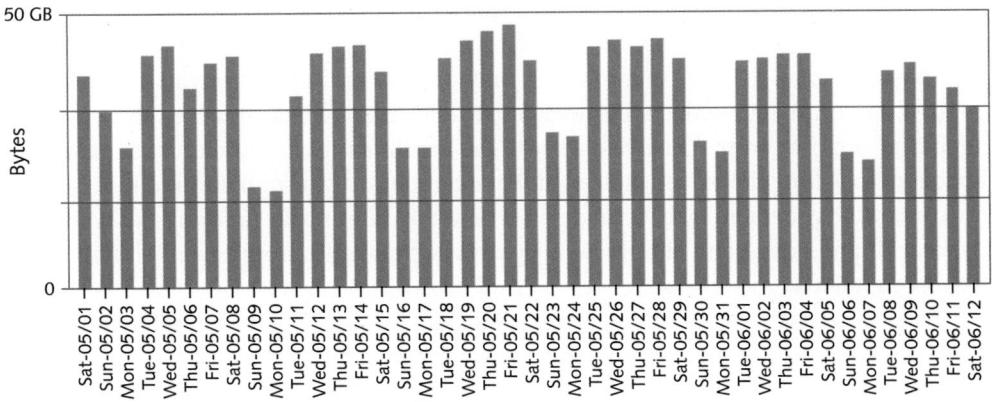

Figure 11-9   Baseline of daily network traffic

Baseline measurements allow you to compare future performance increases or decreases caused by network changes or events with past network performance. Obtaining baseline measurements is the only way to know for certain whether a pattern of usage has changed (and requires attention) or, later, whether a network upgrade made a difference. Each network requires its own approach and a reliable schedule for documenting and reviewing baselines to identify unexpected variations. The elements you measure and monitor depend on which functions are most critical to your network and its users.

For instance, suppose that your network currently serves 500 users and that your backbone traffic exceeds 50 percent capacity at 10:00 a.m. and 2:00 p.m. each business day. That pattern constitutes your baseline. Now suppose that your company decides to add 200 users who perform the same types of functions on the network. The added number of users equals 40 percent of the current number of users (200/500). Therefore, you can estimate that your backbone's capacity should increase by approximately 40 percent to maintain your current service levels.

The more data you gather while establishing your network's baseline, the more accurate your prediction will be. Network traffic patterns can vary considerably over time and must account for two major factors:

- Normal variations throughout the day, week, month, and different seasons. For example, a large retail company will have significantly busier traffic patterns during holiday seasons, and this is completely normal for that network.
- Changes to the network that might be unpredictable in the resulting impact. For instance, the preceding example assumed that all new users would share the same network usage habits as the current users. In fact, however, the new users might generate a great deal more, or a great deal less, network traffic.

How do you gather baseline data on your network? Several software applications can perform the baselining for you. These applications range from freeware available on the Internet to expensive, customizable hardware and software combination products. Before choosing a network-baselining tool, determine how you will use it. If you manage a small network that provides only one critical application, an inexpensive tool may suffice. If you work on a WAN with several critical links, however, investigate purchasing a more comprehensive package. The baseline measurement tool should be capable of collecting the statistics needed. For example, only a sophisticated tool can measure traffic generated by each node on a network, filter traffic according to types of protocols and errors, and simultaneously measure statistics from several different network segments.

Once you've gathered this data, analyze the data for typical rates of utilization and failure. Some of the more common performance metrics include:

- *utilization*—This metric refers to the actual throughput used as a percentage of available bandwidth. No network should operate at maximum capacity. Identify patterns of utilization and ensure that available bandwidth accounts for utilization spikes.
- *error rate*—Bits can be damaged in transit due to EMI or other interference. The calculated percentage of how often this occurs is the error rate.

- *packet drops*—Packets that are damaged beyond use, arrive after their expiration, or are not allowed through an interface are dropped. Packet drops result in delayed network communications while devices wait for responses or have to resend transmissions. Knowing what's normal for your network will help you identify problems when packet drop rates vary.
- *jitter*—All packets experience some latency. When successive packets experience varying amounts of latency, resulting in their arriving out of order, the user experience is degraded. This is called jitter, a problem that can be addressed through traffic management techniques, which we'll discuss next.

Managing Network Traffic

 Certification

1.3 Explain the concepts and characteristics of routing and switching.

3.3 Explain common scanning, monitoring, and patching processes and summarize their expected outputs.

5.3 Given a scenario, troubleshoot common wired connectivity and performance issues.

After you've begun collecting data on your network's traffic patterns and established some reliable baselines, you're ready to monitor your network's status on an ongoing basis and make changes to best meet the needs of your network's users. This process includes two major factors:

- *performance management*—Monitoring how well links and devices are keeping up with the demands placed on them
- *fault management*—Detecting and signaling of device, link, or component faults

To accomplish both fault and performance management, network administrators respond to errors as needed and tweak device and network configurations to optimize performance. Let's look at what kinds of optimizations can be made. Then we'll explore the precautions that can help prevent or minimize the impact of errors and other, more disastrous failures.

Traffic Management

When a network must handle high volumes of network traffic, users benefit from a performance management and optimization technique known as traffic shaping. **Traffic shaping**, also called packet shaping, involves manipulating certain characteristics of packets, data streams, or connections to manage the type and amount of traffic traversing a network or interface at any moment. Its goals are to ensure timely delivery of the most important traffic while optimizing performance for all users.

Traffic shaping can involve any of the following:

- Delaying less-important traffic
- Increasing the priority of more-important traffic
- Limiting the volume of traffic flowing in to or out of an interface during a specified time period
- Limiting the momentary throughput rate for an interface

The last two techniques belong to a category of traffic shaping known as **traffic policing**. For example, an ISP might impose a maximum on the capacity it will grant a certain customer. This prevents the customer from tying up more than a certain amount of the network's overall capacity. Traffic policing helps the service provider predict how much capacity it must purchase from its network provider. It also holds down costs because the ISP doesn't have to plan for every client using all available throughput at all times (an unlikely scenario). An ISP that imposes traffic policing might allow customers to choose their preferred maximum daily traffic volume or momentary throughput and pay commensurate fees. A more sophisticated instance of traffic policing is dynamic and takes into account the network's current traffic patterns. For example, the service provider might allow certain customers to exceed their maximums when few other customers are using the network.

Figure 11-10 illustrates how traffic volume might appear on an interface without limits compared with an interface subject to traffic policing.

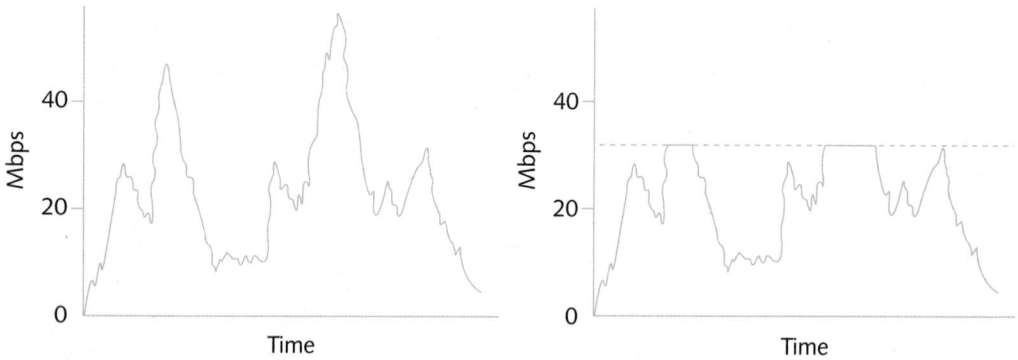

Figure 11-10   Traffic volume before and after applying limits

A controversial example of traffic shaping came to light in 2007. Comcast, one of the largest Internet service providers in the United States, was found to be clandestinely discriminating against certain types of traffic. For users uploading files to P2P (peer-to-peer) networks such as BitTorrent, Comcast was interjecting TCP segments with the RST (reset) field set. These segments were spoofed to appear as if they originated from the accepting site, and they cut the connection as the user attempted to upload files. Soon customers figured out the pattern and used monitoring software such as Wireshark to reveal the forged TCP RST segments. They complained to authorities that Comcast had violated their user agreement. The FCC investigated, upheld the customers' claims, and ordered Comcast to stop this practice. Comcast then chose a different method of traffic shaping. It assigned a lower priority to data from customers who generate a high volume of traffic at times when the network is at risk of congestion.

In the past several years, many ISPs have used traffic throttling to slow down high-bandwidth users. This isn't necessarily a bad thing, so long as all interested parties are aware of what's going on. In fact, some ISPs use traffic shaping to temporarily *increase* a busy user's bandwidth without negatively affecting other users' network activities. To learn more about these practices, search on phrases such as "comcast traffic shaping," "ISP throttling," "net neutrality," and "bandwidth throttling test," which will give you links you can use to test your own Internet connection.

Several types of traffic prioritization—that is, treating more-important traffic preferentially—exist. Software running on a router, multilayer switch, gateway, server, or even a client workstation can act as a traffic shaper by prioritizing traffic according to any of the following characteristics:

- Protocol
- IP address
- User group
- DiffServ (Differentiated Services) flag in an IP packet
- VLAN tag in a Data Link layer frame
- Service or application

Depending on the traffic prioritization software, different types of traffic might be assigned priority classes, such as *high, normal, low,* or *slow*; alternatively, it can be rated on a prioritization scale from 0 (lowest priority) to 7 (highest priority). For example, traffic generated by time-sensitive VoIP applications might be assigned high priority, while online gaming might be assigned low priority (or vice versa, depending on your preferences). Traffic prioritization is needed most when the network is busiest. It ensures that during peak usage times, the most important data gets through quickly, while less-important data waits. When network usage is low, however, prioritization might have no noticeable effects.

Some types of network traffic contribute more significantly to the overall volume of traffic than other types do. When a network is expected to simultaneously support voice, video, and data communications, performance is always a major concern. Let's see what options are available for addressing these concerns.

QoS (Quality of Service) Assurance

You don't want to hear breaks in an online phone conversation or see a buffering message when you watch a movie over the Internet. For that reason, voice and video transmissions are considered **delay-sensitive**. On the other hand, occasional loss of data (skipping video frames, for example) can be tolerated; for that reason, voice and video transmissions are considered **loss-tolerant**. Typical web surfing might not present much of a challenge for available network bandwidth. However, streaming movies, voice or video calls, and online gaming can all place heavy demands on available bandwidth.

To manage these demands, network administrators must pay attention to a network's **QoS (quality of service)**, which is a group of techniques for adjusting the priority a network assigns to various types of transmissions. To do this, network administrators need to be aware of the applications used on a network, including the application protocols they use and the amount of bandwidth they require. For example, variable delays of VoIP packets result in choppy voice quality. A network that handles a lot of VoIP traffic would need to prioritize that traffic in order to avoid problems with jitter.

From the point of view of a person watching a movie online, optimized QoS translates into an uninterrupted, accurate, and faithful reproduction of audio or visual input. For someone competing in online games, high priority on gaming traffic gives quick and accurate responsiveness to game play in addition to a high-quality audio and visual experience. Network engineers have developed several techniques to address the QoS-related challenges inherent in delivering high-bandwidth network services. The following sections describe two of these techniques, both of which are standardized by IETF.

DiffServ (Differentiated Services)

7	APPLICATION
6	PRESENTATION
5	SESSION
4	TRANSPORT
3	NETWORK
2	DATA LINK
1	PHYSICAL

DiffServ (Differentiated Services) is a simple technique that addresses QoS issues by prioritizing traffic at Layer 3. DiffServ takes into account all types of network traffic, not just the time-sensitive services such as voice and video. That way, it can assign voice streams a high priority and at the same time assign unessential data streams (for example, an employee surfing the Internet on his lunch hour) a low priority. This technique offers more protection for time-sensitive, prioritized services. To prioritize traffic, DiffServ places information in the DiffServ field of an IPv4 packet. The first 6 bits of this 8-bit field are called **DSCP (Differentiated Services Code Point)**. (For a review of the fields in an IP packet, refer to Chapter 4.) In IPv6 packets, DiffServ uses a similar field known as the Traffic Class field. This information in both IPv4 and IPv6 packets indicates to network routers how the data stream should be forwarded. DiffServ defines two types of forwarding:

- *EF (Expedited Forwarding)*—A data stream is assigned a minimum departure rate from a given node. This technique circumvents delays that slow normal data from reaching its destination on time and in sequence.
- *AF (Assured Forwarding)*—Different levels of router resources can be assigned to data streams. AF prioritizes data handling, but provides no guarantee that on a busy network messages will arrive on time and in sequence.

This description of DiffServ's prioritization mechanisms is oversimplified, but a deeper discussion is beyond the scope of this text. Because of its simplicity and relatively low overhead, DiffServ is well suited to large, heavily trafficked networks.

CoS (Class of Service)

7	APPLICATION
6	PRESENTATION
5	SESSION
4	TRANSPORT
3	NETWORK
2	DATA LINK
1	PHYSICAL

CoS (Class of Service) is sometimes used synonymously with QoS, but there is an important distinction. The term *QoS* refers to techniques that are performed at various OSI layers via several protocols. By contrast, the term CoS (Class of Service) refers only to techniques performed at Layer 2, on Ethernet frames, and is one method of implementing QoS.

CoS is most often used to more efficiently route Ethernet traffic between VLANs. Frames that have been tagged (addressed to a specific VLAN) contain a 3-bit field in the frame header called the PCP (Priority Code Point). CoS works by setting these bits to one of eight levels ranging from 0 to 7, which indicates to the switch the level of priority the message should be given if the port is receiving more traffic than it can forward at any one time. Waiting messages are cached until the port can get to them, or discarded, depending on the class assignment for that frame.

A network's connectivity devices and clients must support the same set of protocols to achieve their QoS benefits. However, networks can—and often do—combine multiple QoS techniques.

Network Availability

1.4   Given a scenario, configure the appropriate IP addressing components.

1.5   Compare and contrast the characteristics of network topologies, types, and technologies.

2.3   Explain the purposes and use cases for advanced networking devices.

2.4   Explain the purposes of virtualization and network storage technologies.

3.2   Compare and contrast business continuity and disaster recovery concepts.

5.5   Given a scenario, troubleshoot common network service issues.

In the world of networking, the term **availability** refers to how consistently and reliably a connection, system, or other network resource can be accessed by authorized personnel. It's often expressed as a percentage, such as 98% or 99.5%.

The term **HA (high availability)** refers to a system that functions reliably nearly all the time. For example, a server that allows staff to log on and use its programs and data 99.999 percent of the time is considered highly available, whereas one that is functional only 99.9 percent of the time is significantly less available. In fact, the number of 9s in a system's availability rating is sometimes referred to colloquially as "four 9s" (99.99 percent) or "three 9s" (99.9 percent) availability. You might hear a network manager use the term in a statement such as, "We're a four 9s shop." This could be an impressive track record for a small ISP or a school's LMS (learning management system). For a hospital network, however, where lives are at stake, four nines likely wouldn't be enough.

Note 📎

Various cloud services and ISPs offer three nines, four nines, five nines, or better availability, depending on what's defined in their SLAs (service-level agreements). When shopping for cloud services, examine the SLA carefully so you'll know what aspects of a service are guaranteed available.

One way to consider availability is by measuring a system or network's uptime, which is the duration or percentage of time it functions normally between failures. As shown in Table 11-2, a system that experiences 99.999 percent uptime is *unavailable*, on average, only 5 minutes and 15 seconds per year.

Table 11-2 Availability and downtime equivalents

Availability	Downtime per day	Downtime per month	Downtime per year
99%	14 minutes, 23 seconds	7 hours, 18 minutes, 17 seconds	87 hours, 39 minutes, 29 seconds
99.9%	1 minute, 26 seconds	43 minutes, 49 seconds	8 hours, 45 minutes, 56 seconds
99.99%	8 seconds	4 minutes, 22 seconds	52 minutes, 35 seconds
99.999%	.4 seconds	26 seconds	5 minutes, 15 seconds

On a computer running Linux or UNIX, you can view the length of time your system has been running with the command `uptime`. On a Windows 10 system, uptime information is found in Task Manager.

Applying Concepts: Windows Task Manager

Windows 10 provides uptime data, along with a great deal of additional performance information, in Task Manager. Complete the following steps to view this information on a Windows 10 computer:

1. Right-click **Start** and click **Task Manager.**
2. On the **Performance** tab, examine the CPU and Memory utilization statistics. What is the current uptime?
3. Click **Open Resource Monitor** to view additional performance data and graphs. Be sure to take a look at the Listening Ports pane on the Network tab. You'll use this utility again in a Hands-On Project at the end of this chapter.

Fault Tolerance

A key factor in maintaining the availability of network resources is **fault tolerance**, or the capacity for a system to continue performing despite an unexpected hardware or software malfunction. The key to fault tolerance in network design is supplying multiple paths that data can use to travel from any one point to another. Therefore, if one connection or component fails, data can be rerouted over an alternate path.

To better understand the issues related to fault tolerance, it helps to know the difference between failures and faults as they apply to networks.

- *failure*—A deviation from a specified level of system performance for a given period of time. In other words, a failure occurs when something doesn't work as promised or as planned. For example, if your car breaks down on the highway, you can consider the breakdown to be a failure.
- *fault*—A malfunction of one component of a system. A fault can result in a failure. For example, the fault that caused your car to break down might be a leaking water pump. The goal of fault-tolerant systems is to prevent faults from progressing to failures.

Fault tolerance can be realized in varying degrees; the optimal level of fault tolerance for a system depends on how critical its services and files are to productivity. At the highest level of fault tolerance, a system remains unaffected by even the most drastic problem, such as a regional power outage. In this case, a backup power source, such as an electrical generator, is necessary to ensure fault tolerance. However, less dramatic faults, such as a malfunctioning NIC on a router, can still cause network outages, and you should guard against them.

Redundancy

Devices on a network typically have a calculated **MTBF (mean time between failures)**. This is the average amount of time that will pass for devices exactly like this one before the next failure is expected to occur. While any single device might experience a failure much sooner or later, vendors and technicians budget for repairs or replacement of devices based on the advertised MTBF. Once a device fails, there is an average amount of time required to repair the device. This is called **MTTR (mean time to repair)**, and this cost must also be taken into account. Figure 11-11 shows how these concepts are related.

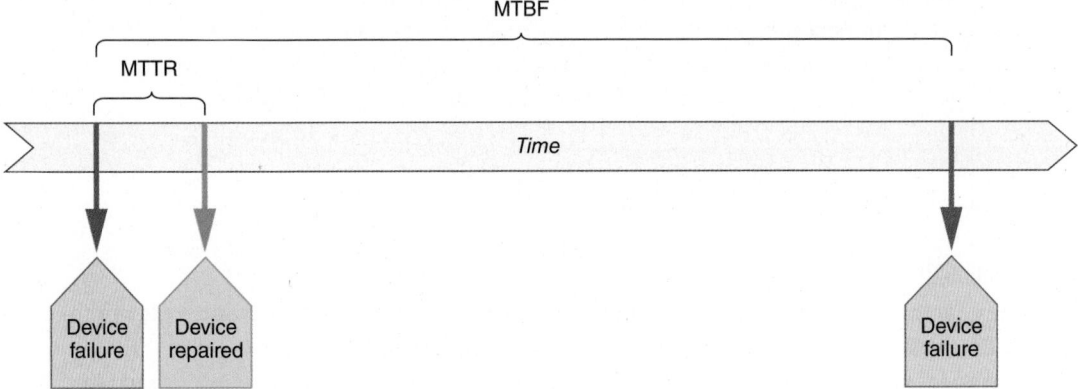

Figure 11-11 Every device eventually fails, it's just a question of when

MTBF, MTTR, and related concepts can all apply to services or systems as well. An ISP service might have an advertised MTBF and MTTR that are defined in the SLA. For example, any time your WAN connection goes down, the ISP might guarantee that it will be back up within two to four hours. Of course, these numbers vary according to provider, connection type, and subscription level, and should definitely be taken into account when selecting WAN service options. You'll learn more about WAN technologies later.

To help protect against faults and failures, networks are often designed with two or more of the same item, service, or connection filling the same role on the network. If one part, service, or connection fails, the other takes over. This is called **redundancy** and refers to an implementation in which more than one component is installed and ready to use for storing, processing, or transporting data. Redundancy is intended to eliminate single points of failure. To maintain high availability, you should ensure that critical network elements, such as your connection to the Internet or your file server's hard disk, are redundant. Some types of redundancy—for example, redundant sources of electrical power for a building—require large investments, so your organization should weigh the risks of losing connectivity or data against the cost of adding duplicate (or triplicate) components.

As you can see, the main disadvantage of redundancy is its cost. Redundancy is like a homeowner's insurance policy: You might never need to use it, but if you don't get it, the cost when you do need it can be much higher than your premiums. Redundant ISP services, for example, can be fairly costly. Compared to the cost to a business of not having Internet access if a trunk line is severed, however, the additional WAN interface might make sense. As a general rule, you should invest in connection redundancies for any connection that is absolutely necessary.

Even when dedicated links and VPN connections remain sound, a faulty device or interface in the data path can affect service for a user, a whole segment, or the whole network. To understand how to increase the fault tolerance of a connection from end to end, consider a typical T1 link to the Internet. Figure 11-12 provides a representation of this arrangement.

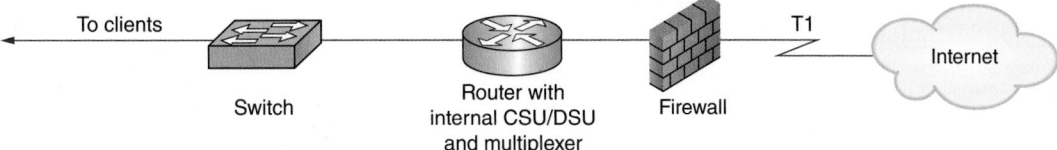

Figure 11-12   Single T1 connectivity

Notice the many single points of failure in the arrangement depicted in Figure 11-12. In addition to the T1 link failing—for example, if a backhoe accidentally cut a cable during road construction—any of the critical nodes in the following list could suffer a fault or failure and impair connectivity or performance: firewall, router, CSU/DSU, multiplexer, or switch. Figure 11-13 illustrates a network design that ensures full redundancy for all the components linking two locations via a T1. (You'll learn more about these components later).

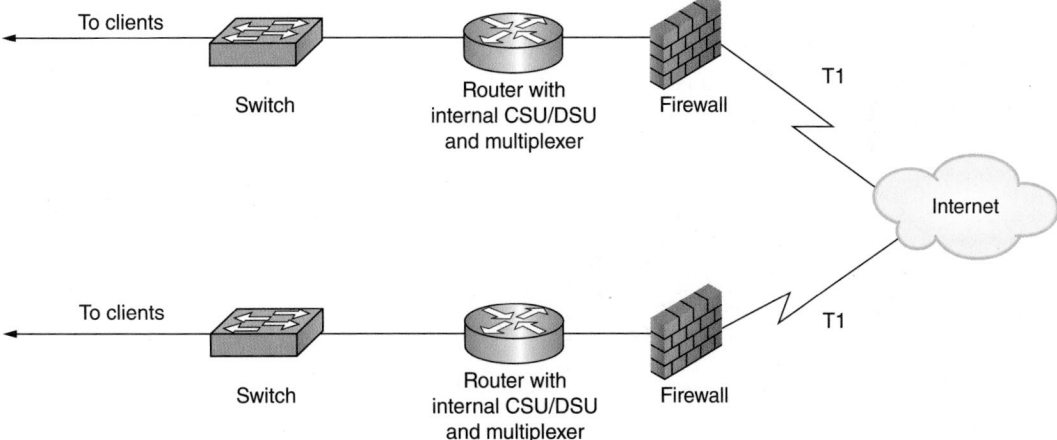

Figure 11-13   Fully redundant T1 connectivity

To achieve the utmost fault tolerance, each critical device requires redundant NICs, SFPs, power supplies, cooling fans, and processors, all of which should, ideally, be able to immediately assume the duties of an identical component, a capability known as **automatic failover**. If one NIC in a router fails, for example, automatic failover ensures that the router's other NIC can automatically handle the first NIC's responsibilities.

In cases where failover-capable components are impractical, you can provide some level of fault tolerance by using hot-swappable parts. Recall that the term *hot-swappable* refers to identical components that can be changed (or swapped) while a machine is still running (hot). There are two approaches to this:

- *hot spare*—A duplicate component that is already installed in a device and can assume the original component's functions in case that component fails.
- *cold spare*—A duplicate component that is not installed, but can be installed in case of a failure. Relying on a cold spare results in an interruption of service.

When you purchase switches or routers to support critical links, look for those that contain failover capable or hot-swappable components. As with other redundancy provisions, these features add to the cost of your device.

Redundant Links

Besides using redundant devices, you can also use redundant connections, or links, between devices. **Link aggregation** is the seamless combination of multiple network interfaces or ports to act as one logical interface, and can help solve problems like network bottlenecks. This implementation is also known by a variety of other terms, such as **port aggregation** on Cisco devices, **NIC teaming** on Windows devices, and a variety of others such as bonding, bundling, or Cisco's EtherChannel. Regardless of the terms used, link aggregation causes two or more NICs to work in tandem handling traffic between two or more devices (usually switches and servers). All the physical links involved in creating the one logical link are called a LAG (link aggregation group), bundle, or team, as shown in Figure 11-14. This configuration allows for three major advantages:

- Increased total throughput
- Automatic failover between the aggregated NICs
- **Load balancing**, which is a distribution of traffic over multiple components or links to optimize performance and fault tolerance

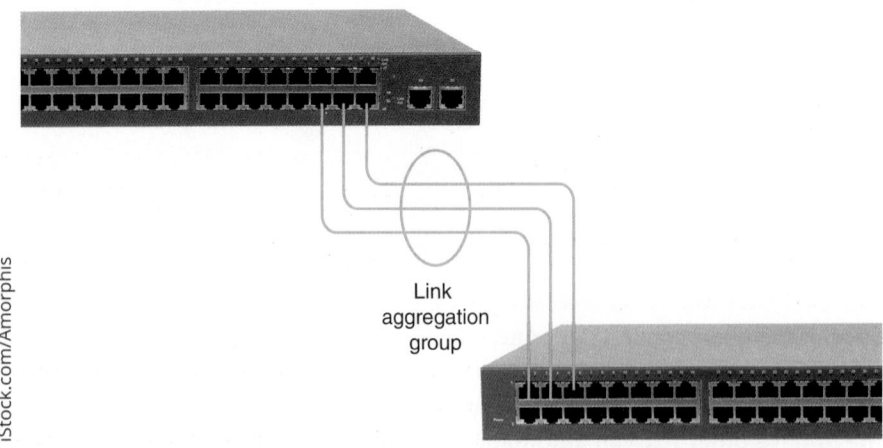

Link
aggregation
group

iStock.com/Amorphis

Figure 11-14 Two switches treat these three physical links as one logical link

Link aggregation isn't about speed of network traffic so much as bandwidth, or total potential to handle more network traffic at one time. Because packets and, generally, sessions, aren't separated between the duplicate connections, the benefits of link aggregation are primarily noticed on busy networks. For example, if a single session is all handled on one of the aggregate connections, that session doesn't reach its destination any faster. However, if two sessions are being transmitted at the same time, one session can traverse one of the aggregated links, and the other session can traverse the other link at the same time. Neither session has to wait on the other (see Figure 11-15).

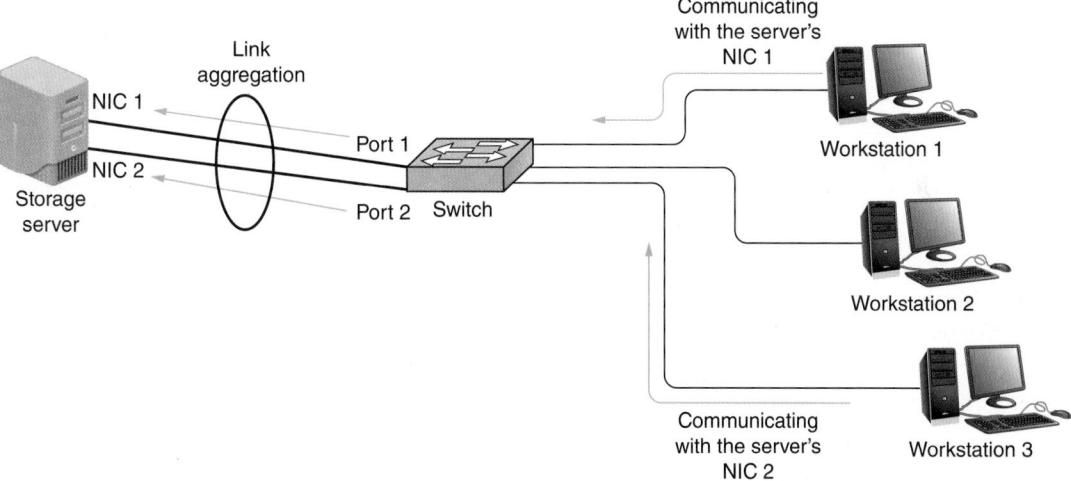

Figure 11-15   Link aggregation allows two workstations to communicate with a server at the same time

For multiple NICs or ports to use link aggregation, they must be properly configured in each device's operating system. For example, all involved interfaces must be configured for full duplex, and have the same speed, VLAN, and MTU settings. Many manufacturers now use **LACP (Link Aggregation Control Protocol)**, which was initially defined by IEEE's 802.3ad standard and currently defined by the 802.1AX standard (notice the change in working group from 802.3 to 802.1). LACP dynamically coordinates communications between hosts on aggregated connections, kind of like what DHCP does for IP addressing. Most of these devices offer similar configuration options, such as:

- *static configuration*—Both hosts are manually configured to handle the division of labor between the redundant links according to particular rules without the ability to compensate for errors.
- *passive mode*—The port passively listens for LACP-defined link aggregation requests, but will not initiate the request.
- *active mode*—The port is set to automatically and actively negotiate for link aggregation using LACP. This allows for fault tolerance should one or more

links fail, as LACP will automatically reconfigure active links to compensate. In reality, this is the most common configuration for all ports involved in link aggregation, and provides the most protection against link misconfigurations or failures.

Figure 11-16 shows the link aggregation options on a SOHO router. Here, you can aggregate two or more of the router's four LAN ports, depending on which ones are currently connected to another device.

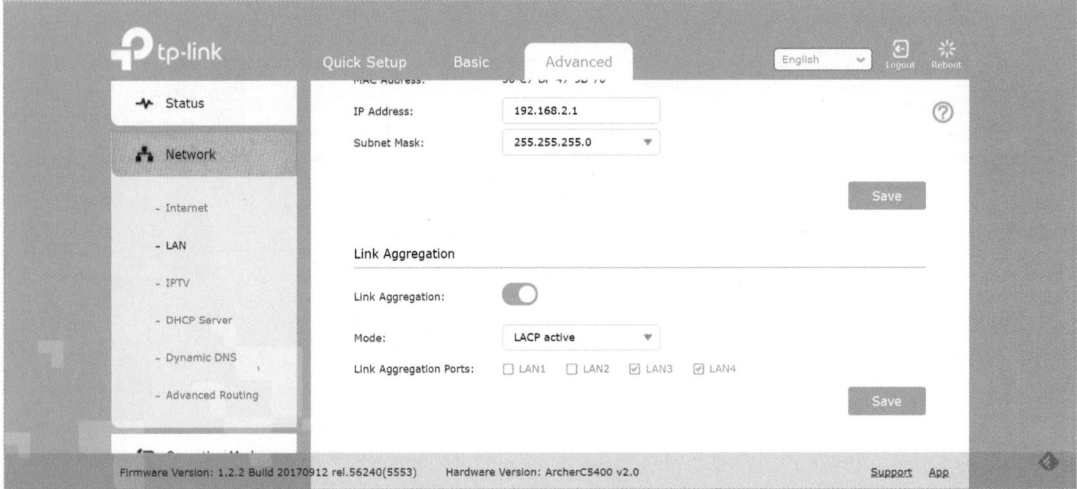

Figure 11-16   Aggregate LAN3 and LAN4 to a network server
Source: TP-Link Technologies Co., Ltd.

More sophisticated load balancing for all types of servers can be achieved by using a **load balancer**, a device dedicated to the task of distributing traffic intelligently among multiple computers. It can determine which among a pool of servers is experiencing the most traffic before forwarding the request to a server with lower utilization. This server pool might be configured as a cluster. **Clustering** refers to the technique of grouping multiple devices so they appear as a single device to the rest of the network. Clustering can be configured with groups of servers, routers, or applications. Although it usually accompanies load balancing, it doesn't have to.

Let's look at an example of how clustering and load balancing might work. Suppose you have two web servers that, together, host a single website (see Figure 11-17). To access the website, web clients direct requests to a single **VIP (virtual IP address)** which represents the entire cluster. To the client, the cluster looks like a single web server. On the back end, though, a load balancer directs traffic evenly between the web servers, and both servers have access to all the data needed to respond to any web page requests from clients. The clients, however, are not aware that two physical machines are at work. As far as a client is concerned, it's talking with a single server.

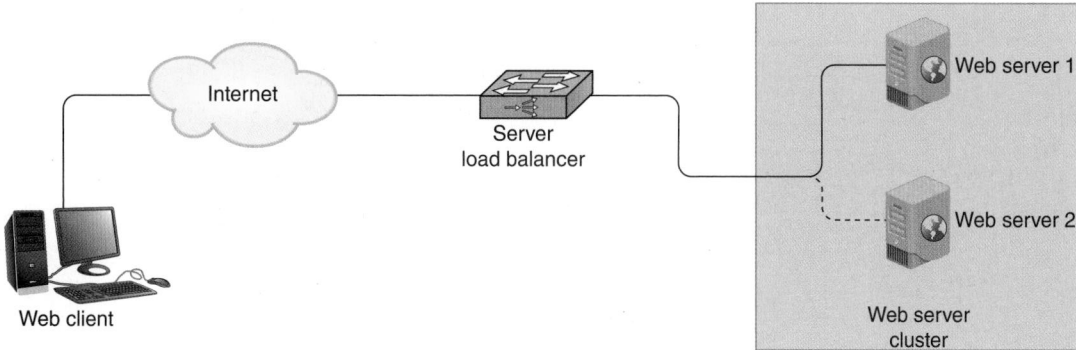

Figure 11-17   **Two web servers work together in a cluster to host a single website**

In this way, a popular website can respond more quickly to the high number of visitors interacting with the site at any one time. Each web server also serves as a backup to the other one. Should one server fail, the other can take over the full load until the malfunctioning server can be fixed or replaced.

Applying Concepts: Add a Virtual IP Address to Windows 10

You can add multiple, virtual IP addresses to a Windows computer. This is not the same use case as previously described with load balancing. Instead, it might be used to assign a different IP address to multiple instances of the same service running on a single machine. For example, you might have three different websites running on one machine, and each website would need its own IP address. To see how to add multiple IP addresses to one network adapter on a Windows computer, complete the following steps:

1. Use Command Prompt to determine your computer's current IP address, subnet mask, and default gateway. What information did you find?
2. Open the **Network and Sharing Center**. Click **Change adapter settings**.
3. Open the properties box for the active network connection. Then open the properties box for TCP/IPv4.
4. Configure a static IP address using the information you gathered in Step 1. Do *not* click OK. Instead, click **Advanced**.
5. On the IP Settings tab, under IP addresses, click **Add**, as shown in Figure 11-18. Enter a second IP address in the same subnet as the original IP address and using the same default gateway. Click **Add**.

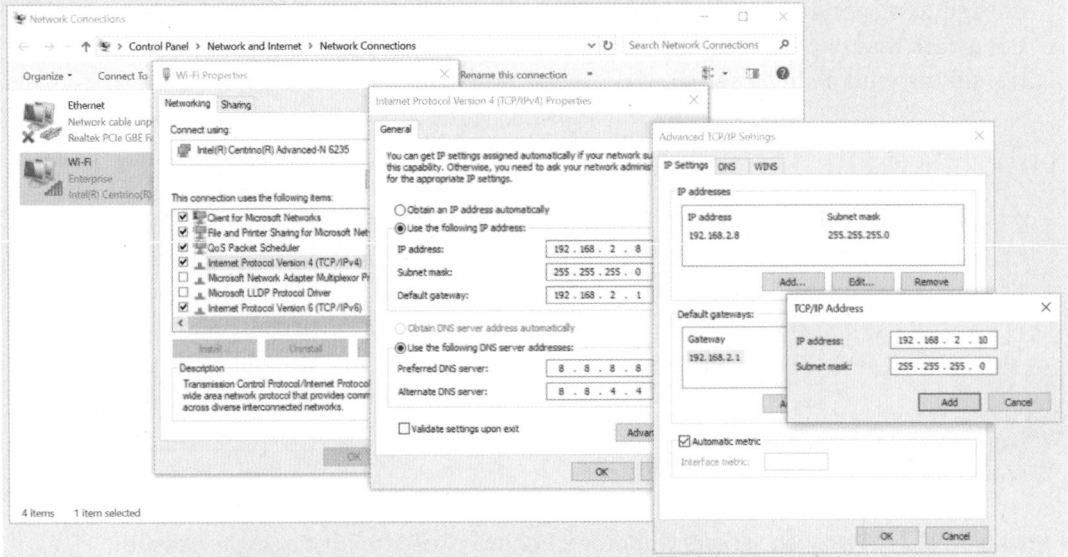

Figure 11-18 Add multiple, virtual IP addresses to a single, physical network connection

6. Click **OK** three times, and close all open windows except Command Prompt. Run **ipconfig** again to determine your current IP addresses, subnet mask, and default gateway. What information is reported this time?

7. Ping your VIP. Was it successful?

8. If you have another computer on this subnet, ping each of the first computer's two IP addresses from the other computer. Are the pings successful? Why do you think this is?

9. What steps do you need to take to return your computer to the IP configuration it had when you started? If desired, do this now.

In some cases, you might have a set of IP addresses to share among multiple hosts. For example, if you have multiple routers that support multiple interfaces, and you want to interlace those routers as a fault-tolerant cluster, you would have a list of several IP addresses pointing to the cluster as a group. This is accomplished with **CARP (Common Address Redundancy Protocol)**, which allows a pool of computers or interfaces to share one or more IP addresses. This pool is known as a group of redundancy or redundancy group. When using CARP, one device, acting as the group master, receives requests for an IP address, then parcels out the requests to one of several devices in the group.

Network+ Exam Tip ⓘ

CARP is a free alternative to **VRRP (Virtual Router Redundancy Protocol)**, or Cisco's propriety version called **HSRP (Hot Standby Routing Protocol)**. Although VRRP and HSRP function somewhat differently than CARP and are used solely for routers, the general idea is the same.

Clustering servers is used in many different ways to pool resources on a network and provide redundancy for fault tolerance. Another scenario is when pooling servers that host VMs. In a server cluster, the VMs are configured with varying amounts of redundancy to provide fault tolerance in the event that one server fails. This can also allow for—and, in fact, necessitates—more efficient networking solutions between the VMs. Recall that VMs connect to a network via a vSwitch (virtual switch) that exists in the host's hypervisor. In a server cluster, a single, distributed vSwitch can service VMs across multiple hosts, as illustrated in Figure 11-19. This is called **distributed switching**. It centralizes control of the VMs, simplifies network operations, and minimizes the chances for configuration errors. To do this, an agent is installed on each physical host and is then controlled by a supervisor module in the distributed switch. Examples of distributed switch products are VMware's VDS (vSphere Distributed Switch) that is native to its vSphere platform, and a variety of third-party products, including Cisco's Nexus 1000v.

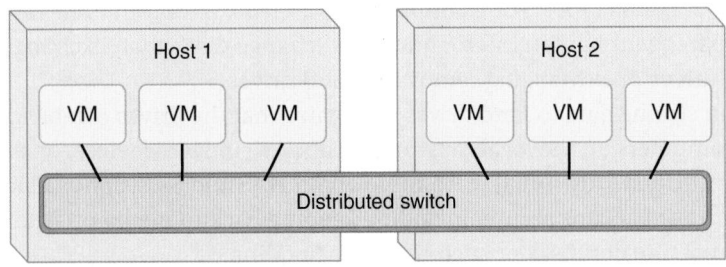

Figure 11-19   Distributed switching centralizes management of VM network connections

Data Backup and Storage

You have probably heard or even spoken the axiom, "If you can't do without it, back it up!" A **backup** is a copy of data or program files created for archiving or safekeeping. Maintaining good backups is essential for providing fault tolerance and reliability.

When designing and configuring your backup system, keep these points in mind:

Step 1:   Decide what to back up. Besides the obvious folders used to hold user and application data, you might also want to back up user profile folders and folders that hold configuration files for your applications, services, routers, switches, access points, gateways, and firewalls.

Step 2:   Select backup methods. Consider cloud backups, where third-party vendors manage the backup hardware and software somewhere on the Internet. In general, cloud backups are more expensive and reliable than other methods. Because cloud backups are not stored at your local facility, you have the added advantage that backups are protected in case your entire facility is destroyed.

For on-site backups, use only proven and reliable backup software and hardware. For your backup system, now is not the time to experiment with the latest and greatest technology.

- Verify that backup hardware and software are compatible with your existing network hardware and software.
- Make sure your backup software uses data error-checking techniques.
- Verify that your backup storage media or system provides sufficient capacity, with plenty of room to spare, and can also accommodate your network's growth.
- Be aware of how your backup process affects the system, normal network functioning, and your users' computing habits.
- As you make purchasing decisions, make sure you know how much the backup methods and media cost relative to the amount of data they can store.
- Be aware of the degree of manual intervention required to manage the backups, such as exchanging backup media on a regular basis or backing up operating systems on servers that run around the clock.
- Make wise choices for storage media, considering advantages and disadvantages of media types. For example, optical media (DVDs and Blu-ray) require more frequent human intervention to exchange disks than exchanging tapes in tape drives or exchanging removable hard drives.
- When storing data to hard drives, recognize that the drives can be installed on computers on the local network, on a WAN, in NAS devices, or even on a sophisticated SAN. You'll learn more about NAS and SAN options shortly.
- Keep your backups secure, including keeping backup media off-site in the event of a major disaster such as fire or flooding.

Step 3: Decide what types of backup will be done regularly (see Figure 11-20):

- *full backup*—Backs up everything every time a backup is done
- *incremental backup*—Backs up only data that has changed since the last backup
- *differential backup*—Backs up data that has changed since the last full backup

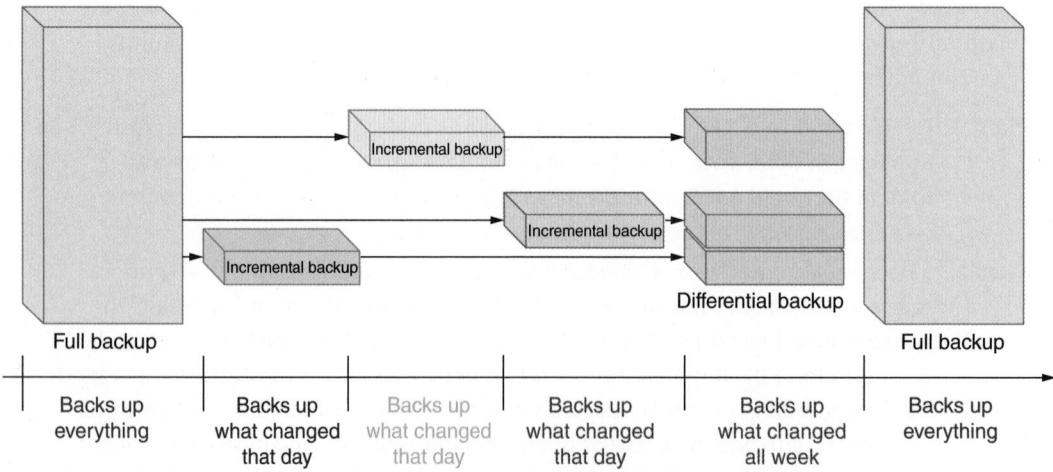

Figure 11-20   Incremental and differential backups demand fewer resources

Note

The OS knows which files to back up for incremental and differential backups because it maintains an archive bit in the attributes for each file.

Step 4:   Decide how often backups are needed. In general, you want to back up data after about four hours of actual data entry. Depending on user habits, this might mean you back up daily or weekly, although, by default, Windows 10 performs incremental backups hourly. Most organizations perform daily backups, which happen in the middle of the night when there's less network activity.

Step 5:   Develop a backup schedule. For example, you might perform a full backup every Thursday night and an incremental backup daily. You might take backup media off-site every Friday and overwrite backups (or destroy or rotate your backup media) every six months. You also must establish policies governing who is responsible for the backups, what information should be recorded in backup logs, and which backup logs are retained and for how long. Be sure to check relevant laws and regulations, as some types of data (such as medical or financial data) must be kept for a number of years.

Step 6:   Regularly verify backups are being performed. From time to time, depending on how often your data changes and how critical the information is, you should attempt to recover some critical files from your backup media. Many network administrators attest that the darkest hour of their career was when they were asked to retrieve critical files from a backup, and found that no backup data existed because their backup system never worked in the first place!

Note

When identifying the types of data to back up, remember to include configuration files for devices such as routers, switches, access points, gateways, and firewalls.

You just learned about three different types of time-delayed backups: full, incremental, and differential. Data protection strategies can employ more granular backup schemes as well, saving changes to files almost immediately after you make them. For example, a **snapshot** is essentially a frequently saved, incremental backup of the data's state at a specific point in time, even as the data continues to be modified by users. Unlike true backups, snapshots typically are not stored in a separate location, and so can't be used to replace a more robust backup system. Sometimes a snapshot only contains information about changes made since the last backup, and so could not fully restore lost data.

Data backups provide a way to recover data that is lost. Backups contain one or more complete copies of the data, are stored in a separate location, and are usually saved in a different format and/or media than the original data (such as on tape storage rather than on a hard drive). This is not the same thing as redundancy, though. Network storage technologies provide hardware redundancy and high-speed access to large amounts of data. Here are some significant differences between data backups and network storage technologies:

- Network storage technologies don't necessarily save multiple copies of the same data.
- Network storage technologies don't usually store data in different geographical locations.
- If there are multiple copies of the data, network storage technologies save those copies in the same format and on the same type of media (such as hard drives).

Let's look at two primary approaches to network storage and the redundancies these systems provide.

NAS (Network Attached Storage)

NAS (network attached storage) is a specialized storage device or group of storage devices that provides centralized, fault-tolerant data storage for a network. You can think of NAS as a unique type of server dedicated to data sharing. NAS devices, such as the one shown in Figure 11-21, offer some significant advantages on a network:

- *optimization*—Compared to a typical file server, a NAS device contains its own file system that is optimized for saving and serving files. Because of this optimization, NAS reads and writes from its disk(s) significantly faster than other types of servers.
- *adaptability*—Because NAS devices can store and retrieve data for any type of client (providing the client can run TCP/IP), NAS is appropriate for networks that use a mix of different operating systems, multimedia types, and even IoT components that require centralized storage space.
- *expansion*—NAS hardware can be easily expanded without interrupting service. You can physically install a new hard drive without shutting down the system. The NAS device recognizes the added storage and immediately adds it to its pool of available reading and writing space.

A NAS server's pool of storage space is provided by multiple hard disk drives. These disks can be configured with a form of RAID (redundant array of inexpensive disks or redundant array of independent disks) for redundancy and improved performance. The four most common types of RAID are:

- *RAID 0*—Data is striped—or written across—multiple disks to improve performance (Figure 11-22). RAID 0 provides no real redundancy, in that only one copy of data is stored.
- *RAID 1*—Data is mirrored—or duplicated—on multiple disks to provide fault tolerance (see Figure 11-23). If one copy is lost, the other copy is still available.

Figure 11-21   Add or replace hard drives inside a NAS

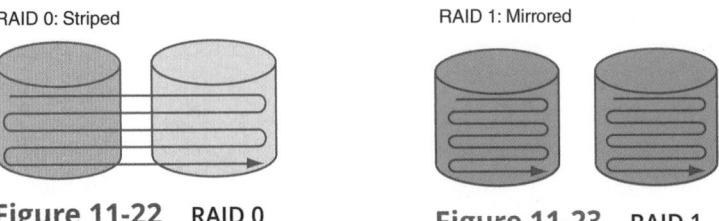

Figure 11-22   RAID 0   **Figure 11-23**   RAID 1

- *RAID 5*—Data is striped across three or more drives, and parity information is added to the data (see Figure 11-24). Parity checking can be used to recreate data from any one drive if that drive fails, even though only one copy of the data is stored.

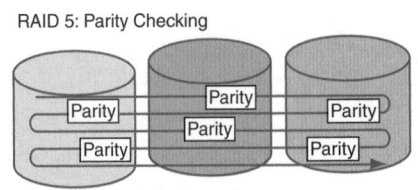

Figure 11-24   RAID 5

- *RAID 10 (pronounced "RAID one zero")*—Using four or more disks, data is mirrored within each pair of disks, and then striped to multiple pairs of disks (see Figure 11-25).

RAID 1: Two pairs of mirrored disks

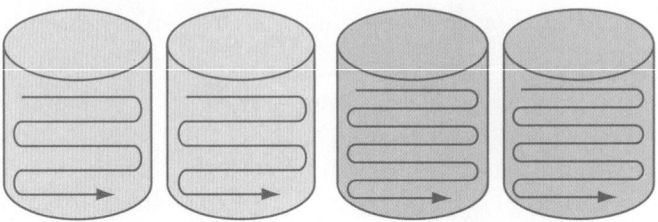

RAID 10: Mirrored and striped

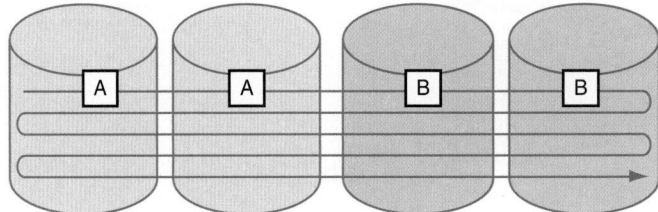

Figure 11-25 RAID 1 and RAID 10

NAS uses file-level storage for its data. This means there must be some kind of file system formatted on the disks—file locations are documented through a directory tree of some kind. This is the same storage architecture that Windows, Linux, and macOS computers use. Files are stored in folders that are stored in folders, and so on.

Like the web and VM servers and routers we discussed earlier, NAS servers can also be clustered. For this to work, the NAS file system is distributed throughout the cluster. Files stored on any device within the cluster can be accessed through the distributed file system and a single connection point.

Due to the organizational structure required to manage data by files, more efficient alternatives have been developed. One of these options is block level storage. While block level storage also has a file system, it's a flat structure, not hierarchical. Data is stored as same-size blocks on storage drives. Systems that use block level storage require different connectivity mechanisms for clients to access the data. Let's look at how this works in SANs (storage area networks).

SAN (Storage Area Network)

Large enterprises that require even faster access to data and larger amounts of storage might prefer a SAN (storage area network) over NAS. Whereas NAS is a device or group of devices attached directly to a network switch, a **SAN (storage area network)** is a distinct network of storage devices that communicate directly with each other and with other networks.

In a typical SAN, multiple storage devices are connected to multiple, identical servers. This type of architecture is similar to a mesh topology, which is the most fault-tolerant type of topology possible. If one storage device within a SAN suffers a fault, data is automatically retrieved from elsewhere in the SAN. If one server in a SAN suffers a fault, another server steps in to perform its functions.

SANs are not only extremely fault tolerant, they are also extremely fast. To do this, SANs use one of these technologies:

- **FC (Fibre Channel)** is a storage networking architecture that runs separately from Ethernet networks to maximize speed of data storage and access. Although FC can run over copper cables, fiber-optic cable is much more commonly used. Fibre Channel requires special hardware, which makes it an expensive storage connection technology. FC switches connect servers with each other and the outside network. Instead of NICs, FC devices communicate through HBAs (host bus adapters). At the time of this writing, FC networks use an alternative to link aggregation called MPIO (Multipath I/O) to achieve speeds as high as 128GFC (Gbps Fibre Channel). Specifications are approved for speeds up to 256GFC, and expected to be available on the market in 2019. Figure 11-26 shows a Fibre Channel SAN connected to a traditional Ethernet network. Besides being expensive, Fibre Channel requires extensive training for IT personnel to support it.

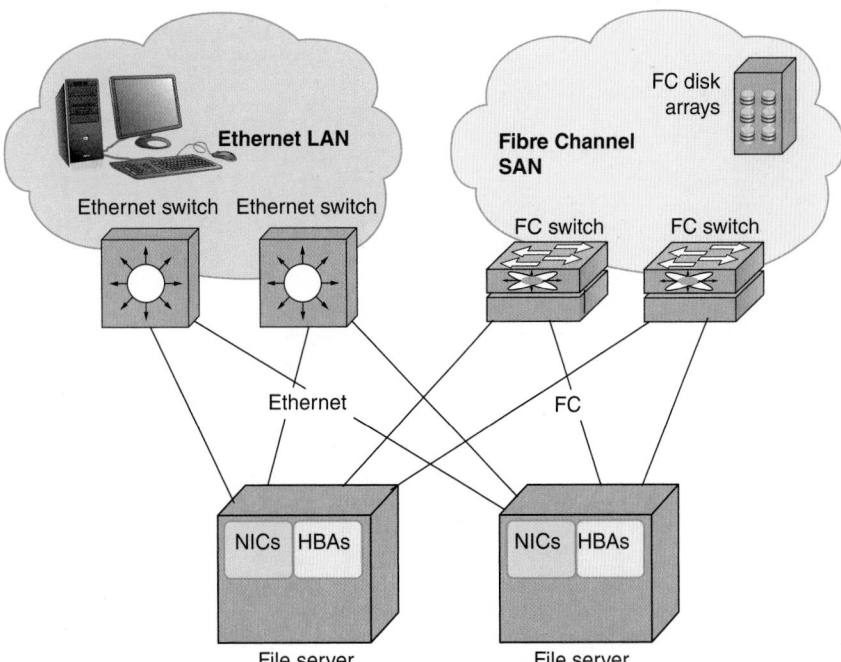

Figure 11-26   A Fibre Channel SAN connected to an Ethernet LAN

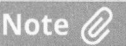

Note

You can get updated information about Fibre Channel and its related technology, FCoE (Fibre Channel over Ethernet), at *fibrechannel.org*.

- **FCoE (Fibre Channel over Ethernet)** is a newer technology that allows FC to travel over Ethernet hardware and connections. To do this, the FC frame is encapsulated inside an FCoE frame, which is then encapsulated inside an Ethernet frame, as illustrated in Figure 11-27. This preserves much of the higher speed capabilities of FC, along with the convenience and cost-efficiency of using existing Ethernet network equipment, as shown in Figure 11-28. With the installation of CNAs (converged network adapters), FCoE switches can connect to network servers and to switches for both the LAN and the SAN.

Figure 11-27 FCoE encapsulation

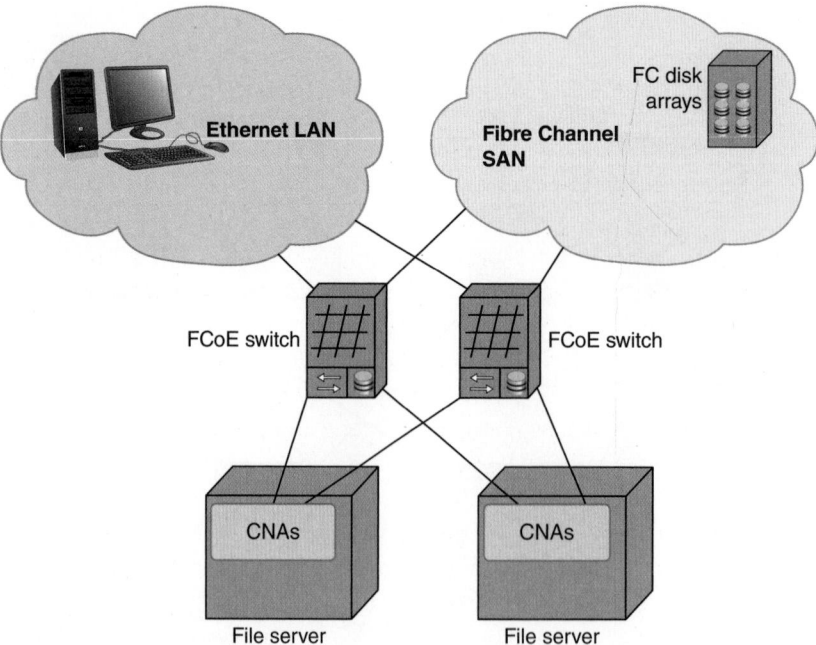

Figure 11-28 A SAN using FCoE to connect to a LAN

- **iSCSI (Internet SCSI)**, pronounced "i-scuzzy," is a Transport layer protocol that runs on top of TCP to allow fast transmissions over LANs, WANs, and the Internet. It can work on a twisted-pair Ethernet network with ordinary Ethernet NICs. iSCSI is an evolution of SCSI (Small Computer System Interface), which is a fast transmission standard used by internal hard drives and operating systems in file servers. The advantages of iSCSI over Fibre Channel are that it is not as expensive, can run on the already established Ethernet LAN by installing iSCSI software (called an iSCSI initiator) on network clients and servers, and does not require as much special training for IT personnel. Some network administrators configure iSCSI to use jumbo frames on the Ethernet LAN. iSCSI architecture is very similar to FC. The primary difference is that Ethernet equipment and interfaces can be used throughout the storage network. In fact, this is the primary advantage of iSCSI over other options, making it relatively straightforward to implement.
- **IB (InfiniBand)**, like FC, requires specialized network hardware. Although it's very fast, InfiniBand tends to serve a few niche markets rather than being widely available. IB falls on the difficult end of the installation and configuration spectrum, and runs on the expensive side as well.

A SAN can be installed in a location separate from the LAN it serves. For example, remote SANs can be kept in an ISP's data center, which can provide greater security and fault tolerance and also allows an organization to outsource the management of its SAN.

SANs are highly scalable and have a very high fault tolerance, massive storage capabilities, and fast data access. SANs are best suited to environments with huge quantities of data that must always be quickly available.

Power Management

Part of managing a network's availability involves managing power sources to account for outages and fluctuations. No matter where you live, you have probably experienced a complete loss of power (a blackout) or a temporary dimming of lights (a brownout). Such fluctuations in power are frequently caused by forces of nature, such as hurricanes, tornadoes, or ice storms. They might also occur when a utility company performs maintenance or construction tasks. Power surges, even small ones, can cause serious damage to sensitive computer equipment and can be one of the most frustrating sources of network problems.

Before you learn how to manage power sources so as to avoid these problems, first arm yourself with an understanding of the nature of an electric circuit and some electrical components that manage electricity.

Applying Concepts: AC and DC Power and Converters

An electric circuit provides a medium for the transfer of electrical power over a closed loop. If the loop is broken in any way, the circuit won't conduct electricity. In a circuit, DC (direct current) flows at a steady rate in only one direction. By contrast, AC (alternating current) continually switches direction on the circuit.

A flashlight, for example, uses DC. The batteries in a flashlight have positive and negative poles, and the current always flows at a steady rate in the same direction between those poles, as shown on the left side of Figure 11-29. AC, however, travels in compression waves, similar to the coils of a Slinky®, alternating direction on the power line back and forth between the source and destination. Just as waves can travel across a huge body of water, power moving in an AC wave pattern can travel efficiently for long distances, as illustrated on the right side of Figure 11-29. Because AC power can be conducted at very high voltages, the source of the current can be far away from the point of use, where it is transformed to lower voltages. Consider the power running a typical laptop computer. AC power comes from the power station through the wall outlet to the laptop's power supply, which converts it to DC before the laptop can use it.

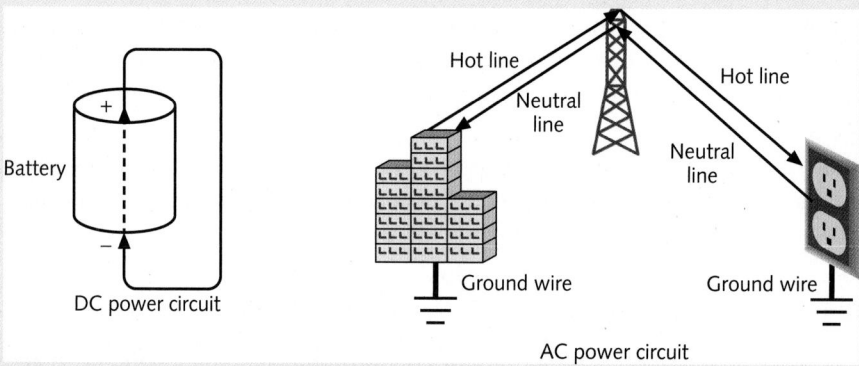

Figure 11-29   DC circuit and AC circuit

Note

For AC power to travel from the electric company to your house, three wires are required. The hot wire carries electricity from the power station to your house. The neutral wire carries unused power from your house back to the power station. A third wire, the ground wire, is used to channel the electric charge in case of a short. These three wires are illustrated and labeled in Figure 11-29.

You're now ready to investigate the types of power fluctuations, or flaws, that network administrators should prepare for. Then you'll learn about alternate power sources, such as a UPS (uninterruptible power supply) or an electrical generator that can compensate for power loss.

Power Flaws

Whatever the cause, power loss or less-than-optimal power cannot be tolerated by networks. The following list describes power flaws that can damage your equipment:

- *surge*—A momentary increase in voltage due to lightning strikes, solar flares, or electrical problems. Surges might last only a few thousandths of a second, but can degrade a computer's power supply. Surges are common. You can guard against surges by making sure every computer device is plugged into a surge protector, which redirects excess voltage away from the device to a ground, thereby protecting the device from harm. Without surge protectors, systems would be subjected to multiple surges each year.
- *noise*—Fluctuation in voltage levels caused by other devices on the network or EMI. Some noise is unavoidable on an electrical circuit, but excessive noise can cause a power supply to malfunction, immediately corrupting program or data files and gradually damaging motherboards and other computer circuits. If you've ever turned on fluorescent lights or a microwave oven and noticed the lights dim, you have probably introduced noise into the electrical system. Power that is free from noise is called *clean* power. To make sure power is clean, a circuit must pass through an electrical filter.
- *brownout*—A momentary decrease in voltage; also known as a sag. An overtaxed electrical system can cause brownouts, which you might recognize in your home as a dimming of the lights. Such voltage decreases can cause computers or applications to fail and potentially corrupt data.
- *blackout*—A complete power loss. A blackout could cause significant damage to your network. For example, if a server loses power while files are open and processes are running, its NOS might be damaged so extensively that the server cannot restart and the NOS must be reinstalled from scratch. A backup power source, however, can provide power long enough for the server to shut down properly and avoid harm.

UPS (Uninterruptible Power Supply)

A **UPS (uninterruptible power supply)** is a battery-operated power source directly attached to one or more devices and to a power supply, such as a wall outlet, that prevents undesired fluctuations of the wall outlet's AC power from harming the device or interrupting its services. A power supply issue may be long in developing, with on-again, off-again symptoms for some time before the power issue finally solidifies and reveals itself. A good UPS in each data closet will help prevent these kinds of problems from affecting the entire network at once. Each critical workstation should also be equipped with a UPS or some other battery backup, which can also help to protect the computers themselves.

UPSes are classified into two general categories: standby and online.

- *standby UPS, also called an SPS (standby power supply)*—Provides continuous voltage to a device by switching virtually instantaneously to the battery when it detects a loss of power from the wall outlet. Upon restoration of power, the standby UPS switches the device back to AC power. The problem with standby UPSes is that, in the brief amount of time it takes the UPS to discover that power from the wall outlet has faltered, a device may have already detected the power loss and shut down or restarted. Technically, a standby UPS doesn't provide continuous power; for this reason, it is sometimes called an offline UPS. Nevertheless, standby UPSes may prove adequate even for critical network devices, such as servers, routers, and gateways. They cost significantly less than online UPSes.

- *online UPS*—Uses the AC power from the wall outlet to continuously charge its battery, while providing power to a network device through its battery. In other words, a server connected to an online UPS always relies on the UPS battery for its electricity. Because the server never needs to switch from the wall outlet's power to the UPS's power, there is no risk of momentarily losing service. Also, because the UPS always provides the power, it can handle noise, surges, and sags before the power reaches the attached device. As you can imagine, online UPSes are more expensive than standby UPSes. Figure 11-30 shows some online UPSes installed on a rack in a data room.

UPSes vary widely in the type of power aberrations they can rectify, the length of time they can provide power, and the number of devices they can support. Of course, they also vary widely in price. UPSes intended for home and small office use are designed merely to keep your workstation running long enough for you to properly shut it down in case of a blackout. Other UPSes perform sophisticated operations such as line filtering or conditioning, power supply monitoring, and error notification. To decide which UPS is right for your network, consider a number of factors:

- *amount of power needed*—The more power required by your device, the more powerful the UPS must be. Electrical power is measured in VAs (volt-amperes), also called volt-amps. A VA is the product of the voltage and current (measured in amps) of the electricity on a line. To determine approximately how many VAs your device requires, you can use the following conversion: 1.4 volt-amps=1 watt (W). A desktop computer, for example, may use a 200 W power

Figure 11-30   Online UPSes installed on a rack

supply, and, therefore, requires a UPS capable of at least 280 VA to keep the CPU running in case of a blackout. A medium-sized server with a monitor and external tape drive might use 402 W, thus requiring a UPS capable of providing at least 562 VA power. Determining your power needs can be a challenge. You must account for your existing equipment and consider how you might upgrade the supported device(s) over the next several years. Consider consulting with your equipment manufacturer to obtain recommendations on your power needs.

- *period of time to keep a device running*—The longer you anticipate needing a UPS to power your device, the more powerful your UPS must be. For example, a medium-sized server that relies on a 574 VA UPS to remain functional for 20 minutes needs an 1100 VA UPS to remain functional for 90 minutes. To determine how long your device might require power from a UPS, research the length of typical power outages in your area.
- *line conditioning*—A UPS should offer surge suppression to protect against surges, and line conditioning (a type of filtering) to guard against line noise. A UPS that provides line conditioning includes special noise filters that remove line noise. The manufacturer's technical specifications should indicate the amount of filtration required for each UPS. Noise suppression is expressed in dB levels (decibel) at a specific frequency (KHz or MHz). The higher the decibel level, the greater the protection.
- *cost*—Prices for good UPSes vary widely, depending on the unit's size and extra features. A relatively small UPS that can power one server for 5 to 10 minutes might cost between $100 and $300. A large UPS that can power a sophisticated router for three hours might cost up to $5000. Still larger UPSes, which can power an entire data center for several hours, can cost hundreds of thousands of dollars. On a critical system, you should not try to cut costs by buying an off-brand, potentially unreliable, or weak UPS.

As with other large purchases, research several UPS manufacturers and their products before selecting a UPS. Make sure the manufacturer provides a warranty and lets you test the UPS with your equipment. Testing UPSes with your equipment is an important part of the decision-making process. Popular UPS manufacturers are APC, Emerson, Falcon, and Tripp Lite.

Note

After installing a new UPS, follow the manufacturer's instructions for performing initial tests to verify the UPS's proper functioning. Make it a practice to retest the UPS monthly or quarterly to be sure it will perform as expected in case of a sag or blackout.

Increasingly, organizations are adding power redundancy—especially for critical servers—by installing **dual power supplies** in their servers, thereby giving each server at least one backup in case a power supply fails. Each power supply is capable of handling the full power demands of the server if needed. Some companies are also running **redundant power circuits** to their data centers so if, for example, a circuit breaker trips, the servers can keep running on the other power circuit. Racks often have multiple UPSes installed as well.

Generators

A generator serves as a backup power source, providing power redundancy in the event of a total blackout. Generators can be powered by diesel, liquid propane gas, natural gas, or steam. Standard generators provide power that is relatively free from noise and are used in environments that demand consistently reliable service, such as an ISP's or telecommunications carrier's data center. In fact, in those environments, they are typically combined with large UPSes to ensure that clean power is always available. In the event of a power failure, the UPS supplies electricity until the generator starts and reaches its full capacity, typically no more than three minutes. If your organization relies on a generator for backup power, be certain to check fuel levels and quality regularly.

Figure 11-31 illustrates the power infrastructure of a network (such as a data center's) that uses both a generator and dual UPSes. Because a generator produces DC power, it must contain a component to convert the power to AC before the power can be released to the existing AC infrastructure that distributes power in a data center.

Before choosing a generator, first calculate your organization's crucial electrical demands to determine the generator's optimal size. Also estimate how long the generator might be required to power your building. Depending on the amount of power draw, a high-capacity generator can supply power for several days. Gas or diesel generators can cost between $10,000 and $3,000,000 (for the largest industrial types). For a company such as an ISP that stands to lose up to $1,000,000 per minute if its data facilities fail completely, a multimillion-dollar investment to ensure available power is a wise choice. Smaller businesses, however, might choose the more economical solution of renting an electrical generator. To find out more about options for renting or purchasing generators in your area, contact your local electrical utility.

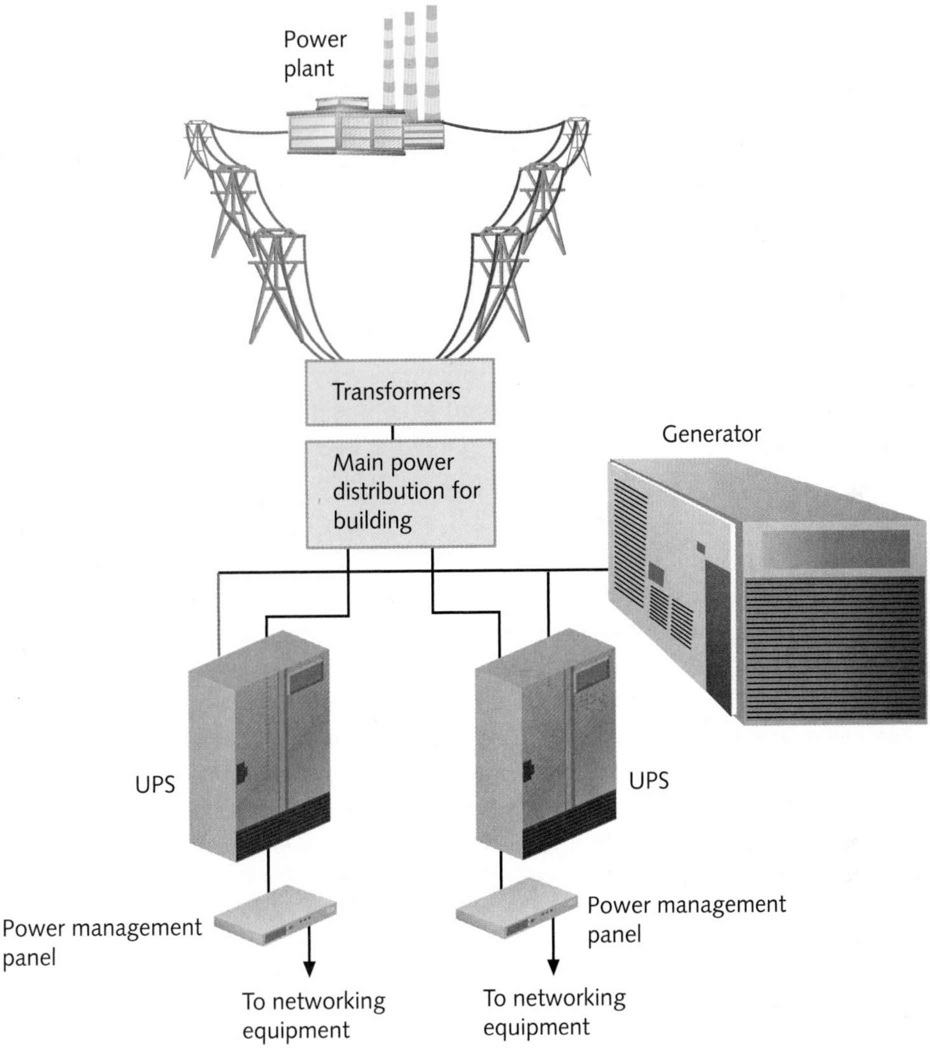

Power plant

Transformers

Main power distribution for building

Generator

UPS

UPS

Power management panel

Power management panel

To networking equipment

To networking equipment

Figure 11-31   UPSes and a generator in a network design

Response and Recovery

 **Certification**

3.2   Compare and contrast business continuity and disaster recovery concepts.

3.5   Identify policies and best practices.

Despite every precaution, disasters and security breaches do happen. Training and preparation can make all the difference in your company's ability to respond and adapt to these situations. In order to be prepared, let's discuss the spectrum of possibilities and how you can anticipate your network's and users' needs in various situations:

- *incident*—Any event, large or small, that has adverse effects on a network's availability or resources. This could be a security breach, such as a hacker gaining access to a user's account, an infection, such as a worm or virus, or an environmental issue, such as a fire or flood.
- *disaster*—An extreme type of incident, involving a network outage that affects more than a single system or limited group of users.

Each of these possibilities requires advance preparation by a team of people, and should have policies in place to reduce the amount of confusion, chaos, and mistakes in handling the event once it occurs. Let's first explore the more general incident response policies, and then we'll look at disaster recovery techniques.

Incident Response Policies

Incident response policies specifically define the characteristics of an event that qualifies as a formal incident and the steps that should be followed as a result. Qualifying incidents take into account the full spectrum of possible events, which might include a break-in, fire, weather-related emergency, hacking attack, discovery of illegal content or activity on an employee's computer, malware outbreak, or a full-scale, environmental disaster that shuts down businesses throughout the city or state. The policy is written with the intent of keeping people safe; protecting sensitive data; ensuring network availability and integrity; and collecting data to determine what went wrong, who is responsible, and what actions should be taken in the future to prevent similar damage.

An incident response is a six-stage process, which actually begins *before* the incident occurs:

Stage 1, Preparation: The response team brainstorms possible incidents, and plans procedures for handling them. This includes installing backup systems, and compiling all the information required to restore the network, such as passwords, configurations, vendor lists and their SLAs, locations of backup data storage, emergency contact information, and relevant privacy laws.

Stage 2, Detection and identification: Because security and environmental alarm systems can detect incidents of all kinds, staff not directly involved with incident response planning are educated about what qualifies as an incident and what to do if they notice a potential problem. Any system or staff alerts are routed to assigned personnel to determine whether the event requires escalation—that is, if it should be recognized as something other than a normal problem faced by IT technicians. Each company will have its own criteria for which incidents require escalation, as well as its own chain of command for notification purposes. Make sure you're familiar with your company's requirements.

Stage 3, Containment: The team works to limit the damage. Affected systems or areas are isolated and response staff are called in as required by the situation.

Stage 4, Remediation: The team finds what caused the problem and begins to resolve it so no further damage occurs.

Stage 5, Recovery: Operations return to normal as affected systems are repaired and put back in operation.

Stage 6, Review: The team determines what can be learned from the incident, and uses this information to make adjustments to prepare for and perhaps prevent future threats.

The response policy should identify the members of a response team, all of whom should clearly understand the security policy, risks to the network, and security measures that have already been implemented. The responsibilities assigned to each team member should be clearly spelled out, and the team should regularly rehearse their roles by participating in security threat drills. Suggested team roles include the following:

- *dispatcher*—The person on call who first notices or is alerted to the problem. The dispatcher notifies the lead technical support specialist and then the manager. He or she also creates a record for the incident, detailing the time it began, its symptoms, and any other pertinent information about the situation. The dispatcher remains available to answer calls from clients or employees or to assist the manager.
- *technical support specialist*—The team member who focuses on only one thing: solving the problem as quickly as possible. After the situation has been resolved, the technical support specialist describes in detail what happened and helps the manager find ways to avert such an incident in the future. Depending on the size of the organization and the severity of the incident, this role may be filled by more than one person.
- *manager*—The team member who coordinates the resources necessary to solve the problem. If in-house technicians cannot handle the incident, the manager finds outside assistance. The manager also ensures that the security policy is followed and that everyone within the organization is aware of the situation. As the response ensues, the manager continues to monitor events and communicate with the public relations specialist.
- *public relations specialist*—If necessary, this team member learns about the situation and the response and then acts as official spokesperson for the organization to the public or other interested parties.

Next, let's look at some specifics on handling extreme incidents and recovering from these disasters.

Disaster Recovery Planning

Disaster recovery is the process of restoring your critical functionality and data after an outage that affects more than a single system or a limited group of users. A disaster recovery plan accounts for the worst-case scenarios, from a far-reaching hurricane to a military or terrorist attack. It should provide contingency plans for restoring or replacing computer systems, power, telephone systems, and paper-based files. The goal of a disaster recovery plan is to ensure **business continuity**, which is the ability of the company to continue doing business with the least amount of interruption possible. Sections of the plan related to computer systems should include the following:

- Contact names and phone numbers for emergency coordinators who will execute the disaster recovery response in case of disaster, as well as roles and responsibilities of other staff.
- Details on which data and servers are being backed up, how frequently backups occur, where backups are kept (off-site), and, most important, how backed-up data can be recovered in full.
- Details on network topology, redundancy, and agreements with national service carriers, in case local or regional vendors fall prey to the same disaster.
- Regular strategies for testing the disaster recovery plan.
- A plan for managing the crisis, including regular communications with employees and customers. Consider the possibility that regular communication modes (such as phone lines) might be unavailable.

Having a comprehensive disaster recovery plan lessens the risk of losing critical data in case of extreme situations, and also makes potential customers and your insurance providers look more favorably on your organization.

Disaster Recovery Contingencies

An organization can choose from several options for recovering from a disaster. The options vary by the amount of employee involvement, hardware, software, planning, and investment each involves. These options also vary according to how quickly they will restore network functionality in case a disaster occurs. As you might expect, every contingency plan necessitates a site other than the building where the network's main components normally reside. An organization can maintain its own disaster recovery sites—for example, by renting office space in a different city—or contract with a company that specializes in disaster recovery services to provide the alternate site. Disaster recovery contingencies are commonly divided into three categories, as compared in Figure 11-32 and described next:

- *cold site*—Computers, devices, and connectivity necessary to rebuild a network exist, but they are not appropriately configured, updated, or connected. Therefore, restoring functionality from a cold site could take a long time. For example, suppose your small business network consists of a file and print server, mail server, backup server, Internet gateway/DNS/DHCP server, 25 clients, four printers, a router, a switch, two access points, and a connection to your local ISP. At your cold site, you might store two server computers on

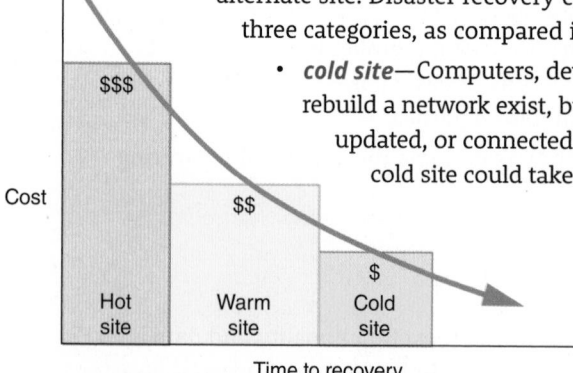

Figure 11-32 The most expensive option also provides the fastest recovery

which your company's NOS is not installed, and that do not possess the appropriate configurations and data necessary to operate in your environment. The 25 client machines stored there might be in a similar state. In addition, you might have a router, a switch, and two access points at the cold site, but these might also require configuration to operate in your environment. Finally, the cold site would not necessarily have Internet connectivity, or at least not the same type your network uses. Supposing you followed good backup practices and stored your backup media at the cold site, you would then need to restore operating systems, applications, and data to your servers and clients; reconfigure your connectivity devices; and arrange with your ISP to have your connectivity restored to the cold site. Even for a small network, this process of rebuilding your network could take weeks.

- *warm site*—Computers, devices, and connectivity necessary to rebuild a network exist, with some pieces appropriately configured, updated, or connected. For example, a service provider that specializes in disaster recovery might maintain a duplicate of each of your servers in its data center. You might arrange to have the service provider update those duplicate servers with your backed-up data on the first of each month because updating the servers daily is much more expensive. In that case, if a disaster occurs in the middle of the month, you would still need to update your duplicate servers with your latest weekly or daily backups before they could stand in for the downed servers. Recovery using a warm site can take hours or days, compared with the weeks a cold site might require. Maintaining a warm site costs more than maintaining a cold site, but not as much as maintaining a hot site.

- *hot site*—Computers, devices, and connectivity necessary to rebuild a network exist, and all are appropriately configured, updated, and connected to match your network's current state. For example, you might use server mirroring to maintain identical copies of your servers at two WAN locations. In a hot site contingency plan, both locations would also contain identical connectivity devices and configurations, and thus be able to stand in for the other at a moment's notice. As you can imagine, hot sites are expensive and potentially time consuming to maintain. For organizations that cannot tolerate downtime, however, hot sites provide the best disaster recovery option.

Data Preservation

During some incidents, data will need to be collected in such a way that it can be presented in a court of law for the purpose of prosecuting an instigator of illegal activity. Some of the forensic data available for analysis can be damaged or destroyed if improperly handled. Ideally, one or more first responders would take charge in these cases. **First responders** are the people with training and/or certifications that prepare them to handle evidence in such a way as to preserve its admissibility in court. However, it's critical that every IT technician in a company know how to safeguard sensitive information, logged data, and other legal evidence until the first responder or incident response team can take over the collection of evidence, as described next:

> **Note**
>
> eDiscovery, or electronic discovery, can reveal a great deal of information, called ESI (electronically stored information) or active data, contained on a computer's hard drives and storage media, such as calendars, email, and databases. Computer forensics is a deeper, more thorough investigation than eDiscovery—essentially a computer autopsy designed to discover hidden data, such as deleted files and file fragments, and who has accessed that data and when. This hidden information is called ambient data.

1. *Secure the area*—To prevent contamination of evidence, each device involved must be isolated. This means it should be disconnected from the network (remove the Ethernet cable or disable the Wi-Fi antenna) and secured, to ensure that no one else has contact with it until the response team arrives. Ideally, you should leave the device running without closing any applications or files. Different OSes require different shutdown procedures to preserve forensic data, so the shutdown process should be left to incident response experts. However, if a destructive program is running that might be destroying evidence, the fastest and safest solution is to unplug the power cord from the back of the machine (not just from the wall). Treat the entire work area as a crime scene. In some cases, such as with a physical break-in, an entire room, or possibly multiple rooms, must be secured to protect the evidence.

2. *Document the scene*—Creating a defensible audit trail is one of the highest priorities in the forensics process. An audit trail is a system of documentation that makes it possible for a third party to inspect evidence later and understand the flow of events. A defensible audit trail is an audit trail that can be justified and defended in a court of law. Document everything you or your team does, noting the time and the reason for each action. For example, if you unplugged the machine because a virus was wiping the hard drive, document the time and describe the symptoms you observed that led you to unplug the machine. Also make a list of everyone found in the area and their access to the computer in question. Make sure no one else enters the area until the response team arrives, and don't leave the area unattended even for a few moments.

3. *Monitor evidence and data collection*—Record all items collected for evidence. Take care to preserve all evidence in its original state. Do not attempt to access any files on a computer or server being collected for evidence, as this action alters a file's metadata and could render it inadmissible in court.

4. *Protect the chain of custody*—All collected data must be carefully processed and tracked so it does not leave official hands at any point in the forensics process. Typically, documentation used to track **chain of custody** describes exactly what the evidence is, when it was collected, who collected it, its condition, and how it

was secured. If at any point in the process you have custody of evidence, be sure to sign off on a chain of custody document, and obtain a signature from the next person in line when you hand over custody of the evidence.

5. *Monitor transport of data and equipment*—Generally, the incident response team is responsible for transporting all evidence to the forensics lab or other authority. Every item should be carefully documented so the exact same configuration can be replicated in the lab. The response team might even have the capability to do a hot seizure and removal, which means they can use specialized devices that transfer a computer from one power source to another without shutting down the computer. This can be especially critical if it's possible that the computer or its data will become inaccessible after power is turned off—perhaps because a password is unknown or data is currently in memory.

6. *Create a report*—Be prepared to report on all activities that you observed or participated in during the course of the incident response. It's best to take notes along the way, and to write your report in full as soon as possible after the event while it's still fresh on your mind. All of this information will likely be included in the final forensics report, so it's important to be thorough and accurate.

Policies alone can't guard against intruders. Network administrators must also attend to physical, network design, and NOS vulnerabilities, as described in earlier chapters.

Chapter Summary

Collecting Network Data

- At its broadest, the term network management refers to the assessment, monitoring, and maintenance of all aspects of a network. It can include controlling user access to network resources, checking for hardware faults, ensuring optimized QoS (quality of service) for critical applications, maintaining records of network assets and software configurations, and determining what time of day is best for upgrading hardware and software.

- A network monitor is a tool that continually monitors network traffic. A similar tool, a protocol analyzer, can monitor traffic at a specific interface between a server or client and the network.

- Virtually every condition recognized by an operating system can be recorded. Records of such activities are kept in a log.

- A list of managed objects and their descriptions is kept in the MIB (Management Information Base), which also contains data about an object's performance in a database format that can be mined and analyzed. The MIB is designed in a top-down, hierarchical tree structure.

- A baseline is a report of the network's normal state of operation and might include a range of acceptable measurements. Baseline measurements are obtained by analyzing network traffic information.

Managing Network Traffic

- Traffic shaping, also called packet shaping, involves manipulating certain characteristics of packets, data streams, or connections to manage the type and amount of traffic traversing a network or interface at any moment. Its goals are to ensure timely delivery of the most important traffic while optimizing performance for all users.
- QoS (quality of service) is a group of techniques for adjusting the priority a network assigns to various types of transmissions. DiffServ (Differentiated Services) is a simple technique that addresses QoS issues by prioritizing traffic at Layer 3. CoS (Class of Service) refers to techniques performed at Layer 2, on Ethernet frames, and is most often used to more efficiently route Ethernet traffic between VLANs.

Network Availability

- The term *availability* refers to how consistently and reliably a file, system, or other network resource can be accessed by authorized personnel.
- A key factor in maintaining the availability of network resources is fault tolerance, or the capacity for a

system to continue performing despite an unexpected hardware or software malfunction.

- A full backup backs up everything. An incremental backup backs up only data that has changed since the last backup. A differential backup backs up data that has changed since the last full backup.
- A UPS (uninterruptible power supply) is a battery-operated power source directly attached to one or more devices and to a power supply, such as a wall outlet, that prevents undesired fluctuations of the wall outlet's AC power from harming the device or interrupting its services. A power supply issue may be long in developing, with on-again, off-again symptoms for some time before the power issue finally solidifies and reveals itself. A good UPS in each data closet will help prevent these kinds of problems from affecting the entire network at once.

Response and Recovery

- Incident response policies specifically define the characteristics of an event that qualifies as a formal incident and the steps that should be followed as a result. Qualifying incidents take into account the full spectrum of possible events.
- Disaster recovery is the process of restoring critical functionality and data after an outage that affects more than a single system or a limited group of users. A disaster recovery plan accounts for the worst-case scenarios. The goal of a disaster recovery plan is to ensure business continuity, which is the ability of the company to continue doing business with the least amount of interruption possible.

- At a cold site, computers, devices, and connectivity necessary to rebuild a network exist, but they are not appropriately configured, updated, or connected. A warm site contains the computers, devices, and connectivity necessary to rebuild a network exist, with some pieces appropriately configured, updated, or connected. At a hot site, computers, devices, and connectivity necessary to rebuild a network exist, and all are appropriately configured, updated, and connected to match your network's current state.

- During some incidents, data will need to be collected in such a way that it can be presented in a court of law for the purpose of prosecuting an instigator of illegal activity. Some of the forensic data available for analysis can be damaged or destroyed if improperly handled. It's critical that every IT technician in a company know how to safeguard sensitive information, logged data, and other legal evidence until the first responder or incident response team can take over the collection of evidence.

Key Terms

For definitions of key terms, see the Glossary near the end of the book.

AF (Assured Forwarding)
automatic failover
availability
backup
baseline
business continuity
CARP (Common Address Redundancy Protocol)
chain of custody
clustering
cold site
CoS (Class of Service)
delay-sensitive
differential backup
DiffServ (Differentiated Services)
disaster
disaster recovery
distributed switching
DSCP (Differentiated Services Code Point)
dual power supplies
EF (Expedited Forwarding)

error rate
event log
Event Viewer
failure
fault
fault management
fault tolerance
FC (Fibre Channel)
FCoE (Fibre Channel over Ethernet)
first responder
full backup
HA (high availability)
hot site
HSRP (Hot Standby Routing Protocol)
IB (InfiniBand)
incident
incident response policies
incremental backup
iSCSI (Internet SCSI)
LACP (Link Aggregation Control Protocol)

link aggregation
load balancer
load balancing
loss-tolerant
managed object
MIB (Management Information Base)
MTBF (mean time between failures)
MTTR (mean time to repair)
NAS (network attached storage)
network management
NIC teaming
NMS (network management system) server
OID (object identifier)
packet analysis
packet drop
performance management
polling
port aggregation
QoS (quality of service)

redundancy

redundant power circuit

SAN (storage area network)

snapshot

syslog (system log)

traffic analysis

traffic policing

traffic shaping

UPS (uninterruptible power
   supply)

utilization

VIP (virtual IP address)

VRRP (Virtual Router
   Redundancy Protocol)

warm site

Review Questions

1. While troubleshooting a recurring problem on your network, you will want to examine the TCP messages being exchanged between a server and a client. Which tool should you use?
   a. Spiceworks
   b. Wireshark
   c. Packet Tracer
   d. VirtualBox

2. One of your coworkers downloaded several, very large video files for a special project she's working on for a new client. When you run your network monitor later this afternoon, what list will your coworker's computer likely show up on?
   a. Top talkers
   b. Top listeners
   c. Giants
   d. Jabbers

3. What command requests the next record in an SNMP log?
   a. SNMP Get Request
   b. SNMP Get Next
   c. SNMP Trap
   d. SNMP Get Response

4. What port do SNMP agents listen on?
   a. Port 161
   b. Port 21
   c. Port 162
   d. Port 20

5. Your roommate has been hogging the bandwidth on your router lately. What feature should you configure on the router to limit the amount of bandwidth his computer can utilize at any one time?

   a. Power management
   b. Port forwarding
   c. Port mirroring
   d. Traffic shaping

6. What field in an IPv4 packet is altered to prioritize video streaming traffic over web surfing traffic?
   a. Traffic Class
   b. Priority Code Point
   c. Time to Live
   d. DiffServ

7. When shopping for a new router, what does the MTBF tell you?
   a. How long until that device fails
   b. How much it will cost to repair that device
   c. How long devices like this one will last on average until the next failure
   d. How long it will usually take to repair that device

8. Which of the following features of a network connection between a switch and server is *not* improved by link aggregation?
   a. Bandwidth
   b. Fault tolerance
   c. Speed
   d. Availability

9. Which power backup method will continually provide power to a server if the power goes out during a thunderstorm?
   a. Online UPS
   b. Generator
   c. Dual power supplies
   d. Standby UPS

10. Which type of disaster recovery site contains all the equipment you would need to get up and running again after a disaster, and yet would require several weeks to implement?
    a. Warm site
    b. Standby site
    c. Hot site
    d. Cold site

11. When you arrive at work one morning, your inbox is full of messages complaining of a network slowdown. You collect a capture from your network monitor. What can you compare it to in order to determine what has changed?

12. What file must be accessed in order to analyze SNMP logs?

13. What kinds of alerts can you program your network monitor to send to IT staff when it detects specific, problematic conditions?

14. Which QoS technique operates at Layer 2 to more efficiently route Ethernet traffic between VLANs?

15. Which fields are modified in IPv4 and IPv6 packets to help prioritize traffic for QoS?

16. What protocol is most often used to bond ports between a switch and a busy server?

17. What type of adapters are required on servers in an FCoE storage network?

18. Why might you want to install two power supplies in a critical server?

19. What are the two main categories of UPSes?

20. What is the primary goal of disaster recovery?

Hands-On Projects

Project 11-1: Work with Data in Event Viewer

In this chapter, you learned how to access and view event log information through the Event Viewer application in Windows 10. In this project, you will practice filtering the information contained in the log.

As in the "Applying Concepts: Explore Event Viewer in Windows" project, you need a computer running Windows 10. Ideally, it should be a computer that has been used for a while, so that the event log contains several entries. It need not be connected to a network. However, you must be logged on to the computer as a user with administrator privileges.

1. Open Event Viewer. In the left pane, click the **Custom Views** arrow and then click **Administrative Events.** A list of Administrative Events appears in the center pane of the Event Viewer window. This log lists Critical, Error, and Warning events.

2. Suppose you want to find out whether your workstation has ever experienced trouble obtaining a DHCP-assigned IP address. In the Actions pane (the pane on the right), in the Administrative Events section, click **Find.** The Find dialog box opens.

3. In the Find what text box, type **dhcp**, and then click **Find Next.**

4. What is the first DHCP-related event you find? When did it occur? What was the source of this event? Read the description of the event in the General tab to learn more about it. Note: If the computer did not find a DHCP event, first make sure the topmost record

is selected before beginning your search to ensure that all the records are searched. If a DHCP event is still not found, search for a different kind of event such as *DNS* or *Service Control Manager*. Otherwise, choose another event at random.

5. Click **Cancel** to close the Find dialog box. Keep the event listing that you found highlighted.

6. Now suppose you want to be notified each time your workstation experiences this error. In the Actions pane, click **Attach Task To This Event.** The Create Basic Task Wizard dialog box opens.

7. In the Name text box, replace the default text with **DHCP_my_computer**, as shown in Figure 11-33, or some other text appropriate for the type of event you're saving. Click **Next** to continue.

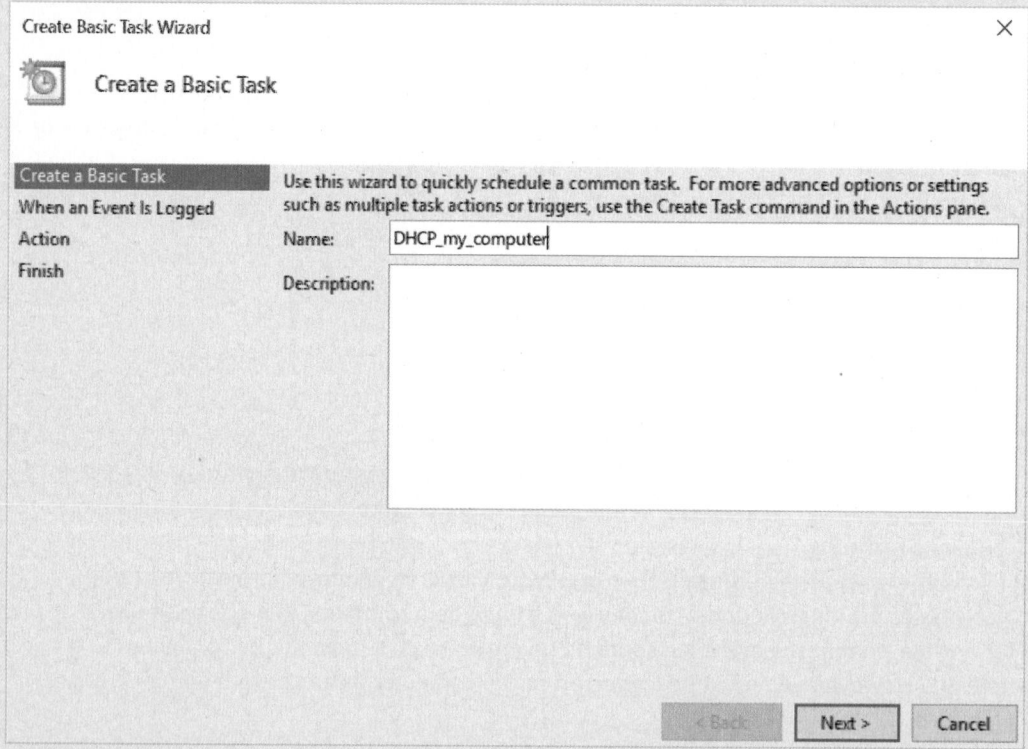

Figure 11-33   Create Basic Task Wizard in Windows Event Viewer

8. You're prompted to confirm the Log, Source, and Event ID for this error. Click **Next** to continue. You're prompted to indicate the type of action the operating system should take when this error occurs. **Start a program** is the only option not deprecated and should be selected by default. Click **Next** to continue.

9. Now you are asked to provide information about the program you want the system to open. Click the **Browse** button and find the cmd.exe file—it should be located in the folder Event Viewer opened by default. Select the file and click **Open**. The default

location for cmd.exe is C:\\Windows\System32\cmd.exe, although your location path might be different. Click **Next** to continue.

10. A summary of your notification selections appears. Click **Finish** to create the task and add it to the actions your operating system will perform.

11. An Event Viewer dialog box opens, alerting you that the task has been created. Click **OK** to confirm.

12. You can see the task you just created by opening Task Scheduler. Press **Win** + **R** and enter **taskschd.msc**.

13. In the Task Scheduler window, click the down arrow next to **Task Scheduler Library,** then click **Event Viewer Tasks**. Select the task you just created, and answer the following questions:

   a. In the lower pane, check the Security options section. Which user account will be used when the task runs?

   b. Click **Run** in the Actions pane. What happens?

   c. What command would keep this task from running without removing it from Task Scheduler?

14. You can now delete this task if you want. Close all open windows.

Project 11-2: SNMP Service in Windows 10

Windows contains an embedded SNMP service, but it's not enabled by default. In this project, you turn on the SNMP service, configure the service to start collecting SNMP messages, and enable the SNMP Trap service. Complete the following steps:

1. Open Control Panel. Click **Programs and Features**, then click **Turn Windows features on or off**. The Turn Windows features on or off dialog box opens.

2. Scroll down and click the plus sign (+) next to "Simple Network Management Protocol (SNMP)." Click the **Simple Network Management Protocol (SNMP)** check box to select it, click the **WMI SNMP Provider** check box to select it, and then click **OK**. When Windows completes its changes, click **Close**.

3. Press **Win** + **R** and enter **services.msc**. Scroll down and double-click **SNMP Service**.

4. In the SNMP Service Properties (Local Computer) window, click the **Security** tab, verify that the **Send authentication trap** check box is selected, and then click **Add** under Accepted community names.

5. Leave the Community rights as READ ONLY, type **public** in the Community Name box, and then click **Add.**

6. Click **OK** to close the SNMP Service Properties (Local Computer) window, then double-click **SNMP Trap**. Near the bottom of the SNMP Trap Properties (Local Computer) window, click **Start**. Click **OK**.

7. Open Task Manager and use the Resource Monitor (on the Performance tab, click **Open Resource Monitor**) to determine which ports the SNMP and SNMP Trap services are listening on, and which protocols (TCP or UDP) the services are using. You'll need to check the **Network** tab and the **Listening Ports** section. What information did you find?

8. Return to the Services window, right-click on **SNMP Service,** click **Stop,** and repeat for the SNMP Trap service. Close all open windows.

Project 11-3: Research Disaster Recovery Solutions

Many companies offer DRaaS (disaster recovery as a service) solutions for all types of IT-related problems. These solutions might include basics, such as off-site storage and access to virtual servers during recovery, or more expensive (but more convenient) options such as customizable backup schedules and single-file recovery, which is the ability to recover a single file at a time rather than an entire drive. In this project, you will research two different disaster recovery solutions and compare the features, cost, and reviews for each. Use complete sentences, good grammar, and correct spelling in your answers. Complete the following steps:

1. Use a search engine to find companies that provide disaster recovery solutions, and select two of these solutions. The more thorough the information provided on the company website, the easier your research will be.
2. For each of your selections, find answers to at least three of the following five questions:
   - What are the key features?
   - Where would the company store your data? In other words, in what geographic areas are their servers located?
   - What kind of encryption does the company use?
   - Which standards are the services compliant with: HIPAA? PCI? SOX?
   - Who audits the company and their disaster recovery services?
3. Find reviews for both solutions. Summarize feedback from at least three customers about these solutions.

Project 11-4: Explore Computer Forensics Investigations

As a network technician, you'll be better prepared to spot security issues if you're already familiar with breaches that have affected other networks in the past. In this project, you will research three computer forensics investigations. Use complete sentences, good grammar, and correct spelling in your answers. Complete the following steps:

1. Using a search engine, find articles, blogs, or videos discussing three different computer forensics cases. Identifying information might have been changed to protect privacy, but be sure the cases are actual cases, not just theoretical ones. Document your source or sources for each case.
2. Answer the following questions for each case:

   - How was the problem discovered?
   - What clues initiated the investigation?
   - What crime was committed or suspected?
   - What evidence was collected using computer forensics?
   - Were there any significant mistakes made in collecting this evidence?
   - What was the final outcome of the case?

Capstone Projects

Capstone Project 11-1: Manage Log Files in Ubuntu Server

Oftentimes it seems that working with Linux operating systems, compared to working with Windows, is like driving a stick shift rather than an automatic. As you've already learned, to configure an installed program in Ubuntu, you must edit a text file. For example, in Capstone Project 5-1, you edited the /etc/vsftpd.conf text file when configuring the FTP program you installed in Ubuntu.

Ubuntu creates various logs to track just about any event, and these logs are stored as text files. By default, most are stored in the /var/log directory. The FTP program maintains its own activity log in a text file that, by default, is /var/log/vsftpd.log. (You can change the default path and filename by editing the /etc/vsftpd.conf file.) This log file is essential to a technician who needs to monitor which users have logged on to the FTP server, when and from where they logged on, and what files they uploaded or downloaded. You can also monitor failed logons, which can tip you off to someone or a robot trying to hack into your system.

Using the installation of Ubuntu Server you created in Capstone Project 4-1 in a VM, follow along to learn how to manage log files in Ubuntu:

1. Start Ubuntu Server and log on with your username and password. Refer to your Last-Pass vault if you don't remember that information.
2. Enter the commands shown in Table 11-3.

Table 11-3   Manage Ubuntu log files

Command	Explanation
`cd /var/log`	Goes to the directory that contains log files.
`ls -l`	Lists all files and subdirectories, and details about each item. Look for log files that have gotten excessively large. If a technician doesn't monitor and control log files, they may get large enough to take up all available hard drive space and bring a system down.
`ls -l vsftpd.log`	Lists details about vsftpd.log. Notice the file is owned by root. Also notice the file size. If it is 0, look for another log file named vsftpd.log.1 that has a nonzero file size. Ubuntu might use rotating filenames in this manner so that one log file doesn't get too large. You might find several vsftpd.log.* files.
`ls -l vsftpd.log*`	Lists all vsftpd.log files—for example, vsftpd.log and vsftpd.log.1. In the next three commands, if the vsftpd.log file is empty, use one that has contents.

(continues)

Table 11-3 Manage Ubuntu log files *(continued)*

Command	Explanation
`sudo less vsftpd.log` and enter your password	Uses the `less` command to view and page through the contents of the file. You must use the `sudo` command to access the file because it is owned by root. How many failed logins are reported?
`q`	Quits the less pager.
`sudo grep "LOGIN" vsftpd.log`	Uses the `grep` command to narrow down a search in a text file for a particular string of text. You must use the `sudo` command to access the file because it is owned by root. The `grep` command is particularly useful for large text files when you're searching for a particular username, event, or command.
`sudo grep "login" vsftpd.log`	Searches for the same text string except using all lowercase letters in the string. How many results do you see?
`sudo grep -i "login" vsftpd.log`	Ignores case when searching. For example, the "login" string now gives the same results as "LOGIN."

3. It's helpful to learn about other log files in the /var/log directory. Search the **help.ubuntu.com** website or do a general Google search on three log files you find in the directory (enter `ls -l` again if you need to see the list again). Write a one-sentence description of the type of information kept in each file and why a technician might find this information helpful.

4. Make some notes on your Wikidot website about your activities for this project.

Capstone Project 11-2: Use Syslog in Ubuntu Desktop

In the Hands-On Project 11-2, you viewed and manipulated log file entries on a computer running Windows. In this project, you will do the same on a computer running the Linux operating system. Because Linux versions vary in the type of GUI application that allows you to open the system log, this exercise uses the command-line method instead.

For this exercise, you need a computer with a Linux operating system installed, such as the Ubuntu Desktop VM that you created in Chapter 2, Capstone Project 2-1. It need not be connected to a network, but for best results, it should be a computer that has been used in the past and not a fresh install. You must be logged on to the Linux computer as a user with administrator privileges.

1. If you are not already at a command-line (or shell) prompt, open a Terminal session now.
2. The syslog file contains information similar to that shown in Figure 11-34. The first step in viewing your Linux computer's system log is to find out where the file is located. Try each of these commands until you find the syslog file that contains information similar to that in Figure 11-34:
```
more /etc/syslog.conf
more /etc/rsyslog.conf
more /etc/rsyslog.d/50-default.conf
```

```
auth,authpriv.*                    /var/log/auth.log

*.*;auth,authpriv.none             -/var/log/syslog

#cron.*                            /var/log/cron.log

daemon.*                           -/var/log/daemon.log

kern.*                             -/var/log/kern.log

lpr.*                              -/var/log/lpr.log

mail.*                             -/var/log/mail.log

user.*                             -/var/log/user.log

uucp.*                             /var/log/uucp.log
```

Figure 11-34   Log files identified in `syslog.conf`

3. The first part of the syslog file appears. In this part of the file, you should see a list of log types and their locations, similar to the listing shown in Figure 11-34. (If you don't see the listing in this part of the file, press the **Enter** or **Space** key until you do see it.)

4. Write down the location and filename of the file that logs all events, as indicated by *.* in the first column. (For example, it might be /var/log/syslog or /var/adm/messages.)

5. Press the **Spacebar** enough times to view the entire log configuration file and return to the shell prompt.

6. Now that you know the name and location of your system log, you can view its messages. At the shell prompt, enter one of the following commands, depending on your log file's location:

   - If your log file is at /var/log/syslog, enter `tail /var/log/syslog`
   - If your log file is at /var/adm/messages, enter `tail /var/adm/messages`

7. The last 10 lines of your log file appear (assuming it is at least 10 lines long). What types of messages are recorded? When did the events occur?

8. Next find out all the types of log files your computer saves. Enter one of the following to change your working directory to the same directory where log files are kept:

   - If your log file is in the /var/log directory, enter `cd /var/log`
   - If your log file is in the /var/adm directory, enter `cd /var/adm`

9. To view a listing of the directory's contents, enter `ls -la`. Notice the types of log files that appear in this directory.

10. Suppose you want to find every message in the system log file that pertains to DHCP addressing. At the shell prompt, enter one of the following:

    - If your log file is named *syslog*, enter `grep DHCP syslog`
    - If your log file is named *messages*, enter `grep DHCP messages`
    - A list of messages containing the term *DHCP* appears, if there are any.

11. Run a new search using a text string that appeared in your results from Step 6. What command did you use?

12. If your operating system is configured to start a new log file each day or each time the computer is restarted, your log file might be brief. Repeat Step 9 and this time, look for other versions of the syslog or messages file in your working directory. For example, Ubuntu Linux will save older system messages in a file called *syslog.1*, *syslog.2*, and so on (see Figure 11-35). If you find a larger, older log file, repeat Step 10 using this log file's name. How do the results differ?

13. Close the Terminal session window. Make some notes on your Wikidot website about your activities for this project.

```
jill@jill-VM2: /var/log
-rw-r-----  1 syslog            adm          0 Oct 19 03:20 kern.log
-rw-r-----  1 syslog            adm     116071 Oct 19 03:16 kern.log.1
-rw-r-----  1 syslog            adm      12951 Sep  8 17:19 kern.log.2.gz
-rw-r-----  1 syslog            adm      14324 Aug 28 18:02 kern.log.3.gz
-rw-r-----  1 syslog            adm      51108 Aug 14 00:54 kern.log.4.gz
-rw-rw-r--  1 root              utmp    292292 Jun 19 00:09 lastlog
drwxr-xr-x  2 root              root      4096 Oct 19 03:20 lightdm
drwx------  2 speech-dispatcher root      4096 Feb 18  2016 speech-dispatcher
-rw-r-----  1 syslog            adm       2043 Oct 19 03:35 syslog
-rw-r-----  1 syslog            adm     193251 Oct 19 03:20 syslog.1
-rw-r-----  1 syslog            adm      21563 Sep  8 17:23 syslog.2.gz
-rw-r-----  1 syslog            adm      24329 Aug 28 18:06 syslog.3.gz
-rw-r-----  1 syslog            adm      22495 Aug 14 00:58 syslog.4.gz
-rw-r-----  1 syslog            adm      60392 Jul 31 22:58 syslog.5.gz
-rw-r-----  1 syslog            adm      21389 Jul 30 13:38 syslog.6.gz
-rw-r-----  1 syslog            adm      21622 Jul 13 23:04 syslog.7.gz
drwxr-x---  2 root              adm       4096 Oct 19 03:20 unattended-upgrades
drwxr-xr-x  2 root              root      4096 May 19  2016 upstart
-rw-rw-r--  1 root              utmp         0 Oct 19 03:20 wtmp
-rw-rw-r--  1 root              utmp      4992 Oct 19 03:15 wtmp.1
-rw-r--r--  1 root              root     29893 Oct 19 03:35 Xorg.0.log
-rw-r--r--  1 root              root     30019 Oct  3 00:52 Xorg.0.log.old
jill@jill-VM2:/var/log$
```

Figure 11-35   Several older syslog files are listed

Source: Canonical Group Limited

WIDE AREA NETWORKS

After reading this chapter and completing the exercises, you will be able to:

Identify the fundamental elements of WAN service options

Compare and contrast Layer 1 WAN technologies

Compare and contrast Layer 2 WAN technologies

Explain the most common wireless WAN technologies

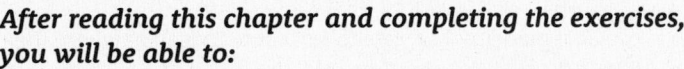

On the Job

The European "cooperative" public Internet exchange model has come to the US in the last few years, changing WAN internetworking considerations related to cloud service access. These days, WAN networking is as much about connecting to cloud services as to far-away offices. A public IX (Internet Exchange) is a less-expensive, cooperative way to directly or near-directly peer with other companies' networks, rather than paying an ISP for expensive Internet bandwidth. In this model, for small fees associated with running the cooperative network at a few data centers in a metropolitan area, we can peer directly with content partners' networks. This requires no ISP in the middle, and makes it possible to route directly to our peers.

Last year, one of our SaaS security software delivery teams advocated for hosting their application at data centers directly connected to a public IX in the United States rather than at our traditional data centers. The SaaS application is very sensitive to Internet latency, and more than 50% of its traffic is exchanged with just a few content providers, including Microsoft, Amazon hosting services, and Google.

At first, I couldn't understand the rationale for adding *more* data center locations, when we already had quite a few. Then the SaaS security team showed me traffic tests. I also ran my own. I learned that the other traffic providers were a hop or two closer when tested from the IX location. More importantly, when connected to the IX network's peering, we saw much faster effective transport speeds with all of our big content partners. Because a peering network allows less expensive Internet transit, some companies might prefer IX routes to routes over the Internet, resulting in better results than the hops saved would suggest.

In a couple of locations, we looked at extending an IX network to our nearby facilities via WAN circuits. But when we compared the cost of the extension to just renting data center space at the IX, it made more sense to host at the location where the IX was already connected, even after buying more network gear.

Public "cooperative" IX examples include:

- AMS-IX (Bay Area Internet Exchange)
- SFMIX (San Francisco Metro Internet Exchange)
- FLIX (Florida Internet Exchange)
- NYIIX (New York International Internet Exchange)

The United States also has some older Internet Exchange providers, but usually their hosting fees are higher, making total cost potentially much higher than in this newer model.

Brooke Noelke
Cloud Service Architect, McAfee

In previous chapters, you have learned about basic transmission media, network models, and networking hardware associated with LANs. This chapter focuses on WANs (wide area networks), which, as you know, are networks that connect two or more geographically distinct LANs. WANs are significant concerns for organizations attempting to meet the needs of telecommuting workers, global business partners, and Internet-based commerce.

The distance requirements of WANs affect their entire infrastructure, and, as a result, WANs differ from LANs in many respects. To understand the fundamental difference between a LAN and a WAN, think of the hallways and stairs of your house as LAN pathways. These interior passages allow you to go from room to room. To reach destinations outside your house, however, you need to use sidewalks and streets. These public thoroughfares are analogous to WAN pathways—except that WAN pathways are not necessarily public.

This chapter discusses WAN topologies and various technologies used by WANs. It also notes the potential pitfalls in establishing and maintaining WAN connections.

WAN Essentials

Ⓠ Certification

1.3 Explain the concepts and characteristics of routing and switching.

2.2 Given a scenario, determine the appropriate placement of networking devices on a network and install/configure them.

2.5 Compare and contrast WAN technologies.

A WAN traverses a significant distance and usually connects LANs. Each of the following scenarios demonstrates a need for a WAN:

- A bank with offices around the state needs to connect those offices to gather transaction and account information into a central database. Furthermore, it needs to connect with global financial clearinghouses to, for example, conduct transactions with other institutions.
- Regional sales representatives for a national pharmaceutical company need to submit their sales figures to a file server at the company's headquarters and receive email from the company's mail server.
- An automobile manufacturer in Detroit contracts out its plastic parts manufacturing to a Delaware-based company. Through WAN links, the auto manufacturer can video-conference with the plastics manufacturer, exchange specification data, and even examine the parts for quality from a remote location.
- A clothing manufacturer sells its products over the Internet to customers throughout the world.

Although all these businesses need WANs, they might not need the same kinds of WANs. Depending on the traffic load, budget, geographical breadth, and commercially available technology, each might implement a different transmission method. For every business need, a few appropriate WAN connection types might exist. At the same time, many WAN technologies can coexist on the same network.

The following list summarizes the major characteristics of WANs and explains how a WAN differs from a LAN:

- LANs connect nodes, such as workstations, servers, printers, and other devices, in a small geographical area on a single organization's network, whereas WANs use networking devices, such as routers and modems, to connect networks spread over a wide geographical area.
- Both LANs and WANs use the same protocols from Layers 3 and higher of the OSI model.

- LANs and WANs may differ at Layers 1 and 2 of the OSI model in access methods, topologies, and, sometimes, media. For example, the way DSL transmits bits over a WAN differs from the way Ethernet transmits bits over a LAN.
- LANs are mostly owned and operated by the companies that use them. On the other hand, WANs are usually owned and operated by telcos (telecommunications carriers), also known as NSPs (network service providers), such as AT&T, Verizon, Spectrum, and Comcast. Corporations lease WAN connections from these carriers, often with payments based on the amount of bandwidth actually used. Alternatively, as you read about in the *On the Job* story at the beginning of this chapter, corporations might connect directly to an IX (Internet Exchange), sometimes called an IXP (Internet Exchange point). This is similar to the difference between buying merchandise at retail prices versus buying products wholesale through a purchasing cooperative. IXes are where the networks of ISPs and other telecommunications providers intersect. By connecting directly into an IX, companies are able to cut out some of the "middle man" expense of WAN connections.

Data Transfer Methods

The individual geographic locations or endpoints connected by a WAN are known as WAN sites. A WAN link is a connection between one WAN site (or endpoint) and another site (or endpoint). WAN links can be point-to-point (connects one site to only one other site) or multipoint (connects one site to two or more other sites). Figure 12-1 illustrates the difference between WAN and LAN connectivity.

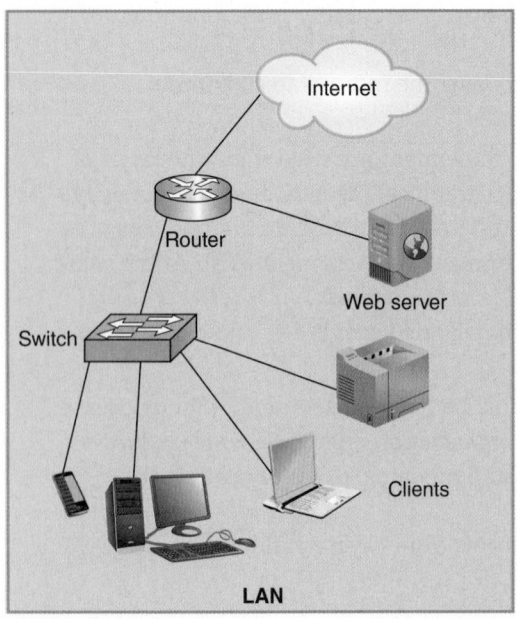
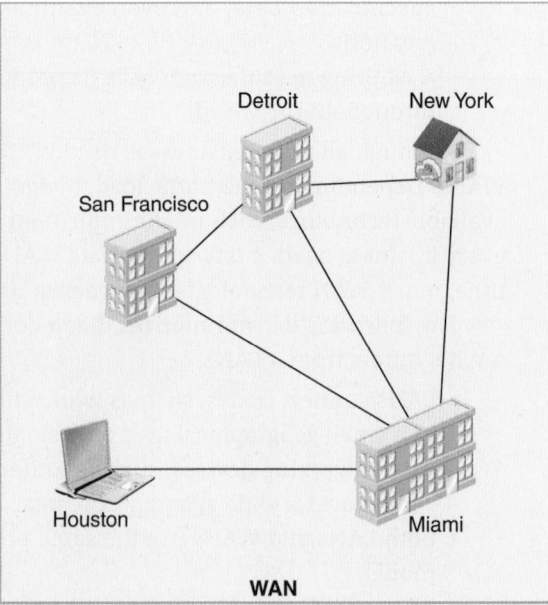

Figure 12-1   Differences in scale between LAN and WAN

The customer's endpoint device on the WAN is called the DTE (data terminal equipment), and the carrier's endpoint device for the WAN is called the DCE (data circuit-terminating equipment). For example, if you have DSL service, you connect a home router with a DSL modem. A **modem** is a modulation/demodulation device that converts between digital and analog signals. In this case, the router is the DTE, usually owned by the customer, and the modem is the DCE, usually owned by the ISP. Figure 12-2 shows this setup, with a router and modem at the customer's site defining the dividing line between each network.

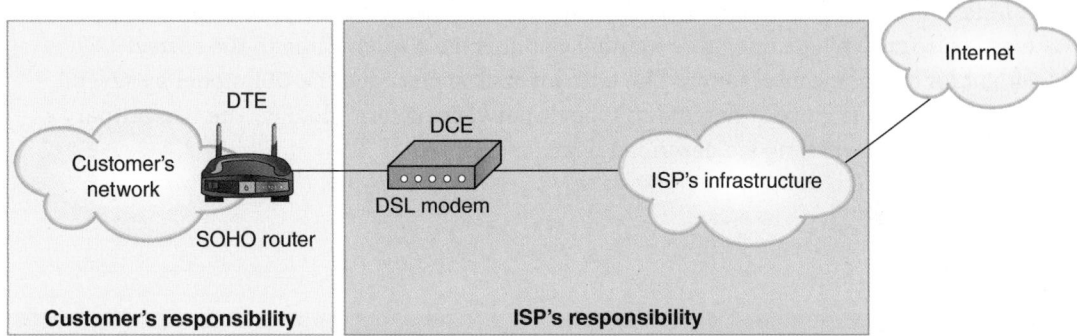

Figure 12-2   A router and a modem define the endpoints where a LAN connects to a WAN

Generally, the DTE is the responsibility of the customer and the DCE is the responsibility of the ISP. The DTE communicates on the LAN, and the DCE communicates on the WAN. Sometimes the DTE and DCE are combined in the same device. For example, a router might have one WAN network adapter, or WIC (WAN interface connector), that connects to a fiber-optic or frame relay WAN and one LAN network adapter that connects to an Ethernet, twisted-pair LAN.

The many possible shapes and forms of WAN connections determine how accessible the WAN link is to the customer, how stable it is, and how much bandwidth it provides. Let's look at the primary categories of WAN connections:

- *dedicated line*—A cable or other telecommunications path has continuously available communications channels and is not shared with other users. Private or dedicated lines are generally more expensive than other options and come in a variety of types that are distinguished by their capacity and transmission characteristics.
- *virtual circuit*—A WAN connection logically appears to the customer to be a dedicated line, but, physically, can be any configuration through the carrier's cloud. One advantage of virtual circuits is that a company can purchase limited bandwidth, and then use the channel only when it needs to transmit data. When that company is not using the channel, it remains available for use by other virtual circuits. Two types of virtual circuits are:
  - *PVC (permanent virtual circuit)*—Connections that are established before data needs to be transmitted and are maintained after the transmission is complete.

Note that in a PVC, the connection is established only between the two points (the sender and receiver); the connection does not specify the exact route the data will travel.

○ *SVC (switched virtual circuit)*—Connections that are established when parties need to transmit, then terminated after the transmission is complete.

Switching determines how connections are created between nodes on a network. Although switching as we know it is a Layer 2 function, the term *switching* here is also applied to Layer 3 when explaining how circuits are created between endpoints on different networks. To understand why this is, think about old telephone switchboards (see Figure 12-3) where operators manually connected a caller's line to the correct circuit for a phone conversation. The term switching preceded the OSI model by several decades, and was grandfathered into today's networking terminology. The two primary approaches to switching are described next:

The Library of Congress

Figure 12-3   A mid-20th century telephone switchboard

- *circuit-switched*—A connection is established between two nodes before they begin transmitting data. Bandwidth is dedicated to this connection and remains available until the users terminate communication between the two nodes. While the nodes remain connected, all data follows the same path initially selected by networking devices. This is similar to telephone circuits created when you make a phone call. As you can deduce, based on your knowledge of how IP packets are assembled and routed, circuit switching is not common today for data networks.
- *packet-switched*—Data is broken into packets before it's transported. Packets can travel any path to their destination because, as you already know, each packet contains the destination address and sequencing information. Consequently, packets can attempt to find the fastest circuit available at any instant. When packets reach their destination node, the node reassembles them based on control information included in the packets. The greatest advantage to packet switching lies in the fact that it does not waste bandwidth by holding a connection open until a message reaches its destination, as circuit switching does. Ethernet networks and the Internet are the most common examples of packet-switched networks.

Whereas a LAN always uses packet-switched connections, a WAN can use either circuit-switched or packet-switched connections, although packet-switched connections are more common. As you learn about various WAN technologies, notice whether they're using circuit-switching, packet-switching, or some kind of hybrid.

WAN technologies differ in terms of speed, reliability, cost, distance covered, and security. Some specifications operate at the Physical layer, whereas others operate at the Data Link layer of the OSI model. Table 12-1 provides a high-level overview of the various wired WAN technologies discussed in this chapter. Note that there are many options other than what is listed here; however, those technologies are beyond the scope of this text.

Table 12-1   Overview of wired WAN technologies

Functions at OSI Layer 1	Functions at OSI Layer 2	Primary media
Dial-up over PSTN	PPP	Copper
ISDN over PSTN	PPP or frame relay	Copper
DSL	PPP, Ethernet, or ATM	Copper or fiber optic
Cable broadband	Cable broadband, Ethernet	Copper and fiber optic
Metro Ethernet	Ethernet, MPLS	Copper, fiber optic, or wireless
T-carriers	PPP, frame relay, or ATM	Copper or fiber optic
SONET	PPP, frame relay, ATM, MPLS	Fiber optic

Troubleshooting an Internet Connection

As a network administrator, one of your primary responsibilities is to keep connections to the WAN working well. With this in mind, there are steps you can take to troubleshoot a problem with a WAN connection before contacting your ISP, and preventive measures you can perform to avoid having the problem in the first place. Normally, we would save the troubleshooting discussion for last. However, in this case, we'll use basic troubleshooting information to lay the groundwork for understanding the variations of WAN technologies.

To troubleshoot ISP problems, you need to know the difference between equipment that belongs to the ISP, and equipment that belongs to the subscriber. Equipment located on the customer's premises, regardless of who owns it and who is responsible for it, is called CPE (customer premise equipment). Equipment belonging to the ISP, despite its location on the customer's premises, should only be serviced by the ISP's technicians, even if it is located on the customer's side of the demarc (demarcation point). Equipment owned by the customer is the responsibility of the customer and will not be serviced by the ISP. The following list describes devices commonly found at or near the demarc:

- *NIU (network interface unit)*—The NIU, or NID (network interface device), at the demarc connects the ISP's local loop to the customer's network. A more intelligent version of an NIU is a **smart jack**, or INID (Intelligent NID), which can provide diagnostic information about the interface. For example, a smart jack might include loopback capabilities. Just like the loopback adapter you use to test a port or cable on your computer, the smart jack can loop the ISP's signal back to the CO (central office) for testing. The ISP is responsible for all wiring leading up to the NIU and for the NIU itself. The customer is responsible for everything past the NIU, unless the equipment is owned by the ISP, such as with a line driver, CSU/DSU, or set-top box.
- *line driver*—Essentially a repeater, a line driver can be installed either on copper lines (in which case, it is called a copper line driver) or fiber lines (in which case, it is called a fiber line driver) to boost the signal across greater distances. The device might be placed on either side of the demarc and, if located on the customer's side, might be owned by either party.
- *CSU/DSU*—Like line drivers, these devices can be owned by either party, depending upon who is responsible for providing this device according to the terms of service. However, the CSU/DSU is typically placed on the customer's side of the demarc, between the demarc and the first router.

When you lose Internet connectivity, a little troubleshooting can help determine the location of the problem and the party responsible for repairing the connection. The following list presents some common issues to look for on your own equipment:

- *interface error*—Misconfigured interfaces, such as an incorrect default gateway or missing DNS server address, can result in interface errors. One possible evaluation technique for bypassing an interface error, which will help confirm that the interface misconfiguration is the issue, is to switch to a different interface on the same device. For example, if your computer's wired connection is having problems, try connecting to the network using the computer's wireless interface.

- *DNS issues*—Correct DNS server information—and a functioning DNS server—are critical requirements for enabling Internet access. Computers can be programmed to use DNS servers on a corporate network or the ISP's DNS servers, or alternatively, they can be pointed to public DNS servers such as those run by Google.
- *router misconfiguration*—Other router configuration issues to consider when Internet connectivity fails might include blocked ports that should be open, speed or duplex mismatches, incorrect IP address range or subnet mask, incorrect default gateway, and STP issues.
- *interference*—Obviously, interference can cause problems with a wireless connection, and you have already learned that interference can wreak havoc with wired connections as well. Intermittent problems, or problems that affect unrelated portions of a network, are common indicators of interference issues.

Applying Concepts: Internet Down

One evening, you're up late working to meet a fast-approaching deadline when suddenly your Internet connection fails. Much of your work requires Internet access for research, but you belay the panic for a few moments to evaluate the situation:

- You try a couple of different websites in your browser, then open a different browser application and try a couple of websites again. None of the sites will load.
- You check all the cable connections between your computer and your network's demarc. Everything looks normal.
- You power cycle the modem and router by unplugging both devices from the electrical outlet, waiting a moment, plugging in the modem, waiting for it to establish a connection with the ISP, then plugging in the router.
- You check the Network Connections status on your computer and confirm that you have a functioning connection with your network.
- You try again to navigate to a website in your browser, but the page still won't load.
- You open a Command Prompt window and ping one of Google's servers at 8.8.8.8. The ping works.
- You ping Google's website at *google.com*, but this time it doesn't work.
- You pull up an outage reporting website for your ISP on your smartphone, and find that a few hundred other people have reported an outage in your area.

With a quick adjustment, you get your Internet service functioning again and continue with your work. Which of the following did you do and why?

a. You switched out the Ethernet cable connecting your modem to your router because the cable was damaged.

b. You used `ipconfig` to release the IP address on your computer and get a new one from your network's DHCP service because your computer had a duplicate IP address.

c. You changed the DNS settings on your router to point to Google's DNS servers instead of the DNS servers of your ISP because the ISP's DNS servers were down.

d. You switched to a different ISP because the former ISP's service was unreliable.

e. You replaced the router with a new router you had ready to go, knowing that the old router had already exceeded its life expectancy and had finally ceased to function.

f. You created an ad hoc network with another computer on your network and used that computer's access to the Internet to continue your research because the Wi-Fi radio on your computer had died and will need to be replaced.

g. You performed a factory reset on your modem so it would reinitiate a connection with the ISP.

h. You updated the default gateway on your computer because it was unable to communicate with the router.

i. You restarted your computer because Windows had updates that needed to be installed.

Now that you understand the basic components that differentiate WANs from LANs, you're ready to learn about specific technologies and types.

Network+ Exam Tip (i)

The CompTIA Network+ exam expects you to know about a variety of WAN connection types and to be able to identify the networking environments that each suit best. For wired WAN technologies, you need to know about ISDN, various leased lines, DSL, Metropolitan Ethernet, cable broadband, dial-up, MPLS, ATM, frame relay, PPP, PPPoE, DMVPN, and SIP trunking.

Layer 1 WAN Technologies

 **Certification**

2.5 Compare and contrast WAN technologies.

7	APPLICATION
6	PRESENTATION
5	SESSION
4	TRANSPORT
3	NETWORK
2	DATA LINK
1	PHYSICAL

As you know, Ethernet is a Data Link layer standard that frames payloads on modern LANs. Ethernet also includes Physical layer components and services that transform Layer 2 frames into transmissions of 0s and 1s that can travel over network cables. USB, Wi-Fi, Bluetooth, and many other Layer 2 protocols also include Layer 1 services. When dealing with WAN technologies, these Physical layer services are generally performed by Layer 1 standards such as DSL, ISDN, SONET, and

T-carrier links. Although these standards might have features that stretch above Layer 1 into higher layers, as you'll see in the following discussions, most operate primarily at the Physical layer to provide auto-negotiation, signaling, carrier sensing, flow control, synchronization, and possibly error control services.

> **Note** 📎
>
> As you learn about Layer 1 WAN technologies, you might notice references to frames at the Physical layer. Normally, we think about framing as being a Layer 2 feature, and it is. However, many Layer 1 standards also use minimalist frames in order to support negotiating connections and exchanging transmissions. Recall that most protocol analyzers like Wireshark can't capture certain portions of a Layer 2 Ethernet frame because that data is removed from transmissions before it becomes visible to most software. Similarly, Wireshark and others can't see Layer 1 frames. It's sufficient to know that most of these Physical layer frames consist simply of a start symbol or a short preamble, a length field, then the Layer 2 payload, occasionally followed by a marker to end the frame.

Some of these Layer 1 standards are called by common names that you might recognize if you've ever shopped around for home or business Internet service or if you've noticed commercials or billboards advertising Internet subscription options. The standards we'll discuss in this section provide the connection between the customer and the ISP, telephone company, or cable company. Most of these connections are made over existing telephone lines. Some, however, are created on the existing cable TV infrastructure or on specialized copper or fiber cables. Later in this chapter, we'll also look at WAN services provided wirelessly.

As you compare WAN technologies, keep in mind one other significant difference between technologies—whether the connection is shared among many customers or dedicated to one customer. The following list explains these two options:

- *broadband*—Especially well-suited for residential customers, the cables (whether telephone, copper, or fiber) and available bandwidth are shared between multiple customers. The ISP makes a "best effort" attempt to provide *up to* the advertised bandwidth, and actual performance varies considerably during busy usage. Bandwidth is also **asymmetrical** or **asynchronous**, meaning download speeds (data traveling from the carrier's switching facility to the customer) are faster than upload speeds (data traveling from the customer to the carrier's switching facility). For a higher premium, businesses can get faster broadband speeds and possibly a static IP address included in the package. However, uptime, service, and bandwidth are still not guaranteed.

- *DIA (dedicated Internet access)*—The cable itself or a portion of its available bandwidth is dedicated to a single customer; this is more common for business customers and comes with an SLA-defined (service-level agreement) guarantee of minimum uptime percentages and maximum recovery times if the service goes down. Bandwidth is **symmetrical** or **synchronous**, meaning download and upload speeds are the same. This is especially important for businesses that back up large amounts of data online. The subscription will also often include a number of static IP addresses.

Applying Concepts: Test Your WAN Connection's Speed

You can test your own WAN connection to see what the current upload and download speeds are using a **bandwidth speed tester**, or a speed test website. During the test, data will be sent to your computer and then requested from your computer in order to measure download and upload speeds, respectively. Complete the following steps:

1. In your browser, go to **speedtest.net**. At the time of this writing, you start the test by clicking **GO**. The test begins, as shown in Figure 12-4.

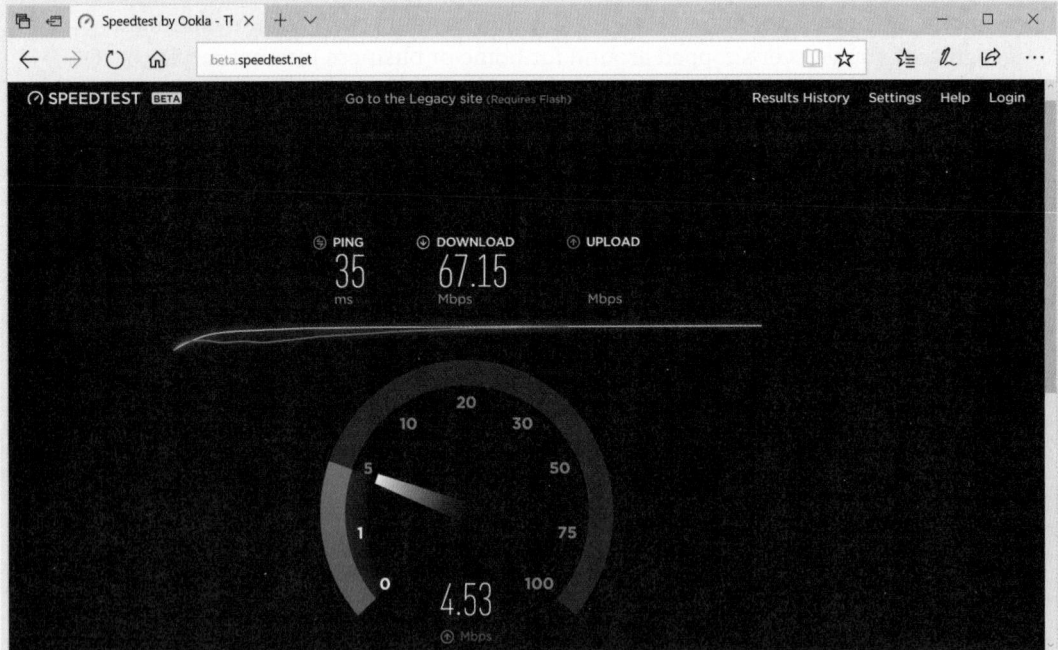

Figure 12-4   Speed test in progress
Source: Ookla Speedtest

2. Wait for the test to complete, then write down your speed test results. What are your current download and upload speeds?

3. Let's try another site and compare results. Go to **verizon.com/speedtest**, start the test (see Figure 12-5), and wait for it to finish. What are the results this time? How do they compare to your first results? Why do you think this is?

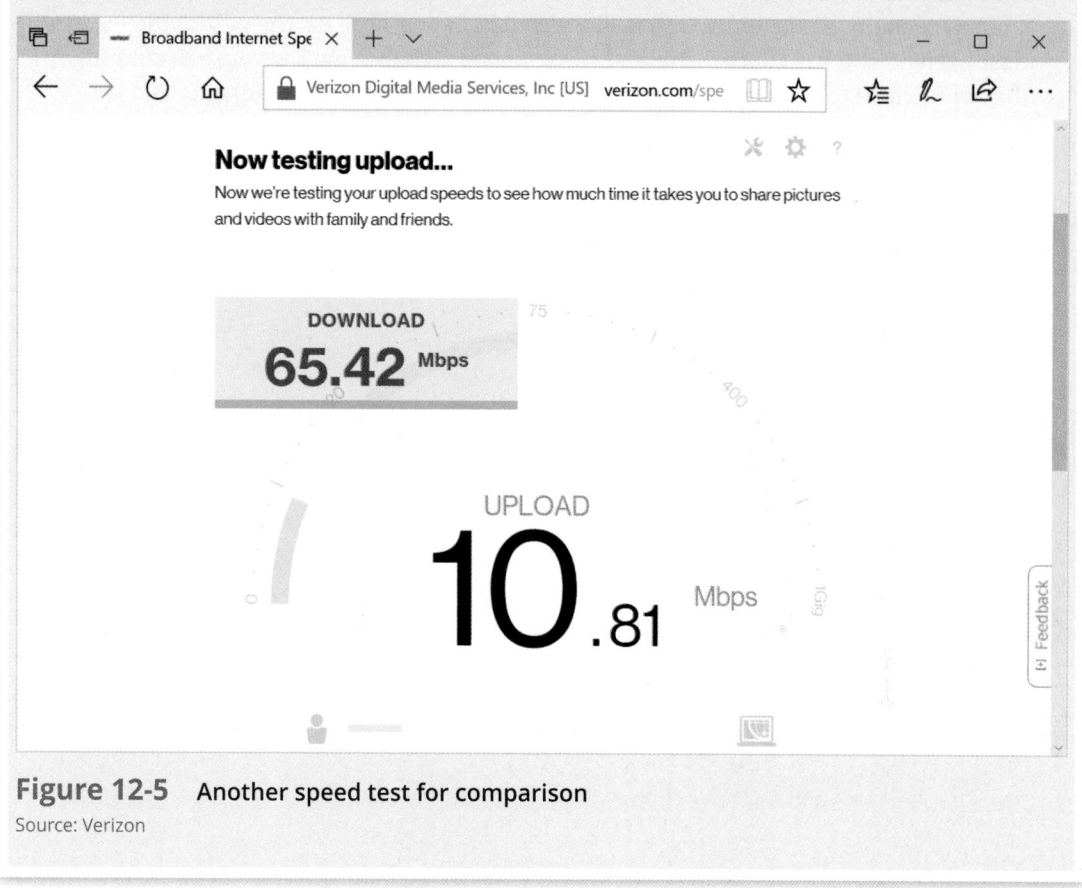

Figure 12-5   Another speed test for comparison

Source: Verizon

We'll begin with a discussion of telephone network-based services. Then we'll look at cable broadband on coaxial cable, and finally we'll explore various dedicated service options.

PSTN (Public Switched Telephone Network)

The **PSTN (public switched telephone network)**, also called POTS (plain old telephone service), is a circuit-switching network of lines and carrier equipment that provides landline telephone service to homes and businesses. Originally, the PSTN carried only analog traffic. All its lines were copper wires, and switching was handled by operators who manually connected calls upon request. Today, switching is computer controlled, and nearly all the PSTN uses digital transmission. Signals may deliver voice, video, or data traffic and travel over fiber-optic or twisted-pair copper cable connections.

The telephone company terminates lines and switches calls between different locations at the CO (central office). The portion of the PSTN that connects any residence or business to the nearest CO is known as the **local loop**, or the "last mile" (though it is not necessarily a mile long), and is illustrated in Figure 12-6. It's the part of the PSTN most likely to still use copper wire and carry analog signals. That's because extending fiber-optic cable to every residence and business is costly. However, fully digital connections are increasingly common, especially for businesses that rely heavily on WANs. No matter what kind of media is used, the end of the local loop—and also the end of the carrier's responsibility for the network—is the customer's demarcation point, where wires terminate at the NIU.

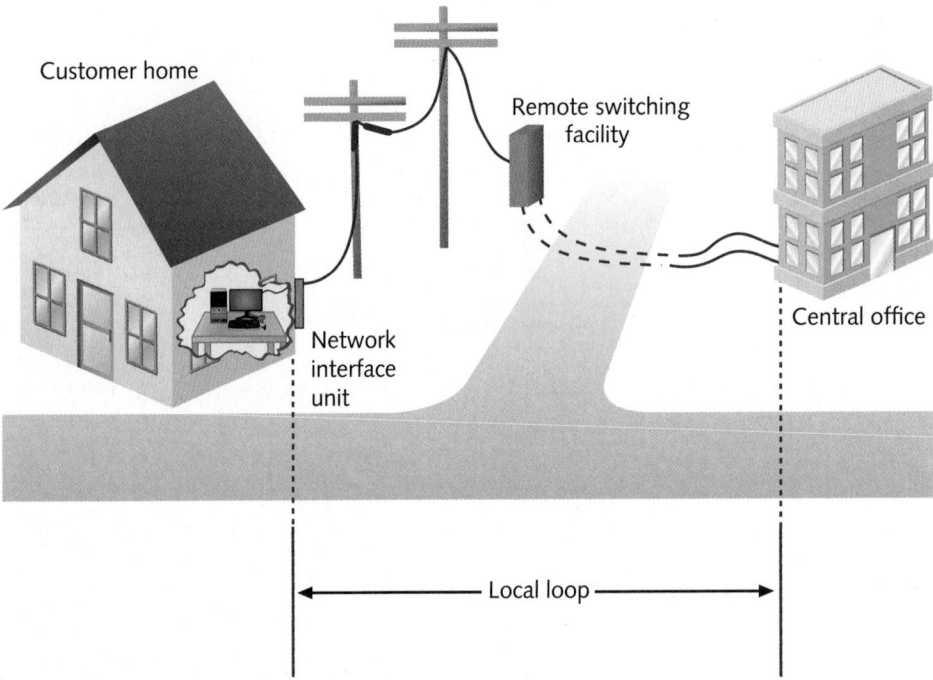

Figure 12-6 Local loop portion of the PSTN

Three examples of PSTN-based network technologies that enable users to connect to WANs are dial-up, ISDN, and DSL. While dial-up and ISDN are mostly obsolete, they're still important building blocks for understanding later technologies, and they're covered on the Network+ exam. Let's briefly discuss each of these two legacy technologies, and then we'll explore DSL in more depth.

Legacy Networking: Dial-Up

When the Internet first became popular in the 1990s, most home users logged on to the Internet via a dial-up connection. **Dial-up** required the user to enter a phone number. The computer then called, waited for a response, and negotiated a connection. To do this, a dial-up connection required the user to plug an RJ-11 phone line into the computer's modem, which could be an internal expansion card attached to the computer's motherboard or an external device that connected to the computer via USB or an older serial cable with a DB-9, DB-25, or RJ-45 connector. The modem then connected to a modem on a distant network and stayed connected for a finite period of time. When the call was terminated, the connection ended. See Figure 12-7.

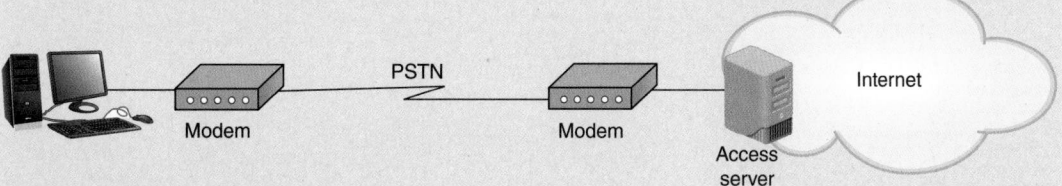

Figure 12-7 **Two modems enable digital communication over the PSTN analog network**

You might still find dial-up services in use to support industrial SCADA (supervisory control and data acquisition) networks—a type of network responsible for acquiring real-time data from a physical system, such as a natural gas pipeline, and managing the physical system in response to that data or presenting data to humans, who monitor and manage the system. Some people also use dial-up to send faxes from their computers. Windows 10 allows you to create a dial-up connection through the Network and Sharing Center, as shown in Figure 12-8. The right side of the figure shows information you might need in addition to the phone number.

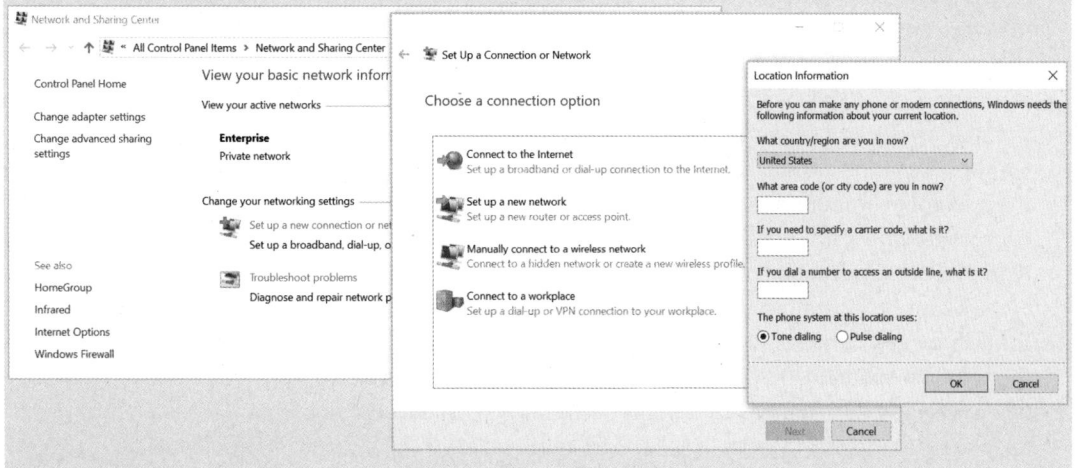

Figure 12-8 **Set up a dial-up connection through the Network and Sharing Center**

As the PSTN became digitized, the technology to bring higher speeds across that last stretch of analog cabling began to emerge. ISDN (Integrated Services Digital Network) was an early attempt with some measure of success.

Legacy Networking: ISDN

ISDN (Integrated Services Digital Network) as an international standard was originally established by the ITU in 1984 for transmitting both digital data and voice over the PSTN. ISDN specified protocols at the Physical, Data Link, and Transport layers of the OSI model. These protocols handled signaling, framing, connection setup and termination, routing, flow control, and error detection and correction. Connections could be either dial-up or dedicated. One disadvantage of ISDN was that it could span a distance of only 18,000 linear feet before repeater equipment was needed to boost the signal. For this reason, it was only feasible to use for the local loop portion of the WAN link.

All ISDN connections were based on two types of channels:

- *B channel*—"Bearer" channel, employing circuit-switching techniques to carry voice, video, audio, and other types of data over the ISDN connection. A single B channel had a maximum throughput of 64 Kbps. The number of B channels in a single ISDN connection could vary.
- *D channel*—"Data" channel, employing packet-switching techniques to carry information about the connection, such as session initiation and termination signals, caller identity, call forwarding, and conference calling signals. A single D channel had a maximum throughput of 16 or 64 Kbps, depending on the type of ISDN connection. Each ISDN connection used only one D channel.

In North America, two types of ISDN connections were commonly used: Basic Rate Interface and Primary Rate Interface. **BRI (Basic Rate Interface)** used two B channels and one D channel, as indicated by the notation 2B+D. The two B channels were treated as separate connections by the network and could carry voice and data or two data streams simultaneously and separate from each other. In a process called bonding, these two 64-Kbps B channels could be combined to achieve an effective throughput of 128 Kbps—the maximum amount of data traffic that a BRI connection could accommodate. Most consumers who subscribed to ISDN from home used BRI, which was the most economical type of ISDN connection.

Figure 12-9 illustrates how a typical BRI link supplied a residential customer with an ISDN connection. From the telephone company's lines, the ISDN channels connected to an NT1 (Network Termination 1) device at the customer's site. The NT1 device connected the twisted-pair wiring at the customer's building with the ISDN terminal equipment via RJ-11 (standard telephone) or RJ-45 data jacks. The ISDN TE (terminal equipment) could include cards or stand-alone devices used to connect computers to the ISDN line (similar to a network adapter used on Ethernet networks).

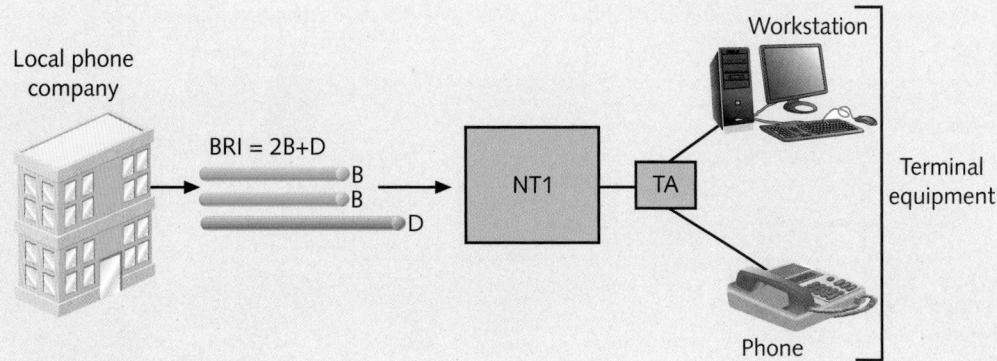

Figure 12-9   A BRI link

Although ISDN is a type of digital transmission, it is sometimes needed to connect to analog equipment, such as a regular telephone. To do so, the digital signal passed through a TA (terminal adapter), which converted it into an analog signal for use by analog devices. (Terminal adapters were sometimes called ISDN modems, though they are not, technically, modems.) For a home user, the terminal adapter was most likely an ISDN router, whereas the terminal equipment could be an Ethernet card in the user's workstation plus, perhaps, a phone.

> **Note** 🖉
>
> The BRI configuration depicted in Figure 12-9 applies to installations in North America only. Because transmission standards differ in Europe and Asia, different numbers of B channels are used in ISDN connections in those regions.

PRI (Primary Rate Interface) used 23 B channels and one 64-Kbps D channel, as represented by the notation 23B+D. PRI was less commonly used by individual subscribers than BRI was, but it was well-suited for businesses and other organizations that needed more throughput. As with BRI, the separate B channels in a PRI link could carry voice and data, independently of each other or bonded together. The maximum potential throughput for a PRI connection was 1.544 Mbps.

PRI and BRI connections could be interconnected on a single network. PRI links used the same kind of equipment as BRI links, but required the services of an extra network termination device, called an NT2 (Network Termination 2), to handle the multiple ISDN lines. Figure 12-10 depicts a typical PRI link as it would have been installed in North America.

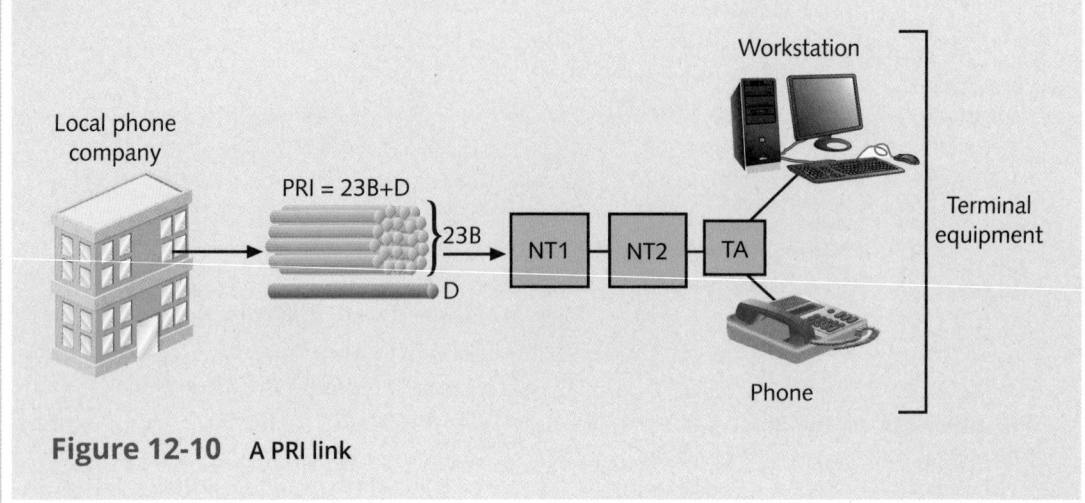

Figure 12-10   A PRI link

DSL (Digital Subscriber Line)

DSL (digital subscriber line) is a WAN connection method introduced by researchers at Bell Laboratories in the mid-1990s. It operates over the PSTN and competes directly with cable broadband and T1 services. Like ISDN, DSL can support multiple data and voice channels over a single line. DSL can span only limited distances without the help of repeaters. Also, the distance between the customer and the central office affects the actual throughput a customer experiences. Close to the central office, DSL achieves its highest maximum throughput. The farther away the customer's premises, the lower the throughput.

DSL uses data modulation techniques at the Physical layer of the OSI model to achieve extraordinary throughput over regular telephone lines. To understand how DSL and voice signals can share the same line, it's helpful to note that telephone lines carry voice signals over a very small range of frequencies, between 300 and 3300 Hz. This leaves higher, inaudible frequencies unused and available for carrying data. Depending on its version, a DSL connection might use a modulation technique based on amplitude or phase modulation to alter the waves at higher frequencies in order to carry data. The types of modulation used by a DSL version affect its throughput and the distance its signals can travel before requiring a repeater.

Types of DSL

The types of DSL vary according to their throughput rates, data modulation techniques, capacity, and distance limitations, as well as how they use the PSTN. The term **xDSL (extended DSL)** refers to all DSL varieties. In each case, the *x* in *xDSL* is replaced by the variety's name (there's that algebra again). The better-known DSL varieties include:

- **ADSL (asymmetric DSL)** has faster download speeds than upload speeds and is the most common form of DSL. In reference to DSL, the term *asymmetric* is typically preferred over the term *asynchronous*. Asymmetrical communication is well suited to users who receive more information from the network than they send to it—for example, people watching movies online or people surfing the web. ADSL and VDSL (discussed next) create multiple narrow channels in the higher frequency range to carry more data. For these versions, a splitter must be installed at the carrier and at the customer's premises to separate the data signal from the voice signal before it reaches the terminal equipment (for example, the phone or the computer). The latest version of ADSL is ADSL2+, which provides a maximum theoretical throughput of 24 Mbps downstream and a maximum of 3.3 Mbps upstream (depending on how close it is to its source). ADSL2+ also extends the reach of DSL to within two kilometers of the provider's location.

- **VDSL (very high bit rate DSL or variable DSL)** is faster than ADSL and is also asymmetric, with faster download speeds than upload speeds. A VDSL line that carries 50–60 Mbps in one direction and 5–10 Mbps in the opposite direction can extend only a maximum of 1.6 km before dropping to speeds similar to ADSL2+. VDSL2 offers throughput speeds nearing 100 Mbps in both directions but drops off quickly at even shorter distances. These limitations might suit businesses located close to a telephone company's CO (for example, in the middle of a metropolitan area), but it won't work for most individuals.

- **SDSL (symmetric DSL)** has equal download and upload speeds maxing out around 2 Mbps. Symmetrical transmission is suited to users who both upload and download significant amounts of data—for example, a bank's branch office that sends large volumes of account information to the central server at the bank's headquarters and, in turn, receives large amounts of account information from the central server at the bank's headquarters. SDSL cannot use the same wire pair that is used for voice signals. Instead, this type of DSL uses the extra pair of wires contained in a telephone cable (which are otherwise typically unused).

Note

Published distance limitations and throughput can vary from one service provider to another, depending on how far the provider is willing to guarantee a particular level of service. In addition, service providers may limit each user's maximum throughput based on terms of the service agreement. For example, in 2011, AT&T capped the total amount of data transfer allowed for each of its DSL subscribers to 150 GB per month. The company instituted the new policy in response to a dramatic spike in downstream bandwidth usage due to Netflix streaming. In fact, in 2010, Netflix accounted for nearly 30 percent of all downstream Internet traffic requested by fixed users in the United States. Today, many providers cap a subscriber's high-speed data usage, although typically the caps are higher now than the one in this example.

Next, let's dissect a DSL connection from a business or residence location over the PSTN to the carrier's CO.

DSL Equipment

This section follows the path of an ADSL connection from a home computer, through the local loop, to the telco's switching facility, as illustrated in Figure 12-11. This describes the most common implementation of DSL, although it's important to keep in mind that many variations exist.

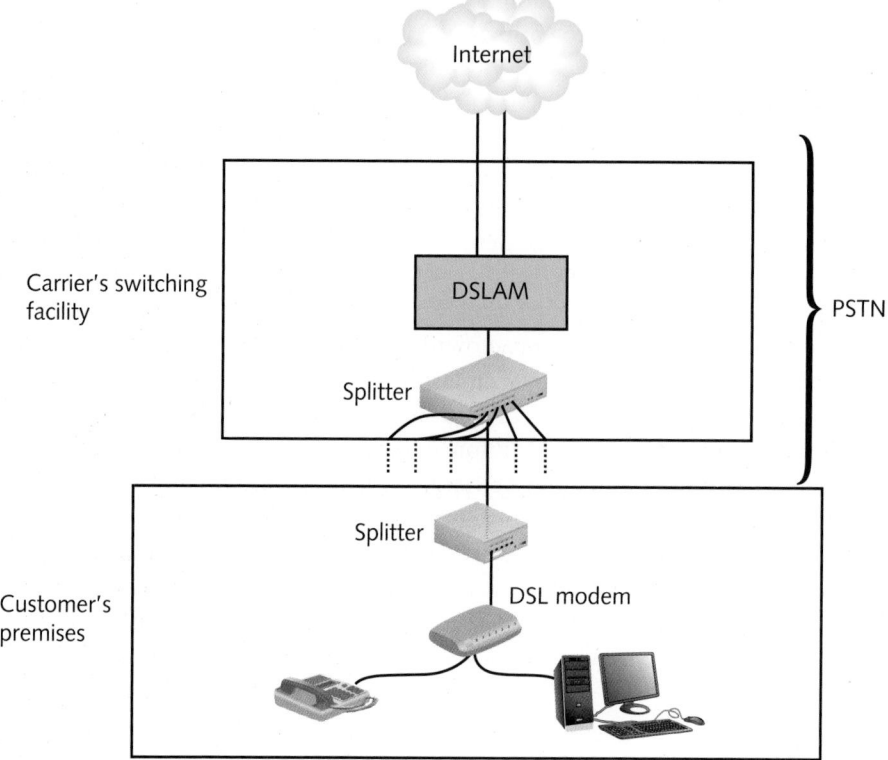

Figure 12-11 A DSL connection

Step 1, *Request connection with web server*: Suppose you have an ADSL connection at home. One evening you open your web browser and request the home page of your favorite sports team to find the game's score. As you know, the first step in this process is establishing a TCP connection with the team's web server. This initial TCP SYN message leaves your computer's NIC and travels over your home network to a DSL modem. A DSL modem, such as the one shown in Figure 12-12, contains ports to connect both to your incoming telephone line and to your computer or network connectivity device.

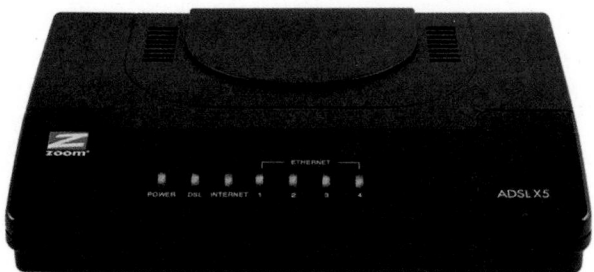

Figure 12-12   A DSL modem

Source: Zoom Telephonics, Inc.

Because you are using ADSL, the DSL modem also contains a splitter to separate incoming voice and data signals. The DSL modem might be external or internal (as an expansion card, for example) to the computer. If external, it might connect to a computer's NIC via an RJ-45, USB, or wireless interface. If your home network contains more than one computer and you want all computers to share the DSL bandwidth, the DSL modem must connect to a device such as a switch or router, instead of just one computer. In fact, rather than using two separate devices, you could buy a router that combines DSL modem functionalities with the ability to connect multiple computers and share DSL bandwidth.

Step 2,   *Send signal to ISP*: When your SYN request arrives at the DSL modem, it is modulated according to the ADSL specifications. Then, the DSL modem forwards the modulated signal to your local loop—the lines that connect your home with the rest of the PSTN. For the first stretch of the local loop, the signal continues over four-pair UTP wire. At some distance less than 18,000 feet, it is combined with other modulated signals in a telephone switch, usually at a remote switching facility. (To accept DSL signals, your telco must have newer digital switching equipment. In the few remaining locales where carriers have not updated their switching equipment, DSL service is not available.)

Step 3,   *Forward to Internet*: Inside the carrier's remote switching facility, a splitter separates your line's data signal from any voice signals that are also carried on the line. Next, your request is sent to a device called a DSLAM (DSL access multiplexer), which aggregates multiple DSL subscriber lines and connects them to the carrier's CO. Finally, your request is issued from your carrier's network to the Internet backbone. The request travels over the Internet until it reaches your sports team's web server.

Barring line problems and Internet congestion, the entire journey happens in a fraction of a second. When your team's web server responds to the SYN message, the data follows the same path, but in reverse.

Telecommunications carriers and related manufacturers have positioned DSL as a competitor for cable broadband and T1 services. The installation, hardware, and monthly access costs for DSL are significantly less than the cost for T1s, but the cost in comparison with cable broadband varies widely by location. At the time of this writing, ADSL costs approximately $35 per month in the United States, though prices vary by speed and location. Generally speaking, DSL throughput rates, especially upstream, are lower than cable broadband, which is its main competition among residential customers.

Cable Broadband

While local and long-distance phone companies strive to make DSL the preferred method of Internet access for consumers, cable companies are pushing their own connectivity option. This option, called **cable broadband** or cable modem access, is based on the coaxial cable wiring used for TV signals. Cable broadband was standardized by an international, cooperative effort orchestrated by CableLabs that yielded a suite of specifications called **DOCSIS (Data Over Cable Service Interface Specifications)**. Cable broadband service is typically offered at asymmetric speeds, such as up to 70 Mbps download and 7 Mbps upload. However, the newest DOCSIS standard, 3.1, allows for full duplex, or symmetric, speeds up to 10 Gbps in both directions, thus rivaling some fiber-optic Internet service options.

In fact, many cable companies employ fiber cabling for a significant portion of their physical infrastructure. As illustrated in Figure 12-13, **HFC (hybrid fiber coaxial)** networks use fiber-optic cabling, which supports high throughput and high reliability, to connect the cable company's distribution center, or head-end, to distribution hubs and then to optical nodes near customers. Either fiber-optic or coaxial cable then connects a node to each customer's business or residence via a connection known as a cable drop.

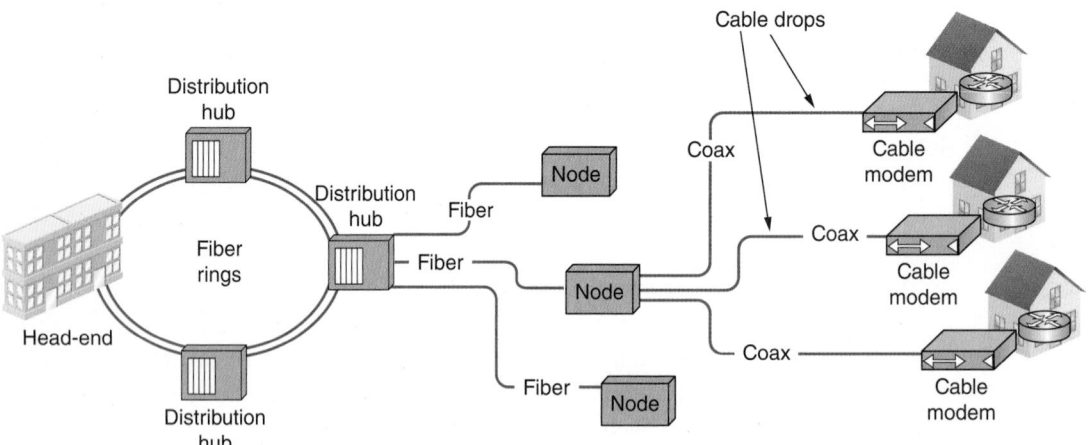

Figure 12-13   HFC infrastructure

Cable broadband connections require that the customer use a special **cable modem**, a device that modulates and demodulates signals for transmission and reception via cable wiring (see Figure 12-14). The cable modem must conform to the correct version of

DOCSIS supported by the ISP. Most newer cable modems use DOCSIS 3.0 or 3.1 and are backward compatible, but ISPs might charge extra when later modem models are used. Table 12-2 presents the versions of DOCSIS along with their specifications.

Figure 12-14   A cable modem

Source: Zoom Telephonics, Inc.

Table 12-2   DOCSIS versions and specifications

Version	Maximum upstream throughput (Mbps)	Maximum downstream throughput (Mbps)	Description
DOCSIS 1.x (1.0 and 1.1)	10	40	Outdated; single channel; throughput was shared among customers
DOCSIS 2.x (2.0 and 2.0 + IPv6)	30	40	Single channel; reduces disparity between upstream and downstream throughputs
DOCSIS 3.0	100	1000	Multiple channels: minimum of 4, no maximum
DOCSIS 3.1	1000–2000	10,000	In 2017, CableLabs published Full Duplex DOCSIS 3.1, which offers symmetrical upload and download speeds up to 10 Gbps

Applying Concepts: Determine a Cable Modem's DOCSIS Version

You can determine the DOCSIS version of a cable modem on a SOHO (small office/home office) network with a little detective work. This project requires a SOHO network serviced by cable broadband and a computer (Windows, Linux, or Mac) connected to the network. Complete the following steps to identify the DOCSIS version of a cable modem:

1. Examine the labels on the cable modem to determine the device's manufacturer and model number. In some cases, the DOCSIS version might be printed on one of these labels. If not, continue with the following steps.

2. Research the manufacturer and model number information online. You might find the DOCSIS information while conducting your research. If not, the minimum information you need is the cable modem's default internal IP address (such as 192.168.0.1 or 192.168.100.1) and admin username and password (if there is one).

3. Enter the default internal IP address in a web browser and log on if necessary. Explore the user interface to locate the cable modem's hardware information. Figure 12-15 shows the hardware information for a cable modem made by ARRIS. What is the DOCSIS version of your cable modem?

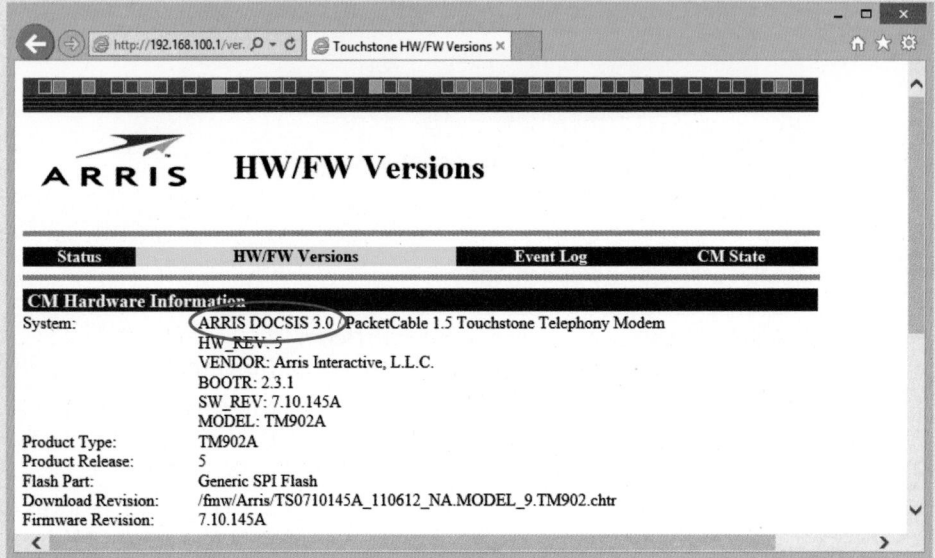

Figure 12-15   This cable modem's DOCSIS version is 3.0

Source: ARRIS

Cable modems operate at the Physical and Data Link layers of the OSI model, and, therefore, do not manipulate higher-layer protocols, such as IP. The cable modem connects to a customer's PC via the NIC's RJ-45, USB, or wireless interface. Alternately, the cable modem could connect to a connectivity device, such as a switch or router, thereby supplying bandwidth to a LAN rather than to just one computer. It's also possible to use a device that combines cable modem functionality with a router; this single device can then provide both the cable broadband connection and the capability of sharing the bandwidth between multiple nodes.

Like DSL, cable broadband provides a dedicated and always-up, or continuous, connection that does not require dialing up a service provider to create the connection. Unlike DSL, cable broadband requires many subscribers to share the same local line, thus raising concerns about security and actual (versus theoretical) throughput. For example, if your cable company supplied you and five of your neighbors with cable broadband services, one of your neighbors could, with some technical prowess, capture the data that you transmit to the Internet. (Modern cable networks provide encryption for data traveling to and from customer premises; however, these encryption schemes can be thwarted.) Moreover, the throughput of a cable line is fixed. As with any fixed resource, the more one person uses, the less that is left for others. In other words, the greater the number of users sharing a single line, the less throughput available to each individual user. Cable companies counter this perceived disadvantage by rightly claiming that at some point (for example, at a remote switching facility or at the DSLAM interface), a telephone company's DSL bandwidth is also fixed and shared among a group of customers.

In the United States, cable broadband access costs approximately $30–$60 per month when bundled with cable TV and/or digital voice services. Cable broadband is less often used in businesses than DSL, primarily because most office buildings do not contain a coaxial cable infrastructure.

Metro (Metropolitan) Ethernet

A growing trend in the ISP offerings for WAN connection services is a fairly recent development in Ethernet technology which began with **Metro (Metropolitan) Ethernet** and grew into a global scale technology called **Carrier Ethernet**. You've already learned about LAN-based Ethernet. ISPs are now developing ways to send Ethernet traffic across WAN connections (called Carrier Ethernet) and MAN connections (called Metro Ethernet), as first standardized by the MEF (Metro Ethernet Forum). The MEF is an alliance of over 220 industry organizations worldwide.

Where available, virtual Ethernet networks can be established across other types of networks using technologies such as Ethernet over SONET (or SDH), Ethernet over MPLS, Ethernet over DSL, and Ethernet over fiber. In metro settings, end-to-end, carrier-grade Ethernet networks can be established via **CET (Carrier-Ethernet Transport)**, which is an Ethernet-based transport solution designed to overcome the inherent weaknesses of implementing Ethernet outside of the LAN environment. As you can see, Carrier Ethernet, therefore, actually spans both Layers 1 and 2 in the OSI model.

For example, where traditional Ethernet, using STP (Spanning Tree Protocol), forwards frames based on MAC addresses, CET adds a transport label to the frame for forwarding purposes and establishes virtual tunnels, or paths, for frames to follow to their destination. Looking back at Figure 10-13, recall that STP blocks certain paths in order to limit potential pathways. CET, on the other hand, predetermines a pathway and tags frames to follow the specified path, as shown in Figure 12-16.

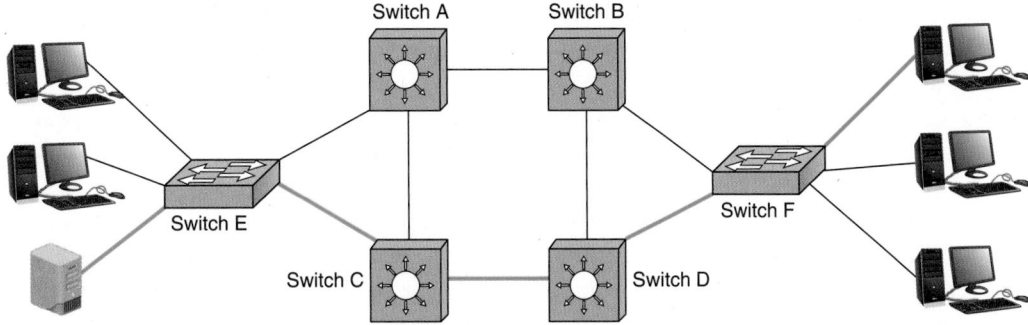

Figure 12-16   CET determines a pathway

Metro Ethernet, as a last-mile service, provides a host of advantages, including:

- *streamlined connections*—Bridging Ethernet LANs with their native Ethernet protocols significantly streamlines the communication processes.
- *cost efficiency*—Metro Ethernet provides higher bandwidth at lower costs than current T-carrier and other options that rely on TDM (such as SONET). Metro Ethernet services at 10 Gbps are available with bandwidths up to 100 Gbps in the works.
- *scalability*—Ethernet services are more easily scaled in finer increments than other high-bandwidth technologies, and can be easily adjusted as subscriber needs change.
- *familiarity*—IT technicians are already familiar with Ethernet protocols and standards, which simplifies maintenance and troubleshooting.
- *hardware*—Ethernet hardware is already widely available and less expensive to obtain the equipment needed for specific situations.

T-Carriers

All the WAN service options we've examined so far rely on cabling that is shared among many customers. **T-carrier** technology, which includes T1s, fractional T1s, and T3s, provides a dedicated logical circuit that is used only by the customer. AT&T developed T-carrier technology in 1957 in an effort to digitize voice signals and thereby enable such signals to travel longer distances over the PSTN. Before that time, voice signals, which were purely analog, were expensive to transmit over long distances because of the number of connectivity devices needed to keep the signal intelligible. In the 1970s, many businesses installed T1s to obtain more voice throughput per line. In the 1990s, with increased data communication demands, such as Internet access and geographically dispersed offices, T1s became a popular way to connect WAN sites via leased lines. The medium used for T-carrier signaling can be specially conditioned copper wire, fiber-optic cable, or wireless links, with fiber-optic being the most common by far.

Types of T-Carrier Lines

As a networking professional, you'll likely work with T1 or T3 lines. In addition to knowing their capacity, you should be familiar with their costs and uses.

- *T1*—Commonly leased by businesses to connect branch offices or to connect to a carrier, such as an ISP. The cost of T1s varies from region to region. Leasing a full T1 might cost anywhere from $200 to $1200 per month in access fees. The longer the distance between the subscriber and the provider (such as an ISP or a telephone company), the higher a T1's monthly charge. T-carrier standards, also called T-CXR standards, use TDM (time division multiplexing) over two wire pairs (one for transmitting and one for receiving) to divide a single channel into multiple channels. Multiplexing enables a single T1 circuit to carry 24 channels, each capable of 64-Kbps throughput; thus, a T1 has a maximum capacity of 24 × 64 Kbps, or 1.544 Mbps. Each channel may carry data, voice, or video signals.

- *T3*—Provides 28 times more throughput than a T1. T3s are more expensive than T1s and are used by more data-intensive businesses—for example, computer consulting firms that provide online data backups and warehousing for a number of other businesses or long-distance carriers (although T3s are losing ground in the marketplace to more modern options). The monthly service fee of a T3 varies based on usage. If a customer uses the full T3 bandwidth of 45 Mbps, for example, the monthly charges might be as high as $10,000 for a longer-distance connection. Of course, T-carrier costs will vary depending on the service provider, your location, and the distance covered by the T3. Some organizations find that multiple T1s—rather than a single T3—can accommodate their throughput needs. For example, suppose a university research laboratory needs to transmit molecular images over the Internet to another university, and its peak throughput need (at any given time) is 10 Mbps. The laboratory would require seven T1s (10 Mbps divided by 1.544 Mbps equals 6.48 T1s). Leasing seven T1s would prove much less expensive for the university than leasing a single T3.

- *fractional T1*—Allows organizations to use only some of the channels on a T1 line and be charged according to the number of channels they use. Thus, fractional T1 bandwidth can be leased in multiples of 64 Kbps. A fractional T1 is best suited to businesses that expect their traffic to grow and that may require a full T1 eventually, but can't currently justify leasing a full T1 right away.

A number of other T-carrier varieties are available to businesses today, as shown in Table 12-3. The speed of a T-carrier depends on its signal level. The term *signal level* refers to the T-carrier's Physical layer electrical signaling characteristics as defined by ANSI standards in the early 1980s. DS0 (digital signal level 0) is the equivalent of one data or voice channel. All other signal levels are multiples of DS0.

Table 12-3   T-carrier specifications

Signal level	T-carrier	Number of T1s	Number of channels	Throughput (Mbps)
DS0	—	1/24	1	.064
DS1	T1	1	24	1.544
DS1C	T1C	2	48	3.152
DS2	T2	4	96	6.312
DS3	T3	28	672	44.736
DS4	T4	168	4032	274.176
DS5	T5	240	5760	400.352

Note

You might hear *signal level* and *carrier* terms used interchangeably—for example, DS1 and T1. In fact, T1 (terrestrial carrier level 1) is the implementation of the DS1 standard used in North America and most of Asia. In Europe, the standard high-speed carrier connections are E1 and E3. Like T1s and T3s, E1s and E3s use time division multiplexing. However, an E1 allows for 32 channels and offers 2.048-Mbps throughput. An E3 allows for 512 channels and offers 34.368-Mbps throughput. Using special hardware, T1s can interconnect with E1s and T3s with E3s for international communications.

Voice Services Optimization

T1s are often used to support voice services to an organization. There are primarily two ways to go about doing this:

- ISDN PRI is essentially a T1 line with the channels slightly reorganized. A regular T1 is formally called a T1 CAS (Channel Associated Signaling) and colloquially referred to as Robbed Bit Signaling because part of each traffic channel is used for signaling. In an ISDN PRI, or T1 PRI, one channel (the Data channel) is dedicated to signaling so the other 23 channels (the Bearer channels) are used purely for voice or data transmission. Similarly, an E1 PRI dedicates two D channels to signaling, leaving 30 B channels for voice transmission. While a T1 CAS, T1 PRI, and E1 PRI can all support both data and voice traffic, the T1 PRI and E1 PRI offer some advantages to voice traffic due to the allocation of channels for different purposes. A huge disadvantage with T1 PRI, however, is that the number of B channels defines how many calls can be supported at any one time. An organization with more than 30 employees, each with his or her own phone number, might need multiple T1s—plus the additional equipment—to keep from running out of phone lines, especially if the business relies heavily on phone traffic. And that doesn't even count the data traffic.
- An alternative to T1 PRIs is a SIP trunk. Recall that SIP (Session Initial Protocol) is a signaling protocol used to initiate connections, such as for VoIP calls. SIP trunking employs VoIP to create virtual connections over an existing data service, whether that's a shared, broadband connection like Metro Ethernet or a dedicated, leased line, such as a T1. With a SIP trunk, the only limitation on the number of calls that can run at any one time is the amount of available bandwidth. All the calls run over the single data line, so it's not necessary to purchase additional equipment to support more channels for more calls. Overall SIP configuration is easier and cheaper than a T1 PRI, and provides greater flexibility.

T-Carrier Equipment

The approximate costs mentioned previously include monthly access, but not connectivity hardware. Every T-carrier line requires special hardware at both the customer site and the local telco's switching facility, as shown in Figure 12-17. This hardware can be purchased or leased, and is described next.

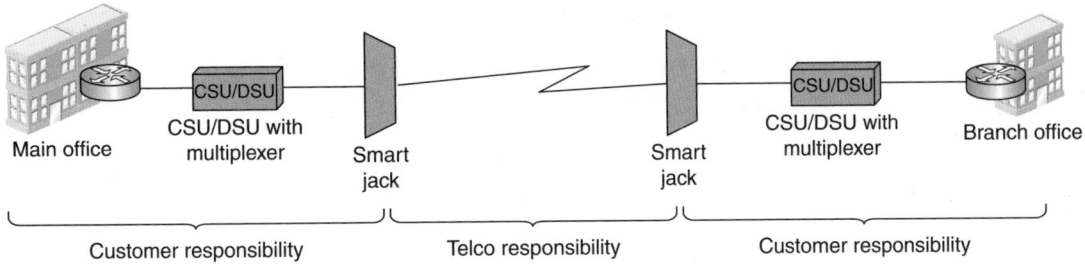

Figure 12-17   A point-to-point T-carrier connection

- *smart jack*—Terminates a T-carrier line at the customer's demarc, either inside or outside the building, and is a type of NIU. The smart jack also functions as a monitoring point for the connection. If the line between the carrier and customer experiences significant data errors, the smart jack will report this fact to the carrier. Technicians can also check the status of the line at the smart jack. Most smart jacks include LEDs associated with transmitted and received signals. For example, a steady green light on the display indicates no connectivity problems, whereas a flickering light indicates data errors. A power light indicates whether or not the smart jack is receiving any signal. Figure 12-18 shows a smart jack (or network interface) designed to be used with a T1. The smart jack is not capable of interpreting data, however, and relies on the CSU/DSU for that purpose.

Figure 12-18   A T1 smart jack

- *CSU/DSU*—Consists of a CSU (channel service unit) and DSU (data service unit) and serves as the DTE (data terminal equipment), or endpoint device, for a leased line. The device can be a stand-alone device, as shown in Figure 12-19, or an interface card.
    - ○ The CSU provides termination for the digital signal and ensures connection integrity through error correction and line monitoring.
    - ○ The DSU converts the T-carrier frames into frames the LAN can interpret and vice versa. It also connects T-carrier lines with terminating equipment. Finally, a DSU usually incorporates a multiplexer. (In some T-carrier installations, the multiplexer can be a separate device connected to the DSU.)

Figure 12-19   A CSU/DSU

Source: Kentrox, Inc.

- *multiplexer*—Combines multiple signals from a LAN for transport over the T-carrier line and separates an incoming T-carrier line's combined channels into individual signals that can be interpreted on the LAN. After being demultiplexed, an incoming T-carrier signal passes on to devices collectively known as terminal equipment. Examples of terminal equipment include switches, routers, or telephone exchange devices that accept only voice transmissions (such as a telephone switch).

On a typical T1-connected data network, the DTE or terminal equipment is a router, which translates between different Layer 3 protocols that might be used on the WAN and LAN. The router accepts incoming signals from a CSU/DSU stand-alone device and, if necessary, translates Network layer protocols, then directs data to its destination exactly as it does on any LAN.

On some implementations, the CSU/DSU is not a separate device, but is an expansion card installed in the router. An integrated CSU/DSU offers faster signal processing and better network performance, and is also a less-expensive and lower-maintenance solution than using a separate CSU/DSU device. Figure 12-20 illustrates one way a router with an integrated CSU/DSU can be used to connect a LAN with a T1 WAN link.

SONET (Synchronous Optical Network)

SONET (Synchronous Optical Network) is a high-bandwidth WAN signaling technique developed for fiber-optic cabling by Bell Communications Research in the 1980s, and later standardized by ANSI and ITU. SONET specifies framing and multiplexing techniques at the Physical layer of the OSI model. Its four key strengths are that it:

7	APPLICATION
6	PRESENTATION
5	SESSION
4	TRANSPORT
3	NETWORK
2	DATA LINK
1	PHYSICAL

- Can integrate many other WAN technologies
- Offers fast data transfer rates
- Allows for simple link additions and removals
- Provides a high degree of fault tolerance

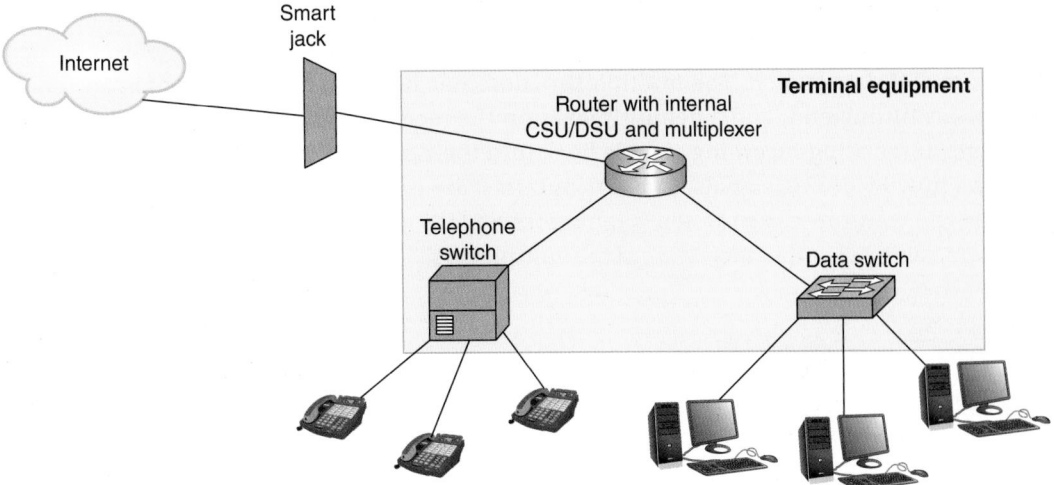

Figure 12-20   A T1 connecting to a LAN through a router

> **Note** 🖉
>
> The word **synchronous** as used in the name of this technology means that data being transmitted and received by nodes must conform to a timing scheme. A clock maintains time for all nodes on a network. A receiving node in synchronous communications recognizes that it should be receiving data by looking at the time on the clock.

Perhaps the most important SONET advantage is that it provides interoperability. Before SONET, telcos that used different signaling techniques (or even the same technique but different equipment) could not be assured that their networks could communicate. Now, SONET is often used to aggregate multiple T1s or T3s. SONET is also used as the underlying technology for ATM transmission, which you'll learn more about later in this chapter. Furthermore, because it can work directly with the different standards used in different countries, SONET has emerged as the best choice for linking WANs between North America, Europe, and Asia. The international implementation of SONET is known as **SDH (Synchronous Digital Hierarchy)**.

Unlike the other Layer 1 WAN technologies we've studied so far in this section, SONET is not primarily used as a last mile service. Instead, SONET more often traverses multiple ISP networks, connecting these networks through the Internet backbone. While SONET functions on fiber-optic cabling, it must interact with other types of media, because transmissions rarely begin and end on fiber.

On the transmitting end, SONET multiplexers accept input from different network types (for example, a T1 line) and format the data in a standard SONET frame. This means that many different devices might connect to a SONET multiplexer, including, for example, a private telephone switch, a T1 multiplexer, and an ATM data switch. The multiplexer combines individual SONET signals on the transmitting end, and a demultiplexer on the receiving end separates combined signals, translating incoming signals back into their original format. Figure 12-21 shows how incoming signals, called tributaries, are merged into a single signal. Along the way, the transmission might cross a plethora of other devices, including routers, switches, repeaters, and more multiplexers.

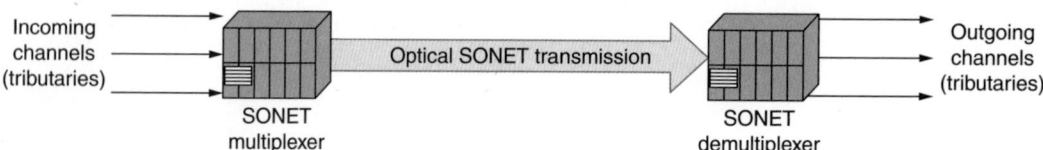

Figure 12-21 SONET tributaries and transmission

SONET's transmissions rely on a carefully orchestrated timing scheme. SONET frames are sent out on a regular schedule, whether or not they contain data. Similar to a city's bus system that continues to run whether passengers are on board or not, SONET's frames will travel without data rather than disrupt the schedule. And yet, it's impossible to keep all SONET devices synced perfectly. Therefore, SONET frames are a consistent size and include information indicating where the payload begins. This overhead information is not collected at the beginning of a transmission like you've seen with other protocols' frames. Instead, the information is interleaved among the data bits, as illustrated in Figure 12-22.

Figure 12-22 The frame's overhead information is interleaved with the frame's payload; the pattern is repeated nine times per frame

The data rate of a particular SONET connection is indicated by its **OC (Optical Carrier)** level, a rating that is internationally recognized by networking professionals and standards organizations. OC levels in SONET are analogous to the digital signal levels of T-carriers. Table 12-4 lists the OC levels and their maximum throughput.

Table 12-4	SONET OC levels	

OC level	Throughput (Mbps)	Notes
OC-1	51.84	Base rate.
OC-3	155.52	Popular choice for large businesses, and is equivalent to 100 T1s. A variant of OC-3 is OC-3c, where the *c* stands for *concatenated*. OC-3c concatenates three OC-1 lines into a single stream.
OC-12	622.08	Used by ISPs for WAN connections and by some large enterprises. Consists of four OC-3s.
OC-24	1244.16	Primarily used by ISPs and large enterprises.
OC-48	2488.32	Primarily used as a regional ISP backbone, and occasionally by very large hospitals, universities, or other major enterprises. Consists of four OC-12s.
OC-96	4976.64	Primarily used by ISPs.
OC-192	9953.28	Used for Internet backbone connections. Consists of four OC-48s.

SONET technology is typically not implemented by small or medium-sized businesses because of its high cost. Instead, it's commonly used by large companies; long-distance companies linking metropolitan areas and countries; ISPs that want to guarantee fast, reliable access to the Internet; or telephone companies connecting their COs. SONET is particularly suited to audio, video, and imaging data transmission. As you can imagine, given its reliance on fiber-optic cable and its redundancy requirements, SONET technology is expensive to implement.

Layer 2 WAN Technologies

 **Certification**

2.5 Compare and contrast WAN technologies.

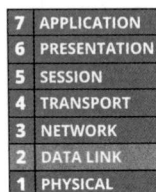

7	APPLICATION
6	PRESENTATION
5	SESSION
4	TRANSPORT
3	NETWORK
2	DATA LINK
1	PHYSICAL

For the most part, the WAN technologies you've learned about so far in this chapter are used for the link between the customer and the ISP. Once the transmission reaches the ISP's network, other Layer 1 technologies come into play, and these are beyond the scope of this text. However, you need to know about some Layer 2 technologies that do traverse the ISP's network in order to connect two or more LANs across a WAN connection. Although there are many more, let's look at the three technologies covered by the Network+ exam that you've not yet learned about in this text: frame relay, ATM (Asynchronous Transfer Mode), and MPLS (multiprotocol label switching).

Frame Relay

Frame relay is a group of Layer 2 protocols defined by ITU and ANSI in 1984. It was originally designed as a fast packet-switched network over ISDN, although today frame relay can be used as the Data Link layer protocol for various virtual circuit interfaces and media. The name, *frame relay*, is derived from the fact that data is separated into variable-length frames, which are then relayed from one node to another without any verification or processing. Routers establish a PVC (permanent virtual circuit) and frames carry an identifier, called a DLCI (data-link connection identifier), that routers read to determine which circuit to use for the frame. Therefore, frame relay is a connection-oriented protocol.

An organization might use frame relay for communication among the LANs at each branch office—each LAN, then, has a PVC from the branch office to the ISP. Frame relay equipment consists of DCE (data circuit-terminating equipment) at the ISP's location and DTE (data terminal equipment) at the customer's location, which might be a frame relay-capable router or switch, or a specialized FRAD (frame relay access device). See Figure 12-23.

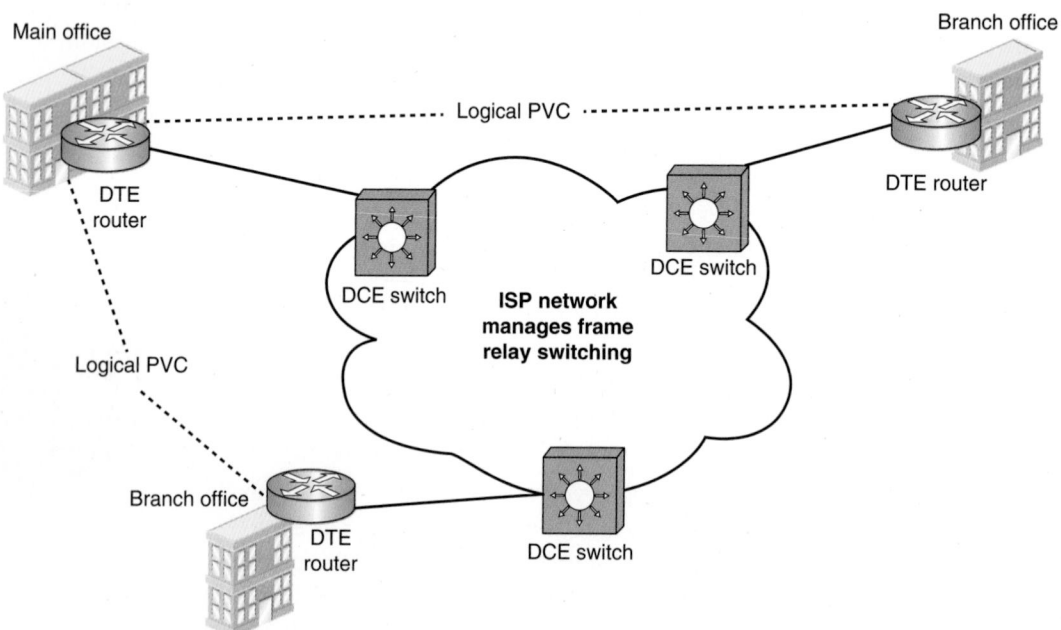

Figure 12-23   Three frame relay connections to the ISP create two different logical PVCs, one between the main office and each branch office

Recall that PVCs are *not* dedicated, individual links. When you lease a frame relay circuit from your local carrier, your contract reflects the endpoints you specify and the amount of bandwidth you require between those endpoints. The service provider guarantees a minimum amount of bandwidth, called the CIR (committed information rate). Provisions usually account for bursts of traffic that occasionally exceed the CIR. When you lease a PVC, you share bandwidth with other frame relay users on the backbone. PVC links are best suited to frequent and consistent data transmission.

The advantage to leasing a frame relay circuit over leasing a dedicated service is that you pay for only the amount of bandwidth required. Another advantage is that frame relay is less expensive than some other WAN technologies, depending on your location and its network availability. However, frame relay has been superseded by newer technologies, and many ISPs no longer support it.

ATM (Asynchronous Transfer Mode)

Along with frame relay, **ATM (Asynchronous Transfer Mode)** is a WAN technology that functions primarily at Layer 2, the Data Link layer, although its protocols can also reach to Layers 1 and 3. Its ITU standard prescribes both network access and signal multiplexing techniques. In this context, **asynchronous** refers to a communications method in which nodes do not have to conform to any predetermined schemes that specify the timing of data transmissions. In asynchronous communications, a node can transmit at any instant, and the destination node must accept the transmission as it comes. This is in contrast to timed, synchronous communications as used by SONET technology.

To ensure that the receiving node knows when it has received a complete frame, asynchronous communications provide start and stop bits for each character transmitted. When the receiving node recognizes a start bit, it begins to accept a new character. When it receives the stop bit for that character, it ceases to look for the end of that character's transmission. Asynchronous data transmission, therefore, occurs in random stops and starts.

Like Ethernet and frame relay, ATM specifies Data Link layer framing techniques. What sets ATM apart from Ethernet on a LAN and frame relay on a WAN is its fixed message size. In ATM, a message is called a **cell** and always consists of 48 bytes of data plus a 5-byte header. This fixed-sized, 53-byte package allows ATM to provide predictable network performance. However, recall that a smaller message size requires more overhead. In fact, ATM's smaller message size does decrease its potential throughput, but the efficiency of using cells helps compensate for that loss.

Like frame relay, ATM relies on virtual circuits. On an ATM network, switches determine the optimal path between the sender and receiver and then establish this path before the network transmits data. The use of virtual circuits means that ATM provides the main advantage of circuit switching—that is, a point-to-point connection that remains reliably available to the transmission until it completes. The use of virtual circuits makes ATM a connection-oriented technology. Because ATM packages data into cells before transmission, with each cell traveling separately to its destination, ATM is also considered a packet-switching technology.

Establishing a reliable connection allows ATM to guarantee a specific QoS for certain types of transmissions. ATM networks can supply four QoS levels, from a "best effort" attempt for noncritical data to a guaranteed, real-time transmission for time-sensitive data. This is important for organizations using networks for time-sensitive applications, such as video and audio transmissions. For example, a company depicted in Figure 12-24 might want to use its ATM connection between two offices located at opposite sides of a state to carry voice phone calls with the highest possible QoS. On the other hand, the company might assign a low QoS to routine email messages exchanged between the two offices.

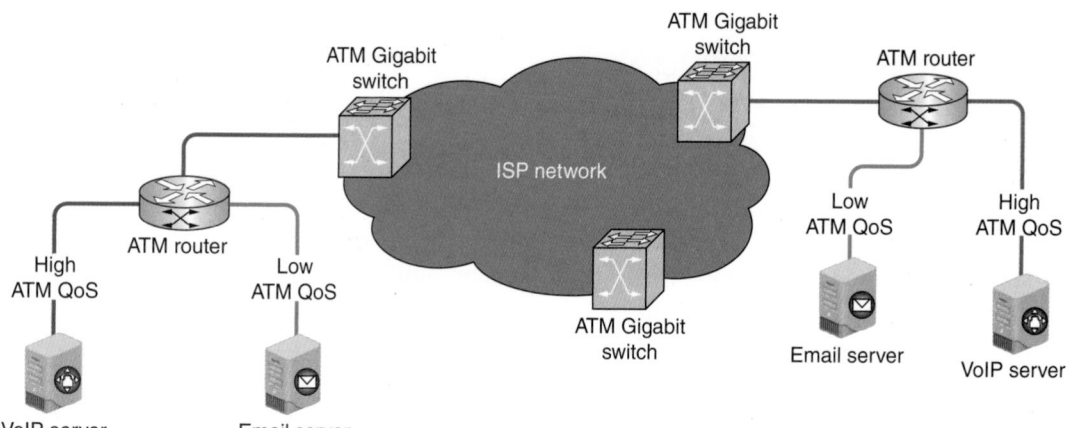

Figure 12-24   QoS can be defined for a point-to-point ATM connection

ATM is relatively expensive, is rarely used on small LANs, and is almost never used to connect typical workstations to a network. Although ATM was popular in the 1990s, it was initially overshadowed by IP and MPLS, and is now being edged out of the market completely by Metro Ethernet, which is cheaper.

MPLS (Multiprotocol Label Switching)

MPLS (multiprotocol label switching) was introduced by the IETF (Internet Engineering Task Force) in 1999. It has some of the strengths of ATM while avoiding its weaknesses, and also combines elements of both circuit-switching and packet-switching. As its name implies, MPLS enables multiple types of Layer 3 protocols to travel over any one of several connection-oriented Layer 2 protocols. MPLS supports IP and all the other Layer 3 and higher protocols used on TCP/IP networks. MPLS can operate over Ethernet frames, but is more often used with other Layer 2 protocols, like those designed for WANs. For these reasons, it's often used by ISPs on their own networks for moving traffic from one customer site to another, and it's becoming the solution of choice for many enterprises to connect their branch offices. For example, in Figure 12-25, an MPLS cloud within the ISP network manages traffic to and from various sites using a variety of Layer 1 technologies.

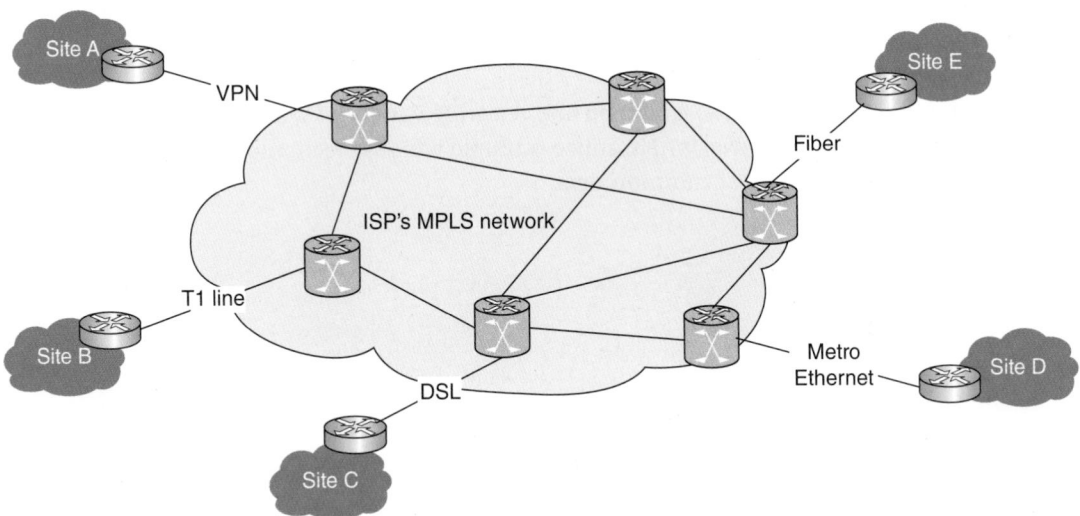

Figure 12-25 An ISP might use an MPLS WAN to move traffic from one customer site to another

One of the benefits of MPLS is the ability to use packet-switched technologies over traditionally circuit-switched networks. MPLS can create end-to-end paths that act like circuit-switched connections, such as VPNs, or it can connect meshed endpoints in an any-to-any scenario.

With MPLS, the first router that receives a message in a data stream adds one or more labels to the Layer 3 packet. Collectively, the MPLS labels are sometimes called a shim because of their placement between Layer 3 and Layer 2 information. For this reason, MPLS is sometimes said to belong to "Layer 2.5." Then, the network's Layer 2 protocol header is added, as shown in Figure 12-26.

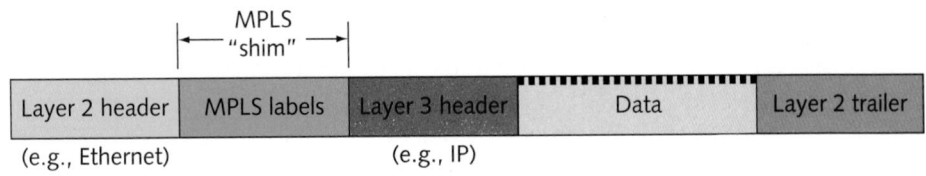

Figure 12-26 MPLS shim within a frame

MPLS labels include information about where the router should forward the message next and, sometimes, prioritization information. Each router in the data stream's path revises the label to indicate the packet's next hop. In this manner, routers on a network can take into consideration network congestion, QoS indicators assigned to the messages, plus other criteria. Network engineers have significant control in setting these paths. Consequently, MPLS offers potentially faster transmission than traditionally packet-switched or circuit-switched networks. Because it can add prioritization information, MPLS can also offer better QoS. These advantages make MPLS especially well-suited to WANs.

So far in this chapter, you've learned about a wide variety of wired WAN technologies. Similar to LANs, WANs utilize multiple wireless technologies as well. We'll look at two of the most common next.

Wireless WANs

 **Certification**

7	APPLICATION
6	PRESENTATION
5	SESSION
4	TRANSPORT
3	NETWORK
2	DATA LINK
1	PHYSICAL

1.6   Given a scenario, implement the appropriate wireless technologies and configurations.

2.5   Compare and contrast WAN technologies.

5.4   Given a scenario, troubleshoot common wireless connectivity and performance issues.

The best 802.11ac signal can travel approximately a quarter of a mile. But other types of wireless networks can connect stations over much longer distances. For example, in large cities, dozens of surveillance cameras trained on municipal buildings and parks beam video images to a central public safety headquarters. Meanwhile, in developing countries, wireless signals deliver lectures and training videos to students in remote, mountainous regions. In rural areas of the United States, elderly patients at home wear medical monitoring devices, such as blood pressure sensors and blood glucose meters, which use wireless networks to convey information to their doctors hundreds of miles away. Such networks can even alert paramedics in case of an emergency. All of these are examples of wireless WANs. Unlike wireless LANs, wireless WANs are designed for high-throughput, long-distance digital data exchange. The following sections describe a variety of ways wireless clients can communicate across a city or state.

Cellular

Cellular networks were initially designed to provide analog phone service. However, since the first mobile phones became available to consumers in the 1970s, cellular services have changed dramatically. In addition to voice signals, cellular networks now deliver text messages, web pages, music, and videos to smartphones and handheld devices. This section describes current cellular data technology and explains the role it plays in wide area networking.

To put today's services in context, it's useful to understand that each leap in cellular technology has been described as a new generation. Each successive generation has brought a greater range of services, better quality, and higher throughputs, as described in the following list:

- First-generation, or 1G, services from the 1970s and 1980s were analog.
- Second-generation, or 2G, services, which reigned in the 1990s, used digital transmission and paved the way for texting and media downloads on mobile devices. Still, data transmission on 2G systems didn't exceed 240 Kbps.
- Third-generation, or 3G, services were released in the early 2000s. Data rates rose to 384 Kbps and data (but not voice) communications used packet switching.
- Fourth-generation, or **4G**, services are characterized by an all-IP, packet-switched network for both data and voice transmission. 4G standards, released in 2008, also specify throughputs of 100 Mbps for fast-moving mobile clients, such as those in cars, and 1 Gbps for slow-moving mobile clients, such as pedestrians.
- Fifth-generation, or 5G, services don't yet exist. However, industry analysts expect 5G devices to offer download speeds of up to 20 Gbps and upload speeds of up to 10 Gbps.

In addition to generation classifications, cellular networks are also grouped by the base technology used to build those networks. Cell phone networks use one of these two competing voice technologies:

- **GSM (Global System for Mobile Communications)** is an open standard that is accepted and used worldwide. Digital communication of data is separated by timeslots on a channel using **TDMA (time division multiple access)**, which is similar to TDM (time division multiplexing). The primary difference is that multiplexed TDM signals all come from the same source (such as a router), while multiplexed TDMA signals come from several sources (such as several smartphones in the same vicinity). First introduced with the release of 2G devices, GSM initially only provided voice communications but added data services with the evolution of GPRS (General Packet Radio Services) and EGPRS (Enhanced GPRS), also called EDGE (Enhanced Data rates for GSM Evolution). GSM networks require that a cellular device have a **SIM (Subscriber Identity Module) card** that contains a microchip to hold data about the subscription a user has with the cellular carrier.
- **CDMA (Code Division Multiple Access)** differs from GSM in that it spreads a signal over a wider bandwidth so that multiple users occupy the same channel, a technology called spread-spectrum. Codes on the packets keep the various calls separated. CDMA networks do not require a SIM card in a cellular device because devices are compared against a white list, which is a database of subscribers that contains information on their subscriptions with the provider. However, some

CDMA networks (such as Sprint's), still require SIM cards for their LTE (Long Term Evolution) features. LTE is discussed later in this section.

CDMA was more popular than GSM in the United States for many years, but an updated version of GSM that replicates some of CDMA's technology is overtaking the global market. In fact, there are many parts of the world where only GSM is available. Although their access methods and features might differ, all cellular networks share a similar infrastructure in which coverage areas are divided into cells. Each cell is served by an antenna and its base station, or cell site. At the base station, a controller assigns mobile clients frequencies and manages communication with them. In network diagrams, cells are depicted as hexagons. Multiple cells share borders to form a network in a honeycomb pattern, as shown in Figure 12-27. Antennas are positioned at three corners of each cell, radiating and providing coverage over three equidistant lobes. When a client passes from one coverage area to another, his mobile device begins communicating with a different antenna. His communication might change frequencies or even carriers between cells. The transition, which normally happens without the user's awareness, is known as a handoff.

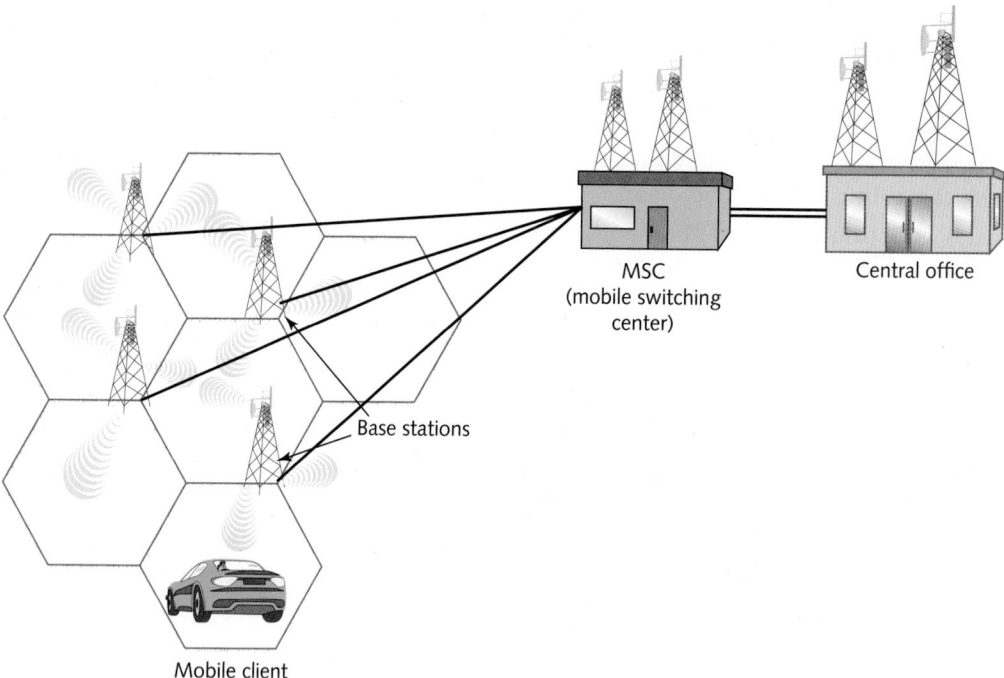

Figure 12-27 Cellular network

Cell sizes vary from roughly 1000 feet to 12 miles in diameter. The size of a cell depends on the network's access method and the region's topology, population, and amount of cellular traffic. An urban area with dense population and high volume of data and voice traffic might use cells with a diameter of only 2000 feet, their antennas mounted on tall buildings. In sparsely populated rural areas, with antennas mounted on isolated hilltop towers, cells might span more than 10 miles. In theory, the division of a network into cells provides thorough coverage over any given area. In reality, cells are misshapen due to terrain, EMF, and antenna radiation patterns. Some edges overlap and others don't meet up, leaving gaps in coverage.

As shown in Figure 12-27, each base station is connected to an MSC (mobile switching center), also called an MTSO (mobile telecommunications switching office), by a wireless link or fiber-optic cabling. The MSC might be located inside a telephone company's central office or it might stand alone and connect to the central office via another fiber-optic cabling or a microwave link. At the MSC, the mobile network intersects with the wired network. Equipment at an MSC manages mobile clients, monitoring their location and usage patterns, and switches cellular calls. It also assigns each mobile client an IP address. With 4G cellular services, a client's IP address remains the same from cell to cell and from one carrier's territory to another. In 3G cellular services, however, client IP addresses might change when the user transitions to a different carrier's service area. From the switching center, packets sent from cellular networks are routed to wired data networks through the PSTN or private backbones using WAN technologies you learned about earlier in this chapter.

Cellular networking is a complex topic, with rapidly evolving encoding and access methods, changing standards, and innovative vendors vying to dominate the market. This chapter does not detail the various encoding and access methods used on cellular networks. However, to qualify for the CompTIA Network+ certification, you should understand the basic infrastructure of a cellular network and the cellular technologies frequently used for data networking, beginning with HSPA+:

- **HSPA+ (High Speed Packet Access Plus)** began as a 3G technology released in 2008 that uses MIMO and sophisticated encoding techniques to achieve a maximum 168 Mbps downlink throughput and 22 Mbps uplink throughput in its current release. To achieve such speeds, HSPA+ uses limited channels more efficiently and incorporates more antennas in MIMO transmission. However, faster and more flexible technologies, such as LTE, are overtaking HSPA+ in popularity.
- **LTE (Long-Term Evolution)** is a 4G technology that uses a different access method than HSPA+. While the latest version, LTE-Advanced, can theoretically achieve downlink data rates of up to 1 Gbps and uplink rates up to 100 Mbps, actual speeds are significantly less. LTE is currently the fastest wireless broadband service available in the United States.

Satellite

In 1945, Arthur C. Clarke (the author of *2001: A Space Odyssey*) wrote an article in which he described the possibility of communication between manned space stations that continually orbited the Earth. Other scientists recognized the worth of using satellites to convey signals from one location on Earth to another. By the 1960s, the United States was using satellites to transmit telephone and television signals across the Atlantic Ocean. Since then, the proliferation of this technology and reductions in its cost have made satellite transmission appropriate and available for transmitting consumer voice, video, music, and data.

Satellite Orbits

Most satellites circle the Earth 22,300 miles above the equator in a geosynchronous orbit. GEO (geosynchronous earth orbit) means that satellites orbit the Earth at the same rate as the Earth turns. A special case of geosynchronous orbit, called geostationary orbit (because it appears stationary from Earth), stays directly above the equator. This is especially common with communications satellites. Consequently, at every point in their orbit, the satellites maintain a constant distance from a specific point on the Earth's equator.

Because satellites are generally used to relay information from one point on Earth to another, information sent to Earth from a satellite first has to be transmitted to the satellite from Earth in an uplink from an Earth-based transmitter to an orbiting satellite. Often, the uplink signal information is scrambled (in other words, its signal is encoded) before transmission to prevent unauthorized interception. At the satellite, a transponder receives the uplink signal, then transmits it to an Earth-based receiver in a downlink. A typical satellite contains 24 to 32 transponders. Each satellite uses unique frequencies for its downlink. These frequencies, as well as the satellite's orbit location, are assigned and regulated by the FCC. Back on Earth, the downlink is picked up by a dish-shaped antenna. The dish shape concentrates the signal so that it can be interpreted by a receiver. Figure 12-28 provides a simplified view of satellite communication.

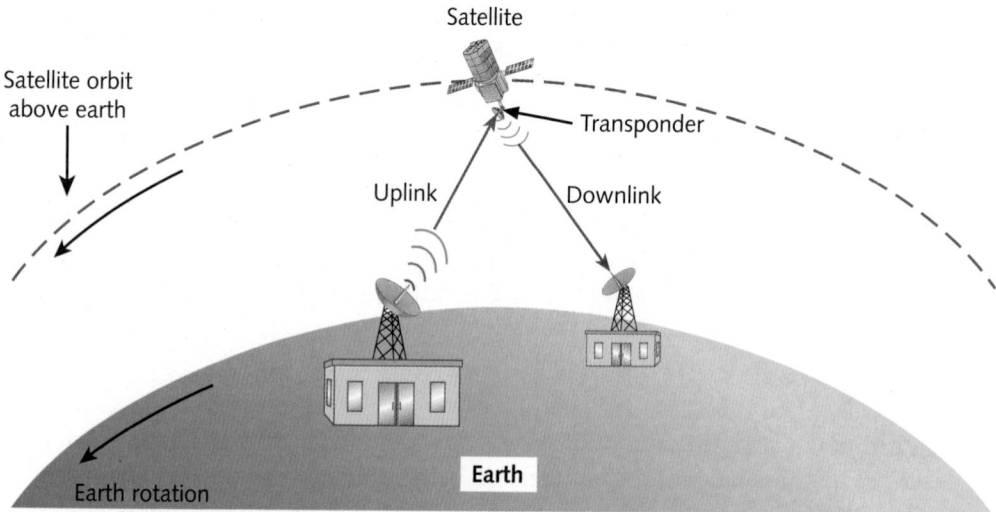

Figure 12-28 Satellite communication

Geosynchronous earth orbiting satellites are the type used by the most popular satellite data service providers. This technology is well established, and is the least expensive of all satellite technology. Also, because many of these satellites remain in a fixed position relative to the Earth's surface, stationary receiving dishes on Earth can be counted on to receive satellite signals reliably, weather permitting.

Satellite Frequencies

Satellites transmit and receive signals in any of the six frequency bands listed in Table 12-5.

Table 12-5   Satellite frequency bands

Band	Frequency range
L-band	1.5–2.7 GHz
S-band	2.7–3.5 GHz
C-band	3.4–6.7 GHz
K_u-band ("K-under band")	12–18 GHz
K-band	18–27 GHz
K_a-band ("K-above band")	26.5–40 GHz

Within each band, frequencies used for uplink and downlink transmissions differ. This variation helps ensure that signals traveling in one direction (for example, from a satellite to the Earth) do not interfere with signals traveling in the other direction (for example, signals from the Earth to a satellite).

Satellite Internet Services

A handful of companies offer high-bandwidth Internet access via GEO satellite links. Each subscriber uses a small satellite antenna and receiver, or satellite modem, to exchange signals with the service provider's satellite network. Clients may be fixed, such as rural dwellers who are too remote for DSL, or mobile subscribers, such as travelers on ocean-going yachts.

Clients are able to exchange signals with satellites as long as they have a line-of-sight path, or an unobstructed view of the sky. To establish a satellite Internet connection, each subscriber must have a dish antenna, which is approximately 2 feet high by 3 feet wide, installed in a fixed position. In North America, these dish antennas are pointed toward the Southern Hemisphere (because many geosynchronous satellites travel over the equator). The dish antenna's receiver is connected, via cable, to a modem. This modem uses either a PCI or USB interface to connect with the subscriber's computer.

As with several other wireless WAN technologies, satellite services are typically asymmetrical and bandwidth is shared among many subscribers. Throughputs vary and are controlled by the service provider. Typical downlink rates range from

2 to 3 Mbps and uplink rates reach maybe 1 Mbps. Compared with other wireless WAN options, satellite services are slower and suffer more latency. In addition, the inconsistent latency causes jitter problems, degrading signal quality. Given these drawbacks, satellite data service is preferred only in circumstances that allow few alternatives or in cases where satellite receiving equipment is already installed.

Chapter Summary

WAN Essentials

- A WAN traverses a significant distance and usually connects LANs.

- The customer's endpoint device on the WAN is called the DTE (data terminal equipment), and the carrier's endpoint device for the WAN is called the DCE (data circuit-terminating equipment).

- To troubleshoot ISP problems, you need to know the difference between equipment that belongs to the ISP, and equipment that belongs to the subscriber. Equipment located on the customer's premises, regardless of who owns it and who is responsible for it, is called CPE (customer premise equipment). Equipment belonging to the ISP, despite its location on the customer's premises, should only be serviced by the ISP's technicians, even if it is located on the customer's side of the demarc.

Layer 1 WAN Technologies

- When dealing with WAN technologies, Physical layer services are generally performed by Layer 1 standards such as DSL, ISDN, SONET, and T-carrier links. Although these standards might have features that stretch above Layer 1 into

higher layers, most operate primarily at the Physical layer to provide auto-negotiation, signaling, carrier sensing, flow control, synchronization, and possibly error control services.

- The PSTN (public switched telephone network), also called POTS (plain old telephone service), is a circuit-switching network of lines and carrier equipment that provides landline telephone service to homes and businesses.

- Dial-up required the user to enter a phone number that the computer called, waited for a response, and then negotiated a connection.

- ISDN (Integrated Services Digital Network) as an international standard was originally established by the ITU in 1984 for transmitting both digital data and voice over the PSTN. ISDN specified protocols at the Physical, Data Link, and Transport layers of the OSI model. These protocols handled signaling, framing, connection setup and termination, routing, flow control, and error detection and correction. Connections could be either dial-up or dedicated.

- DSL (digital subscriber line) is a WAN connection method introduced by researchers at Bell Laboratories in the mid-1990s. It operates over the PSTN and competes directly with cable broadband and T1 services.

- Cable broadband, or cable modem access, is based on the coaxial cable wiring used for TV signals. It was standardized by an international, cooperative effort orchestrated by CableLabs that yielded a suite of specifications called DOCSIS (Data Over Cable Service Interface Specifications).

- A growing trend in the ISP offerings for WAN connection services is a fairly recent development in Ethernet technology which began with Metro (Metropolitan) Ethernet and grew into a global scale technology called Carrier Ethernet. ISPs are developing ways to send Ethernet traffic across WAN connections (called Carrier Ethernet) and MAN connections (called Metro Ethernet), as first standardized by the MEF (Metro Ethernet Forum).

- T-carrier technology, which includes T1s, fractional T1s, and T3s, provides a dedicated logical circuit that is used only by the customer. AT&T developed T-carrier technology in 1957 in an effort to digitize voice signals and thereby enable such signals to travel longer distances over the PSTN.

- SONET (Synchronous Optical Network) is a high-bandwidth WAN signaling technique developed for fiber-optic cabling by Bell Communications Research in the 1980s, and later standardized by ANSI and ITU. SONET specifies framing and multiplexing techniques at the Physical layer of the OSI model.

Layer 2 WAN Technologies

- Frame relay is a group of Layer 2 protocols defined by ITU and ANSI in 1984. It was originally designed as a fast packet-switched network over ISDN, although today frame relay can be used as the Data Link layer protocol for various virtual circuit interfaces and media. The name, *frame relay*, is derived from the fact that data is separated into variable-length frames, which are then relayed from one node to another without any verification or processing.

- ATM (Asynchronous Transfer Mode) is a WAN technology that functions primarily at Layer 2, the Data Link layer, although its protocols can also reach to Layers 1 and 3. Its ITU standard prescribes both network access and signal multiplexing techniques. In this context, asynchronous refers to a communications method in which nodes do not have to conform to any predetermined schemes that specify the timing of data transmissions.

- MPLS (multiprotocol label switching) was introduced by the IETF (Internet Engineering Task Force) in 1999. It has some of the strengths of ATM while avoiding its weaknesses, combining elements of both circuit-switching and packet-switching. As its name implies, MPLS enables multiple types of Layer 3 protocols to travel over any one of several connection-oriented Layer 2 protocols.

Wireless WANs

- GSM (Global System for Mobile Communications) is an open standard that is accepted and used worldwide. Digital communication of data is separated by timeslots on a channel using TDMA (time division multiple access), which is similar to TDM (time division multiplexing). CDMA (Code Division Multiple Access) differs from GSM in that it spreads a signal over a wider bandwidth so that multiple users occupy the same channel, a technology called spread-spectrum.

- Geosynchronous earth orbiting satellites are the type used by the most popular satellite data service providers. This technology is well established, and is the least expensive of all satellite technology. Also, because many of these satellites remain in a fixed position relative to the Earth's surface, stationary receiving dishes on Earth can be counted on to receive satellite signals reliably, weather permitting.

Key Terms

For definitions of key terms, see the Glossary near the end of the book.

4G
ADSL (asymmetric DSL)
asymmetrical
asynchronous
ATM (Asynchronous Transfer Mode)
B channel
bandwidth speed tester
BRI (Basic Rate Interface)
broadband
cable broadband
cable modem
Carrier Ethernet
CDMA (Code Division Multiple Access)
cell
CET (Carrier-Ethernet Transport)
circuit-switched
CSU/DSU
D channel
dedicated line
DIA (dedicated Internet access)
dial-up
DOCSIS (Data Over Cable Service Interface Specifications)

DSL (digital subscriber line)
E1
E3
fractional T1
frame relay
GSM (Global System for Mobile Communications)
HFC (hybrid fiber coaxial)
HSPA+ (High Speed Packet Access Plus)
ISDN (Integrated Services Digital Network)
local loop
LTE (Long-Term Evolution)
LTE-Advanced
Metro (Metropolitan) Ethernet
modem
MPLS (multiprotocol label switching)
NIU (network interface unit)
OC (Optical Carrier)
OC-1
OC-3
OC-12
packet-switched
PRI (Primary Rate Interface)

PSTN (public switched telephone network)
PVC (permanent virtual circuit)
SDH (Synchronous Digital Hierarchy)
SDSL (symmetric DSL)
SIM (Subscriber Identity Module) card
SIP trunking
smart jack
SONET (Synchronous Optical Network)
SVC (switched virtual circuit)
switching
symmetrical
synchronous
T1
T3
T-carrier
TDMA (time division multiple access)
VDSL (very high bit rate DSL or variable DSL)
virtual circuit
xDSL (extended DSL)

Review Questions

1. What is the lowest layer of the OSI model at which LANs and WANs support the same protocols?
   a. Layer 2
   b. Layer 3
   c. Layer 4
   d. Layer 5

2. An organization can lease a private _____ that is not shared with other users, or a _____ that can be physically configured over shared lines in the carrier's cloud.
   a. PVC (permanent virtual circuit), SVC (switched virtual circuit)
   b. SVC (switched virtual circuit), dedicated line
   c. dedicated line, virtual circuit
   d. SVC (switched virtual circuit), PVC (permanent virtual circuit)

3. What kind of device can monitor a connection at the demarc but cannot interpret data?
   a. CSU/DSU
   b. NID
   c. NIU
   d. Smart jack

4. What kind of network is the PSTN?
   a. Packet-switched
   b. Circuit-switched
   c. Virtual circuit
   d. Dedicated line

5. How many channels are in an ISDN PRI connection?
   a. 2B+D
   b. 2D+B
   c. 23D+B
   d. 23B+D

6. What specifications define the standards for cable broadband?
   a. ATM
   b. Digital signal
   c. ANSI
   d. DOCSIS

7. _____ in SONET are analogous to the _____ of T-carriers.
   a. Throughput, digital signal levels
   b. OC levels, digital signal levels
   c. QoS levels, OC levels
   d. OC levels, carrier levels

8. Which DSL standard has the fastest speeds immediately outside the CO?
   a. VDSL
   b. ADSL
   c. SDSL
   d. ADSL2+

9. What method does a GSM network use to separate data on a channel?
   a. SIM
   b. CDMA
   c. TDMA
   d. TDM

10. Where does an MPLS label go in a PDU?
    a. Layer 1
    b. Between Layers 2 and 3
    c. Between Layers 1 and 2
    d. Layer 3

11. What are two types of virtual circuits?

12. What are three examples of Layer 2 LAN or PAN standards that also function at Layer 1?

13. What information is typically included in a Layer 1 frame?

14. Which ISDN channel carries signaling information?

15. What two types of modulation does DSL use to carry data?

16. What device must be installed on a DSL network to protect the sound quality of phone calls?

17. What type of network combines fiber with coax?

18. What is the maximum capacity of a T1 line?

19. Which protocol can provide VoIP services over a Metro Ethernet connection?

20. How large is an ATM cell?

Hands-On Projects

Project 12-1: Research CSU/DSU Devices

Just as you might go shopping for a modem in order to get specific features, you can also shop for a CSU/DSU to meet particular needs when you have a T1 or T3 line. In this project, you will research CSU/DSU devices. Complete the following steps to find an appropriate device for each scenario:

1. You've just been hired by a small company that is ready to lease its first fractional T1 line. Find a Cisco second-generation WIC (WAN interface connector) that can provide a fractional T1 connection. List the product description details that indicate the WIC you found will meet these requirements, and be sure to include the price and the website where you found your device. Find at least three reviews of the product and include that information as well.

2. Your company has grown over the past year, and is ready to upgrade to a full T1 line. You've also decided to upgrade the router at the same time, so you decide to purchase a router-CSU/DSU bundle. Find a device that includes the router and the CSU/DSU capabilities, and that is rack-mountable. List the product description details that indicate the device you found will meet these requirements, and be sure to include the price and the website where you found your device. Find at least one review of the product and include that information as well.

3. Your company has grown even more, and merged with another, larger company. Your new employer is ready to upgrade to a T3 line. You'll need a new CSU/DSU, and this time you decide to get a dedicated CSU/DSU device. Find a device that includes CSU/DSU capabilities for a full-rate T3 line and that is rack-mountable. List the product description details that indicate the device you found will meet these requirements, and be sure to include the price and the website where you found your device.

Project 12-2: Develop a Plan to Troubleshoot a WAN Connection

In this project, you'll research suggestions online for troubleshooting Internet connection problems, and develop your own list of procedures to follow the next time you encounter this type of problem.

1. In a web browser, do a search for tips, tricks, hints, and steps for troubleshooting Internet connection issues. Make a list of ideas from at least three different sources that you can use for future reference.

2. Think about the ideas you've gathered, and consider which steps should be completed first, middle, and last, to narrow down and identify a problem as quickly as possible without a great deal of backtracking. Make sure your troubleshooting steps cover a wide variety of potential problems.

3. Rearrange and edit your list so that the steps would be easy to follow, beginning to end, in a troubleshooting scenario. Draw a troubleshooting diagram using the same style as the troubleshooting diagram in Figure 1-21 at the beginning of this text. Explain why you placed the steps in the order you chose, and list one or more potential problems that each step is designed to detect. Include your information sources with your diagram and explanations.

Project 12-3: Explore WAN Options in Your Area

Selecting a particular WAN solution because its theoretical maximum speed is faster than another solution's theoretical maximum speed won't help much if your local carrier doesn't actually offer service at that speed. Selecting a WAN solution for a corporation requires familiarity with the options available in your area and their actual performance levels relative to each other. Complete the following steps to evaluate the ISP options available to a business in your area:

1. Compile a list of ISPs in your town or city. If you live in a rural area with few options, select a nearby city with more options so that you'll be able to include some of the private WAN technologies in addition to residential WAN offerings.

2. Check the website for each ISP to determine what broadband services they offer in your area, both for residential customers and corporate customers. Include both wired and wireless options. Answer the following questions:

   a. What are their advertised speeds?

   b. How much does each solution cost on a monthly basis?

   c. What installation fees are there, if any?

   d. How far away are you located from their CO? (If you're researching another city besides your own, use a fictional location in that same city.)

   e. What effect will this distance likely have on the actual speeds of each service option?

3. Search online for consumer reviews of each ISP in your list. What kinds of ratings does each ISP receive online?

Project 12-4: Configure TCP/IP in Ubuntu Server

In this project, you will learn to configure TCP/IP in Ubuntu Server. Ubuntu stores TCP/IP configuration settings in the /etc/network/interfaces text file. These settings are persistent, which means they are used each time a NIC reconnects to the network. You can temporarily change TCP/IP settings by using the `ifconfig`, `route`, `nameserver`, and other commands and by editing the /etc/resolv.conf text file. Using the Ubuntu Server VM you created in Chapter 4, Capstone Project 4-1, follow these steps to examine TCP/IP settings and temporarily change these settings.

1. Start the VM and log on to Ubuntu Server.

2. To view the current TCP/IP settings, enter the command `ifconfig`.

3. Write down the IP address, MTU, network mask, and MAC address for the active network connection (not the loopback).

4. To go to the /etc directory, enter the command `cd /etc`.

5. Ubuntu temporarily stores the IP addresses of name servers in the /etc/resolv.conf file. Enter the command `cat resolv.conf` to view the contents of this file.

6. Write down the IP addresses of the current DNS name server(s).

7. To go to the /etc/network directory, enter the command `cd network`.

8. Enter the command `cat interfaces` to view the contents of the /etc/network/interfaces file.

9. What is the name of the primary interface? It might be eth0, enp0s3, or something similar.

10. Enter the command `route -n` to view the IP address of your current default gateway.

11. Recall that 8.8.8.8 is the IP address of one of Google's public DNS servers. Enter the command `ping 8.8.8.8` to verify you have Internet connectivity. To stop the `ping`, press **CTRL+C**.

12. Now let's make some temporary changes to the TCP/IP configuration. Change your IP address to 10.0.0.100 and your network mask to 255.255.255.0, using the following command, and then enter your password:

    `sudo ifconfig <primaryinterface> 10.0.0.100 netmask 255.255.255.0`

13. Most likely, you will no longer have Internet connectivity. To verify that is the case, enter the command `ping 8.8.8.8`.

14. Enter the command `sudo ifdown <primaryinterface>` to release the current TCP/IP settings for the primary interface.

15. Enter the command `sudo ifup <primaryinterface>` to renew the network interface using the persistent TCP/IP settings for that interface.

16. Verify Internet connectivity is restored: `ping 8.8.8.8`

17. Verify DNS works: `ping google.com`

18. Power down your Ubuntu Server VM: `sudo poweroff`

Capstone Projects

Capstone Project 12-1: Create WAN Links in Packet Tracer

You can create several kinds of WAN connections in Packet Tracer. In this project, we'll keep this topology very simple so you can see the process instead of getting mired in the details. You'll create DSL connections between two networks and a web server, which will host your own web page. Complete the following steps:

1. Open Packet Tracer and add the following devices, as shown in Figure 12-29:
   a. Two generic **PCs**
   b. One generic **Server**

c. Two generic **Switches**

d. Two **DSL Modems** (from the Network Devices > WAN Emulation group)

e. One **Cloud-PT-Empty** (from the Network Devices > WAN Emulation group)

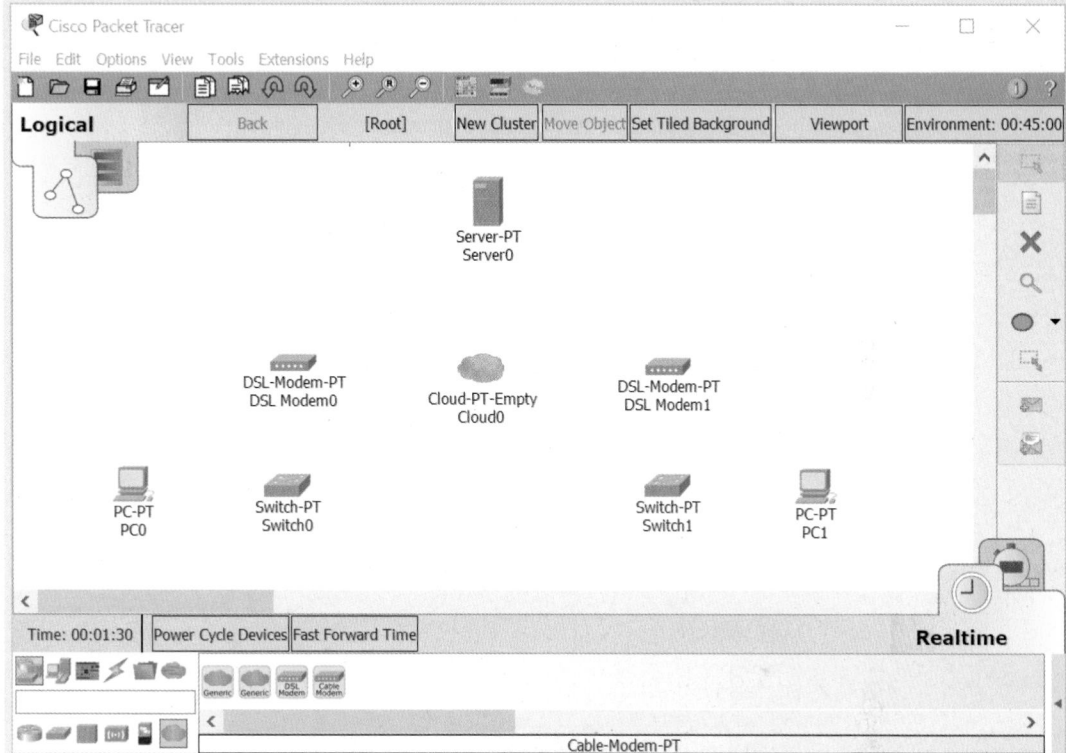

Figure 12-29   Add these devices to your network

Source: Cisco Systems, Inc.

2. Let's first configure the services you need on the Server. Click the **Server** and click the **Config** tab. On the **FastEthernet0** interface, assign the Server the static IP address **192.168.2.100/24**. On the Global Settings page, configure the gateway as **192.168.2.1** and the DNS server as **192.168.2.100**.

3. On the **Services** tab, click **DHCP**. Configure the following information:

   Pool Name: **DSL-lab**

   DNS server: **192.168.2.100**

   Start IP address: **192.168.2.0**

   Subnet mask: **255.255.255.0**

4. Click **Save**, then turn the DHCP service **On**.

5. Click **DNS**, configure the following information, click **Add**, then turn the DNS service **On**:

   Name: **www.cengage.com**

   Address: **192.168.2.100**

6. Click **HTTP**. Next to the index.html file, click **(edit)**. As shown in Figure 12-30, delete the line that says *Welcome to Cisco Packet Tracer. Opening doors to new opportunities. Mind Wide Open*. Replace that text with your own message, such as **Welcome to Jill West's web page!!** (using your own name, of course). Click **Save**, and then click **Yes**. Close the Server's configuration window.

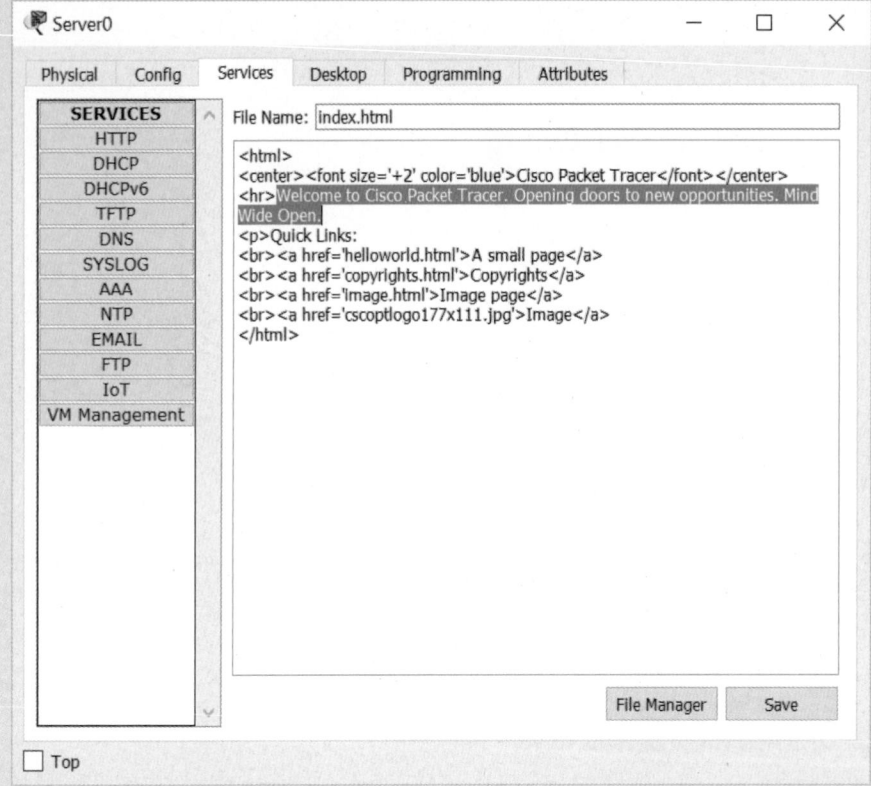

Figure 12-30   Replace this text with your own
Source: Cisco Systems, Inc.

7. Next, add and configure interfaces on the cloud. Click the **Cloud**. Turn off the physical device (scroll to the right to view the Power button if necessary). Drag two **PT-CLOUD-NM-1AM** modules to available slots, then drag one **PT-CLOUD-NM-1CFE** module to an available slot. Turn the physical device back on.

8. Click the **Config** tab and click **DSL**. Make sure Modem3 and FastEthernet2 are showing for the ports, and click **Add**. Then select Modem4 and FastEthernet2, and click **Add** again. Close the Cloud's configuration window.

9. Configure each PC to use DHCP.

10. Connect each PC to its Switch using a **Copper Straight-Through** cable.

11. Connect each Switch to its DSL Modem using a **Copper Cross-Over** cable. Use FastEthernet ports on the Switches, and Port 1 on each Modem.

12. Connect each Modem to the Cloud using a **Phone** cable. On the Cloud, connect to the Modem ports.

13. Connect the Cloud to the Server using a **Copper Straight-Through** cable.

14. Once all ports are up, confirm that each PC received an IP address. What IP address did PC0 get? What about PC1?

15. On each PC, ping the Server. Does it work? If not, troubleshoot the problem.

16. On one PC, ping **www.cengage.com**. Does it work? If not, troubleshoot the problem.

17. On one PC, open a web browser and navigate to **www.cengage.com**. What do you see?

18. Save your Packet Tracer network. Make some notes on your Wikidot website about your activities in this project.

Capstone Project 12-2: Organize Wikidot Website

Throughout this text, you've kept notes on various projects in your Wikidot website. To finish up these projects, let's do some final cleanup and organization so these notes will continue to be useful and easily accessible for you as you move into your other IT classes and your career. You might decide to continue adding notes, pages, and categories, or create new wikis as needed. Using good organization and adding thorough notes could make your wiki a valuable exhibit when applying for your first job in IT. Complete the following steps:

1. Let's first adjust the side navigation menu. On the All Pages page, click **Side Navigation** and then click **Edit**. You should see the text shown in Figure 12-31. Throughout this project, you can ignore any red, squiggly lines in the text unless they indicate a place where you've misspelled a word. Be sure to use correct spelling and good grammar in your wiki's content text.

```
[[div class="text-center" style="margin-bottom: 12px;"]]

[[module Clone]]

[[/div]]


+ Site Navigation

* [[[help:_home|User Guide]]]
* [[[help:first-time-user|First Time User]]]
* [[[main:about|About]]]
* [[[main:contact|Contact]]]
* [[[legal:_home|Legal]]]
* [[[forum:start|Discussion Forums]]]
* [[[system:members|Members]]]


+ Create a Page
[[module NewPage size="20" button="New page"]]
```

Figure 12-31   Side navigation bar coding
Source: Wikidot Inc.

2. Let's change the User Guide link to point to the list of all pages instead. On the User Guide line (the first line under "+ Site Navigation"), edit it to read:

   * [[[system:list-all-pages|All Pages]]]

3. When you're finished, the edited text should look something like what is shown in Figure 12-32 as the first item in the Site Navigation list. Save your changes and test the new link.

```
[[div class="text-center" style="margin-bottom: 12px;"]]
[[module Clone]]
[[/div]]

+ Site Navigation

* [[[system:list-all-pages|All Pages]]]
* [[[help:first-time-user|First Time User]]]
* [[[main:about|About]]]
* [[[main:contact|Contact]]]
* [[[legal:_home|Legal]]]
* [[[forum:start|Discussion Forums]]]
* [[[system:members|Members]]]

+ Create a Page
[[module NewPage size="20" button="New page"]]
```

Figure 12-32   Edited side navigation bar
Source: Wikidot Inc.

Each time you named a page with one part before the colon and another part after the colon, such as Applications:Wireshark, you added that page to a category. The first name, such as Applications, is the name of the category. The second name, such as Wireshark, is the name of the page.

4. To see a list of all categories in your wiki, click the gear icon, then click **Site Manager**, **Appearance & Behaviour**, and **Navigation elements**. Click the drop-down arrow next to *Choose the category*.

The trick now is to find a way to list pages according to each category. To do this, you'll first create a Categories page.

5. Go back to your wiki, and create a new page called **system:All Categories**.
6. Add the text **[[module Categories]]** to your page and save it.
7. Go back to the All Pages list. The All Categories page is listed as "system:All Categories." To list this page as "All Categories" instead, click the **system:All Categories** page, click **Edit**, and change the title of the page to read **All Categories**. The *name* of the page still includes its category (system), but now the *title* of the page will show only "All Categories."

This module automatically creates a list of all the categories and all the pages within each category. If any page is listed in the wrong module, you can't edit the page's title to change its category. When you edit the page, you're editing the title of that page, not its name, which is what defines the page's category.

8. To change a page's category, go to the page and click **+ Options**, then click **Rename**. Change the page's category, which is the name *before* the colon, and click **Rename/move**.

Now let's edit the top navigation bar so it shows one or more categories as an option, and each page within that category as an option.

9. Click the gear icon, and click **Edit Top Bar**. Then click the **Edit** button on this page. You should see text similar to what's shown in Figure 12-33.

```
[[ul class="nav navbar-nav"]]
[[li]][[a href="/main:about"]]About [[span class="fa fa-info-circle"]]@
[[/span]][[/a]][[/li]]
[[li]][[a href="/main:layout"]]Layout [[span class="fa fa-code"]]
@< >@[[/span]][[/a]][[/li]]
[[li]][[a href="/system:join"]]Membership [[span class="fa fa-user"]]
@< >@[[/span]][[/a]][[/li]]
[[li]][[a href="/help:_home"]]User Guide [[span class="fa
fa-exclamation-circle"]]@< >@[[/span]]
[[/a]][[/li]]
[[li class="dropdown"]]
[[a href="#" class="dropdown-toggle" data-toggle="dropdown"]]Help Docs
[[span class="fa fa-question-circle"]]@< >@[[/span]][[/a]][[ul
class="dropdown-menu"]]
  [[li]][[a href="/help:_home"]]User Guide[[/a]][[/li]]
  [[li]][[a href="/help:first-time-user"]]First Time User[[/a]][[/li]]
  [[li]][[a href="/help:quick-reference"]]Quick Reference[[/a]][[/li]]
  [[li]][[a href="/help:creating-pages"]]Creating Pages[[/a]][[/li]]
  [[li]][[a href="/help:editing-pages"]]Editing Pages[[/a]][[/li]]
  [[li]][[a href="/help:navigation-bars"]]Navigation Bars[[/a]][[/li]]
  [[li]][[a href="/help:using-modules"]]Using Modules[[/a]][[/li]]
  [[li]][[a href="/help:templates"]]Templates[[/a]][[/li]]
  [[li]][[a href="/help:css-themes"]]CSS Themes[[/a]][[/li]]
[[/ul]]
[[/li]]
```

Figure 12-33   Top navigation bar coding

Source: Wikidot Inc.

Currently, the only link in the top navigation bar that gives a drop-down menu is the Help Docs link. We want to remove some of the links in the top navigation bar and add a drop-down link for each category.

10. Delete the **Layout** and **Membership** lines in this text.

11. Change the text **User Guide** to **All Categories**. Change its location to **system:all-categories**. The line should now read:

    [[li]][[a href="/system:all-categories"]]All Categories [[span class="fa fa-exclamation-circle"]]@< >@[[/span]][[/a]][[/li]]

12. Change the text **Help Docs** to the name of one of your categories, such as **Applications**.

13. For each sub-item, add the name and location of a page within that category. For example, the Wireshark page would be listed under Applications like this:

    [[li]][[a href="/applications:wireshark"]]Wireshark[[/a]][[/li]]

    It might help to have two browser windows open—one showing the All Pages list for a reference, and the other showing the top navigation menu editing page. Add extra lines if needed.

Notice the small icons next to each item on the top navigation menu, such as an "i" in a circle, an exclamation mark in a circle, and a question mark in a circle. Let's change the icon next to the Applications category to be an "i" instead of a question mark.

14. On the Applications line, change the text that reads "fa fa-question-circle" so it says **"fa fa-info-circle"**.

15. On the About line, change the text that reads "fa fa-info-circle" so it says **"fa fa-question-circle"**.

16. When you've made all these changes, look over it again to see if you can find any typos or missed links. When you're ready, click **Save**. The new Top Navigation bar shows in the page's content area and at the top of the page.

17. Test each link to make sure it works correctly, and troubleshoot any problematic links. To make changes, go back to the **Top Navigation** page and click **Edit**. The edited text should look something like Figure 12-34. Make sure the page addresses are typed exactly right. Replace any spaces in the page's name with hyphens. For example, change "Packet Tracer" to "Packet-Tracer" with the hyphen in place of the space.

```
[[ul class="nav navbar-nav"]]
[[li]][[a href="/main:about"]]About [[span class="fa fa-question-
circle"]]@< >@[[/span]][[/a]]
[[/li]]
[[li]][[a href="/system:all-categories"]]All Categories
[[span class="fa fa-exclamation-circle"]]@< >@[[/span]][[/a]][[/li]]
[[li class="dropdown"]]
[[a href="#" class="dropdown-toggle" data-toggle="dropdown"]]
Applications [[span class="fa fa-info-circle"]]@< >@[[/span]]
[[/a]][[ul class="dropdown-menu"]]
   [[li]][[a href="/applications:hidemeVPN"]]HideMe VPN[[/a]][[/li]]
   [[li]][[a href="/applications:LANSpeedTest"]]LAN Speed Test[[/a]][[/li]]
   [[li]][[a href="/applications:NetStress"]]NetStress[[/a]][[/li]]
   [[li]][[a href="/applications:Packet-Tracer"]]Packet Tracer[[/a]][[/li]]
   [[li]][[a href="/applications:RemoteDesktopManager"]]Remote Desktop
   Manager[[/a]][[/li]]
   [[li]][[a href="/applications:Sandboxie"]]Sandboxie[[/a]][[/li]]
   [[li]][[a href="/applications:SpiceWorks"]]SpiceWorks[[/a]][[/li]]
   [[li]][[a href="/applications:SSH]]SSH[[/a]][[/li]]
   [[li]][[a href="/applications:ThroughputTest"]]Throughput Test[[/a]]
   [[/li]]
   [[li]][[a href="/applications:wireshark"]]Wireshark[[/a]][[/li]]
   [[li]][[a href="/applications:Zenmap"]]Zenmap[[/a]][[/li]]
[[/ul]]
```

Figure 12-34 The edited top navigation bar

Source: Wikidot Inc.

18. Add more categories and pages links, as desired, until you've listed all your categories and pages that you created for projects in this text.

19. On the top navigation bar, add a link to the All Pages page, with an information circle next to it. This link will make the All Pages page accessible directly from the Home page. What line of code must you add to the top navigation bar's code to accomplish this?

20. Edit the Home page text and the About page text to reflect what you've accomplished during this course and to describe the information available through your wiki. Make any other changes you would like to the navigation menus, categories, or pages. You might add screenshots or photos to some of the pages, add more detailed notes, or create new categories for other projects you've completed. If desired, research other editing options, themes, codes, and modules so this wiki reflects your interests and learning progress. Consider that providing a link to your wiki when applying for an IT job could make a strong, positive first impression with a potential employer!

COMPTIA NETWORK+ N10-007 CERTIFICATION EXAM OBJECTIVES

This text covers material related to all the examination objectives for the CompTIA Network+ exam N10-007, which was released by CompTIA (the Computing Technology Industry Association) in 2018. The official list of objectives is available at CompTIA's website, *comptia.org*. For your reference, the following tables list each exam objective and the chapter of this text that explains the objective, plus the amount of the exam that will cover each certification domain. Each objective belongs to one of five domains (or main categories) of networking expertise. For example, comparing and contrasting different 802.11 standards belongs to Objective 1.6 in the "Networking Concepts" domain, which altogether accounts for 23% of the exam's content.

Domain	Percentage of examination
1.0 Networking Concepts	23%
2.0 Infrastructure	18%
3.0 Network Operations	17%
4.0 Network Security	20%
5.0 Network Troubleshooting and Tools	22%
Total	**100%**

As you read through the exam objectives, pay close attention to the verbs used in each objective, as these words indicate how deeply you should know the content listed. For example, an objective that says, "Explain the purposes..." or "Compare and contrast..." expects you to understand the concepts listed, be able to identify those concepts in a scenario, and answer questions about the concepts. However, an objective that says, "Given a scenario, use..." or "Given a scenario, implement..." expects you to be able to put those concepts to work. Any objective that begins with the words "Given a scenario" is much more likely to show up on the exam as a performance-based question rather than simply as a multiple-choice question.

Domain 1.0 Networking Concepts—23% of Examination

Objective	Chapter	Section	Bloom's Taxonomy
1.1 Explain the purposes and uses of ports and protocols.			
• Protocols and ports	1	Client-Server Applications	Understand
○ SSH 22	1	The Seven-Layer OSI Model	
○ DNS 53			
○ SMTP 25			
○ SFTP 22	3	IP Addresses	
○ FTP 20, 21	3	Ports and Sockets	
○ TFTP 69	3	Domain Names and DNS	
○ TELNET 23		(Domain Name System)	
○ DHCP 67, 68			
○ HTTP 80	4	TCP/IP Core Protocols	
○ HTTPS 443			
○ SNMP 161			
○ RDP 3389			
○ NTP 123			
○ SIP 5060, 5061			
○ SMB 445			
○ POP 110			
○ IMAP 143			
○ LDAP 389			
○ LDAPS 636			
○ H.323 1720			
• Protocol types			
○ ICMP			
○ UDP			
○ TCP			
○ IP			
• Connection–oriented vs. connectionless			
1.2 Explain devices, applications, protocols, and services at their appropriate OSI layers.			
• Layer 1—Physical	1	The Seven-Layer OSI Model	Understand
• Layer 2—Data Link			
• Layer 3—Network			
• Layer 4—Transport			
• Layer 5—Session			
• Layer 6—Presentation			
• Layer 7—Application			
1.3 Explain the concepts and characteristics of routing and switching.			
• Properties of network traffic	1	The Seven-Layer OSI Model	Understand
○ Broadcast domains			
○ CSMA/CD			
○ CSMA/CA	3	IP Addresses	

Objective	Chapter	Section	Bloom's Taxonomy
○ Collision domains	3	Domain Names and DNS (Domain Name System)	
○ Protocol data units			
○ MTU			
○ Broadcast	4	TCP/IP Core Protocols	
○ Multicast	4	Routers and How They Work	
○ Unicast	4	Troubleshooting Route Issues	
• Segmentation and interface properties			
○ VLANs			
○ Trunking (802.1q)	5	Copper Cable	
○ Tagging and untagging ports			
○ Port mirroring	6	802.11 WLAN Standards	
○ Switching loops/spanning tree			
○ PoE and PoE+ (802.3af, 802.3at)	7	Virtualization	
○ DMZ	7	Remote Access	
○ MAC address table			
○ ARP table	8	VLANs (Virtual Local Area Networks)	
• Routing			
○ Routing protocols (IPv4 and IPv6)			
▪ Distance-vector routing protocols	10	Network Security Devices	
▫ RIP	10	Switch Management	
▫ EIGRP			
▪ Link–state routing protocols	11	Managing Network Traffic	
▫ OSPF	11	Network Availability	
▪ Hybrid			
▫ BGP	12	WAN Essentials	
○ Routing types			
▪ Static			
▪ Dynamic			
▪ Default			
• IPv6 concepts			
○ Addressing			
○ Tunneling			
○ Dual stack			
○ Router advertisement			
○ Neighbor discovery			
• Performance concepts			
○ Traffic shaping			
○ QoS			
○ Diffserv			
○ CoS			
• NAT/PAT			
• Port forwarding			
• Access control list			
• Distributed switching			
• Packet–switched vs. circuit–switched network			
• Software–defined networking			

Objective	Chapter	Section	Bloom's Taxonomy
1.4 Given a scenario, configure the appropriate IP addressing components.			

• Private vs. public
• Loopback and reserved
• Default gateway
• Virtual IP
• Subnet mask
• Subnetting
  ○ Classful
    ▪ Classes A, B, C, D, and E
  ○ Classless
    ▪ VLSM
    ▪ CIDR notation (IPv4 vs. IPv6)
• Address assignments
  ○ DHCP
  ○ DHCPv6
  ○ Static
  ○ APIPA
  ○ EUI64
  ○ IP reservations
	3
	
	8
	
	11
		IP Addresses
		
		Subnets
		
		Network Availability
			Apply

1.5 Compare and contrast the characteristics of network topologies, types, and technologies.			

• Wired topologies
  ○ Logical vs. physical
  ○ Star
  ○ Ring
  ○ Mesh
  ○ Bus
• Wireless topologies
  ○ Mesh
  ○ Ad hoc
  ○ Infrastructure
• Types
  ○ LAN
  ○ WLAN
  ○ MAN
  ○ WAN
  ○ CAN
  ○ SAN
  ○ PAN
• Technologies that facilitate the Internet of Things (IoT)
  ○ Z-Wave
  ○ Ant+
  ○ Bluetooth
  ○ NFC
  ○ IR
  ○ RFID
  ○ 802.11
	1
	1
	
	6
	
	6
	6
	
	11
		Network Models
		Network Hardware
		
		Wireless Standards for the IoT (Internet of Things)
		802.11 WLAN Standards
		Implementing a Wi-Fi Network
		
		Network Availability
			Understand

Objective	Chapter	Section	Bloom's Taxonomy
1.6 Given a scenario, implement the appropriate wireless technologies and configurations.			

• 802.11 standards
  ○ a
  ○ b
  ○ g
  ○ n
  ○ ac
• Cellular
  ○ GSM
  ○ TDMA
  ○ CDMA
• Frequencies
  ○ 2.4GHz
  ○ 5.0GHz
• Speed and distance requirements
• Channel bandwidth
• Channel bonding
• MIMO/MU-MIMO
• Unidirectional/omnidirectional
• Site surveys
	6
	
	6
	6
	
	12
		Characteristics of Wireless Transmissions
		802.11 WLAN Standards
		Implementing a Wi-Fi Network
		
		Wireless WANs
			Apply

1.7 Summarize cloud concepts and their purposes.			

• Types of services
  ○ SaaS
  ○ PaaS
  ○ IaaS
• Cloud delivery models
  ○ Private
  ○ Public
  ○ Hybrid
• Connectivity methods
• Security implications/considerations
• Relationship between local and cloud resources
	7	Cloud Computing	Understand

1.8 Explain the functions of network services.			

• DNS service
  ○ Record types
    ▪ A, AAAA
    ▪ TXT (SPF, DKIM)
    ▪ SRV
    ▪ MX
    ▪ CNAME
    ▪ NS
    ▪ PTR
  ○ Internal vs. external DNS
  ○ Third-party/cloud-hosted DNS
  ○ Hierarchy
  ○ Forward vs. reverse zone
	3
	3
	3
	
	8
		IP Addresses
		Ports and Sockets
		Domain Names and DNS (Domain Name System)
		
		Subnets
			Understand

Objective	Chapter	Section	Bloom's Taxonomy

• DHCP service
  ○ MAC reservations
  ○ Pools
  ○ IP exclusions
  ○ Scope options
  ○ Lease time
  ○ TTL
  ○ DHCP relay/IP helper
• NTP
• IPAM			

Domain 2.0 Infrastructure—18% of Examination

Objective	Chapter	Section	Bloom's Taxonomy
2.1 Given a scenario, deploy the appropriate cabling solution.			

• Media types
  ○ Copper
    ▪ UTP
    ▪ STP
    ▪ Coaxial
  ○ Fiber
    ▪ Single-mode
    ▪ Multimode
• Plenum vs. PVC
• Connector types
  ○ Copper
    ▪ RJ-45
    ▪ RJ-11
    ▪ BNC
    ▪ DB-9
    ▪ DB-25
    ▪ F-type
  ○ Fiber
    ▪ LC
    ▪ ST
    ▪ SC
      ○ APC
      ○ UPC
    ▪ MTRJ
• Transceivers
  ○ SFP
  ○ GBIC
  ○ SFP+
  ○ QSFP
	2
	
	5
	5
		Components of Structured Cabling
		
		Copper Cable
		Fiber-Optic Cable
			Apply

Objective	Chapter	Section	Bloom's Taxonomy

○ Characteristics of fiber transceivers
  ▪ Bidirectional
  ▪ Duplex
• Termination points
  ○ 66 block
  ○ 110 block
  ○ Patch panel
  ○ Fiber distribution panel
• Copper cable standards
  ○ Cat 3
  ○ Cat 5
  ○ Cat 5e
  ○ Cat 6
  ○ Cat 6a
  ○ Cat 7
  ○ RG-6
  ○ RG-59
• Copper termination standards
  ○ TIA/EIA 568a
  ○ TIA/EIA 568b
  ○ Crossover
  ○ Straight-through
• Ethernet deployment standards
  ○ 100BaseT
  ○ 1000BaseT
  ○ 1000BaseLX
  ○ 1000BaseSX
  ○ 10GBase-T			

2.2 Given a scenario, determine the appropriate placement of networking devices on a network and install/configure them.			
• Firewall • Router • Switch • Hub • Bridge • Modems • Wireless access point • Media converter • Wireless range extender • VoIP endpoint	1 2 3 4 4 5 5	Network Hardware Components of Structured Cabling Domain Names and DNS (Domain Name System) TCP/IP Core Protocols Routers and How They Work Copper Cable Fiber-Optic Cable	Apply

Objective	Chapter	Section	Bloom's Taxonomy
	6	Characteristics of Wireless Transmissions	
	6	Implementing a Wi-Fi Network	
	10	Network Security Devices	
	12	WAN Essentials	
2.3 Explain the purposes and use cases for advanced networking devices.			
• Multilayer switch • Wireless controller • Load balancer • IDS/IPS • Proxy server • VPN concentrator • AAA/RADIUS server • UTM appliance • NGFW/Layer 7 firewall • VoIP PBX • VoIP gateway • Content filter	2	Components of Structured Cabling	Understand
	4	Routers and How They Work	
	6	Implementing a Wi-Fi Network	
	7	Remote Access	
	10	Network Security Devices	
	10	AAA (Authentication, Authorization, and Accounting)	
	10	Access Control Technologies	
	11	Network Availability	
2.4 Explain the purposes of virtualization and network storage technologies.			

• Virtual networking components
  ○ Virtual switch
  ○ Virtual firewall
  ○ Virtual NIC
  ○ Virtual router
  ○ Hypervisor
• Network storage types
  ○ NAS
  ○ SAN
• Connection type
  ○ FCoE
  ○ Fibre Channel
  ○ iSCSI
  ○ InfiniBand
• Jumbo frame
	4	TCP/IP Core Protocols	Understand

	7	Virtualization	
	11	Network Availability	

Objective	Chapter	Section	Bloom's Taxonomy
2.5 Compare and contrast WAN technologies.			
• Service type	2	Components of Structured Cabling	Understand
○ ISDN			
○ T1/T3			
○ E1/E3	7	Remote Access	
○ OC-3 – OC-192			
○ DSL	12	WAN Essentials	
○ Metropolitan Ethernet	12	Layer 1 WAN Technologies	
○ Cable broadband	12	Layer 2 WAN Technologies	
○ Dial-up	12	Wireless WANs	
○ PRI			
• Transmission mediums			
○ Satellite			
○ Copper			
○ Fiber			
○ Wireless			
• Characteristics of service			
○ MPLS			
○ ATM			
○ Frame relay			
○ PPPoE			
○ PPP			
○ DMVPN			
○ SIP trunk			
• Termination			
○ Demarcation point			
○ CSU/DSU			
○ Smart jack			

Domain 3.0 Network Operations—17% of Examination

Objective	Chapter	Section	Bloom's Taxonomy
3.1 Given a scenario, use appropriate documentation and diagrams to manage the network.			
• Diagram symbols	2	Network Documentation	Apply
• Standard operating procedures/ work instructions	2	Change Management	
• Logical vs. physical diagrams			
• Rack diagrams			
• Change management documentation			
• Wiring and port locations			
• IDF/MDF documentation			
• Labeling			

Objective	Chapter	Section	Bloom's Taxonomy
• Network configuration and performance baselines • Inventory management			
3.2 Compare and contrast business continuity and disaster recovery concepts.			

• Availability concepts
  ○ Fault tolerance
  ○ High availability
  ○ Load balancing
  ○ NIC teaming
  ○ Port aggregation
  ○ Clustering
  ○ Power management
    ■ Battery backups/UPS
    ■ Power generators
    ■ Dual power supplies
    ■ Redundant circuits
• Recovery
  ○ Cold sites
  ○ Warm sites
  ○ Hot sites
  ○ Backups
    ■ Full
    ■ Differential
    ■ Incremental
  ○ Snapshots
• MTTR
• MTBF
• SLA requirements
	11
	11
		Network Availability
		Response and Recovery
			Understand

3.3 Explain common scanning, monitoring and patching processes and summarize their expected outputs.			

• Processes
  ○ Log reviewing
  ○ Port scanning
  ○ Vulnerability scanning
  ○ Patch management
    ■ Rollback
  ○ Reviewing baselines
  ○ Packet/traffic analysis
• Event management
  ○ Notifications
  ○ Alerts
  ○ SIEM
• SNMP monitors
  ○ MIB
• Metrics
  ○ Error rate
  ○ Utilization
	2
	
	5
	
	9
	
	10
	
	11
		Change Management
		
		Transmission Basics
		
		Security Assessment
		
		Network Security Devices
		
		Collecting Network Data
			Understand

Objective	Chapter	Section	Bloom's Taxonomy
○ Packet drops ○ Bandwidth/throughput			
3.4 Given a scenario, use remote access methods.			

• VPN
  ○ IPSec
  ○ SSL/TLS/DTLS
  ○ Site-to-site
  ○ Client-to-site
• RDP
• SSH
• VNC
• Telnet
• HTTPS/management URL
• Remote file access
  ○ FTP/FTPS
  ○ SFTP
  ○ TFTP
• Out-of-band management
  ○ Modem
  ○ Console router
	1
	
	7
	7
		Client-Server Applications
		
		Encryption Protocols
		Remote Access
			Apply

3.5 Identify policies and best practices.			

• Privileged user agreement
• Password policy
• On-boarding/off-boarding
  procedures
• Licensing restrictions
• International export controls
• Data loss prevention
• Remote access policies
• Incident response policies
• BYOD
• AUP
• NDA
• System life cycle
  ○ Asset disposal
• Safety procedures and policies
	1
	
	2
	
	6
	
	7
	
	9
	
	11
		Safety Procedures and Policies
		
		Network Documentation
		
		Implementing a Wi-Fi Network
		
		Remote Access
		
		Security Policies for Users
		
		Response and Recovery
			Remember

Domain 4.0 Network Security—20% of Examination

Objective	Chapter	Section	Bloom's Taxonomy
4.1 Summarize the purposes of physical security devices.			

• Detection
   ○ Motion detection
   ○ Video surveillance
   ○ Asset tracking tags
   ○ Tamper detection
• Prevention
   ○ Badges
   ○ Biometrics
   ○ Smart cards
   ○ Key fob
   ○ Locks
	9	Physical Security	Understand

4.2 Explain authentication and access controls.			

• Authorization, authentication, and accounting
   ○ RADIUS
   ○ TACACS+
   ○ Kerberos
   ○ Single sign-on
   ○ Local authentication
   ○ LDAP
   ○ Certificates
   ○ Auditing and logging
• Multifactor authentication
   ○ Something you know
   ○ Something you have
   ○ Something you are
   ○ Somewhere you are
   ○ Something you do
• Access control
   ○ 802.1x
   ○ NAC
   ○ Port security
   ○ MAC filtering
   ○ Captive portal
   ○ Access control lists
	4
	
	6
	
	7
	
	10
	10
	10
	
	10
	10
		Troubleshooting Route Issues
		
		Wi-Fi Network Security
		
		Encryption Protocols
		
		Network Security Devices
		Switch Management
		AAA (Authentication, Authorization, and Accounting)
		Access Control Technologies
		Wireless Network Security
			Understand

4.3 Given a scenario, secure a basic wireless network.			
• WPA • WPA2 • TKIP-RC4 • CCMP-AES	6 10	Wi-Fi Network Security AAA (Authentication, Authorization, and Accounting)	Apply

Objective	Chapter	Section	Bloom's Taxonomy

• Authentication and authorization
  ◦ EAP
    ▪ PEAP
    ▪ EAP-FAST
    ▪ EAP-TLS
    ▪ Shared or open
    ▪ Preshared key
    ▪ MAC filtering
• Geofencing
	10	Wireless Network Security	

4.4 Summarize common networking attacks.			

• DoS
  ◦ Reflective
  ◦ Amplified
  ◦ Distributed
• Social engineering
• Insider threat
• Logic bomb
• Rogue access point
• Evil twin
• War-driving
• Phishing
• Ransomware
• DNS poisoning
• ARP poisoning
• Spoofing
• Deauthentication
• Brute force
• VLAN hopping
• Man-in-the-middle
• Exploits vs. vulnerabilities
	4
	
	6
	6
	
	8
	
	9
		Troubleshooting Route Issues
		
		Implementing a Wi-Fi Network
		Wi-Fi Network Security
		
		VLANs (Virtual Local Area Networks)
		
		Security Risks
			Understand

4.5 Given a scenario, implement network device hardening.			

• Changing default credentials
• Avoiding common passwords
• Upgrading firmware
• Patching and updates
• File hashing
• Disabling unnecessary services
• Using secure protocols
• Generating new keys
• Disabling unused ports
  ◦ IP ports
  ◦ Device ports (physical and virtual)
	9
	
	10
		Device Hardening
		
		Switch Management
			Apply

Objective	Chapter	Section	Bloom's Taxonomy
4.6 Explain common mitigation techniques and their purposes.			

• Signature management
• Device hardening
• Change native VLAN
• Switch port protection
  ◦ Spanning tree
  ◦ Flood guard
  ◦ BPDU guard
  ◦ Root guard
  ◦ DHCP snooping
• Network segmentation
  ◦ DMZ
  ◦ VLAN
• Privileged user account
• File integrity monitoring
• Role separation
• Restricting access via ACLs
• Honeypot/honeynet
• Penetration testing
	3
	
	8
	8
	
	9
	9
	9
	
	10
	10
	10
		Domain Names and DNS (Domain Name System)
		
		Network Segmentation
		VLANs (Virtual Local Area Networks)
		
		Security Risks
		Security Assessment
		Device Hardening
		
		Network Security Devices
		Switch Management
		AAA (Authentication, Authorization, and Accounting)
			Understand

Domain 5.0 Network Troubleshooting and Tools—22% of Examination

Objective	Chapter	Section	Bloom's Taxonomy
5.1 Explain the network troubleshooting methodology.			

• Identify the problem
  ◦ Gather information
  ◦ Duplicate the problem, if possible
  ◦ Question users
  ◦ Identify symptoms
  ◦ Determine if anything has changed
  ◦ Approach multiple problems individually
	1	Troubleshooting Network Problems	Understand

Objective	Chapter	Section	Bloom's Taxonomy

• Establish a theory of probable cause
 ○ Question the obvious
 ○ Consider multiple approaches
  ▪ Top-to-bottom/bottom-to-top OSI model
  ▪ Divide and conquer
• Test the theory to determine the cause
 ○ Once the theory is confirmed, determine the next steps to resolve the problem
 ○ If the theory is not confirmed, reestablish a new theory or escalate
• Establish a plan of action to resolve the problem and identify potential effects
• Implement the solution or escalate as necessary
• Verify full system functionality and, if applicable, implement preventive measures
• Document findings, actions, and outcomes			

5.2 Given a scenario, use the appropriate tool.			
• Hardware tools ○ Crimper ○ Cable tester ○ Punchdown tool ○ OTDR ○ Light meter ○ Tone generator ○ Loopback adapter ○ Multimeter ○ Spectrum analyzer	2 2 3 4 4 4	Components of Structured Cabling Network Documentation Troubleshooting Address Problems TCP/IP Core Protocols Routers and How They Work Troubleshooting Route Issues	Apply

Objective	Chapter	Section	Bloom's Taxonomy

• Software tools
  ○ Packet sniffer
  ○ Port scanner
  ○ Protocol analyzer
  ○ WiFi analyzer
  ○ Bandwidth speed tester
  ○ Command line
    ▪ ping
    ▪ tracert, traceroute
    ▪ nslookup
    ▪ ipconfig
    ▪ ifconfig
    ▪ iptables
    ▪ netstat
    ▪ tcpdump
    ▪ pathping
    ▪ nmap
    ▪ route
    ▪ arp
    ▪ dig
	5
	5
	
	6
	
	9
	
	10
	
	12
		Copper Cable
		Troubleshooting Tools
		
		Troubleshooting Wi-Fi Networks
		
		Security Assessment
		
		Network Security Devices
		
		Layer 1 WAN Technologies	

5.3 Given a scenario, troubleshoot common wired connectivity and performance issues.			
• Attenuation • Latency • Jitter • Crosstalk • EMI • Open/short • Incorrect pin-out • Incorrect cable type • Bad port • Transceiver mismatch • TX/RX reverse • Duplex/speed mismatch • Damaged cables • Bent pins • Bottlenecks • VLAN mismatch • Network connection LED status indicators	2 5 5 5 5 8 11	Components of Structured Cabling Transmission Basics Copper Cable Fiber-Optic Cable Troubleshooting Tools VLANs (Virtual Local Area Networks) Collecting Network Data	Apply
5.4 Given a scenario, troubleshoot common wireless connectivity and performance issues.			
• Reflection • Refraction • Absorption • Latency • Jitter	6 6	Characteristics of Wireless Transmissions Troubleshooting Wi-Fi Networks	Apply

Objective	Chapter	Section	Bloom's Taxonomy
• Attenuation • Incorrect antenna type • Interference • Incorrect antenna placement • Channel overlap • Overcapacity • Distance limitations • Frequency mismatch • Wrong SSID • Wrong passphrase • Security type mismatch • Power levels • Signal-to-noise ratio	12	Wireless WANs	
5.5 Given a scenario, troubleshoot common network service issues.			
• Names not resolving • Incorrect gateway • Incorrect netmask • Duplicate IP addresses • Duplicate MAC addresses • Expired IP address • Rogue DHCP server • Untrusted SSL certificate • Incorrect time • Exhausted DHCP scope • Blocked TCP/UDP ports • Incorrect host-based firewall settings • Incorrect ACL settings • Unresponsive service • Hardware failure	3 4 7 9 10 11	Troubleshooting Address Problems Troubleshooting Route Issues Encryption Protocols Security Risks Network Security Devices Collecting Network Data	Apply

VISUAL GUIDE TO CONNECTORS

Throughout this text, you learned about several different cabling and connector options that may be used on networks. Some, such as RJ-45 connectors, are very common, whereas others, such as MT-RJ connectors, are used only on high-speed optical networks. So that you can compare such connectors and ensure that you understand their differences, this appendix compiles drawings and photos of the connectors along with a brief summary of their uses in two simple tables (see Tables B-1 and B-2). You must be familiar with the most popular types of connectors to qualify for CompTIA's Network+ certification. You can find more details about these connectors and the networks on which they are used in Chapter 5.

Table B-1 Copper connectors and their uses

Specification	Male connector (front view)	Male connector (side view)	Female receptacle (front view)	Application
BNC				Used with coaxial cable for broadband cable connections; also used on old Ethernet networks such as Thinnet
F-connector				Used on coaxial cable suitable for use with broadband video and data applications; more common than BNC connectors
DB-9				One of the RS-232 standard connectors used in serial connections

(continues)

Table B-1 Copper connectors and their uses *(continued)*

Specification	Male connector (front view)	Male connector (side view)	Female receptacle (front view)	Application
DB-25				One of the RS-232 standard connectors used in serial connections
RJ-11 (registered jack 11)				Used on twisted-pair cabling for telephone systems (and some older twisted-pair networks)
RJ-45 (registered jack 45)				Used on twisted-pair cabling for Ethernet (RJ-45) connections
USB A (Universal Serial Bus Type A)				Used to connect external peripherals, such as modems, mice, audio players, NICs, cameras, and smartphones
USB B (Universal Serial Bus Type B)				Used to connect external peripherals, such as printers
USB C (Universal Serial Bus Type C)				Used to connect external peripherals, such as smartphones

Table B-2 Fiber connectors and their uses

Specification	Male connector (front view)	Male connector (side view)	Female receptacle (front view)	Application
ST (straight tip), usually multimode				Uses a bayonet locking mechanism; one of the first commercially available fiber connectors

Table B-2   Fiber connectors and their uses *(continued)*

Specification	Male connector (front view)	Male connector (side view)	Female receptacle (front view)	Application
SC (subscriber connector or standard connector)				Widely used; has a snap-in connector
LC (local connector), single-mode				Most common 2.5-mm ferrule; available in full-duplex mode
MTRJ (Mechanical Transfer Register Jack), multimode				Most common MMF; contains two strands of fiber per ferrule to provide full-duplex signaling

COMPTIA NETWORK+ PRACTICE EXAM

The following exam contains questions that are similar in content and format to the multiple-choice questions you will encounter on CompTIA's Network+ N10-007 certification exam, released in 2018. This practice exam consists of 100 questions, all of which are multiple choice. Some questions have more than one correct answer. The number of questions from each domain reflects the weighting that CompTIA assigned to these domains in its exam objectives. To simulate taking the CompTIA Network+ certification exam, allow yourself 90 minutes to answer all the questions.

1. To ensure that your private network is always protected, you decide to install three redundant firewalls. Which of the following would allow you to assign the same IP address to all three?
   a. SMTP
   b. CARP
   c. SNMPv3
   d. IMAP
   e. NTP

2. What type of network could use the type of connector shown here?
   a. 1000Base-LX
   b. 10GBase-T
   c. 100Base-T
   d. 1000Base-T
   e. 5GBase-T

3. While troubleshooting a workstation connectivity problem, you enter the following command: ping 127.0.0.1. The response indicates the test failed. What can you determine about that workstation?
   a. Its network cable is faulty or not connected to the wall jack.
   b. Its TCP/IP stack is not installed properly.
   c. It has been prevented from transmitting data past the default gateway.
   d. Its DHCP settings are incorrect.
   e. Its DNS name server specification is incorrect.

4. You have been asked to help improve network performance on a store's small office network. The network relies on two switches, two access points, and a router to connect its 18 employees to the Internet and other store locations. You decide to determine what type of traffic the network currently handles. In particular, you're interested in the volume of unnecessary broadcast traffic that might be bogging down shared segments. Which of the following tools will help you identify the percentage of traffic made up of broadcasts?
   a. Port scanner
   b. OTDR
   c. Protocol analyzer
   d. Multimeter
   e. Cable tester

5. Which of the following standards describes a security technique, often used on wireless networks, in which a port is prevented from receiving traffic until the transmitter's credentials are verified by an authentication server?
   a. EAPoL
   b. SSH
   c. RADIUS
   d. Kerberos
   e. CCMP

6. Which of the following ports would be used during a domain name lookup?
   a. 22
   b. 23
   c. 53
   d. 110
   e. 443

7. You are configuring a connection between two backbone switches, and you want to make sure the connection doesn't fail or become overwhelmed by heavy traffic. Which of the following techniques would help you achieve both aims?
   a. Round-robin DNS
   b. CARP
   c. Clustering
   d. Trunking
   e. NIC teaming

8. As a network admin, you have decided to install additional physical security to the main office's data room. Due to the sensitivity of the data held in this room, you decide it's critical to ensure two-factor authentication before granting anyone access to the room. You already have a lock on the door. Which of the following physical security measures would provide 2FA?
   a. Smart badge
   b. Fingerprint scanner
   c. Key fob
   d. Video surveillance
   e. Proximity card

9. You have installed and configured two virtual web servers and a virtual mail server on a physical server. What networking mode will you assign to each server's vNIC to ensure that the virtual machines' clients on the Internet can access the virtual machines?

   a. NAT

   b. Bridged

   c. Host-only

   d. Internal

   e. Grouped

10. At the beginning of the school year, students at your school must configure their computers and other devices to obtain trusted access to the student portion of the school's network. What is this process called?

    a. Authenticating

    b. Remote wiping

    c. Associating

    d. Onboarding

    e. Social engineering

11. When using NAT, how does an IP gateway ensure that outgoing traffic can traverse public networks?

    a. It modifies each outgoing frame's Type field to indicate that the transmission is destined for a public network.

    b. It assigns each outgoing packet a masked ID via the Options field.

    c. It replaces each outgoing packet's Source address field with a public IP address.

    d. It interprets the contents of outgoing packets to ensure that they contain no client-identifying information.

    e. It modifies the frame length to create uniformly sized frames, called cells, which are required for public network transmission.

12. Which of these authentication techniques only encrypts the password when transmitting sign-in credentials?

    a. RADIUS

    b. TACACS+

    c. Kerberos

    d. Single sign-on

    e. Local authentication

13. You are a networking technician in a radiology clinic, where physicians use the network to transmit and store patients' diagnostic results. Shortly after a new wing, which contains X-ray and MRI (magnetic resonance imaging) machines, is added to the building, computers in that area begin having intermittent problems saving data to the file server. After you have gathered information, identified the symptoms, questioned users, and determined what has changed, what is your next step in troubleshooting this problem?

    a. Establish a plan of action to resolve the problem.
    b. Escalate the problem.
    c. Document findings, actions, and outcomes.
    d. Establish a theory of probable cause.
    e. Implement the solution.

14. The software on a firewall you recently installed on your network examines each incoming packet. It blocks or allows traffic based on a set of criteria, including source IP address, source and destination ports, and protocols. What type of system is this? Choose all that apply.

    a. Content-filtering firewall
    b. Stateful firewall
    c. Stateless firewall
    d. Packet-filtering firewall
    e. Application layer firewall

15. Suppose you have created six subnets on a network that leases a group of Class C IPv4 addresses. What subnet mask must you specify in your clients' configurations to adhere to your subnetting scheme?

    a. 255.255.255.6
    b. 255.255.255.128
    c. 255.255.255.192
    d. 255.255.255.224
    e. 255.255.255.0

16. What would the command route del default gw 192.168.5.1 eth1 accomplish on your Linux workstation?

    a. Delete the default gateway's route to the host whose IP address is 192.168.5.1
    b. Remove the assignment of IP address 192.168.5.1 from the eth1 interface
    c. Remove the workstation's route to the default gateway whose IP address is 192.168.5.1
    d. Add a route from the workstation to the default gateway whose IP address is 192.168.5.1
    e. Remove the designation of default gateway, but keep the route for the host whose IP address is 192.168.5.1

17. From your laptop, you need to remote into a switch to make some configuration changes. Which Transport layer protocol and TCP/IP port should you open in Windows Firewall to make this work using Telnet?

    a. UDP, port 23
    b. TCP, port 23
    c. UDP, port 22
    d. TCP, port 22
    e. UDP, port 21

18. Recently, your company's WAN experienced a disabling DDoS attack. Which of the following devices could detect such an attack and prevent it from affecting your network in the future?

    a. A honeypot

    b. SIEM

    c. HIPS

    d. HIDS

    e. NIPS

19. Which of the following routing protocols offer fast convergence times and can be used on both core and edge routers? Choose two.

    a. RIPv2

    b. IS-IS

    c. OSPF

    d. BGP

    e. EIGRP

20. A friend calls you for help with his home office Internet connection. He is using an 802.11n wireless router connected to a DSL modem. The router's private IP address is 192.168.1.1 and it has been assigned an Internet routable IP address of 76.83.124.35. Your friend cannot connect to any resources on the Internet using his new Windows workstation. You ask him to run the ipconfig command and read the results to you. He says his workstation's IP address is 192.168.1.3, the subnet mask is 255.255.255.0, and the default gateway address is 192.168.1.10. What do you advise him to do next?

    a. Display his DNS information.

    b. Change his gateway address.

    c. Change his subnet mask.

    d. Try pinging the loopback address.

    e. Use the tracert command to contact the access point/router.

21. Your organization contracts with a cloud computing company to store some backup data. The company promises 99.999 percent uptime. If it lives up to its claims, what is the maximum number of minutes each year you can expect your data to be unavailable?

    a. Approximately 448 minutes

    b. Approximately 199 minutes

    c. Approximately 52 minutes

    d. Approximately 14 minutes

    e. Approximately 5 minutes

22. Ethernet and ATM both specify Data Link layer framing techniques. How do they differ?

    a. Ethernet uses CRC fields to confirm the validity of the frame, whereas ATM uses no error detection.

    b. Ethernet uses variably sized packets, whereas ATM uses fixed-sized cells.

    c. Ethernet uses synchronous transmission, whereas ATM uses asynchronous transmission.

    d. Ethernet uses frame headers, whereas ATM does not.

    e. Ethernet offers no guarantee of timely delivery, whereas ATM ensures that packets are delivered within 10 ms.

23. What STP configuration ensures that a laptop connected to a switch cannot alter the STP paths on the network?

   a. BPDU filter

   b. BPDU guard

   c. Root bridge

   d. BID

   e. Designated port

24. What is the default subnet mask for the IP address 154.13.44.87?

   a. 255.255.255.255

   b. 255.255.255.0

   c. 255.255.0.0

   d. 255.0.0.0

   e. 0.0.0.0

25. Your CFO has approved installing new backbone cabling on your school's campus. One of the buildings is particularly far away from the others, nearly a kilometer. Which Ethernet standard will reach the distant building without the use of a repeater?

   a. 10GBase-T

   b. 1000Base-LX

   c. 1000Base-SX

   d. 10GBase-SR

   e. 1000Base-T

26. Which of the following is often used to secure data traveling over VPNs that use L2TP?

   a. PPTP

   b. PPPoE

   c. Kerberos

   d. SSH

   e. IPsec

27. You are a support technician working in a data closet in a remote office. You suspect that a connectivity problem is related to a broken RJ-45 plug on a patch cable that connects a switch to a patch panel. You need to replace that connector, but you forgot to bring an extra patch cable. You decide to install a new RJ-45 connector to replace the broken connector. Which tools must you have in order to successfully accomplish this task? Choose two.

   a. Punchdown tool

   b. Crimper

   c. Wire stripper

   d. Cable tester

   e. Multimeter

28. You have purchased an outdoor access point capable of exchanging data via the 802.11n or 802.11ac wireless standard. According to these standards, what is the maximum distance, in meters, from the access point that wireless clients can travel and still reliably exchange data with the access point?

    a. 20

    b. 75

    c. 100

    d. 250

    e. 450

29. Which of the following is a single sign-on authentication method?

    a. IPsec

    b. EAPoL

    c. SSL

    d. Kerberos

    e. CHAP

30. Your organization has just ordered its first T1 connection to the Internet. Prior to that, your organization relied on a DSL connection. Which of the following devices must you now have that your DSL connection didn't require?

    a. Modem

    b. CSU/DSU

    c. Switch

    d. Hub

    e. Router

31. Your friend's printer isn't printing the document she just sent it. In what order should you perform the listed steps?

    a. Follow the OSI model from bottom to top to check possible causes, send a new document to the printer, determine if anything has changed on her network.

    b. Send a new document to the printer, follow the OSI model from bottom to top to check possible causes, ask your friend when the problem started.

    c. Take notes on the outcome, send a new document to the printer, determine if anything has changed on her network.

    d. Determine if anything has changed on her network, follow the OSI model from bottom to top to check possible causes, send a new document to the printer.

    e. Determine if anything has changed on her network, take notes on the outcome, send a new document to the printer.

32. A CEO fires her administrative assistant after the assistant was caught stealing company funds. Over the weekend, the administrative assistant hacks into the CEO's private email account and steals some personal data. What type of attack did the former employee most likely use to accomplish this exploit?

    a. Brute force attack

    b. War driving

    c. Logic bomb

    d. Deauthentication

    e. Man-in-the-middle

33. What is the network ID for a class C network that contains the group of IP addresses from 194.73.44.10 through 194.73.44.254?
    a. 194.73.44.0
    b. 194.73.44.1
    c. 194.73.0.0
    d. 194.73.44.255
    e. 194.1.1.1

34. Your organization is reassessing its WAN connections to determine how much more bandwidth it will need to purchase in the next two years. As a network administrator, which of the following data can you share that will help management make the right decision?
    a. Wiring schematic
    b. Performance baselines
    c. Logical network diagram
    d. Syslogs
    e. Change management documentation

35. You are creating a new Linux server as a virtual machine on your Windows workstation. Which of the following commands will tell you the IP address that is assigned to your virtual server?
    a. ipconfig /all at the Windows workstation's command prompt
    b. ifconfig -a at the Linux server's shell prompt
    c. iptables at the Linux server's shell prompt
    d. ping at the Windows workstation's command prompt
    e. ipconfig /all at the Linux server's shell prompt

36. Which of the following requirements provide multifactor authentication? Choose two.
    a. Iris pattern and typing pattern.
    b. Password and name of first elementary school
    c. Location in a secured closet
    d. Smart card and key fob
    e. Fingerprint and name of first elementary school

37. You are rearranging nodes on your Gigabit Ethernet network. Due to a necessarily hasty expansion, you have decided to supply power to a wireless router in a makeshift data room using PoE. What is the minimum cabling standard you must use to connect this wireless router to the network's backbone?
    a. RG-6
    b. RG-59
    c. Cat 5e
    d. SMF
    e. Cat 6

38. As you're setting up APs in your client's office space, you want to ensure that all work areas and the meeting room have adequate access to the network. What tool will give you the information you need?
   a. Geofencing
   b. Packet sniffer
   c. Bandwidth speed tester
   d. Wi-Fi analyzer
   e. Toner probe

39. Which of the following protocols encapsulates data for transmission over VPNs?
   a. SFTP
   b. L2TP
   c. VNC
   d. TCP
   e. TACACS+

40. Which of the following is a valid MAC address?
   a. C3:00:50:00:FF:FF
   b. 153.101.24.3
   c. ::9F53
   d. FE80::32:1CA3:B0E2
   e. D0:00:00:00

41. Which of the following services would be most important to disable on a Windows workstation?
   a. SSH
   b. DHCP
   c. Telnet
   d. FTP
   e. RDP

42. It's Friday night, and you have just settled in with some hot cocoa and popcorn to watch one of your favorite movies on Netflix. Five minutes into the movie, you realize you're getting more stressed than relaxed, and then you realize the problem is that the movie keeps lagging, buffering, and skipping. What transmission flaw is probably the source of the problem?
   a. Crosstalk
   b. Jitter
   c. EMI
   d. Latency
   e. Attenuation

43. A SIP trunk would most likely work in conjunction with which device?
   a. Wireless controller
   b. VoIP gateway
   c. NGFW
   d. VPN concentrator
   e. Satellite dish

44. Which technology can SIP trunking most adequately replace?
    a. DMVPN
    b. IDS
    c. T1
    d. PRI
    e. DSL

45. Your network manager has purchased a dozen new, dual-band access points and all are configured to use the new 802.11ac standard on the 5-GHz band. These access points will be backward-compatible with older access points that run which of the following standards? Choose all that apply.
    a. 802.11g
    b. 802.11n
    c. 802.11b
    d. Bluetooth
    e. None of the above.

46. You suspect that a machine on your network with the host name PRTSRV is issuing excessive broadcast traffic. What command can you use to determine this host's IP address?
    a. netstat PRTSRV
    b. ipconfig PRTSRV
    c. nslookup PRTSRV
    d. ifconfig PRTSRV
    e. iptables PRTSRV

47. You're installing a network management system and need to install software on various devices. What software must be installed on a managed device, such as a router?
    a. SIEM
    b. OID
    c. NMS
    d. Agent
    e. Syslog

48. You work for a small ISP. Several of your customers have called to complain about slow responses from a popular website. You suspect that network congestion is at fault. Which TCP/IP utility would help you determine where the congestion is occurring?
    a. FTP
    b. Nslookup
    c. Arp
    d. Tracert
    e. Telnet

49. You are a network administrator for a WAN that connects two regional insurance company offices—the main office and a satellite office—to each other by a T3. The main office is also connected to the Internet using a T3. This T3 provides Internet access for both offices. To ensure that your private network is not compromised by unauthorized access through the Internet connection, you install a firewall between the main office and the Internet. Shortly thereafter, users in your satellite office complain that they cannot access the file server in the main office, but users in the main office can still access the Internet. What configurations should you check? Choose two.

    a. Whether the firewall has been configured to run in promiscuous mode

    b. Whether the firewall is placed in the appropriate location on the network

    c. Whether the firewall has been configured to allow access from IP addresses in the satellite office

    d. Whether the firewall has been configured to receive and transmit UDP-based packets

    e. Whether the firewall has been configured to allow Internet access over the main office's T3

50. In IPv6, which of the following is the loopback address?

    a. 1.0.0.1

    b. 127::1

    c. FE80::1

    d. ::1

    e. 127.0.0.1

51. In the process of troubleshooting an intermittent performance problem with your network's Internet connection, you attempt to run a tracert test to *microsoft.com*. The tracert response displays the first 12 hops in the route, but then presents several "Request timed out" messages in a row. What is the most likely reason for this result?

    a. Your network's ISP is experiencing connectivity problems.

    b. Microsoft's network is bounded by firewalls that do not accept incoming ICMP traffic.

    c. The Internet backbone is experiencing traffic congestion.

    d. Your client's TCP/IP service limits the tracert command to a maximum of 12 hops.

    e. Your IP gateway failed while you were attempting the tracert test.

52. You are setting up a new Windows 10 client to connect with your LAN, which relies on DHCP. Which of the following must you do to ensure that the client obtains correct TCP/IP information via DHCP?

    a. Make certain the client's computer name and host name are identical.

    b. Enter the client's MAC address in the DHCP server's ARP table.

    c. Enter the DHCP server address in the Windows TCP/IP configuration.

    d. Nothing; in Windows 10, the DHCP option is selected by default.

    e. Enter a default gateway address in the Windows TCP/IP configuration.

53. Due to popular demand from employees who need to roam from one floor of your office building to another, you are expanding your wireless network. You want to ensure that mobile users enjoy uninterrupted network connectivity without having to reconfigure their workstations' wireless network connection settings as they travel throughout the office space. Which of the following variables must you configure on your new access points to match the settings on existing access points?
   a. Administrator password
   b. Scanning rate
   c. SSID
   d. IP address
   e. Signal strength

54. You have installed a protocol analyzer on your laptop and connected the laptop to a switch on your network's backbone. You want to monitor all traffic on a specific VLAN. Which feature must you configure on the switch to make this work?
   a. Trunking
   b. Port mirroring
   c. Looping
   d. Spanning Tree Protocol
   e. Caching

55. Which of the following does *not* accurately describe TACACS+ in comparison to RADIUS?
   a. TACACS+ relies on TCP, not UDP, at the Transport layer.
   b. TACACS+ is typically installed on a router or switch, rather than on a server.
   c. TACACS+ encrypts all information transmitted for AAA rather than just the password.
   d. TACACS+ was developed for proprietary use on Cisco products.
   e. TACACS+ operates as a software application on a remote access server.

56. You are part of a team participating in a posture assessment of your company's LAN. Which of the following tools or strategies will help you gain a broad understanding of your network's security vulnerabilities?
   a. MIB
   b. War driving
   c. Nmap
   d. DHCP snooping
   e. CCMP

57. Which of the following devices separates broadcast domains?
   a. Router
   b. Switch
   c. Bridge
   d. Repeater
   e. Hub

58. About a year ago, you purchased and installed a new router at one of your company's satellite offices, and you have had nothing but problems with the router since. Today you called the vendor for the third time to have them send a technician to repair the router. They estimate the repair will be completed by the end of business tomorrow. In the meantime, you have decided that you would prefer to replace the router the next time it fails. What factor should you carefully investigate when shopping for a replacement so you won't face this same scenario with the next router?

   a. MTTR
   b. UPS
   c. MTBF
   d. SLA
   e. MIB

59. You have just returned from a business conference and you're anxious to catch up on some projects. First thing in the morning, you unpack your laptop and get to work. Thirty minutes later, your boss calls and asks why you're late to the morning's staff meeting. You know the weekly meeting was scheduled into your calendar on your computer and the reminder has worked consistently for months. What is the most likely reason your computer did not remind you of your meeting?

   a. Windows was unable to connect to the network.
   b. Windows has registered the wrong time zone.
   c. Windows is configured with an IP address that is the same as another host on the network.
   d. Windows is configured with the wrong default gateway.
   e. Windows Firewall blocked the calendar app from communicating with the network.

60. Which of the following figures reflects the type of physical topology most likely to be used on a 1000Base-T network?

   a.

   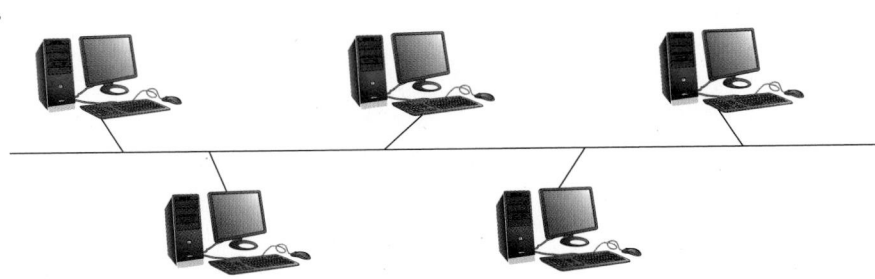

b.

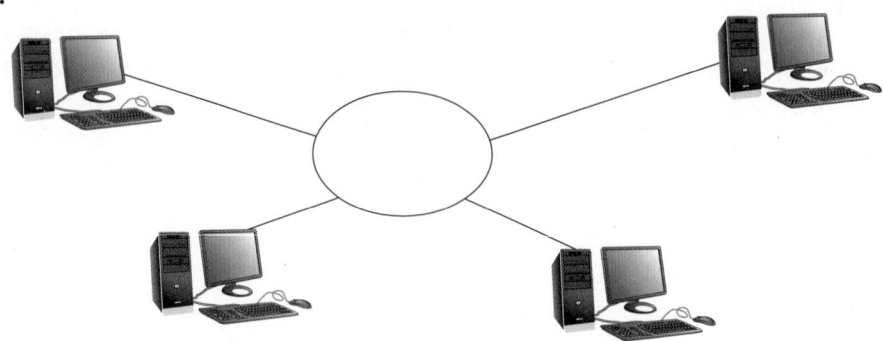

c.

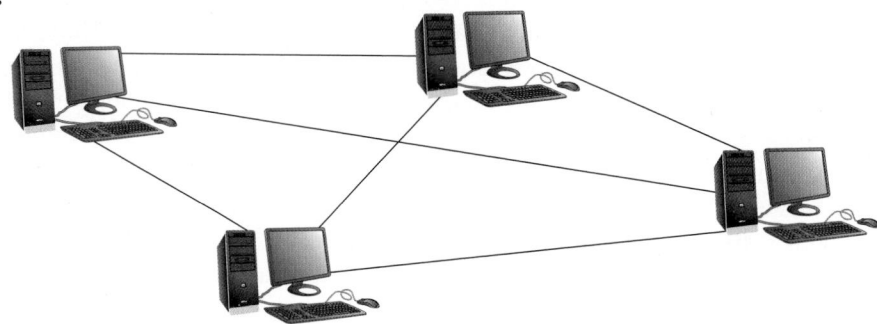

d.

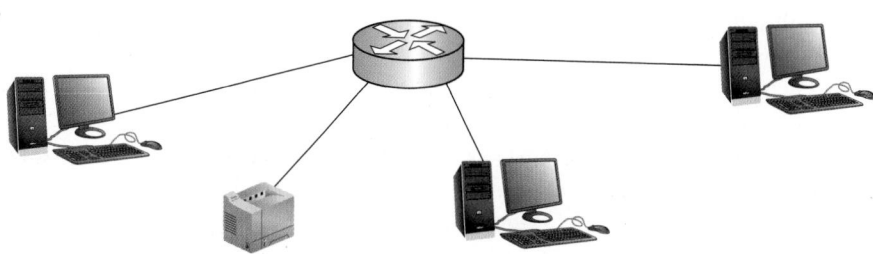

e.

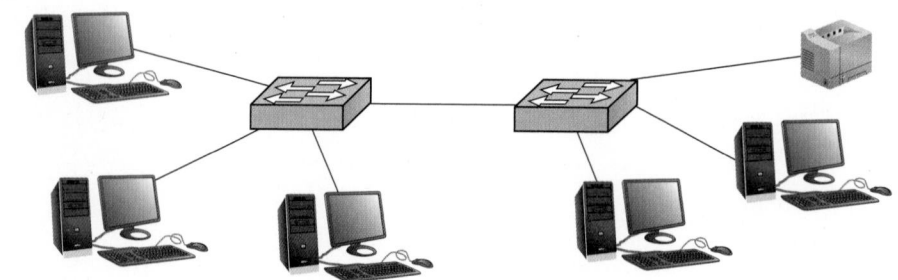

61. Your study partner is trying to access the Internet on her laptop and it's not working. In the browser, you try to go to google.com, and it doesn't work. In a Command Prompt window, you ping google.com, and it doesn't work. You then ping 8.8.8.8, and it still doesn't work. You try to ping the network's gateway, and it fails. You ping your own computer, which is logged onto the same network, and it works. What is the most likely diagnosis of this problem?

    a. Exhausted DHCP scope

    b. Incorrect DNS server

    c. Incorrect gateway

    d. Duplicate IP address

    e. Incorrect netmask

62. You work for a small fashion design firm. Because of a video that recently went viral, your company has received national recognition. Within a few days, your web server crashes. What kind of attack most likely caused the crash?

    a. Phishing

    b. Friendly DoS

    c. Spoofing

    d. Ransomware

    e. Logic bomb

63. You have just installed Linux on an old laptop to bring it new life. Which of the following applications will provide the most protection for the computer when you connect it to the Internet?

    a. Defender

    b. ufw

    c. tcpdump

    d. iptables

    e. Wireshark

64. You are the network administrator for a large university whose network currently contains nearly 10,000 workstations, over 80 routers, 250 switches, and 500 printers. You are researching a proposal to upgrade the routers and switches on your network to primarily use multi-layer switches instead. At the same time, you want to improve the management of your network devices. Which of the following protocols will help automate network management across all the new devices?

    a. TFTP

    b. SMTP

    c. NTP

    d. ICMP

    e. SNMP

65. Which of the following devices operate only at the Physical layer of the OSI model? Choose two.

    a. Hub

    b. Switch

    c. Router

    d. Bridge

    e. Repeater

66. While making some configuration changes to a client's network, you need to connect your laptop to a router's console port. Which of the following connector types might be used for this purpose, depending on the age of the router? Choose two.
    a. RJ-11
    b. DB-9
    c. MTRJ
    d. RJ-45
    e. F-type

67. You have connected to your bank's home page. Its URL begins with *https://*. Based on this information, what type of security can you assume the bank employs for clients receiving and transmitting data to and from its web server?
    a. Kerberos
    b. TLS
    c. IPsec
    d. L2TP
    e. Packet-filtering firewall

68. Which of the following routing protocols has the poorest convergence time?
    a. EIGRP
    b. RIP
    c. BGP
    d. OSPF
    e. IS-IS

69. You need to gather some information about the traffic being broadcast and received on a Linux workstation. Unfortunately, you don't have time to install Wireshark. Which command can you use instead?
    a. tcpdump
    b. pathping
    c. traceroute
    d. dig
    e. nslookup

70. To provide redundancy, you have set up three links from a critical server to two redundant switches, both of which operate on the same subnet. Two connections from the server go to one switch, and the third link connects the other switch to the server. The server is running Windows Server 2016. What feature should you configure on the server to make these redundant links work together for load balancing and failover protection?
    a. Port aggregation
    b. NIC teaming
    c. Bottleneck
    d. Server cluster
    e. Virtual IP address

71. A Windows workstation is configured to use DHCP, but cannot find a DHCP server. You run ipconfig at the Command Prompt. Which of the following IP addresses is most likely reported by Windows?

   a. 129.0.0.1

   b. 255.255.255.0

   c. 192.168.0.1

   d. 169.254.1.120

   e. 172.16.2.18

72. Used side-by-side with Kerberos, what service does LDAP provide Active Directory?

   a. Accounting

   b. Encryption

   c. Auditing

   d. Authorization

   e. Authentication

73. In the following figure, if switch A suffers a failure, how will this failure affect nodes 1 through 3?

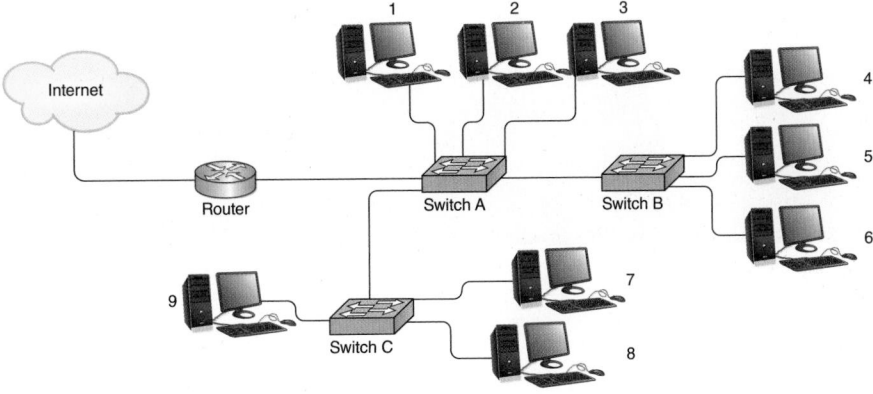

   a. They will be unable to access the Internet or nodes 7 through 9.

   b. They will be unable to access the Internet or any other nodes on the LAN.

   c. They will only be unable to access the Internet.

   d. They will be unable to access nodes 4 through 9.

   e. Their connectivity will not be affected.

74. A file server on your network is running Ubuntu Server. You need to remote into it to make some configuration changes so that a new employee can access a group of files. The files are stored on an encrypted hard drive. Which of the following utilities will give you secure access to the server to make your reconfigurations?

   a. RDP

   b. SSH

   c. SSL

   d. SFTP

   e. Telnet

75. You want to add the five virtual machines that exist on your host machine to the Staff VLAN at your office. Which of the following must your host machine's NIC support?

a. CSMA/CD

b. Channel bonding

c. MIMO

d. Trunking

e. OSPF

76. A regional bank manager asks you to help with an urgent network problem. Because of a sudden and severe network performance decline, the manager worries that the bank's network might be suffering a DoS attack. Viewing which of the following types of network documentation would probably give you the quickest insight into what's causing this problem?

a. Wiring schematic

b. Firewall log

c. Logical network diagram

d. The main file server's system log

e. Physical network diagram

77. While troubleshooting a computer's connection to the network, you enter a command at the Command Prompt and see the following output. Which command did you enter?

```
Default Server:   google-public-dns-a.google.com
Address:   8.8.8.8

>
```

a. nslookup

b. netstat

c. arp -a

d. tracert google.com

e. ping 8.8.8.8

78. Which of the following commands lists active TCP/IP connections on both Windows and Linux computers?

a. nslookup

b. netstat

c. pathping

d. ipconfig

e. iwconfig

79. On which of the following devices should you change the default administrative username and password when adding each device to your network? Choose all that apply.

a. IP security camera

b. Router

c. Programmable thermostat

d. Unmanaged switch

e. Printer

80. Which of the following transmission media is most resistant to interference?

    a. Z-wave transmissions

    b. Fiber-optic cable

    c. STP cable

    d. 802.11ac transmissions

    e. Coaxial cable

81. Which of the following cellular technologies uses time division to separate phone calls and Internet connections on a single channel?

    a. HSPA+

    b. GSM

    c. LTE

    d. CDMA

    e. LTE-Advanced

82. While troubleshooting a printer problem, you figured out the printer's static IP address had not been reserved on the DHCP server and so was mistakenly issued to a workstation. This caused a conflict, and prevented users from accessing the printer. You have now configured the reservation in DHCP. What should you do next?

    a. Document the problem and your solution in your company's knowledge base.

    b. Close the service ticket.

    c. Report your findings to the network admin.

    d. Check that the printer is plugged into the wall outlet.

    e. Confirm that users can now print successfully.

83. How does STP prevent or stop broadcast storms?

    a. It examines the source IP address field in each broadcast packet and temporarily blocks traffic from that address.

    b. It enables routers to choose one set of best paths and ensures that alternate paths are used only when the best paths are obstructed.

    c. It enables switches to calculate paths that avoid potential loops and artificially blocks the links that would complete a loop.

    d. It enables firewalls to keep access lists that name hosts known for high-volume broadcast traffic and block those hosts from transmitting to the network.

    e. It helps routers define the boundaries of a broadcast domain.

84. What is the function of protocols and services at the Network layer of the OSI model?

    a. To manage the flow of communications over a channel

    b. To add segmentation and assembly information

    c. To encode and encrypt data

    d. To add logical addresses and properly route data

    e. To apply electrical pulses to the wire

85. You have created a new web server on a computer running the Linux operating system. Some of the modules aren't loading correctly, and services are encountering errors. Which of the following applications should you check for information on these errors?
    a. Event Viewer
    b. IDS
    c. Packet sniffer
    d. Network Monitor
    e. Syslog

86. Your 1000Base-T network is wired following the TIA/EIA 568b standard. As you make your own patch cable, which wires do you crimp into pins 1 and 2 of the RJ-45 connector?
    a. White with green stripe and green
    b. White with brown stripe and brown
    c. White with blue stripe and blue
    d. White with red stripe and red
    e. White with orange stripe and orange

87. Which authentication technology issues tickets to give users access to network services?
    a. Kerberos
    b. TACACS+
    c. RADIUS
    d. Multifactor authentication
    e. Diameter

88. Suppose your Windows laptop's wireless network adapter is configured to use the 802.11n wireless networking standard. Also, suppose a café you visit has a popular model of an 802.11ac access point. Assuming you have the correct SSID and logon credentials, what will most likely happen when you attempt to associate with the café's wireless network?
    a. Your wireless networking client will be able to see the access point, but will be unable to associate with it.
    b. Your wireless networking client will not be able to see the access point.
    c. Your wireless networking client will be able to see the access point and attempt to associate with it, but the incompatible frequencies will prevent successful association.
    d. Your wireless networking client will be able to see the access point and attempt to associate with it, but the incompatible security techniques will prevent successful association.
    e. Your wireless networking client will be able to see the access point and successfully associate with it.

89. You have just rearranged the access points on your small office network. Now a group of employees complains that they cannot reliably get their workstations to connect with a new 802.11ac access point. You have confirmed that the workstations are using the correct SSID, security type, and passphrase. You have also confirmed that the access point is turned on and functioning properly because when you stand in the computer room where it's located, you can connect to the access point from your smartphone. Which of the following is likely preventing the other users' workstations from associating with the new access point?

a. The users are attempting to log on using incorrect user IDs.

b. The workstations are located beyond the access point's range.

c. The workstations are set to use 802.11g.

d. The users have turned off their wireless antennas.

e. The workstations' wired NICs are causing addressing conflicts with their wireless NICs.

90. With which of these utilities can you require a Windows 10 Professional user to create a password of at least 8 characters?

a. Cmd

b. Devmgmt.msc

c. Virtmgmt.msc

d. Gpedit.msc

e. Netplwiz

91. Which WAN technology uses a fixed message size but does not rely on a specific timing scheme?

a. Ethernet

b. ATM

c. Frame relay

d. SONET

e. MPLS

92. Which of the following is a likely reason for using subnetting?

a. To facilitate easier migration from IPv4 to IPv6 addressing

b. To enable DHCP on a network

c. To limit broadcast domains

d. To reduce the likelihood for user error when modifying TCP/IP properties

e. To reduce the number of routing table entries

93. Which of the following wireless security techniques uses both RADIUS and AES?

a. WPA2-Enterprise

b. WPA

c. WEP

d. WPA-Enterprise

e. WPA2

94. Your company is experiencing a growth spurt and is ready to invest in a more sophisticated disaster recovery plan. Currently the backup plan consists of a few spare computers in a storage closet, and data on the servers is duplicated weekly to an off-site backup service. The company owners have committed to acquiring additional servers to duplicate critical servers in their current network, and they want the servers to be configured identically to the servers now in use. The new servers will be stored at an off-site data center, and updated every time the on-site servers are updated. What type of disaster recovery site is your company creating?

    a. Hot site
    b. Ambient site
    c. Site survey
    d. Warm site
    e. Differential site

95. A virtual switch includes several virtual ports, each of which can be considered a:

    a. Virtual bridge
    b. Virtual router
    c. Virtual gateway
    d. Virtual hub
    e. Virtual repeater

96. Which OSI layer(s) operate differently in wired versus wireless network connections?

    a. Layers 5, 6, and 7
    b. Layers 1, 2, and 3
    c. Layer 1
    d. Layer 2
    e. Layers 1 and 2

97. As a networking professional, you might use a multimeter to do which of the following? Choose all that apply.

    a. Determine where the patch cable for a specific server terminates on the patch panel
    b. Verify that the amount of resistance presented by terminators on coaxial cable networks is appropriate
    c. Check for the presence of noise on a wire (by detecting extraneous voltage)
    d. Confirm that a fiber-optic cable can transmit signals from one node to another
    e. Validate the processing capabilities of a new router

98. You're setting up a wireless network for a coffee shop and want to provide some liability protection for the shop owners when customers use their Wi-Fi Internet access. Which of the following tools will provide this protection while still allowing customers convenient access to the Internet?

    a. ACL
    b. WPA2
    c. MAC filter
    d. EAPoL
    e. Captive portal

99. What type of device does this icon represent on a network diagram?

    a. Router

    b. Multilayer switch

    c. VoIP gateway

    d. vSwitch

    e. IDS/IPS

100. While configuring your new SOHO router, you're given several security options. Which one would provide the most secure encryption of your transmissions?

    a. PSK

    b. AES

    c. WEP

    d. TKIP

    e. RC4

GLOSSARY

1000Base-LX A Physical layer standard for networks that specifies 1-Gbps transmission over fiber-optic cable using baseband transmission. The LX represents its reliance on long wavelengths of 1300 nanometers.

1000Base-SX A Physical layer standard for networks that specifies 1-Gbps transmission over fiber-optic cable using baseband transmission. The SX represents its reliance on short wavelengths of 850 nanometers.

1000Base-T A Physical layer standard for achieving 1 Gbps over twisted-pair cable.

100Base-T A Physical layer standard for networks that specifies baseband transmission, twisted-pair cabling, and 100-Mbps throughput. 100Base-T is also known as Fast Ethernet.

10GBase-T A Physical layer standard for achieving 10-Gbps data transmission over twisted-pair cable.

110 block A type of punchdown block designed to terminate Cat 5 or better twisted-pair wires and typically used to handle data connections rather than telephone connections. The numeral *110* refers to the model number of the earliest blocks.

2FA (two-factor authentication) A form of identity verification where the user must provide something and know something.

4G Fourth-generation mobile phone service that is characterized by an all-IP, packet-switched network for both data and voice transmission.

66 block A type of punchdown block designed to terminate telephone connections. The numeral *66* refers to the model number of the earliest blocks.

802.11a The IEEE standard for a wireless networking technique that uses multiple frequency bands in the 5-GHz frequency range and provides a theoretical maximum throughput of 54 Mbps.

802.11ac The IEEE standard for a wireless networking technique that exceeds benchmarks set by earlier standards by increasing its useful bandwidth and amplitude. 802.11ac is the first Wi-Fi standard to approach Gigabit Ethernet capabilities.

802.11b The IEEE standard for a wireless networking technique that uses DSSS (direct-sequence spread spectrum) signaling in the 2.4-GHz frequency range and provides a theoretical maximum throughput of 11 Mbps.

802.11g The IEEE standard for a wireless networking technique designed to be compatible with 802.11b in the 2.4-GHz frequency range while using different data modulation techniques that allow it to reach a theoretical maximum capacity of 54 Mbps.

802.11n The IEEE standard for a wireless networking technique that may issue signals in the 2.4-GHz or 5-GHz band and can achieve actual data throughput between 65 Mbps and 600 Mbps.

802.1Q The IEEE standard that specifies how VLAN and trunking information appears in frames and how switches and bridges interpret that information.

802.1X A vendor-independent IEEE standard for securing transmission between nodes according to the transmission's port, whether physical or logical. 802.1X, also known as EAPoL, is commonly used with RADIUS authentication.

802.3af The IEEE standard that specifies a way of supplying electrical power (up to 15.4 watts) over twisted-pair Ethernet connections, also known as PoE (Power over Ethernet).

802.3at The IEEE standard that improves upon the older 802.3af by supplying more power (up to 25.5 watts) over Ethernet connections.

A

A (Address) record   A type of DNS data record that maps the IPv4 address of an Internet-connected device to its domain name.

AAA (authentication, authorization, and accounting)   A category of protocols that establish a client's identity, authorize a user for certain privileges on a system or network, and keep an account of the client's system or network usage.

AAAA (Address) record   A type of DNS data record that maps the IPv6 address of an Internet-connected device to its domain name. Pronounced "quad-A record."

access control   One or more security techniques for managing users' access to a network and its resources.

access port   The interface on a switch used for an end node. Devices connected to access ports are unaware of VLAN information.

accounting   In the context of network security, the process of logging users' access and activities on a network.

ACL (access control list)   A list of statements used by a router or other device to permit or deny the forwarding of traffic on a network based on one or more criteria.

AD (Active Directory)   The centralized directory database that contains user account information and security for the entire group of computers on a network.

AD (administrative distance)   A number indicating a protocol's reliability, with lower values being given higher priority. This assignment can be changed by a network administrator.

AD DS (Active Directory Domain Services) The Active Directory service that manages the process allowing a user to sign on to a network from any computer on the network and get access to the resources that Active Directory manages.

ad hoc   A type of wireless LAN in which stations communicate directly with each other (rather than using an access point).

address translation   The process of substituting a private IP address used by computers on a private network with the public IP address of a gateway device or router when these computers need access to other networks or the Internet.

ADSL (asymmetric DSL)   The most popular variation of DSL and offers faster download speeds than upload speeds.

AES (Advanced Encryption Standard)   A private key encryption algorithm that uses a sophisticated family of ciphers along with multiple stages of data transformation.

AF (Assured Forwarding)   A DiffServ forwarding specification that prioritizes data handling, but provides no guarantee that on a busy network messages will arrive on time and in sequence.

agent   A software routine that collects data about a managed device's operation or compliance with security benchmarks, and provides this information to a network management application.

agentless authentication   An authentication process in which the user is authenticated rather than the device. The device is then scanned to determine compliance with access control requirements.

AH (authentication header)   In the context of IPsec, a type of encryption that provides authentication of the IP packet's data payload through public key techniques.

alert   A message generated when a pre-defined event occurs, which is then logged by the system.

alien crosstalk   Electromagnetic interference induced on one cable by signals traveling over a nearby cable.

amplified DRDoS attack   An attack instigated using small, simple requests that trigger very large responses from the target. DNS, NTP, ICMP, LDAP, and SNMP lend themselves to being used in these kinds of attacks.

ANDing   A logical process of combining bits.

ANT+   An open-source wireless technology that gathers and tracks information from sensors typically embedded in heart rate monitors, GPS devices, and other activity monitoring devices.

anycast address   A type of IPv6 address that represents a group of interfaces, any one of which (and usually the first available of which) can accept a transmission. At this time, anycast addresses are not designed to be assigned to hosts, such as servers or workstations, but rather to routers.

AP (access point)   A device used on wireless LANs that accepts wireless signals from multiple nodes and retransmits them to the rest of the network.

APC (Angle Polished Connector)   The latest advancement in ferrule technology that uses the principles of reflection to its advantage by placing the end faces of the highly polished ferrules at an angle to each other, thus reducing the effect of back reflection.

API (application programming interface) call The process an application uses to make a request of the OS.

APIPA (Automatic Private IP Addressing) A service available on Windows computers that automatically assigns the computer's NIC a link-local IPv4 address in the range of 169.254.0.1 through 169.254.255.254.

Application layer The seventh layer of the OSI model. Application layer protocols enable software programs to negotiate formatting, procedural, security, synchronization, and other requirements with the network.

APT (advanced persistent threat or advanced persistent tool) A network attack that continues undetected for a long period of time.

ARIN (American Registry for Internet Numbers) A nonprofit corporation that manages the distribution of public IP addresses for the North American region, including the United States, Canada, and several small islands, countries, and territories in that region (including in the Caribbean). ARIN also services Antarctica.

ARP (Address Resolution Protocol) A core protocol in the TCP/IP suite that belongs in the Data Link layer of the OSI model. ARP works in conjunction with IPv4 to discover the MAC address of a node on the local network and to maintain a database that maps local IP addresses to MAC addresses.

ARP poisoning An attack in which attackers use fake ARP replies to alter ARP tables in a network.

ARP table A database of records that maps MAC addresses to IP addresses. The ARP table is stored on a computer's hard disk where it is used by the ARP utility to supply the MAC addresses of network nodes, given their IP addresses.

AS (autonomous system) A group of networks, often on the same domain, that are operated by the same organization.

ASIC (application specific integrated circuit) A specialized microchip designed to provide customized features to a specific application.

ASP (application service provider) A business that provides software services over the Internet.

asset tracking tag A barcode or wireless-enabled transmitter used to track the movement or condition of equipment, inventory, or people.

association In the context of wireless networking, the communication that occurs between a wireless client and an access point enabling the client to connect to the network via that access point.

asymmetric encryption A type of encryption (such as public key encryption) that uses a different key for encoding data than is used for decoding the cipher text.

asymmetrical A characteristic of transmission technology that offers faster download speeds than upload speeds.

asynchronous (1) A characteristic of transmission technology that offers faster download speeds than upload speeds. (2) A communications method in which nodes do not have to conform to any predetermined schemes that specify the timing of data transmissions.

ATM (Asynchronous Transfer Mode) A WAN technology functioning primarily at Layer 2 that delivers data using fixed-size packets, called cells.

attenuation The loss of a signal's strength as it travels away from its source.

AUP (acceptable use policy) The portion of a security policy that explains to users what they can and cannot do while accessing a network's resources, and penalties for violations. It might also describe how these measures protect the network's security.

authentication The process of comparing and matching a client's credentials with the credentials in a client database to enable the client to log on to the network.

authentication server The authority on computer names and their IP addresses for computers in their domains.

authenticator In Kerberos authentication, the user's time stamp encrypted with the session key. The authenticator is used to help the service verify that a user's ticket is valid.

authoritative server The authority on computer names and their IP addresses for computers in their domains.

authorization The process that determines what a user can and cannot do with network resources.

automatic failover In the event of a component failure, the ability of a redundant component to immediately assume the duties of the failed component.

availability A measure of how consistently and reliably a file, device, or connection can be accessed by authorized personnel.

B

B channel The "bearer" channel that employs circuit-switching techniques to carry voice, video, audio, and other types of data over an ISDN connection.

back door A software security flaw that can allow unauthorized users to gain access to a system.

backbone The central conduit of a network that connects network segments and significant shared devices (such as routers, switches, and servers) and is sometimes referred to as "a network of networks."

backup A copy of data or program files created for archiving or safekeeping.

badge A form of identification that includes the person's name and perhaps a photo, title, or other information.

band A specific frequency range on the wireless spectrum.

bandwidth The amount of data that could theoretically be transmitted during a given period of time.

bandwidth speed tester A website that tests the current upload and download speeds on a WAN connection.

baseline A record of how a network operates under normal conditions.

BCP (business continuity plan) A document that details how an organization intends to maintain business operations during a disaster.

beacon frame In the context of wireless networking, a frame issued by an access point to alert other nodes of its existence.

BERT (bit-error rate test) A test that measures the bit-error rate of a transmission, which is the percentage of bits with errors in a transmission.

best path The most efficient route from one node on a network to another, as calculated by a router.

BGP (Border Gateway Protocol) Dubbed the "protocol of the Internet," this path-vector routing protocol is the only current EGP and is capable of considering many factors in its routing metrics.

BiDi transceiver A fiber-optic transceiver that supports bidirectional transmission on both its ports.

bidirectional A transmission method that allows each fiber cable to carry data in both directions.

biometrics Unique physical characteristics of an individual, such as the color patterns in his iris or the geometry of his hand.

bit rate In digital transmissions, a measurement of throughput and bandwidth that is expressed as bits transmitted per second.

BLE (Bluetooth Low Energy) Also called Bluetooth Smart, a new version of Bluetooth that provides a range comparable to the earlier version of Bluetooth, but that consumes less power.

Bluetooth A low-power wireless technology that provides close-range communication between devices such as PCs, smartphones, tablets, and accessories.

BNC (British Naval Connector/Bayonet Neill-Concelman) connector A coaxial cable connector type that uses a turn-and-lock (or bayonet) style of coupling.

BootP (Boot Protocol/Bootstrap Protocol) An IP network protocol that automatically boots a system and assigns an IP address without user involvement.

border router A router that connects an autonomous system with an outside network—for example, the router that connects a business to its ISP. Also called edge router.

BPDU (Bridge Protocol Data Unit) A type of network message that transmits STP information between switches.

BPDU filter A software configuration that can be used to disable STP on specific ports, such as the port leading to the network's demarc. A BPDU filter prevents access to network links that should not be considered when plotting STP paths in a network.

BPDU guard A software configuration on a switch's access ports that blocks certain types of BPDUs from being sent to or received by the devices, such as workstations and servers, connected to these ports.

BRI (Basic Rate Interface) A variety of ISDN that uses two 64-Kbps B channels and one 16-Kbps D channel, as summarized by the notation 2B+D.

bridged mode A type of network connection in which a vNIC accesses a physical network using the host machine's NIC. The bridged vNIC obtains its own IP address, default gateway, and subnet mask information from the physical LAN's DHCP server.

broadband A WAN technology where the cables and available bandwidth are shared between multiple customers.

broadcast A message that is read by every node on a network.

broadcast domain Logically grouped network nodes that can communicate directly via broadcast transmissions. By default, switches and repeating devices, such as hubs, extend broadcast domains.

Routers and other Layer 3 devices separate broadcast domains.

brute force attack An attempt to discover an encryption key or password by trying numerous possible character combinations until the correct combination is found.

BSS (basic service set) In IEEE terminology, a group of stations that share an access point.

BSSID (basic service set identifier) In IEEE terminology, the identifier for a BSS (basic service set).

bus topology A topology in which a single cable connects all nodes on a network without intervening connectivity devices.

business continuity The ability of a company to continue doing business with the least amount of interruption possible after a major outage or other disaster.

BYOD (bring your own device) The practice of allowing people to bring their smartphones, laptops, or other technology into a facility for the purpose of performing work or school responsibilities.

C

CA (certificate authority) An organization that issues and maintains digital certificates as part of the PKI (public-key infrastructure).

CaaS (Communication as a Service) A service model in which communication services are provided virtually, such as VoIP or video conferencing.

cable broadband Broadband Internet access provided over the coaxial cable wiring used for TV signals.

cable modem A device that modulates and demodulates signals for transmission and reception via cable wiring.

cable performance tester A troubleshooting tool that tests cables for continuity, but can also measure crosstalk, attenuation, and impedance; identify the location of faults; and store or print cable testing results. Also called line tester, certifier, or network tester.

cable tester A device that tests cables for one or more of the following conditions: continuity, segment length, distance to a fault, attenuation along a cable, near-end cross-talk, and termination resistance and impedance.

caching DNS server A server that accesses public DNS data and caches the DNS information it collects.

CAM (content addressable memory) A special kind of high-speed computer memory often used in routers and switches for table lookup functions.

CAN (campus area network) A network of connected LANs within a limited geographical area, such as the buildings on a university campus.

canonical name The true name of a server, such as *www.example.com*, as opposed to one of many alias names a server might have, such as *ns1.example.com*.

captive portal The first page displayed by a client's browser when the client connects to a guest network. This page usually requires the user to agree to a set of terms and conditions before gaining further access to the guest network.

CAPWAP (Control and Provisioning of Wireless Access Points) A proprietary protocol created by Cisco to replace LWAPP. Both LWAPP and CAPWAP make centralized wireless management possible.

CARP (Common Address Redundancy Protocol) A protocol that allows a pool of computers or interfaces to share one or more IP addresses.

Carrier Ethernet A WAN technology that sends Ethernet traffic across long-distance WAN connections.

CASB (cloud access security broker) Software positioned between the local network and cloud-based resources that monitors communications and ensures an organization's security policies are enforced.

Cat 3 (Category 3) An outdated form of UTP that contained four wire pairs and could carry up to 10 Mbps, with a possible bandwidth of 16 MHz.

Cat 5 (Category 5) A form of UTP that contains four wire pairs and supports up to 100-Mbps throughput and a 100-MHz signal rate. Required minimum standard for Fast Ethernet.

Cat 5e (Enhanced Category 5) A higher-grade version of Cat 5 wiring that supports a signaling rate of up to 350 MHz and a maximum throughput of 1 Gbps, making it the required minimum standard for Gigabit Ethernet.

Cat 6 (Category 6) A twisted-pair cable that contains four wire pairs, each wrapped in foil insulation. Additional foil insulation can cover the bundle of wire pairs, and a fire-resistant plastic sheath might cover the second foil layer. The foil insulation provides excellent resistance to crosstalk and enables Cat 6 to support a signaling rate of 250 MHz and throughput up to 10 Gbps.

Cat 6a (Augmented Category 6) A higher-grade version of Cat 6 wiring that further reduces attenuation and crosstalk, and allows for potentially exceeding traditional network segment length limits.

Cat 7 (Category 7) A twisted-pair cable that contains multiple wire pairs, each separately shielded then surrounded by another layer of shielding within the jacket.

Cat 7a (Augmented Category 7) A higher-grade version of Cat 7 wiring that will possibly support up to 100-Gbps throughput and up to 1000-MHz signal rate. ISO standards for Cat 7a cabling are still being drafted and simulations conducted.

catastrophic failure A failure that destroys a component beyond use.

CCMP (Counter Mode with CBC [Cipher Block Chaining] MAC [Message Authentication Code] Protocol) A security method used in WPA2 that helps ensure data confidentiality by providing message integrity and encryption services.

CCTV (closed-circuit TV) A video surveillance system that monitors activity in secured areas.

CDMA (Code Division Multiple Access) A cellular standard that uses spread-spectrum technology, in which a signal is spread over a wide bandwidth so that multiple users can occupy the same channel.

cell In ATM technology, a packet of a fixed size consisting of 48 bytes of data plus a 5-byte header.

CET (Carrier-Ethernet Transport) An Ethernet-based transport solution designed to overcome the inherent weaknesses of implementing Ethernet outside of a LAN environment.

CFP (centum form-factor pluggable) A fiber-optic transceiver intended for 100-Gbps network connections.

chain of custody Documentation that describes evidence, including when it was collected, who collected it, its condition, and how it was secured and transferred from one responsible party to the next.

channel bonding In the context of 802.11n and 802.11ac wireless technology, the combination of two or more adjacent 20-MHz frequency bands to create one 40-, 60-, 80-, or 120-MHz channel.

CHAP (Challenge Handshake Authentication Protocol) An authentication protocol that operates over PPP and also encrypts usernames and passwords for transmission.

checksum A method of error checking that determines if the contents of an arriving data unit match the contents of the data unit sent by the source.

CIA (confidentiality, integrity, and availability) triad A three-tenet, standard security model describing the primary ways that encryption protects data. Confidentiality ensures that data can only be viewed by its intended recipient or at its intended destination. Integrity ensures that data was not modified after the sender transmitted it and before the receiver picked it up. Availability ensures that data is available to and accessible by the intended recipient when needed.

CIDR (Classless Interdomain Routing) A shorthand method for identifying network and host bits in an IP address.

CIDR block In CIDR notation, the forward slash plus the number of bits used for the network ID. For example, the CIDR block for 199.34.89.0/22 is /22.

CIDR notation A shorthand method for denoting the distinction between network and host bits in an IP address.

cipher lock A physical or electronic lock requiring a code to open the door.

circuit-switched A type of switching in which a connection is established between two network nodes before they begin transmitting data. Bandwidth is dedicated to this connection and remains available until users terminate the communication between the two nodes.

cladding The glass or plastic shield around the core of a fiber-optic cable. Cladding reflects light back to the core in patterns that vary depending on the transmission mode.

classful addressing An IP addressing convention that adheres to network class distinctions, in which the first 8 bits of a Class A address, the first 16 bits of a Class B address, and the first 24 bits of a Class C address are used for network information.

classless addressing An IP addressing convention that alters the rules of classful IPv4 addressing to create subnets in a network.

CLI (command-line interface) A graphic-free user interface, such as the Command Prompt application in Windows, where technicians can enter commands more quickly and with more flexibility than in a GUI (graphical user interface) environment.

client A computer or application that makes a request from another computer or application.

client_hello In the context of SSL encryption, a message issued from the client to the server that contains information about what level of security the client's browser is capable of accepting and what type of encryption the client's browser can decipher.

client-server application Data or a service requested by one computer from another.

client-server network model A network where resources are managed by the NOS via a centralized directory database.

client-to-site VPN A type of VPN in which clients, servers, and other hosts establish tunnels with a private network using a VPN gateway at the edge of the private network.

cloud computing The flexible provision of data storage, applications, or services to clients over the Internet.

clustering A technique of grouping multiple devices so they appear as a single device to the rest of the network.

CNAME (Canonical Name) record A type of DNS data record that holds alternative names for a host.

coaxial cable A type of cable that consists of a central metal conducting core, surrounded by an insulator, shielding, and an outer cover. Today coaxial cable, called "coax" for short, is used to connect cable Internet and cable TV systems.

cold site A place where the computers, devices, and connectivity necessary to rebuild a network exist, but are not appropriately configured, updated, or connected to match the network's current state.

collision In Ethernet networks, the interference of one node's data transmission with the data transmission of another node sharing the same segment.

collision domain The portion of an Ethernet network in which collisions could occur if two nodes transmit data at the same time. Today, switches and routers separate collision domains.

colocation facility A data center facility that is shared by a variety of providers. Also called a carrier hotel.

community cloud A deployment model in which flexible data storage, applications, or services are shared between multiple organizations, but not available publicly.

connectionless protocol A type of Transport layer protocol that services a request without requiring a verified session and without guaranteeing delivery of data.

connection-oriented protocol A type of Transport layer protocol that requires the establishment of a connection between communicating nodes before it will transmit data.

console port The type of port on a router used to communicate with the router itself, such as when making configuration changes to the device.

console router A device that provides centralized management of all linked devices.

console server A device that provides centralized management of all linked devices.

content-filtering firewall A firewall that can block designated types of traffic from entering a protected network based on application data contained within packets.

continuity The ability of a cable to carry a signal to its destination.

continuity tester An instrument that tests whether voltage (or light, in the case of fiber-optic cable) issued at one end of a cable can be detected at the opposite end of the cable. Also called cable checker or cable tester.

control plane The process of decision making, such as routing, blocking, and forwarding, that is performed by protocols.

convergence time The time it takes for a router to recognize a best path in the event of a change or network outage.

core A cable's central component that is designed to carry a signal, such as glass or plastic fibers in fiber-optic cable or strands of copper in twisted-pair cable.

core router A router that directs data between networks within the same autonomous system.

CoS (Class of Service) Quality control techniques performed at Layer 2 on Ethernet frames.

CPU (central processing unit) The component of a computer that performs almost all data processing for the computer.

CRAM-MD5 (Challenge-Response Authentication Mechanism-Message Digest 5) An authentication mechanism built on the MD5 algorithm that provides some additional security when communicating over an unencrypted connection.

CRC (cyclic redundancy checking) An algorithm (mathematical routine) used to verify the accuracy of data contained in a data frame.

crimper A tool used to attach a connector onto the end of a cable, causing the internal RJ-45 pins to pierce the insulation of the wires, thus creating contact between the conductors at each wire.

crossover cable A twisted-pair patch cable in which the termination locations of the transmit and receive wires on one end of the cable are reversed as compared with the other end.

crosstalk A type of interference caused by signals traveling on nearby wire pairs infringing on another pair's signal.

CSMA/CA (Carrier Sense Multiple Access with Collision Avoidance) A network access method used on 802.11 wireless networks. CSMA/CA does not eliminate, but minimizes, the potential for collisions.

CSMA/CD (Carrier Sense Multiple Access with Collision Detection)   A network access method specified for use by IEEE 802.3 (Ethernet) networks. In CSMA/CD, each node waits its turn before transmitting data to avoid interfering with other nodes' transmissions.

CSU (channel service unit)/DSU (data service unit)   A device that serves as the connection point for a T1 line at the customer's site.

CVW (Collaborative Virtual Workspace)   A software tool designed to support teams working across geographical distances.

CWDM (coarse wavelength division multiplexing or coarse WDM)   A multiplexing technique used over single-mode or multimode fiber-optic cable in which each signal is assigned a different wavelength for its carrier wave.

D

D channel   The "data" channel that employs packet-switching techniques to carry information about an ISDN connection.

DaaS (Desktop as a Service)   A service model in which desktop services, such as VDI, are provided virtually from a third-party provider.

DAC (discretionary access control)   A method of access control where users decide for themselves who has access to that user's resources.

data breach   Unauthorized access or use of sensitive data.

data frame   An 802.11 frame type that is responsible for carrying data between stations.

Data Link layer   The second layer in the OSI model. The Data link layer, also called the Link layer, bridges the Physical layer's networking media with Network layer processes.

Data Link layer address   *See* MAC (Media Access Control) address.

data plane   The actual contact made between physical devices and data transmissions as messages traverse a network.

datagram   A UDP message at the Transport layer.

dB (decibel)   A unit of sound intensity, signal attenuation, SNR, or antenna gain.

DB-25 connector   A type of connector with 25 pins that's used in serial communication and conforms to the RS-232 standard.

DB-9 connector   A type of connector with nine pins that's used in serial communication and conforms to the RS-232 standard.

DCS (distributed control system or distributed computer system)   A network of field devices in a closed loop system that are distributed throughout the physical system to monitor many aspects of the system.

DDoS (distributed DoS) attack   An attack in which multiple hosts simultaneously flood a target host with traffic, rendering the target unable to function.

deauth (deauthentication) attack   An attack on a wireless network in which the attacker sends faked deauthentication frames to the AP, the client, or both (or as a broadcast to the whole wireless network) to trigger the deauthentication process and knock one or more clients off the wireless network.

decapsulation   Removing a header or trailer from a lower OSI layer.

dedicated line   A cable or other telecommunications path that has continuously available communications channels and is not shared with other users.

default gateway   The gateway device that nodes on the network turn to first for access to the outside world.

default route   A backup route, usually to another router, used when a router cannot determine a path to a message's destination.

default VLAN   A preconfigured VLAN on a switch that includes all the switch's ports and cannot be renamed or deleted.

delay-sensitive   Transmissions that will suffer significantly compromised user experiences if portions of the transmission are delayed, such as with voice and video transmissions.

demarc (demarcation point)   The point of division between a telecommunications service carrier's network and a building's internal network.

device hardening   Preventive measures that can be taken to secure a device from network- or software-supported attacks.

device ID   *See* extension identifier.

DHCP (Dynamic Host Configuration Protocol)   An Application layer protocol in the TCP/IP suite that manages the dynamic distribution of IP addresses on a network.

DHCP pool   The predefined range of addresses that can be leased to any network device on a particular segment.

DHCP relay agent A small application that works with a centrally managed DHCP server to provide DHCP assignments to multiple subnets and VLANs.

DHCP reservation An IP address that is set aside by a DHCP server for a specific network client, which is identified by its MAC address.

DHCP scope The predefined range of addresses that can be leased to any network device on a particular segment.

DHCP snooping A security feature on switches whereby DHCP messages on the network are checked and filtered.

DHCPv6 The version of DHCP used with IPv6.

DIA (dedicated Internet access) A WAN service where the cable or a portion of its available bandwidth is dedicated to a single customer and comes with an SLA-defined guarantee of minimum uptime percentages and maximum recovery times if the service goes down.

dial-up A type of WAN connection in which a user connects to a distant network through a dialed connection over the PSTN, and stays connected for a finite period of time.

dictionary attack A technique in which attackers run a program that tries a combination of a known user ID and, for a password, every word in a dictionary to attempt to gain access to a network.

differential backup A backup method in which only data that has changed since the last full or incremental backup is copied to a storage medium even if earlier differential backups have been made.

diffraction In the context of wireless signal propagation, the phenomenon that occurs when an electromagnetic wave encounters an obstruction and splits into secondary waves.

DiffServ (Differentiated Services) A technique for ensuring QoS by prioritizing traffic.

dig (domain information groper) A utility available on Linux and macOS that provides more detailed domain information than nslookup. Use dig to query DNS nameservers for information about host addresses and other DNS records.

digital certificate A small file containing verified identification information about the user and the user's public key.

disaster An extreme type of incident, involving a network outage that affects more than a single system or limited group of users.

disaster recovery The process of restoring critical functionality and data to a network after an enterprise-wide outage.

distance-vector routing protocol The simplest type of routing protocols; used to determine the best route for data based on the distance to a destination.

distributed switching The centralized control of many VMs' access to a network across a server cluster.

DKIM (DomainKeys Identified Mail) An authentication method that uses encryption to verify the domain name of an email's sender.

DLC (Data Link Control) A service provided at the Data Link layer to manage frames, including error detection and flow control.

DLP (data loss prevention) A security technique that uses software to monitor confidential data, track data access and ownership, and prevent it from being copied or transmitted off the network.

DLR (Device Level Ring) A Layer 2 protocol that enables single-fault tolerance on a network using a ring topology to connect devices.

DMVPN (Dynamic Multipoint VPN) A particular type of enterprise VPN using Cisco devices that dynamically creates VPN tunnels between branch locations as needed rather than requiring constant, static tunnels for site-to-site connections.

DMZ (demilitarized zone) An area on the perimeter of a network that is surrounded by two firewalls— an external firewall that is more porous to allow more types of access, and an internal firewall that is more hardened to provide greater protection to the internal network.

DNAT (Destination Network Address Translation) A type of address translation in which a gateway has a pool of public IP addresses that it is free to assign to a local host whenever the local host makes a request to access the Internet.

DNS (Domain Name System or Domain Name Service) A hierarchical way of tracking domain names and their addresses, devised in the mid-1980s.

DNS poisoning An attack that alters DNS records on a DNS server, thereby redirecting Internet traffic from a legitimate web server to a phishing website.

DNS spoofing An attack in which an outsider forges name server records to falsify his host's identity.

DNS zone A portion of the DNS namespace for which one organization is assigned authority to manage.

DOCSIS (Data Over Cable Service Interface Specifications) An international, cooperative effort orchestrated by Cable-Labs that standardized cable broadband service.

domain In the context of Windows Server NOSes, a group of users, servers, and other resources that share account and security policies.

domain local group A group of workstations that is centrally managed via Active Directory for the entire network.

domain name The last two parts of an FQDN, such as *mycompany.com*. Usually, a domain name is associated with the company's name and its type of organization, such as a university or military unit.

DoS (denial-of-service) attack An attack in which a legitimate user is unable to access normal network resources because of an attacker's intervention. Most often, this type of attack is achieved by flooding a system with so many requests for services that it can't respond to any of them.

DR (designated router) In the context of OSPF, a router normally selected automatically to serve as a central collection point for routing information on a network.

DRDoS (distributed reflection DoS) attack A DoS attack bounced off of uninfected computers, called reflectors, before being directed at the target.

DSCP (Differentiated Services Code Point) The first 6 bits of the 8-bit DiffServ field in an IPv4 packet which indicates to network routers how the data stream should be forwarded.

DSL (digital subscriber line) A WAN connection technology that operates over the PSTN and can support multiple data and voice channels over a single line.

DSSS (direct sequence spread spectrum) A modulation technique that, like other spread-spectrum technologies, distributes lower-level signals over several frequencies simultaneously.

DTLS (Datagram Transport Layer Security) A variant of TLS designed specifically for streaming communications.

dual power supplies Power supply redundancy.

dual stacked A type of network that supports both IPv4 and IPv6 traffic.

duplex A type of transmission in which signals may travel in both directions over a medium simultaneously.

DWDM (dense wavelength division multiplexing or dense WDM) A multiplexing technique used over single-mode or multimode fiber-optic cable in which each signal is assigned a different wavelength for its carrier wave.

dynamic ARP table entry A record in an ARP table that is created when a client makes an ARP request that cannot be satisfied by data already in the ARP table.

dynamic IP address An IP address that is assigned to a device upon request and may change when the DHCP lease expires or is terminated.

dynamic routing A method of routing that automatically calculates the best path between two networks and accumulates this information in a routing table.

E

E1 A digital carrier standard used in Europe that offers 32 channels and a maximum of 2.048-Mbps throughput.

E3 A digital carrier standard used in Europe that offers 512 channels and a maximum of 34.368-Mbps throughput.

EAP (Extensible Authentication Protocol) An authentication mechanism that provides the framework for authenticating clients and servers. It does not perform encryption or authentication on its own, but rather works with other encryption and authentication schemes to verify the credentials of clients and servers.

EAP-FAST (EAP-Flexible Authentication via Secure Tunneling) A form of tunneled EAP developed by Cisco that uses PACs (Protected Access Credentials), which are somewhat similar to cookies that websites store on a user's computer to track their activities.

EAPoL (EAP over LAN) *See* 802.1X.

EAP-TLS A form of EAP that uses TLS encryption to protect communications.

edge router A router that connects an autonomous system with an outside network—for example, the router that connects a business to its ISP.

EDNS (extension mechanism for DNS) A mechanism that expands DNS parameters, thereby increasing the protocol's functionality.

EF (Expedited Forwarding) A DiffServ forwarding specification that assigns each data stream a minimum departure rate from a given node.

EGP (exterior gateway protocol) A type of routing protocol used by edge routers and exterior routers to distribute data outside of autonomous systems. BGP is the only modern example of an exterior gateway protocol.

EIA (Electronics Industries Alliance) A former trade organization composed of representatives from electronics manufacturing firms across the United States that sets standards for electronic equipment and lobbies for legislation favorable to the growth of the computer and electronics industries. EIA was dissolved in 2011 and its responsibilities transferred to ECA (Electronic Components, Assemblies, Equipment & Supplies Association), but the standards brand name, EIA, will continue to be used.

EIGRP (Enhanced Interior Gateway Routing Protocol) An advanced distance-vector protocol developed by Cisco that combines some of the features of a link-state protocol and so is sometimes referred to as a hybrid protocol.

elevated Command Prompt A Command Prompt window with administrative privileges.

emergency alert system A system that typically generates loud noise and flashing lights in response to a fire or other environmental threat. The system might also be able to send alert messages to key personnel or make network-wide announcements.

EMI (electromagnetic interference) A type of interference that can be caused by motors, power lines, televisions, copiers, fluorescent lights, or other sources of electrical activity.

encapsulation The process of adding a header to data inherited from the layer above.

encryption The use of an algorithm to scramble data into a format that can be read only by reversing the algorithm—that is, by decrypting the data—to keep the information private.

entrance facility The location where an incoming network service (whether phone, Internet, or long-distance service) enters a building and connects with the building's backbone cabling.

error rate The calculated percentage of how often bits are damaged in transit.

ESD (electrostatic discharge) The transfer of electrical charge between two bodies, such as when a technician touches a computer component.

ESP (Encapsulating Security Payload) In the context of IPsec, a type of encryption that provides authentication of the IP packet's data payload through public key techniques and encrypts the entire IP packet for added security.

ESS (extended service set) A group of access points and associated stations (or basic service sets) connected to the same LAN.

ESSID (extended service set identifier) A special identifier shared by BSSes that belong to the same ESS.

Ethernet II The current Ethernet standard. Ethernet II is distinguished from other Ethernet frame types in that it contains a 2-byte type field to identify the upper-layer protocol contained in the frame.

Ethernet port The type of port that connects devices on a LAN; it uses an RJ-45 connector.

EUI-64 (Extended Unique Identifier-64) The IEEE standard defining 64-bit physical addresses. In the EUI-64 scheme, the OUI portion of an address is 24 bits in length. A 40-bit extension identifier makes up the rest of the physical address, for a total of 64 bits.

event log The service on Windows-based operating systems that records events.

Event Viewer A GUI application that allows users to easily view and sort events recorded in the event log on a computer running a Windows-based operating system.

evil twin An exploit in which a rogue access point masquerades as a legitimate access point, using the same SSID and potentially other identical settings.

exhausted DHCP scope A shortage of available IP addresses on a network so that no new clients can connect to the network.

exploit In the context of network security, the act of taking advantage of a vulnerability.

extension identifier A unique set of characters assigned to each NIC by its manufacturer.

exterior router A router that directs data between autonomous systems, for example, routers used on the Internet's backbone.

F

fading A variation in a wireless signal's strength as a result of some of the electromagnetic energy being scattered, reflected, or diffracted after being issued by the transmitter.

fail close System default that denies access during a system or network failure.

fail open System default that allows access during a system or network failure.

failure A deviation from a specified level of system performance for a given period of time.

Fast Ethernet A type of Ethernet network that is capable of 100-Mbps throughput.

fault The malfunction of one component of a system.

fault management The detection and signaling of device, link, or component faults.

fault tolerance The capacity of a system to continue performing despite an unexpected hardware or software malfunction.

FC (Fibre Channel) A storage networking architecture that runs separately from Ethernet networks to maximize speed of data storage and access.

FCoE (Fibre Channel over Ethernet) A technology that allows FC to travel over Ethernet hardware and connections.

F-connector A connector used to terminate coaxial cable that transmits television and cable broadband signals.

FCS (frame check sequence) The field in a frame responsible for ensuring that data carried by the frame arrives intact.

FDM (frequency division multiplexing) A type of multiplexing that assigns a unique frequency band to each communications subchannel. Signals are modulated with different carrier frequencies, then multiplexed to simultaneously travel over a single channel.

FDP (fiber distribution panel) A device on a rack where fiber cables converge, connect with each other, and connect with fiber-optic terminal equipment from the ISP.

ferrule The extended tip of a fiber-optic cable connector that encircles the fiber strand to keep it properly aligned and ensure that it makes contact with the receptacle in a jack or other connector.

FEXT (far end crosstalk) Crosstalk measured at the far end of the cable from the signal source.

FHSS (frequency hopping spread spectrum) A wireless signaling technique in which a signal jumps between several different frequencies within a band in a synchronization pattern known to the channel's receiver and transmitter.

fiber-optic cable A form of cable that contains one or several glass or plastic fibers in its core. Data is transmitted via a pulsing light sent from a laser or LED (light-emitting diode) through the central fiber or fibers.

FIM (file integrity monitoring) A security technique that alerts the system of any changes made to files that shouldn't change, such as operating system files.

fire suppression system Any system designed to combat the outbreak of a fire. A fire suppression system might include an emergency alert system, fire extinguishers, emergency power-off switch, and/or a suppression agent such as a foaming chemical or water.

firewall A device (either a router, a dedicated device, or a computer running special software) that selectively filters or blocks traffic between networks.

firmware Programs embedded into hardware devices.

first responder A person with training or certifications in handling evidence in such a way as to preserve its admissibility in court.

FM (frequency modulation) A method of data modulation in which the frequency of the carrier signal is modified by the application of the data signal.

forward zone A DNS lookup file that holds A records.

forwarding DNS server An optional server that receives queries from local clients but doesn't work to resolve the queries.

FQDN (fully qualified domain name) A host name plus domain name that uniquely identifies a computer or location on a network.

fractional T1 A service option that allows a customer to lease only some of the channels on a T1 line.

fragmentation A Network layer service that subdivides packets into smaller packets when those packets exceed the maximum size for the network.

frame The entire Data Link layer message, including the header, payload, and trailer.

frame relay A group of Layer 2 WAN protocols that separate data into variable-length frames, which are then relayed from one node to another without any verification or processing.

frequency hopping A process performed by some wireless devices to help reduce interference by quickly hopping between frequencies within a given band of frequencies.

FTP (File Transfer Protocol) An Application layer protocol used to send and receive files via TCP/IP.

FTP bounce An attack in which an FTP client specifies a different host's IP address and port for the requested data's destination. By commanding the FTP server to connect to a different computer, a hacker can scan the ports on other hosts and transmit malicious code.

FTPS (FTP Security or FTP Secure) A version of FTP that incorporates the TLS and SSL protocols for added security.

full backup A backup in which all data on all servers is copied to a storage medium, regardless of whether the data is new, changed, or unchanged.

full-duplex   A type of transmission in which signals may travel in both directions over a medium simultaneously; also called, simply, duplex.

G

gateway   A computer, router, or other device that a host uses to access another network. Gateways perform connectivity, session management, and data translation, so they must operate at multiple layers of the OSI model.

gateway of last resort   The router on a network that accepts all unroutable messages from other routers.

GBIC (Gigabit interface converter)   A standard type of modular interface that may contain RJ-45 or fiber-optic cable ports (such as LC, SC, or ST). They are inserted into a socket on a connectivity device's backplane. Pronounced *jee-bick*.

Gbps (Gigabits per second)   A unit for measuring data transfer rate.

geofencing   An authentication restriction that determines a client's geographic location to enforce a virtual security perimeter.

Gigabit Ethernet   A type of Ethernet network that is capable of 1000-Mbps, or 1-Gbps, throughput. Requires Cat 5e or higher cabling.

GLBP (Gateway Load Balancing Protocol)   A protocol that allows a pool of interfaces to share one or more IP addresses and also provides load balancing services.

global address   An IPv6 address that can be routed on the Internet. These addresses are similar to public IPv4 addresses. Most global addresses begin with the prefix 2000::/3, although other prefixes are being released.

global routing prefix   The first four blocks or 64 bits of an IPv6 address that normally identify the network. Also called site prefix.

GPG (GNU Privacy Guard)   An encryption software program that provides an alternative to PGP.

GRE (Generic Routing Encapsulation)   A tunneling protocol developed by Cisco that is used to transmit PPP data frames through a VPN tunnel.

grounding   Connecting a device directly to the earth so that, in the event of a short circuit, the electricity flows into the earth rather than out of control through the device.

Group Policy (gpedit.msc)   A Windows utility that is used to control what users can do and how the system can be used.

GSM (Global System for Mobile Communications)   An open standard for cellular networks that uses digital communication of data separated by time slots on a channel.

guest   In the context of virtualization, a virtual machine operated and managed by a virtualization program.

guest network   A separate wireless network created through a Wi-Fi router or access point to protect a private network while still providing guests with access to the Internet.

H

H.323   A signaling protocol used to make a connection between hosts prior to communicating multimedia data. H.323 has largely been replaced by SIP, which is easier to use.

HA (high availability)   A system that functions reliably nearly all the time.

hacker   Traditionally, a person who masters the inner workings of computer hardware and software in an effort to better understand them. More generally, an individual who gains unauthorized access to systems or networks with or without malicious intent.

handshake protocol   A protocol within SSL that allows the client and server to authenticate (or introduce) each other and establishes terms for how they securely exchange data during an SSL session.

hardware address   *See* MAC (Media Access Control) address.

hashing   The transformation of data through an algorithm that generally reduces the amount of space needed for the data. Hashing is mostly used to ensure data integrity—that is, to verify the data has not been altered.

HDLC (High-Level Data Link Control)   A group of Layer 2 protocols that can provide either connection-oriented or connectionless service for data transfer between nodes.

HDMI (High-Definition Multimedia Interface)   A standard connector used primarily for video or audio data transfer.

header   An area at the beginning of a payload where protocols add control information.

HFC (hybrid fiber coaxial)   A physical infrastructure where fiber-optic cabling connects the cable company's distribution center to distribution hubs and then to optical nodes near customers; either fiber-optic or coaxial cable then connects a node to each customer's business or residence.

HIDS (host-based intrusion detection system) A type of intrusion detection that runs on a single computer, such as a client or server, to alert about attacks against that one host.

HIPS (host-based intrusion prevention system) A type of intrusion prevention that runs on a single computer, such as a client or server, to intercept and help prevent attacks against that one host.

honeynet A network of honeypots.

honeypot A decoy system isolated from legitimate systems and designed to be vulnerable to security exploits for the purposes of learning more about hacking techniques or nabbing a hacker in the act.

hop The trip a unit of data takes from one connectivity device to another. Typically, hop is used in the context of router-to-router communications.

hop limit The number of times that an IPv6 packet can be forwarded by routers on the network; similar to the TTL field in IPv4 packets.

host (1) Any computer or device on a network that provides or uses a resource such as an application or data. (2) In the context of virtualization, the physical computer on which virtualization software operates and manages guests.

host ID The portion of an IP address that identifies the host on a network.

host name The first part of an FQDN, such as *www* or *ftp*, which identifies the individual computer on the network.

host-based firewall A firewall that only protects the computer on which it's installed.

host-only mode A type of network connection in which VMs on a host can exchange data with each other and with their host, but they cannot communicate with any nodes beyond the host. In host-only mode, VMs use the DHCP service in the host's virtualization software to obtain IP address assignments.

hot site A place where the computers, devices, and connectivity necessary to rebuild a network exist, and all are appropriately configured, updated, and connected to match a network's current state.

hot-swappable A component that can be installed or removed without disrupting operations.

HSPA+ (High Speed Packet Access Plus) A 3G mobile wireless technology released in 2008 that uses MIMO and sophisticated encoding techniques to achieve a maximum 168-Mbps downlink throughput and 22-Mbps uplink throughput in its current release.

HSRP (Hot Standby Routing Protocol) Cisco's proprietary standard that assigns a virtual IP address to a group of routers.

HT (high throughput) A relative term indicating more efficient data transfer.

HTTP (Hypertext Transfer Protocol) An Application layer protocol that formulates and interprets requests between web clients and servers.

HTTPS (HTTP Secure) The URL prefix that indicates a web page requires its data to be exchanged between client and server using SSL or TLS encryption.

hub An outdated connectivity device that belongs to the Physical layer of the OSI model and retransmits incoming data signals to its multiple ports.

HVAC (heating, ventilation, and air conditioning) A system that controls the environment in a data center, including the temperature, humidity, airflow, and air filtering.

HVD (hosted virtual desktop) A desktop operating environment hosted virtually on a different physical computer from the one the user interacts with.

hybrid cloud A deployment model in which shared and flexible data storage, applications, or services are made available through a combination of other service models into a single deployment, or a collection of services connected within the cloud.

hybrid routing protocol A routing protocol that exhibits characteristics of both distance-vector and link-state routing protocols.

hybrid topology A physical topology that combines characteristics of more than one simple physical topology.

hypervisor The element of virtualization software that manages multiple guest machines and their connections to the host (and by association, to a physical network).

Hz (Hertz) A unit of frequency. One Hz equals one wave cycle per second.

I

IaaS (Infrastructure as a Service) A service model in which hardware services are provided virtually, including network infrastructure devices such as virtual servers.

IANA (Internet Assigned Numbers Authority) A nonprofit, U.S. government-funded group that was established at the University of Southern California and charged with managing IP address allocation and the Domain Name System. The oversight for many of IANA's functions was given to ICANN in 1998; however, IANA continues to perform Internet addressing and Domain Name System administration.

IB (InfiniBand) A storage networking architecture that serves a few niche markets and falls on the difficult end of the installation and configuration spectrum.

ICA (Independent Computing Architecture) A proprietary protocol used by Citrix's XenApp and other products to standardize data transfer between servers and clients.

ICANN (Internet Corporation for Assigned Names and Numbers) The nonprofit corporation currently designated by the U.S. government to maintain and assign IP addresses.

ICMP (Internet Control Message Protocol) A core protocol in the TCP/IP suite that notifies the sender when something has gone wrong in the transmission process and packets were not delivered.

ICMPv6 The version of ICMP used with IPv6 networks. ICMPv6 performs the functions that ICMP, IGMP, and ARP perform in IPv4. It detects and reports data transmission errors, discovers other nodes on a network, and manages multicasting.

ICS (Internet Connection Sharing) The use of one device's Internet connection to provide Internet connectivity to one or more other devices.

ICS (industrial control system) A group of networked computers used to manage a physical system of industrial processes.

IDF (intermediate distribution frame) A junction point between the MDF and concentrations of fewer connections— for example, those that terminate in a data closet.

IDS (intrusion detection system) A stand-alone device, an application, or a built-in feature running on a workstation, server, switch, router, or firewall. It monitors network traffic, generating alerts about suspicious activity.

IEEE (Institute of Electrical and Electronics Engineers) A professional society that develops national and international standards in a variety of technical areas.

ifconfig An interface configuration and management utility used with UNIX and Linux systems.

IGMP (Internet Group Message Protocol) A Network layer protocol used on IPv4 networks to manage multicast transmissions.

IGP (interior gateway protocol) A type of routing protocol, such as OSPF and IS-IS, used by core routers and edge routers within autonomous systems.

IGRP (Interior Gateway Routing Protocol) A Cisco-proprietary routing protocol designed for use within autonomous systems.

IKE (Internet Key Exchange) One of two services in the key management phase of creating a secure IPsec connection. IKE negotiates the exchange of keys, including authentication of the keys.

IKEv2 The current version of IKE that offers fast throughput and good stability when moving between wireless hotspots.

IMAP4 (Internet Message Access Protocol, version 4) A mail retrieval protocol that allows users to store messages on the mail server. The most current version of IMAP is version 4 (IMAP4).

implicit deny An ACL rule which ensures that any traffic the ACL does not explicitly permit is denied by default.

in-band management A switch management option, such as Telnet, that uses the existing network and its protocols to interface with a switch.

incident Any event, large or small, that has adverse effects on a network's availability or resources.

incident response policy A document specifically defining the characteristics of an event that qualifies as a formal incident and the steps that should be followed as a result.

incremental backup A backup in which only data that has changed since the last full or incremental backup is copied to a storage medium.

infrastructure A type of wireless network in which stations communicate through an access point and not directly with each other.

insider threat A security risk associated with someone who is or was trusted by an organization, such as an employee, former employee, contractor, or other associate.

interface A network connection made by a node or host on a network.

interface ID The last 64 bits, or four blocks, of an IPv6 address that uniquely identify the interface on the local link.

interference Degradation of a wireless signal caused by electromagnetic waves in the atmosphere.

interior router A router that directs data between networks within the same autonomous system. Also called core router.

internetwork To traverse more than one LAN segment and more than one type of network through a router.

InterNIC (Internet Network Information Center) More recently known as the NIC (Network Information Center), a predecessor to ARIN in the oversight and management of multiple Internet resources, such as IP address allocation in North America.

inventory management The process of monitoring and maintaining all the assets that make up a network.

IoT (Internet of Things) Any device connected to the Internet.

IP (Internet Protocol) A core protocol in the TCP/IP suite that operates in the Network layer of the OSI model and provides information about how and where data should be delivered. IP is the subprotocol that enables TCP/IP to internetwork.

IP address A unique Network layer address assigned to each node on a TCP/IP network. IPv4 addresses consist of 32 bits divided into four octets, or bytes. IPv6 addresses are composed of eight 16-bit fields, for a total of 128 bits.

IP exclusion One or more IP addresses used for static IP assignments and excluded from the IP address pool so the server doesn't offer those IP addresses to other clients.

ip helper-address A robust Cisco command that can be configured to create and send helper messages that support several types of UDP traffic, including DHCP, TFTP, DNS, and TACACS+.

IP reservation An IP address that is set aside by a DHCP server for a specific network client, which is identified by its MAC address.

IPAM (IP address management) A standalone product or application embedded in another product, such as Windows Server, that provides a way to plan, deploy, and monitor a network's IP address space.

ipconfig The utility used to display and alter TCP/IP addressing and domain name information in the Windows client operating systems.

IPS (intrusion prevention system) A stand-alone device, an application, or a built-in feature running on a workstation, server, switch, router, or firewall that stands in-line between an attacker and the targeted network or host, and can prevent traffic from reaching that network or host.

IPsec (Internet Protocol Security) A Layer 3 protocol that defines encryption, authentication, and key management for TCP/IP transmissions. IPsec is an enhancement to IPv4 and is native to IPv6.

iptables A command-line firewall utility for Linux systems.

IPv4 (Internet Protocol version 4) The Internet Protocol standard released in the 1980s and still commonly used on modern networks. It specifies 32-bit addresses composed of four octets.

IPv6 (Internet Protocol version 6) A standard for IP addressing that is gradually replacing the current IPv4. Most notably, IPv6 uses a newer, more efficient header in its packets and allows for 128-bit source and destination IP addresses, which are usually written as eight blocks of hexadecimal numbers, such as 2001:0DB8:0B80:0000:0000:00D3:9C5A:00CC.

IR (infrared) A wireless technology that uses a bandwidth just below the spectrum that is visible to the human eye, with longer wavelengths than red light.

ISAKMP (Internet Security Association and Key Management Protocol) One of two services in the key management phase of creating a secure IPsec connection. ISAKMP works within the IKE process to establish policies for managing the keys.

iSCSI (Internet SCSI) A Transport layer protocol used by SANs that runs on top of TCP to allow fast transmission over LANs, WANs, and the Internet.

ISDN (Integrated Services Digital Network) An international standard that carries both digital data and voice over the PSTN.

IS-IS (Intermediate System to Intermediate System) A link-state routing protocol that uses a best-path algorithm. IS-IS was originally codified by ISO, which referred to routers as "intermediate systems," thus the protocol's name.

ISP (Internet service provider) A company that provides Internet connectivity.

IT (information technology) The study or use of computers and other telecommunications equipment.

iterative query A DNS query that does not demand a resolution, which means the server provides the information only if it already has that information available.

ITS (Intelligent Transportation System) Innovations in transit and traffic management.

IV (initialization vector) The initial, arbitrary number used to randomize the encryption process.

iwconfig   A command-line utility for viewing and setting wireless interface parameters on Linux and UNIX workstations.

J

jitter   A transmission flaw caused by packets experiencing varying amounts of delay and arriving out of order. Also called PDV (packet delay variation).

jumbo frame   A setting on Ethernet network devices that allows the creation and transmission of extra-large frames, as high as 9198 bytes.

K

Kbps (Kilobits per second)   A unit for measuring data transfer rate.

KDC (Key Distribution Center)   In Kerberos terminology, the server that issues keys to clients during initial client authentication.

Kerberos   A cross-platform authentication protocol that uses key encryption to verify the identity of clients and to securely exchange information after a client logs on to a system.

key   A series of characters that is combined with a block of data during that data's encryption.

key fob   A device or app that provides remote control over locks and security systems.

key management   The method whereby two nodes using key encryption agree on common parameters for the keys they will use to encrypt data.

knowledge base   A collection of accumulated insights and solutions to the problems encountered on a particular network.

KVM (keyboard, video, and mouse) switch   A device that connects the equipment in a rack to a single console to provide a central control portal for all devices on the rack.

L

L2TP (Layer 2 Tunneling Protocol)   A VPN tunneling protocol that encapsulates PPP data for use on VPNs.

LACP (Link Aggregation Control Protocol) A protocol currently defined by IEEE's 802.1AX standard that dynamically coordinates communications between two hosts on aggregated connections.

LAN (local area network)   A network of computers and other devices that typically is confined to a relatively small space, such as one building or even one office. Each node on a LAN can communicate directly with others on the same LAN.

latency   The delay between the transmission of a signal and its receipt.

Layer 3 switch   A switch capable of interpreting Layer 3 data and works much like a router in that it supports the same routing protocols and makes routing decisions.

Layer 4 switch   A switch capable of interpreting Layer 4 data, which means it can perform advanced filtering, keep statistics, and provide security functions.

Layer 7 firewall   A firewall innovation that monitors and limits the traffic of specific applications, adapts to the class of users or user groups, and adapts to the context of various applications, users, and devices.

LC (local connector)   The most common 1.25-mm ferrule connector, which is used with single-mode, fiber-optic cable.

LDAP (Lightweight Directory Access Protocol)   A standard protocol for accessing network directories.

LDAPS (Lightweight Directory Access Protocol over SSL)   A version of LDAP that uses SSL to encrypt its communications with network directories and clients.

lease time   A time limit on the validity of a DHCP-issued IP address.

LEC (local exchange carrier)   A local telephone company.

LED (light-emitting diode)   A cool-burning, long-lasting technology that creates light by the release of photons as electrons move through a semiconductor material.

light meter   A device that measures the amount of light power transmitted on a fiber-optic line. Also called OPM (optical power meter).

licensing restrictions   The portion of a software license that limits what a product can be used for.

link   Any LAN (local area network) bounded by routers.

link aggregation   The seamless combination of multiple network interfaces or ports to act as one logical interface.

link local address   An IP address that is automatically assigned by an operating system to allow a node to communicate over its local subnet if a routable IP address is not available.

link-state routing protocol   A type of routing protocol that enables routers to share information beyond neighboring routers, after which each router can independently map the network and determine the best path between itself and a message's destination node.

LLC (Logical Link Control) sublayer A sublayer of Layer 2 that is primarily concerned with multiplexing, flow and error control, and reliability.

LLDP (Link Layer Discovery Protocol) A Layer 2 protocol used by nodes on a network to advertise their identity and capabilities.

load balancer A device that distributes traffic intelligently among multiple computers or connections.

load balancing The distribution of traffic over multiple components or links to optimize performance and fault tolerance.

local link Any LAN (local area network) bounded by routers.

local loop The part of a phone system that connects a customer site with a telecommunications carrier's switching facility.

logic bomb A malicious program designed to start when certain conditions are met.

logical topology A characteristic of network transmission that reflects the way in which data is transmitted between nodes, including how access to the network is controlled and how specific resources are shared on the network. A network's logical topology may differ from its physical topology.

loopback adapter A troubleshooting tool that plugs into a port (for example, an RJ-45 or fiber-optic port) and crosses the transmit line with the receive line, allowing outgoing signals to be redirected back into the computer for testing. Also called a loopback plug.

loopback address An IP address reserved for communicating from a node to itself, used mostly for troubleshooting purposes.

LOS (line of sight) A wireless signal or path that travels directly in a straight line from its transmitter to its intended receiver.

loss-tolerant Transmissions that can tolerate occasional loss of data without compromising the user experience.

LSA (link state advertisement) In the context of OSPF, a message type sent by routers to communicate information about the network's topology.

LTE (Long-Term Evolution) A 4G cellular network technology that, in its latest version (called LTE-Advanced), can theoretically offer 1 Gbps throughput, although actual speeds are significantly less.

LTE-Advanced The latest version of LTE, with theoretical downlink rates of up to 1 Gbps and uplink rates

up to 100 Mbps, although actual speeds are significantly less.

LWAPP (Lightweight Access Point Protocol) A wireless protocol created by Cisco that makes centralized wireless management possible.

M

MaaS (Mobility as a Service) A service model in which public or shared transportation services are accessed virtually, such as through a phone app.

MAC (mandatory access control) A method of access control where resources are organized into hierarchical classifications, such as "confidential" or "top secret," and grouped into categories, perhaps by department. Users, then, are also classified and categorized. If a user's classification and category match those of a resource, then the user is given access.

MAC (Media Access Control) address A 48- or 64-bit network interface identifier that includes two parts: the OUI, assigned by IEEE to the manufacturer, and the extension identifier, a unique number assigned to each NIC by the manufacturer.

MAC address table A database configured manually or dynamically that stores MAC addresses allowed on a network.

MAC filtering A security measure that prevents an AP or a switch from authenticating any device whose MAC address is not listed by the network administrator as an approved device.

MAC reservation An IP address that is set aside by a DHCP server for a specific network client, which is identified by its MAC address.

MAC sublayer The lower portion of the Data Link layer that is specifically involved with managing MAC addresses in message frames.

magic number In the context of calculating subnets, the difference between 256 and the interesting octet (any octet in the subnet whose value is something other than 0 or 255). It can be used to calculate the network IDs in all the subnets of a larger network.

malware A program or piece of code designed to intrude upon or harm a system or its resources.

MAN (metropolitan area network) A network of connected LANs within a limited geographical area, such as multiple city government buildings around a city's center.

managed object Any characteristic of a device that is monitored, including components such as a processor, memory, hard disk, or NIC, or intangibles such as performance or utilization.

managed switch A switch that can be configured via a command-line interface or a web-based management GUI, and sometimes can be configured in groups.

management URL A web-based user interface where the user can make changes directly to a device.

Mbps (Megabits per second) A unit for measuring data transfer rate.

MBps (Megabytes per second) A unit for measuring data transfer rate.

MDF (main distribution frame or main distribution facility) Also known as the main cross connect, the centralized point of interconnection between an organization's LAN or WAN and a service provider's facility.

MDI (media dependent interface) A connector used with twisted-pair wiring on an Ethernet network.

MDM (mobile device management) Software that automatically handles the process of configuring wireless clients for network access.

media converter A device that enables networks or segments running on different media to interconnect and exchange signals.

mesh A wireless network in which multiple APs work as peer devices on the same network, thereby providing more fault-tolerant network access to clients.

mesh topology A type of network in which several nodes are directly interconnected and no single node controls communications on the network.

Metro (Metropolitan) Ethernet A WAN technology that sends Ethernet traffic across MAN connections.

MFA (multifactor authentication) An authentication process that requires information from two or more categories of authentication factors.

MGCP (Media Gateway Control Protocol) A protocol used for communication between media gateway controllers and media gateways.

MIB (Management Information Base) The list of objects managed by an NMS, as well as the descriptions of these objects.

MIMO (multiple input-multiple output) In the context of 802.11n/ac wireless networking, the ability for access points to use multiple antennas in order to issue multiple signals to stations, thereby multiplying the signal's strength and increasing their range and data-carrying capacity.

MitM (man-in-the-middle) attack An attack that relies on intercepted transmissions. It can take one of several forms, but in all cases a person redirects or captures secure data traffic while in transit.

MLA (master license agreement) A contract that grants a license from a creator, developer, or producer, such as a software producer, to a third party for the purposes of marketing, sublicensing, or distributing the product to consumers as a stand-alone product or as part of another product.

MMF (multimode fiber) A type of fiber-optic cable containing a core that is usually 50 or 62.5 microns in diameter, over which many pulses of light generated by a laser or LED (light-emitting diode) travel at different angles.

MOA (memorandum of agreement) A document that describes a partnership or other cooperative relationship for a specific project or scenario.

modal bandwidth A measure of the highest frequency of signal a multimode fiber-optic cable can support over a specific distance. Modal bandwidth is measured in MHz-km.

modem A modulation/demodulation device that converts between digital and analog signals.

motion detection Technology that triggers an alarm when it detects movement within its field of view.

MOU (memorandum of understanding) A document presenting the intentions of two or more parties to enter into a binding agreement, or contract. The MOU is usually not a legally binding document (although there are exceptions), does not grant extensive rights to either party, provides no legal recourse, and is not intended to provide a thorough coverage of the agreement to come.

MPLS (multiprotocol label switching) A type of switching that enables multiple types of Layer 3 protocols to travel over any one of several connection-oriented Layer 2 protocols.

MSA (master service agreement) A contract that defines terms of future contracts.

MS-CHAP (Microsoft Challenge Handshake Authentication Protocol) An authentication protocol provided with Windows operating systems that uses a three-way handshake to verify a client's credentials and encrypts passwords with a challenge text.

MS-CHAPv2 (Microsoft Challenge Handshake Authentication Protocol, version 2) An authentication protocol provided with Windows operating systems that follows the CHAP model, but uses stronger encryption, uses different encryption keys for transmission and reception, and requires mutual authentication between two computers.

MSDS (material safety data sheet) Instructions provided with dangerous substances that explain how to properly handle these substances and how to safely dispose of them. Also called SDS (safety data sheet).

MTBF (mean time between failures) The average amount of time that will pass before the next failure of a device or service is expected to occur.

MTRJ (Mechanical Transfer-Registered Jack) The most common type of connector used with multi-mode fiber-optic cable.

MTTR (mean time to repair) The average amount of time required to repair a device or restore a service.

MTU (maximum transmission unit) The largest IP packet size in bytes that routers in a message's path will allow without fragmentation and excluding the frame.

multicast Transmissions in which one host sends messages to multiple hosts.

multicast address A type of IPv6 address that represents multiple interfaces, often on multiple nodes.

multimeter A simple instrument that can measure multiple characteristics of an electric circuit, including its resistance, voltage, and impedance.

multiplexing A form of transmission that allows multiple signals to travel simultaneously over one medium.

MU-MIMO (multiuser MIMO) In the context of 802.11ac wireless networking, the ability for access points to use multiple antennas in order to issue multiple signals to different stations at the same time, thereby reducing congestion and contributing to faster data transmission.

mutual authentication An authentication scheme in which both computers verify the credentials of each other.

MX (Mail Exchanger) record A type of DNS data record that identifies a mail server and that is used for email traffic.

N

NAC (network access control) A technology solution that balances the need for network access with the demands of network security by employing a set of network policies to determine the level and type of access granted to a device when it joins a network.

name resolution The process of discovering the IP address of a host when the FQDN is known.

NAS (network attached storage) A specialized storage device or group of storage devices that provides centralized fault-tolerant data storage for a network.

NAT (Network Address Translation) A technique in which IP addresses used on a private network are assigned a public IP address by a gateway when accessing a public network.

NAT mode A type of network connection in which a vNIC relies on the host machine to act as a NAT device. The virtualization software acts as a DHCP server.

native VLAN An untagged VLAN on a switch that will automatically receive all untagged frames.

native VLAN mismatch A configuration error where switch ports on each end of a trunk are configured with different native VLAN assignments. Also called a VLAN mismatch.

NCP (Network Control Protocol) An obsolete ARPANET protocol that provides remote access and data transfer.

NDA (non-disclosure agreement) The part of a security policy that defines what confidential and private means to the organization.

NDR (non-delivery receipt) A notice of a failed email delivery.

neighbor Two or more nodes on the same link.

neighbor discovery A process whereby routers learn about all the devices on their networks. On IPv4 networks, this process is managed by ARP with help from ICMP. On IPv6 networks, NDP (Neighbor Discovery Protocol) automatically detects neighboring devices and automatically adjusts when nodes fail or are removed from the network.

NetBEUI (network basic input/output extended) An extension of NetBIOS that provides standardization for the frame format used during data transport on small networks. Pronounced *net-booey*.

NetBIOS (network basic input/output system) A protocol that associates NetBIOS names with workstations.

netmask In IPv4 addressing, a 32-bit number that helps one computer find another by indicating what portion of an IP address is the network portion and what portion is the host portion.

netstat A TCP/IP troubleshooting utility that displays statistics and details about TCP/IP components and connections on a host. It also lists ports, which can signal whether services are using the correct ports.

network   A group of computers and other devices (such as printers) that are connected by and can exchange data via some type of transmission media, such as a cable, a wire, or the atmosphere.

network-based firewall   A firewall configured and positioned to protect an entire network.

network diagram   A graphical representation of a network's devices and connections.

network ID   The portion of an IP address common to all nodes on the same network or subnet.

Network layer   The third layer in the OSI model. The Network layer, sometimes called the Internet layer, is responsible for moving messages between networks.

network management   The assessment, monitoring, and maintenance of all aspects of a network.

network policy   A rule or set of rules that determines the level and type of access granted to a device when it joins a network.

network service   A resource the network makes available to its users, including applications and the data provided by these applications.

NEXT (near end crosstalk)   Crosstalk that occurs between wire pairs near the source of a signal.

NFC (near-field communication)   A form of radio communication that transfers data wirelessly over very short distances (usually 10 cm or less).

NFS (Network File System or Network File Service)   A client-server file system protocol for use on a NAS.

NFV (Network Functions Virtualization)   A network architecture that merges physical and virtual network devices.

NGFW (Next Generation Firewall)   A firewall innovation that monitors and limits the traffic of specific applications, adapts to the class of users or user groups, and adapts to the context of various applications, users, and devices.

NIC (network interface card or network interface controller)   The device that enables a workstation to connect to the network and communicate with other computers. NICs are manufactured by several different companies and come with a variety of specifications that are tailored to the workstation's and the network's requirements. NICs are also called network adapters.

NIC teaming   The seamless combination of multiple network interfaces or ports on Windows devices to act as one logical interface.

NIDS (network-based intrusion detection system)   A type of intrusion detection that protects an entire network and is situated at the edge of the network or in a network's DMZ.

NIPS (network-based intrusion prevention system)   A type of intrusion prevention that protects an entire network and is situated at the edge of the network or in a network's DMZ.

NIU (network interface unit)   The point at which the ISP's local loop connects to the customer's network.

nm (nanometer)   A microscopic unit of distance.

Nmap   A scanning tool designed to assess large networks quickly and provide comprehensive, customized information about a network and its hosts.

NMS (network management system) server   A server or workstation that collects data from multiple managed devices at regular intervals.

NNTP (Network News Transport Protocol)   A protocol used by newsgroups on a network to share news articles between servers or clients.

node   Any computer or other device on a network that can be addressed on the local network.

node ID   The portion of an IP address that identifies the node on a network.

nonpersistent agent   Agent software that remains on a device long enough to verify compliance and complete authentication, and then uninstalls.

NOS (network operating system)   The software that runs on a server and enables the server to manage data, users, groups, security, applications, and other networking functions. Popular examples of network operating systems are Windows Server, Ubuntu Server, and Red Hat Enterprise Linux.

notification   A message sent to IT personnel via email, text, or some other method that is triggered by the occurrence of a predefined event.

NS (Name Server) record   A DNS lookup file that indicates the authoritative name server for a domain. It's mostly used for delegating subdomains to other name servers.

nslookup (name space lookup)   A TCP/IP utility that allows a technician to query the DNS database from any computer on the network and find the host name of a network node by specifying its IP address, or vice versa. This ability is useful for verifying that a host is configured correctly and for troubleshooting DNS resolution problems.

NTP (Network Time Protocol)   A simple Application layer protocol in the TCP/IP suite used to synchronize the clocks of computers on a network. NTP depends on UDP for Transport layer services.

O

OC (Optical Carrier) An internationally recognized rating that indicates throughput rates for SONET connections.

OC-1 The base rate of a SONET connection's potential throughput, providing a maximum 51.84 Mbps.

OC-12 SONET throughput service that provides a maximum 622.08 Mbps.

OC-3 A popular throughput rate for SONET services, providing a maximum 155.52 Mbps.

OCSP (Online Certificate Status Protocol) A protocol applications can use to determine the revocation status of a digital certificate.

octet One of 4 bytes that are separated by periods and together make up an IPv4 address.

off-boarding The reverse process of on-boarding, involving the removal of programs that gave a device special permissions on the network.

OID (object identifier) A number assigned each managed object.

omnidirectional antenna A type of antenna that issues and receives wireless signals with equal strength and clarity in all directions.

on-boarding A process of configuring clients for wireless access to a network.

open circuit A circuit in which necessary connections are missing, such as occurs when a wire breaks.

open source Software whose code is publicly available for use and modification.

OpenVPN An open-source VPN software that is available for multiple platforms.

OPM (optical power meter) A device that measures the amount of light power transmitted on a fiber-optic line. Also called light meter.

optical loss The degradation of a light signal on a fiber-optic network as it travels away from its source.

OS (operating system) Software that controls a computer.

OSA (Open System Authentication) An insecure form of authentication used by WEP where no key is used at all.

OSHA (Occupational Safety and Health Administration) The main federal agency charged with regulating safety and health in the workplace.

OSI (Open Systems Interconnection) reference model A model for understanding, developing, and troubleshooting computer-to-computer communication and was developed in the 1980s by ISO. It divides networking functions among seven layers: Physical, Data Link, Network, Transport, Session, Presentation, and Application.

OSPF (Open Shortest Path First) An IGP and link-state routing protocol that makes up for some of the limitations of RIP and can coexist with RIP on a network.

OTDR (optical time domain reflectometer) A performance testing device for use with fiber-optic networks which can accurately measure the length of the fiber, locations of faults, and many other characteristics.

OUI (Organizationally Unique Identifier) A 24-bit character sequence assigned by IEEE that appears at the beginning of a network interface's physical address and identifies the NIC's manufacturer.

out-of-band management A dedicated connection (either wired or wireless) from the network administrator's computer used to manage each critical network device, such as routers, firewalls, servers, power supplies, applications, and security cameras.

P

P2P (peer-to-peer) network model A network in which every computer can communicate directly with every other computer. By default, no computer on a P2P network has more authority than another.

PaaS (Platform as a Service) A service model in which various platforms are provided virtually, enabling developers to build and test applications within virtual, online environments tailored to the specific needs of a project.

packet The entire Network layer message, which includes the segment (TCP) or datagram (UDP) from the Transport layer, plus the Network layer header.

packet analysis The examination of information contained within packets to identify protocols, errors, and misconfigurations.

packet drop Packets that are damaged beyond use, arrive after their expiration, or are not allowed through an interface.

packet sniffer A software package or hardware-based tool that can capture data on a network.

packet-switched A type of switching in which data is broken into packets before being transported.

paired A term used to describe two Bluetooth devices that are communicating with each other.

PAN (personal area network) A network of personal devices, such as a cell phone, laptop, and Bluetooth printer.

PAP (Password Authentication Protocol) A simple authentication protocol that operates over PPP.

password policy Minimum requirements defined on a system for user passwords.

PAT (Port Address Translation) A form of address translation that assigns a separate TCP port to each ongoing conversation, or session, between a local host and an Internet host.

patch A correction, improvement, or enhancement to part of a software application, often distributed at no charge by software vendors to fix a bug in their code or to add slightly more functionality.

patch cable A relatively short section (usually between 3 and 25 feet) of cabling with connectors on both ends.

patch management The process of monitoring the release of new patches, testing them for use on networked devices, and installing them.

patch panel A wall- or rack-mounted panel where cables converge in one location.

pathping A Windows utility that combines the functionality of the tracert and ping utilities to provide deeper information about network issues along a route; similar to UNIX's `mtr` command.

payload Data that is passed between applications or utility programs and the operating system, and includes control information.

PC (personal computer) A freestanding computer designed for user productivity.

PCM (phase-change memory) A high-speed form of non-volatile RAM that changes the physical structure of the material used to store the data.

PDoS (permanent DoS) attack An attack on a device that attempts to alter the device's management interface to the point where the device is irreparable.

PDU (protocol data unit) A unit of data at any layer of the OSI model.

PEAP (Protected EAP) A tunnel-based form of EAP that creates an encrypted TLS tunnel between the supplicant and the server before proceeding with the usual EAP process.

penetration testing A process of scanning a network for vulnerabilities and investigating potential security flaws.

performance management The ongoing assessment of how well links and devices are keeping up with the demands placed on them.

persistent agent Agent software that is permanently installed on a device and that can provide robust security measures such as remote wipe, virus scanning, and mass messaging.

PGP (Pretty Good Privacy) A key-based encryption system for email that uses a two-step verification process.

phishing A practice in which a person attempts to glean access or authentication information by posing as someone who needs that information.

physical address *See* MAC (Media Access Control) address.

Physical layer The lowest, or first, layer of the OSI model. The Physical layer is responsible only for sending bits via a wired or wireless transmission.

physical topology The physical layout of the media, nodes, and devices on a network. A physical topology does not specify device types, connectivity methods, or addressing schemes.

ping (Packet Internet Groper) A TCP/IP troubleshooting utility that can verify TCP/IP is installed, bound to the NIC, configured correctly, and communicating with the network. Ping uses ICMP to send echo request and echo reply messages.

pinout The pin numbers and color-coded wire assignments used when terminating a cable or installing a jack, as determined by the TIA/EIA standard.

PKI (Public-key Infrastructure) The use of certificate authorities to associate public keys with certain users.

platform The operating system, the runtime libraries or modules the OS provides to applications, and the hardware on which the OS runs.

plenum The area above the ceiling tile or below the subfloor in a building.

PoE (Power over Ethernet) A method of delivering up to 15.4 watts to devices using Ethernet connection cables.

PoE+ A method of delivering more current (up to 25.5 watts) than PoE does to devices using Ethernet connection cables.

polling A network management application's regular collection of data from managed devices.

PoP (Point of Presence) A data center facility at which a provider rents space to allow for dedicated connection services.

POP3 (Post Office Protocol, version 3)
An Application layer protocol used to retrieve messages from a mail server. When a client retrieves mail via POP, messages previously stored on the mail server are downloaded to the client's workstation, and then deleted from the mail server. The most commonly used form of POP is POP3.

port   A number that identifies a process, such as an application or service, running on a computer. TCP and UDP ports ensure that data is transmitted to the correct process among multiple processes running on a computer.

port aggregation   The seamless combination of multiple network interfaces or ports on Cisco devices to act as one logical interface.

port forwarding   The process of redirecting traffic from its normally assigned port to a different port, either on the client or server.

port mirroring   A monitoring technique in which one port on a switch is configured to send a copy of all its traffic to a second port.

port scanner   Software that searches a server, switch, router, or other device for open ports, which can be vulnerable to attack.

posture assessment   An assessment of an organization's security vulnerabilities.

POTS (plain old telephone service)   The network of lines and carrier equipment that provides wired telephone service to most homes and businesses.

PPE (personal protective equipment)   Wearable equipment such as goggles that might be required in the workplace to increase safety of workers.

PPP (Point-to-Point Protocol)   A Layer 2 communications protocol that enables a workstation to connect to a server using a serial connection such as dial-up or DSL.

PPPoE (PPP over Ethernet)   PPP running over an Ethernet network.

PPTP (Point-to-Point Tunneling Protocol)   A Layer 2 protocol developed by Microsoft that encapsulates PPP data frames for transmission over VPN connections.

Presentation layer   The sixth layer of the OSI model. Protocols in the Presentation layer are responsible for reformatting, compressing, and/or encrypting data in a way that the application on the receiving end can read.

PRI (Primary Rate Interface)   A type of ISDN that uses 23 B channels and one 64-Kbps D channel, represented by the notation 23B+D.

primary DNS server   The authoritative name server for an organization, which holds the authoritative DNS database for the organization's zones. This server is contacted by clients, both local and over the Internet, to resolve DNS queries for the organization's domains.

principal   In Kerberos terminology, a user or client.

principle of least privilege   A security measure that ensures employees and contractors are only given enough access and privileges to do their jobs, and these privileges are terminated as soon as the person no longer needs them.

private cloud   A deployment model in which shared and flexible data storage, applications, or services are managed on and delivered via an organization's own network, or established virtually for a single organization's private use.

private IP address   IP addresses that can be used on a private network but not on the Internet. IEEE recommends the following IP address ranges for private use: 10.0.0.0 through 10.255.255.255; 172.16.0.0 through 172.31.255.255; and 192.168.0.0 through 192.168.255.255.

private key encryption   A type of key encryption in which the sender and receiver use a key to which only they have access. Also known as symmetric encryption.

privileged user account   An administrative account on a device or network that gives high-level permissions to change configurations or access data.

probe   (1) A repeated trial message transmitted by the tracert and traceroute utilities to trigger routers along a route to return specific information about the route. (2) A small electronic device that emits a tone when it detects electrical activity on a wire pair. When used in conjunction with a tone generator, it can help locate the termination of a wire pair. Also called a tone locator. (3) In 802.11 wireless networking, a type of frame issued by a station during active scanning to find nearby access points.

propagation   The way in which a wave travels from one point to another.

protocol   A standard method or format for communication between network devices.

protocol analyzer   A software package or hardware-based tool that can capture and analyze data on a network.

proxy server   A server acting as an intermediary between the external and internal networks, screening all incoming and outgoing traffic.

PSK (Pre-Shared Key) An authentication method for WPA or WPA2 that requires a passphrase for a device to be authenticated to the network.

PSTN (public switched telephone network) The network of lines and carrier equipment that provides wired telephone service to most homes and businesses.

PTP (point-to-point) A point-to-point network topology.

PTR (Pointer) record A type of DNS data record that is used for reverse lookups, to provide a host name when the IP address is known.

PUA (privileged user agreement) A document that addresses the specific concerns related to privileged access given to administrators and certain support staff.

public cloud A deployment model in which shared and flexible data storage, applications, or services are managed centrally by service providers and delivered over public transmission lines, such as the Internet.

public IP address An IP address that is valid for use on public networks, such as the Internet.

public key encryption A form of key encryption in which data is encrypted using two keys: One is a key known only to a user (that is, a private key), and the other is a key associated with the user and that can be obtained from a public source, such as a public key server. Public key encryption is also known as asymmetric encryption.

punchdown tool A pointed tool used to insert twisted-pair wire into receptors in a punchdown block to complete a circuit.

PVC (permanent virtual circuit) A point-to-point connection over which data may follow any number of different paths.

PVC (polyvinyl chloride) A flame-resistant material used to manufacture cable jackets because it produces less smoke than regular cable coating materials.

Q

QoS (quality of service) A group of techniques for adjusting the priority a network assigns to various types of transmissions.

QSFP (quad small form-factor pluggable) A fiber-optic transceiver that complies with the 802.3ba standard, squeezing four channels in a single transceiver and supporting data rates up to 40 Gbps (4 x 10 Gbps).

QSFP+ Generally the same technology as QSFP while supporting data rates over 40 Gbps.

quarantine network A network segment that is situated separately from sensitive network resources and might limit the amount of time a device can remain connected to the network.

R

RA (router advertisement) A message from a router in response to a client's solicitation and provides DHCP information.

rack diagram A drawing that shows the devices stacked in a rack system and is typically drawn to scale.

radiation pattern The relative strength over a three-dimensional area of all the electromagnetic energy an antenna sends or receives.

RADIUS (Remote Authentication Dial-In User Service) A popular protocol for providing centralized AAA services for multiple users.

range The geographical area in which signals issued from an antenna or wireless system can be consistently and accurately received.

ransomware A program that locks a user's data or computer system until a ransom is paid.

RARP (Reverse Address Resolution Protocol) An obsolete protocol used by network clients to request an IP address.

RAS (remote access server) A server that runs communications services enabling remote users to log on to a network and grant privileges to the network's resources.

RBAC (role-based access control) A method of access control where a network administrator assigns only the privileges and permissions necessary for a user to perform the role required by an organization.

RC4 (Rivest Cipher 4) An insecure encryption cipher that is still widely used.

RDP (Remote Desktop Protocol) An Application layer protocol that uses TCP/IP to transmit graphics and text quickly over a remote client-host connection. RDP also carries session, licensing, and encryption information.

reassociation In the context of wireless networking, the process by which a station establishes a connection with (or associates with) a different access point.

recursive query A DNS query that demands a resolution or the response that the information can't be found.

redundancy The use of more than one identical component, device, or connection for storing, processing, or transporting data.

redundant power circuits Multiple pathways for providing power to a data center.

reflection In the context of wireless signaling, the phenomenon that occurs when an electromagnetic wave encounters an obstacle and bounces back toward its source.

refraction In the context of wireless signaling, the way in which a wave alters its direction, speed, and wavelength when it travels through different transmission mediums.

registered port The TCP/IP ports in the range of 1024 to 49,151. These ports can be used by network users and processes that are not considered standard processes. Default assignments of these ports must be registered with IANA.

remote access A method for connecting and logging on to a server, LAN, or WAN from a workstation that is in a different geographical location.

remote application An application that is installed and executed on a server, and is presented to a user working at a client computer.

Remote Desktop Services A feature of Windows Server 2008 and later editions of Windows Server that allows technicians to manage remote applications.

remote wipe A security procedure that clears a device of all important information, permissions, and programs without having physical access to the device.

repeater A device used to regenerate a digital signal in its original form. Repeaters operate at the Physical layer of the OSI model.

resource record The element of a DNS database stored on a name server that contains information about TCP/IP host names and their addresses.

reverse zone A DNS lookup file that holds A records where the IP addresses must be stored in reverse—with the last octet listed first—plus the domain *.in-addr.arpa*. For example, the IP address 1.2.3.4 would be stored in a PTR record as *4.3.2.1.in-addr.arpa*.

RF (radio frequency) Electromagnetic signals generated from radio or TV antennas.

RFI (radio frequency interference) A kind of electromagnetic interference that can be generated by broadcast signals from radio or TV antennas.

RFID (Radio Frequency Identification) A wireless technology that uses electromagnetic fields to store data on a small chip in a tag, which includes an antenna that can both transmit and receive, and possibly a battery.

RFP (request for proposal) A document requesting that vendors submit a proposal for a product or service that a company wants to purchase.

RG-59 (radio guide 59) A type of coaxial cable characterized by a 75-ohm impedance and a 20 or 22 AWG core conductor, usually made of braided copper and used for relatively short connections.

RG-6 (radio guide 6) A type of coaxial cable with an impedance of 75 ohms and an 18 AWG core conductor. RG-6 is used for television, satellite, and broadband cable connections.

ring topology A network layout in which each node is connected to the two nearest nodes so that the entire network forms a circle. Data is transmitted in one direction around the ring. Each node accepts and responds to packets addressed to it, then forwards the other packets to the next node in the ring.

RIP (Routing Information Protocol) The oldest routing protocol that is still widely used. RIP is a distance-vector protocol that uses hop count as its routing metric and allows up to only 15 hops.

RIPv2 (Routing Information Protocol version 2) An updated version of the original RIP routing protocol that generates less broadcast traffic and functions more securely than its predecessor. However, RIPv2's packet forwarding is still limited to a maximum 15 hops.

RJ-11 (registered jack 11) The standard connector used with unshielded twisted-pair cabling (usually Cat 3) to connect analog telephones.

RJ-45 (registered jack 45) The standard connector used with shielded twisted-pair and unshielded twisted-pair cabling.

rogue access point An unauthorized access point in the same vicinity as a legitimate network.

rogue DHCP server A DHCP service running on a client device that could be used to implement a MitM attack by configuring the attacker's IP address as the victim computers' default gateway or DNS server.

role separation In the context of role-based access control, a security technique that allows a user to be a member of only a single user group at a time in order to perform any tasks.

rollback The process of reverting to a previous version of a software application after attempting to patch or upgrade it.

root bridge The single bridge on a network selected by STP to provide the basis for all subsequent path calculations.

root guard   A restriction that prevents switches beyond the configured port from becoming the root bridge.

root server   A DNS server maintained by ICANN and IANA that is an authority on how to contact the top-level domains, such as those ending with .com, .edu, .net, .us, and so on. ICANN oversees the operation of 13 clusters of root servers around the world.

route command   A command-line tool that shows a host's routing table.

router   A Layer 3 device that uses logical addressing information to direct data between two or more networks and can help find the best path for traffic to get from one network to another.

routing cost   A value assigned to a particular route as judged by the network administrator; the more desirable the path, the lower its cost.

routing metrics   Properties of a route used by routing protocols to determine the best path to a destination when various paths are available. Routing metrics may be calculated using any of several variables, including hop count, bandwidth, delay, MTU, cost, and reliability.

routing protocol   The means by which routers communicate with each other about network status. Routing protocols determine the best path for data to take between networks.

routing table   A database stored in a router's memory that maintains information about the location of hosts and best paths for forwarding packets to them.

RPO (recovery point objective)   A metric that defines how much data loss is tolerable, depending on what backup methods and schedules are in place.

RS (router solicitation)   A message from a client to a router requesting network configuration information.

RSA (Rivest, Shamir, Adelman)   An encryption algorithm.

RSH (Remote Shell)   Software that enables a user to run shell commands from another user's account.

RSTP (Rapid Spanning Tree Protocol)   As described in IEEE's 802.1w standard, a version of the Spanning Tree Protocol that can detect and correct for link failures in milliseconds.

RTO (recovery time objective)   A metric that defines the maximum tolerable outage time for an application or network service.

RTP (Real-Time Protocol)   An Application layer protocol used with voice and video transmission.

RTS/CTS (Request to Send/Clear to Send)   An exchange in which a source node requests the exclusive right to communicate with an access point and the access point confirms that it has granted that request.

RTSP (Real-Time Streaming Protocol)   A protocol used to create and manage media sessions.

RTT (round trip time)   The length of time it takes for a packet to go from sender to receiver, then back from receiver to sender. RTT is usually measured in milliseconds.

S

SA (security association)   The relationship created between two devices for the purposes of establishing a secure connection.

SaaS (Software as a Service)   A service model in which applications are provided through an online user interface and are compatible with a multitude of devices and operating systems.

SAN (storage area network)   A distinct network of storage devices that communicate directly with each other and with other networks.

SC (subscriber connector or standard connector)   A connector with a 2.5-mm ferrule that is used with single-mode, fiber-optic cable.

SCADA (supervisory control and data acquisition)   A network that acquires real-time data from a physical system and manages the physical system or presents the data to humans, who monitor and manage the system.

scalable   The property of a network that allows an administrator to add nodes or increase its size easily.

scanning   The process by which a wireless station finds an access point.

scattering   The diffusion, or the reflection in multiple directions, of a wireless signal that results from hitting an object with a rough surface or small dimensions compared to the signal's wavelength.

scope option   Specific configuration information, such as a time limit and a default gateway IP address, that is shared from a DHCP server along with an IP address assignment.

SCP (Secure Copy Protocol)   A method for copying files securely between hosts.

SDH (Synchronous Digital Hierarchy)   The international equivalent of SONET.

SDLC (software development life cycle)   The time it takes to plan, create, test, and deploy a program or application.

SDN (software-defined networking)   A centralized approach to networking that removes most of the decision-making power from network devices and instead handles that responsibility at a software level.

SDN controller   A product that integrates configuration and management control of all network devices, both physical and virtual, into one cohesive system that is overseen by the network administrator through a single dashboard.

SDP (Session Description Protocol)   A standard for creating multimedia sessions.

SDSL (symmetric DSL)   A variation of DSL that provides equal throughput both upstream and downstream between the customer and the carrier.

secondary DNS server   The backup authoritative name server for an organization.

security audit   An assessment of an organization's security vulnerabilities performed by an accredited network security firm.

security policy   A document or plan that identifies an organization's security goals, risks, levels of authority, designated security coordinator and team members, responsibilities for each team member, and responsibilities for each employee. In addition, it specifies how to address security breaches.

security token   A device or piece of software used for authentication that stores or generates information, such as a series of numbers or letters, known only to its authorized user.

segment   (1) A TCP message at the Transport layer. (2) A part of a network.

server   Any computer or application that provides a service, such as data or other resources, to other devices.

server_hello   In the context of SSL encryption, a message issued from the server to the client that confirms the information the server received in the client_hello message. It also agrees to certain terms of encryption based on the options the client supplied.

session   An ongoing conversation between two hosts.

Session layer   The fifth layer in the OSI model. The Session layer describes how data between applications is synced and recovered if messages don't arrive intact at the receiving application.

SFP (small form-factor pluggable)   A standard hot-swappable network interface used to link a connectivity device's backplane with fiber-optic or copper cabling.

SFP+   A type of SFP that can send and receive data at rates of up to 16 Gbps.

SFTP (Secure File Transfer Protocol)   A protocol available with the proprietary version of SSH that securely copies files between hosts.

SGCP (Simple Gateway Control Protocol)   A predecessor to MGCP that was used in VoIP systems.

SHA (Secure Hash Algorithm)   A hash algorithm originally designed by the NSA to eliminate the inherent weaknesses of the older MD5 hash. The most recent iteration is SHA-3, developed by private designers for a public competition in 2012.

short circuit   An unwanted connection, such as when exposed wires touch each other.

SIEM (Security Information and Event Management)   Software that can be configured to evaluate data logs from IDS, IPS, firewalls, and proxy servers in order to detect significant events that require the attention of IT staff according to predefined rules.

signature   Identifiable patterns of code that are known to indicate specific vulnerabilities, exploits, or other undesirable traffic.

signature management   The process of regularly updating the signatures used to monitor a network's traffic.

SIM (Subscriber Identity Module) card   A microchip installed in a cellular device to hold data about the subscription a user has with the cellular carrier.

SIP (Session Initiation Protocol)   A signaling protocol that is used to make an initial connection between hosts but that does not participate in data transfer during the session.

SIP trunking   Virtual connections over an existing data service to provide VoIP services.

site prefix   The first four blocks or 64 bits of an IPv6 address that normally identify the network. Also called global routing prefix.

site survey   In the context of wireless networking, an assessment of client requirements, facility characteristics, and coverage areas to determine an access point arrangement that will ensure reliable wireless connectivity within a given area.

site-to-site VPN   A type of VPN in which VPN gateways at multiple sites encrypt and encapsulate data to exchange over tunnels with other VPN gateways. Meanwhile, clients, servers, and other hosts on a site-to-site VPN communicate with the VPN gateway.

SKA (Shared Key Authentication)   An insecure form of authentication where all wireless access clients use the same key, which can then be used for encrypted transmissions.

SLA (service-level agreement) A legally binding contract or part of a contract that defines, in plain language and in measurable terms, the aspects of a service provided to a customer. Specific details might include contract duration, guaranteed uptime, problem management, performance benchmarks, and termination options.

SLAAC (Stateless Address Auto Configuration) The process by which an IPv6 client collects the basic information required to configure its own IPv6 address on a network.

SLIP (Serial Line Internet Protocol) An obsolete Layer 2 communications protocol that enabled a workstation to connect to a server using a serial connection such as dial-up or DSL.

smart card An electronic access badge.

smart jack An intelligent type of NIU located at the customer's demarc that can provide diagnostic information about the interface.

SMB (Server Message Block) A protocol for communications and resource access between systems, such as clients and servers.

SMF (single-mode fiber) A type of fiber-optic cable with a narrow core of 8 to 10 microns in diameter that carries light pulses along a single path from one end of the cable to the other end.

SMS (short message service) A service that transmits text messages.

SMTP (Simple Mail Transfer Protocol) An Application layer protocol responsible for moving messages from one email server to another.

snapshot A frequently saved, incremental backup of the data's state at a specific point in time, typically containing only information about changes made since the last backup and not capable of being used to fully restore lost data.

SNAT (Static Network Address Translation or Source Network Address Translation) A type of address translation in which a gateway assigns the same public IP address to a host each time it makes a request to access the Internet.

SNMP (Simple Network Management Protocol) An Application layer protocol in the TCP/IP suite used to monitor and manage devices on a network.

SNR (signal-to-noise ratio) The proportion of noise to the strength of a signal.

SNTP (Simple Network Time Protocol) A simplified version of NTP.

SOA (Start of Authority) A record in a DNS zone about that zone and the records within it.

social engineering The act of manipulating social relationships to circumvent network security measures and gain access to a system.

socket A logical address consisting of a host's IP address and the port of an application running on the host with a colon separating the two values.

SOHO (small office/home office) network A network consisting of fewer than 10 workstations.

SONET (Synchronous Optical Network) A high-bandwidth WAN signaling technique that specifies framing and multiplexing techniques at the Physical layer of the OSI model.

SOP (standard operating procedure) The steps defined for a specific process within an organization in order to maintain consistency and avoid errors.

SOW (statement of work) A document that details the work that must be completed for a particular project, including specifics such as tasks, deliverables, standards, payment schedule, and work timeline. An SOW is legally binding, meaning it can be enforced in a court of law.

SPB (Shortest Path Bridging) As described in IEEE's 802.1aq standard, a descendent of the Spanning Tree Protocol that keeps all potential paths active while managing the flow of data across those paths to prevent loops.

spectrum analyzer A software tool that assesses the characteristics (for example, frequency, amplitude, and the effects of interference) of wireless signals.

speed and duplex mismatch A problem that occurs when neighboring devices are using different speed or duplex configurations and results in failed transmissions.

SPF (Sender Policy Framework) A validation system that helps fight spam by identifying the email servers allowed to send email on behalf of a domain.

SPI (Stateful Packet Inspection) The inspection by a firewall of each incoming packet to determine whether it belongs to a currently active connection.

spoofing The act of impersonating fields of data in a transmission, such as when a source IP address is impersonated in a DRDoS attack.

SPS (standby power supply) A UPS that provides continuous voltage to a device by switching virtually instantaneously to the battery when it detects a loss of power from the wall outlet.

SRV (Service) record A type of DNS data record that identifies the hostname and port of a computer hosting a specific network service besides email, such as FTP or SIP.

SSH (Secure Shell)   A connection utility that provides authentication and encryption. SSH is often used to log onto a host, execute commands on that host, and copy files to or from the host.

SSID (service set identifier)   A unique character string used to identify an access point on an 802.11 network.

SSL (Secure Sockets Layer)   A method of encrypting TCP/IP transmissions—including web pages and data entered into web forms—en route between the client and server using public key encryption technology.

SSO (single sign-on)   A form of authentication in which a client signs on once to access multiple systems or resources.

ST (straight tip)   A connector with a 2.5-mm ferrule that is used with single-mode, fiber-optic cable.

star topology   A physical topology in which every node on the network is connected through a central device.

star-bus topology   A hybrid topology in which groups of workstations are connected in a star fashion to connectivity devices that are networked via a single bus.

stateful firewall   A firewall capable of examining an incoming packet to determine whether it belongs to a currently active connection and is, therefore, a legitimate packet.

stateless firewall   A firewall that manages each incoming packet as a stand-alone entity without regard to currently active connections.

static ARP table entry   A record in an ARP table that someone has manually entered using the ARP utility.

static electricity   An electrical charge at rest. When that charge is transferred between two bodies, it creates an electrostatic discharge, or ESD.

static IP address   An IP address that is manually assigned to a device and remains constant until it is manually changed.

static routing   A technique in which a network administrator programs a router to use specific paths between networks.

STDM (statistical time division multiplexing)   A type of multiplexing that assigns time slots to nodes (similar to TDM), but then adjusts these slots according to priority and need.

STP (shielded twisted pair)   A type of copper-based cable containing twisted-pair wires that are not

only individually insulated, but are also surrounded by a shielding made of a metallic substance such as foil.

STP (Spanning Tree Protocol)   A switching protocol defined by the IEEE standard 802.1D that functions at the Data Link layer and prevents traffic loops by artificially blocking the links that would complete a loop.

straight-through cable   A twisted-pair patch cable in which the wire terminations in both connectors follow the same scheme.

structured cabling   A method for uniform, enterprise-wide, multivendor cabling systems specified by the TIA/EIA 568 Commercial Building Wiring Standard. Structured cabling is based on a hierarchical design using a high-speed backbone.

subnet   A smaller network within a larger network in which all nodes share a network addressing component and a fixed amount of bandwidth.

subnet ID   The 16 bits, or one block, in an IPv6 address that can be used to identify a subnet on a large corporate network.

subnet mask   In IPv4 addressing, a 32-bit number that helps one computer find another by indicating what portion of an IP address is the network and subnet portion and what portion is the host portion.

subscription model   A service model in which software is provided by subscription.

supplicant   In EAP, the device requesting authentication.

SVC (switched virtual circuit)   A logical, point-to-point connection that is established when parties need to transmit, then terminated after the transmission is complete.

switch   A connectivity device that logically subdivides a network into smaller, individual collision domains.

switching   The determination of how connections are created between nodes on a network.

symmetric encryption   A method of encryption that requires the same key to encode the data as is used to decode the cipher text.

symmetrical   A characteristic of transmission technology that offers the same download speeds as upload speeds.

synchronous   (1) A characteristic of transmission technology that offers the same download speeds as upload speeds. (2) A communications method in which data being transmitted and received by nodes must conform to a timing scheme.

syslog (system log) A standard for generating, storing, and processing messages about events on a system.

system life cycle The process of designing, implementing, and maintaining an entire network.

T

T1 A digital carrier standard used in North America and most of Asia that provides 1.544-Mbps throughput and 24 channels for voice, data, video, or audio signals.

T3 A digital carrier standard used in North America and most of Asia that can carry the equivalent of 672 channels for voice, data, video, or audio, with a maximum data throughput of 44.736 Mbps.

TA (terminal adapter) A device used to convert digital signals into analog signals for use with ISDN phones and other analog devices.

TACACS+ (Terminal Access Controller Access Control System Plus) A Cisco proprietary protocol that provides AAA services.

tag A VLAN identifier added to a frame's header according to specifications in the 802.1Q standard.

tamper detection Sensors that can detect physical penetration, temperature extremes, input voltage variations, input frequency variations, or certain kinds of radiation.

T-carrier Standards that specify a method of signaling using TDM (time division multiplexing) over two wire pairs to divide a single channel into multiple channels, which enables digital data to be transmitted at high speeds over the PSTN.

TCP (Transmission Control Protocol) A core protocol of the TCP/IP suite that makes a connection with the end host, checks whether data is received, and resends it if it is not.

TCP/IP (Transmission Control Protocol/Internet Protocol) A suite of networking protocols that includes TCP, IP, UDP, and many others. TCP/IP provides the foundation for data exchange across the Internet.

tcpdump A free, command-line packet sniffer utility that runs on Linux and other UNIX operating systems.

TDM (time division multiplexing) A method of multiplexing that assigns a time slot in the flow of communications to every node on the network and, in that time slot, carries data from that node.

TDMA (time division multiple access) A method of multiplexing in which signals from several sources on a channel are separated by timeslots.

TDR (time domain reflectometer) A high-end instrument for testing the qualities of a cable.

telco (telecommunications company) A provider of telecommunications services, including telephone and Internet access.

Telnet A terminal emulation protocol used to log on to remote hosts using the TCP/IP protocol.

TFTP (Trivial File Transfer Protocol) A TCP/IP Application layer protocol that is seldom used by humans. Computers commonly use it as they are booting up to request configuration files from another computer on the local network. Unlike FTP, TFTP relies on UDP at the Transport layer using port 69.

three-way handshake A three-step process in which Transport layer protocols establish a connection between nodes.

throughput The amount of data that a medium transmits during a given period of time. Throughput is usually measured in megabits (1,000,000 bits) per second, or Mbps.

TIA (Telecommunications Industry Association) A subgroup of the former EIA that focuses on standards for information technology, wireless, satellite, fiber optics, and telephone equipment. EIA was dissolved in 2011 and its responsibilities transferred to ECA (Electronic Components, Assemblies, Equipment & Supplies Association), but the standards brand name, EIA, will continue to be used. Probably the best known standards to come from the TIA/EIA alliance are its guidelines for how network cable should be installed in commercial buildings, known as the "TIA/EIA 568-B Series."

TIA/EIA 568A A standard pinout for RJ-45 plugs required by the federal government on all federal contracts.

TIA/EIA 568B A standard pinout for RJ-45 plugs commonly used in homes and businesses.

ticket In Kerberos terminology, a temporary set of credentials that a client uses to prove its identity has been validated by the authentication service.

TKIP (Temporal Key Integrity Protocol) An encryption key generation and management scheme used by WPA.

TLD (top-level domain) The last part of an FQDN and the highest-level category used to distinguish domain names—for example, .org, .com, and .net. A TLD is also known as the domain suffix.

TLS (Transport Layer Security) A version of SSL standardized by the IETF (Internet Engineering Task Force). TLS uses slightly different encryption algorithms than SSL, but otherwise is very similar to the most recent version of SSL.

TMS (Transportation Management System)   Software that tracks inventory as it is transported between locations, such as between a warehouse and a storefront.

tone generator   A small electronic device that issues a signal on a wire pair. When used in conjunction with a tone locator, it can help locate the termination of a wire pair. Also called a toner.

tone locator   A small electronic device that emits a tone when it detects electrical activity on a wire pair. When used in conjunction with a tone generator, it can help locate the termination of a wire pair. Also called a probe.

toner   *See* tone generator.

toner and probe kit   A two-piece tool that includes both a tone generator and a tone locator. Used together, they can help locate the termination of a wire pair.

toner probe   *See* toner and probe kit.

topology   How the parts of a whole work together.

TOS (Type of Service)   A field in an IPv4 header that currently serves as the DSCP field and the ECN (Explicit Congestion Notification) field.

TPM (Trusted Platform Module)   A chip on a motherboard that holds an encryption key required at startup to access encrypted data on the hard drive.

traceroute   A TCP/IP troubleshooting utility available in Linux, UNIX, and macOS systems that sends UDP messages to a random port on the destination node to trace the path from one networked node to another, identifying all intermediate hops between the two nodes.

tracert   A Windows utility that uses ICMP echo requests to trace the path from one networked node to another, identifying all intermediate hops between the two nodes.

traffic analysis   The examination of network traffic for patterns and exceptions to those patterns.

traffic policing   A traffic-shaping technique in which the volume or rate of traffic traversing an interface is limited to a predefined maximum.

traffic shaping   Manipulating certain characteristics of packets, data streams, or connections to manage the type and amount of traffic traversing a network or interface at any moment.

trailer   Control information attached to the end of a packet by a Data Link layer protocol.

transceiver   A modular interface that can be inserted in a switch to connect its motherboard with an external, fiber-optic cable.

Transport layer   The fourth layer of the OSI model. The Transport layer is responsible for transporting Application layer payloads from one application to another.

trip hazard   Items such as extension cords or tools lying on the ground in walkways that can cause someone to stumble.

trunk port   The interface on a switch capable of managing traffic from multiple VLANs.

trunking   The aggregation of multiple logical connections in one physical connection between connectivity devices. In the case of VLANs, a trunk allows two switches to manage and exchange data between multiple VLANs.

TTL (Time to Live)   A field that indicates the maximum duration that an IPv4 packet can remain on the network before it is discarded. Although this field was originally meant to represent units of time, on modern networks it represents the number of times a packet can still be forwarded by a router, or the maximum number of router hops remaining.

TTLS (Tunneled Transport Layer Security)   A variant of TLS that provides authentication like SSL/TLS, but does not require a certificate for each user. Instead, TTLS authenticates the server end of the connection by certificate, and users are authenticated by password only or some other legacy method.

tunneling   The process of encapsulating one type of protocol in another. Tunneling is the way in which higher-layer data is transported over VPNs by Layer 2 protocols.

twist ratio   The number of twists per meter or foot in a twisted-pair cable.

twisted-pair   A type of cable similar to telephone wiring that consists of color-coded pairs of insulated copper wires, each with a diameter of 0.4 to 0.8 mm. Every two wires are twisted around each other to form pairs, and all the pairs are encased in a plastic sheath.

TX/RX reverse   A problem caused by mismatched pinout standards, resulting in near end crosstalk.

TXT (Text) record   A type of DNS data record that holds any type of free-form text. It might contain text designed to be read by humans regarding network, server, or accounting issues.

Type 1 hypervisor   A hypervisor that installs on a computer before any OS and is therefore called a bare-metal hypervisor.

Type 2 hypervisor A hypervisor that installs in a host OS as an application and is called a hosted hypervisor.

U

UC (unified communications) The centralized management of multiple types of network-based communications, such as voice, video, fax, and messaging services.

UDP (User Datagram Protocol) A core protocol in the TCP/ IP suite that does not guarantee delivery because it does not first make the connection before sending data or check to confirm that data is received.

UNC (universal naming convention) Notation that identifies files or peripheral devices shared on a network.

unicast address A type of IPv6 address that represents a single node on a network.

unidirectional antenna A type of antenna that issues wireless signals along a single direction, or path. Also called a directional antenna.

unmanaged switch A switch that provides plug-and-play simplicity with minimal configuration options and has no IP address assigned to it.

UPC (Ultra Polished Connector) A type of ferrule in which the tip has been highly polished, thereby increasing the efficiency of the connection.

upgrade A significant change to an application's existing code, typically designed to improve functionality or add new features while also correcting bugs and vulnerabilities.

UPS (uninterruptible power supply) A battery-operated power source directly attached to one or more devices and to a power supply (such as a wall outlet) that prevents undesired fluctuations of the wall outlet's AC power from harming the device or interrupting its services.

upset failure Damage that can shorten the life of a component and/or cause intermittent errors.

URL (Uniform Resource Locator) A string of text that uniquely identifies a file available on a network.

USB (universal serial bus) A connector used for peripheral devices.

utilization A measure of the actual throughput used as a percentage of available bandwidth.

UTM (Unified Threat Management) A security strategy that combines multiple layers of security appliances and technologies into a single safety net.

UTP (unshielded twisted pair) A type of copper-based cable that consists of one or more insulated twisted-pair wires encased in a plastic sheath, which does not contain additional shielding for the twisted pairs.

V

VDSL (very high bit rate DSL or variable DSL) A variety of DSL that provides higher throughput than its predecessor, ADSL.

VIP (virtual IP address) A single IP address that represents a cluster of devices.

virtual circuit A connection between network nodes that, although based on potentially disparate physical links, logically appears to be a direct, dedicated link between those nodes.

virtual firewall An installation of a firewall's operating system in a VM.

virtual router An installation of a router's operating system in a VM.

virtual switch A logically defined device that operates at the Data Link layer to pass frames between nodes.

virtualization The emulation of all or part of a computer or network.

virus A program that replicates itself to infect more computers, either through network connections when it piggybacks on other files or through exchange of external storage devices, such as USB drives, passed among users. Viruses might damage files or systems or simply annoy users.

VLAN (virtual local area network or virtual LAN) A network within a network that is logically defined by grouping ports on a switch so that some of the local traffic on the switch is forced to go through a router, thereby limiting the traffic to a smaller broadcast domain.

VLAN hopping An attack in which the attacker generates transmissions that appear, to the switch, to belong to a protected VLAN.

VLAN mismatch A configuration error where switch ports on each end of a trunk are configured with different native VLAN assignments. Also called a native VLAN mismatch.

VLSM (Variable Length Subnet Mask) A subnetting method that allows subnets to be further subdivided into smaller and smaller groupings until each subnet is about the same size as the needed IP address space.

VNC (Virtual Network Computing) Software that uses the cross-platform protocol RFB (remote frame buffer) to remotely control a workstation or server.

vNIC (virtual NIC)   A logically defined network interface associated with a virtual machine.

VoIP (Voice over IP)   The provision of telephone service over a packet-switched network running the TCP/IP protocol suite.

VoIP endpoint   An end user device or application that gives the user access to VoIP services on a network.

VoIP gateway   A device that converts signals from a campus's analog phone equipment into IP data that can travel over the Internet, or that converts VoIP data from an internal IP network to travel over a phone company's analog telephone lines.

VoIP PBX (private branch exchange)   A dedicated telephone switch or a virtual switching device that connects and manages calls within a private organization, and manages call connections that exit the network through a VoIP gateway.

VPN (virtual private network)   A virtual connection between a client and a remote network, two remote networks, or two remote hosts over the Internet or other types of networks, to remotely provide network resources.

VPN concentrator   A specialized device that authenticates VPN clients, establishes tunnels for VPN connections, and manages encryption for VPN transmissions.

VRF (virtual routing and forwarding)   A routing technology that allows a router to maintain multiple versions of a routing table.

VRRP (Virtual Router Redundancy Protocol)   A standard that assigns a virtual IP address to a group of routers.

VTC (video teleconference)   An application that allows people to communicate in video and voice.

VTP (VLAN Trunk Protocol)   Cisco's protocol for exchanging VLAN information over trunks.

vulnerability   A weakness of a system, process, or architecture that could lead to compromised information or unauthorized access to a network.

vulnerability scanning   A technique to identify vulnerabilities in a network, with or without malicious intent.

W

WAF (web application firewall)   An Application layer firewall that monitors web traffic on a server.

WAN (wide area network)   A network that spans a long distance and connects two or more LANs.

WAP (Wireless Application Protocol)   A standard that defines how mobile devices access data over a mobile wireless network.

WAP (wireless access point)   *See* AP.

war driving   The act of driving around an area while running a laptop configured to detect and capture wireless data transmissions.

warm site   A place where the computers, devices, and connectivity necessary to rebuild a network exist, though only some are appropriately configured, updated, or connected to match the network's current state.

WDM (wavelength division multiplexing)   A multiplexing technique in which each signal on a fiber-optic cable is assigned a different wavelength, which equates to its own subchannel.

well-known port   The TCP/IP ports numbered 0 to 1023, so named because they were long ago assigned by Internet authorities to popular services and are, therefore, well known and frequently used.

WEP (Wired Equivalent Privacy)   A key encryption technique for wireless networks that uses keys both to authenticate network clients and to encrypt data in transit.

Wi-Fi   The IEEE standards and their amendments, extensions, and corrections for wireless networking.

Wi-Fi analyzer   Software that can evaluate Wi-Fi network availability as well as help optimize Wi-Fi signal settings or help identify Wi-Fi security threats.

wiki   A website that can be edited by users.

wireless bridge   An access point used to create remote wired access to a network.

wireless controller   A central management console for all the APs on a network.

wireless range extender   A device that extends the reach of a wireless signal by repeating the signal from a closer broadcast point.

wireless spectrum   A continuum of electromagnetic waves used for data and voice communication.

wiring schematic   A graphical representation of a network's wired infrastructure.

WLAN (wireless local area network)   A LAN that uses wireless connections for some or all of its transmissions.

WMS (warehouse management system)   Software that manages the resources in a warehouse.

WPA (Wi-Fi Protected Access or Wireless Protected Access) A wireless security method that dynamically assigns every transmission its own key.

WPA2 A wireless security method that improves upon WPA by using a stronger encryption protocol called AES.

WPAN (wireless PAN) A purely wireless version of a PAN.

WPS (Wi-Fi Protected Setup) A user-friendly—but not very secure—security option available on some consumer-grade APs.

WSL (Windows Subsystem for Linux) A Linux shell CLI in Windows that allows users to interact with underlying Windows functions and system files.

WWN (World Wide Name) The unique identifier assigned to a manufacturer of storage technology devices.

X

XaaS (Anything as a Service or Everything as a Service) A type of cloud computing in which the cloud can provide any combination of functions depending on a client's exact needs, or assumes

functions beyond networking including, for example, monitoring, storage, applications, and virtual desktops.

xDSL (extended DSL) A generic term used to refer to all varieties of DSL.

XFP (10 Gigabit small form-factor pluggable) A type of SFP that can send and receive data at rates of up to 10 Gbps.

XML (eXtensible Markup Language) An alternative to HTML that provides rules for formatting documents.

Y

Z

zeroconf (zero configuration) An automatically configured IP network.

zero-day exploit An attack that takes advantage of a software vulnerability that hasn't yet or has only very recently become public.

Z-Wave A smart home protocol that provides two basic types of functions: signaling, to manage wireless connections, and control, to transmit data and commands between devices.

INDEX